Also by the Same Author

Shenfan

Secker & Warburg   London

SHENFAN

WILLIAM HINTON

First published in England 1983 by
Martin Secker & Warburg Limited
54 Poland Street, London W1V 3DF

PHOTOGRAPHS COPYRIGHT © 1980 BY RICHARD GORDON

MAPS BY ANITA KARL/JIM KEMP

BOOK DESIGN BY LILLY LANGOTSKY

ISBN: 0-436-19630-1

Printed in the United States of America

For
WANG CHIN-HUNG
and
CHANG WEN-YING

Two Long Bow peasants who embody so many of the fine qualities
long displayed by the Chinese people—capacity for hard work,
frugality, tenacity,
curiosity about everything that breathes,
moves or revolves, vision, creative drive,
warmth and courage. Add two attitudes that are as new as
they are rare in the world—faith in
the tillers next door, commitment to
cooperation as a way of life. To the extent that the
Chinese people and their leaders trust
and encourage men like Wang and women like Chang
will China prosper.

I believe that some day it will be found that peasants are people. Yes, beings in a great many respects like ourselves. And I believe that some day they will find this out, too—and then! Well, then I think they will rise up and demand to be regarded as part of the race, and by that consequence there will be trouble!

MARK TWAIN, *Recollections of Joan of Arc*

Acknowledgments

First of all I want to thank the people of Long Bow village for the hospitality they have extended to me over so many years and for the goodwill and patience they demonstrated as I tried to grasp the tortuous course of their community's history and at the same time learned to wield a Chinese hoe. The officials of Horse Square Commune, Changchih City, the Southeast Shansi Region and Shansi Province also deserve heartfelt thanks. Without them I could never have carried out my investigations in Long Bow village or learned about the social, political and economic relations that surround, support and are in turn supported by life at the grass roots.

At the national level Premier Chou En-lai had the vision and the courage to invite me back to China at a time when many of his colleagues regarded *Fanshen* as a very controversial book. A true internationalist, he treated me, my wife and my children like members of one world family, as did the indomitable Hsing Chiang, who planned our far-flung travels. After Premier Chou's death it was the staff of the Chinese People's Association for Friendship with Foreign Countries and its wise chairman, Wang Bing-nan, who welcomed the continuation of my efforts and made possible so many subsequent trips to Southeast Shansi. Both Chang Hsueh-liang and Kuo Tse-pei served as exemplary guides and interpreters and showed the kind of love and respect for peasants and peasant life that made them comfortable companions. The beautiful headquarters of their Association, across the street and around the corner from the Peking Hotel, is a delightful refuge for any weary traveler.

Back home I have to thank Random House for patient support over many years, years when it sometimes looked as if no book would be forthcoming. Toni Morrison, a most sympathetic and devoted editor, has given me tremendous encouragement to keep plugging away at what often seemed a task that had no end. Without her enthusiasm and keen sense for the order and fitness of various sequences, not to mention the order and fitness of words as such, I might well have bogged down long ago. Thanks also to Dotty Seidel of Topton, Pennsylvania, and Eileen Ahearn of Random House for being able to produce clean typed pages from the overcorrected, illegible drafts that I constantly turned over to them.

I owe more than I can hope to repay to my daughter Carma, who accompanied me through two long sojourns in Long Bow, who translated endlessly for me and, on her own, dipped into aspects of village life that I would not ordinarily have access to. Her in-depth, intuitive sense of the realities of Chinese life and her mastery of Chinese literature and culture have opened many a door for me and saved me from many an error. Carma Hinton and Richard Gordon took thousands of pictures of Long Bow scenes and people. From their rich harvest I have selected a few shots that seem most likely to illuminate the text.

My heartfelt thanks go also to Wu Hung, a Peking student of philosophy, now studying at Harvard, for suggesting *Shenfan* as the title for this book and pointing out the various levels of symbolic meaning that the word may take on.

Finally, I want to thank the rest of my family for the patience they have shown for more than a decade in the face of the crankiness generated by literary frustration, and also for their calmness in the face of the financial austerity that a work too long in progress inevitably entailed. I gave up farming to complete this book and gave up lecturing to gain more time for it. Although we never doubted that the next meal would be forthcoming, we did sometimes wonder when we would pay the oil bill and how we would pay the taxes. Debts also piled up. I hope Joanne, Michael, Alyssa and Catherine will decide that it has all been worthwhile.

Shenfan

Shenfan is a common word in the Chinese countryside. It means deep tillage, deep plowing, a deep and through overturning of the soil. Between the completion of the fall harvest and the onset of winter people go out to turn the earth. Side by side, armed with mattocks or spades, they dig the wide fields in preparation for next year's planting.

During the Great Leap of 1958 *Shenfan* came to stand for the vast, grass-roots movement to increase farm production that swept the hills and plains. People believed that the deeper they dug into the ground, turning both soil and subsoil, the more grain they would reap. They also believed that, in the absence of machinery, they must depend on their own hands to till the soil as deeply as possible, thus laying the foundations for a bountiful harvest.

Attributing to the word symbolic meaning, *Shenfan* suggests all the painstaking effort peasants are willing to make once they own their own land, and it can express the hope they have for their land. It may also express the spirit of the cooperative movement by means of which people, working together, try to fashion a new way of life on ancient fields.

Overall *Shenfan* stands here as a symbol for the drastic changes that have taken place in Chinese society since 1949. These changes have, after all, been brought about by incessant "deep-digging," by "turning" and "overturning" China's social foundations in a rigorous search for a bright road to the future. *Shenfan,* it is clear, inevitably follows on the heels of *Fanshen.*

All the Chinese words in this book are spelled according to the familiar Wade-Giles system. In China this has been superseded by a new, official Pinyin (phonetic) system, which many authors and publishers outside China are already using. I have chosen to stick with the old Wade-Giles system, primarily because *Shenfan* is the sequel to *Fanshen,* in which all the Chinese spellings are Wade-Giles. Most of the place names and the personal names in the new book would differ sharply from those in the old if I adopted the new official spelling. Since these names are confusing enough to the Western reader, it seemed best to maintain continuity and hew to the familiar.

Preface

*There is nothing more difficult to take in hand, more
perilous to conduct, or more uncertain in its success,
than to take the lead in the introduction of a new order
of things.*

Niccolò Machiavelli

I assembled the raw material for a contemporary history of Long Bow
village with some difficulty, over a long period of time, fighting a battle or
two to obtain various components and a battle or two to hold onto them.
I digested the material slowly and molded it even more slowly into its
present shape, challenged always by the unfolding complexity of the subject.
Note-by-note, skirmish-by-skirmish, page-by-page, the project lured me
into an unpremeditated life work.

Between the time I gathered my first notes in Long Bow village and the
time *Fanshen* appeared in print, eighteen years passed. Between the time
Fanshen appeared in print and the time *Shenfan* is scheduled to appear,
another seventeen years will have rolled by. A final volume, *Li Chun,* may
well consume two more. The best that can be said for these delays is that
the longest of them were dictated by circumstances beyond my control.
After I left Long Bow in 1948 I spent five years teaching farm mechanization
to Chinese peasants, hence found no time to write. When I returned home
in 1953 the U.S. Customs seized my notes and turned them over to Senator
Eastland's Committee on Internal Security. I won them back in 1958 only
after a protracted and expensive lawsuit. With notes in hand at last, it took
me six years to write the book and two years to find a publisher courageous
enough to print it. The publisher was Monthly Review Press, headed by
Paul M. Sweezy and the late Leo Huberman. They brought out *Fanshen*
in 1966.

Long before I finished *Fanshen* I made up my mind to go back to Long
Bow to learn what happened to its citizens following land reform. Unfortunately at that time I could not implement the decision. I was not allowed to travel. Because I stayed on in China after 1949 and spoke
favorably of the Chinese revolution after I came home, Mother Ship-

ley* at the State Department denied me a passport. For fifteen years I could not venture beyond Canada and Mexico, two countries that do not require passports of American citizens.

Neither the landmark 1958 Supreme Court decision in the Rockwell Kent case, which held that the Secretary of State could not withhold passports because of a citizen's political beliefs or associations, nor the pivotal 1964 decision in the Aptheker case, upholding the right to travel even for such people as leaders of the Communist Party, solved the problem for me. The Passport Division, using regulatory harassment to circumvent the law, continued to deny me a passport, knowing that I wanted to travel to China, a country still on its restricted list.

In 1967 I finally threatened legal action of my own against Secretary of State Dean Rusk. Only then did the Passport Division relent and issue a passport to me, my wife and my two-year-old daughter, Catherine. Unfortunately they stamped the long-withheld documents "not valid for travel in China." What would happen if we went to China anyway? We made inquiries and found that officials of the People's Republic circumvented the regulation by the simple expedient of stamping entry visas on blank pieces of paper. Technically Americans did not have to use their passports to enter or leave the country. Reassured, we flew to London, England, early in 1968 and requested, through the Chinese Embassy there, permission to go on to Peking and Shansi.

We waited many weeks for China's reply. When it came it expressed sincere regret. "It is inconvenient for us to receive you at this time." We felt that it was inconvenient, indeed, for us to return home after coming so far, but we had no choice. We did not learn until several years later that armed fighting had broken out in and around Changchih City and that even People's Liberation Army soldiers could not travel to Long Bow without risking their lives.

In 1970, after armed struggle had died down and the people had reestablished relatively stable local governments throughout the hinterland, China's capacity to welcome foreign visitors revived. Mao Tse-tung and Premier Chou En-lai decided to break their nation's dangerous world isolation by renewing contact with the American people and the American government. One of their first moves was to get in touch with three writers whose books dealt in some depth with the Chinese revolution: Edgar Snow, Jack Belden and myself. They invited Edgar Snow, Mao's old friend and biographer, to come in 1970. He was already in Peking interviewing Mao once more when I received word that I and my whole family should come, stay as long as possible, and travel at will. We were still winding up our affairs at home and making travel arrangements when the Ping-Pong diplomacy of April, 1971, startled the world. We arrived in Peking on April 30 and stayed in China for seven months. We would have stayed longer if we had not been worried that our children would fall behind their peers in their

*Mrs. Ruth B. Shipley, State Department Passport Division Head. When she retired in 1955, Secretary of State Dulles appointed a like-minded successor, Frances Knight, who continued to deny passports to people with "suspect" beliefs and association.

Kutztown, Pennsylvania, primary school. Throughout our stay my daughter Carma, born in Peking in 1949, accompanied us. Chinese by culture and education but competent in English, she helped us penetrate layer after layer of Chinese life and thought. If some of the complex texture of reality comes through in these pages she, more than any other, is responsible.

In those seven months we saw a great deal. Premier Chou En-lai unlocked doors for us everywhere: at the Peking locomotive works, where we spent five weeks and I worked for a time on the shop floor; at Tsinghua University, where we spent eighteen days talking to members of the rival student factions; at Tachai Brigade, Central Shansi, where we lived through the heat of July, joined field work, climbed mountains, and talked many times with brigade leader Ch'en Yung-kuei; and finally at Long Bow village, where we attached ourselves to a work team responsible for Party rectification and stayed right through to the end of the fall harvest and the deep-digging that set the stage for the next year's crops.

We found it impossible to absorb everything we saw and heard on that trip. Delving into the Cultural Revolution alone was enough to occupy every waking moment. We were trying to understand that extraordinary upheaval and at the same time catch up on the whole sweep of history since 1949. I came away with ten thick books crammed cover to cover with handwritten notes and a mind crammed temple to temple with words and impressions, many of them contradictory.

When I returned home I wrote a book about the Cultural Revolution at Tsinghua University, *Hundred Day War,* that focused on two short years of bizarre factional struggle. I also put five interviews with Chou En-lai together in one small volume, *Conversations with Americans,* but the Long Bow material proved more difficult to assimilate. We had listened to a torrent of rhetoric from local officials, which did not seem to coincide with the reality around us or with the rhetoric we heard elsewhere. The polemics of the Cultural Revolution led almost invariably to serious erosion of the integrity of words, to widespread conceptual embezzlement. People used and misused all the key words and phrases in the Marxist lexicon to a point where they became mere fig leaves for atrocious betrayals of principle. The "proletariat" came to mean me and my friends; the "bourgeoisie," you and your friends, a group that had obviously degenerated into a "gang." To "make revolution" meant for me to take power. If you took power that was "counterrevolution." Whoever held power, however briefly, seemed able to justify, in the most glowing revolutionary jargon, what he or she planned to do. Later, the change in personnel might be complete, but the tone of righteous commitment remained intact, and the theoretical integument that sheathed all arguments appeared impermeable. The protagonists had read their Marx and their Mao and they knew how to select the most convincing quotes. I found it hard to develop a coherent framework for appraising what had happened, not to mention a suitable form for telling the story. I wrote a few chapters about the early, post-land-reform period, then bogged down in rhetoric of my own.

In 1975 I had the good fortune to travel again to China, this time as a board member of the U.S.–China People's Friendship Association. The trip lasted one month. Although I did not have a chance to go to Long Bow,

I met two of the brigade leaders in Peking and talked with them for hours. In 1977 I went back to the village and settled in for a two-and-a-half-month stretch. In 1978 I spent two weeks in Long Bow, in 1980 another two weeks and in 1981, ten days. With the perspective and insights acquired on these subsequent visits, the 1971 material began to fall into place. By that time the Chinese Party and people had begun to reevaluate what had happened during the so-called "lost decade." Their discussion helped me define a series of historical stages and the most complex of these, the Cultural Revolution, began to lose some of its mystique if not much of its surreal, Catch-22 quality. By 1978 an atmosphere conducive to analysis, as opposed to rhetoric, replaced the frenzied milieu of earlier years and some people found the courage to call follies follies, frame-ups frame-ups and murders murders. Although the political pendulum soon swung so far to the right as to jeopardize objectivity from that extreme, the very act of swinging helped put things in perspective.

The prosperity achieved by the people of Long Bow after 1973 also helped. With production going well and the quality of life improving, brigade members were willing to talk about the past more freely and sum it up with less bias. Without any need to target scapegoats whom they could blame for failure, people learned to relax and even to laugh when telling about their assorted misfortunes. Some people, however, afraid of rekindling factional bitterness, still preferred to leave history strictly alone. Why talk about the past? Words could only reopen old wounds.

Shenfan continues the story of Long Bow village, Shansi Province, China, that *Fanshen* began. *Fanshen* (turn over, stand up) told of the liberation of the community from Japanese occupation and of the land reform that smashed several millennia of landlord domination. *Shenfan* (deep plowing, deep overturn) tells of the cooperative movement that peasants have been building in the Chinese countryside ever since every family gained a share of land.

In contrast to the land reform, a once-and-done-with grass-roots upheaval that drastically redistributed property and set the stage for community self-rule, the cooperative movement has developed as a "100-year great task," advancing discontinuously, veering left then right, reeling back in disorder, even coming to rest at times, only to recover momentum and roll on to truly remarkable achievements such as one thousand percent increases in yield for some units and even some counties and the doubling of grain output nationally since 1952.* Sharp conflict, uneven development, qualitative leaps alternating with stagnation and sudden collapse have characterized the process from the beginning. While about a third of the units have done well in recent years, feudal style, despotic rule, extreme leveling or just plain bad management have prevented another third from catching up. Many in the bottom third require massive loans or state subsidies to

*China claims a threefold increase since 1949, but 1949 was an exceptionally bad year. By 1952 the peasants restored normal production at the 150-metric-ton level. Since then they have increased it to a stable level of more than 300 million metric tons, which amounts to a generous doubling of output.

carry them through from one year to the next. In spite of all difficulties, national leaders have, until recently, upheld at least a facade of firm resolve to solve all problems, objective or subjective, that stand in the way of collective agriculture. Over the years they have marshaled a vast army of rural cadres and peasant activists who have devoted their lives to making the system work. Most of the men and women whose stories fill these pages are volunteers in that army.

Shenfan tells how, starting with spasmodic mutual aid, Long Bow producers learned to work together; pooled land, livestock and implements to create a viable cooperative; and how they joined their cooperative to others to form an association called a commune. It tells how, once collective labor became universal, Long Bow peasants attempted a great leap—cast iron ingots from local ores; built dams, reservoirs and railroad beds by hand; and deep-dug their land in expectation of record-breaking yields, only to suffer crop failures and sideline bankruptcies as drought seared the land and huge, centralized work units foundered for lack of sound management.

Shenfan goes on to tell of a retreat toward private enterprise in the early sixties, of the resurgent cooperative organizing that followed, and of the mobilization of Long Bow peasants to "bombard the headquarters," overthrow all established leadership and go all out to change the world, in the Cultural Revolution; a drive that split the community, created diehard factions bent on power for power's sake, and pushed dedicated militants into all-out civil war. It tells how Liberation Army soldiers imposed a warped peace and how Party leaders tried, with marginal success, to unite people and cadres, reestablish normal life at the grass roots, and spark new production drives.

Shenfan ends in the fall of 1971 at a time of deep crisis, both locally and nationally. With the Cultural Revolution aborted, Mao old and ailing, Lin Piao dead, and Chou En-lai under attack from an ultraleft faction centered on Mao's wife, factional strife subsided in and around Long Bow, but ill will remained. As "class struggle" alarms fanned up new confrontations, the common people dragged their feet into the new decade.

By 1980 these problems all came to a head and some of them found resolution. A third book, *Li Chun,* will tell how Long Bow peasants reorganized their community once more; how a combination of new and old activists brought people together, analyzed the roadblocks to production, and led their cooperative unit to a remarkable breakthrough in crop culture, farm mechanization and small-scale industry; how, from a troubled, split-prone backwater, Long Bow transformed itself in a few short years into a very successful brigade. *Fanshen, Shenfan* and *Li Chun,* taken together, will add up to a provisional history of one small North China village from 1945 until today.

During the three decades it took for Long Bow to evolve the viable new form it now enjoys, China, formerly the "sick man of Asia," transformed herself into a major, independent, self-reliant new force on the world stage, a force with which our country must not only come to terms, but one with which it must seek common ground if we Americans are not, in our turn, to end up in dangerous isolation in the world. This imperative lends urgency to a book such as this. Seeking common ground demands, first of all, some understanding.

My overall goal in investigating and describing events in Long Bow remains what it was when I wrote *Fanshen*—to reveal through the microcosm of one small village something of the essence of the continuing revolution in China. A question arises as to whether Long Bow is a microcosm typical enough to reveal any such thing. Has Long Bow's development been universal or unique? The answer must be, as it was in the days of land reform, that it has been something of both.

In 1945 Long Bow shared a common class structure, from landlord to hired laborer, with most of rural China, and suffered consequently from a typically severe land tenure problem. At the same time it stood out as a village with a large Catholic minority, a village that suffered occupation by the Japanese, and a village liberated overnight from both foreign conquest and indigenous gentry control—a transition so sudden that no one was prepared for it. These features created tensions that few other villages had to face. In the post-land-reform period all three became rapidly less important as influences on development, to be replaced by features far more unsettling—industrialization and urban sprawl. Long Bow lies only twelve miles from Changchih City. The surrounding countryside boasts huge reserves of coal and substantial deposits of iron ore. After 1949, higher leaders decided to turn Changchih into an industrial center. They redrew county boundaries to give the city control over several important coal fields and over level plains on which to build new industries, both heavy and light, together with highways and railroads that could link them to the rest of China. Since then industrial output in the city has expanded several thousand percent. Because Long Bow, once a part of Lucheng County, lies practically in the middle of Changchih's new industrial zone, the development of this zone has profoundly influenced every facet of village life. Long Bow peasants have lost two-fifths of their land but they have gained enormous assets in the form of night soil and kitchen waste from industrial workers, a front-gate market for all the bricks they can make and all the vegetables they can grow, endless opportunities for transport work, freight handling, contract work in industrial plants and contract work on industrial products. For many years now the nonagricultural income of the community has far outweighed the income derived from the land.

If in 1948 Long Bow could be called typical of the isolated Chinese countryside, today it can be called typical of the rapidly changing industrial outskirts of the nation's burgeoning cities, and that may place it somewhat closer to the essence of what is happening in China as a whole than any pristine farming village can claim to be. If the land reform, a manifestly rural movement, set the tone in Long Bow in the past, all the complex crosscurrents of China's modern industrial upsurge buffet the community today. The Cultural Revolution demonstrated this most strikingly. Starting in the universities of Peking, spreading to colleges and middle schools in urban centers, then leaping to factories everywhere, it tended to lose momentum and dissipate its forces when it hit the countryside. In Long Bow, by contrast, because the village had already linked up with suburbia, because a middle school had moved into the old Catholic orphanage at its center, the Cultural Revolution exploded within a few hours after it first surfaced in the nation's capital and dominated the community for years. When the working class of the Changchih industrial zone took up the movement, Long Bow peasants joined whatever factions controlled the mines and mills that hired them for contract work, and they brought factional differences home with them as soon as such differences appeared. The village served as a battleground for contending student and worker militants who fought with "hot" weapons such as pistols, rifles and hand grenades. For self-defense, if for no other reason, many Long Bow peasants built up arsenals of their own.

Reflecting the general rule that the peasants of suburban communes participated more continuously and more actively in the Cultural Revolution than peasants living deep in the countryside, Long Bow ably served as a window on the kind of commitment and the kind of conflict that stamped their arcane, medieval signature on the times.

Special as Long Bow most certainly is today, it is still at its core a farming village, a community of peasants, family-centered, tradition-bound, yet richly creative and passionately committed to change. I can't help feeling satisfaction with the historical accident that sent me there in 1948, rather than to some other place. I chose it because it was the "basic village" (work-team location) nearest to Northern University. I could walk to village meetings in the morning and teach classes back on the campus in the afternoon. A few weeks after I first set foot there, the university moved hundreds of miles away. I stayed behind long enough to see the land reform story unfold in full, and this was long enough to become deeply attached to the place. I have followed the fortunes of Long Bow people ever since with as much interest and concern as I follow the fortunes of my closest friends and neighbors back home. Furthermore, as a farmer, I have been able to make some contribution to the technical transformation of agriculture that most Long Bow peasants yearn for. Together we have built grain driers, center-pivot irrigation equipment, new tillage implements and a complete system of mechanization for corn. On my trip in 1981 I brought the Party Secretary a small cable hoist, a device that we call a "come-along." After forty experiments Long Bow mechanics solved the technical problems involved in its manufacture and began to produce it for the market. They now send advertising material across the country to promote what they call their "Stalwart Zebra." Because our relationship has always been two-sided, our rapport has deepened year by year, people have opened their homes and their hearts, and I have been able to assess not only the outer contours of their lives but some of the emotional wellsprings that shape those contours from within.

The special relationship that I have with Long Bow, the very warp on which this book is woven, has created its own special drawback. Social studies are influenced, it seems, by a variant of the Heisenberg principle that makes it impossible to measure both the speed and the mass of a subatomic particle. Just as in physics to measure a particle changes it, so in social science the very act of studying a community inevitably brings on alterations. In the case of Long Bow, the alterations have mainly been due to intervention from above. Ever since the community won renown as the site of *Fanshen,* higher authorities in Changchih City, the Southeast Region and Shansi Province have paid special attention to Long Bow, sending work team after work team there in an effort to break the impasse in politics and production that plagued the village in the sixties and early seventies. Before our visit in 1971 they suddenly replaced key village leaders, mobilized the whole community to build up the mud-prone streets with cinders from the railroad yards, and paint courtyard walls with whitewash. They also prevailed on scores of families to buy and raise pigs. They wanted to present us with a model community, but except for a few firmer streets, a score of glistening walls and an extra pig or two, they failed. The people of Long Bow happily went on being themselves, a trifle lethargic in production perhaps, but brilliant as actors on the stage of their local theater. The cadres sent in from outside did not possess enough practical knowledge to analyze, not to mention overcome, the real roadblocks to production. What the work teams accomplished was to allow all the members of the community a chance to air their grievances, thus giving us deeper insight into their problems and their state of mind. When the people of Long Bow finally got their act together they did it from within, with their own resources, and they applied creative solutions to their problems that higher authorities had never even thought of. If intervention failed in the long run to transform the village into a model, it did manage nevertheless to influence it in many ways that are hard to measure. I cannot claim that the community we studied was the same one that would have existed had *Fanshen* never appeared. Nor, given the inevitable intervention, can I claim immunity for the individuals whose lives are so freely examined in these pages.

Since idle gossip can generate unwarranted embarrassment for miles around, and since truth can bring down on individual heads various forms of official harassment, I have reluctantly changed the names of most of the Long Bow citizens who appear in this account. Only the men and women of the older generation whom the public already knows from reading *Fanshen,* and a few of their sons and daughters whose antecedents are important to the story, retain their real names. All the other people in the community, all the members of the younger generation who have taken the lead in recent years, bear pseudonyms. The same holds true for some of the higher-level activists who played a big role in the factional confrontations of the Cultural Revolution. Since all accounts of those extraordinary times carry built-in bias, I hesitate to jeopardize careers by linking real names to extreme acts. Less controversial commune, city, regional and provincial personalities appear as themselves. In regard to national leaders, controversial or otherwise, anonymity hardly applies. In any case, I have little to report about them that others have not already revealed, and so I have decided to let the chips fall where they may.

Neither abnormal intervention from above nor any of the other special circumstances surrounding Long Bow is reason enough, in my opinion, to rule it out as a fruitful place to study the development of peasant life in China or at least a suburban variant of it. Nevertheless, one may well ask how penetrating and valid a picture of any community can be compiled by means of interviews, observations and sporadic participation in community life and construction. In the preface to *Fanshen* I wrote that if the history contained in that volume was not accurate in every detail, its main content and spirit nevertheless contained the truth. To make the same claim sixteen years later for the content of *Shenfan* is not so easy.

What I have finally managed to assemble here is certainly not any definitive history of Long Bow, but rather a history compiled from a series of recollections voiced by an assortment of common people and cadres, most of them lowly, who lived through and played an active part in the tumultuous years of rural reconstruction after 1949. Since each informant brought to light his or her own experience and point of view, the versions of events recorded here sometimes clash. Since the time span covered by the book is long, quite a few gaps appear. Since I could not reconcile all the differences or fill in all the gaps, the story may seem at times disjointed; nevertheless each segment reflects an important aspect of remembered reality. Several factors make it difficult to claim that these segments add up to the truth in the same all-around sense that similar material compiled during the land reform movement did.

For one thing, the canvas on which *Shenfan* is painted dwarfs the canvas that served *Fanshen*. In order to make the internal politics of Long Bow comprehensible, I had to describe, if possible, what was going on in the surrounding areas, in the city, the region and even the province. The wider the focus the more room there is for distortion and also for omission. I could not get as detailed or rounded a view of the region, not to mention the province, as I could of the village itself.

For another thing, as stated above, the time span covered by *Shenfan* is long, several times longer than that covered by *Fanshen*. Over time, political winds shifted and people changed their attitude about what had happened to them—or at least what they were willing to say about what had happened to them. Policies that appeared admirable when the Party as a whole pushed them suddenly appeared less admirable when the Party turned against them. Conflicting versions of events, therefore, came not only from different individuals, but from the same individual after his or her attitude or willingness to speak out changed.

One reason attitudes shifted so much over time was the lack of consensus in China over the proper road to follow after land reform. This contrasted sharply with the situation during the earlier democratic revolution, the great popular movement that, over a period of a century, overthrew feudalism* and smashed foreign intervention in China. In the course of the

*Many scholars use the word *feudal* to describe only the vassal-lord, serf-and-manor system characteristic of medieval Europe. In this book, as in *Fanshen,* the word is used in a broader sense to describe a society in which a ruling class, basing its power on the private ownership of and control over land, lived off a share of the produce extracted from that land by a class of laboring people. The latter, though neither slaves nor serfs, were still so closely bound to the land they cultivated as to make them little better than serfs of the landed proprietors. It was a society, furthermore, in which these two classes constituted the main social forces and determined the contours of development. Recent developments in China suggest that the centralized bureaucratic state, originally created by the landlord class, acquired such cohesion, autonomy and power that it became much more than a democratic revolution a series of brilliant leaders, culminating in Mao Tse-tung, laid the theoretical foundations for a broad united front of hundreds of millions of people from all walks of life, who wanted to get rid of land rent and venal gentry on the one hand and free China's economy and culture from imperialist domination on the other.

Even though right and left swings distorted policy as cadres tried to implement consensus politics (*Fanshen,* at one level, is primarily a running account of the political swings that buffeted land reform), clarity on such questions as the enemies to attack and the friends to win over, the feudal property to expropriate and the capitalist property to protect, the feudal culture to abandon and the new democratic culture to create, sharpened year by year. Anyone trying to sum up what happened during the postwar civil war and the land reform could tap a huge reservoir of common experience brought into focus with the aid of a shared theoretical lens. I did not have to create a coherent philosophical framework for *Fanshen.* The Chinese people and their leaders, in the course of a century of conflict, had already created one, and it reflected reality as I experienced it.

Starting with 1949 no one has been able to forge a similar political consensus. After the victory of the new democratic revolution Mao led the whole country immediately into a new stage called "socialist revolution," but apparently he never won a majority of his colleagues to the view that he had named the stage correctly or had prepared an appropriate program for it. It seems that he never won a true working majority of the Chinese people to this view either. It is my impression that most peasants in the countryside took Mao's "socialism" enthusiastically to heart, but there is evidence to indicate that beyond the confines of the Liberated Areas of the North, where land reform created a new society as early as 1948 and cooperation developed step by step on its merits, the response was often brittle and sometimes hollow. Throughout the south, cadres flooding in from old wartime bases beyond the Yellow River tended to push cooperation too soon, too fast and too rigidly to ensure full popular acceptance and self-sustaining growth.

Lack of strategic consensus has had an incalculable influence on the reconstruction of China since 1949. The right and left swings that constantly distorted policy in the post-land-reform period were nothing new, but in the absence of consensus the swings tended to be far more extreme and far more destructive than they had been before. Foot-dragging by an important section of the leadership that disagreed on strategic goals often served to undermine and slow down political initiatives. But by taking the opposite tack, these same leaders could, if they felt like it, speed up those initiatives and carry them to extremes for the sole purpose of discrediting not only the initiatives themselves, but the overall direction of the movement. Once ultraleft errors make radical programs look absurd, the substitution of

---

servant, an executive committee for that class. State functionaries crystallized as a self-perpetuating class above classes, the most important and stable component of Chinese civilization, able to reconstitute itself historically, over and over again, and apparently, even to survive the expropriation and destruction of the landholding gentry who for thousands of years served as its social base.

conservative alternatives becomes easy. Whether or not anyone ever consciously carried out such devious maneuvers, objectively the ball clearly bounced that way.

After 1949 unprincipled struggle over power also intensified right and left swings. At stake was not simply the right to lead the revolutionary movement, as was the case before Liberation, but the right to rule the nation. This qualitative difference introduced an acrimony into conflicts between individuals and cliques that soon became lethal. Such conflicts occurred with increasing frequency as the new apparatus of government took on all the attributes of China's traditional bureaucracy—centralized, all-powerful and responsible to no one outside its ranks. In a well-established hierarchy ambitious individuals base their decisions less on what is good for the country and more on what is good for their personal careers. The important thing is not to solve problems but to please superiors. If higher authorities call for dissolving shaky cooperatives, lower authorities dissolve cooperatives wholesale, the sound along with the unsound, as proof of their eagerness and competence. If higher authorities call for taking grain as the key link, lower authorities push for grain only, neglecting forestry, fisheries, livestock and side occupations, as proof of their activist spirit.

Thus a slight corrective puff, when translated into policy at the village level, can turn into an irresistible hurricane that blows down everything in its path. When higher authorities, let us assume in good faith, try a compensating puff, a new hurricane, generating from another point of the compass, sweeps in turn across the wasteland left by the previous storm. In China they call this "one stroke of the knife." When the knife falls, even lowly team cadres feel constrained to practice bureaucratic one-upmanship. Little wonder peasants conclude that to be "objective" one must first decide what direction the wind is coming from.

Political analysts in China today blame past policy failures and irrational swings on the remnants of "feudal ideology" that still influence the minds of so many individuals, especially individuals who hold power. They allege backward thought to be part of these officials' "peasant" inheritance. What seems obvious to an outside observer is that living, institutional feudalism in many forms and disguises daily reinforces "feudal ideology." Here one must grant pride of place to the enormous government apparatus that responds to problems almost exactly as earlier imperial governments responded. Priority number one always has to be the consolidation of power and maintenance of official prerogatives. It may even be argued that the principle source of antagonism in China today is this government apparatus, a modern reincarnation of scholar-gentry rule, riding herd on everything in sight; but this is a theory too painful to contemplate for a generation that has known nothing but revolutionary upheaval. It is much more comfortable to blame backwardness and stagnation on the peasants, on "peasant mentality" carried into the government by cadres from the countryside, and to postulate modern education as the cure.

Mao, of course, tended to blame everything on the bourgeoisie and their representatives inside the Party. He thereby raised a whole set of knotty theoretical questions too vast to examine here.

My point, in any case, is that there is confusion about what has happened and what is happening in China, that sharp conflict within the country over past, present and future policy persists. The conflict concerns not simply tactical questions, but basic strategic questions: What stage of revolution is China going through? What kind of society does China now have and what kind of society should China build? What classes and strata can working people count on as allies and what classes or strata, if any, should they target as enemies?

To write a definitive history of the last thirty years one would have to distill some order out of this intellectual disarray; one would have to develop a theory comprehensive enough to account for the facts—all of them. Clearly such a theoretical tour de force is beyond me and beyond the scope of this book. It may well take a whole generation of Chinese and world scholars to sift the true meaning of these three decades. The best that I have been able to do is to listen carefully to what people have told me, try not to let the biases inherited from past experience interfere, then write down what seems most significant. What this amounts to, in traditional Chinese parlance, is "throwing out a few bricks, in hope of attracting some jade." I would consider it a great accomplishment if my flawed and, in Chinese eyes, possibly preposterous account of Long Bow village provoked somebody in China to produce a community chronicle as it should be produced —by a native of the community described, by someone tied to his or her own village by a thousand invisible threads, aware of every nuance in the complex network of its relationships, of every warp, twist and bend in its forward progress, or, as could well happen, its relapse into stagnation.

In the meantime, I am concerned about the future of the cooperative movement and the destiny of its vast peasant membership. At the present time, just as some scattered units, including Long Bow village, reach new levels of success, the movement as a whole, plagued by commandism, corruption, apathy and stagnation, has suddenly broken ranks and slid into headlong retreat. Tachai Brigade, for years the model for self-reliance and public spirit, is being denounced on questionable evidence as a subsidized fraud. People who once looked upon cooperation as the road to salvation now damn it as sharing poverty, "people eating out of one big pot." The dream, born in 1949, of liberated tillers marching together toward socialist prosperity has given way to an old principle from which hundreds of millions suffered grievously in the past, the principle that "a few must get rich first."*

At the close of land reform I could truthfully write that the peasants were gradually learning the central lesson of our time, "that only through participation in common struggle can any individual achieve personal emancipation, that the road to *Fanshen* for one lies through the *Fanshen* of all." Now, three decades after the first scattered peasant families in North China spontaneously organized cooperative production around "three legs of a donkey" or "five washed-out gullies," national leaders, seizing on backcountry inertia, are calling into question the very concept of collective work.

*"A few must get rich first" is not the same as "distribution based on work performed," a basic principle for rewarding members of cooperative units and for calculating the income of cooperative units competing against one another.

They are pushing hard for new production systems that stress material incentive as cure-all. They are urging producers to contract land, animals and implements for individual production, then take sole responsibility for the profits and losses incurred. Some thirty percent of the peasants, displaced by the contract procedures wherever they have taken hold, are scrambling to set up home crafts or are taking to the open road as peddlers. When peddlers crowd each others' heels, can beggars be far behind?

In the wake of this sudden reversal of official priorities in China, *Shenfan* and *Li Chun* may well turn out to be, not the challenging epic of an earthbound people learning to substitute cooperation for competition, to place their faith in community action, to put "public first and self second" that I conceived it to be when I first began work on it so long ago, but rather, a disconcerting chronicle of the rise and decline of a cooperative dream, a story of stagnation and decay for what has been, from the start, probably the boldest, certainly the most massive, social transformation of all time.

WILLIAM HINTON

Fleetwood, Pennsylvania
February, 1983

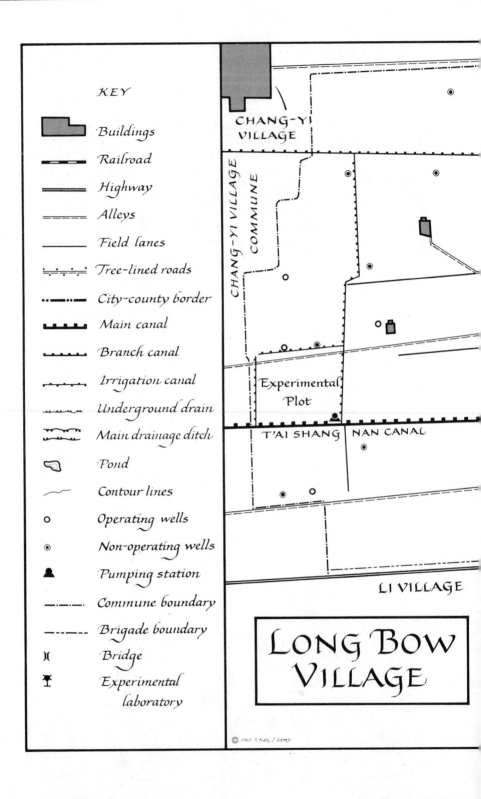

KEY

Buildings

Railroad

Highway

Alleys

Field lanes

Tree-lined roads

City-county border

Main canal

Branch canal

Irrigation canal

Underground drain

Main drainage ditch

Pond

Contour lines

o Operating wells

⊙ Non-operating wells

▲ Pumping station

Commune boundary

Brigade boundary

)(Bridge

⚲ Experimental laboratory

CHANG-YI VILLAGE

CHANG-YI VILLAGE COMMUNE

Experimental Plot

T'AI SHANG NAN CANAL

LI VILLAGE

LONG BOW VILLAGE

© 1983 · J. Kari, J. Kemp

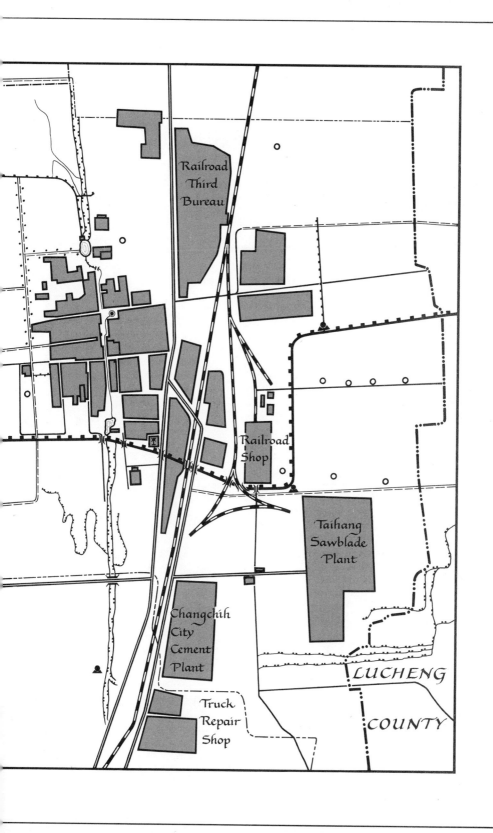

Contents

A villager touches up one of the characters that spell out the name of Long Bow on a building along the main road past the town.

Opposite page: An old Catholic grandmother, dressed in her finest winter clothes, beams at a grandchild in her family courtyard. This lady still has bound feet.

A survivor of Japan's war with China, in a peaceful moment with a village child.

This little boy is doing his best to fill a bucket of water, which probably weighs more than he does.

Opposite page: Although there are spigots in Long Bow for drinking water, the villagers use a trench that runs down Main Street for washing. The water is runoff from a nearby hill.

The beautiful handsewn and embroidered hat worn by this child illustrates the enormous pride the Chinese take in their children.

Elementary-school children reciting lessons in a village classroom. They hold their hands behind their backs as a sign of respect for the teacher.

Children on their way to school. Sometimes small groups of children get together and march in step on their way to school.

A bride is prepared for her wedding.

A grandmother feeding her grandchild. The chickens are picking up the scraps.

A woman spinning thread in her courtyard while her granddaughter looks on. Clothmaking is a rare craft in today's Long Bow because manufactured cloth is cheap and readily available.

Children playing with a homemade "balloon." The red banner on the wall is a certificate for outstanding work issued by the commune.

Opposite page: A young girl feeds noodles to a friend at a "one-month-old" birthday party. The pants the little boy is wearing are common throughout China.

An elderly lady at home. Her feet, bound as a girl, have been unbound and are only half normal size.

A funeral procession in which the mourners wear traditional white robes.

A woman preparing saw handles for saws to be exported to Tanzania.

Worker welding the frame of a corn drier designed by the brigade chairman.

Shaping bricks with a wooden plank before they are baked in a kiln.

Two stilt dancers made up to perform in a satirical skit about the deposed Gang of Four. One *(at top)* represents Chiang Ch'ing (widow of Mao Tse-Tung). Another *(below)* represents Chang Ch'un-ch'iao, the leading ideologist of the clique.

Banned for almost ten years during the Chinese Cultural Revolution, the ancient art of stilt dancing has now been revived. From left to right they represent: Wang Hung-wen—he carries a hatchet to signify his ruthlessness; Chiang Ch'ing (Mao's widow)—she holds a deck of cards to imply a decadent life-style; Chang Ch'un-ch'iao—the fan is an old Chinese symbol of cunning and deceitfulness; Yao Wen-yuan—the brush symbolizes his domination of the propaganda apparatus during the Cultural Revolution.

Girl demonstrates stilt walking to her young friend.

The leader of the Women's Association of Long Bow. She has one of the few marriages in China in which the husband cooks and serves the food while she entertains the guests.

A Long Bow woman and her father crush soy flour with one of the old grindstones still scattered around the village. Though cheap electric grinders are available, some villagers still prefer the taste of stone-ground flour.

Some villagers have become full-time fishermen recently, since the country built a large reservoir several miles from Long Bow. Before the reservoir was constructed, hardly anyone in this area had ever eaten fresh fish.

A woman threshing millet.

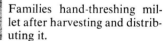

Families hand-threshing millet after harvesting and distributing it.

A bride, in traditional dress, wears the much-admired Western sunglasses.

A groom. One of the standard features of Long Bow weddings is a procession on horseback. In addition to this wedding, the couple will have a secular wedding, complete with posters of Mao Tse-tung in the background.

Introduction

SHANSI, LAND OF THE OXHIDE LANTERNS

*Door after door, gate after gate, mountains on the out-
side, mountains on the inside.*

Old Shansi proverb

In ancient times it was said, "He who holds the Shangtang [Shansi's south-
eastern plateau] holds the world." Shansi Province, fortresslike and impreg-
nable behind its mountain walls, has always been easy to defend and hard
to conquer. To fight one's way up through the many-tiered ridges and
towering peaks to dominate their heights is all but impossible, but to drive
down out of them and raid the plain below is a routine exercise in military
prowess. The strategic advantage thus offered by Shansi's mountain massif
has attracted empire builders throughout the ages.

With a rich central valley producing surplus grain, with loess badlands
on all sides supplying an endless stream of conscripts, with the bedrock
underfoot yielding coal, iron ore and precious metals, Shansi has been both
a tempting prize and a formidable redoubt. More than one conqueror,
content to let the world fend for itself, has tried to turn this mountain
fastness into an independent kingdom.

Independent or not, Shansi displays the most regular outline of any
Chinese province. With two sides parallel and two ends that slope away to
the southwest at roughly the same angle, it forms a parallelogram. This
shape is dictated by the mountain ranges that run from north to south, side
by side, ridge upon ridge, in unbroken succession from the edge of the
coastal plain in the east to the great gorge of the Yellow River in the west.

The whole scheme is rather like that formed by the Appalachian chain
in the eastern United States, where the ridges, starting in the Poconos of
northern New Jersey, sweep in one great arc westward into Pennsylvania
and then south through Maryland, Virginia and the Carolinas to Georgia.
Following this same grand design the mountains of North China, rising out
of the sea at Shanhaikuan, sweep westward around Peking, then southward
all the way to Honan. South and east of this arc lie lowlands that resemble
those of the Atlantic Seaboard, while to the north and west multiple ranges
back each other up just as they do across Pennsylvania and all the highlands
of Appalachia.

But if the geography of the mountains is similar, the mountains them-selves are not. The mountain peaks of Shansi, at least those of the eastern ranges known as the Taihang, are unlike most peaks seen elsewhere in the world. They tower like medieval fortresses. Sheer cliffs at the base rise to brush-covered shelves that generate sheer cliffs once more so that the whole mass thrusts skyward in a series of giant steps, like a set-back wedding cake scaled for the gods. Whereas most mountains slope gently at the bottom and grow steeper as they ascend—a form universal in the Appalachians—Tai-hang peaks rise perpendicularly, tier on tier, to domelike summits that often appear to be more massive than the foundations that uphold them. This top-heaviness gives them an extraordinary, otherworld appearance more suited to the moon or Mars than to earth.

The mountain wall that divides Shansi from Hopei rises out of the plain with the same starkness that marks not the Appalachians but the Rockies west of Denver. In China, however, the contrast between plain and moun-tain is more striking than in Colorado because there is no continental slope rising in steady undulation for hundreds of miles to reach mile-high alti-tudes before the rock peaks loom suddenly to twice that height. In North China the great alluvial plain barely rises above sea level as it approaches the mountain escarpment, that mighty fortress of rock that thrusts skyward to heights of nine or even ten thousand feet, creating a barrier more formi-dable than anything to be encountered in the Rockies.

On the west side of that barrier, running almost its entire length, lies Shansi, a province that can be reached only by seeking out one of the rare gaps in the line of cliffs and peaks that guard the border. These cliffs and peaks are actually the front parapets of a tableland that is far less rugged than its outlying defenses. Threading their way through awesome canyons, a few access roads climb steadily up out of the mountains into an elevated world where mile-high peaks shrink to mere foothills when measured from their origins in the plateau around them.

Halfway across the province the tableland breaks up and one descends, through awesome canyons once more, into the valley of the Fen, a river that divides lower Shansi into more or less equal parts. The Fen flows southwest-ward through a rich, agricultural valley that ends in the inaccessible gorges of the Yellow River. West of the Fen lie the Luliang Mountains, a set of ranges higher and wilder than the Taihang in the east. The Fen River valley thus forms a thin ribbon of fertility twisting through a desert of rock that would be virtually uninhabitable if it were not for the blanket of loess that now covers large sections of it. (Loess is windblown soil from the deserts of central Asia that has been deposited over the centuries in layers that vary in thickness from a few inches to several hundred feet. It produces fine crops whenever enough rain falls to germinate seeds and nurse seedlings to matu-rity.)

Taiyuan, the capital of the province, lies on the upper reaches of the Fen surrounded by irrigated ricelands, orchards and vineyards on the mountain slopes, with enormous seams of coal underground. In Shansi all roads lead to Taiyuan, but the roads that radiate out of Taiyuan in every direction lead nowhere. Downriver the Yellow River gorges block access to the highlands of Shensi; upriver the peaks of the Luya, Wutai and Meito mountains cut off Mongolia. No matter what direction one takes, only by traversing numerous passes can one finally come out into thickly settled, civilized regions.

The most recent aspirant to an independent kingdom in Shansi was the warlord Yen, whose given name, Hsi-shan, sounds like a palindrome of *Shansi,* but actually means "tin mountain." He ruled the province for thirty-eight years, defying first Yuan Shih-kai, then Chiang Kai-shek and finally the Japanese. When the Japanese drove him out of Taiyuan he maintained jurisdiction over several southern counties, then returned as conquering hero after the surrender of the invaders. But the peasant warriors of the People's Liberation Army, backed up by the landless, the landpoor, and the independent smallholders of the loesslands, used Shansi's mountains to greater advantage than any warlord could, and by 1949 they were strong enough to smash old Yen. He fled to Taiwan, taking with him several planeloads of gold bars. The planes flew right over Chihsien, Hopei, where I was ploughing up wasteland with the students of the first Liberated Areas Tractor Training Class. As the students watched the planes go, happy to see the last of Yen but angry that he was able to make off with so much of the region's wealth, they shook their fists at the sky.

Yen Hsi-shan left Shansi in the hands of the "old hundred names," the poor-and-middle peasants, the miners and the railroad workers, who were led by the Communist Party and its regional strategist, Po Yi-po. Commissar Po, according to his detractors, then proceeded to fashion Shansi into an independent kingdom of his own!

Independent kingdoms provide fertile ground for cultural innovation. Behind their mountain walls the people of Shansi have created a life-style as original, as intriguing and, some say, as perverse as the terrain that dominates it.

Party Secretary Po Yi-po told Jack Belden, "The mountain people . . . are known as Cow Skin [Oxhide] Lanterns, meaning that outside they are dark but inside, bright. For the past two thousand years, their chief characteristics have been frugality, diligence and a capacity to bear hardship. From their outside appearance, they are not bold, but soft, shrinking and timid. In the past, the rest of China has looked down on them, contemptuously calling them 'Old West.'

"In reality, however, these people are far from timid. They are skillful in business and exceptionally far sighted. They do not make plans for one year or two years, but for their whole lives."*

The way these Oxhide Lanterns build houses reflects their long-term outlook. They build bigger, better, longer-lasting homes than people elsewhere and think nothing of saving their whole lives through to repair the house they live in or finally to build a new one. "If Hopei people have an extra coin they spend it on something to eat. If Shansi people have an extra coin they save it for a new house," so goes the old folk saying. And experience bears it out. Shansi people would not keep pigs in the low adobe

*Jack Belden, *China Shakes the World* (New York: Harper & Brothers, 1949), p. 49.

huts that many Hopei people live in. Terrain, of course, is decisive here. Floods constantly menace the Hopei plain, submerging, even washing away, whatever structures people build. In the mountains a stone set on another stone remains in place.

Many Shansi homes rise a story and a half. The "half" consists of a loft where one can stand erect. In some villages peasants have always lived in two-storied stone structures that only landlords could hope to own elsewhere. In Hsiyang County, taking their lead from Tachai Brigade, peasants now build vaulted cave homes out of hand-cut granite blocks. When they set these caves, tier on tier, on top of a ridge or mountain summit, the completed edifice resembles some modern-day acropolis, as beautiful as it is enduring. When we asked the builders how long they thought these linked and layered vaults would last they said, "2,000 years." I saw no reason why they should not last 10,000.

Loving their houses, Shansi people prefer to stay home, a preference which, when put into practice, accentuates isolation and fosters eccentricity. Some Shansi customs strike one as bizarre; others are downright dangerous. According to Chou En-lai, by 1971 Shansi alone, of the eighteen provinces in China proper, failed to reach twenty million inhabitants. This was due primarily to methods of childbirth that took the lives of both mothers and newborn children. Since then medical teams have been trying to persuade the women of the hill counties that sitting upright to give birth and fasting on broth for ten days afterward invite disaster.

Even in the ways food is prepared, one notes eccentricity coupled with danger. Shansi people subsist for the most part on millet and ground corn; nevertheless, their homeland is known as noodle country. They prefer noodles, especially for feast days, and have devised at least 100 different ways to produce them. One of these, often talked about but seldom demonstrated, is to place a large hunk of dough on top of one's head and slice chips off it with a cleaver in such a way that the chips fall into boiling water. *La mien,* drawn noodles, require equally spectacular techniques. The cook holds the dough like a piece of rope between his hands. He then throws the center of the rope at the floor with lightning speed. Just before the loop of dough hits the dirt, he crosses his hands, causing the two sides to wind up on themselves to form a single rope again. This throwing and twisting kneads the dough into proper shape to be drawn—that is, pulled out, doubled back, pulled out and doubled back again until it forms long strands that can be cut loose and dropped into a waiting pot.

When Shansi people tire of noodles, they can choose among many forms of wheat cakes, the most spectacular being *shuai ping,* or thrown cakes. To form these, the cook flops a small pat of kneaded dough back and forth through the air with a tapered wooden dowel until it is as large and thin as an Italian pizza, whereupon he slaps it onto a sizzling griddle, then serves it with donkey meat.

No one in Shansi eats noodles, wheat cakes, donkey meat or anything else without adding a generous dollop of vinegar, a vinegar that is as dark and thick as crankcase oil and smells like molding hay. Such vinegar cannot be obtained anywhere else in China. When Shansi people travel they take a bottle of vinegar along and wind up their journey when they have used all the contents. They consider the aroma of native vinegar to be irresistible. According to folklore, if a Shansi woman is suffering through a difficult delivery, one has only to uncork a vinegar bottle nearby. The child will come out forthwith.

The soldiers of Warlord Yen Hsi-shan's provincial armies won notoriety for the three things they carried at their waists—hand grenades, cartridge belts and vinegar bottles. Thus outfitted they were formidable on the battlefield. Deprive them of vinegar and their bullets missed their targets, their hand grenades fell short, and the desertion rate rose to catastrophic proportions.

Because in China to "eat vinegar" means to be cuckolded, Shansi people suffer endless teasing. This has had no noticeable effect on their eating habits, however, nor is there any evidence to prove that Shansi wives are less faithful than wives elsewhere.

Going your own way in glorious isolation is called "taking a stand on the mountaintop." Here lies a whole province committed to mountaintopism!

"High mountains are the home of demons, steep peaks the lair of fiends." No one should be surprised, then, if the worst rogues of Shansi refuse to yield pride of place to evildoers elsewhere. For folly and depravity who can surpass the revolutionary bandit Yang Ch'eng-hsiao, who dallied with concubines while hit squads cut down his rivals, or that most political of officers, Chief of Staff Li Ying-k'uei, who entertained guests at Ping-Pong while he fanned up factionalism with false charges against his rivals?

In ancient times the notorious Tsao Tsao fought in Shansi. He was the most talented and successful of the many adventurous condottieri who led their bands of mercenaries in dismembering the Han empire. According to Balazs they transformed it in one generation from a powerful, unitary state into something close to a vast cemetery. "A vile bandit in times of peace, a heroic leader in a world of turmoil," wrote the chronicler of the Hou-Han book.*

In the days of the Republic there was H. H. Kung, the banker from Shansi's capital, Taiyuan, who boasted descent directly from Confucius and fancied himself the wealthiest man in all China. During World War II his wife cornered the market on penicillin and made a fortune hoarding the drug while uncounted soldiers died of septicemia.

Legend has it that high mountains also produce good spirits like Princess Shyblush and Crown Prince Natha, two immortals who helped the Monkey King cross the Himalayas so long ago. Truly the best of Shansi is exemplary beyond compare. Citizens of Weitsutsai, not far from Long Bow, claim that martyred hero Pi Kan lies buried on their soil. More than a thousand years before Christ this faithful court minister angered the Shang emperor with forthright criticism of his sovereign's rapacious social policy. "The hearts of sages," Emperor Chou Wang said, "are supposed to have seven orifices.

*Etienne Balazs, *Chinese Civilization and Bureaucracy*, trans. H. M. Wright, ed. Arthur Wright (New Haven: Yale University Press, 1964).

Let's see how your heart measures up." With that he ordered his guards to cut open Pi Kan's chest. The chronicle fails to state how many orifices he found on the slain man's vital organ.

In 1947 at Yunchohsi Village, Wenshui County, the brave peasant girl Liu Hu-lan suffered more conventional martyrdom. She refused to give information about her comrades in the Liberation underground. The troops of Yen Hsi-shan led her before a fodder chopping knife in the middle of the village square where the corpses of two comrades already lay dismembered in pools of half-dried blood.

"Don't you regret having lived only to the age of fifteen?" asked her executioner.

"I've lived fifteen years," said Liu Hu-lan. "If you kill me, in another fifteen years I'll be as old again as I am now."

One stroke of the knife sufficed to chop off her head.

For comic relief Shansi provides petty scoundrels like Shen Liu-chin (Whiskers Shen), of Long Bow, who never did an honest day's work in his life. Blessed with an analytic mind, he could sniff out the weak link in any social arrangement and turn it to his advantage. Where cadres had prestige he posed as a cadre; where veterans had prestige he posed as a veteran; where soldiers had prestige he posed as a soldier and thus claimed for himself many a free ride, many a free meal, an occasional gullible maiden, and every once in a while a well-deserved beating.

In Shansi, during the Cultural Revolution, political confrontation degenerated into armed struggle earlier than elsewhere in China, and armed struggle, in the form of festering civil war, lasted longer there than elsewhere. The battle of Changchih broke out in December, 1967, and did not come to a halt until March, 1968. The battle of Chieh-hsiu County broke out in midsummer, 1969, and did not wind down until early 1970. Violence, once unleashed, burst all bounds and the wounds that factionalists inflicted on each other still smart.

One image burned into my mind by local storytellers is that of the peasant activist Ch'en Yung-kuei, shouting into the darkness from the ramparts of P'ingyao's ancient wall.

Some local leaders, worried about Ch'en's safety, said, "We'll find a place for you to hide."

But Ch'en said, "I won't take the dog's road. I'll take the broad highway."

So he went right up to the highest point of the wall and called out, "I was sent by the Central Committee to stop all this fighting. Whoever opposes should shoot this way. Shoot here where you hear my voice!"

The response: silence.

It took three brigades of Liberation Army troops to rescue Ch'en from P'ingyao.

The political extremes indigenous to Shansi have a tendency to rub off on outsiders assigned to work there. It would be hard to find a quarrel that outdid in bitterness the one between Liu Ke-p'ing, the venerable Moslem from Hopei, and Chang Er-ch'ing, the model Long March commander from Peking's Headquarters Guard. Entrusted with the task of uniting Shansi, they fell to quarreling over who would be top man. Each raised an army against the other and refused to make peace even when confronted by a series of ultimata from Peking. In the end disillusioned colleagues forced both of them out of the province in disgrace.

In writing about Shansi it is hard to avoid exaggeration. But exaggeration, after all, contains a core of truth. Shansi is a land rich in variety, contrast and conflict. These give the province a special measure of vitality, a lively creative impulse, a disregard for precedent—qualities that deserve to endure.

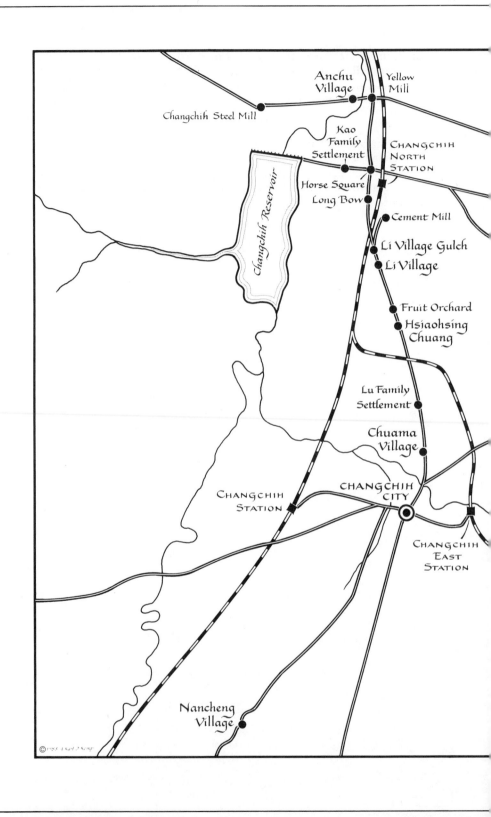

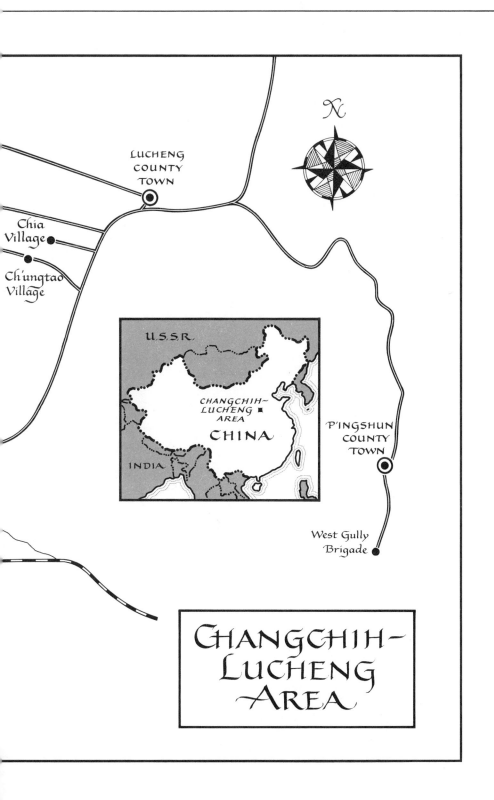

LUCHENG
COUNTY
TOWN

Chia
Village

Ch'ungtao
Village

N

U.S.S.R.

CHANGCHIH~
LUCHENG
AREA

CHINA

INDIA

P'INGSHUN
COUNTY
TOWN

West Gully
Brigade

CHANGCHIH~
LUCHENG
AREA

Volume

One

TRANSITION
TO SOCIALISM

The serious problem is the education of the peasantry. The peasant economy is scattered, and the
socialization of agriculture . . . will require a long
time and painstaking work. Without socialization of
agriculture, there can be no complete, consolidated
socialism.

Mao Tse-tung, June 30, 1949

Part 1

RETURN

I know you want to visit Long Bow village, but I don't know if it can be arranged. You see, we don't know which class holds power down there.

Chou En-lai

RETURN TO THE SHANGTANG

 For seven years prior to 1971 the weather over Southeast Shansi remained abnormally dry. People remembered 1965 and 1970 for searing droughts that stunted crops throughout the mountains and sent thousands of people south into Honan to buy dried sweet potatoes. In the years between some rain did fall but rarely enough to make up for the long deficiency and never more than the parched soil could absorb. As one arid summer followed another, the peasants who lived in the deep valleys of the Taihang range began to reclaim land in the gullies and the river bottoms. They first put into place massive stone dikes, dragons' tails of boulders, to hold the meager but erratic runoff on a predetermined course. Then they carried in soil by mulecart, pushcart and carrying pole and spread it out behind the dikes to a depth of two feet or more. They scraped this soil from the hills wherever a small pocket could be found and concentrated it in the gullies and on the valley floors to create the first large fields that many communities had ever known. Millions of man-days went into this effort without any counting of costs. The newly created land—level, well drained and easy to irrigate—produced excellent crops. People shrank from no sacrifice that could help lay foundations for high, stable yields to come.

P'ingshun County led the way. Peasants there built 5,000 acres of new land. Their labor converted a tributary of the Chang River that had been nothing but a wasteland of boulders into a gardenlike giant staircase of corn, sorghum, soybeans and squash, interspersed here and there with small orchards of apple trees where the fruit grew larger than a pair of clenched fists. At several places in the valley hand labor threw up high dams that blocked the main river. The dams formed deep, green lakes where mist hung like a veil between the hills at dawn and the sunlight at noon set ripples shimmering.

The city of Changchih, having taken over parts of Lucheng County for industrial development, had organized the construction of a huge dam on the main branch of the Chang River. It stretched more than a mile across the valley and created a lake six miles long that, when seen from a distance, shone blue like the sea. When the wind blew out of the west it stirred up waves more than two feet high. Such a lake had never been dreamed of in the mountain regions. Raised without water skills, local peasants had to send to Kiangsu for low-country men who could stock it with fingerlings, then catch the fish that grew.

In the course of thirteen seasons this lake never filled its artificial basin. During the seven dry years the water level shrank back sharply from the three-quarter mark that had been reached earlier. Recovery was so slow that engineers discounted the possibility of flood and took their time about building a secure spillway through the bedrock at the east end of the dam. By 1971 they had completed only half of the vital emergency overflow system.

On August 15, 1971, the skies over Southeast Shansi suddenly reversed themselves. A storm of unprecedented ferocity dropped from three to six inches of water over vast areas in a matter of hours. Nobody expected the inundation; nobody had prepared for it. Least prepared of all were the Shansi provincial cadres assigned to accompany me back to Long Bow. By coincidence August 15 was the day they chose for me, my wife, Joanne, and my daughter Carma to drive in a convoy of jeeps south out of Taiyuan and up through the mountains to the heart of the Shangtang Plateau that I had left, traveling eastward on foot and by mulecart, twenty-three years before.

Our route lay through Wuhsiang, where, much to our delight, a great rural fair dominated the county seat. Thousands of peasants from outlying districts had left home that morning in ordinary summer clothing and had walked to town to buy, sell, see, be seen and celebrate the completion of the summer harvest. The weather was everything any fairgoer could wish for —bright, clear, warm, even hot, with a dazzling sun in an azure sky. When a few clouds drifted in around noon some pessimists predicted showers, but even they made no move to speed up final purchases. If a few drops did fall the sun would soon dry things out again.

By two o'clock most of the back-country visitors had started on a lei-surely trek homeward, their progress slowed by the weight of everything they had bought at the fair and by the fact that almost all the roads leading out of Wuhsiang ran uphill. As we pulled out of the local guesthouse, with the driver of our jeep pressing frantically on his horn button to clear a path through the departing multitudes, the sky turned dark and rain began to fall. Those peasants who could reach nearby trees took shelter under them. Those who could find no trees threw whatever outer garments they had over their heads and continued to climb. For a minute or two the rain fell fast and hard, then eased off. The sun found a hole in the clouds and relit the whole valley with glowing, exuberant light. It was a moment of false prom-ise followed by disaster. Suddenly the clouds closed in again, black and menacing, a strong wind came up, and the rain returned in earnest. Not drops, but sheets of water enveloped the mountainside, each sheet following the one ahead as if driven by the one behind. The surface of the road disintegrated quickly, causing our jeep to lurch toward a ditch that already overflowed with mud-laden water. The driver, jerking the wheel, almost hit a peasant who had fallen down in the mud. The people under the trees soon abandoned them as useless and began to rejoin that long procession of those who had never stopped walking. Together they almost blocked the right of way. By now most of these pedestrians had removed their cloth shoes and were holding them over their heads for protection. But shoes were no more effective than trees at warding off water. The rain quickly soaked through summer clothes and all the precious purchases made at the fair.

We reached the height of land south of Wuhsiang just as the first contingents of this bedraggled army "turned the mountain" and started down the other side. As we pulled ahead onto an empty road at last, all the dry gullies, small creeks and meandering watercourses of the drought years transformed themselves into raging torrents, but torrents so clogged with silt that they looked and behaved more like flowing oil than water. Waves, breaking on the ledges in their path, gurgled rather than hissed, releasing dark globules of slime instead of white spray. At every sharp bend in the channel this heavy slurry piled up against the outside bank in such a manner that its midstream crest rose above the level of the road we were traveling. Over and over again we had to look up rather than down at the flood. It was a fearful sight. The silt gave the current a power, a ferocity, a lethal cutting edge that surpassed anything I had ever experienced, even the terrible New England flood and hurricane of 1938. Whole sections of road disappeared behind us. Bridges on side streams collapsed as we watched. Mud-laden currents swept pigs, chickens, sheep, stacks of straw and waterlogged manure piles into midstream and propelled them toward the valley at awesome speeds.

As we approached the lowlands, only slightly ahead of the crest of the flood, signs of impending disaster multiplied. Fields, village streets and family courtyards already lay awash in menacing brown liquid. All traffic came to a halt behind an ancient arched bridge that now dammed instead of spanned the stream that flowed beneath it. With a huge lake forming on the upstream side, the raging slurry pressed against the bridge with such pressure that the dark fluid shot out from below like a jet from a giant hose. Local authorities, on hand to direct traffic, gave the bridge, after a life-span of centuries, no more than half an hour to stand. We left our vehicle, dashed across on foot, then waited anxiously while jeep drivers risked their lives behind steering wheels to join us.

Over the next range of hills the highway itself plunged into water that was placid in some places, swift-running in others, but still shallow enough to drive through. Later, as we approached the great coal mines at Wuyang, we found the whole valley blocked by the lake created by a railroad embankment that had been designed with only one small culvert at its midpoint. Our route ran into this lake at a place where rows of corn, standing ten feet tall, disappeared under water, tassels and all. To our right, as we came to a halt, the adobe walls of a sheep pen collapsed. The frightened sheep lunged for higher ground, then sniffed gingerly at the already bloating body of one of their number that had drowned a short while before. Behind us on the highway trucks, mulecarts, jeeps and buses assembling miraculously out of nowhere came to a halt, creating a line of vehicles that stretched over the hill and out of sight.

And still the rain poured down.

By four o'clock the volume of the cloudburst declined slightly, then faded stage by stage. Toward evening the level of the lake in front of us dropped sufficiently to enable us to pass through without going under or floating away. It was almost dark when we reached the Changchih plain. A line of low hills stirred some chords of memory as we sped southward in the gathering gloom, but the asphalt highway, tree-lined and ditch-drained, gave no further hint as to where we might be. It wasn't until we reached the imposing, three-storied guesthouse in the middle of a completely reconstructed, unfamiliar Changchih City that I was told we had already driven right past Long Bow village.

"Didn't you see it?"

"No, nothing at all . . . only those hills. Were they the hills at Li Village Gulch?"

"Yes."

"I'll be damned!"

Thus it was that I returned to Southeast Shansi in the midst of the worst natural disaster to plague the region in many decades. The destruction wreaked by the storm overwhelmed the population. Half the new land in P'ingshun County had disappeared in the course of a few minutes, and with that soil, so laboriously set in place over many years, had gone the finest crops in living memory. Losses elsewhere mounted in proportion. Laboring people in the high valleys of half a dozen counties walked outdoors the next day in tears, as stunned and depressed as the peasants of Long Bow had been after the great hailstorm of 1948.

For those in the highlands the worst dangers, at least, had passed. All that remained was to survey the damage, weep, and plan a recovery. For the peasants in the lowlands the dangers went on building. Lowland waters were rising and at the great Changchih Reservoir cracks had begun to appear on the face of the dam. The concrete tower, the sluice gates and the conduit under the dam that had been designed for ordinary overflow proved grossly inadequate to cope with the flood that kept pouring down from the hills. Already water lapped at the crest of the small coffer dam that had been built at the upper end of the half-completed spillway. This coffer dam was leaking badly, and threatened to burst at any moment. If either dam gave way the consequence would be disastrous all the way to Tientsin, 500 miles away on the shores of the Yellow Sea, for that was the direction in which the Chang River flowed. Any flood in the mountains threatened the whole northern section of the great North China Plain.

Cracks in the face of the big dam and leaks penetrating the body of the little one at a time when the flood waters were still rising, created a crisis for all the villages and towns downstream. It also created a crisis for the administrative offices upstream in Changchih City Hall and in the headquarters of the regional government. Leading cadres took it for granted that they would get no sleep that night or for many nights thereafter. They had to mobilize the army, the militia and rotating platoons of ordinary peasants to reinforce the big dam, raise the level of the little dam and open, if possible, some channel in the neglected spillway so that it could handle an explosion of water.

As if this were not trouble enough for the officials to face, I presented them with a disturbing request: I wanted to walk to Long Bow village. Somehow, I had always imagined that if and when I returned to the village it would be on foot as I had first come to it, as I had returned to it so many times in the past, and as I had finally left it in August, 1948. I wanted to proceed slowly, walk up the road and take in the familiar sights, sounds and smells of the Shansi countryside. Thus tempered I would feel ready to enter Long Bow village itself.

Regional leaders did not welcome my suggestion. In fact, they responded to it with alarm. Trying to conceal their acute misgivings, they presented me with a series of arguments against walking. The road to Long Bow, they said, was no longer a dirt track but a heavily traveled, blacktop highway, both dangerous and boring to traverse on foot. We had already traveled down it on our way to the city, what could possibly be gained by walking back up the same route? Consider also, they added, the twelve-mile distance. We would be overtired, overheated, hungry and thirsty by the time we reached the village. After wasting half a precious day walking we would waste half of another precious day recuperating. What possible benefit could there be in that? Why not accept a pleasant ride in a new Peking-made jeep?

But I was adamant. The closer I came to the village the more important it seemed to me to plant two feet firmly on the ground and walk there step by step. Commander Li Ying-k'uei, the squint-eyed, gnomelike, witty Cantonese who was vice-chairman of the regional government and the man directly responsible for our visit, finally agreed.

"All right, you can walk! What time do you want to start out?"

"Eight o'clock," I said.

At eight the next morning I, my wife and my daughter walked out onto the street. Our appearance caused a public commotion as overwhelming as it was sudden. As soon as we emerged from the guesthouse gate children came running from near and far. Behind them came men, women, women carrying children, men carrying children, children carrying children, workers on foot, workers on bicycles, soldiers, militiamen, peddlers, students. Soon the street, both behind and in front of us, filled up with cheerful, animated, curious humanity. By the time we reached the main north-south thoroughfare it became apparent that the whole population of Changchih had been alerted to the fact that the big-nosed Americans had walked out in broad daylight. The main street, like the side street we emerged from, soon filled with people, bicycles, handcarts, mulecarts. Here and there a few cars and trucks merged with the tide. People on bicycles ran into each other as they strained to catch a glimpse of us over the heads in the crowd. Little children tripped, fell down, and were almost trampled as their elders rushed for a clearer view. Truckdrivers, unable to move either forward or backward, blew their horns in annoyance. But when they discovered that American visitors had caused the traffic jam on the street, they jumped out of their trucks, abandoned them wholesale, and joined the delighted crowds that swept northward up the avenue around us.

So intense was the curiosity, so tumultuous the welcome, and so dense the crowd that we could not help worrying. We were disrupting the work of the whole city, we were tying up traffic, we were causing accidents, maybe even injuries. I began to wonder if it had not indeed been foolish to insist on walking to Long Bow. This mass turnout had probably been anticipated by Commander Li and other regional leaders. They no doubt had feared for our safety in the crush and also for law and order in the city. But they had been too polite to talk about it. They had swallowed their objections and bowed to our arrogant insistence.

Once we were out on the main street it was too late for second thoughts. We could do nothing but stride boldly forward and hope for the best. In the meantime, as the crowds grew to unmanageable proportions, the city police mobilized all available manpower, including worker and student deputies, in an effort to maintain some semblance of order. We passed more than one young woman, red armband in place to signify emergency police power, urging the young people packed around her to go back, to return to work, to let the foreigners proceed in peace. But such efforts had no visible effect at all. If anything, they slowed the forward movement of the crowd and escalated the crisis.

The offices of the regional Revolutionary Committee and Regional Communist Party occupied ground at the northern end of the avenue. Most of the spectators assumed that we were walking from the guesthouse to one or another of these important power centers. They were determined to walk with us, relishing every minute of our extraordinary but brief public appearance. When we failed to turn in at either gate, but strode on at a rapid pace, some of the crowd began to fall away. By the time we reached the northern limits of the city only a few thousand young people still kept up with us. In the course of the next mile, when it became clear that we were going to walk right out into the countryside, most of these last-ditch enthusiasts also fell away. Attrition finally reduced our group to three Americans and four Chinese hosts. For the first time we had the road more or less to ourselves.

I had been so busy making my way through the crowds, worrying about the near riot we were causing, and wondering if the congestion would ever thin out, that I hardly had time to look at Changchih City. I caught only fleeting glimpses of imposing three- and four-story buildings facing tree-lined avenues that obliterated the past. The ancient wall, a formidable brick-faced fortification that had always been the most prominent feature of the town, enclosing it completely, seemed to have disappeared without a trace. The Changchih I had known so well in 1948, that ruined county seat with its dilapidated yamen, its huddled clusters of homes and its abandoned temples, scattered and all but lost in brick-strewn, pockmarked, empty space, was now a thriving complex of urban congestion with all the paved roads, modern buildings and public utilities typical of such great cities as Peking. If Peking, to the Western visitor, seemed backward and still rural in spirit, here was one of the reasons. The wealth of new China, instead of flowing into a few large cities, stimulating them to abnormal, mushroomlike growth, was spreading more or less evenly over the whole country. County towns and regional centers could already boast almost every facility, service and convenience that the advanced centers had long taken pride in. What slowed the growth of Peking clearly sped the growth of Changchih.

If Changchih seemed unfamiliar, the countryside that we walked into on leaving the city proved even more so. I saw almost nothing that I could recognize. Instead of the dirt track that I had followed so often in the past, we found a modern two-lane highway paved with asphalt. The plain, remembered for its moonlike barrenness, was now ornamented by serried rows of trees that had been planted on both sides of the right of way. The canopy of leaves supported by the slim trunks almost met overhead. Other lines and groves of trees could be seen on either side of our route. Each marked some new construction. On our left we passed several large factories, then on our right the imposing buildings of the regional Normal College. Farther on, on the right, we came abreast of the Changchih airfield, where several small planes took off, flew around and landed again in continuous rotation, as if their pilots were in training. Not far from the airfield we passed over a large irrigation canal, then crossed a well-maintained railroad track. A branch line splitting off from it ran into a freight depot where six-wheeled trucks loaded coal.

In revolutionary China one expected to see new construction—new factories, schools, highways, railroads, even an airport or two—but I hardly expected to find them all together here on the road to Long Bow. Nor did I expect to find half the population of each village en route waiting by the roadside to greet us as we passed. We no sooner left Changchih than word spread through the countryside that we were coming. The people in the villages on either side then made for the highway even in places where they had several miles to walk. Unlike the townspeople we had left behind, these rural sightseers were content to look and not to follow. After passing each cluster of animated, laughing peasants we found ourselves alone in the fields once more. Some people in almost every group recognized me and called out to their neighbors.

"There's Old Han."

"How he has aged!"

"Look, his hair is white."

"That's the one. I talked to him at the mutton soup stall."

Clearly, I still had many friends in the villages on the plain.

Meeting the people was one thing. Trying to adjust to the transformation of the area was another. Whatever adjustment I was able to make in the course of our triumphant progress northward did not really prepare me for what I saw on reaching the height of land at Li Village Gulch, where the highway, the railroad and the strung-out village itself all competed for space in a narrow ravine between Great Ridge Hill and Little Ridge Hill.

I could hardly contain my excitement as I climbed toward a spot on the flanks of Great Ridge Hill where neither trees nor tall summer crops obscured the view. I finally stepped out on a small terrace planted to millet from which the whole broad valley to the north could be seen. I stood and looked, and looked again, and saw nothing that I recognized.

During the many years I had been away, and especially during the years that I worked on the book *Fanshen,* I had constantly re-created Long Bow in my mind's eye, and that imagined village had come to have an existence of its own that was for me more real than the Long Bow that remained in China. What I expected to see when I looked down was a view that corresponded to the image in my head. I expected to see the whole of Long Bow stretched out on the flat plain like a map, with the tall, square tower of the

Catholic church, that abiding monument to foreign intervention, dominating the center and the gullylike main street splitting east from west. The polarization of the old village society had always been clearly revealed by its architecture. The adobe huts of the poor peasants and hired laborers with their roofs of mud and straw had always contrasted sharply with the high brick dwellings of the landlords and rich peasants with their roofs of tile. Before the land reform gentry families had occupied whole courtyards while poor peasants had bedded down in whatever tumbledown sections of walled enclosure they could find. Parts of these walls had fallen down and the paths of the poor had penetrated them at random in gross violation of the orthodox, north-south orientation so dear to the Confucian mind. In 1948, in spite of revolutionary reapportionment, all this could still be clearly seen.

But what I saw that day from the flank of Great Ridge Hill had no relation whatsoever to any remembered scene. Now all that met the eye where the village was supposed to lie was a forest of green trees. The tower of the Catholic church had vanished and there was no way to tell if the trees had grown so tall that they hid the tower or if, in fact, that imposing structure had been torn down. Trees also obscured whatever architectural contrasts might still remain. Their undifferentiated greenery could stand, perhaps, as a symbol of the social equalization that had been the primary thrust of the years of land reform, and of all the years that followed.

Equalization showed most strikingly in the fields around the woods. Long Bow land no longer exhibited that patchwork, postage-stamp fragmentation that had been typical of peasant farming since ancient times and had, if anything, been accentuated by a land reform that gave every family its share of scattered plots. Now, instead of countless small plots, each planted to a different crop in haphazard profusion, great fields of corn interplanted with beans alternated with equally great fields of millet, white potatoes or sweet potatoes.

This was an extraordinary change, a reversal of 4,000 years of history. It was a change that brought land use into line with the state of agricultural art in the Western world and set the stage for mechanization. It was a change that I had anticipated, counted on, and rejoiced over even before I confirmed it by coming here. But there was another change that I had not expected and was not prepared for, a change that dominated the view and made everything else, including the woods and the large fields, seem almost unimportant by comparison. That change was industrialization, an industrialization that had begun with transportation, then spread to every home and shop through electrification, and was now exploding in an open-ended drive for mine, mill and plant construction as crude, irreverent and vigorous as anything that had marked the industrial revolution in nineteenth-century Europe or America.

The highway we had been walking on all morning ran right past Long Bow's eastern edge. Beside it, running parallel, as far as the eye could see, was the railroad that came from Chengchow in Honan and would soon link through to Taiyuan the provincial capital, then on to Peking. Beside the railroad, just opposite Long Bow's east-west street, lay the main locomotive shop of the region with all the storied buildings, smoking stacks, water towers and spur tracks that such a shop required.

As if this were not disruption enough to an erstwhile peaceful scene, a huge cement mill dominated the land between the railroad shop and Great Ridge Hill. A vast chunk of the hill itself had been cut away to supply limestone to the mill. On the leaves of corn and beans nearby one could see a coating of rock dust, a by-product of crushers and kilns that ground and burned raw limestone twenty-four hours a day.

Looking up the railroad, past Changchih North Station, a new town in its own right, I could see in the distance the coal-fired power plant at Yellow Mill pouring black smoke on the wind, and to the northwest, across the swollen and still rising waters of the Changchih Reservoir, the dim outlines of the blast furnaces at Changchih Steel. Behind them on the hill that blocked the horizon more huge mill buildings and towering smokestacks marked the location of the coal mines at Shihkechieh and Wuchuang.

The shock of this galloping industrialization involuntarily brought to mind Blake's poem *Milton*:

> And did those feet in ancient time
>   Walk upon England's mountains green?
> And was the holy Lamb of God
>   On England's pleasant pastures seen?
>
> And did the Countenance Divine
>   Shine forth upon our clouded hills?
> And was Jerusalem builded here
>   Among these dark Satanic Mills?

What I hoped to find in Long Bow in 1971 was what I had left behind in 1948—an isolated, rural community where the social transformation brought on by revolution could be traced and understood as a microcosm of the social process in China as a whole. This time, of course, I hoped to study and understand not land reform but how a whole people had gone from individual to collective farming. Nevertheless, the requirements, in terms of an ideal community, were the same. Industrialization was something that had not entered my conception of the task. It now, quite clearly, threw all previous estimates into disorder.

On the Shangtang Plateau something much more complex than I had dreamed of was happening. I felt ill-prepared intellectually or emotionally to cope with it. The Long Bow world that I was returning to had been so drastically transformed as to seem, at the moment, quite alien. I felt keen disappointment, even resentment. But these feelings were followed, almost immediately, by surprise that I could feel such alienation, that I could ever slip into rejection of the variety, complexity, creativity of the real world. Long Bow village had never been typical. In the early forties the large Catholic minority, the Japanese occupation, the sudden Liberation, all had made it unique as a peasant community in North China. Why should it be any more typical today? Furthermore, what reason was there to believe that rural isolation typified modern China? Perhaps Long Bow represented a much more important and universal trend. The collision of the old with the new, the integration of industry with agriculture, the urbanization of the countryside—wasn't this the future direction of all China? Urbanization might make my work more complicated, but it could hardly make it less interesting or less significant.

As I climbed down from the terrace to rejoin my wife and daughter and our Chinese companions, I wondered if the village itself would seem as strange as its surroundings. Would there be anyone left whom I knew and who knew me? Would there be any common ground on which to renew our relationship after almost a quarter of a century?

Feeling like a modern-day Rip Van Winkle, I took a deep breath and walked down the mountain.

2

DO YOU
REMEMBER ME?

 I rejoined my companions on the road at the top of the pass and we started down the long, gentle slope toward Long Bow village. At a certain point the road veered sharply westward, crossed the railroad on a wooden bridge, then turned northward once more, leaving the steel tracks in a deep cut in the hill to our right. Since every step we took led downhill it didn't take long to draw near the village. As we did so we became aware of a crowd of people moving rapidly up the highway in our direction. We met head on and found ourselves immediately surrounded by familiar faces. A dozen hands reached out to take mine. Chang Hsin-fa,* Wang Wen-te, Hu Hsueh-chen, Chang Kuei-ts'ai,* Kuo Cheng-k'uan, Chang Ch'ün-hsi, Shih Ts'ai-yuan—almost the full roster of the village leadership of 1948 stood before us, alive, healthy and eager to welcome me back from across the sea.

I was amazed at how easily I recognized them. Some, like Hsin-fa, had hardly changed at all. He strode forward with characteristic military bearing, shaven head shining, handsome profile held high. Twenty-three years might have passed, but he was still a youthful and vigorous man, able to hold his own in the field or on a construction job. Cheng-k'uan likewise seemed unchanged. He had always seemed older, quieter, more pensive, more considerate than the others. Now those same qualities shone through as he looked me in the eye, held my hand and would not let go. Cheng-k'uan's own eyes carried a hint of sadness, of prolonged suffering. Could it have been caused by the chronic bronchitis that wracked his chest and interrupted his sleep at night? Or was it some reflection of the trouble he had been through in the Cultural Revolution? Of all the Long Bow leaders he was the most *lao shih* (genuine), a deeply honest, straightforward person who absorbed new things slowly but, once having decided on a course, never looked back.

Others had noticeably aged, among them Hu Hsueh-chen. Though she had never been a beauty, her broad face, set in a frame of jet-black, bobbed hair, had radiated health and strength. Now it expressed fatigue. She had

*The names are given here as they appear in *Fanshen*. Chang Hsin-fa is really P'ei Hsin-fa; Chang Kuei-ts'ai is really Chao Kuei-ts'ai.

allowed her short locks to grow out so that they could be gathered, folded back, and fastened at the nape of her neck with a comb in a style appropriate to a married countrywoman. This style accentuated an unexpected leanness in her face and added years to her appearance.

Chang Kuei-ts'ai had also aged quite shockingly. He had shrunk to a lean wisp of a man with his head thrust forward on a scrawny neck laced with tendons, a chin that receded to the vanishing point and upper teeth that stuck out in so bold a manner that they had become the most prominent feature of his face. He looked like a bantam rooster in molt. Kuei-ts'ai had been sick, very sick with stomach ulcers. At times he had not been able to eat at all. When he ate he spat blood. But he was tough, wiry and determined, still the master of his fate, and not too sick to serve as the secretary of the Communist Party Branch, a position that made him, after all these years, the leading person in the village.

We shook hands, we embraced, we laughed, we wiped away tears. Little children danced around us as they always had in Long Bow and soon hundreds of people whom I didn't know so well or had never known at all pushed in on us from every side. Then this rapidly expanding cluster of happy, chattering, excited people began to surge back down the highway and into the village. As it did so a young man of thirty strode up to me, put his palms before his face as if in prayer, then quickly slid his fingers into a position such that the middle fingers of each hand lay back to back and, standing out from his clasped palms, wiggled to and fro in the air as if they were on a single shank. Though this strange signal completely mystified most people nearby, I knew immediately that here was one of the "little devils" with whom I had played so much in 1948 when they were only six or seven years old. I had taught them all this finger trick and they had not forgotten it. Now the ability to perform this sleight of hand was a sure sign that the individual had been one of that little clique of children that had always gathered round me after meetings, played games that I took an active part in, brought their school slates for me to repair, or exchanged Chinese words for English.

During the next few weeks I was to meet five or six of these fully grown "little devils," some male, some female, and each time their finger trick, inducing an automatic countertrick from me, stimulated uproarious laughter in all who saw it. At this first encounter the laughter was most contagious and widespread. Though I had no idea who he was, I put my arm around the man and we walked down the street together to a point where the adobe roof of a shed came to within six feet of the ground.

"When I was little you put me up on this roof and I couldn't get down," he said.

Again uproarious laughter. People pressed in from all sides, recalling incidents from the days of the Liberation War and testing my memory for names and faces. This young man, it turned out, was now the village doctor, Chi San-chiang (Three Gingers Chi). His father, long dead, had been a successful practitioner of herbal medicine and a devout Catholic. His mother, still alive, greeted me with particular warmth, as if somehow my arrival from "Christian America" reestablished for her a link to a mother church that was still her most precious association.

Having entered the village from the east, we came finally to the main
north-south thoroughfare and walked up it to the right, toward the gate of
the old mission compound where, I had been told, we were to live. Since
these were the same quarters I had lived in so many years before, this was
to be, in every way, a homecoming. But looking up the street I couldn't tell
where the compound was. Things did not look the same. It did not take me
long to understand why. The whole tower of the church had been torn
down. The hall behind it, which had seemed so huge in the old days, had
already been matched by an even larger structure across the street, and the
trees growing everywhere topped even the tallest roofs. It was no longer
possible for any single building to dominate the street.

We had walked northward toward the mission compound only a few
paces when an old woman on bound feet stepped across the ditch that
flanked the road and placed herself squarely in front of me.

"Do you remember me?" she asked.

There she stood, arms akimbo, looking intently up into my face, her
mouth wide open to form an amused smile that fully revealed two gums bare
of teeth.

I looked and looked again. The toothless, wrinkled face, the thin gray hair
—who could this be? There was something about the thrust of her shoulders, pugnacious, bold. Of course, I thought, of course . . .

"You're Old Lady Wang!"

"Yes, Old Han," she said and grasped my hand firmly in both of hers.
"We've been waiting for you. We thought you'd never come. Back in April
when you arrived in China we saw your picture in the paper. We all said
you'd come here but it has been many months."

She looked at me quizzically, shook her head. "Old Han, you've aged.
Your hair is white. You've grown old. You've grown old!"

"Yes. I have grown old," I said. "But you, you're still young and
healthy!"

"I'm seventy-two," said Old Lady Wang proudly. "I've never been sick
a day in my life. I've never been to see a doctor. I've never taken any
medicine and I've never even had an injection since the day I was born! And
this is Jen-pao," she said, turning to introduce me to her son, a slight figure
of a man in his early forties who looked far from well. "He's a Communist.
He's a member of the brigade Party branch. Our new society, it's really
marvelous, really marvelous," she said and the marvel was that a son of hers
could aspire to be a member of the leading core of the community.

"I still work," she went on without a pause, even to catch her breath. "I
work 150 days each year in the fields and earn work points like anyone else."

We left Old Lady Wang standing beside her gate, the same gate that had
been hers ever since, as a famine refugee from Honan, she had arrived in
the village as the bought and paid-for bride of Old Man Wang.

We moved on up the street to the mission compound. This street, Long
Bow's main thoroughfare, no longer served as a gully down which the
summer torrents rushed after every rain. The villagers had filled it in with
two or three feet of cinders from the fireboxes of the locomotives at the
railroad shop. They had thus transformed it into a good, all-weather road,

crowned and well drained by deep ditches cut on either side. They had likewise filled in the two small streets that led eastward to the highway. Since the ground to the west was slightly higher and less subject to flooding, this cindering and ditching had pulled the whole village out of the mud. Peasants had done the job in the spring of 1971, only a few months before we came, effecting a striking improvement that was particularly important in the aftermath of the storm of the day before. If they had not rebuilt the village streets, we would have been walking in water.

Construction crews hired by the region had vastly expanded the mission compound which we then entered, accompanied only by cadres. The huge crowds remained in the street behind us. The crews had added row on row of new structures on the east side. These included a large meeting hall, built to house first a middle school run by the regional government and then a medical school attached to the army. The medical school still occupied the site.

The crews had also converted the old church into an office building for the medical school. They had not only torn down the tower, they had divided the cavernous interior, so impressive in the days before land reform, into two ordinary floors, with classrooms and offices on both. They had thus done away with any resemblance to a church that the building might still possess.

As part of a more recent remodeling, new crews had walled off that part of the compound butting on the main street to the west, where the Catholic fathers once lived, and had converted it into a hostelry for distinguished guests—for me, my wife, my daughter, for the cadres that had accompanied us from Peking and Changchih, and for the staff that would take care of us. We numbered, altogether, some fourteen people.

When the cadres showed us to our rooms it became clear that my daughter Carma was to sleep in the room which Hsieh Hung and I had shared in 1948. My wife and I shared a much larger room one door to the east, where the other cadres of the 1948 work team had lived and where we had so often met either as a team or as part of the village leadership. This compound, though recognizable, had nevertheless changed a great deal. Renovators had torn down or moved walls, put up inside partitions where none existed before, cleaned and swept the whole place and whitewashed it so that it gleamed. They had put curtains on the windows, a luxury even the Catholic fathers had never indulged in, and, most striking of all, had installed electric lights everywhere, in every room, in the courtyard, and in the large multiple privy. Between our rooms and the cookhouse-dining room, which now occupied a long shed across the open ground, stood an outdoor sink made of concrete. The tower in the railroad yards supplied it with running water. Later investigation disclosed that while electric lights graced all of the houses in the village, running water flowed from only two of three outlets in Long Bow. Most of the people still lifted their water from wells with buckets.

We no sooner entered the small inner courtyard that was to be our home than our hosts shut and locked the gates at both ends, barring out the world and making it impossible for us to leave without finding a custodian with a key. This upset me, but unpleasant as it was, it proved to be necessary because as soon as word got out that Old Han, his wife and daughter had returned from across the sea, crowds began to gather in the streets. The people came not only from Long Bow, but from every village within walking distance, which meant a radius of twenty to thirty miles! They came on foot, by cart, by bicycle, on crutches, leaning on canes, hobbling on bound feet, with children in their arms or on their backs. They came when the sun shone and they came in the rain. They came by the hundreds, by the thousands, and once they came they would not leave until they had caught a glimpse of us. We had arrived in the middle of the rainy season on the heels of the worst storm in years and even though that storm was over it went on raining almost every day. Crowds of men, women and children, most of them without any water-resistant clothing, stood in the rain from dawn until dark—friendly, good-humored, patient, but persistent. They would not leave until they had seen what they came to see—the three Americans. Bowing to the inevitable we went out into the street at least twice a day, sometimes more often, to greet the multitudes, make short speeches, and exchange some questions and answers. These "audiences" satisfied the people and most of them, having had a look and heard us speak, went home. But not all. Some stayed for a second or even a third appearance and some, having returned home, came back with aunts, grandmothers, visiting relatives or simply neighbors to show off the foreigners to an ever-widening circle. It was an extraordinary outpouring of friendliness and curiosity by a people who had not seen travelers from abroad for more than twenty years, most probably since I left the area in 1948. Many had not seen a white face since the Dutch priests left after the start of the Anti-Japanese War. Those born after the Liberation had not, of course, ever seen a white face at all. Here we were offering them not only white faces but a black one as well, a black face topped with an Afro. They all thought Joanne was wearing some sort of a woolen hat! The tremendous attention she generated was more than she could bear. Having seen Long Bow and met all its outstanding citizens as well as most of the population of several surrounding communes, she arranged to return to Peking as soon as possible.

Even after she had gone the people still crowded in in great numbers. For at least a week they jammed the street outside the old mission compound each day. Then gradually the pressure subsided. The crowds dwindled until finally we were able to go out without attracting any more attention than the stares and smiles of a few village children.

Considering all the commotion that we had created in Changchih, on the highway and later at Long Bow, I decided that it was a mistake to have insisted on walking to the village. But the people of Long Bow did not agree. We heard from several sources several times over that our action had pleased the people of the region very much. After we arrived they all had but one demand, and that was to see us. By walking twelve miles from the guesthouse in Changchih to the village of Long Bow we had made it possible for tens of thousands to see and greet us. They deeply appreciated this. For us to have dashed in and out of the city in side-curtained jeeps would have been an affront to the public. Their opinion was that we had followed the "mass line."

Learning of the people's reaction forced me to do some hard thinking. My action had not been influenced by what the people might feel. I had been concerned only with recapturing something of the past and with absorbing something of the present through a long walk in the countryside. It had not occurred to me that central to the reality of the present were hundreds of thousands of people eager to meet and greet the foreigner, eager to establish contact. This long walk, so ordinary for the forties, but so unusual for the seventies, made a deep impression on the people of the Shangtang. Years later they still talked about it, and laughed about it too. What caused amusement was the fact that the officials who walked with us were so exhausted by their exertions that every one of them had to rest up for two or three days afterward. What many peasants still did as a matter of course —walk to Changchih and back in a day—the regional officials no longer even thought of doing. Apparently it was not the prospect of the crowds and the disorder in the streets that had most alarmed them when I suggested walking, but the prospect that several of them would have to join the trek in person. This at least was what the peasants said.

As for the crowds that came to see us, I could remember no precedent for them.

I had wandered around Lucheng County alone many times in 1948, and though I had attracted some attention, particularly the attention of children, I had never gathered the kind of crowds that now waited for us and followed us everywhere. It seemed to me there were two reasons for this. First, in those days the people did not trust any foreigner—they had suffered too much from foreign intervention. They did not assume that a white man with a big nose was a friend. Children followed me out of curiosity, but adults tended to maintain their distance, not sure just what sort of an attitude to take. The second thing was that in those days people were under great pressure to survive economically. Land reform had been completed, but intense labor was required to wrest a living from the small plots of soil which the peasants had won. Each family depended on its own labor to live. A day or an hour lost from work could spell trouble, especially in the critical spring and summer period. So even if he or she had been curious and friendly the average peasant would have thought twice about standing all day in the rain to see a foreigner; there were many other demands on his or her time. By 1971, with collective farming universal in the region, peasants had won basic economic security. The well-being of the populace, their income, depended not on individual effort alone, but on the combined effort of the work team and the brigade. Whether one individual worked today or not did not really matter. As a member of the collective each would get a share of the crop in any case. He or she might lose a day's work points, but this was a small fraction of the year's income. The crop itself was unlikely to suffer. Someone else would do whatever crucial work that day required. The new collective system freed a certain number of the people to leave home in order to see and greet the foreigners. No matter how long it took, no matter what the cost in time, wet clothes and exercise, they determined to carry their mission through. I, on my part, felt that I had indeed come home. Although on the surface I was annoyed that I had to see and greet so many people, deep down I felt an abiding bond with these multitudes. I knew they were the salt of the earth, the driving force behind the revolution on the Shangtang, the very force I had come so far to study and to understand.

3

UNEXPECTED TWISTS

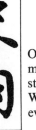

On meeting so many old friends in Long Bow I directed my first questions toward clearing up the many unfinished stories of 1948: Had Shen Hsien-e won her divorce? Had Wang Wen-te ever "passed the gate"? Had the authorities ever discovered Little Ch'uer's assailant?

The answers to these questions contained surprising twists, twists which I had never even dreamed of as possible alternatives.

Shen Hsien-e was the beautiful young woman whose father had forced her into a prearranged marriage while she was still below the legal age limit. In 1945 her fiancé, Wang Wen-te, captain of the village police, and his father, Wang Yü-lai, in charge of security, had the power to bend the law. This father-and-son pair, both members of the Communist Party, threatened to charge Hsien-e's father, a Catholic, with counterrevolutionary aid to the escaped priest, Father Hsin, if he did not agree to an early marriage. Once Hsien-e moved into the Wang home, both Wangs treated her very badly, forced her to work long hours and often beat her. Rumor had it that her father-in-law demanded sexual favors from her, whipped and beat her when she refused, then beat her even more fiercely when she threatened to expose what was going on. In August, 1948, during a period when all Communist cadres had to appear before the people to be examined on their work, Hsien-e finally got up courage enough to go to the Women's Association for help. She agreed to accuse her husband and father-in-law in public if the authorities granted her a divorce, which would enable her to leave their home and thus escape retribution.

Hsien-e's courage in facing two men who had become new-style local bullies, and her testimony on life in their home, turned the tide in the confrontation between the people of Long Bow and this pair. Once Hsien-e spoke out, everyone else in the village who had grievances against the police captain and the head of security dared to voice them. In the end Wang Wen-te and Wang Yü-lai had to bow their heads in front of the people and vow to reform their ways.

But when I left Long Bow in August, 1948, county leaders had not settled the question of a divorce for Hsien-e. They had sent her husband, Wang Wen-te, off to a special training class for Communists who could not "pass the gate" (i.e., win the approval of the populace as Communists and cadres) while Hsien-e remained at her father's home, where she had been living ever since she made contact with the Women's Association. From her point of view this was no solution. Even if Wen-te did reform as a Communist and a police captain, she did not want to continue her marriage to him. Without an approved divorce, she would have to live in a social limbo, a married daughter in her father's house, a nonbeing with no status at any level and no right even to remarry. In spite of Hsien-e's earnest demand for a legal solution to this problem, the district officials put off any decision in her favor. No divorce had ever ended a marriage in Long Bow. Most people still opposed divorce, any divorce, on any grounds, on principle. Among them were peasant mothers-in-law who habitually mistreated their daughters-in-law and were appalled at the idea that a young woman could walk out at will, get a divorce, and marry again. The revolutionary officials had to support justice, they had to support women's rights, but at the same time they could not get too far ahead of the people as a whole. Where no consensus prevailed in the community in favor of divorce, it behooved them to move slowly, do more educating, and wait until public opinion caught up with the requirements of the time. That was the "mass line."

Such was one argument for moving slowly. A second argument had to do with the ultraleft tendency that distorted the whole Party rectification campaign in 1948. Once the regional leaders raised the prospect of public examination and criticism of the Party members by the people, as a means for educating and reforming the Communists who were leading the revolution at the village level, some people blew up a sharp wind of hostility to these local leaders. By raising the demand that land and property be divided absolutely equally, and that every poor peasant family receive enough property to make it self-sufficient—a demand that was impossible to achieve since there was not enough property in the whole area to satisfy all—these people made the land reform movement seem a failure and the activists who led it appear incompetent, even venal. They attacked the activists as enemies and treated them as if they were landlords and counterrevolutionaries. In this atmosphere higher cadres perpetrated many injustices against village cadres. They punished people who deserved criticism with removal from office, and punished people who deserved removal from office with arrest and trial. Once this wind blew up nobody could control it, in part because the rank-and-file did not have any experience in confronting officials. They did not know how their criticisms would be taken. They feared the possibility of retribution. To many it seemed better to knock people right out of office than to criticize them and leave them with power. If they still held power they might take revenge on their critics.

In the summer of 1948, a period when the Party set out to correct the worst abuses brought about by this situation, no one wanted to rush into granting a divorce for Hsien-e. At a minimum Party leaders ought to review the whole situation. Perhaps the young bride had exaggerated. Perhaps there was some positive side to her marriage. And perhaps Wang Wen-te, if he finally confronted the mistakes he had made in public work and private life, might change enough to win Hsien-e's respect and reestablish his marriage. Since he categorically opposed the divorce and regarded it as a severe punishment, it was best to go slowly. No one wanted to add to the long list of excesses that had been imposed on village cadres since rectification began. This was, after all, a contradiction among the people and not one between the people and their enemies. Contradictions had to be handled according to their overall nature and the concrete circumstances of each particular conflict. Responsible cadres ought at least to study the circumstances well.

Such was the second argument for moving slowly. In the end, in spite of the fact that Wang Wen-te did confront his mistakes at the cadre school, did return to Long Bow as a Communist in good standing, did "pass the gate" there and did resume his post as head of the village police, the authorities granted a divorce to Hsien-e. They granted it because, even though Wen-te opposed it to the end, his wife had a legal right to it. They did not consider the divorce a punishment, but only a logical consequence of the fact that Wen-te had mistreated and alienated his unwilling bride. Thus this story had a happy ending.

Hsien-e eventually met and married another peasant who lived in Horse Square. There she bore and raised three children. Since I had been so impressed with her beauty and had written about her with such enthusiasm one of the Commune officials became curious. What sort of woman could so impress a foreign friend? He sought her out to his great disappointment. At forty years of age the mother of three was not beautiful at all. She looked to him like any other hardworking Shangtang peasant wife. Clearly he doubted my assertion that in 1948 Hsien-e had been an exquisite young bride.

But that is not the whole of the story about Long Bow's first divorce. The county granted Hsien-e a divorce and she remarried. Wang Wen-te, divorced against his will, also remarried and his choice of a mate came as a complete surprise. Wang Wen-te married Hu Hsueh-chen, the chairman of the Women's Association and the woman responsible, more than any other, for the mobilization of Hsien-e as a public witness against her husband, the woman responsible for Hsien-e's divorce. It was because Hu Hsueh-chen supported the divorce and won the majority of the Women's Association to her point of view that county officials granted it in the end.

That Hu Hsueh-chen should then turn around and marry the notorious police captain was one of those truths that are stranger than fiction. How had such a match come about? Wasn't Hsueh-chen older than Wen-te? Wasn't she his severest critic? Wasn't she, after all, already married? Yes, Hsueh-chen was married but she was married to a doctor who was serving at the time on the staff of Resistance University. He was a member of the People's Liberation Army. When the army moved on he moved with it. He ended up in Peking and wrote Hu Hsueh-chen to join him there, but this she did not want to do. She didn't want to leave her home in Long Bow and travel to distant Peking as an army bride.

Such a decision seemed perverse. There were and still are millions of young women in China who would give anything for a chance to leave their village homes and go to Peking to live and work. There are hundreds of thousands of men working in Peking who cannot get permission for their wives to join them in the city. They work in Peking with special permits while their wives and children have to stay behind in the brigades they grew up in or married into. If there were no such regulations new immigrants would overwhelm Peking, straining housing and commodity supplies to the breaking point.

With so many people longing to move to Peking why did Hsueh-chen refuse? Was it simply that she loved Long Bow and didn't want to leave home? That was probably a factor. Shansi people are well known as homebodies, perversely loyal to their native place. They are not easily persuaded to leave those solid houses, built at such great expense in money and in time. But the real reason, it seemed, for Hu Hsueh-chen's reluctance was a reservation about the character of her new husband. She told me that he treated her well, that he even did the cooking at night so that she could attend meetings freely. But rumor had it that he had a roving eye. He was a ladies' man who, when not near the one he loved, tended to love the one who was near. As the army moved so did the object of his attentions, and so Hsueh-chen's second marriage was not as ideal as I had presented it in *Fanshen*. Rather than move to Peking and suffer through such a relationship, Hsueh-chen asked for and won a divorce.

And so there were, after several thousand years of enforced stability in marriage, not one but two divorcees in Long Bow. Both Hsueh-chen and Wen-te were Party members. From the point of view of the Party leaders the next step was not only logical but well-nigh inevitable. Why should two divorced Communists avoid each other? Party leaders talked it over with Hsueh-chen and Wen-te. They agreed, and in the end married. No one ever claimed that this was a very happy union, but no one called it a disaster either. Hsueh-chen assured us that Wen-te never beat her and Wen-te assured us that Hsueh-chen was an efficient housekeeper who took good care of him. Whether any affection ever blossomed between them was hard to determine. In 1971 one could not discern anything from the way they acted toward each other. They seemed to ignore each other's existence but that was normal public behavior for all peasant couples. At that time Hsueh-chen was ill. She had not been feeling well for many years and had completely retired from political activity. Wen-te was the head of the Fifth Team Garden, a vegetable project that covered more than six acres. To supervise and protect his plants he usually slept in a hut in the field and ate his meals there, too. There was little opportunity for these two to quarrel. They rarely saw each other at home, which was perhaps what each preferred.

Stranger even than the outcome of Hsien-e's divorce case was the question of Little Ch'uer's assailant. Had he ever been discovered? The answer was a bizarre yes and no!

In March, 1948, several Catholic peasants found the work team cadre Chang Ch'uer bound, gagged and semiconscious beside a well on one of Long Bow's back streets. Apparently someone had ambushed him, stuffed a towel in his mouth, tied him up, and dragged him toward the well with the intention of throwing him in, and then for some reason had dropped him a few feet short of this goal and fled.

Little Ch'uer was a member of the Fifth District Work Team, Lucheng

County. An activist in his home village, he had been assigned to Long Bow to help review the status of land reform and carry through the Party rectification movement. Any lethal assault on a land reform cadre had to be seen as a counterrevolutionary crime. The evidence, circumstantial at best, pointed toward four village cadres whom many people had reason to fear, even to hate. These four included Wang Yü-lai, the head of public security, and his son Wen-te, captain of the police, the Wangs involved in the divorce case; Li Hung-er, captain of the village militia; and Wang Hsi-yu, vice-chairman of the village government. County police arrested the four and held them in the county jail for several weeks, but finally released them for lack of evidence. When they returned to the village in June all four swaggered defiantly through the streets, threatening harm to all those who had brought evidence against them. One of these was Wen-te's battered wife, Hsien-e. She had identified the towel removed from Little Ch'uer's mouth as being exactly like the ones Yü-lai kept at home.

When I left Long Bow in August, 1948, the work team had pronounced the four cadres innocent and had arranged their release. The team members had not solved the case. They had not apprehended any other suspect. I assumed that some of the dissident Catholics who found Ch'uer beside the well that night and who so busily assembled evidence against Yü-lai and his cronies must be the guilty parties, but no confirmation of these suspicions ever came from the village or the county authorities. Now, on my return, I learned that the case had been solved several days before the four cadres were released from the county jail and months before I left Long Bow. The solution was *extraordinary*. It involved no assailants, because there had never been any assault. Little Ch'uer bound, gagged and beat himself, then threw himself beside the well.

County authorities discovered the truth when Little Ch'uer, on his own, broke down and confessed. They didn't want to publicize this surprise ending because they were afraid of what the four cadres might do. After all, when Little Ch'uer was found gagged beside the well police had arrested the four, held them for weeks, and had beaten them badly.

Wang Wen-te said to the guards at the Lucheng County Jail, "I don't care how much you beat me, you can beat me to death. I'll never confess to this crime. I had nothing to do with it, and I don't know anything about it." His father, Yü-lai, and the other two cadres also stood firm. In the end the county had to release all four as innocent victims of an attempted frame-up. If they now found that no one had attacked Little Ch'uer, that he had done this to himself, who could control their anger, who could head off their revenge?

County leaders decided to let the matter ride for a while. After tempers cooled and memories faded, after they assigned Little Ch'uer to work in some other place, they could announce the news and hope all concerned would take it calmly.

But why had Ch'uer done this to himself? The answer was straightforward. He wanted to avoid being sent south as a member of one of the civilian work teams that accompanied the People's Army into newly liberated areas in the Yangtze Valley. Like Hu Hsueh-chen, he loved his home and didn't want to leave it. He also felt that by going south, into the war zone, he might be risking his life. His self-assault served as a form of draft-dodging. If he could simulate victimization by counterrevolution here in Long Bow, he might avoid real victimization by counterrevolution elsewhere, and he could pose as something of a hero to boot. A cadre in Li Village Gulch had already carried out a similar plan. He remained safely at home, a renowned casualty of the class struggle.

Little Ch'uer did achieve his primary goal—survival. No one ever sent him to the wartorn south or any other danger zone. His hopes of surviving as a hero, however, collapsed. His confession badly tarnished his record as a Communist. Party leaders suspended him for a long period. When they finally reinstated him, they assigned him to menial work.

Other unexpected twists of fate greeted us on our arrival.

Chang Kuei-ts'ai, the young district cadre who quit public service in disgust in 1948 because "policy changes so often" and because, deep in his heart, he felt that with land of his own, some implements, a pig in the sty, a wife at last and a child on the way, the revolution was over for him—this same Chang now served as Secretary of the Communist Party Branch.

In the meantime Chang Hsin-fa, the leading Communist in the village in 1948, the man who had served as Party Secretary for many years thereafter, no longer held any office. After leading Long Bow through the whole period of land reform in the forties and then through the land pooling and cooperative movement of the fifties, he stooped to speculation in the sixties. He learned how to buy and sell houses at a profit, was charged with misuse of public funds, and was removed from office. The brigade assigned him to the task of raising communal pigs.

Thus the anomaly—the man who led the village through a decade of drastic reform ended in a modest production post, and the man who "quit the revolution" to enjoy a happy, independent life assumed all the burdens of this large and complicated collective.

Here again, truth was stranger than fiction. Who could have predicted such a reversal of roles?

During the course of our discussion that day and in the days to follow informants filled in other gaps in the land reform story and corrected some questionable reports. When Chang Kuei-ts'ai and Chang Hsin-fa found out how important a role I had given to Chang T'ien-ming in my book, they laughed. I had described him as the first Communist Party member in Long Bow, as a key organizer of the first village government after Liberation, and as the one responsible for the mobilization of the peasants when they first accused the landlords of crime.

"But T'ien-ming didn't play that big a role," said Hsin-fa.

"He definitely wasn't the first Party member in the village," protested Kuei-ts'ai.

"But he told me that he was," I said.

"No. It's not true. That's what comes from listening too closely to one person. In fact, Shih Ts'ai-yuan was the first member. But all of us played a role in setting up the first branch and organizing the accusation meetings. T'ien-ming was one of several. We had no *Fanshen* heroes."

Their protest over this seemed reasonable, but even so it was hard to get the facts. Each person interviewed naturally stressed his or her own role and tended to downplay that of others. T'ien-ming, after playing a very active role from 1945 through 1948, had reassumed the post of Communist Party Secretary in 1949; he had not led the village well, had quarreled with almost all the other key leaders, and had then stepped down. He later got a job in an industrial plant in Changchih and spent most of his time in the city. When he got the job in the factory he transferred his Party membership to the factory branch and became politically active as a worker, not as a peasant. Though he maintained his home in Long Bow and left his family there, he himself only returned on Sundays and holidays. Only after his retirement as a worker, almost thirty years later, did he resume an active part in village affairs. He took up the job of political director to the Second Production Team.

In the meantime Chang Hsin-fa, Shen T'ien-hsi, Kuo Cheng-k'uan and other early members of the movement in Long Bow led the village into the socialist period. Decades later they recollected T'ien-ming as a man who played a minor role in land reform, then dropped out of village affairs altogether. I found no way to verify this further. Recollections obviously conflicted.

All those whom I talked to agreed about another incident described in *Fanshen*—the reform of Ken-pao, the peasant dissident who denounced the land reform, attacked Village Chairman Ch'un-hsi and badly wrenched his thumb, then escaped twice from the village lockup. I reported that on the day after the new Village Congress started to function in July, 1948, Ken-pao accepted its censure of his behavior and peacefully went off to work the next morning on the private land of a soldier's family. To make amends for his bad behavior the Congress required him to do fifteen days of work for the family of a young man who was off fighting at the front. I saw Ken-pao walking off to work that morning and assumed that he had, on his own, recognized the authority of the elected village government and decided to abide by the law.

Hsin-fa, Kuei-ts'ai, Cheng-k'uan and others all laughed at this notion.

"Ken-pao had no change of heart," said Hsin-fa. "What really happened was that the night before he went out to work so docilely Ch'un-hsi and Wang Man-hsi 'repaired' him. They gave him a serious beating. They beat him because he assaulted Ch'un-hsi and almost broke his thumb, and because, when they locked him up, he refused to stay put and broke out twice. They lost patience with him, decided that words were not much use, and gave him a good beating instead. Because he didn't want another beating he decided to do as he was told!

"In fact, at the very moment they were beating him—it was out behind the brigade office in the old orphanage compound—I came by and discovered what was going on. I didn't stop them. I just said, 'Be careful, don't break any bones and above all don't kill him.' "

Clearly I had overestimated the power of moral persuasion in Long Bow in 1948. An experiment in village democracy had begun. People had taken part in the first real elections in history and had chosen a council of dedicated people who had both prestige and authority. But a gap still separated the democratic process as it was set up to function and the actual process of governing the village, in particular the maintenance of law and order. The chronic violence of old rural China did not easily yield to education, persuasion and due process of law. Sad to say, the problem remains to this day.

4

LOOKING AROUND

 The first thing we did when we left our locked and guarded compound was to take a long walk through all the sections of the village and then out into the surrounding fields. The damage wrought by the previous day's storm confronted us everywhere. Across the street from the mission compound a courtyard wall had collapsed into the street and the roof of an old adobe house had caved in. We saw an emergency crew of militiamen shoveling the remains of the shattered adobe into flatcarts. They would haul the bits to a nearby field as fertilizer. At several other spots in the old center section of the village walls and roofs had collapsed. If it continued to rain, more would follow them down. Successive downpours had so thoroughly soaked the ground that nothing underfoot remained firm.

Also, if it continued, no one could guarantee even the crops in the fields. Water already stood ankle deep in numerous hollows. As water levels rose these spots spread and merged until whole areas flowed together as temporary lakes.

In the face of this impending disaster we found it hard to concentrate on the sights of Long Bow village, but some of them were impressive enough to focus our attention momentarily on progress rather than destruction. On the ruins of the old Japanese blockhouse the villagers had built a school that housed 400 students and employed thirty teachers. Opposite the village pond, on the site once occupied by Ts'ai-yuan's store, stood an enclosed community center with a meeting hall larger than the nave of the old church, a row of brigade offices, a barbershop, a clinic and dispensary, and a control room for incoming electricity. These units were evenly spaced around four sides of an open courtyard, with the brigade offices facing the meeting hall and the barbershop facing the dispensary. Behind all this lay a second, smaller yard where mills, powered by electricity, ground, cleaned and sifted the grain that had traditionally been processed on stone mills powered by human muscle.

At the crossroads south of the brigade office stood the new cooperative store, a long one-story building, clean and sparkling. A counter ran the whole length of the partition-free structure and behind it, along the back wall, shelves reached from floor to ceiling. They were well stocked with cotton cloth in many colors, thread, sewing equipment, pots, pans, Thermos flasks, canned fruits, cooking oil, biscuits, bicycles, bicycle tires—everything necessary for the daily life of a thriving peasant community. Nothing even remotely comparable to this had existed in Long Bow in 1948. Ts'ai-yuan's store had carried only cloth, cooking oil and a few hard biscuits. In those days, unless one wanted to wait for the annual autumn fair, the commercial high point of the year in Long Bow, one had to travel all the way to Changchih City to buy a needle or a thimble.

Even more impressive than these community projects were all the new houses that peasants had built privately since 1948. Two hundred and fifty-one families had built 1,015 sections of new dwelling space (a section was ten feet, the distance between the standing timbers that held up the roof). This was roughly equal to all the housing in the village at the time of land reform. The new houses were almost all large, story-and-a-half structures with brick foundations, wooden door and window frames and glass windows. All visible woodwork shone with fresh bright blue or red paint. These were the kind of solid, ample dwellings that landlords and rich peasants had once fashioned as soon as they became prosperous. Now this "gentry" model set the standard for all new construction.

In courtyards new and old, flowers proliferated. They bloomed in many colors, converting the hidden recesses of the village into an unexpected series of floral displays. I could not remember seeing flowers in the village in 1948.

Flowers expressed something about the quality of life and so did trees. As early as 1953 the brigade had established its forestry group. On land set aside for a tree nursery group members raised tens of thousands of saplings. They transplanted them to both sides of all public thoroughfares inside the village and beyond to the limits of the land owned by the brigade. These saplings, most of them a species of poplar, grew fast. Many of them had already reached a height of thirty feet. They crowned the whole area with a leafy shield that transformed the barren, windswept atmosphere so typical of the Shangtang of old. Trees converted the desolate, sunbaked, semiruined earthworks of pre-Liberation times, open to all the violence of heaven, into a shaded, gardenlike complex of interlocking streets, alleys and courtyards that offered protection against the extremes of all seasons.

Striking as they were, trees and flowers made up only a small part of the total vegetation in the village. Every courtyard of any size boasted, in addition, a vegetable plot of corn, beans, melon and Chinese cabbage plants that responded to the rains with vigorous growth. Cornstalks as tall as the courtyard walls served as climbing poles for masses of green beans, while melon vines covered the ground in between and almost buried the cabbages from sight.

Even though many families received important supplementary income from these gardens, they did not count as the private plots guaranteed to the peasants by the cooperative charter, but simply as courtyard space, each house being allowed several hundred square feet. People held their private plots in the fields beyond the confines of the village, but they had long since pooled them for collective cultivation. What private plot land now amounted to was a certain portion of the collective fields set aside on the record books. The state demanded no taxes or sales of grain from this portion. Long Bow people saw the fractional remission of taxes and quota sales as an important fringe benefit. But as for private cultivation of the plots in question, people had voted against this. Most people preferred to let their team grow the crops on private plot land just as they did in the fields at large.

When we finally left the confines of the village we moved westward toward the new reservoir, then swung south through the best land and ended up at the brick kilns halfway up the slope leading to Li Village Gulch. We then turned northward once again along the gully that had been the old cart track and this brought us back to the south end of the main street.

This tour of the fields revealed several remarkable changes. We took for granted the disappearance of small plots and their merger into large fields. Nevertheless the size of the fields—ten, fifteen, even twenty acres thrown together—and their adaptability to machine cultivation surprised us. And just as people merged their fields, so had they merged their threshing floors. They had abandoned dozens of small, hard-packed areas adjacent to the village and developed six large ones in their place, one for each production team. Each of these had some buildings where team members kept tools and implements or stored sizable amounts of threshed grain. In addition to these threshing floors each team had a livestock yard where it housed and fed its horses, mules, cattle and donkeys. These were not linked to the threshing floors, but were incorporated as large cleared areas amidst the small court-yards of the people on the edge of the village.

Our route through the fields took us across the large irrigation canal that brought water from the new reservoir. It ran westward straight as an arrow for several miles. Nearby we found several branch irrigation systems, many sluices and one large pumping installation, which was called the Secondary Pumping Station (the primary one lay at the edge of the reservoir). This station, still under construction, butted on fields that had not been leveled or ditched. Behind this failure after ten years of mobilization lay a long and complicated story which we were to unravel in the coming weeks. Nevertheless, if people of Long Bow had not yet irrigated much land, the big news was that they had brought irrigation water, in ample amounts, to the village from a vast reservoir that had been nothing more than a dream in 1948. We found no objective reason why Long Bow land should ever again suffer from drought unless the drought was so prolonged that the reservoir itself dried up.

Drying up was hardly the problem during those critical days. As we returned to the village in the gathering dusk we saw platoons of Liberation Army men with shovels and picks on their shoulders dogtrotting north-ward. Their mission was to save the coffer dam at the spillway site. The water in the reservoir had risen to within six inches of the top of this temporary structure and all the labor of the local troops and peasants mobilized nearby had been unable to build it up fast enough to keep ahead of the rising waters. Main force Liberation Army units were rushing to the scene to reinforce the emergency effort. An air of anxious suspense lay over the whole North Changchih District.

If no more rain fell, the dam and coffer dam would probably hold. But what if the clouds opened up again, as they appeared on the verge of doing? The thought disturbed every waking moment.

The crops in the fields looked promising, though a far cry from the bumper harvest in the making that we had seen at Tachai, the outstanding brigade in Central Shansi, which we had left only a few days before. One of Long Bow's chronic problems was that the stands of corn and sorghum were too thin—there just were not enough plants to push yields beyond thirty bushels—and the interplanted beans were also thin. Furthermore, the heavy rains, while stimulating growth in some fields, had already slowed growth in others because of waterlogging. Over large areas near the highway corn and kaoliang stalks already stood in water one to two feet deep. If the peasants did not quickly find some means to drain this surface water away, they would lose their whole crop. If corn and sorghum stands were thin, so were those of millet. The millet had beautiful heads, but there were not enough of them. We also saw thin stands in the sweet potato fields. Plant populations seemed to be Long Bow's most pressing technical problem. Kuei-ts'ai, the brigade leader who led us on this walk, criticized the Second Team—which was his own—for failure to treat the sweet potato seedlings with fungicide. Disease had completely wiped out the first planting. The second planting, set out much too late, had suffered from a period of drought in the spring.

We estimated that with good weather in the next period the whole brigade might possibly harvest forty bushels of grain, thereby reaching for the first time the goals laid out in the national charter of agriculture for areas north of the Yellow River. Previously the highest average had been twenty-seven bushels.

Our last stop before returning to the village was at the brick kilns in the south. These were under the direction of Wang Man-hsi, that terror of the gentry, who had gone on to beat up so many ordinary peasants after the completion of the land reform. Now middle-aged, he showed hardly any of the physical superiority that had once made him so formidable. Far from towering over his fellow workers, he was now shorter than most of them. His whole frame seemed to have shrunk to less than normal size. In the process his neck had all but disappeared, leaving his head jammed on his shoulders like a cabbage on a board. Only a pair of abnormally long arms still marked him as somebody to reckon with. Two long arms and two very big ears set Man-hsi apart, these and a pair of small pig's eyes that peered out from under a brow as heavy as that of Peking Man.

In character Man-hsi was still the stolid, uncultured rustic I had left behind in Long Bow so many years before. Time had not developed in him any of the sophistication or the political maturity that so many peasant Communists acquired. We soon learned that he was no longer a Communist. The Party had expelled him almost twenty years earlier for raping a young woman without even a shadow of an excuse. Man-hsi's female victims in the land reform period had either been women of the dispossessed gentry whom everyone hated, or the daughters of "struggle objects," poor and middle peasant collaborators, whom nobody cared to defend. For forcing his attentions on women like these he had been severely criticized in 1948, and he had promised to reform. But in 1952 he stepped completely out of line by raping one of his neighbor's daughters. This shocked the whole community and the Party branch, convinced that criticism could no longer help, expelled him.

Man-hsi, however, was still a leader of sorts and he had a following among some of the tougher young men who admired his physical prowess. He had the ability to command. In the absence of anyone better qualified he had been put in charge of brickmaking. As we might have anticipated, on the day that we met him again, Man-hsi was in serious trouble. His troubles, like everyone else's that week, sprang from the weather. The hard downpour of August 15 had made it all but impossible to make bricks. The many mud blocks that had been formed and stacked to dry, prior to being placed in the kilns for baking, had not dried out at all. Some of the stacks had simply collapsed. Like the water-soaked walls in the village center they rapidly returned to their original state as amorphous piles of mud. These mudpiles took up space that was needed for new stacks, but some of the Sideline Team members, wanting only to earn points as rapidly as possible, were pressing and stacking new blocks wherever they could find an empty spot. They refused to clean up the piles of mud that lay in everyone's way.

Under direct orders from Man-hsi, most of the recalcitrant young men finally switched their efforts. They began a cleanup. But one man, Chin Ken-so, went right on making bricks as if nothing had happened. This so angered Man-hsi that he seized a carrying pole and attacked him, causing an uproar that soon spread to the whole brigade. When I finally met him again Man-hsi was under fire from all sides, just as he had been throughout most of my stay in Long Bow in 1948, and he had that same hangdog, hurt expression on his face. He was not quite able to understand why an action taken in the interest of work, of production, an action designed to advance the revolution, had aroused such a storm of criticism and opposition.

If Man-hsi looked hurt and downcast, so did the whole brickmaking operation. Water half-filled the clay pits and flooded all paths and hollows. Collapsed stacks of unbaked bricks were scattered far and near, and one of the kilns stood in imminent danger of cave-in. All hands, including those of the defiant young troublemaker, were currently working on shoring up the endangered kiln. Their clothes were covered with mud, and their feet were soaked. Truly, brickmaking was no "soft spot" where work points came easily.

As we walked back into the village, skirting a veritable lake of flood waters at the southern entrance, we came across Kuo Yuan-lung in the street. I recognized him almost at once. Tall, thin-faced, permanently dour, he nevertheless greeted us warmly. We exchanged a few words and passed on. I remembered him as a very promising young man from the southwest corner of Long Bow who had played an active role in 1948. He had helped man the gate, opposed taking revenge on cadres who had done wrong, and generally helped to push ahead the work of the team sent in to check up on the land reform. But Kuei-ts'ai said that Yuan-lung was also in trouble. He no longer had any status in the village or any post of leadership, for he had been exposed as a member of the Legion of Mary, an underground Catholic organization accused of counterrevolutionary crimes.

If Man-hsi's troubles and Yuan-lung's disgrace left us somewhat taken aback by the complexity and persistence of all kinds of problems in Long Bow, our spirits revived at the last stop made that day—the grain mill behind the brigade office.

When families needed fresh supplies of wheat flour and cornmeal, which was usually several times a week, they dipped into their stores of whole grain and took whatever amount they wanted ground to the *chia kung ch'ang,* or "processing plant." There it was processed at so much a catty by three young women who stayed on duty night and day. The morale of the three millers was obviously high. Their leader, the sister of the brigade's new accountant, was provocatively attractive. Buxom, healthy, red-cheeked and vivacious, she worked with a mischievous twinkle in her eyes. Her two companions, both plump and plain, were kindred spirits who fully made up in energy and good humor whatever they may have lacked in grace. Their mill was a natural gathering place where sooner or later everyone showed up. No one needed an excuse to hang around because it was obvious that until each portion of grain had been extruded from the mill its owner had reason to tarry.

The social potential of the situation had not been lost on the three young millers. They developed their workplace into an informal community center where light-hearted banter, serious debate, practical jokes and compassionate advice to the lovelorn, the hurt and the scorned all had their function in a sort of three-ring circus that refused to be drowned out by the roar of the mills. Having vowed never to shut down their mill until they had ground all the grain brought in, the operators of this "processing club" often kept it open until eleven or twelve at night. Anyone dropping in could count on lively company, something to laugh at and something to listen to—a welcome contrast to the silence of the street once the sun went down.

5

STATISTICAL SUMMARY

We returned to the brigade office to drink some tea. While we sipped the fresh brew made by pouring boiling hot water from a Thermos flask onto a few tea leaves in the bottom of each cup, Shen Chi-ts'ai, former brigade accountant and now vice-chairman of Long Bow, gave us some figures that summed up two decades of change. He recited them in his dour, pedestrian fashion, as figures to be proud of, a series of socialist successes. In absolute terms these figures certainly demonstrated progress, but when one analyzed them in the light of the swollen population of 1971 the progress seemed badly diluted. On a per capita basis production in Long Bow had barely held its own.

In 1948 there were 960 people living in 252 households. By 1971 there were 1,637 people living in 398 households—a 70 percent increase in population and a 58 percent increase in the number of family units. Together these 398 families tilled 3,405 mou (567.5 acres) of land. This was 2,220 mou (370 acres) less than the land tilled in 1948. Combining this 39 percent decrease in land area with a 70 percent increase in population cut the per capita land share from 5.86 mou (almost one acre) to 2 mou (one-third acre), a drastic reduction that brought Long Bow holdings more or less into line with the rest of North China. For people used to reaping marginal crops from surplus land, the sudden shift to minimum holdings had been traumatic.

The total labor power available in Long Bow was reckoned at 532, a figure devised by adding together the full and fractional labor power of more than 600 people, some of them old, some of them sick and some of them too young to count as fully able-bodied. This labor manned six agricultural teams, one sidelines team, and a small tree-planting group. The agricultural teams, working hard on the land throughout the growing season, had produced in 1971 some 236 catties of grain per mou (26 bushels per acre). This was more than twice the average yield obtained in 1948, but given the great increase in population and the reduced land area, the grain available per capita had actually declined from 586 catties (10.7 bushels) in 1948 to 485 catties (8.89 bushels) in 1971. This was a drop of 101 catties (1.85 bushels) per person.

Such a drop in grain per capita would have brought about a serious deterioration in the standard of living if it had not been for two things: truck gardens that supplied vegetables for all and the development of side occupations. They filled the gap and raised combined per capita incomes considerably above what they had been at the time of the land reform. Long Bow sidelines consisted of the truck gardening and brickmaking that we had seen, mule and pushcart transport on the highway, and contract labor in local industries—unloading freight at the railroad station, cutting steel bars at the steel mill, shaping metal at the milling machinery plant. Income from these sources in 1971 amounted to 102,523 yuan, substantially more than the value of the staple crops. Assuming an average price for grain of .09 fen per catty, all the wheat, corn, millet and sorghum raised in Long Bow was worth 72,322 yuan. Thus grain income had fallen to 41 percent of the total as compared to sidelines including vegetables, which had risen to 59 percent.

When added together all these sources of income came to 174,845 yuan. This was twice the total income earned by the brigade in 1948. On a per capita basis, however, income had gone up only from 91 to 105.5, an increase of 14.5 yuan. This could hardly be called a major increase, but when one considered the large increase in the population and the drastic reduction in the land area available for tillage, the 16 percent rise still had to be regarded as a significant achievement.

These figures did not give a complete picture of post-land-reform progress because they left out the private income which many families received from kitchen gardens and various home crafts. In some cases this income was substantial, adding 25 percent or more to the total.

While statistics showed only small per capita gains in twenty-three years, the great increase in capital goods and equipment owned by the community as a whole indicated that the true position of the population should not be judged by such figures alone. There were electric lights in every home, loudspeakers in almost half of them and one large community loudspeaker on a pole in the center of the village. The brigade office boasted a telephone. Other electrical equipment included 3 transformers and 38 electric motors; they powered 5 grain mills, 2 crimping mills, 2 fodder choppers, 23 water pumps, 8 water wheels, and a large pumping station. The smaller pumps pulled water from 22 wells dug at strategic points in the fields. They were capable of irrigating some 1,100 mou (183 acres) of land. Another 700 mou (116.6 acres) could be irrigated from the trunk canal that linked Long Bow to the Changchih Reservoir.

For transport work the brigade had acquired 2 large rubber-tired carts suitable for long-distance hauling and 65 small carts made for short hauls. Mules, at least three to a hitch, drew the large carts, and donkeys or men the small carts. In spite of the increase in carts, draft animals had no more than held their own. There were 88 on hand in 1971 as compared to 75 before. On a per capita basis this was a sharp decrease.

Sheep and goats now numbered 250 and pigs 176 head, 50 of which resided in the collective sty managed by Chang Hsin-fa. Although this represented a substantial increase in the total number of livestock, the number per capita had decreased.

Implements, large and small, had increased to 3,100. This figure included a large number of mattocklike hoes which were still, as they had been for thousands of years, the main tool for tilling the soil. On a per capita basis, implements, like livestock, had decreased.

The above items were all classified as means of production. There was another category called personal property. The totals here showed significant increases not only absolutely, but on a per capita basis. The brigade members owned privately 148 bicycles, 7 radios, 13 watches and 37 sewing machines. In 1948 there had been only 2 bicycles in Long Bow and no radios, watches or sewing machines at all. In addition to these "hard" items, the per capita supply of "software," particularly quilts to sleep under and felt mats to sleep on, had increased sharply. These things had been so scarce in 1947 that families quarreled over who would get which quilt in the distribution. Rivals had torn more than one piece of bedding in half. Now everyone had quilts and mats to spare.

If one compared Long Bow's achievements with those of the whole region they looked impressive, even in the field of agricultural production. Long Bow's yields per acre were almost three times as high as they had been in 1948, while in the region as a whole, yields had been raised only 60 percent. But when one compared Long Bow's achievements with the rest of the commune to which it belonged the figures did not look so promising. In spite of level land, large fields, plenty of irrigation water, a surplus of labor power and increasing quantities of night soil from the growing industrial population in the neighborhood, Long Bow produced the lowest average yields in the whole commune.

Five of Horse Square's twelve brigades had already "crossed the Yellow River," that is to say, they had achieved or surpassed the goal of 55 bushels per acre set for the provinces between the Yellow and the Yangtze rivers. Two of the five had already harvested as much as 75 bushels per acre, and these had raised the average of the commune as a whole to just under 40 bushels, a level of production significantly higher than Long Bow had ever been able to reach. There were teams in Long Bow that had reaped 40 bushels or more, but the brigade as a whole had never done that well, and still produced at a rate that was far below the standard set by the Central Committee for areas north of the Yellow River. This standard was 44 bushels to the acre.

If one compared Long Bow's achievements not only to the best in Horse Square Commune but to the best in Shansi, the outcome looked even worse. Model brigades like the one at West Gully in mountainous P'ingshun County to the east, or Nancheng in hilly Changchih County to the south, or Tachai in the slashed and eroded badlands of Hsiyang County to the north, in spite of unfavorable natural conditions, had all pushed average yields above 100 bushels to the acre, and each year broke new records as they strove to match or even surpass the best world levels in grain production. They had multiplied pre-Liberation yields ten times over, and on a few fields here and there as much as twenty times over.

Of course, one could not take agricultural production as the sole criterion for judging the transformation and progress of a community; total income, the development of side occupations, the adequacy of housing, the quality of medical care, the quality of education, the stability of the leading core, the policies followed by this leading core—all these entered into the picture when appraising a brigade. But when we compared Long Bow with its neighbors along these lines the comparison was still shocking. In Horse Square Commune Long Bow was lagging, not to mention in Shansi Province as a whole.

I was relieved to learn that this had not always been so. In the middle fifties Long Bow had done fairly well, had even been looked up to by nearby brigades as a place to emulate. But starting at about the time of the Great Leap Forward in 1958 and continuing through the Socialist Education Movement and the Cultural Revolution, Long Bow people had to a certain extent lost their way, failed to concentrate on crop production, and consequently failed to raise yields significantly above the levels attained a decade earlier.

As early as 1963 Long Bow had harvested a grain crop of 26 bushels per acre. By 1969 the average yield had reached 30 bushels per acre, but by 1970 this had fallen back to 26 bushels. In fact the summer crop, wheat, had done so badly that the brigade had to ask the State Grain Company to send back 10,000 catties (183 bushels) of grain that had already been sold and shipped so that its members could get through until the corn and millet harvest in the fall.

Confronted by stagnation in production and by the possibility of recurring grain deficits, the higher authorities had decided to send a team of cadres to intervene in Long Bow once more.

In a sense, then, the situation had come full circle. In 1948 I had come to this place because a work team was engaged here checking up on the results of the land reform. It had been sent to Long Bow, not because the community was doing well, but because so many problems remained unsolved. Now, in 1971, another work team (this time called a propaganda team) was engaged in Long Bow checking up on the results of the Cultural Revolution. And once again the team had been sent not because Long Bow had something to teach others, but because so many unsolved problems remained. In 1948 Long Bow had been known throughout the region as an "old, big, difficult" place. In 1971 it was still known as an "old, big, difficult" place, and I was on hand, as before, to see what could be done about it.

We no sooner arrived in the village than an incident occurred that brought home to everyone just how "old, big and difficult" Long Bow's problems were.

6

THE BLACK GANG

 In the middle of the night the militiaman Tseng Kuo-fan walked down the main street from north to south singing at the top of his voice. What he sang was an aria from *Ma Tien* (The Curse in the Hall). This is an opera about a confrontation that occurred 1,000 years ago, after Chao K'uang-yin, the general who founded the Sung Dynasty and became Emperor T'ai Tsu, died (A.D. 976). The climax of the opera takes place in the Audience Hall of the Imperial Palace at Kaifeng as the widowed Queen Ho accuses her brother-in-law, Chao K'uang-yi, now Emperor T'ai Tsung, of usurping the throne that should have gone to T'ai Tsu's son, not to his brother. Before the assembled court Chao K'uang-yi has just driven the legitimate heir, young Teh Chao, to suicide. Queen Ho, in shock, unleashes a torrential curse, one of the famous maledictions of Chinese opera and one much beloved by Shansi mule drivers. She calls K'uang-yi more wicked than any of the shameful connivers of the past and, without mentioning her husband, a notorious usurper in his own right, spits all their names on the air. She demands that K'uang-yi yield the throne to her surviving boy child, Teh Fang.

It is an overwhelming scene, charged with pain, hatred and, above all, daring, for the Emperor, with a snap of his fingers, can settle the poor woman's fate. She is, after all, guilty of *lèse-majesté*. But the points made by Queen Ho, in rapid-fire succession, are so telling that K'uang-yi, after threatening to execute her, closes his eyes and pretends to be both deaf and dumb. Taking their cue from the man on the throne, all members of the court follow suit.

That a Long Bow peasant knew this aria surprised no one. It had roots in local history. Queen Ho's husband, Emperor T'ai Tsu, was no stranger to the Shangtang Plateau. After he usurped the throne of Chou in 961, two rival generals in Shansi rebelled against his illegitimate rule. The Emperor assembled a mighty force, marched into the Shansi highlands, drove his rivals from Luchou (now Changchih) and finally defeated them in a major battle at Tsechou (now Chincheng), the town where militiaman Tseng Kuo-fan was born.

That a Long Bow peasant would dare to sing this aria in public in 1971 was, however, astonishing. To sing a part of any old opera was itself an act of defiance. Ever since the Cultural Revolution began in 1966 all traditional themes had completely disappeared from the stage. They had been replaced by the eight revolutionary model works (five operas, two ballets and one symphony) sponsored by Mao's wife, Chiang Ch'ing. To challenge these works in any way, even by humming an old tune on the street, was a reprehensible political act, a reactionary slap in the face to all right-thinking people.

To sing this particular aria was much worse. The words had direct political significance. By shouting out "Curse in the Hall" Tseng Kuo-fan was clearly denouncing the people in power in Long Bow Brigade. To use the past to denounce the present was an old Chinese custom. The whole Cultural Revolution had begun as a debate over a play about the historical figure Hai Jui, who had been dismissed from office by a Ming emperor. The official position in 1971 was that the play had been written as an attack on Mao Tse-tung for dismissing General P'eng Teh-huai from his post as Commander of the People's Liberation Army. The author of the play, Wu Han, had been denounced as a counterrevolutionary, then detained. Could Tseng Kuo-fan's challenge, so similar in form, be ignored?

This was a difficult question. Tseng Kuo-fan, in his own right, didn't amount to much. He was not, after all, the vice-mayor of Peking, but only a well-known lumpen-element in Long Bow who had few rivals as a womanizer and brawler. People said the pockmarks on his face reflected the holes in his heart. He looked like an old-time rural bully, the kind of man the landlords used to hire to carry guns, beat people up, and collect overdue rents. All that was needed for his face to recall the thirties, the days of local tyrants, private gunmen and summary executions on the street, was a felt hat with a wide brim that could be pulled down over his eyes. It was a face disfigured by smallpox, with here and there a mole from which a single hair protruded. His skull, closely cropped at all times, was covered with scars, bare patches and at least two ugly lumps, not to mention an alarming depression left over from a crushing blow he had received when he fell off a swing as a child. Another lump, like an unlanced boil, disfigured the back of his neck.

His clothes, always tattered and frayed, were discolored by layers of grime, especially at the collar and cuffs. They were the clothes of a bachelor who looked after himself and didn't waste much time on niceties. He walked with a limp, his left foot splayed out, almost as if it were clubbed. A bone growth on his left heel made every step painful unless he held his foot askew, and because he almost always held it that way we called him Splayfoot. His twisted foot and peculiar gait caused his cloth shoes to wear out faster than most men's, so that a toe or two could usually be seen through the ragged upper. In spite of his limp, Splayfoot Tseng moved with power and grace, like a natural-born athlete who expends no more effort than necessary but can, in an emergency, unleash overwhelming might. His opponents in many a fight could vouch for that. He had bulging shoulders and long arms but short legs. All the muscles of both torso and limbs were lean and fit, tempered by a lifetime of labor and conflict.

A strange historical echo added an ironic touch. Splayfoot's name, Tseng

Kuo-fan, was also the name of the general who defeated the Taiping Rebellion in 1864 and recaptured Nanking for the Emperor. General Tseng was a member of the Hunanese scholar-gentry, a famous reactionary in Chinese history.

On the night he sang the provocative aria Splayfoot was, if not drunk, at least somewhat befuddled by drink. Under ordinary circumstances it didn't make much sense to take the words of a tipsy brawler seriously. But in this case evidence came to light of circumstances that were far from ordinary. It turned out that Splayfoot had spent the evening in the home of a young man named Li Ts'eng-pao and that another young man named Chin Kuei-pao had joined them there. The three men had spent the time talking and drinking, and when Splayfoot Tseng left for home, with enough liquor under his belt to make him careless of the consequences, it was not hard to imagine that the song that poured from his lips expressed not only his deepest feelings, but those in the hearts of his companions as well.

And what was this feeling in their hearts? It was deep resentment at having been removed from office only three months earlier. Up to that time Li Ts'eng-pao, whom everybody called Swift Li, had been Party Secretary of Long Bow Brigade for almost five years, while Chin Kuei-pao, whom everybody called Fast Chin, had been captain of the brigade militia for almost eight years. Since the names of both these men ended in Pao (gem), people, not without sarcasm, called them the "Two Gems." Suddenly, only a few months after the propaganda team arrived, team cadres charged the Two Gems with gross mismanagement of brigade affairs and set them aside. Their departure from power threw into question the careers of a whole group of young stalwarts like Splayfoot Tseng, Ch'en Liang-t'ien and Li Shou-p'ing, who had been their most active supporters, served as the backbone of the militia, and carried out all orders that came from the brigade office.

These young men had all been members of the same faction in the Cultural Revolution. Their leader, Swift Li, had been Vice-Party Secretary when the struggle began and his brother Lu Chin-jung had been Party Secretary. In 1967 a group of rebels from the south end of the village, stigmatized as "running dogs" of the landlords, rich peasants and Kuomintang reactionaries, had overthrown the two party leaders. In the nick of time Swift Li rallied a large group of supporters and seized power again, thus saving the revolution, so he felt, for the poor and lower-middle peasants. He forgave rank-and-file members of the rebel units as "hoodwinked masses" but arrested the leaders of the uprising as counterrevolutionaries, beat them severely, and drove them from the village. One older man, a party member and head of the Sidelines Team, backed the rebels. The cadres who had climbed back to power made him their principal target. They beat him until he left the village. When he returned months later they beat him again and put him under surveillance by the militia. In the end they expelled him from the Communist Party as a counterrevolutionary. He lived on in disgrace as an ordinary member of the Fourth Production Team, working every day in the fields and holding his tongue.

But the young men who had returned to power, Party Secretary Swift Li and Militia Captain Fast Chin, did not lead well. Higher cadres charged that the two spent far too much time suppressing the rebel faction and far too little time developing production. They also charged that although irrigation water was available for Long Bow land, these two failed to have the land leveled and ditched so the water could be used. They concentrated instead on sidelines, on contract work for nearby industries and on profiteering—selling hemp at illegal prices in Honan and buying dried sweet potatoes there for import into Shansi without the required permits.

As to their personal lives, the charge continued, power had gone to their heads, just as it had at first to the heads of the young leaders of the liberated brigade in 1945. Rumor had it that Swift Li had entered into liaisons with eight different women, thus driving his wife to attempted suicide, while Fast Chin took up with his neighbor Shih Kui-hsiang, the notorious "songbird of Long Bow."

Reacting to all this adverse information, both rumor and fact, the propaganda team, after months of investigation and deliberation, removed Swift Li and Fast Chin from office. They then backed Chang Kuei-ts'ai, first chairman of the village after Liberation, Shen Chi-ts'ai, an honest and steadfast accountant, and Li Kuang-ching, a demobilized Liberation Army company commander, as the new leading group.

The reorganization of the village, which took place in May, 1971, did not produce any remarkable results. In spite of a vast political mobilization, production remained slack. Whole fields of sweet potatoes failed to sprout because of prolonged dry weather, and now that the rains had come blight was invading the corn. The Two Gems, Swift Li and Fast Chin, denounced the decision of the Party branch to remove them and slipped away to Changchih to protest to the City Committee. Defiant, they mounted a counteroffensive, disrupting whenever they could.

They publicly defended their administration, refused to admit any serious mistakes, made sarcastic remarks about the new leading group, and proudly adopted the label "Black Gang" which the propaganda team had placed on their heads. When one of Swift Li's neighbors asked if he would sell any of the new litter of pigs that had just been born to his homegrown sow, he answered with impatience, "I don't have enough piglets for the members of my 'black gang,' what makes you think I'd share them with the likes of you?"

People hardly had time to absorb the implications of these remarks when Splayfoot Tseng escalated the whole conflict by walking down the street in the middle of the night shouting out his "Curse in the Hall."

The midnight incident created a serious problem for the propaganda team. It put pressure on them to make a decision about the character of Swift Li and his group. Was this just a group of misguided young men who resented demotion and hoped to reverse it? Or was this a group of counterrevolutionaries trying to disrupt the socialist revolution in Long Bow and turn back the clock to pre-land-reform days?

At first glance this might seem to be an outlandish question. Why would young peasants want to launch a counterrevolution? But in the atmosphere of 1971, with the emphasis placed by the Cultural Revolution on class struggle, two-line struggle, the socialist road and the capitalist road, every conflict had to be examined for its underlying class significance. Mao's warning, "Never forget class struggle," had been reprinted, reproduced and repeated a hundred times a day, as had his remark that "the Cultural Revolution is a continuation of the struggle between the Communist Party and the Kuomintang." Mao had also said that the "fundamental question of revolution is political power. To have political power is to have all. To lose political power is to lose all."

Anyone who took these quotations seriously tended to put one question ahead of all others—the question of class power. On arriving anywhere cadres first asked, "Which class is in power here?" Any time one group tried to unseat another the question had to be, "Who represents which class?" In order to find the answer cadres tried to "take the lid off the class struggle," which meant they tried to find those bad elements, those counter-revolutionary wreckers responsible for creating all the trouble, then settle accounts with them.

Disorganized crop production, low yields, financial irregularities could all be indicators that hidden wreckers were active. If a brigade was doing poorly it was taken for granted by many that class enemies must be responsible. Landlords, rich peasants, bad elements and counterrevolutionaries were assumed to be setting people against one another, warping the correct line of the Communist Party, and wrecking socialist production.

Since Long Bow was doing poorly the answer seemed obvious. The time had come to "take the lid off the class struggle" and expose the long-hidden sinister conspiracies underfoot. Propaganda team cadres saw Splayfoot Tseng's loud "Curse in the Hall" as a crack in the lid. All that remained was for them to pry that lid wide open and confront the enemy, now presumed to be the Two Gems and their "Black Gang."

To call Swift Li and his followers a "Black Gang" was easy enough. To prove a case against them was something else. All of them shared impeccable credentials as poor peasant activists.

The deposed Party Secretary, Swift Li, had been abandoned in a field by his poor peasant mother on the day that he was born because she saw no prospect of feeding him in a famine year. Picked up by a foster mother who was soon widowed, Li labored in the field, from the age of twelve, to support his new family. The weight of the carrying pole on his shoulders bent his spine down and forced his neck forward, making him appear forever after slightly *t'o,* or humpbacked.

Fast Chin was also the son of a poor peasant. He labored in the fields most of his life until he joined the People's Liberation Army for a three-year stint as a soldier. Then, as a demobilized veteran, he returned to Long Bow to become captain of the militia.

As for Splayfoot Tseng, he had come to Long Bow as a famine refugee at the age of five. His mother, a resident of Chincheng, some fifty miles to the south, had sold him to a child broker for one peck of grain. His purchaser, at the other end of the line, was the impoverished caretaker of Long Bow's North Temple. This ill-starred man and his common-law wife eked out a precarious living on a small plot allotted to the temple. His death, when Splayfoot was twelve years old, forced the boy into the field to work when he should have been in school. By that time the land had been divided and pooled. Splayfoot went to work as a junior member of the Second Production Team and remained a member in good standing in spite of the reputation he soon earned for not showing up.

How could these three be accused of a conspiracy to restore feudalism?

The case against them rested primarily on the liaison established between Fast Chin and the seductively attractive Shih Kui-hsiang, who lived next door. Kui-hsiang was the niece of the notorious Shih Ho-fa, an ordained Catholic priest who had served for years as an elected delegate to the People's Congress of Yellow Mill. In 1966, as a result of exposures brought about by the Socialist Education Movement, city police arrested Shih Ho-fa as a director of the underground Catholic organization, the Legion of Mary. The court accused him of complicity in fomenting a Catholic rebellion in Taiyuan that year, denounced him as a counterrevolutionary, and imprisoned him for life. The court charged his brother, Shih Kui-hsiang's father, with membership in the Legion of Mary and placed him under supervision by the masses.

Kui-hsiang herself came to Long Bow as the bride of a man named Pei Chi-fa, a worker in the cement plant. Pei was half brother to Pei Liang-shun, leader of the Second Production Team. His courtyard was situated alongside that of his half brother, Liang-shun, Fast Chin's other neighbor. Chi-fa's bride turned out to be no ordinary peasant girl. She dressed with a special flair, rode her bicycle to work in the fields at a breakneck speed, and sang Shangtang Bang-tzu, the local brand of Chinese opera, so skillfully that she had long been known as the "Songbird of Horse Square." After her marriage she was called by some the "Flower of Long Bow." She caught Fast Chin's eye as soon as she moved into the village and he apparently caught hers. As captain of the militia he felt no need to conceal the liaison that developed and openly spent long hours in her home. Who dared criticize him? Who dared confront him?

Not Kui-hsiang's husband, it seemed. Outsiders who visited the courtyard reported that Pei Chi-fa could usually be found sharing his meal and his wine with Fast Chin, while Kui-hsiang waited on both. If he resented the militia captain's attentions to his wife there wasn't much he could do about it. The man was too powerful to defy. Why defy, in any case? There were advantages to be gained by cooperating with those in power.

But now all the terms of the equation had changed. The Two Gems no longer held power. Now the question of the militia captain's links to a notorious Catholic counterrevolutionary through a liaison with the man's niece raised the specter of class struggle. Now the question was, could this seductive woman be dragging Fast Chin and Swift Li down into the swamp of reaction? The very thought sent a shiver of dread through the community. Everything the Two Gems had ever done began to take on sinister meaning.

7

LIN T'UNG

The case of the Two Gems fired the imagination of Lin T'ung, a representative of the Foreign Ministry who traveled with us, made all necessary arrangements, and tried to help us to understand what was happening in China. Lin T'ung was a mature woman, the mother of two sons and the wife of an official in the Foreign Ministry whose name she refused to divulge. She was short in stature, plump, round-faced and vigorous. As a traveling companion she was both endearing and exasperating; endearing because she was so efficient, so cheerful and so tireless in her efforts to make good arrangements everywhere and solve all problems quickly; exasperating because she was so dogmatic, so impatient and so often arrogant. Lin T'ung's good qualities tended to dominate. Under an imperious front she hid a warm heart. She was enthusiastic about China's future and deeply involved in what she was seeing and doing. She enjoyed travel, however arduous and tedious, and often found ways to enliven the day by arranging small surprises, like a picnic lunch at some beautiful spot along the road. In preparation for such diversions she ordered up lunch boxes filled with bread, biscuits, boiled eggs, apples and orange soda—that ubiquitous orange soda that was always too sweet and too warm. On one trip by jeep from Taiyuan to Changchih she picked out a certain reservoir as an ideal spot for a picnic. When that body of water finally came into view it proved to be far from ideal. The water level had fallen drastically; wide banks of mud sloped toward a residue of opaque, stagnant water. Undaunted, Lin T'ung personally reconnoitered the site, picked out the least objectionable spot, spread out a white cloth, and proceeded to preside over a picnic appropriate to the grounds of Windsor Castle.

Lin T'ung loved fine food, both to eat and to talk about. Food talk often served as a means of avoiding more controversial subjects. Her taste ran unerringly to fish, and when fish appeared on the menu all the great fish of the past came up for review. Meanwhile Lin T'ung finished off whatever was on the plate in front of her; this included the fish head, eyes and brains. She specialized in fish heads and knew where to find the bone from the head of one species of fish that, when extracted and cleaned, would stand erect on three points. This was known as a lucky bone. It was held at arm's length, then dropped onto the table. If it landed on the three points and stood up your wish was granted. If it fell over you were out of luck!

Lin T'ung came from a great coastal city, where she graduated from a high school run by missionaries. While still quite young she joined the Communist underground, then somehow survived the dangerous years before Liberation when exposure meant torture and often death. Her selfless dedication to the cause of the Liberation of China took tremendous courage. Outwitting the Kuomintang police took equally great skill. Hers was a record that inspired awe.

In the mission school Lin T'ung acquired a good command of English. She spoke with more fluency and understood more of what she heard than any of the interpreters assigned to our group. But she would not, if she could help it, allow herself to be put in the position of translator. She was a foreign service officer, not a language officer, and she resented any implication that her duties might include translation.

This attitude originated in another facet of her character that was exasperating: her respect for hierarchy, her reverence for rank. She always made clear that she came from *Central,* that she was no mere interpreter, and that accompanying a foreign guest through China was for her a temporary assignment. This acute sense of status and its prerogatives surprised no one whom we met on our travels. Hierarchy is basic to the organization of life in China and has been for millennia. Every citizen, high or low, takes rank and status for granted, giving no more thought to justifying it than is given to the air in the atmosphere. Even so, not everyone parades his or her own superior rank before others in a blatant manner. It was this latter tendency on Lin T'ung's part that was distasteful.

Lin T'ung combined reverence for rank, especially her own, with political rigidity. Her appetite for dogmatism rivaled her appetite for fish, and the opinions she held at any given moment tended to be absolute. The fact that they might be in direct contradiction to opinions held earlier or to other opinions held simultaneously did not seem to bother her. What mattered was her interpretation of the Party line at the moment and she held to it tenaciously, as if the slightest adjustment, the slightest doubt, had the capacity to throw her whole world outlook into question. I suspected that her outward certainty concealed an inner uncertainty. The less secure she felt about a position the more dogmatically she asserted it. Others said of Lin T'ung, "She is so afraid to be wrong that she is wrong!" But that, of course, she would not admit, even to herself.

For Lin T'ung the outstanding fact about Long Bow was that it was a *backward* brigade. This backwardness she automatically attributed to political disruption. To look into the ordinary weaknesses and mistakes of peasant leaders, to question the way they had applied policy directives from above, seemed irrelevant. To question the validity of the policy directives themselves never even occurred to her. The important thing was to uncover those who were wrecking the work, isolate them and deal with them, harshly if need be. Once this was done the brigade could quickly pull itself together and realize its potential.

Lin T'ung felt certain that by concerted effort, in the course of a month or two, she herself could "pry the lid off the class struggle" in Long Bow.

She came, after all, from Peking, from *Central*, as she never tired of remind-ing us. If a *Central* cadre could not see through the twists and turns of a village conspiracy, quickly expose the guilty parties and solve the problem, who could? All that was required was concentration and energy—investiga-tive energy.

Lin T'ung lost no time in launching her own personal investigation. In doing so she made several assumptions. The first of these was that the new brigade leaders deserved support, that they represented revolution.

Propaganda team members had selected the men after intense consulta-tion at all levels. They had installed them in office in June, 1971, with the full approval of the Brigade Party Branch, the Party leaders of Horse Square Commune, and the Changchih City Committee. To attack them meant to attack the Communist Party itself, the Party of the working class, the vanguard of the Chinese revolution. Since Party decisions were by definition revolutionary, opposition could hardly be considered a legitimate expression of an alternative viewpoint. She saw it rather as a counterrevolu-tionary challenge that was particularly dangerous in this case because power was involved—administrative power over the brigade.

How could a struggle over power like this be anything other than class struggle? If it was class struggle, then two classes must be contending. Who represented which class? There didn't seem to be much room for doubt. Three levels of Party leaders had recommended the new brigade leaders after a thorough investigation of their class origin, past behavior and cur-rent outlook. Surely they represented the working class. Whoever opposed them must represent some other class. In the absence of any bourgeoisie in Long Bow this class had to be the overthrown feudal remnants, the land-lords, the rich peasants and their running dogs. Hence the importance of the Catholic "songbird" Shih Kui-hsiang. Since the men were all of poor peasant origin only Kui-hsiang provided a possible link to reactionary classes and reactionary forces. The whole structure of Lin T'ung's case rested on this one attractive, mysterious, provocative link.

8

THE PROPAGANDA
TEAM

 Our arrival galvanized into renewed action a propaganda team that had, over the course of many months, lapsed into relative passivity. Lin T'ung, with her single-minded determination to expose class enemies, greatly strengthened the hand of those who shared her viewpoint. Prior to our arrival the team had split over its appraisal of the real nature of the situation in the village. One group, proudly "radical," maintained that there was some sort of conspiracy afoot in Long Bow; a second group, made up of middle-of-the-roaders, had no fixed opinion on the subject; a small group, whom the radicals labeled "rightist," maintained that if class enemies did indeed exist in Long Bow they had not played much of a role in the development of the community. The dissension there was rooted in contradictions among the people; that is to say, problems and conflicts between various groups of working people, none of whom could be called enemies but who had rather a wide community of interest.

Lin T'ung, carrying with her the prestige of a *Central* cadre, greatly strengthened the hand of the radicals. So did the intermittent presence of a young man named Fan Wen, whom we called "Smart Fan," a key figure of the General Affairs Office of the Changchih City Committee, who had been assigned by that body to supervise the visit of the foreigners to Long Bow.

Smart Fan was a "helicopter cadre," a man who rose miraculously from the ranks in a short period of time just as a helicopter rises vertically into the air. Before the Cultural Revolution he had served as an office clerk in the Changchih City Bureau of the State Grain Company. The Bureau supervised the work of some 450 people employed primarily at the various grain stations in the communes and at city grain shops. After the university students began writing militant posters in Peking he posted a declaration at the Grain Bureau that challenged the way it was run. Soon afterward he helped overthrow the Party leaders of the Bureau and rank-and-file members elected him chairman of the Revolutionary Committee that replaced them. Then the City Committee ordered him into the front lines as editorial adviser to the *Changchih Daily Paper*. Seizing on this position Smart Fan organized a group of rebellious newspaper workers who could serve as a political base. He next established liaison with the most radical students in the schools and colleges of Changchih as well as with a number of wandering student groups from Peking and Tientsin who came to make connections with their provincial brethren. In spite of the fact that his organization never enrolled more than a handful of members, Smart Fan led it into the coalition that seized power in Changchih City on January 25, 1967, and emerged as a key member of the Revolutionary Committee that replaced the old city leadership. He simultaneously acquired a position on the City Party Committee, and organized eighteen people at Party headquarters into an action group called the *Second Headquarters of the Red Column*. After a series of the most complex and bizarre maneuvers that aligned him with the winning side in the three-month civil war that fractured Changchih in early 1968, he rose to the top as Secretary of the General Affairs Office of the Changchih City Committee, a strategic post at the very center of power in one of the fastest-growing industrial areas of China. By that time, according to his own account, his organization had grown to thirty-two members.

The man who could parlay leadership of a "mass" organization of eighteen into a leading post in a city of 350,000 had to be an astute politician. Smart Fan certainly looked the part. A very high, broad forehead was the most prominent feature of his face. It suggested a brain both quick and competent, attributes confirmed every day by the brilliance of his conversation and the flexibility of his tactics. In action he released a great deal of nervous energy, and lit one cigarette from another in endless succession. His right hand was never without one; the thumb and first two fingers on that hand were stained deep brown from tobacco.

Chain-smoking reinforced the air of sophisticated ennui that Smart Fan radiated. His expression bore the stamp of chronic exhaustion, as if he stayed up all night, every night, in some smoke-filled room, but he nevertheless remained alert and in full command not only of himself but of the whole situation. Anyone who wanted to get the better of Smart Fan had to be very wide awake indeed, because, although his eyelids drooped and his mouth hung slightly open, he was capable of intense concentration, penetrating analysis and swift action. Smart Fan might be a helicopter cadre but it wasn't because someone had pulled him into place from above. He had jumped into the stratosphere by his own effort. He had talent enough to reach the top and talent enough to stay there, at least for the time being. We learned only later that he was subject to epileptic fits.

One method of staying on top was to make a good impression on Lin T'ung, and through her on *Central*. This Smart Fan proceeded to do energetically and systematically. From the very first day he treated her with respect, briefed her with inside information on the local scene, and spent long hours in serious consultation. Lin T'ung, both charmed and flattered by so much attention, responded in kind. Smart Fan, she decided, was a rising cadre of great promise. He could not only play a key role in unraveling the mysteries of Long Bow but might well in due time move on to the national scene. On Lin T'ung's initiative these two formed a team that conferred far into the night, jointly launched interviews and investigations, and collaborated on long written reports about the developing class struggle in the brigade.

That Smart Fan actually agreed with Lin T'ung about the true situation in Long Bow may be doubted. After all, he belonged to the same region-wide faction in the Cultural Revolution as Swift Li, the deposed brigade Party Secretary, and could hardly be expected to view the young peasant leader as a counterrevolutionary enemy. Nevertheless, since Lin T'ung had taken up this battle, and since she provided a heaven-sent opportunity to establish personal ties to the center, to the government and the Party in Peking, it was advantageous to support her, to play along with her. Thus it was that Smart Fan adopted the class struggle rhetoric preferred by Lin T'ung and helped direct the whole team into a hunt for evidence of counterrevolutionary words, ties and activities on the part of Swift Li and his "Black Gang."

But Smart Fan was not so dull-witted as to risk his whole future on any single throw of the dice. While taking a public stance alongside Lin T'ung in condemning the Two Gems and exposing "class struggle," he quietly took Swift Li aside and told him not to worry too much. True, he had helped to overthrow the Party Secretary, but when this wind blew itself out and things calmed down he would help him get back on his feet again. Swift Li could count on that.

In the meantime the "class struggle" wind continued to blow with considerable force. The Smart Fan–Lin T'ung alliance so strengthened the radical group in the work team that they were able for a time to dominate its decisions and set the tone of all political work.

The propaganda team of 1971 represented as typical a cross section of Southeast Shansi society as had its forerunner in 1948. In the intervening years the society of the area had grown considerably both in size and in complexity. In keeping with this the team was larger, more sophisticated and more varied than the other team had been. On the whole its members were also quite a bit older.

The team leader was Kao Lu-sheng, forty-eight years old. He was a cadre of middle-peasant origin who had grown up in North Street, one of the villages inside the Changchih City wall whose inhabitants farmed the abandoned soil there.

When Changchih was liberated in 1945 Kao Lu-sheng helped lead the land reform movement, was recruited into the Communist Party, and took office as vice-head of his village. When North Street merged with the City of Changchih as it filled out to and overflowed its ancient walls, he became the head of the village, now a ward of the city. In 1948 he won promotion to the financial department of the municipal government and finally, in 1951, to the Changchih People's Court, where he served as a judge right through until 1969. In that year, as a result of the Cultural Revolution, the city set up a school for the reeducation of its staff. It was one of those May Seventh Cadre Schools, named for the date on which Mao Tse-tung called for the universal reeducation of cadres in special institutes that combined work and study. Sent there for education, Kao had gone out to do rural organizing in a nearby commune and in September, 1970, had finally won assignment to the propaganda team in Long Bow. Judge Kao was steady, hardworking, soft-spoken and devoted, 100 percent devoted, to the work assigned. What he lacked in intellectual brilliance he made up for in perseverance. If he had any fault it was his habit of talking too long when he held the floor. He often reviewed facts and summarized policies that were already familiar to all his listeners, but he plodded through his discourse anyway.

The vice-chairman of the team was Li Chin-tung, forty-six, soft-spoken, gray-haired and tired, a man who had been manager of the Changchih City Theater until transferred to rural work in September, 1970. He was a follower, not a leader, and made very little impression at all on the team, on Long Bow or on us.

Far more forceful, but not necessarily wiser, was the tall, lean-faced man of forty-one named Chi Li-te, a nonparty man of the Hui nationality (Moslem) who had served in General Chen Keng's Second Field Army in the South Shansi campaigns of the Liberation War. Badly wounded in 1949, he was demobilized and given land in Chincheng, at the southern edge of the Province. After graduating from a school for administrative cadres in 1951 he worked in various Changchih City posts, finally ending up in 1969 in the Tax Collection Section. He entered the May Seventh Cadre School along with Judge Kao, but instead of working on the school farm and studying with the majority of the cadres, he won assignment to a propaganda team in Yellow Mill, where, because of his experience as an accountant, he undertook to investigate special cases involving graft and corruption. It was as a special-case investigator that he came to Long Bow in 1971.

Also on the Long Bow Team was a forty-eight-year-old army veteran named Wang Ching-ho. Born on South Street in Changchih, he joined the Eighth Route Army in 1939 at the height of the National Liberation War against Japan. Taking part in the race to the Northeast after Japan's surrender, he fought in the decisive Liao-Shen campaign as a Company Political Director in the Forty-Fifth Army of Huang Yung-sheng, a unit of Lin Piao's Fourth Field Army. In the Peking-Tientsin Campaign he was badly wounded in the mouth, head, arm and back; he returned to Changchih to recuperate in 1949. His left arm never fully regained its function and because he could not do heavy labor he received a small subsidy as a wounded veteran. Since coming home, Veteran Wang had worked for twenty years in the rural areas of Changchih municipality and was a walking encyclopedia on the development of the cooperative movement from its very beginning. Though born a poor peasant, he had attended four years of primary school and this made him one of the more literate members of his army unit, if not of this work team. "In those days," Wang said, "anyone who had been to school for as long as one year was considered to be a Confucius by his battlemates."

A fifth member of the Long Bow Team was Wang Hsin-mao, or Donkey Meat Wang, as he was affectionately called. He was a Changchih-born "worker" from the meat-packing industry; his parents had once owned a small independent business specializing in a brand of cured donkey meat that was famous far and wide for quality and flavor. During the period of socialist transformation the Wang family meat shop had been merged with others into a large cooperative which the municipal meat-packing industry later absorbed. Thus Wang was transformed from an independent butcher into a packing-house worker. On the Long Bow team he had the lowest "cultural level," as the Chinese like to call ability in reading and writing, but perhaps the most developed sense of humor. His slow, wry talk and deep, chronically hoarse voice almost always made us laugh. His long, thin, leathery and deeply creased face was donkeylike enough to go with the voice, and we often teased him about his nickname.

The political director Shen An-huai, thirty-four years old, was among the younger members of the team. He was a handsome, lively fellow from a poor peasant family at home on Changchih's South Street. With the exception of a four-year stint in the army, he had spent his working life as a policeman. Joining the Changchih Security Bureau as a messenger in 1955, he went to the People's Liberation Army (PLA) in 1957 only to return to the Security Bureau in 1961 as an officer in charge of residence cards for the Western Section of the city. On the eve of the Cultural Revolution the city transferred him to Horse Square Commune as Security Officer for the whole commune and as secretary of the commune Youth League. This meant that he had to leave the city police system with its fixed salaries for work points as a commune member.

During the Cultural Revolution the group that led an uprising in the commune chose Shen as its leader. On February 4, 1967, he became political director of the Horse Square District Revolutionary Rebel Seize Power Headquarters, the group that actually took over direction of the commune. When he and others finally established a revolutionary committee, he became a member of its standing committee. He also became a member of the Horse Square Commune Party Committee.

Shen was outgoing and talkative, taking considerable interest in the personal foibles and errant ways of various Long Bow residents. He had been in the village longer than any other member of the team, having been included on two previous teams that had failed to solve village problems. He had first come to Long Bow in June, 1970, as a member of the core group of the commune. He came to carry out the movement known as the "one blow, three oppose." He left again in September when he had a chance to visit Tachai with other commune travelers. He returned to Long Bow in October of the same year with a team organized by the city administration, only to leave again in March when the team, stalemated in its work and unable to unite internally, withdrew in the face of a barrage of hostile posters. At that time, after four days of study in the city, Shen returned to Long Bow with a new team of fifteen, the team that we now had joined.

Other members of the team included a technician from the Changchih City Construction Company—white-haired Chao Fu-kuei, forty-three—and three workers from Changchih Steel: Huang Chia-huan, thirty-one, a fitter from the pipe maintenance section; Cheng Huai-hsin, forty-two, also a fitter; and P'ei Ping-ch'uan, thirty, an accountant. P'ei and Huang had both joined the PLA in 1961 and as members of the same battalion had fought in the Sino-Indian Border War.

The two women members, Li Shen-tai and Ch'ien Shun-ying, both thirty-one, had been classmates at the Peking Normal School and came to Changchih together to teach at the First Middle School. One taught Russian, the other mathematics.

The oldest member of the team was Chi Wei-ho, fifty-five, a middle peasant from Hukuan who had joined the PLA in 1946, was demobilized in 1954, and then worked many years in various construction and industrial organizations in Changchih City. He had come to settle permanently in Long Bow, or, in other words to *ch'ia tui,* to squat, to attach himself to the brigade. He and his wife had become ordinary members of the Third Production Team, but while the propaganda team remained in Long Bow old Chi worked as a part of this outside group.

Security Officer Shen led the "radicals" on the team, and Chi the Moslem, Huang the pipefitter and P'ei the accountant backed him up. Judge Kao and Theater Manager Li stood more or less in the middle supported by the two women school teachers and the technician, Chao Fu-kuei, while the wounded veteran Wang Ching-ho and Donkey Meat Wang formed the opposition that others saw as rightist. This alignment wasn't as clear-cut as described because people tended to shift back and forth on the issues; there were many issues where no one drew clear lines and others on which the team united. Nevertheless, two poles of opinion kept recurring and almost invariably Security Officer Shen could be found arguing one side while Veteran Wang argued the other. With Lin T'ung and Smart Fan backing the security officer, the veteran often found himself isolated.

9

CONTRADICTIONS

The most intensive debates occurred every morning at dawn as the propaganda team gathered for an hour or two of study. All its members usually came together in the Lu family courtyard where Security Officer Shen and his roommate, Donkey Meat Wang, had rented one large room. This room was at the west end of a long, story-and-a-half peasant house that had brick foundations, adobe walls and a tile roof. The house itself was in good repair, but the wall that enclosed the yard had crumbled badly under the heavy August rains. Several sheds and small outbuildings attached to the wall leaned rakishly, as if about to fall. The privy, in the southwest corner of the yard, posed no danger, for it had no roof. It was a deep cistern dug in the ground and overlaid with two large stones set a few inches apart at the center. By placing one foot on each stone one could squat and relieve oneself. A three-sided adobe wall had once provided privacy, but this wall, like the one around the yard itself, had suffered serious erosion. It was now so low that the head and shoulders of anyone squatting there could easily be seen. In summertime this didn't really matter because the main part of the yard had been planted with corn and sunflowers that had grown so tall that they dominated the whole space and arched over the entrance path as trained vines might do. Bean, pumpkin and squash seeds had been planted between the tall stalks and as the stalks shot upward the vines climbed apace, throwing out leafy clusters that created an impenetrable green jungle. Foliage of many shapes and shades completely screened the privy and the courtyard walls from sight.

Closer to the house lay an open well equipped with reel, rope and bucket. As we rubbed our eyes and exchanged morning greetings a succession of peasants came and went drawing water. Obviously this well served more than the Lu family that owned the courtyard. With the wall in the west broken out in several places there was nothing to prevent neighbors who had no well of their own from coming across.

The morning air chilled us to the bone. A low, rolling mist blocked the sun and carried dampness and cold right into the house where Shen and Wang slept on an old brick platform, or kang. The heavy rains of the last few days had raised the water table to unusual heights. Dirt floors sweated visible drops while adobe walls, even when they sat on brick foundations, slowly changed color at the base as the ground water rose in them, threatening the whole building with collapse.

Since the inside air was so stale and damp we took our stools, chairs and assorted bricks saved for seats into the yard outside. There, hunching our shoulders against the fog, we launched into the required daily study. To get off the damp ground and generate more heat Donkey Meat Wang used to squat rather than sit on his little wooden footstool. He looked rather curious sitting there several inches off the ground, knees against his chest, arms around his shins, more like some bird perched on a wilderness rock than a man at his lessons.

The sight caused Veteran Wang to recall how rural cadres behaved when they first came into the city. In 1948 the office of the Regional Party Headquarters in Changchih boasted upholstered sofas complete with clean white covers. After one peasant cadre sat down to make his report, he pulled first one foot, then the other, up onto the cushion, thus reestablishing his customary village squat. In doing so he ground some good, yellow Shangtang earth into the pure white sofa cover. No one ever succeeded in washing out the stain.

From the adjoining sections of the house came the sounds of the Lu family rising. Soon Wang Yü-mei, whom we knew as the young woman behind the counter in the dispensary, and as the star of the local drama group, appeared in the doorway to begin her morning chores. Her long hair, as yet unbraided, fell to her waist, black, sleek and surprisingly alluring. She first drew several buckets of water from the well and carried them home, her slight figure straining under the weight of a shoulder pole and two wooden buckets fully laden. Then she went to the cook shack along the east wall to light the morning fire. While she rushed to prepare the family breakfast her husband's sister, a full-grown teenager, sat in the doorway combing and recombing her hair.

Each day's study began with a text. Sometimes it was a passage from the Shansi provincial paper, sometimes a new directive from the regional government. More often it was a selection from the writings of Mao Tse-tung. This morning Judge Kao had chosen a section of Mao's essay, *On Contradiction.* Teacher Li, picked for the task because her level of literacy was the highest of any team cadre, read it aloud. She no sooner put down her book than a lively discussion began about the contradictions that team members saw all around them, contradictions such as those between husband and wife.

Security Officer Shen, who lived in the courtyard and had a chance to study the host family carefully, watched Yü-mei as she came by for her third bucket of water.

"There's an example for you," he said. "Wang Yü-mei has a problem. She is oppressed in her husband's home and has ended up at bay. She doesn't even dare fight back."

"How can you say that?" said Judge Kao, astonished. "She's not the one who is ruled in that family."

"Maybe she's not ruled," intervened Veteran Wang, "but can you say that she rules them? Who in fact holds power in the next room? Obviously it's the old lady!"

"But there has to be someone in charge," countered Judge Kao. "You can't have everyone in charge, even in a family."

"Well, of course," Veteran Wang replied, "someone has to be in charge. But that person doesn't have to be a dictator. Wang Yü-mei doesn't dare resist."

"Lu Shu-yun, chairwoman of the Women's Association, is in the same position in her family," said Security Officer Shen, joining in again. "There is no equality there either."

This Judge Kao would not allow.

"Nowadays in families, everyone has equal rights."

"In theory maybe, but in practice how can you speak of equality?" asked Shen. "Neither Shu-yun nor Yü-mei has any equality at all."

"But Yü-mei earns her own money and spends it where she likes. She wears good clothes and eats the same food as the rest. Why isn't she equal?"

"Why? Because she ends up doing all the work, as you can see for yourself. As for living standards, there are at least two or three in the family who earn money. Any girl could eat and dress well in such a household. You can't judge her situation just by looking at her clothes. They wouldn't let their daughter-in-law run around in rags. She is on display, so to speak. They want to show off what a good daughter-in-law they have. But she still does all the work."

"Well, isn't it right that she should work?" asked Judge Kao, upset by the trend of the argument. "Does that mean that she is oppressed?"

"No, of course not," said Donkey Meat Wang, throwing in his two cents. "She should do her share. But that doesn't mean she should work 365 days a year while some others never lift a hand to help."

"Well, you still have to investigate what's going on," said Judge Kao. "Maybe the old lady is unable to work."

"That old lady is healthy enough," declared Security Officer Shen. "And her seventeen-year-old daughter is even healthier. But she hasn't carried a single bucket of water since we've been here. It's all left to Yü-mei. Wang Yü-mei is afraid of her husband and her father-in-law is afraid of his wife!"

"But surely they talk such things over inside that family," said Judge Kao, unwilling to yield.

Living in the room next to Yü-mei, Security Officer Shen overheard what went on between the family members day in and day out. "Consultation is nothing but a formality there," he said. "Yü-mei has no right to speak. If she wants to say a single word she has to ask for permission, and every time she goes to cook a meal she has to ask her mother-in-law what should be put in the pot. It's as if she were one of the servants of old."

"But she looks happy," protested Judge Kao.

"You call that happy," said Shen in disgust. "Do you think it makes her happy to be able to wear a sweater?"

At this point Teacher Li, the young mother on the team, broke in. "Happy! What do you mean happy? Comrade Kao, you had better do a little investigating before you jump to conclusions."

"Well," said the team leader, on the defensive, "I just don't agree that she is oppressed. There aren't enough facts to prove it. What I see is this: when they eat noodles she eats noodles, too."

"Come off it," protested Huang the pipefitter. "Her father-in-law eats two eggs every day. She never has a chance to taste even one."

"Well, maybe that's a special need that the old man has," said the Judge.

"But she has her special needs, too," said Shen, indignant. "Why can't she have her share?"

"I agree," said Veteran Wang. "There's a lot of feudal thinking there and some oppression, too. You can't say it's exactly the same as feudal oppression, but it's oppression all the same!"

Unable to agree on the question of Yü-mei, Judge Kao changed the subject to the central problem they were all wrestling with—the contradiction between the members of the Long Bow Brigade and the Two Gems. Was it a contradiction among the people or one between the people and sworn enemies?

This topic unleashed intense discussion and some strong emotions.

Security Officer Shen was very critical of the deposed Party Secretary Swift Li.

"He won't accept criticism because he thinks he was on the right side in the Cultural Revolution. But many people who were on the right side at first committed terrible mistakes later. Look at Kuai Ta-fu of Tsinghua University! Look at Liu Ke-p'ing of Shansi!"

"He won't criticize himself," said pipefitter Huang, "and he won't criticize anyone who stood on his side in the Cultural Revolution. He sees himself as a beautiful flower, while everyone else is bean curd. If anyone criticizes him, he counterattacks—this one has made a line mistake, that one is a bad element—how can they criticize me? But he himself has two ways of looking at things. Who does he rely on? Some really dubious characters. But he judges them leniently because they support him. Then he applies a class line, very strict indeed, toward those who are critical."

"Swift Li is really slippery. First he answers back, then he weeps," said Security Officer Shen.

"Yes, when I talked to him yesterday he wept," said Lin T'ung from *Central*. "I told him straight out: you think there are people who will stand behind you, people who won't betray you. But how can you rely on them? Your problem now leads right to Heaven [to *Central*]. The only way out is to make an honest self-criticism.

"His problem is very serious," she continued. "We have to deal with him. I only met him for the first time yesterday but I got a very bad impression. False tears. Red eyes. 'I have made such big mistakes,' he said. 'I can't hold my head up before the comrades who are trying to help me.' What nonsense. Long ago I learned to see through people like that!"

"We have to be careful not to put too big a cap on him," said Judge Kao. "His main problem is one of pride. He comes from a poor peasant family. He joined the Communist Party in the middle sixties as a clean young cadre of the new generation. He came to power as the leader of a correct faction in the Cultural Revolution. He led the village for five years with some success. He thinks his record is good. This makes him proud and conceited. Why should he bow his head?"

"It looks to me like a contradiction among the people," said Veteran Wang. "But a contradiction like that, if not resolved, can turn into something else."

"If Swift Li won't criticize himself, if he continues to defy our team, the brigade, the commune and the city leadership, he could turn this contradiction into an antagonistic one," said Donkey Meat Wang.

"That's true," said Judge Kao. "Up to now he hasn't recognized his mistakes. He thinks anyone who criticizes him is just reviving the factionalism of the past, while those who support and flatter him are his true friends. With such an attitude, that criticism comes only from enemies, he can never hope to remold himself and take a new road."

"You all think it's not so serious," said Lin T'ung, alarmed by their leniency. "But maybe there is more to the story. How much do we know about Swift Li's best friend, the militia captain Chin? What is behind his relationship with Shih Kui-hsiang? Her relatives are counterrevolutionaries. Her uncle actually took part in the Catholic uprising in Taiyuan. Chin's whole family is also Catholic. Perhaps there is a political side to this infatuation? Perhaps it is not only a question of a decadent life-style? How can we be sure there isn't someone standing behind this woman, urging her to get close to Long Bow cadres in order to pull them down into the mud?"

"Yes, when you look at all this you have to ask some questions about Swift Li," said Security Officer Shen. "How is it that as soon as Li comes to power in the Cultural Revolution he links up with questionable people who in turn link up with counterrevolutionaries, who, in turn, proceed to pull everyone down into the mud? It looks as if Swift Li is being pulled over by Fast Chin, who is being pulled over by Shih Kui-hsiang, who in turn is being pulled or pushed by some very questionable forces. These things should make us vigilant."

This gave Lin T'ung just the opening she was looking for.

"Swift Li looks like a double-dealer to me. He's just like any other May 16 conspirator," she said as if she could detect counterrevolution on sight, as old Wang Yü-lai claimed to be able to do in 1945. "He really puts on a show. He says he can't be blamed. All the blame must be pinned on others. But who, if not he, beat sidelines director Shen? Who, if not he, ate and drank at Militia Captain Fast Chin's house? Who, if not he, seduced the daughter of that counterrevolutionary, Old Man Wu Kuo-fan? And who, if not he, protected Fast Chin at every turn? Why protect Chin if he himself is not implicated?"

Prodded by Lin T'ung, the team members decided to investigate thoroughly all the ties that linked the Two Gems to each other and to the world at large.

While the propaganda team concentrated on this disturbing issue I decided to go back to the beginning, to the conclusion of the land reform in 1948. I wanted to trace how Long Bow had come to this strange turning point. I wanted to understand, first of all, how Long Bow village had transformed itself from a community of more or less equal smallholders, each farming his or her own scattered plots, into the large-scale, cooperative brigade of today where the peasants carried out all major production in common. Also, how could a question about the leading group and the policies it followed generate such deep interest and such intense struggle?

Part II

GET ORGANIZED

People do not truly believe in anything new until they have had actual experience of it.
Niccolò Machiavelli

THE FOUR
FREEDOMS

 We met in the courtyard of the old Catholic orphanage under the arches where, so many years before, the land reform work team and the village activists had often discussed problems late into the night. Chang Kuei-ts'ai, Chang Hsin-fa and Shen T'ien-hsi, who had joined those gatherings as young militants, now came together once more as middle-aged parents, grandparents and community elders to try and recall for me what happened after the land reform movement concluded. With them came the propaganda team cadre Wang Ching-ho (Veteran Wang), wounded warrior of national and civil war, who had spent the last twenty years in the Rural Work Department of the Changchih City Government. What the Long Bow Brigade members failed to remember Old Wang was sure to recall. From his vast experience in every corner of the suburban area he was able to re-create the local context in which the events in Long Bow unfolded.

Whenever we could, we sat on chairs and stools out in the brick-paved courtyard, but as often as not, during those first days of my return, it rained and we had to retreat to the damp shelter of the cavernous mission buildings.

Chang Hsin-fa was, as in the past, the most vocal of the three peasant leaders. As he began to tell about some of the problems that beset the organization of mutual aid groups in 1949 he warmed to the task.

> One of the advantages of mutual aid was the prompt settlement of obligations. There were lots of labor-swapping and animal-swapping arrangements among individual peasants, but sometimes, when a person failed to return the labor owed or failed to pay up by other means, it was hard for families to collect. In our organized group the members had more leverage.
>
> We had a new member, Sun Chiu-fa, who refused to pay what he owed to others. We hoed his land for him several times and piled up labor credit with him that he never returned. To make payment easy we calculated his debt in millet but he never paid the millet either. He claimed that he didn't have any. Finally we said, "Pay up, or get out of the group," but that didn't move him. In the end we took our quarrel to the District Office right here in this building. We

sent Sun Chiu-fa in to see Party Secretary Chu. Sun went in at a very busy moment and Secretary Chu told him to wait in the next room.

Then Secretary Chu became so absorbed in his work that he forgot there was anyone waiting to see him. When lunchtime came he walked out, locking the door behind him. Sun found himself sitting in an unused back room full of fleas. Ravenous for human blood, they attacked him by the hundreds. When he could stand it no longer he ran for the door, only to find that it was locked. He decided then that he was under arrest. The fleas, having tasted blood, followed him from one room to the other, biting viciously. He became frightened, pounded on the walls, kicked at the door, and yelled for help. But nobody heard his cries.

When Secretary Chu finally returned Sun was beside himself. He volunteered to pay his debt to the group right away. Anything was better than detention in that den of fleas. He never learned that the whole episode was unplanned—an accident.

With this story of Sun Chiu-fa and the fleas we launched into the history of collectivization in Long Bow, a history which is the central theme of this book.

Toward the end of *Fanshen* I wrote a paragraph that tried to sum up the situation in Long Bow after the completion of land reform in 1948:

"Land reform, by creating basic equality among rural producers, only presented the producers with a choice of roads: private enterprise on the land leading to capitalism, or collective enterprise on the land leading to socialism. The choice between them still had to be made, and there was as yet no unanimity on the question. Only the most advanced among the peasants had even considered it."

Judged in the light of all that has happened since, this summary stands up well. In 1948, not only had most peasants, in or out of the Party, never considered the choice that lay before them, but many Communist Party leaders had not seriously considered it either. With civil war raging across the land, the policy of the Party at the time was to guarantee production, to make sure that the vast upheaval brought about by land reform did not prevent people from tilling every square foot of land and harvesting bumper crops wherever possible. That is why the land reform team leader in Long Bow, Ts'ai Chin, before he left for other work, told the peasants: "In the future we will not love the poor. We want everyone to strive to work hard and become a new rich peasant. With the land question solved there is nothing to prevent us all from becoming as rich as Li Hsun-ta [the P'ing-shun County labor hero]."

This idea was later summed up in two provocative words: "Enrich yourselves." These words recognized the essence of the situation in the countryside of North China at the time: the peasants, in possession of the land at last, would have no one to blame but themselves if they did not make the most of the opportunity. They were on their own in an absolute sense, without any crutch or prop, even such a venal one as a rich peasant to borrow seed from, or a landlord to stake them to a season's supply of millet.

Each family had to take charge of its own fate, put arms and hoes to work, and force the land to produce. There was no guarantee as to the outcome, no "fixed grain ration," no "iron rice bowl" that could provide some subsistence minimum for man, woman or child. Subsistence had to be wrung from the soil by sweat and toil. Everything depended on the peasants taking up this challenge with enthusiasm and pursuing it to the end.

Since, out of historical necessity, what prevailed in the sphere of ownership was private property, what prevailed by way of motivation was self-interest in the narrowest sense. To satisfy this, the government had to guarantee that initiative would be rewarded, that the fruits of toil would belong to the toiler, and that these fruits could be freely spent on the improvement of individual lives, or freely invested in further private production.

To that end the Communist Party restated the *Four Freedoms* of New Democracy and thoroughly implemented them. They were:

1. Freedom to buy, sell or rent land.
2. Freedom to hire labor for wages.
3. Freedom to lend money at interest.
4. Freedom to set up private enterprises for profit.

These *Four Freedoms* formed the basis for the development of private enterprise in countryside and city and ensured, insofar as possible, that people would use what resources they had to produce all they possibly could, thus enriching themselves on the one hand, and on the other supplying ample food, fiber, handcrafts and manufactured products for vast liberated areas crippled by decades of invasion, civil war and social upheaval. Only if peasants produced these supplies could the war ever be won.

Furthermore, even after the war was won, it would take several years for the economy to recover, several years of reconstruction before any basic reorganization of society as a whole could begin. Throughout that whole period private production must predominate. The *Four Freedoms* provided the key to a whole stage in the revolution.

To support the *Four Freedoms* during the reconstruction period did not mean, however, to overlook the negative aspects of private production for China and especially for the Chinese countryside. There were literally millions of peasants who did not win enough land, draft animals and implements to carry on any viable form of small-scale production, not to mention enriching themselves. To call on every peasant producer to become a rich peasant was a contradiction in terms. A rich peasant was by definition an exploiter who prospered through hiring the labor of others. Only a few families in any community could hope to become rich by hiring labor, buying land, lending money at interest and setting up small private enterprises. If some families bought land other families must sell. If some families hired labor others must hire out. If some lent money others must borrow it and pay the interest. For every family that went up the economic ladder, several must go down.

For those on the way down, a way out had to be found. The way out advocated by Mao was to organize, first in mutual-aid groups where people helped one another with labor, implements and animals, but each took home his own crop; and second in cooperatives where people pooled land, implements and livestock for joint tillage and joint sidelines, then shared the common crop and other common income.

Organization, at whatever level, to be viable, must be voluntary. Mutual-aid groups and cooperatives, freely joined by those who recognized the benefits, would have to crystallize out of a sea of private operators who still practiced, for better or for worse, the *Four Freedoms*. Only after cooperation became a dominant form could these freedoms and the remaining private production be challenged.

It was in 1943 that Mao first raised the slogan "Get Organized." He raised it then in order to stimulate production, to bring people with scattered and inadequate means of production together so that they could more effectively cope with nature, wrest larger returns from the soil, and guarantee victory in the war against Japan. But by 1948, with land reform already completed over wide areas of North China, getting organized began to take on a new, deeper meaning as a challenge to the old way of life. Organization began to be promoted not simply as a more effective way to produce, but as a first skirmish in the battle to determine the shape of the society to come—whether China would develop as a capitalist or a socialist country.

Now that on the mainland the power of the landlords, the compradores and their overseas backers verged on collapse, the heart of the social struggle in China began to shift to this new level where the target would no longer be the traditional feudal rulers but the modern bourgeoisie—a multilayered class that had, in the great battle for national survival, been an ally.

As the Communist Party mobilized people to create socialist forms of production, Mao foresaw a great new class struggle arising, but a struggle that would take forms far more subtle than the armed confrontation that preceded it.

Once the Kuomintang suffered defeat, once the industrial and commercial holdings of its leaders had been confiscated, once land reform spread to the whole of China, there would no longer be a question of overthrowing a dominant exploiting class. The problem would be to restrict and control the development of capitalist enterprise in city and countryside so that no such dominant class could arise. In the countryside this meant building functioning collectives that could weld producers together, mobilize their full productive power, and ensure the prosperity of all members.

The alternative was clearly accelerated polarization, the growth of a rich peasant economy, which in ten years could bring China to the same impasse that faced the Soviet Union in the thirties. There, after 1917, a rich peasant (kulak) economy developed such strength on redistributed land that what amounted to a second civil war became necessary in the name of rescuing the poor from peonage. In the course of the struggle not only rich peasants but middle peasants became targets, and good relations between the countryside and the city suffered lasting damage.

In China, Mao warned, all the conditions existed for just such a class differentiation. If the Party allowed it to develop too far, serious conflict could hardly be avoided. To start with, land distribution, in spite of its tremendous leveling effect, had not abolished classes in the countryside. The primary target of the land revolution, wherever it had been carried out, had been that bastion of feudalism, the landlord class. Landlords had been thoroughly expropriated. But from 1949 on only the surplus property of rich peasants could legally be confiscated, leaving them in about the same position as the middle peasants who had all along received protection. Down below, although large numbers of poor peasants gained enough to establish themselves as independent producers, a strong minority of former tenants and hired laborers still remained poor because there was not enough property to go around. In spite of the fact that the whole peasant population now consisted of laboring people, peasants entered the post-land-reform struggle for survival on unequal terms, with the deck stacked in favor of those with superior means of production.

These differences, inherited from the past, could only be intensified by the policy of *laissez-faire*, the equal application of the *Four Freedoms* mandated by the overall situation. While a large number of families in the middle managed, for a while, to hold their own, some of the better-off immediately began to move up as the worst-off started to slip down. This polarization seemed destined to accelerate with time. The end result could only be a new class society, at best one dominated by rich peasants, at worst a replica of the traditional gentry system.

Looking at Long Bow village in the light of these warnings one had to ask:

1. Did classes, in fact, still exist?

2. Were new classes being formed through polarization and, if so, on what scale?

3. What difference did these things make in the way individuals thought and behaved?

LONG BOW FACTS
AND FIGURES

Between 1946 and 1948 (the years of the land reform) 169 families of poor peasants and hired laborers with 605 members took over 2,077.7 mou (346.3 acres) of land. This doubled their holdings and brought their average per capita share to 5.8 mou, or just under 1 acre. Seventy-six families of middle peasants with 341 members lost 480 mou (80 acres) but still held 6 mou, or a full acre per capita. Rich peasants and landlords who had originally owned two to three times the amount of land held per capita by middle peasants, and who dominated, through their control of religious and clan institutions, an additional acreage almost as large, lost 914 mou (152 acres) of private land and 650 mou (108 acres) of church, temple and clan land and ended up with a meager 4.6 mou apiece.

What was true of land was also true of the other productive property such as draft animals, carts and farm implements, and of personal property such as houses, clothes, cooking utensils and storage vessels. The Peasants' Association had distributed everything owned by landlords and rich peasants and a small portion of the property of middle peasants so that the whole population enjoyed almost equal shares of productive equipment, housing and the other necessities of life. In addition the Association had reallocated all the wells and privies so that every family had the right to draw water from a designated well, to relieve themselves at a designated privy, and to share the fertility stored there.

In spite of this massive redistribution of wealth some inequalities remained. There were still 29 poor families with 82 members who did not receive enough to give them each an acre of land. They held 5.1 mou apiece, or 10 percent less on the average than everyone else. Their share of draft animals, carts, implements and even housing was also somewhat deficient. These families were still classed as poor peasants. In contrast, 140 families who received slightly more were classed as new-middle peasants. They held 5.8 mou per capita. Somewhat more prosperous than these new-middle peasants were the 70 families of old-middle peasants. The 341 people so classed owned exactly an acre apiece, and were somewhat better off in regard to draft animals, implements, carts and housing. Five families of former landlords and rich peasants with 12 members in all held significantly less than any other group—4.6 mou per capita, or 20 percent below the average.

As directives from Party leaders made clear, and as the experience of the Long Bow peasants themselves confirmed, there was no acceptable way to bring the 29 deficient families up to the average by distributing existing wealth. Local property for distribution could have but two sources: middle peasant families who had carried a heavy burden of debt in the past and had acquired what property they did own only through hard labor, and the remaining expropriated rich peasants and landlords whose holdings had already been reduced below the standards set for the rest of the community. No more property could be taken from them without forcing many of them onto the road as beggars. If this occurred the burden of supporting them through handouts would have returned to the shoulders of the working peasants who had previously underwritten their easy life by paying rent and interest and by providing cheap hired labor.

With the only obvious sources of distributable wealth ruled out, 29 families of poor peasants not only remained poor, they were severely handicapped when it came to "enriching themselves." They constituted a social force interested in cooperative rather than individual solutions to the problem of survival.

In the next category one had to list the former poor peasants and hired laborers who had in fact *fanshened.* Many of them also looked to cooperation as a way out. True, they had acquired enough land and other property to earn the label of new-middle peasant, but they had no experience of prosperity as petty producers and few illusions that the meager holdings they had acquired in land reform could really solve problems of livelihood. In relation to the projected class struggle to come they were recognized by the Party leadership as poor peasants still, with demands that were objectively revolutionary. Their commitment to private property was relatively weak and could well be shaken by a viable, collective alternative.

A section of the middle peasants themselves, the lower-middle peasants, augmented this group of poor and formerly poor peasants. It was made up of families who in the old society had generally been drifting downward in the social scale, falling deeper into debt each year, losing land and livestock and staring bankruptcy in the face. They, too, held few illusions that the small holdings left to them could guarantee a prosperous future. In Long Bow these groups added up to some 209 out of 250 families, with 786 out of 960 people. Together they made up that new class category put forward at the time by the Central Committee—the poor and lower-middle peasants; it was a solid majority unlikely to do well on the capitalist road. On it Mao based his hopes for a socialist transformation of the countryside.

With 209 poor and lower-middle peasant families, with 36 old-middle peasant families who owned but a fraction more real property per capita than the former, with 4 families of ex-rich peasants and 1 family of ex-landlords, most of whom owned even less, on the average, than the poorest remaining peasants, the class situation in Long Bow could hardly be called extreme.

A detailed study carried out by the Regional Party Committee in five nearby villages found a high level of homogeneity as much as five years later. In 1951 middle peasants, new and old, made up some 95.02 percent of the total, with rich middle peasants amounting to only 2.22 percent. Rich peasants developed after land reform occupied 0.6 percent, hired laborers 3.84 percent and miscellaneous other categories only .44 percent.*

If one conceived of class status simply as a function of the relationship between people and their productive property, if one took holdings alone as the standard, one could conclude that, for all practical purposes, only one class existed in Long Bow and the neighboring villages and that the world outlook of its members must be uniform. In reality two major factors made such a conclusion unrealistic.

First, one had to take into account the influence of previous class status on people's minds. There were obviously remnant exploiters in Long Bow who considered the restoration of past holdings to be far more important than anything else, certainly more important than plans for increased production based on hard labor. There were also a number of old middle peasant families whose members wanted only to be left alone to prosper as they had usually managed to do in the past. Here were at least two groups with perceived interests left over from history that diverged from those of the majority.

A second influence, even more powerful than the mental warp built in by previous class status, was the process of polarization that constantly transformed the status quo. Statistics showed that for quite a few families winning land and productive property only marked the start of renewed change in the family fortune. They began either to rise or fall. The direction of movement tended to influence the outlook of every family member more profoundly than the starting point. Those on the way up viewed individual effort with growing satisfaction, while those on the way down suffered increasing disillusionment.

The regional study of 1951 revealed that after five years some 96 peasant families in the five villages surveyed had sold 284.11 mou of land, primarily to raise money for wedding or funeral expenses, while 99 peasant families in the same communities had bought land. Thus the number who, because of natural or man-made calamity, had lost land and were headed toward poverty was balanced by at least an equal number who were prosperous enough to expand. Party analysts estimated that those who faced serious difficulties as independent producers numbered as high as 37.7 percent, but only about half of these saw the problem clearly and took organizational steps to help themselves. And 42.3 percent, who were somewhat better off, still definitely preferred to go it alone.

For this group, a portion of whom were on the way up, new things and new ways made life increasingly interesting. Young men were planting new varieties of crops in the fields; young women were bobbing their hair. Young and old could count on each season to bring unexpected surprises and delights. A rhyme, celebrating all this, spread throughout Southeast Shansi.

> Early each morn
> Cook Golden Queen corn.
> At noon repeat
> With One-Six-Nine wheat.

*These are the official figures listed in Wang Ch'ien's report.

At night take a whirl
With a short-haired girl.

The regional Party Secretary, Wang Ch'ien, used these couplets in his report to the Central Committee on post-land-reform conditions. He felt constrained, however, to substitute "glass beauty," a new variety of millet, for the "short-haired girl" that enlivened the night. This change made the poem more consistent, but removed much of its spice.

The poem came to stand as a symbol for "new democratic" thinking, an attitude of mind that was quite satisfied with the state of the nation after land reform and saw no need for further struggle or transformation. Those who thought this way included many Party members. The theory they consciously or unconsciously adopted was the theory of "the success of the revolution," the idea that with land reform the revolution was over and the thing to do henceforth was to bury one's head in production, prosper and enjoy life.

Three families in Long Bow, by burying their heads in production, did particularly well after 1948.

The most prosperous of these was made up of the Shih brothers. Shih Ts'ai-yuan, an Eighth Route Army veteran and a leading member of the Communist Party Branch; Shih Fu-yuan, another Communist Party member who worked as a District Cadre after 1947; and little brother Shih Er-chih, who concentrated on tilling the fields at home. They had been middle peasants prior to the land reform, but they had suffered exploitation and oppression and had grievances to settle with Long Bow gentry. Both Ts'ai-yuan and Fu-yuan became activists before Liberation, joined the Party early, and served in leading posts as cadres. Strategically situated politically, they received generous amounts of property in the distribution and emerged from the land reform period with 70 mou (11.7 acres) of land, two donkeys and two carts. During the busy season, particularly at harvesttime, they hired labor to get their work done. As long as they remained healthy, as long as all three brothers could work hard, the family was bound to prosper.

Chang Hsin-fa, secretary of the Communist Party Branch in 1948, was another leader who prospered. Originally a bare-poor peasant, a man who had worked all his life as a hired man, he emerged from land reform with 15 mou (2.5 acres) of land. Soon thereafter he acquired a donkey and then a mule. In the prime of life, with only three mouths to feed, he could look forward to a surplus at the end of each year.

The third prosperous family was that of Li Chüan-chung, known to everyone as Li-the-Fat. He had joined the militia early and had become a squad leader. In 1949 he joined the Party. When the old distillery worker Wen Tui-chin died, Li succeeded him as chairman of the village People's Congress. He came from a family so poor that in the famine year they sold a son for a few quarts of grain. Li-the-Fat himself lost 4 mou of his land to the rich peasant Kuo Ch'ung-wang, then had to rent it back from him on shares. After the crop failure of 1942 Ch'ung-wang, in lieu of rent, took the whole crop, all the clothes and all the household goods that the Li family owned. But in the course of the land reform Li-the-Fat reversed his fate.

For a family of five he received 5 good acres and half a donkey. In the prime of life, he worked hard. Soon he had saved enough to buy another acre. This came from a Linhsien peasant who sold out his holdings in order to return home. Soon after that Li-the-Fat bought a mule, and then bought over the other half of the donkey. Thus he became sole owner of two draft animals. By hauling coal that was in demand for household fuel and by plowing for various neighbors he put many families in his debt. When he needed help on the land it was always available from those who owed him money and preferred to work off their debts. His method was to demand help from eight or ten people after every rain and thus get his land hoed within twenty-four hours while the soil was still soft and the weeds still vulnerable. He always settled wage accounts promptly, offering three to four sheng of millet for a day's work, and he always fed people well when they worked on his land. Thus he had no problem finding help. Once he became a cadre, prestige and power worked in his favor. People, especially young people, found it hard to refuse any request made by a cadre.

Li-the-Fat did so well with new animals and new land that he was soon in a position to buy more houses. He bought six sections in his home courtyard from a poor peasant with many children who could not make ends meet and had to sell housing won in the land reform. As Li-the-Fat's children grew up and got married he bought new sections of housing for each of them in turn. His ambition was to acquire the whole courtyard in which he lived. These purchases did not exhaust his resources. He often had enough left over to lend grain to poorer neighbors. It was said that he did not charge interest on such loans. If so it was only because Party members were not allowed to.

From the very beginning, because his brother had joined the People's Liberation Army, Li-the-Fat got help on the land as a soldier's relative. Later, when his brother came home wounded, this help increased. The family got 90 yuan in cash twice a year from the government as a disability payment while the community continued to contribute 150 labor days a year to the family crops.

The wounded brother, Li T'ai-p'ing, did so well that he hired a full-time laborer and provided housing for him and his family. This laborer was Chou Cheng-fu, a poor peasant who had won land of his own but managed it so poorly that he could not survive as an independent producer.

Li-the-Fat continued the expansion of his holdings by setting up a small flour mill. During the busy season he hired the poor peasant Shen Shui-sheng to work there by the day. Shen Shui-sheng had a family so large that he could not feed them on the small amount of land he won in the land reform. He had to hire out to ensure "salt turnip for his wife and children to put on their millet."

It is clearly not possible to write about those who prospered without mentioning those who failed and ended up working for others, such as Chou Cheng-fu and Shen Shui-sheng. Another person who failed was Chin Ch'en-hai, a nephew to old Kuo Ch'ou-har, who had played such a role in the struggle against police captain Wang Wen-te in 1948. Ch'en-hai's father won 20 mou in the land reform, a house, half an ox and half a cart. When the old man fell ill and could no longer work, his son was only fourteen. He did not count as a full labor power and could not handle heavy work on the land. He was also somewhat lazy. Unable to survive as an independent peasant he sold half his holding, his house and his share in the ox and the cart to old Ch'ou-har, his uncle. Then, without any means of support, he went to work in the fertilizer plant set up by the Regional Government outside Changchih City. As a worker Ch'en-hai did well. He earned good wages, saved part of them, eventually married, and again bought a house in Long Bow. By that time the village had become a cooperative brigade in Horse Square Commune. Ch'en-hai rejoined it as a full member.

An important factor contributing to the rise of some families while others slowly went under was the possession of draft animals. As Veteran Wang pointed out, a peasant who owned two good draft animals could get by without working at all. He had only to feed and care for his animals, and hire them out to receive in return enough labor from others to grow his whole crop.

This was made possible by the relatively high value placed on animal power as compared to human labor power. An able-bodied man working all day could earn 4 sheng of millet (1 sheng is equal to 1½ pints, 3 cups, or approximately 1 quart). To hire an animal to plow 1 mou cost 5 sheng of millet. Two animals paired could plow 8 mou in a day at a cost of 40 sheng. Any peasant who invited a man and team to plow for a day had to work 8 to 10 days to pay the debt. In terms of the crop (with yields at 20 bushels to the acre) plowing costs equaled 5 percent of the total.

The owner of draft animals not only benefited from the high cost of animal power as compared to human labor power, he was also in a position, because of the scarcity of draft animals and the critical nature of the spring and autumn rush when draft power was most needed, to twist every other facet of the exchange to his benefit.

Hsin-fa described the process in some detail.

> A man can break up one mou a day with a hoe, but the labor is heavy. He would rather wait for draft power if that is at all possible. But when the animal is finally brought in the soil is turned only to a depth of four inches, less than can be done with a hoe. The owner of the animal plows his own land deeply but is not so conscientious on the other fellow's land. Also, when he plows his own land he does it when the land is just right, neither too wet nor too dry. But when he plows for his neighbor he comes when he can, when the land is hard and dry or when the land is still muddy. What you receive in such an exchange is plowing of sorts, but what you have to pay back could be any kind of labor, and no matter what you do, no matter how hard the labor, it only counts as one day. You may have to haul coal, thin millet, move soil for brickmaking by wheelbarrow or carrying pole. And all of these are very hard work, certainly harder than driving a team hitched to a plow. The animal owner has another advantage: he not only disposes of the animal's productive power but he also owns the manure produced by the animal. And this goes on his own crops.

So a peasant without a draft animal has to beg for help every time. In the spring he can't get the compost to the field on time. In the fall he can't get his crop home. But the owner of a draft animal does everything on time. He finishes his own work first, then helps others. His land is nice and neat. Everything is in order. He who lacks an animal can only wait for favors from others.

The man without an animal has to talk to the animal owner far in advance. "Whatever work you have to do, I'll do it," he promises. "Then when I need you and your mule you'll help me out? OK?".

All this has to be done early. Above all the offer must look attractive to the animal owner. Everything that follows is arranged according to his convenience. When his harvest is ready he calls on all those who are obligated to him to come at once, no matter how busy they are or how short the supply of labor is. They come, they do the job quickly. His wife cooks one meal for them, one big harvest meal. It is all very convenient. But if you should dare say that you are busy and would prefer to come some other time, you won't get any big harvest meal. You may not get any meal at all, and the next time plowing season comes around he won't plow for you either!

A peasant is not in the same position as a worker. He does not earn money. He swaps his labor for labor or services that jump up and down in price. There is always a problem of equivalent exchange. There is busy season labor and slack season labor, heavy labor and light labor. The money paid for various types of labor at various seasons of the year varies widely. Thus a poor peasant without an animal, when he agrees to swap labor for plowing at a fixed rate, will have to give far more than he gets in return, especially in terms of hours expended.

What seemed apparent from this discussion of draft animals was that animal power often commanded more than its value in exchange, particularly in the busy season, while human labor often commanded less than its value. Such a situation could only arise because of a temporary scarcity of draft animals due to the ravages of war, the wanton slaughter of animals for meat by Japanese troops, and the difficulty of raising replacements in a period of social disruption and short crops.

But even as the supply of animals increased, bringing the price of animal power in line with the cost of its reproduction, a draft animal still represented a substantial capital investment. Those families who disposed of enough funds to make such an investment were in a position to take advantage of their neighbors, just as, in the American countryside, the owner of a big tractor or combine can take advantage of his neighbors through custom work.

During the post-land-reform period of prosperity for some, decline for others, several Long Bow residents abandoned farming and set up private businesses as their sole means of support. Chi Kuei-sheng first left home to work as a clerk in a state-operated store. But when he saw that the *Four Freedoms* were actually enforced in the economy he returned home and set up a small shop. In time competition from the community-owned cooperative store proved too much for him. He sold out and went to work for the branch of the cooperative that operated in Horse Square.

Another old resident, Ch'ien Er-ching, moved back to Long Bow all the way from the Northeast to set up a shop. A newcomer, Chin Ta-ch'uan, of Linhsien, Honan, moved in to the village to set up a flour mill.

The small but persistent trend toward class differentiation, so well documented in Long Bow village, permeated the whole region. Another survey made by the Regional Party Committee in 1950 covered 15 villages with 3,394 family units. It revealed that 13.7 percent of the families had sold land, 9.6 percent were already selling labor power, while 4 percent were hiring labor. In 13 villages there were already 28 new-rich peasant families, families who were earning the major part of their income from other people's labor. They made up less than 1 percent of the population. Most of these new exploiters were from families that had been bare-poor before the land reform; they had learned how to enrich themselves in the short period since.

A second survey examined the state of handcrafts in the villages of three counties. Altogether 50 families who owned small cottage industries had become exploiters. Together they employed 142 workers, slightly less than three per family, but enough to make them dependent on hired rather than family labor.

12

MUTUAL AID—
SOME EXAMPLES

Obviously the implementation of Ts'ai Chin's slogans,
"Every family strive to become a new rich peasant," "The
Communist Party no longer loves the poor," and finally,
"Enrich yourselves," brought prosperity to some in Long
Bow village. At the same time it forced others into bank-
ruptcy. As for the majority, who managed to hold their own, they did so
under increasing economic pressure. Some of the more farsighted responded
as Mao had so often urged peasants to do, by organizing.

The first step in the organization process was mutual aid—the sharing of
labor power, draft animals and implements on a small scale by groups of
neighbors willing to enter into such arrangements. What made people willing to give mutual aid a try was not primarily exhortation on the part of
Communist leaders, at whatever level, but immediate economic advantage.
In spite of the thorough way in which all productive property had been
redistributed, there simply were not enough donkeys, oxen, carts, seeders
or even iron hoes to go around. When these were distributed as fractional
shares (one leg of a donkey, one wheel of a cart) people had to cooperate
in order to produce at all. When one family got one necessary item, such
as a donkey, but not another, such as a cart, they also had to share. The
alternative was to put themselves at the mercy of some enterprising middle
peasant or one of the new-rich peasants who were beginning to emerge.

Furthermore, unless one went in for custom work in the style of a
new-rich peasant, owning livestock and implements could represent over-
capitalization.

One good mule could farm 20 acres. But no family owned as much as
20 acres, and few had half that much. The largest holding in all of Long
Bow, after land reform, was a little more than 11 acres for a family of nine
people. Even such a large family could not effectively use all the productive
capacity of one mule. If they had tried to keep a mule, a cart, a plow, a
harrow and a seeder, the capital investment would have been grossly out
of proportion to the production possible on 11 acres of land. Therefore the
family that owned a mule was not likely to own the other essential implements, not even a cart, even though the latter was used as much for transportation on the roads as it was for agriculture.

Since there were not enough draft animals and implements to go around and since the landholdings were too small to engage efficiently any complete set of equipment, all but the most ambitious in the end found it advantageous to swap and share what they had, and to help each other out.

All the economic pressures that pushed people toward mutual aid during and after land reform had existed for thousands of years. They had produced labor exchange on a spontaneous and limited basis, but this had never developed into a mass movement or crystallized out in any permanent form, primarily because of class differences. Cooperation is very difficult when producers are unequal in their holdings and productive power. The rich peasant does not swap labor with the poor peasant; he hires him and realizes surplus value from the transaction. In the old society the owners of oxen or mules that could be used as levers to extract unpaid labor from poor neighbors were not likely to swap labor with such people for mutual benefit. It was only after land reform had created a community of approximately equal smallholders with several families sharing an ox or a plow that wide-scale sharing of labor, draft animals and implements became possible.

A further factor leading people to try mutual aid was the phenomenal success of certain outstanding examples. In Shansi Province there was one very famous unit, a group in West Gully led by Li Hsun-ta. Li Hsun-ta started a mutual-aid team with six neighbors in 1943. They hitched themselves to a plow and opened up wasteland in an abandoned ravine high in the mountains of P'ingshun County. Some of this land they planted to cotton. Li Hsun-ta's mother cut down a tree, fashioned a spinning wheel, and taught the women of the group how to spin cotton thread. Cooperative effort led to high yields on the land and high productivity in cottage industry. In 1944 Li Hsun-ta was invited to a conference of model producers and returned home an elected labor hero of the whole Shansi-Hopei-Honan-Shantung Border Region. After that West Gully became a household word in North China.

Not so well known at the time, but very famous later, was the *Old and Young Team* led by Ch'en Yung-kuei of Tachai.* Ch'en Yung-kuei lived in a desolate wasteland of loess soil and rock on the northern slope of Tigerhead Mountain, in Hsiyang County, Central Shansi, a place comparable in American geography to one of the isolated hollows on the western slope of the Appalachian chain in West Virginia, North Carolina or Tennessee. He arrived there as a child in a basket slung at one end of his father's carrying pole. They were famine refugees from more fertile regions to the south.

Tachai territory consisted of eight ridges and seven ravines running down from the barren summit of Tigerhead, a slope so steep and so cut up that the 100 acres of tilled land there were divided into 4,700 bits and pieces. Most of them were narrow terraces on the ridges formed by piling up stone walls and filling in the space behind with earth.

No one filled the ravines, because they were subject to washouts. Sixty families of bare-poor people farmed these badlands. Most of them paid rent

*Ch'en Yung-kuei and Tachai are now under attack in China. In my opinion, the attack is politically motivated and unjust.

to one absentee landlord and three rich peasants who rarely set foot in this godforsaken place if they could help it.

A high proportion of the residents of Tachai were ex-beggars who were able to settle on Tigerhead Mountain because the land there had been abandoned. No sooner did they reclaim a small terrace or two, however, than landlords who had forgotten about the place suddenly resurrected their land deeds and moved in to collect rent. As long as Tachai remained a wasteland no one cared about it, but as soon as anyone produced something there everyone wanted a share.

Tachai peasants talked of three *poors* and five *manys*—poor people, poor land, poor village; many shepherds, many hired hands, many beggars, many children sold, many suicides. Sometimes they added a sixth, many calamities. When it didn't rain their crops withered on bone-dry terraces. When it rained the terraces washed into the gullies, carrying crops, soils and terrace walls into the valley below. No one ever supposed that there was a way out. The three *poors* and the six *manys* added up to fate.

But the Japanese War ended in victory. It was followed by land reform. And land reform, having brought the peasants together in struggle, led to organized production–mutual aid. When forming groups for mutual aid people took it for granted that "soldiers match soldiers, officers match officers," i.e., that people with equal labor power should get together. Twelve families with young men in the prime of life formed the *Stalwarts* group. Four families of older people without sons and six families of widows with young children formed the *Old and Young Team*. The rest continued to farm on their own.

Ch'en Yung-kuei, who had been an activist in the anti-Japanese underground and a leader of the land reform movement, joined the *Stalwarts*. But he was ill at ease. Forty-two young men, his comrades in arms in the War of Resistance, had been killed by the Japanese. Twenty others had joined the People's Liberation Army to defend the fruits of victory. Their parents, wives and children had formed the *Old and Young Team*. How could he, a man in the prime of life, join with the strongest and best producers of the community and leave the dependents of his dead comrades and the army volunteers to shift for themselves?

"All the families that were short of labor power were left stranded," Ch'en said. "In these families only women, children, and old, sick and weak people remained."

" 'What about us?' they said.

"They were all poor and lower-middle peasants. I heard their complaints and I couldn't help thinking, Where did the labor power of these families go? Some were killed by the Japanese. Others joined the People's Liberation Army. Now who will care for their dependents?

" 'We have *fanshened,*' they said. 'But nothing has changed. We still can't live. We have no animals, no tools, no labor power, so what use is the land to us? We can't eat the land.'

"I didn't think in terms of line then. I only thought, These are poor peasant brothers and sisters. I am also a poor peasant. They suffered in the old society. So did I. *Isn't their problem my problem, too? The road we take must solve everyone's problems, not just those of a few.*

"I withdrew from the *Stalwarts* group and joined the group of children and old people. The youngest of the old people was sixty and the oldest of the young people was twelve. If any of these worked hard it would ruin his health. I was the only able-bodied member in the prime of life. I'm not boasting. It is a fact. I was strong as an ox.

"The children and the old people welcomed me. They had never dreamed of such a thing. They didn't say I was stupid. It was the *Stalwarts* who said I was stupid,

" 'Now Ch'en has really *fanshened*,' they said. 'He has old men who can't mount a horse and children who can't pull a plow.' "

A rich peasant took Ch'en's wife aside. "In the past you had nothing to eat or drink. And now you are in the same boat. What does Ch'en get working with that rabble? The oldest of the young people is twelve and the youngest of the old men is sixty! Mao has called on us to organize, but what sort of organizing is that?"

But Ch'en had an answer for everyone.

"The old have experience. The young will grow up. If we listen to the voice of the Communist Party we'll be on the right road."

So Ch'en swapped labor with old people and children who could not do a fraction of the work he was capable of. Ch'en made two big baskets for his carrying pole that could hold 200 catties (220 pounds), while four children between them carried 100, and day after day they worked together. The old people and the children wondered what motivated Ch'en. They talked about him behind his back and they decided that he felt sorry for them, that he was a kindhearted man. But after the rich peasants started slandering the group, called Ch'en stupid, and asked, "What sort of a fine opera is this?," they began to understand that Ch'en worked with them because of class feelings, out of solidarity for the poor against the rich.

"Bit by bit their consciousness rose, more and more they supported my views. They worked with me all day, then went home to eat, but once they had their bowls filled they brought them back to my house and had supper with me. Both old and young did this. We united as one person."

And to the astonishment of all, and especially the *Stalwarts* group, the *Old and Young Team* produced better crops than anyone else.

"Why? How could we achieve so much, that very first year? We had so little labor power, yet we beat the *Stalwarts* in production. It was because of our unity. It was because we were determined to take the collective road."

As for the *Stalwarts*, they got together in the spring but dispersed in the summer, stayed away in the autumn worrying about their own harvests, and fell apart in the winter. In fact, they practiced mutual aid for only a month or two in the spring, then went their separate ways and failed to increase their yields beyond the 10 bushels per acre average that was traditional in Tachai.

But the *Old and Young Team* organized well, discussed everything democratically, made joint decisions, helped one another, stuck together, and increased their yields substantially. For seven years they stuck together, increased their crop yields each season, and attracted new members until by 1953 they had 49 families who harvested 27 bushels to the acre, almost triple the yields that anyone had wrested from Tigerhead Mountain in the past.

Central to their success was the decision made by Ch'en Yung-kuei to disregard the basic principle of mutual-aid organization—matching labor power against labor power. He could then swap his able-bodied labor without demanding equivalent exchange for the work of children and worn-out old men.

Everyone thought he was crazy. "Nobody with half a catty of grain at home would ever choose to be 'king' of these people," said the critics. But Ch'en took no such narrow view. "Isn't their problem my problem, too? The road we take must solve everyone's problem." On the one hand he felt sympathy for those older men who had worked all their lives for landlords, as he himself had done since the age of eight, and for those children whose fathers and brothers had been killed or now risked their lives at the front. *Fanshen* should have been a great liberation for them; their weakness should not be allowed to turn it sour. On the other hand he had a vision of what cooperation could do. With the rich experience of the older people and the enthusiasm of the young, with unity forged through hard work and open discussion, could they not unlock the riches of Tigerhead Mountain and change their fate? Ch'en Yung-kuei believed that they could, and this belief set him apart from the thousands of other peasant activists who saw in mutual-aid organization some immediate benefits for themselves and their neighbors, but hardly recognized it as a road to the transformation of society.

It is doubtful if in those days Ch'en himself ever consciously formulated such a view. Collective action simply seemed right to him. It made sense for the long pull and he did not feel compelled to make that close calculation of immediate personal gains and losses that so typified peasant mentality. He carried this attitude with him through each stage of development.

"We didn't have the little *Red Book* to read then," said Ch'en. "I had never heard of 'Serve the People' or 'The People are most precious' or 'The socialist road versus the capitalist road.' Even to this day I cannot memorize any quotations from Mao Tse-tung. But I did have class feelings, and I knew that we did not have enough people to do all the work that needed to be done. We had to get together and we had to work together. And when we did that we transformed our lives."

13

FIRST STEPS
IN LONG BOW

 As Li Hsun-ta expanded his West Gully aid group into a team that took on a whole mountain valley, as Ch'en Yung-kuei built his *Old and Young Team* into a village-wide unit, Long Bow peasants, determined to catch up, consolidated and expanded the experimental labor exchange groups that had formed during the first months after land reform.

The most successful of these groups was the one led by Yang Chung-sheng. He brought together twenty-two families who farmed 80 acres of land.

Starting with several friends who had confidence in one another, this group prospered because it carried out the principles for mutual aid laid down by Mao Tse-tung. These principles, summed up from the experience of thousands of successful groups, were three: 1. voluntary participation; 2. equal exchange of labor and value; 3. democratic operation—clearly a lower level of commitment than that which motivated Ch'en Yung-kuei. Yang Chung-sheng's group also avoided the three common mistakes: 1. mutual aid in everything; 2. large-scale groups; 3. complicated organization.

As described in *Fanshen,* the twenty-two families under Yang's leadership "met often, discussed every problem thoroughly and worked out a good system of keeping records so that the exchange of labor time balanced out in the long run. Yang never tried to tell the group what to do. When they met they talked things over and only when they agreed did they act. They always tilled the land of soldiers' dependents first, asking only their meals in return. Families without manpower paid wages for all work done, but the group did not demand that these wages be paid at once. Those who had no grain could wait until after the harvest to settle up. A committee of four was elected to report on all hours put in and on all exchanges of implements and draft power. One member who could write and figure on the abacus was appointed to tally up the accounts. At the end of every period—that is, planting, hoeing, harvesting, etc.—a balance sheet was drawn up and a settlement made. Everyone paid up what he owed except those who were in difficult circumstances and needed more time. This satisfied all participants and helped to maintain morale at a high level.

"The group met briefly every evening to plan the next day's work. When the cocks began to crow before dawn, no time was wasted in consultation. Everyone went straight to the field without having to be called. When the six animals possessed by the group members were not needed in the fields, they were taken by their owners on transport work that was individually planned and executed. In other words, the group did not try to pool all the activities of its members. They worked together where the advantage was greatest and went their separate ways where that was more suitable. To add to their winter production they pooled resources to set up a bean-curd plant."

Yang Chung-sheng, after representing Long Bow at a regional meeting of model peasants and workers, expanded the activities of his group to include a cooperative carpentry shop. Its thirteen members built tables, chairs, wooden shovels, cart bodies, wheel hubs and finally cartwheels complete with iron rims. In order to ensure adequate supplies of wood this group journeyed to the Western Mountains, bought standing trees, cut them, hauled them home, and sawed their own lumber.

By 1948 these cooperative efforts were so successful that many new families applied to join the group. Chung-sheng wisely turned them down, encouraged them to form new groups, and stabilized the organization under his leadership at twenty families.

The second successful mutual-aid group in Long Bow was led by the Secretary of the Communist Party Branch, Chang Hsin-fa. Hsin-fa, as described earlier, was doing very well on his own, but Party leaders demanded that village Communists take the lead in organizing production, so Hsin-fa took up the task. He did it out of Party loyalty and political conviction, not because he faced production problems himself.

According to the principle of "soldiers match soldiers, officers match officers," Hsin-fa brought together several of Long Bow's *Stalwarts,* men in the prime of life, well endowed with labor power and each in possession of an ox, a mule or a cart. The group consisted of ten families: Yang Li-sheng, Kuo T'ai-shan, Yang Yü-so, Wang Kuei-pao, Tai Ta-kuan, Chang Ch'i-fa (Hsin-fa's brother) and Chang Hsin-fa himself. Only Kuo T'ai-shan, a thirteen-year-old without a father, contributed less than full labor power to the group.

"Most of the work was too heavy for him," Hsin-fa recalled. "He only had strength enough to pour night soil on the corn hills at planting time. We really carried him for years. We did it because his mother was a widow. He had all his father's land to take care of and couldn't handle it all. Yang Yü-so had been a close friend of his father's and they had suffered the life of poor peasants together. Out of loyalty to T'ai-shan's father we took the son in. In fact we did express some class feelings for this family. They had no draft animal. We hauled coal for them. We plowed for them at a time when T'ai-shan couldn't even carry a loaded sack. But he did whatever he could and by the time we decided to form our coop he was a big, strong boy."

T'ai-shan's security as a member of this group stood in contrast to the vulnerability of young Chin Ch'en-hai mentioned earlier, who was too young to work the land his ailing father owned, failed to link up with any group, and had to sell out most of his holdings to survive.

"To be truthful, I was also a burden to the group," said Hsin-fa. "As Party Secretary, I had to go to so many meetings. But when I went off they did my work first so I had nothing to worry about. We practiced democracy in the group. We decided all questions through discussion and we held together through thick and thin. Yang Li-sheng was our group leader. He always told the members to work on my land first when I was away and to work on other members' land later. With such a good leader the contradictions between individual members didn't show up very much and we never had any big quarrels!

"Li-sheng himself kept the records—which family the team worked for, who came, and how much work they did. Then after every agricultural season we settled up. We settled up with millet. If the amounts owed were about equal, then it was OK, things balanced out, but if one had done more labor than another he had to collect millet for the extra work. We never quarreled over the quality of the millet; most millet is the same anyway. Besides, we would have been embarrassed to quarrel over such minor things as that."

"What if a family couldn't afford the millet they owed?"

"That never came up in our group," said Hsin-fa. "We were all more or less equal, so the amount of millet that changed hands was really very small. As a side occupation our group opened an inn where carters hauling freight down the road could stay. The main purpose of this inn, insofar as the group was concerned, was to collect manure, the manure produced by the cart animals that stayed overnight. Of course there was also some cash income. We called our establishment Horse Cart Inn."

Soon a third functioning group of half a dozen families, all headed by strong, able-bodied workers, came into being, organized by Shih Ts'ai-yuan, the demobilized veteran. Like Hsin-fa, Ts'ai-yuan was in an especially favorable position to prosper as a new-rich peasant. It was Party pressure that set him on the cooperative road. However, no amount of pressure could persuade him to abandon the principle of matching labor power against equal labor power. He would not accept old people, widows or orphaned children. Nor did he favor people without skills. His group included a number of carpenters who worked out by the day for wages while other group members tilled their land. This was matching labor power with money. Some of the cash earnings from carpentry were used to pay for the labor that was put in on the carpenter's land. The crops from each family's land went into its own storage jars.

Some of the old, the widowed and the children unable to do a full day's work, who were rejected by these three groups of stalwarts, came to Peasants' Association leader Kuo Cheng-k'uan for help. They begged him to form a group that they could join. Soft of heart and anxious to serve the people well, he created a fourth year-round mutual-aid group in Long Bow, that could well have been called *The Weak, the Halt and the Blind*.

In addition to four year-round groups, at least ten seasonal groups, generally called "plowing teams," were formed. Plows were an expensive and relatively scarce item of equipment that few families could afford. In the busy season clusters of eight or ten families tended to crystallize around each implement. These clusters might just as well have been called "honey cart groups." The large, barrellike wooden tanks mounted on wheels that were used to haul liquid night soil from the deep storage cisterns to the fields were even more expensive and certainly scarcer than plows. In the whole village there were only thirteen honey carts. This alone could well account for the fact that there were, in the busy season, some thirteen labor-swapping groups.

All the peasants spoke enthusiastically about mutual aid as long as it was organized on a voluntary basis and democratically led. The Communist Shen T'ien-hsi praised working together. "When we work together we get more done," he said. "Whenever I stay up late at a meeting I would sleep through half the morning if the aid-group leader didn't come to call me. And I get very discouraged whenever I have to go out all alone and face a big stretch of land. With others there to tackle the job, the work goes fast. We talk, laugh and keep each other's spirits up."

T'ai-shan's widowed mother confirmed this. "When I am alone in the field I often look up and wonder if it is noon. But when we work together, noon comes and goes, and we don't even notice it. Soon the work is done."

T'ai-shan was equally enthusiastic. "It was 1950 when we joined the group. Before that we had a hard time. My mother was old and I was young and we had to call on other people for help.

"After we joined the group my mother could choose light work. I was the youngest member. We took turns helping each other so that all the land got planted and nothing went to waste. But I was always falling behind in the field. We would go out together but I would fall behind. Then Hsin-fa would encourage me, saying, 'It's only because you are younger,' and he would come up the row and help me finish."

Mutual aid, because it solved problems, grew and developed in Long Bow village, in Southeast Shansi, across North China and, finally, throughout the country wherever land reform prepared the ground. But it contained within itself many contradictions.

Short-range disputes arose over such problems as whose field to plant first after a rain. A good team leader usually said, "Do mine last." But some would hedge on this with the excuse, "My land is nearest, let's do it now and get it out of the way." By the time the group got to the last fields the soil had dried out. Seeds sown in dry clods had less chance for germination. Then the unfortunate owner of the neglected land had to ask the team to carry water to his plot. But this meant expending many more man-hours of labor on the last plots than on the first. Some members always objected, causing quarrels that split groups apart. Then each member had to go his own way and work his plot as best he could, with his wife and children all out laboring from dawn until dark.

Long-range disputes arose in part because mutual aid did not fundamentally change the relationship between those who owned large amounts of productive capital and those who owned little or none. This was particularly true in the case of draft animals. Those who owned them, particularly those who owned them outright, could still command the labor of others, as Li-the-Fat discovered. Once he joined the Communist Party he was not allowed to hire out animals for money. Such hiring was proscribed as a form of exploitation, and Communists were not allowed to exploit others. But as a member of Ts'ai-yuan's mutual-aid group his charges for animal power were recorded as workday credits to be balanced against workdays performed by others. With such an arrangement Li-the-Fat's donkey and mule rolled up a big credit backlog. He didn't have to do any work at all for his neighbors. They, on the other hand, worked many extra days for him in order to even the account.

Hiring out animals, either directly or in this disguised form, brought big returns, but it should not be supposed that the transaction always went smoothly. When the driver of the animal was not the owner he tended to beat it on uphill grades. How else could one get more work done in a day? But if the owner saw this he wanted to protest.

"Your mother's ———! What are you beating my mule for? You haven't laid out any money for him."

The protest was sure to provoke an angry response and the quarrel that followed could threaten the stability of the group.

Nevertheless, for those without draft animals, mutual aid had distinct advantages. The remaining poor peasants were almost always better off inside an organized group than outside, on their own.

This was because within the group there was a commitment, mutually agreed upon, that all the work of all the members would be completed. There was also usually an agreement that those fields needing the most work would be attended to first, regardless of ownership. Furthermore, the rates at which labor was to be swapped for animal power were fixed in advance and not subject to sudden, seasonal overcharges. A day's work inside the mutual-aid team was usually fixed at 4 sheng a day. It did not rise to several times that amount during the harvest rush, then fall to almost nothing in the slack season. By the same token rates for animal power also remained stable. Inside the mutual-aid groups there was some measure of collective control over all aspects of production; the thrust of this control was toward equalization rather than toward a differentiation that favored those with capital assets. Equalization included the prompt settlement of accounts. This could cut both ways, but often as not it was the better-off peasants who refused to settle what they owed. They could afford to pay, but they didn't want to.

I have already told how Sun Chiu-fa, devoured by fleas in the Party Secretary's office, agreed to pay what he owed to his aid-team colleagues. This lesson, learned behind locked doors, didn't last very long, however. Old Sun was soon in trouble again. As a prosperous peasant with five acres to till, he looked on the mutual-aid group as a labor pool set up for his personal convenience. A few weeks after the flea episode the time came to settle up once more. Hsin-fa went to Sun's house to collect the grain that was due, but the old man said he had no millet, no millet at all.

"If you don't have millet, then wheat will do."

"But I don't have any good wheat either," he said.

He uncovered a large jar full of wheat. Green mold covered the surface.

"That's all the grain I have. As you can see, it's not fit to eat."

"Dump it out," said Hsin-fa. "Maybe there is some good grain underneath."

"It's no use," said Sun. "It's rotten right to the bottom."

But Hsin-fa didn't believe him. He tipped the jar over and, sure enough, most of the wheat that tumbled out was in excellent shape. He took 5 sheng for each day of labor that Sun owed the group.

"Later," said Hsin-fa, "we held a meeting to discuss Sun Chiu-fa's case and we decided to expel him because he was wasting so much of our time with quarrels. Life was too short to spend getting mad at him all the time. We really had no choice."

14

QUARRELS AND HESITATIONS

"Actually, the mere threat of expulsion was often enough to settle most questions," said Shen T'ien-hsi.

He was a big man, with great reserves of strength. That strength had made him a formidable opponent as a militia-man in the critical days before the land question was settled in 1948. In the intervening years T'ien-hsi had received a blow in the right eye that damaged it permanently and gave him a sinister squint. With his muscles bulging under his coat, his right eye half shut, his left eye inflamed, and a dark stubble covering his cheeks and chin, he looked quite fierce. But he told a humorous story about the three Shih brothers, Ts'ai-yuan, Fu-yuan, and Er-chih, all of whom belonged, as a family, to the same mutual-aid group as T'ien-hsi.

One spring the members decided to dig a well for irrigation water. They made good progress until about the third day, when Shih Er-chih went into the hole first to do his share. After he disappeared underground no signal came for the other men to pull up the basket. Time passed. Finally Chang Kuei-ts'ai got upset at the delay and started to swear.

"If you're so good at it why don't you come down and dig?" retorted Er-chih, from the bottom of the well.

With that he climbed into the basket himself and signaled the others to pull him out.

"To hell with this," said Shih Er-chih, as he reached ground level. "I don't want to have anything to do with this group anymore."

"All right," said T'ien-hsi. "If you don't want to work with us, then quit."

Young Shih went striding off but he didn't go very far. He took a few steps toward the village and then sat down. He sat, in deep thought, for several hours while the rest of the crew went on digging. His brother Ts'ai-yuan finally went over to where the young man was sulking. He criticized him for making such a big issue over so small an incident.

In the end Er-chih came back.

"I'm wrong," he said.

Then he shouted down to Kuei-ts'ai, who was taking his turn at the bottom of the hole, "You come up. I'll go back down. I don't really want to leave the group. I'll try my best from now on."

Because personal adjustments were difficult, mutual aid did not suit some people. In spite of repeated calls from Party leaders for Communists to take the lead in organized production, not even all the Communist Party members joined.

One notorious case in Long Bow involved Tai San-tsai, a young man in the prime of life who had *fanshened* well. His father, Tai Chia-kuei, was a bare-poor peasant from Linhsien who had nothing to his name when he came to Long Bow as a famine refugee. Although by 1945 he had acquired 2½ mou of poor land, he did not even have a house to live in. Active in the land reform movement, Chia-kuei became a group leader of the Peasants' Association while his son San-tsai joined the militia. Since one was a minor cadre and the other a militiaman, and since both pushed hard for their own self-interest, they received somewhat more than most when land and other property was distributed. They won more than 20 mou of good land, 8 sections of house (five of them one and a half stories high) and sole ownership of an ox.

The ox was large and strong. It could haul 1,200 catties on the road. Where others earned 3 tou of millet a day hauling goods, Tai could earn 6. Thus he felt hemmed in by mutual aid. If the group decided on field work he had to delay his transport work and thus lose cash. On his own he felt he could set a separate pace and earn much more.

T'ien-hsi repeatedly tried to mobilize him. "Look around you. In every field but yours there are eight to ten people working together. Here you and your father are all alone. Don't you feel lonesome? Morale is much better when you work together."

But San-tsai still felt that it was better to go it alone, free to turn his hand to whatever profited him the most. Finally, because the Party leaders insisted on it, he did join the mutual-aid team. But this was in name only. He only came out with the rest when it suited him. Most of the time he still worked by himself.

Behind San-tsai's unusual stubbornness lay an acute personal problem. Even though prosperous, he had not been able to find a wife. He was untidy, careless in his habits, and had a reputation for selfishness. Nobody could get along with him. It was not surprising, therefore, that he could not find anyone willing to marry him. He sought a bride high and low but to no avail. The Catholic community, composed of those who still went to worship every Sunday with the priest in Horse Square, took note of his plight, and one day a go-between approached him with a deal. A certain family was willing to promise their daughter to him if he would pay 20 tan of millet and join the church!

Unable to find a wife any other way, San-tsai accepted the offer. But it meant somehow earning and saving 20 tan of millet, an impossible task as a member of the mutual-aid group. By working long hours on his own on the highway San-tsai did, in time, accumulate this hoard of grain. He got a marriage license at the county office and then went to the church in Horse Square to be wed. After that he developed close relations with the Catholic priest there. As a militiaman who often stood guard in Long Bow he was in a position to tell the father when it was safe to come and go in his home village. Standing there with his rifle he appeared to be looking out for the interests of the people. Actually he was protecting the Catholic father and allowing him a free hand in organizing the Legion of Mary.

In the case of Tai San-tsai, one could say that it was not routine self-interest that pushed him out on the "capitalist road," but desperation in regard to his single state.

Other prosperous peasants, already married, opposed mutual aid on principle. Some of them went out of their way to condemn it.

Yang Ching-shun's father, an old-middle peasant, said, "No one in Long Bow can manage even one household well. How can anyone manage several families all crowded together in one unit?"

Chief of Staff Hsu's relative, Hsu Hung-ye, the man who had hidden 3,000 silver dollars for the Kuomintang officer until an indiscreet letter exposed his scheme, sneered, "We'll see what this mutual aid will ever amount to."

"Aren't you pleased with Chairman Mao's great call?" asked his neighbor, Chang Kuei-ts'ai.

"Have I said something wrong?" asked Hsu, lowering his voice to a whisper.

After that he did not openly attack organized production, but he made sure that four-line verses like these made the rounds of the village:

> Pooling private property,
> Pooling land thrives.
> Next pool children,
> Then pool wives?

This verse played on people's fears. Once cooperation started, where would it end? What did the Party really have in mind? Was it true, as another verse said, that all peasants would wind up eating out of one big pot?

An ambitious experiment in collective farming that was far in advance of the times added fuel to worrisome speculations. During the period when mutual-aid groups were still feeling their way, at a time when more stable cooperative forms had hardly been tried, Soviet experts suddenly appeared in Changchih to help set up a collective farm.

The main criterion put forward was technical; the experts wanted a large, flat piece of land suitable for tractor and combine operations. City officials selected such a tract on the plain outside the north gate of the city and southeast of the airport. Taking Kuan Village as the center, Changchih leaders drew a line around seven adjoining villages and called it the "Sino-Soviet Friendship Farm." It was also known as the "Kuan Village Collective Farm."

In one leap the villagers there went from part-time mutual aid to an advanced collective organization that was made up at the base of fifty to sixty field teams. They received directives from a management department that was in turn responsible to an overall Collective Farm staff headed by an appointed chairman and vice-chairman. The state (in the form of the Southeast Shansi Regional Government) provided imported tractors, combines, tractor plows and other large implements and also sixty horsecarts. It was hoped that with this large organization and high level of mechanization great production records would be set.

But things did not work out that way. The whole project departed from the principle of self-reliance and voluntary participation. Since the state initiated this "great leap" the rank-and-file expected the state to carry it through. Seeing all that expensive equipment they thought, we'll just sit here and get rich. People came from miles around to watch the machines at work, but the combines left a lot of grain on the ground, the cultivators left a lot of weeds standing, and there were no machines at all to thin the millet. Soviet experts stayed only a few weeks. Baffled technically, without experienced leadership and without strong personal commitment, the local people went through the motions of farming. When the crops fell short of expectations they demanded and got relief funds from the state. Time and again Changchih City leaders sent cadres, middle-school students and soldiers into action to thin, weed and harvest, but even this extra help failed to ensure normal yields, to say nothing of bumper harvests. As officials from the region and the Rural Work Department of Changchih City withdrew in the face of failure, local men took more responsibility, but the project went deeper and deeper into debt.

As Veteran Wang said, "What we had here was organization without an ideological base, machinery without developed consciousness. These large-scale Soviet methods just did not work. Our people had no experience and no tradition for such a thing. The whole effort, so highly subsidized, only encouraged people to lie back in the arms of the state and rock their way through life."

Nevertheless, Changchih City never openly abandoned this collective farm. Six years later, when peasants established communes all over Southeast Shansi, Nanshui Commune absorbed the Kuan Village unit as a single brigade. This eased budget problems because the teams down below no longer had to pay salaries to top-level managers. Managerial functions were taken over by the new commune leaders. They were on the state payroll and thus outside the collective sphere, a relationship that was duly noted by the populace.

While this collective experiment gradually fell apart in Kuan Village, another attempt at large-scale organization took shape in the mountains nearby. Several villages, with the aid of state funds, set up a forestry project that was called a State Farm. After some initial successes it, too, bogged down; six years later it quietly dissolved itself by becoming a brigade in a local commune.

In the euphoric days following nationwide victory in the civil war and the establishment of the new government in Peking, people had high hopes for mechanization. Machines would not only make collective farms and state farms possible, they would transform farming at the grass roots as well. But efforts to promote even the simplest of new implements and machines often suffered the same fate as the large-scale projects. Some cadres supported innovation with enthusiasm but the people were slow to react.

Veteran Wang told how waterwheels first came to Changchih and the surrounding districts. These waterwheels were actually chain pumps, a mechanism by which rubber discs on a chain were pulled upward through a pipe as a donkey or several people walked in a circle around the well opening. The flow of water raised in this way far surpassed whatever could be raised by other muscle-powered methods. These waterwheels made irrigation practical. But when they first appeared people wouldn't buy them. Frustrated, Wang's work team tried to force the pace.

"We met with the peasants at the stage [opera platform] on the west side and explained the new waterwheels. But nobody offered to buy one. 'If you don't buy a wheel you can't leave,' I said. This ultimatum stretched the meeting far into the night. Toward morning a few families gave in. They were allowed to depart. The rest we held there until the meeting broke up at dawn. When asked about this later the peasants said, 'We spent the whole night at the Yellow River Tower,' an allusion to a famous incident in the tale of the Three Kingdoms when Liu Pei was told not to leave the tower on the Yellow River until relief came.

"What held people back that night was the fact that few families had a block of land large enough to make use of one such wheel. With a wheel the water from one well could be distributed over several mou, north, south, east and west. But unless you owned the land, or the other owners agreed to share expenses, it was no use setting up the equipment. The reluctant owner of a single strip could disrupt the whole scheme. Only after mutual aid brought people together on a wider scale did these waterwheels succeed."

By that time members of mutual-aid groups could go to the state bank and borrow money at very low interest rates to purchase the wheels. Individuals in Long Bow borrowed altogether over 8,000 yuan for this purpose, money which was never paid back. The state bank canceled the debt, thus in effect presenting the waterwheels to Long Bow residents and to residents of many other brigades as well.

Soon research units and cooperative factories produced other improved implements, among them a one-handled plow and a small gas engine designed to run on marsh gas. Although manufactured in great numbers and enthusiastically promoted, neither succeeded in winning support from peasants. A local poet summed up their fate:

> The small gas engine,
> The one-handled plow
> Committed suicide.
> Where are they now?

Somewhat later the same thing happened to the double-bottomed horse-drawn plow. Whenever we walked to the southern edge of the village we passed one such plow abandoned and half buried in a small grove of trees. Rust covered those parts that remained above ground. One local poet had apparently seen many such sights.

When it's time to buy machines
Our Party Chairman intervenes.
But when formalities are done
They lie exposed to wind and sun.
Allow a year or two to pass,
They're nought but scrap iron in the grass.

Orders from above could not put machinery to work, nor could they bring mutual-aid groups to life. In the Rural Work Department of Chang-chih City there was a well-known cadre named Liu Fa-tzu. He was a rough-and-ready old peasant who couldn't write his own name. But "word blindness," as illiteracy was called, didn't inhibit him in the least. He made long speeches, directed cultural events, and organized production.

One day, disregarding his advice, a group of peasants refused to form a mutual-aid group. He called them all "potatoes."

"Old Liu, don't curse us now," protested one.

"Who's cursing?" retorted Liu. "Aren't you just like potatoes? Put you on a hill together and you'd all roll off in different directions."

"Well, if we're potatoes what are you?" they asked.

Sometime later another village wanted to put on a stage show. Liu limited each performance to an hour—no more, no less. People protested, saying, "Some of these acts last only half an hour. Others, like the opera, take more."

"Never mind," said Liu, "the short ones must be stretched."

"And the long ones?"

"They must be cut back."

And he meant it.

When one group refused to get off the stage after an hour he stepped in and kicked their drum away.

When it came to making speeches himself, Liu lost track of time. Since he was illiterate, he never made notes or even an outline of what he meant to say. Once started he often forgot what he had already said and repeated himself. At one meeting he started things off right by saying, "I won't talk at all. Let other men talk." That was fine with those present, but after everyone had finished he suddenly changed his mind. He said he wanted to make a few final points. Starting with both hands in his pockets, he brought his right hand out for "point one." Then he brought his left hand out for "point two." Finding a chair in front of him he placed his right foot on it for "point three."

He soon ran out of feet and hands but the points proliferated effortlessly. Midnight came and went but Liu Fa-tzu talked on. Nobody could get up and leave because he was standing right in front of the door. Those who knew him best started counting the points. By tallying them with five-stroke *chen* ideographs they eventually recorded more than sixty. By that time dawn was breaking in the east. Several people had fallen asleep. Those who were still awake were angry.

Liu's topic was Mao's three-part call, "Let the army advance at the front, behind the lines strengthen discipline, and raise production one inch." Examining this slogan from every angle Liu Fa-tzu droned on and on.

Finally an angry voice broke in from the back of the room.

"Let's finish off this meeting. It's already grown a foot, not to mention an inch."

Liu Fa-tzu's public career ended when the Regional Committee started looking for recruits to send south for political work. They decided to test the cadres for literacy. When Liu Fa-tzu failed in every category they asked him to go to school. He refused point-blank, rolled up his quilt, put it on his back and stalked off homeward. Now he works as a carpenter in his native brigade. The city administration lost a devoted cadre.

Liu Fa-tzu exemplified what the Chinese call "peasant narrowness." When contrasted with the high-handedness and dogmatism of the bureaucrats who later intervened in his district, however, his faults seem almost like virtues.

15

A FIVE-VILLAGE SURVEY

In spite of difficulties, quarrels and hesitations in organizing production, the economy surged forward between 1945 and 1951. Peasants quickly restored and surpassed prewar levels of yield per acre, and surpassed them in some places by as much as 25 percent. They also repaired or rebuilt buildings neglected or destroyed during the war years and replaced smashed agricultural implements and slaughtered livestock. As the economy recovered, the purchasing power of the peasants showed growth. In 1951 the local coop sold 155 percent more woven cloth, 881 percent more raw cotton padding, 142 percent more salt, 43 percent more kerosene and 215 percent more sodium bicarbonate than in 1949.

The rising prosperity had a marked effect on education, culture and public health. In 1951 the Regional Party Committee surveyed social progress in five villages near Long Bow. In these villages 82 percent of the school-age children attended school, a figure that far surpassed any prewar experience. Many children, including girls, were already traveling to comprehensive primary schools established in Changchih and some of the larger market centers. Some even enrolled as boarders in secondary schools, a thing unheard of before the war. Volunteers promoted adult education through so-called "people's schools," as well as through newspaper-reading teams, village libraries and picture or cartoon exhibits. Eighty-three percent of the young adults were attending the "people's schools." Twenty-nine percent of all adults had already learned to recognize 200 written characters, 13 percent up to 500 characters, 18 percent up to 900 characters and 10 percent over 1,000 characters. Assuming that being able to read 900 characters made one literate, it was calculated that the literacy rate among adults had already reached 28 percent.

Young people were particularly keen on literacy. Young men said, "If we can read we can do anything we want." Young women said, "If we don't lag behind in study we can marry literate people." Father and son, mother and daughter, and husband and wife models in the literacy movement proliferated. Keeping diaries and calligraphy notebooks developed into a mass movement.

Newspaper-reading teams developed into a lively, spare-time activity. Various units in the five villages subscribed to 30 newspapers and selected readers, each one reading aloud to from twenty to thirty people. Although only one village boasted a library, this stocked some 320 books and 70 readers visited it daily. Picture exhibits traveling widely drew vast numbers of viewers.

The most popular form of entertainment, as in prewar years, was Chinese opera. If any one village put on an opera, peasants from all the nearby villages around went to see it, thus crowding all available space. In addition to the old operas, peasants wrote and produced their own new plays. In each village there were twenty to thirty local actors and actresses, and three to five people who wrote and directed plays. The new plays did not draw as large an audience as the old operas but their popularity was growing. Over the slack season each village collected money to buy costumes, engage opera teachers, and organize new productions. In addition, there were many varieties of storytelling, slide shows, yangko dance troupes, stilt walkers and musical bands competing for attention. The most popular games were Chinese chess and poker, the most popular sports Ping-Pong, gymnastics and stilt walking. With the development of recreation old-style gambling all but disappeared.

Sanitation and health care also improved quickly. Before land reform, it was reported, 39 percent of the families in Suku never washed their eating bowls or their cooking pots, and 35 percent of the families never swept or washed their living quarters. By 1951 only four families remained who neither washed nor cleaned. In Hsiats'un washing clothes and sunning bedding had become routine for all peasants. In one-third of the families women already used scented soap purchased at the coop, and some men had also begun to do so. Hsiats'un organized village-wide cleanups twice a month.

During menstruation women were beginning to use clean cloths instead of socks or old rags. In Hsiats'un the young women cut up new cloth for sanitary napkins, then washed the cloth thoroughly before reuse. Such measures protected the ability of women to bear children and the number of live births went up sharply. With the aid of state-trained midwives the incidence of umbilical tetanus fell sharply. Health workers gave smallpox vaccinations and immunization shots every year in three of the five villages. Hsiachuang even made a contract with one local hospital to give all peasants a periodic medical checkup. Each participant agreed to pay a small annual fee, and by 1957 42 percent of the families had signed up.

Rising prosperity and the new marriage law greatly improved the position of women, who, since the land reform, had owned their share of land and joined in field labor, thus winning a measure of independence. Whereas, in the past, women had only five weapons of defense—crying, scolding, feigning sleep, fasting and committing suicide—now they had the right to divorce, and had exercised it 79 times in the five villages since the marriage law was passed. In the same period 274 couples married, and 48 percent of them married by free choice. People who worked together on the same mutual-aid team, or read newspapers in the same group, or took part in cultural activities together could get acquainted, fall in love, and get married without parental introduction.

Unheard-of things, such as boys and girls writing letters to each other, young women washing clothes and sewing for their fiancés, mothers-in-law making dumplings for their sons-in-law, all began to be accepted as right and proper. Couples going steady before marriage worked together in the fields, studied together, criticized each other and argued on different sides of issues in public.

The possibility of free choice in marriage improved relations between the sexes and between husbands and wives. Before the war 342 men and women had been involved in irregular sex relations—illicit affairs, prostitution and rape. Now irregularities had fallen by 74 percent. While some older people still carried on illicit affairs, the young tended to apply high moral standards. "In the old days," the young men said, "there was no way to make a living. People like us could not afford a wife. Therefore they did questionable things. Now there is freedom of marriage. We feel good about it. We would be ashamed to do anything disgraceful." No one wanted a bad reputation, especially those not yet married, for it would harm their chances of finding a suitable mate.

Young people still had to struggle for the freedom to marry. Men who doubted their ability to win a mate complained, "In the past if one had money one could have a wife. Now I can't find one." Others said, "You have raised women too high. No one dares cross a woman anymore. If you do they ask for a divorce." But the women were delighted. They said, "Now that divorce is possible there is no need to die."

The new land system, the new marriage law, free choice in marriage and the right to divorce greatly improved relations within families. Of the 105 pairs of new mothers-in-law and daughters-in-law in the five villages, the vast majority enjoyed harmonious relations. Only 24 percent still quarreled and only 2 percent of the daughters-in-law still suffered abuse from their mothers-in-law. Open-minded mothers-in-law said, "The world is getting better. Young people attend meetings and understand things. They weave, spin, and work in the field. They are more capable than we. They can learn well without supervision." Thus many older women were willing to give up their "authority." When they refused to do so daughters-in-law said, "I too want to eat, have clothes to wear, and do productive work. You must not oppress me." The days when "the mother-in-law farted and the daughter-in-law had to collect the gas" faded away.

Relations between husband and wife were also improving. Of 311 husband and wife pairs interviewed, 73 percent shared housework equally; 9 percent of the women had become heads of households. Only 17.7 percent were completely dependent on their husbands and only one still received regular beatings from her husband.

All signs indicated a rising status for women. Nobody drowned girl babies anymore. Parents sent their girls off to primary schools, even middle schools, an unheard-of thing in the past. Nevertheless, they still preferred boy children. Other factors being equal, the boy always got the best food at home and always got the first chance at going off to school. Without boys people thought they could have no descendants. But if there were no boys, the girls had the right of inheritance; this was something entirely new.

Fathers were also beginning to treat sons better. Whereas in the past "even if there were a thousand people in the family there was only one head" and "while the father still lived the son could not claim to be illustrious," now fathers often handed family affairs over to their sons, fathers and sons often consulted and mutually accounted for all income and expenses. Many fathers encouraged their sons to study and to labor well. Very few continued the old practice of beating them.

When peasants compared the past with the present they said, "In the past there were many opium smokers, gamblers and thieves. Now there are many model workers. In the past there were many bachelors and many loose women. Now there are model couples with children. In the past there were many hired hands. Now there are many cadres and students boarding in schools. In the past many went without food and clothing. Now many eat white flour and wear fine, machine-made cloth. In the past what we had plenty of was pawn tickets. Now we have plenty of cash."

While it seems doubtful that social progress after land reform ever reached the levels described in the regional report, no one could deny that for most people the quality of life had improved greatly. Improvement was all to the good, but the basic direction of the rural economy had yet to be determined. As mutual aid grew, so did polarization. Meanwhile speculation and the free market favored sharp practice over honest trade.

16

TRYING OUT COOPS

Peasants remembered 1952 and 1953 as the golden age of the free market. At that time, if you asked a father or mother whom they preferred as a son-in-law—a worker, a soldier or a cadre—there was only one answer—a speculator! It was considered glorious and not at all shameful to marry a speculator. For was he not, after all, the smart one, the man who knew how to work the system, the man who lived without hard labor? *Kao t'ou-chi* (buy and sell, make a profit)—these were good words. The successful speculator had talent. Every family hoped for a son-in-law with such talent!

In those days landlords and rich peasants who still had some capital would show off by sitting outside their doors eating noodles (a relatively expensive dish) and dangling them enticingly from their chopsticks.

"Look at us," they would say. "We are private operators. See how prosperous we are. Going it alone is the road to wealth."

They wanted everyone to believe that it was their efforts on the land that enabled them to eat noodles, but actually buying and selling brought in the cash. This influenced the middle peasants. They were torn between the two roads—between go-it-alone and cooperation—and many waited to see which road would win out.

Ch'en Yung-kuei of Tachai reported on the strength of this tendency:

> Landlords, rich peasants and some ordinary peasants thought they would get rich fast by doing something other than working the land. To do that they had to go into trade and try their hand at speculation (*t'ou chi tao pa*). A person could buy cotton in Hopei Province and sell it in Shansi Province, then buy other things in Shansi and sell them in Hopei. The rich peasants led the way in this, the rich peasants and the landlords. They had done a lot of trading before the land reform. They didn't like working hard in the fields. They were always pushing for a chance to go out and do a little trading instead. Some Party members supported them in this. At that time, though I didn't think it was a very good idea, I didn't resist it as I should have.

One of the rich peasants from Tachai set up a trading station in Hsingt'ai County, Hopei. He collected merchandise there, then brought it into Shansi by donkey. When he had collected enough material for a shipment he would call up the village and we would send men and donkeys to haul it back. Once we sent six men and twelve donkeys. The poor peasant Chia Jiu-shen and I were in charge. In the morning when we arrived in Hsingt'ai, the sun was already well up, but the rich peasant was still fast asleep in the local inn. We had traveled all night and now the sun was high in the sky, but this rich peasant was still snoring away.

Chia knocked on the door, *ka tsa, ka tsa,* over and over again, and called out, *"San yeh yeh, san yeh yeh."* (They shared the same family name so the poor peasant called him "Third Grandfather," a very respectful term.) He called and knocked for more than ten minutes before that bastard woke up and opened the door.

I felt terrible. Here landlords and rich peasants sleep while poor peasants stand outside calling *"San yeh yeh."* This is the way it was before Liberation. How come such a thing is happening now?

The rich peasant finally opened the door and we went in. What a sight! There he was sleeping under a silk quilt on a heavy felt mat. And the room was very fancy indeed. When we saw this we really felt angry. We were disgusted. Here he was, even more comfortable than before Liberation, and we had walked the rough road all night. I thought to myself, Who, after all, is leading whom?

We loaded the donkeys and hauled the cotton back to Shansi. We hauled it back to the trading coop in our village. Each donkey could carry 120 catties (132 pounds), so altogether we brought back about 1,440 catties of cotton (1,584 pounds). No sooner did we pile the cotton in the coop yard than a group of members began to blow water on it to make it heavier. The next day some forty people went out to peddle it from door to door. Lots of people went in for this. Each family had its own scale. They went down the mountain to sell cotton. They exchanged the cotton for melon seeds, then took the melon seeds down to Hopei to sell. The idea was to get the proper amount of melon seeds first, and put them in your pocket, then hand over the cotton and leave. The buyer squeezes the cotton and finds water in it. He yells but it is too late. You're already gone. He yells, "There's water in the cotton, there's water in the cotton"—but you are already long gone.

I thought, Why should all this be going on now?

I didn't know any theory that said peasants neglecting farming and going in for trade was the wrong line. But I thought, We are farmers, we work on the land. Why go in for all this? Are we peasants, or workers, or merchants? What are we, after all, that we do all this?

In December, 1951, the Central Committee of the Chinese Communist Party, after studying the experiences of millions of mutual-aid teams and of 500 agricultural producers' cooperatives that already existed, issued its "Decisions on Mutual Aid and Cooperation in Agricultural Production." This document, primarily a call for a mass mutual-aid movement, instructed local administrations all over the country to set up, in an experimental way, land-pooling producers' cooperatives. In the next few months over 13,000 coops appeared.

In Southeast Shansi these included the coop set up by the labor hero Li Hsun-ta in West Gully, and the coops set up by the citizens of Purple Vegetable Farm and Sung Family Settlement, two of the six natural villages inside the Changchih City wall. Wounded Veteran Wang, of the Long Bow Propaganda Team, was Party Secretary of the hsiang administration responsible for these six villages. In forming these coops (two collective islands in a sea of private enterprise) Wang ran into many problems, but these proved to be minor compared to those he encountered in holding them together throughout the year. This latter task required all the ingenuity and energy that Wang possessed.

For the first step, land pooling, he mobilized Party members to take the lead, but not all of them found it easy to do so. Some of them had personal reservations. Others couldn't convince family members to go along. Sometimes these two phenomena were linked. Party members who were not ready to make such a drastic move put the blame on the rest of the family.

"Here," said Veteran Wang, "is a Communist who doesn't want to join the cooperative. He knows that Party members must take the lead so he says, 'I am anxious to join.' Then he adds the sad information, 'My wife doesn't agree. My father doesn't agree.' When this has sunk in he says, 'But I am resolute. I'll join anyway. I'll divorce my wife. I'll break with my father. I'll do whatever has to be done.'

"'Oh, you better not do that,' says the Party leader. 'That's carrying things too far. Since you can't convince the others, you had best stay out yourself for the time being.' And he leaves this Communist out of the organizing plans, which is, of course, what the man counted on all along.

"Another option is to step in with one foot but not the other. Here is a reluctant Communist who wants the best of both worlds. He divides the family holdings. He turns the best land, implements and draft animals over to his brother and enters the coop with some third-rate plots and a 'tattered' donkey. He calculates that if the coop fails he can always retreat by reestablishing a partnership with his prosperous brother.

"Of course family pressures can also work the other way."

Sometimes, children played a big role. Children liked cooperation because so many people would go out to work together. They often laughed and played games in the fields. When Security Officer Shen was small he urged his family to join up because he liked all that excitement. Later there was a big drive to form coops. A joining wind blew up and those who opposed it lost face. This made them vulnerable to pressure from their children, who wanted to be in the swim, so to speak.

To get people to join coops, leaders made concessions at first to individual needs and demands. Few new members felt any embarrassment about expressing self-interest. Such thinking was normal in those days, especially among middle peasants, and nobody had yet called it "capitalist road thought." If, on joining a coop, a middle peasant earned less than he had previously made on his own, the other members would sometimes grant him a bit of a subsidy so that he would not lose out.

This was to counter the influence of the independent peasants, who fanned up strong countercurrents. They tried hard to show off the "superiority" of their way of life. Copying the landlords and rich peasants, they, too, often sat outdoors in a very conspicuous place eating noodles. "Say, Old Chang, look at me. Look at these beautiful noodles. I can go to the fields whenever I want, or I can stay home when I feel like it and eat like this, too."

The go-it-aloners were, nevertheless, extremely interested in the yields reaped on cooperative fields, and if their own yields fell short they spread rumors that the coop figures were false.

"There was a whole lot of bourgeois thinking then," said Veteran Wang. "Self-interest was as thick as cement!"

Coops made concessions to middle peasants because it was difficult to farm without them. They had the best implements and the best animals. Every effort had to be made to include middle peasants in the leadership. Administrative policy stressed *Three Thirds*—a poor peasant, a middle peasant and a Communist Party member sharing power on the cooperative council. In order to bring in those with more land, groups divided 60 percent of the crop on the basis of the land contributed to the common pool, while only 40 percent went to cover the work points earned.

As soon as people joined a coop they began to earn labor days. But they didn't really know what a labor day was, what it meant in terms of their share of the crop, and they got worried. They wanted something in hand that they could hold. To satisfy this demand some of the coops, in addition to marking down points on the record sheet, issued slips of paper that they called work tickets. For each day worked peasants earned a ticket with its point value written on it. At harvesttime they turned these in for the amount of grain the ticket represented.

But prior to the actual distribution even these tickets didn't solve the problem. People didn't know what the tickets were for, or if they really could be exchanged for grain. Some people felt that only grain and land were truly worth having and they complained, "Since the land belongs to the coop now, what's the use of these little pieces of paper?"

A satirical poem appeared:

> Work all day, limbs worn out,
> Nighttime comes, paper they flout!
> Ass to the sky, face to the ground,
> Work till you die, papers abound!

When people lost faith in paper altogether, they wanted to get out of the coop. At one point Sung Family Settlement Coop shrank to six families, three of whom were talking about leaving.

"We sent Kuo Ch'uan-te and two others there to keep things moving," said Wang. "Our instructions to them were, 'Hold the red flag up. Under no circumstances must this coop be allowed to collapse.' Old Kuo had ability and he also had determination. He said, 'Whoever lets this coop collapse will be kicked out of the Communist Party. Each of us can carry two families. We'll work with one family today and with the other family tomorrow and see this thing through to the end!' "

At the Vanguard Coop in Purple Vegetable Farm the vice-secretary of both the coop and the Communist Party branch, one Yang Huan-yü, was one of those who wavered. In the land reform he had won good land and had also found a wife. Since he was in the prime of life there was nothing to stop him from prospering on his own. When the coop ran into difficulties he decided he wanted to leave. He thought he could make a killing buying and selling on the open market.

Since he didn't dare say this openly, he went around quietly urging other people to withdraw. He thought this would bring the whole coop down. He planted doubts everywhere. But Wang countered them vigorously and won enough support to isolate Yang. Seeing that the coop was not going to collapse, Yang finally came forward and said he personally wanted to get out.

"But you're the vice-secretary of the Party," said Wang. "You can't leave just like that."

"Yes I can," said Yang. "The Central Committee Directive clearly states that cooperation is voluntary."

Wang saw this as a serious challenge. If Yang Huan-yü left the coop, many other waverers might also leave. The future of the Vanguard Coop was at stake. He sounded out the other Party members and found that most of them wanted to stay in. So he decided to hold a public meeting to consider Yang's withdrawal. He asked Yang to come to the meeting with his mule.

There in front of the whole village Wang made a rousing speech about following Chairman Mao down the socialist road. With bold strokes he painted a picture of the socialist future. He ended by saying that anyone who wanted to go against Chairman Mao was free to do so.

Wang felt that Yang Huan-yü, thus confronted in public, would not dare go through with his plan. It would mean the loss of too much face.

But Yang Huan-yü was stubborn. He mounted the platform and said, "Cooperation is voluntary, I can join and I can leave. Now I want to leave."

Tall, well dressed, with a clean white towel on his head, he proudly read out, ". . . according to the directive of the Central Committee."

His attitude angered Wang.

"OK. Leave. But if you leave you cannot be our Party vice-secretary. Take your mule and go."

"Get out. Go. Take your mule and go home," several people shouted all at once.

Huan-yü's face fell. He took the mule by the halter and started to walk away.

The coop members stood there shocked and dismayed. The activists clapped and cheered, making fun of Yang, celebrating his decision to leave with mock applause. Meanwhile ex-landlords and rich peasants hung around the edge of the crowd, waiting to see what would happen.

"You can't just let him leave like that," said several of the Party members. "What about his Party membership?"

Wang took a quick poll.

All the other members present said, "Throw him the hell out. Expel him from the Party."

There was no such policy at the time, but Wang made up a policy to suit the emergency.

"On behalf of the Communist Party of the Hsiang, I hereby expel Yang Huan-yü from his post as Party Secretary of our coop, from his office as vice-secretary of our coop and from our Party branch as a member. Next year we can reconsider his case, but only as a candidate member."

Yang Huan-yü buried his face in his towel for a moment, then threw the towel across his shoulders, took his mule by the halter and walked out alone.

The ex-landlords and rich peasants poked each other in the ribs and smiled. "Stick around. Let's see if they don't all walk out and finish this coop off for good."

But Wang was one jump ahead of them. He had already mobilized as many Party members and rank-and-file peasants as possible to stand up and express support. Confidently he called out, "Yang Huan-yü has left the coop. Since he is a Communist and a cadre, we no longer want him. But you are free to speak up. You can get out or stay in. Whoever wants to leave should leave now. Whoever wants to stay can stay. How about you, Yang Ying-ch'eng?"

"I'll stay even if I am the only one left," said Ying-ch'eng.

All the other Party members and Youth League members spoke up in turn. After two-thirds of the rank-and-file members also declared that they were staying, the other third, those who were wavering, decided to stay also.

Someone in the crowd spoke out with enthusiasm. "Let's make a plan. Let's show by your action tomorrow what the coop can do."

All those who had been standing there hoping for a mass exodus showed their disappointment. The ex-landlords and rich peasants walked home crestfallen.

Veteran Wang's quick action totally defeated Yang Huan-yü. But that was not the end of trouble for the Purple Vegetable Farm cooperative. There were two clans in the village. Members of one of them lived to the east of the public toilet, members of the other to the west. Right across the road from the toilet sat the village office. It sat on the dividing line between the two clans.

As the New Year approached, village leaders planned a single lantern festival, but each clan wanted to make its own arrangements and soon the people fell to quarreling over which clan was best. What began as a fistfight between a few hotheads developed into a village-wide riot. When this split the village, Yang Huan-yü again became active. He advocated dividing the coop.

Wang felt that this would be the first step in its dissolution. He publicly criticized Yang for the second time. This stabilized the coop temporarily, but even so a new problem came up every few days. Contradictions popped up like weeds in a cabbage patch. None of the higher cadres of the city or the hsiang wanted to visit Purple Vegetable Farm. Coops, they said, were easy enough to start, but they were very hard to consolidate. People quarreled over work points not because the problems were so knotty but because they had never liked each other to begin with. Many thought that once the harvest was in it would be better to dissolve the whole thing. The weather had not been any too favorable and some of the coop fields looked worse than the private fields nearby.

Yang Ying-ch'eng, who was determined to stick it out, went to Wang. "Mao Tse-tung must find a solution," he said. "He can't just leave us here with all these problems. Maybe we can get rid of the voluntary principle. Let them come in of their own free will, but once they're in tell them they can't get out. Then the thing'll work."

"That can't be," said Wang. "The voluntary principle has been established by the Party leaders. We can't change it on our own."

Nothing Wang could say would cheer up Yang Ying-ch'eng.

"Never mind," said Wang. "Mao Tse-tung will give us a method. He'll find a solution. We don't know what it is but it will come."

Wang's faith was justified. In the fall of 1953 the Central Committee decided on the unified purchase of grain by the state, a state monopoly on the buying and selling of grain. As explained by Vivienne Shue, this was "probably the single most powerful step taken to restrain rural petty capitalism at this stage, because it quite simply eradicated the peasant's own control over the disposition—and most particularly, over the marketing—of the crop that was harvested. . . . Land reform had sharply limited the profit to be made by renting out land; Mutual Aid Teams made it more difficult to make a profit with hired labor; . . . Credit Coops and low-interest government loans were, at the same time, making it harder to make much money by lending money; and now, sales quotas and set prices were to make it virtually impossible to do any better than anyone else in the marketplace.

"This created conditions in which the only remaining way to increase income was to increase output. . . . Unified Purchase and Supply in effect decisively closed off what was in most cases the last significant option available to peasants for getting rich through independent action, and consequently made cooperativization, when it came, much less of a sacrifice than it otherwise would have been.

"From the point of view of village politics, the success of Unified Purchase went a long way toward diminishing the major outstanding differences in interest between middle peasants and poorer peasants, and thus it helped to reestablish a basis for class unity in the coming confrontation with rich peasants. In this way it helped create a broad village constituency for rapid collectivization."*

As Unified Purchase and Supply of grain went into effect, everything fell into place. All the advantages of cooperation began to show their strength, and private farming became more and more difficult. Up to that point the leadership had always said, "Block the capitalist road, plug the capitalist loophole."

*Vivienne Shue, *Peasant China in Transition* (Berkeley: University of California Press, 1980), pp. 214–15.

"But how could we plug this hole?" asked Wang. "To talk of plugging the hole with our little pile of grain was to talk nonsense. But once the state took over the grain trade people began to come around in large numbers asking, 'When will the coop take me in?'

"In our hsiang all six villages formed coops and the whole atmosphere changed. When people went to visit their relatives all the conversation turned to coops."

"Have you joined yet?"

"Have you?"

"In Huang Nien the coop is even bigger than ours!"

"Even in backward Chia Village there is already a coop."

More than 80 percent of the people joined the coops then and ex-landlords and rich peasants, left out in the cold, sent envoys to ask if they too might join. Some were for letting them join on probation. Others said, "Let them go it alone."

"Going it alone" became a form of punishment, for there was no longer any bright path to wealth through speculation. If you weren't in a coop by that time it was clear that there was something wrong with your class origin.

Among those asking to come in was a much-chastened Yang Huan-yü. He had more land than he could work alone. He couldn't hire anyone to work for him, for his peasant neighbors were all either members of the coop or busy on their own land. His crop yields fell off but his taxes and his quota of sales to the state remained fixed.

"I've lost my position in the Party and in the coop," he said. "But I am willing to be a probationary member and start all over again."

But the people shouted, "Don't let him in! Don't let him in!" Some really meant it. Others just joined in to make him feel uncomfortable.

The Party leaders finally decided to let Yang Huan-yü return to the coop as a probationary member. As this was quite punitive, since it was the treatment meted out to ex-landlords or rich peasants, Wang suggested that he be welcomed back as a regular member. But the masses would not agree. "Let him stay on probation. Didn't he walk out of his own free will, with his mule and all? Let him come back and prove himself!"

"How things had changed!" said Wang. "Now it was a matter of shame if you were not in the coop. To be forced to go it alone meant that there was something wrong with you."

When the national government formed the State Grain Company, thus taking responsibility for the purchase of grain nationwide, it also set up a nationwide grain rationing system to control the distribution and consumption of grain and guarantee to all nonfarming people a fair share of staple food. This was a most far-reaching and influential measure which affected the future development of China in the most radical fashion. For what it accomplished, in fact, was to divide the population into two segments, into two categories of people—those with ration books, who were guaranteed a certain standard amount of grain at a controlled price regardless of crop or season, and those without ration books, who had to depend for grain on what they could raise themselves.

In the first category belonged all city residents, all workers, professional people and government cadres—the vast majority of whom were already employed by the state. The independent capitalists and their employees also covered by this system were, within a few years, also absorbed into the state-owned economy. In the second category fell all the peasants in the countryside. They were left on their own to provide themselves with the basic necessities of life.

At the same time the government set up its rationing system, it initiated a nationwide system of residency permits. The residency permits matched the two categories of people already established. City permits entitled one to live in the city, receive a ration book, and buy grain from the State Grain Company. Rural permits restricted those possessing them to dwelling in the countryside, ruled out ration books, enforced self-reliance, and made it impossible for their holders to leave the countryside without first winning the approval of the local leadership (the Communist Party Secretary of their unit) on the one hand, and concurrently the approval of the leadership (the Communist Party Secretary) of some urban unit on the other hand. This unit must guarantee employment, sponsor issuance of a ration book from the local police, and thus make possible a permanent transfer to urban life.

These far-reaching measures permanently divided the people of China into two groups—an urban group with guaranteed employment and gua-ranteed subsistence—the famous "iron rice bowl"—and a rural group in direct confrontation with nature, fending for itself to the best of its ability and unable to leave the land except by invitation.

Within both these spheres there was some freedom of movement. Urban employees could apply for alternative industrial service, or professional jobs, and with the approval of their superiors (the Communist Party Secre-taries of their respective units), move about from job to job within the urban or the state sphere. Such mobility was minimal but it was possible, particu-larly for those with influence and connections—the famous "back-door" which had plagued Chinese administration from time immemorial.

Rural residents, on their part, could apply to move from one village to another within the rural sphere. Any transfers, however, had to be approved by the Secretary of the Communist Party where the individual resided and by his or her counterpart in the community to which the individual wished to move. Once these regulations went into effect there was no such thing as picking up and leaving at will to look for something better. Every move had to be planned, not only by those directly involved, but by both of the communities affected by the transfer. In spite of this requirement many people did manage to move from one place to another. But it was almost always because they had relatives to speak for and sponsor them in their new home and thus had some inside track through which to influence the leaders of the new community.

Such transfers within the rural sphere were not considered "back-door" only because movement from one rural community to another was not considered to be any great privilege. No one could gain a ration book thereby, nor any sinecure, but only the right to till the land or labor at a sideline in some new place. Of course the land and other conditions for making a living were far better in some communities than in others. People who enjoyed obvious advantages in regard to fertility of the soil, natural resources such as coal for heat or clay for bricks, transportation facilities or other coveted amenities, were not in the habit of opening their doors to any and all comers. Hence some communities were much harder to move into than others.

However, the barriers erected between communities could never be compared with the barriers that blocked the leap from the rural to the urban sphere. Without approval from both sides this leap was all but impossible. (The only exception that I am aware of is certain rural construction gangs that have found ways to live for years illegally in Peking.) To make the leap one had to acquire a ration book, a book that could not be obtained without an urban residency permit. Without a ration book one could not buy grain and therefore one could not survive away from home for very long.

Of course, with the economy growing rapidly, with millions of peasants being recruited each year to join expanding industries and help construct them, many people were able to transfer to urban life through approved channels. But those who were accepted in the cities fell far short of those who applied. There were enormous pressures in the countryside, primarily economic ones, pushing people to leave, but once these regulations came into effect they bottled up those pressures. In the main, people had to stay where they were and make the best of the resources, whether agricultural, handcraft or industrial, that were available to them in the countryside.

Measures restricting movement had both positive and negative effects. On the positive side they prevented a vast exodus of destitute people who could not really hope to find useful employment in the cities, but would under other circumstances have left home anyway in hopes of bettering their conditions. Such an exodus would have created enormous shack towns around every major city and every major industry such as are so commonly seen in other parts of Asia, in Latin America, the Middle East and Africa. Because Chinese peasants, after 1953, could not leave the land freely, shack towns were not built. Only those who were actually assigned to existing jobs could leave the rural areas. They were absorbed, more or less according to plan, in the cities and on industrial construction sites.

Since only those with jobs could enter the cities, the whole process of urbanization became subject to plan. Theoretically, at least, housing, water, sanitation, health care and education could all be provided in advance for new city residents. There was no need for the appearance of slums, not to mention shack towns populated by the teeming dispossessed. The primitive level of much urban housing in China certainly makes many districts resemble slums, but the gainful employment, social organization, services, education and health care available make clear that these places are not truly the last refuge of the destitute.

Since the bulk of the peasantry had to remain on the land, they were forced to apply their energy and ingenuity to developing rural resources, and this did happen on a fairly wide scale, inspired by such outstanding examples as West Gully and Tachai in Shansi. Had rural people been free to leave home, such places might well have been completely abandoned. As it was, local residents had to find ways to prosper where they were and some of them succeeded in ways that no one could have imagined a decade earlier. Others, of course, without such obvious resources as the piled-up loess at

Tachai, or the reforestable slopes of West Gully, found no new resources to tap, raised poor crops, and left home in large numbers to beg when winter came round each year.

On the negative side, these regulations divided the Chinese into two categories of citizen, one of which, the urban category, was secure and privileged and the other, the far larger rural category, remained at the mercy of nature and weather and was in most respects underprivileged. Judged by almost any standard—income, food, clothes, medical care, education, cultural opportunity—rural life was inferior. Only in the realm of housing did country people generally have more room and more comfort than urban workers.

The fact that rural people were unable to leave home perpetuated one of the primary aspects of feudalism—bondage to the land—which had plagued Chinese peasants over the ages. Under the new regulations this bondage was much more severe, in fact, than it had been under the old regime because Chinese peasants had not traditionally been serfs bound by contract to feudal manors or castles. Their bondage was the bondage imposed by debt, and was more logically classed as peonage than serfdom.

But under the old regime this peonage was only partial, spotty and unevenly persistent. Millions of peasants felt free to come and go as they pleased, walking over the face of China as beggars or itinerant laborers, seeking whatever work could be found. Even those crushed by debt could sometimes escape its bondage simply by running away. Social order was so chaotic that there was little likelihood that their landlord could track them down.

After 1953, on the other hand, every rural resident was bound to the land, bound to the village into which he or she had been born or married. The result was to guarantee a certain minimum level of security as long as the crops grew moderately well but the price was to give up mobility, the freedom to move on and look for something better.

When this system was inaugurated it met the needs of China's new society for stability and social order. It was supported, on the whole, by the Chinese people in both city and countryside. But in the long run it gave the new administration of the country exactly what the old imperial bureaucracy had always striven for—complete control over the whole population, especially the rural population. It fostered tendencies toward rural stagnation and played into the hands of those numerous officials at the middle level who "with little concept of time or efficiency, stick to old ways, easily fall into a rut and are given to procrastination. . . . Every day some cadres eat their fill and do nothing, they are quite satisfied with things as they are and just muddle along idling away their time at their official posts."

The fact that rural people are not allowed to leave home means that much less attention must be paid to their problems than would otherwise be the case. A bureaucratic state can muddle along for decades with what amounts to a crisis in the countryside as long as the peasants are tied to the land and have no choice, short of revolt, to make demands known. And this, it seems to me, affects not only the attitudes of those born procrastinators in the middle level of the administration, but also the thinking of many otherwise capable and energetic leaders at the very pinnacle of power.

There is an assumption, widely held in China, that as long as the peasants are busy on the land with their hoes, all is right with the world. And this holds true even though people with hoes may well be producing less per capita than their ancestors did in the Han Dynasty some 2,000 years ago.

In 1953 the decision of the state to take over the grain trade and parcel out grain by ration book to all urban residents made sense. Almost everyone, with the exception of the professional speculators in China, supported it, and it made possible the orderly, impressive economic development that followed. The full implications of this extraordinary two-pronged policy are only now being felt.

17

LONG BOW ORGANIZES A COOP

Long Bow residents took their first step toward cooperative production in the fall of 1953 at about the same time that the central government established its monopoly of the grain trade. Attitudes throughout the countryside toward speculation on the one hand and cooperation on the other were undergoing a rapid transformation. Throughout the old liberated areas of the north, where land reform had been completed for at least four years, the Communist Party prepared the way by holding large, marathon rectification meetings, expelling diehard individualists and calling on the more advanced members to take the lead in forming trial cooperatives. In Lucheng County, Secretary Wang Ting-mo, who had helped lead the land reform movement to a successful conclusion, led a month-and-a-half-long meeting.

Wang Ting-mo was so short in stature that he had to stand on a stool every time he made a speech, so that the people at the back of the audience could see him. Craning one's neck was a small price to pay to hear him talk. He was a popular speaker with a voice as big as his body was small. He had learned to minimize generalities and maximize concrete examples. This lively style captured attention and won support.

This time Wang Ting-mo attacked selfishness, all tendencies toward capitalism in the countryside after land reform, the whole concept of "getting rich quick" with good land and strong animals. This was the winter of the Three-Anti and Five-Anti campaigns in China as a whole—the campaign against corruption, waste and the bureaucratic spirit among the cadres; and the campaign against bribery, tax evasion, fraud, theft of government property and theft of state economic secrets on the part of those in private industry.

A number of leading Communists from Long Bow attended the meeting. These included Hu Hsueh-chen, the leader of the Women's Association; Chang Hsin-fa, the Party Secretary; Shih Ts'ai-yuan; and Li-the-Fat. It was somewhat ironic that all three of the men were already well known in Long Bow as new-rich peasants. To be called upon to take the lead in pooling land and forming a cooperative posed problems for each of them.

"The way the County Party Secretary put it, we had no choice," Hsin-fa said. "As Communists we had to jump in and pool our land for joint tillage.

As far as I was concerned it was no problem. What did I have to lose? All I had was 2½ acres of land, and one-third of a donkey. I had only two dependents—my wife and my daughter. So I slept very well that night. But the same could not be said for Ts'ai-yuan and Li-the-Fat; they were really worried about their freedom. Ts'ai-yuan had a lot of land and it was all good. He also had two draft animals, a horse and a donkey. Why should he join together with people who had poor land and no livestock? For him it would really mean a loss. He had twelve mouths to feed at home. By hiring extra help he was able to feed them because his land was good. But suppose he joined up in a cooperative. He would only earn labor shares. Since at that time Ts'ai-yuan didn't know about land shares or livestock shares he thought that in a cooperative he would be cut back to two labor shares and this looked like a disaster. With brother Fu-yuan working out, he and Er-chih alone would have to support twelve people. The women did not count as labor power because the custom at that time was to leave women out of field production, hence as he foresaw things only he and his brother could expect labor income.

"Li-the-Fat was in the same position. He had everything he needed for prosperity except labor power. He himself was the manager of the supply coop. Brother T'ai-p'ing was a disabled veteran who made up for his own weakness by hiring Chou Cheng-fu full time. Little brother Ch'i-shun was at best but half a labor power. By planting a few mou himself he could raise enough to eat, but when it came to earning labor days in a cooperative his prospects seemed bleak indeed. In a cooperative Li-the-Fat himself would be cut back to one labor share. How could that ever equal the earnings he made with his mule on the road? The Li brothers all thought that if they tried to live off labor shares they would really suffer.

"Li-the-Fat and Ts'ai-yuan hardly slept at all that night. The advantages and disadvantages of cooperation reeled through their minds. But they always came back to one thought: 'We are Communists. Communists are expected to take the lead on the socialist road. If we don't start, who will or can?' In the end, when they got back to Long Bow, they called their mutual-aid group members together and formed a land-pooling coop with twenty families as founding members."

That was Hsin-fa's version. When Kuo Cheng-k'uan, still head of the Peasants' Association and leader of the Fifth Production Team, heard this he smiled.

"Hsin-fa says he had no problem with the idea of a cooperative. But that's not true. He wasn't just a poor peasant with a few mou and one-third share in a donkey. He was well known as one of the four new-rich peasants of Long Bow. After that county meeting he didn't sleep well either. Of course he went through a mental struggle. But the Party presented land pooling as a revolutionary task. The Party leaders in the village had to lead the cooperative movement, so Hsin-fa went along.

"It was even harder for the Li brothers but in the end they helped build the first coop because Li-the-Fat was a Party member and he pulled the others in; he pulled the whole family in against its better judgment."

As for Hu Hsueh-chen, she described her own views as follows:

"I agreed to join right away. Mao Tse-tung wanted us to take the cooperative road and I felt we would be better off, so I wanted to join right away. Wen-te, on the other hand said, 'Why not wait and see?' He wanted to stand aside and see if the coop would work first. But I opposed this. I saw people joining, people with many burdens. 'With only three in the family what have we to be afraid of?' I said. 'We have always followed Mao Tse-tung before, so how can that be wrong now?' "

All but two of the members of Hsin-fa's mutual-aid team joined this first coop. Yang Yü-so, who had spoken for the poor peasant delegates at the "gate" that confronted Long Bow's Party members in 1948, decided to wait a while. "I want to see how it goes," he said.

Wang Kuei-pao, the first peasant to be classified by the Poor Peasant League in 1948, the man about whom there had been no doubt—"he's been a poor peasant all his life, and a poor peasant he remains"—also hesitated. He had a loom at home and worked hard, day and night, at weaving. Ten feet of handwoven cotton cloth brought about 5 sheng of millet on the market. In a day Kuei-pao could weave from 20 to 30 feet, thus earning as high as 15 sheng of millet. That was more than he could earn in the fields. When Wang Kuei-pao hesitated, the other members of the group didn't press him very hard. They looked on his weaving as a sort of capitalist tail (free enterprise!). They thought that his labor power, insofar as heavy farm work was concerned, was marginal and that his land was, on the whole, pretty poor. So it was better to let him stay outside the coop anyway.

But if two members of the original group stayed out, ten new families joined to bring the total strength of that new coop to twenty.

Many of the members brought in their livestock. Lu T'ai-p'ing brought his cow, Chang Kuei-ts'ai also brought a cow, Yang Ching-shun brought a donkey, Li-the-Fat a mule and Wang Wen-te a donkey. Altogether the group, from the very beginning, boasted five donkeys, two cows, one horse and one mule, all of them good strong animals in the prime of life. With each of these animals came a cart—the old-style carts with wooden wheels and iron tires. Between them these same members contributed four iron plows. Those who had no livestock, carts or plows to contribute brought their hoes with them.

Very important—members of the group also owned two night-soil carts, one belonging to Ts'ai-yuan and one to Hsin-fa's brother Ch'i-fa.

Between them the twenty families pooled eighty pieces of land, or four to a family. Chi Shou-hsi, for example, contributed five pieces of 4, 4, 2, 15 and 5.5 mou respectively.

The original group of cooperators included a high proportion of village cadres. After Hsin-fa, Li-the-Fat and Ts'ai-yuan came back from the Lu-cheng County meeting, they led a discussion on the whole question of coop formation inside the Long Bow Party branch. The branch leaders decided to start small, do well, and expand slowly on the basis of confirmed successes. They urged all Communist Party members to jump in and take the lead. Even though some of them had misgivings concerning loss of freedom and their own ability to operate a successful coop, the consensus was that "If we want to continue to make revolution we can't hang back. We have to go ahead, make a start, and carry it through."

Most of the leading members of the Party branch, all of them also holding important posts in the village administration, joined the new coop. Shih Ts'ai-yuan became the Party leader in the coop while serving as Secretary of the Long Bow Party Branch. Hsin-fa resigned as village chairman to become chairman of the coop. Kuo Fu-shu, clerk of the village, resigned that post to act as chief accountant for the new collective. Chi Shou-hsi, in charge of public affairs, Wang Wen-te, in charge of security, Lu Shui-ch'ang, captain of the militia, all joined the coop but retained their posts in the village. The Party branch decided that Shen T'ien-hsi should stay out of the joint tillage organization and lead the production work of the non-cooperators. But T'ien-hsi wasn't at all happy with this. He went to the District Party office to protest. He demanded membership in the coop, and in the end won his point.

As a result, cadres made up 70 percent of the membership. It was a coop full of tigers—all generals and no troops. No one would defer to anyone else. How could they ever get along? What could such people do together?

"In truth," said Hsin-fa, "we quarreled every night."

Nevertheless, looking at this coop in an all-around way, the conclusion had to be that it was sound. It joined together poor peasants and middle peasants in balanced proportions. It was well supplied with Party members and experienced cadres. It could command, as members' property, draft animals, carts, manure carts, large implements and good land. This coop had every reason to succeed. As if to confirm this, the name chosen for it by its members was the "Advance Coop."

In order to ensure, insofar as possible, that this pioneering effort would start on a sound basis a work team came from the county seat to give advice and help. This team was headed by a man named Shen Shuang-fu (Double Wealth Shen), an experienced accountant. He had studied the regulations of model cooperatives already established elsewhere and was familiar with the kinds of problems that almost always arose between people as they pooled their land to work together. He helped the Long Bow group with every step. Teams like this, composed of one or two people, went out to all the villages in the winter and spring of 1954 to help get the producers' cooperative movement off the ground.

18

THE DRAFT
CONSTITUTION

 Double Wealth Shen brought with him a model "Draft Constitution for an Agricultural Producers' Coop" that had been approved and passed down by the provincial Party leadership.* This was a comprehensive document in twelve sections: 1. general principles; 2. members; 3. land; 4. means of production other than land; 5. share funds; 6. production; 7. organization of work and labor discipline; 8. payment for work; 9. financial management and distribution of income; 10. political work, cultural and welfare services; 11. management; 12. supplementary rules.

The general principles, contained in the first ten articles, constituted an excellent summary not only of what agricultural producers' cooperatives were but why they were needed, how they should be organized, what stages they would pass through, what tasks they should accomplish, and how they should accomplish them.

CHAPTER ONE

GENERAL PRINCIPLES

ARTICLE 1　An agricultural producers' cooperative is a collective economic organization formed on a voluntary and mutually beneficial basis by working peasants with the guidance and help of the Communist Party and the People's Government. In such a cooperative, the principal means of production such as land, draft animals and farm tools owned privately by members are put under a single, centralized management and gradually turned into their common property; members are organized for collective work and the fruits of their labor are distributed according to a common plan.

The aim in promoting agricultural producers' cooperatives is step by step to end capitalist exploitation in the countryside, to overcome the backwardness of small-peasant farming and develop a socialist agricul-

*Quoted material here is from *Model Regulations for an Agricultural Producers' Cooperative,* adopted by the Standing Committee of the National People's Congress on March 17, 1956. The Draft Constitution used in Shansi Province in 1953 contained most of the same articles, with some difference in wording.

ture which will meet the needs of the nation's socialist industrialization. That is to say, steps must be taken gradually to replace private ownership of the means of production by collective ownership by the working masses, and small-scale production by large-scale mechanized production, so as to create a highly developed agriculture bringing prosperity to the peasants as a whole and satisfying the ever-increasing demands of society for agricultural products.

ARTICLE 2   Agricultural cooperation is the only clear road which can lead the working peasants to the final elimination of poverty and exploitation; that is why all working peasants must be gradually enrolled in the agricultural producers' cooperatives, to bring about the complete victory of socialism in the countryside. To do this, cooperatives must on no account resort to coercion in dealing with the peasants remaining outside; they must persuade and set an example to them so that they become willing to join when they realize that far from suffering loss, they can only benefit by joining.

The agricultural producers' cooperative should be an association bringing mutual benefits to all the working peasants, especially as between the poor and middle peasants. The only way to ensure that the peasants take the road of cooperation voluntarily is by adherence to the principle of mutual benefit. In promoting agricultural producers' cooperatives the rule must be to rely on the poor peasants and unite firmly with the middle peasants. The cooperative must not violate the interests of any poor peasant, or of any middle peasant. When the cooperative has reached the advanced stage at which all the chief means of production are turned into common property and the peasants as a whole prosper, there will no longer be any distinction between poor and middle peasants.

ARTICLE 3   Agricultural cooperation proceeds through two stages —the elementary and the advanced. At the elementary stage, the cooperative is semisocialist in character. At that stage part of the means of production is owned in common and members are, for a definite period of time, allowed to retain ownership of land and other means of production, which they have pooled for use under centralized management, and to receive an appropriate return on this property.

As production develops and the socialist understanding of members grows, the dividend paid on land pooled by members will be gradually abolished. Other means of production brought by members for use under centralized management will, as need arises and with the approval of the owners, be gradually converted into common property, that is, property collectively owned by all the members, after paying the owners for them or taking other mutually beneficial measures. In this way the cooperative will pass step by step from the elementary to the advanced stage.

At the advanced stage the cooperative is entirely socialist in character. In such a cooperative, all the land pooled by members and other means of production needed by the cooperative will become common property.

Household goods of members, small plots of household land, small holdings of trees, and poultry, domestic animals, small farm tools and tools needed for subsidiary cottage occupations will not be made common property in cooperatives, either of the elementary or advanced type.

ARTICLE 4 The cooperative must bring about a steady expansion of productive activities, raise the level of agricultural production, make its members more efficient and increase yields.

The cooperative must work to plan. It should draw up plans both for the production and sale of products in the light of its own conditions and gear these plans to the production and purchase plans of the state.

With its land under centralized management and by working collectively the cooperative should, as circumstances permit, start using better farm tools, constantly improve farming skills, and, with the assistance of the state and working class, bring about the gradual mechanization and electrification of agriculture.

The cooperative should do everything possible to take full advantage of organized collective work, promote labor emulation, encourage and urge every member to work hard, and make vigorous efforts to create wealth both for the community and for each individual member.

ARTICLE 5 In paying members for work, the cooperative must stick to the principle "to each according to his work—that is, more work, more pay."

ARTICLE 6 The cooperative must not practice any form of exploitation. It must not hire farm laborers for lengthy periods, rent out land, lend money out for a profit, or engage in commercial exploitation. No one is permitted to bring farm laborers into the cooperative upon joining it.

The cooperative may engage technical personnel; it may hire a small number of farm laborers for short periods if an urgent need arises. Those employed by the cooperative must get proper treatment.

ARTICLE 7 In dealing with its economic problems, the cooperative should stick to the principle of giving due consideration to both public and private interests, so that the interests of the state, the cooperative and individual members are properly integrated.

The cooperative must set an example in fulfilling its duties to the state. In paying the agricultural tax it must observe the state's requirements regarding quantity, quality and delivery dates; it must sell its products in accordance with the state plan for unified purchase of agricultural produce and prior contracts for purchase of products concluded with state purchasing agencies.

In distributing the fruits of labor, the cooperative should, while giving each member his due, set aside funds needed to expand production and improve public welfare and amenities.

With the expansion of production, the cooperative should gradually improve the material well-being of members and enrich their cultural life.

ARTICLE 8 The cooperative should live up to the principles of democracy and strive for unity and constant progress.

The cooperative should manage things in a democratic way. Officers of the cooperative should keep in close touch with members, discuss things with them thoroughly, and rely on the members as a body to run the cooperative well. They must not abuse their authority and position or restrict democratic rights.

The cooperative should take any measures that will effectively strengthen internal unity and foster comradely relations among members. There must be no discrimination against members who belong to national minorities, members who come as settlers, new members or women members.

The cooperative should take any measures which will bring about a steady rise in the level of political understanding of members; it should give them regular education in socialism and patriotism, and see to it that every member abides by the laws of the country. It should be ready to respond to the call of the Communist Party and the People's Government, and lead its members in the advance to socialism.

ARTICLE 9 Close contact should be established between agricultural producers' cooperatives, and between them and supply and marketing cooperatives, credit cooperatives and handicraft producers' cooperatives, as well as the state economic agencies in the villages, so that each can help the others to carry out their economic plans and join in the common effort to implement the state economic plan.

The cooperative should make a big effort to unite with working peasants still outside its ranks—those who have joined agricultural producers' mutual-aid teams and those who still work individually—and do all it can to help them increase production and take the cooperative road.

ARTICLE 10 The cooperative should carry on the struggle against the rich peasants and other exploiters so as to restrict and gradually abolish capitalist exploitation in the countryside.

It was no accident that chapter two of the model regulations took up the question of membership. Who could join a land-pooling cooperative, and on what basis, was a most crucial question influencing the form and the future development of the movement. The Party regarded the membership question as a class question. What class or class interests should the cooperative serve?

The membership provisions stated that all working peasants, men and women sixteen and over, who wanted to join could become members once the general meeting accepted their applications.

Some guidelines for approving members followed:

1. No restrictions should be placed on admittance of poor peasants; no middle peasant shall be prevented from joining the cooperative.

2. Demobilized soldiers, dependents of people killed in the course of the revolution, dependents of soldiers and of government workers, and new settlers should be actively drawn in. The aged, the weak, the widowed and the orphaned should find a place.

3. The coop should not accept former landlords and rich peasants as

members for the first few years. (The document outlined special procedures for admitting individual landlords and rich peasants whose status had been officially altered.)

4. Persons deprived of political rights should not be admitted.

These four points bear some examination.

Point one implied some difference in attitude toward poor peasants as compared to middle peasants. While it placed "no restrictions" on the admittance of poor peasants, no middle peasant should "be prevented" from joining. This was the reflection in the model regulations of the basic political position that in the organization of cooperatives members must "rely on the poor peasants and unite with the middle peasants." It seemed to say, "Get the poor peasants in by all means and open the doors to all middle peasants who want to join them."

Point two urged the cooperatives to make special efforts at drawing in certain types of people, most of whom were, by definition, deficient in labor power. Of the nine special categories mentioned, only demobilized soldiers (if they were not disabled) and new settlers could be presumed to be able-bodied. The dependents of martyrs, soldiers and government workers; the aged and the weak; the orphaned and the widowed were all categories that would find it difficult to maintain life working on their own, and by the same token must become dependent, to some extent, as members of a cooperative group. From a narrow, short-term point of view, working peasants could not serve their mutual interests by collectively assuming the burden of support for such people. But looked at from a different perspective, all people, as children, start weak at first. They grow strong, grow old, and become weak again. Any person may die leaving orphans or a widow, may join the army, may die in battle, or may become a government worker, so that to look after these categories of people and to subsidize them, to the extent that they cannot support themselves, is really only a form of social insurance or social security, doing for friends and neighbors what one would hope they would certainly do for you under the same circumstances.

Point three addressed itself to a problem that prevailed throughout the Chinese countryside during and after land reform. The gentry—the landlords and rich peasants—had long dominated education, culture and government administration, even business and commerce, so that they had a superior cultural level, wider social experience and more developed administrative talent than most poor or middle peasants. Once overthrown as the rulers of their respective communities, they had the capacity, if given an opening, to move into the new organizations of the people, especially village governments and cooperatives, and to try to twist them in their own favor. They often used their position in the coops either to enrich themselves, or to disrupt and discredit whatever the revolutionaries were trying to build in order to turn back the clock and lay the groundwork for a restoration of former privilege and power.

Thus the people justly feared allowing any rule to the gentry.* But they

---

*"Gentry," as used here, does not refer to "degree holders under the old examination system," a common usage in works on Chinese society, but to the rural elite, the exploiting landlords and rich peasants who were the country squires of China.

did not treat the gentry as absolute, unchanging, reactionary quantities. They made provision in the law for individuals who had joined for lengthy periods in productive labor and had transformed their life-style and their ideology to change their class status and claim full political rights. Hence point three went on to say:

"Former landlords whose status has been changed according to law, and rich peasants who have for many years given up exploitation, may be admitted individually into the cooperative, but only when the cooperative in question is firmly established and when over three-quarters of the working peasants in that particular township and county have joined cooperatives, and after a general meeting of members has examined their cases and approved their applications, and this decision has been examined and sanctioned by the county people's council."

In other words, the model regulations made clear that a cooperative could absorb ex-landlords and rich peasants individually once the unit had established itself well and developed enough strength to forestall sporadic disruption from within.

Communities such as Long Bow, from which many landlords and rich peasants originally fled, were glad to get rid of them at the start. But later, large numbers of dispossessed gentry living from hand to mouth in the cities, and then taking jobs as industrial workers of uncertain class and social background, became a serious problem. Advanced communities like Tachai then made a point of seeking out and tracking down their runaway gentry, bringing them back to their native communities and placing them under community supervision where they could do little harm. These returned gentry became working members of established coops, but without the right to vote or to assume posts inside the organization.

Article 13 of the model regulations described the rights of members, Article 14 the duties. The four basic rights balanced the four basic duties:

RIGHT: To take part in the work of the coop and receive the payment which is due.

DUTY: To observe the regulations of the cooperative; to carry out decisions of the general meeting of members and of the management committee.

RIGHT: To take part in the activities of the cooperative, put forward suggestions and criticisms concerning its management and participate in supervising the management of affairs; to elect the leading personnel of the cooperative and to be elected, and to be appointed to certain posts in the cooperative.

DUTY: To observe labor discipline in the cooperative and punctually fulfill the tasks assigned.

RIGHT: To engage in subsidiary cottage occupations on condition that this does not interfere with participation in the work of the coop.

DUTY: To care for state property, property owned in common by the cooperative and property owned by the members but turned over to the cooperative for public use.

RIGHT: To enjoy the benefits of all public services and amenities provided by the cooperative.

DUTY: To strengthen the unity of the cooperative and resolutely oppose all activities aimed at undermining it.

Article 15 guaranteed free withdrawal from the cooperative and defined how land pooled and property sold should be returned to the individual.

Article 16 set the conditions for punishment, the most serious of which was expulsion, and similarly provided for the return of property pooled or sold to the group.

The central feature of a producers' cooperative, was, of course, the pooling of land for joint tillage. Since different individuals and families, in the aftermath of land reform, still owned differing amounts of land, the important problem to be solved in regard to pooling was how to overcome these differences so that mutual benefits could accrue to all, so that neither those who put in large amounts of property or those who contributed only their labor power would lose out.

The draft model regulations resolved the problem of unequal land contributions by means of a dividend plan which allowed a certain percentage of the annual income to be allocated according to land shares, with the balance allocated according to labor contributed. Since the work of its members, not their ownership of land, created the income of the coop, the draft recommended that the total amount paid in dividends be less than the amount paid for agricultural work, but that, at the same time, these dividends should not be set so low as to discourage people with relatively large holdings or members with considerable land but little labor power from joining.

These regulations called for fixed dividends. As productivity and income increased, the amount of these dividends would inevitably drop as a proportion of the total; then the coop could allocate an increasingly large fraction of total income to payments for work performed or to investment in new common property.

Where people found fixed dividends hard to establish, the draft recommended a percentage rate so that a certain percentage of total income could be allocated to land shares, while the remainder could be distributed as payment for work. This was the method adopted in Long Bow village. At the start the members agreed upon 40 percent for land shares and 60 percent for labor shares, but they soon cut this to 20 percent and 80 percent. When they moved on to the higher stage coop, they dropped land share payments altogether.

If the pooling of land constituted the central aspect of a producers' coop, the pooling of means of production came next in importance.

The draft model regulations called for the cooperative gradually to take over all major means of production other than land—draft animals, carts, large implements, et cetera—essentially through various forms of lease–purchase. Since at the start these valuable means of production belonged to individual members, the draft allowed the coop to hire or rent them without further obligation.

Section 1 of Article 26, referring to draft animals, said:

1. Members may retain the ownership of their draft animals and feed the animals themselves, in which case the cooperative hires the beasts at the fees

normally paid in the locality. This method of private ownership and rearing of animals and their collective use is in general suited to a newly established cooperative. Owners may use their draft animals hired to the coop when they are not needed by the latter; they may also hire them out or lend them to others. But such owners cannot sell their animals without consent of the cooperative.

This was the method Long Bow residents originally adopted.

A second method was for the coop to feed and care for an animal that still belonged to the individual peasant, and pay a suitable amount for its use. A third method was for the coop to buy the animal outright from its owner and turn it into common property. Long Bow residents adopted this third method later and by doing so raised their coop from a lower to a higher stage.

In order to finance each season's farming operations and to acquire common property such as large implements, carts or draft animals, the draft called for two kinds of share funds: 1. the production expenditure share fund, and 2. the common property share fund. These could be called, respectively, the operating capital share fund and the investment capital share fund.

Both these share funds were made up of contributions based on the amount of land each member brought into the group. Members who pooled little or no land in the cooperative contributed to the share funds in part or entirely on the basis of the amount of labor they were expected to contribute to the joint effort. Members who were too poor to pay their full contribution could apply for state loans through a special fund known as the "poor peasants' cooperation fund."

The total amount of the production expenditure share fund equaled the sum required for crop expenses—seed, fertilizer, fodder—under ordinary conditions. Members were expected to pay it in full in cash on joining.

The total amount of the common property share fund equaled the amount needed by the cooperative to buy the necessary means of production such as draft animals, carts and large farm implements from members. The coop credited the value of the means of production sold to it by members toward their share in the common property share fund. If the value of the property sold exceeded their share the coop paid the difference in cash or kind; if it fell short of their share the coop made up the difference with loans to be paid off in future years.

As a general rule the cooperative had three years to pay for means of production and members had three years to come up with their share of the common property fund. Provision was made for members to pay interest on back payments at the rate customarily paid on money deposits by credit cooperatives or credit unions.

Just as the draft compensated for the inequalities in land holding by the mechanism of a land dividend, so it compensated for inequalities in capital contribution both for operating expenses and for investment through the method of the share fund. Without such mechanisms it would have been impossible for large numbers of peasants to pool their property and work together to bring "mutual benefits to all the working peasants, especially as between the poor and middle peasants" as called for in Article 2 of the general principles. Only if the coop truly recognized differences and made material adjustments so that nobody gained or lost too much by joining the pool, could pooling actually proceed.

The purpose of pooling land and other means of production was, of course, to increase production.

In the chapter on production the model regulations call on the cooperative and its members to increase production through rational use of arable land, irrigation works, improvement of farm tools, the breeding and improved care of draft animals, improved strains of crops, accumulation of manure and fertilizer, improved tillage and cultivation, erosion control, reclamation of waste land, afforestation and the development of aquatic products. All these should be combined with suitable side occupations. The coop should mobilize all members for work, help them to overcome obstacles and physical disabilities, encourage them to study, acquire scientific knowledge, and master skills. Finally it should plan production and draw up seasonal, annual and long-term plans in coordination.

All of this was common sense. This chapter said nothing controversial or unexpected, but it presented, in capsule form, an excellent digest of the production possibilities confronting the Chinese peasants and challenged them to undertake the all-around development of their productive resources collectively, something they never could have done individually.

Next to the problem of pooling land and means of production, which, after all, however complex, may only be done once, the most difficult part in building and carrying on a cooperative was the organization of labor and payment for work.

The model regulations called for a division of labor and a definite organization of work based on the formation of approximately equal production teams (called brigades in the original document), on a year-round permanent basis, and the appointment of certain people as bookkeepers, technicians, stockmen, supply clerks, etc. Each team was to take responsibility for a definite area of land for cultivation and definite numbers of animals and equipment. Each team was also supposed to allocate jobs clearly and keep a proper record of the jobs accomplished and the credit due each person *each day.*

The draft detailed four rules of labor discipline:
1. members shall not absent themselves from work without good reason;
2. they shall carry out instructions when they work;
3. they shall bring their work up to the required standard;
4. they shall take good care of common property.

The draft listed criticism, fines, reduction of workday credits, payment for damage done, removal from post and finally expulsion as proper responses to violations of labor discipline.

Chapter eight, Payment for Work, generated the most controversy. Most of the struggle in the cooperative movement later swirled around this point.

The model regulations issued in the early fifties tended to be patterned after Soviet examples and based their work-point and payment schemes on relatively sophisticated piecework norms according to the overriding principle "to each according to his work—that is, more work, more pay," with equal pay for equal work, applied to men and women alike without exception.

The regulations required cooperators to set norms for each job and reckon these norms as workdays, each workday being equal to ten points. "The cooperative must make a correct assessment of the number of workdays a member is entitled to for fulfilling the norm for each job. There must be a suitable difference in the number of workdays awarded for fulfilling different kinds of norms. Such differences, however, should be neither too small nor too large. On the one hand uniformity must be avoided in order to be fair to members doing difficult jobs; on the other hand, rate of payment for certain jobs must not be set so high that everyone wants to do them, nor should rates for other jobs be set so low that nobody wants to do them."

Article 51 described a method of "fixed rates with flexible assessment," recommended for use before the various norms and rates of payment had been settled through experience and discussion.

"Each member is assigned a definite number of work points based on his skill or capacity for work. This number is subject to revision after a discussion of the work the member actually does for the day. If a good job has been done it may be increased; if otherwise, decreased. In this way the actual number of work points earned for the day is settled. This method, however, wastes time, and payment for work actually done by each member cannot be accurately calculated by it. The cooperative must therefore fix norms and rates of payment for various jobs as soon as it can, so as to avoid confusion regarding payment for work done and consequent losses in production."

Article 55 linked piecework with a system of responsibility for a particular job so that if a job was assigned to a particular team the number of workdays required for completion was specified. Regardless of how much time the team actually used to complete the job, it earned only the specified workdays. If the team did a poor job and completed the work late, it stood to lose workdays.

Article 56 extended this fixed responsibility system from short-term jobs to year-round responsibility. It demanded, for example, a certain crop from a certain piece of ground, expected certain supplies to be consumed, and certain means of production to be used. The regulation credited teams which overfulfilled these norms with additional workdays while it penalized those which fell below 90 percent of completion by loss of workdays.

The article called for awards to members who overfulfilled output norms, as well as prizes for outstanding work or innovation. "If the cooperative, as the result of good leadership, overfulfills its production plan, those responsible for its management should also be given suitable prizes."

What a workday was actually worth to the individual who earned it depended on the annual income of the cooperative as a whole. "As a general rule, what remains of the total income of the cooperative in a particular year, both in kind and in cash, after deducting production expenses, the reserve fund, welfare fund and dividends on land, will be divided by the total number of workdays worked by the cooperative during the year. The result is the value of each workday.

"Thus, the greater the annual income of the cooperative the more each workday is worth. When the annual income of the cooperative drops, the value of each workday drops, too. Therefore if the cooperative member wants a bigger income he must make an effort to earn more workdays; at the same time, each member must do his best to increase the total income of the cooperative so that the value of each workday increases accordingly. In this way the personal interests of each member are correctly combined with the collective interests of the cooperative."

These paragraphs summed up the essence of the payment scheme. Cooperative members shared in the total income of their coop after making all necessary deductions, and they shared in proportion to the number of workdays each contributed. How many workdays a member could earn on any given job depended on the norm allocated to that job and whether the member fulfilled the norm both quantitatively and qualitatively. The basic principle was "to each according to his work—that is, more work, more pay." The model regulations thus set up a system of direct material incentive based on piecework that appeared to be quite clear and straightforward. The problem, in Chinese agriculture, however, was the multiplicity of jobs, the variety of conditions, the wide variation in possible standards depending on these conditions, and therefore the difficulty of setting up suitable norms, judging whether or not they had been realized, and keeping proper records of the same. Thus from the very beginning the work-point system developed into the most controversial part of the whole cooperative setup and remains so to this day.

One thing, however, these regulations made clear: To pool land in an agricultural producers' cooperative was in no sense to give up individual interest, to enter into a share-and-share-alike arrangement where everyone ate out of one big pot and slept under one big quilt. From the very beginning the cooperative movement in Chinese agriculture took seriously the principle of payment according to work performed and all along proposed to reward the peasants in proportion to the effort made by each. Various ways of evaluating, recording, and rewarding this effort supplanted one another, but none of them departed in theory from the basic principle that he who does more work should receive more pay. In practice, however, various forms of "leveling" often obliterated differences.

In this summary I have so far left out one major facet of the payment system and that is payment to leaders, to those involved in managerial work who do not actually, day in and day out, move their hands in production, but who, nevertheless, play an essential role in it.

Article 53 covered this problem.

"Those engaged in managerial work for the cooperative and who take a regular part in actual productive work will receive a suitable number of additional workdays as compensation according to the amount of managerial work done and the contribution made by them; the amount of compensation will be decided once a year by a general meeting of members.

"The amount of compensation received by the chairman of the cooperative, added to the value of the workdays he earns by taking part in productive work, should, as a general rule, be higher than the value of the average number of workdays earned by the average member of the cooperative. The earnings of a bookkeeper, or of the chairman and other staff of a fairly large cooperative, who are not able to take part at all in production, must also be decided by a general meeting of members; such earnings must, as a general rule, correspond to, or be higher than, the value of the average number of workdays earned by the average member."

The remaining chapters of the model regulations covered a series of subsidiary problems.

Chapter nine dealt with the intricacies of financial management—budgets, managerial expenses, bookkeeping, cash handling, supervision of accounts, the allocation of funds such as the agricultural tax, various production expenses, reserve funds, welfare funds, dividends on land shares and advances to members. The final article of this chapter, Article 68, stated that a withdrawing member could not take away any of the common property of the cooperative.

Chapter ten provided for education in politics, particularly collective consciousness and spirit; for the study of reading and writing and of science; for recreation and cultural programs; for safety, sanitation and health care; for nurseries, aid to pregnant women and other people with special needs.

Chapter eleven dealt with management, the organizational structure of the cooperative where the highest body was the general meeting of members. Once a year this general meeting elected a management committee of five to fifteen members, a supervisory committee of three to nine members, and a chairman.

This chapter listed the functions and powers of the general meeting of members under eight headings, the most important being 1. to approve or amend the regulations; 2. to elect and remove from office the chairman and committee members; 3. to decide on the amounts to be paid for means of production, contributions to the share fund and the distribution of income; 4. to examine and approve of the production plan and the budget, the norms for work and important contracts signed with other parties; 5. the approval of new members and problems of discipline and expulsion.

I decided to reprint here the general principles of the Draft Constitution in full and to continue with a discussion in some depth of the twelve sections and eighty-two articles of this document because this Draft Constitution provided then and continued until recently to provide the basic framework, the bones and sinews underlying the economic, social, political and cultural relations of rural China. Complex, sophisticated, flexible and democratic in spirit, it spelled out a method for adjusting the often contradictory, multiple and multilayered interests of rural producers at all levels of prosperity, so that they could pool labor power and capital and thus bring to bear on the transformation of nature a much greater leverage than any individual or community of nonintegrated individuals could do. The 740,000 cooperatives built on these lines went through many upheavals, combinations and permutations, but the principles outlined in the Draft Constitution defined the essence of the social contract that bound peasant families together in the functioning artels that have for decades been the womb, the cradle, the life hammock, old-age home and grave for hundreds of millions.

19

PROBLEMS
AND ADJUSTMENTS

Cooperative farming, by pooling land, wipes out borders and unnecessary paths between fields and so brings more land under cultivation (5 percent more on the average).

Cooperative farming makes it possible to carry out water conservancy projects, water and soil conservation, and land and soil improvement on a large scale. Cooperative farming makes it possible to transform arid land into irrigated fields, and barren and waste land into fertile soil.

Liao Lu-yen, "Some Explanations on the Draft National Program for Agricultural Development (1956–1967)," 1956

 When Double Wealth Shen first called the prospective members of Long Bow's coop together to discuss the model regulations he stressed two points. First, that private landholdings would not disappear. The stone markers in the fields that divided one plot from another would remain even though peasant members pooled their fields and worked them in common. Furthermore, the landholdings themselves would yield income through the device of the land dividend, and this dividend would reflect the proportionate amount of land pooled by each family.

Second, he stressed the principle "He who works more gets more." In various ways, over and over again, he explained that "the more you produce, the more you sell, the more you store and the more you eat." He reiterated the four "mores"—produce more, sell more, store more, eat more —as the basic goal of the coop, and also as an illustration of the relationship between the collective and the individual. By taking care of their collective interests the members would also take care of their individual interests.

"These policies," said Shen, "will not change. When this coop moves from small to big, even if all the families in the village join it, the basic principles will still be the same."

These model regulations were well thought out and comprehensive. Quite obviously they did not spring from Chinese experience alone, but were based on the kind of rules and regulations that had long been worked out and applied on the collective farms of the Soviet Union. In the early fifties the Chinese made an intense study of Soviet experience and launched earnest attempts all over China to apply what Soviet "elder brothers" recommended.

Right from the beginning, however, problems arose with the work-point system based on a concept of refined piecework that purported to be able to measure objectively the actual amount of work performed by every cooperative member. Linked to this was an accounting system recommended by Soviet experts that in its turn purported to be able to measure objectively the real costs of every facet of the production process. The work-point system led to prolonged struggle, which will be described in subsequent chapters. The accounting system was tried, found wanting, and rather quickly laid aside. Hsin-fa gave this report:

> Right at the start we tried to study Soviet experience. Soviet experts came to the region and led a training school in cost accounting. This was a disaster. They gave everything a value and then depreciated everything according to formulas that our accountants found hard to understand or to use. Since their prestige was so high everyone tried to study their methods seriously, but really, they weren't practical for us.
>
> Double Wealth Shen, the cadre who came from Lucheng to advise us, was nobody really. He was just a rank-and-file cadre. He blurted out his objections.
>
> "How do you depreciate a tree?"
>
> "Well," said the Soviet expert, "a tree has a fixed life-span. It has to be figured as a capital asset, and then depreciated according to its estimated life. Every tree must eventually die."
>
> Double Wealth thought this was ridiculous. He responded with an old saying, "A thousand-year-old pine, a ten-thousand-year-old eucalyptus, taken together they can hardly match an old poplar taking a rest. Yet the poplar still has to call the persimmon grandfather!"
>
> By this he meant that length of life is not the only criterion for judging a tree. Furthermore, trees live so long—how can one estimate rational depreciation?
>
> The way the Soviet experts did cost accounting one could never afford to dig a well for irrigation. The well cost so much that the increased crops would never pay for it. They could prove, with figures, that digging the well was not worthwhile.
>
> The way they did cost accounting we couldn't even afford to make compost. In estimating the value of the crop the corncobs, the cornstalks and everything else that went into the compost had to be given a value. They were counted as costs in compost and consequently in crop production. When one figured costs this way the compost became as expensive to use as pig manure. Furthermore the whole thing was too complicated. The accountants of the Southeast Region couldn't cope with it, they couldn't handle all the mathematical formulas involved. The whole system obviously tied people's hands.

The peasants set the Soviet accounting system aside, but the same could not be said for the refined piecework system. They made serious attempts all over Southeast Shansi to establish the norms, keep the records, and award the work points that people actually earned in 150 different farming jobs.

Long Bow peasants recalled vividly a quarrel over work points that almost broke up their first cooperative a few months after it was established. Since at this stage fixed norms had not been worked out, the twenty-family coop that Hsin-fa chaired applied the "fixed point, flexible appraisal" method of fixing work points.

> Each day we worked [explained Hsin-fa] we put down a labor day but how much this day was worth depended on how much we actually got done. Shih Er-chih was the one who kept the records. On that particular day his brother Shih Fu-yuan had lagged a few dozen steps behind. That night when it came to record the points several people said, "Never mind, just give him the same as everyone else." But Er-chih wouldn't agree. He insisted on cutting Fu-yuan back. He argued that lagging behind in this way should not be allowed to slide past without penalty. "If we allow this then everyone will start to dawdle. We must give him less. He came out late and he never caught up with the rest of the group all day." The discussion that began with Er-chih in opposition to the group degenerated into a personal quarrel between Er-chih and his brother Fu-yuan. The older brother, Shih Ts'ai-yuan, who was secretary of our village Party branch, could not stand the tension.
>
> "To hell with it," he said. "Let's break it up. If this is the way it's going to be it's not worth it!"
>
> When I heard this I said, "You're the Party Secretary, if you dare dissolve our group, I do too," and I stalked off.
>
> Actually I had no intention of dissolving it. I went to Yang Li-sheng, our production leader, and told him to plan for work as usual and I visited the members and told them to report the next morning for work, and to do as Li-sheng directed. Then I went to the hsiang office to find Double Wealth Shen, the cadre from the county.
>
> "They're fighting," I said. "I can't lead them anymore."
>
> Double Wealth was alarmed.
>
> For a coop to fall apart was easy enough at that time. Conditions weren't like what they are now with everything long merged and nobody able to find his own land anymore. At that time it was just a question of each man taking his ox home and going out to work on his own plot.
>
> "No, no," he said. "You mustn't let the group dissolve."
>
> He immediately wrote a letter to the hsiang government. The hsiang government called Ts'ai-yuan in. I knew that the next thing would be, he'd come along to find me. So the next morning I just lay in bed. Sure enough, Ts'ai-yuan came and called out, "Get up, get up! We can't dissolve this coop. We'll be blamed personally if it folds. I'm the number one culprit and you're number two."

"Not on your life," I called back from the kang. "Don't try to pin any blame on me."

"Get up, get up!" Ts'ai-yuan called out again.

"Go along," I said. "It's none of my business what you do."

He went away distraught.

A little later the District Party Secretary showed up. By that time I was up and had had a bite to eat. He came to the door with Ts'ai-yuan in tow.

"Where are the members? We can't find anyone," they both said at once.

"Why, they're in the fields. Where would you expect them to be?"

"I thought you said you washed your hands of the whole thing. I thought you didn't make any arrangements for today."

"Who told you that?" I asked. "I made all the work assignments long ago."

Ts'ai-yuan felt great relief. He was so relieved that his appetite revived. We all had something to eat together.

The District Chairman said, "Ts'ai-yuan, if you let this thing fall apart you'll die and I'll be finished."

"Look, Ts'ai-yuan," I said. "Just because your brothers quarreled and you can't decide between them, you want to throw the whole thing over. What sort of an attitude is that?"

"OK, OK, I was wrong," said Ts'ai-yuan. "Let's forget it. Pretend I never raised the issue."

"No, I can't do that," I said. "We'll have to have a membership meeting tonight and you'll have to explain your actions to everyone."

So we held the meeting.

District Secretary Chang Ch'uan-pao joined in and we all criticized Ts'ai-yuan.

Chang said that what was really going on here was two-line struggle. The poor peasants and the lower-middle peasants were taking one line and the middle peasants were taking another. The middle peasants (like Ts'ai-yuan) always feel that they have lost something when they cooperate because their land and equipment is complete as it is. They feel they are pooling their efforts with paupers. So when they meet with problems they easily give up and want to go back to private production.

"Ts'ai-yuan," Chang said. "You must go on. You are the Communist Party Secretary. You can only do a good job. You cannot fail. If you fail I'll have to remove you as Party Secretary. Mao Tse-tung has called on us all to take the collective road. If you choose, instead, to go down the road of class differentiation you'll have to start worrying about your position in the Party!"

We criticized Ts'ai-yuan all day long. He apologized and criticized himself. I criticized myself also. I said that in the future we ought to think more before we talked.

That was our most serious quarrel, the quarrel that became a court case; that is, a quarrel that had to be taken to the leadership and was only resolved by intervention from above.

After that meeting we set up a rule. Every ten days we decided to meet, make criticisms and self-criticisms, and exchange opinions about work. Once we had this system we corrected most small mistakes on time and we did well in production.

Hsin-fa recalled another quarrel that involved the Shih brothers. This time it was not about work points.

One evening Fu-yuan and Er-chih asked Yang Li-sheng, their pro-duction leader, where they would be working the next day. Li-sheng looked skyward, thought a moment and then said, "I haven't figured it out yet."

The two Shih brothers took this for arrogance.

"Who do you think you are? You are production leader for a few days and you mount the horse just as you did when you were a puppet policeman!"

It looked as if they were making a case for refusing his leadership because he had been a puppet policeman for a while under the Japanese.

"Hold on, wait a minute," said Hsin-fa. "Are you trying to over-throw him?"

This made the older brother, Ts'ai-yuan, angry and he threw his support to his two brothers.

Another long meeting had to be held to resolve the issue.

"Look," said Hsin-fa, "we all elected Yang Li-sheng. Why should we bring up this puppet police problem now? We knew when we elected him that he had been a policeman under the Japanese. But we elected him anyway because he is skillful in production. So now we must listen to him and follow his instructions. How else can we proceed?"

In the end Ts'ai-yuan apologized to Li-sheng and so this problem, too, found resolution.

If the coop members quarreled quite a bit, they always felt relieved when the quarrels were settled for they very much wanted their coop to succeed. There were some in the village who reacted quite differently, however. There were those who felt delighted whenever a quarrel disturbed the coop. One of these was the old upper-middle peasant Li Hung-jen. He called the Advance Coop the "Quarrel Coop." "With so many cadres together it's nothing but boss meets boss. Why should anyone listen to anyone else? Why should anyone yield? Since no one is afraid of anyone else it's bound to be a mess. How could it work out otherwise when scum get together?"

This Old Li had no desire to join the group. All his land was in one fine piece—40 mou and a vegetable plot right outside the village and right alongside his own house. He could sit in his doorway and look at his wealth. He also owned a horse and a cart. What benefit could cooperation have for him? He was the last in the whole village to join. He joined after everyone else and in the end died of disappointment over the surrender of his autonomy. After joining he carried his hoe to the field ever so slowly, one foot in front of the other and the familiar rhyme went through his mind:

> Ass to the sky,
> Face to the ground,
> Work till you die,
> Papers abound!

Hsin-fa had this to say about Old Li:

I often walked past his door. I found him there staring out at the land that used to be his.

"You shouldn't look at it like that," I would say. "Everyone has a share in it now!"

"Ha," he would say, slapping his thigh. "Don't remind me of it!"

My words really shocked him. He would be sitting there daydreaming, recalling his visions of wealth. Then suddenly, "Everyone has a share!"—the phrase sent a chill through him.

He never did get used to the idea. His great loss plagued his mind day in and day out. Eventually it affected his brain. It got so he didn't have enough brain to use.

Before Old Li finally joined the coop he had challenged its members to a yield contest. As the corn seeds sprouted his field looked good.

"Look," he said proudly. "My sprouts are better than yours."

But the coop members had not exhausted their bag of tricks. They went to work and side-dressed their whole field with liquid manure. When harvesttime came their yields topped Li's by quite a margin.

The old middle peasant slapped his thigh once more in anger.

"Done for, done for," he said in despair.

Old Li Hung-jen had long been a symbol of single-minded selfishness in Long Bow. Even before Liberation he had a reputation for trying to cheat whenever he could. In the old days when the clan elders called on everyone to contribute grain to the temple he used to add weight to his share by mixing sand with the millet.

After Liberation his self-interest grew to the point of mania. He had a young son. His brother Li Yü-nien had a young son. One day while the boys were playing in the fields, a wolf attacked them. The wolf dragged one of them off. When the people came running to tell Li Hung-jen he didn't even rise to his feet.

"Which one was taken?" he asked.

Which one! If it was his own son he meant to do something, but if it was his brother's son he wasn't going to bestir himself.

"Stop worrying about which boy it is," said Hsin-fa. "Hurry up and help us find the victim."

The search party found only the bones of the wolf's prey. The bones belonged not to Li's son but to his nephew.

How could such a man be expected to have a collective spirit? Before Liberation, even though he was a middle peasant, he never did any work. Since he was the elder brother in the family, the senior male member, he sat around playing chess while everyone else worked hard. After Liberation and the land reform he never joined mutual aid. He joined the coop only when it became all but impossible to farm on the outside. Then, before the members shared out the crops in 1956 he lost his mind. No one could treat him as normal after that, and just before Long Bow people merged their coops into one big unit and joined the commune in Horse Square, he died.

Li Hung-jen's younger brother, Li Ch'ang-chih, was a political liability. He had served as a member of the puppet district police and had defended the fort at Nantsui. One night the Eighth Route Army had surrounded the fort. When they withdrew they left behind a wounded soldier, whom they thought to be already dead. Ch'ang-chih discovered that this soldier was alive, shot him dead, and stole his pistol and two bullets. Later, when the Liberation Army entered Nantsui, Ch'ang-chih retreated with the reactionary forces (the Chin-Sui Army of Yen Hsi-shan). After the war, when he finally returned home he turned in his gun to the District Government. The District officially closed his case, but his neighbors could not easily forget his past. They considered the whole family reactionary.

Dispossessed landlords and rich peasants did not always just sit by and wring their hands when they saw the cooperative movement succeeding. They did not all die of broken hearts like Old Li. At Tachai in 1954 coop members distributed the first collective harvest which averaged out at 270 catties per mou, or a 30 percent increase over the mutual-aid team's best efforts, on a threshing floor that lay outside an old rich middle peasant's window. As the clerk called out individual shares this man, Li En-ho, listened carefully and wrote down the amounts. Then he came to the harvest celebration and startled everyone by saying:

"What's 270 catties per mou? I harvested 300 per mou on my land."

Coop Chairman Ch'en Yung-kuei didn't believe this and figured out a method for exposing his lie. Since the unified state purchase of grain had already gone into effect, all families had reported their consumption needs for the year. After setting aside reserves and investment funds, they had promised to sell the balance of the grain to the State Grain Company.

"Fine," said Ch'en Yung-kuei to this rich middle peasant. "Your 300 catties are fixed. You can keep what you stated as your needs. Sell the balance to the state."

This was too much for Li En-ho. He began to beat his own face and admitted to all that he had lied about his yields, hoping that some members might quit the coop and go to work for him. If he added all the straw and stalks from his crops he could not possibly get a figure of 300 catties. It turned out that he had harvested 150 catties per mou. Had he sold this amount to the state he would have had no grain left at all.

Cases like those of Li En-ho and Li Hung-jen were extreme, but they were not the only peasants to go through mental struggle over the question of cooperation.

It was true that the private land did not disappear when the coop was formed, and that the land contributed brought in income. At this stage the peasants were not asked to give up the land which they had so long dreamed of owning and had struggled so hard to seize. Nevertheless, the coop still asked them to surrender the essence of ownership, which is the right to decide on use, and the exclusive right to the produce of the land. Personal stories about the first steps toward cooperation in Long Bow illustrate that these things were indeed hard to give up.

Old Chi Sheng-mao, a lifelong hired laborer for the landlords in the old days, spoke to Kuei-ts'ai in the field one day when nobody was about.

"I want to ask you something," said Old Chi.

"Go ahead," said Kuei-ts'ai.

"What are we intending to do in this coop?"

"Why, we intend to go to socialism in this coop," said Kuei-ts'ai.

"But," said Old Chi, "it looks like I've *fanshened* right back into the feudalism. I don't have my land anymore. My donkey works for everyone and here I am laboring in the fields with nothing at all just as I did in the past."

The coop had been formed in the winter. The previous fall Old Chi, like everyone else, had harvested his own crops and had accumulated quite a pile of manure. Now that spring had come he had been asked to send his manure to another man's field.

"I had the best manure in the village, but now it's all on someone else's land. All my life I worked for the landlords. Then Mao Tse-tung gave me land and a house. But with this coop I have nothing left. No land. No manure. What is going to happen to me?"

"Wait until fall," said Kuei-ts'ai. "Wait till fall, and you'll see. We'll all share more grain than ever before. You mustn't worry. Working together we'll all do well. That's the socialist way."

But Old Chi could not think it through. He was almost seventy. In his mind he found it hard to round the corner to socialism. He worried so much that he got sick. His legs stopped functioning.

Because of the doubts expressed by people like Old Chi the leaders met often for discussion. They decided that they needed special measures to relieve people's minds. They decided to divide the beans and the squash that had been harvested right away, instead of waiting until everything could be totaled up. In that way coop members could carry something home that very day and have something concrete to show for their labor other than their workday tickets. If the members harbored many backward thoughts and made many adverse remarks, they also held many meetings to discuss and solve problems. But in spite of everything people still worried.

PROBLEMS AND ADJUSTMENTS, CONTINUED

Cooperative farming makes it possible to use the full abilities of all men and women, those who are able-bodied, and those who are not fully able-bodied, and those who can do light tasks, enabling them all to engage in many fields of work to help develop production in agriculture, forestry, cattle breeding, subsidiary occupations and fishing.

Cooperative farming makes it possible to have single management of the farm, to cultivate crops best suited to the various types of soil, to put more labor power into improving the land, to improve cultivation by deep plowing and careful weeding, better techniques of sowing and planting; to improve the organization of field work and increase yields per mou.

Liao Lu-yen, "Some Explanations on the Draft National Program for Agricultural Development (1956–1967)," 1956

Former poor peasant Yang T'u-sheng joined the group early in spite of serious doubts as to its ultimate success. One day, just at harvesttime in the fall, he and Chang Kuei-ts'ai, vice-chairman of the Advance Coop, went out to haul manure to a field that was earmarked for wheat. The coop's crops were still in the field unharvested, piled on the threshing floor unthreshed, or lying in heaps undivided. But some of the independent peasants had already harvested and threshed out their own fields and were busy hauling their produce home.

Seeing this, T'u-sheng sat down by the side of the road and wept.

"All those people are hauling their grain home, but we don't have a thing, not a thing!"

"Look ahead, not back" said Kuei-ts'ai. "Look how good our crops are. After they have all been harvested and threshed think how large your share will be. You'll have much more than before. You won't be crying, you'll be laughing. You'll even be singing opera!"

But T'u-sheng still worried.

"How much do you think we'll get? What will our share be?"

"At least 400 catties per head," said Kuei-ts'ai, confidently.

"Not that much?"

"Just you wait. You'll see. It'll be at least that much."

T'u-sheng stopped crying but he still could not suppress his anxiety.

Former poor peasant Lu Shui-ch'ang, now captain of the village militia and a Communist, also worried as he waited for his share. He saw the individual peasants grinding new corn and even eating corn-on-the-cob for supper.

"Your mother's ———," he cursed. "I don't even have a single grain of corn for my children."

Then he, too, began to cry.

"Others are already eating their harvest. We have nothing!"

When he got home he cursed his wife and beat his children but even this was not enough to rid him of his frustrations.

When the coop members finally completed the harvest and had threshed all the grain, they piled it before the stage at the village opera theater, a covered platform that was all that remained of the old North Temple. Then as the families came to draw their share the coop officers weighed out 400 catties for each person, 400 catties as their labor share alone. When they figured up the land dividends and the payments for the use of animals, the average per capita share came to over 700 catties. T'u-sheng and his father learned that they had together earned over 900 labor days. This translated into a veritable hill of grain. When delivered, the corn alone almost filled their whole courtyard. Even T'u-sheng's wife, a born pessimist, had to admit that the coop had done well.

Lu Shui-ch'ang also expressed delight. On his own he had never harvested more than 350 catties per person and out of this he had had to pay his agricultural tax. Now his coop share, without counting the returns from his private plot, amounted to over 600 catties. It was almost twice what he had earned before. With no idea of the size of the pile of grain that this would make he was amazed when it filled all the jars in his house. When he saw that all the jars were full and that there was still grain left over he suddenly began to clap his hands.

"Peasants," said Hsin-fa, "are very practical, very realistic. Before they have the harvest in hand they worry. But once the coop fills their jars and storage mats they become sold on it."

At the end of that first year the crops truly surpassed expectations. When, on the order of the coop committee, members piled all the grain at the site of the old North Temple, the whole population was able to see exactly how much had been reaped. As the pile grew, as the heavily laden carts rumbled through the dusty lanes and past the village pond, independent peasants along the route pressed forward. They grabbed beautiful ears of corn off the carts, ears that were much bigger than anything they had grown on their own, and they called out, "How about letting us in?"

The rich harvest not only satisfied the twenty member families, but it provided over 25,000 catties that could be sold to the state. This was 1,250 catties per family. At the same time coop members, with their jars and mat tuns full, all had enough grain to last until spring.

Some of the independent families, on the other hand, ran out of food by the time the Chinese New Year came around. They had to apply to the county government for relief. This was in part the result of tax policy.

The taxes paid both by individuals and cooperatives were based on the estimated average yield of the land, not on the actual crop harvested. Since the coop quite easily raised its yields, the percentage of the crop that went for taxes usually fell. In the case of a poor crop, the state changed the method of calculation and asked coops for a reduced percentage of the actual crop harvested. This was because coops made their yield figures public; they were well known to all and could hardly be disputed as to accuracy. The individual, however, still had to pay a tax based on the estimated average yield, because there was no way that the government could check up on individual yields. For this reason taxes on individual producers tended to remain constant except in years of general crop failure when the tax office approved some reduction all across the board. For the individual producer with a poor crop, taxes could grow into a real burden. They might leave the family without enough grain to pass the winter.

Surprisingly, the very act of weighing grain caused hesitations and doubts on the part of some ordinary peasants who either stayed out of the coop or worried a great deal after joining. They had never really weighed their grain before. They thought in terms of tan (a long, lean bag) or tou (a peck measure) but not in terms of catties. When, in response to their question, "How much will we get?" their coop chairman told them, "At least 450 catties," this did not mean anything. Like Shui-ch'ang, they had no idea what size pile 450 catties would make. Since the crop on their own land, which they knew so well, no longer belonged exclusively to them, and since it was hard to visualize what any share of the total crop would be, they felt uprooted, cut loose from all past experience, adrift in an uncomfortable limbo, where promises and small early season shares of beans and squash could hardly hope to establish full confidence.

The bumper crop of 1954 turned attitudes around.

People who had stayed out because they thought that was in their interest now suddenly criticized the coop members for excluding them. "You who have joined together don't care about us anymore," they said. "Now that your crops are so good you don't want us."

With go-it-aloners suddenly clamoring to get in, recruiting became easy. The coop grew quickly from twenty to ninety families, and coop members became adept at explaining how they had been able to raise production so quickly.

"We had a division of labor so that everyone counted. We all worked together, checked on each other's work and compared. Since each had a skin to save, all tried hard. The private operators didn't set such high goals and didn't work as hard as we. We decided who should go out on sideline work and concentrated the majority of our members on the land hoeing, thinning, side-dressing manure, and we took the time to spread the manure more evenly than before. In a family operation, if the chief laborer goes off on sideline work, others can't help but neglect the land and all these extra tasks get slighted.

"As the old saying goes, 'When three people unite yellow dirt changes to gold!' 'Three stinking shoemakers make a Chu-ke Liang!' "*

As the Advance Coop grew to ninety members, a second coop, based on Yang Chung-sheng's mutual-aid group of twenty-two families, sprang into being. Right from the start forty families joined in, twice the number the Advance Coop began with. Actually there were fifty families in the neighborhood but Yang turned down ten of them on various grounds.

The basic factor in the sudden shift toward cooperation was, of course, the size of the crop harvested by the Advance Coop. As knowledge of this sank in, a pro-coop wind began to blow down mainstreet. Three old men, who had up to that time been very skeptical, helped fan it. These three were Wang Kuo-fan, Yang Te-hsin and Shen Yuan-chen. Too old to work, certainly too old to work full time, these three spent much time squatting in the village streets spreading gossip. From the way people gathered around them wherever they held forth, it was obvious that they represented something important in the community and that they had influence. The problem was that they spread whatever they heard. They spread what was good and they spread what was bad. When Ts'ai-yuan threatened to walk out on the coop they spread a rumor that the coop was about to break up. They repeated middle peasant Li Hung-jen's slanderous assertion that the coop leaders were a bunch of bosses who could never get along and they called the coop the "Quarrel Coop."

But once the coop brought in a fine crop that fall, they changed their tune completely and began to praise it to the skies. "After all, the collective way is good," they said to all who would listen. "Everyone should join up." North, south, east and west they propagated this view. Their words were more effective than any words spoken by cadres, for people really believed what they said.

More effective than words was the fact that, after mobilization by Ts'ai-yuan and Hsin-fa, the old men joined the coop themselves and never wavered in their praise of it. When others hesitated in the face of difficulty, they argued strongly for sticking together. "As long as there is a cart ahead of us there is a track and we can follow it," they said. By their words and actions they influenced a large number of people, and thus the Advance Coop quickly grew from twenty families to ninety, while Yang Chung-sheng's Liberation Coop soon reached a membership of forty.

The experience of the next few months even demonstrated that "a bunch of bosses" could be an asset rather than a liability. The Advance Coop had almost all the cadres in Long Bow as members, the Liberation Coop had only one, Chang T'ien-ming. The Advance Coop functioned smoothly, pioneered some new methods, and solved problems quickly.

It had been the custom, when there were only twenty members, for the Advance membership to meet every night to evaluate the work done and

*A famous Three Kingdoms strategist, military genius, wise man, who could solve any problem; a favorite Chinese hero.

record work points. As the group grew from twenty to ninety, members found that it was enough for the team leaders to meet with the record keeper, who at one sitting gathered the figures on all the work, whether by night or by day. Later with the accumulation of experience, they held these meetings once in five days or even once a week, thus sharply reducing the time spent on record keeping.

The Advance Coop concentrated enough capital to set up a mill for milling wheat. One day the manager discovered that some bran was missing. The coop leaders made an investigation and soon traced the missing bran to the home of Wang Hua-nan, the middle peasant who had been expropriated at the time of land reform when he helped his brother Hsiao-nan to bury a landlord's horde of silver. Some thought that Wang hid the bran in an effort to disrupt the coop and that this was in retaliation for the beatings he had received so many years before. In any case, Hua-nan admitted having taken the bran and people criticized him openly at a large public meeting. The quick, thorough handling of this incident impressed the whole village.

At harvesttime Li Shu-huai, the production leader, spent much time sorting out the ears of corn and setting the best ears aside. Everyone thought that he was selecting seed corn for the next year. But when the checker at the scales called out for Li Shu-huai's share, he put all those big ears on the scale. Dozens of people immediately rushed up to protest.

"What right has he to do that?"

"We are all equal here, what's his claim to special treatment."

"Who said he could pick the best?"

Hsin-fa, as chairman of the coop, stepped in and threw the whole basketful of big ears back onto the common pile.

"He may pick them out," said Hsin-fa, "but he can never haul them home. If he tries to he'll never join our production work again."

This, too, impressed people. Many said, "When all is said and done, the cadres are more able."

The three old men, well known for their gossip, put the sentiment into rhyme:

> With cadres the coop went up,
> Without cadres the coop broke up.

Yang Chung-sheng certainly agreed. He found it hard to manage Liberation Coop with the help of only one cadre, Chang T'ien-ming. But that was in part because T'ien-ming did not get on well with people. The same qualities that made him aggressive and fearless under the Japanese occupation seemed to make him subjective and dogmatic as a coop member. He always knew best, always wanted to have his way. He divided rather than united the group. With these problems at the leadership level, the Liberation Coop lagged in solving problems, spent much time over work points, and in the end reaped less grain than Advance. Among its members a demand grew for a merger.

At the same time most of those peasants who had stayed out of the two coops, or had not been allowed to join, began demanding entrance. Some of them, like the ten rejected by Yang Chung-sheng, were shunned by both groups either because they were politically unpalatable or because they could not uphold their end of the work.

People still considered all peasants who had been targets of struggle, beginning with the antitraitor movement of 1945, to be political liabilities, even those who had suffered unjust attacks. One could understand, perhaps, some reluctance to allow Kuo Hung-chun into any coop. He was the son of Kuo Fu-kuei, the village head who served under the Japanese. But he was, after all, the son, not the puppet village leader himself, and his father was already dead. Hung-chun lived with his wife and mother, and did moderately well on a normal holding of land. For a long time he did not even ask to join.

Discrimination against Wang Hsiao-nan's son was harder to understand. Hsiao-nan, it was true, had hidden silver dollars for a landlord in North Market who was his brother-in-law, and had been beaten to death. But he was not a landlord himself. The whole hunt for buried wealth had since been called a mistake by Party leaders. They had apologized to his brother Hua-nan for the killing and for the attack on the family and had repaid him for all goods confiscated. In spite of this people still called Hsiao-nan's son an *object of struggle* and refused him admission to the Liberation Coop.

Chin Shao-heng met the same rebuff for even less reason. In 1947 the Peasants' Association had expropriated him as a rich peasant. By 1948 village leaders had reclassified him as a middle peasant. They had also restored his expropriated property. Yet in 1954 no one invited him to join the coop because people still thought of him as an *object of struggle.*

Both Hsin-fa and Kuei-ts'ai openly admitted that they were unwilling to make a distinction between improper *objects of struggle* and proper *objects of struggle.* As far as they were concerned, rightly or wrongly, these people had been targets and targets they remained. Their response was similar to that of the cop on the Philadelphia Red Squad.

"Don't beat me, I am not a communist. I am an anticommunist," cried his victim.

"I don't care what kind of communist you are," said the cop, "you're under arrest."

In fairness to the Long Bow leaders it must be added that most of the middle peasants expropriated in the first flush of land reform were, in fact, collaborators, people who had compromised with the Japanese occupation. Even if, from a class point of view, they should never have been expropriated, in the minds of Kuei-ts'ai and Hsin-fa and most of the people in the village, they were guilty of serious betrayal and deserved whatever they got.

When it came to rebuilding society after land reform, the class analysis on which the land reform was based created numerous and sometimes insoluble contradictions. As Veteran Wang said, there was a difference between being a landlord "element" and being of landlord origin. A landlord "element" is the landlord himself. His son had a chance to be, instead, a person of landlord origin. But whether or not the son could actually escape being called an "element" could only be determined by his age at the time when the family lost its holdings. If he was of working age he, too, must be called an "element" because he too had lived the life of an exploiter. Otherwise he was a person of landlord origin.

All this seemed clear enough, but there was also the question of what year a person came of age. In order to establish a limit on classification in an unstable society, in order to prevent going back three generations to discover landlords, in which case millions of bankrupt descendants of landlords would not be able to escape the classification, the Communist Party had, in 1948, set the three years prior to Liberation as the base period on which every family should be judged. This led to such strange reversals as that of the peasant who had worked ten years as a hired laborer for a landlord who in 1948 was finally classed as a poor peasant, while the laborer himself was classed as a middle peasant. In the last three years before land reform the landlord had taken to smoking opium and had gone bankrupt. At the same time his hired laborer, sober and industrious, had prospered and bought some land. When the time for class analysis came along, the former employer classed out lower than the former hired man.

"I can't think it through," said the new middle peasant. "For ten long years I worked for that bastard and now he's a poor peasant!"

Several other families found themselves unwelcome in the coop for completely different reasons. They lacked labor power. One of these was the coal miner Yang Kuang-sen. He worked his ten mou of land as a sideline in the time he had at home after his shift underground. His neighbors felt he would not uphold his end of the collective labor. Shen Yün-peng had very poor land and was notoriously lazy. Nobody wanted him. Chia Ch'eng-lan was a widow without labor power. She lived with her old mother-in-law. Between them they owned twenty mou, most of which they abandoned to weeds. On the few parcels that they did manage to scratch up and plant, the millet heads grew about as big as a man's little finger. Chia Ch'eng-lan was willing to hire seasonal help, but just when help was most needed nobody wanted to come; so her work was always done late.

"We were afraid our coop would collapse with people like this," said the accountant for Liberation Coop. "Since we wanted the coop to show real results we didn't dare take on too many burdens. Furthermore, there were so many things we needed to buy. We decided to bring in only those with some property."

This discrimination, whether on political or economic grounds, violated policy, for the policy of the Communist Party in the countryside was to depend on the poor peasants and unite with the middle peasants. The model regulations specifically stated that "no restriction shall be placed on admittance of poor peasants" and "no middle peasant shall be prevented from joining the coop." Furthermore, "the aged, the weak, the orphaned and the widowed who can take part in subsidiary work should also be absorbed . . . according to plan."

All this was well known. At the same time higher authorities put great pressure on the first coops to succeed. County cadres knew they would be judged by whether the coops under their jurisdiction flourished or failed. They had faith in middle peasants because they had farming experience, land, animals and labor power and rarely made trouble. Landlords and rich peasants behaved with even greater docility. They had suffered expropriation and they were afraid. Poor peasants, on the other hand, brought nothing but problems. They lacked this, they lacked that, and they lacked the other. At the same time they wouldn't listen to anybody or follow any instructions because, as everyone knew, poor peasants held power.

If the coop didn't succeed people could say that the county cadres were incompetent. Also, once a coop folded it was very hard to start it up again. So why not play it safe? Avoid those poor peasants who would only drag things down. Pick good workers with good land and ample equipment, then the new coop had a chance to do well. And so, in reality, during that first year or two, higher cadres often violated the basic class policy of the Communist Party in the name of expediency.

Fortunately the very success of the early cooperatives brought a solution to the problem. As they grew and merged they very soon absorbed as members all the families in the village—those with merit and those without merit, those with labor power and those without labor power, those with impressive means of production and those with very meager means of production. Once the whole community came in there was no turning back. For better or for worse everyone had to sink or swim together and the problem of "the aged, the weak, the orphaned and the widowed" as well as those that were the objects of struggle and ex-landlords and rich peasants became problems for the agricultural producers' coop rather than problems for the village administration, for the two had merged—there was no longer any distinction between them.

In Long Bow village the great merger occurred in the fall of 1955 after the summer crops had been harvested. First the Liberation Coop led by Yang Chung-sheng merged with the Advance Coop led by Chang Hsin-fa. Then all those families who had previously been refused admittance and all those who had been reluctant to apply were invited to join. Within a short period of time they all did so without exception. Even the most obdurate holdouts finally joined up when they saw the scale of the movement. What future could there be for private farming with all available land pooled and all poor peasants fully employed? With no labor available for hire and no land available for sale, there would be no place to invest a surplus, no way to expand. Bowing to the inevitable, they, too, became cooperators.

But if the cooperative expanded to encompass the whole community, it remained organizationally at the elementary, semisocialist stage and some exploitation continued within it just as it had inside the mutual-aid teams. The cooperative was formed by pooling productive capital, primarily land, and by allocating workday credits for the use of livestock and major implements. Thus even though all members worked together on common enterprises their incomes could differ quite widely depending on the land dividends and fees received. In fact, during this elementary cooperative stage it was still possible for an individual to live without labor if his land share was big enough or if he owned at least two sound draft animals.

In other places there had already been conflict over such issues. In Tachai the poor and lower-middle peasants who built the local cooperative complained, once it became village-wide, that they were still being exploited by the big shareholders. After the brigade paid land dividends, animal rentals, and fees on carts, implements and tools, it didn't have much left for division on the basis of work. Those families who had contributed less land, few implements and no livestock saw their wealthier neighbors getting prosperous through the manipulation of "iron rice bowls" (capital shares with assured income) while they themselves, after a year of work, felt like a peeled sorghum stalk—"nothing left but pith."

The unrealistic evaluations that some people had put on their land when it was pooled aggravated this problem. One member reported harvesting forty bags of grain a year when in reality he had only harvested twenty. When the coop added payments for land of this quality, plus payment for livestock and implements to his labor share, he received so much grain that it overflowed all the storage crocks in his house and spilled over onto the floor. After joining the coop he got 4,000 catties more grain than he had ever received while farming alone even though, he admitted himself, he didn't work very hard. Another peasant, Chia Chang-yuan, in contrast, put less into the coop, told the truth about what he put in, worked very hard for a whole year, and earned less than enough to feed his family. Neither of these peasants felt satisfied with the coop—young Chia because he got so little for his labor and the other man because he was not free to do exactly as he liked in the coop. He remembered his land as being very good and convinced himself that his large share had all come from his former holdings. If he had been tilling it alone, he thought, he might have harvested even more!

Seeing these problems Ch'en Yung-kuei took the lead in cutting back the value placed on land shares. His own land, which everyone knew yielded thirty-two bags of grain, he reported at eighteen. The accountant, Chia Chen-jang objected, saying, "No one can alter the books at will." But Ch'en Yung-kuei said, "Give me the writing brush. This is no mistake. I'm not adding, I'm cutting back the value of my land. You're opposed because you're afraid you'll have to follow suit and do the same."

With that Ch'en wrote eighteen bags in the land column after his name and Chia, ashamed, cut his yield figure in proportion. Following this example many other party members reduced their yield figures and with them their capital dividends. But not all the coop members agreed to do this, and so when harvesttime came around the next year the Party leaders really felt the pinch. Like young Chang-yuan they felt that there was "nothing left but pith." It was this sense of unfairness in the arrangements that caused everyone, and particularly those leaders who had cut back their shares, to favor moving on to a higher-stage coop where land shares would no longer be a factor, all animals and large implements would be purchased by the cooperative, and income would be based on workday points alone.

Many other places also saw conflict over what proportion of income to allocate to labor days as against capital shares. In order to get middle peasants to join, many early cooperatives had to offer a sixty-forty split on capital and labor. But such a split soon alienated those who brought in the most labor. As yields went up it became clear that it was not the land and implements that created the increases but more intensive labor. Those who supplied the latter resented turning over the major portion of the income to holders of capital shares. At year's end the members renegotiated contracts to achieve fifty-fifty splits, even forty-sixty splits and in some cases, after a year or two, twenty-eighty splits.

In Long Bow none of these problems became as acute as they often had elsewhere because the community came out of land reform with approximately equal per capita landholdings. Land pooling brought no one any particular advantage in part because it occurred at a comparatively late date, after the state had taken over the grain market, and after other units had settled some of the sharp contradictions that arose over labor and land shares. As a consequence Long Bow's cooperative began with a forty-sixty land-labor split and soon reduced this to twenty-eighty. No one could really complain that land shares were tipping the wheel of fortune and polarizing the population.

Unfortunately, the same could not be said in regard to the ownership of draft animals, which had always been the most divisive local issue. The only comprehensive solution to this was to move to a higher stage of cooperation, a collective farm where land, draft animals and other means of production became the property of the community as a whole and members divided the crop on the basis of labor contributed.

In Long Bow village the leap to a higher stage took place not long after the merger of the Advance and Liberation cooperatives, and not long after the merged coop expanded to include the whole community. When they made the great leap to full collectivization in the fall of 1955, Long Bow peasants learned from the experience of Chiu Village, a nearby suburban brigade.

21

MOVING TO A HIGHER STAGE

Chao Ken-tzu owned not only the finest animal in Chiu Village, he owned the finest animal in the whole area administered by Changchih City—a mule. Chao's mule was solid black in color and his coat shone like polished stone. You could place four bricks on the ground, set one of the mule's feet on each brick, then let children run back and forth under his belly and he would not move. What a mule! Changchih had never seen his like before. Chao Ken-tzu claimed that his animal was worth 1,200 yuan.

Just to think about a fair price for this mule gave everyone a headache. Most people agreed that cooperatives were good but this pricing question was a terrible stumbling block. If Chiu Village was to move to a higher stage of cooperation, draft animals had to be pooled along with the land. Before this could happen, the animals had to be priced, and all prices in Chiu Village, it was clear, would depend on the price of the best, Chao Ken-tzu's mule, an animal that was worth at least seven or eight donkeys. If this mule went high, oxen and donkeys would go high. If this mule went low, oxen and donkeys would go low; the question affected everyone.

All those who owned animals, whether old or new middle peasants, wanted to see a high price because that would raise the price of their stock. Those who didn't own animals wanted to see a low price, because that would reduce the amount of capital that they had to raise as a group. There were both middle peasants and poor peasants on the management committee, a forty-sixty split. When Chao asked for 1,200 yuan the middle peasants supported him. But the poor peasants opposed him resolutely. They said his price was far too high.

Chao Ken-tzu tried to resolve the conflict by a generous offer. "I'll sacrifice 200 yuan," he said. "I'll take 1,000, even, for my mule."

But the poor peasants balked at this, too. A whole series of meetings failed to bring the two sides together. Either everyone talked at once, so that nobody could hear anyone else, or both sides fell silent, too angry to talk at all. Finally a poor peasant said, "Let's stop quarreling about it and find someone to settle the question. Let's go to the county marketplace and find a tooth expert [an animal appraiser] and let him name a price; then we'll all abide by it."

By that time the price of Chao Ken-tzu's mule had become an issue for the whole suburban area, including Long Bow village. Chao Ken-tzu was chairman of Chiu Village, his brother Chao Lien-tzu was vice-chairman. They owned the mule together. If they took the lead in working out a fair price, their example would influence not only the price of the other 179 animals in Chiu Village but of all the animals in the suburbs of Changchih, which in turn could influence the whole region. Without anyone willing it, this struggle had developed into a turning point for the cooperative movement in Southeast Shansi. It was a test case that would determine how middle peasants would make out when property was pooled. Some of the middle peasants already had grievances. They were summed up in a couplet that was as blunt as it was brief:

> In the coop poor peasants have clout.
> In the coop middle peasants lose out.

The heart of the issue was the question of share capital, a financial arrangement originally devised to equalize sacrifice, to make sure that those with more property did not suffer unduly through pooling, and that those with little property also ended up owning a share, a material stake in the cooperative. As outlined in Article 26 of the Draft Constitution, all the animals and large implements to be pooled must be appraised and the total value of this productive capital must be divided by the total labor power available to the group. This calculation determined what each family, based on the units of labor power supplied, had to pay into the capital fund in the form of capital shares. Any family contributing an animal, a cart or a plow got share credit for each item. Any value above the share capital required of them must be paid back in cash. Those who had little or nothing to contribute in the way of real property had to buy their shares with cash.

It was this direct link to share capital that made pricing so important and pushed those in possession of capital items into demanding high prices, while those without possession of capital items demanded low prices. Obviously those without capital to contribute were under heavy pressure in such an arrangement. When problems came up the middle peasants never failed to ask, "Where are your capital shares?" Where could poor peasants find the cash to "buy in," so to speak? Where indeed? Since very few had any cash reserves there were only two sources: workday earnings withheld by the coop committee or loans from the state bank. Obviously shares bought with earnings could not be paid for in one year. The time had to be extended. After much discussion most coops set up their share funds on a three-year basis, as suggested in the Draft Constitution. Those owing money had three years to pay in full. Those to whom the coop owed money would likewise be paid in three years.

Thus to the controversial issue of price an issue of time was added. Middle peasants with property to contribute feared not only that the prices offered would be too low, but that time payments might never be honored. People were asking them to turn over living, breathing animals at prices set by someone else for cash payments that represented only one-third of total value. Promises alone covered the other two-thirds. Most peasants thought cash in hand was worth much more than the most solemn promise. Who could guarantee that the coop would last for three years? No one was surprised when some people suddenly sold animals and implements privately at bargain prices.

From the middle peasant point of view the poor peasants seemed to get the best of this deal. They had the use of the animals from the very first day they were pooled, yet were allowed to pay in installments over three years. What guarantee was there that the payments would ever be made? If the poor took loans from the state bank, the middle peasants were assured of getting their money back, but the same could hardly be said for the bank. Bank agents never pressed very hard for compliance. Many poor peasants never paid back what they owed and in the end the banks canceled the loans. Thus society as a whole subsidized the formation of the higher cooperatives.

The prices set for draft animals and implements played a central role in the whole share capital scheme. To set them too low would place the middle peasants, old and new, in a position of subsidizing the poor peasants. To set them too high would saddle the poor peasants with a burden of debt that only the state could alleviate.

In this context the price of Chao Ken-tzu's mule took on extraordinary importance. The leaders of Changchih City paid special attention to the question, thinking that if it were well settled the whole movement would go smoothly. On the one hand, they called in Chao Ken-tzu and his brother Chao Lien-tzu to impress on them the importance of a reasonable settlement. On the other hand, they met with the animal appraiser to urge caution and fairness. They also set up a committee to aid the appraiser in his work. It was composed of a Rural Work Department team member, a representative of the Management Committee of the coop and a representative-at-large of the people.

When the day came for the big event the central street of Chiu Village took on the appearance of a major livestock market. All the animals in the community were staked out for public viewing. To make sure that no favoritism influenced any decision, the owners stayed away from their livestock. Instead of a family name, each beast bore only a number. On the number slip there was room for various suggested prices and a big blank space for the final price. The whole community turned out to watch—wives, children and family members, not to mention the anxious family heads themselves. They all waited, hardly daring to breathe, for the first decision —the price of Chao Ken-tzu's mule.

Some committee members said, "1,000." The tooth expert himself said, "900." Finally Chao Ken-tzu stood up before the whole crowd and said, "I'll accept 800."

Some people cheered, others were so dismayed they could hardly speak. Chao Ken-tzu had undercut the price of every animal on the sheet. A cousin named Chao Chi-tzu had a mule that he thought was worth 600 yuan. But if Chao Ken-tzu's mule brought only 800, he could hardly hope for more than 400.

"Chao Ken-tzu has ruined the whole game," complained Chao Chi-tzu. "If he gets that kind of pittance, I'll get next to nothing."

Committee members, feeling the pressure, said, "Give him 900." The tooth expert repeated his original figure—"900."

But Chao Ken-tzu stood firm. The city cadres had convinced him that he must lead the way, so lead he did with 800, and stuck to it. When Chao Ken-tzu's 800 went on the books it forced the others to trim their prices. At the time it looked like a victory for the cooperative movement, but some people thought in the long run the results were not so good. Low prices upset the middle peasants and undermined their morale.

The price of Chao Ken-tzu's mule depressed animal prices throughout the suburban area. When Long Bow peasants met to set prices, they felt great pressure to set them low. Anticipating this, Li Lung-pi, one of the members of the local Party branch, took his ox and cart to a distant market and sold both for cash. In doing so he took at least 15 yuan less than he would have received from the coop, but Lung-pi was satisfied because he got the full price in cash right away. He didn't like the idea of being paid in three installments. He wasn't sure if the cooperative in Long Bow would last and he wasn't sure that the currency would maintain its value under inflationary pressure. What made him happy was cash in hand. Since no move to price and pool livestock had yet taken place in Long Bow it was hard to prove that Lung-pi had sabotaged the movement. Livestock sales occurred all the time.

Taking their cue from the experience in Chiu Village, Long Bow leaders organized an appraisal committee made up of delegates elected by each team and the same tooth expert from the county market who had led the way on Chao Ken-tzu's mule. This man was a professional broker who had made a lifelong study of livestock, livestock prices and market conditions. Before Liberation he had been much in demand as an impartial arbitrator, consulted by buyers and sellers alike. After Liberation he found an additional employer, the commercial department of the city government charged with the responsibility for holding official prices in line and setting reasonable limits on free market prices.

While the brigade leaders were forming this committee, they also sponsored neighborhood meetings to mobilize activists, announce policy, alert people against attempts to sell animals privately on the side, and persuade animal owners to accept reasonable offers. They paid particular attention to Communist Party members who owned valuable stock. They reasoned that if Party members led the way, ordinary coop members would follow and the whole process would go smoothly.

Finally the day of decision came, early in November. The brigade chairman announced over the loudspeaker that all draft animals, carts and large implements should be brought to the open space beside the village pond and that all cooperative members should assemble for mass meeting. Once the stock and implements were in place and the people had gathered, Shih Ts'ai-yuan, the local branch secretary, announced that Long Bow would henceforth reorganize as a higher-stage coop. As a first step the coop members would have to price all animals and implements. They would then turn over these assets to the collective as capital shares. The collective would make cash payments to those whose contributions surpassed the standard.

"We will be fair and just," said Ts'ai-yuan. "We will appraise everything according to its true value. We will price good things high, fair things lower, and poor things lower still."

Proceedings began with a hard look at Shen T'ien-hsi's horse. This was a fine "four tooth" (young) specimen sound in every respect. Shen had bought him only a few months before by trading off an aging donkey and throwing in some cash. His goal had been to earn more credit for draft power in the lower-stage coop. Now the experts appraised this horse at 224 yuan. It was not a high price, but in relation to the price asked for the marvelous mule from Chiu Village it was within reason.

Shen swallowed hard and said nothing. As a Communist, how could he object?

The next animal belonged to Chang Lao-pao, the man who, everyone said, always got the worst of everything. He was the dirty towel on whom everyone wiped his hands, and he resented it. Lao-pao's horse was not as good as T'ien-hsi's. When the committee priced it at 200 yuan Lao-pao flew into a rage. He insisted that his horse was just as good in every way as the animal that had gone before, and no amount of persuasion would calm him down. The argument went round and round. The appraisers held adamantly to their price. Chang Lao-pao hardened his stand in opposition. It looked as if the whole meeting would founder over this one horse. Finally the appraisers offered a concession. They would give Lao-pao another 4 yuan. To everyone's surprise he accepted, so his animal was listed at 204.

Next in line was Li Ta Hung-er, the former militia captain, famous as a ladies' man, who had intimidated so many people during the Party rectification movement of 1948. Although his Party colleagues had tried to persuade him to be cooperative, he absolutely refused to accept the 120 yuan offered for his donkey and flatcart; he wanted 150. When the committee refused this, he picked up his whip, turned his donkey around and drove both donkey and cart home.

"You can't sell it anywhere else, you can only sell it here," shouted people in the crowd. "If you sell it outside we'll throw you out of the coop."

But Hung-er was adamant. He drove off home as if he had not heard a word.

This act of defiance disrupted the meeting. People began to quarrel over prices that had not even been determined yet. Neighbors who had been friends for years fell out, too angry to speak. It was all Ts'ai-yuan could do to call the meeting to order. When he finally got a measure of quiet he scolded the whole village.

"Why are you looking so hard at these few donkeys, horses, oxen and carts?" he asked. "Once our coop develops we will all share in the wealth, and we'll all be far ahead, far, far ahead. Let's not lose sight of our goal quarreling over a few yuan. If prices are reasonably fair between one animal and another, shouldn't that be enough?"

With this argument he won almost everyone over. The appraisal process started up once again and continued late into the evening.

In the meantime Li Jui-hsiang, inspired by Ta Hung-er's defiance, drove his mule and cart off toward the Western Mountains, his old home. When he first came to Long Bow in 1948 he passed himself off as a poor peasant but actually he had been a rich peasant in the West. Now he said he had to go home to pick up some personal belongings. When he returned the next day on foot, it became clear that "personal belongings" were nothing but his excuse for driving away. He had sold his mule and his cart.

Brigade leaders called a second mass meeting to criticize Li Jui-hsiang. Everyone said that if Li Ta Hung-er had not defied the committee and driven his donkey home Jui-hsiang would never have dared to dispose of his mule. By the end of the afternoon, as Jui-hsiang stood in silence before the crowd, unable to defend his action, Li Ta Hung-er suddenly appeared, driving his mule and cart. He had talked it over with his father, he said, and he was ready to accept 120 yuan.

Everyone agreed that turning over the animals was the hardest single step in the whole cooperative process. People who possessed a good draft animal and cart considered it to be "half of the family." This was because they could always earn money transporting goods on the road. If all else failed, transport work could fill the gap. People also became emotionally attached to their animals. They usually kept them in the front room of the house, a sort of stable and utility area, while they themselves lived in the back. Through intimate association they came to regard their animals as members of the family.

Ch'ien Jui-lin, who had been bare-poor before Liberation, bought a calf in 1947, then raised it in his anteroom into a full-grown ox. One day, after he sold it to the coop on that famous November afternoon, the ox broke a horn while at work. Chien's wife, when she heard the ox had been hurt, started to cry. She found some old rags and went out to bandage her erstwhile pet. She was afraid that the wound wouldn't heal, that infection might set in. "Someday the old ox may return to us," she said. If it had belonged to someone else she would not have cared at all, but since she had raised it, it would always be, in her mind, a member of the family.

Lu Pu-fang felt the same way about his donkey. He had raised the little devil from birth, feeding it by means of a piece of cloth soaked in gruel. He only broke it in after it was well grown and fully able to work. Even then he never overloaded it. He never piled more than 500 catties on the flatcart and never rode on the cart shaft himself. On appraisal day he almost cried. His beloved donkey brought only an average price, then was turned over to team members who saw nothing unusual in front of them.

After that when Pu-fang heard someone shout, "Take out Pu-fang's donkey," he winced. There they go, hitching up my good donkey again, he said to himself. If it comes back injured or worn out it won't be my good donkey anymore! It particularly upset him when he saw the cart loaded to a peak with 800 catties of manure, rock or coal, and the driver sitting jauntily on the right-hand shaft to boot.

Out of deference to the original owners of the livestock the coop committee decided that during slack periods old owners could borrow the animals they had sold. Pu-fang wanted to take his wife to her old home over the New Year holiday of 1956. So he borrowed his beloved donkey for his wife to ride and set off to see his in-laws. On his return, before he returned it to the coop stable he looked all around for something nice to "give to my donkey."

Li Shun, an older man, did not survive the sale of his animal. He was another bare-poor peasant who, after the land reform, saved money for several years to buy some draft power. Only six months before the leap to a higher-stage coop, he finally realized his life's dream, bought an ox and a cart, and immediately began to earn steady money on the road as a private hauler. He never joined a mutual-aid team and only entered the lower-stage coop at the very last moment. Within a few weeks the coop priced his ox and cart and took control of it. The shock was too much for him; he sickened and died. Everyone said the cause of death was grief, grief over the loss of his ox.

Most people, however, recovered quickly after the sale of their stock. In fact, after a few months, they began to enjoy life without an animal in the front room that had to be fed, watered and cleaned up after. Income improved quite quickly once the higher-stage coop began to function. With their extra earnings people bought bicycles and sewing machines, while the coop bought electric mills for grinding grain. With a bicycle one could visit relatives in distant places without sitting astride an animal, and with electric grain mills one could grind all the grain any family needed without an animal in front of the millstone. With 80 percent of the members doing better than before, owning animals didn't seem nearly so important as it once had. People began to remember Ts'ai-yuan's words, "Once our coop develops we will all share in the wealth. . . . Let's not lose sight of our goal quarreling over a few yuan."

Moving to the higher-stage coop meant selling livestock to the collective. It also meant giving up all private land and getting rid of land markers. In the old days a piece of cut stone some three feet long, one end of which was buried two feet or more in the ground, marked each plot of land. After land reform, peasants tended these markers carefully; as long as they farmed their land individually, no one dared plant along the line between stones. During the first stage of cooperation crops obliterated the property lines but nobody moved the stones. After all, the land remained private property. But the coop members planned to pool the land in perpetuity. They would call in tractors and they would plant rows in any direction. They had to move the markers and liberate the fields.

The coop committee decided that each family should move its own land markers. Most people went out, pulled up the stones and discarded them, but quite a few, lacking faith in the future of the cooperative, went out and buried the stones deep in the corners of the field. If, in the future, the coop should collapse, they could still prove that a given plot of land was theirs.

"What did you say to your wife, Hsin-fa, the night before you pulled the stones?" I asked.

"Say? That's a strange question. I'm a cadre. I wouldn't ordinarily talk to anyone about the real thoughts running through my head. If I did, my wife would be the last person I would talk to. What a notion!"

"Well, what do you think about it now?"

"The way things have been since 1956 no one can find his old plot of land. Everything is in big fields and even the rows run in a different way, right across the old property lines. Even so, sometimes when I pass a certain well, I take a look around, north and south, that whole familiar view, and suddenly I realize that this is the land I used to own."

"And what does that mean to you?"

Hsin-fa shrugged his shoulders. Obviously he felt no strong attachment to his former holding, but still . . .

"Some people found it hard to get used to," he said after a long silence. "For months after we turned the land over to the coop we never called it 'our land,' and the same was true of the animals and the implements. We used to say, 'I am going out to Hung-er's land,' 'I'm going to load Wang's cart,' 'Harness up T'ien-hsi's mule.' That's the way we used to speak. I can't really remember when the word 'our' took over. But it must have been at least a year later, perhaps more."

22

TO EACH ACCORDING TO HIS WORK

 It was one of those clear October days when the sky seemed less a vault than a veil that just managed to obscure the infinity of space. The bright emptiness above temporarily dwarfed the mountains ringing the Shangtang plain, and everything between them seemed closer together than usual, even the two ends of the long field in which the women were working—a cruel illusion, for it took a whole day to work from one end of the field to the other. The ripe corn had been cut with sickles and laid down in rows so that all the tassels pointed south while the butts pointed north. Two women on each row were picking off the ears and leaving them in small piles. Most of the women formed one ragged line across the field. If one pair did temporarily move ahead, others soon caught up and left that pair, for an interlude, a few feet behind. But there were two women who lagged so far back that they broke ranks entirely and found themselves alone. One of them was Li T'ien-hu's wife and the other was Yang Kuei-lin's wife. The two women had a lot to say to each other, and they talked almost without pause for breath as they moved down the row. As the sun sank toward the mountains, the mountains seemed to rise to meet the sun. Then large parts of the plain fell into shadow. Finally, just before darkness overwhelmed everything, the loudspeaker on the roof of the meeting hall burst forth with that orchestral rendition of "The East Is Red" that announced the end of the working day. By that time the women in line had reached the end of the field. They rose slowly to an erect position, stretched, adjusted their tunics, brushed off their pants with their hands and started for home. T'ien-hu's wife and Kui-lin's wife, even though they were forty or fifty meters behind, even though they had not finished their row, quit at the same moment.

The next morning team leader T'ien-hu scolded the two laggards sharply.

"How come the others all finished and you didn't? If you weren't able to finish your row, you should have reported to me. Instead you just walked off."

"Our row had many more stalks than the others," said T'ien-hu's wife. "We did just as much work."

"Let's not quarrel about it," said a companion. "Let's just get back to work."

But team leader T'ien-hu had already lost his temper and would not let the matter drop.

"Your mother's ———! What kind of a stinking thing are you? Get out of here, get out of my sight."

That was no way to talk to any woman and certainly no way to talk to his wife, but T'ien-hu was responsible for production, for production norms and work points, and the responsibility made him irritable. How was he to know if one row was thicker than another? Who had time to investigate that? Maybe the women were so busy talking they forgot to work. Why couldn't they just stay a few minutes longer and finish things up neatly like everyone else? Then there would have been nothing to argue about. Everyone would have met the same standard.

Once the coop took over all work, attention invariably centered on work points—how to set them, how to measure them, how to record the measurements and how to reward people for work points earned. Over the years various methods were tried, but none of them proved truly satisfactory, just as no wage system, flat-rate system or salary system has ever proved to be truly satisfactory in the United States.

Behind the tension in the wage system of the West lies the exploitation at the heart of it—how much surplus value the investor will siphon off, how much real value the workers will take home with them. In a Chinese cooperative, direct exploitation of this sort has been done away with; nevertheless some people always feel that the system is biased against them, and those responsible for enforcing it always feel that enforcement is difficult, if not impossible.*

The work-point system adopted by the Long Bow coop came originally from the Soviet Union and was suggested by Double Wealth Shen of the Rural Work Department of the Changchih City Committee. Shen called it the "fixed point, flexible appraisal" method and based it on piecework rates. By this method coop leaders allotted *fixed points* to each individual based on his or her normal working capacity. They held an average day's work to be worth 10 points. They rated a person who normally accomplished 10 points' worth of work at 10. They could rate an extra good worker at 11 or even 12, and someone less good at 9, 8 or 7. The term *flexible appraisal* referred to a daily judgment as to whether the worker had met the standard. The team leader and sometimes several members of the team committee looked over the job and confirmed, added or deducted points depending on what they saw.

*Even though no individual siphons off personal wealth from a well-run cooperative (the emphasis here has to be on "well-run"), insofar as wealth still flows from country to city, from agriculture to industry in China as a whole, one cannot say there is no exploitation. The rural-urban transfer is accomplished not through a system of taxes and rents as in the days before Liberation, but through a price scissors that sets the market value of agricultural products low and the value of industrial products high. Throughout China, in spite of recent readjustments, the price scissors remains wide open and the peasants certainly carry more than their share of the burden of national development.

In order to apply this system coop members had to establish a time frame. They split the day into five periods. They called the hours from dawn until breakfast one period; those from breakfast to lunch, two periods. They counted the hours from the end of the lunch break (which usually lasted through the heat of the day until about three o'clock in the afternoon) until darkness set in once again as two periods. In order to earn full points one had to work through all five periods.

Within this time frame leaders rated the various jobs according to how much ought to be accomplished by an able-bodied, mature male. They made some of the calculations in a relatively straightforward manner. Hoeing, for instance, they measured by the mou, with 1.5 mou of corn and 1.2 mou of millet taken as the standard. On any given field they counted the number of rows that covered 1.5 mou or 1.2 mou and required people to hoe a certain number of rows. Appraising other jobs, such as plowing, was more complicated, since the grade of the soil, its relative hardness, had to be taken into account. Coop members delineated three grades of soil from easy to hard. Then they took into account the quality of the draft animals. They divided the animals into three grades. With a first-grade animal on first-grade soil they set the standard for plowing at 5 mou (not quite an acre) a day. With a second-grade animal they set the standard at 4.5 mou and with a third-grade animal at 4 mou per day. For harrowing, with a first-grade animal and a double harrow, they set the standard at 15 mou per day.

Coop leaders found setting standards for hauling manure and compost to the field to be an especially complicated matter. There were near fields, middle distance fields and far fields. The quality of the animal and the size of the cart also entered into the equation. They came to expect that each worker with a standard flatcart and healthy donkey would haul 25 loads of 10 baskets each to nearby fields, 18 loads of the same volume to middle distance fields, and 15 loads to far fields. A man with a carrying pole could carry only two baskets to the field at one time or one-fifth as much as a man with a donkey and a cart. Hence on this job nobody tried to earn work points with a carrying pole.

At the start the committee members worked out some seventy standards for various farm jobs. This proved to be too few and by the late fifties they had classified as many as 160 jobs. They worked out the final standard for any job in part on the basis of custom. Generally accepted norms already existed for many kinds of work. Coop leaders tested these norms by going out and performing various tasks for one or several working days. They took reasonable rest breaks but worked hard in between. Then they took the figure of the work accomplished per man to a coop membership meeting for evaluation. After the members had thoroughly discussed all suggestions and objections and had arrived at a reasonable consensus, they fixed the standard.

Once the standard was set and people went to work, each team leader checked on accomplishments and each record keeper recorded them with a notation about the time worked, the quantity completed and the quality of the job. In order to take some of the burden off the team leader, each team elected a "check and review" group that periodically took over the task of inspection. In addition to this each team held membership meetings for comparing work done, for choosing labor models and for criticizing lazy workers and sloppy work. Those chosen as models not only got credit for the work points earned, but won prizes such as a new ax, a new hoe or a new sickle, and honorable mention in the city newspaper. Those who fell short suffered criticism in public. Furthermore, the team leader had the right to ask anyone whose work failed to come up to standard to do the job over again without any additional points.

Good workers usually felt quite satisfied with the standards, but lazy people always complained that the rates had been set too high, that it was too hard to earn a day's credit. They quarreled with the team leader and the record keeper, and they always earned criticism. "You are just as tall and strong as the rest of us, you eat just as much if not more. How come we can do the job and you can't?"

Needless to say, this upset the lazy ones.

On the whole the system worked quite well. In the fifties people did not know of any other and they kept refining their "fixed point, flexible appraisal" method in hopes of overcoming all the various contradictions that arose. But quarrels about the standards and the quality of the work never ceased. "Why would people quarrel if there weren't contradictions in the system?" asked Hsin-fa. Contradictions arose in part because, no matter how finely various jobs were measured, the measurements could never truly reflect the complexities of the real situation.

If, for instance, for the purpose of judging hauling rates, one divided the fields into three zones—near, middle and far—what could be done about the near and far edge of each zone, the near and far end of each field, and trips that started at compost piles at the near and far edge of the village? The actual distance traveled to and from each zone could vary greatly, yet earnings remained the same within it. As soon as the committee set any dividing line, that line quickly revealed its arbitrary nature.

Furthermore, if the committee set twenty-five trips as a standard day, some people would try harder and make thirty trips. They would earn more than a day's points while those who made twenty-five trips would earn credit for one day only. The leaders praised the thirty-trip man but actually he might have overworked his animal, or he might have loaded his cart less heavily. Even if he had not done so others often suspected that he had. They tended to argue about it and quarrels began.

In order to make extra points some people worked the animals so hard that mares did not come in heat, never got bred, and hence never reproduced. Or if they did come in heat and got bred they had miscarriages. Those who valued the collective and took good care of the animals earned fewer points while those who didn't care and only wanted to make a good showing and collect big earnings earned more points.

No matter how carefully the coop committee set its standards, when people had a choice between different jobs they tended to choose the lighter rather than the heavier job, the job nearby rather than the job far away. There were always jobs where one could earn points more easily as compared to jobs where one found the points harder to earn. Team leaders had to persuade people to take the difficult jobs and persuasion often led to friction.

After many years of experience with the "fixed point, flexible appraisal" system Long Bow leaders summed up its weaknesses under eight points:

1. The system put work points rather than political consciousness in command. People tended to work only for immediate personal gain and lose sight of long-range goals and benefits.

2. The system rewarded only actual physical accomplishment, each day's work done, but did not reward creativity, collective spirit, a cooperative attitude, all of which in the long run had great potential for raising output.

3. Since the primary standard set only measurements for quantity, quality suffered. People worked only for points and did only what was necessary to create an outward appearance of points, even when, in fact, they did not do the job well.

4. In their drive for points people overworked the animals. This hurt production in the long run.

5. Since both animals and implements belonged to the collective, people tended to neglect them and abuse them.

6. No matter how precise the standards were, some unfairness always remained.

7. Working out standards, inspecting work done and adjusting complaints took up an extraordinary amount of the coop leader's time. Problems which in fact could only be resolved through a higher level of political consciousness tied up the cadres night and day and in the end nobody was happy anyway.

8. Record keeping became so complex that no ordinary person could do the job. The recording clerk had to be skilled at juggling figures and at working an abacus.

Hsin-fa commented on the system.

> We saw all these problems with the system. We thought of discarding it and trying something else, but we didn't know what to replace it with, so we didn't dare throw it out and try something new. The central problem with work points in command was that people tended to be passive. They didn't go to work until the team leader roused them from their houses, or even from their beds; in the field they tended to quarrel a lot over what to do and how much to do in order to get credit; as noon approached they spent a lot of time listening for the dynamite blast at the rock quarry that was our signal for twelve o'clock.
>
> The quarrymen at the cement mill drilled holes and placed dynamite all morning, then at noon they cleared the area for their big daily blast. In the afternoon they moved whatever rock had been blown loose. These points are summed up in a rhyme that was popular in the fifties:
>
>> Seven o'clock, eight o'clock by our team leader harassed,
>> Nine o'clock, ten o'clock quarrels come thick and fast,
>> Eleven o'clock, twelve o'clock await the quarry blast.

Why is it that in each rectification movement the people had so many criticisms of the coop cadres? It was because this work-point system locked the people and the cadres into a contradiction, and this contradiction was hard on both. It certainly was hard on the cadres. People constantly accused them of having a bad working style, but the system drove them to such a style. When confronted with lazy people they could only threaten them with the standards, threaten to dock their earnings. It was *kuan, k'a, ya*—supervise, dock and oppress. There was no other way.

During those years we all felt that it was very hard to be a cadre. In the spring you were a "big red person" [a hero]. Both the leaders up above and the people down below looked to you to organize and lead the coming year's work.

As the summer harvest ripened, people already began to criticize you and before the fall crops had been reaped they charged you with being lazy, a good-for-nothing who had spent the whole season agitating, checking, recording and reporting, a shirker who had not done a single stroke of hard work all year.

By the time winter set in the annual Party rectification movement made you its target. You were a ne'er-do-well with a roster of mistakes as long as a man's arm.

What seemed clear from all this was that you had not grasped the central thing—the education of people in the Thought of Mao Tse-tung. You had not developed their revolutionary consciousness, their enthusiasm for transforming the world, but had, instead, ridden herd on them and enticed them with a system of material incentives—the stick-and-carrot method. Since you hadn't grasped the root of the problem, since you had neglected political education, even though you wanted to do well you couldn't do well. You worked yourself to the bone but everyone was dissatisfied with you. It was called "make an effort and mess things up."

People treated you just like the father-in-law who carries his daughter-in-law across the creek. He puts forth a great effort but gets nothing but curses in return. Why? Because he is suspected of wanting to take the daughter-in-law in his arms, of wanting to embrace her. The daughter-in-law considers the old man to be fresh, and the son thinks his pop is taking liberties with his bride!

That's just the way things go with a coop cadre. He works hard at organizing, checking up, mediating quarrels, solving problems. He gets up early and stays up late. He attends one meeting after the other and then in the end people accuse him of pursuing self-interest, of avoiding physical labor, of bureaucratic arrogance and endless other mistakes and crimes. We have a rhyme about that too:

> Work hard the whole year through,
> Till the harvest fills the bins,
> Those above will surely find fault,
> Those below will curse your sins.
> Go home to your wife in dismay,
> Not a word to you will she say.

Many changes in leadership reflected the difficulty that various peasant activists had leading Long Bow village through the fifties. In the ten years from 1948 to 1958 seven different people tried their hand at being Party Secretary, the central post in any revolutionary village, while the post itself changed hands nine times. All seven aspirants found the post very difficult, several were relieved of their duties because they could not satisfy the demands either of those below or of those above, others were transferred to more important work outside or shifted to other posts in the village in the hopes that a readjustment would help things run more smoothly.

When I left the village in 1948 Chang Hsin-fa was Party Secretary, having replaced Chang T'ien-ming, who transferred to district work in 1947. In 1949 the village again chose Chang T'ien-ming as Party Secretary but replaced him in 1952 with a returned PLA veteran, Sun Chiu-hsiang. Later people accused Sun of having betrayed a revolutionary fighter during the Anti-Japanese War. The county committee investigated his crime, found him guilty, removed him from his post, and expelled him from the Party altogether.

In 1953 Chang Hsin-fa then returned to the post for about a year. When the coop was formed, Hsin-fa became chairman of the coop and Shih Ts'ai-yuan, another Liberation Army veteran and the first Long Bow peasant to join the war against Japan, became Party Secretary.

In 1956 Ts'ai-yuan transferred to a managerial post in the Horse Square Cooperative Store and Wang Wen-te became Party Secretary. Because Wang Wen-te still had a bad style of work, a short temper and a rough manner, Party members asked him to step down late in 1957 and chose Kuo Cheng-k'uan, the Chairman of the Peasants' Association, as their local branch Secretary.

Kuo Cheng-k'uan, because he was too honest and blunt, soon alienated support from above. Commune leaders replaced him with Hsin-fa once again in 1958.

Hsin-fa's third tenure lasted only ten days. He found it impossible to keep up with all the reports on yield figures, storage figures, sales figures and miscellaneous figures that the commune authorities required, and he resigned in favor of a young man who was literate—Lu Chin-jung. This new secretary remained in the job until a group of rebels threw him out when they seized power in 1967 in Long Bow.

Through all these various changes the one constant factor was the leading role played by Chang Hsin-fa. He stepped down as Party Secretary to head up the first cooperative unit. When the coop expanded to include the whole village he remained coop chairman and hence chairman of the village. It was not until 1964, during the Socialist Education Movement, that a work team from Changchih City discovered irregularities in his finances, and removed him from office after almost two decades of active leadership in the community. In 1973 Long Bow village again elected Chang Hsin-fa to high office and he serves to this day as a member of the Long Bow Brigade Committee.

23

CONTROVERSIES AND CONFLICTS

In Long Bow the development of cooperation from small, seasonal mutual-aid groups to a village-wide brigade replete with seven teams, six for agriculture and one for sidelines, proceeded relatively smoothly. The community made steady progress from small to large and as it reached each new level, production responded. By the mid-fifties grain harvested per mou was almost twice as much as had traditionally been harvested on the Shangtang Plateau. Housing, education, culture, health care, trade, personal possessions and savings all developed year by year and people looked back with satisfaction on what had been truly a decade of progress. But in the country as a whole cooperation had not developed so smoothly. The decade following Liberation, particularly during the years from 1953 through 1957, had been marked by conflict at the highest level over the need for collectivization and its pace. Mao Tse-tung had repeatedly pushed for accelerated coop formation and the development of coops from lower to higher forms, while other leaders, notably Liu Shao-ch'i and the Minister of Agriculture, Teng Tzu-hui, had several times called for a slowdown, a pause to consolidate gains, and even a drastic reduction of coop numbers. They advocated getting rid of many weaker organizations on the grounds that the movement had outrun popular consciousness, popular support and its potential material base.

Mao Tse-tung, focusing on the poverty and frustration of many poor and lower-middle peasants as independent producers, believed cooperation was the only way out for them, and warned that unless the Communist Party helped them to take this road they could well lose faith in its leadership—a loss which would have disastrous consequences for solidarity between workers and peasants, two classes regarded as the political core of the New Society. Liu Shao-ch'i, focusing on the reluctance of the more prosperous middle peasants to pool land and property, emphasized that efforts to bring them into cooperatives against their will, before the benefits had been proven, could cause them to lose faith in Communist leadership, thus rupturing the worker-peasant alliance from the other side.

Mao was quite aware of this problem. He not only opposed dragging upper-middle peasants into cooperatives, he advised leaving them out for the time being, to make things easier for those inside. But at the same time he discounted their political opposition on the grounds that well-to-do middle peasants who were heading in the direction of capitalist enterprise would not in any case be pleased with Communist leadership. "We shall never be able to satisfy their demands unless we intend to take the capitalist road."

At this turning point in history Mao urged the Party to "get on" the horse of cooperation and ride boldly forward. Liu Shao-ch'i urged caution. Some units should "get off" the horse of cooperation, at least temporarily, lest it founder.

"There is a difference of only a single word here," said Mao. "One says 'off' while the other says 'on'—yet it demonstrates the difference between two lines."

In 1953, when there were fewer than 14,000 semisocialist cooperatives in China, certain Party organizations, apparently on Liu's initiative, dissolved hundreds of them on the grounds that they were shaky and could not be consolidated. Large blocks of members had joined only under pressure and now wanted to get out, it was charged. In 1955 after Party committees had organized several hundred thousand cooperatives, they suffered a second drastic reduction. Members dissolved tens of thousands of newly formed coops on orders from above.

In July of that year Mao sharply criticized "reduction." "An upsurge in the new, socialist mass movement is imminent throughout the countryside," he said. "But some of our comrades, tottering along like a woman with bound feet, are complaining all the time, 'You're going too fast, much too fast.' "

Mao blamed the Party for falling behind the mass movement and urged its cadres to jump in, take the lead, and learn how to build cooperatives by building them, not dissolving them.

Mao saw the essence of the matter as the desire of the overwhelming majority of the peasants to build a cooperative movement in the countryside, and he stressed the ability of the Party to lead such a movement successfully. Mistakes in the course of the movement, difficulties, doubts and retreats he saw as side currents, nonessential minor aspects. True, they could not be overlooked, they had to be dealt with one by one, but they should never be taken as the main content of the times.

In order to build confidence and show the way forward Mao personally selected and edited a huge volume of reports from all over the country about how cooperatives, both semisocialist and socialist, had been successfully organized. This volume presented both positive and negative experiences, what to do and what not to do, but the chief thrust of the material centered on the enthusiasm of the mass of the peasants for taking the socialist road and the tremendous gains that had been made by those who had done so wisely and well.

Mao's comments on the Wang Kuo-fan cooperative in Tsunhua County may stand as typical of the spirit of the whole volume:

"The Wang Kuo-fan cooperative originally consisted of twenty-three poor peasant families and a three-quarter share in the ownership of a donkey [they owned three of its four legs—W.H.]. It was nicknamed 'The Paupers' Coop.' But, relying on their own efforts, in three years' time its members accumulated a large quantity of means of production. They 'got it from the mountains,' they explained. Some of the people visiting the cooperative were moved to tears when they learned what this meant.

"Our entire nation, we feel, should pattern itself after this coop. In a few decades, why can't 600 million 'paupers,' by their own efforts, create a socialist country rich and strong? The wealth of society is created by the workers, the peasants, the working intellectuals. If they take their destiny into their own hands, use Marxism-Leninism as their guide, and energetically tackle problems instead of evading them, there is no difficulty in the world which they cannot overcome."

"Evading problems" was the response of many Communist cadres when confronted with the complexities of cooperation. "Because they do not understand and are afraid of being asked questions, they make a detour around the coop," Mao wrote. "So-called 'drastic compression'—the issuing of orders to dissolve whole batches of cooperatives—is also a manifestation of 'making a detour around the coop.' But its advocates do not limit themselves to mere passive evasion. Rather, with one sweep of the knife, they 'cut down' (to use their own expression) a great many cooperatives, and in a highly diligent manner. They take up their knife and—chop!— another troublesome problem out of the way. They are always telling you how difficult it is to run a cooperative. According to them their hardships are simply inconceivable."

"Drastic compression" did not reach Long Bow village. The Party leaders of Lucheng County never sent cadres down to urge dissolution of the cooperative chaired by Chang Hsin-fa. But the Changchih City Party Committee did mobilize Veteran Wang, working in the rural affairs department of the city, to dissolve coops that he himself had helped set up. He recalled this, in 1971, as a bitter experience.

> When asked to organize coops we were determined to get them running well. We all worked hard and did good work. When higher-ups suddenly ordered us to do the opposite, to go out and dissolve coops, we went out with a heavy heart. But we went. We obeyed the orders of our leaders. If anyone expressed any doubts the response was always, "Don't you think the leadership knows better than you?" As soon as the leaders put anything before us as a Communist Party task, most of us automatically worked very hard at it. We were the sort of "docile tools" advocated by Liu Shao-ch'i.
>
> Dissolving coops was the final outcome of a movement called the "Anti-Blind Adventurist Movement." Village Communists whom we had told to take the lead in forming coops we suddenly had to ask to take the lead in getting out of them. The City Committee asked Kuo Ch'uan-te, who had so enthusiastically upheld cooperation in Sung Family Settlement, to take charge of liquidating that same unit. But he refused. He said, "I can't talk out of both sides of my mouth. When we set up the coops I talked day and night about how good they were. Now you want me to go out and tell people to abandon them. I can't do it."

Since Kuo refused, the City Committee decided to send Hsiao-ch'uan instead. He was a pliable fellow, always willing to do whatever was asked of him. To the surprise of the Committee members Hsiao-ch'uan also refused. "Whoever built the coop should go out and dissolve it," he said. But since Old Kuo wouldn't go and the City Committee kept after him, Hsiao-ch'uan finally agreed. He went out reluctantly to do what had to be done to prepare Sung Family Settlement for dissolution. When he came back he reported that all the necessary steps had been taken. But in fact, behind his back, the members of the coop defied him. They maintained their accumulation fund, the heart of their collective. On the surface they dissolved their cooperative, but in reality they retained it.

The P'ingshun County Party Committee put great pressure on labor hero Li Hsun-ta's West Gully coop, which by 1955 had expanded to include such neighboring settlements as Nan Tsai, to break into smaller units. A work team sent by the Province demanded a reorganization. In Li Hsun-ta's absence (he was away attending a meeting in Peking), the team leaned heavily on the other local leaders, but they and the people of West Gully refused to abandon what they had already built. "We joined together of our own free will," they said. "If we split that must also be voluntary. Nobody can force us to separate."

Just as the struggle reached its height Li Hsun-ta came back from Peking with Mao's July report urging more, not less, cooperation. Instead of breaking up, the peasants of West Gully and Nan Tsai proceeded to transform their lower-level coop into an advanced socialist collective.

The struggle at the Central Committee level over the pace and scale of the cooperative movement in the countryside was in reality only one facet of a more fundamental struggle concerning the whole course of the revolution. Mao Tse-tung and Liu Shao-ch'i disagreed on the basic question of what stage the revolution had reached. Liu Shao-Ch'i took the position that the New Democracy that had been built in the liberated areas during the course of the long struggle, against Japan and then the Kuomintang, the New Democracy that had since 1949 been extended to the whole country, must be a prolonged stage in the Chinese revolution, a period of a decade at least, perhaps several decades, a period during which the wartorn economy would recover and then gather strength for an eventual transition to socialism. He foresaw that the mixed economy of public, joint public-private, collective and private ownership would extend many years into the future and with it the political coalition—the class alliance between peasants, workers, petty bourgeoisie and national bourgeoisie—that had been forged to liberate China from feudalism. He projected a rapid economic buildup under the New Democratic framework—the industrialization and modernization of the country. Once industry, both private and public, had reached a certain level, the conditions would be ripe for a transition to socialism in city and country, a socialism solidly based on a new technology. This was Liu's famous thesis, later summed up, as far as the countryside was concerned, as "mechanization before cooperation."

The prospect of a prolonged New Democratic stage after Liberation seemed to be consensus politics and throughout the four-year period after 1949 that I lived and worked in China I never heard anyone question it. But during those years Mao Tse-tung developed quite a different thesis. The victory over the Kuomintang, Mao decided, represented the final victory of the New Democratic revolution and the beginning of the socialist revolution.

The New Democratic revolution was a special historical stage made necessary by the semifeudal, semicolonial nature of Chinese society. During that stage the principal contradiction was between the Chinese people— peasants, workers, petty bourgeoisie and national bourgeoisie (native capitalists) on the one hand and the landlord class and the bureaucratic capitalists (officials monopolizing investment) backed up by imperialism on the other. The military victory of 1949 thoroughly resolved this contradiction, Mao said, thus bringing the New Democratic stage of the revolution to an end. A new contradiction, one that had always been secondary in semifeudal, semicolonial China, now moved into the central position—the contradiction between the Chinese people and the capitalist class. Even though, out of necessity, the *Four Freedoms* must be allowed for a while, even though for the time being private entrepreneurs must be allowed to develop their industry and commerce, the socialist revolution designed to abolish capitalism once and for all had begun. Strict limits would be placed on all capitalist enterprise and trade. The state would begin the process of buying into capitalist units and would eventually buy them out completely and absorb them into the state-owned and -operated economy. In the countryside, even though private production must predominate after land reform and the state must allow some peasant families to prosper and become rich peasants, still the state must soon undertake a massive drive to collectivize the rural economy. This would make possible not only a prosperous future for the 70 percent or more of the peasants who still had to be considered poor, but would also guarantee increased production and larger supplies of market grain, a necessary condition for the socialist industrialization of the country. That other great section of petty producers in China—the shopkeepers, handicraftsmen and tradesmen—would also, in due course, merge their efforts in cooperatives and thus complete the socialization of the economy. After a period of development the socialist economy would be able to supply the technology and machinery for a technical transformation of agriculture and thus introduce a third great revolution in the countryside —mechanization. This was Mao's famous thesis, later summed up, as far as the countryside was concerned, as "cooperation before mechanization."

There is no question, even today, about the sharp divergence between these two points of view. They reflected two very different approaches to China's problems and called for the implementation of very different policies. The question that is now raised does not concern the divergence, but whether or not it had a class nature. Were these the views of two antagonistic classes, or were they an honest difference of opinion about the best path toward socialism? For decades the answer given in China was clearly the former.

Until recently Party documents described Chinese history in the fifties

and sixties as a gargantuan struggle over the future shape of Chinese society
—whether the country would take the capitalist or the socialist road. They
defined the struggle as a class struggle between the bourgeoisie and the
working class and predicted decisive battles fought out inside the Communist Party between "Party people in authority taking the capitalist road"
and proletarian revolutionaries who wanted to build socialism. They said
these two class forces had crystallized out as two headquarters, a bourgeois
headquarters led by Liu Shao-ch'i and a proletarian headquarters led by
Mao Tse-tung. They denounced Liu's call for the consolidation of the
system of New Democracy as a reactionary platform for the restoration of
capitalism, while they lauded Mao's call for the swift transformation of the
New Democratic system as revolutionary, a platform for the realization of
socialism.

In the course of the reevaluation that has taken place since the death of
Mao and the arrest of his wife and her collaborators (the notorious Gang
of Four), new Party documents have begun to question the class nature of
the differences. Everyone still concedes, of course, that the Chinese peasants
and the Chinese people as a whole faced a choice of roads in 1949. Theoretically it was possible, once the land had been divided, for China to develop
as a capitalist country. If things had been allowed to drift, capitalist relations of production could well have blossomed at the village level and
eventually dominated everything. It was also possible, given astute leadership and vigorous intervention from the center, for socialist relations of
production to be introduced step by step until a full-blown socialist society
flowered and bore fruit.

What is not so clear, at this point, is that Liu Shao-chi's thesis, the call
for the consolidation of the New Democratic system, was in fact a call for
building capitalism. Some people now insist that a prolonged period of New
Democracy, with its mixed economy, might have provided a more secure
and rational base for building up productive forces and creating the conditions for a transition to socialism than the rapid socialization of all the
means of production that Mao called for and succeeded in carrying
through. In the long run the peasants did have to choose between the
capitalist and the socialist roads, but the socialist road probably could not
be reduced to a simple question of socialist cooperation now, versus polarization leading to capitalism later, as projected by Mao and those who
followed him with such enthusiasm.

By laying such major emphasis on the danger of "capitalist restoration"
—a meaningless term in a countryside where capitalism had never had a
chance to develop—critics now say that Mao's policy tended to bypass
serious questions concerning feudalism, the dominant system for thousands
of years, and how it was to be uprooted administratively, ideologically and
culturally after a land reform which smashed some feudal economic relations at the village level but did not resolve many other questions left over
from the old society, questions such as how to guarantee autonomy to rural
units; how to make use of market forces to stimulate production; how to
ensure democratic control.

The domestic target of the Chinese people during the New Democratic period was feudalism. The domestic target during the period of socialist construction inaugurated by decree in 1949 was ostensibly capitalism. But after almost thirty years of struggle against "bourgeois tendencies of all kinds" many people have come to the conclusion that the main roadblocks to progress in China are still such vestiges of feudalism as dogmatic, absolutist modes of thought and an abnormally swollen, centrally directed bureaucracy, both autocratic and patriarchal, both hierarchical and privileged. Under the radical sloganeering of the Cultural Revolution these intensely conservative feudal vestiges proliferated at an alarming rate. One hapless victim of burgeoning bureaucracy was democracy, the civil liberties of the Chinese people, a fragile enough sprout in any case, but one which must flower vigorously if the creativity of the people is ever to be given enough free play to enable China to enter the modern world.

It makes sense, therefore, to consider whether a prolonged period of New Democracy, focusing its attention on the thorough destruction of feudalism, might not have played a more useful role in the transformation of China than the abrupt shift to socialist goals that actually took place, bringing central planning and central power to every level and into every nook and cranny of the country, too often with negative results.

Thinking along these lines, China's new leaders give sympathetic consideration today to Liu Shao-ch'i's views on New Democracy, on the *Four Freedoms,* on tolerating a rich peasant economy and on the positive role of family contracts and other direct forms of material incentive in a transition period. Because so many stubborn problems remain, because per capita productivity in agriculture remains where it was thirty years ago, they have brought state policy in many respects around full circle and are busy carrying out what surely deserves to be called a new "drastic compression" of functioning cooperatives.

Looking at the results this time around one is forced to conclude that, after all, Mao was right. Land reform gave mutual aid and cooperation a momentum among the former poor and hired that made it possible for new collective relations of production to sweep the countryside. Mao seized the opportunity and led the movement through to completion. Had he not done so he would have missed a unique historic opportunity and would have doomed the countryside to the kind of fragmentation and polarization that is now once more running rampant. Today's leaders predict that after a period of go-it-alone, prosperous peasants will again chose cooperation. But cooperatives, once abandoned, cannot easily be revived. After his great fall all the king's horses and all the king's men couldn't put Humpty-Dumpty together again. The same may well prove true of collective agriculture.

In the middle fifties doubts about the value of cooperation failed to dampen enthusiasm. With the tremendous development of cooperation after Mao's July, 1955, speech and the publication of "Socialist Upsurge in China's Countryside," Mao's program won a decisive victory. In spite of the "drastic compression" blamed on Liu Shao-ch'i and the alleged liquidation of 200,000 coops, 550,000 new coops were formed in 1955, bringing the total by midyear to 650,000. This figure grew to 1,300,000 by 1956, and although in 1958 only 740,000 coops were reported, they had grown in size from a few dozen to 160 families each, on the average. This meant that the entire peasantry of Han China had pooled property and taken up socialist forms of production.* Not only that, by 1958 the majority of these coops were no longer semisocialist, land-pooling associations but fully socialist collectives with all land, draft animals and large implements held as joint property and all income divided on the basis of labor contributed.

This has to be considered the most massive transformation of a way of life ever carried through in world history. Within the short space of five years, from 1953 to 1958, hundreds of millions of peasants abandoned their age-old, individual mode of production for socialist cooperation. And this was done, on the whole, without bloodshed, without any significant destruction of property and without any major lapse in productivity.

The collectivization of the countryside paralleled a massive and equally rapid collectivization, in name at least, of small enterprises, handcrafts and trade in the cities. By 1958, outside the minority areas, where special conditions prevailed, very little private production remained in China. It was this tremendous, rapid, triumphant but too poorly consolidated socialist transformation that led up to the extraordinary events of 1958—the formation of communes and the Great Leap Forward.

As things worked out it was more than a week before we were able to ask about these developments which ushered in the second decade of Long Bow's Liberation. A week in Changchih City, to attend a municipal cadres' meeting, interrupted our interviews.

---

*Minority nationalities in autonomous areas moved more slowly toward cooperative forms.

Part III

GREAT LEAP—
GREAT FALL

With iron pick for pillow and feet against a rock,
With earth beneath for mattress and sky my bedding
*   quilt,*
The north wind woke me, but I turned over and said:
*   "Blow there! Blow the moon down!*
You won't blow me off the hill till our dam is done."
*   Poem from Shantung in Anna Louise Strong,*
            Rise of the Chinese People's Commune

24

FLASH FLOODS
AND FEUDALISM

 While I talked with Long Bow's peasant leaders, trying in a few days to grasp the history of decades, it continued to rain. As the rainfall accumulated in the lowlands the crisis at the dam on the Changchih Reservoir deepened. If one walked out to the highway east of the village at almost any time of day or night, one could see small detachments of troops marching northward on the double to reinforce the manpower already present at the damsite. Thousands were already working there round the clock trying to cope with the widening cracks in the main dam, and adding height to the small coffer dam at the uncompleted spillway.

We asked Commander Li Ying-k'uei if we could visit that critical spot. He quickly assented and came in person with a Peking-made jeep to escort us there in the waning light of a heavily overcast afternoon. The dam impressed us with its great height and length. Over a mile long, straight as a die, it divided the valley into two worlds—a southern world of water, sullen, silt-laden, dotted with the flotsam and jetsam of distant counties, and a northern world of lowland fields, orchards, fishponds and sandpits, shrouded in mist and swept by rainsqualls. In the deepening gloom we could see that the water in the lake was only a foot or two from the top of the big dam and only inches from the top of the frail earth-and-sandbag barrier that protected the northeast corner by the spillway. There soldiers, militiamen and civilians elbowed each other in confusion as they rushed forward with new materials to reinforce the coffer dam. They moved more quickly but with far less coordination than was normal on big projects.

A few weeks earlier I had marveled at the slow rhythm of earth moving on the lower reaches of the Hai River. From the highway bridge where I stood I could easily see 300,000 people with one glance. The calm but steady flow of handcarts and carrying poles in both directions, back and forth, had merged into a stately dance of cosmic proportions, the choreography of which could only be conceived on the plains of Asia. Here, in contrast, I saw frenzied, haphazard motion, a burst of restless energy fueled by the knowledge that another foot of water without another foot of dam could spell unprecedented disaster.

"Can it hold?" I asked Commander Li.

"Things look better this evening," he said. "I've been told the water is no longer rising. If it doesn't rain tonight or if the rain is light our dam will hold."

On the way back to Long Bow we threaded our way through the flooded countryside on roads that were all but submerged. Ribbons of mud barely maintained cohesion in a sea of slurry. Horse Square turned out to be an island of rain-soaked ground surrounded on all sides by rising water. As we approached it from the north we saw a newly assembled labor force starting work on a huge ditch that could carry local water into the river below the dam.

How strange it all seemed, a flood on the Shangtang, the highest tableland in all North China, the homeland of drought. For this place to drown seemed a contradiction in terms, but there was the water, all around us, restless, unpredictable, menacing. Who was responsible, after a dozen years, for an unfinished spillway? In the gloom that evening it seemed a criminal oversight, an inexcusable blunder.

"Our mistake," said Li Ying-k'uei, "was that we forgot to give the water a way out. We violated Mao Tse-tung Thought. Chairman Mao always said to give the opposition, including class enemies, a way out. Even landlords should get some land to till, a chance to work. Do not force anybody to the wall. But we forgot to give the water a way out."

This thought reminded the Commander of a bizarre episode from the last days of the civil war. He laughed aloud. When we asked why, he told us a story about a "way out" that should never have been granted:

There was a young battalion commander named Iron Egg Hsieh. He was only twenty-three. He surrounded, fought, and defeated a Kuomintang battalion in a brilliantly planned night attack. He captured the enemy force intact—weapons, stores, kitchen utensils and all. Among those captured was the Kuomintang commander, also young and very proud.

The Kuomintang commander protested that the tactics used by Commander Iron Egg were unfair. What sort of military prowess could be demonstrated by a surprise attack under cover of darkness? In a fair fight in broad daylight he would have held his own, he would have prevailed, in fact.

This claim offended Iron Egg Hsieh. "You mean I can't defeat you in a head-on battle in daylight? Of course I can."

To prove it he released the captured commander, all his troops and all his arms. Then the two battalions fought it out again under the full glare of the sun. In the end Iron Egg Hsieh prevailed once more. He routed the Kuomintang force and captured its commander a second time. In the course of the battle a lot of his men fell wounded and several of them were killed —a stiff price to pay for one commander's pride.

This story, like a flash of heat lightning, illuminated the times. China still lived in the shadow of the Middle Ages. In the midst of a bitter class war two knights-errant had joined the joust. Long live chivalry!

As we reached the highway at last and drove southward between serried ranks of Canadian poplars, now threatened by the water flooding the ditches on both sides of the right of way, night fell. The jeep driver switched on his headlights and in their glare we could see raindrops shining. God help us all. God help North China tonight. It was beginning to rain again in earnest.

When we got back to the village we found the propaganda team cadres sitting in their quarters talking at random. The talk that night threw more light on a feudalism that was supposed to be dead.

"They used to say, if you honored Confucius you could learn to read," said Donkey Meat Wang. "But I honored Confucius for a long time and never learned a single ideograph. It didn't help at all."

"So what are you, a primary school graduate?" asked Veteran Wang.

"Who? Me? No. I'm a primary school nongraduate," said Donkey Meat Wang.

"When I was in school," mused Veteran Wang, "they taught me to use the abacus. There were so many rules in rhyme to remember, *er yi tien tso wu* [two into one, bring down five],* and the like. 'What does that mean?' I asked the teacher. 'Stupid ass,' came the reply, 'how could two into one equal four?' He never explained any reason for anything, just cussed me out and made me memorize.

"In those classes none of the children wanted to learn. We were bored to death. And the rules were so strict! Why, even to go to the toilet you had to get a *p'ai-tzu* [a block of wood that served as a pass and was held by the teacher]. Of course the child carrying it often dropped it into the toilet cistern, and not always by accident. Then two students had to go and fish it out. This always took a long, long time. It was a good excuse to get out of class.

"Those teachers weren't at all devoted. They did as little as they could. I well remember, one told us to memorize a certain essay before noon. Then he went to the back of the room and lit up his opium pipe. As the sun approached its zenith he returned to the front and demanded a recitation. Those who failed to repeat the essay word for word were punished. The teacher took his ruler, wide at one side, narrow on the other, and hit them across the hands.

"This was formalism in education. It bred the worst kind of apriorism."

Apriorism—the concept that mind preceeds matter, that thoughts precede experience—was familiar to them all because they had been studying philosophy, dialectical materialism, the Chinese phrase for which, directly translated, means "the theory of material things, how they change through conflict."

"Speaking of apriorism," said Judge Kao, "in the old days we used to think that talent (called heavenly skill) just existed, a sort of gift from God. Some people do indeed just seem to have it. Take that carpenter who made the martyrs' monument here in Long Bow. He is illiterate. He has had no training anywhere; but he is able to build whatever he wants to build. When he decided to build that memorial he went to study an old building in Changchih. Then he came back and built this little templelike structure. If

---

*On an abacus, "one" in the left column represents ten. To halve it, you bring down five in the column to the right.

he made any mistake at all it was that the roof corners do not turn up quite enough. Also the stone monument itself should stand on a platform. It should stand a little higher so that one can read the names without leaning over. But these are minor points. On the whole he did a beautiful job.

"It was the brigade leaders who messed it up. They put all their names on the stone, just like the gentry of old. To celebrate twelve martyrs they added the names of twenty cadres. No one wanted to be left out. So the question arises—who has been memorialized?"

"Such a temple would have honored a god in the old days," said Donkey Meat Wang. "When I was little we had a god for everything. In the county town there was the god of the town and in the village there was the god of the earth (the Great Father God). Where the roads crossed in the middle of the village there was the 'five-road temple' and each courtyard had its 'door god.' In the yard there was the 'heaven and earth god,' and in the house there was the 'oven god,' the 'stove god' and the 'pot god' who watched over all cooking arrangements.

"During the second week of the first month all those gods rose up to heaven to report to the Great Father God, the Lord of Heaven. They reported on the behavior of everyone in the family. Just to make sure that they wouldn't tell bad things about everyone, we made a kind of candy out of wheat and covered it with taffy. If the gods ate enough of this candy their jaws got stuck together and they couldn't tell the Lord of Heaven what we had been up to.

"We children always wanted to know how far it was to heaven. So the adults said, 'Just figure it out. They go up there on the ninth and they come back on the fifteenth, the last day of the New Year celebration, at the fifth call [just before dawn].' So we all began to count and we counted just seven days for the round trip, which meant that it was three and a half days each way. But then, of course, we had to leave some time for the reports, so make it three days each way."

I couldn't help thinking how like the old imperial capital, or for that matter modern Peking, heaven proved to be. Traveling by train from the farthest reaches of the nation, it still takes two or three days for an official to reach the capital and make his annual report to the highest level. That level is still referred to throughout the land as "heaven." As the saying goes, "Heaven is high and the emperor far away."

The New Year story reminded Veteran Wang of an experience from his own youth.

"When I joined the PLA I was only about thirteen. They were recruiting young Communists into the Party branch secretly. I was on guard duty outside of the Commander's door. Peering through the crack, I saw people standing in front of an oil lamp. On the wall was a flag with a hook on it [sickles in China are straight, not crescent-shaped, so the symbol meant nothing to a peasant boy] and beside it a picture of Mao Tse-tung.

"I ran to the cook and asked, 'What are all the people doing raising their fists in front of the hooked flag? Are they burning incense to some god?'

" 'Where did you see anything like that?' asked the cook.

" 'I looked through the door,' I said.

Later the Commander came and asked me if I had seen any Communists anywhere.

" 'No,' I said.

" 'Communists are frightful,' he warned, trying to put me off the scent. 'They are covered with green slime and they have fangs. Spare yourself and never look through that crack again.'

"So I never dared take another peek.

"Later, of course, I learned about the Communist Party. But for a long time it was very secret."

In Long Bow the Party came out from underground in 1948. Six months earlier Liu Po-ch'eng's troops had driven victoriously across Honan to new bases in the Great Difference Mountains and forced the Kuomintang onto the defensive. No longer afraid of a military counterattack in the Taihang, the Party went public so that people could criticize its members. Public criticism of officials undermined feudal custom, but Party leaders always found it hard to mobilize people to speak out honestly. As long as the officials held power they could always retaliate. Who could guarantee the future? In 1971 the propaganda team in Long Bow undertook to allay these fears once more. No one believed any longer that Communists were covered with green slime, but as for fangs with which to settle old scores, that was a different matter.

25

CITY CADRES MEET

On the night we returned from our visit to the dam we learned that the Changchih City Committee had called the propaganda team, all its leaders and members, to a city-wide meeting that would review past work. What the team was preparing for at the time was a Party rectification movement at the grass roots. The city-wide meeting would check on the progress made so far and set the course of the whole movement for weeks to come.

This was a gathering equivalent to the Lucheng County land reform meetings that I had attended in 1948, and I was very eager to take part. At these big conclaves of cadres from the whole county or city administration one could get some idea of the overall situation, hear summaries of experiences from many communities, and learn what the line and policy of the Communist Party really was.

Knowing from past experience that it was not just attendance at meetings that was important, but actually living at the conference site and taking part in the meals, the recreation and the spontaneous discussions, I asked if we could join the meeting as I had done before, as regular participants from beginning to end. At first our hosts did not approve. Smart Fan told us that we could live in the Regional Guest House and attend the conference sessions, held in another building, by traveling back and forth for the morning and afternoon sessions. We protested this, but feeling that some participation in the conference was better than none, prepared to accept it. Then suddenly, at the last minute, the regional leaders changed their minds. As we were leaving Long Bow to drive to the city Smart Fan said that we could live at the conference site throughout the period, sleep in the dormitories along with the cadres from the teams, eat in the mess hall with everyone else, and merge our lives completely with theirs.

This was welcome news, and it made all the difference, both at that conference and later as we stayed through the autumn in Long Bow, between being guests looking in from the outside and being actual participants in the movement. Once we established ourselves in regular attendance at all meetings and discussions in the city-wide conference, the propaganda team automatically included us in all activities after we returned to Long Bow and thus we were able to attend not only brigade mass meetings, team meetings, cadre meetings and Party meetings but also all meetings of the propaganda team itself, whether for study or for work, whether formal or informal.

I had no idea what to expect at the conference. What I carried in my mind's eye were the conferences in half-destroyed Lucheng County Town in 1948 where the cadres slept on straw spread over the floor in several abandoned temples, and twice daily cooked and served millet in huge iron cauldrons in the open air. Plenary sessions met in the stripped-down great temple, while small groups met outdoors in any corner of the rubble-strewn ruins that they found convenient. I assumed that once again people would be sleeping on the floor and eating out of open cauldrons under a hot August sky. Instead, we lived in style in a modern multistoried building that was designed to house, feed and otherwise accommodate gatherings of cadres, however large they might be. It was called the Changchih City Guest House.

This was a new structure, rather handsome in gray brick. Over the main entrance a small balcony jutted a foot or two from the wall and ran on around the corner of the building. The balcony railing, formed in concrete, re-created an intricate Chinese design, similar to the designs peasants made when putting lattice work on the windows of their loess caves. The inside of the building had the stark decor typical of most government structures in China: bare concrete floors, blank white walls and unadorned window apertures without curtains, draperies or shades of any sort—a no-nonsense building, strictly functional, barren throughout, cold and damp even in summer, yet striking because it was so massive.

On the ground floor we found kitchens and a huge dining room that also served, once the meals were cleared away, as a meeting hall. On the two upper floors we explored bedrooms, large and small, some holding as many as eight or ten beds, others holding only one or two. The beds were fitted out, not with bare boards, but with springs, mattresses and pillows. While the rank-and-file cadres had to supply their own quilts, the Guest House provided us with government quilts, each encased in a clean cotton cover. In the dormitory rooms each bed had a writing table beside it. Chairs for general use surrounded a large table in the middle of each room. A recreation room with a Ping-Pong table and two large washrooms, one for men and one for women, completed the layout of each floor. Each washroom had a cement sink along the wall for washing hands and brushing teeth. Lavatories built into the floor flushed into a central sewage system. We noted all these details because they were so unusual, such a marked improvement over the Spartan lodgings of the past, and so far beyond anything that most people enjoyed at home.

I was assigned to a room on the second floor at the far corner of the building. Seven other cadres of the Long Bow Propaganda Team shared the space. Our north windows looked out on the Transportation Building, which had been held by a small group of *United* faction people during the armed siege of Changchih in 1968. From our high vantage point we could plainly see the scars inflicted by artillery shells on the brick walls of the structure. Just up the street stood the four-sided compound of the Fourth Transportation Company, where the *Red* faction had held twenty-six mem-

bers of the regional Revolutionary Committee after seizing them in the
infamous street ambush of January 20, 1968. These were episodes of the
Cultural Revolution that I was eager to learn about, but since Party rectification was the business at hand, rectification had to come first.

The Changchih Guest House was by no means as romantic or exotic a
setting for a conference as the Lucheng County Party headquarters had
provided in 1948. Nor were the participants as colorful and heterogeneous
as the participants of the peasant and student gatherings of that pre-Liberation year. Here were assembled some 250 members of the propaganda teams
working in all the factories, mines, work units, bureaus and brigades of the
urban and rural area administered by Changchih municipality. Not one of
them wore peasant garb. All were uniformly clad instead in cadre uniforms,
soft cotton jackets and pants of faded blue, olive drab or light green, with
blue predominant. Here and there, because someone had removed a jacket
in the heat, a spot of white gleamed from shirt or undershirt. No one wore
a towel on his head after the manner of the Shansi peasants, and very few
wore caps. By and large the conference participants ate, played and met
bareheaded, with their hair closely cropped, even shaved, for coolness.
Exceptions to this rule included, of course, the women, who numbered
fewer than 5 percent of the crowd.

In comparing these men and women with their forerunners of 1948 several other differences immediately became apparent. On the whole the
individuals were older—fully twenty years older—than the militants of land
reform days, a circumstance that could surely have been anticipated after
twenty-three years of revolutionary transformation. Not only were they
older but they were far more literate. Almost everyone present had a
notebook in hand and displayed one or more pens in a front jacket pocket.
While listening to major reports or joining in discussion meetings they
almost universally took notes and, when they spoke, often spoke from notes.

One should not assume from this, however, that they were all full-time
political or administrative cadres from various municipal and Party organizations. If there were many such cadres present, there were also many
rank-and-file workers from the steel, transportation and food industries and
a scattering of teachers from higher educational institutions like the Changchih Normal School. If outwardly they seemed, because of more or less
standardized dress, cast from one mold, in fact they represented a genuine
cross section of Southeast Shansi society, and their histories varied as much
as the diverse population of the region.

The Long Bow team—with a non-Party Moslem, a wounded veteran, a
donkey meat butcher, a commune police officer, a city theater manager, a
judge from the people's court, two steelworkers, an accountant, two high
school teachers and an old-middle peasant—could stand as a typical example of this diversity in age, background and interest.

On the morning of our arrival a printed folder of quotations from Mao
Tse-tung provided the topic of study. All the quotations had to do with
problems of Party rectification. Many of them were well-known selections
from the little *Red Book* or the *Selected Works* but there were several new
or hitherto unpublished paragraphs that aroused great interest. Of these I

reproduce here a lively discourse about the transformation of people through education. The substance of it was summed up as the third requirement for revolutionary successors in the Ninth Response of the Sino-Soviet exchange of 1962, but it was printed in our folder in the fullness of Mao's original version for the first time.

> One ought to be able to unite with the majority of the people. To unite with the majority means to include those who have wrongly opposed you, no matter what "mountaintop" they belong to. Do not hold grudges. We cannot have the policy of "when the emperor changes the whole court changes." Our experience teaches that without a correct policy for forging unity our revolution could not have succeeded. Of course we have to pay attention to people who plot and scheme—for instance, in the Central organs there were people like Kao, Jao, P'eng and Huang. But all phenomena conform to the principle that one breaks into two. There are some who just have to hatch schemes. Since they have such a compulsion what are we to do? Today there are still some who continually hatch schemes. The existence of schemes and plots is an objective fact which depends not one jot on whether we like it or not. All matter follows the law of the unity of opposites. There are five fingers on our hands, but one is opposite the other four, and only because it is opposed can we grasp things. There is no such thing as absolute purity, but this fact has not been digested by a lot of people. Impurity is what makes the world of nature and of society. With complete purity neither nature nor society could be created. That would violate the law of dialectics. Impurity is absolute, purity is relative—this reflects the unity of opposites. Take sweeping the floor; you can sweep it for twenty-four hours, right through the day and the night, and there will still be some dust on the floor. Take the history of our Party. Was there any time, any year, when it was absolutely pure? No. But we did not collapse. Neither the imperialists nor the revisionists emerging from our Party were able to make us collapse. After Liberation we had Kao, Jao and P'eng. Were they able to ruin us? No. It is not easy to ruin us. That is our historical experience.
>
> Human beings can change, but there are a few who will not change. Even when their stomachs are full they still go right on cursing. There are a few of this type in every province. But they make up a very small minority. It's all right if they don't change. Let them curse to their hearts content. Meanwhile, in dealing with those who have made mistakes, we should persuade them to change for the better, help them correct themselves, so to speak. As long as they are sincere about changing we shouldn't go on criticizing them endlessly.

To unite with the greatest possible number, even with those from other mountaintops, even with those who have personally opposed us, even with those who have wrongly opposed us—here indeed was something to ponder over. Uniting all those who could be united was clearly no simple task.

The eight o'clock study sessions hardly had time to exchange views on these Mao quotes when the call came through the building to assemble for a major report. We trooped down to the dining room, where the tables had been arranged in long rows, running the full length of the hall, at right angles to the speakers' table. There we were introduced to Comrade Ts'ui Sheng-ho, a PLA commander who was vice-chairman of the Changchih City Revolutionary Committee, and vice-secretary of its Party Committee.

Ts'ui was a plump officer with a ruddy face and a self-satisfied air. He was well used to public speaking and well versed in the vocabulary not only of the Chinese Revolution in general, but of the Cultural Revolution in particular. Overused, one could truthfully say abused, political phrases rolled off his tongue one after another, and so fast that it was difficult for Carma to translate them. Her difficulty stemmed in part from the fact that his words bored her.

"This CP rectification study opens its meeting under the direction of Mao Tse-tung's Communist Party building line." "The situation inside and outside the city, based on a growing victory for the Party rectification work, is proceeding according to the Regional Plan." "Raise high Mao Tse-tung's Thought, put politics in command, develop achievements, correct mistakes, and carry the fight through to the end! . . .

"Under Mao Tse-tung's Party-building thought and line, under the leadership of the Regional Communist Party Committee and the Communist Party organizations of various levels, we have raised high the banner of Mao Tse-tung's Thought, put politics in command, and carried out our work in accord with Mao Tse-tung's Thought, setting forth the stages of the Cultural Revolution through struggle-criticism-transformation. . . .

"Closely following Mao Tse-tung's strategic plan, on the basis of clearing the class ranks, we have proceeded for one year—two winters and one spring—and have basically completed the low-level Party rectification. Our achievements are good, the situation is excellent. . . ."

Through clouds of rhetoric some facts began to emerge:

Party leaders had set up new leading bodies in 21 lower Party Committees in the City, 11 Commune Committees, 47 general branches and 711 basic branches. They had expelled 110 party members (0.9 percent of the total) and recruited 805 new members (6.7 percent of the total). With the ranks thus purified and educated and with a high tide in the study of Mao Tse-tung Thought, the region had exceeded its 1970 industrial plan by 11.1 percent and its agricultural plan by 1.5 to 2 percent, and this in spite of many natural disasters—wind damage, drought, flood and pests. Average yields for the communes under the city administration had reached the standard for North China: 400 catties per mou.

Comrade Ts'ui then went on to make five recommendations for the future:

1. Put ideological revolution in first place.
2. Persist in the mass line.
3. Set up a good leading body.
4. Weed out the old, take in the new.
5. Revolutionize the propaganda teams themselves.

Under the first point he stressed education in line struggle and began with Mao Tse-tung's thesis that in order to correct organizational weaknesses one must first correct ideological weaknesses by struggling against bourgeois ideology. This idea he nailed down with the ninth selection in the pamphlet of Mao quotes:

"There are many Party members who have joined the Communist Party organizationally but have not yet joined the Party wholly or at all ideologically. Those who have not joined the Party ideologically still carry a great deal of the muck of the exploiting classes in their heads, and have no idea at all of what proletarian ideology, or Communism, or the Party is. Proletarian ideology? they think. The same old stuff! Little do they know that it is no easy matter to acquire this 'stuff.' Some will never have the slightest Communist flavor about them as long as they live and can only end up leaving the Party. Therefore, though the majority in our Party and in our ranks are clean and honest, we must in all seriousness put things in order both ideologically and organizationally if we are to develop the revolutionary movement more effectively and bring it to speedier success. Putting things in order organizationally requires our first doing so ideologically, our launching a struggle of proletarian ideology against non-proletarian ideology."

To advance ideological education Comrade Ts'ui outlined five methods: study Mao Tse-tung Thought; remember past bitterness and compare it with the good situation of today; expose problems; repudiate bad tendencies; repudiate bad people.

In this context he reviewed what all the Party members had studied. For several months already all the Communists in Changchih City and its suburbs had been reading about and discussing several themes—to wit: Mao's theory of continuing revolution under the dictatorship of the proletariat; Mao's basic line for socialist construction; Mao's theory on Communist Party rectification and construction—the famous fifty-word sentence; Lin Piao's Ninth Congress Report; the new Communist Party constitution; and the history of two-line struggle in the Communist Party (July 1 Editorial). As negative examples all members had also studied Liu Shao-ch'i's six rotten theories; apriorist philosophy as expounded by Liu and Wang Ming; the reactionary theory of the productive forces; the theory that class struggle was dying out, as well as the rotten feudal and bourgeois concept of humanism (the essence of which is the denial of class struggle). They had also studied the question of capitalist tendencies in rural and urban policy; the question of bourgeois factionalism—the unprincipled struggle for personal power which had developed so feverishly during the Cultural Revolution; and the phenomena of anarchism which had also developed during the Cultural Revolution.

For a positive example of proletarian line they had studied the history of the Tachai Brigade.

"All this," said Ts'ui, "has raised the consciousness of the rank-and-file Party members in regard to class struggle, line struggle and continuing the revolution under the dictatorship of the proletariat."

Bringing things from the abstract to the concrete level, Ts'ui spoke of the results of this education in the Party branch of the Paiho Brigade of Nanshui

Commune, where, prior to the movement, nine out of twenty-two Communist Party members wanted to leave the Party and thirty-two out of thirty-five cadres wanted to quit work and become rank-and-file peasants once more. The local propaganda team had made a detailed appraisal of the seven Party Secretaries who had led the brigade in its twenty-three-year history and concentrated its criticism on the fifth of these, who had neglected grain as the key link, stressed material incentives, concentrated on sideline production, and allowed production to fall to about twelve bushels per acre in 1964.

A new secretary named Chia, elected in 1965, reversed the downward trend by conscientiously learning from Tachai; he raised production to about fifty bushels per acre in 1965. But this success apparently went to his head, for he later relaxed, ignored class struggle, failed to criticize shortcomings or praise good work. As a result production stagnated until 1969 when the Party mobilized the people to criticize him. Chia's problem, they decided, was "New Democratic Thinking," that is, the concept that the revolution basically ended with land reform—the great goal of the new Democratic Revolution—and that it was enough, in the following period, to be honest, hardworking and loyal, even if one did not grasp what the socialist transformation was all about and dig in to carry it through. Even though our yields are lower than the advanced brigades, Chia thought, they are still higher than those of the backward ones; so he was satisfied. "Even if I haven't made big contributions to the revolution, still I have made some small ones every year," he rationalized, and consequently his brigade slipped into stagnation. Right next door other brigades facing the same natural conditions produced almost twice as much grain per acre.

Criticized for his complacency and his "wrong line," Chia had made a great change in his own thinking and in the course of the movement the nine Party members and the thirty-two cadres who wanted to quit all decided to hang in and devote their lives to revolutionary transformation.

"The crux of the matter," stressed Ts'ui, "is ideological education, consciousness in regard to line struggle."

Under the topic of "mass line" Ts'ui outlined the need for open-door rectification, for inviting the masses in to criticize the cadres and the Communists, and for listening seriously to the masses. "This is not a question of method but a basic question of principle, a question of whether or not one has grasped the spirit of the Party," Ts'ui said. As an illustration he told of a branch secretary who personally gathered opinions about his work from sixty families in his brigade, then made such a thorough self-criticism that the members reelected him to his post in spite of serious past mistakes.

In regard to the third point, the importance of a good leading body, Ts'ui declared that this was the main issue on which the propaganda teams would be judged—had they or had they not helped establish a strong, line-conscious, leading body in their assigned unit? Very few cadres, he said, were really bad. One such, Li Yeh of the Kucheng Brigade, Kucheng Commune, was a rotten profiteer, gambler, superstitious element and factionalist. He had been removed from office. More typical of those with problems was a man like Chao Kan-tse of Shihchiach'eng Brigade, Hsingchung. "He is a good person with serious mistakes. His mistakes are mainly spinelessness

—an 'old good fellow stance.' He opens his eyes but can't see the direction. He uses his nose but can't tell a rotten stench from sweet perfume. He holds power but doesn't make decisions. Meeting a problem he mixes everything up. If he can postpone a decision he does so. If not he runs away! He doesn't really hate class enemies or love the people. He doesn't praise good things or attack bad."

But even this man, after education, developed consciousness and won reelection to his Party branch.

In addition to finding strong principled leaders, Ts'ui went on, it was essential to try and develop a three-in-one combination—that is, choose young, middle-aged and old people so that each group could bring to the work its special strength. In the 700 branches set up by July 1, some 10 percent of the members were old, 70 percent middle-aged and 20 percent young. This was a satisfactory percentage.

Ts'ui picked out for praise as outstanding new Communist Party organizations the Party Committee of the Changchih Transportation Company; the Party branch of the Battery Factory; the Party branches of three rural brigades Hsinchiu, Nanhsia, and Tahsingchung; and the Party branch of the Changchih Department Store.

Under the fourth point, "weed out the old, take in the new," Ts'ui discussed the question of dropping and recruiting members. Of course we must expel enemy agents, class enemies, renegades and diehard capitalist roaders, he said, but we should simply persuade others who have lost their Communist spirit and can never really play a vanguard role in the future to drop out. The figure of 110 expelled or dropped members included many in this latter category—people who did not really want to continue as Communists and withdrew after talking things over. Toward such people Ts'ui advocated a cautious policy so that their withdrawal would not lead to bitterness that might cloud their future progress and their future work. When the Party expelled or punished people, every effort was to be made to see that they understood the reasons behind the move and the possibilities for the future. "A negative attitude is hard to penetrate," said Ts'ui.

In summing up this point Ts'ui stressed, "Pay attention to policy, do careful ideological work, make a clear distinction between contradictions among the people and contradictions with the enemy, and thus avoid measures that are too harsh or too lenient. We should not draw in our favorites and throw out those against whom we are prejudiced, we should not throw a lot of people out and recruit a lot of new faces, nor should we adopt a policy of not throwing anybody out and not recruiting anybody either."

Ts'ui's fifth point had to do with the revolutionization of the propaganda teams themselves. "Without this it is not possible to do good work." He reserved his highest praise for the team in Yellow Mill, Horse Square Commune, which had put self-transformation high on its priorities. "Work means hardship," they all said. The political officer of this team, Chao Hsiao-kuan, and the vice-political officer Chang Ch'ang-fu, took the lead in daily study, spoke out at meetings and tried to transform their world outlook in practice. In the coldest winter weather they led the way into the water to help construct a dam that could irrigate 400 mou. Hsiang Chih-p'ing, even though sick, worked all day in the wind and snow. The whole propaganda team labored together with the peasants before the ground froze and dug 4,000 mou of land to a depth of one foot. Right on the work site they repudiated bad working style and bad elements. The transformation of the leadership pushed forward the transformation of the whole team and the whole village. The masses said, "This team is full of cadres with heart." Under leadership like this people worked ten months as if it were a day!

At the same time Ts'ui also found some tendencies requiring criticism. "One divides into two," he said "and there are still some ideological problems. Some people want to leave their propaganda teams. Having been on detached service for the better part of a year, they demand a change of shift. They are afraid they will fall behind technically at their original places of work. Since some have already been reassigned, others feel maybe they have lost their chance. Hence there is a growing tendency to fear hardship, to fear going to new places and to fear taking up new political work."

Ts'ui criticized several individuals for arrogance, subjectivity, lack of attention to policy, and slack discipline—such as going home without asking leave, not showing up for study, or avoiding assignments.

"All these problems we hope to solve at this meeting," he said.

The taproot of these weaknesses, Ts'ui continued, was failure to recognize the protracted nature of rectification work. In the first place there were still units where a good leading body had not yet been established. In the second place, in the majority of units where good leadership had been found and consolidated it was not possible to say that the work was finished, because education, class struggle and line struggle still had to be carried forward. Since overall the results were uneven, there was still a great deal to do. The cadres must be prepared for serious protracted effort.

In the course of his report Comrade Ts'ui mentioned Long Bow village several times. When talking about the importance of a strong leading body he mentioned Long Bow's former Party Secretary, Swift Li, as a good person with serious mistakes, who, after coming to power, stressed sidelines and speculation as the road to prosperity. Under him, Ts'ui charged, per mou production fell from 270 catties to 250 catties to 237 catties in three years, and life for the people became progressively harder. "He lost his class stand, took up with people who had political problems, and gave up working in the fields. But his class background is good, he took a correct line in the Cultural Revolution and upheld principle, so we say he is a good person with mistakes. Our Long Bow Team should strengthen his education, help him recognize mistakes, do a thorough self-criticism, and then help restore him to leadership. So far he has accepted none of these things!"

Party Secretary Swift Li's case remained unsettled because Li himself had not recognized his own shortcomings or done anything about correcting them. As for Fast Chin, the former militia captain, the authorities could not settle his case because the facts were not clear. They had not yet determined whether this was simply another contradiction among the people or a contradiction with an enemy.

In regard to Long Bow's new leading body, Ts'ui said that it lacked strength because, although Chang Kuei-ts'ai, the new Party Secretary, was strong, the second and third in command were not very outstanding.

26

TARGET: SWIFT LI

 I sat through Comrade Ts'ui's whole report feeling vaguely dissatisfied. It seemed to me that it was rich in rhetoric and generalizations and lean in concrete analysis of the real problems of the Communist Party in Chang-chih City and its administrative environs. It certainly suffered by comparison with the reports given at the cadre meetings in Lucheng County in 1948. At that time one came away from each session feeling that one had gained a clearer picture of the overall situation in the county, of the progress, the problems, the contradictions and their resolution. Comrade Ts'ui evidently felt somewhat dissatisfied, too, because he concluded his speech with the following words: "This is a shallow and rough summing up. We should have much more lively facts and figures. What I have done is throw out a brick to attract jade, the jade of a mass summing up. From the mass of the cadres will come lively facts and living experiences. We are not content with summing up the principles of the rectification movement; we must express the concrete reality of it."

As soon as Ts'ui finished his report the participants rearranged the long rows of tables so that chairs could be set around them, thus transforming the meeting hall into a dining room. Then the guesthouse staff served a good meal of piping hot steamed bread and vegetables such as eggplant and Chinese cabbage with a sprinkling of fine-chopped pork. They topped this off with millet gruel, all that anyone could want, ladled from several very large metal pots. Scores of cadres and team members seated themselves round the tables as they wished and ate with hearty appetites. As stomachs began to fill up, talk began and soon a loud cacophony of mutual exchanges and laughter filled the air.

After eating, one and all retired to their dormitory rooms on the upper floor, stretched out on their clean beds and fell asleep until three. This custom of a noontime siesta was universal in China among peasants, students and government cadres. Only in industrial plants, where shift work began again after a noontime break for food, did people fail to rest in the middle of the day. Of course, in the rush of the harvest season peasants often worked right through the daylight hours and in emergencies so did cadres, but under normal conditions the siesta proved to be as fixed a part of Chinese life as it traditionally has been of Mexican or Spanish.

At three o'clock the Long Bow Propaganda Team assembled in one of the smaller dormitory rooms for study and discussion. The quilts on the beds had been rolled up at one end and each member found a place on one of the cotton-covered mattresses to sit or lounge through the long afternoon session.

Talk almost always began in a low key, with one member summing up his or her experiences in the light of the report that had just been heard. Had the people of Long Bow raised their awareness in the course of the movement? Had they actively involved themselves in the study of Mao Tse-tung Thought? What were the main problems in the brigade or on the team to which the individual had been assigned? How did one assess the leading group—the Party and Revolutionary Committee leadership? And how did the speaker himself feel about assignment to this protracted rural work?

Some of these reports rambled aimlessly. Listeners closed their eyes and almost seemed to fall asleep. Others took notes, faithfully, endlessly. This, of course, I too was doing, with the help of Carma, who translated for me tirelessly, hour after hour.

All called Long Bow an "old, big, difficult place," where political work was complicated by the fact that the people had come from all over North China—"from thirteen provinces and twenty-three counties," as the saying went—so individual class origins were not always clear. Within the community an unusual amount of marrying also mixed up class lines. In most ordinary villages, where one or two family names predominated, everyone traced relationship to everyone else through the paternal side, hence marriages had to be arranged with outsiders, local girls leaving to marry men in other villages and girls from other villages marrying local men. But in Long Bow, because people had drifted in from so many places, it was possible to arrange suitable matches between unrelated individuals, with the family next door or the family down the lane, and thus a network of maternal relationships developed that linked landlords to peasants, former Kuomintang reactionaries to militant revolutionaries, thieves and lumpen-elements to respected community elders, until, as Security Officer Shen said, no one could claim to be clean all around. If one wanted to find a weak spot in the political armor of the local cadres it was always possible to dig up some aunt or uncle, some sister-in-law or brother-in-law of questionable origin or unsavory reputation. On whom, then, should one rely? Who were those "basic masses" on whom the Party rectification, the production movement and the socialist transformation must depend?

"When we first came to Long Bow," said Shen, "we took a curved road. We didn't dare rely on anyone. Whenever we chose some man or woman to work with, others always turned up with some unfavorable story; this one was a former Catholic, that one's father was a KMT [Kuomintang] official, this one had indulged in immoral liaisons with various women. We were shocked and drew back and didn't know where to turn for activists. When we mobilized the masses for criticism of the leading group, hundreds of posters went up, but we didn't know which ones to believe or how to check them out, we had no clear line.

"Chin Fu-ch'uan looked like a very honest sort, but people said that he was a 'movement element' who always became active whenever some new campaign was brewing, but then fell quiet and did nothing until the next campaign. So how could we rely on him? And who else was there?

"Actually, as it turned out, Chin Fu-ch'uan withdrew last winter because his wife fell sick and all the chores at home fell on him. But when the propaganda team left in March he stood up for principle and opposed bad tendencies. So one cannot just accept what people say.

"In Long Bow there are always side winds and countercurrents. It is customary to attack whoever is active. And this can't help but influence the team members. People wonder about the sincerity of activists!"

Wang, the wounded veteran, agreed. "In Long Bow everyone is related. He is this one's nephew. She is that one's daughter-in-law. No one is free of bad connections. We thought of relying on Hsin-fa, but everyone said he had once been a bandit. So we hesitated. But in the countryside there is no such thing as a person without any problems at all. Even the best of the activists aren't completely consistent. He or she may be active on one front and passive on another. All of this is very difficult to analyze.

"Also," Wang went on, "some members of the team pay no attention to contradictions among the people. They are constantly looking for class enemies who can be blamed for everything that has gone wrong. Instead of trying to resolve internal contradictions they are on the lookout for Kuomintang agents to knock down!"

This was why Mao's statement on purity, which all had studied that morning, emerged as something important. One had to take the world as it was and work with the people who actually existed and not demand some abstract revolutionary purity as a condition for unity and action.

Another problem that loomed large as the team members carried on their discussion was the presence in the village of a handful of scoundrels, ne'er-do-wells or lumpen-elements, people like Splayfoot Tseng, Whiskers Shen, Li Yü-ken, his son Li Shou-p'ing and Ch'en Liang-t'ien. The escapades of Whiskers Shen alone were enough to fill a book. Splayfoot Tseng and Ch'en Liang-t'ien had framed a fellow production team member, Ts'ui Chin-tso. They stole some corn, hid it in a stack of corn fodder, and blamed it on poor Ts'ui; they then drove Ts'ui from their team.

Li Yü-ken was said to have hit his wife in a fit of anger, thus causing her death. His daughter had drowned in a deep privy cistern and some believed that Li had pushed her in. Here, all agreed, was a man with all five vices —ch'ih, he, p'iao, tu, chueh hsiao t'ai t'an ke tsui (eat, drink, whore, gamble and smoke opium and throw in a little stealing on the side).

That such people inhabited the countryside surprised no one. This was no cause for alarm. The problem in Long Bow was that a number of these unsavory characters were said to be close friends of Swift Li's and Fast Chin's, had served the two well as leading members of the brigade militia when the Two Gems were in power, and still met together with one or the other or both of the ex-leaders to drink, gossip and commiserate over their loss of power and prestige since the arrival of the third city propaganda team in March.

The charge was that Swift Li had used people like this to listen in on propaganda team meetings, then had encouraged them to throw bricks at rectification activists as they returned home after dark. When all this failed to stop the team's investigations, Swift Li, it was said, had taken advantage of the big character poster campaign, launched for the purpose of repudiating bad people and bad tendencies, to mount a counterattack against the team and all those who cooperated with it. When this, too, failed the Two Gems, so it was charged, had resurrected two controversial incidents out of the past, the *Little Four P'ei Case* and the *Reverse Land Reform Case,* to divert everyone's attention away from the real issues, which were said to be the quality of Li's leadership and the political line pursued by him and his cronies during the five years that they held power.

This third ploy worked well for a while. So great was the outcry generated by the Two Gems over the death of P'ei Hsiao-szu (Little Four), a suicide ten years earlier, and over those who were said to reject the land reform settlement of 1948 by questioning the killing of Wang Hsiao-nan twenty-four years earlier, that the propaganda team wasted two weeks looking into both matters from every possible angle. In the end they had to conclude that neither case merited attention. After a long detour into these stale charges the investigation had to come back to the main question once more: What had the Two Gems done with their power?

At this point Swift Li and Fast Chin abandoned the offensive, reversed the field, and beat a swift retreat. In the middle of the night they teamed up with Splayfoot Tseng and Wang Wen-te, two secondary targets of the rectification movement, and headed on foot for Changchih City.

Alerted by the propaganda team, commune headquarters sent people out to look for the four runaways. They checked out the bus station first because they thought the four might have taken the bus to Taiyuan, but nobody there had seen anyone from Long Bow. The next day the commune cadres went over to the offices of the City Committee, but no one there had seen Long Bow men either. They were about to leave empty-handed when the four came straggling up the stairs.

Smart Fan and Comrade Ts'ui received them and reviewed the charges against them—stressing sidelines at the expense of grain; refusing to study Tachai as yields dropped; depending on degenerates for support, thus throwing their class stand into question; leading corrupt and hedonistic lives; and defying the rectification movement.

The four, it was said, could not answer these charges and so stood silent. In the end Comrade Ts'ui persuaded them to go back to Long Bow.

A few days later, the leaders of the City Party Committee decided to remove the Two Gems from office and hold elections for a new Party Secretary and a new Revolutionary Committee to lead the brigade. So much for the old leading group.

In the long study sessions in the upstairs dormitory at the City Guest House, the cadres next turned their attention to the *new* leading group in Long Bow. The central aim of the Party rectification movement was to develop a leading core of individuals in each community who would take the lead in building socialism, not just maintain the status quo, and not foster "capitalism" by default. This, Ts'ui made clear, was the primary issue on which the work of the team would be judged. Discussion revealed that no one was too happy about the results so far.

"I'm not very pleased with the new leading group," said Judge Kao. "It's far from ideal, but the fact of the matter is that old Chang Kuei-ts'ai, Shen Chi-ts'ai and young Li Kuang-ching are the best people we can find for the job. There simply aren't any better cadres or activists who have been over-looked. They are hardworking, they are honest, and they have some prestige with the people. Who is there that could take their place?"

"Kuei-ts'ai is staunch in defense of the poor peasants," said Security Officer Shen. "He is not at all selfish and does not dream of taking personal advantage of any situation. But his cultural level is low, he is always behind in study and he is slow to grasp new things."

"Probably the main problem with Kuei-ts'ai is his short-sighted outlook, his 'Democratic Revolution' ideology," said Veteran Wang. "It shows up all the time. He thinks, As long as we don't steal, graft or speculate, what is there to be afraid of? What fault can anyone find? But this shows a low level of consciousness, because line problems are central now. Even if you don't steal, graft or speculate, if you don't grasp line questions, you can make even more serious mistakes by leading the whole community down the capitalist road.

"Also Kuei-ts'ai makes too many decisions alone without consultation and without all-around consideration of circumstances and policies. The leading cadre of a brigade should sum up the correct opinions of the masses, make correct decisions, and stand firmly for these decisions. Kuei-ts'ai can stand firm enough but he doesn't always think things through. And even when he is correct he can't always explain why and thus win people over. He doesn't consult enough with others. The other cadres, when problems are brought to them, say, 'Go and ask Kuei-ts'ai.' Thus we get one-man rule."

"In handling problems Kuei-ts'ai has some rough and ready methods left over from land reform days," added Judge Kao. "In regard to one stubborn case he said, 'Just give him a good beating, that'll take care of him!' When we discuss someone who won't do self-criticism, won't answer questions, and won't help clear up problems he is apt to say: 'Send him to me. I'll solve the whole thing in one night!' meaning, I'll educate him by beating him. This is *peasant realism*. Very practical! But this is no way to solve problems among the people."

All agreed that strong ultraleft tendencies swayed the population and the cadres. As a result many of Kuei-ts'ai's decisions tended toward the extreme.

Long Bow's new leading group had drawn up a set of regulations governing labor discipline, crop distribution and membership rights. Several of these regulations were questionable. One of them required that anyone who failed to perform his or her basic labor days and thus earn his or her share of per capita grain should pay a two-yuan fine for each missing day. This regulation was impossible to carry out, had not been enforced, and smacked of sheer material incentive or its opposite. Problems of slack work must be solved ideologically, not through rewards and punishments.

Another regulation required women who married outside the village to leave home and take their residence book to their husband's community or unit. This meant that their per capita grain had to come from elsewhere and their children's per capita grain had to come from elsewhere, thus relieving Long Bow, a community chronically short of grain, of this burden.

"But," said Veteran Wang, "this violates the marriage law and denies women their rights. You can't even call it 'New Democratic' thinking; it is feudal thinking! A woman does not have to move to her husband's house. She can make her own decision on this."

This regulation forced people to move by denying per capita grain to the second child of married women who stayed in Long Bow and did not earn enough labor days to cover the grain consumed.

"But in such cases one can only use persuasion, not force," said Wang. "Once a woman has married, the villagers want her to leave right away because they only have a couple of mou per capita. But you can't cut people off from grain just because they have more than one child. That's like condemning them to starve."

"Such a regulation," said Judge Kao, "concerns not simply one person, or one family, but the whole community and the line. Instead of solving problems of livelihood through increased production they are trying to solve them by exporting people! A leading body should look at a problem from all sides, take a broad view, and understand basic policy. But Kuei-ts'ai and his comrades tend to look at problems one by one and propose regulations that violate the spirit of socialist transformation."*

Tachai, everyone said, best exemplified the spirit of socialist transformation in 1971. But Long Bow cadres, though they had twice been to Tachai to see for themselves, had not grasped what that leading brigade was all about.

To study Tachai meant to put politics in command—that is, to study Mao Tse-tung Thought and apply it in daily life and work. It meant to adopt a policy of self-reliance and hard work; to transform nature and transform social relations; and it meant to put concern for the collective and concern for the state—that is, the country as a whole—in first place. Concern for the collective meant concern for collective property, for collective accumulation and collective investment, concern for full payment of taxes in support of the country as a whole and concern for full sales of grain to feed the cities.

But the ruling ideology in Long Bow, said Theater Manager Li, seemed to be, "Cheat the collective, cheat the state, and collapse the family seed" —that is, run through the wealth accumulated by one's ancestors.

What indicated this? Well, for one thing, lack of concern for collective tools. In the spring one team left their night-soil buckets in the field. In the fall, after the corn harvest, the commune tractor plowed up the remains of several buckets. People broke, misplaced and lost tools. So many losses caused people to meet to discuss how their attitude differed from that of Tachai. The cadres realized that they hadn't understood the Tachai spirit,

*Communist Party policy has since changed. Regulations now punish families for a third child or a child born out of order in violation of community plans.

so they arranged several visits to Tachai. But these visits failed to bring the Tachai spirit back to the people.

"Learn from Tachai" remained empty rhetoric. No one really grasped what Tachai was all about. The first time that Long Bow cadres visited Tachai they brought back the advanced work-point system where every brigade member was judged once or twice a year on his or her quality as a worker and assigned a fixed number of points for each labor day. Under this system, no matter how much you actually did on a given day, you got the same number of points. Impressed by this system, the Long Bow cadres did away with their old, clumsy, piecework system and adopted the Tachai method, only to find that people did less work each day than ever before.

The second time they went to Tachai they looked at all the solid stone caves and decided to build bigger and better houses in Long Bow, houses that soon began to rise like mushrooms on the outskirts of the village, even as crop production slipped.

What they failed to grasp was Tachai's political line: how to make grain production the key link and develop around that all viable secondary crops and sidelines; how to aim high for better, faster, more economical results based on hard labor, self-reliance and collective action.

To follow Tachai a community had to have a stable core of enlightened leading cadres. But it was exactly here, in the handling and promotion of cadres, that the "left" cast of thought that plagued Long Bow had shown up most harmfully. The brigade still would not use middle peasants who were Communist Party members as political officers of production teams or as team leaders because of their "hard" class origin. Only former hired laborers, poor peasants and lower-middle peasants would do. What happened, then, to the policy of uniting with middle peasants?

The Long Bow Brigade also summarily dismissed cadres who had made mistakes, even when the mistakes were not so serious. The policy of the Communist Party was to educate and remold people, help them overcome their mistakes, and give them a chance to do better. But the practice in Long Bow seemed to be to remove cadres wholesale and replace them with other, less-experienced cadres who soon made the same or worse mistakes. Had Lu Chin-jung done better than Chang Hsin-fa? Had Swift Li done better than Lu Chin-jung? To ask the question was to answer it. Instead of developing a seasoned leading core of mature, conscious cadres, Long Bow had changed leadership twelve times in twenty-three years and this had had a marked effect on progress.

"Once someone makes a mistake," said Security Officer Shen, "he is removed from office. But everyone must make some mistakes. Especially some of the younger people; as they come to leadership they are prone to make mistakes. If you remove them immediately it influences others, who then become less daring in their work. And year after year it goes on like this. Each year the leading core changes. In the spring they lead the planting, in the fall they preside over the harvest, and in the winter they resign under fire. There are so many one-year team and brigade leaders in Long Bow's history! And so the masses have come up with a saying, 'In the spring a *big red person* [everybody's favorite], in the fall a harassed bureaucrat, in the winter a struggle object!'

"As a result of this Party rectification it's a fact—most team leaders and brigade leaders don't want to work anymore! 'Left' in form, 'right' in essence is not just a thing of the past. It still lives and breathes!"

In truth many of the members of the propaganda team weren't so anxious to continue working either. When the discussion came around to the revolutionization of team cadres everyone had his or her list of complaints.

Security Officer Shen, who had been in Long Bow the longest and had played an active role on three successive cadre teams, admitted that he had not been so happy when he was sent back there in March, 1971. "We worked so hard and so long, but in the end they rewarded us with a Class III brigade [an old, big, difficult place] once more."

The new members, on the other hand, knowing that a Grade 13 cadre, a leading member of the Changchih City Committee, who had led one of the early teams, had failed to solve the problem, said, "If high-level cadres haven't been able to achieve a breakthrough, what can we hope to do about it? Long Bow is like a bowl of half-cooked rice. We are expected to come out and eat the mess they left behind."

The obvious answer to this was, "Of course Long Bow is a hard place to work; if it weren't why would they send a team here? After all, what is work? Work is struggle, Mao Tse-tung says, and so the thing to do is pull ourselves together and go out and 'feel the bottom,' as the saying goes."

Others admitted that they were somewhat tired of struggle, especially in the countryside, where the conditions were so hard. "If conditions weren't easier in the cities who would want to go to the cities?" asked Veteran Wang.

They agreed that for commune and detached service cadres who were working in the countryside anyway, service in Long Bow was more or less routine, but for the factory workers, office workers and city cadres who had come out, the adjustment was difficult.

"City life is much easier. We have eight-hour days, Sundays off, and in our regular work we don't have to cudgel our brains nearly as hard as we do here. Staying here a long time makes us tired and we want to go back to our regular jobs," said one of the workers.

"You're also afraid that you'll fall behind technically and can't advance to a higher grade when the time comes," said Security Officer Shen.

"Well, we don't make a big issue of that."

"Perhaps not, but still it counts."

"But the real problem is that in the countryside the work is harder," said one steelworker. "There are no regular hours. We work in the fields all day and meet all night. One has to be selfless and work every night until midnight and then get up at four in the morning when the first cock crows. So we get only three or four hours of sleep. Then when we still can't solve problems we get discouraged!"

"Yes," said Shen, "we learn firsthand about the *three waters*. Every day, the peasants say, there are three waters—'dew in the morning, sweat all day and rain all night.' "

Lest this thought depress everyone too much, Security Officer Shen suddenly jumped up.

"Anyone for Ping-Pong?"

Carma responded enthusiastically and soon they were playing through a hotly contested singles match in the recreation room. At least half of the Long Bow team stood by to watch, several members ready to challenge the winner as soon as he or she emerged.

One regional cadre, the journalist Tai Chin-chung, was especially good at Ping-Pong and it was he who ended up playing Carma. When he beat her, one of the steelworkers challenged him, and so it went, far into the night.

Ping-Pong, at least, had the capacity to divert our minds from that "old, big, difficult" place called Long Bow.

27

BASTARDS TO THE END

 On August 25, after breakfast and morning study, all the participants of the conference assembled once again to hear a major political report, this time by T'ien Yuan-feng, a PLA commander who was the secretary of the Changchih Party Committee. T'ien's report was, if anything, more abstract and theoretical than Ts'ui's. In three long hours he said little or nothing that Ts'ui had not already said and gave no concrete examples of anything that had happened during party rectification either in the area administered by the City of Changchih or any other area.

"Our work is part of the class struggle, part of the ever-present line struggle. In order to do it well we must all see it as a great task. . . . We must raise our consciousness and unite our thinking . . . we must depend on the people and unite with the people. . . . When we study the role of a Party branch we should ask ourselves: Does the leading core carry out Mao Tse-tung's line? . . . Has the movement raised the awareness of Communist Party members, causing them to play a vanguard role? . . . Do the Communist Party members distinguish between the capitalist and the socialist line? . . . Is the leading body in the hands of people boundlessly loyal to Chairman Mao? . . . Does the leading body put politics in command? . . . Have we got rid of bad people and admitted advanced good elements? . . . Has the new leading body promoted the study of Tachai, Taching and the People's Liberation Army? . . ."

After a long-winded review of these seven criteria for judging Party branches he went on to outline the work of the next period—a checkup on results. The checkup, he said, would concentrate on rural areas. Team members who had been working in one place would be transferred to other places to carry it out. In the next two weeks, August 30 through September 15, they were to look into the whole situation in their new community, bring out unresolved problems and solve them, then wind up the Party rectification wherever it was possible to say that the seven standards had been met, or met in the main. In doing this they were to involve the people and depend on the people, listen to all sides, and strive for all-around understanding. He singled out two of the seven questions for emphasis:

1. Has the movement raised the awareness of the Party members, causing them to play a vanguard role?

2. Has the leading core carried out Mao Tse-tung's line?

"One standard for judging all this is whether things have gone well on the production front. Consciousness may be transformed into matter and matter into consciousness. Since the rectification movement has gone through the whole farming season, we should take a look at the crops. If we put politics in command and carry on class struggle, production will be high. It is impossible to have good politics and poor crops!'"

Since no one challenged this dubious statement, he went on to give advice, much of it trite, as to how, having answered these questions, the team members should proceed. They should make distinctions between the actual situation found in one brigade as compared to another and tackle different problems differently. Where the work had gone well and the seven standards had been met, the movement should be carried to a still higher level. The remaining weak spots should be exposed and the remaining problems solved. Where the work had gone poorly and the seven standards had not been met, or only met in part; where the class situation was not clear; where the stale had not been rooted out and the fresh brought in; where Mao Tse-tung Thought had not been well studied or well grasped—in such places the team members would have to launch the movement again after the fall harvest. At that time special teams would assemble for remedial work.

"Where the work has been well done, look for weaknesses. Where the work has been poorly done, look for strong points," said T'ien. "In this way one can bring into play the enthusiasm of all, for one cannot just walk into a community and point out all the bad things that have happened. One must stress whatever strong points there are and bring all positive features into play."

The checkup was to be carried out in four stages:

1. mobilization;
2. study of documents;
3. investigation of the situation on the spot;
4. solution of problems.

Lest anyone should assume that all this was too much trouble, T'ien described what he considered to be some of the negative "living thoughts" in the minds of the rank-and-file team members.

"Some think that rectification is important, but the checkup really doesn't amount to much," said T'ien. "They think: One movement after another! Where will it ever end? What if there are some problems left? Is that such a big deal? So they don't take the checkup seriously, especially those who have done some of it. 'What's the use? What does it matter?' they say. They lack enthusiasm.

"Another living idea is, 'Pass the test, pass the gate.' That is, make a good appearance in order to get by without going deeply into things. In order to pass more easily they try not to expose contradictions but cover them up and smooth them over, thus giving the appearance that all is well. Now this is very wrong, because the problems will surface sooner or later and it is wrong not to expose and solve them.

"A third living idea is, 'One thing at a time.' Since now everybody is very busy with farm work, with the fall harvest coming up and the wheat planting around the corner, they think the checkup should be put off until later. But this is very wrong. It slights the importance of the checkup. We have to give it proper weight in our own minds!

"A fourth living idea is that 'it's time to leave.' Some cadres are fed up with the work. When they were assigned to the rural brigades they were told it would be a job for two seasons [six months], but now they have been down in the countryside for over a year. They want a transfer. They want to get back to their original jobs. They fear hardship. They are glad when praised but very gloomy when criticized. But all ideas of quitting are wrong. This movement is a chance to test and temper ourselves. We should make up our minds to see it through to the end!

"After all, this checkup is not something local. It is a task that came down to us from the provincial level and it is going on right now all over Shansi. So we must all do our best!"

T'ien ended his report with some general advice:

"Be careful. Don't exaggerate. Pay special attention to expulsions and recruitments. Expulsions must be approved by the City Committee and recruitment must be approved by the next higher body, which means when there is no general branch, the City Committee. But first the team members must agree. If you haven't agreed among yourselves don't bring the problem to us!

"Finally: sum up your experiences, both positive and negative. These experiences are our precious wealth."

The Party Secretary's report, like that of the vice-secretary's a few days before, lasted all morning. After lunch and the noon siesta, the discussions began once more in the dormitories and continued all afternoon and evening.

Long Bow team members expressed serious doubts over the effectiveness of this "checkup."

"To understand conditions in Long Bow in the space of two weeks is hard enough," said Chi the Moslem, "not to mention solving problems. How can a new team be expected to solve problems that have baffled us for so long?

"What sort of leading group does Long Bow now have? Is it soft, hard, bad, good? Who can really say?

"Has the lid been taken off the class struggle in Long Bow? I doubt it!

"Can anyone answer these questions in two weeks? I doubt it!"

"When you come to the bottom of it," said Wang, the wounded veteran, "the problem in Long Bow is the problem of the Two Gems. Has it been solved? No. Do we really understand it? No. Is there still factionalism in Long Bow? Yes. It is inherited from the Cultural Revolution. I attack you, you attack me! Can this be solved in three or four days? I doubt it!

"In addition to the Two Gems there is the problem of Wang Wen-te and the problem of Shen Chin-ts'ai, Little Shen, leader of the 'seize power' faction. Wang Wen-te has not passed the gate and Little Shen has been expelled from the Party, unjustly perhaps. Can we say we really understand these problems? No. First we have to decide what category they fall into. Are these contradictions among the people, or contradictions with enemies? Then we have to find an appropriate method to solve them. We can't just let them slide and slide. We can't leave them hanging in the air indefinitely!"

"If we really look into it, if we grasp it tightly, we can find a solution for Little Shen," said Judge Kao, the team leader. "But as for Swift Li, Fast

Chin and Wang Wen-te, the crux of the problem lies with them. They refuse to recognize their faults, they refuse to do self-criticism. What more can the team do?"

"We can mobilize the masses to repudiate them," said Theater Manager Li. "Sooner or later they will have to come round. There is no such thing as 'bastard to the end.'"

"How can you say that?" retorted Chi the Moslem. "If there is no such thing why is there such a category in the Party instructions? 'Bastards to the end' are to be tried and punished. Certainly there are 'bastards to the end'!"

This assertion started a major argument during which everyone began to talk at once. Some, for whom Chi the Moslem spoke most eloquently, maintained that there were persons who simply could not be touched by criticism or repudiation, and others, led by Wang, the wounded veteran, maintained with equal eloquence that most people could be reached and that the fault in this case lay with the team and not with the obstinate cadres.

"Well, in regard to Swift Li," said Theater Manager Li, "it would be a 'left' mistake to expel him and punish him at this point. But it's up to him to recognize his mistakes. He won't. He thinks he's completely revolutionary and no one has the right to criticize him! He's too stubborn! That's not our fault. We can't make his self-criticism for him. We've done all we can do."

"But there are still two sides to this," replied Veteran Wang. "The suspended cadres have to make proper self-criticism, that's true, but the propaganda team has to do its work well also. We have to find a way to reach them."

"Two sides, I'll admit," said Li, "but the two sides aren't equal. The main problem lies with Swift Li. We've done our best. He's to blame."

"Well," said Veteran Wang, "I doubt if we've done our best. You must admit that our work also has shortcomings. Even on this question we can still improve!"

"But the problem still lies with the men themselves," Li insisted once more. "Swift Li thinks that out here in the countryside there is not that much pressure. He figures we'll leave eventually and his supporters in the village will remain. He'll be reinstated in the Party and in some leading office and that will be that. When all is said and done, he thinks, I am not a counterrevolutionary, so they can't do anything about me. I'll outlast them!'

But Veteran Wang would not give in. "I think the main problem is that our team members are not united. We don't have a uniform understanding of this case. If we did we could solve it."

"How can you say we disagree on it," said Security Officer Shen. "We all agree it's a contradiction among the people. We all agree that the Two Gems made line mistakes. We all agree that they should recognize their mistakes and criticize themselves. So where's the disunity?"

"Well, there's some doubt about Fast Chin's class stand, his relationship with the singer Shih Kui-hsiang. Can we say we have gotten to the bottom of the case? And as for Wang Wen-te, it's clear we have no unity."

"What makes you say that?"

"Well, after he was brought before the masses and made his self-criticism, the team members had nothing to say. The whole thing was left up in the air. We had nothing to say because we couldn't agree."

"I deny that," said Security Officer Shen. "Our attitude is clear. Wen-te is not a class enemy. We have made mistakes in working style. We discussed our conclusions in the leading group. The problem was we failed to tell everyone, so it seemed we had no position."

"Well, it certainly seemed to me that the propaganda team was not united," said Wang, "and that's why his criticism was so poor and there has been no solution."

"No! No! No!" said Shen excitedly. "That was not decisive at all. The problem was not that we weren't united. The problem was with Wen-te himself."

"That's right," said Li, jumping in, in support of the Security Officer. "The team may have made some mistakes in method, but the crux of the matter is Wen-te's attitude. The masses won't press him because he never changes—and it's his fault, not ours!"

Once again the debate became very lively, with people interrupting one another and several people talking at once. As in the case of the Two Gems the issue was, Who is to blame, the stubborn cadres themselves, or poor work on the part of the team? The lineup in the debate clearly turned out to be those who had been there a long time, defending their work and their effort, against those who had come more recently. The old-timers charged that the latecomers had not attended the crucial meetings, didn't really understand what had happened, and didn't realize how much patient work and explanation had gone into the reform of the obstinate cadres. The latecomers, on their part, kept insisting that that was all very well, but since the problem hadn't been solved, more work must be done and perhaps it could be improved.

To me the debate seemed strangely familiar and I suddenly realized why. Twenty-three years before, when Wang Wen-te, his father, Wang Yü-lai, Li Hung-er, the village militia captain, and Wang Hsi-yu returned from the county jail in a defiant mood, the Long Bow Work Team had conducted a very similar debate, with my assistants, Ch'i Yun and Hsieh Hung, demanding drastic action against stubborn cadres who refused to criticize themselves. Hou Pao-pei, leader of the work team, had insisted that the men were not class enemies, that he could not simply slap them down, that he had to do more patient education and mobilization work.

What made this debate, so old and yet so new, so singular, even uncanny, was the central role Wang Wen-te still played in it, and for the same basic reasons as before. He had been proud and stubborn in the past and had refused to bow his head before the people who accused him of arrogant and oppressive work as captain of the police. After a long period of suspension and reform he had resumed work as captain of the police, as the man in charge of village security, and now once again was under fire for arrogant and oppressive ways. True to form, he proudly and stubbornly refused to criticize himself except in the most superficial way.

As Security Officer Shen said in disgust, "After hours of mass criticism what does Wen-te do? He steps forth and says, 'I welcome your criticism,' then proceeds to ignore it!"

Perhaps no such thing as "bastard to the end" existed, but there certainly were some very stubborn cases. Wang Wen-te was one of these and so, apparently, were the Two Gems. A fourth was the man at the brick kiln, Wang Man-hsi. Since the latter was not a Party member he was not a major issue for the Party rectification movement, but because he was serving as a cadre, as the head of a Sidelines Team, he created a problem, especially since Man-hsi, as everyone well knew, had recently beat up one of the brick kiln workers for refusing to clean up after a heavy rain.

"Don't tell me he did it in the interest of the work," said Chi the Moslem. "Such a working style cannot be tolerated. The beating, instead of advancing the work, completely disrupted the work. How can Man-hsi still serve as a cadre? He'll never change!"

But others disagreed. Even Man-hsi, they said, could change. "Change is a process from not recognizing error to recognizing error and it is sometimes very slow."

Part of the problem, it seemed, was the way in which everyone treated Man-hsi. When he made serious mistakes the brigade shoved him aside and criticized him heavily, but then when the brigade needed a loyal, hardworking person to spark some work, it called him back to lead the way. "We push him off the stage when we are mad at him and pull him back into the act when we need him again," said Veteran Wang. All this created confusion. It did not help in the remolding of Man-hsi.

Once again I was aware of an echo out of the past. For was it not the case in the land reform struggle that when the village needed an activist, Man-hsi had led the way in beating the landlords and won great respect from all, only to lose it when he began to beat ordinary people as heartily as he did people's enemies? But when the confrontation occurred between the Village Congress and the rich peasant widow Yü Pu-ho, suddenly everyone thought of Man-hsi again as the man to take direct action.

Could it be said that all the education of the intervening years had failed to have any effect? I think not, for Man-hsi had mellowed considerably. But he still had a hot temper, and he still lost his head occasionally, especially when some young person obstructed the brigade's work. I, for one, was ready to grant Man-hsi some potential for growth.

Not so Chi the Moslem.

"How can we use a man like him as a cadre! Why, right in the middle of the Cultural Revolution he stole a board. He's rotten inside. His style is impossible. If he's not doing something lecherous, he's stealing something!"

Once again, as was the case with the Two Gems and Wang Wen-te, two lines emerged in the propaganda team, a hard line toward errant cadres and a soft line. The extended discussion at the City Guest House in August did not lead to a meeting of minds. The differences persisted and built toward a climax in the days to come.

But on one thing all agreed: a two-week checkup by a completely new team would be of questionable value. Carma and I agreed with this and added our own urgent argument for continuity in Long Bow. If a completely new team appeared and all the people who had been there for months and even years were transferred out, how would we ever come to grips with the real situation in Long Bow? To whom could we turn for the story of its recent history and an evaluation of its cadres and ordinary people?

Chang Ch'ang-fu, vice-leader of the Revolutionary Committee of Ma-chang Commune, who sat in on the discussions of the Long Bow team, brought both the team's doubts and our own objections to the City leaders and they worked out a compromise. Half or more of the Long Bow team would leave, but a solid core of the people who had been there longest, plus Veteran Wang, the man most experienced in rural work, would stay. Several newcomers would join them, and together they would carry through the checkup. It was a happy solution, at least for Carma and me. When we returned to the village, the propaganda team with whom we had lived, eaten and met morning noon and night accepted us as completely and warmly as that land reform work team had accepted me in Long Bow twenty-three years before.

As the discussions continued it became more and more apparent that the whole conference lacked decisive leadership. Since the keynote speeches had not illuminated concrete problems the participants found it hard to achieve cohesion. The major weakness of Party Secretary T'ien's speech was its abstract content. Vice-secretary Ts'ui had called for lively examples, firsthand experiences that could give flesh to the bare bones of his political rhetoric. But after two days of extended discussion and exchange, T'ien's report emerged leaner and drier than the one that preceded it. One had no sense, from attending this meeting, of the true situation in the municipal area. What main contradictions plagued the various brigades and units? What principal shortcomings marred the work of the Party members and the Party branches? What sort of rotten people had the branches found and removed, and what sort of healthy new forces had they recruited? What concrete manifestations of the projected struggle between the "capitalist" and the "socialist" roads in Changchih City had shown up and how could one defeat the former and carry the latter to victory?

Party Secretary T'ien presented no analysis, no summary, no estimate that could explain the local situation, while down below the team members wandered through a veritable thicket of concrete problems which seemed to pile one on the other until they weighed everyone down. The Long Bow Team had at least raised some basic questions: In the case of the Two Gems, were they dealing with a contradiction among the people, or were they dealing with class enemies? If there were "bastards to the end," how did one judge them, and short of that, what constituted an adequate effort to reach and reform people? If a brigade neglected grain production to concentrate on sidelines, how did one determine the proper role of sidelines in such a rapidly growing industrial area? What were the conditions in the outskirts of Changchih that made this problem so acute? Were private peddlers and private repair shops for bicycles, watches and other household goods wrong in principle? If not, how should they be judged? Was it exploitation for craftsmen to charge money for repairs? And what about all the ultraleft

policies and tendencies discovered by the propaganda team in Long Bow
—the revolving door for cadres who had committed small mistakes; the
reluctance to use anyone of middle peasant origin; limited rights for people
who had been expropriated, even though unjustly; limited rights for all
second-, third- and fourth-generation landlord and rich-peasant children;
and the denial of per capita grain to children born of married mothers who
refused to move away?

The notion that in the persons of Swift Li and Fast Chin one might be
dealing with an enemy contradiction rested on their relationship with Shih
Kui-hsiang, the niece of a leading Catholic reactionary, now under supervision. The leading Catholic's crime was his role in the so-called "Catholic
Uprising" of 1966. But surely, if there were some reactionary Catholic
movement afoot, its ramifications must spread way beyond Long Bow.
There must be some evidence of agitation in the municipality, the surrounding counties and the Southeast Region as a whole. Surely the secretary of
the City Party Committee could come up with some framework of conspiracy or lack of it which could aid people at the village level to judge the
phenomena they were dealing with. But no such analysis ever surfaced.
T'ien talked only in generalities—"class struggle," "line struggle," "Mao
Tse-tung Thought," "weed out the stale, bring in the fresh."

Factionalism ran like a troublesome thread through every facet of local
life. Even though the army had suppressed open fighting more than four
years ago, the persistence of mutual hates and grievances, stemming primarily from the Cultural Revolution, continued to divide the whole population.
But on factionalism T'ien said not a word. In the face of massive evidence
to the contrary, he spoke as if the whole phenomenon no longer existed.

T'ien could have made the same speech in Tientsin or Heilungkiang.

After the conference broke up, but before we left our quarters to return
to Long Bow, the leading comrades of the City Committee came to my
dormitory room to say goodbye. They asked me what I thought of the
five-day meeting.

After some embarrassing hesitation I finally said to Ts'ui, "It seems to
me that there is a gap here between theory and practice; that up above there
is a rather abstract theory of Party rectification and down below there is
a morass of concrete problems untouched by theory. Up above, some rather
grand rhetoric, and down below, an intricate maze of contradictions without any clear picture as to what is significant and what is not."

I could see from the faces of the Long Bow team that this was a welcome
opinion. I caught, out of the corner of my eye, a fleeting smile on Shen's
face and a flash of enthusiasm in Kao's eyes. But the army comrades met
the opinion with stolid silence. They did not say yes, they did not say no.
They dropped the subject and returned to the pleasantries of our farewell.
Perhaps they had not really expected to get an opinion. Or perhaps they
recognized that there was something to it and did not know how to respond.
As always, it seemed to be very difficult to get any kind of exchange going,
to talk man to man, comrade to comrade, about any real problem with
higher cadres. They seemed reluctant to take a stand, at least one that could
be presented to a foreigner.

28

YAMENS,
NEW AND OLD

 On our way home to Long Bow, as I mulled over the lessons of the conference, it occurred to me that there was something wrong with the very building in which it was held. I wondered if the new government had really thought through the question of an architecture suited to a people's democratic state.

Under the feudal order architects designed government buildings, such as the county magistrate's yamen, to inspire awe and obedience. Cut off from the street by massive walls and moats, their entrances manned by fierce guards, they caused even the boldest of ordinary citizens to think twice before entering. The whole layout expressed overwhelming centralized power.

The offices manned by Communist revolutionaries during the decades of civil and national war, prior to 1949, expressed just the opposite principle. Under guerrilla conditions the government usually functioned far from any county or regional capital. The officials made their homes and offices wherever they could, often taking over the courtyards of some local landlord who had been expropriated and, like as not, sharing it with a newly *fanshened* peasant family or two. With chickens and pigs underfoot and a donkey braying nearby, they conducted official business out of a dispatch case. Security guards, young Eighth Routers with Lugers on their hips, merged with the population, helped with the morning chores, carried water for the cadres and for their peasant hosts, and could usually be found early in the morning sweeping the courtyard along with the mother of the family and her eldest daughter.

Thus the officials lived close to the people, rubbed shoulders with them at home and on the street, and made themselves available to everyone who had a grievance or a suggestion. Shared quarters obliterated, or very nearly obliterated, the traditional great gulf between official and common man. People thought of their revolutionary cadres as they did of the soldiers recruited from their midst—as a brother-and-son, sister-and-daughter force. Truly the people served as the water in which the cadres swam like fish.

All this was dramatically expressed by Anna Louise Strong in a description of a visit to the Yenan cave where Mao Tse-tung lived:

I went to Mao's home by autotruck, slithering down the steep bank, bumping over boulders in the water, climbing the far shore at a dangerous angle, and passing the gate into Yang Family Village, the narrow ravine where the headquarters of the Central Committee was located. We dismounted a short distance up the ravine, climbed a steep path between cornstalks and tomato vines, and came to a ledge from which a score of caves opened.

Four of these caves, set close among the neighbors, were the home of Chairman Mao. . . .

We sat on a flat terrace under an apple tree while the late afternoon wore on and sunset glorified the arid hills. Mao's fascinating, dark-haired wife sat beside us for a time and then went in to arrange a meal. Their small daughter, in a dress of bright-figured cotton, played around her father's knee. . . .

In the early part of the conversation I noticed a movement in the grass higher up the hill, some fifty feet above Mao's caves. "Who is up there?" I asked, thinking how easily a bomb could be dropped on our terrace and wondering if there were guards about protecting the chairman's home.

"Just another family," replied Mao. "Their children are curious about my foreign guest."

Seldom have I seen a man so happily and sociably set in his environment. Living like a peasant, he did not even demand the privacy that most intellectuals think necessary for their work. What privacy he needed was given by the respect in which his neighbors held him. The children above peeped down but made no noise. . . .*

With liberation of the whole country and the regularization of government, with the establishment of a new structure of power in the very centers where power had been wielded of old, much of the informality and accessibility of the guerrilla regime crumbled or was crushed. If the new county and municipal organizations did not move back into the old seats of power, the thick-walled feudal yamens, they built imposing new government structures, modern office buildings surrounded by equally high walls that were often topped by barbed wire or even broken glass embedded in cement. The soldiers who guarded the gates stood stiffly at attention, with automatic rifles slung across their bellies. Certainly the ordinary citizen must hesitate more than a little before entering such imposing portals to seek out an official in his second- or third-story office. While not unmindful of the problem of security for cadres in a period of sharp class struggle such as the socialist transformation of the last twenty years, it seemed to me that most city and county offices and officers could have done business on the ground floor of buildings built like ordinary stores along the main street or the side streets of county seats and regional capitals, offices so constructed that ordinary people could feel welcome as they walked in off the street to

*Anna Louise Strong, *The Chinese Conquer China* (New York: Doubleday & Company, Inc., 1949), pp. 39–41.

consult over taxes, grain purchases, marriage licenses or whatever other business they might have to contract.

To spend so much money on imposing public buildings seemed to me to be not only wasteful, but also unfortunately symbolic of the reestablishment of that great gap between people and government which cursed old China. Such buildings cut cadres off from people and people off from cadres so that the former easily fell into elitism and commandism, and the latter easily fell prey to feelings of inadequacy and suppliance.

Even at the brigade level modern headquarters were walled in. In Long Bow village there was only one entrance to the large courtyard that housed the offices of the Revolutionary Committee, but this entrance, though covered, dispensed with guards. Inside the walls the brigade's leading officials shared their grounds with the accountant's office, the doctor's clinic, the dispensary, the community barbershop, the electrician's shop, the power switchboard, a warehouse and a large meeting hall. People used the hall for rehearsals, dramatic performances and an indoor carpentry shop, as well as for mass meetings of the brigade members. Hundreds of people had business here every day and they came freely in and out as the spirit moved them. Since all brigade officials worked at least half-time in the fields as members of various production teams, and since they lived in houses and courtyards in no way different from those of their fellow brigade members, their life-style tended to resemble the old, easy integrated relationship between officials and populace that had so impressed the peasants in guerrilla war days.

Once one reached the commune level, however, the old official habits began to reassert themselves, as the sketch on page 203 of Machang Commune headquarters shows. Here in one large walled compound, all the offices of the district were concentrated. The seat of the government, the headquarters of the Revolutionary Committee, stood at the back as in a yamen of old. That ordinary people entered this commune complex reluctantly was by no means certain. With a proper attitude on the part of the commune leaders, peasants might always feel welcome here. But the architecture suggested exclusiveness, it walled the cadres into an official enclosure, and if their attitude ever wavered they could easily turn to abusing their power.

Between form and content there is always an intimate relationship, and the form here seemed out of keeping with the equalitarian content which China's new leaders had set out to create.

Along with imposing offices, the new government continued the old feudal practice of making papers and decrees, correspondence, invoices and receipts official through the use of seals. These large handcut wooden or stone stamps carried the name of the organization. The higher the level, the larger the stamp, until they reached four by four or six by six inches in size. An order stamped with an official seal using ink in the color of authority —red—commanded universal respect. To control a seal meant to wield real power. To seize a seal meant to seize real power. An official seal exerted more social leverage than a platoon of troops. Starting out as symbols of power, seals came to embody real power because people stood in awe of them. In the new society, as in the old, seals attained the stature of true

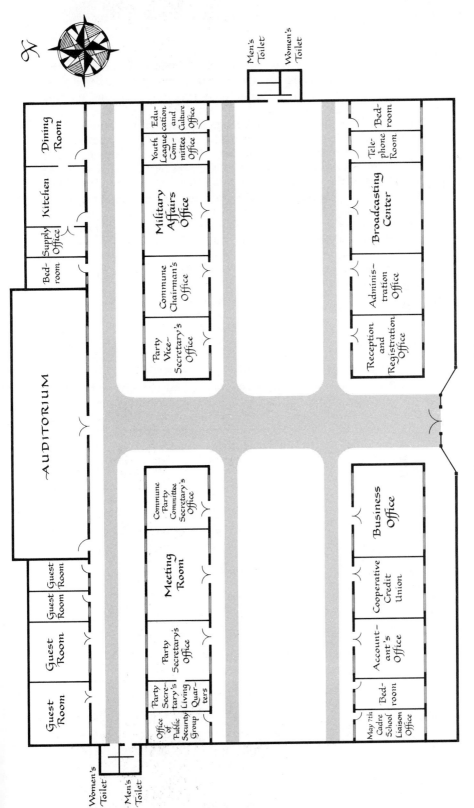

HORSE SQUARE COMMUNE HEADQUARTERS

N

Men's Toilet
Women's Toilet

Women's Toilet
Men's Toilet

Dining Room
Kitchen
Supply Office
Bed-room
AUDITORIUM
Guest Room
Guest Room
Guest Room
Guest Room

Education and Culture Office
Youth League Committee Office
Military Affairs Office
Commune Chairman's Office
Party Vice-Secretary's Office

Commune Party Committee Secretary's Office
Meeting Room
Party Secretary's Office
Party Secretary's Living Quarters
Office of Public Security Group

Bed-room
Tele-phone Room
Broadcasting Center
Adminis-tration Office
Reception and Registration Office

Business Office
Cooperative Credit Union
Account-ant's Office
Bed-room
May 7th Cadre School Liaison Office

fetishes, objects irrationally reverenced, objects imbued with independent life. Surely seal fetishism inhibited the emancipation of the mind that must open the way for democracy. It is doubtful, however, that anyone in China ever gave this matter a thought.

These were the thoughts running through my mind as we returned to the village by jeep, but I had little chance to share them with anyone. As soon as the team members arrived in Long Bow they began to reorganize their ranks. Theater Manager Li, Moslem Chi, Steelworker Cheng, Accountant P'ei and Teacher Ch'en all prepared to leave. Two new members, Wen Liang-yü and Liu Shu-wang, appeared to make up, in part, for the loss. Security Officer Shen stepped into the position of team leader, while Judge Kao dropped down a notch to the position of vice-leader. He was joined there by Pipefitter Huang, who won promotion to the same level. As if to confirm my worst fears about official behavior, Pipefitter Huang no sooner became a vice-leader than he shed his worker's modesty, put on his old military uniform, and began to behave like a platoon sergeant in the army. As his opinions became more dogmatic, he expressed them ever more loudly. When he dealt with peasants, he seemed always to be barking commands.

After spending one long afternoon evaluating the work of the departing comrades and listening to their suggestions for future work, the remaining team members plunged into the task at hand—mobilizing the members of the local Party branch for the study, discussion and self- and mutual criticism to come. Carma and I attended some of the preparatory meetings but in the intervals between them we continued to meet with the old cadres like Chang Kuei-ts'ai and Chang Hsin-fa to dig out the rest of the story about what had happened in the last two decades.

The second decade after the completion of the land reform began with the "Great Leap." Participants spoke of it with enthusiasm.

29

THE GREAT LEAP

"Those were the days. Whenever I sit at home and think about it I feel happy again. I was only twenty-one at the time. What was so great? The fact that so many people came together. Their discipline was marvelous. Everyone came to work on time and all joined in with a will. No line divided village from village, people from here and people from there! We'd never even seen iron made before, but here we were making it ourselves.

"As we waited for the iron to pour out we got more and more excited. I had nothing to do but watch over the diesel engine in my care. As long as it was running well I could go and look around. Thus I hung around the various furnaces taking everything in. One day I dug some big grooves in the sand spelling out "Let the whole people smelt iron." When the molten metal ran out it filled all the channels I had carved, casting these words in solid metal. We hung this up." (Chao T'ung-min, Peasant Technician)

"When we first marched off to work on the dam at Hsiying many of us had second thoughts. We assumed we were going far away to a place of hardship and hunger. As we said goodbye to family and friends we wept. But from the very first moment we set foot in their village Hsiying people treated us well. They let us stay in their best cave homes. We always had plenty of millet to eat and every third day we had mutton. We ate so well and enjoyed it so much that when it came time to leave no one wanted to go home." (Chang Kuei-ts'ai, Party Secretary)

"One hundred thousand laborers worked on the dam at Hsiszuho. Red flags flew all over the place. At night electric bulbs outnumbered the stars. They made the night as bright as day. All the cadres went down to work among the people and everybody worked with great determination.

"With 100,000 people in three shifts there were people everywhere. If you stood on the hill and looked down, you saw seas and oceans of people." (Shih Ts'ai-yuan, Director, Consumer Coop)

"On the railroad construction project everyone worked hard. All strove to be heroes and nobody lagged behind. People were enthusiastic and easy to lead. Whenever I called a meeting they all came to take part. Leadership was easy in those days.

"We launched all sorts of competitions. There was a woman from Tienshih named Miao Wen-ying. She could haul 1,000 catties of stone in a cart uphill or down. Men liked to work with her because she put all her strength into her work. Sometimes we staged races, one commune against the other, to see which could move the most dirt to the embankment. Miao Wen-ying carried two big baskets on her carrying pole and no man could beat her. Not even Chao Ta-yuan, a sixty-year-old, who always came out first in competitions between men. She took on ten different men, one at a time, and defeated them all. Finally I volunteered to give it a try. Everyone warned me that I'd never beat her. I tried, but she defeated me, too." (Wang Wen-te, Leader, Fifth Team Vegetable Garden)

Thus Long Bow people spoke about the Great Leap, a mass movement of a few months' duration that served, without doubt, as the high point of their lives between the land reform of 1947 and the Cultural Revolution of 1966. The Great Leap of 1958 and the movement to form communes were organically linked. In some places, notably in Honan Province, communes were formed by merging cooperatives; on the basis of this new, large-scale organization, a great leap in production was launched. In other places, in order to join the production movement that was already sweeping the nation, people quickly formed communes through mergers. The two movements stimulated each other and reinforced each other. Between them they fanned up a nationwide reorganization of rural society and a nationwide movement to remake nature, build industries throughout the countryside, and smelt iron and steel everywhere.

It is best to begin with the organization of communes. In the winter of 1957–58 the Party launched a big drive to bring water to hitherto dry lands, especially in Honan. With all the peasants of that province already organized in higher stage coops, it was thought that rural people had already found an organizational form with the strength to carry out whatever tasks needed doing. But as the drive developed it became clear that the small scale of the cooperatives, each containing from 100 to 200 families, stood in the way of rational progress. There were too many conflicts of interest between groups over land use, rights of way and water rights, and there were too few people under coordinated command. These problems were most easily resolved by a leap to a higher stage of cooperation that brought all the groups of a single township, even all the groups in a county, together. By pooling all land and all resources and by allocating labor power on a large scale, projects hitherto undreamed of suddenly became practical. Out of the needs of the moment large associations of cooperatives were born. Mao Tse-tung called them *communes* after he inspected what was going on in Honan and Shantung. Very quickly the idea of the commune developed far beyond a simple association for carrying out capital construction in the land. Since the communes were as big as townships and sometimes as big as counties, they soon took over the functions of government. They became responsible not only for agricultural production but for small industries also, then widened their powers to direct all administration, trade, banking, education, medical care and culture. In the end they took over military affairs, the organization and direction of the militia, as well.

"In the present circumstances," said the Central Committee resolution of August, 1958, "the establishment of people's communes with all-around management of agriculture, forestry, animal husbandry, side occupations and fisheries, where industry (the worker), agriculture (the peasant), exchange (the trader), culture and education (the student) and military affairs (the militiaman) merge into one, is the fundamental policy to guide the peasants to accelerate socialist construction, complete the building of socialism ahead of time, and carry out the gradual transition to Communism."

The sudden introduction of the concept of "Communism" here was startling. What stood in the way of true equality, what blocked the road to Communist sharing, many felt, was the persistence in China of three great differences: the difference between city and country, between worker and peasant, and between mental and manual labor. Communes, with the resources to bring about a technical revolution in every branch of production, with the strength to build industries in the countryside and at the same time to develop all-around education, medical care and cultural life, could tackle these differences, raise the countryside up toward the level of the cities, turn peasants into workers, at least part-time, and develop people capable of both mental and manual labor. Each of these steps was a step on the road to Communism, a hitherto distant goal, which suddenly appeared on the horizon as a social stage possible to achieve in a decade or two, certainly in the lifetime of the people discussing the problem.

The Sputnik Coop, in Suiping County, Honan, showed how communes should actually be organized to accomplish these goals. The merger of twenty-seven smaller coops, all of which had been engaged in overlapping and conflicting water conservancy projects before they joined to pool resources and labor power, brought Sputnik into being in April, 1958. Sputnik's constitution, the first to be published anywhere in China, set the tone for the movement to come. It codified an advanced and large-scale collective way of life that brought together some 9,000 households in a multifaceted cooperative conglomerate. Members pooled not only all the productive property of their original collectives but also such private holdings as garden plots, house sites and trees, distributed income through a monthly wage system instead of the seasonal division of the crop, and guaranteed each individual a free supply of grain. They organized public dining rooms, nurseries and sewing teams to take over women's work, thus freeing women to join production. To facilitate capital construction on the land and the building of industries, they pooled and put under unified control all material and financial resources and all manpower. This huge coop soon merged with the township, so that the congress delegates, council members, chairman and deputy chairman of the township assumed equivalent posts in the commune. Commentators interpreted this merger of state and cooperative as the disappearance of the lowest level of state power, a first step toward the disappearance of the state under Communism as predicted by Marx and Engels.

After the peasants formed the first communes in Honan, and after Mao Tse-tung, on a tour of Shantung, told a reporter that "communes are good," communes formed rapidly throughout China. As they formed, they began reclamation projects large and small as well as all sorts of industrial construction, with the accent on iron and steel. Out of this the Great Leap emerged. Feeling that the cooperative movement as a whole and the sudden leap to the large commune form had unleashed enormous new forces of production, Mao revived a slogan first coined in 1956 and once again called on the whole nation to "go all out, aim high for greater, faster, more economical results in the building of socialism."

It must be admitted that there was at the time some basis for thinking that China could move rapidly forward economically and socially. There truly were enormous forces of production that had never been mobilized and enormous resources that had never been tapped. Tens of millions of peasants had always been underemployed, working hard only during the height of the crop season, then idling throughout the slack season for lack of alternative employment. The average days worked per year before cooperation had been something like 100 to 150. Cooperation raised this to over 200. It was thought that communes could ensure 300 or more workdays per year, many of them in capital construction that would greatly increase the productivity of the land, and create new industries capable of employing millions.

If millions of peasants had always been underemployed, huge reserves of minerals, water, wastelands, range lands and forests had always been under-utilized. Held back first by a stalemated landlord-tenant system, then by a fragmented individual economy, China's vast labor power had never been able to come to grips with the wealth of the country. Now, it was argued, the labor power of the people, liberated from private property, could at last go to work. In a very short time, this power, once activated, could transform the economy. The slogan "Catch up with and surpass Britain in fifteen years" fired the imagination.

Surpassing Britain was in some ways a modest demand for a country of China's size and resources. Britain was not, after all, a superpower. The home islands produced only forty million tons of steel and generated some 450,000 million kilowatt hours of electricity per year. For China, however, producing at that time only five million tons of steel and generating only 40,000 million kilowatt hours of electricity, surpassing Britain in fifteen years loomed as a serious challenge.

The excellent crop maturing throughout the length and breadth of the nation in 1958 gave everyone cause for optimism. Partly because of the extensive conservation measures that had been undertaken the previous year, but primarily because of a stretch of excellent weather that brought neither prolonged drought nor serious flooding to any large section of the country, the season promised an unprecedented harvest. Given abundant food at last, the Chinese people considered no task too great to accomplish. They launched a "drum-beating, cymbal-clashing" mass exodus from the routines of normal life. People went out by the millions from quiet villages and carefully tended fields to build dams in the wilderness, dig canals that changed the course of rivers, open mines wherever ore or coal could be found, and smelt iron and steel on the spot. With full stomachs, high hopes and infectious zeal, they challenged nature. Never had China's future seemed so bright.

"Now our enthusiasm has been aroused," said Mao Tse-tung. "Ours is an ardent nation, swept by a burning tide. There is a good metaphor for this: our nation is like an atom . . . when this atom's nucleus is smashed the thermal energy released will have really tremendous power. We shall be able to do things which we could not do before."

30

POLITICAL PREPARATION

Changchih City, with its suburban districts, took up the challenge of the new movement early. A city-wide debate on the socialist road versus the capitalist road had prepared the way. Called the "big four" debate—big subject, big wind, big character posters, big controversy—all struggle centered on the question of cooperation versus private farming. The sharpest conflict took place inside the Communist Party, where a new rectification movement was in progress to clarify policy, criticize weaknesses and mobilize all positive factors for building socialism.

Wang, the wounded veteran on the Long Bow Propaganda Team, recalled vividly the course of the debate at Yellow Mill, where he went to work as a Changchih City cadre that year. Because Yellow Mill served as a concentration point, Long Bow Brigade members also attended the sessions. For a five-day period cadres encouraged the people to speak out all their grievances. Many problems, large and small, came to the surface. From among those who spoke critically the debate committee chose three whose complaints brought out most sharply the question of the old society versus the new. One was a former puppet district head who attacked the new society head-on. "The pig will always die at the hand of the slaughterer," he said. The second was the son of an upper-middle peasant who claimed that since cooperatives came on the scene he had not been able to get enough to eat. The third was an ex-Communist who had once been a beggar. Since Liberation two of his brothers had died in their prime. He reacted bitterly to this and had come to resent the discipline of collective work. To anyone who would listen he recalled, with nostalgia, the "free" life of his days as a beggar.

The committee asked these three to speak before public meetings. Large crowds gathered in the street to hear them and refute them.

The son of the upper-middle peasant proved no match for the people. The per capita grain distributed that year in Yellow Mill amounted to 450 catties. He claimed this was not enough.

"Before Liberation I could buy all the grain I wanted. Now I only get this small share."

"What, then, is your idea of enough?" asked one.

"Is 500 catties enough?" asked another.

"No," said the critical young man.

"How about 800?"

"800? Maybe. 800 is better."

This immediately isolated him from his listeners. The per capita distribution of 450 catties had created a grain surplus for most families. True, a single person might need as much as 500 catties, but there was always additional food and income available from the private plots. To demand 800 catties surpassed all reasonable expectations. Confronted with these arguments, the young man could not hold out for long. After a couple of hours he "gave up the gun" and agreed that he was wrong.

The people found the ex-beggar who had once been a Party member more difficult to deal with. They debated with him for five days. The clash proved important, because he expressed the private thoughts of a certain minority of honest people who really had reservations about the new collective way, all those adjustments in life-style that people had to make in order to be able to work well together.

This man began with the history of his family, how he had grown up with his two brothers, sometimes working, sometimes begging. During the Anti-Japanese War all three became Communists.

One brother joined the Eighth Route Army and died in battle. The other became a full-time cadre, worked hard, fell ill, and died at home. Socialism, concluded the lone survivor, is not as good as that which existed before. "Soldiering killed my older brother. Overwork killed my second brother. I'm the only one left. In the old society my older brother wouldn't have joined the army and my second brother wouldn't have worked himself to death. Furthermore, being a laborer is better than owning one's own land. When I worked for others harvesting wheat, I ate five meals a day. Now all I get is three. What were those five meals? On rising we ate corn dumplings. At midmorning our employer sent steamed bread to the fields. At noon we ate noodles. In the afternoon we had steamed bread again and in the evening it was porridge and vegetables. Even when I had to beg, it wasn't so bad. Whenever I got hungry I just asked for something to eat. When I wasn't hungry I slept under a tree. I lay there and watched the ants climbing up and down the tree. I enjoyed myself. When I needed food I got it. If you had money you could get what you needed. Now, whatever they have, whatever they offer, you have to eat it."

People found it hard to hear this man out. As soon as he finished they asked him, "Is it true that in the old society you could eat all you wanted? In those days there were sharks' fins, swallows' nests, sea slugs and fish. Did you ever eat any of these?"

"I didn't have any money" said the ex-beggar. "If I had had money I could have eaten them."

"Well, why didn't you have any money?"

The man hesitated.

"Speak up, speak up," shouted the people.

"It was because I couldn't earn any."

"But you said you ate five meals a day!"

"No. That was only during the harvest season, during the wheat harvest."

"Well, why wouldn't the landlord give you five meals a day the rest of the time?"

"There was no harvest work. Why should he hand out five meals then?"

People easily refuted the idea that this man ate well in the old society, but the idea that he could, when he wanted to, just lie under a tree and enjoy himself intrigued some. It was his main argument in favor of being a laborer in the past rather than a master in the coop of today.

"If I wanted to work I worked. Otherwise I just quit and did nothing."

"If the old society was all that good, how come you went begging?"

"Well, in the busy season I worked. In the slack season nobody wanted me. I had to go begging."

"When there was work how many days did you work?"

"Every day, from morning to night."

"Why didn't you just quit?"

"That wouldn't do. No work, no money. No money, no food."

"So how many days do you work now?"

"200."

"That means you can rest 100 days and more?"

"I guess so."

Having forced him into this much of a retreat, his questioners bored in.

"Were you allowed to criticize in the old days?"

"How could I? I just did whatever I was told."

"Did you ever get sick in the old days?"

"Yes."

"When you got sick could you get any help from a doctor?"

"No. Where could I find a doctor?"

"What if they grabbed you and put you in the army? Could you refuse in those days?"

"No. But there weren't so many people in the army in those days either."

"But everyone in the ranks was poor. Isn't that true? They were all poor people like us."

"Yes, they only grabbed the poor."

Again and again the people forced him to the wall, figuratively speaking.

"So now you work only 200 days, you eat every day, you can speak out what is on your mind, if you're sick you can see a doctor, the army doesn't grab anybody—so how do you think your life is now? How does it compare with the past?"

"Speak up, speak up so everyone can hear," the crowd shouted.

"This man is too stubborn," said a few. "He's forgotten his origin. Let's give him a good licking."

But the Party leaders decided to treat him as a confused poor peasant. The discussion went on.

Finally the man said, "I can't debate anymore. I've lost. I'll admit there are some advantages to being a member of the coop."

The third target, the old puppet district head, stood before them as a class enemy. What he meant by "the pig will die at the hands of the slaughterer" was "the Communist Party will do the people in." Kao, the Party Branch Secretary, made him stand high on a stool so that everyone could see him, but his very presence angered the crowd. The members of the work team were afraid that the confrontation might lead to physical assault. They wanted to get the man down and away before the situation got out of control. Simply to ask him to step down, however, was too transparent. Everyone present would resent it.

"Never mind," said Kao. "I have a method."

He stepped to the front of the crowd.

"Quiet. Quiet. Listen to me. His words are vicious, are they not?"

"Yes," shouted the people, almost in unison.

"Then how can he be allowed to stand up here above the crowd? He ought to climb down and stand on the ground."

"Yes, make him come down," shouted the people.

So Kao ordered the man to step down. After a few brief exchanges the work team members led him away. Thus they defused a violent incident.

These debates, carried forward all over the county in 1958, helped to clear up some confusion. Since the organizers made a clear distinction between vicious attacks on the new society and the doubts and reservations in the minds of honest people, the movement united the vast majority who wanted to develop cooperation and isolated those diehards who preferred to go it alone.

In Long Bow village the debates that followed the events in Yellow Mill centered on the three Li brothers, Li Chüan-chung (Li-the-Fat), his wounded veteran brother, Li T'ai-p'ing, and young Li Ch'i-shun.

These three formerly poor peasants were all Communist Party members. Li-the-Fat was by this time a cadre of the hsiang or township government that administered twelve villages, including Long Bow, from Horse Square (roughly equivalent to the old Fifth District of Lucheng County). T'ai-p'ing served as a village officer of Long Bow, while Ch'i-shun remained a rank-and-file Party branch member. I have already described how these three prospered as new rich peasants after land reform, and how, once they joined the new agricultural producers' cooperative, they still managed to take advantage of their neighbors because of the large capital shares they contributed. In 1957 their fellow coop members criticized them because of the arrogant manners they had developed. Most people dared not cross them. To say nothing of the masses, these three brothers cursed their fellow cadres and everyone else. Now posters went up saying, "In the old days the landlords bullied us. How come you are bullying us now? Before Liberation you were modest and hardworking. How come you are so arrogant now?"

The real issue in the case of the Li brothers was, of course, not their attitude, but their line, the road of individual gain and profit which they managed to follow whether outside of the collective or inside it. But their attitude was what people saw most clearly and resented most keenly. The public could only approach their overall role through criticism of their attitude and of their working style.

Under a barrage of criticism Li-the-Fat had no ready answers. He squatted at the back of the room in silence, while neighbor after neighbor cursed him.

A few days later these same neighbors exposed Sun Chiu-hsiang, who had served for a time as Party Secretary of the Long Bow Branch, as a renegade.

During the Anti-Japanese War he had tipped off the puppet administration about the whereabouts of an underground fighter. The fighter was captured by puppet police and killed in the fort. When this story came to light the Party expelled Sun Chiu-hsiang from its ranks.

The debate served to expose two other coop members as counterrevolutionaries. One of these, Lin Ho-shun, had been a company commander in General Yen Hsi-shan's warlord army. His job in the coop was to operate the bean-curd mill, but he mismanaged it. Many pigs, ostensibly fattening on the by-products of the mill, died. The mill always lost money. The members accused Lin of wrecking collective property.

Coop members also exposed Yang Kuang-hung as an ex-Kuomintang member. He had once shared a courtyard with a KMT Party official. During the land reform movement the peasant Lu Ch'ing-fa won this courtyard as his new home. He tore down a wall for more room and there in a crack found some KMT membership cards. One bore Yang Kuang-hung's name. Yang would admit to nothing but his neighbors claimed the cards to be irrefutable evidence. The man was labeled counterrevolutionary.

Overall, the big debate at this time cleared up some questions about the old and the new, capitalism and socialism, and set the stage for the Great Leap to come.

31

THOSE WERE THE DAYS

When the news of Mao's support for the communes in Honan reached Southeast Shansi, cadres and activists everywhere took up the idea with enthusiasm. They formed huge commune organizations overnight. Long Bow first joined Yellow Mill Commune, a hastily constructed cooperative federation that encompassed large parts of both Lucheng and Changchih counties. Some time later this huge commune split, leaving Long Bow to link up as a brigade (a new term that year) with the new East Wind Commune that covered about half of Lucheng County. East Wind Commune embraced four sections, each comprising roughly one of the old administrative districts of Lucheng. Long Bow was in the southernmost district that centered on Horse Square. In 1959, in a further drastic reorganization, these sections became separate communes and Long Bow ended up as a brigade of Horse Square Commune. By that time the regional government transferred this whole section of Lucheng County to the Changchih City administration. The transfer came about because the area was so industrialized and included the main railroad yards of the region. This final move gave the city a rather large northern hinterland that included a fair amount of agricultural as well as industrial production. But here I am getting ahead of the story, which must begin with 1958.

In 1958 three converging movements drastically transformed life in Southeast Shansi. First came the sudden organization of the communes; second came a nationwide call for everyone to go out and make iron and steel; third came the growth on local land of an enormous crop, the fruit of hard collective work and very favorable weather. The crop, estimated to be twice as large as any that had been grown before, lifted morale, undercut conservatism, and made it possible for large numbers of people to leave home for long periods with ease of mind. As a result things began to happen at a pace and on a scale that nobody had foreseen.

Veteran Wang spoke of that year with awe:

> I was on my way to a village. I saw corn lying on the ground. I asked a peasant why he didn't pick it up.
> "Why don't you pick it up yourself?" he shot back.
> "At least you could use it for popcorn," I said.

"Who needs it?" replied the peasant.

That was the attitude some had.

Grain lay all over the place that year. There just wasn't enough transport to haul away the public grain. It was piled up beside the highway. If an empty truck came along the crew loaded some of it on. Transport regulations did not allow truckdrivers to drive empty trucks, so if the trucks went out loaded, they picked up state grain on their return. Some trucks hooked two or three, even seven or eight, trailers behind them and came down the highway looking for all the world like freight trains on a track.

In those days every commune set up little factories of all kinds. They also organized construction teams, hospitals, repair shops. The money for steelmaking came from funds transferred from the brigades down below. The East Wind Commune had tractors, a bicycle-and-cart-repair shop, a fishpond and a horse farm. The Commune also made firebrick.

With an independent income the Commune became powerful as an organization. Its cadres could concentrate labor power and wealth whenever and wherever they wished. They could requisition up to 10,000 yuan from any affluent source. If there was a good carpenter working somewhere, they could transfer him. A slip could come at noon saying that your tractor must report for work far away at 4:00 P.M. If there was a pile of bricks sitting somewhere, whoever needed it hauled it away. How were producers paid back? It was done through self-report. Example: A peasant piled 200 bricks beside the highway. Someone hauled them away. Later, through self-report, he made his loss known. Then the various units sorted out their accounts and paid for everything, or should have.

No one dared resist an order for the transfer of property. Whatever the cadres demanded, people gave—money, grain, materials, everything. The Communist Party could expel as a rightist anyone who dared resist.

Before the iron smelting started, its organizers held a mobilization meeting for cadres in Changchih. I went there representing the Rural Work Department. Speakers who represented the industrial department called on every individual and every department to support the iron and steel drive wholeheartedly.

I said, "You make steel. What has that got to do with me?"

But they ignored my question and asked instead: "How many electric motors do you have? How much wire? How many diesel engines?"

"What for?"

"You dare not conceal the facts. How much can we transfer out for iron and steelmaking?"

"Transfer! What do you mean? I came here to ask you for such things. You're one department, I'm another. How can our stuff be yours?"

"Never mind how. You go and list your power equipment and report back to me this afternoon."

The Party Secretary demanded that we transfer all our power machinery to the new drive.

I went back to my office immediately.

"They want all our machines!" I complained to our department head.

"Then don't go to their meeting!"

"But they'll come looking for me. They'll demand that I go. They'll say, 'You dare to arm-wrestle with steelmaking!' "

With all decks cleared for the new drive, my department head told me I'd better take a trip to Honan. I left just in time, just before the city-wide mobilization. The Party Secretary himself spoke to the people. I was gone, not to Honan, but to Hantan, in Hopei. Furnaces already dotted Hantan. They all sprang up within a week, all along the railroad, all along the highway—everywhere.

But even though I was gone Changchih cadres started transferring the power equipment set aside for agriculture to iron smelting sites. Since it was already autumn the effect wasn't so bad. By spring most of the stuff came back. The bulk of the people came home before the Chinese New Year, so things worked out.

The movement was tremendous. Each brigade competed against every other for records in production. Cadres high and low took part. Secretary Shih, of the East Wind Commune here, worked day and night at the furnaces along with the rest of the people under the slogan, "Temper the people along with the steel."

If it hadn't been for 1958, the Great Leap and the iron smelting, we wouldn't have the Changchih Reservoir, because the iron smelting broke the barriers that stopped people from going out. Before that, people wouldn't leave home. But once they went out to make iron and steel, everything became possible. Projects, big projects, sprang up everywhere.

We all ate well during the smelting drive—bread and noodles at midnight for all hands. Huge pots next to every furnace provided the noodles. Who can ever forget it? And then there were the skits, the drama teams, the films! All the barriers between people broke down.

"Those were the days," said Chao T'ung-min, the first member of Long Bow Brigade to join the iron smelting effort. He had gone to Taiyuan one year earlier to study the operation and maintenance of small diesel engines. On August 13, 1958, he loaded the diesel engine under his care on a horsecart and took it to T'iensheng, a brigade some dozen kilometers to the north, where the members had already set up furnaces. This diesel helped power fans that blew air for the furnace fires. As Chao T'ung-min described it:

Two to three thousand people gathered there from many different communities. They came with horsecarts, baskets and carrying poles. The smelting started with two or three furnaces. Later we built so many that we lost track of the number. At first we built them with brick from the ground up, but later we dug them as caves in the loess banks on the flanks of the hills. Either way, the overall shape of the furnaces was the same—squat and round. We filled them with coal and ore in alternate layers. We launched a big contest to see who could make the most iron in one day. Our slogan was, "Send up sputniks." That whole place turned into one big iron smelter. Smoke billowed down the valley. When we needed fuel we just went to the mine and hauled away whatever coal we saw. The miners were striving for high production. Their slogan: "Coal is the grain of industry."

As many women as men went there to work. They helped smash ore. At night we put oil lamps all over the place and lit up the countryside. At night, or whenever our iron makers went off shift, we helped the local people on the land. We helped them harvest peanuts and ate our fill. The brigade leader told us to help ourselves.

Without permission no one touched anything. Discipline was very strong. No one took a single sweet potato from the field beside the road. If anyone took as much as one potato others would criticize him or her at a mass meeting.

Only three or four of the technicians there had studied diesel engines in Taiyuan. We taught others. Since we lacked skilled people, we chose able young men and trained them. That way lots of people in the village learned a skill—how to run a machine or hook up an electric wire. These people later formed the work force for commune industries. We needed skilled people everywhere and these iron smelting projects trained them.

In those days it was easy to get people to come out and work. Nobody worried at all about their livelihood. They didn't care where the next meal was coming from. They just marched off. I went to T'iensheng. My wife went to Shihhui. We just locked our door and took off. Were we afraid of losing anything? No! Who wants anything from anyone else anyway? In those days nobody thought of taking anything. Starting in 1958 people paid little attention to private property. They just went wherever they were sent and didn't worry about anything in the world.

We combined work and military training. All militia members trained every morning. We were all young people. We kept our rifles at the worksite. When the bugle blew for practice we all assembled at once.

Those were great days! Great days!

Soon it was impossible to count the people that overflowed the worksite. The villages all emptied out because all the people went to make iron.

City people came out in busloads from middle schools, primary schools and offices. The schoolchildren carried ore in their kerchiefs or they stuffed their pockets full. The cooks who came with them set up their pots and fires beside the road.

Everywhere you go in Shansi there is coal and iron. We had everything we needed so we did not worry about raw materials. Even the firebricks we made ourselves. We were self-sufficient. We had coal-digging teams, ore-digging teams, clay-digging teams, lime-digging teams and transportation teams.

At midnight each night the coordinators held a telephone conference. "Tomorrow," they would decide, "we need 400 people at such and such a place." And tomorrow all 400 would be there.

When I first went out I thought it would take at least twenty days to prepare the site. But in a few days we finished the first furnaces and the iron began to run out. I thought we would build the project up gradually. But *ai ya!* Soon we fired furnaces all over and found the people to tend them. I had in mind that I would rest every now and then, but *ai ya!* that was impossible. I had no time to stop, and no time to return home. Who would have thought it?

Every time I recall those days I am filled with happiness.

Soon after Chao T'ung-min went to T'iensheng with his diesel engine more than 100 Long Bow people—men, women and children—went to another spot, Shihhui, to make iron. Wang Wen-te, Kuo Cheng-k'uan and Shih Ts'ai-yuan all led this contingent at various times. That same week Chang Kuei-ts'ai led a second group of ninety to Hsiangyuan County to work on a new reservoir at Hsiying, on the north branch of the Chang River. Shihhui was only seven kilometers north of Long Bow but Hsiying was fifty kilometers farther up the line.

The first 100 volunteers at Shihhui proved to be too few for the tasks at hand so delegates went back to the village to organize a general exodus. With summer hoeing completed and the fall harvest yet to come, no major farming tasks loomed ahead. Everyone who could work went out. Old women with bound feet who had never before traveled as far as Changchih City went off to the mountains to haul ore. Mothers with children only five years old took them with them. Other new mothers, as soon they could wean their children, left them with older relatives and joined the exodus. Only the very old, the pregnant women and women nursing babies stayed behind, together with a skeleton staff of village caretakers—one leader from each team, a storekeeper, an accountant, a few cooks for the community kitchen and a few people to feed the draft animals. The only able-bodied people left were the six team leaders. When the old man Chu Hung-shun died, all six had to carry his coffin. A heavy coffin ordinarily requires sixteen men. Somehow the six managed the job.

Each production team sent a group out to make iron. Each group took its own grain, its own set of cooking pots and its own system of supply. Each found a suitable camping spot and immediately built a big mud stove. At first the members slept on the ground in the open. They covered the bare dirt with reed mats or set out bricks, laid boards on the bricks and covered the boards with mats. Later, when it began to rain, the commune headquarters issued canvas tarpaulins that could be strung over the mats to form makeshift tents. Although each unit set up its own kitchen, each kitchen made hot food available to all who came along. No one planned for breakfast, lunch or supper. The hungry, regardless of unit, just stopped at the nearest kitchen and ate their fill. Kitchens lined the highway from south to north and anyone could eat out of any pot. No one kept any records. The commune committee guaranteed grain supplies to all. Behind the commune stood Changchih City. This was the solid material base behind the call, "Let the Whole People Make Iron and Steel."

At first each village contingent set up a complete production unit that did everything from mining to smelting. With each unit producing its own iron, the leadership could make comparisons and see how well each passed the test. The iron makers made low furnaces, about six feet high, and lined the floor with firebrick. They piled dry wood at the bottom, then a layer of coal, then a layer of ore, coal, ore, coal and ore until the pit was full. Then they lit it from below. There was not enough power equipment to go around so most of them fanned the flames with winnowing baskets. After about three days they could tap the furnace. As soon as iron poured out they notified the Commune Committee to come and check the results. At Shihhui the results weren't always good. The goal was to tap two tons from each heat but usually they got only one and a half. The iron was too low in quality to process directly and had to be sent on to the mill at Changchih Steel to be reworked. As could be expected, there were a lot of accidents. One furnace was powered by an electric blower. One day the power supply failed, the fire went out, and the whole molten batch in the furnace solidified. It took twenty days to hack the metal out. At another furnace the man assigned to watch the fire fell asleep. His nap almost ruined another batch.

"Right in the middle of the Great Leap, with everyone working so hard he falls asleep!" said Cheng-k'uan, still indignant after a dozen years. "Since he was a Communist it was very bad. We held a big meeting at the worksite to repudiate him. People called on the Party to expel him. But he made a self-criticism. He said he was sorry and he asked the people to forgive him. In the end they thought he had recognized his mistake, that the meeting had educated both the culprit and the masses, so they did not demand expulsion."

From the descriptions of the pace of work at this time it is hard to see how anyone kept awake. "As long as I worked at the iron smelting I made no distinction between night and day," said Wen-te. "We began working shifts, but soon abandoned that and just worked straight out, two or three days at a time."

All accounts confirmed that work was continuous. What kept people going was the food. If there was one facet of the Great Leap that everyone remembered it was the food.

"We lived well," said Wen-te. "We ate a lot of meat. It was considered revolutionary then to eat meat. If you didn't eat meat it wouldn't do. At New Year's we got ten catties of meat and assigned each family the task of eating that quota. People even vied with each other to see who could eat the most."

"Teams on shock work could stop and eat anytime, anywhere," said Ts'ai-yuan. "And they could eat all they wanted to."

The system of each village or brigade making its own iron was soon abandoned, in part to assure better quality. Movement leaders reorganized the work so that each brigade concentrated on a particular task. Since the ore at Shihhui was relatively poor, they abandoned this site in favor of

T'iensheng. There they rebuilt the furnaces to gain greater efficiency with greater height. After that the people from Long Bow dug and hauled ore that others smelted. It was one kilometer from the digging face to the furnaces. They carried the ore by cart, by carrying pole or simply by hand. Some old women just carried lumps of ore in their hands or on their backs. If the lump was too big for one person, then two people carried it.

At that time, with the first big push completed and the work reorganized, lots of people went back to the village. The original team of 100 stayed on until November, when most of them also returned home to tackle the corn harvest. But even at harvesttime several dozen stayed behind. They continued to make iron for more than a year. A few of this group never did return to their home brigade. The reorganized installation at T'iensheng with its tall furnaces took the name "East Wind Commune Steel Mill." Only in 1961, when the commune broke into four sections and Long Bow remained with Horse Square, did this steel mill break up. Then local managers converted it into an agricultural implement repair station.

Later, most of these small enterprises shut down. City and county leaders cut many small industries, which some thought should have continued, back to nothing. "The wind that blew then was an individual wind," said T'ung-min. "Industry got down off the horse. When the cutback came the cuts went all the way." And people blamed the debacle on Liu Shao-ch'i.

In summing up the technical side of this whole experience T'ung-min said, "Our East Wind iron wasn't bad. The quality was fair, unlike some other places. How much did we make? We don't really know. We only provided the people. The commune leaders were in charge and they tried to keep track. Of course some machines broke down at that time. But later we either fixed them and returned them or we paid for them."

Cheng-k'uan led the main group back to Long Bow for the corn harvest. By that time it was already late in the season. "We no sooner got back than it snowed, a very heavy snow. So we had to get the corn out of fields covered with snow. Right after we got the harvest in, a call came for a group to help build the Shimen Reservoir. Lu Chin-jung led a new group out while I stayed in the village to organize deep-digging on the land and a drive to gather fertilizer."

32

TWO DAMS
AND A RAILROAD

 By the time Lu Chin-jung and Ts'ai-yuan led their group out to work on the local dam, Kuei-ts'ai with a crew of ninety had already been working at Hsiying for more than two months. They were to stay there until the Lunar New Year, a five-month stint in all.
Kuei-ts'ai spoke of it with enthusiasm:

At first we all lived in a little village at the top of a mountain. The people loaned us their cave homes temporarily. These caves were better than Long Bow houses. All the walls were decorated with paintings. It was the custom there to pay as high as five tan of millet per cave to an artist who specialized in wall painting. All the old fairy tales were illustrated there, the villains and monsters of ancient legends, the heroes of the Three Kingdoms and also the leading characters in modern tales like *Hsiao Er-hei Gets Married*. We had never seen walls that beautiful before.

We lived in their best caves while we dug cave quarters of our own. We made them big, big enough to sleep twenty people each. Within a few days we completed our caves and we set up housekeeping on our own.

Altogether, counting the Long Bow unit, 500 of us went there from Lucheng County. Since work on the new dam didn't begin for three or four days, we volunteered to help the local people pick their cotton. We picked it all in one day. Delighted, the local people returned the favor by sending us meat. For 500 people we had organized three kitchens. When the Hsiying people saw this set up they sent each kitchen a big goat "to improve your life!"

At the worksite we tried to win awards for the fastest workers and the fastest teams. These awards consisted of extra grain. Our basic ration was 1.2 catties per person per day and this we brought with us from Long Bow. For each cubic meter of earth we moved we got another 3 catties of grain. Of this 40 percent was wheat flour. In addition we earned a 45-fen cash subsidy for extras such as salt, soy sauce and vinegar. Because we worked so fast we took in more money than we could use. And because we helped the local people harvest cotton they helped us with food whenever they could. One day the local brigade leader showed me a cave full of pumpkins. "We can't give you these for nothing," he said. "But if you give us 5 yuan you can eat all the pumpkins you want." When we needed another goat "to improve our life," they sold us one for 8 yuan. We got 30 catties of meat from it. We killed the goat on our rest day, and what with the goat meat, the pumpkins and plenty of onion greens we made some fine dumplings.

Once again, what the people remembered most vividly was the food. The good food made up for all the hardships of late fall and midwinter work. Frozen ground provided the most serious challenge. The people put their heads together to think of some way of breaking up the solid icy crust. Dynamite would do the job, but dynamite was expensive. By lighting a large fire they could melt a small circle of the frozen soil. Once they dug this away, they could enlarge the circle by digging under the frozen crust. After the crust was undermined it could be broken up with heavy hammers and carted away. But the process, once started, could not be interrupted. Any unattended land froze solid in half an hour. So work went on around the clock. If one shift went off before the next one arrived, those who were leaving covered the land with their quilts, layers of quilts, so that it would not freeze until digging could begin again.

Under conditions like this the earth movers made slow progress and some of them lost heart. A rich peasant named Ch'eng Chin-lung tried to discourage the whole Long Bow group by spreading a rumor that because of the difficult conditions the project would last several years. No one, he said, would be allowed to go home until they completed the last cubic meter of work. This so affected morale that Long Bow peasants averaged only one cubic meter per shift while others did two. At mealtime Kuei-ts'ai noticed that some of the women were crying and that the men were eating their millet with their heads down.

"What's the matter," he asked. "Why are you all so gloomy?"

"We're gloomy because we can't go home. We can't even go home at New Year's."

"Who says so?"

"Ch'eng Chin-lung," said Yang Chung-sheng, half aloud.

"That's a lie," said Kuei-ts'ai. "Don't listen to that rich peasant bastard. We'll all go home at New Year's."

Kuei-ts'ai called a meeting to confront Ch'eng Chin-lung. He had to stand before the people of his brigade, bow his head, hold his hands high behind his back, and listen to the accusations as they piled up by the dozens. He stood there until the sweat ran from his forehead.

"He said this work will go on for years! He was trying to wreck the dam. He was trying to wreck socialism," said Kuei-ts'ai.

"Yes," shouted the crowd in response. "He told us that."

"He told us more than that."

"Poor peasants and landlord bastards can never share the same spirit!"

Yang Chung-sheng became so angry he took off his shoe and ran up to beat Chin-lung with it, but Kuei-ts'ai stopped him. The bitter words of the crowd were punishment enough, he said. The meeting went on until very late that night. In the course of it the people recovered their enthusiasm, their determination to go forward regardless of difficulty. Within a day or two they caught up with and even surpassed some of the other brigades. Then a poster went up at the command post on top of the hill commending Long Bow. The poster said Long Bow people were working really well. This made everyone think and they cursed Ch'eng Chin-lung once more.

"Long Bow people never lost face before," they said. "If it hadn't been for this rich peasant bastard we wouldn't have fallen behind in the first place."

The goal set for each brigade for the week was 190 cubic meters of soil. This was for frozen soil on the north side of the mountain. Long Bow people finished their quota in six and a half days. They were the first to finish. Fu Village came in second. Some other brigades hadn't finished after eight days. Once Long Bow forged ahead, Fu Village and Changkung Settlement couldn't earn as much as Long Bow. Since these three communities all cooked together in one big pot, this created a problem. Quarrels broke out between Long Bow people, who were getting extra rations, and those from other brigades who were not. Long Bow people were eating too much while the others weren't eating enough. In the end Fu Village and Changkung Settlement borrowed 700 yuan from Long Bow to even things out. But they never repaid the debt.

"Of course that debt has been canceled," said Kuei-ts'ai. "We wrote it off."

By that time, when Kuei-ts'ai went from cave to cave to sound out the sentiment of his comrades, most of them said, "We are doing so well, we won't go home even if they send us back."

"Our work went so well and our living conditions were so good that General Headquarters invited me to come and talk about our experiences," said Kuei-ts'ai. "Since there were 8,000 people in our division altogether and several hundred team leaders attended the meeting, I was reluctant. What did I really have to talk about? What I finally said was that we didn't have any good experiences except those that we pulled out of bad ones. So I told them how we had exposed Ch'eng Chin-lung and repudiated him. The team leaders all studied this and soon other brigades pulled out a few bad apples. They painted black rings on their faces, put tall dunce caps on their heads and paraded them around the worksite. One of the Changchih brigades found two wreckers in their midst. They made hats for them out of straw mats that were six to eight feet tall and painted flower designs on their faces.

"This political struggle woke people up, it inspired them to work well. If you want to lead effectively you must grasp class struggle."

Pulling out "wreckers" raised morale, competition consolidated it. In addition to the regular record keeping that showed the relative standing of the brigades in production, special contests pitted teams against one another for prizes. For example, each company chose five very strong young men to compete in digging a cubic meter of earth out of the ground. Stakes marked out the exact areas, one meter square each. The competitors, lightly clad in shorts and T-shirts, wore numbers on their backs. Under the supervision of higher cadres, checkers stood by to measure the depth of the cut. At a given signal every man began to dig as fast as possible. They used all the strength they had. Some worked so hard they spit blood. Some worked too hard and fell ill. Record performances were posted on bulletin boards all over the worksite: such and such a member of such and such team dug a cubic meter in one hour and ten minutes. The best record Kuei-ts'ai could remember was one cubic meter in fifty minutes.

Kuei-ts'ai's tales of dam building at Hsiying soon merged with Ts'ai-yuan's recollections of the work on the Shihshaho Reservoir, on the south branch of the Chang River just west of Long Bow village.

> Our committee organized supplies well. During the night shift cooks served hot soup twice and all of us could drink our fill. They sent the soup out in carts that rode the tracks along which we moved the earth. We worked three shifts altogether. The whole project was organized like an army at war, with regiments, brigades and companies.
>
> Loudspeakers sounded all over the place announcing immediately whatever happened on the site. Leaders used them to direct the work, to issue instructions to the regiments, brigades and companies. At other times, when we struggled against bad people or bad tendencies, they wrote the incidents into plays or long rhyming poems, and broadcast them for all to hear. As if the loudspeakers were not enough, we had blackboards and big character posters everywhere as well.
>
> And this was only a part of our cultural life. Almost every day Changchih City sent out a new play or a film while we created local plays and skits right at the worksite. Each regiment had its own drama group that concentrated on living people and immediate problems. Unfortunately, when the big commune dissolved and the local administration split up, much of this written culture got lost. It was dispersed, misplaced, even burned. That is too bad.
>
> To get the complete story on the construction project [Ts'ai-yuan said], you would have to go to a man like Liu Yao-wen, one of the assistant leaders of the Changchih City government. He headed up the General Headquarters of the construction project and is still the manager of the reservoir. He is very able and he ran things firmly but well. You couldn't be soft on a job like that. He had a reputation for being li hai [fierce]. Because of this, rebels overthrew him during the Cultural Revolution, but he is back on the job again now. Each team, such as ours from Long Bow, only fulfilled a task and then went home. None of us knew what happened before or later. But Liu Yao-wen at General Headquarters still has the records of the whole project, how many people took part, how much earth they moved.
>
> All 100,000 of us lived in villages near the dam. We lived in tents, mat sheds and temporary shelters of every kind. Villages as far as ten li [3.3 miles] from the worksite served as dormitories. Many

people moved out of their houses to let dam workers move in. Our method was to go for a month, then come home for fifteen days and then go back for another month, two periods of work alternating with one period of rest. But the cadres from the city worked on a different schedule. They went out for a week at a time every three or four weeks. Thus they could still carry on their work in the city.

The spirit of the people was so high that they did not even notice the cold. Once I saw two people lying on the frozen ground under their quilts. "Aren't you cold?" I asked. "Not at all," they said. But how could that be?

One reason for such high morale was the competition. We had a *Liu Hu-lan* team of young women and a *Flying Cart* team of young men. They ran down the 100-meter dam face as fast as lightning. The way this is done, the carter climbs up on the rear of the cart pressing the end beams of the frame into the dirt to act as a brake. The cart then takes off under the pull of gravity and plunges on a wild ride to the bottom. It's like being hitched to a runaway horse.

The older women had a *Shih T'ai-shun* team, named after the famous woman warrior of the Sung Dynasty who could box and fight as well as any man and bore eight sons, all of whom became generals. They also had a *Tung Hsun-jei* team, named after a hero of the Liberation War who blew up a strategic bridge by holding dynamite against the abutment with his hands. And there was a *Lao Hua-chung* team, named after a famous general of the Three Kingdoms.

Even though they *were* old, the women would not admit any such thing. Their slogan was:

> Block the Chang river,
> Irrigate the Shangtang land.

They wrote this slogan of theirs large on straw mats, each five by seven feet, two mats to an ideograph, and placed it on the face of the dam.

This spirit helped the people, old and young, create many new things. At first people pulled the carts uphill by hand. Later they worked out a system of winches and ropes so that as the full cart went down, it hauled the empty cart up. The original rule about tamping was that a three-inch layer had to be tamped to two. But the people learned to flood the new earth with water so that they could tamp it much tighter than that and so made the whole dam firmer and safer.

We went out to build the dam in midwinter and when we came back it was already fall. Some of us immediately went out again to work on the railroad under Wang Wen-te. This time the work began close to home, across the highway, in fact, from the entrance to our village. Engineers set up the headquarters for railroad work right in Long Bow in the old orphanage grounds that now house the medical school.

Work on the new railroad that thrust its way up onto the Shangtang Plateau from the old railhead at the huge coalmine of Chiaotso in the Yellow River Valley went on for three years. Many Long Bow people went out for a period and then came home as others took their places. But Wang Wen-te, who took charge of the railroad construction crews supplied by the whole district, now called Horse Square Commune, stuck with the work for thirty-six months. At any given time he had under his command some 500 workers. They labored on the railroad embankment, section by section, from West Changchih Station all the way north to Wuyang, the village in Hsiangyuan County that in 1971 served as the northern terminus of the line. This line has since been pushed through to Taiku on the central Shansi plain where it joined the old rail line running from Taiyuan, the Provincial Capital, to the very southwest corner of Shansi at Fenglingtu. The new railroad reversed the order of construction undertaken by the Japanese, who with forced labor pushed a narrow-gauge line south from Taiku to Changchih in the early forties. Guerrillas completely tore up this line during the Liberation War (1947–50). Since the new standards for grade, curve and radius were much more demanding than the old, the new broad-gauge line frequently departed from the old Japanese route.

Wang Wen-te, still as dour and lonely a man in 1971 as he had been in 1948, was a hard person to interview. Under a cloud of criticism and unable, for the time being at least, to "pass the gate" in the Party rectification then underway, he usually answered only the immediate question put to him, and then only with a few short sentences. The subject of the Great Leap, however, transformed him. The Great Leap had quite obviously been the high point of his life. Once we got on the subject of railroad work, he talked without prompting for the better part of an afternoon, eyes shining, hands waving.

"I hesitated to take on such a big job," Wen-te said. "It meant being responsible for 500 people. But the commune leaders said they couldn't find anyone else. So I agreed and stuck with it for three years. To all of us who worked that long at it they offered permanent jobs when the Wuyang sector was completed, either as railroad workers or steel mill workers. But I still didn't want to leave home. I came back to Long Bow to work as a local cadre.

"They paid us according to a piecework system. They marked each stretch of the embankment based on the number of people available. They calculated the distance between stakes on the basis of each person moving about two cubic meters a day. Once a group piled up its quota of earth and tamped it down, their pay was calculated according to the total cubic meters completed. All our pay came as money, no grain, no grain coupons. Men and women did the same work and got the same pay. Actually, the railroad administration only paid each team for the total amount of earth moved and tamped. The team then divided the money among its members depending on their workday units.

"Why did things go so well then? Under Mao Tse-tung's leadership once the cadres take hold, the masses follow. If the cadres don't take hold but only shout orders and tell the masses what to do, then of course it doesn't work. On the railroad, whatever we had to do we discussed with everyone. We cleared everything through the people.

"In some places the digging was much harder than in others. The teams working at such places always fell behind and couldn't make their quotas, while those digging at the easy spots surpassed theirs. Then we would meet, discuss and decide on new quotas for the hard spots. With everything decided fairly, the people were happy and did their best. Even at New Year's we didn't go home. We just rested one day and then on *open door red* [the day after New Year's Day] we went right back to work.

"I got a lot of experience with dynamite during those years. We had to use dynamite to get rock for Erkangshan. We learned how to drill holes with one person holding the bit and two wielding hammers. We drilled the holes two meters deep, sometimes even three meters, then blew a little blast to enlarge the hole before blowing the main blast. Once we made our hole just right, loaded it just right, and with one blast brought down 500 cubic meters of rock. In regard to blasting, we met often to report how much rock we had moved and to exchange experiences. It would never do to have some do well while others did badly and then not compare notes.

"At one point we came on a gully that had to be filled. The time for completion of that section of the line was almost up. A hill overhung the gully. We only had to move the hill into the gully to solve the whole problem. We decided to do the job with dynamite. We dug a cave in the hill, filled it with explosives, and with one blast leveled the gully."

33

PUBLIC NURSERIES, PUBLIC DINING ROOMS

The East Wind Commune, created at the time of the Great Leap, had the power to allocate labor power, draft animals and equipment across half the county. The commune served as the accounting unit and distributed the income of every individual member from the center, as a monthly wage. This newly created collective power made possible the great iron smelting drive and the dam and railroad building projects that broke down such old habits as always staying at home, distrusting outsiders, and "mountaintopism" (local sectarianism). These massive collective efforts outside the traditional village community opened the way in turn toward experiments in collectivization inside the community. Most important were the nursery schools and community kitchens that freed women for productive labor outside the home and enabled them, for the first time in history, to "hold up half the sky."

The expansion of the village school from a three-year to a seven-year school liberated women further by putting most of the children in the community under collective care for the better part of each day. In order to supply the community kitchens with vegetables, teams pooled the private plots retained by each family as team vegetable gardens. This diverted hundreds of man-hours from private to collective production, rationalized vegetable growing, and further liberated women from home-related chores. The new-type diesel engines that came to the village in January, 1957, and the small steam engines that came that same year in July, made possible the large-scale vegetable growing of 1958. These engines could pump enough water to irrigate several acres, and that stimulated the teams to open up vegetable land even before the Great Leap began. During the Great Leap iron smelters commandeered the engines, as we have seen, but by that time Long Bow had hooked into the electric power supplied to the new cement mill across the highway and replaced the small engines with electric motors. Prior to 1958 no one had dared ask for power from the cement plant. The plant and the village collective functioned in two entirely separate organizational spheres, two different administrative worlds. Furthermore, electricity was regarded as high technology, a mysterious field reserved for trained electricians only. Ordinary villagers would not dare tamper with it. The Great Leap broke down both the administrative and the mental barriers.

Long Bow peasants requisitioned wires from commune headquarters, strung them across the road, hooked into the generators at the cement plant, and lit up the whole village. Soon every house had a light, and it became possible, with small electric motors, to grind the daily grain at a central mill instead of pushing the old stone mills around by hand as the women of each family had done since time immemorial. This constituted another step forward in the liberation of women.

The community gathered funds for all these innovations from several sources. Long Bow peasants went to work as contract laborers in the cement mill, in the railroad yards and in the railroad repair shops that sprang up across the highway to the east. The wages earned were paid to the commune, not to the individuals who did the work. The money went into the general fund, while workers earned work-point credits. The value of the credits was always lower than the industrial wages. Out of the difference the commune accumulated investment funds.

The railroad and the cement plant settled for the land they occupied with a lump sum payment to the commune. They did not call this transaction a sale, but simply a transfer for industrial use. The compensation paid amounted to the value of three years' average crops from the land. Thus the commune, though it lost the use of some land, gained some working capital.

New investment backed up by the abundant crops of 1958 put *seven guarantees* on the agenda. The seven goods and services that many communes supplied to all were food, fuel, education, medical care, housing, marriage and burial expenses. The East Wind Commune never went that far, but it did undertake to supply the first and the third—food and education. These guarantees, whether two or seven, gave people an unprecedented sense of security. Many stopped saving against illness, old age and burial expenses and began to spend money on the four jewels instead—bicycles, sewing machines, wrist watches and radios.

The saying had always been:

> When young save for a house,
> When grown save for a bride,
> When old save for a coffin.

Now the whole attitude toward savings began to change. People thought more about things they needed and wanted and less about possible catastrophes. A brisk rural market in consumer goods developed. Daily life underwent a profound temporary transformation. Even though the commune movement failed to consolidate these guarantees and most of them collapsed within a year or two, they made a lasting impression on peasant consciousness.

The huge East Wind Commune spanning half the county and disposing at one time of most of the labor power, implements and capital of forty villages according to a central plan, split into four parts by 1959. The nursery schools in Long Bow folded soon afterward. The public kitchens carried on for another two years but failed to survive the third year of poor crops in 1961. After commune accounting collapsed, village-wide cooperatives, now called brigades, took over all bookkeeping. Large collective gardens, power pumping, electric milling and electric light in every home survived and developed as brigade projects. Then, in 1973, commune leaders began to criticize brigade accounting as overly centralized and premature. Production teams of sixty to one hundred families took over the books and shared income and expenses at a much lower level than commune organizers had dreamed of. The retreat was widespread and precipitous.

While the nursery school in Long Bow lasted, local women welcomed it. Hu Hsueh-chen spoke of it enthusiastically.

"We set up the nursery when we joined the commune. The commune paid all expenses and provided schooling free for all children. In fact, we set up the nursery in two centers, one in the south and one in the north. In the south we used Chin Pao-pei's house and in the north Chang Kuei-ts'ai's old courtyard, the yard that now belongs to Lu Ho-jen. Two women took charge of each center. Chia Ching-shun's wife and Li Hsiao-mer headed the southern center. Sun Ch'uan-ying assisted them. Each center cared for from seventy to eighty children, but the numbers varied a lot depending on the season. The busier the work on the land, the more children showed up at the nurseries. Even so, a lot of parents never brought their kids. If they went out to work they left them instead with grandmothers or aunts.

"Most parents who used the school brought their children after the morning meal and then went to the fields. They picked them up and took them home at noon to eat, then brought them back in the afternoon when they went to the fields again. The children ate their main meals at home, but the nurseries still served food, corn dumplings and hot soup prepared by the public kitchens. They served these as snacks between meals.

"Our nursery was really successful. We taught the children to sing. We taught them to read a few characters and how to play games. Many visitors came to see how we ran things, and we visited nurseries elsewhere. At that time nurseries dotted Southeast Shansi. In order to learn from one another, nursery staff members and parents did a lot of mutual visiting. They went to see who was doing the best job."

When I asked why Long Bow women abandoned their nursery in the end, Hu Hsueh-chen said, "When winter came and the weather turned cold, many parents didn't want to send their children. Our nursery was a busy season project that continued through two seasons, but folded in the end."

Altogether the nursery lasted about a year. It collapsed in the winter of 1958–59 when the East Wind Commune broke up and could no longer supply funds.

The community dining room, set up at the same time as the nursery, lasted much longer, through July, 1962. At first each of the six teams in Long Bow opened a dining room but later they paired off, two teams sharing one. Thus three public kitchens operated throughout most of the period. At the start, in spite of mobilization meetings to explain the advantages of collective dining, only a minority of the peasants ate there. Any family that could spare a member to do the cooking at home did so. But later, as the food and the service improved in the dining rooms, almost everyone came.

The cooks made every effort to vary the menu according to plan. Their slogan was, "Make coarse grain fine by cooking well." Every few days a meal of wheat flour replaced the standard fare of corn and sorghum. Special dishes marked the holidays. Dining room managers competed with one another to provide the best food and the most variety. They organized two-way visits and on-the-spot meetings to discuss improvements. At the municipal level (after Changchih City took over Horse Square Commune) a vice-secretary of the City Party Committee took responsibility for improving the living conditions of the people. His sole job was to solve the problems that arose in the daily lives of peasants and workers, including food problems.

One of the three kitchens in Long Bow, the North Kitchen, was set up in the yard at the brigade headquarters. The second, the South Kitchen, operated in Shen Yün-peng's courtyard. The third took over rooms in the South Temple. Each of these establishments occupied ten sections of housing, not to mention the living quarters for the cooks (two or three per kitchen). Each contained a big stove, a large pot, electric blowers for the fire, a small stove or two and small pots for special food. Each also assembled equipment for making steamed bread, and power machines to cut vegetables. To supervise all this and buy all needed supplies each kitchen appointed a full-time supply officer. When this supply officer planned well, things went well.

What made the dining rooms so popular, once they got on their feet, was, first, convenience and, second, free supply. The convenience was at its height during the busy season, when many meals had to be eaten in the field. Then two or three cooks efficiently supplied hot food for the members of all six teams. All the team members had to do was send someone to pick it up. Without such a collective kitchen the teams had to send a porter with a carrying pole through the lanes ringing a bell and collecting food from each family in individual pots. Since it was rare for so many families to have food ready at the same designated time the bell-ringing carrier always had to wait for the late starters. The food that was prepared on time inevitably cooled off by the time it reached the field. Cooking food collectively saved labor and the food was more apt to be hot when it arrived in the field.

Even in the slack season many families found the kitchens convenient because all they had to do was send someone around with a container and bring home the meal. For single people and people with large families this was important. Others tended to put more stress on variety, on individual taste, on special food for the sick, on meals at odd hours and other special demands which the collective kitchens found hard to meet.

The peasants supported cooked meals as an item of free supply at first. In 1958 and 1959 the dining room food was actually half free and half financed by family contributions. That is to say, the collective (first the commune and later the brigade) held back from distribution enough grain and enough money (20 percent of the money income) to supply the dining rooms for half a year. Each family then supplied the grain and money needed for the balance of the year out of their share of the annual crop distribution. From 1960 through 1962 the brigade held back enough grain and money to support the dining rooms year-round and gave to each family as food one-half catty of grain per capita per day. Obviously this was not free food in any ordinary sense. Long Bow people ate no grain stocks produced by other people's labor. They consumed no foods that were not paid for with money they themselves had earned. The more food and money they allocated to the dining rooms, the less food and money was distributed as family shares. What free supply meant in this context was that the food was supplied, in part or in whole, equally to all on a per capita basis without regard to work points earned, that is, in part or in whole on the basis of need and not on the basis of work performed. In regard to food, then, the community jumped partway and then all the way to the Communist principle of distribution according to need. It was a form of leveling that gave every individual in Long Bow an equal share of food regardless of age, sex, health, strength or other criteria. Some peasants obviously welcomed this more than others, and more welcomed it widely in years of abundant crops, when ample food was taken for granted, than in years of scarcity, when food supplies posed a serious problem and the harvest did not necessarily go around. Under the latter condition those who worked the hardest and contributed the most tended to resent sharing the fruits of their labor with less productive families and individuals and slacked off in their work. The least productive, with food guaranteed, did not necessarily put forth their best effort in production either.

Free supply, by allocating equal shares to all, also brought on some waste, since families tended to take home their full share of prepared food even if they didn't mean to or could not eat it all.

In the period of reorganization and retrenchment that followed the Great Leap, cadres from Changchih City came to Long Bow more than once to look into the whole question of food distribution and the public dining rooms. They called mass meetings to gather opinions and listened to many complaints. The dining rooms, some charged, were not flexible enough with regard to mealtimes or menus. They made no special food available to the sick. They also wasted some food. Having voiced these criticisms, some peasants withdrew from the dining rooms, but a large group stayed on. The dining rooms finally collapsed during the movement to oppose the "five winds" of exaggeration, commandingness, leveling and transferring, boasting and blind directives. This came in 1962, along with a revised charter for the organization of rural communes which came to be known as the Sixty Points.

Obviously the dining rooms set up in 1958 answered a real need. Many social innovations created during the Great Leap collapsed long before public dining rooms did. They lasted longer in Long Bow than in many other brigades. In at least one other brigade under the Changchih administration they never collapsed at all. In 1971 Hsiao-sung still supplied free food prepared in public kitchens to all its members without regard to work points.

34

THE COMMUNIST WIND

In Long Bow, to this day, the Great Leap has its supporters. They look upon it as an inspiring interval, as a time when everyone ate his fill and went out to do important work imbued with high hopes and equally high spirits. What undermined the Great Leap, caused it to falter and in the end collapse, was bad weather on the one hand, and on the other, the Communist Wind. Bad weather brought crop failures, food shortages and even famine in some places. Without abundant food the population could not easily sustain big projects. The Communist Wind destroyed incentive, turned activists passive, and undermined whatever production remained after the weather turned hostile.

The Communist Wind, an irresistible push for complete equality, became the excuse for deploying labor power and capital goods on a vast scale by decision from on high without regard for property rights, even the collective property rights of production teams and brigades, and without regard for mutual benefit. Higher bodies asked large numbers of people to supply materials for and work on projects that brought no benefit at all to their local communities.

This was called *ping-tiao* (leveling and transferring). The transfer of material goods and labor power from one community to another was supposed to even out differences and guarantee an equal share to every village. In fact some received treatment that was blatantly "more equal" than the treatment received by others. Within villages the same thing happened. Village leaders often expanded free supply from free food to the seven basic requirements of life—food, clothing, childbirth expenses, education, medical care and marriage and funeral expenses. In some places they added extras such as housing, fuel for winter heating, baths and haircuts, even plays and films. With so many things on the free supply list, brigades had very little wealth left to distribute on the basis of work performed. Need became the sole criterion for income and as a result hard work developed into its own reward. The chances were good that almost anyone benefited more than the person doing the work.

Actually the Communist Wind soon developed into something more than a simple drive for equality. It generated four side drafts or adverse currents with disastrous effects on the Great Leap. Whenever the "Level and Transfer Wind" blew, the "Blind Directive Wind," the "Commanding Wind," the "Exaggeration Wind" and the "Boasting Wind" were sure to follow. With these winds all blowing together, extreme equalitarianism became almost a side issue. Cadres reported crops that never grew, allocated grain that did not exist, undertook projects that had no hope of success, and when the projects failed they reported them as triumphs. Anyone who questioned the figures, anyone who hesitated, won denunciation as a right opportunist, risked public criticism, even punishment by removal from office, demotion or arrest.

Of the "Four Winds" that blew up in 1958 perhaps the most vigorous and far-reaching was the "Exaggeration Wind." Here, in the words of Ch'en Yung-kuei, was what happened when that wind struck Tachai:

The Big Leap played an important role in Tachai. In the fall the region called a meeting for all advanced units. I went to the meeting representing Tachai. The people were happy to send me because they all felt that we had outstanding achievements; we had increased our per-mou production by over 200 catties in one year. Our total production for 1958 was 150,000 catties above that of 1957. Each person had produced 500 catties more grain than the year before. The poor and lower-middle peasants of Tachai were very pleased, their happiness was like *Chiang Fei te hutzu manlien* [their faces were as full of happiness as Chiang Fei's face is full of hair; Chiang Fei is a legendary hero who had a bushy beard].

But as it turned out, the meeting was not at all what we expected. The wind of exaggeration was blowing very hard. Anyone who had actually harvested 100 catties would report 1,000. I had no idea that things like this were going on. As a result of the all-out effort we made, we had harvested 540 catties per mou. Yet all the others reported more than that. There were "sputnik" brigades and whole counties with over 1,000 catties per mou. They said to us, "You Tachai people call yourselves advanced. But you only harvested 540 catties per mou. That's not even enough to get on the list! There is nothing good about you!"

One "sputnik" brigade reported 33,000 catties per mou. Reports came in from a 1,000-catty county and a 10,000-catty commune. Truly, Tachai was not even on the list. "Who cares for your 540 catties?"

The old Party Committee of the county and the region tried to come to our aid. They urged us to change our figures to 2,000 catties per mou. Only by such a move could we hope to get on the list! What should we do? Should we change the figures or not? If we changed them, we could get on the list. I thought about it very hard. I thought, I am a peasant. Don't I know how much the land can produce? If we change our figures, we can hold up the flag of an advanced brigade. But if we change them, all the class enemies in our village—landlords, rich peasants—what will they think of us?

At that time I thought, If I lie, if I make an empty boast, what will the landlords get out of it? They know we only harvested 540 catties. And I also thought about myself, over forty years old already. If I reported 2,000 catties, how could I ever make things square with the poor and lower-middle peasants? Even by the time of my death I would never be able to do it. I also thought, Communists can't tell lies. I can't do that.

The members of the Party Committee spoke with anger. They said, "If you don't change your figures, you can't get on the list." I said, "If you make a false report and get on the list, you will still fail." They demanded that I go and learn from those "advanced" units. I said, "Fine. I'd love to learn from them." These leaders believed that these "advanced" units had really produced such yields. They said we must learn from others, but actually they were just trying to make people change their figures to please the upper leadership.

They got all the "advanced" units together, dozens of them. Those of us from the so-called backward units who couldn't get on the list went to learn from them. Some of the supposedly backward units had much respect for these "advanced" units. They studied them enthusiastically—how they plowed, how they planted, how many seeds, et cetera. But I had ch'ing hsü [I felt upset]. I didn't ask anything. I just sat with my head back and kept my eyes shut. One corn "sputnik" claimed that they planted 3,000 plants per mou and harvested 33,000 catties, more than 11 pounds per stalk. I thought, That kind of production, no matter how you study, even if you kill yourself, you can't get it. I'm not a wai hang—a novice outside the profession—I'm a peasant. I may not know much about other things but at least I know something about corn.

So they criticized me. They saw that I was not learning and they said I was too proud to learn. They didn't actually name me. They just said, "There are some people who are too proud to learn. While some study enthusiastically, others are so proud that they don't know how high heaven is."

All the "advanced" brigades got t'e teng chiang [special awards]. The committee awarded twelve trucks in our county. It gave out tractors in even greater numbers. And all these units sent delegates to Peking to join the heroes' meeting. All those with awards went —such excitement! But I wasn't even on the list. I felt very gloomy [hui liu liu te, a streak of gray]. I wanted so much to see Chairman Mao. I had never met him. But they left me behind. Leaders of Hsi Ts'ai Commune in our county, who claimed that they had produced 3,800 catties of oats per mou, got to go. They claimed the title of "Oat King" and they went to Peking to the heroes' meeting. To comfort the "backward" units who were left behind, committee members organized a get-together with city workers, a kung nung lien huan. They elected me as head of the peasant delegation to go and celebrate with the workers. I wouldn't go. I wanted to be on the delegation that went to Peking to see Chairman Mao, but our merits were not enough. I had to go back to Tachai to earn more merit so our delegate could see Chairman Mao in the future. I was very dispirited. One of the cadres tried to reason with me. He said, "You shouldn't be so disgruntled. Those units have achieved things, that's why they were chosen." He was a member of the old Party Committee.

I said, "It's all false."

"Don't say that," he said. "You'll mess things up."

I knew him well, so I said, "Well, I'm only telling you. Don't tell anyone else."

Clearly I didn't always resist wrong things as well as I should have.

Ch'en Yung-kuei enjoyed meeting people, particularly people who were interested in the Chinese countryside. He had so much to say, it rolled out in a flood of stories, self-criticisms, exclamations, philosophical musings. He acted out each part. His hands moved, bracketing ideas. His face changed expression swiftly and completely, a rough-hewn face, craggy as the rock on Tigerhead Mountain, yet completely mobile. It reminded me of Fernandel, the great French comedian, so serious, even tragic, at one moment, yet creased with laughter the next. On his head he always wore a white hand towel tied behind in typical Taihang Mountain fashion. He wore this towel even in Peking, even while attending the national People's Congress. When Ch'en went to the city, the countryside held its own, no doubt about that.

Ch'en's voice was deep and gravelly, his vocal cords no doubt as stained with nicotine as his fingers from smoking too many cigarettes and lighting one from the other. He spoke as if he had called too often to the people breaking rock in the next ravine. His accent was pure Hsiyang, broad yet angular. Not too many tones. Shansi people don't speak in the tones of Peking. And his vocabulary—it was as rich as any vocabulary I ever heard, not only rich in words but rich in images, in colloquialisms, in imitative sounds; a knock on the door—*ka tsa, ka tsa;* depression—*hui liu liu te;* dismay—*ai ya, ai ya;* empty-handed—like a kaoliang stalk, nothing but pith inside; glory—the whiskers of Chiang Fei (legendary hero) all over our faces; pride—a tail in the air that nobody dares to touch; a plot—the weasel says Happy New Year to the chicken. No English translation can ever be more than a pale reflection of a conversation with Ch'en Yung-kuei.

In 1958, along with the "Exaggeration Wind" came the "Commanding Wind" and the "Blind Directive Wind." Ch'en Yung-kuei described their searing breath.

In 1958 we had a sharp run-in with the cadres at the commune level. Our commune leaders set aside 14 mou of land [2.3 acres] to build a 10,000-pig sty. It took a lot of labor to do the job but the commune didn't have any pigs. The only way to get pigs was to transfer them from the brigades. All the brigades that had pigs gave pigs. Tachai had 300 pigs. They wanted us to give thirty or forty. We didn't agree. After this they had to have grain; since they had pigs, they needed grain to feed them. They had no grain production at the commune level, so they wanted grain from the brigades. Once, after I had been away, I came back into the room in time to hear Chia Cheng-jang say over the telephone, "Tomorrow we will certainly send it." He turned to me and said, "We are the only ones left who have not given grain for the pigs." But I took the telephone, and said, "We're not going to give one catty of grain. Once we have sold grain to the state, the commune level cannot ask for more grain on their own."

"Comrade Ch'en shouldn't resist so firmly," one of the members said to the Party branch meeting. "He shouldn't oppose them like this. It will only bring trouble to the brigade."

But, in this struggle, if we had failed to be firm we would have gone under. Other brigades did what they were told. They sent all the pigs and all the grain they were asked to send. But we sent not one single pig, not one catty of grain, and this was based on principle. A commune is a big collective that includes several brigades or small collectives. If the large one takes from the smaller ones in a way that does not increase production but merely transfers property from small to large, we have to oppose it.

Since we refused pigs and grain, the commune leaders said, "Ta-chai cadres are *chao ao te pu te liao* [arrogant beyond belief]. No one can lead them. They are so proud they won't listen to anybody. They hold their tails straight up in the air and nobody dares touch them."

But what we did was not linked to pride in any way at all. It was a matter of line. When they wanted this and wanted that [unwarranted transfer of collective property], we refused to give it.

They reported back to all levels about us, how we had refused to listen to the leadership.

Such people knew nothing about production, yet they went around directing it, giving orders of all kinds, and throwing everything into a mess. They said you can get high yields by putting dry chopped cornstalks in with the seeds as they are planted. They spread this experience all over the county. During that week I was at a cadre meeting in Yangch'uan. Our brigade sent a comrade to call me home. He said, "We can't hold out against this if you don't return. The order says we must plant 200 mou by this method in so many days. If we don't do it there will be a big beating of drums while they send away the red flag now held by us. The county leaders say we have already fallen behind at this task, so they have ordered 300 people from Tachai to take the flag to another brigade."

"I can take the flag myself," I said. "Don't send 300 people for that."

In very low spirits, I excused myself from the meeting and got ready to go home. They didn't want to let me go. It was right in the middle of the hard years. At the cadre meeting the food was of poor quality. I was so angry I couldn't eat. They thought it was the food. "What's wrong with your health?" they asked. "Can't you eat this food?" And they asked the cook to make something special for me. But I said, "I don't need good food. My stomach is full of *ch'i* [anger]." All along the road on the way back I saw people putting chopped stalks in with the seed as they planted.

"Why are you doing it that way?" I asked.

"We were ordered to," they said. "We're not like you Tachai people. We don't dare resist."

When I got back to Tachai our people were also planting in the same way. I told them to stop immediately. We had to do the planting all over again. We covered all the holes and planted again, according to our original plan. I pointed out that some leaders were giving wild directives, blind directives, and that we had to use our own heads.

I found out later that as soon as I left the meeting a Yangch'uan cadre had called our commune leaders and told them to get the red flag from Tachai quickly themselves. They were afraid I was going to take the flag into my own hands and turn it over to the next brigade in person. So when I got there no red flag waved anywhere.

But when the repudiation of this wrong directive came along, these same cadres turned on the other brigades and criticized them for not being able to resist as Tachai had!

Such bureaucrats!

The exaggeration wind could not have started from down below among the peasants. In August, 1958, the Provincial and the Regional Committees criticized us, saying, "You don't read the papers. All over the country there are 'sputniks' reaching the sky but you are not even moving." People down below said, "Don't believe it." But some people above said, "We watched the harvest and took part in it. How can the reports be false?"

The slogan was *yi ma tang hsien, wan ma ben t'eng* [one horse in the lead, 10,000 horses gallop along]. Grain was the leading horse, and everything else was to follow. Our county was criticized at the provincial meeting. Cadres said, "You have neither one horse in the lead nor 10,000 horses following." In order to follow this slogan, some people made false reports full of empty talk.

People from above came down to more advanced brigades fanning up the wind, pushing for more and more exaggeration. Those people in the brigades who were slavish followed their lead and did whatever they were told to do.

Take the brigade that was given the title of "Oat King." My sister lives there. I asked her whether they really harvested 3,800 catties per mou [1 catty is about 1.1 pounds]. She said, "No, not even 380." She said that a piece of land that had belonged to her before the cooperative was formed, the best land near the river, had yielded only 200 catties. If you could get 240 catties of oats per mou, that would be good. But some people from above blew the exaggeration wind all summer. They reported how much land had produced so much, adding more each time, each trying to outdo the other, all exaggerating shamelessly. First, they demanded that the land produce 5,000 catties per mou. When the commune members said they couldn't do this, they finally compromised on 3,800!

Another method was for certain provincial cadres to find an advanced place, then publish false production figures in the paper.

Then people would say, "If others can do it, why can't we?" They built *yüeh chin ma* [Great Leap Horses: replicas of flying horses made out of bundles of millet or wheat], bigger and bigger, until they were so large they couldn't even be pulled in a cart. And these were supposed to represent the horse in the lead.

If this didn't come from above, where did it come from? It damaged the enthusiasm of the people and brought great harm to the national economy. All the grain they reported did not exist—empty figures. The whole state plan got messed up. Factories and other units depended on real grain for their production, not just figures on paper. Why in the end did the higher cadres conduct a checkup in 1959? Because they came down to look at grain that wasn't there. Then they had to look into the matter. Where had all the grain gone?

People who had pushed exaggeration figures damaged the planning of the whole national economy. They advocated close planting of rice and reported close planting that was so thick that a person could walk on top of the rice growing in the field and not sink in. They said there were wheat fields so thick that an egg placed on the heads of the wheat would not drop through to the ground. Propaganda of this kind cannot come from down below. The people below are peasants. They know reality. How could they have said things like this? Only bureaucrats behind closed doors can say things like this. The practical people down below would never think up such things, or dare to say them. What happened to us in Tachai also shows that this came from above. We harvested 540 catties per mou but they tried to make us change the figure to 2,000. They put pressure on us to adopt the change. All these examples show that the exaggeration wind came from above. The masses down below opposed it. But those above were so bureaucratic that they didn't care and only came down to find out the truth when grain deliveries fell short. What did they accomplish by all this? Only harm, no advantage at all.

Some people were afraid of losing their positions. They didn't dare stick up for what was right, didn't dare struggle against these wrong things. In the meantime these blind directives kept flooding down. "Spread advanced experience! Sow 500 catties per mou!" People below opposed this. Then they were criticized from above. Officials told them not to be so conservative. "To plant 500 catties of seed per mou is a good thing. If you plant 500 catties of seed and harvest in return only three catties for each one planted, you'll still reap 1,500 catties per mou."

When this wind blew so hard, it swayed us a little, too. We didn't completely resist it. We had been criticized too much. We had to do something. So we tried this kind of planting on a fifth of a mou. With our old seed drill, we couldn't even get 200 catties per mou onto the land, not to mention 500. So we just plowed the land and poured seeds all over it as if we were using an open field as a storage bin. We planted another tenth of a mou by scattering wheat on the soft ploughed ground in a thick layer. This amounted to 200 catties per mou. The harvest we got from this was 90 catties per mou. We thought this was a lot of crap to begin with, but now, after trying it out with less than half of their 500 catties we were more convinced than ever that these people knew nothing about agriculture, to say the least. But to see it in this simple way was to give them the benefit of the doubt. Looking at it from a different angle, one had to ask if they were all really so stupid. Weren't there some who deliberately set out to wreck?

From all these ridiculous examples I have mentioned here, you can see that blind directives came down like hail in our county at that time.

35

THE 10,000-MOU SQUARE

Tachai is in Hsiyang County, Central Shansi. But the same winds blew in Changchih City, Southeast Shansi, and in every other region. The Communist Wind, once it started to blow, not only seared all of Shansi, it blasted the whole nation.

"Political winds blow all the time in China," said Veteran Wang Ching-ho of the Long Bow Propaganda Team. "They blow with special intensity in periods of mass upsurge. People, on the whole, tend to go along with them, whichever way they happen to blow. It's like the situation at any big funeral. Watch closely. The horn-blower marches in front. Behind him come the family members, weeping. At the corner the street is all but blocked by neighbors who have come out, not to pay their respects to the dead, but to hear the music. They cheer and applaud the maestro on the horn. Those who are there to weep can hardly keep a straight face. In the end they, too, are drawn into clapping for the musicians. A little boy sobs, takes a cucumber out of his pocket and bites off a big chunk, then suddenly claps. When mourning is in order everyone mourns. But if applause takes over, everyone applauds."

"But if people are getting hurt, surely somebody starts complaining?" I objected.

"Down below there is muttering, but when the leaders say, 'Let's bring the problems out in the open,' the rank-and-file cadres say, aghast, 'Who? Me? Oh no. I don't want to raise any questions. I'll be called a right opportunist. I'll be labeled as backward. I'll shout when everyone else shouts, not before. I'm not going to stick my neck out.'

"The fact of the matter is," said Wang, "these tendencies such as the 'blind directive' wind usually started in a small way, as when the commune leaders called on the people to raise more chives. At the very tail end of a production meeting last summer the Party Secretary suddenly said, 'Chives are very important. Now is the time to plant them. We have ample seed. All brigades should send in for their share.'

"No study, no discussion followed. People were not clear about when to plant, where to plant, how much to plant. Some brigades had no open land to plant on in any case. So a lot of the seed never got planted, some of it never came up, and much that did come up didn't grow well. That often happened with general calls. Without concrete plans suited to the place and time they could hardly bring about a good result.

"The next spring the commune leaders called on everyone to dig wells. In Long Bow people dug several wells, then let them sit. The call came to dig wells to increase irrigation, but in spite of the wells, they made no effort to irrigate. They hadn't leveled the land, for one thing. They spent a lot of money on each well. They used as many as 20,000 bricks to line one, but they never used the new wells for water. First a big mobilization, the people dug the wells, then everything fizzled out. Nobody really cared what happened as long as the call met a response. That's called *loa min shang ts'ai* [people used, money spent]. But in the end there is nothing to show for it."

It was not easy to fix any exact point when the Communist Wind began to blow through Long Bow. It gathered momentum all through the fall of 1958 and reached its height in the spring of 1959 when the brigade attempted a 10,000-mou square, a 10,000-pig farm, excessive deep-digging and extreme close planting all at once and all on a grand scale. The effort ended in a fiasco. But even though these schemes collapsed in 1959, yields did not drop disastrously because the land had reached a high state of fertility in the preceding decade. It was 1960 before crop failure became widespread in the region, and this was due as much to severe drought throughout the mountains as it was to the excesses of the Communist Wind.

What Long Bow people remembered most vividly was the scheme for a 10,000-mou square (2½ square miles). The idea behind the square was to concentrate the labor, the implements, the manure and the expertise of a given area where they would do the most good, on the best and most fertile land. Some technicians thought that such concentration would bring about a breakthrough in yields and a larger total crop than the traditional, dispersed effort so common to the village system.

This idea came originally from the Luliang Mountains, the badlands east of the Yellow River, where the people, tired of harvesting only eight bushels an acre, stopped tilling the worst lands and concentrated all their efforts on the best. The results fully justified the method and it won publicity on a nationwide scale as the "basic farmland plan"—cut acres to increase crops.

Changchih City cadres saw an application of this plan in Chishan County, South Shansi. A whole group of city, county and brigade cadres, including Lu Chin-jung of Long Bow, went to South Shansi to look at public health and sanitation work. On the way they passed right through the middle of a specially treated 10,000-mou square at Chishan. They were impressed by the extraordinary crops and well-tended appearance of the project. When they got back they called a big meeting at the city level. There the participants decided that the East Wind Commune should try such a square.

In order to create a block of land 10,000 mou in size, commune leaders treated Long Bow, Horse Square, Kao Family Settlement and Wangkung Settlement as a single unit. To start with they recommended concentrating all the energy of the laboring people and all the productive resources of these four villages on 2,000 mou of the best land at the very center of the square. They thought that an average yield of 1,500 to 2,000 catties of grain per mou could be achieved there, and this would more than make up for land abandoned elsewhere.

They asked Long Bow people, together with the people of the other three brigades, to send their accumulated manure to a large, level stretch of land that centered on Kao Family Settlement.

"None of this land was ours," said Hsin-fa. "We didn't really want to ship our manure away but we had no way out. We thought, If 2,000 catties are actually harvested from each mou there, then we'll rely on that. In the meantime we'll plant what we can at home, just in case. But the commune leaders said, 'Never mind planting crops at home. If any village is short of anything we'll see that the shortage is made up.'

"We said, 'So be it, if we fall short we'll ask the commune for grain.'

"No one really believed that the square would produce that much. But we had to ship our manure up there because they divided up the square, gave each village a section of it, and then checked up to see how much manure and compost finally got there. There was no way to get out of it. So we organized six manure hauling teams and by midwinter had hauled almost everything away."

Soon after the peasants completed this great transfer of fertilizer the whole scheme collapsed. Two weeks after the Chinese New Year a directive came down from the Central Committee in Peking that all communes should be organized on three levels—teams, brigade, commune—and that responsibility for production should lie primarily at the team level. At this point the East Wind Commune split up and along with it all the grandiose schemes for large-scale collective projects. Each brigade pulled back to its own land and resources.

"In Long Bow," Hsin-fa continued, "we scraped what night soil we could find out of the village cisterns, carted this to the fields, and planted whatever land we could, in whatever way we could!"

Official figures presented by Changchih City cadres showed that Long Bow harvested 205 catties per mou that year. Brigade accountant Shen Chi-ts'ai's report said they reaped only 160 catties. Results in 1960 were even worse. Average yields fell to 138 catties due to severe drought throughout the area. This was little more than the pre-land-reform level.

Kao Family Settlement, which benefited from all the outside manure, didn't have anything remarkable to show for it either. Even though manure was plentiful, the land could not be irrigated and the crops all suffered from lack of water. Of the eight measures specified in the agricultural charter—soil improvement, rational application of fertilizer, water conservancy, improved seed, rational close planting, plant protection, field management and improved farm tools—only one reached optimum levels—the application of manure. As a result, instead of 1,500 catties, Kao Family Settlement harvested only 240 catties per mou.

At about the same time that the commune initiated its 10,000-mou square, it issued a directive about a 10,000-pig farm. If concentration would produce record-breaking crops, it should also produce record-breaking pigs. The idea was to concentrate most of the pigs of the East Wind Commune in one place, give them the best food, veterinary care and supervision, and thus break out in one leap from atomized family production to large-scale livestock raising worthy of the name "socialist."

Since there were very few pigs in Long Bow or any of the neighboring brigades and no tradition of pig raising such as caused almost every family in Tunliu (20 kilometers away) to raise at least one brood sow, no one did much about the 10,000-pig farm. Suddenly a high-level inspection group made up of provincial and regional cadres descended on the area. In the middle of the night Chia Feng-jung, Party Secretary of the East Wind Commune, called Long Bow's Party Secretary Kuo Cheng-k'uan and demanded that something resembling a pig farm be created before six the next morning.

"Put up a gate, anything! Show that we are moving on it."

Cheng-k'uan sent to Peishih for a professional stage builder who for 10 yuan (about ten-days' wages for the average peasant) worked all night lashing poles together to form a great arch. Brigade members decorated this arch with red silk cloth, slogans, posters, bundles of wheat straw and red lanterns, and christened it "Great Leap Gate."

At five o'clock in the morning, when Cheng-k'uan saw the arch standing there at last, he went home to bed. He no sooner fell asleep than a commune cadre woke him up. "They will be coming soon," said the cadre. "Better check the whole village and make sure everyone gets out to the fields. It won't make a good impression to have anyone standing around here."

At six Chia Feng-jung called.

"Is everything ready?"

"Yes."

A truckload of well-fed cadres left commune headquarters at about eight, drove south through Horse Square, and then turned off toward Kao Family Settlement. It passed through a section of the 10,000-mou square and right in front of the Great Leap Gate, but bypassed Long Bow village itself.

"This," said Chia, with a grand sweep of his hand, "is our 10,000-mou square, and this is the entrance to our 10,000-pig farm."

The truck did not even slow down, not to mention stop. Nobody apparently even thought of getting down to walk through the archway to see what might be behind it. They accepted Chia at his word and disappeared down the highway in a cloud of dust.

Soon word came from commune headquarters: "Take the arch down." Cheng-k'uan went out with a crew and dismantled it. But this was not the end of the 10,000-pig farm. Long Bow peasants actually built some pens in the field where the Great Leap Gate had stood. When they couldn't find any pigs to inhabit them, they abandoned the pens, whose adobe walls gradually crumbled away.

"These visitors from on high," said Hsin-fa, "they sit in the commune office and listen to an impressive report: 10,000-mou square! 10,000-pig farm! Then they eat a big meal and depart! This is the ill wind that Liu Shao-ch'i blew up."

Because this wind blew so hard at the time, Long Bow sent two of its best mares to the 10,000-horse farm at Yellow Mill. The two mares stayed away for a year and a half. During that period one of them had a foal. When the horse farm broke up it sent three horses back to Long Bow, instead of two.

In 1959 not only did the call go out to concentrate compost and pigs, the call went out to concentrate plants as well. Commune cadres asked every brigade to set aside land for experimental plots; first and foremost among the experiments came close planting trials. "Plant 100 catties and reap 10,000! Plant 200 catties and reap 20,000," said the call.

"The people called this a lot of hot air," said Cheng-k'uan. "How could 10,000 catties ever grow on one mou? But no one dared oppose the idea publicly. If you did so you'd be called a right opportunist. We never planted very much at those rates, however. The peasants opposed it too strongly. In the spring the millet shoots came up like the hairs on your head. We told the people to thin it. But even after they did so, the millet never grew."

Along with close planting came the idea of deep-digging. This was an advanced technique recommended by a brigade in Honan. Veteran Wang had gone to Honan to see the results. There the people had taken shovels and turned the top six inches of soil out over the land beside it as a plow would turn a furrow. Next they had turned over the exposed subsoil to a depth of one foot. Then they turned the adjoining strip of topsoil over onto this stirred subsoil, as a plow would turn it, and exposed a new strip of subsoil. In this manner they turned the whole field and stirred it to a depth of one and a half feet without bringing subsoil to the surface or moving it laterally. The result was said to be a sharp rise in yields that could be attributed to increased aeration, water percolation, root penetration and other favorable factors brought on by deep tillage. In Honan the people planned to dig one-third of their land by this method each year and thus ensure high yields for a long time to come.

While Wang was investigating this deep-digging in Honan, word came that in Shansi people had already learned to till to a depth of three feet, not just a foot and a half. When Wang asked the Honan people about this they expressed surprise. They had never heard of digging three feet. But when Wang got back to Changchih colleagues told him a foot and a half was considered backward indeed. The slogan now was, "Dig three feet and harvest 10,000 catties per mou!"

To show the way at East Wind Commune a team of Changchih cadres came out to dig beside the highway. The land belonged to Long Bow. They dug and turned the soil to a depth of one meter, but were not very careful. They left a lot of subsoil on top. Fortunately they never finished the first field. They had dug only a few mou when the call came to build the 10,000-mou square. They dropped everything and rushed off to help lay out the big square and haul manure to it. This project no sooner got well underway then the call came for the 10,000-pig farm. The Changchih cadres then went there to start building pens.

"I remember the confusion clearly," said Kuei-ts'ai. "I took part in it all. First we were digging three feet deep along the highway. Then we rushed to the 10,000-mou square to dig out cornstalks to make ready for plowing. We no sooner got there—some people were in fact still on the road—when the call came to go to the 10,000-pig farm.

"Plans couldn't keep up with changes and changes couldn't keep up with the telephone calls!"

At the height of the euphoria of 1958 people dared to think impossible thoughts. No goal seemed beyond the capacity of an aroused peasantry.

One brigade secretary proposed that his unit purchase a truck. Sometime later, when he was criticized for conservative thinking, he said, "Well then, let's buy an airplane."

The Party Secretary of Purple Vegetable Garden decided that since he and his collective were on the way to Communism they ought to go modern. He bought a car for his personal use. It was a Polish car, shipped all the way from Warsaw. He bought it to show how prosperous his brigade had become. But he never dared drive out in it because even the secretary of the City Party Committee didn't have a car that could match it. Since he couldn't risk putting others in a bad light by using it, he finally decided to sell it.

Old Tsao, the Party Secretary, suffered teasing about that car for many years.

"Old Tsao, loan me your Warsaw car," said a voice from the New Year's crowd in 1959.

"Who said that? Why don't you get lost!" retorted Old Tsao.

He hoped everyone would forget his Polish car, the sooner the better.

When regional cadres first proposed the Changchih Reservoir, they talked a lot about all the fine buildings they would build on its shores. In the end none of them was ever built, but the people of Horse Square did decide to build a Great Hall of the People. Cadres asked each family to bring a piece of wood for this project. Thus they transferred a lot of private timber to the public domain. They wanted to build their Great Hall beside a lake. Under the direction of the Commune Committee hundreds worked hard to dig out an artificial lake and stock it with fish. They threw up a high brick wall around the water and completed it with four gates, each facing one of the cardinal directions. Unfortunately they undertook all this in the middle of winter. In the spring, when the ground thawed, the wall fell down.

36

THE BIGGEST CASUALTY

 During the high-pressure days of the Communist Wind, cadres stretched truth to the point of exaggeration and expanded exaggeration to the point of lying. As the popular rhyme put it:

> Reports that glow
> To your leader show;
> The more we show,
> The brighter the glow;
> The brighter the glow,
> The more we show.

Commune leaders cursed Long Bow's Kuo Cheng-k'uan as a "rightist lump" because he always gave honest answers. In 1958 one of these leaders took some visiting cadres from Changchih City out to see the results of some deep-digging.

"This land," the commune man announced, "has been dug a foot and a half deep."

Cheng-k'uan put his hand down into the soil, felt around, and said that the depth couldn't possibly be more than six inches. This caused the commune leader to lose face. He got angry. Once the higher cadres left, he criticized Cheng-k'uan severely.

Back at brigade headquarters Hsin-fa also criticized Cheng-k'uan.

"Why on earth did you tell him it had been dug only six inches deep?" asked Hsin-fa.

"It was the truth."

"But if he says it's one and a half feet you should agree. Why make trouble?"

"But I was only telling the truth!"

"If you insist on telling the truth you'll only earn curses."

Hsin-fa's prediction came to pass when the Commune Party Secretary called in the spring to ask how much manure had been hauled out per mou.

"We hauled all our manure to the 10,000-mou square," said Cheng-k'uan. "There's nothing left to haul to the fields here."

"Why tell him that?" remonstrated Hsin-fa, lowering his voice to a whisper. "Just tell him you have hauled out plenty, a big amount. No one will ever come to check. Just give him a big figure. You can't afford to tell him the truth. He's at the other end of the telephone line and will never know the difference. Just tell him we sent out 5,000 to 6,000 catties per mou. If you go against him like that you'll get yourself in trouble. He's a big potato. We're only little village chips."

"But I'm telling the truth. I'm objective."

"Ha," said Hsin-fa. "Objective! The first rule of objectivity is to take notice of the wind. Figure out which way the wind is blowing and sail the boat accordingly. If he plays the game of truth with you, you can play it with him. But if he comes up with empty stuff, you should come up with empty stuff in return."

Cheng-k'uan, however, was stubborn. He clung to his own idea of "objectivity." He went to a meeting at the commune office to discuss increased sales of grain to the state. Even though Long Bow had already sold all the grain that the quota called for, Secretary Chia, reading from a prepared list, asked Long Bow for another 30,000 catties.

"We won't sell any more. We can't sell any more. If we do we won't have enough to get through," said Cheng-k'uan.

He arrived home in a very bad mood. Hsin-fa asked him what had happened.

"They asked for another 30,000 catties," said Cheng-k'uan, "but I refused."

"How could you do that? If they ask for it you can't resist!"

"Well, I won't give any more," Cheng-k'uan said. "And I won't go to the next meeting either."

"Well," said Hsin-fa, "someone has to go."

In the end it was Hsin-fa who went.

Secretary Chia asked if he had prepared the grain for shipment. Hsin-fa assured him that he had, but after the meeting he went to Chia's house.

"What have you come for?" asked Chia.

"Well, the 30,000 catties you are asking for, we have it, but that's all we have to eat."

"How much will you sell?"

"Well, we can sell some. Maybe 10,000 catties."

"It's got to be at least 20,000, no less."

"That's too much."

"15,000. I absolutely won't settle for less."

"10,000."

"Get out of here."

Long Bow Brigade leaders finally agreed to sell 15,000 catties. They agreed to sell that much, but when they calculated how much they would need at home before the summer harvest they found that they would fall 40,000 catties short.

"In the end they had to send us 40,000 catties," said Hsin-fa. "They couldn't let us eat less per capita than the year before, so they had to send back 40,000. At first they didn't believe that there was no more grain here. But later, when it became clear that we didn't have enough to eat, they gave the grain back."

Thus Hsin-fa accomplished by a roundabout route what Cheng-k'uan could not do directly. Because he fell out with Secretary Chia so often Cheng-k'uan lost his job as Brigade Party Secretary. Chia transferred him to the Blacksmiths' Cooperative at Yellow Mill. Since this was a commune-level enterprise the people of Long Bow thought that he had won promotion. Actually Chia set him aside because the commune leaders considered him a "rightist."

Chia then appointed Hsin-fa to Cheng-k'uan's post as Party Secretary of the Long Bow Brigade, but he served in the post only ten days.

"At that time," said Hsin-fa, "work was different from what it is today. You couldn't lead anything if you couldn't make financial estimates. Comes a phone call, you give a figure. Comes a higher cadre, you give a figure. It's figures here and figures there. No one goes to the fields to check. But if you can't make estimates you get trampled on.

"A call came to spread 100 tan of compost per mou. If the call was for 100 we'd offer 90. They would then say, 'Hang up and make up the ten.' We would do absolutely nothing. Then they'd call again and ask 'Have you enough now?' And we'd say, 'Yes, everything is OK now.'

"Every day I had to report figures to the Commune Party Secretary. He wanted production figures, yield figures, storage figures. Sometimes he wanted them over the telephone and sometimes he wanted them in person. Then I had to go Horse Square to report. In the end I told him, 'I can't report all these figures.' 'Who can?' he asked. 'Lu Chin-jung,' I said.

"So they sent for Lu Chin-jung. He served as Party Secretary until 1966.

"But Chia trusted me all the way," said Hsin-fa. "I always told him what he wanted to know. I never got in his way. Of course, we didn't dare exaggerate on too large a scale. We had to estimate our harvest carefully. If we estimated low we could be accused of being rightists, but if we estimated high then we had to sell a lot more to the state, so naturally we didn't want to report figures that were too high. We'd prefer to report less rather than more. It is the higher cadres who don't have to come up with their own grain who tend to inflate the figures. In those brigades that reported high figures the peasants had to hand over grain that had already been divided out to individual families."

More serious than the collapse of any of the big schemes dreamed up under the influence of the Communist Wind was the collapse of the morale of the peasants. They saw little else but conflicting orders, emergency tasks and finally chaos. First consolidate, then divide; first send manure, then plant at home; first enjoy free supply, then take whatever you can find. After the collapse of the 10,000-mou square, members of the Long Bow Brigade planted a few catch crops at home, then more or less gave up. They no longer had any reason to work hard. Half a year's hard work had already gone down the drain.

Bad as this was, in the long run the biggest casualty of all was the habit of telling the truth.

As the summer crops, such as they were, ripened, some people began stealing right out of the fields. The public kitchen still operated, but all that one could get there was a few ounces of watery gruel. If one wanted more grain there was only one way—to take it wherever you could find it.

The old Catholic, Shen Ch'uan-te, justified this with a little rhyme:

> 100 people,
> 100 flowers bright,
> Stealing from your neighbor
> Never can be right.
> But stealing from the public
> Brings no shame.
> If you don't do it,
> You have only you to blame.
> However hard you work,
> You will never make it.
> The only way out is
> When you see it, take it.

Long Bow, by going along with the 10,000-mou consolidation scheme, had really suffered. Other brigades such as Anyang refused to pool animals or land, resisted the Communist Wind, and came through intact. But the commune cadres made life very hard for Anyang's Wang Hsin-nien. (His parents named him Hsien-nien, which means New Year, because he was born on New Year's Day.) Old New Year Wang insisted that Mao Tse-tung's view of a commune could not justify random transfers. "You people are just blind. You follow with blind loyalty. Mao Tse-tung never said that the land will produce as much as people dare to think about." When he refused to give away horses, pigs and land, they pinned some labels on him, called him a rightist, and took what they wanted anyway. Anyang's horses and pigs had to be seized, but Long Bow gave away everything voluntarily, including its precious manure. People ended up with nothing to put on the land.

"So that year our people just lay down on their kangs and wouldn't move," said Hsin-fa. "They didn't care whether they produced or not. 'Let the commune feed us,' they said."

A mental attitude of depending on the commune and on the Changchih City government spread widely that spring. "If we harvest more we won't get to see it anyway because the state will purchase more. If we harvest less and run short, the state will come to our aid," people said. They stopped worrying about whether the crops grew well or not and harvested whatever the land gave. If higher cadres came down to inspect, they took them to see the best land. If they had to pass some poor land on the way they said, "That land belongs to the village over there."

These attitudes had first appeared at the beginning of the Great Leap when the East Wind Commune instituted a wage system. At that time each member of the huge collective received three meals a day and 2½ yuan in wages regardless of work done, even if he or she did no work at all. This method, known as the "three guarantees," held sway for about a month. Then the commune ran low on grain and money and the whole system collapsed. But word had already spread that the equalitarianism of the "three guarantees" was "Communism." In response the peasants began to develop an attitude toward "Communism," and that attitude was skepticism. Since everyone could eat free of charge and everyone who lay at home all day got paid, those who had always been most active began to slow down. If one could eat and earn whether one worked or not, why work?

Now, long after the wage system had collapsed and the brigade members were, in fact, back on their own, this attitude still dominated their approach to collective production. When it came to private enterprise—well, that was a different story.

Ironically, in the midst of all the calamities of 1959, Long Bow peasants earned a higher return per workday than they had ever earned before or were to earn for many years thereafter. In cash terms each workday that year brought 1.35 yuan. This was the result of completely unforeseen circumstances that amounted to profiteering in the face of adversity—a foray down the capitalist road that the cadres and people of Long Bow launched by default, so to speak.

What happened was this: After the collapse of the 10,000-mou square, several half-hearted attempts to plant crops without manure, and a spreading drought throughout the area, the commune (now reduced in size to the Horse Square section of the original East Wind giant) called a meeting for the purpose of salvaging whatever could be salvaged from the impending debacle. Cadres allocated interim production tasks to various brigades. They asked Long Bow, because it already had some wells and a few acres of irrigated gardens, to concentrate on turnips, cabbages and other vegetables. They also asked Long Bow to expand brick production at the already existing kiln. As a result of this conference Long Bow assigned a large number of people to brickmaking. The second and fifth teams pooled resources and planted 300 mou (50 acres) of vegetables, while other teams planted another 50 mou (8.3 acres).

These enterprises all paid off handsomely. With new construction still proceeding everywhere, bricks were in great demand. Long Bow peasants earned money not only for making bricks but for transporting them. At the new cement mill just across the highway bricks brought 60 yuan a thousand. Vegetables, in scarce supply throught the Southeast Shansi Region, did even better. Eggplant that usually sold for 12 fen a catty in city markets brought 50 fen right in the field. Cabbages and turnips brought the same high price. Individual members resold the vegetables distributed to them in small lots at even higher prices.

Not only did prices soar that year, no one controlled weight or quality. At the kiln workers stacked bricks 250 to a pile, but these piles included half bricks as well as whole ones. Those who hauled the bricks didn't care. After all, the bricks were for public construction. Those who received them didn't raise too many objections either. With bricks so scarce, they overlooked a short count, even numerous half bricks. Builders welcomed building materials at almost any price.

Sellers usually weighed vegetables, but in 1959 neither buyer nor seller took time for that. Long Bow people simply piled their turnips, cabbages and eggplants on the ground and estimated the weight by the piles. "This plot has 10,000 catties, that plot has 6,000." Even though they always estimated high, never low, the buyers paid the price and hauled the goods away without asking too many questions. There were plenty of other buyers scouring the countryside looking for food in any form. Some approached the brigade through the "back door," offering black-market prices that far exceeded the public price of 50 fen.

"Our collective consciousness wasn't very high then," said Hsin-fa. "If we could earn money for the brigade selling bricks and turnips, to hell with the factories, to hell with the consumers. We'd collect what the traffic would bear. Now we know that this attitude is not correct. With the education that we have today, we look back and see that lots of things were wrong. Today everyone has to tell the truth. There is no place for exaggeration or lying."

I took his words as a statement of the way things ought to be, of what the authorities wanted me to hear, and not as any summation of the real state of affairs. Exaggeration and lying could not, after all, disappear that quickly.

And so it was that in 1959, that year of retrenchment, disorganization and drought, Long Bow peasants enjoyed a most prosperous season. With brigade accounting, the high income from brickmaking and vegetable growing benefited all teams equally. The return of 40,000 catties of grain from the State Trading Company also assured adequate grain rations. Slowly the situation stabilized, life improved, and spirits rose.

"That Communist Wind really got us in trouble," said Cheng-k'uan. "If we had continued down that road we would have died of starvation in the end. In nearby villages scores of people did starve to death. Another two years and things would have been worse than in the old society. Chairman Mao sent us some relief grain and saved our lives."

Attributing the arrival of relief grain to Chairman Mao was purely figurative on Cheng-k'uan's part, a statement automatically equating the Chairman with the Communist Party and the Central Government. Actually, by the time relief became necessary in 1959, Mao Tse-tung had already relinquished his post as Chairman of the Republic and had gone on the defensive politically, facing the most serious challenge to his leadership since the thrities.

In 1958 it was Mao, acting on his own and relying on his prestige as supreme leader of the revolution, who seized the initiative, launched the Great Leap, spurred the tempestuous formation and expansion of communes, and called into being the nationwide drive to smelt iron and steel in backyard furnaces. These movements no sooner got underway than serious disproportions developed throughout the economy. While, on the one hand, local cadres launched many great works of capital construction, and small collective enterprises sprang up like mushrooms, on the other, they misdirected vast amounts of capital, squandered countless man-days, and bankrupted numerous enterprises soon after they set them up. Bumper harvests lay in the fields unharvested because everyone had gone off to more glamorous projects. In an atmosphere of euphoria that caused people to exaggerate every achievement, production in many places, far from going up, actually went down. When the Central Committee met at Wuhan in

November–December, 1958, the disarray was already serious enough to force a reappraisal of commune structure, a criticism of rampant equalitarianism, and a reaffirmation of the principle of payment according to work. Colleagues prevailed upon Mao to resign as Chairman of the Republic and Liu Shao-ch'i assumed the post.

By the time the Central Committee met again at Lushan in July–August, 1959, bad weather had escalated the consequences of disproportion and mismanagement to the level of disaster, driving some regions to the brink of famine and others beyond the brink. The crisis in agriculture spilled over into industry, causing shortages in almost every item of daily use. The Central Committee could hardly avoid calling Mao to account for the miscarriage of his grand design.

The Chairman's foremost critic at Lushan was General P'eng Teh-huai, vice-chairman of the State Council, Minister of Defense and a prestigious old soldier who in 1928, at the age of twenty-seven, had led an independent uprising in the army of the Hunan warlord Ho Chien and set up a workers' and peasants' government in an isolated section of Hunan. P'eng had then gone on to link up with Mao Tse-tung and Chu Teh. Together they formed the Red Army on Chingkang Mountain. Two years later, as commander of the Fifth Red Army Corps, a force of 8,000 men, he routed 60,000 of Ho Chien's troops, took the city of Changsha and held it for ten days. On the Long March he led the First Army Corps to Yenan and, as resistance mounted against Japan, took this corps eastward across the Yellow River all the way to Southeast Shansi, where he set up a base in the Taihang Mountains flanking Changchih. This base was later expanded into the Shansi-Hopei-Honan-Shantung Border Region, an area with a population rivaling that of France. The young men of Long Bow, such as Shih Ts'ai-yuan, who joined the Eighth Route Army in 1938, actually joined P'eng Teh-huai's Eighteenth Group Army. They were recruited into Regiment 688 (old Red Army Regiment 35) of the 129th Division commanded by Liu Po-ch'eng, with Teng Hsiao-p'ing as their political director.

When Lin Piao retired as commander of the Chinese Volunteers early in the Korean War, it was P'eng Teh-huai who replaced him and successfully directed the Chinese military effort until the cease-fire was negotiated in 1953.

P'eng owed his position in the Party, the army and the government to no patron. He earned his rank and status by meritorious service; his prestige, both among the people and the rank-and-file of soldiers, was enormous, in part because he lived a simple life not only before but after Liberation. As a commander he shared weal and woe with his troops; as an administrator he kept in close touch with the life lived by ordinary Chinese citizens. Everyone agreed that he had the common touch. Of the various leaders who came to Double Bridge to visit the tractor school while I taught there, only P'eng Teh-huai insisted on taking a ride on a tractor. I arranged for it myself.

In the course of thirty years of fighting and building, General P'eng also made his share of mistakes, the most serious being the launching of the 100 Regiments Campaign in the Taihang Mountains in 1939. It was a premature effort at all-out mobile warfare that led to serious defeats and set back the resistance movement several years. Perhaps it was this painful lesson that made General P'eng particularly sensitive to premature, ill-prepared offensives and influenced him to take the chaotic, often disastrous results of the Great Leap more to heart than others. Perhaps because of this he dared voice objections and, when Mao took him on, dared talk back. "If Chairman Mao can yell at me, why can't I yell at him?" he asked his wife. Mao's version of what P'eng Teh-huai said was, "You fucked my mother for forty days, can't I fuck your mother for twenty days?" On the Central Committee P'eng considered himself, with reason, an equal among equals.

At the Lushan meeting P'eng circulated a memorandum that summed up the post-Leap crisis as "three parts natural calamity and seven parts man-made disaster." The disaster he attributed to "subjectivism" and "petty bourgeois fanaticism," an attempt, through sheer willpower and enthusiasm, to leap to higher levels of production without regard for the limitations of the material base, the productive forces available.

There is no question that P'eng's criticism had merit. He had wide support from other Party leaders for his views and the facts cited were obvious to all. A few years later Mao summed up the Great Leap in almost the same terms. Unfortunately, debate on the issue was cut off. The very validity of P'eng's criticism created a crisis inside the Party, for it raised the question of a line mistake on the part of Mao Tse-tung. If Mao agreed to settle the issue on its merits and assumed responsibility for the disarray in the country it would seriously compromise his ability to lead China, perhaps even force his retirement. In a country less subject to feudal formality and reverence for rank and status, such a policy failure would almost certainly have brought new faces to power. But this neither Mao nor many other old comrades were prepared to accept.

Confronted with a dangerous challenge to his authority and prestige, Mao prevailed on Liu Shao-ch'i and Teng Hsiao-p'ing, who had already assumed responsibility for the day-to-day operations of the Party and state, to join him in an all-out counterattack on P'eng Teh-huai. In return for a free hand to revise national policy as they saw fit, Liu and Teng agreed to what can only be called a frame-up of P'eng Teh-huai. They eased Mao into semiretirement with all possible honor, while they sent P'eng packing in disgrace.

Party documents called P'eng a right opportunist leading a clique against the Party, the people and socialism. They attacked his much admired candor and frugality as feigned, a ruse to win support so that he could split the revolutionary ranks. They denounced him as a hypocrite, a careerist and a conspirator who represented the bourgeois enemy in its protracted struggle against the proletariat. All these slanders circulated through the Party, not simply in the form of speeches and written articles, but as the content of a resolution of the Eighth Plenary Session of the Eighth Central Committee meeting on August 16, 1959. The condemnation could not have been given any greater authority. Significantly, the chairman of this conference was Lin Piao, and when on September 17 the Central Committee dismissed P'eng Teh-huai as Minister of Defense, it appointed Lin Piao in his place.

Revolutionary leaders settled the confrontation at Lushan by a deal in the imperial tradition, one that saved face for the supreme ruler by making a scapegoat of his foremost critic, and one that, at the same time, usurped some of his power. This deal resembled other curious compacts in China's long history, especially the deal by which the Ming emperor Chia Ching removed Councillor Hai dui from office, a parallel that was not lost on P'eng Teh-huai and his peers. It also had a certain resemblance to the prewar compact made by Chiang Kai-shek in Hsian, the compromise that united China for resistance to invasion from Japan.

In 1936 Chiang Kai-shek went to Hsian to force Generals Chang Hsueh-liang and Yang Hu-sheng to mount an offensive against the Communist-held base area in the Yenan region. But the generals, who were tired of fighting other Chinese, demanded a chance to strike back at Japan instead. They turned on Chiang, arrested him, and threatened him with death. Mao Tse-tung saved Chiang by sending Chou En-lai to negotiate his release. Chiang agreed to call off his anti-Communist drive. The Communists agreed to give up their land revolution. Together they agreed on a common front against Japan. But to save face, to preserve his prestige, Chiang was allowed to take Chang Hsueh-liang back to Nanking with him as a prisoner. In spite of the fact that General Chang was absolutely right about the situation in China, right to challenge the Generalissimo's civil war orders and right to demand that Chiang reverse his priorities and take on the Japanese, he had to be punished for insubordination. It was a case of *lèse-majesté*. If Chang had not submitted, Chiang Kai-shek would have found it difficult to maintain his footing as China's head of state. For the young general from the northeast the surrender was a tragedy. Chiang Kai-shek never released him. When Nanking fell to the People's Liberation Army in 1949 he was taken to Taiwan, still under guard. He continued to live there in detention for thirty years.

The sacrifice of P'eng at Lushan enabled Mao to maintain his image as supreme leader, hold on to his most important post, that of Chairman of the Communist Party, and prepare for a comeback to full power at a later date. Liu, Teng and other leaders went along presumably because upholding Mao's prestige seemed, at the time, most necessary for stability and unity and was therefore in the best interests of the nation. They also went along because Mao had enough support and political sagacity to throw the whole Party and government into prolonged upheaval if his minimum demands were not met. Mao is reported to have threatened to return to the country-side and raise a new guerrilla army if the Central Committee upheld P'eng. On his part, Mao had to surrender the day-to-day leadership of the nation and go into semiretirement.

It is possible, all things considered, that both Mao and those who collaborated in this deal, reluctantly or otherwise, chose the best of several bad options. The prestige of a national leader, especially one of Mao's stature, can never be lightly jettisoned. Nevertheless, the price paid was extraordinarily high. It undermined democracy inside the Communist Party, violated party by-laws, and betrayed decades of commitment to the principle of "seeking truth from facts," which Mao had always publicly upheld. P'eng had done nothing against the norms of Party behavior. He had not operated behind anyone's back. He was well within his rights in voicing criticisms and suggesting solutions. His criticisms, furthermore, had to be taken seriously because they were grounded in reality.

Unfortunately the legitimacy of P'eng's actions and the validity of his views became irrelevant as soon as it became clear that they threatened Mao's position. Mao's role in the crisis could not be debated without rocking the foundations of the state. With the chickens coming home to roost, the majority of the Party united to drive them away by lifting Mao onto a pedestal where he retained little administrative power and by denouncing P'eng Teh-huai. They preserved Mao's image, but they badly mauled the credibility of the Party built up over many decades and undermined the whole process of reform through self- and mutual criticism. After Lushan it became difficult for any Party member to speak candidly about himself or anyone else. Who could be sure of a fair hearing? Preserving the prestige of power holders could always take precedence over the need to study facts and solve problems. "Which way does the wind blow?" could not help but climb toward the forefront as the first criterion of truth.

The ultimate consequences of this retreat from principle are impossible to estimate. In the course of the Lushan meeting Mao shed a lot of democratic clothing, the garments of a comrade, in order to don, layer by layer, the vestments of a sovereign. He climbed the stairs toward a life apart, where he would be exempt from the rules governing ordinary mortals. As Mao rose, his colleagues fell from the status of companions to that of subjects, and with this shift China came perilously close to closing that circle that had so often been closed before—the establishment of a new dynasty on the ruins of the old through peasant rebellion.

One cannot avoid the conclusion that what happened at Lushan was a power play, but that does not mean, as alleged by Simon Leys,* that the protagonists had no policy differences. Mao disagreed on principle with the Party leaders who challenged him. A running battle over policy enlivened the fifties, sixties and seventies, right up to Mao's death, and still continues to this day. The tragedy of Lushan occurred when the imperatives of power overwhelmed policy differences, forcing the deal makers on each side to justify the shoddiest actions and the flimsiest explanations on the grounds that these preserved their power to act for the common good. Even P'eng, under duress, sullied his integrity with a shameless confession of guilt and a plea for a second chance. It would be naïve to think that policy questions can ever be disentangled from questions of power. Without power no one can put ideas into practice. Nevertheless, there are, surely, degrees of entanglement and disentanglement. At Lushan the contest for power so dominated the arena that questions of policy became virtually irrelevant. Settling anything on its merits became impossible, and the surreal, Catch-22 atmosphere created by the clash influenced the whole future. Once the revolution created its own "throne," all that was needed was a crisis that called into question the mandate of the occupant. Then events immediately thrust China back into a familiar pattern summed up so well by Sun Yat-sen:

"The imperial throne has always been fought over, and all the periods

*The Chairman's New Clothes (New York: St. Martin's Press, 1977), pp. 101–7.

of anarchy which the country has gone through have their origin in the struggle for the throne. In China there has for the last few thousand years been a continual struggle around the issue of who is to become emperor."

Interpreting the deal struck at Lushan as a face-saving maneuver on Mao Tse-tung's part, with negative consequences that have still not played themselves out, one is still left with the question of the validity of Mao's vision for the Great Leap. Just because Party cadres carried the movement initiated by him to extremes of leveling and to heights of euphoria that brought on disaster, one need not conclude that the original impulse was wrong or impractical. Why shouldn't China's greatest resource, her vast reserve of labor power, be mobilized in down-to-earth fashion to achieve "better, faster, more economical results in the construction of socialism"?

At every juncture in China's modern history sound policies put forward by Mao and others veered in practice either to the right or to the "left." Those who carried the wartime alliance with Chiang Kai-shek to the point of "all unity, no struggle" led the New Fourth Army into danger in 1939. Those who practiced "all struggle, no unity" also courted destruction through isolating themselves. In the post–World War II land-reform period, those who hesitated to divide the land or curried favor with the landlords by leaving them in possession of both land and wealth seriously undermined the political mobilization of the peasants. But those who carried land distribution to the point of absolute equality, insisting on the division of the last bowl and chopstick, undermined the mobilization of the peasants even more seriously. They set various peasant strata against one another and drove the middle strata toward the enemy camp.

In each case spontaneous tendencies carried sound policy to absurd lengths, but conscious manipulation cannot be entirely ruled out as a contributing factor. If, for instance, a certain leader opposed land reform, no more effective method of sabotage existed than that of pushing expropriation and distribution to such extremes that even the landless poor had to draw back. By the same token, if some leader opposed the Great Leap, no better way to bring it down existed than to fan up a "level and transfer wind," "a blind directive wind," "an exaggeration wind" and a "boasting wind." Anyone capable of fanning up such winds could make prophecies of disaster self-fulfilling. Then, with an "I told you so," the vindicated prophet could lead a headlong retreat toward the other extreme—production for private profit. The shrill polemics published by Mao's supporters in the Cultural Revolution accuse Liu Shao-ch'i of pushing the Great Leap to "left" extremes in order to destroy it. Unfortunately the polemics are so clumsily contrived and poorly documented that they cannot easily be confirmed or denied. One thing is clear: they never ask one of the central questions posed by each great "leftward" swing since 1949—why was it that Mao repeatedly launched mass movements to correct right deviations but never tried to mobilize against even more lethal "left" deviations? In the course of revolution swings are inevitable. A successful leader ought to be prepared with effective remedies, regardless of the direction of the swing.

Part IV

WHAT IS THE SOCIALIST ROAD?

The agricultural cooperative movement has been a severe ideological and political struggle from the very beginning. . . . After a cooperative is established, it must go through many more struggles before it can be consolidated. Even then, the moment it relaxes its efforts it may collapse.

Mao Tse-tung, 1955

37

MEDICAL EMERGENCY

On September 14, 1971, just as dawn began to break in the east, the powerful loudspeaker on the roof of the meeting hall sprang to life. First it simply crackled, showing off its latent electronic power, then suddenly that ubiquitous hymn "The East Is Red" blasted out toward all eight points of the compass, drowning the community in an enormous wave of harsh, triumphant sound—"The east is red, the sun rises, China sends forth a Mao Tse-tung. . . ."

Even though the army band introduced the theme with instruments alone, the words sprang automatically into the mind of every listener, only to be repeated as a mighty chorus of human voices added its effort to the trumpets and the horns—"He is the people's great saving star, he has performed outstanding service. . . ."

The hymn woke everyone in Long Bow—man, woman and child—for it was impossible to shut the sound out. In some homes a small loudspeaker hanging in the corner and hooked directly to the turntable in the broadcasting room brought words and music to the listeners' ears slightly ahead of the sonic boom that emanated from the rooftops. This gave the song a curious double emphasis, a dissonance produced by split-second delay and magnified by proximity. But most homeowners had long since disconnected the wires to the brigade center. Only one cataract of sound poured down from heaven to notify all laboring people that it was time to rise and start the new day.

"The East Is Red" burst upon the airwaves each morning courtesy of the brigade accountant, who somehow arose, minutes ahead of time, and placed the much-abused record on the turntable. It was followed by the first news of the day, broadcast directly from Peking, picked up and amplified by every local radio station in China, and rebroadcast by every brigade with a sound system, which meant—on the Shangtang Plateau, at least—every brigade ever organized.

The news from Peking always began with a quotation or two from the works of Mao Tse-tung, and the most common of these in the fall of 1971 was, "In agriculture learn from Tachai, in industry learn from Taching, people of the whole country learn from the Liberation Army." Some directive concerning Party rectification usually followed. Most popular was

Mao's fifty-ideograph summary of the nature of the Party, "The Party organization should be composed of advanced elements of the proletariat; it should be a vigorous and vital organization of vanguards which can lead the proletariat and the revolutionary masses in struggle against the class enemy." The broadcast then went on to tell about setting up new Party committees in various cities and provinces, about outstanding achievements in industrial and agricultural production, about the latest national sports contest and the day's most important development in world affairs—a people's victory in Vietnam or Nixon's impending China visit.

On September 14 the loudspeaker burst in upon our sleep earlier than usual, but instead of "The East Is Red" we heard the voice of the brigade doctor, Three Gingers Chi, announcing an emergency.

"Attention, everyone! Everyone pay attention! Two Long Bow children have been stricken with encephalitis. We sent them to the hospital last night. This disease is spread by mosquitoes. We are launching a massive campaign to kill mosquitoes, clean up all mosquito breeding spots, and inoculate all young children. We want everybody out. Kill every mosquito you see. We will spray every house with DDT, treat every toilet cistern with 666,* put chlorine in the pond, sweep up and carry off all trash, and dry out and fill in every puddle. Please bring all children under six to the brigade clinic. And please report any suspicious symptoms to me immediately.

"The symptoms of encephalitis are severe headache, vomiting, high fever, stiff neck and stiff limbs. If you lift the arm the whole body rises. If you see anything like this it could be serious. Everybody out. Let's get started."

The announcement sent chills up and down my spine. My sister Joan and her husband, Erwin Engst, had arrived the day before from Tachai, bringing with them my three children aged six, eight and ten. An encephalitis epidemic was about the worst thing that could happen, not only to my family, but to the entire community of Long Bow.

Carma and I jumped out of our beds and left our quarters for the brigade office without taking the time to wash, brush our teeth or comb our hair. The street already bristled with people armed with shovels, brooms, baskets and whatever else might be useful in a grand cleanup of the streets and courtyards.

All the people under supervision in the brigade—landlord and rich peasant widows, former Kuomintang members, a rich peasant settler who had misappropriated funds—were busy cleaning out the ditch on the right side of the main street under the watchful eye of All Here Li, Long Bow's security chief.

"Make Long Bow healthy, keep Long Bow clean," shouted Li; then he cursed the "bad elements" under his breath. "These people are supposed to be out here every morning cleaning up the street, but if you don't keep after them they don't do it. Well, they're going to have to do it today. Let's get busy there. Get busy. Old Lady Kuo"—it was Kuo Ch'ung-wang's wife —"don't leave any leaves behind."

All Here Li looked fierce indeed, and just to make sure that his charges took his words seriously he carried a rifle slung over one shoulder.

*666 is the insecticide lindane, now banned, as is DDT, in many parts of the world.

Militiaman Lu An-ho, rifle in hand, stood beyond the old women in the ditch and added his threats to those of his chief. "We're checking on everything today. Whoever doesn't do a good job will have to do it over again. If you had kept the street clean it wouldn't be such a mess today. When are you bastards going to learn to be honest?"

Two of the women tottered along on pitifully small, bound feet. They moved as if on stilts and barely seemed able to wield the big flat brooms made of pressed fire bushes that were standard equipment for sweeping down streets, alleys and earthen courtyards. The men, piling leaves into wicker baskets, also seemed barely able to lift their shovels as they shuffled forward in the post-dawn chill. A more miserable collection of cowed individuals could hardly be imagined. These "bad elements" and remnants of the old ruling class, in no position to threaten anybody, were practicing the only form of resistance left to them—slow motion.

Fortunately the cleanup did not depend on the motley crew under supervision. Dr. Chi's words had brought out the flower of the community's labor power. People went to work with such enthusiasm that they soon raised a cloud of dust.

We found Dr. Chi in the clinic busy preparing his inoculation equipment. He said several cases of encephalitis had been reported from Horse Square early in the month. One of the stricken Long Bow children was the son of a railroad worker who had gone to play with friends in Horse Square and had been bitten by a mosquito there. He had been sent to the hospital run by the Railroad Bureau at Changchih North Station, one mile to the north. The other Long Bow child was the son of the brigade electrician, Li Chung-lu. Chung-lu had recently wired his own home, leaving all doors and windows open while he did so. Mosquitoes, enjoying free access to the interior, had bitten his child. As soon as the symptoms of encephalitis showed up, the boy had been sent to the Changchih Hospital.

Dr. Chi was preparing shots not only against encephalitis but against tetanus, whooping cough and malaria as well. He had stocked a triple-threat serum just a few days before and was taking advantage of the emergency to make sure that all children received treatment. In the meantime he had ordered all homes sprayed with DDT, all privies treated with the chemical 666, and the pond sterilized with chlorine. He said adults could immunize themselves against encephalitis with a soup made from Kuanchung grass. As he explained this, an attractive young woman in a long white smock and white cap came in with more serum. She was Dr. Chia Shu-hsien, thirty-six years old, Long Bow–born and trained in medicine by Dr. Chi himself— an apprentice turned colleague.

Three Gingers Chi, short in stature, energetic, always smiling, was one of Long Bow's most noteworthy citizens. As a child of six he had been part of the gang that hung around with me, learned the finger trick, and memorized a few words of English. One day while roughhousing, I had placed him on the roof of a low building and he had not been able to get down on his own. He hollered until I took him down. He had always loved music, poetry, drama and gala affairs where he specialized in setting off fireworks. He kept a collection of all the folk songs, marching songs and revolutionary

battle songs of the Anti-Japanese War and the civil war and knew most of
them by heart. When he found that I remembered some of them too, he
liked to sing duets with me:

Taihang Mountains, high, oh high!
One hundred times ten thousand men
Take up the cry.
Young men of the soil,
Fear not shell or knife.
Each shot we fire
Takes an enemy life.

On top of all that he was a good doctor, well versed in the traditional
medicine he had learned from his father, Chi Ping-k'uei, and also at home
with some of the basic knowledge and techniques of modern Western
medicine, which he had learned in the course of many training sessions at
the commune and city level.

"I studied under my father," said Three Gingers Chi. "He practiced
Chinese medicine for years and was very skillful. In 1958 the commune
opened a district clinic. My father was invited to attend but he decided that
he was too old and sent me in his place. I was just seventeen. What we
learned and practiced there was also Chinese medicine. But on Saturday
afternoon we had classes in Western medicine, so I added some of that to
my arsenal and later went to whatever short courses came along. One step
at a time I increased my knowledge. Now I can even do minor surgery, but
I can't open stomachs or anything like that."

From the point of view of skill Dr. Chi was much better qualified than
the average brigade medical officer. We thought Long Bow was lucky to
have him and wondered why he had remained there when by rights he
should have been practicing in one of the largest hospitals nearby.

Then we learned that Dr. Chi had once been a doctor in the commune
hospital at Kao Family Settlement. One of his duties had been to supervise
childbearing in the surrounding villages. When the family was Catholic, Dr.
Chi, who came from a dedicated Catholic family, helped them find a good
Christian name for the child and, on the quiet, helped christen the child
with two names—an ordinary Chinese name for official use and public
consumption and a Christian name like Peter or Mary for family use and
use among Christians. When the Four Clean Movement exposed this activity, the hospital fired Dr. Chi and sent him back to Long Bow in disgrace.
The commune's loss was the brigade's gain. Long Bow acquired one of the
best native doctors in the area. The clinic at Long Bow became popular not
only with the local brigade members but with a large part of the working
population in the vicinity; so popular, in fact, that fees from nonmembers
supported the entire clinic, enabled it to earn a profit, and in the long run
treat Long Bow brigade members free.

According to the cooperative medical system that was established during
the Cultural Revolution after a June, 1966, directive from Chairman Mao
Tse-tung, each resident of Long Bow was supposed to pay one yuan a year
into the medical fund and was then entitled to free professional service at

the clinic, including diagnosis, acupuncture, injections, minor surgery, prenatal care and childbirth. The clinic charged only for medicines, which it sold to members at half price. Clinic staff members made most of the medicines at home from Chinese herbs, but the dispensary also stocked such antibiotics as penicillin, tetracycline, Terramycin and streptomycin, and some of the more effective drugs such as sulfanilamide and sulfaguanidine.

In order to maintain low prices Dr. Chi and Dr. Chia raised domestic medicinal herbs in a special garden and spent much time on nearby mountains gathering wild herbs. After the two doctors succeeded in finding samples of the herbs they needed most, they instructed village youngsters in herbal identification and then sent large crews of people out to look for them. Whenever they collected any herb in quantity they dried it, packaged it, and sent it to the Drug Company in Changchih City, where raw herbs could be exchanged for processed medicines at prices far below the usual retail prices. Wang Yü-mei, the brigade's star actress, manned the dispensary. She kept Western medicines on a set of wooden shelves; dried herbs and herbal concoctions were kept in small wooden drawers—hundreds of drawers in cabinets set side by side across the back of the room.

Wang Yü-mei confirmed Dr. Chi's description of prices. She said that herb medicines in the Long Bow clinic generally sold for half market price while Western medicines had fallen to about half the prices of a decade ago. Whereas in 1958 penicillin sold for 3 yuan an ampule, the price was now 1 yuan; tetracycline, which had formerly sold for 10 fen per pill, now sold for 5 or 6 fen.

Dr. Chi and Dr. Chia trained people to gather herbs and also trained medical assistants to take care of emergencies in the field. These assistants they called "barefoot doctors." They were assigned to regular field work with the agricultural teams, but studied medicine in their off-hours and carried simple first-aid kits when on duty. In the slack season they attended regular classes and studied acupuncture and simple herbal remedies such as cabbage-root for headaches. They also learned how to splint broken limbs, stop bleeding, and restore breathing with artificial respiration.

The barefoot doctors earned only standard work points from their field work. The three full-time people on the medical staff earned work points for every day spent on medical work—10 points for Dr. Chi, 8 points for Dr. Chia and 7 points for Wang Yü-mei, the pharmacist. The points assured them a share in the total grain crop harvested by the brigade and in the cash earnings, including, of course, the cash earnings brought in by the clinic and the pharmacy, both of which amounted to profitable brigade sidelines in their own right.

Remembering the terrible toll taken by navel ill, or tetanus of the umbilical cord, and how of the eight children born in April, 1948, only one lived, I asked Dr. Chi about midwives and childbirth. He said that midwives, because their methods were so unsanitary, no longer found customers among Long Bow people and no longer practiced their "art." One of the old midwives had gone to school to learn sanitary methods. She had helped with childbirth until she died. Then Dr. Chi trained Dr. Chia to take charge of all maternity problems and she quickly learned to handle them well. In the last few years not one child who was alive at parturition had been lost.

Even those who could not breathe had been revived with artificial respiration and heart massage. One reason for this excellent record was the periodic examination of pregnant women. Those carrying children in abnormal positions were sent to the local hospital in good time. Thus last-minute emergencies were avoided.

Dr. Chia taught expectant mothers a method of painless childbirth that included muscle and breathing exercises. She had a kit with everything necessary for normal birth, and took it along to the mother's home when called. If the painless methods didn't work, she used acupuncture to induce anesthesia. She also used acupuncture to ease the pain of post-birth uterine contractions.

In the old days a shockingly high rate of infant mortality held the population of Long Bow in check. Now that every child lived, what would hold the population down? we asked.

Dr. Chi described a complete program for birth control—propaganda, advice, the pill, uterine rings, condoms, tube tying and vasectomies. But still the age-old pressure to have at least one male child made many families grow. From on high came propaganda for the two-child family, but when the first two were girls almost all couples kept trying until they had at least one boy. Dr. Chi's wife first gave birth to three girls. So she tried again and had a boy. Then she felt that a single boy would lack a playmate, so she decided on another child and that, too, was a boy. Thus the Chi family, which ideally should have been limited to two children, grew until there were five.

Even those families that started off with boys often had more children because they hoped to have at least one girl. In a cooperative brigade girls were not nearly as much of an economic drain on the family as they had once been considered to be. As soon as they were old enough to work they could go out, earn work points and begin to contribute to the family income. It was even possible for a girl to bring a man into the family through marriage. In the old days girls almost invariably married out, but now, since Long Bow enjoyed such a favorable location beside the highway and the railroad, people from outlying districts wanted to move to Long Bow and establish residence there. One way to do it was to marry into the brigade.

Given all these influences, it did not look as if the birth rate in Long Bow would fall very fast. With infant mortality almost eliminated and with life-spans lengthening because of better diet and medical care, the population seemed certain to leap.

Dr. Chi assured us that he had brought under control almost all of the infectious diseases, from syphilis and gonorrhea to smallpox, infantile paralysis and whooping cough. He just didn't worry about them anymore. With a little more effort he expected to make encephalitis disappear. Since preventive medicine and prompt treatment had been so effective, we asked why there were so many "minor" ailments around, scalp and skin diseases like impetigo, for instance, and eye ailments like conjunctivitis and trachoma. Dr. Chi said skin diseases were particularly common in Long Bow because the village was so damp. Ever since the completion of the reservoir during the Great Leap in 1958, the water table had stabilized at four feet below the ground, the earthen floors in the homes suffered chronic dampness, and the dampness even climbed the walls, weakening them and causing them, occasionally, to collapse. Some kinds of skin ailments could be treated with penicillin, but not all children could take penicillin shots. Those who couldn't had to make do with Chinese remedies such as dandelion soup or dandelion juice applied to the skin, a treatment that took a long time to prevail over the infection.

One problem, said Dr. Chi, was that people paid very little attention to skin ailments and put off coming in for medical care as long as they could. Only if their blisters covered the whole face were they moved to do something about it. By that time the condition was hard to cure.

The same thing was true of eye ailments. People with trachoma tried to ignore it, or they washed their eyes out with chrysanthemum water. They only sought out a doctor when their eyes were already damaged beyond repair.

Dr. Chi said that acupuncture was effective against conjunctivitis and such things as flash burn, but here again, people were reluctant to ask for professional treatment, so the diseases often continued unchecked.

On the morning of September 14 Dr. Chi and Dr. Chia inoculated all the children under six, then went out to see how their antimosquito war was going. A quick round of the village indicated progress on all fronts, pools filled in, ditches cleaned, trash swept up, most homes already sprayed and toilets treated. The doctors came back to the clinic well satisfied.

The annihilation of mosquitoes was evidently complete. No more cases of encephalitis showed up, and the two children who had earlier contracted it were released from the hospital as cured after a few days. The contrast between the medical system of 1971 and that of 1948 was striking. If there had been progress in no other field, the progress here would have justified the revolution.

38

HUSBANDS AND WIVES, WIVES AND HUSBANDS

The next morning, as we gathered at Security Officer Shen's lodgings for political study, the topic was, as it had been for several days, Mao's essay *On Contradiction*. The contradiction that was bothering Judge Kao was the one that was tearing the family of poor peasant Little Lin apart. Little Lin quarreled with his wife because his wife quarreled with his mother. The two women had not been getting along for some time, so Judge Kao had arranged for Little Lin's mother to move out of her own house, which she was sharing with the young couple, and into separate quarters in another courtyard. Unfortunately, this move had not solved the problem. Little Lin's wife was still mad at her husband because he gave his mother 5 yuan a month to live on. She thought the sum was much too munificent.

"Well," said Veteran Wang, hunching the fur collar of his new coat around him, "there are lots of contradictions, but the economic one is the principal one."

"I agree that their income is small," said Security Officer Shen. "But that shouldn't prevent Little Lin from giving her a hand around the house. He could help her, but he won't do a thing. Everything falls on her shoulders."

"It's still economic," said Wang, warming to the discussion. "If his wife earned 80 yuan a month he would hover around her and pay her no end of attention. He would flatter her and not ignore her."

"But really, it's the ideas in their heads that are important," said Judge Kao. "The contradiction between the old and the new in their consciousness, old ideas of women's place and new ideas of women's equality."

"But politics and economics, consciousness and material welfare can't be separated," retorted Wang. "Economics is still the base."

If this sounded a bit like revisionist "productive forces theory" to Shen, he still had to admit that it fit the case of Little Lin. "Each of them wants to spend more money than there is," he said. "Little Lin only earns 40 yuan a month at the truck repair depot. Twenty yuan of this goes to repay a debt. For a long time the family ate brigade grain. Then Lin borrowed money from a neighbor to pay the brigade back. Now he has to pay the neighbor 20 yuan a month until the debt is cleared. This leaves him only 20 yuan to live on. He gives his mother 5 for herself and the child of his first marriage, who lives with her. He spends another 5 yuan for his own grain at the worksite. This leaves only 10 yuan for his wife, and she thinks it's far too little. One month, because he lost three days' work, he gave her only 8 yuan. His wife thought he had cheated her and had given the balance to his mother—either that or he had hidden it, split it with someone, or spent it recklessly."

"Isn't that just as I was saying?" said Wang. "No matter what family you want to talk about, if there's a quarrel it's rooted in economics."

"But economics is only the appearance, politics is the essence," said Kao.

"How can that be? Economics is the base. If it isn't, what is?" protested Wang.

"At bottom it's still a thought problem," said Kao.

"But where does their thinking come from—not out of the sky, surely?"

"You say it's because they don't have enough money, but even if they had a lot more money they would still quarrel over what to buy with it. So isn't that a thought problem?" asked the Judge. "In my view husband-and-wife quarrels are left over from the old society and they are getting less and less."

"What do you mean, less and less?" objected Shen, abruptly. "I see plenty of them."

"And most of them are rooted in poverty," said Wang, sticking stubbornly to his original point.

"Well," retorted Kao, "will the problem be any less when everyone earns 100 yuan a month?"

"Yes and no," said Wang, thinking it over carefully. "That will solve some of the problem but the contradiction will develop to a new stage. With higher incomes there will still be economic contradictions and there will be contradictions in ways of thinking also."

"Lu Shu-yun's problems don't seem to be rooted in poverty," said Shen.

Lu Shu-yun was the young woman of twenty-five who headed the Brigade Women's Association. Slight of build, plain, sad-eyed and without color in her cheeks, she wandered unhappily about the village and seemed to have only marginal success in rallying the women for production or study, two tasks which the Brigade Party Branch counted on the Women's Association to perform.

"Why is Lu Shu-yun so forlorn?" asked Carma.

"Well, for one thing, she's living in her husband's house, just like the pharmacist, Wang Yü-mei. She has to do most of the work for her mother-in-law and never sees her husband. He is a worker in a transistor factory in Tat'ung [at the northernmost border of Shansi] and only comes home for twelve days once a year. Furthermore, he doesn't really care for her that much. He's interested in some girl in Tat'ung."

"I'd have a long face, too, under those circumstances," said Teacher Li.

"Well, why did they get married in the first place? Don't young people marry whom they want these days?" asked Carma.

"Yes, they do, but in this case true love didn't run very smooth," said Security Officer Shen, who always seemed to know the inside story of every peasant's personal relations. "Lu Shu-yun is pretty well educated. She went to primary school for four years here, then went to higher primary school for four more years in Horse Square. After she graduated at fourteen she came back to Long Bow to look after her brother's children, then joined the Sixth Team for field work when she was sixteen. Two years later, during the Socialist Education Movement, she joined the Party but she hadn't been a member very long when she was suspended because she fell in love with Li Te-jui."

"Isn't that her husband?"

"Yes."

"Well, how could she be suspended for falling in love with him?"

The story turned out to be a complicated one.

Li Te-jui was the boy the wolf did not kill. His father, the upper-middle peasant Li Hung-jen, was the man who died of a broken heart after he pooled his land in the coop. He died when Te-jui was nine. His brother Li Yü-nien brought the boy up. The whole family suffered from the reputation of another brother, Li Ch'ang-chih, who had once killed an Eighth Route Army soldier and stolen his gun, then fought in the Chin Sui Army of the warlord Yen Hsi-shan.

Li Te-jui went through primary school with Lu Shu-yun, then on to the Regional Middle School in Long Bow. The two fell in love when the boy was a middle school student and they got engaged. After graduation Li Te-jui went off to Changchih to study electricity and then on to Chungking in far-off Szechuan. From Chungking he won a transfer to the provincial capital, Taiyuan, where he worked in the arsenal. He became interested in another woman there and suggested breaking off the engagement. Shu-yun got very upset. "We got along fine before. How come you suddenly don't want me?" she wrote.

"If you want to come here, then come," he wrote back. "It's easy enough to come, but not so easy to return home. Think about it. What class am I? What class are you? How can we marry?" Obviously he didn't want to go on with the engagement, and the real reason was that he had found another girl.

Just at that time the movement to "clear class ranks" began. Some brigade members accused Li's dead father of a serious crime. They said that during the Anti-Japanese War he had gone into the blockhouse to report on underground activity and had leaked information that led to the capture and execution of several resistance fighters. Suddenly Li Te-jui's father, who had gone south after the nationwide victory as a land reform cadre, became a collaborator responsible for the death of fellow villagers. With this accusation added to the charges against Uncle Ch'ang-chih, the future of the whole family looked dark indeed.

Chang Kuei-ts'ai, on behalf of the Party Branch, called Lu Shu-yun in and tried to get her to call off her engagement. "You're a Party member. What do you want to carry on with the son of a man like that for?" When Shu-yun refused to give up her marriage plans, the other Party members would not allow her to pass the rectification "gate." They suspended her pending a change of heart.

Under heavy pressure from the Party leaders and angry at the prospect of being jilted, Lu Shu-yun wrote the arsenal in Taiyuan about her fiancé's background. Brigade leaders added a letter of their own raising questions about the entire Li family. Cadres at the arsenal decided they had better not take any chances. They transferred Li Te-jui to a civilian factory in Tat'ung.

The Taiyuan girl young Li had fallen for dropped him forthwith. She didn't want anything to do with a security risk. And so Li Te-jui, jilted in his turn and under a political cloud, arrived in Tat'ung. Marriage to Lu Shu-yun didn't look so bad after all. Just then he received a letter from his uncle. Class ranks were being cleared in Long Bow. Charges were being hurled about like chicken feathers. "It's hard for us. If you don't marry Lu Shu-yun things could get worse. She is a Communist. She is a member of the Brigade Committee. By linking up with her you can cover up 100 dark spots."

That tipped the scales. Young Li came back to Long Bow and begged Lu Shu-yun to marry him. By that time she had already taken up with a worker at the truck depot. But in her heart she still loved Li. She ditched the depot man and married Li Te-jui. But instead of living together happily thereafter, her husband returned to Tat'ung as a worker and soon found another girl who interested him.

A marriage like that didn't seem to offer very much hope for the future. From the man's point of view it was a marriage of convenience. From the woman's point of view it was a love match, but in the anguish of rejection she had taken a step that cast a pall over her loved one's career, and now she had to live with the consequences. What a mess!

And all to no purpose. The charges against Li Te-jui's dead father were only charges, nothing more. Even if they had been true, the alleged incident happened long before the boy was born. Could he be held responsible? The real difficulty was his upper-middle peasant origin. In Long Bow that was hard to live down. After the heat of the class ranks movement had passed, after the marriage became a reality, the whole problem faded away. The Party reinstated Shu-yun and the women of Long Bow elected her chairman of the Women's Association. Outwardly, it seemed, everything had turned out for the best. But inside the young woman's heart deep wounds refused to heal.

Carma and I talked to Lu Shu-yun about women's work.

"We lead women in the study of Mao Tse-tung Thought and in collective labor," she said. "Women can do whatever men can do."

"Do the men agree to that?"

"Yes. We study at the same sessions and we speak out at meetings, and we speak out just as men do. In the busy season—wheat planting, harvest-time—we organize all the able-bodied women to join in. We get the older women to look after the children and we all go out to the fields."

"Why don't you organize a full-time nursery?"

"It's not really necessary. We set one up for the busy periods. Then dissolve it again. We have no permanent site, no fixed staff. Our arrangements are flexible and no one is tied down. The busy season never lasts very long. When it's over the women with children stay home, cook and make clothes."

"It still seems as if a permanent nursery would fill a need."

"One of the problems is work points. When others look after your kids you have to give work points. Most people don't feel it is worth it. If grandparents and old people do it temporarily, that's one thing. But to give work points, that is something else."

Carma asked her about the new regulation that women who married outside the village would not get per capita grain for their children if they stayed in Long Bow.

Lu Shu-yun argued in favor of it.

"Two years ago the rule was that the women could stay here. But all the young married women wanted to stay. The village got very crowded, so we decided not to give residency permits for any children here if their mother had married outside. Then we didn't have to supply grain either. Our problem is, we have too many people. Too many are eating and not enough are working. When they marry out we try to convince them to leave."

"Can their husbands come and settle here?"

"No. The men can't come here, not since the Four Clean Movement. If we let them all come we would have too many. Of course, if a family only has daughters and no sons, then they can arrange for one of the husbands to come. But if they have sons they can't bring in sons-in-law."

"Isn't that pretty unequal? Women must go. Men can't come."

"Well," said Lu Shu-yun, doleful as always, "we have to have some restrictions. Life is so easy here, if we didn't block the way everyone would flock to Long Bow and load up the place."

"Why do they want to come here?"

"Our conditions are so good. Level land, flat road. This whole area attracts mountain people. When you step out the door there is no slope, up or down. If you want to go somehwere you just get on the bus. When you have to haul something you just put it on a cart. No carrying poles. When you need water it is only a few feet down. Also there are plenty of factories going up. You can get work. If you marry one of the workers you want to find housing here. Industry, construction—all this makes a difference."

Her words sounded enthusiastic but her mouth refused to smile. Whatever life in Long Bow meant to others, it apparently meant something else to her.

The vice-leader of the Women's Association was Yang Lien-ying, thirty-nine. She was always as happy as Lu Shu-yun was sad.

"I encourage all the women of the Third Team to go out and work. Women are the majority on our team, and my work is to mobilize them. In Long Bow Lu Shu-yun and I take responsibility for getting the women out."

Yang Lien-ying laughed. She obviously enjoyed working with the women. She obviously enjoyed her life.

"If there are two or three working members in a family, then the women feel they should not go out. That's because there's too much housework to do. If they don't do it nobody will."

"The men won't help out?"

"No. Most of them won't. They're not like my husband. When he comes home he does all the work."

She laughed again, her broad face deeply wrinkled, her bobbed hair glistening. Almost all the married women in Long Bow wore a braid down the middle of the back—even Hu Hsueh-chen, the once bold leader of the women in land reform. But not Lien-ying. She bobbed her hair, smoked cigarettes, and drank hard liquor, downing one thimble cup after another as if it were water. When you went to a peasant home in Long Bow you ate with the men, while the women busied themselves in the cookhouse. They entered the front door only to bring food. But not at Lien-ying's. When you ate at her house she did the honors, poured the liquor, and matched toast with toast. Her husband manned the cookhouse, brought the food, and only sat down to eat after his guests had eaten their fill.

Yang Lien-ying was born in 1931 in a small hamlet in the mountains west of Changchih. Her father was a hired laborer who rented two small rooms to live in and sought work where he could find it, often staying away for days at a time until he earned enough to bring something home. When work was slack he went into the high mountains to reclaim wasteland and succeeded in taming about half an acre on which he planted grain.

When Yang Lien-ying was only eighteen months old her mother died. Her father despaired of raising her and brought her to Long Bow, where his sister had married one of three Wang brothers. This sister had borne three sons but no daughters, so her brother thought she would take in a daughter, especially since her last-born had fallen into a well and drowned. But by the time old Yang brought little Lien-ying to Long Bow, his sister Yang Feng-wen had already adopted another son, whom she called Yu-fu (has wealth, possessing wealth) and neither her husband nor her husband's brothers would agree to taking in a little girl. What use would it be to adopt a girl? A girl amounted to nothing. People all wanted boys who would look after them when they got old. Who wanted a girl? Nobody!

One of the brothers who vetoed the adoption was Wang T'ao-yuan, the notorious heroin peddler and wife-broker who had such difficulty in getting accepted into the Peasants' Association during the land reform. He was the man who, after telling the association members about the sale of his wife and the death of his donkey, wept uncontrollably. "Well, you sold her," someone said, "and now you weep about it." "I'm not weeping for my bartered wife. I'm weeping for my dead donkey," he replied. Another brother who vetoed the adoption later fathered a son whom we knew as Li Chung-lu, the brigade electrician. Chung-lu would play an important role in the village life of the seventies.

When Aunt Yang Feng-wen refused to take in the little girl her father, in desperation, took her to the Catholic orphanage, turned her over to the nuns and went home weeping. Four days later he came back and asked for her. He could not bear to leave his only daughter in the hands of a foreign church. He took her to Tunliu instead, and tried to give her to her paternal grandmother, but this old lady wouldn't accept her no matter how he pleaded. In the end he had no alternative but to keep her in his own house. There Lien-ying and her brother, who was only five at the time, survived somehow, cooking and caring for themselves while their father was away. Because he had two children the father could not take a year-round job that required living in somewhere. He continued to find odd jobs wherever he could, cooked at home as much as possible, and tried to be both father and mother to his children. Finally, when Lien-ying was nine, her father married again. She had a mother at last. But bringing a stepmother into the home did not make life any better for the girl. The stepmother treated her very badly. She soon found herself wishing that her father had never remarried.

"Whenever I think of the past, I weep," said Lien-ying. "It was so very bitter. I was small and there was no one to look after me. I had no padded clothes in winter, and often had nothing to eat. After I moved to Long Bow I often talked about the old days with my aunt Feng-wen. And sometimes my father joined in. He always said he had had a narrow escape. If Yang Feng-wen had actually taken me in I wouldn't have been his daughter anymore and he wouldn't have the right to receive the small gifts and the money that I have been able to give him from time to time as he gets older. Who could have foreseen that in those days?"

After Liberation life improved. Lien-ying's father won 20 mou of land. He and his son worked the land while Lien-ying and her stepmother cooked and kept the house.

Yang Lien-ying met her husband-to-be, Wang Ch'i-fa, for the first time in the fall of 1948, when she was seventeen. On that occasion she paid no more than passing attention to him. She had come to stay for a while in Long Bow with her aunt, Feng-wen. Wang Ch'i-fa, who was twenty-two, had already been working at the Chincheng Arsenal, some fifty miles away, for several years, but he was at home on vacation at that time. He was the eldest of old Wang Yü-lai's four children. The next two, Kuei-ying and Liu-hua, were daughters. The last was Wen-te, the ex-police captain, so notorious for his bad temper and for being the first person ever to be divorced by a wife in Long Bow history. "But don't jump to conclusions," said Yang Lien-ying. "Ch'i-fa was the brother with the good disposition. He was always good-natured, just the opposite of his brother Wen-te. In our marriage I was the one with the bad temper."

At the age of sixteen Ch'i-fa left home under duress. He was conscripted by the Japanese and ordered out to Tunliu County to work on a new railroad embankment. As soon as the Japanese surrendered he returned to Long Bow and joined the PLA. Instead of sending him to the front they sent him to the Chincheng Arsenal as a worker in uniform. In 1950 he was transferred to the Huai-hai Arsenal in Changchih City, then mustered out. He stayed on as an arsenal worker.

That Lien-ying ever met Ch'i-fa a second time was a matter of chance. Lien-ying's stepsister had a friend who went to the family quarters at the Huai-hai Arsenal to work as a wet nurse. While there she heard that the worker Wang Ch'i-fa was looking for a wife. She brought this news home and Yang Lien-ying, hearing the name, concluded it must belong to the man she had met in Long Bow two years earlier. She expressed interest, so her stepsister undertook some arrangements. On the day of the fall festival, word was sent to Wang Ch'i-fa to wait outside the arsenal gate. He was there, according to the plan, when Lien-ying came by. They talked and agreed to meet again. At their second meeting they decided to get married. This big decision was no sooner made than they went off to the supply coop and bought some cloth to be made into clothes for Lien-ying, a transaction that sealed the deal for both sides, it would seem.

New cloth in hand, they went to the offices of the municipal council, taking Lien-ying's stepsister along as a witness. There they got a marriage certificate and a clerk pronounced them man and wife. Without time to make any wedding clothes, without time for Wang's fellow workers even to organize a party, they got married in that bare public office, then went out to find rooms to live in. They found some vacant space in the house of a Changchih City family and set up housekeeping that night. Weeks later Lien-ying's stepsister helped sew some wedding clothes that never attended any wedding.

The young couple consummated their marriage without the consent of the parents on either side. Old Wang Yü-lai didn't even know about it until Ch'i-fa brought his bride home to take part in the fall festival on August 1, lunar calendar. That was months after the wedding. Lien-ying's father knew about the match but was opposed to it. He refused to sanction it and would not see his daughter for more than a year after it took place. He was angry because long before the Liberation (1945) he had already arranged a match for Lien-ying. He had chosen a landlord's son. He thought it was an excellent idea for a laborer's daughter to marry a landlord's son and thus link her fortunes to a family of great wealth. The prospective landlord father-in-law was killed during the land reform struggle, but this didn't matter to old Yang. He was determined to uphold his side of the bargain. "But after Liberation how could I step out on that old road?" asked Lien-ying. "I couldn't marry that man's son. Not in a hundred years!"

Yang Lien-ying took Liberation seriously, both as a Chinese and as a woman. She chose her husband without advice from her father and didn't ask a single thing from her husband's family. She was married in clothes she had made herself out of cloth bought by her fiancé with his own wages. At each stage in this affair she was self-reliant and self-motivated. There is no indication that this was the result of any deep, uncontrollable fascination with Ch'i-fa as a man. She had met him, she liked him and considered him suitable as a husband, but there was nothing about their relationship to suggest romantic love. Certainly she never hinted at any such thing later on. And long after Ch'i-fa died, when she married again, it was clear that she married not for love, but by rational choice, in an effort to create a home environment that added to her security and at the same time ensured her liberation, that allowed her to function better both as a private person and as a public figure. It seemed to me that from a very early age Lien-ying must have been self-assured, purposeful and calm. Yet she was not cold; far from it. Personal relations moved her deeply. She really cared about the sufferings of others and she was loyal, almost too loyal, to her friends, to her comrades and to all those who depended on her.

After her marriage Yang Lien-ying lived in Changchih City for almost twelve years. She bore a daughter there in 1952. In 1958 she got a job in the Huai-hai Arsenal kitchen. But in 1962, because the arsenal laid off many workers it also cut back on the kitchen staff. She lost her job and had to decide what to do next. She could have remained in the city as a nonworking wife, but Mao Tse-tung had called for surplus personnel to return to the countryside to work. She decided to move back to her husband's home in Long Bow instead. That meant moving into the same courtyard with Old Wang Yü-lai and his son Wen-te. Lien-ying got two sections of house for herself and her daughter while Wen-te, his wife, children and father lived in three sections next door. In 1964 they tore the old house down. Lien-ying got the material from her two sections and built another house in a new location. She swapped land with another family.

Unlike some others who returned to the countryside against their will, Lien-ying moved to Long Bow because she liked the idea. "I came back here because I like life in the village. The countryside is a wide world in itself. I wanted to come back and take part in labor on the land. I could have stayed in the city as a factory wife, but I didn't want to."

Soon after returning to Long Bow Lien-ying gave birth to a son, but as soon as the boy was able to crawl she became active in brigade affairs. She assumed a leading role on the Third Team and was elected to the committee of the Women's Association.

Wang Ch'i-fa died of cancer of the throat in 1966. Widowed, Lien-ying remarried in 1970.

"I married a power plant worker. He is the cook at the power plant in Anyang. He is forty-three. His wife died. He has one married son, twenty-one years old. The friend who introduced us said, 'Why cook alone? You need someone to help out on Sundays. You need company. When you are old you'll need someone to look out for you. I know a man who won't interfere with your life. And you won't interfere with his.' So she introduced us.

"I had many reasons to marry again. My son is still young. My daughter will soon marry and I'll be alone with the boy. In the old days my brother-in-law, Wang Wen-te, would not have let me remarry. I wouldn't have been allowed to bring another man here. If I wanted to marry again I would have had to leave and I would have had to leave my son and my house behind. I would have had to depart all alone and they would have had to burn some straw in the house to show that I was gone—gone completely, no trace left. But now the attitude toward remarrying is different. Those old feudal ideas no longer hold sway.

"Every year since I came back I have worked at least 200 days in the field. My daughter is not at home. She is a teacher in the primary school. So I cook for myself and do all the housework; then I go to the fields. I also cook for my daughter because she is so busy teaching, preparing lessons, going to study classes. But on Sundays my new husband comes home. Then he cooks for me."

As a young bride Yang Lien-ying must have been truly beautiful, though not in the classical sense. She was not one of those slight, willowy, porcelain-doll women so celebrated in Chinese art and culture, but a strong, healthy peasant girl with a finely proportioned broad face and a vigorous, athletic body; well formed, mature and at the same time distinctly feminine. She projected both vitality and confidence, and it was hard to say which of these was her most attractive feature. Obviously they reinforced each other. One had a feeling, being near her, that life's potential had expanded, that with her as a center all manner of new ideas and actions were in a continuous process of creation. With this quality she easily assumed leadership. People brought her their problems as a matter of course, depended on her for moral support, and looked to her for some way out of whatever difficulty pressed them. Yang Lien-ying cheerfully assumed the burdens thrust upon her by this faith and this dependence and seemed to thrive on struggle.

Yang Lien-ying, a liberated woman and a natural leader, lived at ease with herself and at ease with the world. Without her Lu Shu-yun would not have been able to rally the women at all or even perhaps collect her own spirits long enough to do any work.

39

FAITH IN THE LORD OF HEAVEN

 A few days later, while we were eating breakfast, Judge Kao came in with a message.

"An old friend of yours is coming!"

"Who is it?" I asked.

"Wang Ting-mo. He was vice-secretary of the Lucheng County Party Committee in 1948. Do you remember him? He made several reports to the land reform cadres."

"Yes, I remember him. What has he done since?"

"He was promoted to Party Secretary after you left. Then he transferred to Central Shansi. When the Cultural Revolution began he was Party Secretary of Yangch'uan, the big coal-mining town on the railroad. Red Guards from Peking and a group of rebel miners overthrew him. Now he is a cadre again in the Southeast Region."

As Judge Kao talked, Carma began to smile.

"His name is Wang Ting-mo?"

"Yes."

"Why, he's the man we all attacked. He was the big 'revisionist' of Yangch'uan. I helped throw him out," said Carma, shaking her head. "What will he think when he sees me?"

It did not take long to find out. Wang Ting-mo came striding in a few moments later. He was a very short man, slightly overweight, with a round, red face and a lively smile.

Wang Ting-mo greeted me warmly, then turned to shake hands with Carma.

"I was one of the Red Guards from Peking who attacked you in 1967," Carma said.

"Is that right?" said Wang, smiling broadly. "I heard there was a 'big nose' in the crowd, but I never had a chance to set eyes on you. At last we meet."

He began to laugh. Carma laughed with him. The two erstwhile antagonists laughed with such enthusiasm that we all began to laugh.

What a strange world! First you overthrow a man. Then he greets you as a welcome guest.

"I guess I owe you an apology," I said when things quieted down. "I produced a daughter who made a lot of trouble for you."

"It wasn't her fault," said Wang, still chuckling. "That was the wind of the times. People were seizing power everywhere. Why shouldn't they seize mine?"

We were off to a good start. We talked with Wang Ting-mo for the rest of the morning. Security Officer Shen had already told us that Wang Ting-mo was a famous man throughout Southeast Shansi. He was one of the most skillful anti-Japanese guerrilla fighters in the province. His was a name that struck terror in the heart of the enemy. But what did that matter to the young Red Guards? The movers and shakers of the Democratic Revolution were the "capitalist roaders" of the Socialist Revolution, and the bigger they were, the harder they fell.

Since Wang Ting-mo had led Lucheng County for several years after 1948, I asked him about that early period, and especially about the problem posed by the Catholic Church and all the devout believers in Horse Square and Long Bow. What happened to them? How had he persuaded them to give up the faith?

> Horse Square [Wang Ting-mo said] was an example of something bad turning into something good. At the time of land reform 100 percent of the people there were Catholic. A Catholic clique controlled the entire brigade and prolonged backwardness. Production teams harvested only 100 catties per mou. A local rhyme described the situation:
>
> > Church in the middle,
> > Pond at each end,
> > Virgin bless our griddle,
> > To heaven we'll ascend.
>
> Machang peasants thought if they didn't worship God every day they would be in trouble. A picture of the Virgin Mary hung in every home. Before eating they all sat down to pray. Before sleeping they all knelt to pray. They had a prayer for everything and because they prayed all the time they didn't have any time left for revolution or, it seems, production.
>
> The leader of the entire Catholic community was the priest, Shih Ho-fa. He was in charge of Anyang, Horse Square, South Temple, and Kao Family Settlement. All of these places were the same. Any peasant who didn't join the church couldn't make a living. They isolated non-Catholics and drove them out.
>
> We made sure that in Horse Square two Communists assumed power as Party Secretary and village chairman, but over and over again people reported to me that they, too, really worked for the church. On instructions from the church they drew a line down the middle of main street. The Party Secretary took charge of all affairs to the east of that line and the village chairman took charge of all affairs to the west of that line. It was the old pastoral division established by the missionaries to facilitate the work of the church.
>
> These two Communists followed the orders of the priest, Shih

Ho-fa. As a community leader the priest served on the County People's Congress as a deputy. But he never stopped working on loyal Communists who had been Catholics, hoping to break them down and welcome them back into the fold. He even broke down Liang Ma-tou, a famous *fanshen* here who had led the whole community in the struggle against the landlords. But that was because we made a serious mistake. We launched a rectification movement against extra privileges for cadres. We made Liang Ma-tou, since he was so well known, a natural target and registered all sorts of complaints against him. We used him as an example and treated him much too harshly. The whole thing slipped too far to the left; it was unfair. Shih Ho-fa took advantage of this, gave Ma-tou support, and reconverted him. When I saw what was happening I tried to correct the mistake. I gave him a lot of ideological education but I never won him back. He never became active again.

Our policy was to grant religious freedom. I thought it was a class question, and a serious one at that, but Wang Ch'ien, who was Party Secretary of the region, stressed the religious rights of the people and was reluctant to interfere. I thought he was a rightist, while he said to me, "How left can you get?"

Every time we came up with a policy the priest had his own interpretation. When we introduced the unified purchase plan for grain our standard was to ensure 380 catties for every person. People were supposed to sell any receipts above that to the state. But People's Deputy Shih said that God had given the 380 catties to every individual. "What if we harvest enough to grant everyone 400 catties?" asked another deputy. "It's still God who gives the grain," said Shih.

He knew that the constitution granted freedom of religion and he played on that to the hilt. Once we started a campaign to educate people about all forms of superstition. Shih immediately came round to ask me what sort of campaign we expected to have. "I don't know," I said. "I don't know either," he said, "but one thing I do know, we haven't done anything to violate the constitution." "Nor have we," I said. "We haven't violated the constitution either." Then Old New Year Wang of Anyang said, "The constitution guarantees freedom of religion. You have freedom to believe. We have freedom to oppose."

That upset Deputy Shih. He ran immediately to the Secretary for Religious Affairs and complained about Old New Year Wang. After that the Party Secretaries held back. They were afraid they would make mistakes.

But we came into conflict with the church anyway. I once went into Shih's room in Kao Family Settlement and looked at all the written material on his table. He even had some material in English that I couldn't read! That upset everyone.

We wanted to mobilize the masses for production, but he wanted to hold religious services. It was spring planting time, time to get busy in the fields, but he insisted on a huge parade [Easter procession] with all the Catholics, wearing white clothes, marching in from

Kao Family Settlement, South Temple, Horse Square and Long Bow. So we sent one of the Party Secretaries, Tu Shen-wang, to ask if he wouldn't call the parade off. It was no use. Shih said, "No. The people demand this procession. We must have it."

We decided to hold a mass meeting to oppose it, but none of the Party cadres wanted to speak. They were afraid they would violate policy and get criticized. Secretary Hsiao of the Changchih City Party Committee said, "What's wrong with all of you? Are you afraid to take on the Catholics?"

"If it's so easy, then why don't you do it," we replied.

In the end he persuaded Veteran Wang to make the speech, and we coached him about what to say. Old Wang Ching-ho got up and said:

"I'm a Communist. I don't believe in God, but I respect the constitution. We have our freedom, you have yours. But all freedom has its limits. According to the constitution our country is led by the working class in alliance with the peasants. Thus it is a people's democratic state. Our freedom is freedom under Communist Party leadership. There is no other freedom. But you people violate the constitution. You call on all Catholics to obey the reasonable regulations of the government. But what regulations of the government are unreasonable? All our regulations are reasonable.

"Our marriage law is reasonable, but you violate our marriage law because you don't allow people to get divorced—that violates the constitution."

Wang refuted Catholic practice on point after point. When the meeting was over Shih had to give way. He said he'd listen to the government, and he called off his procession. We made a big issue of it and he called it off.

In 1951 a serious incident took place. We held a countywide meeting to prepare for spring planting. Over 1,000 cadres came from villages far and near. Wang Shen-pao, the head of security in South Temple, a poor peasant and former Catholic, criticized the church sharply. "Every year we try to organize our people for production," he said, "but every year the church sabotages our efforts. Under the cloak of carrying on Catholic activities they resist all mobilization." When he got home he found a poisonous snake in his bed. Neighbors told him that word had gone out that he was a devil, and that God wanted to settle accounts with him. On his third day at home after that meeting neighbors found his body at the bottom of a well.

The death of Wang Shen-pao marked a turning point. In retaliation we launched a drive against the church. The first step was to catch and confront the priest, but we never even saw him. The people of the community gave him protection. They had cellars under their adobe huts and they linked the cellars, one to the other, with tunnels. When we came into the village the priest simply went into a cellar, then went from house to house underground. We couldn't find him. Sometimes, when he suddenly appeared in Kao Family Settlement or South Temple, Communist sympathizers notified us. But by the time we got there the priest had gone underground again and we couldn't find him. He had organized the whole community to stand watch. The women, sitting on the doorsteps, looked as if they were only sewing shoe soles. Actually they were lookouts who reported our arrival as soon as we stepped onto the street.

This game of hide-and-seek went on for three or four years. We never solved the murder case. In the end we let the matter drop. Church activity gradually wound down. Deputy Shih came out from underground and took up life in the village as an ordinary peasant. We thought the Catholic question had more or less been solved. I transferred to a new post.

But then, in 1966, the great Catholic uprising took place near Taiyuan. The Catholics had built an organization called the Legion of Mary. That year they spread the word that the Virgin Mary would perform a miracle on a mountain near Taiyuan. Members came from miles around, from other counties and even from other regions to observe and take part. Thousands came, tens of thousands, to stand in the darkness and watch the top of the mountain. As they watched a beam of light shone forth, proof that the Virgin had come at last.

Wang Ta-jen was in charge of provincial security. He vowed to break this case. He did a thorough investigation and then, one night, led a group of security men to the mountaintop. There they found a man with a flashlight turning it on and off to create the "miracle" beam. They arrested him and exposed the whole plot to the people.

One of the organizers of this affair was Shih Ho-fa. The authorities here arrested him for complicity and sent him to jail. They searched his home, seized all sorts of personal and religious material, and then prepared an exhibit to expose his underground activity. There was material in English, and a photograph of him sleeping with his niece, Shih Kui-hsiang, a well-known local opera star.

It turned out that all the time he was living that quiet life he was trying to corrupt the cadres and the activists, threaten people and spread "change of sky thought." He never took to the street himself, but used other people to carry out his plans.

During the Four Clean Movement after we exposed the miracle on the mountain at Taiyuan, we broke up the Legion in this area. Most of the Catholics repudiated their imperialist religion. Then production began to rise. Last year in Horse Square the harvest amounted to 600 catties per mou. So that's why I say something bad turned into something good. Change took place internally, propelled by help from outside, by a work team that concentrated hard on this problem. Because Horse Square was 100 percent Catholic we did a lot of work there and turned the situation around. Because Long Bow was only one-third Catholic, not so much attention had been paid to the problem here. So there are still believers here. They still meet and they still pray.

Wang Ting-mo apologized for the fact that he didn't have more material on the question. All his records, it turned out, had been seized by the Red

Guards when they threw him out of office in Yangch'uan. They seized complete files of material on the Catholic Church in Lucheng and destroyed them. For that, we decided, Carma had to shoulder a share of the blame.

In the years since 1971 it has become increasingly clear that Wang Ting-mo overestimated the results of his campaign to eradicate Catholicism in Horse Square. By the time the Communist Party held its Twelfth Congress in 1982, Party and government leaders had convinced most people that they would again allow freedom of religion. Catholics who had for years been meeting secretly for worship, or who had not dared meet at all, began to hang pictures of the Virgin Mary on their walls, quite often on the wall opposite a portrait of the still-revered Chairman Mao, and dared attend Sunday services in the open. Horse Square today is as solidly Catholic as it was at the time of liberation in 1945, while the Catholics of Long Bow can still claim about one-third of the population as believers.

After Wang Ting-mo left us on that September afternoon in 1971 we met once more with old Secretary Chang Kuei-ts'ai, Chang Hsin-fa and Shen T'ien-hsi to pursue the history of the village. After the Great Leap and the collapse of so many grandiose schemes, they said, the Southeast Shansi countryside witnessed a political and social retreat.

40

RETREAT

Hand back the land, our crops will flourish.
Hand back the animals, fat stock we'll nourish.
Hand back the tools, they'll never break.
Hand back sideline enterprises, money we'll make.

This poem was recited enthusiastically by Shen Ch'uan-te and Li Ho-jen, who still met for worship every Sunday as active members of the dwindling open Catholic group in Long Bow. By "hand back" they meant to hand back pooled property to individual, private owners. This was not only the demand of a few maverick peasants in Long Bow, it was the essence of the policy pursued by the Central Committee of the Chinese Communist Party under Liu and Teng as they tried to salvage something from the debacle of 1959. With the collapse of the Communist Wind, the collapse of the huge equalitarian organizations which that wind had fostered, and along with this the collapse of much of the production that had made both temporarily possible, the reorganized Party now led a retreat all the way back to individual production and property, including land, allocated to private use.

"On the question of knowing which form of production is best [collective or individual], the following attitude must be adopted," said Teng Hsiao-p'ing. "The best form of production is that which, within the framework of local conditions, is most likely to restore and develop production. . . . We can only progress if we temporarily accept the need to take one step backward first. . . . To build individual enterprise as a basic political line would be a mistake, but it could be used temporarily to cope with an urgent situation. . . . For the time being the most important problem is to increase food production. Insofar as individual enterprises can further this production they are a good thing. It is not important whether the cat is black or white as long as it catches mice."

The slogan Teng advocated was *san szu yi pao* (three freedoms, one contract). First, enlarge the area set aside for private plots; second, expand free markets for private buying and selling; third, increase the number of small enterprises responsible for their own profits and losses; fourth, let each family, as a production unit, contract to farm a certain amount of land and raise a certain quota of crops.

In agriculture there were to be four *send-downs,* or *returns*—the return

of land, draft animals, small livestock and groves of trees to private ownership. In industry there were to be five *adjustments*—cut back, close up,
transfer, merge and transform collective units. This meant converting
many of them back to private ownership. To many people this did not
look like a program for reordering, correcting and consolidating collective
agriculture and industry. It looked more like a program for liquidating
both. Since the critics of the Great Leap considered the failure to be
"seven parts man-made disaster," corrective efforts concentrated on those
social and economic relationships that were too advanced to be consolidated, equalitarian relationships which had brought about "acute contradictions" in the worker-peasant alliance. Wherever the problems were
most serious the suggested way out was to dissolve the larger cooperative
forms and put production back into fewer hands, even into individual
hands, if necessary.

In Southeast Shansi, Party Committees began to study the experience of
Anhui, where crop failures had led to people leaving home in large numbers
to beg. Brigades in Anhui had parceled out collective land, torn down
pigpens and divided up the collectively owned pigs, even destroyed several
dams and reservoirs in order to redistribute the land reclaimed from the
water. Soon Anhui "experiences" were being reproduced in Southeast
Shansi. Wuhsiang County collectives sent 7,000 out of 15,000 draft animals
back to their former owners. Regional leaders presided over the dissolution
of some 3,000 commune industries. They left untouched only the small
industries in West Gully, home of the famous labor hero Li Hsun-ta, and
in Linchuan County's Fuchang Commune. Li Hsun-ta was too famous to
flout directly. Fuchang was the home village of Wei Heng, Party Secretary
of the Southeast Region. Old friends and neighbors there made a personal
plea for the production facilities they had set up with so much sweat and
sacrifice. In the end Wei Hung made an exception for them.

Changchih City exerted strong pressure on the communes under its
jurisdiction to carry out "three freedoms, one contract." Wounded Veteran
Wang, then a cadre in the Rural Work Department, recalled in 1971 that
he had resisted the call.

"Of course," said Wang, "when this policy of *pao ch'an tao hu* [each
family contracts its crop] came down, we all wavered. How could we go
against a policy from above? On the other hand, how could such a policy
come from above? Without actually opposing it we did our best to prevent
people from taking that road.

"Some said, 'They've already started in Honan. We'd better hurry.' But
I said, 'This is really a strange policy, let's slow down a little.' Just then a
relative of mine came from Honan. He said it really was so. Each family
had been given five mou of per capita consumption land—that is, land for
subsistence—and five mou of public grain land where the crop was contracted to the state.

"The contracts were supposed to ensure that the crop actually got to the
State Grain Trading Company. For example, there was a brigade in our
commune that grew a lot of peanuts. But every year the peasants took so
many peanuts home that there were none left for the brigade to harvest.
Now with their land under contract the families, not the brigade, would

have to turn in the crop. They could hardly steal from themselves, so the problem would be solved.

"But, I thought, this isn't so good. What if people still don't turn any peanuts in? You can't use force against them. You can't execute them. The crime is not serious enough to warrant jail sentences. How, then, can this problem be solved? If you raise the slogan 'the family contracts the crop,' isn't this the same as saying 'the peanuts go home'? If we take this road we'll be making a big mistake.

"My colleagues said, 'They are already advocating this method up above.' But I replied, 'We won't do it by this method down below.' The fact of the matter was that we didn't think this policy was correct. We knew it was a wind blowing hard from somewhere, but we figured if we followed it we'd be criticized later, maybe even punished."

In Long Bow Chang Kuei-ts'ai also claimed to have been shrewdly alert. As he recalled that period, he said, he saw the new policy as a form of entrapment. "Promote 'three freedoms, one contract,' let all these people hop up and take the capitalist road. Then knock them down later!"

This was evidently a genuine response. When they heard the rumors about Honan, the brigade leaders of Long Bow met to discuss it. They decided that if Mao Tse-tung himself asked for the land to return to the families they would do it, but not otherwise. So in Long Bow no one split up any land. The commune broke up into four communes, as we have seen. Most communities abandoned brigade accounting in favor of team accounting, but they maintained the three-level system—commune, brigade, team—with the basic unit of production at team level. People continued to farm together as they had since 1956.

At the same time they returned draft animals to family care and encouraged individual sideline production.

The return of the animals did not reestablish the old system of private ownership. Animals sent down to be individually cared for were fed with grain and fodder supplied by the brigade, a form of "public ownership, private care" that worked only if the individual involved cared for the collective. Some people fed the animals as if they were their own. Others, as soon as collective property fell into their hands, wrecked it. Long Bow gave Shen T'ien-hsi a horse that was slick and plump. Six months later it remained so. Long Bow also gave the notorious rascal Whiskers Shen an ox. This ox did so poorly that people began to ask where all the food was going. When they saw Whiskers Shen's pig they knew. Before long the ox died but Shen's pig grew to be the fattest one in town.

When the ox died people got angry. They launched a public struggle against Whiskers Shen and demanded that he pay for the ox. But Shen, as usual, had no money. It made no sense to lock him up. So in the end he received only criticism.

"It is Mao Tse-tung's policy to repudiate and educate, but not to punish too much. So we were lenient," said Kuei-ts'ai.

Under the policy of encouraging individual sideline production lots of small enterprises appeared—individual shops, home weaving, other crafts and special services such as watch repair, lock repair and bicycle repair. In

Long Bow two family heads, Ch'in Lai-ts'ai and Wu Shuang-hsi, repaired watches. Each had a complete set of tools; Ch'in, Wu and other operators of family enterprises did so well that they stopped going to the fields. Whenever there was a fair or a market, far or near, they went there to set up booths. They repaired flashlights, pens, watches—anything that the people commonly owned. Since they didn't put any sign on their door they didn't officially engage in any business, but they did business just the same. In 1971 this was looked upon as a serious breach of collective norms.

The most enterprising village craftsman was Chin Shou-yi. He started with a small bicycle repair shop and developed it into a handcart manufacturing plant complete with forge and oxyacetylene welding equipment. By devious means Chin acquired an oxygen tank from a state industrial unit. A donkey cart driver, whose job it was to haul oxygen tanks from the plant in Changchih to the power station at the coalmine, always passed Long Bow at about the same time of day. Chin Shou-yi plied him with cigarettes and in return won permission to use some oxygen for welding—but never so much as to arouse suspicion. Later this driver found an extra tank at the plant and left it at Chin's house. Chin claimed the tank as his own.

As private crafts and services multiplied, the brigade leadership made some attempt to regulate them through a concession system. The brigade authorized craftsmen and repairmen to go out in its name, turn in the bulk of their earnings, and earn in return work-point credits that determined their share of the semiannual distribution. In other words, their earnings were pooled as cash income due the coop as a whole and then shared out through the same workday credit system that regulated the distribution of income to all members.

The method chosen was a flat-rate method with a built-in incentive to individual effort. Each craftsman who turned in 40 yuan each month earned credit for 20 workdays. On the surface this seemed to favor the brigade because the craftsmen were turning in 2 yuan for each workday credit when in fact the cash value of the average workday at its highest (1959) was 1.35 yuan and in normal years was usually closer to 1 yuan. Actually, the system favored the craftsmen because most of them could earn more than 2 yuan a day outside the brigade and most of them worked more than 20 days a month. They treated the 40 yuan as a sort of fee paid for the privilege of working out, a fee that enabled them to earn an income substantially larger than could be earned by those who only shared in the brigade pool.

Under this system Chin Shou-yi accumulated substantial capital in the form of tools and equipment. His earnings usually exceeded his expenditures and he reinvested the surplus. If he had been allowed to continue in this way he would soon have piled up more productive capital than his own labor could manipulate, thus creating the need to hire others. He could easily have transformed himself into an employing entrepreneur.

The craftsmen with their small shops and repair services actually contributed productive labor to society. They were creators of wealth. The same could hardly be said of all the traders and speculators who also took to the road at this time. The Second Plenary Session of the Eighth Central Committee (August 16, 1959) approved the reestablishment of free markets and the freedom to buy and sell throughout the countryside, with one proviso: Communist Party members and cadres could not participate. Such trade had in fact already begun. The Central Committee directive only legalized an activity that was already widespread. It was legalized because, temporarily at least, neither the state nor the vast consumer cooperative movement could provide all the things that people needed for their daily lives. Insofar as traders, and even speculators, did facilitate the circulation of much needed goods, they also made some contribution to society, but the returns were often way out of proportion to the contribution. Many of the most backward elements of society bestirred themselves, mobilized whatever cash they could find, bought small carts or bicycles, and took to the roads, buying cheap wherever they could and selling at whatever the traffic would bear, often for windfall profits. Young women again cast eyes on speculators as the most desirable husbands. All of this had a demoralizing effect on those honest peasants who stayed at home and tried to raise what crops they could on collective land.

Kuei-ts'ai went to the meeting in Changchih that announced the reopening of free markets. When he came back he told the whole community, "From now on whatever you want to sell you can sell. We Communists, however, will not take part." (This did not, of course, include grain, oil, machine-made cloth, pork or coal, which were rationed.)

In speaking of this later Kuei-ts'ai said, "All I could guarantee was that I myself would not trade in any free market. I was powerless to dissuade others. Since the Party leaders had called for free markets but had banned Communist Party members, I myself could not get involved, but I would let others do as they pleased. I said to Hsin-fa, 'They are calling for this now, but surely it will be changed later. Since we Communists are not allowed to join we'll certainly be called to account if we start buying and selling. There is bound to be a rectification movement!' At the same time I expected all the freaks and monsters would crawl out of their holes, and sure enough they did."

Former upper-middle peasants Chin Fa-wang and Chin Ta-hung, former rich peasants Chin Chung-fu and Shen An-lung, all bought handcarts and went out at night to profiteer. If all went well they could make 7 or 8 yuan in one night.

Yang Szu-ho went to Hsinhsien on his bicycle, bought 100 catties of turnip seed at 5 yuan per catty, and sold them in and around Long Bow for 25 yuan a catty. He made several hundred dollars in one night.

Chin Shou-yi, who traveled widely to find parts for his bicycle repair business and his handcart making, used these trips to do speculative buying on the side. He traveled south to Chengchow, Hankou and even Shanghai. He traveled north to Hantan and Peking. He bought bicycle tires and sold them back home at three times their cost. He bought bicycle spokes for 10 fen apiece and sold them for 1 yuan. Everywhere he went he bought silver coins from anyone who would sell them. He paid peasants 1.20 yuan for old coins and sold them in Hankou for 3 yuan apiece. This was an illegal but very profitable trade, which the Hankou police once brought to an abrupt halt. They confiscated all of Shou-yi's coins. It turned out that he had not even paid for them but had taken the coins on consignment to be paid for when sold. The people who entrusted their silver to him lost out completely;

they didn't dare bring any complaints against him because they were not supposed to have any coins in the first place. They were supposed to have turned them in for People's Currency during the Korean War, eight years earlier.

More widespread even than private trade and speculation and more damaging to collective solidarity was the reclamation of wasteland for private use. This was linked to the development of the free market because the products grown on the reclaimed private land (with the exception of grain) could be sold privately. This not only disrupted collective production in the countryside but also, to a certain extent, industrial production in and around the cities. Cadres and workers, enticed by the high returns, went home to reclaim wasteland and grow whatever was most in demand, such as tobacco, eggplant or turnips.

In Long Bow some peasants began to neglect the collective fields in favor of small plots of unclaimed land that could be found where larger fields met roads or canals, or on the banks of the roads and canals themselves. Whoever opened up such land could claim it for personal use. It was quite common for such "wasteland pioneers" to enlarge their small patches at the expense of the collective fields. In one notorious case a peasant even usurped the dry bed of an irrigation canal. It was the former rich peasant Chin Chung-fu who, not content with the profits made by pulling his handcart at night, opened up wasteland wherever he could, and finally planted a big plot in the bed of the main trunk canal which lay temporarily unused because land leveling work in Long Bow had fallen behind and the water level in the reservoir had fallen too low for pumping.

Chin Yi-jen, a former puppet street captain who had been targeted as a collaborator, said, "I'm too old to work collective land." He pulled out of his production team altogether and found, up on the mountain, not far from the highway, some small plots that added up to five or six mou.

The land reclaimers were not all former rich peasants and struggle objects. Wang Wen-te, a member of the Communist Party and successful leader of the railroad construction brigade for three years, opened up five or six mou of road and canal bank land. In his eyes this was not the same thing as trading or speculating. He justified it as production, increased production, and was able to raise 500 to 600 catties per mou on his own land at a time when the collective fields were still yielding only 200. Li Lin-feng also raised 500 to 600 catties per mou on reclaimed land.

Private land yielded well because intense effort went into it. People got up early, stayed out late, and skipped their rest at noon to till these plots. If they had any manure in the privy at home or any compost in their pigpen they took it to this private land instead of turning it over to their team for work points. They didn't do it openly, in the daytime, but late at night when most people were asleep. And they didn't take it out with carts that rumbled but walked out quietly with carrying poles. They worked so hard on private land at night that when they turned up for collective work in the daytime they were worn out. They worked slowly and found it necessary to lie down frequently for long naps.

During this period when the wind of private enterprise blew so hard,

Whiskers Shen, the rascal who starved the ox, had his finest hours. A vagrant before Liberation, Shen followed the garrison troops, looting and stealing. Fifteen years later, completely unmoved by the transformation of society, he still maintained his reputation for shiftlessness. He shrewdly analyzed the new social relations, took advantage of the trust that most people naturally placed in others, learned how to pose as a most admired soldier, militiaman or cadre, and fleeced people out of small goods and services over and over again.

Soldiers, militiamen and cadres all enjoyed certain privileges based on the contributions they ostensibly were making to the well-being of the people and the nation. By impersonating one or another of these categories Whiskers Shen found that he could enjoy all these privileges to the hilt without danger of immediate exposure. Public trust had become so prevalent after land reform remade rural society that people forgot to watch out for impostors as they always had before Liberation.

Cadres in the militia were entitled to haircuts at headquarters expense. In a barbershop in Lucheng County Town, Whiskers Shen claimed to be from militia headquarters. The barber cut Shen's hair, expecting to collect his fee from the militia commander, Tung T'ien-fu. As luck would have it, Tung T'ien-fu walked in as Whiskers Shen walked out.

"Since when did he join your militia?" asked the barber.

"Who?"

"The man who just walked out."

"That's not one of our men," said Tung. "That's Long Bow's Whiskers Shen. Don't you recognize that rascal?"

Next time, perhaps, the barber would. In the meantime he was out the price of a haircut.

As far as Shen Liu-chin was concerned, the world was wide. There were lots of barbershops. It was unlikely that he would try the same trick in the same place twice.

Penniless in Changchih one day, Shen approached the driver of a horsecart.

"I'm the head of the supply department of the middle school in Long Bow. Will you take me there?"

The man agreed, transported Whiskers Shen right to the door of the middle school, then asked for 2 yuan for his services. Whiskers stepped into the school gate, saying he had to get the money, and never came back. Finally the cart driver went inside himself, found the school office, and announced that the supply chief owed him 2 yuan for a trip from Changchih.

"But our supply chief has been here all day," said the surprised office clerk.

When the cart driver refused to accept this information, he called in the whole staff—cooks, helpers, supply chief, everyone. None of them looked in the least like the stranger who had ridden the man's cart.

Finally a student said, "I saw Whiskers Shen run out the back gate half an hour ago."

That solved the mystery but not the problem of the cart driver's fee.

"Didn't you recognize that rascal?" asked the supply officer, incredulous.

"If I ever see him again, I'll give him a thrashing," replied the driver. But Whiskers gave this particular cart a wide berth thereafter. The thrashing is long overdue.

One day in Peishih Whiskers Shen got very hungry. An attractive young woman caught his eye as she made her way home from the coop store. By the door of her home hung a plaque that said, "Soldier's Family." She had no sooner entered than Shen knocked loudly.

"Don't you know me?" he said, when she opened the door. "I was in your husband's platoon throughout the campaign."

Unwilling to offend an old comrade-in-arms of her husband's, the young wife invited Shen in.

"Are you afraid I'm going to eat your noodles?" he asked.

"Oh, no." She laughed. "Please have some."

So Whiskers Shen sat down and went through two bowls. As he started on his third, the woman's husband came home. Suspecting some sort of liaison he started to scold his wife for inviting an unknown man into the house. She, in turn, scolded her husband for not telling her his old army buddy was in town. In the midst of this fray Whiskers Shen quietly finished his third bowl of noodles and sneaked away.

The quarrel between husband and wife continued so hot and heavy that finally the neighbors had to intervene.

"But that was Whiskers Shen from Long Bow," said one. "Didn't you recognize the rascal?"

Shen Liu-chin didn't always get away unscathed, however. Once the workers at Shihkechieh Coal Mine caught him stealing coal. They painted his face, put a tall dunce cap on his head, and set him high on the top of a great pile of coal.

Shen kept shouting, "I'm from Shihtienkung. Shen Lai-ch'ing is my name."

But Shihtienkung people all said, "That's nonsense. That's Whiskers Shen from Long Bow. Don't you recognize the rascal?"

The mine workers apparently did, because after they brought him down from the coal pile they gave him a good thrashing.

Another time Shen went to Hsiwang to haul coal and stole some iron rods while there. Other Long Bow peasants saw him do it; when they got home they went to the brigade office to report the incident. The brigade chairman called Shen in, and as usual, Whiskers denied everything. Finally, after being forced to confront several eyewitnesses, he admitted his guilt. He had buried the rods on the road to Kao Family Settlement. He was sent out under guard to dig them up. When he got back he was brought before a large public meeting. He had to hold the bars high overhead while the people discussed his case. They struggled against him all afternoon. The meeting exposed scores of his venal tricks but it didn't do a bit of good.

A few days later this renowned rascal volunteered to act as matchmaker for a railroad worker who had been divorced by his wife. Whiskers said that he had a contact, an interested party; he needed only 70 yuan to close the deal. The desperate divorcé paid out 70 yuan to Shen. In due course the wedding took place. Only then did the poor man learn that neither his new wife nor her family had ever asked for or received anything in the way of payment. Whiskers, of course, had already spent the money. There was no way to force him to repay it.

"Since Liberation," said Kuei-ts'ai, "Whiskers Shen has been beaten up more than twenty times, but he never learns anything!"

It was during the years of retreat, with its erosion of collective life, that Chang Hsin-fa, chairman of the Long Bow Brigade, initiated a series of private transactions that involved housing. In the course of buying, repairing and selling four different houses over a period of eight years, Hsin-fa at one point borrowed several hundred catties of public grain from the village warehouse, then failed to repay them. In the end, this misappropriation led to his removal from public office, a traumatic eclipse for the single most important peasant leader in Long Bow. Leading Party committees came and went, Party Secretaries replaced one another (six times from 1948 to 1966), but Hsin-fa served at the center of the storm of village life from the middle of the land reform until the eve of the Cultural Revolution. Hsin-fa became Secretary of the Long Bow Party Branch in 1947 when Chang T'ien-ming, the first branch secretary, left to do district work. Hsin-fa held this post until 1949, then again for a year in 1953. In 1954 he resigned in favor of Shih Ts'ai-yuan, in order to become chairman of the new coop. When the coop expanded to include the whole brigade, Hsin-fa became brigade chairman and held this post until he was removed in 1965. Throughout those years he held important positions on the executive committee of the Party branch, most often serving as vice-secretary, and this was the Party post he held at the time of his disgrace in the housing scandal. Although nominally the Party Secretary held the key post at any level of organization in China after Liberation, Hsin-fa in fact led Long Bow even when he didn't hold that post. By virtue of seniority, ability and political experience he dominated the Party Committee regardless of its composition at any particular moment, and regardless of whoever might be serving as the nominal head. At different times, for short periods or long, Chang T'ien-ming Sun Chiu-hsiang, Shih Ts'ai-yuan, Wang Wen-te, Kuo Cheng-k'uan and Lu Chin-jung all served as Party Secretary, but each of them looked to Hsin-fa for advice and support and each of them followed his lead most of the time. He was the most stable factor in an otherwise shifting leadership and provided continuity that was otherwise minimal. Whatever successes Long Bow achieved had to be credited, in part, to his leadership. Whatever failures Long Bow sloughed through had to be blamed, in part, on him. It seems quite clear from the record that he did not have vision enough and was not clearheaded enough to set Long Bow firmly on the path to collective prosperity and keep it there. Over and over again, at important points in the life of the community, he did lead the way forward toward a viable cooperative community, but at the same time he did not fully grasp what socialism could mean in a wider sense. He submerged himself in solving petty problems, avoided conflict whenever possible, sought ways for the community to get by, and finally fell into a rut of personal enrichment through speculation in housing.

Hsin-fa, like the other poor peasants and hired laborers of Long Bow, won a house in the land reform movement. It was up against the Catholic Compound wall. This compound was turned over to the Regional Luan Middle School in 1950. In 1952, when the middle school sought to expand, Hsin-fa sold his house to the school, acquired a new plot of land, bought materials, and built another house up against the middle school wall. Later the middle school expanded again and bought the second house as well. With the proceeds from this sale Hsin-fa bought five sections of house in the south end of the village from his brother, Ch'i-fa. (Ch'i-fa's share at the time of land reform had been the famous Western Inn. When the brigade chose this site for its headquarters, it gave Ch'i-fa property of equal value in the south.) After Hsin-fa bought Ch'i-fa's house he fixed it up, and sold it, at a profit, to Yang Ch'eng-tao, a rich peasant settler from the Western Mountains who was related to the new Party Secretary, Lu Chin-jung. He then loaned some of the money to his brother Ch'i-fa, so that the latter could build a new house. Not long after Ch'i-fa completed this house, Hsin-fa bought it from him for 600 yuan, enlarged it, then turned around and sold it for 2,000 yuan. With this 2,000 yuan Hsin-fa built the solid one-and-a-half-story structure that he called home in 1971.

While it might be questionable for a leading Party member and chairman of the brigade to become so deeply involved in real estate transactions, there was nothing illegal in all the buying and selling that Hsin-fa did. If he had financed these many deals himself they might never have become an issue in Long Bow. The sad truth was that Hsin-fa did not have enough personal resources to both buy and fix up these various houses. From time to time he borrowed grain from the brigade pool and in the end failed to pay it all back. It was the private expropriation of public wealth that made Hsin-fa the target of an investigation when the Socialist Education Movement began in 1964. Altogether over a period of several years, and they were the hard years from 1959 to 1962, Hsin-fa borrowed over 900 catties of grain that he never repaid. He was able to do this because he was brigade chairman. Team leaders had a personal interest in working along with him, in maintaining good relations with him. When he asked to borrow a little grain they went to their team threshing floors and said, "The brigade needs three bags," or "The brigade needs five bags." Team members did not object because they assumed that careful records were being kept. If they did realize that the grain had been loaned out privately, they assumed that it would be paid back. Short of a major settling of accounts such as occurred in the Socialist Education Movement, they did not follow through on all the bookkeeping from month to month, or even, for that matter, from year to year. Thus Yu Pao-chan of the Third Production Team, Li Hsiao-fan of the Fourth Production Team, and Sun Chiu-hsiang of the Fifth Production Team all helped Hsin-fa out from time to time. They knew how much grain had been loaned to him. The team accountants also knew, but because he was brigade chairman they did not press him or hold him strictly to account. As the case broke open they all became targets along with Hsin-fa, who was designated a "Party person in authority taking the capitalist road." He became the central target of the Socialist Education Movement in Long Bow.

ALL HERE LI
DEFENDS HIS RIGHTS

Hsin-fa also played a leading role in the complex case that arose out of the disposition of Li Lai-ch'uer's house. This story is worth telling because it throws light on so many facets of the impact of socialism on village life—the anomaly of private property in housing at the heart of a socialist collective; the pressures toward favoritism exerted by relatives and in-laws; the reluctance of people in power to move in a case involving one of their number; the boldness of an aggrieved peasant in demanding a redress of grievances; and the strong emotional commitment to upholding the results of land reform which, in the end, had the power to carry everything before it.

To understand this case one must go back to the days of the Anti-Japanese War when Long Bow was a garrison point held by a detachment of Chinese puppet troops under Japanese command. The middle peasant Tseng Chung-hsi owned a small courtyard with two houses of four sections each, facing each other across a narrow strip of ground. After the Japanese occupied the village, local collaborators pressed Tseng into service as a street captain working directly under Company Commander Wen, leader of the puppet detachment that ruled the community. Tseng was an opium smoker and a small-time dealer. He supplied Commander Wen with opium and they spent many hours together, smoking opium side by side. During these intimate sessions Commander Wen pumped Chung-hsi about the affairs of Long Bow village, and particularly the underground resistance movement. It was information supplied by Chung-hsi, the Party leaders said, that led to the arrest and execution of Shen So-tzu, a leader in the underground.

After Liberation, during the first wave of struggle against collaborators, the aroused peasants attacked Tseng Chung-hsi and expropriated his property. They took his land, his courtyard and eight sections of housing. The Party later evaluated collaboration as a social phenomenon that had to be distinguished from feudal exploitation through land ownership and therefore had to be handled differently. Peasants' Association cadres automatically applied expropriation against landlords and rich peasants regardless of their social behavior, even against those who were revolutionary activists. They saw it as a class measure applicable to families as a whole, which could terminate their feudal-style land ownership and liquidate them as a class. Collaboration, on the other hand, they treated as an individual criminal activity to be punished according to degree; execution, imprisonment, heavy fines might all be used, but not the expropriation of property. They ruled out expropriation as a suitable response because it punished whole families for the crime of an individual and reduced middle peasants and poor peasants to beggary. Even expropriated landlord families had a right to land to work and houses to live in on a per capita basis. Should the relatives of collaborators, many of whom were middle peasants and even poor peasants, be treated worse than landlords? The answer was obvious.

As the movement developed in Southeast Shansi, cadres returned property even to people like Tseng Chung-hsi. In Tseng's case, they returned most but not all of his housing. The community retained four of eight sections as fruits to be distributed to others on the grounds that, as a puppet street captain, he had profiteered at the expense of the people and should give up something. The four sections of housing seized from Tseng were given to Li Lai-Ch'uer, a young activist who joined the Communist Party in the sixties; during the Cultural Revolution he became vice-secretary of the village Communist Party Branch.

Roughly translated his given name, Lai-ch'uer, means "all here." Since Lai-ch'uer had a habit of arriving late for meetings the joke on the street was that when he arrived the meeting could begin, the crowd was "all here."

All Here Li found living in the courtyard with Tseng very difficult. The quarters were crowded. The four sections housed not only All Here, his wife and children, but his aging mother, his brother and his brother's wife and children as well. For several years All Here's brother served away from home in the People's Liberation Army. When he came back he fell ill and lay bedridden at home for a long time.

Since both the house and the courtyard were small, the Lis and the Tsengs often got in each other's way. This led to quarrels. The quarrels were particularly unpleasant because Tseng always insisted on an indignant last word.

"You struggled against us and seized our property, and now you still want to oppress us," he would say.

"You struggled against us once. Are you going to attack us again and take the rest of our house?" his wife would add in her high, shrill voice.

Unwilling to live like this indefinitely, All Here Li looked around for other quarters and finally rented a few sections of house in the northern end of the village from the doctor, Chi San-chiang. At first homeowner Chi asked for a lump sum of 100 yuan in lieu of rent. Later he returned the 100 yuan to All Here and asked for 50 fen per section per month. This was later raised to 1 yuan a month and finally, after so many workers moved into the area because of the railroad yards and the brick plant, to whatever rent plant workers customarily paid for village housing.

Li found paying rent to be a burden, but the worst problem, again, was getting along with the neighbors, in this case the Chi family who owned the house. In 1965 All Here joined the People's Liberation Army himself. During the five years that he was gone his brother and his mother quarreled many times with Three Gingers Chi and particularly with Chi's mother. These quarrels reached a climax over the death of a pig. Chi's two baby pigs were always escaping from the courtyard. One day one of them was found dead on the street. Chi's mother blamed All Here's mother for the death of the pig. She threw the dead carcass in front of All Here's door and demanded payment. When All Here's mother refused she ordered her to vacate the house. To emphasize the point she made off with the front door and the frame of the main window.

With All Here away in the army and her second son away working on the reservoir, Old Lady Li did not dare resist. She moved out of the house and took refuge with a friendly neighbor. At the same time she registered a complaint with her nephew, Shen T'ien-hsi, a member of the security forces in Long Bow.

"These quarrels never end," she said. "Whenever the pigs ran away I went out to look for them. I even brought them home more than once. Now that one is dead she blames me. If you don't solve this problem for me I can't go on living here."

Shen T'ien-hsi conducted a thorough investigation, concluded that All Here's mother was not at fault, and warned Chi San-chiang's mother not to blame people at random in the future. After that the contradictions in the courtyard eased a little, but by no means disappeared.

When All Here was demobilized and learned about all these problems, he decided to ask the brigade for some land on the outskirts of the village. He wanted to build a new house and live in peace. As soon as his request was approved, he tore down the old house in Tseng Chung-hsi's courtyard and used whatever material could be salvaged to build afresh. There wasn't too much that was serviceable. After the establishment of the commune in 1958 the four sections had been heavily used as one of the three public dining rooms of the brigade. They were in a state of near collapse.

No sooner had All Here torn his old house down, than Tseng Chung-hsi began to build a shed on the spot. This really upset All Here. In his view the plot had become public land. The brigade had given him a new plot of ground. His old plot should therefore revert to the brigade. He went to Brigade Chairman Hsin-fa to protest.

"My old plot is now brigade property," he said. "The brigade can use it or you can give it to some poor peasant for personal use, but for Tseng to occupy it amounts to settling accounts with the land reform."

"Never mind," said Hsin-fa. "You have a place to live now. Why worry about the old place?"

All Here complained to Hsin-fa over and over again but Hsin-fa said, "Tseng is only going to build a cowshed there, what's all the excitement about?"

The excitement was about reversing the land settlement of 1948. The excitement was also about favoritism. Lu Chin-jung, the new secretary of the Brigade Communist Party Branch, had married Tseng Chung-hsi's daughter. Lu Chin-jung was allowing his father-in-law to reoccupy land that had been confiscated from him during the land reform and he was letting Hsin-fa take responsibility for it, since it was unseemly for him openly to favor a relative.

When All Here pressed the issue Hsin-fa said, "This matter is out of your hands. The brigade has already decided the question."

"Who made such a decision?"

"Sun Jing-fu and Kuo Fu-shu" (two other members of the Party Committee).

"I don't care who made it," said All Here. "I won't let Tseng build there."

"Whether you let him or not, the shed will be built. It's been decided."

Angered by the arrogance of this reply All Here tried one last ploy.

"It's as plain as the nose on your face. Lu Chin-jung has a hand in this!"

"Not on your life," said Hsin-fa. "Don't drag him into this. I'm handling this matter."

Blocked at every turn, All Here decided to wait until Tseng Chung-hsi had almost completed his cowshed, then appeal to the commune leadership.

Tseng Chung-hsi mobilized all his relatives, including Lu Chin-jung, to build the new building as fast as possible. Soon they put the roof beams in place and smeared the adobe walls with a final coating of mud.

Then All Here sought out Hsin-fa again.

"I want to protest the building of this shed."

"He can build there if he wants."

"I don't think so," said All Here. "Give me a letter saying that the brigade made such a decision and I'll take it to the commune office."

"Your mother's———!" said Hsin-fa. "You'll get no letter. Go to Horse Square if you want. See if you don't run six li for nothing. It won't get you anywhere."

"All right, don't give me a letter. What you've said will do. I'll go and find out."

Off went All Here to the commune headquarters. Knowing that Lu Chin-jung was a "big red person" (a favorite) in the eyes of the commune committee, he was prepared for a rebuff. Instead of asking for action, he asked for a letter of introduction to the Changchih Party Committee.

"Let's be patient," said the cadre on duty that day. "There are no responsible comrades here right now."

"How can I be patient?" asked All Here. "If you wait any longer the shed will be finished. It will be a fact. Do I have a case or not? If you can't do anything, I'm off to the city."

The commune cadre hesitated.

All Here got angry.

"You're all tied in," he shouted. "Has Party policy changed? Have I no right to speak? If you are so powerful, then take away my veteran's card. My brother and I are both poor peasants. We have both served in the army. But now, it seems, we don't even have a right to breathe."

The cadre looked at the veteran's card that Lai-ch'uer was waving under his nose.

"Take it easy. Don't get angry."

"I was calm enough when I came here," said All Here, "but there isn't much time. If you can't do anything, I'm off to the city right now."

Finally the cadre said, "Tell me the details once again."

As All Here spoke the commune official wrote his words down. Then he wrote a letter and stamped it with the official seal. The letter ordered Tseng to stop building until the matter could be investigated.

This was what All Here wanted. He ran the whole way back to Long Bow, sought out Li Chung-lu, the head of public affairs, and thrust the letter into his hands.

"See here, the commune has issued an order. If you don't act right away I'll make an issue of that."

Li Chung-lu ran out to Tseng's courtyard and ordered all work stopped.

"What's all this?" asked Chung-hsi. "Am I allowed to smoke a cigarette?"

"Smoke whatever you like, but read this letter."

He read the letter and passed it around.

Tseng said, "Let's finish the building."

But Lu Chin-jung said, "No. Let's stop. We'll have to stop."

Stop they did.

After three or four days they got together again and tore down what they had built. The land reverted to the brigade. The brigade, in turn, turned it over to the Third Production Team. The Team's best builders then put up a five-section house on the site to serve as a meeting and study center.

All Here Li was happy. He was willing for some other poor peasant to use the land. He was willing for the Third Team to use it. But he was not willing to see it revert, by default, to the man from whom it had been taken as fruits in the land reform.

Since Tseng Chung-hsi was a middle peasant and had been wrongly expropriated in the first place, I asked, was it absolutely wrong to let him have this land back? The answer was yes, it was wrong. It was wrong because the brigade leaders had settled the case back in 1948. They had returned most of Chung-hsi's buildings, land and other property to him after the second land reform conference in Lucheng County. They had not returned everything because he had profiteered as a puppet street captain. All Here held that this decision was just and should not be lightly overthrown by Lu Chin-jung, Chang Hsin-fa or anyone else.

Thus the case of All Here's house became an issue in the early sixties. All Here raised it as a grievance in the Socialist Education Movement, a grievance against Lu Chin-jung and against Chang Hsin-fa. In front of the "gate" held at Anch'ang Village, Hsin-fa made a startling admission. Lu Chin-jung, he said, *had* come to him for help in getting Chung-hsi's shed built. Since Chung-hsi was his father-in-law, he couldn't very well press the matter himself, so he came to Hsin-fa seeking a favor and Hsin-fa agreed. The two men as community leaders were natural allies, interested in mutual support. They underestimated All Here Li and they underestimated the very strong feelings that everyone still had about the final settlement made through land reform. Those feelings came to the fore again during the Cultural Revolution, fanned up by the same cadres who had ignored them in the Tseng Chung-hsi case, and they led to unforeseen consequences.

Even though it got him into trouble of the sort stirred up by All Here Li, Hsin-fa found it hard to refuse people when they came and asked him for favors. This was understandable when colleagues like Lu Chin-jung, the new Party Chairman, approached him. When the people were complete strangers, it was harder to explain. During the fifties and early sixties Hsin-fa proved to be somewhat lax in regard to new settlers who wanted to move into Long Bow.

Since he was himself from Lin County in Honan, he welcomed other settlers from Honan and did not always check thoroughly enough into their background. As a result some upper-middle peasants and even rich peasants settled in Long Bow as poor peasants.

In addition to those who came to Long Bow from Linhsien there were several who came from the Western Mountains. Between 1948 and 1950 travel passes had been abolished but rationing books and residence permits had not yet been issued and people could still move about freely. Li Jui-hsiang, his brother and his brother-in-law Hsiao Fu-lai were all dispossessed rich peasants who fled their homes in the Western Mountains and came to Long Bow seeking resettlement as poor peasants. Hsin-fa did not check out their background thoroughly, accepted their story that they had left home because of the goiter endemic in the mountains, and found land and housing for them. As resettled poor peasants they later received substantial state aid. Hsiao Fu-lai became storekeeper for the Fourth Team, but he was not as honest as he should have been, misappropriated goods worth several hundred yuan, and faced charges during the Four Clean Movement.

Lu Chin-jung, the new Party Secretary, also made errors in handling new settlers. He allowed his aunt's husband, Yang Ch'eng-tao, to move to Long Bow and accepted the man's word that he was a poor peasant. Actually, he was a man under supervision as a rich peasant in his home village of Changtzu. Later Lu Chin-jung recommended him for the position of buyer for the Sidelines Team. As sidelines buyer, Yang Ch'eng-tao grafted over 800 yuan, covered his tracks poorly, and so became a target in the Four Clean Movement.

Lu Chin-jung also used poor judgment in appointing Sun Chiu-hsiang as vice-team leader for the Fifth Production Team. Sun Chiu-hsiang was the same man who had served as Party Secretary to Long Bow in 1952 but had been removed from office and expelled from the Party when it became clear that as a soldier in the puppet garrison command he had supplied information to the enemy that led to the death of Ch'ing-to, an underground worker. With such a record Sun should not have been appointed to any new post, but Lu overlooked the man's past because he was an uncle. Sun Chiu-hsiang's appointment as vice-team leader also became an issue in the Socialist Education Movement, a powerful political wind fanned up by Mao Tse-tung to counter the *laissez-faire* policies of the recovery years, and reassert socialist collective values and customs.

This review of the years following the Great Leap reflects the political climate of the fall of 1971 when I talked to the Long Bow peasants and the Changchih City cadres. While they did not gloss over the disasters generated by the Great Leap, they concentrated much more fire on the derangements that arose from the corrective policies subsequently applied. In reality the collapse of highly centralized collective forms, the retreat to small group and family production control, the development of individual crafts and services, and the revival of free rural markets probably played some positive role in stimulating a modest recovery throughout the country in the early sixties.

That Long Bow village shared in this recovery is illustrated by the production figures for the years 1958 to 1964:

Average yields in catties per mou

1958	169	1962	209
1959	205	1963	251
1960	138	1964	210
1961	193		

By 1971, however, after going through both the Socialist Education Movement and the Cultural Revolution, cadres automatically condemned private production, regardless of scale, and sharply attacked family contracts, noncooperative buying and selling (generally castigated as speculation) and uncontrolled public markets. They piled up negative evidence on the "bourgeois" thrust of the times and never broached the possibility of positive economic or social consequences. Everyone at least paid lip service to the view that in the early sixties backsliding brought out the worst in Chinese society; some went to great lengths to prove that they had never really approved of any policies that came down from above that in any way threatened the viability of collective production.

By 1980 all this had been reversed. In the wake of the economic dislocations brought about by the Cultural Revolution and the rise of the "Gang of Four," the Central Committee revived policies identical to, or closely parallel to, those of the early sixties. New decrees extended a form of "market socialism" to the whole of China; private plots, free markets and enterprises responsible for their own profits and losses all won support from on high and promotion at the village level. Higher cadres began to condemn commune accounting in those few places where it existed, force brigade accounting onto the defensive, stress team accounting, and pressure many large teams to break up into smaller, multifamily units. In areas where farm production remained fragmented and scattered they promoted family production contracts, even an occasional "go it alone" nuclear unit as legitimate and necessary.

By 1981 it became apparent that the government favored family contracts or individual labor contracts not only in isolated mountain areas but as a basic form applicable to all farm communities everywhere. Flying over South Hopei in July of that year I saw vast areas of level plain that had been divided into ribbonlike strips. People from the area said that some of these strips were so narrow even a horse cart could not pass along them. Peasants were selling animals and carts and taking up their carrying poles. The new contract system had already led to a degree of land fragmentation unusual even in the days before land reform.

If today one were to ask the questions about the 1960s that I asked in 1971, the thrust of the answers might well be quite different, at least at higher levels of the administration. The facts have not changed but official attitudes toward them have, and this colors what people say, particularly those for whom career advancement takes precedence over all other considerations. Teng Hsiao-p'ing's "seek truth from facts" notwithstanding, for many bureaucrats in China the first article of objectivity still is, "What way is the wind blowing?"

42

THE NATIVES RETURN

 In the fall of 1962, perhaps the most difficult year in China's post-Liberation history, a young couple dressed in ordinary workers' garb got off the train at Changchih North Station and set out to walk the three li southward on the highway that would bring them to Long Bow. By carrying on their backs quilts that bulged with personal possessions, both had freed their hands to cope with numerous unruly packages and bundles that could not be tied up behind. As was the custom, the man walked ahead down the road, while his wife dutifully brought up the rear, afraid of falling behind, but even more afraid of saying anything about slowing down, lest her husband respond with some sharp retort.

In appearance the man was quite striking. His high, wide forehead gave him a brain case larger than average. Bullet heads, pointed heads, pin heads and flat heads are all quite noticeable in China, where so many men shave off all their hair, but this young man, shaven like the rest, exhibited a skull that was just the opposite in form. The top of his head was extremely broad and well rounded, like an egg large end up. It gave his whole face a spherical fullness. His eyes repeated the pattern. They were unusually large and round. They were also unusually bright. Perhaps, in themselves, they were no brighter than those of other young people, but because he was so obviously inquisitive, so eager to see and to learn, and so quick to absorb all the impressions that came his way, he radiated an exceptional vitality that was expressed first of all in his eyes, and caused people to notice them.

This unusual head commanded a body equally unusual in a negative sense. It was slightly deformed. His shoulders had been depressed and his neck pushed forward, apparently by too much work with a carrying pole, to the point where he was clearly *t'o* (camelbacked or humpbacked). It was not that he carried a great protruding lump on his back, but rather that his upper spine, slightly compressed and bent forward, caused his neck to thrust out instead of straight up and this in turn caused his head to precede him slightly. This suggested, as he walked, that he was most eager to get where he was going and was looking somewhat anxiously for some quicker way to his goal.

The man's deformed back did not seem to affect his health, however. He carried a big load and walked swiftly and steadily down the road.

The young woman who struggled to keep up with him was a petite beauty whose most striking feature was also a very round face set off by two round eyes almost as large and bright as her husband's. Her hair was bobbed, cut off abruptly just below the level of her ear lobes, a style that made her seem particularly vivacious and perky, like a teenager off to school for the first time. Her feet, clad in cloth slippers, were exceedingly small and gave the only clue that a delicate, well-proportioned body might be concealed under the sloppy blue jacket and baggy pants of the power plant workers' uniform that hung on her like a sack.

The young man was Li Ts'eng-pao, the individual who became the central target of the rectification movement nine years later. Just nineteen at the time, he was returning to Long Bow because his job as a power plant construction worker had been abolished. The young woman, his wife of only a few months, was Kuan Hsiu-ying, eighteen. Her job as an electrical instrument technician had also been abolished. Both these young people had been laid off as a direct result of the Sino-Soviet split that by 1960 brought about the abrupt withdrawal of all Soviet experts and the termination of all Soviet aid.

Nineteen sixty had been a year of real crisis. All over China crops failed owing to adverse weather and the dislocations of the Great Leap. At the height of the crisis the Soviet Union, in an effort to force China into line on questions of world policy, ordered its experts home. When they left they took with them many of the blueprints for the construction projects on which they had been working. They also halted shipments of machinery and materials necessary for the completion of these projects. These abrupt moves generated severe maladjustment throughout the whole economy, and threw the five-year plan into confusion. The Chinese government had no choice but to slow down and eventually halt many large projects. The shutdown did not occur all at once, but in the months that followed the Soviet pullout, major construction projects gradually ground to a halt.

As construction slowed project managers laid off workers first by the hundreds, then by the thousands, and finally by the tens of thousands. Those laid off included not only the construction workers on field projects but production workers in the native industries supplying these projects. Key machinery, especially heavy machinery, had been ordered from the Soviet Union, but light machinery and many other items and supplies had been ordered from domestic factories. As the orders were cut back workers were laid off. The layoffs were hard on many people who had left their native villages a few years earlier to enter the main stream of national construction with high hopes, only to find themselves suddenly going homeward with no prospects at all other than a life of hard labor wielding a heavy iron hoe.

But these individual setbacks also had a positive side. Hundreds of thousands of people with skills and experiences that could never have been acquired in the deep countryside suddenly found themselves thrust back into their home environments. They brought with them a significant accumulation of advanced culture, custom and technology. From the point of view of their home communities they were a windfall which no one had anticipated or planned on. Those who adjusted well to this sudden return often played a major role in the transformation of society at the village level. The Cultural Revolution later sent millions of educated urban youth into the countryside, but many of them were unwilling to go and many of the communities they settled into had difficulty absorbing them. On the whole, the results were questionable. The Sino-Soviet break, in contrast, sent large numbers of job-trained youth back to a countryside where most of them had always fit in well. Their home communities had little trouble absorbing them. In many cases they made full use of the skills and talents that the young people brought back with them, and elected them to responsible posts.

This was true, in the long run at least, of Long Bow, where the most important returnee was Li Ts'eng-pao (Swift Li).

Swift Li, though born in Long Bow, had not been born into the Li family. His father was named Lu Chin-shun, and he was the eldest of four brothers who prior to 1948 owned not one sliver of land or section of house among them. All they could boast of were some skills as carpenters and a few tools of the trade. They picked up work where they could find it. When there was no work they went hungry. They moved from Long Bow to Kao Family Settlement when buildings were going up there, but in the famine year (1943) no work could be found anywhere. Lu Chin-shun, on his own, moved back to Long Bow. That was the year Swift Li was born. His mother had already borne two sons and two daughters. There was not enough food in the house for two adults, not to mention five children, and the mother's breasts were dry.

Chin-shun and his wife offered their newborn son to his aunt, his mother's younger sister, who had married a Long Bow middle peasant named Li. She had already given birth to two daughters and very much wanted a son. But just as little Ts'eng-pao was born, she herself gave birth to a third daughter. Since she could not nurse two infants at once, she reluctantly turned the offer down. Lu Chin-shun and his wife, seeing no other alternative, abandoned the boy in a cornfield.

Aunt Li, who still wanted a son more than anything in the world, made a drastic decision. She took her newborn third daughter to the Catholic orphanage in the center of the village and turned her over to the nuns. Then she picked up Ts'eng-pao in the field and brought him home to nurse in the little girl's place. Thus Ts'eng-pao grew up in the Li family, and never knew, until many years later, that his real mother was the kindly "Aunt Lu," who lived on the other side of the village.

By that time Lu Chin-shun had become quite prosperous. He not only received land in the land reform but he signed up as one of the original members of the mutual-aid carpentry shop set up by Yang Chung-sheng. After some severe economic difficulties in the first few years, this shop began to prosper in the fifties. All its members did well. In the meantime the middle peasant household of the Li family fell on hard times. When Swift Li was two, his foster father died. Soon afterward his foster mother fell ill with a tumor in her womb. The growing tumor forced her to work less but her financial burdens never ceased to multiply. In addition to Swift Li, she had to support her husband's old mother and two young daughters. The family never had enough of anything in the household to go around. When Swift Li was eight he started out to school but didn't have enough money to buy books, paper, pencils or slates. Since he often went to play at "Aunt Lu's" house, his true mother was well aware of his problems. She fed him when he was hungry, gave him money to buy the school supplies he needed, and paid half of the tuition required by the school. The men at the carpentry shop, where his father, Lu Chin-shun, worked, kidded the boy when they saw him. "That's a nice slate you have. But you don't seem to know how to address the woman who gave it to you!" "What do you call the one who bought those books?" "Who gave you those pencils?" Every day they had questions. After a while it dawned on the boy that "Aunt Lu" was really his mother.

When he asked Aunt Li about it, she admitted that she had picked him up in the cornfield, but had been afraid to tell him because she thought he wouldn't stay in the family, wouldn't support her in her old age as a true filial son automatically would.

Swift Li's life improved a little when he was ten. That was the year people began pooling land and setting up producer cooperatives in place of mutual-aid teams. Widow Li contributed her land to the coop as her capital share. Her donkey went to work every day and earned work points. After two years the cooperative finally bought the animal. Then Widow Li got cash.

As coop members with an able-bodied donkey, the family members were better off than they had been farming on their own without labor power, but they were still very poor.

In 1955, when Swift Li graduated from the junior primary school, he passed the exam for entering the senior primary school but couldn't gather together enough money to enroll. The school was in Nantsui Brigade, several miles away. He had to move there to live and supply not only the grain he ate himself but also grain for tuition and books. The higher school charged fees well above those required by the junior primary school and neither Li's foster mother nor his real mother and father could afford them.

He finally solved the financial problem by borrowing 7 sheng of millet from a neighbor, Chang Ch'ün-hsi, the elected head of the village in 1948. Li's older brother, Lu Chin-jung, who was already earning work points and owned a bicycle, put Li on the frame of the bike, hung the millet in a sack from one side of the baggage rack behind, tied his bedroll on top of it and set off to the school in Nantsui. Somewhere on the way the sack came loose and fell against the revolving spokes of the wheel. When they got to Nantsui the millet was gone. The spokes had worn a hole in the bag and all the grain had run out.

This created an impossible dilemma for Swift Li. He had already registered for entry in the school. He hoped to be able to make payment some other way so he stayed on, ate grain provided by the school, and started to attend classes. But he found no way to borrow anything more. Once he ate school grain he was not allowed to leave until he paid for it, but since he had no grain to give in return he had to stay, eating more grain. Each day his situation became more impossible, more desperate. Finally his oldest brother, Lu Chin-fa, came back from Peking, where he was a student at the Aviation Technical School. Having saved a little money of his own, he went to Nantsui, paid off Swift Li's debt, picked up the boy and his quilt, and brought them both home. That was the end of Li's formal education. He was twelve years old.

Since he was unable to go on with school, Li started to work as a member of the coop. He drove a small donkey cart hauling manure, compost, grain and crop residues. Although he worked all year the family ended up 6 yuan in debt to the coop. His second sister, who was old enough to work, married and left home. The tumor in his foster mother's belly grew to the point where it bled night and day. Her face turned pale—a mask of white. Then his foster-grandmother died. Swift Li had raised two pigs to a weight of 80 pounds. He sold them for 47 yuan, borrowed another 20 yuan from the coop, bought a coffin, and buried the old woman. But after paying for the grain which he and his foster mother ate and paying the other expenses of the funeral, he didn't have enough money to pay the coop back in full.

As 1957 began Swift Li had to work even harder. He hauled manure by cart and by carrying pole, poured night soil into the seed pockets at planting time, weeded the sprouts as they grew, and in addition to all this physical labor kept the work-point records for his production group. That year things went better financially. He paid off all the family debts and came out ahead. He had 40 yuan in cash.

Swift Li then began to take an active part in the social and political life of the brigade. He learned to walk on stilts and took part in stilt parades. He joined the drama group and played roles on the stage during "cultural" evenings. He began to attend the political night school and took part in political discussions. In September he joined the Youth League, the Party-led group for young activists who wanted to play a political role.

That same year he underwent some physical changes. The heavy labor, particularly the work with the carrying pole, began to press his shoulders down and push his neck forward. Soon people were saying that he looked like a camel.

Swift Li never knew whether this slight humpbacked condition was the result of too much hard labor while he was growing, or whether he had inherited a curved upper spine. His older brother, Chin-jung, showed the same tendency after similar labor as a teenager, but there were many others in Long Bow who worked just as hard, or almost as hard, who showed no sign at all of back trouble.

Anyway, it was a question whether this could be called trouble, since it didn't seem to affect Li's general health. He ate well, slept well, worked hard and played hard, and had more energy and stamina than most young people of his age. At worst, being t'o made him stand out as slightly deformed, clearly unique, and certainly not as beautiful as a youth approaching his prime should be.

In 1957 the state built a power station in Anyang, a few miles to the north. This station was designed not only to supply power to local industries but to light up the villages as well. Young people were chosen by all nearby brigades to go to the power station to study electricity, then come home, put up wires and install lights in every peasant's home. Long Bow Brigade leaders chose five people, three women and two men, to go. One of these was Swift Li. After studying for three months they did come home to wire the village, but they had all done so well in their courses and made such a good impression that the Capital Construction Bureau of the Power Department of Shansi Province recruited them as permanent workers. One young women was assigned to electric meter repair. Two men and another young woman were assigned to electric generation, while Swift Li was assigned to work as a crane operator in power plant construction.

These assignments were made in March, 1958. One year later, after he had learned the trade, Swift Li traveled to Paotou, in Inner Mongolia, where the huge Paotou Iron and Steel works was then under construction. The power plant at Paotou generated electricity with steam to spare. The job at that time was to lay pipes so that steam could be supplied to the huge new Furnace #1, at the steel works. When this job was completed Swift Li helped install a second large boiler and steam turbine for the Thermal Electric Company. One incident that he remembered most vividly was watching, from high on the boiler, a convoy of official cars on inspection tour, driving up to Furnace #1. The lead car carried Premier Chou En-lai. That glimpse of the Premier, if only from a perch in the sky, made Li feel that he was taking part in a project of true national importance.

"Working outside like that widens your vision and stretches your mind," Li said years later. "If you use your mind you can learn a lot just by looking and doing. There are also good people from whom you can learn. At first I knew nothing and understood next to nothing. But just as, by visiting a place, you can begin to understand it, so I began to make some sense out of what I saw.

"The first time I pulled into Taiyuan Station I saw locomotives and freight cars everywhere. So many of them. And this was only one province. How many must there be in the whole country? How large our country is, and how wealthy overall! I felt that China was really tremendous; so many good things and so much wealth. I looked at this great city full of people, and then thought of the whole country, spotted with cities. How big! How full! How glorious!

"The very first day that I reported to work the master worker in charge put a safety belt on me and sent me thirty meters in the air. Looking down from that height I saw only great disorder. There were people coming and going in all directions, apparently without coordination or plan. But then I learned that each one had a task and a purpose, and that there really was central management on that construction job. And I contrasted that to the way we had always done things in the countryside, our haphazard, relaxed ways. On the job we had strict maintenance, repair and depreciation schedules. Why not apply the same standards at home? A piece of machinery, if it is just used and never repaired, will disintegrate quickly. And the same goes for crops in the field. You have to hoe, side-dress and spray on time or you lose out and get nothing. One can learn a lot from the way industries are managed, particularly in regard to the whole question of personal responsibility."

Swift Li's job as a crane operator made him part of a crew of fitters who were responsible for putting all the heavy pieces of a power plant together —the boiler, steam turbine, generator rotor and generator housing—and then linking all these up with pipes and tubes. Everything had to be exactly placed, level and in line. The pieces were heavy (the boiler alone weighed fifty tons) and required careful handling. Swift Li worked under the direction of a veteran fitter who acted as foreman and showed the new men how to fasten their cables, how to operate the crane with a light, sure touch, and how to line things up without error. In addition to lifting and placing heavy pieces, this crew had to build the frames that held the boiler upright and join miles of pipe. This they did by welding, using both electric and acetylene torches, often at dizzy heights. Swift Li left his crane from time to time to join the welders and added that skill to his arsenal.

Using the construction job as a sort of "university," Li kept a flexible steel ruler and a notebook in his pocket. Whenever he saw something interesting, something new, something useful, he measured it, made a sketch, and wrote out a simple description.

"In those days I had nothing else on my mind," Swift Li said. "When I saw something that I liked I put it all down in my notebook. If you write things on loose pieces of paper it is easy to lose them. So I always carried a notebook, and a ruler. I used to have a steel tape but I lost it. Then I bought a tailor's measuring tape and that was even better. It's so soft, you can put it right around any object. If I saw even a simple table that was well proportioned I'd measure it and write down all the dimensions—width, length, height and what material it was made of. If I saw a generator I'd measure both the drive and the driven pulley, the V-belt pulleys, and figure out the reduction ratio.

"That way I not only learned technology, but I polished up my writing and reading ability. I retained the level that I already had and even improved. If I had remained in the countryside and worked every day in the field I could easily have forgotten the ideographs that I knew. But because I kept writing things down I got better in time. Now I can even write a small essay and not be ashamed.

"A construction job is a great place to learn because there are so many different trades and skills involved—boilers, pipes, machine shops, welding, surveying. Every unit is complete and many-sided, with its own transportation, its own power, everything. And then, if you move from job to job you see even more. The more places you go the more things you see—the types and the sizes of the machinery, and different ways of doing things.

"If I had stayed at Paotou I would have seen only one set of methods, but I was transferred from there to Linfeng, then to the power plant at Anyang, and then to Chincheng, Yungcheng and finally to Taiyuan and the Hohsi #1 Power Plant there. Everywhere I went I learned something new.

"In addition to all that I learned on the job, I attended study classes that raised my level. First I studied electricity for three months, then later on the job I signed up for technical courses. If we worked with electricity we had to study it. Even so, I never worked with high voltages. In our construction work we set up everything without power. Once we completed the plant we turned it over to the permanent crews and we moved on. So, although we installed those huge transformers and erected those giant power poles and hung the high tension wires, we never coped with high voltage ourselves. The highest voltage on the crane was 380.

"I studied a lot of technology, I increased my level of literacy and I learned to admire the outlook and the strong points of the old workers. From them I learned to value state property, to come to work on time, to be responsible for my work and always to work hard. At a height of thirty meters, in bitter winter weather, they went all out to do a good job. This made a deep impression on me.

"When we erected a scaffold of wooden poles we had to use a lot of steel wire to tie the poles together. Then when we took the scaffold down we always had a lot of leftover, short pieces. Instead of throwing them away the old workers saved them, welded the ends together to make wire rings, and then used these rings to bind the poles together the next time. That worked really well. As the poles sank down the rings tightened on the wood and held everything firmly. Higher leaders learned about this and praised our crew for this economic innovation.

"In those days everyone wanted to be a hero like Hsiang Hsiu-li, the Canton girl who lost her life trying to save state property when the factory she worked in caught fire. She saved property but lost her life. We read books dedicated to Hsiang Hsiu-li and other heroes of construction, and we had cards with quotations from Mao Tse-tung such as, 'Fear neither hardship nor death.' We sent books and cards home to brothers, sisters, classmates and friends."

Living conditions on the construction jobs were crude. Workers always had to live in temporary houses—adobe and reed shacks, or even tents. When he worked in Paotou Swift Li lived in a Mongolian yurt. It was covered with canvas outside but had a layer of traditional felt inside. Li earned a meager pay to start with. As an apprentice he got 12 yuan a month. After six months this was increased to 17 yuan and after a year to 19 yuan. After two years he won promotion to the level of First Grade worker and earned 34 yuan. Then in 1961, at the start of his fourth year, he won promotion to the Second Grade and earned 40.5 yuan a month.

Swift Li drew his pay according to his grade regardless of the actual work done. While at Paotou he played an active part in Youth League work and took part in the Youth League Congress. After he was transferred to Linfeng, Shansi, in October, 1959, he was assigned work in the office of the Youth League. He spent four months doing secretarial jobs, registering letters, writing letters of introduction for people transferring to new places, collecting Youth League dues, sending out notices to other branches, copying documents and reports, paying out the salaries to the staff and other miscellaneous duties. When he arrived in Taiyuan in 1960 the Central Trade Union office took him on as a staff member. He was assigned to workers' welfare, which meant distributing relief funds to families in need during the daytime and showing films in recreation halls at night. The film team had two projectors, one 35 millimeter and one 16 millimeter. Swift Li's job was to order the films, schedule the showings, sell the tickets, collect the tickets, and operate the projectors. When the worker in charge of this team fell ill and retired, Li took command of the whole operation. Thus he became a skilled projectionist and organizer of cultural events.

Altogether, for Swift Li the years 1957 through 1962 were extraordinary years of travel, study, on-the-job learning, hard work, challenge and personal growth. In addition to all this he met a girl, became engaged, and before he was laid off and sent home, got married. The girl, Kuan Hsiu-ying, was not, in fact, any stranger to Li. Although she came from Chang-yi Commune, she had attended the training class at Anyang where Li studied electricity. After graduation she was assigned to meter repair, and their ways parted, but one year later she ended up in Linfeng working for the Youth League just as Li did, and it was then that he began to take notice of her. The secretary of the local Youth League, one Chang Ken-tse, was a native of Changchih, and knew both the Long Bow young people. They were obviously fond of each other, were beginning to see a lot of each other, and would soon fall deeply in love. Chang Ken-tse stepped in at the right moment to serve as a matchmaker. One day he called in Swift Li and said to him, "A young fellow like you really needs a wife. I'll introduce you to someone from your own area, Kuan Hsiu-ying. Then if you ever have to go back, you can go back together. If you meet and marry someone from outside and you are transferred home, you may lose her. She may not want to go back to some far-off village with you."

With an official introduction from the head of the Youth League, it became possible for Swift Li and Hsiu-ying to formalize their relationship. Once Secretary Chang broke the ice they became officially engaged. They could easily have arranged an engagement without his help, but Li liked to hide behind the formality of that official introduction. He was not the type of person ever to admit that he had taken the initiative in a romantic matter, or had on his own, without proper introduction, fallen in love. In this respect, in spite of being so modern, so scientific and so enlightened, Li still harbored many feudal notions. This was a common contradiction in the character of young militants in China. They exhibited a most advanced outlook toward politics, technology, national and world affairs, but often in regard to family matters and other intimate personal relations they unconsciously honored Confucius.

After Swift Li and Hsiu-ying were engaged, their work took them to different cities. He was transferred to Anyang while she went off to Yun-cheng. They kept up a correspondence. Two years later the layoffs which Secretary Chang had warned about suddenly occurred. All the apprentices recruited in 1958 received termination notices. With the Soviet withdrawal there was not enough work left for the older construction workers, not to mention the new recruits. The man in charge of the Trade Union Office in Taiyuan where Swift Li worked wanted to keep him. "I can keep one person here, and I've decided to keep you." But he could not persuade the power department to go along with that decision. They wanted to keep the people in the operating divisions and dismiss those in construction. The Trade Union Office could do nothing about it, so Li was laid off. But not before the office sponsored a gala wedding for him and Hsiu-ying, and loaded them both with presents to take home.

Swift Li and Kuan Hsiu-ying were married at the Trade Union Head-quarters in Taiyuan. Large red posters announced the wedding and in the evening the guests came. The chairman of the city trade unions served as master of ceremonies. He formalized the wedding by announcing it to the assembled company, urged both the young people to study well and help each other out, and then recounted the whole story of their romance, how they met, how they were introduced and how they later corresponded. Swift Li and Hsiu-ying then, of course, had to answer questions about their affair and cope with all the teasing and suggestive talk that young couples in China are subjected to on their wedding day.

What seemed to stick in Li's mind the most, at least when he talked of this occasion in later years, was the economic advantage of a wedding in the provincial capital sponsored by an important organization like the Trade Union Headquarters. The year 1962, that notoriously difficult year, was a year of shortages, even hunger in some areas; not only were grain, cloth, oil, coal and pork rationed, but cigarettes and sugar as well. The Party Secretary of the organization said, "Give them ration tickets. Let them buy clothes, blankets, candy. Make it possible for them to set up housekeeping when they get home." All these things were cheaper in Taiyuan than they were in Long Bow, and what the young couple couldn't afford to buy the organization gave them. Whatever money they themselves had saved they could spend on household needs because all travel expenses for returning home were paid by the organization. That was part of the layoff procedure. To top it all off Li's mother sent him a new quilt. When the pair got home they had no trouble setting up an independent household.

Back in Long Bow both of the returnees immediately found work closely related to the fields in which they had been trained. Hsiu-ying became the telephone operator at the commune headquarters in Horse Square and Li became the electrician for Long Bow Brigade. He worked as electrician for the next three years, but Hsiu-ying soon became pregnant, began bearing children, and had to withdraw from active work to rear them. Her work outside became less and less regular.

Politically Swift Li remained active as a Youth League Member. In June, 1965, on the recommendation of Hsiao Chia, Political Director of the Military Department of Changchih City, and leader of the Socialist Education Movement Work Team sent to Long Bow, Li was promoted to the post of Youth League Secretary. Soon after that he joined the Communist Party and immediately on joining became the vice-secretary of the Party branch that was headed by his brother Lu Chin-jung. The Party did not subject Swift Li to any period of probation or testing. It recruited him as a full member in good standing and appointed him to the post of vice-secretary of the branch all in one day. This was a somewhat irregular, if not an unusual procedure, and led to charges, by those who were not too happy with the way the brigade was being led, that Long Bow had become a "Lu Family Kingdom," that the "Lus" held decisive power in the community and arranged things to their satisfaction, regardless of the wishes of others. In terms of village politics Swift Li had become, without any plotting on his part, a "helicopter cadre," an individual who rises rapidly without apparent merit or effort, straight up into the sky. What propels the helicopter, of course, is influence—personal influence.

Nineteen sixty-two, the year Swift Li came home, was also the year that Yang Lien-ying, future vice-leader of the Women's Association, came to Long Bow. Laid off as a cook at the Huai-hai Arsenal due to cutbacks linked to the Soviet withdrawal, she came to Long Bow not because it was her hometown, but because it was the place her husband had settled into as a child when he came with his parents as a famine refugee from Honan. Nevertheless, as described earlier, she no sooner arrived than she began to play an important role and in time assumed two leading posts. Lien-ying's rise, unlike Swift Li's, had little resemblance to that of a helicopter, however. It was, rather, a steady progression made possible by hard work and devotion to the public good.

Coming to Long Bow to live and work in the same year, both Swift Li and Yang Lien-ying strengthened that group of activists that had run the affairs of the village more or less from the beginning. Li functioned as part of the leading group that included not only his brother Lu Chin-jung, but also Chang Hsin-fa, former Party Secretary and now chairman of the brigade; Chang Kuei-ts'ai, former chairman of the brigade and now a key member of its Party Committee; and Wang Wen-te, in the early sixties still responsible, as he had been in 1948, for security. Yang Lien-ying, as the wife of Wen-te's brother, Wang Ch'i-fa, automatically fitted into this group and was accepted both by the brigade leaders and the rank-and-file as a natural addition to it. All this would become significant later as the Cultural Revolution split the community and mobilized a whole body of people, who had never shared leadership, to challenge all incumbent village officers.

The careers of Yang Lien-ying and Swift Li struck me as being remarkably similar. Both of these young people, born in the disastrous years before Liberation, were unwanted children who survived only through luck. Both had to go to work almost as soon as they learned to walk. Had there been no Liberation, no land reform and no cooperative transformation, they would most probably have succumbed to war, disease or famine. If they ever had, by chance, managed to grow to maturity, they would have lived out their lives as illiterate, voiceless laborers whose ill-rewarded services went unappreciated, unrecorded and unnoticed. They would have shared the common fate of countless millions in the generation that preceded them. As it was, they lived to play extraordinary roles in their community, roles which came to have a meaning far beyond Changchih City, and eventually, at least in Swift Li's case, far beyond Shansi Province.

These two people returned to Long Bow just as Mao Tse-tung proposed a new mass movement designed to reverse what he considered a wholesale retreat from socialism after 1949. He was also determined, apparently, to reverse the setback that he had personally suffered at the Lushan meeting that same year.

43

MAO LAUNCHES A COUNTERATTACK

 In 1962 at the Working Conference of the Central Committee at Peitaiho and at the Tenth Plenary Session of the Eighth Central Committee held in Peking in August and September, Mao Tse-tung, still Chairman of the Communist Party but no longer responsible for administrative duties in the country, launched a counteroffensive against all those individualistic, profit-oriented, *laissez-faire* tendencies that developed so strongly in the aftermath of the Great Leap. The way Mao analyzed the problem, these were not isolated phenomena that sprang spontaneously from the activity of peasants who were still at heart smallholders. They were part of a coordinated offensive launched by hostile class forces, feudal remnants and bourgeois elements, both old and new, against the general line proposed by the Central Committee. As he described it, this offensive was not confined to the grass roots, but permeated the whole of society and expressed itself most dangerously inside the Party as a high-level attack on the fundamental goals of the revolution, the socialist cause itself. The slogan raised by Mao at Peitaiho was, "Never forget class struggle."

"Throughout the historical period of proletarian revolution and proletarian dictatorship, throughout the historical period of transition from capitalism to communism (which will last scores of years or even longer)," Mao said, "there is class struggle between the proletariat and the bourgeoisie and struggle between the socialist road and the capitalist road. The reactionary ruling classes which have been overthrown are not reconciled to their doom. They invariably attempt a comeback. At the same time, bourgeois influence, the force of habit of the old society, and the spontaneous tendency toward capitalism among sections of small producers all continue to exist. Consequently there are still some people who have not yet undergone socialist remolding. They constitute only a tiny fraction of the total population, but they always try to depart from the socialist road and turn to the capitalist road whenever the opportunity arises. Class struggle is inevitable under these circumstances."

To back up this statement Mao listed nine phenomena said to be common in the countryside that demonstrated the pervasive nature of class struggle:

1. The overthrown exploiting classes, the landlords and the rich peasants, invariably attempt a comeback. They seize every opportunity to counter-

attack, to take class revenge and to attack the poor and lower-middle peasants.

2. The overthrown landlords and rich peasants try in a thousand and one ways to corrupt the cadres and grab leadership. In some communes or teams leadership has actually fallen into their hands. Their agents have also seized some positions in other organizations.

3. In some places the landlords and rich peasants try to restore feudal clan rule. They make counterrevolutionary propaganda and form counter-revolutionary organizations.

4. The landlords, rich peasants and counterrevolutionaries make use of religion and reactionary secret societies to deceive the masses and engage in criminal activities.

5. In many places various kinds of sabotage by reactionary elements have been discovered, such as the destruction of public property, the stealing of information and even murder and arson.

6. In the field of commerce, speculation and profiteering are quite serious, and in some places flagrant.

7. Exploiting hired labor, usury and the buying and selling of land have also occurred.

8. Besides the old bourgeois elements who continue to engage in speculation and profiteering, new bourgeois elements have appeared who have amassed considerable wealth through speculation and exploitation.

9. In government organizations and in the sphere of collective economy, there have appeared a number of grafters, thieves, speculators and political degenerates. They collude with the landlords and rich peasants in committing misdeeds. They form a section of the new bourgeois elements or are their allies.

"What do all these facts tell us?" asked Mao.

"The most profound lesson they have taught us is that at no time must we forget class struggle, forget the dictatorship of the proletariat, forget to rely on the poor and lower-middle peasants, or forget the policy of the Party and Party work."

On May 20, 1963, Mao called for a Socialist Education Movement among all cadres and Party members that would "strengthen their proletarian class stand and correct mistakes running counter to this stand, so that they may correctly lead the overwhelming majority of the people in class struggle and in struggle between the two roads."

In issuing this call Mao made clear that for him it was not just a question of going forward more quickly or more slowly, a question of making socialism a little stronger or a little weaker; it was a question of life or death for the revolution.

"Class struggle, the struggle for production and scientific experiment are the three great revolutionary movements for building a mighty socialist country. These movements are a sure guarantee that Communists will be free from bureaucracy and immune against revisionism and dogmatism, and will always remain invincible. They are a reliable guarantee that the proletariat will be able to unite with the broad working masses and realize a democratic dictatorship. If, in the absence of these movements, the landlords, rich peasants, counterrevolutionaries, bad elements and ogres of all kinds were allowed to crawl out, while our cadres were to shut their eyes to all this and in many cases not even differentiate between the enemy and ourselves but collaborate with the enemy and become corrupted and demoralized; if our cadres were thus dragged into the enemy camp or the enemy were able to sneak into our ranks; and if many of our workers, peasants, and intellectuals were left defenseless against both the soft and the hard tactics of the enemy; then it would not take long, perhaps only several years or a decade, or several decades at most, before a counterrevolutionary restoration of capitalism on a national scale would inevitably occur, the Marxist party would certainly become a revisionist party or a fascist party, and the whole of China would change its color. Comrades, please think it over: what a dangerous prospect this would be!"

But even though Mao described the coming conflict as a matter of life or death, a conflict in which the very survival of the revolution was at stake, he stressed that the new movement was, as its name implied, still educational.

"The present struggle is one to reeducate people. It is to reorganize the revolutionary class forces for waging a sharp tit-for-tat struggle against the capitalist and feudal forces which are brazenly attacking us, in order to crush their counterrevolutionary arrogance and ferocity and to transform the overwhelming majority of the persons involved into *new people.* It is also a movement in which the cadres take part in productive labor and scientific experiment together with the masses, to make our Party more correct, greater and more glorious and our cadres into really good cadres, who are both politically good and professionally efficient, who are both 'red and expert,' who are not bureaucrats or lords floating above the masses and isolated from them, but cadres who are at one with the masses and supported by them."

The May 20 Directive, entitled "Decision of the Central Committee of the Communist Party of China on Some Current Problems in Rural Work," stressed that in carrying out the Socialist Education Movement Party cadres must rely on the former poor and lower-middle peasants and must therefore organize anew within the communes, brigades and teams of the collectivized countryside, organizations of former poor and lower-middle peasants who would elect all their representatives, committee members and chairmen and play a full role in assisting and supervising the commune, brigade and team management committees. The impetus for reform would thus come from below.

The main immediate task of these new organizations must be to conduct an all-around, thorough checkup on the previous years' accounts, inventories, public property and work points (known as the "four checkups") and also on all purchases made with state investment funds, bank loans and credits from commercial departments. Such a checkup would help resolve the widespread contradiction between local cadres and the people arising out of the confusion over accounts, inventories, public property and work points. Mao saw this contradiction primarily as one among the people and urged all cadres to "take a bath in warm water," "receive a preventive injection in time," so that they could lay down their burdens, correct run-of-the-mill mistakes, reestablish unity between themselves and the people, and return to their work at ease.

At the same time, since big grafters, diehard profiteers and political degenerates were exposed, Mao saw the movement as serious class struggle, a struggle to defeat and crush the "brazen attack of the capitalist forces."

By enabling minor transgressors to "wash their hands, take a bath in warm water" and lay down their burdens, the movement could ensure that all the good and comparatively good cadres united with the people against a few diehard enemies, thus "uniting 95 percent of the people and the cadres to fight against the class enemy. . . ." In other words, by helping to resolve contradictions among the people, this campaign should bring about a great unity among the people, a great unity among the cadres, and a great unity between the people and the cadres so that they could successfully handle the antagonistic contradictions that remained in society and blocked the development of socialism.

Point nine of the directive stressed the importance of all cadres taking part in productive labor on a regular basis. "The fact that Party branch secretaries are taking part in collective productive labor in accordance with the established rule shows that our Party cadres are ordinary workers, and that they do not lord it over the people. By their participation in collective productive labor, the Party branch secretaries will be able to maintain the widest, most constant and closest contact with the masses, to have an up-to-date understanding of class relations, the problems of the masses and the production situation, and to have timely discussions with the masses and thus solve problems by the mass line."

The directive called on commune- and county-level cadres to join productive collective labor on a regular basis and urged fewer and better-organized cadre meetings so that more time would be open for labor together with the people. Hsiyang County, home of the Tachai Brigade, was cited as a model in this respect.

At Mao's insistence this directive both began and ended with some basic Marxist theory. The introduction was Mao's essay on the theory of knowledge entitled "Where do correct ideas come from?" and the concluding or tenth point consisted of some comments on the Marxist scientific method in investigation and study. Both stressed the importance of practice, of joining the people in class struggle, the struggle for production and scientific experiment, "getting down off the horse," going deeply into primary units, living there and gaining systematic and fundamental knowledge on important questions. First comes perceptual knowledge, using the eyes, ears, nose, tongue and body; then, after the accumulation of enough perceptual knowledge, comes the *leap* to conceptual knowledge, the formulation of ideas; finally there is the testing of this knowledge in social practice, which alone can provide the criteria of truth. "Often," writes Mao, "a correct idea can be attained only after many repetitions of the process from matter to consciousness and back to matter—that is, from practice to knowledge and back to practice. Such is the Marxist theory of knowledge, the dialectical materialist theory of knowledge. . . . It is necessary," Mao continued, "for our comrades to study the dialectical materialist theory of knowledge so that they can correct their thinking, be good at investigation and study, can sum up experience, work better, overcome difficulties and commit fewer mistakes. . . ."

Why stress at this point that the source of knowledge lay in practice? Most probably because rote learning, formalism and jargon threatened to reassert their age-old dominance over Chinese political life.

Stressing practice could undercut that tendency, so deeply embedded in traditional culture, toward philosophical idealism, toward revealed truths, fixed, absolute and so faithful in their reflection of the hierarchical nature of Chinese society and the Chinese state—"the magistrate in his yamen, the peasant in the field with his hoe, all's right with the world." Without remolding their way of thinking could Chinese ever rebuild their lives?

Why stress, at the same time, the tortuous, back-and-forth nature of learning? Mao sought, perhaps, to prepare both people and cadres for long years of combat to come. His argument could also serve to refute those who, disturbed by the excesses of the Great Leap and the sharp setback to the economy that resulted, were repudiating the Leap altogether and along with it the People's Communes and the Party's General Line for Socialist Construction. To those who charged that the Great Leap was a disastrous exercise in voluntarism, Mao seemed to reply that no great social experiment could ever be conceived a priori. The way forward had to be tested out by plunging into practice, summing up experiences, adjusting and amending plans, then plunging back into practice once more.

While willing to admit enormous mistakes—"the chaos caused was on a grand scale and I take responsibility"—Mao was not willing to negate the Leap altogether. He spoke with bitterness about those critics who always emphasized the losses by putting them first; "while there is a loss, there is also a gain." "The fact that they put the word 'gain' second is the result of careful consideration," he complained. "Is it [the Great Leap] mainly a failure? No. It's only a partial failure. We have paid a high price. A lot of 'communist wind' has blown past, but the people of the whole country have learned a lesson."

No matter what others said, Mao was not willing to withdraw the central slogan first adopted for the production drive of 1956 and later reemphasized as the inspiration for the Great Leap. "Go all out, aim high, achieve greater, faster, more economical results in socialist construction." Nor was he willing to say that mobilizing the whole Chinese people for a great mass movement in production was wrong. Mao saw the mistakes as side currents, reverse eddies in a main stream that flowed majestically in the right direction. For him the central thing was not that so many mistakes had been made, but that hundreds of millions of people had pitched in with enormous enthusiasm to transform China and that neither they, nor China, would ever be the same again. The central thing was not that so many experiments had failed but that the people had successfully completed tens of thousands of experiments, both social and scientific, pushing the frontiers of the possible back a step. Against the cost of the Great Leap in social confusion, misdirected labor, material waste and dashed hopes, Mao balanced the appalling potential cost of "antiadventurism," "the sad and dismal flatness and pessimism of the bourgeoisie." Unwillingness to try, muddling along in the same old rut, failing to seize the time, failing to take the initiative, not daring to test the capacity of the Chinese people in the new conditions created by the socialist transformation of the economy in the middle fifties —what would such philistinism cost in the long run?

Now that retrenchment had repaired the ravages of the Communist Wind to a certain extent, had temporarily stabilized the situation and set the economy once again on an upward curve, Mao moved to stem the precipitous retreat from collective practice that Liu and Teng's emergency measures had initiated on so wide a scale. He moved to block the wind of private profit that was turning that retreat into a rout in so many places.

The method chosen was a new Party rectification movement, an open-door confrontation between Party members and a fully mobilized people. In the course of it, the honest majority of cadres could "wash their hands and take a bath," repudiate all capitalist mistakes and tendencies, and unite to go forward on the socialist road. Mao described it as a movement to bring the many together and oppose the very few, a movement to cure the disease and save the patient, and in the process educate both people and cadres in the choice that confronted them—as Mao saw it—the choice between capitalism and socialism.

Unfortunately, the Socialist Education Movement, as launched by Communist leaders in Shansi, had little resemblance in spirit or in form to the program outlined by Mao. The impetus came not from below, with the organization of the poor and lower-middle peasant masses, but from above, with the organization of huge teams of higher cadres who came down to ride herd on those beneath them.

44

TACHAI ON THE DEFENSIVE

"*K'e liao pu te* [terrible]!" exclaimed Ch'en Yung-kuei, the Party Secretary of Tachai. "Thousands came. They were *hsiao chang chi le* [arrogant in the extreme]."

The Hsiyang County Work Team, 5,000 strong, sent 300 cadres to Tachai alone. Since the total population of the brigade numbered less than 400, this was almost one functionary per capita.

The following pages tell the story of the work team's sojourn in Tachai and Hsiyang as Ch'en Yung-kuei reported it.

The work team cadres hardly had time to put down their bedrolls before they announced that they had come to look for worms in the flagpole (the rotten people holding office in the brigade). They promised to unite with whoever voiced complaints about the local cadres. They labeled all who opposed them counterrevolutionaries and said that the fruits of this movement (property siezed back from corrupt cadres) would amount to more than the fruits of land reform (the property expropriated from rich peasants and landlords) in 1946.

When Ch'en Yung-kuei heard their program, and particularly the point about uniting with all who had complaints about local cadres, he became alarmed.

There is something wrong here, he said to himself. These people have no class analysis. You may rely on whomever you like, thought Ch'en. I'll gather the proletarian forces. You gather the bourgeois forces, and we'll fight it out.

To his comrades he said, "Awake the whole village. Prepare for battle."

On that very first day team leader Chang Tzu-yi, a section head in the organization department of the Regional Party Committee, called the people together and set them to studying a document known as the "Peach Garden Experience." This was a summary, written by Liu Shao-ch'i's wife, Wang Kuang-mei, of the investigation and rectification movement she had personally led in a Hopei village. Her methods deviated sharply from those advocated by Mao Tse-tung.

"Why are you studying 'Peach Garden' so hard? Why don't you study Mao Tse-tung Thought?" asked Ch'en Yung-kuei.

"Old Ch'en," said Chang Tzu-yi, "you're still the smartest one. You understand." Then, turning to the others he smiled. "Look at you. You're so dumb. Ch'en sees the essence right away. It's quite clear, we mean to have some achievements [i.e., exposures]. If not, how could we report to the top?"

"You'll never get anywhere," said Ch'en.

But for a period Chang Tzu-yi and the work team had everything their own way. Ch'en had to leave for Peking to attend the Third National People's Congress as a delegate from Shansi. The Congress lasted forty days. In Ch'en's absence the work team set aside the brigade leaders, assigned team members to do their work, and brought charges not only against all the cadres themselves but also against most of the working members of their families. First of all they attacked Ch'en Yung-kuei. They said he and all his relatives were the same shade of red—a bad shade. They suspended Ch'en's son, Ming-chu, a leader of the Tachai Youth League. They charged Ch'en's daughter-in-law, a clerk in the commune cooperative store, with misappropriating funds, then closed the store down. They charged Ch'en's wife with stealing pig feed at the brigade pig farm where she worked. They did the same with the other brigade leaders. They labeled all of them members of a "Ch'en clique" and set out to prove how thoroughly power had corrupted them.

The work team cadres tried to build up damaging dossiers by applying an old principle of bureaucratic control—divide and rule. They called in Chia Cheng-jang and told him that Sung Li-ying had exposed all his misdeeds. Then they called in Sung Li-ying and told her that Chia had revealed her many transgressions.

They went to Chia's second brother and asked him to give evidence against several Communists in the Party branch.

"I won't do anything that is against my conscience," he said.

"If you oppose us you'll be classed as a counterrevolutionary," they threatened.

"I can't accept that," he retorted. "Just as a man who has never stolen can resist being called a thief, I can resist being called a counterrevolutionary."

As a last resort they told the Tachai cadres: "None of you can compare with Ch'en Yung-kuei. He has made a clean breast of things in Peking."

To prove it they piled documents on the table that they said contained all the material revealed by Ch'en in the capital.

But even this did not work.

"In other places," said Ch'en, "a work team could take a Communist Party member aside and tell him they had heard all sorts of charges against him or her from other comrades. The reaction would often be, 'That bastard, he spoke against me, I'll speak against him.' But when they tried these tactics in Tachai, the Party members didn't fall for them. 'No one would say a thing like that about me,' they said, and so they refused to hit back. It was impossible to set one of us against the others.

"So they spread rumors that we were proud, so proud that we couldn't be touched. How could other people study us when these work team members were so busy spreading bad rumors about us? When they applied pressure and we refused to submit to it, their anger blew sky high. 'Your mother's ————!' they said. 'We've never seen a Communist Party Branch as solid as this one.' "

Work team cadres under Chang Tzu-yi attacked the Tachai leaders individually and tried to pit them against one another. They also attacked the brigade as a whole in an attempt to destroy its vanguard reputation. First and foremost, they seized on the question of crop yields. Tachai that year had harvested over 600 catties per mou (72 bushels to the acre). Since not even the most prosperous villages on the Hopei plain had achieved such yields, the team leaders challenged the figures and began a hunt for discrepancies. Their first thought was "hidden land." Tachai people must be farming more acres than they recorded. Any crop divided by a low mou figure would come out with a high average. "800 mou!" they sneered. "Why, twice 800 mou would not suffice to cover the area you farm." Work team members, unwilling to trust Tachai peasants, went to all the surrounding communities—Chinshihp'o, Kaochialing, Wuchiaping, Chinke—asking people to point out which of the border fields Tachai farmed. Then they measured every field and every terrace from the boundaries of the neighboring villages to the top of Tigerhead Mountain. They came up with a figure well short of 800 mou. When this was rejected at the county seat on the ground that newly reclaimed land must have increased the total area, they surveyed the land again, this time making sure not to leave out even the smallest shelf at the highest reach of the seventh ridge. The total still came to only 796 mou—six mou short of the 802 that Tachai people had all along claimed.

This made the Tachai people angry indeed. The work team had lost six mou for them. They demanded those six mou back. As for the idea that reclaimed land must have added to the acreage of grain crops, they pointed out that the creation of new fields in the gullies had allowed them to retire some poor land on the ridges, and here they had planted trees. As a result their tilled acres had remained the same.

Since the work team couldn't find any extra land they decided that the crop itself had been exaggerated. They weighed all the grain stored in people's homes, and all the grain stored in the brigade warehouse. Then they checked all the figures of sales to the state. Everything checked out to the last catty. Not a single grain of Tachai's crop had been counted twice.

Then someone remembered that there was a regulation regarding moisture content. In corn that was not fully dry 1.25 percent of weight had to be deducted for each percentage point of moisture above 15.5 percent. This was a national regulation that Tachai people had never heard of. When told of this, they denied that it was applicable, since Tachai crops had been weighed and distributed after the lunar New Year. By that time the corn had dried well and certainly did not contain more than 15.5 percent moisture. Furthermore the State Grain Company had tested the corn delivered to the state by Tachai and had not reported high moisture.

But the work team pressed hard on moisture. They tried to carry the issue to the people. "Your leaders have their own Central Committee. They make their own policy in regard to moisture. You think you are getting a fair share of the crop, but actually 20, 30, even 40 percent must be deducted from the weight you think you have because of moisture. They have been cheating you."

Some people wavered, but others set the record straight. "We didn't deduct for moisture because our corn was dry. Aren't we getting bigger crops than ever before? Aren't you all getting larger shares than ever before? Of course. But they are telling you that we aren't harvesting big crops on the one hand and on the other they are telling you that we cadres have misappropriated so much that when it is divided up you'll get more than you ever got in the land reform! Does that add up?"

Fought to a standstill on the question of land measurement, total yield and moisture content, the work team cadres had to retreat. But they soon began a counterattack on the question of work points for cadres. "Your cadres," said the team, "have been reporting work points that they never earned."

All Tachai cadres indignantly denied this. "We have never reported a single point that we didn't earn," they said. But here a work team member tripped them up. He had been in Tachai long before with a high cadre of the Provincial Agricultural Department. This man had demanded full reports on many subjects, and so the cadres had reported to him during their noon break and at night after working hours. On the day that he left they still had not completed their reports. They talked through and beyond their noon hour, so that nothing would be left out and reported for work one hour late. All this the team cadre had recorded in his notebook—year, month, day, hour. But brigade records showed full work points for everyone that day.

The Tachai cadres had to criticize themselves then. They indeed had all received credit for an hour not worked. But the brigade rank-and-file didn't agree that this was cheating. They said, "You were late because you were working for the brigade, not for yourselves." And they asked the work team cadres point-blank: "When you work in your office eating the people's millet, have you ever been one hour late to work? Have you never been off sick for a day? Have you ever paid for medical care? You say you don't miss an hour a year? What nonsense! Not ten, not one hundred would be enough to cover what you yourselves miss!"

The team continued to find fault with the work-point system. Tachai people had always given work points to those who cleared away snow in winter. Since the brigade's winter work involved remaking one gully after the other, people had to get to the fields, haul rock and move earth regardless of weather. Without snow removal crews none of this could be accomplished. People considered snow removal as important as any other work. They allocated work points to it just as they would for any other work. If there were two brothers in a family and one went to build retaining walls while the other went to sweep away snow, they both earned the same amount. The work team cadres said this should not be. They had never heard of "snow removal" work points. They considered sweeping snow to be light work that people ought to do in their spare time. Under pressure from the work team the Tachai Brigade dropped snow removal from its work plan and abandoned all points awarded to it.

Having made some inroads on the issue of work points, the work team moved to a vigorous attack on Tachai's method of allocating the basic grain ration. The Sixty Point Charter entitled every brigade member to 300 catties of grain for subsistence, regardless of age or physical condition. Within this overall framework Tachai Brigade had worked out a system for graduated allocation that gave children under six 180 catties, those between six and ten 240 catties, and adults 300 or more depending on the nature of the work they undertook. The total amount of grain allocated per capita was 300 times the population, but children who could not possibly eat 300 catties received less. This created a surplus that could be allocated to those who needed it most because they worked the hardest. It also ensured that grain allocated to, but uneaten by, children would not find its way into any black market. No family received substantially more than it consumed, hence no family had a surplus to sell.

The work team cadres called this an unwarranted distortion of policy. They again accused Tachai cadres of setting up a Central Committee of their own in order to cheat the masses.

In fact there was not much about Tachai that pleased Chang Tzu-yi and his team. Its members criticized the new long rows of solid stone housing that Tachai people began to build after the flood washed out their loess cave homes as impractical. "There's no place to put a pig sty or plant a few tobacco plants," said the team. They also criticized the lack of a free market. "No free market? With life so bitter you haven't encouraged buying and selling? Isn't this suppressing the people?"

Some of the criticisms were well founded. Tachai housing did not allow for home-raised pigs or kitchen gardens. Other criticisms could at least be debated. Not even the Central Committee had reached a consensus on the question of rural markets, how large, how frequent and how free they should be. A few criticisms were patently ridiculous. An art worker from Taiyuan tried to ferret out what happened to the income realized through selling the offspring of the brigade mules. He suspected graft until he learned, to his surprise, that mules do not reproduce. Another city-bred team member wanted to know why Tachai cornstalks, unlike those he had seen elsewhere, grew so thin. He was looking at tall sorghum plants, known in China as kaoliang, and not at corn at all.

"Why did work team cadres attack Tachai like that?" asked Ch'en Yung-kuei. "Because Tachai was prosperous while the other brigades lagged behind. Knowing Tachai, one could make comparisons. One could launch a study movement. But they didn't start a study movement because Tachai had Ch'en Yung-kuei, and he could make trouble. Therefore Tachai was no good. They did their utmost to oppose Tachai and suppress that troublemaker, Ch'en Yung-kuei. Every day they came up with new schemes and designs to suppress Ch'en."

One official who considered Ch'en Yung-kuei a diehard troublemaker was Po Hung-chung. Po, leader of the 5,000-man Hsiyang County Work Team, came from the nearby village of Hotung. He was the son of one of the county's most powerful landlords. In 1945 landless peasants had completely expropriated his father's estate. By that time Po Hung-chung had already been a Communist for several years. He joined the Party during the Anti-Japanese War and rose quickly in its ranks. In 1964 he represented not only the Central Shansi Party Committee, but the Shansi Provincial Party Committee as well.

Sent down from the provincial level to lead this great rectification movement in his home county, he began by suspecting everyone, denouncing everyone and pressing everyone to confess crimes. He showed such vindictiveness toward all rank-and-file cadres, most of whom were poor peasants who had taken the lead in breaking up the feudal land system in Hsiyang, that they began to suspect him of seeking revenge on behalf of the landlord class. He could not have behaved worse if he had been a member of the Home Return Corps, they reasoned.

Home Return Corps units were irregular armed groups of landlords and landlord henchmen who came back to take charge of their native districts whenever the Kuomintang Army managed to recapture any territory from the People's Liberation Army during the post–World War II civil war. They seized back from the peasants whatever had been expropriated, hunted down and killed Communists and activists, and instituted white terror wherever they held sway.

Under the circumstances it hardly seemed unfair when the peasants began calling Po Hung-chung "Home Return Corps" Po.

"Home Return Corps" Po knew Ch'en Yung-kuei well. He had clashed with him only a few months earlier but, much to his chagrin, had not been able to intimidate him. The clash occurred during what was known as the "October Incident," a frame-up case that developed after one county head replaced another. The old county head, Chang Huai-ying, had inspired and led most work well. Under him cadres habitually joined in manual work, writers and actors crowded local stages with new plays and skits, and peasants created grain surpluses that stimulated investment in new industries. In spite of this record, Chang Huai-ying had to yield his post in 1961 to a man with a similar name but quite different politics—one Chang Jung-huai. The new county head proceeded to reverse all the basic policies initiated by his predecessor. He neglected collective production, praised reclaimers of wasteland for private use as "wasteland pioneers," encouraged private trade and individual enterprises for profit, and even advocated blowing up the main dam on the river so that he could redistribute the flooded land. When the people vetoed this he sold the dam to Yangch'uan City. As a result most of the brigade cadres in Hsiyang opposed his leadership.

In October, 1964, just before the Socialist Education Movement began, Chang Jung-huai announced that he had uncovered an anti-Communist plot in the county. He fingered eighty county-level cadres and 400 brigade-level cadres as participants. Some he labeled "counterrevolutionary" and jailed. Others he labeled only "anti-Party." He sent them to work at new posts to redeem themselves. Some twenty from all three levels of the administration—brigade, commune and county—he brought before the Regional Party Committee as special cases. The chief investigator in charge of the special cases was "Home Return Corps" Po. He accused the twenty of serious crimes, ordered them beaten, and questioned them until they broke down and admitted guilt. As soon as they admitted something, he had them beaten again until they admitted more. In the end, unable to find any way out, they could only lie in their quarters and weep.

All of Po's efforts failed to develop a satisfactory case, however. In the end, he labeled Ch'en Yung-kuei an anti-Party activist and called him in to confirm the charges against those accused. Angry because so many of his old comrades had been beaten, Ch'en rolled up his sleeves and prepared to fight.

"I called you here to expose them," said Po. "If you protect them instead, I'm going to press charges against you."

This angered Ch'en Yung-kuei further. He prepared to take on the whole Regional Committee.

"Why did I fight back so?" asked Ch'en Yung-kuei later. "Because they were not carrying out Mao's policy. If cadres had made mistakes they should be helped to learn from them. 'Cure the disease and save the patient.' But they were dealing merciless blows, even beating some people to death! They were hitting hard at the many to protect the few. I figured that even if they put me in jail someone would come along and let me out."

Unwilling to move decisively against anyone so well known as Ch'en, Po backed down and sent him home as fast as a return trip could be arranged.

In October, 1964, Po Hung-chung sent Ch'en Yung-kuei home, but he did not forget the resistance the peasant leader had offered. When he arrived in Hsiyang a few weeks later as head of the county work team, he focused primary attention on Tachai and saturated the brigade with hostile investigators.

It would be wrong to assume, however, that the style, tone and direction of the work team's efforts grew out of personal animosity alone. All the teams sent out to deal with brigades in the county acted in the same way. Following directives from Liu Shao-ch'i and An Tse-wen in the capital, all of them concentrated almost exclusively on economic questions, on the financial integrity of the peasant leaders at the village level, and adopted divisive tactics to force confessions.

45

HUNTING BIG TIGERS

"What the work team in Hsiyang County really went after was graft and corruption," said Ch'en Yung-kuei. "The more illegal money and grain they could report, the bigger their achievement, the greater their merit. That was all they were concerned about. They never mentioned two-line struggle, the socialist road or the capitalist road. So they didn't teach the masses anything."

On the question of graft team cadres did not proceed from reality, from on-the-spot investigation of real problems. Instead, they made charges based on the number of years a cadre had been serving and his or her relative had access to money. At a time when the total income of the brigade hardly amounted to 12,000 yuan, they accused Tachai's eight leaders of grafting over 12,000 yuan, without any evidence whatever. They accused Wang Hua-chou, the outstanding Party Secretary of Houchuang Brigade, of embezzling 4,000 yuan. They herded him into isolation together with all those cadres of his unit whom they had doubts about, twenty-four out of a total of twenty-seven, and watched them day and night. They allowed them out during daylight hours to work under surveillance but shut them in again at night under heavy guard.

Team members searched the cadres' homes and questioned their families sharply. They summoned Wang's wife again and again. They told her and her children that Wang was a "four-unclean" cadre and that his family must expose all the double-dealing he had been involved in. Wang's third daughter, only eight years old, had just started going to primary school. Team members called her in, demanded evidence, then pushed her back and forth between them until she fell and cut her head on a stone. They prevailed on Wang's second daughter, a boarding-school student at a distant middle school, to write a letter calling on her father to confess.

The work team cadres also went to all those willing to speak against Houchuang's leaders and called them together for accusation meetings. Most of them were ex-landlords and rich peasants who had lost property at the time of land reform. Of course they had ideas against the revolutionary leaders of the community. Wang admitted glaring at them, even cursing them. Why wouldn't he curse class enemies? But he steadfastly refused to plead guilty to any of the charges brought against him.

The work team found a man in the county who had been a buyer for a unit handling pottery. He had bought many large jars from the Houchuang kiln. He testified, under pressure, that he had once paid 800 yuan directly into Wang Hua-chou's hands and he signed a statement to this effect. Here, said the work team, was proof of graft. They called Wang in and asked him to admit the charge. For three afternoons and two nights running they made him stand, while they pressed for a confession. They shouted at him, banged on the table, pushed him against the wall, threatened him. But Wang stood firm.

"If this were true," he said, "I would ask to be expelled from the Party. I would ask to have my head cut off."

In the end the issue split the work team. The team member who had forced the buyer to give evidence admitted that he had fabricated the charge. The team leader transferred him in disgrace to another team, and dropped the matter of the 800 yuan. But he did not drop the attack on Wang Hua-chou. If he could not charge Wang with graft, he could still charge him with anti-Party activity. He could send him as a special case to a countywide meeting where cadres from three levels—brigade, commune and county—underwent investigation. The meeting charged Wang with anti-Party activity because he had opposed the County Party Secretary, Chang Jung-huai. For seven days and seven evenings the proceedings focused on Wang alone. At night two guards stood beside his kang while a third watched his door. "In order to go to the privy I had to ask permission of all three guards and they went with me, watching me every minute."

Wang had indeed opposed Chang Jung-huai. He had not only opposed him, he had played a leading role in organizing the forty votes cast against him as Party Secretary in 1963. He opposed Jung-huai because that cadre opposed Wang's own three-year plan for remolding Houchuang along lines pioneered by Tachai. According to Jung-huai, Houchuang lacked any resources that could be transformed by winter labor. When Wang refuted this and worked for the Secretary's defeat, Jung-huai labeled him a ringleader of the opposition, a secret conspirator who opposed the Party. Wang admitted opposing Jung-huai, but never admitted that he had ever opposed the Party.

"If it were not for Chairman Mao, I wouldn't even be alive. How could I oppose the Communist Party?" he asked.

All over Hsiyang County the work team led by "Home Return Corps" Po put local cadres under extraordinary attack. He held them under house arrest, mobilized their families against them, harassed them in endless meetings, charged them with serious corruption and even counterrevolution. A few of his less stalwart victims, unable to withstand the pressure, committed suicide. Many others seriously considered killing themselves.

When Ch'en Yung-kuei finally returned from the Third National People's Congress in Peking, he walked into a crisis at home. Even though the members of the Tachai Party Branch had stuck together and refused to bring charges against each other, some of the brigade members had submitted to pressure and raised false grievances against their leaders. Landlords and rich peasants living in the brigade under supervision had also raised grievances. These the work team had compiled, worked into reports, stamped with their official seal, and sent to T'ao Lu-chia and Wei Heng, leaders of the Shansi Party Committee who reported directly to Liu Shao-ch'i. With these reports in hand Liu concluded that Tachai was much worse than the Peach Garden Brigade where Wang Kuang-mei had overthrown everyone in power. Orders went down to step up the pressure to push all charges of graft and malfeasance and to carry the Four Clean Movement through to the end.

These orders flatly contradicted the conclusions of the National People's Congress where Premier Chou En-lai had praised Tachai as a model for the whole country to follow. At the Congress Ch'en had not only talked with Chou, he had attended Mao Tse-tung's birthday party and had exchanged a few words with the Chairman himself. Much encouraged, Ch'en Yung-kuei had departed for home, expecting to find that the work team had dropped its slanderous attacks. He found, to his dismay, that the team was pressing all charges with renewed vigor.

"The day I got home none of the ordinary members dared come near me. The cadres, gathered at my house, wept all afternoon. They shook hands, clutched my shoulder and said, 'The only reason we're still here is because we've been waiting for you. If it hadn't been for that we'd have found a way out long ago. Now that we've seen you we can depart in peace.'"

These old comrades were talking about suicide. Their talk stunned Ch'en. He needed a rest and time to think. He told them to go home and wait. Then right after supper he stormed into the work team office and demanded that the good name of the Tachai cadres be restored. The office was full of high officials, provincial level cadres, regional level cadres, department heads and vice department heads. One of the latter, a Yu-tzu County man named Liu, was on duty. He was looking over some documents, confident and serene, when Ch'en suddenly walked in and began pounding the table with his fist.

"You sit there calmly reading documents while my cadres are destroyed! Restore their good name for me. Restore their good name now!"

This confrontation so startled Liu that he jerked his head back, strained his neck and had to be sent to the hospital.

Having confronted and denounced the work team, Ch'en Yung-kuei went home and called the Tachai cadres together.

He asked about the rich peasants and landlords—what were they saying?

"They don't say very much."

"What about the people, then?"

"They've been badly frightened. They only meet up in the gully after dark."

"What kind of Communists are you," asked Ch'en, "that you can't stand struggle? You have to fight back. If you kill yourselves they will say you are guilty, that you killed yourselves out of remorse. Go back and struggle. Without struggle you can never win. Let's go and meet with the people. We won't die in their hands. We'll ask them if they want us to live or die."

He led his old comrades up onto the mountain where the people had gathered to move earth. The work team, getting wind of this, sent some cadres to watch.

Ch'en asked no one for permission to speak, as cadres under suspension were supposed to do.

"Here are all the Tachai cadres," Ch'en said. "Have they committed crimes that deserve death?"

The people stood silent. Many turned to look at the work team members who were glaring at them.

"No," shouted Ch'en. "Look here, look at me. No matter what crimes they have committed they don't deserve death. But this work team has tried to drive them to their graves."

In less than ten minutes Ch'en won the people over. Soon they were all talking at once.

"The work team deceived us and spread lies about the cadres."

By that time the work team cadres had gathered in force. Some of the activists deserted their leaders, joined the people, and started to attack the work they had been led to do.

It was getting dark. Ch'en turned to one of the team leaders and asked, "Can you accept this or not?"

The team leader shook his head.

Clearly the battle would go on.

Late that same evening an old friend, Wang Po-li, Party Secretary of Hsiaszulu, knocked on Ch'en's door.

"Old Ch'en, I have come in secret to see you. The work team has me under guard, but I came anyway. I came to say goodbye. I am going to kill myself."

"How can you think of such a thing?" Ch'en asked, in anger. "Are you a man or not? Before, when the enemy occupied Hsiyang, they couldn't kill us. But now you want to kill yourself!"

"They've pinned all these crimes on me," Wang replied. "How can I face anyone anymore?"

"Do the masses agree with these charges?"

"They don't dare speak out. But all the riffraff are active."

"This is exactly what's wrong," said Ch'en. "The masses don't dare speak out. Class enemies run wild and you, you want to kill yourself! You are wrong. If you dare kill yourself I'll mobilize the people of the whole county to repudiate you. As long as the work team doesn't chop your head off with a sword, you have to stay alive. If they put you in jail never mind. Sit there. Someday your case will be reversed."

Thus Ch'en shamed Wang Po-li into fighting back.

"As you can see the struggle was very fierce, both inside and outside the brigade," said Ch'en. "Fierce struggle was good, it educated us. It taught us to be cautious and careful when handling all struggle. What do I mean by that? In this kind of fierce struggle, if you fail to handle one point well, it will be used against you. We had to stress tactics. We had to unite all the cadres and rely on the masses again and again.

"This made the work team cadres stop and think. How could they ever accomplish their task? They kept reading about how teams in other places had such great achievements, how they had found so many big grafters, so many corrupt cadres. Since they had found nothing of the kind here they became nervous.

"Thus they educated us again and again. And we made even greater efforts to rely on the masses. If you don't have truth on your side you can't stand firm in struggle. We also feel strongly that unity is important. Without unity your group can be influenced. It can be split and broken up."

"We feel now," said Ch'en, "that Liu Shao-ch'i and his cohorts in the province, the region and the county, when they pressed us down, did a good thing. If they hadn't pressed us down so hard we wouldn't have become so tough. We were pressed into steel. They really suppressed us terribly. Suppress, suppress, suppress. We were very unhappy at the time. But when we look back now, we feel that it wasn't so bad. It turned into a good thing."

After his return Ch'en Yung-kuei served as a catalyst that united Tachai people and people all over the county for a counterattack. They fought one battle after another. One of the first occurred over snow removal.

Ever since Mao Tse-tung had called on the whole country to study Tachai, visitors had started coming to the six ridges and seven gullies of Tigerhead Mountain by the hundreds and the thousands. In winter, if the peasants did not clear away recurring snowfalls, the visitors could hardly move around. At times they could not even reach the Tachai Brigade from Hsiyang County Town. Once a particularly important group of 5,000 announced that it would arrive the next day. Higher authorities asked the work team to ensure that the visit went smoothly. In the middle of the night a foot of snow fell, blocking all roads. In a panic the team cadres went to the brigade leaders for help. "Clear the snow," they said.

"We can't," said the Tachai people. "There's nothing in the plan for clearing roads. You insisted that we cut all points for that. You'll have to clear the roads yourselves."

Confronted with what amounted to a sit-down strike, the work team had to reverse its position and approve work points for snow removal.

Seeing the power of collective *non*cooperation, the cadres of Houchuang were impressed. When the time came, they surprised the work team assigned to their brigade with a new variety of passive resistance that was as effective as it was unexpected. Their power to disrupt depended on a regulation that no work team could complete its assigned task and leave a village without first establishing a functioning Party branch. Wherever Party branches had been disbanded, all suspended members first had to renew their Party registration; then they could be readmitted and the branch reconstituted. Since almost all of Houchuang's Communists had been charged with graft, anti-Party activity or counterrevolution, and since few of these charges had been withdrawn and even fewer had been adjudicated, the Party members, led by their secretary, Wang Hua-chou, refused *en bloc* to register. Their action effectively marooned the work team on Houchuang's high hill and guaranteed that all unsettled cases would soon receive attention at the highest level.

The resistance sparked by Ch'en Yung-kuei's return came none too soon. Eighty percent of the cadres in the county had been labeled bad. Forty individuals had already committed suicide.

While Ch'en Yung-kuei mobilized resistance down below, members of the Central Committee began asking questions up above. Chou En-lai examined the "black material" sent up by "Home Return Corps" Po and decided that something was wrong in Hsiyang County. He sent a top-level group headed by Li Hsueh-feng to make an on-the-spot investigation.

When this group got to Tachai they asked Ch'en Yung-kuei to report on production.

"Production!" said Ch'en. "How can I report on production? The big problem here is the Four Clean Movement. Through the civil war, the land reform and the Great Leap we all survived. But now, after a few weeks of this work team, already forty people have died by their own hand."

The members of the work team, Ch'en said, confronted with these facts, became so nervous that their hands shook. A few days later Peking ordered the team to withdraw and sent a new team in its place.

The work team under Chang Tzu-yi was withdrawn from Tachai just as a new directive from Mao Tse-tung, known as the Twenty-three Article Document, came out. The new team came with a fresh mandate, based on the new document. One important clause required teams to handle advanced brigades by relying on and working through their existing Communist Party branches. Grass-roots cadres could no longer be set aside at the whim of a team leader.

"But when the new work team came, its members did not do what they had promised to do," Ch'en said. "They went back to the advanced brigades and started messing them up again. Once again they said, 'Advanced brigades have the most problems,' and they brought out that old 'Peach Garden Experience.' Wang Kuang-mei, what a bad apple! If I ever see her I'll bite her. At the meeting they said they wouldn't use Wang Kuang-mei's 'experience.' But when they came that's just what they used. And they did the same in Hungtung County. There they fought a second battle of annihilation! Later, at big meetings I often complained about our sufferings at Tachai, but the Hungtung people always said 'We got it worse!'"

In 1966 after the Cultural Revolution had already started, a third work team arrived in Hsiyang County. The members immediately began to attack for a third time all the cadres who had been the targets of the Po Hung-chung team. This sparked a rebellion that led to the overthrow of the County Party Committee and the whole county administration. Ch'en Yung-kuei took over the post of County Party Secretary. Then the brigade cadres and the people of Tachai, Houchuang and all the other communities that had suffered so much from Four Clean distortions demanded that the leading cadres of the Po Hung-chung team be brought back for criticism and reeducation.

Chang Tzu-yi had to return to Tachai. They put him to work in the fields during the day and at night held mass meetings to criticize him. Since he had led the massive survey that measured Tachai's land and had come up with six mou less than Tachai people themselves claimed to farm, they demanded that he fix up six mou of new land before leaving.

"Where is our six mou? You lost them; you had better find them. Fix up six mou for us or you can't go!"

"But" said Chang, holding out his soft white hands, "it takes 300 labor days to fix up a mou of land. I couldn't make six mou in less than five years!"

"Who cares how long it takes?" they replied.

They kept him at hard labor for a month.

"Our iron hands. His soft hands. He got a nice tan. Finally he wrote a deep self-criticism," said Brigade Chairman Chia.

The people of Chinkou Brigade, a part of Tachai Commune, once ordered Po Hung-chung himself to appear before them. Ch'en Yung-kuei walked over to attend the meeting. He wanted to make sure that the people really spoke out. He was afraid that it might be a relaxed affair, and sure enough, when he got there he found Po Hung-chung listening happily to a succession of mild criticisms.

"What kind of repudiation is this?" asked Ch'en, launching into a description of all the "Home Return Corps" crimes that Po Hung-chung had committed. As he spoke he became more and more angry, waved his hands, and pointed accusingly at Po. Ch'en's words and gestures galvanized the audience. People rushed up, seized Po by the arms and forced him to bow his head and raise his hands behind his back in the "airplane" position.

Po cried out in pain.

"What are you yelling about?" asked Ch'en. "Do you call this suffering? Have you forgotten how many people committed suicide when you led the work team?"

And so a pattern of sharp struggle, even physical attack on provincial and regional cadres emerged. Local leaders and rank-and-file peasants demanded the return of at least a dozen key members of Po Hung-chung's team, made each of them do the "airplane," then beat up those they hated most.

"The beatings were my mistake," said Ch'en. "If I hadn't pointed so accusingly at Po to start with, nothing like this would have happened in the whole county. But once the attacks began in my presence, it was hard for me to stop them."

The arrogance, high-handedness and perverse political bias of the work team in Hsiyang fostered a violent response. Like a black squall that heralds a major line storm, these beatings served as portents of serious disturbances to come.

46

TO PEACH GARDEN INCOGNITO

From Ch'en's account of the Socialist Education Movement in Hsiyang County it seems clear that it failed to define, isolate or overcome any real political errors or any real class enemies. It also failed to reeducate people, reorganize the revolutionary class forces in the countryside, or transform cadres into "new people."

Instead of helping the average cadre to "wash hands, take a bath" and put down whatever burden might be holding him or her back, the movement tended to fasten burdens more and more firmly on cadres' backs by indiscriminately attacking all mistakes and shortcomings as if they were serious crimes, setting cadres aside for such "crimes," and not allowing them to stand up and resume work after suitable self-criticism. Instead of a movement to unite 95 percent of the cadres and 95 percent of the people, it developed into a movement that split the people from the cadres, fostered antagonism against cadres, and set the cadres against each other. Four Clean work teams victimized almost all the cadres at the brigade and commune level because almost all of them, at one time or another, had confused public and private property, had eaten an extra meal at public expense, had taken an ear of corn or a piece of rope home from the collective fields, or had eaten an apple from a collective tree. Focusing on minor transgressions, the work team lost sight of the positive contributions many cadres had made.

In 1971 all blame for the distortion of Mao's original proposal, and consequently for the warped direction of the movement, centered on a set of supplementary regulations for rural work issued in the name of the Central Committee by Liu Shao-ch'i and Teng Hsiao-p'ing. These regulations came out as a supplementary ten points to the original ten points. I was never able to find a copy of those points but critics said they focused almost entirely on economic questions. Instead of setting out to clear up minor economic transgressions so that cadres and people could unite against those corrupting forces of private enterprise that were presumed to be on the offensive, the new directives concentrated on the irregularities themselves as the primary target. They defined the contradiction in the countryside not as a class contradiction between socialism and capitalism, a clash over the direction of development, but as a contradiction between those who were "clean" in four ways and those who were "unclean" in four ways, between those who had grafted and those who had not. Furthermore, they described the contradictions inside the Communist Party and those outside the Communist Party as overlapping or intertwined, which meant that both Party members and non-Party members were unclean, that grafters could be found both inside and outside the Communist Party, and that all should be cleaned up. This had the effect of equating Party members, who held primary power, with non-Party members who held secondary power or no power at all, and thus took the Party and Party members off the hook. A movement that was meant to focus on the central problem of the time, defined rightly or wrongly as "the socialist road versus the capitalist road," turned into a shotgun attack on economic irregularities and graft wherever these appeared. If work-team cadres could not find any big grafters they assumed, not that the community was "clean," but that the movement had failed.

Commander Tsao of the Shansi Provincial Revolutionary Committee said: "This inside-outside formula shifted the aim away from the Party people in authority at whom Mao had directed the arrow. Capitalist roaders inside the Party had power. If you didn't knock them down you couldn't solve the economic problem no matter how many cases you solved. Therefore it was not permissible to enlarge the scope of attack by saying you were after graft, per se, and that it didn't matter whether it was inside or outside the Communist Party. Such a position put the arrow on the masses, on the rank-and-file of rural cadres, because almost all of them had made a few mistakes, especially in the hard years.

"For instance, according to the regulations, subsidized work points for cadres (that is, payment for public work) could not exceed 2 percent of the total labor days worked by any team or brigade. In order to survive, cadres had to join·collective labor. They had to go to the fields along with everybody else most of the time. So if the cadre arrived late, ate an extra meal at public expense, took a slightly larger personal share, or feigned illness once or twice, this became an economic crime. Focusing on such 'crimes,' we didn't discuss his political line, what he stood for, how he led people, but only his mistakes, and we used them to show that he had a contradiction with the masses, with all the honest forces.

"Instead of trusting 95 percent of the people and 95 percent of the cadres we ended by mixing everything up—class struggle, line struggle, contradictions of all kinds. As a result we attacked all the poor and lower-middle peasant cadres. Having done so, we could not help but deduce that everything was extremely dark in the countryside, that in the villages there was nothing but one unrelieved network of crime. So the conclusion had to be that we had failed. If most cadres were, in fact, bad, then we had failed! We must therefore concentrate our forces for decisive battle."

Based on the assumption that most cadres were bad, the Party developed "human sea" tactics and stressed the importance of outside leadership. The Central Committee sent non-Shansi people into Shansi to give overall direction. Within the province these outsiders recruited cadres primarily from centers where no movement had yet been launched and concentrated them in the eight "problem" counties chosen for the first "engagement." The counties chosen included Changtzu in the Southeast, Yangko, Hungtung and Hsiyang. The leaders concentrated huge forces for training sessions in July, then sent them out to the target areas in October. On the average they sent one team member for every twenty families in the local population. They sent 7,000 cadres to Changtzu and 5,000 to Hsiyang. Of the latter, 3,000 were from outside the province.

All the teams, as soon as they arrived, set local Communists and cadres aside and began a search for material that could be used against them. They did this by "striking roots, making contact, and carrying out secret investigations" in the community. It was thought that if outside cadres were used and they did not reveal their real names, they would feel free to look into problems actively and be immune to all mutual protection and cover-up schemes.

Teams based their strategy on the "Peach Garden Experience." Liu Shao-ch'i's wife, Wang Kuang-mei, had entered the East Hopei village of T'aoyuan or Peach Garden with a Four Clean work team incognito. Declaring the democratic investigative methods used by Mao Tse-tung in Hunan in 1927 to be outmoded, she bypassed the Communist Party Branch and the people's organizations in the village and conducted secret, one-to-one interrogations. Our Shansi informants said she found one particularly vocal dissident in the village, believed him, depended on him, brought him to power, and suspended all other Party members and all the other cadres. Then, in an effort to help Peach Garden surpass Tachai in production, she recommended massive financial, material and technical help from above. Since the man she brought to power as brigade leader was an opportunist who gathered round himself a small clique of like-minded sycophants, he was unable to put "public first, self second," take agriculture as the base and grain as the key link, or unite the whole village for the large-scale transformation of nature. Instead of relying on the people of Peach Garden and on their enthusiasm for constructing a new socialist community, he relied on aid from the state, or loans, subsidies and outside experts, and as a result was not able to put to good use the material aid that was made available. The people, taught to expect help at every juncture, did not mobilize themselves, did not "go all out, aim high for better, faster, more economical results," but instead lay back and waited for others to solve all problems for them. Such, people said, was the final outcome of the real Peach Garden Experience. But Wang Kuang-mei, flushed with enthusiasm for the complete turnover of personnel that her efforts had caused in Peach Garden, and for the many "crimes" large and small that she and her colleagues had discovered there, wrote a report on Peach Garden that became the guide for the Four Clean Movement all over the country. Her report was reproduced and distributed as study material for work teams, village Party branches, and ordinary people everywhere.

The parallel between Wang Kuang-mei's Peach Garden Experience and the first guidelines followed by the land reform checkup team in Long Bow village in 1948 struck me as unusually close. In Long Bow at that time, because many poor peasants had obviously not *fanshened* (turned over), the land reform was declared to have been a failure. Since it was a failure the

Communists in the village must be to blame. Most of them must be bad, either class enemies, embezzlers and grafters corrupted by power, or "old good fellows" who went along with them. If land reform had failed and most cadres were bad, then the picture was dark indeed. The situation in the countryside was critical and the Party had to mobilize for a decisive battle. Work team members were told that they must either serve the people wholeheartedly like an ox or be sent to the slaughterhouse. Even though this threat was not meant to be taken literally, it was ominous. When they got to the village they set all the Communist Party members and non-Party cadres aside. They relied heavily on dissident opinions without too much regard for their source and tended to believe the worst about all the village leaders. As a result a number of opportunists and dishonest people cut a wide swath temporarily, the morale of honest people and honest cadres and Party members dropped to a very low level; for a time, at least, the movement bogged down in a round of investigations and self- and mutual-criticisms that could not find any way out. Truly if all the cadres were to be replaced, they must be replaced with people less dedicated, less experienced and less apt to maintain integrity while holding power than they themselves were.

In both these cases, in the land reform and in the Four Clean Movement, the instructions that came down from above could be accurately characterized as "left" in form but "right" in essence. They were "left" in form in the sense that they were couched in militant rhetoric and proposed drastic solutions to contradictions regarded as antagonistic. In a dark situation, with bad cadres everywhere, a great campaign would be launched to investigate all, overthrow all, and solve the problem once and for all.

They were "right" in essence because they raised ordinary contradictions to a level of antagonism that had no justification, no roots in reality. In fact, the situation was not as extreme as claimed. Most of the cadres remained good, or comparatively good. Attacking them all created a level of contradiction between them and the people that was artificial and destructive. Calling some of them enemies, when they were not enemies at all, split the cadres, split the people, and encouraged real opportunists and real enemies to raise their heads and make trouble. All this was a setback for the revolution that, if not corrected, could lead to disintegration and collapse.

Such tactics as these, which could be summed up as "attacking the many to protect the few," came to the fore over and over again at crucial times in the course of the Chinese revolution and served to divert the thrust of various campaigns. Each time the leaders unreasonably expanded the scope and range of their criticism they converted educational campaigns into broad attacks on the majority of cadres and, through them, on the people themselves. At the same time, they consolidated their own positions, thus "protecting the few."

47

TAKING A BATH

Cadres in Southeast Shansi insisted that before they launched the Socialist Education Movement at the village level, in key spots such as Yellow Mill and Long Bow village, they had corrected the excesses that had so marred its initial phase in Changtzu and Hsiyang Counties. They said they had abandoned "human sea" tactics for more traditional methods, had dispersed work teams, had rejected undercover investigations, and had banned blanket charges of wrongdoing. The movement nevertheless administered a traumatic jolt to the brigade cadres of the region, both the "clean" and the "unclean," for no one escaped its harsh impact.

In areas under the administration of Changchih City the Socialist Education Movement came late and in two waves known as the "Little Four Clean" and the "Big Four Clean." The Little Four Clean reached Long Bow in the winter of 1964 at about the time that the huge provincial work team left Tachai under criticism. To carry out the movement not 300 but three cadres arrived from the city: Chang Ken-hu, Po Kuo-hsiang and a man named Liu. Liu soon departed, leaving a team of two to carry on the work.

Long Bow's Four Clean team first called a brigade-wide mobilization meeting to explain the coming campaign and then set up a series of small meetings for "back-to-back" exposure of the cadres' mistakes and wrongdoing. "Back-to-back" meant that the accused did not face their accusers. The accused, and this included all Party members and cadres without exception, met separately at "unload the burden" meetings where they could hear the accusations, speak out their own shortcomings and crimes, expose the shortcomings and crimes of others, and, if they did this thoroughly, become activists at a later stage of the movement.

Once the bulk of the charges against the cadres had surfaced through "back-to-back" meetings, and the cadres had responded in isolated "unload the burden" meetings, the cadres confronted the people directly at what were known as the "bathtubs." In Long Bow there were two of these, one in the South and one in the North. Each "bathtub" was supervised by one of the Changchih City cadres and was manned by the former poor and lower-middle peasants of that section. They examined the cadres who lived in their neighborhood.

All these meetings went on at night. During the daytime the people and the cadres reported for work as usual. The atmosphere was tense and the questioning sharp. Team cadres Chang and Po did not make any presumption of innocence; quite the contrary. They suspected every cadre of wrongdoing, if not of substantial graft or misappropriation, then at least of having eaten an unfair meal, or of having used an unfair share of public wealth or property. They spread the idea that everyone must have at least one smudge on his face and that this should be exposed.

"I can tell from your face that you have problems," said Chang Ken-hu to the storekeeper of the Fourth Team, Hsiao Fu-lai, a former rich peasant who came from the Western Mountains to avoid goiter.

Hsiao's face flushed.

"See! See! What did I tell you?" said Chang.

Hsiao began to sweat. He wiped his brow.

"You had better speak out. Your problems cannot be small!" shouted Chang, pressing his advantage.

Under this offensive Hsiao cracked and admitted, one after the other, some of the dishonest things he had done.

The main accusation against Hsiao Fu-lai was that he had misappropriated several bushels of wheat from the storehouse under his care. When he admitted this he implicated Kuo Yuan-lung, the Catholic poor peasant who had defended Long Bow's Party members in 1948 as "good" and had served as a delegate to the first Village People's Congress.

Kuo Yuan-lung had fallen under a cloud in 1954 when he confessed to being a member of the underground counterrevolutionary Catholic organization, the Legion of Mary. The Communist Party member Meng Fu-lu, the wartime puppet village head Kuo Te-yu, the loquacious poor peasant Shen Ch'uan-te, the poor peasant Chi Yung-nien and the carpenter Li Ho-jen had all been exposed as fellow members. But because, once exposed, they spoke frankly about the organization and revealed everything they knew, they were not prosecuted, only criticized. Isolated for a while, they all gradually reentered the life of the community. Kuo Yuan-lung eventually served as a cadre for the Third Production Team. He first took charge of public affairs and did well enough at that to run for Third Team accountant. With this promotion he got in trouble again. He became known as one of the "eat more, use more" cadres, who could always be counted upon to show up at a wedding, or a housewarming, and eat their fill. At one point, when he could not balance his accounts, he said he had locked some cash in his drawer and lost it. Many people suspected that he had spent it. In the Four Clean Movement it turned out that he had shared the wheat that Hsiao Fu-lai took from the Fourth Team warehouse. Shocked by all these charges, his teammates removed him from office and returned him to the status of rank-and-file member.

Another production team accountant, Li So-tzu, recorded work points in a freewheeling manner. He wrote down extra points for his friends and recorded points for himself on days that he did not even report for work. In one year he gave himself eighty extra workdays. He also arranged extra grain shares for people whom he liked. As soon as the wife of one friend became pregnant he allocated a per-capita share for the baby that was as yet unborn, but kept no record of this in the Production Team book. Like Hsiao Fu-lai and Yang Ch'eng-tao, Li So-tzu was a new settler in Long Bow and the brigade leadership did not have any clear idea of his class background or his history. He said he was a middle peasant from Payi. Investigation revealed that he was from an upper-middle peasant family that had been unjustly deprived of property in the land reform movement. In the period of readjustment that followed, Payi cadres apologized and restored the family property at least in part, but the stigma of "struggle object" still clung to all family members.

Yang Ch'eng-tao, a rich peasant "struggle object" from Changtzu, who had been allowed to settle in Long Bow without any check on his past because he was married to Party Secretary Lu Chin-jung's aunt, was also exposed at this time. As the buyer for the Sidelines Team he handled more money than any other cadre in Long Bow. He bought reeds, wood, coal and anything else needed for the brick kilns, the contract work, and the other enterprises of the Sidelines Team. He kept sloppy accounts, failed to collect many "accounts receivable," and himself misappropriated large sums of cash. He so muddled the sideline financial records that no one was able to straighten them out again. As late as 1971 there were still 1,000 yuan in uncollected bills outstanding and it was thought that Yang Ch'eng-tao had grafted at least another 1,000 yuan. Long Bow sent him back to Changtzu under supervision and he remains there to this day.

Brigade members charged another accountant on the Sidelines Team, Niu Pao-shan, with having grafted over 1,000 yuan in the course of several years' work and removed him from office.

Another big case of the Little Four Clean involved Kuo Fu-shu, who was the chief accountant for the whole brigade. He had served in this post for nearly twenty years and was suspected of having embezzled large sums. Instead, his accounts were found short only 600 yuan, of which he was charged with misappropriating only about 100 yuan. This was enough, however, to bring about his removal from office, not because the sum was large but because it had been misappropriated by a former poor peasant who had served during the Anti-Japanese war as captain of the puppet police. It was this bad history, combined with a small breach of trust, that brought about a decision to set him aside.

When Kuo Fu-shu lost his post as brigade accountant, Shen Chi-ming's second son, Shen Chi-ts'ai, a Communist Party member and an activist, took his place. Under Kuo Fu-shu he had held the post of *chu-na*—cashier in charge of receipts and expenditures. Shen Chi-ts'ai's promotion left the post of *chu-na* open and a young man of twenty, Hu Wen-fa, stepped into that post, with disastrous results that will be described later.

It seems clear from these cases that the Changchih City cadres did not misdirect the policy of "suspect all, suspend all" that they brought to Long Bow as atrociously as their provincial colleagues had in Hsiyang County. Where graft and corruption existed, their suspicious attitude could lead to real exposures and the resolution of some cases. But at the same time, because no one mobilized the people politically or educated them about basic goals, the movement failed to go deeply into affairs. Investigations tended to scratch the surface only and produce evidence that was not always firm. Thus some cadres could pass the gate of the people, the "bathtubs," by giving false reports.

"Whatever you admitted," said Wounded Veteran Wang, "whether it was true or not, it enabled you to pass, if the masses were satisfied. If you couldn't satisfy the masses, then you couldn't 'go downstairs' [return to normal life] and you remained a target. The theory was that in the ranks of the cadres everyone had problems and everyone must speak out. But even if this was done, would all the problems come out? On the surface it looked as if all the problems were exposed, but actually very big problems might well slip by. This whole method was 'a left in form, right in essence' method. The people were never taught to understand and repudiate the Communist Wind of 1958–59, or the *San szu ye pao* [three freedoms, one contract] Wind that followed. So the work teams and the people only grabbed the 1,000-yuan grafters and the 10,000-yuan grafters. To judge whether or not the movement had succeeded they only looked to see how many grafters they had exposed. What this amounted to was using economic struggle to cover up class struggle. Since the team never mobilized the people to analyze or to expose the line that various power holders followed, none of the criticism or the self-criticism touched on line questions. Thus economism was used to avoid class struggle."

In 1971 cadres like Wang automatically equated policy differences known as "line struggle" with class struggle on the assumption that the different lines put forward were the lines of different social classes. While these assumptions are being challenged today, they were all but universal prior to Mao's death in 1976.

"Competition developed between work teams in different brigades. Wang continued. "One team would say 'We have found three 1,000-yuan grafters.' The other team would admit shamefully that they hadn't found any.

" 'You can't find any!' exclaimed the first team. 'Perhaps you are rightists?'

"Afraid of being called rightists, everyone looked very hard for big grafters and sometimes put 'grafting caps' on people even though the evidence was insufficient or even nonexistent."

Even with the best of motives and the most careful work it was not easy to uncover the truth about many complex cases. Veteran Wang, who had been in charge of special cases in the outskirts of Changchih during most of the movement, outlined some of the problems. In the first place the investigators had to make sure that they found the right person.

"We investigated a man named Hsi Lun. He was supposed to have knowledge of a certain transaction. But when we asked him to write down what he knew, he refused point-blank. We thought he was very stubborn, and we began to suspect him of bad motives. We went to talk to him many times but it was all to no avail. Finally it turned out that the man who knew about all these things was not Hsi Lun at all, but Lun Hsi. When we found Lun Hsi he cleared everything up in short order."

It was also important to keep accurate records of places visited, people interviewed and statements made. It was easy to run all over the place for nothing.

"There was a case of goods," said Wang. "The receipt said it had been bought in Houchuang. But there were three Houchuangs. We checked out all three but found no record of any such sale. One investigator who came back empty-handed was asked where he had been. He said he didn't know. He only knew that he had gone by bus to Hantan, a long day's drive to the east, and then out to some county town nearby.

" 'Where, exactly?'

" 'I don't know. Ask the other fellow who went.' "

How could anyone get to the bottom of anything with that attitude? Yet getting a complete story was very important.

In Hsipaitu Commune word spread that rich peasants had put donkey manure in the cooking pot at the community dining hall.

"Can such dastardly class revenge be allowed!"

Investigation showed that the story was not quite accurate.

Two old ladies were busy preparing dough for some steam bread. There was a strong wind blowing. One old lady warned the other to be careful and cover the dough well so that the wind would not blow dust or perhaps even donkey manure from the courtyard outside into the food.

A busybody outside the door overheard this remark, or part of it, and rushed to report that rich peasants were plotting to contaminate the food.

When an investigation showed that "it was just two old ladies taking pains to keep the food clean," the work team leader didn't believe it.

"Tell me another," he said. "I know what happened."

The city sent a second investigator to expose the class enemy. But in the end he could only conclude that the cooks were planning a good deed, not a bad one.

Long Bow's notorious Whiskers Shen stole a brass bearing, took it to the coop, and sold it. Rumor had it that this piece weighed as much as nine catties. People were indignant when they heard about it. But Shen wouldn't admit to any such sale.

"I don't care how great the anger is," he kept saying. "My crime is not great."

That was typical of his *hun tan* (mixed-up) logic.

" 'What do you mean, the anger is great but the crime is not great?' we said. 'Where does the anger come from if you have committed no crime?' "

A work team member went to the coop and returned with a slip written out by the sales clerk that said a man by the name of Shen had come in and sold a brass bearing that weighed eight or nine catties. But Whiskers Shen continued to deny the transaction. He admitted that he sold a pound or two of broken brass, but not any such thing as a shiny new bearing weighing nine catties.

Since he freely admitted many other crimes, some of them much worse than this, another member of the work team became suspicious. He decided to go back to the coop and look into the matter further. It turned out that right from the beginning the young woman who was the sales clerk had denied buying any such bearing. So the first investigator had gone to the coop manager. The manager said, "How can she remember? It was a long time ago." So he called her in and persuaded her to sign a statement. Now, she insisted she had signed the paper under duress. When the second investigator went to the manager with this information he said, "She's an unreliable element. She often makes false statements."

The second investigator finally came home with a statement proving that the first statement was false.

When people covered up for each other like that it was very hard to get at the truth.

Work team members put a Communist Party Branch Secretary under investigation. (Other members of his family had already been proven corrupt.) Under prolonged questioning he admitted that he had made 10 yuan through speculation. The details? He spelled them out—the goods he bought, the buying price, the selling price and the coop store where the transaction took place.

Repeated checks with the clerk of this store failed to reveal any corroborating evidence. Finally the clerk, under heavy pressure, wrote an affidavit that the transaction was exactly as the Party Secretary had said. In the end the Secretary admitted that he had made up the charge to get the work team off his back, and the clerk admitted that he provided the evidence for the same reason!

The work team in Long Bow made Shen T'ien-hsi, the big militiaman who had served as brigade storekeeper after 1961 on, a major target.

In a back-to-back session Wu Shu-lin said that he and T'ien-hsi had taken eight bags of wheat from the storehouse and unloaded it in T'ien-hsi's courtyard. Wang Wen-te and Lu San-kuei said they saw the grain enter T'ien-hsi's gate. T'ien-hsi admitted having kept the grain in his house overnight. This was because it had been loaded too late in the day to deliver it anywhere. But he insisted that he had delivered the grain to the State Grain Company the next morning. This was confirmed by Lu Yu-sheng, who hauled it away. But Yu-sheng had been untruthful in several other matters, so no one believed him. No one considered the fact that all the warehouse records balanced as conclusive. Since three people swore that the grain had entered T'ien-hsi's gate and only T'ien-hsi and the unreliable Yu-sheng said that it had been shipped on, the city cadres took the position that "there is no evidence that he didn't keep the grain." They demanded that T'ien-hsi pay back at least six bags. They would have demanded eight but for the fact that T'ien-hsi was feeding two brigade-owned mules at the time. Since the mules were sleek and fat it was assumed that they had consumed some of the stolen grain.

T'ien-hsi insisted on his innocence and appealed this decision to the commune leaders. They reserved judgment and the case dragged on until the Big Four Clean that began in August, 1965.

One result of the Little Four Clean that seemed unimportant at the time was the return to Long Bow of old peasant Shen Chi-ming's firstborn son, Shen Chin-ts'ai. Because his name was exactly the same as that of a distant relative, usually called "Big Shen," everyone called Chin-ts'ai "Little

Shen." When the checkup began in 1964 Little Shen had been working for several years as a staff member of the commune-run Credit Union at Horse Square. A thorough review of the Credit Union accounts revealed some sloppy bookkeeping. Little Shen was charged with misappropriating funds and was sent home under a cloud. For a Party member and a commune cadre it was a serious blow. Little Shen had embarked on what appeared to be a promising career. He was tall, strong, good-looking, literate and competent. To find himself suddenly home again, assigned to work on the Sidelines Team, embittered his heart. He felt certain that he had been destined for a greater role. He had ancestors who had made their mark, not only in the district, but in Lucheng County when Long Bow was part of Lucheng, and he was determined to do the same. Though raised as a poor peasant, Little Shen could not forget that his grandfather had been a *hsiu ts'ai,* a scholar who had passed the imperial exams, taught Chinese at the higher middle school in the county seat, and acquired thirty mou of land, a substantial estate on the Shangtang Plateau. The fact that Little Shen and his father, Shen Chi-ming, had been cut out of their inheritance by a grasping stepmother and forced into a life of hard labor had cast a cloud over his childhood, but by dint of diligent study in school and political activism in his spare time he had made a favorable impression on the brigade leaders, had been recruited into the Party, and finally won promotion to the level of a commune cadre. Now, through no fault of his own, he was back at the bottom again. Little Shen was not in the habit of judging himself harshly. It was possible that he had taken advantage of a deal or two, but in his eyes the deals were legitimate. The confusion in the coop books was certainly not his fault. He felt he was being used as a scapegoat for others who had misappropriated funds, then put the blame on him to protect themselves.

His career seemed to parallel that of his grandfather, the *hsiu ts'ai,* who, Little Shen Chin-ts'ai convinced himself, was too honest to prosper in the corrupt environment of old Lucheng. Grandfather Shen found himself matched at every turn against another *hsiu ts'ai* named Li, who also came from Long Bow. The latter's grandson, Li Kuang-tsung, still lived down the street. In the old days both men had the right to collect county taxes, but when Li collected them he always took twice as much grain as the government required and put the surplus away in his own granary. *Hsiu ts'ai* Shen, ostensibly because he felt sorry for the cheated peasants, denounced *hsiu ts'ai* Li to the police. But the head of the police bureau sided with Li. A long quarrel ensued. Exasperated, *hsiu ts'ai* Shen waylaid the head policeman and beat him up. This offense led to an indictment and a court trial in the course of which both *hsiu ts'ai*s mobilized all possible influence to guarantee a favorable verdict. Stalemated in Lucheng, the case went to the provincial capital, Taiyuan, where *hsiu ts'ai* Li had more clout. *Hsiu ts'ai* Shen lost the case, and soon thereafter died, whether from heartbreak or a flogging remains unclear.

When *hsiu ts'ai* Shen died, his grandson, Little Shen Chin-tsai, was one year old. The child soon discovered that as a descendant of the old scholar's first wife he had been born into the wrong branch of the family. His paternal grandmother had borne a son, Shen Chi-ming, and two daughters, but when she died her husband married again. He took as his new mate the daughter of a well-to-do veterinarian. The woman, spoiled by wealth, immediately took command of the household. She treated her grown stepchildren like servants. When her second child was born and her breasts ran dry she forced her daughter-in-law to nurse it, thus depriving Little Shen of his mother's milk. When *hsiu ts'ai* Shen died in Taiyuan, she connived with her father to divide her husband's property in such a way that she and her own two children got the lion's share while her stepson, Shen Chi-ming, and his children got only nine mou, three sections of house and a big slice of the old man's debts. Shen Chi-ming had to sell land and house to pay off creditors. He sent his wife and Little Chin-ts'ai back to Tunliu, where his maternal grandmother had inherited twenty mou. Then he himself went to Taiyuan to pull a rickshaw. After a year of hard labor he managed to save a little money to send home, but the messenger he chose to deliver the cash to Tunliu stole every cent. He worked another year, saved more, and this time returned to Tunliu himself. After that he hired out to a landlord as a hired laborer. When Little Shen Chin-ts'ai was thirteen he joined his father in the field during the busy season, then took to the road with a wheelbarrow in the off-season, hauling clay pots, cotton and any other freight that came his way. By that time a younger brother, Shen Chi-ts'ai, grew strong enough to join them. Laboring together, the father and two sons finally saved enough to buy back the nine mou and three sections of house they once owned in Long Bow. They returned home in time to take an active part in the land reform. After they won twenty-nine additional mou of land and half ownership in a mule, their life improved greatly. Both sons learned to read and write at a level sufficient for rural leadership, both joined the Communist Party, and both became cadres. When the elder, Little Shen, went out to work full time as an official of the Commune Credit Union, the younger, Chi-ts'ai, became an accountant, first for the Fourth Team and finally for Long Bow Brigade.

On the rise, Little Shen viewed the future with confidence. Success seemed to come easily both in the field of commerce, where he found that his affable manner and shrewd business sense made possible one fine deal after another, and in affairs of the heart, where he found that his good looks and promising career impressed women favorably. Chasing women got him into trouble more than once. His most serious scrape occurred in 1960 when he was courting a local beauty in Yellow Mill. The woman's husband resented the liaison and challenged Little Shen to a fight. Little Shen, almost six feet tall, easily vanquished the poor man, beating him so badly that he landed in the hospital. This was too much for the man's relatives and friends in Yellow Mill. They took the matter to the police, who promptly arrested Little Shen and held him for two months. In the end the principals settled the case out of court. County authorities never brought Shen Chin-ts'ai to trial. They released him, with his reputation as ladies' man and fighter much enhanced, but with his career record tarnished by an arrest and a jailing.

Shortly thereafter Little Shen became interested in a young woman who lived down the street. She was the widow of Chin Ts'ai-pao, the brother of Fast Chin, the militia captain. Ts'ai-pao's widow was famous for her good looks and her domestic skills. She was one of the best cooks, seamstresses and all-around housekeepers in the brigade. When her husband died many bachelors sought her hand. Foremost among them was her brother-in-law, Fast Chin. She reacted favorably to go-betweens sent by Chin and led them to believe that she intended to marry him. In the meantime she secretly received Little Shen in her home, fell in love with him, and suddenly, without warning, married him. Fast Chin, taken by surprise, was deeply offended and angry. He vented his spleen not on his sister-in-law, who had jilted him, but on Little Shen, who had so cleverly outmaneuvered him. From that time forth he carried a deep grudge against Shen Chin-ts'ai who was, after all, from the southern end of the village, had clan ties to the South Temple, and thus represented an opposition group that had always been in conflict with the people of the north who rallied around the North Temple. In Chin's eyes it seemed that his intended bride had been stolen by one of the enemy, something akin to the conquest of Juliet, a Capulet, by Romeo, a Montague.

Little Shen's return to Long Bow under charges of financial irregularity set the stage for conflict. In spite of the fact that the brigade, mindful of his commercial skills, soon placed him in charge of all sidelines, he considered the work to be demeaning. He had, after all, been a commune cadre. His level of literacy and his social experience left him better prepared for leadership than anyone else in the community, yet he was not elected to any brigade-level post but was relegated instead to a mere team. This was a loss of authority and prestige which Little Shen found hard to take, especially since he rationalized the charges brought against him in the Credit Union to be a frame-up, one that by implication replayed the injustice done to his grandfather more than a score of years before. That he and the whole family might also have rationalized that earlier frame-up could not be ruled out. Everyone always made the best possible case for his own side. In the flux and flow of official life in China, if a man didn't defend himself and his ancestors, who would?

As if demotion to a team cadre was not misfortune enough, Little Shen's new post put him at the mercy of Militia Captain Chin, who in name served the brigade chairman, Lu Chin-jung, but in fact acted as a law unto himself. Considering the hatred which Fast Chin had for Little Shen because of the matter of the "stolen bride," Shen anticipated nothing but trouble.

Little wonder, then, that when the Cultural Revolution came to Long Bow and Little Shen saw a chance to reverse the tables on those in power, he was ready and willing to act.

48

MAO'S TWENTY-THREE POINTS

The Big Four Clean began after Mao had launched a counterattack on the supplementary ten points issued by Liu Shao-ch'i. Mao deplored the way the Four Clean Movement was being used as a broad attack against the great mass of the cadres. A National Working Conference called by the Political Bureau of the Central Committee of the Communist Party in January, 1965, summed up its discussions with a document entitled "Some Questions Now Raised by the Socialist Education Movement in the Rural Areas." This document, divided into twenty-three sections, came to be known as the Twenty-three Article Document, or the Twenty-three Points.

It challenged the narrow economic orientation of the movement as conducted by Liu Shao-ch'i and focused squarely on the question of the class struggle alleged to be raging throughout the country. "In China," said Article One, "serious and sharp class struggle exists both in the cities and the countryside.

"Since the basic completion of the socialist transformation of the system of ownership, the antisocialist class enemy has been trying to restore capitalism by means of 'peaceful evolution.' Such class struggle is bound to be reflected within the Party. The leadership of some communes, brigades and enterprises has been corrupted or has been usurped. Our work is still confronted with many problems in its forward movement. But practice proves that it will not be hard to identify and to solve many of the problems in the cities and the rural areas, so long as our whole Party continues to implement all the decisions of the Central Committee on the Socialist Education Movement more deeply and more correctly, grasps the class struggle as the key, grasps the struggle between the road of socialism and the road of capitalism as the key, relies on the working class, the poor and lower-middle peasants, the revolutionary cadres, the revolutionary intellectuals and other revolutionaries, and pays attention to uniting more than 95 percent of the masses and to uniting more than 95 percent of the cadres."

Article Two directly attacked Liu Shao-ch'i's conception of the movement itself. Mao asked, "What is the nature of the movement?" and he came up with three alternatives:

1. There is the contradiction between being clean and being dirty on the

four questions (no longer simply accounts, inventories, public property and work points, all of which had to do with transactions in the economic sphere, but rather four categories of behavior: political, economic, organizational and ideological).

2. There is the intertwining of the contradictions inside the Party and of the contradictions outside the Party; and there is the intertwining of the contradictions between the enemy and ourselves, on the one hand, and of the contradictions among the people on the other.

3. There is the contradiction between socialism and capitalism.

The first two formulations came directly from Liu Shao-ch'i's Ten Points. Mao rejected them as classless and ahistorical. The third, said Mao, is "a Marxist-Leninist formulation" in accord with the basic thesis put forward in 1949 that "throughout the transitional period, class contradictions, the class struggle between the proletariat and the bourgeoisie, and the struggle between the road of socialism and the road of capitalism will continue to exist."

Mao then formulated for the first time very clearly what the main target of this movement was to be: "Party members in leading posts who take the capitalist road." The target, then, was not simply grafters, not simply bureaucrats, not simply people with mistakes, but Party members in power who followed a bourgeois line, promoted careerism, individualism, private enterprise and private gain, and undermined the socialist system of ownership and the socialist system of production and exchange.

Mao went on to describe, in general, who these Party members in leading posts taking the capitalist road might be. . . .

"Some act on the stage while the others operate behind the scenes.

"Of those who support these elements, some are in the lower levels and the rest are in the higher levels.

"Of those in the lower levels who support these elements, there are landlords, rich peasants, counterrevolutionaries and other bad elements who have already been identified as such, and there are landlords, rich peasants, counterrevolutionaries and other bad elements who escaped being identified as such.

"Of those in the higher levels who support these elements, some are antisocialist elements working in the organs of the communes, districts, counties and prefectures and even in the provincial and central departments. Among them there are some who have always been alien class elements; others are degenerates; and still others are persons who have received bribes and are collaborating in violating the law and discipline.

"Some are persons who have failed to draw a line of demarcation between the enemy and ourselves, have abandoned their proletarian class stand, or have shielded relatives, friends and old colleagues who are engaged in capitalist activities.

"The overwhelming majority of our cadres want to take the socialist road. But among them there are persons who do not have a clear understanding of the socialist revolution, do not assign people correctly or do not conscientiously check up on their work, and thus commit the error of bureaucratism."

As this summary list made clear, those accused of taking the capitalist road and their supporters were made up of two categories of people: 1. old alien class elements who had always opposed socialism, but who were not all necessarily publicly known as such; 2. revolutionary elements who had changed, "degenerates," "persons who have received bribes," "persons who have failed to draw a line of demarcation between the enemy and ourselves," and "persons who do not have a clear understanding of the socialist revolution." The latter group could be, and later were, more precisely designated as "new bourgeois elements" to distinguish them from the leftover alien class elements such as landlords, rich peasants and capitalist entrepreneurs.

Clearly, as this was stated in 1965 and then repeated many times over as the Socialist Education Movement developed into the Cultural Revolution, most people had no real concept of who these "new bourgeois" elements might be. Since no one in China possessed private capital, such objective criteria as the ownership and control of productive property and income from exploitation could no longer serve to demarcate classes. What remained were subjective criteria, judgments concerning belief and behavior, estimates of politically significant line and policy differences. Giving undue emphasis to material incentives, producing goods for profit, even by a collective, stressing technology and neglecting politics—all these were considered "capitalist road." But since Mao all along made clear that material incentive had its place, that in production output should surpass input, and that technique must be mastered in order to modernize the country, making these distinctions became a balancing act of great complexity. In the last analysis what remained were individual opinions. How could one choose between them? As Ye Chien-ying said in October, 1979, "The Cultural Revolution was launched with the aim of preventing and combating revisionism . . . but no accurate definition was given of revisionism."

Given these difficulties, it was always much easier to place the emphasis on leftover, alien class forces, on people of landlord or rich peasant background, on people with ties to the old Kuomintang or on people who had served the Japanese as puppets. Concerning people like these one could gather hard negative facts. They could then be placed in an "enemy" category. Since cadres found the "new bourgeois" hard to define, they tended to set aside the whole question in favor of minute reexaminations of the class origin and past affiliation of more traditional targets.

Just as Mao's Twenty-three Points challenged Liu Shao-ch'i's formulations regarding the purpose of the movement and its targets, so they also challenged the criteria used to measure the success of the movement. Whereas Liu emphasized primarily the question of being clean or unclean on the four questions, and these four tended to boil down to one—economic propriety—Mao posed six criteria that included economic propriety, but by no means stopped there. Mao's six were:

1. Whether or not the poor and lower-middle peasants are really aroused.

2. Whether or not the problem of dirtiness on the four questions among the cadres has been solved.

3. Whether or not the cadres take part in manual labor.

4. Whether or not a good leading nucleus has been established.

5. When the disruptive activities of landlords, rich peasants, counter-revolutionaries and other bad elements are discovered, whether they are dealt with by passing the contradictions on to the higher organs or by arousing the masses to control these elements strictly and reform them on the spot.

6. Whether output is increasing or decreasing.

To counteract the early emphasis on secret investigations and the tendency of such investigations constantly to broaden the target—"attacking the many to protect the few"—Mao issued a series of instructions on working methods. "The work teams," said Mao, "must rely on the majority of the people and the majority of the cadres; they must be above-board and open from the very beginning, and explain to the people at large their purpose in coming and the policies to be followed. They must arouse the poor and lower-middle peasants, organize their class forces, cultivate activists, form a representative nucleus and work with it. They must not work mysteriously among a small number of people. At the same time they must pay attention to production and to the distribution of income and not allow the movement so to take precedence that questions of livelihood go by the board."

In their zeal to uncover economic crimes and make a good record for themselves by piling up exposures, work teams guided by earlier directives had used crude methods, including force or extreme social pressure, to extract confessions. Mao strictly forbade this, even forbade the use of confessions as evidence.

Distrusting all indigenous cadres, Liu's forces had brought people from outside to man the work teams; in order to wage battles of annihilation they had concentrated huge forces at selected spots. Mao stressed that every province and municipality should have the right to assign forces, and opposed "human sea" tactics that concentrated overlarge teams in a county, commune or brigade.

In order to overcome the common policy of setting aside large numbers of cadres and of inflating small errors and mistakes into large crimes so that those accused could never hope to be reinstated, Mao stressed "learning from past mistakes to avoid future ones," and once again "curing the disease to save the patient." He also said "those Party members and cadres who have made mistakes but can still be educated and are different from incorrigibles should all be educated and not abandoned, whatever their class origin." The policy toward cadres with mistakes should be "persuasion and education, helping them to wash their hands and take a bath and to lay down their burdens, and uniting with them against the enemy," and "starting with a desire for unity, resolving contradictions through criticism or struggles so as to achieve a new unity on a new basis."

Mao emphasized that those who had made small mistakes in regard to the four questions, or those with many problems who had genuinely recognized them, should be "liberated" (restored to active political life) early. At the same time, "Necessary and proper disciplinary measures shall be taken against some cadres who have made mistakes. This is for the purpose of educating and reforming them. *So long as they are willing to take the socialist road,* the Party and the masses will unite with them."

Significant, in the light of the widespread power seizures from below that occurred in the Cultural Revolution, was point number seven in the article on cadres. "In cases of a serious nature, where the leadership has been seized by alien class elements or degenerate elements, struggles should be waged to get it back. First struggle with them, and then remove them from office."

There is no hint here that this might occur simply by action from below. These are instructions to work teams sent by the Party leaders. A power seizure of this kind was seen as an action engineered by the work team in consultation with its higher leadership, and with the support of masses mobilized for the purpose. Certainly very few imagined that within a year or two groups of rebels organized at the grass roots would be seizing power from alleged "capitalist roaders" all over China. Whether or not Mao Tse-tung had such seizures in mind in 1965 is difficult to say. All the elements of the strategy that later emerged in the Cultural Revolution are there in the Twenty-three Points: Party members in leading posts (the famous "Party people in authority") taking the capitalist road; mass organizations of the rank-and-file mobilized to rectify the Party; a two-line struggle between the working class and the bourgeoisie that will determine the fate of the revolution. But there is a world of difference between people taking things into their own hands and seizing power from below without any approval from above, and people led by a work team sent by higher administrative bodies removing people with mistakes from office and temporarily ruling in their place. The latter had occurred many times in the course of the revolution—for instance, in the Taihang during the great land reform checkup in 1948. The former had not occurred at all in areas under the leadership of the Communist Party. To find examples of such a thing one had to go back to the overthrow of Kuomintang authority by small groups of Communist rebels during two decades of struggle prior to the Liberation of China.

With the distribution of Mao Tse-tung's new Twenty-three Article Document, the Little Four Clean Movement in Long Bow and the other rural brigades under the administration of Changchih City slowly wound down, and finally came to a halt altogether just before spring planting. The city withdrew its cadres, set them to studying the Twenty-three Article Document, and then concentrated them in Changtzu Village to try out new methods. Although many problems had been exposed and a few problems had been solved, the departing cadres left the brigade in a state of suspended animation, with many Party members still under charges and no ongoing effort to review their cases.

49

BIG FOUR CLEAN

It was August, 1965, potato-digging time in Long Bow, when the next wave of rectification, the Big Four Clean Movement, got underway. At that time a new work team composed of fifteen city-level cadres arrived. Hsiao Chia, assistant political director of the Changchih City Militia, chaired the team. A man named Pi Min served as political director. A vice-chairman and twelve rank-and-file members made up the balance of the group. Thus there were two outside cadres for each Long Bow production team working under a three-man leading committee.

These city cadres had studied the Twenty-three Points of Chairman Mao. On the surface, at least, they came to Long Bow imbued with a "class" approach and announced that they were looking for people in power taking the capitalist road, not just grafters.

But in fact they applied again a policy of looking primarily at individual finances with a policy of "suspect all, suspend all." They did not approach any of the cadres in Long Bow, arrange to take any meals in their homes, or even speak to them. They set them all aside and appointed work team members, two to a production team, to take charge of the daily administration of the brigade. They called together the Peasants' Association, an organization that existed on paper but had been defunct for some time, and charged it with the task of examining the cadres. They allowed no cadres or members of cadres' families to join the resurrected Association or take part in its activities. They warned the cadres not to "cross heads and bite ears" when they met—that is, not to carry on any private conversations or consultations. To ensure that these warnings were heeded, they called on Association activists to supervise the cadres day and night, note everything they did and said, and to whom they said it. They even asked the activists to report on what the cadres said in their sleep.

After a few days the team concentrated all the cadres from all the brigades at commune headquarters in Horse Square Commune and kept them there for twenty days. This gathering was called "Wash-the-face, take-a-bath, put-down-the-burden-on-your-back" meeting, or more simply, the "three-level cadres' meeting." It included a few "activists" from each brigade who were there to confront the cadres "face to face" on behalf of the Peasants' Associations back home. The Association rank-and-file, for their part, were busy gathering materials "back to back" in each brigade.

For a while nobody knew what was going on. The "activists" wondered why they were included, people with serious problems worried night and day, and people without serious problems also worried. The work team finally explained that the "activists" would present material, that minor problems would be quickly solved so that the people accused of them could also become "activists," and that major problems would be solved in due course, taking into account the attitude of the people involved. This explanation eased the tension.

The work team asked the cadres to speak out one by one: first brigade accountants, then brigade storekeepers, then team accountants, then team storekeepers. As problems came out, everyone present discussed them. If someone said, "Last year I got five catties of squash free," others would immediately ask, "Are you sure it wasn't ten?"

The work team divided the cadres from each brigade into two groups, with a leader and an assistant leader for each. After everyone had made a first, tentative self-criticism, those with minor problems rose to positions as group leaders. The groups then assumed collective responsibility for the living conditions and safety of all members. They undertook to enforce discipline and ensure that nobody went home, and that those with serious problems neither ran away nor committed suicide. They also reported all unusual or suspect behavior to the work team.

Once the work team established this structure, it concentrated all efforts on what were deemed to be "major cases." During the day the team members met with suspects individually. In the evening the latter went before large group meetings or combined group meetings. If the group was not satisfied with the way they spoke, they returned to the Four Clean office for further consultation. The large meetings usually ended at about eleven o'clock, but were followed by an hour or two of individual mobilization, where leaders explained Communist Party policy and urged suspects to speak out more frankly in order to earn lenient treatment.

Listeners judged the quality of each self-criticism against the material brought to the commune meeting from the mass meetings in the brigades. If a cadre did not cover everything that the people at home had brought up, he was urged to say more. The leaders sent a summary of what each cadre had said back to his home brigade to be checked against the knowledge accumulating there.

Team members urged each cadre to recall his or her own past, to remember how poor he or she had been before, how he or she had been saved by the Communist Party and now, having come to power, had taken advantage of the collective to enrich him or herself. Weeping, they were supposed to make clear how much they had grafted.

Once the work team cadres were satisfied that the truth had been revealed, they would announce their verdict and decide if the treatment should be harsh or lenient.

"So-and-so spoke well. He grafted 100 catties of grain and 1,000 yuan. But he made a clean breast of it, so the amount he must repay will be reduced."

They held out Huang Hsiao-yuan of the Anch'ang Brigade as an example. He had taken several hundred catties of grain and several hundred yuan. Both his uncle and his mother came to the meeting to expose him. They recalled their bitter past life and blamed him for forgetting his origin. "Now he wants to exploit the people," they said. They called on the Communist Party to educate him and punish him severely so he wouldn't do anything like it again. But his own criticism was so thorough and sincere that team members asked him to repay only a proportion of everything. They recommended no other punishment. Hsiao-yuan himself was happy and grateful. In group meetings his case was discussed. "See how well Hsiao-yuan spoke! Look at the treatment he got!" By such means other people were encouraged to speak out and not hold anything back.

Small groups met together every day. If any cadre did not speak frankly to his small group, leaders convened larger meetings to hear him. This they called "heating things up." If the larger meeting brought no change, they arranged a still larger meeting. Thus leaders relentlessly pursued the question of graft. They brought heavy pressure indeed on the cadres.

All Here Li had been a vice-team leader in Long Bow for half a year and a team leader for a year. He had done nothing irregular. Work team members called him before them and threatened him all the same. "We know your problems already. The people have thoroughly exposed you, so don't think we don't know all the facts. You must wage a conscious struggle for revolution and tell us exactly how much grain you have taken."

"But I haven't taken any grain, or any money either," said All Here.

"All right. If you dare guarantee your own honesty, we may accept that, but you had better go and think about it some more."

Further thought did not change All Here's story at all. Since the work team had, in fact, no bad reports about him, they appointed him a group leader.

Kuo Fu-shu, brigade accountant, found himself in All Here's group. After facing a large meeting, Fu-shu came back to his quarters in tears.

"Why are you weeping?" asked All Here.

"I can't get my problems straightened out," sobbed Fu-shu, as he chewed on a large chunk of steamed bread. (Every day the commune kitchen came up with some different fare, well prepared.) "The food here is good, but I can't pass the gate. I have no real problem, but they keep saying that I have," and he wept for a long time.

Since he had been Long Bow's chief accountant for almost twenty years and before that had served as captain of the puppet police, some people in the brigade and some members of the work team refused to let him go. The Little Four Clean had found him 100 yuan short. Now the Big Four Clean leaders insisted that he had misappropriated thousands. The fact of the matter was that Pi Min, political director of the Long Bow work team, wanted credit for exposing a "big grafter" in Long Bow and Kuo Fu-shu looked like a likely target. In the end all efforts to pin large crimes on Fu-shu failed.

Frustrated, Pi Min turned his attention to Shen T'ien-hsi and the eight bags of wheat.

Unfortunately for T'ien-hsi, Wu Shu-lin, the man who had carted four of these bags, had been chosen as one of the peasant activists by the Long Bow Peasants' Association. As a man who had exposed a number of big problems he enjoyed high prestige. At a face-to-face meeting with Shen T'ien-hsi present, Wu repeated his charges.

"Eight bags of wheat were delivered to T'ien-hsi's courtyard. I drove one cart. T'ien-hsi drove the other. Each cart carried four bags."

Then Wang Wen-te and Lu San-kuei stood up and said, "It's true, we saw it."

"You say there is nothing to this," said Pi Min, turning to T'ien-hsi, "but here are people giving evidence against you."

On Pi Min's initiative the meeting went on like this all day. Finally T'ien-hsi had enough.

"Yes. I did it. I took the grain."

"How much did you eat, and how much did you feed your animals?"

Looking around for some reasonable reply, T'ien-hsi said, "We wasted a lot. I ate all I wanted and I threw a lot into the mules' trough. That's why the mules are so fat."

"And how much do you have left?"

This was a more difficult question. Since he had taken no grain in the first place, how could he report that there was some left? He would be asked to produce it.

When T'ien-hsi made no clear reply, they adjourned his case for the day. Pi Min asked him to think it over. When no better answer ever emerged, he charged T'ien-hsi with misappropriating eight bags of grain and asked him, as before, to repay six.

Outraged by this decision, disillusioned by the handling of this whole case, T'ien-hsi withdrew from the Communist Party. He refused to register when the Party branch was reestablished, and in 1971 still remained outside the Party.

While Pi Min pursued doubtful targets such as Kuo Fu-shu and Shen T'ien-hsi, some real graft occurred right under his nose.

When Kuo Fu-shu stepped down as brigade accountant and Shen Chi-ts'ai took his place, Chi-ts'ai's previous job, that of cashier, went to twenty-year-old Hu Wen-fa. At about the same time another young man, Shen Ta-li, took over the accounts of the Sidelines Team. In the seven months that elapsed between the Little Four Clean and the conclusion of the Big Four Clean, these two young men, working together, embezzled ten times as much money as Kuo Fu-shu was suspected of embezzling in twenty years. The people of Long Bow had such confidence in them that they elected them both as "activists" representing the Peasants' Association at the three-level cadres' meeting in Horse Square. The two young cadres apparently regarded this as perfect cover for escalating their efforts. They made off with the money paid into the brigade account by all those who had settled up for past abuses of trust during the Little Four Clean. They also made off with the 40 fen a day that the state paid to all cadres attending the Horse Square Meeting. These funds were paid into the brigade account to be distributed as part of the cash share earned by everybody as work points. When it came time to settle accounts in the fall, no one could find either the cash settlement money or the per diem money. Hu and Shen Ta-li had expropriated it all.

"They really surprised us," said All Here Li. "Especially Hu Wen-fa. He was born right here. He was only twenty years old and had always been honest and active. He had just graduated from school. We wanted to give him a chance, to help him develop. We appointed him after the Little Four Clean had made graft stink throughout the county, and he only held office seven months. In that short time he embezzled more money than any other Long Bow cadre before or since!"

As Veteran Wang said, when a work team bogged down in a search for graft, big problems could easily slip by. By the same token, a small problem could easily be blown into a major affair, and this, it seemed, is what happened in regard to Chang Hsin-fa, the Chairman of the Long Bow Brigade and vice-chairman of its Party branch. The three-level meeting in Horse Square laid bare all his real estate deals and totaled up the loans he had received from three different production team leaders. It branded Hsin-fa and the three team leaders a "grafting clique" and held them up as an example for the education of all. Hsin-fa appeared before mass meetings more than ten times. He made a self-criticism, listened to opinions from the people, then met with the work team cadres and criticized himself some more. After these criticisms were reported to the people for discussion, Hsin-fa talked privately with the work team cadres and then spoke before a mass meeting again. Then the people split into small groups for discussion, and came forward with new charges. So the movement went, round and round.

In the course of this campaign against him Hsin-fa became known as the big "capitalist roader" of Long Bow, the central case in the whole Four Clean Movement. The brigade punished him by removing him from office. He had speculated in the housing market; borrowed public grain without repaying; engaged in banditry prior to Liberation. In regard to the third point, it had been thrashed out many times before. The incident occurred in the famine year, 1942. As landlord Yang's hired man, Hsin-fa had once joined his employer in a night raid on a granary, had helped haul the stolen grain home, and had been paid off with a share of it. Such a pre-Liberation "crime" only became significant when a cadre fell into new trouble. Then investigators dragged up everything in his past that could possibly be held against him in order to make the case more convincing. But no matter how much they blew up this whole case, it was hard to make Hsin-fa into a major criminal or diehard reactionary. The total amount of money involved was too small. They charged Hsin-fa with misusing only 180 yuan of public money. Since he spoke honestly about it and seemed sincerely to regret having betrayed the people's trust, they reduced his debt to the brigade by 80 yuan. By selling his bicycle and his radio he was able to realize the remaining 100 yuan and pay off everything he owed. The team never sent his case to court. Party leaders never punished him inside the Communist Party. In the end everyone felt that he had received lenient treatment.

But the fact remained that one of Long Bow's leading cadres, a man who had been in office for twenty years, who had led the brigade through land reform, mutual aid, cooperation and the Great Leap, was summarily dismissed as a capitalist roader and lived in disgrace for many years thereafter, all because of 180 yuan.

At about the same time Hsin-fa, who had always longed to have a son and had already adopted one of his brother's sons to ensure a male heir, became the proud father of a boy. His wife gave birth prematurely to a baby that weighed hardly more than a pound. Both mother and child were very sick for a long time after that, and Hsin-fa, in disgrace, did nothing outside of his regular field work but hang around home and look after his threatened family. He managed somehow to hire an herb doctor who lived in his house and gave constant attention to the two sick ones. Slowly his wife recovered and his son took a lease on life that could not be denied. This surprised everyone, including Hsin-fa, who called the boy Ke-chi (Little Chick) because he was so small. Though small, Ke-chi grew into a normal child in every other respect, and once he learned to walk, accompanied his father everywhere. Hsin-fa was so fond of the boy that he almost never let him out of his sight and gave him everything he wanted without exception. No one had ever spoiled a Long Bow child as Hsin-fa spoiled little Ke-chi. He was in a position to do so because he no longer held any public post. He had time on his hands.

A man of Hsin-fa's caliber could hardly be set aside indefinitely, however. A few years later, when the brigade leaders decided to set up a pig farm, they asked Hsin-fa to take charge of it. He once again took up a public post, unpretentious as the post might be.

In the course of the investigation, work team members accused Hsin-fa of many things that he had nothing to do with. One of these was the death of Little Four P'ei. Little Four P'ei was a young member of Long Bow Brigade accused of stealing tools and iron bars at the cement plant shortly after that plant began operating. Plant guards caught him carrying stolen goods. They turned him over to the commune police officer, who questioned him, then released him. Shortly thereafter a peasant found P'ei's body at the bottom of a Long Bow well. Changchih City security officers, called in to investigate the death, came up with a verdict of suicide. They found no welts or other marks of violence on the body. No one had beaten or bound Little Four, they concluded. He had simply jumped into the well.

Ordinarily an official announcement of this kind would have ended the case. But not so this time. For some reason many people did not accept the verdict of the security forces. Thereafter, every time a movement arose to rectify the Party or overcome problems in the leadership of the brigade, someone always brought up the death of Little Four P'ei. In the Big Four Clean Movement several people suddenly declared that Chang Hsin-fa had beaten Little Four to death and thrown his body in the well.

The accusation deserves mention in this history only because it started a trend. With each change in administration that followed, someone invariably accused the leading cadre of the brigade of having killed Little Four P'ei.

Over the years this strange, somewhat bizarre death of a young man caught thieving became a convenient "club" with which to beat people. The "outs" used it as a preferred weapon in every campaign to discredit the "ins." In the political infighting that developed during the Cultural Revolution, factions used "clubs" like this as a matter of course. From the history of the Little Four P'ei case it should be clear that such "club" wielding was not something new in Long Bow's political life.

If, during the Four Clean Movement, Chang Hsin-fa stood accused as the main "capitalist roader" in Long Bow, he was by no means the only one. The work team called suspected embezzlers like Kuo Yuan-lung, Kuo Fu-shu, Hsiao Fu-lai, Shen Tien-hsi, Hu Wen-fa and Shen Ta-li "capitalist roaders," and applied the same label to all peasants who had taken advantage of the "three freedoms, one contract" wind of 1960–64 to set up individual enterprises. In order to ensure that these "entrepreneurs" returned to their production teams and did their fair share of work in the fields, city cadres wiped out the concession system. They no longer allowed anyone to follow the fair circuit in the name of the Long Bow Brigade, even if they paid a cash sum for the privilege. Nor did they allow anyone to repair things quietly at home for a fee. They ordered the brigade to confiscate all the tools of trade. If city cadres set a policy that was extreme indeed, brigade cadres made it worse by applying it unevenly. They took tools away from watchmakers like Ch'in Lai-ts'ai and Wu Shuang-hsi, but allowed Chin Shen-yi, who operated on an even bigger scale, to hang onto his welding equipment. They even allowed Wang Jen-pao, Old Lady Wang's son, a middle school graduate and a Communist Party member, to set up a new bicycle repair business.

As the work team slowly worked through its case load of "capitalist roaders" the City Committee introduced a new dimension to the Four Clean Movement by calling once more for the classification of every family in the village. This was considered necessary for two reasons: 1. the Twenty-three Article Document said that there were landlords, rich peasants, counterrevolutionaries and bad elements who had escaped being identified as such; 2. this same document called for reorganizing the Peasants' Associations with the poor and lower-middle peasants as the core. Without a thorough investigation into the class background of all doubtful families it was impossible to say whether there were, in fact, still some landlords or rich peasants posing as ordinary citizens, and without a community-wide review of all class backgrounds it was equally impossible to say who the lower-middle peasants really were. After the great classifications of the land reform period, the job had been done once again in 1954–55, but a lot of social experience had accumulated since then, and by 1965 people had a much clearer idea of class standards than they did when the concept was first introduced.

At the time of the land reform some eighteen years earlier the people had classed their neighbors as hired laborers, poor peasants, middle peasants, upper-middle peasants, rich peasants and landlords according to the relationship that various families had had to productive property during the three-year period prior to Liberation. Since the crucial question at that stage of the revolution had been to draw a line between friends and enemies, and since middle peasants were considered to be friends and rich peasants enemies, the most careful work and the greatest time had been spent on the dividing line between the upper-middle peasants, on the one hand, and the rich peasants on the other. As I wrote in *Fanshen,* cadres drew this line very carefully, so that any family that depended on its own labor for half or more of its income earned classification as a middle peasant, while any family that earned less than half of its income through its own labor and depended for the rest on the exploitation of hired labor, land rent or lending money at usurious rates earned classification as a rich peasant.

The emphasis on this problem in 1948 was certainly necessary. But after land reform a new problem arose; the big question now was on what part of the peasantry could the Communist Party and the working class depend in building socialism. Here Mao came up with a new formulation: "Depend on the poor and lower-middle peasants, unite with the middle peasants to build socialism." This formula introduced not only a new category—lower-middle peasant—but by making this category part of the "basic" masses, it created a new, significant dividing line, the line between lower-middle and ordinary-middle peasant.

The category "lower-middle peasant" consisted of two groups—the old lower-middle peasants and the new lower-middle peasants. The former were defined as families who prior to the land reform owned enough land, draft animals and tools to be more or less self-sufficient, but still suffered exploitation because they had to work out, at least part-time, and also had to borrow money on which they paid heavy interest. Furthermore, in the course of the land reform movement, they did not receive enough productive property to make them completely self-sufficient.

The latter, the new lower-middle peasants, were defined as poor peasant families who received only enough property in the land reform to bring them to approximately the same level as these old lower-middle peasants.

In addition to these two "still-not-well-off" categories, there were many former poor peasants who, although they had received land in the land reform, continued to have difficulty because of shortages of labor power, draft animals and farm implements and could not yet be considered middle peasants in any true sense. They were the "still-poor."

The "still-poor" and the "still-not-well-off" together comprised from 60 to 70 percent of the rural population. "These sections of the people," said Mao Tse-tung, "are fairly close to each other in economic position. . . . Therefore they all have an active desire to organize cooperatives. . . . So the first thing to do is to divide those who are poor or still not well off . . . into groups according to their degree of understanding, and, in the next few years, to get them to organize themselves into cooperatives, and then go on to absorb the well-to-do middle peasants."

Such were the instructions Mao gave in July, 1955. Acting in accord with these instructions, the Party undertook a reclassification of the peasantry throughout China so that all poor and lower-middle peasants could be brought together to form cooperatives. Now, ten years later, after the Great Leap, the Communist Wind, and the "capitalist resurgence" of the "three freedoms, one contract," a new drive to consolidate the cooperative movement again placed major emphasis on its social base—the poor and lower-middle peasants—and set out to reexamine exactly who made up this category. In 1965 Southeast Shansi cadres interpreted the standards more leniently than before—that is, they tended to drop people into lower categories, thus enlarging the basic group of poor and lower-middle peasants and cutting back the number of middle peasant allies and landlord-rich peasant enemies.

Once again peasants used the method of self-report and public appraisal to achieve consensus. In Long Bow they now called many families who had formerly been classed as upper-middle peasants simply middle peasants, and called quite a few families formerly classed as middle peasants lower-middle peasants. Lu Ho-jen, Li P'ing-ting, Wang Shu-pao, Chao Pao-ch'eng and Chao Chin-hung all dropped from upper-middle to middle peasant, while Yang Fu-sheng and Lu Ch'ing-fa dropped from middle peasant to lower-middle peasant.

Dropping a grade in class status had a favorable effect on morale. Everyone wanted to be considered part of the "basic masses."

At the same time about twenty people who had been passing themselves off as belonging in class categories well below the one they rightly belonged to suddenly rose up. They were all new settlers who had come to Long Bow after the land reform. Among them were upper-middle peasants who said they were middle peasants, and rich peasants who said they were poor peasants. This group included Hsiao Fu-lai, his brother-in-law Li Jui-hsiang and Li Jui-hsiang's brother, all from the Western Mountains. They said they had abandoned the mountains because of the goiter endemic there, when in fact they left because they had been expropriated as rich peasants. The group also included a number of Kuos from Linhsien, all relatives of the brigade accountant Kuo Fu-shu, who himself had come from Linhsien in the famine year of 1942. With Hsin-fa's help (Hsin-fa was also from Linhsien) Kuo Fu-shu found land for them in Long Bow even though they never made their class status clear. Chin Fa-wang, Chin Wan-liang, Chin Hsi-sheng and Chin Ta-hung all turned out to be former upper-middle peasants, a status that made them barely acceptable in Long Bow.

As the classification inside the brigade proceeded by the method of self-report and public appraisal, all the new settlers had to produce official documents from their home communities certifying their class origin. Some of them, like Li Jui-hsiang, seemed very reluctant to do so. Although Li went back to the Western Mountains several times during the winter, he said he was unable to get any document—the cadres there were not home, they were too busy, he had missed them. Finally he produced a document certifying that he was a poor peasant. Ch'in Lai-ts'ai, a new settler living right in his own courtyard, had forged it. But the brigade leaders didn't trust this unusual document. The more they thought about it, the more they thought there was something irregular about Li Jui-hsiang. Finally they sent two people to his home village to check everything out. Far from being poor peasants, as claimed, Li Jui-hsiang, his brother and Hsiao Fu-lai turned out to be rich peasants and "struggle objects" to boot.

This information embarrassed the brigade leaders because they had chosen Li Jui-hsiang as a brigade activist representing the poor peasants of Long Bow at the Big Four Clean meeting in Horse Square. They had also given him thirty yuan, three catties of raw cotton and fifteen feet of cloth as a state subsidy. The government introduced state subsidies for the poor at the time of the Four Clean Movement as a show of support for the "basic masses," and as an attempt to make up for some of the abuses of the past when state aid had been available but had been given out to many undeserving people because class lines had been blurred and a wind of private enterprise had been blowing.

When the brigade leaders learned that Li Jui-hsiang was really a runaway rich peasant, they asked him to pay back what he had received in state subsidies. When he was unable to do this because he had spent or consumed it all, they confiscated his house, put a price on it, and asked him to buy it back in installments. He had received this house free as one poor peasant's share of the fruits of land reform. Now, as a rich peasant, he would have to buy it.

The passage of time and fundamental changes in the system of ownership created additional classification problems that had not existed in 1955, problems such as what to call landlords' children. People who had themselves been landlords and actually collected rent and interest for a living continued to be called *fen-tzu* ("elements"). But this term could hardly be applied to young people who had never owned land in their own name or ever collected or spent any unearned income. These young people, who had labored in mutual-aid groups or the production teams of Long Bow Brigade all their lives, were finally called *wei yeh lao tung chih*—"laborers without profession."*

Another problem arose over the classification of people like Kuo Cheng-k'uan's wife, who had previously been married to a Kuomintang officer, the former puppet district leader Meng Hsien-chung. After Hsien-chung was killed as a collaborator, Kuo Cheng-k'uan married the man's widow even though she had been classed as a landlord. Now, having behaved well and worked hard for many years as the wife of a poor peasant, she had earned the right to be reclassed. Brigade leaders called her a poor peasant. At the same time they warned Cheng-k'uan to pay attention to his ideology. It was possible that his wife still harbored some landlord thoughts that could influence him.

When it came to the change of class status through marriage, the directives of the Communist Party still embodied serious sex-based discrimination. A landlord's widow or daughter who married a poor peasant could earn poor peasant status after a period of good behavior. But a landlord's son who married a poor peasant girl did not get the same consideration. No matter how many years he labored, he still carried the label *wei yeh lao tung chih*. This was because inheritance traditionally passed through the male line. Women married "out," and in the popular mind quickly assumed the class status of their husbands and their husbands' families. Men, on the contrary, brought wives "in," and gave them new status without in any way altering the status they themselves brought to the marriage. And the status they inherited they passed on to their sons.

*This is my own translation of an obscure term unfamiliar outside Southeast Shansi.

50

A ZIGZAG ROAD

 Trying to sum up the wide array of information, conjecture and reminiscence that poured out when people discussed the Socialist Education Movement, I asked everyone interviewed to say whether or not the movement had been conducted in a proper manner (proper being defined at the time as "in accordance with the directives issued by Mao Tse-tung") and whether it had solved the problems it was supposed to solve.

Commander Li Ying-k'uei, Chief of Staff of the People's Liberation Army forces stationed in Southeast Shansi, gave what today must be called an extreme "Gang of Four" view. He unconditionally denounced the early stages of the movement. According to him, "bad people"—"counterrevolutionaries," in fact—had led it.

Commander Li called Wang Hsiang-chih, the head of the big work team responsible for Changchih City and its surrounding rural areas, a "renegade." He called both Ch'en Hsiu-chuang, the political officer of this team, and Chang Hsing-fu, the political officer of the Wuhsiang County team, Kuomintang agents. Chang Hsing-fu had been a member of the Standing Committee of the Southeast Regional Party Committee and head of the Provincial Level Liaison Group for eight years. But Commander Li charged that before Liberation he had headed the Kuomintang Party organization in Licheng County and still served it secretly.

Commander Li further charged that the son of the biggest landlord in Licheng County had headed the 7,000-man work team in Changtzu. He called this man, Lou Han, a "Kuomintang agent" who "infiltrated the Communist Party during the Japanese war."

According to Li Ying-k'uei the Party had accepted all these "bad people" as members in compliance with Liu Shao-ch'i's policy of "recruiting renegades and traitors," that is, "taking in people who surrendered to the Communist forces and thus became renegades to the Kuomintang." In Li's view none of these recruits had really renounced their Kuomintang ties. They were false converts to revolution who played the role of "special agents" inside the Communist Party and People's Government of the Southeast Region.

Since, during the Anti-Japanese War, the Communist Party had recruited a large number of patriotic students, many of them sons and daughters of gentry (who else made it to the university in those days?), Li Ying-k'uei had no trouble digging out damaging material on the class origins and previous connections of these and many other outstanding cadres. In his hands the strongest element of the Party's wartime program—the united front policy that brought together people from all walks of life for armed resistance to Japan—turned into an Achilles' heel, into an excuse for whole-sale attacks on all who lacked ironclad "proletarian" credentials. Ironically, Li himself had joined the army as a university student. His own class background could hardly allay suspicion, and that perhaps was one explanation for the vindictiveness of his offensive.

Be that as it may, Li spread the thesis that, as soon as Liu Shao-ch'i issued his abysmal ten points, the "agents" in the Region gathered together 7,000 cadres and sent them to Changtzu County to carry out a line "left in form, right in essence." Responsible cadres hid their real names, adopted secret methods of work and fanned out like a human sea to "strike roots and make contact." Suspecting all, denying all, they attacked the majority of honest cadres to protect a small handful of turncoats. Only after Mao Tse-tung issued his Twenty-three Points was it possible for real Communists to turn the movement in the right direction. Even then they succeeded in correcting only a few of the early mistakes.

Ch'en Yung-kuei of Tachai, by 1971 already Chairman of Hsiyang County and vice-chairman of Shansi Province, never charged that Kuomintang agents led the Four Clean Movement, but he condemned work team methods and policies as forcefully as Commander Li.

"Before Mao came forward with his Twenty-three Points," said Ch'en, "the way party leaders carried out the Four Clean was wrong. After Mao intervened, work teams corrected some mistakes but they corrected them only on the surface. If the work teams had gone deeply into problems, they would have been forced to struggle against themselves, so actually they did not correct their mistakes."

Commander Tsao, vice-chairman of the Shansi Provincial Revolutionary Committee, had a more charitable opinion. He stressed positive results while blaming Liu Shao-ch'i for all that had gone wrong.

"After the Twenty-three Points came down," he said, "the movement took a correct direction in the main. But there was some poison left over. For example, the work teams were still quite large. Even when they abandoned the 'strike roots and make contact' method of Wang Kuang-mei, they still used some very complicated work methods. They constantly used Liu's viewpoint to twist Mao's line and put all emphasis on economic problems.

"What we say is, the main direction was correct. Liu Shao-ch'i tried to obstruct it and wreck it. Each time Mao took the initiative to clarify the problem, he raised the consciousness of most of the cadres. In each battle over line Mao's line won out. During the Cultural Revolution some people tried to deny the achievements of the Four Clean entirely and to reverse all the verdicts on the people overthrown. But the Central Committee has endorsed the Four Clean in the main. The problems must be seen in the light of the concrete conditions in the countryside at the time. Those cadres and rank-and-file people who made mistakes were primarily people who were not clear about Mao's line. Most of them were good people who made mistakes. Clear up these mistakes, do a good job of self-criticism, and you can take up new work.

"But no matter how well people solved the problems down below they could not root out Liu Shao-ch'i up above, and this meant that down in the counties there were people who couldn't be thrown out either. Higher cadres protected them. Do what you will at the village level, there are people up above who are manipulating everything, so that the problem can't really be solved. That's why Mao Tse-tung raised the idea of the Cultural Revolution."

This view was not so different from the one put forward by Premier Chou En-lai, who in 1971 summed up the Socialist Education Movement as a sharp struggle over political line between two centers in the Party. This was the official position of the Central Committee that year and remained so until challenged by Teng Hsiao-ping in 1980.

> In 1963 [Chou said], Mao Tse-tung issued Ten Points to guide the Socialist Education Movement. Liu Shao-ch'i countered with a second ten points, complicated and full of meaningless detail, an exercise in scholasticism. Liu opposed coming to grips with capitalist roaders as directed by Mao. He proposed instead to differentiate between being clean-in-four-ways and being unclean-in-four-ways (economics, politics, organization, ideology). Everyone, holding a big job or a small job, inside the Communist Party or outside it, could be knocked out of office if he or she was unclean in any of the four spheres.
>
> With such a program, the scope of attack could not help being greatly enlarged. Among the cadres in the countryside petty selfishness does exist, such things as taking a little collective property for private use. If such acts as this make them bad elements, then almost all the cadres in the countryside, with only a few exceptions, must be overthrown. For instance, suppose something is left in the field (a basket, a sack, or a length of rope). A cadre takes it home for his own use. Is he a grafter or not? If all this is called serious corruption the consequences are hard to estimate. It would be *pu te liao* [an awful mess]!
>
> Liu Shao-ch'i looked on Communist Party and government cadres as no good, as all rotten. He attacked many, many. When he or his group went to a village to "squat" [to make an intensive investigation and solve problems], they did secret work. "Put down roots and make contact," they called it. After fifteen years of state power they still did secret work? How could this come to any good? "Put down roots, make contact, carry out secret investigations" —all this departs completely from the mass line.
>
> Liu Shao-ch'i never implemented the Socialist Education Movement as a two-line struggle. He turned it into a clean-in-four-ways, unclean-in-four-ways contradiction among the cadres—did they graft or didn't they graft?—or into the intertwining of the contradictions inside the Communist Party and outside the Communist Party,

or into a struggle between "good" people and "bad" people. Outwardly he applied no class line at all. To treat the Socialist Education Movement in this way was completely out of step with the theory of class struggle, of two roads, two lines.

With this method of Liu's, one removes great groups of cadres and brings new groups into power. One turns the Socialist Education Movement into an unprincipled struggle over who is to be in power. This opens the road to capitalist restoration. It is very dangerous.

Chou En-lai concluded his discussion with some advice about how to study this question:

"If you go to Peach Garden to investigate, you should stay there for a period and get it all clear. Tachai, Long Bow, Peach Garden—these three villages are three points for concentration. Tachai is taking the socialist road pointed out by Mao Tse-tung. Under Liu Shao-ch'i and Wang Kuang-mei, Peach Garden took the capitalist road. What the condition is in Long Bow today I do not know. Long Bow went down a zigzag road."

None of these comments came to grips with what looks today like the outstanding difference between Mao Tse-tung and Liu Shao-ch'i in their approach to the Socialist Education Movement. Mao repeatedly called for a mobilization of the peasant masses down below. He wanted the people to judge, criticize and supervise the Party and state apparatus, hence demanded the revitalization of poor and lower-middle peasant associations. Liu, it seems, saw such a bottom-up campaign as a threat to stable government and bureaucratic power. Wherever possible he replaced mass mobilization at the village level with top-down rectification of the errors of local leaders. As Maurice Meisner points out, "Whereas the original Maoist directive emphasized that the first step was 'to set the masses in motion,' Liu Shao-ch'i insisted that 'to launch the Socialist Education Movement at any point requires the sending of a work team from the higher level. The whole movement should be led by the work team.' "*

A movement built primarily around work teams could hardly target "capitalist roaders" in the higher echelons of leadership, the very target Mao considered most important. The two approaches serve to illustrate a fundamental divergence in outlook—Mao always looking to the people as the final repository of wisdom, as the arbiter of last resort, and counting on the people to overcome the political and ideological impurities plaguing the party; Liu, in contrast, looking on the party leadership as all-wise, as capable of overcoming through internal rectification all deficiencies and mistakes down below. For Liu, the Party, or at least its Central Committee, loomed as an absolute. For Mao, the only absolute was the people and their interests—as he defined them, of course. Whenever the Party moved in ways that seemed wrong to him, Mao appealed over the heads of other Party leaders to the people themselves, thus bypassing the whole institutional framework of the revolution and filling the hearts of most functionaries with anxiety and dismay.

*Mao's China (New York: The Free Press, 1977), p. 291.

On one point all commentators agreed—the Socialist Education Movement, otherwise known as the Four Clean, never came to an end. In 1966 it merged with and was submerged by a most bizarre, gigantic, complex and unprecedented struggle, the Great Proletarian Cultural Revolution. In the course of the enormous factional struggle over government power and position that ensued, the issues raised so sharply in 1963 never found resolution. No consensus ever emerged on whether authority resided in the people or in the Party, and no consensus ever emerged on what constituted "the socialist road." As far as the countryside was concerned, no one ever spelled out the proper balance between public and private, individual and collective, earned income and free supply, individual rights, socialist norms and Communist sprouts, which alone could adjust and reconcile the diverse interests of assorted brigade members so that they could unite with ease of mind and forge ahead.

The Cultural Revolution, which brought tens of millions of people into action on the political stage, fanned up instead a new "Communist Wind" that stressed the public, collective, free-supply, Communist-sprout side of the equation and carried the peasants back toward equalitarian excesses reminiscent of the Great Leap of 1958—a near policy debacle.

As a rectification movement for the reform of individual cadres, the Cultural Revolution also foundered. Instead of "uniting over 95 percent of the masses and of the cadres to fight against the class enemy . . ."* it broke the ranks of both people and cadres into hostile factions and set them to fighting each other over who had the right to hold power.

Looking at these results, we began to wonder if we had been asking the right questions. We needed to know, not only if the Four Clean Movement had been carried out in accordance with the directives issued by Mao Tse-tung, but also if the directives issued by Mao Tse-tung constituted a valid program for rectifying the Party and building up China in the sixties.

To answer such a crucial question we had to look beyond the Socialist Education Movement. We had to look into the Cultural Revolution itself and try to understand what happened and why. We were already beginning to sense that this struggle most resembled, not some revolutionary conflict of the modern age, but one of those massive upheavals typical of mankind's feudal past, the Hundred Years' War in France, perhaps, or the Wars of the Shogunate in Japan. But before we had a chance even to explore the grass-roots level of the conflict, we got involved in the mobilization of Long Bow's peasants for wheat planting and in a new Party rectification campaign that the propaganda team members superimposed on this and all other fall tasks.

*Quoted from "Decision of the Central Committee of the Communist Party of China on Some Current Problems in Rural Work (Draft)," May 20, 1963, p. 12.

Part V

RECTIFICATION AT THE GRASS ROOTS

Bourgeois society makes fun of us, saying, "You Communists only talk about the public as if there were no self." But this is not true. We hold that without individuals there is no collective. What we advocate is putting the collective first—public first, self second.
Chou En-lai, 1971

51

WHEAT PLANTING

 A rare afternoon, clear sky, bright sunlight, an unobstructed view of distant mountains; fifty people on a five-acre plot organized into squads, each with a special job to do. One squad of women, somewhat scattered and working the land ahead of the rest, uses wooden mallets on long handles to break up the clods left behind by tractor plows and harrows. This last-minute improvement to the seedbed ensures even germination of the wheat.

To the east of the women, carters, hauling compost from the Fourth Team's compost ground, come and go continuously. Keeping a dozen carts in motion, they dump their loads, pile by pile, in a straight line across the field. Since some have to load while others haul and dump, no more than one or two move across the worksite at any one time. Interspersed between the compost carts come the "tankers" hauling liquid night soil. These tank carts with their barrellike wooden containers, being fewer in number than the compost carts, establish a timetable of their own. They dump their loads into temporary pits designed to hold the precious "black gold" of the village cisterns, while a special crew enriches the local product with chemical urea poured from plastic bags, two or three bags to the pit.

The cart drivers and the plastic bag crew just manage to keep ahead of the demands of the wheat planters themselves, a large group of men and women organized into four platoons. First the furrow diggers, using a team of horses and a specially adapted plow, easily open enough furrows in a few minutes to keep everyone else busy for half an hour. Behind them a dozen or so night soil distributors, working at full speed, dip the stinking privy fluid from the pits with buckets slung on shoulder poles and pour it evenly along the prepared furrow. Next a second dozen, with baskets instead of buckets on their poles, spread and mix in an appropriate amount of dry compost. As the final step a pair of sowers, highly skilled at distributing an even layer of seed along the enriched soil of the furrow bottom, keep just ahead of several followers who cover the seed with topsoil to a depth of one inch.

In this complex operation, each separate task emerges out of its preparatory task, as it sets the stage for the task to come. The participants, like dancers in some pastoral ballet, create a skein of diverse motion that blends without apparent effort into a single rhythm as they progress, furrow by furrow, across the field. Scores of individuals, each working at his or her own speed, move as a unit from west to east, leaving in the newly inoculated soil an important part of next year's livelihood.

From a stout pole set proudly in the open ground not far from the mud track that leads from Long Bow to Changkungchuang, the Fourth Team's red banner flaps in the wind.

Moments like these manifest the underlying power of Long Bow's collective life. Here, instead of a disorganized array of go-it-aloners struggling to scratch a living from pitiful small plots, stands an organized attack force applying a new method of wheat planting over a large area, enriching the land with predetermined quantities of night soil and compost, even adding chemical urea, sowing improved seed from tested stocks of the best varieties available in the region, and standing ready, once the wheat comes up, to irrigate the whole expanse with water pumped from a reservoir that is itself the collective creation of tens of thousands of neighbors. How can this be equated in any way with the past?

As the work stops for a break and the people sit down to rest, the team leaders, one or two brigade leaders and some cadres from the Municipal Propaganda Team hold a spur-of-the-moment meeting to discuss problems. Are the furrows wide and deep enough? Is the seeding rate sufficient? Will the night soil hold out for the full expanse of the field? How much urea can the wheat tolerate without burning? Can soil trampling be reduced? If three stinking shoemakers can equal a Chu-ke Liang, this group of earnest consultants ought to be able to surpass that ancient hero and call him "grandson."

It seems clear that this consultation adds a significant dimension to the strength of the collective. It includes not only the local peasants responsible for this field, but the leaders of their whole community and representatives of the city as well. The members of Team Four on the front line of production have their cooperative, their commune and their city behind them. Behind these, in turn, stand the province and the nation. What happens here is not being ignored, forgotten, neglected or dismissed. Everyone seems to regard it as a fragment of one battlefield in the overall war to transform and remold China. Up and down the chain of command there are evidently people who care.

The impressive collective power applied to the wheat fields that we experienced that fall did not arise spontaneously. It developed as a result of hard organizing work at the highest echelons in the city and at every level down below, reaching finally into every production team and every family unit.

Fortunately, since July the weather had improved enough to make the organization of fall work effective. In the beginning of September the rain eased off.

Even though the season continued to be wetter than usual, runoff from the mountains began to subside. As it subsided the water in Changchih Reservoir stopped rising. The badly cracked main dam still stood, and so, miraculously, did the coffer dam that had been continually raised and reinforced ever since the cloudburst of August 15. This improvement in the weather came none too soon, for the flood waters literally lapped at the top of both dams and the runoff from another inch of rain would have burst all temporary earthworks regardless of their height.

As soon as the water in the reservoir stabilized, everyone began to relax. Conversations turned from flood control to more mundane subjects such as why some people let their domestic pigs run wild, why cart drivers so often ran down growing crops, and who, during the busy fall season, would pick the scattered castor beans that had been planted where nothing else would grow?

The pig problem was most acute. When people did not properly pen their pigs, the animals got out and sooner or later found their way to the fields, where they celebrated by rooting around in the ground for undug sweet potatoes, knocking down cornstalks to get at the ears, and even making forays into the carefully tended truck gardens to eat eggplant and tomatoes. Not knowing where their charges were did not seem to bother the pig owners at all, and the reason was obvious. By allowing their pigs to roam they were getting something for nothing, they were fattening private pigs on collective land. What could be more "bourgeois" than this? Word went out through the brigade that pigs had to be kept at home. In the future if private pigs found their way into the fields, brigade leaders would do something drastic. They might even confiscate the pigs.

The problem of the carts running down the crops was more universal and more difficult to solve. Team members everywhere planted their crops right up to the edge of any road or path so that no land would go to waste. But whenever it rained two things always threatened the crops. The first was the tendency of tall crops like corn and sorghum to lodge as the soil softened. Even a moderate breeze could blow corn down on the road. Then the cart drivers, who were always in a hurry to increase their work points, would drive right over the stalks and tramp them into the mud. When they saw downed stalks they were supposed to take time to right them, tie them back if necessary, so that the grain could develop normally, but most drivers counted on someone else to save the grain. Their problem was to get down the road and back as quickly as possible.

The second threat to the crops occurred whenever and wherever the road got so soft that the carts sank in. Cart wheels created enormous ruts in the wet spots and it became harder and harder for the donkeys, mules and oxen to pull their loads through. Whenever ruts made the original road impassable, the drivers pulled off to the left or the right, straight into the crops, and ran them down to create a temporary bypass. This destroyed much more grain than the crops ever lost through lodging; no matter how often or how stridently leaders condemned the practice of "bypassing," their words never slowed it down. In the old society the owners of private plots used to dig ditches beside the road to prevent anyone from turning out; this created a form of war that was all-against-all, as the cart drivers and the plot owners struggled over the sanctity of the right of way. Now that people owned and managed their land collectively, no one cared enough about any given stretch to fashion defenses against the carts, so the destruction expanded year by year. This year, because the rains lasted beyond their normal season, the problem was worse than ever. Party Secretary Chang called it to the attention of the whole brigade. Even though most brigade members tried hard not to destroy the source of their own work points, the problem continued because many carts from other brigades and from nonagricultural factories and units used the same roads and no local appeal touched their self-interest.

As for the castor beans, in 1971 brigade members had made a special effort to plant them along the edges of the roads, on the banks of the canals, and in any other small space that could not be cultivated on the usual scale. Now that the castor beans were getting ripe, the bolls that covered them were splitting open, spilling the beans onto the ground or into the ditches, where running water carried them away. With big jobs like wheat planting coming up, how could the brigade save the castor beans? Party Secretary Chang decided to call on the older women, the mothers with small children and the children of the brigade themselves to go out in a planned way for the castor bean harvest. By picking a certain weight of beans they could earn a definite number of work points. Chang's call worked and soon, at almost any time of day, one could see old women and children with baskets, shawls or some other makeshift carrier, picking and collecting the beans which would supplement the income of the whole community. Peasants pressed the beans for oil, a valuable resource in a countryside where cooking oil always ran short and efforts to raise flaxseed and rape had so far failed to fill the gap.

Pig control, carts and castor beans added up to a diversion only. The big task that confronted the peasants of Long Bow remained the *san ch'iu,* or "three fall" for short. The "three falls" were wheat planting, harvesting the summer crops, such as field corn and beans, and preparing the land for next year's crops. This last included land leveling, irrigation ditch construction, irrigation ditch repair and fall plowing.

Because these three tasks crowded on each other's heels and had to be completed before the onset of winter, autumn turned out to be the busiest time of year, the time that required the most labor power, the most animal power, the most equipment and the most material support.

Wheat planting came first and created great tension because, for reasons that I never clearly understood, the wheat had to be in the ground before the end of September. Whereas in Pennsylvania winter wheat can be planted through the middle of October and even into November, throughout most of North China farmers must plant wheat at least one month earlier to ensure adequate yields.

The challenge posed by the need to get wheat into the ground early was taken up first by the Communist Party Organization and the government of the whole province, particularly by those responsible for agriculture at every level. The Provincial Committee mobilized the regions, the regions mobilized the cities and counties, and these in turn mobilized the communes. Higher cadres called meetings, issued directives and reported progress day by day in the press, in the form of battle communiqués on the "three fall" front.

This mobilization reached Long Bow in the form of a conference at Horse

Square Commune attended by Brigade Party Secretary Chang Kuei-ts'ai and vice-Party Secretary Shen Chi-ts'ai. At this conference commune leaders asked Long Bow to plant 800 mou (133 acres) of wheat, two-thirds of it on irrigated land by a new wide-furrow method and one-third of it on dry land by well-known conventional methods. On the irrigated land 130 tan of organic compost and 30 tan of raw night soil scooped from privy cisterns applied to every mou ought to produce a yield of 38 bushels per acre. On dry land 160 tan of organic compost applied to every mou ought to produce a yield of 28 bushels per acre.

These goals did not seem to be very high, but when we heard what had been harvested in 1971, we understood why nobody was willing to set them higher. The previous season had been disastrous for wheat from the very beginning. A severe drought at planting time had cut back germination. An open winter without snow allowed heavy frost to kill many of the sprouts that did come up. A dry spring stunted the few plants that remained, and so Long Bow had harvested less than 10 bushels to the acre in late June.

Certainly no one expected renewed drought at planting time this year. They feared waterlogging instead. But just in case the coming year came off dry, all plans centered on irrigation. And this was something new where wheat was concerned. The peasants had always considered wheat to be a low-yield crop, a catch-as-catch-can effort. Traditionally, they spread whatever compost was available, turned the soil over, and sowed seed in rows about fourteen inches apart, then left the crop alone to make whatever heads would grow. They never tried heavy applications of fertilizer, careful soil preparation or irrigation on wheat because the yields they expected could not justify such outlays and such effort.

Now, from above, the word came down that wheat, when properly cultivated, was a high-yield crop. By using new, intensive methods Tachai, West Gully, South City and other advanced brigades had reaped 50, 60, even 100 bushels per acre. Long Bow, the authorities said, could do the same. The problem was really one of attitude. If people made up their minds that wheat could equal any other crop and took the necessary steps to ensure that result, all local records could easily be broken, and the brigade could cross the Yangtze (reap 80 bushels per acre) with wheat alone. This was an intriguing thought and one which the peasants were not willing to dismiss out of hand.

The method proposed by the commune leaders was called the wide-furrow method. Instead of sowing a thin trickle of wheat in rows that were close, peasants were urged to open up widely spaced furrows at least four inches across and enrich them with fertilizer. They were to mix organic compost, liquid night soil and chemical urea into the soil below, then plant wheat across the whole width of each furrow in a band and cover it lightly. If they made the bands at least two feet apart they could bring in irrigation water to drench the whole field, and in the spring they could plant corn in this space, thus doubling up on crops and intensifying the use of the land. Even if the wheat only yielded 40 bushels, if the corn yielded 60, then each acre produced 100—something unheard of in Long Bow in the past.

Not satisfied with irrigation and wide-furrow planting, the commune leaders also suggested that as much land as possible be prepared by "deep-digging." This was a method for turning the land over to a depth of a foot or more with long-bladed, long-handled shovels known as "Tachai" shovels, after the Tachai Brigade in Hsiyang County. With a Tachai shovel the top six inches of soil could first be set to one side all down the edge of the field. The soil exposed by this removal could then be turned over in place. The next strip of surface soil, one shovel wide, could be deposited upside down in the disturbed trench, filling it up and creating a new trench adjacent to it with the subsoil again exposed. The whole process was similar to the kind of job that would be done by a plow if, after the plow turned each furrow-slice, the tractor driver used some power instrument to stir the subsoil beneath it. Behind this labor-intensive method of tillage lay the idea that loosening, turning and aerating the soil increased yields, and that the deeper this was done, the better the results would be. Trials indicated that by dint of hard work from dawn to dusk one able-bodied person could "deep-dig" one-third of a mou (1/18 of an acre) a day.

Chang Kuei-ts'ai and Shen Chi-ts'ai listened carefully as commune leaders explained all this. If they had any objections, they did not voice them. The new, wide-furrow method sounded good, even if it had never been tried on Long Bow soil. They were willing to adopt it wherever irrigation water could be brought in. They knew that a large amount of compost and raw night soil from privy cisterns was available. They could send buyers out to find chemical urea, and they could mobilize team members for deep-digging. The brigade leaders failed to agree only on the suggested acreage. Long Bow did not have 133 acres free of crops that could be planted to wheat. No matter how they counted, they could come up with only 108, of which some 76 could be irrigated while 32 must remain dry. When Chang and Shen offered 108 acres, the commune leaders objected, but they had to agree in the end. They had no alternative; no one could find any more land.

On returning to Long Bow Kuei-ts'ai and Chi-ts'ai called the leaders of all the production teams together to discuss wheat planting and convince team members to try the new methods. In order to make the discussion easy, they prepared mimeographed sheets with the total planned acreage broken down team by team—how much irrigated wheat, how much dryland wheat, how much wide-furrow wheat and how much deep-digging. The delegates from each team engaged in some very lively exchanges, then reported to the whole meeting on what they proposed to do.

Lu Ho-jen, captain of the militia and political director of the Second Team, reported first. Because of the impending Party rectification and the criticism he was sure to receive, his morale had sagged in recent weeks, but wheat planting seemed to inspire him and he reported enthusiastically on his team's response to the plan.

"We will mobilize our members by studying Mao Tse-tung Thought and will firmly take hold of irrigation work and manure handling. We will put politics in command, praise good things and repudiate bad, and fix up the necessary irrigation channels. Eight are needed. We already have four, so we'll fix four more as soon as we have dug up the sweet potatoes that now occupy the land. The land will be leveled in squares that are one-tenth of a mou in size so that water can be uniformly distributed. We will deep-dig all our irrigated land to a depth of one foot. We have thirty-five Tachai shovels. If thirty-five people each prepare one-third of a mou per day, we can do the whole job in seven days. While one crew digs, another will level the land. Then we'll harrow it. We have twenty smoothing harrows. Ten days of work should make everything ready, including the canals. But we still don't have enough compost. We'll have to start gathering wild grass and weeds right away. If we do that, we can guarantee fifty tons of compost and twelve tons of liquid night soil per acre. In the spring we'll add twenty tons of compost and 120 catties of chemical nitrogen per acre. It won't matter if it rains or not. If it doesn't rain, we'll water the wheat five or six times. If it does rain, we'll water it twice."

Having said all this in a rush, barely pausing for breath, Ho-jen stopped suddenly, let his proposal sink in, then added, "We guarantee 38 bushels per acre."

Sad-eyed Kuo Cheng-k'uan reported for the Fifth Team. He displayed little of Ho-jen's enthusiasm. This was not because he disliked the furrow method or had no faith in deep-digging, it was because the Fifth Team had lost 50 mou of their best irrigated land to the Taihang Sawblade Works. In order to plant the 100 mou of wheat suggested in the plan, they would have to put 70 on the dry-land hill terraces, and no one could guarantee any 38-bushel yield there.

The Sixth Team had also lost land to the Sawblade Works, but only 30 mou. They felt able to make this up somewhere else and so guaranteed more than 80 mou of irrigated land. The First and Third teams accepted their share of the plan without objection, but the Fourth Team found that it had fallen way behind in the accumulation of compost. By launching a concerted drive to cut grass and weeds that would rot quickly because they were green, and by cleaning out all the sheep- and pigpens managed by the team and its members, Yang Chi-wang, the team leader, thought the deficiencies could be made up. His team members would deep-dig all irrigated land and would level it carefully. He, too, guaranteed 38 bushels per acre.

The Sidelines Team, not to be outdone, guaranteed to send out manpower in the evening to help whatever team fell behind. After a full day at the brick kiln or at the railroad yards unloading freight, its members would cut grass, haul compost to the fields, or deep-dig land wherever needed.

Judge Kao, very pleased with this meeting, congratulated the teams on their spirit of hard work and self-reliance, then closed the session with a short talk on the topic, "Put politics in command." He advised all teams to reserve some time for political study each day and suggested that they should pay particular attention to Mao's words on "seizing the time," on "manure as the grain of field crops," on "irrigation as the lifeblood of agriculture," on "the importance of deep-digging the land well" and on "the source of correct ideas."

The proposal for planting the wheat in wide furrows did not impress me, in particular that part about leaving room for corn between the wheat rows and for wheat between the corn rows. Carma and I had worked with the Fifth Team preparing wheat land planted to corn and found that this intercropping made every aspect of production several times more difficult than straightforward single-cropping ever had.

On days when we foresaw free time in the afternoon we sought out Cheng-k'uan at breakfast and asked him to come and get us after four. Then we joined whatever work the majority of the members of the Fifth Team were doing. In September we almost always ended up in the intercropped field. The first step there was to hoe all the land between the corn rows to a depth of six inches and break up the clods that the hoes turned up. By the time we finished this job others had dumped great piles of compost at the upper end of the field. Since the compost carts could not drive down between the rows of corn we had to carry the compost to every part of the field with baskets slung on carrying poles. All this carrying so compacted the soil that we had to hoe the whole field a second time as soon as we finished spreading the manure.

We then had to form lateral ditches for irrigation water. This we also did with hoes, taking great care to avoid uprooting corn plants. Since the laterals ran at right angles to the corn rows, some of them ran right into corn plants. These we cut and carefully laid aside in hopes that the ears already formed might still ripen as the stalks dried. In the course of constructing the laterals our feet packed down a lot more land and this we had to hoe for a third time.

Finally, as we planted the wheat in hastily formed wide furrows, fertilized it with compost and wet it down with liquid night soil, we trod down and packed more land. This we had to loosen with hoes before we could leave it, and this hoeing counted as the fourth in less than ten days.

All of this hoeing, transport by carrying pole, hand shaping of ditches and hand planting used up a tremendous amount of labor. Some fifteen people worked for days on that one three-acre field. Carma and I hoed some of the same land at least three times, and all because we had to save a few cornstalks that could not possibly yield more than 20 bushels to the acre. Had it not been for the interplanted corn, we could have plowed the field with a mule or a tractor, delivered compost and manure by cart, opened furrows with animal or machine power, and transported seed by wheeled vehicle to the spot where we wanted to sow it. But because a few cornstalks had not yet ripened, we poured endless man-days of labor into the plot. Cheng-k'uan and his teammates got up early, ate both breakfast and lunch in the field, and worked from before dawn until after dark in hopes of wresting a high yield of wheat from the soil.

It was obvious to everyone that all this extra work was not worth the value of the corn they were protecting by doing it. But they kept at it out of sheer stubbornness. In the spring they had decided to intercrop and they were determined to carry that experiment through to the end no matter what difficulties arose. The effort brought Cheng-k'uan to the verge of complete exhaustion. The chronic bronchitis that had plagued him for years grew worse. His house was just across the wall from the mission compound and he made it hard for us all to sleep, by coughing the night away.

"Why don't you rest up for a day or two?" I asked.

"I'm getting old. I would really like to eat warm food at home, quit earlier, rest longer, and do easier work. But how can we catch up with

Tachai like that? If the team leader doesn't show the way, how can he expect others to follow?"

Driven by this logic he forced himself up before dawn and spent each long day in the field at the head of his team. When he put down his hoe after dark he still had to eat supper and after supper he still had to lead team meetings. He was lucky if he got more than a few hours of sleep twice a week. Thus he proved his quality as a man and a revolutionary. He was sick, he was always overtired, he was usually cold. He was illiterate, a deficiency that made political leadership difficult because he could not scan the paper, decide what should be read at field breaks, or read it out loud to his teammates—but he never gave up.

After seeing him in action day after day, we found it impossible not to respect and admire Cheng-k'uan. Peasants such as he would never rest as long as they could stand up. They did not know the word "defeat." They were convinced that they had their shoulders up against the wheel of history, and they meant to push it forward if they could.

I saw intercropping in other places that held out more promise than the Fifth Team plot offered. Cheng-k'uan's mistake had been to plant far too little corn. On the other hand, perhaps he planted a lot and very little survived. In any case the stand was poor. With a good corn crop growing between the beds of wheat all that extra labor would not have seemed so useless. Even so, I questioned the value of the method. When it came time to harvest the wheat, team members would have to haul all the grain and all the straw out of the field by carrying pole just as we had hauled the compost in, and in the process the pole carriers would pack down the land a fifth time. Was all that extra labor and all that abuse of the soil worth even a 60-bushel corn crop? Since it was clearly possible, with a pure stand of corn, to get 100 bushels per acre, or even more on irrigated land, the answer had to be no.

The optimistic plans for raising a bumper crop of wheat and turning it from a low-yield to a high-yield crop served to mobilize an impressive effort throughout the brigade, and all the teams achieved their planting schedules, at least in the main.

What they failed to accomplish was all the deep-digging. The team leaders and later the team members based their digging guarantees on good, that is dry, weather. To level the land for irrigation, then deep-dig it, distribute huge amounts of compost, and finally plant the wheat in wide furrows on a bed of compost leavened with liquid night soil, all within two weeks, depended on at least ten days of good weather, which did not materialize. The rains of August had been particularly heavy, and just as drought had generated drought, so rain had generated rain. With the whole Shangtang Region soggy from excessive downpours, one after the other, every time the sun came out huge amounts of water vapor moved skyward, only to form once again into clouds and come pouring down as rain once more. The days when the peasants could work the land in the fields were few and far between, and so they had to cut back some of their grand plans. For the most part it was deep-digging that was slighted, but even some of the land leveling was abandoned as the season moved toward planting time. The brigade leaders decided to plant whatever land was ready, or even half ready, then fix up additional tracts if the weather allowed. If, in the end, no one had time to prepare for irrigation, then they should plant the tracts by ordinary methods.

While these preparations were underway Party Secretary Chang made a trip to a far county to investigate new varieties of wheat for seed. While there he studied over 200 different wheats and finally selected three—East Is Red #1, Changchih #515 and Nanfu Nungtai. He brought back enough improved seed to plant all the brigade's wheat land, and advised the teams to choose whatever variety they liked best. When asked about another good wheat that brigade members had seen doing well in and around Changchih City, he opposed it on the ground that it required exceptionally high levels of fertility, the kind of heavy supplies of night soil that only a city population could provide. Long Bow, he said, could not hope to match such efforts. Secretary Chang further recommended that all the new seed be chemically treated for smut and other seedborne diseases. He sent out a buyer to find suitable chemicals.

The scene in the fields as the work went forward never failed to inspire us. As we joined in each day, we felt a constantly renewed sense of collective power. Beneath all the splits and quarrels, the rivalries and the dissatisfactions that plagued the village, solid foundations for collective consciousness seemed to have been laid. People showed respect for their community and relied on group action. Whatever the troubles of this new era might be, they did not replay the troubles of the past, and rejection of that past was all but absolute. Even those who, like the Two Gems, had been accused of taking the "capitalist road," could hardly be accused of defying the collective framework of their village. They took the superiority of this framework for granted. They had no desire to undermine it, but only plans for prospering within it. That certain forms of personal prosperity might be a threat to the system was something they apprehended but dimly. They took the life of their cooperative for granted without perhaps fully understanding the need for daily and hourly reinforcing and refining it.

We felt that same sense of collective power, of relaxed satisfaction with cooperative life, one evening at the height of the harvest when we went out to pick eggplant and hauled it home to the Second Team threshing floor for distribution. Representatives of all the families on the team crowded round the flatcarts to get their share. Holding baskets, bags and nondescript containers of all sorts, little children clung to the backs of bigger children, nursing mothers stood in line with sweat-stained cart drivers and stinking privy cleaners. Team cadres distributed eggplant at so many catties per head to everyone on the team, old or young, sick or well, hardworking or lazy, as part of that category "Free Supply" so attractive to the multitude and yet so controversial overall. The good humor, the infectious laughter, the sense of community solidarity overwhelmed us.

From the threshing floor we returned to brigade headquarters and there all the impressions of the evening were renewed and expanded. On one side of the courtyard several meetings of cadres filled the rooms; on the other side the brigade barber was giving a peasant a haircut. In the meeting hall at the south end scores of young people were rehearsing new dances and skits, while in the dispensary to the east Wang Yü-mei the druggist, whose hair fell so provocatively below her waist when she let it down, was making up a prescription. On the far side of the wall, behind the village office, the brigade flour mill was roaring and shaking, its three women attendants all too busy to talk. Men, women and children of all sizes and shapes waited for their grain to be ground—laughing, joking, teasing, playing. It was impossible not to feel a sense of fitness, of rightness, a sense of deep fellowship permeating the scene on both sides of the wall. How better could an earthbound people organize a community like this, how better face the future?

Sensing the tremendous strength that cooperation demonstrated that fall and the positive effects of leadership from the city level, we underestimated, perhaps, the negative consequences of too much input from above, input that often came down as arbitrary intervention in the complex process of crop production. As time went on we became aware of many painful episodes arising out of "official meddling." Over the years "meddling" increased to the point where regulations tied peasants hand and foot. But this kind of intervention was as yet only a cloud on Long Bow's horizon. It could not cancel out the strong sense of competence and future potential generated by a rationally led, vertically integrated society.

As the field work went forward the Fourth Team seemed to pull ahead. This was due in part to the fact that the young men in charge had found a way of attaching a block of wood to their mule-drawn plow. It broke a wide ditch in the ground instead of turning a furrow. This saved hoeing time, so that many people who might have been tied up at this task could concentrate on spreading night soil and compost. With compost piles well spaced and night soil pits conveniently located, the planting went ahead rapidly.

The Third Team, working the land on the other side of the irrigation ditch, seemed to lag behind. Third Team members, led by that remarkable woman Yang Lien-ying, spent much more time leveling their land than did their rivals; though their compost piles seemed somewhat bigger, their planting methods lagged badly. The furrows they dug out with hoes, in contrast to the plowed furrows of the Fourth Team, ran in uneven lines, as if an old woman with a shaky hand had drawn a comb through the field. Their daily progress across the vast expanse of land seemed minimal. Since they fell so far behind we tended to ignore them and never did walk out to see what they were doing, or how they were doing it.

When the sprouts came up, however, it was Third Team wheat that emerged dark green, vigorous and healthy, while Fourth Team wheat showed pale and thin. In their hurry to get the job done the Fourth Team members had used only half-rotted compost in the furrow; the night soil hauled from the deep cisterns of the village homes, though plentiful in volume, turned out to be low in fertility due to the flooding of the cisterns in the heavy August rains. Even the chemical urea dumped in to make up the deficit had failed to solve this problem.

In practice the flashy Fourth Production Team, with its young, creative leadership and its organizational drive, had done less well than the stolid Third Team with its plodding perseverance. The final results, of course, were not yet in. There was still time for the Fourth Team to side-dress its wheat and ensure fertility wherever this was low. Much would depend, also, on the irrigation water next spring. But here again the Third Team seemed to have an edge because they had taken much greater pains to make their land level.

52

WORK AT DAWN, MEET AFTER DARK

With the whole community mobilized to plant wheat during daylight hours, the Party rectification demanded by the municipal conference took place at night. One might have thought that wheat planting was enough for the peasants to cope with and that they deserved to rest in the evening. Obviously many people had just such inclinations. That is why the propaganda team cadres, as they organized the interminable meetings that were the heart of the rectification process, began every speech by denying that there was any contradiction between political and production tasks.

But no matter how often they repeated this, they could not convince Party Secretary Kuei-ts'ai.

"At the start people will come," he said, "but since they will get more and more tired in the field each day they may not come back night after night."

"Didn't you have a lot of meetings during spring planting?" asked Smart Fan.

"That was different. The people were in high spirits then."

"Well, grasping revolution should promote production, not hold it back," said Smart Fan. "Weren't there more meetings this year than before? And didn't production go better? Meetings don't block production. To arrange meetings well is the responsibility of the leaders. You have to urge people to come early and get through early."

At one meeting half of the people fell asleep, the other half left early for home. Undaunted, Judge Kao said, "Some people think these meetings conflict with production, but that's wrong. There is no contradiction between meetings and production. The day is short. The night is long. We can get up a little earlier in the morning. Some say that when things are busy we should stop studying. But just the opposite is true. The busier we are the more attention we should pay to study."

Fortunately for the big meeting that inaugurated the campaign, rain fell on September 2. If the continuing rains threatened the dam, harmed the crops and delayed the harvest, they nevertheless gave a boost to political work. Since it was raining so hard that no one could go to the fields, the propaganda team "seized the time" and called for a brigade-wide meeting in the assembly hall. Somewhat curious as to what might be afoot, people jammed the hall from wall to wall and from back to front, right up to the edge of the raised platform that served as a stage. All elements of the village population showed up—old, young, young adult and middle-aged, married, single, divorced and widowed. They brought lots of children, children just learning to walk and nursing babies who gurgled and cried. When babies cried too much, cadres ordered their mothers to carry them out. Some of the most beautiful girls in the brigade, dressed in their very best, sat in the front row on some bricks they had found stacked along the south wall. They wore their hair in long braids, even those who were married, and sported much brighter tunics than any woman in Peking would dare put on— flowered prints or bright checks in contrasting primary colors. They were much more interested in watching Carma and me than in anything that went on at the meeting, talked constantly among themselves and giggled by turn.

A few rows back sat Shen Hsi-le, the old Catholic who was the father of the abused bride of 1948, Hsien-e. This was the first time we had seen him since returning. In the intervening years he had grown an impressive gray beard. Near him, on a little stool, perched a rather handsome older woman who never took her eyes off us. This was the mother of Chi San-chiang, the village doctor. She was a confirmed and open Catholic believer.

Since there were no permanent seats in the hall, everyone had to bring his or her own stool, block of wood or brick. Since it was also raining lightly and no one could stand outside in comfort watching the proceedings through the window, the whole audience had to squeeze into the hall proper. This took some time and a lot of pushing and rearranging. One of the propaganda team cadres counted 370 participants, all told. They were jammed into a building designed for 200.

Judge Kao delivered his report seated at a large wooden table on the stage. Behind him on the wall hung a huge portrait of Mao Tse-tung. The judge, who was noted for long speeches, did nothing to damage his reputation that day. He began with a review of the charges against the Two Gems, which explained their removal from office. He then spoke of the lively production drive that had been mounted by the new leading group in the spring. He listed in detail the outstanding achievements of outstanding individuals, crediting both to higher levels of consciousness acquired through study and struggle. This demonstrated, he said, how ideas could be transformed into material wealth.

All of this was by way of introduction to the main point, which was the need to examine critically the role of the new brigade leadership and carry out a popular review of the Party rectification process. He repeated the seven standards for judging party members that had been laid down at the municipal meeting and explained the "open-door" nature of the Party meetings to come. The rank-and-file were to hear and criticize the Party members who belonged to their respective production teams.

The rectification plan proposed by Judge Kao called for five days of mobilization and study, five more days for the individual review of each Communist, ten days for an all-out effort to appraise the policies and performance of the new leading group and to settle, if possible, the cases of those still under suspension, and finally five days for reviewing all the regulations and arrangements governing the life of the brigade. On this question it was hoped that all members would definitely speak out.

After Judge Kao finally finished, the director of the General Affairs Office of the City Party Committee, Smart Fan, took the floor to reinforce what had been said and make a strong plea for active participation on the part of the people.

"Every day," he said "we talk of the struggle between two lines and of Mao Tse-tung's line. But the basic difference between the two lines is whether or not you trust the people. According to Mao each Party branch must be rooted among the people. That is why the rectification movement is an open-door movement, and that is why the checkup that we want to begin today is an open-door movement, a public affair. The people have to discuss whether the work of the brigade is well done or not and what still needs to be done. Mao Tse-tung wants us to take part. That is a sign of his trust in us. If we don't respond with active participation, we must beg his pardon!

"So anyone who does not show concern for this movement is not listening to Mao Tse-tung. Everyone must overcome fear of revenge, fear of being hurt through speaking out.

"Some hesitate to annoy others by talking frankly. Why?

"Because in previous movements some cadres did not follow Mao Tse-tung's line and they used the strength of their faction to take revenge. They enlarged small problems, or manufactured problems that did not exist and they found ways to hit back with fewer work points, or unattractive assignments.

"So some people think, To hell with it, we'll be silent.

"But now everyone's consciousness has been raised. We have a new set of leaders in our Communist Party Branch. We can trust them and we can speak out with ease of mind.

"Another reason why some hesitate is self-interest. People have their own shortcomings. They would rather let well enough alone lest they be criticized in turn. But that is a shortsighted attitude. In the long run we should all face up to our weaknesses and unite to transform Long Bow.

"As for annoying people, if they are class enemies, who cares? If they are not class enemies, there are still many ideas and acts that we have to struggle against. If we let them pass, the whole collective will suffer. Isn't that what happened with the Two Gems? Both were poor peasants without any serious problems in their history. They were elected to office because they were good people. So how come they turned out so badly? It's because we did not give them proper supervision. Whenever any new leading group is set up there is always the problem of relying on the people to supervise it. We have to check up on them every few months. The key to everything is the leading body. The key to keeping them moving forward is constant criticism from the masses and the key, as far as the leaders are concerned, is listening to mass opinions. If you want the masses to follow you, you must first follow Mao Tse-tung."

Having made this point as forcefully as possible, Smart Fan went on to clarify a few specific issues that were causing confusion in people's minds.

One of these was that hardy perennial, the *Little Four P'ei Case*. Now that Chang Kuei-ts'ai had again become the Party Secretary of Long Bow, rumors were starting to circulate that the death of the young thief who had been found in the bottom of a well ten years earlier was the fault of Kuei-ts'ai.

"Why is this case constantly revived?" asked Fan. "Is it because there is a misunderstanding? No. This is an outbreak of class struggle. There are those who wish to suppress living people with people who are already dead.

"We want rectification. This will eventually hit these people, so they raise the case of Little Four P'ei. They want to divert attention and throw us off the track. Every time we have a movement this happens. Who starts this every time? Certainly not anyone good."

Going on to the question of unsettled cases, Smart Fan said, "Some people want to use this checkup period to demand a quick settlement of their cases. But settling cases has two sides. Anyone who wants a case settled quickly must first speak out honestly and bring out all the facts. Then it will be easy to settle the case."

Finally Fan brought up the problem of brigade unity.

"Some people are trying to undermine our unity. They keep cursing the brigade leaders for small mistakes. This cursing-the-cadres wind is nothing but a wrecking wind. Consider what Fast Chin said the other day. He said, 'Sure, we are a Black Gang. Let's see your Red Gang do any better. How long will it be before the people start cursing you?'

"Fast Chin, what kind of a remark is that?"

Since the rain continued, the people met again all afternoon to discuss the movement. This time they met team by team. Carma and I went to the Fifth Team headquarters in the southeast corner of the village. It turned out to be a broken-down building in a crumbling courtyard behind the huge mat shed that housed the Liberation Army tank unit. The building consisted of three sections of a one-story adobe house that was completely empty except for a few bricks piled up along the walls to serve as seats and a battered old desk in the corner. On the middle wall opposite the door hung a portrait of Chairman Mao. Above it a photograph of Mao and Lin Piao had been pasted. On each side hung citations for the work of the Long Bow militia; one from the regional administration citing the Fifth Platoon (the Fifth Team's unit) for excellence, another from the municipal administration citing the First Squad (a subunit under the Fifth Platoon). On the north wall there was a further citation for the First Squad from the Revolutionary Committee of Horse Square Commune.

Children were playing outside in the courtyard. We could hear their shrill voices and laughter clearly because there was no glass in the delapidated window frames. A team carpenter had fashioned them out of unplaned sticks. He had closed in the bottom of one window by nailing a fiberboard panel across the frame but the panel was too short for the window and failed to close it completely at either end.

The people straggled in one at a time. The team leaders sent runners out to round up laggards. When a few finally came they said they hadn't known there was a meeting. This meant that they had paid very little attention, for Judge Kao had made the announcement and repeated it at the mass meeting and broadcast it over the loudspeaker throughout the noon hour. The roundup effort was not too successful. It delayed the start of the meeting, and as everyone waited for more people to arrive, several people who had come early got up, left, and never did show up again.

Wang Wen-te came, with his pants rolled up above his knees to keep them dry. His calves were so lean the tendons stood out on them like rope. On his head he wore a towel, tied in traditional fashion. It was the only head towel present. In contrast, Wang Kuei-pao wore a white skullcap. All the younger men wore visor caps, cadre-style tunics and pants, and ankle-high rubber boots. Some wore shirts made of striped cloth. The white and blue stripes ran horizontally across their chests and backs. They smoked cigarettes, one after the other. The older men still smoked pipes, but instead of the traditional flint and steel they lit them with modern, thumb-activated lighters.

The political director of the team, Li Yü-hsi, opened the meeting by reading passages from the July 1 editorial in the *Shansi Daily,* reviewed the main goals of the Communist Party Rectification, and called for a discussion on the importance of the checkup as a stage in the rebuilding of the Party. But the meeting went very badly. The topic was apparently too abstract. Nobody had anything to say.

In order to break the silence team leader Chin P'ing-kuei said a few words. Chang Chiang-tzu, sitting in for the commune, took up the cue and said a few words also, but after that there was silence again. The slow drizzle, all that remained of the morning's rain, eased off. Seeing this, Wang Wen-te got up and went out into the courtyard. Within a few minutes about a third of the people followed him out. Soon a lively conversation developed outdoors. Annoyed, Yü-hsi went out and drove the people back with a tongue-lashing. But Wen-te never did come inside again. He sauntered off homeward instead. The one man who most needed rectification, the one Fifth Team member whose Party membership had been suspended, thought too little of the gathering to honor it with his presence.

The meeting degenerated into a fiasco. Since nobody had anything to say, Li Yü-hsi had no alternative but to adjourn the session.

Affairs went little better elsewhere. At the Second Team meeting only Splayfoot Tseng, the alleged "rascal" who was the Two Gems' most vocal supporter, and Fast Chin, the main target of rectification, spoke out. Splayfoot Tseng rushed actively from group to group, sparking one conversation after another, but avoided speaking out before the meeting as a whole. When he finally did take the floor, he voiced nothing but complaints. Ever since the new group came to power in the brigade, he said, things had really been dead in the village.

Second Team leaders found it impossible to hold the crowd. People kept drifting out and could not be persuaded to come back. Most of them could not even be found to listen to persuasion of any sort. In the end, when Chin decided to speak, many did come back, not because they necessarily supported him, but because they were curious to hear what this notorious "black ganger" would say. How they knew that he was about to speak was a mystery.

What Chin actually said was that the reports made by the propaganda team leaders at the big meeting were one-sided, that he had tried several times to reach them them in order to talk things out, but that they had failed to meet. He sandwiched this criticism of the team leadership between some facile self-critical remarks such as "the rectification movement is good. If I had been the leader it would not have been so well done. I should study Mao well, criticize my mistakes, bow my head and admit my crimes, and ask the comrades to criticize me." But since in fact he made no substantive criticism of himself, his words resolved nothing.

As a starting point for a major mass movement, these meetings were not auspicious. Discussions on the importance of Party rectification were too abstract and theoretical to arouse interest. As soon as the process moved on to the next stage, the actual confrontation between team members and Communists, the participation of rank-and-file peasants picked up somewhat, but even at its height the movement never developed into anything more than a pale reflection of the Party rectification that had so stirred everyone in 1948.

Stirring or not, the pace of the rectification accelerated with each passing day. Team meetings, branch meetings, joint branch and propaganda team meetings, meetings of representative poor peasants and meetings of poor peasant women crowded whatever waking hours the peasants and the cadres had left after their long days in the field. All these meetings were designed to draw out the opinions of the rank-and-file on the one hand and prepare the Communists and cadres for serious self- and mutual criticism on the other.

53

GATHERING OPINIONS

A meeting of ten representative poor peasant men who came together in Security Officer Shen's headquarters on September 10 was lively and fruitful even though the opinions expressed struck at random like buckshot, exposed only minor problems, and were hard to summarize.

The willingness of team leaders, most of them Communists, to tackle problems and criticize people kept recurring as a topic. Team members criticized those who avoided such struggle, while they praised those who stepped in to solve problems, even at the risk of offending people.

On the Sixth Team two members of the vegetable group, while picking produce for the team as a whole, set aside the best vegetables for themselves. This led to a quarrel that was brought to team leader Liu-shun. He arranged a special meeting to discuss vegetable distribution, criticized the two offenders, and solved the problem. This pleased the other team members because they had been reluctant to protest lest they be victimized as troublemakers and forced to accept the poorest vegetables in the future. Who wanted to risk that? If, on the other hand, the team leader took action, he won respect. No one could call him a troublemaker.

Li Lin-kuang, a long-faced older man from the Sixth Team, elaborated on this point. "When the team leader is there the people work one way, but when he leaves they work in another. Some people just get lazy and don't work well. I always say what is on my mind. Even though nobody listens, I speak right out. I have always knocked slack work, but no one listens to me. They only listen to the team leader or the political director.

"Of course some people agree with me. But some of these young, fresh characters just go right on fooling around and raising hell. Chin Er-k'uei is the ringleader. He's a bad apple. He's not serious about anything. Last year when Yen-hsin criticized the way he was hoeing the corn, leaving weeds and uprooting plants, he beat him up right on the spot. When it came time to elect the daily work-point recorder, Er-k'uei didn't even want to discuss the matter. We should have elected the best possible person, but Er-k'uei said, 'Whoever gets elected will serve,' and following his lead none of the young people said anything about who would be best.

"When we set work points each feels that as long as his or her rate is OK then it is best to shut up and not care about the others. Even if someone else doesn't deserve high points, they still won't raise any objection for fear of retaliation later. Maybe their own points will be cut down. So it's better not to speak out.

"All this leads young people to carelessness in work. Young girls say to me, 'Look, you did a row and I did a row.' But they pay no attention to the quality of the work. Some of them hoe three rows at a time, but they don't hoe between the plants in the row, so the weeds still grow there. Or they just pile dirt up around the corn and bury the weeds. Now it's all right to hill up the corn but it should be hoed well, all around, first.

"These young people all say, 'Three rows at a time is very efficient.' In their view it's only the old conservatives who go up and down the field row after row. If the team leader were there, the young people wouldn't act like that. If there were a set quota for the day, then they would do better. But if there is no quota they just drag along and don't get anything done.

"It's the same on all the teams. To learn from Tachai is not easy. If you don't get rid of old-good-fellow thinking you'll never learn from Tachai. As for me, as I said, I like to speak out. It has got so, when the young people see me they say, 'Look, the old bastard is here again!' "

"Do you notice any change in the field work this year?" asked Judge Kao.

"No, no change," said long-faced Li dolefully.

"But you still have to say it's better than other years," objected Lu Shui-ch'ang of the First Team. "You can't say it hasn't improved at all. Before, if the team leader criticized they just answered back and went their own way. Now they at least listen to the team leader if to no one else. That's why the brigade has to support the team leader. If the team leader criticizes people and offends them, and if the brigade doesn't support the leader, then he has no prestige on the team anymore and can't stand on his feet.

"The way it was before, when you met a problem at the team level and you went to the brigade for help they just said, 'Good, good,' but never did a thing. They just sat there and 'mixed mud' all day. So under conditions like that you could never get rid of old-good-fellow thinking.

"We can start to do something only when we get rid of the fear of offending others. We must dare resist whoever is wrong."

"That's right," broke in Chi K'uan-shun of the Sixth Team. "But team leaders only dare fight when they have brigade support. Even when you have a team leader who is not afraid to ruffle feathers, if the brigade leaders don't back him up, then he can't go on for long. He is bound to end up passive."

"I agree," said Judge Kao, speaking for the work team. "Brigade and team should be unified and give each other mutual support. The brigade leaders should back up the team leaders. But of course they should never back up a team leader doing bad things, but only one carrying out Mao Tse-tung's line. We should never repeat those incidents in the past where the brigade backed team leaders in doing wrong."

Long-faced Li Lin-kuang was still not convinced that things had improved that much in 1971. "When Sun Jing-fu and Chi Ch'eng-en are in the field, people work well. But if Yen-hsin alone is there they pay no attention to him at all. People just don't listen to Yen-hsin. He has no prestige. Ever since he got beaten up last year and nobody at brigade level stuck up for him, everyone bullies him at will."

"But perhaps," said Judge Kao, "people don't listen to certain team leaders because of the way they work when they are out there."

"Well, that's true," said Li Lin-kuang. "Yen-hsin doesn't work as well as he might. He has plenty of problems at home and often comes late to the field. Then if others are late he can't very well criticize them. In the morning, people sit around in the field saying, 'The team leader hasn't come, so why should we begin?' And this happens much too often."

"On our team there is a problem with Kuo-liang," said Shui-ch'ang of the First Team. "He tends to pick out the easy jobs. When he takes manure up the hill he doesn't block off the back of the cart. As he goes up, the manure spills out. By the time he gets to the top only half the load is left. Sometimes, when he hauls manure he puts ashes on the bottom of the load, then fills out the top with heavy pig manure. Thus the whole load is lighter. But he says this is done out of concern for the animals."

"But the Party members on the Sixth Team play a better role than that," said Chi K'uan-shun, breaking in. "Take Chi Hu-lan, for instance. She used to pay attention to nothing but her own family. She was beaten up once and never wanted to take any responsibility after that. But now it is just the opposite. Now she speaks up whenever she sees anything wrong."

"And I speak up, too," said Wang Kuei-pao of the Second Team. "One day when we were hoeing, the team leader left everything rough. I had to rake everything twice just to get it smooth. I told him about it. Several people asked me how I dared raise such a thing with the team leader. But I said, 'If he weren't in the wrong, I wouldn't say anything. But if he does something wrong, it's not a mistake to mention it.' "

The participants at this meeting agreed that though the atmosphere was better than before, with many people daring to speak out on some things, and many team leaders daring to give some leadership, still there was a lot of room for improvement. The brigade leading body, they said, continued to be too soft. Good decisions made at meetings often did not get carried out, or at least were not carried out by all the teams. When the brigade leaders made a decision, some teams acted on it while other teams didn't, and the brigade still did not follow through. Thus, even though the brigade leaders decided to spread all available manure and compost in preparation for planting wheat, a lot of manure still lay around the village, and the Third Team and the Sixth Team even quarreled over the manure that had already been spread.

Right on the heels of the representative poor peasants' meeting, the Party members themselves came together for a briefing on what was expected of them in the open-door meetings to come.

Security Officer Shen explained that the movement required not just a self-criticism but a *chang-yung*, an overall evaluation of strengths and weaknesses as exhibited in past work, and of progress since the beginning of the rectification movement. They should also express their resolve for the future. Both those Party members who were in good standing and those four who still remained under suspension should make this evaluation.

Those in good standing should stress an all-around appraisal, while those set aside should concentrate on self-criticism, since it was mainly because they had, until now, failed to recognize their serious mistakes that they still could not win reinstatement.

In regard to the standards by which the members should judge themselves, Shen stressed first the fifty-character sentence from the New Year's editorial of 1968, which quoted Mao Tse-tung as saying, "The Party organization should be composed of advanced elements of the proletariat; it should be a vigorous and vital organization of vanguards which can lead the proletariat and revolutionary masses in struggle against the class enemy."

As to what might constitute an advanced element, Shen urged that everyone study the five requirements for Party members laid down in the 1969 Constitution of the Communist Party:

1. Carry on living study and application of Marxism-Leninism and Mao Tse-tung Thought.
2. Work for the Chinese people and the people of the world.
3. Unite with the majority and even with those who oppose you.
4. Consult the masses on all problems.
5. Dare to conduct criticism and self-criticism.

In regard to the work of the branch as a whole, Shen said the team would judge it by how well it had carried out the five tasks set for Party branches in the new Party Constitution:

1. Lead the Communist Party and the masses in the study and application of Marxism-Leninism and Mao Tse-tung Thought.
2. Conduct class education and education in two lines; lead the Communist Party members and the masses in struggle against the class enemy.
3. Propagate and carry out Communist Party principles.
4. Establish close ties with the masses.
5. Admit new vanguard members. Get rid of the stale and take in the fresh.

The Party members responded to Security Officer Shen's talk with passive general agreement to such a public evaluation. They said it should be done in good time, and often, so that Communist Party members could avoid mistakes.

At this point, Fast Chin, still outside the "gate," made another remark that soon became an issue throughout the brigade.

"Learning from Tachai means hard work. I'll just work hard. Isn't that OK?" he asked.

Early on the morning of September 11 the work team cadres met to sum up their work so far. They had some interesting comments to make about various Party members.

Li Yü-hsi (Fifth Team leader): Very steady, down to earth. Hardworking. He doesn't like to blow the horn or beat the drum.

Li Fu-wang (First Team): Always says OK. Always agrees with higher leaders. Then goes back and does whatever he did before.

Chin Er-k'uei (Sixth Team): Truly hard to deal with. Like a knot in a plank he's hard to plane smooth.

Sun Jing-fu (Sixth Team leader): Able. Whatever he says, he does. Dares to struggle. No good-fellow thought. But he is prickly when criticized. He works hard himself, then says, "This is what I have done. If you can't do the same, you can't pass muster." This makes some people unhappy. The method is too rough.

Liu-shun (Sixth Team): Also quite able.

All Here Li: He's still always the last to get to a meeting. When he arrives the people have *lai ch'uer* (they're "all here"). But he has done better lately. Even though his leg is badly swollen he works hard. He led a shock brigade to work on the canal until 1:00 A.M., then reported for work early that same morning!

Wan-fu: Has not done so well since his divorce. The divorce upset him. It's an ideological problem. He has let go of the leadership of the Second Team.

Lu Ho-jen (Second Team): Has conflicts with the team leader Pei Liang-shun. Worked hard in April but has now slacked off. Why? Too many rumors being spread? No. Too many negative people. Too few supporters. He can't overcome the adverse wind.

Speaking of adverse wind, when the Second Team publicly criticized Fast Chin's paramour Shih Kui-hsiang, the people asked Splayfoot Tseng, still a suspended Party member, to stand up also. But he refused. "I won't stand up with her! What sort of creature is she anyway?" All present thought this was a case of the pot calling the kettle black. Splayfoot Tseng's case, as a Communist, was much more serious, after all, than the case of the young bride Shih Kui-hsiang.

"But," said Judge Kao, "that's typical of the Two Gems' clique. They always answer back. They always have something to say in defiance of popular demand. They should listen to mass criticism but they never do. They always answer right back!"

This meeting no sooner concluded than the team called an enlarged branch meeting to help the Communist Party members prepare for the confrontations scheduled for that evening.

Judge Kao started off the meeting with a short statement. "We should talk about the changes since the start of the rectification movement and use Tachai to judge Long Bow, and thus find our weak points. To demonstrate resolution for the future we should make concrete plans. We should look for the faults in our work and not just find fault with the people, for by that method you simply look back and forth and finally conclude that the masses are backward and there *is* no way out."

One after another the leading Communists spoke and all of them contrasted the enthusiasm of the spring planting period with the apathy of September.

"This spring," said Lu Ho-jen, political director of the Second Team, "there was a great change. We grasped class struggle. The masses aroused themselves and quickly finished all the work left over from the winter. We praised the good in time and struggled against the bad. Work went well. But now everything has slacked off. When we have directives about the work we don't check up. It's not a question of ability, it's a question of *kan chih* [enthusiasm] and of study. We got things off the ground, in the spring. Why not now?

"To tell the truth, we haven't done any deep-digging for the wheat even though we promised to. The land was too wet. We only used our hoes. Perhaps we dug a little deeper than usual, but not much. On the other hand, we did haul more fertilizer."

All Here Li said the same thing. "We have achieved something as compared to the past, especially in the spring. We repudiated mistaken thinking as it appeared. We hauled manure to the fields, repaired the canals, and set up shock brigades. We even hauled manure to the fields at night without asking for extra points. We all worked hard and were happy and at ease." He spoke of this with real feeling and the more he thought about it the faster his words came. "Our spirits were really high then. More and more people turned out. Even old people. Some young workers said to an older man, 'Don't carry that, it's too heavy for you.' But the old man refused to put the load down. 'I want to do my part,' he said.

"At first my shock brigade had only young people, but soon old people turned out in large numbers. We had socialist competition. People came early and left late. All was going fine!

"So now, since a few of us have just returned from Tachai, we should fan up such a spirit again. We are people just like those at Tachai and our natural conditions are much better than theirs. If we can't do well it is shameful."

Smart Fan sat in on this meeting; after listening to all the individuals talk, he put in a final word of advice.

"Whether or not you can move the people to criticize you or not depends on your attitude. If you are honest and really welcome criticism, it will be forthcoming. When talking of your achievements leave a little room to maneuver. If you have ten points, talk about eight or nine. Don't lay out all ten. If you do the people won't like it. But when it comes to shortcomings, expose them all. Don't hide a single one."

54

A TEAM
LEADER SPEAKS

 That night we once again attended the meeting at Fifth Team headquarters. The people, tired after a hard day's work planting wheat, did not assemble until after 9:00 P.M. That was when they finally finished eating supper after coming in from the fields when the sun went down. A single electric light, hanging from the ceiling at the end of two hot wires, illuminated the Fifth Team's stark headquarters.

According to the custom, where self-criticism was concerned, that the most important cadre lead off, Kuo Cheng-k'uan stood up first. He spoke very seriously. It was obvious that he had given the matter deep thought; his words came from the heart. Of course some of the things he said smacked of routine; he used many of the stock phrases that people naturally repeated when making a political statement in China, but it was obvious that Cheng-k'uan, rather than simply repeating phrases, was sincerely trying to give expression to his feelings of the past period, to lay bare his shortcomings and show that he meant to take hold with renewed determination in the future.

On formal occasions Cheng-k'uan always began his remarks with some quotes from Mao Tse-tung. This time he repeated haltingly from memory the first selection from the first page of the *Red Book:* "The force at the core leading our cause forward is the Chinese Communist Party. The theoretical basis guiding our thinking is Marxism-Leninism." He followed this with "Grasp revolution, promote production," "Unite to win still greater victories," and "In agriculture learn from Tachai."

Cheng-k'uan had to memorize the Mao quotes because he couldn't read. In the fifties the brigade had sent him away to a literacy class, but although he stayed away for two and a half years he never even learned to write his name. When he got back, friends and neighbors asked how many ideographs he had memorized. His answer was, "None. The state invested in me for nothing!"

"For all that millet you should have been able to buy at least one ideograph," they taunted.

"Forget it," said Cheng-k'uan, blushing. "Just forget the whole thing."

Now, in a voice hoarse from years of chronic coughing, he began to speak, slowly and haltingly at first, but with increasing fluency as his ideas started to flow.

"I want to talk about my own understanding of the Communist Party rectification and learning from Tachai. I went to Tachai this year for the second time. I lived with an old man and talked with him and I feel deeply that we are falling farther and farther behind. So I also want to speak about my resolve in regard to the future.

"I'm a poor peasant, an old Communist and an old cadre. I've been a cadre for twenty years and lately I've been tempted to retire. But with the work I've done I really can't hold up my head before Mao Tse-tung and the poor peasant masses.

"The cadres of the Fifth Team have not united well in the past and I didn't play the role I should have played as a Communist and a political director to solve this problem. I have never really learned to read and so I haven't studied well. What I learned about line struggle during this movement made me ashamed of my past work.

"I decided to quit thinking about retiring and to jump in to carry the revolution on. Since then I have led the team in study by asking those who can read to read aloud.

"In the spring our cadres were united in the movement to accumulate manure. We decided to raise production on the Fifth Team, and we decided to concentrate on compost and night soil. In the past when we sent 80 tan per mou [27 tons per acre] to the field we used to report 100 or 110. But that was an exaggeration. That's not living up to Communist standards, and after all, we were only cheating ourselves. Manure is the grain of the crops, so we had to think about how to get more. After we had spread everything available, we decided it still wasn't enough, so we cut weeds, swept the courtyards, scoured the neighborhood and piled up more. In the end we had 120 tan per mou. In this campaign we led the masses to work very hard, for if you don't grasp manure you can't grasp grain."

From manure he turned to irrigation:

"We talked about irrigation every year but we never really succeeded because we hadn't leveled the land. This year, at last, we tried to level the land and build all the little field canals that make irrigation possible. Those we had made the year before had been washed out by big rains flooding the trunk ditches. So this year we decided to make it work whether the rains were heavy or light. Thus our labor would not be wasted as it had so often been in the past.

"Since our new irrigation system is west of the highway, we fixed up the land in the west, 180 mou, and most of it works. If you can't make irrigation work, you can't resist drought.

"As to the land in the east, we watered it in two days but because it hadn't been leveled properly some was flooded while the rest remained dry. We fixed all this also, because the cadres took the lead. First the cadres have to work hard themselves, then they can criticize those who are lagging. Since my only aim is to promote higher production, why should I hesitate to criticize weak points or praise strong points in team-mates?

"When we hoe and we have finished a row, as we reverse ourselves, I look to see if the land has been well done. It's easy to see who has been doing well and who poorly. Without investigation one has no right to speak but after I look everything over I can speak. If I didn't check it myself but only listened to others, I could make serious mistakes.

"All through the spring I led in repudiating Liu Shao-ch'i in the fields. We carried on two-line struggle—grasped class struggle and also production—from plowing to hoeing we grasped it. But then some bad thinking cropped up in my mind. I'll talk about it and ask for help, since others can see my shortcomings better than I can.

"I thought our crops were doing better than last year. All the sprouts had come through, the skips had been replanted and both millet and corn were doing well, not like last year, when one field of millet was empty in the middle. This year was a different story and especially the millet planted by the wide-furrow method and irrigated; it was growing well. I felt proud. What more could we ask?

"But pride leads to failure. One should never be proud. I thought our crops were pretty darned good. When the propaganda team leader asked me if we could harvest 400 catties I said, 'It won't be short by much!' I wasn't very modest.

"And in study I relaxed also. I found it so much trouble to ask this one and that one to read, so sometimes we just sat and took a rest. Embarrassed because I couldn't read, we just passed the time of day. And sometimes it was like this for two or three days in a row. Then, remembering that we hadn't studied for a while, I'd organize some study quickly.

"If we don't lead the masses to study Mao Tse-tung's line, it's bound to cut back production. But there is this bourgeois, self-interest thinking. I feel if we start study I'll have to put out my pipe. What a nuisance! Better just sit and be comfortable. But study depends on the leader and if the leader calls for it everyone will fall to. But I didn't make a firm resolve or a big enough effort. So I couldn't lead the masses well, and besides I thought the crops weren't half bad. So this was part of it, too."

It was almost as if Cheng-k'uan were alone in the room, thinking out loud. There was not a stir, or even a cough from the audience, which sat huddled in semidarkness along all four walls of the room and in groups dispersed across the floor. The team leader's trip to Tachai had really made an impression. He turned to talk of it once again.

"Now I have just come back from Tachai. Last year I also went. This year their corn is even bigger than last. Last year we went up the east side and came down the west. This year we went up the west side and came down the east, so we saw it all again. We met on Tigerhead Mountain and the local people introduced us to each gully and told us how it had been fixed up. The way the crops are growing there, if they say they'll harvest 1,000 catties per mou, that's no mistake. All the corn ears were the same huge size and all the millet heads were of the same great length. When you come back here and take a look, it's obvious that our crops are not half as good. Our crops are so uneven. Some stalks have no corn at all, and as for millet, there are more short heads than long. But there each millet head is 12 to

13 inches long. They speak of 1,000 catties. It's no myth. It's really happening!"

Cheng-k'uan paused to let this idea sink in. Then he went on to try and explain it.

"There the cadres take the lead. They send two meals to the field every day and people go out early and come back late, after dark. One old peasant of Hsiyang County told us that he used to get less than 200 catties off his private plot. Everyone worked hard all year and still went hungry. Then they visited Tachai and their leading people got themselves together. In three years they raised yields to 700 catties and higher. This old man got 600 catties of grain as his personal share. And his dumb son, so dumb he couldn't even find a wife, got 800 catties. And they got potatoes besides. What does this show? Once the cadres stiffen up, production goes up. They get to the fields at 4:00 A.M., they eat breakfast and lunch there. They plan well, send three to do three people's work, and they keep track of quality. No one gets a point unless the work is well done!

"After listening to this old man I feel we leaders must blame ourselves and not the people. This year we have taken all our meals at home and that's because the cadres wanted to eat at home. If the cadres stay home, the people stay home. Tachai is on our lips, but not in our actions.

"As for me, I am getting old. I feel I need a good rest. Go home, get a good rest and then work hard. But this is lazy thinking. Since when have I been afraid of hardship and hard work? How can we ever make a revolution this way? How can we ever catch up with Tachai this way?

"And we went to Hsikoupi, a village of 1,200 people who cut a channel through a mountain. They built a dam 200 meters long and made 50 mou of flat fields that yield 1,000 catties per mou. How did they do it? They studied Mao Tse-tung Thought well. Why can't we do it? Are we afraid of hardship, we cadres? Or are we conservative?"

Cheng-k'uan paused again to let this sink in and also to decide how to finish up. Wang Wen-te lit his pipe. Shen Shun-ta coughed. Outside some children, still wide awake, laughed as they played in the darkness.

"Based on this visit to Tachai," the team leader continued, "I want to tell everyone my resolution. This fall on the two plots of high-yield wheat land we will concentrate 200 tans of compost and 40 tans of night soil. And we will plant by the wide-furrow method to guarantee irrigation. Our poorer land on the hill doesn't have enough fertilizer. We must add more, and I discussed this with Li Yü-hsi tonight.

"In the fall harvest we guarantee that every grain gets back to the threshing floor. We can't spill it all over the roads and the fields as we did last year. Whoever violates the rules will be criticized. And we promise to eat our meals in the fields. We'll put this into practice right away. Thus we can seize the time during the harvest season. In making compost we should chop up 80 percent of our cornstalks, then mix them with night soil and chemical fertilizers as they do at Tachai. And after the harvest we must deep-plow or deep-dig 80 percent of the land. In study we have to seize the time also and should never be lazy. To be lazy in this means not to make revolution. Stealing time to be lazy means stealing time from the revolution.

"Going to Tachai costs a lot. The State pays for it. So if we can't learn something we can't face Mao Tse-tung. Tachai earns glory for Mao Tse-tung and the people of the world. Without grain, talk of overthrowing imperialism is nothing but empty talk!"

When Cheng-k'uan finished, Judge Kao asked if anyone had fallen asleep along the back wall.

"No, we're all awake here," came the answer out of the gloom.

But several people had slipped out the door to light up their pipes in the cool night air.

"Those outside had better come in," said Judge Kao. "Whoever skips out ought to be called back to fight-self [make a self-criticism]. Let's divide into groups and discuss Cheng-k'uan. Has he made a good estimate of his strengths and weaknesses?"

Some people floated in from the courtyard, while inside the room discussion groups formed hesitantly. Discussion was slow at first and in low tones.

A man with very heavy, protruding lips spoke to those around him at the far end of the room.

"Each cadre talks better than the last but no one does all that well. If you don't do well yourself, how can others follow?"

"You mean Cheng-k'uan?" asked a young militiaman.

"Yes. He blows hot and cold. He's always shouting, learn from Tachai, learn from Tachai, but it's all from the lips. Everyone talks too much while doing too little."

"What bothers me," said Yang Kui-lin, "is the hot and cold. You can't just remember to be up to standard one day in order to pass the test, and then the next day forget and relax."

"Nor will it do just to criticize the honest ones," said the man with thick lips, "and not take on the prickly ones. Whatever the honest one does that is wrong he gets criticized, but the prickly ones never get criticized because they answer right back and they're hard to handle."

Most of the team members were not ready to go along with this. Chin P'ing-kuei said, "Cheng-k'uan has shown improvement during the movement. In study he tries hard even though he can't read. He dares to criticize and struggle with anyone who doesn't do well. He takes the lead in all labor."

And Wang Wen-te concurred. "Cheng-k'uan studies well. He can arouse enthusiasm for work. He dares to criticize. Whatever he turns his hand to he is serious about and carries it through. He has patience to carry on. In irrigation he sticks to it until it works!"

It was readily apparent that the peasants thought well of Cheng-k'uan. The one critical theme that kept recurring was that he sometimes relaxed in study but, "In the main he leads the study well."

While everyone else spoke of Cheng-k'uan, Hsin-fa made a short speech about fixed tasks. "If we don't refine the tasks people can't work well," he said. "Without a task or a quota they just rub and grind and let time pass. The ones with watches look at their watches, the ones without watches look at the sun! We are just too lazy here. We have such good natural conditions, but no one wants to work the land. At Tachai they have to carry their crops home by carrying pole. We can haul everything home on a cart. Not only do we carry our load on the cart, the cart driver sits down and gets a free ride as well!"

Since no one raised serious criticisms of Cheng-k'uan, Judge Kao summed up what had been said and called on Li Yü-hsi, the vice-team leader, to talk. Yü-hsi spoke in much the same vein as Cheng-k'uan; he had relaxed the lead in political study, he had not planned well, he had not worked hard enough, and he tended to let problems slide rather than criticize people. He vowed to do better, to set high standards for himself as a Communist, and to live up to them.

A number of people spoke up with criticisms, the most serious being that Yü-hsi was impatient with people. When there was something to correct or criticize, his manner was rough.

"He should do patient ideological work."

"Only through discussing patiently can he do well."

"He criticizes—that's all to the good—but he should be careful of his attitude."

On the whole, though, the people approved of Yü-hsi and thought that for one so young he had done well.

It was already very late, certainly after eleven o'clock, so Judge Kao decided to wind up the meeting before everyone fell asleep where he sat. The main problem was that people had not really spoken out actively. In part this was due to the lateness of the hour, but in part also because people were still hesitant to speak their minds, not being certain what might come of it in the long run.

Judge Kao was aware of the problem. In his closing remarks he tried to confront it.

"There are nine Communists on our team," he said. "We have only done two. We have to be more efficient. Tomorrow night please come earlier. Let's start at eight-thirty.

"The discussion hasn't been very lively. If you speak out, that is a political act. If you don't speak, it is also a political act; it is liberalism. Some groups have discussed well, others not so well. Some people say they don't have an opinion. But who can believe that? You all live together and work together. How can you say you don't have an opinion? To think like that is wrong. Long Bow can never be transformed with that kind of thought!"

As the meeting dispersed Yü-hsi outlined his plan for wheat planting the next day and called for seven carts. He named the drivers. But there was some doubt as to how many people heard him. They were drifting off home in the darkness by twos, threes and fives. It was very late at night. And it was very dark.

We had chosen the Fifth Team because we felt close to Kuo Cheng-k'uan. He was the man we ate with when we took our bowls out on the street, and he was the man we worked with whenever we had time to go to the fields. So it was natural to join the Fifth Team for the rectification movement as well. While Carma and I joined the Fifth Team, Lin T'ung, our companion from Peking, attended the Second Team meeting. She returned from the experience with tales of a sharp struggle, which she reported in detail.

At the Second Team meeting the leader also spoke first, but in this case the leader was notorious for his reticence and came up with probably the shortest self-criticism in Long Bow annals.

"I don't know how to talk," said Pei Liang-shun. "I'm like a teakettle with its spout knocked off. I don't fight bad people and bad things because I can't speak out. So I'm no locomotive for the team. As for my strong points and my weaknesses, you all know them as well as I do, so what's the use of discussing them? Just speak out what is on your minds."

Now his strong point, as was well known, was his skill as a farmer and his conscientious devotion to his task. He was always the first one up and the first one to fall to at the task. It was he who rang the bell to summon the team to work every morning, and it was he who led the work in the fields, being usually the first to finish the row he was hoeing, the pile he was turning or the ditch he was digging. He was also good at deciding on the key task for each period, and though the Second Team's crops had never been outstanding it was generally conceded that no other team leader was better qualified than Pei.

His major weakness was his "old-good-fellow" attitude, his lack-of-struggle spirit, his reluctance to criticize anyone who did wrong or even to praise anyone who did right. Under normal circumstances this was a serious fault for a team leader. On the Second Team in 1971 it came pretty close to being a disaster because Fast Chin with his hurt pride and his sarcastic mood tended to dominate the team and was able to rally round him such henchmen as Splayfoot Tseng and Li Shou-p'ing and checkmate any positive effort from any other quarter. The main forward drive came from the young political director of the team, Lu Ho-jen, who was also the captain of the Long Bow Militia, a post in which he had succeeded Fast Chin and thus assured for himself the latter's undying enmity. Lu Ho-jen was eager, hardworking and brave, but he lacked both social and technical experience and tended toward a simplistic dogmatism politically. Worst of all, given the situation on the Second Team, was that he frequently overslept and showed up late for work in the morning. These lapses made him an obvious target for criticism and tended to undercut all the mobilization and high-minded revolutionary exhortation that he engaged in. The many late meetings he had to attend as team political director and brigade militia captain and all the sleep he lost as a result did not provide a valid excuse for his being late. In fact, just because he was so prominent everyone expected him to set a good example for others regardless of the cost to himself.

When Pei Liang-shun, the team leader, asked for criticism, Fast Chin led his group in praising him, but when Lu Ho-jen had said his say, Fast Chin led the group in a sharp, sustained attack on the young political director. They called him lazy, ignorant and unfit for political leadership. They drove him close to tears. Ho-jen told the propaganda team afterward that he was unable to sleep that night and developed a very severe headache that would not go away.

Team members thought the attack by Chin's clique was very one-sided and unfair, for Lu Ho-jen had done much good work since his assumption of office in the spring. During the planting rush he had organized a shock team of young women or "Iron Girls," named after the Shansi anti-Japanese heroine Liu Hu-lan, and a second shock team of older men called the "Tough Bone" team. He had not only helped formulate a scientific plan for the crops for the year but had also organized some experimental plots with signs explaining the treatment, the seed, the amount and kind of fertilizer. He had led the whole team in land leveling and the creation of irrigation channels as well as in study in the field. For all this the propaganda team had cited the Second Team as outstanding.

It was only later, toward the end of hoeing, that Lu Ho-jen had relaxed his efforts, met less with the other team cadres, began to quarrel with team leader Liang-shun, began to worry about offending people with criticism, and lapsed into an indecisive and subjective mood. For all this he deserved criticism, but not in such a way as to negate his achievements.

55

THE BRIGADE
LEADER FOLLOWS

Lin T'ung from *Central* described the situation of the Second Team to us as a place where the two lines and the two conflicting forces in the village manifestly confronted each other. In short, this was the place where the "class struggle" had broken into the open. We decided to drop the Fifth Team temporarily and follow the proceedings of the Second Team for a day or two.

On the evening of the twelfth we finally found time to attend the Second Team meeting. It was held in the building where a section of the primary school met each day because the big new school building at the site of the old Japanese fort could not hold all the children. This was a neglected adobe structure of three one-story sections very similar to the Fifth Team headquarters. There were no frames at all in the wide-open windows and no door at the open doorway. A few battered desks and benches served as furniture for the daytime scholars, but most of the team members could find no seats and had to bring their own bricks or stools to sit on as usual. If the Second Team had an office of its own, no one mentioned it. This schoolroom seemed to be the only meeting hall available.

On this evening the main speaker turned out to be Kuei-ts'ai, the brigade leader, who still registered as a member of the Second Team because he lived here, in Second Team territory, and had worked as a Second Team member before being elected brigade leader. According to a recent decision, he was supposed to do his field labor from now on with the First Team and thus serve as their daily contact with the leading group. But since he had not worked with them in the past, it made no sense for him to speak before them or listen to criticism from them. With Kuei-ts'ai on the stand and brigade affairs the topic, there was no sharp confrontation, such as had made the meeting so lively one day earlier. We saw little evidence of Chin's "clique" in action and so missed out on the "class struggle" that had so alerted Lin T'ung.

Nevertheless, since Kuei-ts'ai was the brigade's leading cadre, we were eager to see what he would say and what people would say about him.

As was the custom everywhere we went in Shansi in 1971, Kuei-ts'ai began with several quotes from Mao. He chose two sentences that stressed the protracted nature of the struggle for socialism:

"In China the struggle to consolidate the socialist system, the struggle to decide whether socialism or capitalism will prevail, will take a long historical period."

"Classes and class struggle exist throughout the stage of socialism. This class struggle is long and complex and at times very acute."

That these quotes had been chosen with care became apparent as he launched into his presentation, for the first point that he stressed was the same as that stressed by Kuo Cheng-k'uan at the Fifth Team meeting the night before—what Kuei-ts'ai called his "half-revolutionary thought."

"Before this rectification movement I thought of not working anymore. The objective reason for this? I can't read. I am getting old. Political work demands so much care nowadays. It's not like our rough-and-ready style after Liberation. So I got to thinking half-revolution. Also my family is doing better than ever before. I have built a new house and our standard of living is rising. So I start thinking like a half-revolutionary and find that I am not so eager to serve as before. Now that is quite wrong. Lots of illiterate people are doing well. Tachai and Hsikou both have illiterate leaders who are older than I, so my thoughts make no sense. Nevertheless, that's what I am thinking.

"Now the movement has gone on for a year and I have done some more thinking. I studied the advanced examples of Yang Hsi-ts'ai and Chao Yü-lü. I now realize that if you don't continue the revolution you can turn against the revolution. It's wrong not to carry the revolution through to the end. All I have to do is compare the old society with the new. I was a shepherd and a hired laborer. Now I am a Communist and a cadre. If the people want me to be their servant, how could I face Mao Tse-tung if I refused? I ought to use 120 percent of my strength.

"If the people ask me to serve I should be a good ox for the people and I should never worry about earning enough labor days to live well. It should be simply: Serve the people and raise production so that all can eat.

"So now I no longer calculate backward or forward. My thinking is, If they need me for a day I'll work hard for a day. When I die that is the end. I resolve to transform Long Bow's backward face so that I can die at ease.

"This year I did less work in the fields. I didn't join enough in collective labor. Also I have been subjective. On several questions I didn't consult with others but just made decisions on my own. I don't discuss enough with the cadres and the masses and so I get divorced from the masses.

"And lately I also became rather proud. I thought this year's crops were growing well and so we were much better off than before even if we didn't reach 400 catties per mou. But this is not a good way to think, for once we feel satisfied we can't go forward. The fact of the matter is we are way behind in Horse Square, not to mention Shansi Province or the nation. One mile to the north they are harvesting 400 to 500 catties and we haven't reached 300 yet! As for Tachai and Hsikou, we can't even catch the tail of their yields.

"Taking less part in collective labor is the main sign of divorce from the people. I belong to the Second Team but have not worked with them much or met with them much. Ch'en Yung-kuei [the Tachai Brigade leader] goes

to the field whenever he has an hour or half an hour. Why shouldn't I go
to the fields before breakfast?

"Some of the problems of the Second Team are my responsibility. Mao
Tse-tung says wherever there is difficulty there we should go. If there are
problems they must be dealt with. But I didn't solve many problems for the
team. I heard that they had burned out an electric motor but I didn't look
into it. This is bureaucratic. I have so few achievements and so many
shortcomings.

"So this is what I have to say about myself tonight. Hereafter I'll work
together with the people whenever I have time and I will consult on problems. I will carry out the 'Learn from Tachai Movement.'

"At another time I must criticize myself before the Communist Party
Branch and the whole brigade. Please criticize me; it's not easy to see the
dirt on one's own face but others can see it quite clearly. If you don't point
out my shortcomings, I might think I was correct. I have been using Mao
Tse-tung's fifty-word quotation as a standard. I'm all for it, but I realize that
I don't have the necessary vitality.

"That's all. I welcome criticism from you. If you don't criticize, you harm
me!"

Considering the importance of Kuei-t'sai's job, the Second Team members made only mild and quite general comments. Instead of raising their
grievances directly, people talked about them indirectly. Chou Cheng-fu,
for instance, who was Kuei-ts'ai's brother-in-law, and was involved in a
bitter quarrel with his own brother Chou Cheng-lo over property lines in
a courtyard they had inherited from their father, said:

"We should act according to State Council policy. All public interest and
self-interest has to go according to the policy of the State Council, and the
—how many are there? is it sixty points?—I don't remember, but anyway
according to the points laid out."

Obviously he thought that in the case of his property rights his brother
had violated the sixty-point charter.

The main target, Fast Chin, when he finally spoke up, said Kuei-ts'ai
should learn to unite with people with whom he had differences. This was
an important point in Mao Tse-tung's rectification guidelines. Though Chin
did not spell it out, it seemed obvious that he meant Kuei-ts'ai should learn
to work together with the speaker, Fast Chin himself, and all his followers.

"Why is it," asked Chin, "that Second Team people chat freely among
themselves as they cut weeds but when you appear they fall silent? You
should learn to listen to different opinions. You should listen to all view-
points and learn more."

Here again, without naming any names, Fast Chin was telling Kuei-ts'ai
to take his own group into account.

Chin also said that Kuei-ts'ai talked a great deal over the loudspeaker
system, but that that system should give more time to the voice of the
Central Committee, more time to explaining national and local policy.

All of this indicated that there were grievances simmering under the
surface that people were not willing to speak plainly about, but if one took
into account the speakers it also indicated that these grievances were special

cases involving individual mavericks and not basic problems concerning Kuei-ts'ai's leadership.

Most of the speakers felt that Kuei-ts'ai was doing a good job as brigade leader. They liked and trusted him as a person and found him approachable, especially since the beginning of the rectification movement. They especially liked his presence there in front of them and his willingness to listen to criticisms. The biggest question they raised concerned subjectivism. Their brigade leader had a tendency to make decisions off-the-cuff, without adequate consultation or investigation. His declaration that room rent for workers' families should be 1 yuan per room was an example. How could a flat rate cover good rooms and bad? Another was his decision that the third child of married women who refused to move to their husband's villages should get no per capita grain. On complex matters such as these, Kuei-ts'ai tended to make decisions that violated national policy or ignored the interests of one or another segment of the people. In regard to some other questions the problem was simply that he had given no adequate explanation to the people. A case in point was the distribution of the emergency grain borrowed by the brigade to tide the community over until the fall harvest. No one made clear that this grain was for hardship cases only. Many people thought there would be a per capita distribution. When this did not take place they voiced many complaints, but all were due to a misunderstanding of the basic policy behind the grain loan.

Another problem, raised by Shen Shih-yu, the only surviving son of Shen Ch'uan-te, the loquacious Catholic who played such a dubious role in 1948, seemed to me to be of special importance.

"Since you are number one, I want to say that the main problem here isn't fertilizer but faith in scientific methods. We've grasped fertilizer and irrigation but the soil itself remains a problem. When we water it, it gets hard. This must be solved. There is also the question of the best seed for this soil. How to improve our soil and breed the right seed—these are the most important questions."

Here, it seemed to me, *was* a crucial question. There had to be some reason why, with a huge reservoir of irrigation water available and the basic trunk canals long since completed, Long Bow peasants had not yet prepared all their land for irrigation. And that reason had to lie with the response of the soil itself to water. This soil was known locally as "fall salt" land. This meant that in the fall, as the rainy season came to an end, heavy evaporation carried salt from the lower layers of the soil profile and turned the land into hard, concretelike clay that was all but impossible to work. To respond to the national calls for irrigation and manure proved woefully inadequate for the situation in Long Bow. The technical problem here went beyond fertility and water supply to questions of soil structure, soil drainage and internal percolation. But instead of tackling this problem the brigade cadres, the commune cadres, and the municipal cadres all considered Long Bow's low yields to be a political problem, a line problem, a "capitalist road" problem. Their solution was to stress collective consciousness, Tachai self-reliance, Tachai hard work, more manure and more water. And since repeated campaigns to stress these things had not succeeded—the people had been very reluctant to extend irrigation canals and to level land for proper irrigation—the cadres tended to regard the people as backward, stubborn and perverse. And since, of course, it was an article of faith in the Chinese Communist movement that the people are not backward, the only other conclusion had to be that the cadres were backward, stubborn and perverse.

Now, of course, in a most basic sense the problem could be called political. A dedicated socialist leadership would long since have put farming in first place in Long Bow and would have objectively analyzed the technical problems standing in the way of high yields. Without accepting at face value the general solutions coming from above—more manure, more water—such a leadership would have studied Long Bow's peculiar soil conditions and made experiments to overcome this "fall salt" land. A sound political attitude would most certainly have led to a sound technical solution. Instead, faced with low yields, shrinking acreage and a rapidly rising population, the brigade leadership had taken the easy way out and stressed sidelines while, in the meantime, all the efforts of higher bodies to get Long Bow on the track by concentrating on more manure and more irrigation met with passive resistance from the peasants. Knowing that water made the land hard and almost ensured that next year's crops would not come up, they continued to farm in their traditional way and refused to break their backs constructing irrigation systems.

When Long Bow peasants heard that one mile away Horse Square was doing much better with crops, they discounted the news. They knew well that Horse Square soil was not as difficult to work as Long Bow soil and was probably not "fall salt" land at all.

This problem, which was to come up again and again as time passed, brought no response that night. What people concentrated on instead was the crucial role that Fast Chin played in the conduct of the meeting. He seemed to be in control of the pace of the proceedings. When he said, "Let's discuss," general discussion ensued. When he decided that the discussion had gone on long enough, the discussion ended. His personality seemed to dominate the whole group while his henchmen, men like Splayfoot Tseng, played an active role, speaking more often and more loudly than anyone else. At one point Fast Chin ordered, not asked, Lu Ho-jen to get him a cup of water, as if Ho-jen, political director of the team, were some sort of servant, and Ho-jen complied.

It seemed obvious that Fast Chin and his group were operating with some sort of predetermined plan.

On the very next night Fast Chin asked Donkey Meat Wang if he could make his own self-criticism.

"If I talk only of mistakes can I speak?"

"I'll have to consult the leadership," Wang said. "The original decision was that only those who have recovered their Party life can speak before the team meetings."

"But everyone knows me here," said Chin. "How I work. What I do. What harm is there in my talking before my team?"

"I'll have to take it up with the leadership," said Wang once more.

This upset Chin so much that he strode back into the crowd, picked up his stool and stomped out.

This high-handed attitude, this attempt to dominate the team meetings and control their course, without even the slightest sign of a self-critical attitude, caused people to feel that Fast Chin was acting wildly and had broken down all controls. When to his general stance of resistance he added some sarcastic remarks about wheat planting rates and the distribution of emergency grain supplies, he himself set the stage for a major struggle directed against him.

Once Fast Chin left, the regular meeting of the Second Team proceeded on a more even keel. The group heard two Communists evaluate themselves: the old comrade Ch'en Wan-t'ien, who had joined the Party in 1945 at the age of nineteen, and the young woman Li Lian-p'ing, who had been recruited during the Four Clean Movement in 1964.

Ch'en was apologetic about his work with the draft animals, especially his failure to get the mares bred according to plan, but claimed some success in keeping up with the young people on the shock brigade during the spring rush and told proudly of having loaned his quilt for the night to eight PLA men who were passing through. "They had only four quilts among them. I gave them my quilt and boiled water for them. That's no more than a Party member should do. It was my duty."

Li Lian-p'ing, who kept the records for the Second Team, felt she had not studied steadily enough or hard enough and that she lacked struggle spirit. "I don't struggle against bad people, and I don't really understand two-line struggle." She did not mention the fact that as a young mother, with a new baby, she had not been able to take an active part in the rectification movement.

Team members discussed these two actively and made pointed criticisms.

"Remember," said Lu Ho-jen, the team political director, "we have standards for a Communist. A Communist can't be judged like any old-hundred-names! I think Ch'en Wan-t'ien has changed a lot. He cares more now for public property. When some part of the cart he is driving breaks he doesn't ask for help from the team, he uses whatever he finds around home and fixes it in his own spare time so that no time is lost from work. He also takes the lead in production. He led the cart drivers in fixing up the irrigation canal.

"His weakness shows in class struggle. There he plays no leading role. Illiteracy is, of course, an excuse. It's hard for him to study, but you don't have to know how to read and write to repudiate a class enemy. Bad people and bad things should always be exposed. He could improve in this respect."

P'ei Hsin-min agreed with Ho-jen about Ch'en Wan-t'ien. Speaking from a corner of the room so that his voice came disembodied from the darkness, P'ei said, "Wan-t'ien has improved this year. He used to work in the grain mill. Now he drives a cart. He is very responsible. He takes whatever animal is assigned to him, good or bad, and works with it. If anything breaks he fixes it in his spare time. But his weak point is, he takes no initiative in class struggle. No matter who is up for criticism, he never speaks out!"

"It's a selfish attitude," chimed in Sun Shu-te. "He has no struggle spirit and that is really selfishness. He should really criticize himself and stand up and fight bad people and bad things."

They criticized Li Lian-p'ing for the same weakness, but in regard to her work as record keeper they all praised her. "Very responsible." "Demonstrated in the course of a few days that there were no mistakes in her work." "Explains problems patiently." But, "She never reports to the leadership about people's complaints and criticisms. Instead, she complains along with them." "In class struggle she is an old-good-fellow." "She's a good record keeper, but she's an old-good-fellow."

When the meeting adjourned and the rank-and-file had left, the Party members stayed on to discuss what they should do about the criticisms.

P'ei Hsin-min at first said, "The thing to do is just dig in and work!"

"That's right," said Ch'en Wan-t'ien. "Whatever they brought up, we'll correct."

"But we shouldn't just follow blindly behind the people," said Hsin-min. We should really take the lead. Then team decisions should be carried out to the end. No half measures! Let's set a quota for the day's work. Five rows is five rows. Don't just do four, then look at the setting sun, see everyone ready to quit, and leave the field."

"Right," said Lu Ho-jen. "Even though we now have only two mou per person. There are so many factories and the railroad yards nearby. We can get all kinds of night soil. If we can't get this land to produce there is no excuse. But our people are still going out at three in the afternoon when they should be in the fields by two."

"The ones who are the slowest are those without wives at home," said Wan-t'ien. "During the fall harvest we won't even come home to eat at noon."

"I have a suggestion," said Hsin-min. "There's a place near the Railroad Third Bureau where many people have already moved in and no one has arranged for the night soil. Furthermore, the PLA right here in the village has no place to go with its pig manure. We should contact both places, build a privy near the Third Bureau and contact the PLA about the pigpens."

"To say it is to do it," said Donkey Meat Wang.

"I'll contact them tomorrow," promised Hsin-min. "Do we have any more big jars?"

With the water level so high due to unusually heavy rains, it was impossible simply to dig a privy; one had to bury an earthen jar for the proper collection of human waste.

Lu Ho-jen said he knew where there was one, then added a thought about criticism. "Criticism from the masses doesn't always sound sweet. We have to treat them all correctly. We must not feel angry or resentful. That wouldn't meet the standards for a Communist. We have to take the lead in labor, work hard, and not just complain about the tasks set by the leadership. Each person can play an important role on his own."

As a final piece of business Pei Liang-shun brought up the problem of the carts that were running down crops.

"If an animal runs away and some crops get run down, we can't blame the driver too much," said Ch'en Wan-t'ien. "But some people just sit on their carts and watch a whole row go under the wheel, especially some of the young people. They don't care and they never listen!"

They decided to call a team meeting to discuss this and also make further plans for sowing wheat by the new wide-furrow method.

56

ORDINARY MEMBERS
TAKE THEIR TURN

 On September 15 the teams met again for Party rectifica-
tion. At the Fifth Team headquarters Old Lady Wang's
son, Wang Jen-pao; Chang Hsin-fa, former Party Secretary of the brigade; and Hu Hsueh-chen, former leader of
all women's work in Long Bow, took the floor.

Wang Jen-pao raised an important question. He started off by saying that
he had been poisoned by Liu Shao-ch'i's line. This was a pretty big "hat"
to put on, but after he explained it we began to see what he meant. Jen-pao
was a skilled mechanic. Taking advantage of this, he had set up a bicycle
repair shop at the edge of the highway. The shop, housed in a ramshackle
adobe hut, bore the title "Longbow Fifth Team Repair Station." Actually,
Jen-pao ran it as a private concession linked to the team through a licensing
arrangement. Before he opened the shop the brigade office discussed the
matter and decided that he should turn in 1.8 yuan a day to his team and
get in return credit for the days worked. Twice a year, when the team
divided its income, he would get his share based on the total number of
workdays earned. Since workdays had never been worth much more than
1 yuan per day, the arrangement was profitable to the team. They were
taking in 1.8 yuan per day and paying out 1. But the arrangement was also
profitable to Jen-pao because he could almost always earn more than 1.8
yuan a day in the shop and anything in excess of the daily fee stayed in his
pocket as personal income. Furthermore, he only had to return 1.8 yuan
twenty days a month. For every day worked beyond this quota, he retained
100 percent of the take. By applying himself throughout the month Jen-pao
could earn much more than those who were assigned to the fields, sometimes as much as two or three times more. Sharp criticism had convinced
Jen-pao that this was not very fair and certainly not proper for a Communist.

"This rectification has raised my consciousness," he said. "I see it now
as a line question. Am I working for myself or am I working for the
collective? I'm a poor peasant. I *fanshened* with the help of the Communist
Party. I think it's wrong to set up private enterprises like this. I've taken
the wrong road."

What Jen-pao now proposed was an ambitious new plan to set up a
combination machine shop, foundry and repair shop under the direct aus-

pices of the Long Bow Brigade. Such a shop, in addition to repairing bicycles, could build and repair farm implements, transport equipment or anything else needed by the brigade. With the acetylene welding equipment already on hand, with the iron, steel and other materials already collected, a strong foundation existed for such a collective effort. The brigade would finance the project and the staff would earn only workdays in their respective teams. Any profit above expenses would go to the brigade as a whole. Why not start this enterprise right away?

The idea was enthusiastically received. Everyone praised Jen-pao and encouraged him to begin as soon as possible.

The next Party member to take the floor was Chang Hsin-fa. We were more than eager to hear what he would say. For twenty years he had virtually commanded Long Bow village, only to fall into disgrace during the Four Clean Movement because he had speculated in houses. After he was removed from office he felt that his prestige fell below that of an ordinary field worker. He decided to look out for himself first of all, pay attention only to the well-being of his family, and lead as comfortable a life as possible.

He didn't study. He didn't set himself any political goals. Assigned to build up a collective pig-raising enterprise, he worked at it methodically, without vision or inspiration. He was afraid that he couldn't do well, afraid that if he failed the brigade would blame him and severely criticize him again. But in spite of his negative attitude things had gone really well in the last twelve months. The three sows with which he started had multiplied. He now had fifteen. In addition, he and his helpers were feeding forty fat pigs with the leftover material from their corn noodle plant. If each sow now farrowed a living litter of six, they could look forward to 200 pigs in 1972, a great leap in any sense of the word.

Success with pigs and the challenge that came with Party rectification had caused Hsin-fa to reevaluate his life. "If capitalism ever takes over, I can never guarantee a prosperous life for my family," he said, so he decided to step out and become active once more.

Fellow team members welcomed this decision. All said Hsin-fa had done wonders with the pigs and they hoped he would be able to supply piglets for private pigsties in the future as well as raising several hundred head collectively.

Rectification had not meant as much to Hu Hsueh-chen. In evaluating herself she said very little. She stressed only that she had lots of shortcomings and no good points, no achievements. She had done nothing in production work or in Party work because her health was so bad.

Several people asked her why she couldn't organize among the people as she used to do. Why not teach Mao Tse-tung Thought to the women?

In reply she said she had made up her mind to do what she could for the Party in the future, but privately she told Security Officer Shen that work was difficult because her husband, Wang Wen-te, never paid the least attention to anything she said.

"Why?"

"Because I am four years older than he is. He likes to recite the old rhyme:

With a wife older by four
A man's wealth will soar.

Fact is, he has never been very happy about it."

"Don't let it worry you," said Shen. But he knew just as well as she did that the poem was a way for Wen-te to save face. Shen told us later than when the lovely Hsien-e sued for divorce Wen-te lost the wife he really wanted. "So now he comforts himself with this stupid couplet."

If Hu Hsueh-chen rivaled the Second Team's Pei Liang-shun for the brevity of her self-criticism, Shen Tung-liang of the Fourth Team outdid them both. Shen, who taught blacksmithing at the primary school, contented himself with three sentences: "I haven't played a role. I would like to do better. I will try to do better in the future."

At this, those listening all laughed.

People in his team, nevertheless, had a good opinion of him. They thought he had improved in both his attitude and his work since the rectification began and they urged him to "raise high the flag of Mao Tse-tung Thought and make revolution your whole life long."

Shen Tung-liang had not previously been noted for combativeness. Once, when he came across some neighbors posting critical opinions about Wen-te, he tried to stop them.

"You dare write about him! Put up 1,000 posters against me, what does it matter? But don't try writing about him."

"In the past," said Security Officer Shen, "if you fired on Shen Tung-liang with three cannons he still wouldn't speak out. When he was team leader he once went knocking on doors early in the morning to rouse people for work. After a few minutes, when nobody showed up, he went to the field all by himself!"

If some Party members lacked "struggle spirit," others evidently carried it too far. Chi Feng-teng saw class conflict where it didn't exist and constantly attacked Han Man-wen for no reason. Han Man-wen was one of six Communists on the First Team roster. His parents had collaborated with the Japanese before 1945, had lost property because of it when the land reform began, and thereafter bore the stigma "struggle object." Man-wen, on his part, joined the Liberation Army in 1953 and, while serving as a soldier, joined the Communist Party. After he returned to Long Bow in 1956 he became an active member of the brigade Party Branch. However, when the Cultural Revolution began he was attacked as the son of a "struggle object" and decided to withdraw from politics altogether. No amount of persuasion would deter him. Now the style of the rectification convinced him that Mao Tse-tung Thought was back in command. He began to be active again and take the lead in work. For every four cart-loads of manure that others hauled to the fields he hauled six. Where others required an extra hand to push heavy liquid manure carts over slight rises, he loaded his so that one man could do the job. Team colleagues praised him highly for this.

But Chi Feng-teng, the leading Communist on the team, was very critical. He accused Han Man-wen of unloading his manure at the near end of each field, thus making an impressive record on paper, while shirking long hauls and neglecting distant land.

"Two different classes, two different lines!" said Feng-teng. "The poor peasants choose the hardest tasks while the middle peasants sneak by with the easiest."

Thus Feng-teng raised a slight disagreement with Man-wen to the level of antagonism.

Other team members said such accusations were unjust. The only difference between the work of the two men was that one began unloading at the near end of each field while the other began at the far end. As the land was covered each moved his dumping spot so that in the end the whole field was fertilized. He who began at the far end ended up at the near and he who began at the near end ended up at the far. The hauling turned out, in the end, to be equal.

People said that Feng-teng was much too hard on others. They advised him to pay more attention to his own work. In 1964 the team had given him sixty goats to look after. Four years later there were only eighteen goats left. "You criticize others' faults but can't even see your own," they said. "Instead of educating other people in the Thought of Mao Tse-tung, you just get angry and curse."

Feng-teng, it seemed, always had something to curse about. If his points were low he made a big fuss. If he ran out of grain he blamed the whole team. Proud of his own class background, he tended to look down on anyone whose parents had been more prosperous than his.

"He thinks he's a beautiful flower, while others are nothing but bean curd."

Another Party member who made things hard for his teammates was Shen Ch'i-ch'ang. He was known as "Comrade Three Too Much." He complained too much, talked nonsense too much, and thought about himself too much. His thinking was backward, his work was poor, and at times he even stole. This time criticism brought rapid improvement and he became an activist, not only on the Sidelines Team, where he pitched in to help the team leader, but at home, where he raised pigs and piled up enough compost to earn an extra hundred workdays.

If some were not combative enough, while others carried chips on their shoulders, still a third group of Communists, it was said, dared to tackle problems in a principled way. One of these was Shen Hsü-wen of the Third Team, who was the brigade accountant.

Accepting a post as accountant in itself involved conflict because Hsü-wen's parents felt that anyone who kept financial records was bound to get into trouble. They advised him to take no part in it. As the saying went:

> One two, one two,
> One two three,
> Under the light bulb
> The accountant we see.
> Flicking his abacus
> Diligently.

He makes no distinction
Between night and day,
But when the "gate" comes
Can he pass? No way!
Better by far
A plain member be,
Working hard, in the fields,
But honestly.

Shen Hsü-wen didn't agree. How could the revolution succeed without accountants? It was not accountants who couldn't pass the "gate," but people who violated Mao Tse-tung's line, people who put self before public and took advantage of their position. Shen Hsü-wen, according to his own report, took up the position of brigade accountant with a clear conscience.

When the propaganda team first came, it set up a special case investigation group, a group to look into all books, all accounts; a group dedicated to the exposure of graft and corruption in the brigade at whatever level.

The group invited Shen Hsü-wen, with his good head for figures, to join the work. Once again his parents opposed the move. How could it lead to anything but trouble? Of course, to expose graft and corruption was a good thing, but it was easy to make mistakes, follow false leads and make dubious accusations that could only alienate people. Then, instead of striding out on a straight road, you could walk into a brick wall. Much better to play it safe, leave well enough alone, and keep your nose clean.

But once again Hsü-wen disagreed. How could the revolution succeed if no one was willing to stick his neck out and fight graft and corruption? Of course he might make some mistakes, but if he made mistakes he would correct them. Good people would understand. If criminals were offended by his work, so be it. How could that block his road?

Shen Hsü-wen dared to take on problems, people agreed. But since he became an accountant and an investigator, he had found little time for work in the fields. With all those calculations in front of him it was easy to say, "I'm busy." But wasn't it more truthful to say that he had become a little lazy and that by withdrawing from labor he had created a gap between himself and the rank-and-file?

Shen Hsü-wen had to agree that he should organize his work better and show up more frequently for work in the fields.

The Party rectification, which had gotten off to so slow a start, never did develop into an enthusiastic mass movement. Nevertheless day by day, meeting by meeting, it built up a certain momentum, so that attendance at meetings grew rather than diminished and people spoke out more fully and more freely instead of gradually saying less and less. None of the self-evaluations seemed in themselves spectacular. None of the criticisms standing alone could shake the brigade, or even startle any individual member, yet as the days passed the atmosphere in the village improved somewhat. In the fields people began to talk about rectification when ordinarily they would have discussed the weather or the crops. Informally they reviewed the record of each Communist again and again.

"Who dared criticize the Party members in the past?" said many, forgetting the many movements of the fifties and sixties when Party members stood before the "gate" just as now. "Party problems were handled at the brigade level for years. But now it's back to the masses. This ought to be a regular thing—once a month, once every two months. Then we would all have close ties."

The Party members, finding people's opinions reasonable and far from vindictive, tended to feel better. Having entered on self-criticism with hesitation, for fear of being kicked down, they found on the contrary that the community upheld them; expected a great deal from them, but nevertheless upheld them. This raised their spirits somewhat. Accepting criticism could be refreshing, like taking a hot bath and emerging scrubbed and clean. Positive results showed up right away in the fields. Both Lu Ho-jen and Pei Liang-shun of the Second Team, where morale had surely been the lowest, turned out for work at the end of the week, each with a crew in high spirits.

"The Party members have taken a step forward and so have the masses," said Judge Kao.

No one disputed Judge Kao's statement, but no one took it very seriously either. Clearly the movement had failed to inspire the community as a whole. In trying to analyze why, I decided that the novelty of reasoned confrontation, of self- and mutual criticism, which had so fascinated everyone in 1948, had long ago worn off. One could hardly expect that after repeated immersion in this process people would approach it with the same verve and enthusiasm they had shown twenty-three years earlier. Mao's thesis that Liberation marked only the first step in a 10,000-li Long March, and that the difficult and complex task of building a new society must take not only decades but perhaps centuries, had been confirmed by events. This being so, no one suffered under the illusion that any single movement could miraculously transform the community, its Communist Party members or its Communist leaders. Long Bow must go through the process again and again, year in and year out, from one decade to the next, in order to keep moving forward.

Nevertheless, if the community did indeed make progress with each rectification, people should take up the task with some enthusiasm. Knowledge that the long struggle for a good crop must begin again next year had not in any way dampened the morale of those responsible for this year's cultivation of the soil. Why, then, did peasants approach the cultivation of social relations with so little commitment? They were going through the motions of Party rectification without devoting either their hearts or their minds to it. The whole process lacked "soul." Having looked forward to progress as dramatic as that achieved by the "gate" of 1948, I was disappointed. I sensed that something more serious than overexposure held people back, but I could not define what it was.

I hardly had time, however, to digest first impressions, not to mention arrive at any conclusions. The wheat planting, moving toward its climax, dominated every daylight hour. After long shifts in the field I found it hard to stay awake through meetings that crowded midnight. I was not alone. One or two peasants, leaning back against adobe walls, almost always fell asleep before the last speech ended. The whole community, it seemed, had mobilized to full capacity and could hardly be expected to undertake anything more. It never occurred to me that, at this busiest of times, Long Bow would rise to meet not one but two new challenges.

57

COUNTRY FAIR

When the mid-September sun set, cool air caused a mist to form around the pond in the center of Long Bow. By morning the mist had spread outward in every direction until it enveloped completely all the neighboring lanes and courtyards. When we got up, a little after dawn, to join the propaganda team members in study, the sun shone faintly through a white miasma, suffusing the whole area with tender, glowing light. This light converted lanes, walls, trees and courtyard gates into ethereal forms that more closely resembled stage props for an imagined village than the mundane landmarks we had come to know so well.

Several sheds made of bamboo poles and reed mats intensified our sense of fantasy because they had materialized mushroomlike, in the middle of the night, to occupy hitherto empty space. They were propped against the wall at the northern edge of the square. Smoke from several cooking fires floated lazily upward through and around the mats. In the absence of even the slightest breeze, the smoke merged with the mist at treetop level and hung there, motionless.

These sheds were the first booths of Long Bow's annual autumn fair. We rubbed our eyes, looked, and looked again, incredulous. The fair, we had been told, would not take place. Li Szu-yuan, the vegetarian vice-chairman of the Southeast Shansi Region, had announced only a few days before that such a diversion would interfere with wheat planting. To enable everyone in Long Bow to concentrate on this central task, and to prevent friends, relatives and casual acquaintances from coming from miles around to enjoy the hospitality of Long Bow families, thus disrupting their work, the fair that had been held every year as long as anyone could remember, had been officially canceled. Let everyone do without three days of socializing, petty trading, snacks, drama, barter and fun. Let everyone get on with the business at hand, the great challenge of the "three fall" season. Let them show how serious they were about studying Tachai.

Yet here in the predawn mist the first booths of the fair had already been set up. Even as we watched, more individuals and groups arrived, some claiming only a few square feet of ground on which to spread their wares, others assembling booths, large and small, each tailored to the merchandise or service its builder planned to offer.

From one of the fires a delightful aroma of highly spiced donkey meat wafted our way. Since the thought of great chunks of stewed donkey meat so early in the morning repelled Carma and me, we gravitated instead toward a second fire where an old man was preparing *shuai ping* (thrown cakes). We watched with fascination as he tortured a piece of dough into a thin tortilla ready for cooking. Instead of flopping the dough back and forth as was usual on the Shangtang, he whirled it freely in the air around his stick, making it larger and larger and thinner and thinner with each revolution until it reached the exact size and shape of his griddle. Then, at just the right moment, with a masterly flourish, he flopped it on the hot metal to fry.

While this cake absorbed heat, he applied castor bean oil to a second griddle with his left hand and simultaneously twirled another piece of dough around the stick held in his right hand. As soon as it was ready he flipped it deftly onto the empty griddle, then, with a flick of the wrist, turned the cake on the first griddle completely over, revealing a delicious brown crust on the upturned side. When the cake was ready to eat, we bought it for a few cents and divided it.

The virtuosity of this vendor's performance, similar to the skill of a veteran pizza maker in Italy, impressed us greatly and we would have watched the art several more times if we had not suddenly remembered our study hour. Afraid of missing some important lesson, we reluctantly moved off. As we did so, other early risers materialized out of the mist in search of the source of the irrestistible aromas that were spreading through the whole village.

By the time we finished our morning study, the mist had burned off, revealing one of those incandescent sunlit days for which the Shangtang is famous. As the morning wore on, the air warmed up, then grew hot, hot enough for August, but without the humidity of the rainy season.

On returning to the square we found that the booths opened before sunrise constituted only the starting nucleus of an extensive array of sheds and sales locations that stretched up and down both main streets, completely surrounded the pond, and overflowed into several side alleys. To the east, all the way to the highway, but concentrated on the south side of the street, stood tethered donkeys, mules, cows, oxen and horses, most of them already surrounded by buyers and curious onlookers. As the booths and the livestock proliferated, so did the people. At its height that day the fair attracted 5,000 people. They came on foot, by bus, by animal-drawn cart and by bicycle. Bicycles propped against trees, stacked against gate posts or laid sideways on the ground, wherever a free space could be found, cluttered the byways. One of the marks of prosperity in the Chinese countryside after land reform was the steady increase in the number of bicycles. Whereas formerly only the wealthiest landlord or the most prosperous peddler could hope to own a bike, now almost every family boasted at least one, and some had a bicycle for every adult member.

We saw in the crowd some extraordinary back-country individualists, flamboyantly decorated with colored scarves and sashes, yet perfectly at ease in their splendor, as if the occasion required extravagant dress and everyone else had failed to respond. We also saw cripples, idiots and quite a few people with terrible diseases of the eye. Considering the efficient medical care provided by the Long Bow clinic and the even more proficient services available at the Commune Hospital and the Railroad Hospital nearby, it was hard to understand why there should be so many eye problems in the area. But there the people were, large as life, striding through the fair with eyes half destroyed by trachoma or conjunctivitis. We could not help noticing them because all visitors from outside Long Bow were fascinated by the appearance of Americans on the street and followed us wherever we went, staring, staring without end. If it was disconcerting to be stared at by healthy people, it was much worse to look back into a face where one eye discharged gray fluid while the other—red, inflamed and half closed—seemed already beyond repair.

As the fairgoers crowded the narrow streets and moved up and down between the booths, they stirred up clouds of dust. By noon, dust hung like a pall over the whole village, occupying much the same space as the mist had earlier done. The dust, needless to say, had none of the charms of the mist it replaced. Nevertheless it added its own unique atmosphere to the scene. It reminded us, if reminder was needed, that we were still in North China.

The variety of goods lying on the ground, displayed in the booths or hawked on the street by peddlers, fascinated us. There were hoes, shovels, forks, rakes, brooms, winnowing baskets, flour sifters and sifter screens, all used in farm production. There were booths full of cloth, both the machine-made variety that required ration coupons and handspun, handwoven cloth that was not subject to rationing. Some of the handmade cloth showed the delicate tawny color of natural brown cotton. Much of the rest was an undyed white. But we also saw some homespun that had been dyed with commercial colors, then woven into striking plaid patterns.

Other vendors displayed vegetables grown on private plots or in home gardens, such things as eggplant, Chinese cabbage and late summer beans. Some had large baskets of fruit, especially the thorn dates and pears native to this region and the apples that had been recently introduced. Strings of dried persimmons were also on sale. In some locations the vendor had only one basket of produce to market. When he or she sold out, the space was vacated, only to be quickly occupied by someone else. Not all of these locations represented individual sales effort. Many of them were staffed with people sent by a brigade or production team. The income from their sales would go into the brigade or team pool to be distributed as cash shares at the end of the year.

We learned that the *shuai ping* booth and the donkey meat counter were collective efforts, as were many of the stands selling candy and candied fruit. Right in their midst a confirmed individualist, an itinerant dentist, had cleared a space and laid out on a piece of red cloth a gruesome display of hundreds of the teeth pulled by him in past years. What he advertised was painless dentistry. This he guaranteed by massive injections of Novocaine applied with an equally massive, if not too sanitary, syringe and needle. The final extraction he accomplished by means of a vicious collection of chisels, hammers and pliers. Not the least of the attractions of this "jaw clinic" was its open public nature. Whenever a tooth was about to be pulled a large crowd gathered to encourage both dentist and patient. Total cost per tooth —1.50 yuan (75 cents).

Booths and locations selling hardware and other manufactured items were numerous; some of them were devoted to watches and watch repair, others to bicycle and tire repair, while still others concentrated on flashlights, damaged Thermos flasks, pens or broken chinaware. Repairs, for the most part, were done while the customer waited.

Perhaps the liveliest section of the whole fair was that part of the street at the north side of the pond that offered weaned pigs for sale. They had been carried to the fair in large wicker baskets tied to the rear racks of heavy-freight bicycles, and now they were laid out in groups on the ground, each with its front legs tied, one to the other, by a rope across the top of the neck. Back feet, meanwhile, were tied together behind. Trussed in this manner, the little pigs could roll and twist across the ground for a few feet but could not possibly get up and run away, and so they lay squealing, grunting, twisting and turning, waiting for a buyer to select them and remove them from the hot noonday sun. Whenever a buyer picked one up it screamed as if it were stuck with a knife. Most of the pigs were black, but some had white spots and some were reddish with black spots. The sellers squatted alongside, talking with the customers. From time to time they flipped an errant pig back toward the center of the group from which it had managed to squirm or roll away.

One of these vendors, a middle-aged peasant in a very clean tunic, told us he came from Wuhsiang, a county town to the north that was forty miles away. Pigs such as these, in plentiful supply there, brought only 80 fen a catty, while here, in the suburbs of Changchih, where pig breeding had been neglected, they were worth 1 yuan per catty. Since the pigs averaged ten to twelve catties in weight, this was an increase of 2 yuan per pig. Between sunrise and sunset a man with a bicycle could easily transport ten, fifteen or even twenty pigs by bicycle all the way to Long Bow, and sell them. The earnings for one long day could be as much as 30 or even 40 yuan, which was far more than a person could earn by hard work in the fields in a month.

The question that arose in our minds was, Is this a form of profiteering? Or if this price was fair, what was there to prevent weaned pig prices from climbing higher day by day, especially since a public campaign was just then getting underway to expand pig raising? The answer was that a ceiling had been set on the per catty price of pigs. It had been established by the administrator of the fair. This man was an official from the economic department of the City Administration. He was there to enforce ceilings not only on the price of pigs but on all other important commodity prices as well. This fair, it turned out, was not a free market in the classical sense, a place where supply and demand found their own equilibrium, but a marketplace where privately or collectively owned commodities and property could be brought for sale, subject to price controls enforced by the State.

If any buyer felt that there was price gouging going on, he could seek out the market administrator and register a complaint. The offending vendor would then have to answer for his prices and presumably lower them. This policing of the market proved to be a very important factor at the Long Bow September Fair of 1971, because right in the midst of the fair the Long Bow Brigade suddenly launched a mass campaign for the purchase of pigs by its members.

After seeing the entire fair and trying to take it in, I was amazed that vice-chairman Li Szu-yuan had tried to cancel the event. According to this well-known "anti-revisionist" vegetarian, the fair had to be postponed so that it would not interfere with wheat planting and other "three fall" tasks. But quite obviously the fair was a boon to fall work. Almost everything that anyone took to sell there, and almost everything that anyone went to buy there, had some bearing on production, either direct or indirect. The fair had a significant, even decisive, economic function to perform.

The most important of these functions was the exchange of livestock, primarily draft animals—the horses, mules, donkeys, oxen and cows needed for the heavy work yet to come. Brigades and teams with animals to sell sought out the few remaining autumn fairs on the Shangtang Plateau even when these fairs opened scores of miles away. By the same token, brigades and teams that needed animals sent buyers to fairs in distant counties even when it took several days to walk their purchases home. Without a few fairs moving from community to community in predetermined seasonal pattern, it was difficult to see how sellers could find buyers, or buyers sellers. Perhaps a lively section in the regional newspaper devoted to "for sale" and "want" ads could have accomplished the same purpose, but there was no such section in the paper and, even if there had been, a newspaper ad was a poor substitute for animals in the flesh, lined up side by side for all to see, compare and bargain over.

In the livestock department the other great exchange that went forward in September was, of course, the sale of weaned pigs. This was also closely linked to "three fall" production because it was on the grain and fodder reaped from the summer crops that the weaned pigs to be marketed the following year would be raised, and it was on the pig manure and compost created by this batch of new pigs that next fall's wheat planting would depend. Since most fat hogs went to market in the fall, now was the time to buy replacements. For counties with surplus pigs and little grain, the Long Bow fair was as important as it was for counties with surplus grain and few pigs. In Wuhsiang, forty miles to the north, pig breeding had become a major enterprise, both private and collective. There everyone kept sows but did not raise enough grain to feed all the pigs farrowed. On the outskirts of Changchih, in contrast, few sows were kept but grain and grain products were relatively abundant. The fair was the place where Wuhsiang sellers and Changchih buyers met to the great advantage of both, and mutually assured the future of pork and grain production in the mountains and on the plain.

If livestock was the most important product exchanged at the fair, it was by no means the only important one. To put livestock to work the peasants needed harnesses, halters, bridles and whips, horseshoes and horseshoe nails. To plant, harvest and process grain they needed seed sacks, seeders, manure buckets, carrying poles, hoes, shovels, sickles, winnowing baskets, brooms, flour sifters and sifter screens, to mention but a few items. All these could be found in one booth or another.

Even the cloth on sale was important to production, at least for those families whose clothes were already worn out. It was especially important for families who had run through their cloth ration. Machine-made cloth could always be bought at the coop store, but the unrationed homespun, handwoven cloth could rarely be found there. The rough products of home spinning wheels and handlooms were brought to the fair directly by the families that made them, or by a few peddlers who specialized in such goods.

One could even argue that the booth manned by the itinerant dentist, with his gruesome display of last year's extracted teeth, was a link in the production cycle, for who could devote proper energy to wheat planting or the fall harvest with a nagging toothache?

If there had been no fair where small quantities of vegetables and fruits could be sold, few peasants would take the trouble to raise them, garden plantings would be restricted to what each family itself could eat, few fruit trees would be set out, and those fruit trees that already bore fruit would often be neglected. In a fully developed collective society the cooperative store must certainly handle such items, but in 1971, so far as I could determine, none of the village supply cooperatives handled perishable produce.

There remained the booths selling delicacies like *shuai ping,* donkey meat and candied apples. These, of course, were luxury foods that people did not need to consume in order to produce. They were not only luxuries, they were expensive, and the people who bought them could hardly be called anything but self-indulgent. Nevertheless, it seemed obvious that the whole question of rest, recreation and moderate self-indulgence could also be linked to production, for people cannot "keep their noses to the grindstone" day in and day out, week in and week out, month in and month out, the whole year through and still maintain enthusiasm for their work. There must be some ebb and flow, some period of rest and relaxation, some fun. For Long Bow village and the surrounding communities this September Fair provided one of the infrequent but highly prized traditional periods of rest and celebration. The moon festival in August and the ten-day New Year holiday provided others. On the grounds of recreation alone it seemed that the Long Bow fair had an important role to play.

That city, commune and brigade officials had called off the fair without any discussion of all these factors was hard to understand. To cancel a major facility for exchange of commodities necessary for fall work without providing some viable alternative could only be considered a sectarian extreme. Yet it was easy to see how higher cadres and even propaganda team members fell into this. Their attention was concentrated on production. Buying and selling smacked of bourgeois opportunism, of speculation and profit mongering. The whole question of free markets, to what extent they should be encouraged, to what extent they should be controlled, what commodities they should handle, and what limits should be imposed on prices—all these questions had never been really settled. They had divided Party leaders for years. On the one hand, there were those who advocated unrestricted trade, private exchange and the profit motive as a stimulant to production in the countryside. In 1971 these were regarded as "right opportunists." On the other hand, there were those who advocated doing away with free markets altogether, condemning them as bourgeois, reactionary and subversive to socialist construction. Riding high in 1971, they have since been called "left dogmatists."

Neither of these positions seemed satisfactory to me. To give free markets unfettered reign was to encourage all the speculative forces in the countryside and place unnecessary strain on collective production and exchange. To do away with free markets altogether, however, was impractical. Neither the state commercial departments nor the cooperative supply societies were able to handle the intricate variety of commodities and services that undergirded a flourishing rural economy.

In practice, government policy had swung from enthusiastic promotion of free markets to severe restriction without ever allowing them to develop their full potential, on the one hand, or ever completely doing away with them on the other. At any given stage of development there was presumably some optimum role for the free market to play, but this role had not been easy to determine and so the fortunes of the market had been blown first one way and then another, depending on which wind predominated in society as a whole.

What predominated in Changchih City and Horse Square Commune in 1971 was an antifree-market wind that ignored all the links which the Long Bow fair had to the production tasks of the "three fall" period. All the arguments against the fair had to do with its disruptive effect on three days of wheat planting, without any recognition of the fact that the wheat planting, not to mention the fall harvest and the fall plowing, all depended to a large extent on animals, implements, supplies and commodities available at the fair.

Fortunately the peasants understood the relationship more clearly. Even though officials canceled the fair, it took place on schedule and on a scale rarely seen in the past, a scale that reflected the development of the economy and the vitality of production in the preceding years. All that the ban from on high accomplished was the elimination of the dramatic performances that alone could have given the occasion some political content. At fair time Long Bow's leaders had always brought in the best amateur dramatic groups from the surrounding area and had also hired, at considerable expense, a professional theater troupe. The troupe had staged major dramatic and operatic productions both afternoon and evening. For three days running a continuous selection of operas, plays, skits, dances and songs had been offered free to all who wished to come. Most of these performances had carried some timely or timeless political message, some celebration of a past revolutionary victory, some agitation for more determined efforts in socialist construction, some criticism of backward ideology and action, or some praise for advanced thought and behavior.

Once the fair was officially canceled, the brigade could not appropriate a budget for entertainment, thus aborting the traditional political content of the event. While spontaneously, from below, the economic function of the fair surged to new heights, it had no directed political function to perform, no explicit message to impart. This meant, of course, that commercial politics reasserted themselves by default; "me first" ideology promoted a traditional selling and buying spree. In the absence of any other political message commercial advantage took command.

Here was an illustration of the way in which "left dogmatism" inevitably played into the hands of "right opportunism." Under the influence of ultraleft thinking, higher cadres canceled the fair. Since this was a blow to the local economy that peasants could not tolerate, the fair took place anyway. At the same time, the whole cultural side of the event, the celebration of socialist ideology, which always depended on the higher leadership to organize and inspire, collapsed, a prime casualty of the decision to cancel.

Meanwhile, the lively market in weaned pigs that burgeoned at the very center of the village challenged Long Bow's peasants to do something about pig raising.

58

ALL ABOUT PIGS

 As hawkers and vendors counted their cash, sorted their goods and rolled up their mats after a record day of business on Long Bow's main street, the single bulb in the Fifth Team meeting room suddenly lit up. It cast a dim light on a score of bone-tired peasants who had gathered to discuss an unprecendented demand: every family must buy at least one pig.

The meeting had hardly begun when Old Er-lui got up to leave.

"Where are you going?" asked Kuo Cheng-k'uan, the team leader.

"Stop."

"What are you leaving for?"

"We've just begun."

The protests came thick and fast from the old man's neighbors.

"I'm going home to drink my supper," said Er-lui angrily. He used the word "drink" because his supper was gruel.

"But what about pigs? Aren't you going to buy one?"

"I haven't put anything in my stomach since noon."

"You ought to raise fewer dogs and support Chairman Mao by buying a pig," said a voice from the darkness of the corner.

But Er-lui paid no attention. Since he had stomach trouble, he raised dogs because dog meat was "hot" and he could digest it. Pork was something else again.

In defiance of his teammates he walked out into the night muttering, ". . . don't even give a man a chance to drink his supper! Buy a pig! On an empty stomach!"

"That Er-lui," said Cheng-k'uan. "He's too stubborn! Such a huge courtyard, all those dogs and not one pig!"

It was Smart Fan, with his tobacco-stained fingers, the General Affairs Secretary of the City Party Committee, who alerted the brigade to its dismal record in pig raising. On the first day of the September Fair weaned-pig buyers from distant places such as the Workers' and Peasants' Commune and Big Star Brigade had come to stock up. When Smart Fan asked the man from Big Star how many pigs his brigade raised, it turned out that by National Day (October 1) Big Star families would average two pigs apiece, and the supply of fine young piglets at the Long Bow fair made this possible.

The contrast with Long Bow was striking. Smart Fan well knew that Long Bow Brigade, with over 400 families, had on hand only 165 pigs and 53 of these were in the collective pig-breeding project under Hsin-fa's direction. Less than a quarter of Long Bow's peasant families raised any pigs at all. In the light of the national goal of raising one pig per family, and taking into consideration that some of the more advanced brigades in Shansi were already raising one pig per capita, it was a miserable record.

Smart Fan immediately called together the propaganda team and brigade leaders and urged them to mobilize the village for a pig-buying campaign that would enable Long Bow to reach if not surpass the national goal. With a good crop in prospect, with the promise of extra grain from the state grain company, with weaned pigs from all over Southeast Shansi right there on their doorstep, it was folly for Long Bow people to continue in their lackadaisical way, raising a pig here and there as it suited the fancy of some individual householder, without any brigade goals, without any brigade campaign.

That night when the production teams met in their various meeting halls, it was not Party rectification that held the spotlight, as had been the case ever since the August cadre meeting in Changchih City, but pig raising.

In the dingy room behind the Liberation Army tank park where the Fifth Production Team met, less than half the family heads showed up. After sending assistant team leader Li Yü-hsi out to round up the laggards Judge Kao, leader of the propaganda team, opened up the subject.

"Mao Tse-tung has called on us to develop pig raising on a wide scale. This is a question of principle," he said, raising his voice to emphasize the point. "Whether or not you are loyal to Mao Tse-tung will be demonstrated by whether you raise a pig or not. Here the weaned pigs have been brought to our front door. Buyers from other brigades have traveled long distances to buy them, while we sit on our hands. What we want to discuss tonight is how we are going to buy pigs tomorrow. Brigade and team cadres and Communist Party members must take the lead and the rest of the people should demonstrate their attitude. Since so many people are absent, we will have a special meeting before going to the fields tomorrow, for all those who did not come tonight. We want everyone who does not already have a pig to buy one tomorrow at the fair!"

"Of course there are some practical problems. Some people don't have any place to keep a pig. We suggest that they place their pigs at the brigade sty until they have built pigpens of their own. Some people don't have enough money to buy a pig. We suggest that they borrow the money from the brigade, and pay it back later. Shen Chi-ts'ai and Chao T'ung-min, accountants from the brigade office, will be out on the street tomorrow to solve the problem of financing for all who can't come up with the cash. If there are any other problems, you had better bring them up right now. We want a pledge tonight from every family that it will buy a pig tomorrow and raise it this fall. Who will speak first?"

Lu Kuang-han, an older man with extremely thick lips, spoke first. He was a pig-raising enthusiast. "Buying pigs is great," he said. "How can you possibly lose by it? You help yourself and you help the country. Why should anyone hold back?"

Team leader Cheng-k'uan, on the other hand, was self-critical. "As team leader I should have set an example in pig raising, but in the past I never paid much attention to this. When I went to the commune this afternoon for a meeting, Comrade Fan, the Party Secretary, asked me if the fair was on. When I told him that it was, he asked how many pigs Long Bow people had bought. I couldn't give him any answer. But I did know that out of seventy-one families on our team only eight have pigs. And of the twelve pigs they own, five belong to one member—Swift Li. He has a sow that just gave birth to four piglets. Yet all we have done about the matter is distribute to each family a copy of the Central Committee's directive on pig raising. Well, yes"—he paused, and thought a bit—"We've discussed it a number of times also but we haven't taken any action. The main problem is that we leaders haven't taken the lead."

"Let's make a list right now. Who will buy a pig? I'll be the first. Put me down for one."

"I'll buy one," said Shen Shun-ta, the six-footer whom everyone called "Short Shen."

"Put me down for two."

"One."

"Mark my name down."

For a moment it looked as if the campaign would quickly snowball into a mass movement, but then someone spoke out pessimistically from the back wall.

"I was thinking of raising a pig long ago but I haven't any place to put it."

Silence greeted this declaration. Some low grumbling came from the opposite corner. Then again—silence.

Judge Kao broke the stillness by reading off a list of pigs already present or promised in the community.

"Swift Li, 5; Shih Ts'un-hsi, 3; Chin Ta-hung, 1; Li So-tzu, 2 (bought at the fair this very day); Lu Kuang-han, 2; Chang Hsin-fa, 2; Li Hsing-rui, 1; Wu Chung-shu, 2. Even with tonight's volunteers less than a third of the families are on the list. Who else will join?"

Li Hsueh-jen's wife said gloomily, "What would I feed a pig with, even if I did buy one?"

"We're going to provide feed," said Judge Kao.

"Well, I haven't got a pigpen either," she said.

"You should worry about a pen, with a yard as big as yours is," said Cheng-k'uan.

"All right, write me up for one, then," said the woman hesitantly.

"I don't have any place for a pig either," said Chin Hsi-sheng.

"The brigade will find you a place," said Judge Kao.

"But the people will get mad," said Chin, despondent.

He had just been through a big struggle about a spot for a family privy and didn't look forward to another such battle. Since there had been no room in his courtyard for a privy, the brigade had given him some public land out on the street. But the privy he actually built took up more room than had been agreed upon, so the neighbors got angry and cursed him.

"Now they'll start cursing again," he said.

"Let them curse," said Judge Kao. "What does it matter if they get a little upset? They may be angry today, and may still be angry tomorrow, but after a while they'll get used to it and they won't be angry anymore."

"Maybe," said Chin, unconvinced.

"Whoever doesn't have a pigpen can temporarily lodge his pig with a neighbor or give it to the brigade to care for," said Cheng-k'uan, coming up with a constructive solution. "The brigade will also set up a system for allocating pig feed. The harvest will provide both husks and stalks. The brigade will build a fermentation station and the fermented fodder will be divided as needed."

After pausing long enough to let this sink in, Cheng-k'uan continued with an even more important proposal concerning pig manure.

"We will solve the problem of payment for pig manure along the lines tried out by the Third Team. They used to pay for pig manure by the basket, but everyone had to take time out to dig the manure out of the pens and thus lost labor time in the fields. Since the price per basket was set very low, they lost income and no one wanted to take an active part in producing and delivering pig manure. Now the Third Team gives labor days for pig manure. Five carrying poles of the first grade, ten carrying poles of the second, are equal to a labor day. Shen Ch'i-ch'ang and Kuo T'ai-shan have each earned over 100 labor days already this year delivering pig manure.

"Pig raising is loaded with benefits. Why can't every family afford to do it? The pig can be sold for money, you can keep some pork to eat, you can earn work points by delivering pig manure, and the manure will raise yields so that everyone's share will be bigger. All this is clear. So what we have to do now is solve the practical problems like feed and pens. The rest is easy. The real problem is in our minds. Like me, you have probably been thinking, 'This pig business is too much trouble.' For the last two years I haven't raised a pig. But now I have thought it through and so should you. Once you make up your mind the rest is easy. Who else will buy a pig tomorrow?"

Several more immediately signed up.

Whereupon Short Shen, the six-footer, raised a problem that no one else had thought of.

"If we all go out just like that and buy pigs tomorrow the prices will go sky high. The sellers are individuals with only a few pigs each. If buyers remain few, the prices sag. But if there is a rush on pigs, the prices can go out of sight!"

"Well, why can't we get around that by having one or two people do the buying?"

"You mean let one person pick out the pigs for the rest of us?"

"Yes, why not?"

"That's a good idea!"

"Here's a plan," said Cheng-k'uan. "We'll buy all the pigs that have been spoken for. We'll bring them here with a price tag on each. Then you can each pick out the pig you want."

"I've got a better idea," said Swift Li. "Why not add up all the pigs by weight? Average the weights and sell the pigs by the catty?"

"That's too much trouble!"

"Better do it the first way."

And so it was decided. The Fifth Team chose a delegation consisting of Kuo Cheng-k'uan, Li Ch'i-shun and Li P'ing-ting to do the buying. This had the added advantage, as Li Yü-hsi pointed out, of allowing the rest of the team's manpower to return to the fields for wheat planting; thus the main work of the season would not be neglected.

Judge Kao closed the meeting by summarizing the results.

"Eight families originally had pigs. Now twenty-five have signed up to buy. This makes thirty-three, but it's not even half. We must inform all those who did not come and try to reach our goal: a pig per household!"

Before leaving, the team members sang in unison, "Sailing the Seas Depends on the Helmsman." Then they dispersed into the night.

All seven production teams (six agricultural, one sidelines) of Long Bow Brigade conducted similar meetings on the evening of the eighteenth, and most of them chose a few buyers to select all the weaned pigs that the team members had promised to raise. As a result of this unprecedented mobilization, the pig market was by far the liveliest spot at the fair throughout the following day. Long Bow buyers alone bought 150 head, which was almost the whole of that day's offering. This put a lot of pressure on the market and the same type of pigs that had sold the day before for 1 yuan a catty quickly shot up to the market administrator's ceiling of 1.20. If it had not been for the ceiling, prices would have soared much higher. With the ceiling those who had quality to sell got hurt because even the worst pigs brought 1.20 per catty, while the best pigs were held to the same maximum. On the whole, though, both buyers and sellers were happy. Sellers found a market for every pig they brought in at prices higher than the day before, and buyers got all the pigs they bargained for at a fair price—in some cases at a bargain price, if one considered quality.

That night, when the teams met again in their separate headquarters, the great pig purchase was the first order of business. Protracted moral pressure was brought to bear on those families who had not yet agreed to go along.

At the Fifth Team meeting Yü-hsi read out the names of all those who had not yet bought pigs, then went on to say, "If you haven't bought a pig, you still have time to buy one. But we can't always just speak fine words and rest content with ideological work. If you don't buy a pig the team will buy one for you and deliver it to your door. So don't turn this glorious opportunity into an embarrassment. Cover yourselves with glory and buy a pig now."

Even those families who had already bought a pig became targets for further persuasion. Cheng-k'uan urged on them the idea of two. "If, when the pigs reach 30 to 40 catties, you can't afford to go on feeding both, you can turn one into the brigade and raise only one to maturity."

This second night of mobilization brought results equal to the first. Fifth Team buyers went forth the next day with orders for at least fifty pigs.

As the propaganda team met for morning study on September 20, pig buying and pig raising dominated the conversation there as it had for two evenings at the production team meetings. Security Officer Shen came up with a little rhyme which illustrated an old habit of thought—the idea that until grain production reached a certain point it was useless to talk about increasing pig numbers:

> Pigs are alive, they grow each day,
> Each day more grain must go their way!
> A bigger harvest is the vital link,
> Without it pig raising is bound to shrink!

"What is missing here," said Shen, "is the realization that pig raising promotes grain production. We have to understand the relationship between the two. Of course pigs eat some grain, but they also eat a lot of wild grasses and waste materials."

"They do if people gather this stuff for them," said Wang. "It means a lot of extra work."

"That's why single men and widowers, not to mention widows, are reluctant to undertake the task," said Shen. "They don't have the time for it."

"And then there is the problem of state policy," said Veteran Wang. "We've seen it happen already. Once pig production reaches a certain level, suddenly the local buying office lowers the grades and messes everything up. The state is supposed to pay 48 fen for first-grade pork, 46 fen for second-grade, 43 fen for third-grade and 40 fen for fourth-grade. But if they back off on this and people don't get what they have been promised then pig raising goes into a tailspin."

"Well, they ought to carry out policy just as strictly as anyone else," said Judge Kao. "There's too much at stake. What's the point of all these benefits —extra grain on credit, credit for the purchase of pigs, brigade mobilization to supply fermented feed, mobilization to build pigpens—if the buying office doesn't hold up its end and maintain steady prices?"

"We should make sure that they do," said Donkey Meat Wang.

"How?"

"Raise the problem with them anyway," said Wang.

Everyone on the propaganda team was elated by the sudden burst of activity on the livestock front. A few days before, pigs had not even been on the agenda. Suddenly, due to Smart Fan's prodding and the September Fair, pig raising in Long Bow had embarked on a revolution. It was possible the brigade would never be the same again. But Veteran Wang, as was his wont, brought the matter into perspective.

"To start like this is easy enough, but to go on is harder. In the long run no one can say that pig raising is solidly grounded in Long Bow unless the people raise and keep brood sows and supply their own weaned pigs. All we've done this time is to transfer pigs from one brigade to another. We haven't added a single pig to the face of China.

"Furthermore, to feed the pigs we have bought won't be so easy. People bought them with borrowed money, and have been allowed to purchase 60 catties of state grain per head to start them on. These incentives are very attractive but some people, as soon as they get the grain, may well turn around and sell the pig and we'll be back where we started from."

"That's right," said Donkey Meat Wang. "One member of the Second Team bought a pig yesterday morning and sold it in the evening. His wife refused to help with it. She won't work outside the house, even in her own courtyard. She just messes around all day on the kang with her baby. So he sold the pig already!"

As if to emphasize the point, the difficulty of consolidation, Shen Ch'uan-te's son, Shen T'ien-yu, suddenly appeared in the doorway.

"My pig ran away," he reported sorrowfully.

In contrast to his dead father's efficient, pompous manner, the younger Shen always seemed to be but half awake. He was clad in a sleeveless cotton tunic that was only half buttoned across his chest. In the chill morning air the skin on his arms was peppered with goosepimples, but he seemed oblivious to everything but his loss. Shoulders drooping, jaw slack, he leaned against the doorpost.

"You've lost your pig already?"

"Yes. It jumped the wall and ran into the fields. I know where it is, but I can't catch it. It's much too fast for me."

"But that is one of the best pigs bought all day," said Judge Kao, incredulous.

"Yes. I paid top money—17 yuan. I'll go back and keep an eye on it if someone will go to Horse Square after that pig dog."

In Horse Square, it seemed, there was a dog that could catch pigs and hold them without harming hair or hide until the pig's two-legged pursuers caught up. But Security Officer Shen didn't trust any dog around pigs.

"Never mind the dog," he said. "You just go back out and keep an eye on the pig. As soon as we get through our meeting we'll all turn out and help catch it."

At that young Shen cheered up and ambled off, his shoulders straighter than usual.

Shen had no sooner left the scene than another peasant arrived with an equally grave problem. He had bought a pig on a promise from the brigade leaders that a spot would be found for a pen. They had chosen a large yard nearby. The owner of the yard had protested strenuously but Kuei-ts'ai had overruled him.

"If you try building here I'll lie right down on the spot," said the outraged peasant.

"Go right ahead," said Kuei-ts'ai. "You lie there and we'll build a wall right around you and turn the pigs in with you."

This silenced the man temporarily, but once Kuei-ts'ai left he raised a huge fuss. Work on the pen still had not begun.

Security Officer Shen promised to look into the matter.

"Old Chou Cheng-fu is having pen trouble, too," said Donkey Meat Wang. " 'I don't have a pigpen, how can I raise a pig?' he shouts. 'What I want to know is, does this new leading body want *me*, this member of the masses? If they do, let them find me some land for a pen. I listen to you cadres. I listen to the Communist Party, but no one ever listens to me. No one ever solves *my* problems!' "

" 'What are you shouting for?' says Splayfoot Tseng. 'I'm not only raising one pig, I'm raising two. I'm a single man. I work overtime, but I can still raise two pigs!' That's Splayfoot's method for stalling our criticism. On this front he suddenly plays a positive role. But old Cheng-fu messed up the whole meeting, the way he carried on. I finally asked him if he would build a pen along the south wall of the yard he shares with his brother. 'If the leadership says so, I will,' he says, 'but if this problem isn't solved I won't raise pigs at all.' What he really wants to do is build a pen right beside that cookhouse he built to spite his brother. We haven't settled the cookhouse quarrel yet, and Cheng-fu is ready to start another one!"

"Kuei-ts'ai says, 'In Chou Cheng-fu's family there's not a single member that is any good!' " said Security Officer Shen, laughing.

"He ought to know; he married the man's sister," said Donkey Meat Wang.

"These pigs are really shaking this town up," said Veteran Wang.

We were all looking forward to the big pig chase once the study session was over. It was just what we needed to warm us up. But, just as we started out, Shen T'ien-yu came running back to tell us that he and his buddies on the Second Team had caught the pig. One problem, at least, had solved itself.

What with peasants selling pigs the day after they bought them, with pigs jumping out and running away, and with families quarreling hotly over where to build new pens, I began to wonder if Smart Fan's brilliant plan might not be characterized as adventurous. On September 21, the last day of the fair, families that obviously didn't really want them bought fifty additional pigs. How much trouble would they go to in building tight pens and in finding the roots, weeds and waste that could supplement the grain diet? And even with the best will in the world how could Long Bow people suddenly find grain, grain by-products and waste matter for 212 more head than they had ever raised before? Wouldn't it have been better, I wondered, to have set more modest goals—say, the addition of 100 pigs with the stipulation that at least a dozen of these would be raised as brood sows?

But things turned out better than I anticipated.

Sudden sales and wild escapes subsided along with property line quarrels. Three weeks after the great pig purchase only four pigs had died. One met its fate on the highway, crushed under the wheels of a truck. One had died of ulcers of the mouth. Two others escaped into the fields and were devoured by wolves. Only a few gnawed bones rendered mute testimony to the fate of pigs that would not stay home.

One reason that things turned out so well was a set of policies to stimulate pig raising that had been adopted by the national government. Given the tenor of the times, none of these policies involved "material incentives." They depended instead on "reasonable rewards."

To start with, the State Grain Company had set aside substantial amounts of grain for the campaign. For each breeding boar or sow kept, a family was allowed to buy 120 catties of grain. For each fat pig raised, a family was allowed to buy 60 catties of grain from the state and 60 catties of grain from the brigade. In addition to that, for each pig raised a family got extra cotton cloth coupons and extra cooking oil coupons. Finally, for each pig sold the family could retain 10 catties of pork for home consumption.

On the surface these measures did not appear to be very attractive: in return for raising pigs the peasants were allowed to *buy* grain, cloth and oil and eat some of the meat. In fact, this was an important concession because the peasants had no grain ration books. They could not legally buy grain in any market and they were restricted to very tight rations of cloth and oil. Raising a pig provided the only method, short of relief, by which a peasant could go out and buy more grain than had been earned through workdays in the cooperative, and more cloth and oil than the ration allowed.

The grain sold by the state under this system did not have to be fed to the pig. Family members could eat the grain and feed something else to the pig. But if the pig failed to grow and never reached the market, the right to buy this grain could not be renewed. For that reason, if for no other, everyone tried hard to keep his pig alive and growing. A family might feed the pig none, some or all of the grain purchased. For the most part, though, people ate the grain and found other materials to fatten pigs on.

What really put pig raising on a sound basis in Long Bow was the invention, by a soldier in the Liberation Army, of a new kind of yeast which, when added to finely ground cornstalks, corncobs, millet straw or other fodder, transformed it in such a way that pigs could digest it and grow on it. This process of fermenting fodder in earthenware crocks amounted to placing a rumen, such as cows, sheep and goats already have, outside an animal without any rumen, and predigesting coarse feed for them, coarse feed that they could not ordinarily eat, or could gain little from if they did eat it. In a grain economy such as China still had, where all grains were needed for human consumption, meat animals had always been raised on wasteland (cattle, sheep and goats) or on waste materials (pigs and chickens). Whatever edible scraps, human feces, garbage or other wastes the pigs and chickens could find about the village, plus whatever materials were left over from the processing of grain into liquor, flour or noodles, these were the primary feeds. The amount of material available for scavenging, and the by-products of noodle making and liquor making, had always been limited, hence pig raising and poultry raising had also been limited. With increases in grain production, there had, of course, been increases in grain by-products. With local grain surpluses there had even been some whole grains left over for pigs in certain places, but these increases could not be large because the total grain situation in proportion to population was still so tight. It was the discovery of the new fermentation process that opened the way to large-scale pig raising and the possibility of transforming China's traditional grain economy into a new type of grain-fodder-livestock combination.

Chang Hsin-fa, who was responsible for Long Bow's brigade-financed pig-raising project, showed us how corncobs, kaoliang and cornstalks could all be ground, placed in jars, and processed with yeast to yield valuable pig feed. In addition, he supervised a plant making corn and bean noodles. Both these products were made from finely ground corn or beans. When placed in jars of water the heavier noodle material sank while the lighter by-products floated, were skimmed off, and fed to pigs. Because pigs easily digested the floating wastes, noodle plants and pigsties went together all over China.

Next to feed, internal parasites posed the biggest problems for Chinese pig raisers. In Long Bow, the fat pigs and breeding stock of the brigade unit suffered severely from parasites, which caused the animals to grow slowly, if at all. Everywhere we went in North China, including Tachai, we found the same problem. Only a few pigs waxed fat and healthy. Most had the lean shanks and swollen bellies of the worm-ridden. To this rule we found only one exception—the brigade piggery at Nancheng, south of Changchih. There all the pigs seemed unusually healthy. In part this was due to the extraordinary measures Nancheng pig raisers took to ensure balanced rations, but they must also have controlled parasites in some way. Unfortunately, I didn't inquire into this.

Raising pigs one or two at a time in household pens tended to reduce the problem of parasites because the pigs were isolated, a new generation was introduced only once a year or every year and a half, and much voided infectious material was rendered harmless by the passage of time. It was also possible, when raising only a pig or two at a time, to start each set in a new, parasite-free pen. It was probably for this reason that home-raised pigs tended to do better than communally raised pigs—and consequently leaders pushed the "one pig per family" slogan even more vigorously.

That pigs actually served as fertilizer factories, an article of faith in the Chinese countryside at the time, and one that had been promoted across the length and breadth of China by none other than Mao Tse-tung himself, was doubtful. A living, growing pig added nothing to the material that he ate that could give it more fertilizer value than it already possessed. In fact, the very process of digestion and elimination undoubtedly destroyed some of the nutrients in the material consumed by the pig that might otherwise become fertilizer for plants. It has always seemed self-evident that if the peasants directly composted their waste material it would yield more in the way of plant food than it could possibly do when fed to a pig and then composted as pig manure. So why did the Chinese put such great faith in the slogan, "Raise pigs, accumulate manure!" (yang chu, chi fei)? And why did they insist that raising pigs increased crop production?

The only plausible answer, it seemed to me, was that when they raised a pig they took great pains to collect waste materials and bring them to the pigpen where, even if they were not digested and processed by the pig, they were trampled and mixed together with pig manure and urine into a useful compost that no one without a pig would ever have bothered to assemble.

The benefits of this kind of a program were obviously limited, especially if, in fact, the pigs destroyed some of the nutrient value of the material they processed. To increase pig numbers first to one pig per family, and then to one pig per capita, and then to still higher figures, must inevitably yield sharply diminishing returns once most of the usual waste materials had been gathered up. China produced, after all, only a certain amount of waste material, a certain amount of fodder and a certain amount of by-product grain. To increase pig numbers beyond the limit that China could thus support would in the long run cut into the grain supply itself because the pigs would have to start eating whole grains instead of waste materials; in the process, from beginning to end, pigs would not create a single new pound of nitrogen, phosphorus or potash. In the long run, grain production cannot depend on pig raising, but only on the massive growth of a fertilizer industry, and the massive propagation of nitrogen-fixing legumes.

In fairness to the plans of Chinese agricultural leaders, I should record that they were also building a fertilizer industry as rapidly as possible by the "walking-on-two-legs method"—that is, by using small-scale indigenous processes as well as large-scale modern industrial processes. China did not depend on pig raising alone to increase grain yields, but worked to develop all possible sources of plant nutrients, from the meticulous collection and processing of waste materials in pigpens to the fixation of nitrogen from the atmosphere with coal, gas and electric power.

59

BATTLES—NORTH, SOUTH AND AT HOME

On the last day of the fair a cold front blew across the Shangtang Plateau, dropping the temperature into the low thirties. Security Officer Shen and Donkey Meat Wang were the only members of the propaganda team with a kang, a mud platform with built-in flues that could be heated. After shivering through the final hours of daylight in the pig market, we all gathered in their room to sit on the kang and absorb some of its gentle warmth.

Cold weather always made Veteran Wang's shattered left arm ache. As he rubbed it he began to talk about his life in the army, a life which he recalled with nostalgia. Nostalgia for the past seemed universal among those who had fought their way through the thirties and the forties. Those, apparently, were simpler times, days of extraordinary national unity that brought members of all classes together in resistance first to foreign conquest, and then to continued Kuomintang rule.

Veteran Wang, once started on the Liberation War, could hold forth for hours:

> The battle for Tientsin was big. Of course we were all scared. But in those days nobody asked, "Are you scared?" The only question was, "Can you carry out your task?" If you couldn't carry out your task, the commander had to find someone who could, then transfer you somewhere else.
>
> Commanders and political directors had to take the lead. While everyone else took shelter we had to stand up. I was standing up, looking through my binoculars, when a bullet blasted my hat from my head. Then I felt the blood running down. A fragment of that bullet still remains in my skull. It's right on top and it hurts sometimes.
>
> Later, my arm was hit. A fusillade whipped it backward. Eighteen bullets struck my arm at the same moment. Some of them are still there. Other bullets hit my leg and back. When it rains or comes off cold, all the old wounds ache. I feel pain in half my body.
>
> How did I get out of there? I don't know. I was unconscious. I

don't know what happened or how I survived. After the whole country was liberated I still lay in the hospital in Tientsin.

We didn't have much anesthesia then. What we did have we saved for the seriously wounded. When the doctor took the bullets out of my arm he just poured salt water on the wound, then went in after them.

In that operating room there was a "little devil" [messenger boy] with a bullet in his rump. The doctor went to cut it out.

"Does it hurt?" he asked.

"Yes, it hurts," said the boy.

"You mean a Liberation Army soldier, a follower of Mao Tsetung, can feel pain?"

"Certainly not," said the boy.

So the doctor cut the bullet out and the boy never said another word.

In that battle for Tientsin one of our soldiers flung an explosive charge into a dugout. An enemy inside flung it right out again. The soldier, calm as you please, picked up the charge and flipped it back into the dugout. That charge blew the wall all to hell, opened a hole in the enemy line, and our troops went charging through.

The soldier earned a triple merit badge.

"How come you were so brave?" I asked him.

"I was just trying to carry out my assignment," said the man. "In the past I was a no-good bastard. I smoked opium, chased women and wasted my life. Now the People's Army has given me a chance. How would it look if I didn't carry out my assignment?"

"When the charge came flying out, why did you pick it up?"

"If I hadn't I'd have been killed when it went off."

"So you just threw it back again?"

"Yes."

That's the way heroes behaved.

I liked the way they showed the soldiers in the film *Fighting North and South*. We really were like that. Some of the later films aren't so good. When I see that film I feel as if I'm seeing what we really did in those days. Later films never caught our style, the essence of our life.

That soldier, a lifelong no-good suddenly turned hero, moved me. If I had been a writer I could have written him up. But I can't write. So many things happened. No reporter could begin to write them all down. Before going into battle we always swore an oath to stick together through life and death. That was real unity. Political work was easy in those days. You gave a short speech, no extra words, and everyone did his best. I remember once, before a battle, the political director called everyone together.

"Do you want to live or do you want to die?"

"We want to live."

"Then follow me," he shouted and charged forward into a hail of bullets.

That's all there was to it.

We wrote simple reports, too.

"Arms, ammunition, men and horses received. Patrols sent out . . ." period.

But was it so easy to be a cadre in those days? It wasn't that easy. You had to make all decisions on your own. And you had to solve your own supply problems, too. There weren't any documents to study or any forms to fill out. So how did we get our supplies?

We raided the landlords' homes. And each day each man got a yuan and a half in cash. We had a poem:

> Life hard,
> Meet it with a laugh
> Every day
> Spend a yuan and a half.

Our soldiers were sassy, too. They thought nothing of talking back. I remember once, we passed members of a propaganda unit stationed beside the road. They were trying to cheer up the troops and get them to move faster.

"Are you tired?" they called out to our men.

"No," we shouted back.

"Not any of those on horseback, anyway," said one smart-aleck kid.

But even though the youngsters spoke like that they went into battle bravely. They fought like tigers and no one found fault with the way they talked.

Our literacy level was really low. I went to primary school for four years only. Even so, I was Confucius in my unit. Our theoretical level was also low. We just did whatever we were told. We didn't pay attention to strategy but only looked at tactics, how to win the battle we were in. But after the Shihchiachuang campaign the leaders decided to practice democracy in the army and discuss all their battle plans with the troops. That upset some of the commanders. They couldn't imagine talking everything over with foot soldiers. They thought our level was too low. "If that's the way it's going to be," they said, "I won't lead men into battle anymore!"

It's funny how our thinking changed over the years. During the Anti-Japanese War we thought like this: Drive out the Japanese devils, then go home and get a good night's sleep.

After the Japanese surrender Liu Shao-ch'i talked about an era of peace. Lots of us went along out of wishful thinking. The Chungking agreements called for a reduction of forces. We cut our Eighth Route Army back to nine divisions. We transferred some units to local forces and completely demobilized others. Many fighters were unhappy about that, but they were told that the time had come to put on civilian clothes, the clothes of the "old hundred names" [the common people].

When the press announced the Chungking truce agreement in October, we jumped with joy. We relaxed our vigilance. We thought,

Now at last we can take off our clothes at night and sleep soundly. But the ink no sooner dried on the documents than the attacks began. After the first high tide of clashes, fighting tapered off but it began again at New Year's. We were still paying our mutual New Year's respects when the Kuomintang attack came. Our scouts had reported signs of an offensive but none of us paid any attention because we didn't want to. After all, we had signed a truce, hadn't we? But the Kuomintang attacked anyway and we had to pull out on very short notice. The unprepared got left behind.

Those were the days of the truce teams—three-in-one combinations of U.S., Kuomintang and Eighth Route Army officers. But fighting raged on all fronts anyway.

Once we attacked across the railroad at night. We stashed our armbands and moved off quietly, but we didn't have leather shoes like the Kuomintang forces and some bastard snapped pictures of our straw sandals. At one of the meetings he produced them as evidence of a truce violation.

When the Kuomintang surrounded us the truce teams never showed up. But as soon as we surrounded the Kuomintang the teams came right away to help them get out of the trap.

During the Liberation War our thinking changed again. We began to think about surviving. "Will I still be alive when we capture Chiang Kai-shek and liberate the country?" By that time we had all seen great cities and beautiful regions and we asked, "Will I be around to inherit all this? Will I ever see home again?"

These questions implied that the revolution would come to an end. In our minds the problem of carrying the revolution to a higher stage had, for all practical purposes, been rejected.

Veteran Wang's stories stimulated other men's memories. Huang Chia-huan, the steelworker, informed us he had fought in Tibet.

"When we went into Tibet we faced Tibetan soldiers commanded by a living Buddha. We heard they weren't afraid of death because no bullet could touch them. But as soon as the artillery started to fire, the living Buddha ran away and hid in a ditch. We all ran up to catch a glimpse of this famous god. He was nothing but a little boy, ignorant, illiterate, cowering in a ditch, frightened to death."

Buddhas reminded Secretary Chang Kuei-ts'ai of the charms members of the peasant Red Spear Society used to make. "When the Anti-Japanese War began we wrote ideographs in white on yellow paper. Then we burned the paper and dissolved it in water. If you drank that water neither spears nor bullets could touch you. That's what people said. But actually the bullets went right through you, and real fast, too!"

"Japanese soldiers used to carry a little carving of Buddha hung on a string around their necks," said Veteran Wang. "Before they went into battle they took it out, and bowed down before it. We surrounded a Japanese soldier once. He took out his little Buddha, bowed, and pulled the pin on a live grenade. The explosion finished him."

"The Japanese treated their wounded cruelly," Wang continued. "A

soldier badly hit became a burden to his comrades. They burned him alive.
They just poured gasoline on him and ignited it."

"That's right," said Secretary Chang. "Once when I was working as a
laborer for the Japanese one of the guards got his kneecap blown off. They
laid him on his back on a wooden bench and poured gasoline over everything. The soldier wept. His comrades wept. Then he took out his Buddha
and nodded his head while the flames burst out all around. After the fire
died down we had to take his bones and grind them into powder. His
comrades wrapped them in paper and sent them back to Japan."

Huang Chia-huan surprised us by saying that he had fought not only in
Tibet, but also on the Sino-Indian border. He had marched all the way to
the tea plantations of Assam, at the foot of the Himalayas:

> On October 18, 1962, the attack order came. As we moved out each
> of us carried enough rations for seven days. But our commander told
> us these rations must last for two weeks. So we cut back to two meals
> a day and ate the second meal very late, sometimes at midnight.
>
> But a strange thing happened. We encircled an area shrouded in
> mist. Machine guns fired from an enemy strongpoint across the
> ravine. We tried to silence them but several of our men got hit, so
> our commander ordered artillery. The artillery shells smashed the
> machine gun nests. Then we took the whole place. But the Indian
> command didn't know that. They thought the area still belonged to
> them. Planes came over, circling low. We took cover thinking they
> would bomb us, but they dropped supplies by parachute instead. We
> shot down two of the planes. The pilot of the third saw that some-
> thing was wrong. He tried to gain height quickly, but another com-
> pany farther down the line shot him down. The planes came with
> supplies for their own men—rice, kerosene and warm clothes. They
> didn't know we had already taken the area. After that we had plenty
> of food and fuel. We got everything we needed from that airdrop.
>
> We captured so many prisoners everywhere. Our group alone
> captured 900. Another unit surrounded three whole brigades. We
> captured all their officers except General Kaul. He got away.
>
> Their men were tall, much taller than we were. They never
> thought that we would roll over them like that. I am tall for a
> Chinese but I had to look up at them. They were bearded, bearded
> Sikhs. We surrounded whole Sikh units. They abandoned their
> weapons and scattered up the slopes. Then we had to go and round
> them up. We found some crouching with their heads buried in holes,
> rumps up, arms out, holding wristwatches in the air as much as to
> say, "Don't kill me, take my watch!"
>
> We took their watches, got them to their feet, then put their
> watches back on their wrists. We took them to the rear, found warm
> clothes for them, and food. Supply troops took them from the front
> to base camps farther back where supplies were more plentiful. In
> those freezing mountains lots of them had only summer uniforms.
> Their feet froze. Their feet turned purple and they couldn't walk.
> Four of us carried one cripple up a steep mountain trail. It was hard

enough to climb without any load. Four of us could hardly carry him up. Once we got our prisoners to safety we gave them the best of everything, padded cotton coats, padded shoes, padded caps.

Our drive took us all the way down to the foot of the mountains. Then we got orders to pull back. We had to pull back and return everything we had captured. We couldn't understand why. Our leaders insisted, saying it was policy. We were fighting a political battle and we had to pull back. As in the film *Fighting North and South* we had to make a strategic withdrawal. We gathered all the captured weapons together, including the fancy Soviet rockets, and fixed them all up, even polished them. Then we invited the Red Cross to come and check them out. After we withdrew the Indians came and got the stuff.

As for the prisoners, we sent them back, too. When it came time for them to go, some of them didn't want to leave. They cried. They wanted to stay with us. They were afraid they would be punished for surrendering, afraid for their lives if they went back. They were conscripts. So we had to persuade them and reassure them. We had to convince them that nothing would happen to them.

"Well, I never fought North or South," said Secretary Chang, "but I saw plenty of action nevertheless. Long Bow was a complicated place. In the morning, at the crack of dawn, the Japanese would come along demanding grain. They threw sacks on the ground and demanded that we fill them up. Then in the afternoon Kuomintang bandit units came through looking for grain, clothes and money. They thought nothing of taking the clothes right off a man's back. Once my mother made me a new pair of shoes. They took my shoes off, hit me across the face with them, and strode away. If they found the village head they tied his hands behind his back, bound his ankles together, put a rope around his neck, and threatened to throw him in a well unless he came up with grain and money.

"The people really hated those Kuomintang bandits. After the Japanese surrendered we captured a middle-level puppet commander, General Swen Fu-ch'uan. He had killed twelve Long Bow men, including the only two sons one woman had. When we brought him here women attacked him with scissors. They cut off his ears, his nose and his lips. Then they cut out his tongue. They stabbed him with the awls they used to make shoe soles. Then they crushed his skull with rocks.

"Han Shao-wen commanded a puppet platoon under the Japanese. In the course of the war he killed more than 300 people. He used to say, 'If three days go by without somebody to kill, my palms began to itch!' We sent fifteen militiamen to find him. They finally caught up with him in Hantan and pinned him against the wall with two bayonets, one through his right shoulder, and one through his left. They pinned him but they spared his life so that they could bring him back for punishment. Here in front of a mass meeting they tied him to a table, piled cornstalks all around it, and set them afire. Han Shao-wen burned to death.

"As for Wen Ch'i-yung, commander of the entire Lucheng puppet garrison, the regional forces didn't know what he looked like so we sent militiamen out to round him up. We brought him before a huge mass meeting in Horse Square. The crowd was out for blood. They wanted to kill him. I was standing on the steps only a few feet from him. The way he glared back angered me. I jumped behind him, grabbed my gun with all my might and jammed the bayonet into his back. The blade went right through him and dumped him, spread-eagled, onto the floorboards. Other people rushed forward with their knives and bayonets and finished him off. They stabbed him hundreds of times.

"I had a reputation as a tough customer. In regard to Long Bow the Landlords' Home Return Corps spread the word, 'First get Man-hsi, then get Kuei-ts'ai.' They gave Man-hsi top billing because he beat more people, but I was the Party leader who stood behind him and I went into action when necessary."

These tales, so enthusiastically told, brought out aspects of the past that contrasted sharply with the present. The speakers had no trouble distinguishing friend from foe. They took it for granted that they had fought and triumphed in a just cause. On the Indian border Chinese soldiers treated rank-and-file prisoners as class brothers, just as they had always treated captured conscripts from the armies of Chiang Kai-shek. On the home front landlords, "running dogs," collaborators and turncoats stood out as enemy targets against whom everyone could unite. Nobody talked about taking the lid off the class struggle. The oppressors themselves did an excellent job of calling attention to that.

In the seventies friend and foe no longer stood forth so clearly. Without foreign invaders, local tyrants or rent-gouging gentry to mobilize against, Party leaders raised the specter of hidden agents bent on counterrevolutionary wrecking. Every time a problem came up, every time a conflict arose, every time someone committed a questionable act, they called for revolutionary vigilance, for unmasking class enemies, for uncovering class struggle. But these calls seemed strangely unrelated to the reality before us.

At the conclusion of the Long Bow fair, when the brigade leaders reported back to the propaganda team, team leaders asked them to sum up all the evidence of "class struggle" that had come to their attention. Under this heading they lumped all negative phenomena, large and small—everything that harmed the community or violated its mores.

Stealing incidents made up the largest single category. Stealing was classified that fall as harvest wrecking, as primarily a political rather than an economic act. Yet there seemed to be no lack of thieves or thefts. Each team reported numerous incidents.

A peasant named Chu Chiu-ch'ang had planted two squash plants in his yard. Each of these had produced a huge, twenty-catty squash. Before he got around to pick them they disappeared. Everyone said that 80 percent of the squash stealing in Long Bow was the work of that rascal Whiskers Shen. People had seen Shen eyeing these two monstrous squashes several times in the past week. Hence he was suspect number one.

Ch'en Shen-nien had lost five ears of corn. Someone cut them right off the stalks in his frontyard. Who could it be?

Old Wu Wan-t'ien raised date trees in his yard. One day he woke up to find himself locked in his house. When he finally managed to break out, scores of ripe dates had disappeared. So Wu said, at any rate. But other people said that he ate the dates himself, then spread rumors about thieves. As for Wu having been locked in, that no one disputed.

Soon afterward Lu Hsien-hui, the widow, found herself locked in her room. When she got her door open at last she thought surely she would find things missing from the yard, but everything was in order. She thought that was because in the courtyard next door drama practice had gone on late into the night. With so much light, and so many people coming and going, the thief had not dared to move farther.

Shen Hu-ch'en lost several peaches from his tree.

The Third Team grew corn near the vegetable garden at the edge of the village. They lost seventy ears, all cut with a knife. A whole row vanished.

The Fifth Team also reported a vanishing row of ear corn. They suspected some stranger coming down the highway on foot or one of the railroad workers who lived by the tracks. East of the railroad peasants often found their cornstalks standing without ears. One man reported that he saw an off-duty train crew roasting fresh corn over a fire. Where had those ears come from?

Complaints made to the Railroad Third Bureau (construction headquarters) always provoked countercharges that Long Bow peasants had been doing some stealing of their own. Hadn't there been a steady loss of coal from the yards at night? Hadn't Lu Yuan-hai made off with two buckets of charcoal? And hadn't five children of the Tai, Han and Yen families taken five shovels from the Third Bureau warehouse? Rumor had it that another child, Shen Liu-hai, had stolen a chain and sold it at the market in Chang-yi. More serious, someone had stolen two telephone poles from the Third Bureau Communications Yard.

With all this stealing going on one had to be careful. A branch from a neighbor's tree stuck over the wall into Chi Yu-hsin's yard. It rubbed against the electric lines, but Yu-hsin didn't dare cut it off until he notified Donkey Meat Wang. He was afraid he would be charged with theft.

Attacking village cadres, making things difficult for them, developed into a second category of "class struggle."

Fourth Team leaders had complaints against Chi Tseng-chien. He went up and down the street cursing them out. Shepherds were supposed to get 8 points per day, but the team gave his son only 7.5. When they divided relief grain the Chi household got only sorghum and no corn. After Chi worked for several days in the Fourth Team garden the team leader's brother cheated him of his work points.

"Yang Chi-wang, your whole family is against me," yelled Chi, jumping up and down in his frontyard. "Low work points for my son, no work points for me, and all we have to eat is sorghum!"

"Maybe Yang's brother just forgot your work points," suggested a neighbor.

"No, they're against me. I'm going to the commune office to press charges."

When Yang Chi-wang's brother heard this he said, "OK, if you tell on me you'll get even fewer points in the future."

That same week Chi Tseng-chien's wife and Chi Wan-ch'ang's wife both got mad at team leader Yang Chi-wang's wife. Tseng-chien's wife was called "Little Airplane" because she talked so fast and walked so fast. Wan-ch'ang's wife was called "Potato" because she was short and round. On the basis that everyone had to do her share, Little Airplane and Potato had been hustled out to pick castor beans against their will, but the team leader's wife never showed up.

"We knew she wouldn't come," said Potato. "She's too busy supervising the building of that big new house so she can rent rooms out to workers and get help from them with baby-sitting."

With that she let out a stream of curses, the kind of original curses she was famous for.

Why was all this included under "class struggle"?

Because Potato's husband was a rightist under supervision by the people, just as his father had been before him. People knew the father, Chi An-hsing, as "three sides red"; that is, he made out well under three different regimes. When Yen Hsi-shan ruled Shansi, he collected rent as a landlord. When the Japanese came, he ran through a fortune smoking opium. By the time the Eighth Route Army liberated Southeast Shansi, he had impoverished himself to the point where he received land in the land reform. How lucky could one get?

Chi An-hsing's wife was called "Big Black Bean." She pushed son Wan-ch'ang's marriage to Potato even though he was under attack for his ancestry and his record. He had been a medical service man for Yen Hsi-shan. When captured, he joined the Eighth Route Army, but came home still carrying a rightist label. In the Cultural Revolution he linked up with a group called the *Stormy Petrels*. When they seized power he "jumped very high." But the *Stormy Petrels* didn't hold power very long and the disappointed Wan-ch'ang complained, "Now you are sitting on the power I once held." Nobody could get along with him. When he disliked someone it showed on his face, which was always looking up because he was so much shorter than others.

The Sixth Team earned notoriety for Chin Er-k'uei, who beat up his vice-team leader Yen-hsin. Chin always criticized the team leaders. He told anyone who would listen that none of the leaders, at team or brigade level, spoke the truth anymore.

The question was, Why were the rank-and-file of the Sixth Team so inactive? Were there bad elements operating behind the scenes? Troublemaker Chin Er-k'uei's membership in the Communist Party made this question urgent.

The Sixth Team also included the eighteen-year-old orphan Shen Shou-sheng. He lived alone in the house inherited from his parents and often stayed up all night. When his married sister, twenty-one years old, came home, which was often, groups of rowdy railroad workers dropped in to party until dawn. What sort of goings on were these?

If certain team leaders came in for abuse, brigade leaders also got their share. Some of the work team members planted corn on unused land by the highway. To prevent its being stolen they harvested it prematurely, husked it in the brigade office quadrangle, and threw the husks into the brigade office privy.

When some members of the Second Team came to haul away the night soil, they found the privy was full of semidecayed cornhusks.

"Why so many husks?" asked one.

"They're from the brigade office, obviously," said another.

"So that's where all the corn goes," said a third.

"Why does this shit stink so much?" asked a fourth.

"Because it's not made from dried sweet potatoes," came the answer. The remark implied that unlike the average Long Bow family, now subsisting on dried sweet potatoes from Honan, the brigade leaders were feasting themselves nightly on nourishing fresh corn.

When it came to Fast Chin, not only the brigade leaders but the Revolutionary Committee leaders of the commune itself served as targets for his scorn.

When Secretary Chang walked down from commune headquarters to look over the preparations for the wheat planting, he told Chin to be sure and spread the compost heaps evenly over the fields so that the wheat could come up and grow evenly. In response Chin turned his head and spat on the ground.

Later Chin and team member Kuo worked together sowing wheat. Chin applied about fifteen catties of seed per mou. Kuo questioned whether this was enough. "According to the Commune directive the wide-furrow method requires twenty catties."

"If you just open your hand a little you can apply sixty," replied Chin. What kind of a remark was that?

Some propaganda team members thought it was counterrevolutionary. The Commune Party Committee had decided on twenty catties. Now Fast Chin was casting doubt on their directive. What did he want to do? Set up his own Central Committee? Wasn't he trying to wreck the fall sowing, wreck the brigade and wreck socialism?

On the very next night something even more shocking occurred, for that was the night that Splayfoot Tseng, drunk and staggering slightly, walked the full length of the main street from north to south singing "Curse in the Hall" at the top of his lungs. With this song he launched an attack not only on the brigade leaders, but on the cadres of the commune and on the City Party Committee. Had they not selected and approved the new leading body in Long Bow?

This time, Lin T'ung said, Splayfoot had gone too far. It was time to take the lid off the local class struggle and settle accounts with all class enemies. She proposed a confrontation with the Two Gems, their gang and all like-minded wrongdoers. Smart Fan, Security Officer Shen and Huang Chia-huan, the steelworker, backed her up with enthusiasm. Judge Kao demurred, but Veteran Wang, supported by Donkey Meat Wang, opposed the action as premature. Wang was loath to lump so many diverse phenomena under any single label. He wanted time to investigate.

Veteran Wang felt that the team leaders, by piling all these incidents together as "class struggle," undermined the meaning of the concept. Most of the conflicts looked more like "contradictions among the people"—

personal animosities, family frictions, gripes and grievances blown up to the point of confrontation. Bad as stealing was, it was primarily the work of the children of the poor, of a few railroad workers out for a treat, or of a few well-known rascals who hadn't done an honest day's work since before Liberation. As for singing "Curse in the Hall," perhaps Splayfoot had a legitimate grievance.

Why call all this "class struggle"?

It was important to call things by their right names, Wang argued. If cadres failed to call things by their right names, how could they ever understand the problems that faced them, much less solve them? How could they develop self- and mutual criticism? How could they use rectification to right wrongs?

Perhaps the lack of enthusiasm shown by the peasants for the whole rectification process had its roots in opposition to the loose way leaders had of tossing dangerous accusations about. People might well be tired of endless movements, protracted self- and mutual criticism, repeated rectification, but maybe what they really rejected was overblown rhetoric that turned misdemeanors into crimes, dissent into counterrevolution, old friends and allies into enemies, and lumped all negative phenomena, whether lethal or benign, into one big heap labeled "class struggle."

Were these distortions inadvertent excesses, annoying ripples on the broad river of an ongoing revolution? Or were they the burgeoning expression of a wrong political line that could bring the whole revolution to a halt?

At that point, halfway through our stay in Long Bow, we could barely formulate the question, much less arrive at an answer. What we felt was a deep unease about the direction the movement was taking, an unease that grew into alarm in the weeks that followed.

Volume
Two
THE CULTURAL REVOLUTION

By January, 1965, having analyzed capitalist restoration in the Soviet Union and the bitter post-leap struggle within the Chinese Party, Mao concluded that the Chinese revolution was in jeopardy and the enemy was those in authority in the party leadership taking the capitalist road. The Great Proletarian Cultural Revolution was about to begin.

Mark Selden, *The People's Republic of China: A Documentary History of Revolutionary Change*

Part VI

THE ABSOLUTE
CORRECTNESS
OF THE PRESENT

The tension between action *and* belief *is far better
understood than the tension between* belief *and* doc-
trine. . . . *Where the belief and the propaganda of a
ruling class differ significantly, the class becomes the
victim of a cynicism which inevitably penetrates
throughout society.*

Michael Szkolny, *"Revolution in Poland"*

60

STOP, THIEF!

A dozen young women in bright flowered tunics, embroidered aprons and dark silk slacks sprang forward in unison, took a short step, brought their hoes down as if to split the ground, then swung them overhead in preparation for another rhythmic blow. As their hoes flew upward the dancers fell back half a step, shifted to the left, then sprang forward once more as if working their way across the top of a barren mountain. Each advance brought a new slice of soil under symbolic attack. One could see in this pattern, perhaps, the origin of the Yangko, that basic four-step figure of North China's rock step—a right-left forward drive, then a soft right-left retreat. As they leaped and swung their hoes, the women sang at the top of their voices a song called "K'ai Huang" (Opening Wasteland). With its words and rhythm they created an illusion of joyous urgency, energy and commitment, as if the only thing in the world that mattered was turning over the soil and celebrating it in song.

In real life Long Bow youth had not distinguished themselves in this or any other form of farm production, but when it came to dramatic presentations that was a different matter. Talented singers, dancers and actors emerged from every courtyard on occasions such as this, an evening of local theater staged to compensate for the lack of entertainment that had marred Long Bow's great seasonal fair. These young performers had the power to lift their audience right out of everyday life into a magic world that even someone as skeptical as I had no trouble believing in.

The star of the group was the twenty-year-old daughter of Pei Liang-shun, leader of the Second Production Team. Medium in height, plump and broad of face, she didn't have the svelte figure one might expect of a lead performer, but as soon as she began to dance she dispelled all negative impressions by the grace and coordination of her movements, each of which flowed so smoothly from the one preceding it that she seemed to float above the stage without effort or design. She captured the attention of the audience so completely that many could not say who else performed before them. It was not that one could find fault with any of the other dancers, it was simply that none of them could begin to match the overpowering stage presence, the perfection of timing and motion, that young Pei so effortlessly displayed. Her rounded limbs and torso, her brightly rouged and powdered face, defined her as a model of rural health and happiness, a poster-style symbol of modern collective life such as an artist might paint for the magazine *China Reconstructs*. Her voice, sustained in high register, blended with the chorus, yet stood out enough to form a central pillar of sound around which the other voices clustered in support. I found it hard to choose between her singing and her dancing. Both seemed beyond reproach that night.

Next to Pei's magnificent daughter, the most appealing personality on the stage was the descendant of one of Long Bow's expropriated gentry, the landlord Sheng Ching-ho. Though she moved and sang and smiled along with the rest, I detected in her face a hint of the pain and sadness that a "hard" class origin must bring to the life of any offspring of a "struggle object." Most of the time she succeeded in covering her feelings with a noncommittal, masklike set of the eyes and other features, but now and then her control lapsed, revealing an inner self not quite certain of welcome, not quite at ease among colleagues who, by contrast, felt completely in tune with each other, with the music and with the audience. Knowing the depth of the discrimination applied to second-generation landlords and rich peasants, knowing how often fellow villagers must have flung the "feudal tail" of her ancestry in her face, I was surprised to see the young woman performing in public at all. Apparently she had found in Long Bow's Theater Group a place where, temporarily at least, she might be judged by her talent and not by her grandfather's landholdings. Nevertheless it took a special brand of courage to come out, to practice, to dress up and to perform before the whole community. Others of her origin and generation had given up. They rarely left home except to report for work.

The "Opening Wasteland" dance was followed by a solo from the throat of a willowy thirteen-year-old who stepped out alone and unafraid. A long face, a miniature mouth and a receding chin, features that taken singly were not very appealing, all combined in the graceful singer to create astonishing beauty. She captivated the audience almost as completely as Pei's daughter had. Her high, thin voice, clear as a bamboo flute at dawn, expressed intense emotion. I found the emotion hard to analyze. It was joyful, yet nostalgic, lively and at the same time lonely, revealing the inner tension felt by a young woman just beginning to be conscious of the world beyond her village, wanting to step forth with exuberance and hope, yet not quite sure of the shape of the future and therefore still reluctant to abandon childhood.

The stillness that pervaded the hall as the teenager sang lingered on after she finished, only to be suddenly shattered by six young men who came stomping onto the stage like a bunch of wild steers. Their sudden appearance before us in perfect alignment, staring expectantly as if we and not they were about to perform, brought the entire audience to uproarious laughter. By playing a gang of self-absorbed bumpkins, uncertain as to why they had come or what might happen next, they plunged us into a comic world as convincing as the romantic one they had so rudely destroyed, and our willingness to go along enhanced not only the excitement of the plunge but the depth of our enjoyment once they got their act underway.

One verse form in China requires each participant to start out with the last word uttered by the preceding speaker and to create a new verse based upon it as rapidly as possible. By custom the humor is supposed to become broader and more biting with each effort and those who are waiting to speak are free to add whatever flourishes, instrumental sounds or back talk they desire.

Suddenly the six on the stage launched into such a rhyming contest. They must have memorized it beforehand, but they spoke as if making it up on the spot. Each young man stood with absolute solemnity, waiting his turn, then fired off his lines with staccato precision and ended up saying *teng per ch'ang* in imitation of a drum and cymbals, while the next speaker held forth with his lines. Each imitated drum and cymbal with a straight face, but with anger in his voice, as if the mere creation of the sounds gave pain, as if surprised at having to use his vocal cords at all instead of beating out the real sounds with instruments. This sequence brought rollicking laughter from the audience and sustained applause when it was over.

The young men followed up the rhyme, called an "add on," with a short skit in rhymed couplets about the importance of studying Tachai. After each verse the six participants did a little dance in unison—one step forward, one step sideways and one step backward. They performed these steps, like the *teng per ch'ang*s of the previous number, with appropriate solemnity and with a certain studied clumsiness, as if they had just emerged from a compost pile and were shaking the manure off their feet. The dance brought down the house. I found myself laughing uncontrollably along with everyone around me. Yet the young men on the stage never so much as smiled as they went through each succeeding verse and the comic foot routine that followed. What made this act particularly delightful was the knowledge that the performers were not really clumsy, that this uncouth, compost-pile step was something they had created to instill in us a vision of back-country rustics just learning to dance. Not incompetence but art had set the theme.

While the audience still labored to catch its breath after this hilarious version of "Learning from Tachai," the young men launched into a little play called "Four Carrying Poles of Turnips." A quartet of stalwarts strode onto the stage, each individual weighed down with two large baskets of garden produce hanging from the opposite ends of a carrying pole. They sang:

> "Out of the east fresh winds whirl,
> In turbulent air red flags unfurl.
> To our motherland the winds of spring
> A new upsurge of change will bring.
> Upon this stage we four will tell
> Of four poles of turnips we hope to sell."

"What the devil is there to tell about four poles of turnips?" asks one of the players, temporarily stepping out of his role as a young man on the way to market.

"Comrade, don't get uptight! Stop worrying," responds another. "There's plenty to tell about these turnips. What with all the twists and turns we'll be lucky to get through it. And the point of the whole thing is that class struggle on the economic front is not as simple as it looks."

"Well, what do you know!" says the doubter. "Let's get on with it then."

And so the play begins, with an old poor peasant named Wang, rising before dawn, to lead his three companions, all heavily laden with turnips, to the market at the county seat. Soon they come across a shadowy figure lurking at the crossroads in the morning mist. *Kuei kuei sui sui* (devil devil, evil evil) speaks the man, obsequious as a beggar.

"Could you tell me if, by any chance, those turnips might be for sale?"

"What do you mean, for sale?" respond the four, shocked.

> "Take it easy, don't shout.
> There's nothing to fight about.
> Sell to me, I'll make it plain,
> Fifty cents a pole you'll gain!"

Incensed at this speculative offer outside the market, Old Wang calls on his cohorts to hurry onward. But the "devil devil, evil evil" speculator is not so easily shaken off. Running ahead, he again intercepts them and this time offers eighty cents above the market price.

"Stop," says Old Wang. "Put your baskets down."

The speculator is overjoyed. "Flowers bloom in his heart." He digs a pack of Heavenly Gate cigarettes—China's most prestigious brand—out of his coat pocket and offers Old Wang a smoke, repeatedly passing the pack under the old man's nose so that he will not miss the overwhelmingly attractive aroma.

But!

> "Old Wang is such a wonderful man,
> Divert him from socialism no one can!
> With a face full of anger dark
> And a voice full of thunder stark
> He announces on the spot creation
> Of a meeting for repudiation.
> Smash all cow devils and snake gods
> Who cheat the state and twist the odds!"

Right there at the crossroads the unreformed exconvict turned speculator, for so he proves to be, is treated to a mass denunciation joined by all who happen to pass by. After "shaking this criminal like a sifter screen and looking right through him, hole by hole," Old Wang shoulders his pole of turnips and leads his three companions down the road to the vegetable market.

> "The sun now rises from its eastern bed,
> Ten thousand li all bathed in red,
> As we journey toward the morning sun
> Heroic feelings our hearts overrun!"

The audience greeted this play, performed with such gusto by the Long Bow youths, with equal gusto. It challenged the conscience of the community. Many remembered the summer of 1960, when, having sent all their manure to the "10,000-Mou Square" in the north, they had nothing left with which to grow crops at home. Long Bow peasants, in despair, put in a catch crop of turnips and reaped an enormous harvest. Because of the general shortage that year, they sold it all at speculative prices. In the midst of general disaster turnips brought them the highest per capita earnings in the brigade's history. But if Long Bow residents prospered that year, the city and the region did not, and this kind of dog-eat-dog, devil-take-the-hind-most spirit did nothing to revive production or construction. In the long run it could only spell disaster for everyone, including the temporarily prosperous Long Bow residents. "Four Carrying Poles of Turnips" was a raw polemic against the speculative fever that so permeated Southeast Shansi in 1960 and still infected many individuals ten years later. As they watched, people recognized both their past and their present. They appreciated the play immensely and gave it more applause than they offered to any other production that night. But whether that was because they took its message to heart or simply enjoyed the verve with which it was performed was hard to determine.

By the time "Four Carrying Poles of Turnips" began, Long Bow residents had packed the meeting hall in the brigade compound. Not only had most of the brigade's own members showed up with their families, but many of the railroad and construction workers who rented lodgings in Long Bow had also crowded in. Most of them could not find room to sit down. Even those who came early, bringing their own stools and bricks, had to stand in the end because as soon as the dances and skits began the people in front stood up to see better, forcing everyone behind them to stand up in order to see at all.

Under the clear night sky a spectator could remain outside the hall and watch everything through the central doorway or one of the window openings on the north wall. Since no one had ever fitted the doorway with a door or any of the windows with frame or pane, all openings served equally well for going in and coming out. They also served as vantage points for onlookers, standing shoulder to shoulder six or eight deep, as they craned their necks to follow the action on the stage. On this occasion almost as many people stood outside, looking in, as sat or stood inside under the roof, a tribute to the popularity of the performers.

The plays, skits and songs provided a diversion, an interlude of "culture" before the real business of the evening began. The real business turned out to be the continuation of the Party rectification campaign. The propaganda team had called the whole brigade together to hear brigade Party Secretary Chang Kuei-ts'ai repeat his self-criticism.

Chang made essentially the same points he had already made, a few days before, in front of the Second Team. As he talked the audience began to dwindle. A large number of nonbrigade members, workers and their families who had come for the drama left, as was expected, as soon as the entertainment was over. But Kuei-ts'ai had not talked very long before quite a few brigade members, for whom the self-evaluation of their chosen leader was an important political event, or should have been, also began to leave.

Either he made too many general and unfocused remarks—he himself said, "I may put the back in the front and the front in the back"—or people did not consider his leadership a serious issue in the village. Whatever the reason, by the time the Party Secretary finished, only half the people who should have heard him out remained.

As soon as Secretary Chang sat down, Judge Kao stepped forward and began to talk about class struggle. At that point another third of the audience left.

"What is there to show that we still have to confront class struggle?" asked Kao. "Well, it's obvious. Class enemies are going around doing damage and spreading rumors. And they are also doing a lot of stealing. They are stealing corn right out of the field. Some of the thieves aren't so young, they are thirteen or fourteen years old. One of them is even twenty years old. I heard a rhyme:

"Stealing from the public brings no shame
If you don't do it, you have only you to blame.

"What I say is: All stealing is wrong. We can't excuse it. We must protect our harvest and stand guard over it. Mobilize the masses. Catch the thieves. Repudiate them. . . ."

Just as Judge Kao said these words, Security Officer Shen rushed to the middle of the stage.

"Hold everything," he shouted at the top of his voice, "We have been robbed! Somebody has broken into Li Tien-ch'i's house and has stolen his trunk! Militia squad leaders report at once to the brigade office."

Shen's announcement almost finished the meeting. All those left on the floor started to talk at once. Militia squad leaders sprang to their feet and rushed toward the door or the nearest window. A lot of other people, taking advantage of the interruption and not too interested in "class struggle" anyway, did likewise.

Judge Kao and Security Officer Shen tried to hold things together. Kao went on with his speech as if nothing had happened, but the action had shifted to the brigade office where Smart Fan and Pipefitter Huang had called the militia squad leaders together and were trying to decide what to do about the daring robbery.

Nobody had much information to go on.

Investigators called first on the victim, Li T'ien-ch'i's mother, for a lively blow-by-blow version of the incident that led nowhere in terms of identifying the culprit.

The old lady, according to her own account, rarely went out. But this evening, tempted by the skits and plays, she broke precedent and departed for the brigade hall. As she locked the door to her house she said to an old neighbor in the same yard, "We are all going out. Please listen for trouble. Keep an eye peeled." Then she stepped gingerly on bound feet into the gathering gloom and joined her son, her daughter and her daughter-in-law in the crowd before the stage.

As soon as the last performance concluded she and her son left the hall. Young Li hurried home, saw nothing amiss in the courtyard, entered his own quarters and lay down to sleep. The old lady, walking very slowly down pitch-dark streets and lanes, arrived home somewhat later.

"Who's there?" her son called out.

"Me," said the old lady.

Painstakingly she opened the door with her key and lay down on the kang, worn out. Before dozing off she felt, out of habit, for her precious wooden box. She kept many small valuables and over 200 yuan in cash concealed in it. Her hand felt only empty space.

"We've been robbed!" she shrieked. "We've been robbed!"

Her son ran in. "What's the matter?"

"The box! It's gone."

"No. That can't be," said young Li. "Was the lock in place on the door?"

"Yes. I unlocked it as usual, just now."

"Then maybe you've misplaced the box?"

"How could that be? What do you take me for? It's gone, I tell you, it's gone!"

Li searched frantically. When he couldn't find any box, he examined the door. When he pulled the door chain, it fell apart. One link in the chain had worn out long ago. He had replaced it with several strands of looped wire. The thief had cut the wire with pliers and removed the chain, padlock and all. On leaving he had looped the chain in place and refastened the wire with a twist of the pliers. Thus the padlock remained untouched.

As his mother began to weep and wail at the top of her voice, Li ran off to the brigade office to report disaster. Within a few minutes not only the militia squad leaders but many militia men and women came pouring out of the meeting, ready for action.

Militia leaders discussed three possibilities:

1. The thief had already carried the box home. If this was the case, he must soon carry it out again because he would not dare to keep so large a piece of evidence around.

2. The thief had carried the box out into the fields for temporary concealment. If so, he would have to carry it back into the village later.

3. The thief had already taken the box somewhere else. But even if he had, he couldn't have taken it far because the thief must be local. No outsider would know that the whole Li family had gone off to see the plays. No outsider would know that they possessed a box with something valuable inside.

Smart Fan suggested mobilizing every member of the militia, posting guards at or near the home of every possible suspect, and at the same time surrounding the entire village with sentries so that no one could enter or leave the fields without being seen. Security Officer Shen and Pipefitter Huang issued all the orders necessary for carrying out such a strategy. Then Smart Fan, Shen, and the rest of the propaganda team cadres returned to the meeting, leaving law and order in the hands of Militia Captain Lu Ho-jen.

In the meeting hall Judge Kao was still holding forth on the question of class struggle. His audience, now drastically diminished, found it hard to settle down. As the Judge droned on, private conversations, some of them very animated, rippled across the floor.

"The struggle for high yields of wheat," Judge Kao declaimed, "is also class struggle. We want high yields. But there are some who are content with low yields. Isn't this in opposition to the study of Tachai? Isn't this a class question? Two classes, two lines! Our enemies have not suddenly become honest, they haven't given up. So we have no alternative but to battle it out.

"We are asking for furrowed wheat that can be irrigated. For wheat like this we have to sow twenty catties per mou. That is the standard set by the commune leadership. But on the Second Team we found people who were only sowing fifteen. A lively discussion of sowing rates developed and one team member said, 'All you have to do is loosen your fingers a little and you can sow sixty catties.'

"What sort of words are these? These are reactionary words, wrecking words. They are not the words of a good person. They are spoken by someone who hopes we will do wrong. We are aiming at a 500-catty harvest and he is unhappy.

"Such words, such wrong thoughts have to be exposed wherever they show their heads. Wives should not cover up for husbands, children for parents, or parents for children either. To protect wrongdoing only helps the wrongdoer develop into a real criminal, perhaps into a class enemy. If you make a mistake and don't recognize it, it can turn into an enemy contradiction, and you can develop into a class enemy. In time you can go from good to bad."

Judge Kao's serious warning had no apparent effect on what remained of his audience. The random conversations on the floor continued, even expanded, with five or six people putting their heads together to gossip about the disappearance of the Li family box. Security Officer Shen, upset by the equanimity of the peasants, jumped onto the stage and took the floor, intent on driving home the point about class struggle which Judge Kao had raised with such indifferent results.

"We have to grasp class struggle," shouted Shen, his voice carrying forcefully to the four corners of the room. He was not lecturing like the Judge. He was declaiming.

"People are destroying crops and stealing grain. Just now somebody stole a trunk, broke the lock on the door of a home, and stole a trunk. Someone else sang 'Curse in the Hall' on the street. What was he cursing? It was not the deed of a good person. It was the deed of a dangerous element. He doesn't admire the Eight Model Works. He admires the old operas."

Security Officer Shen suddenly switched from anonymous charges and called out:

"Fast Chin, is he here?"

No answer came from the floor.

"No. He doesn't even come to important meetings. But he's the one who said, 'Just open your hand and you can sow sixty catties.' What is this if not a scheme to wreck the 'three-fall' tasks, to wreck learning from Tachai? Reasonable close planting is scientific planting, but who ever heard of sixty catties per mou. What is this if not class struggle?

"And then there is Lin Yao-lung. He cursed the oil pressing plant because the machine broke down. But why curse? If you have criticisms take them up with the leadership. What was behind all that cursing? Wasn't it an effort to wreck relations between our Sidelines Team and the oil-pressing plant? After all that cursing the plant didn't want our people anymore and they had to come home.

"Because we ran out of grain we had to get 10,000 catties back from the state. It was supposed to go to those who needed it most. But class enemies fanned up dissatisfaction. They went around saying, 'He got some, why not you?' Some people fell for it and got very upset. 'I've worked for the revolution but now I don't get any grain.' What kind of consciousness is that?

"In the surburban area a dance troupe has issued a call for dancers and actresses. Some Long Bow peasants just dropped their wheat planting and ran over to try out for a part. The troupe has a good goal—to propagate Mao Tse-tung Thought—but if you run off in the middle of the wheat planting how does that fit in with Mao Tse-tung Thought? Almost twenty people ran off. They had no discipline at all. We have to grasp class struggle."

The more Shen talked, the more serious the class problem loomed in his mind. Class struggle, it seemed, permeated everything.

"Tonight, as long as the plays were on the stage, our hall was full. But as soon as the performers retired many people left. We ought to check up and see who it was that ran off. There is a saying, 'Before doing anything, first look at the line [the political meaning].' When people walk out on a meeting just because the play is over, doesn't it show a very low level of political consciousness? And what about all those people who persist in carrying out their little meetings on the floor? What about those who bring their sewing and their knitting? Even when they are criticized they go right on sewing, doing what they have been doing all along.

"We can't go to sleep with the red flag flying over us and not pay attention to the enemies sharpening their knives. Class struggle is sharp. We must be vigilant. Lots of strange things are happening. Why? Because we have relaxed, we haven't carried the struggle to the enemy in on-the-spot meetings that stop them in their tracks."

At this point Shen realized that perhaps he had gone a little too far. He had attacked every person in the room. The very fact that these people were still there meant that they were the vanguard of the community. The less conscious, the less disciplined, had long since departed for home. He abruptly changed his line of thought and his tone.

"Class struggle means to attack the bad, but it also means to praise the good. We ought to praise people like All Here Li, who worked at cart repair several nights in a row although his leg was badly swollen, and Kuo Cheng-k'uan, who maintains enthusiasm for production even though he is getting old."

Coming at last to the conclusion of his speech, Shen dropped class struggle altogether and went back to wheat planting.

"Let's repudiate the theory that wheat is a low-yield crop. To think this way is to think at a low level. If we raise the level of our thoughts, we will raise the level of our yields. Now I want to propose a *six don't* policy.

> "Without 200 tan of compost per mou, don't sow wheat.
> Without leveling the land, don't sow wheat.
> Without selecting good seeds, don't sow wheat.
> Without close planting, don't sow wheat.
> Without irrigation, don't sow wheat.
> Without careful weeding don't sow wheat."

It was getting very late. The people on the floor stirred restlessly. Some more of them began to leave.

Shen finally concluded his remarks with an order to all team leaders and political directors:

"Write down the names of all those who left the meeting early and send them in."

With that everyone vacated the hall.

In the meantime the militia completely surrounded the village. Where the houses stopped and the fields began, a militiaman stood guard at every 100-foot interval.

The strategy worked.

Near midnight one of the sentries, Shen Er-chiang, young Li's brother-in-law, heard a rustling noise in the castor bean field west of the village and saw a slight figure of a man, carrying a box, walk out. He followed what he took to be the thief right into the village and straight to the courtyard of one-armed Ch'en San.

"Who goes there?" he shouted, rushing up.

"Me."

It was Chi Chung-ch'i, Ch'en's son, a twenty-year-old whom no one had thought to suspect.

"What do you have there?"

"A box."

"Where did you find it?"

"In the castor bean field."

"Give it to me," said Shen Er-chiang, grabbing the box out of Chi's hands and striding off with it.

Chi stood silently in the middle of the courtyard.

"Aren't you coming?" asked Shen without slackening his pace and without turning back.

Chi gave no answer. He watched the militiaman disappear in the darkness, then went into his room and lay down.

Shen carried the box triumphantly to his mother-in-law's home.

"Where's the thief?" asked the old lady.

"He didn't come," said Shen.

"But without the thief you can't prove anything!"

"Who cares?" said Shen Er-chiang. "How can he get away? It's Chi Chung-ch'i. I can find him anytime I want."

That proved to be true. Half an hour later, when Er-chiang and a fellow militiaman, Dog Child, went to the Ch'en courtyard to look for Chi Chung-ch'i, they found him fast asleep on his kang.

They pulled him rudely to his feet.

"What do you want?" asked the startled sleeper.

"You're under arrest for stealing a box," said Shen.

"What box? I don't know anything about a box," said Chi.

They hustled him off to the brigade office nevertheless, assigned a man to guard him, then went to find Security Officer Shen and other members of the propaganda team.

When the two militiamen came back with several cadres, Chi was gone.

"Where did he go?"

"He went to the toilet," said the guard.

But the toilet proved to be empty. Chi had climbed the compound wall and run away.

Once again Shen alerted the entire militia. In the middle of the night 100 men combed the village and the surrounding fields for Chi Chung-ch'i, but to no avail. At four in the morning most of them gave up and went to bed.

"We'll look for him in the morning," Shen said.

As he said it Chi appeared, hands bound, with the militiaman Dog Child behind him, pushing him along.

"Where did you find him?"

"Take a guess."

"No use guessing."

"He went home again. He was asleep on his kang."

Poor Chi Chung-ch'i. The future looked dark for him. Everyone said he could hardly avoid becoming a thief. The Chi family had buried an ancestor in a "thief's head grave." Chis had been thieves in the past and, because of the position of the grave, they would be thieves in the future. If one stood in front of the ancestral grave and looked eastward toward the Taihang Mountains, one could see the distant peaks clearly. If one then went into a squat, the mountains disappeared altogether. But if one rose to a half-standing position, one could see the tip of one mountain and a tree. This half-squat, half-standing position was said to be the stance of a thief, hence the grave was a thief's head grave, and everyone descended from the men buried there would surely end up a thief.

But, some objected, Chi Chung-ch'i was not a male line descendant. His father's name was Ch'en. Only his mother was a Chi. How could the grave determine his fate? Only because he had changed his name, said the geomancers. His mother's brother had posthumously adopted him so that he could inherit the dead man's house. To be an heir he had to take the man's name. Having taken the name, he inherited the fate that all Chis must bear because of their ancestor's thief's head grave. Geomancy, like astrology, took pity on no one.

61

VICTIM VICTIMIZED

 On the evening of September 20, after another long day in the fields, we dropped by the brigade office to catch up on the news. There we found Judge Kao pacing soberly up and down while the thief, Chi Chung-ch'i, wrote out a description of his crime. Chi was a stunted youth, lean to the point of emaciation, with an ashen face and the dark stubble of an incipient beard on his chin. He looked closer to fifteen than twenty years old and clearly must always have had trouble holding his own at field work. We were told that he could earn only seven points a day, while his peers earned ten. With two dependents his standard of living could not possibly be anything but meager.

On the table beside Chi lay many assorted bits of hardware that had been found in his home. We could see light bulbs, a crescent wrench with "Pig Farm" burned into the handle, a folding knife, some box wrenches, a few bicycle tools, some small armatures, a big electric motor casing and a grease fitting on the end of a flexible tube. On the floor sat the now famous Li family box, 15 by 15 by 20 inches in size. It was made of brown, unpainted wood. A small metal lock secured the lid.

Some of the items on the table seemed to match losses reported that day by various peasants who had come to the brigade office to blame Chi Chung-ch'i for everything that had disappeared around the village during the last month. Articles they now said they missed included two new bicycle tires, a canvas breeching strap, eight assorted carpentry tools, electric wires for the new pumping station, a set of wrenches, a pair of pliers and a light bulb from the pig farm.

Instead of questioning the suspect about each of these articles, Judge Kao demanded that he write a new confession. If the young man's arrest and daylong interrogation had accomplished its purpose, there would be no need to confront him with further evidence. He would list everything himself.

While Chi Chung-ch'i sat in the dim light of a single, low-powered bulb writing each ideograph with painstaking care, Judge Kao told us what had happened since Chi escaped from the village lockup in the middle of the night.

At four in the morning the militiaman, Dog Child, found the suspected thief asleep once more on his own kang. He arrested him for the second time and escorted him back to the brigade office. There Security Officer Shen and Smart Fan questioned him until daylight, but for a long time Chi strongly denied knowing anything about the Li family box that militiaman Shen Er-chiang had taken right out of his hands.

"I was at the performance from beginning to end," said Chi. "When Shen announced that a box had been stolen I ran out along with everyone else, to help find the thief. If you don't believe me ask my friends Ho Kuei, Meng Ta-nien or Wu Pao-pei. I was with them the whole time."

When questioned young Ho confirmed this story but the other two weren't sure. True, they had all gone to the performance together, but when they got there the hall was so crowded they split up and found seats wherever they could. After the performance, as Secretary Kuei-ts'ai started to speak, young Meng went out. He found Chi Chung-ch'i squatting on his haunches beside the door. But Meng could not affirm that Chi had been there all along.

Chi's story sagged further when it turned out that he could describe in detail only the first three of the seven plays and skits that had been per-formed. He could recall only the general outline of the last four and could not say who had performed what part. (In the meantime, militiamen search-ing his home found many articles, tools and odds and ends that appeared to have been stolen.) Pursuing the advantage, Shen made clear to Chi that he could win lenient treatment by talking frankly but would be punished severely if he remained defiant. Just as daylight began to dispel the darkness in the courtyard outside, the youth broke down, wept profusely and admit-ted stealing the Li family box.

The next day, about noon, Judge Kao took over the questioning.
"Name?"
"Chi Chung-ch'i."
"Age?"
"Twenty."
"Class origin?"
"Lower-middle peasant."
"How many in the family?"
"Three. My father, my younger brother and I."
"Their ages?"
"My father is seventy, my younger brother fourteen. He's in school."
"Have you been to school?"
"I went about one year to Horse Square Primary School. But my mother died when I was quite young, so I came home to work in the brigade."
"How many years have you been working?"
"Five or six."
"Do you belong to any organization?"
"Not really. But in the Cultural Revolution I joined the *Guard the East Regiment.*"
"We heard that your mother gave you to her brother."
"Yes."
"What is your father's name?"
"Ch'en, but my uncle's name was Chi, so that's the name I have."

"How many people in your uncle's household?"

"None. I never saw any member of the family that adopted me. My uncle was dead before they gave me his name and made me his heir."

This unusual answer puzzled Judge Kao. When he asked around he found that Chung-ch'i's mother and her brother Chi En-te had arranged for the boy to become the child of an older, childless brother so that his house would remain in the family. By taking his dead uncle's name, Chung-ch'i became the son of the deceased and inherited half of his house. The other half went to Uncle Chi En-te's adopted son, Chi Ta-hung, a delinquent and habitual thief. Ta-hung didn't like the arrangement. As the nearest male heir on the paternal side he expected to inherit the whole house. He ignored Chung-ch'i's claim and went to the brigade leaders for permission to sell the property. This angered the dead uncle's widow, who felt that once her nephew sold the house the family would break up and the family name would disappear. There would be no offspring on hand to look after the ancestral graves. She accused Chang Hsin-fa, then brigade chairman, and Chang Kuei-ts'ai, then vice-chairman, of selling out Chi family interests for a few cigarettes, eggs and other small gifts which she said Ta-hung had showered on the brigade leaders in order to win their approval. When they refused to listen to her complaint, she took the case to the Changchih City court.

Judge Lin summoned Hsin-fa and Kuei-ts'ai before him and asked crossly just what they had received from Chi Ta-hung in return for favors rendered.

Chang Kuei-ts'ai lost his temper. "Your mother's———," said Chang to the Judge. "You sit on this court and eat the people's millet, but for what? Since you already know that I have been bought off, you had better tell me how it happened, tell me what my price is. As far as I'm concerned I don't give a damn. I'll piss all over you. I dare you to arrest me here and now."

Chang's outburst brought Chief Judge Chin to the scene. He had once served as a liaison officer in the Fifth District of Lucheng County. He knew Kuei-ts'ai well, knew that he could not easily be bought, and asked Judge Lin to apologize. After Judge Lin apologized to Kuei-ts'ai, Kuei-ts'ai apologized to Judge Lin for his belligerent attitude and foul words. They then settled the case amicably. The court drew up a legal document stating that while Ta-hung owned half the house, Chung-ch'i owned the other half, and that each had the right to sell as he wished. In the end it was Chung-ch'i who sold, receiving 380 yuan for his two-section share. He continued to live with his true father, Ch'en, and his younger brother. But the Chi family name hung heavy on his head. For 380 yuan he had inherited a thief's head grave to tend, and destiny as a thief into the bargain. Half the community fully expected him to come to no good and their scorn helped ensure that the prediction would come true.

Unlike some of Long Bow's native sons, however, Judge Kao had no use at all for the ominous influence of the thief's head grave. He assured the young man that the village would be lenient to anyone who spoke frankly and made a clean breast of the past.

"You are young. You come from a lower-middle peasant family. If you cooperate with us you will have a bright future."

"The way I see it, I'm done for," said Chi Chung-ch'i gloomily. "My whole future is dark. I have this stain on me. How can it ever be washed out?"

"One stain can't ruin your whole life," said Kao. "As long as you learn a lesson from this, your future is whatever you wish to make of it. No one can avoid a mistake or two, the important thing is to learn from mistakes, correct them quickly, and avoid them in the future. So you had better say what you have been thinking about in the last few hours. We are concerned for your future. You should be concerned for it also. What road have you chosen?"

At this point Chung-ch'i broke down. Tears welled in his eyes. "I can't face Mao Tse-tung. I can't face the poor peasants, I can't . . ." his voice trailed off.

"Well you had better tell us exactly what happened."

"Last night, as the show began I saw Li Tien-ch'i's mother in the audience. This meant that there was probably no one at their home. I had often been there and knew where they kept their things. So I slipped out, broke into the old lady's room, took the box, hid it in the field, and came back to the meeting. When word came that someone had robbed the Li house, I rushed out to investigate the matter along with everyone else."

"Were you alone when you broke in?"

"Yes."

"Did you use pliers?"

"Well, when I left the meeting I first went home after the pliers. They had replaced one link in the chain with wire. I cut it and went in. I took the box and hid it in the field. Later, after everything had quieted down in the village I went out to bring the box home. But Er-chiang saw me, grabbed the box and ran off. He called back, 'Aren't you coming?' but I said, 'No,' and went on home. I tried to go to sleep and that's where Dog Child found me."

"Just when did you slip out of the meeting hall?"

"After the third skit."

"Wasn't there anyone at home when you went to get the pliers?"

"My father was there."

"Did he know what you were up to?"

"He knew that I came in but he didn't know what for."

"Which pair of pliers was it?"

"The one with the green handles."

"Where did you get such a pair?"

"My brother brought them home and gave them to me."

"Where did you leave them last night?"

"On top of the chicken coop, on the bricks there."

"Did you know what was in the box you took?"

"No."

"Why steal it, then?"

"Well, I saw that it had a lock on it and figured there must be something valuable inside!"

"Are you telling the truth now?"

"Yes, of course."

"You wouldn't try to fool anyone now, would you?"

"Certainly not. That's all that happened. I swear."

Judge Kao turned the conversation to a new tack, the motive behind the act.

"Why do you have this capitalist 'get rich quick, get something for nothing' attitude? Have you been thinking about this for a long time?"

"No. Li was a good friend of mine. I often visited there."

"Did they ever open the box while you were there?"

"No."

"Then why did you choose it?"

"There were two boxes, but that one, the small one, had a lock on it."

This did not satisfy Judge Kao. He wanted a self-analysis. "You must tell us when you started to think about stealing. You must get to the roots of this in your own mind; otherwise you won't be able to change. What first put the idea in your head?"

Chung-ch'i didn't answer right away. He thought for a while, then spoke hesitantly. "Li has a sister. I thought, She must have some clothes. In my house there was nothing to lock away. There are only the three of us."

"But what does that have to do with it? What would you want with women's clothes? You couldn't wear them. Besides, they get the same cloth ration that you do."

"But the Li family has more people working than we do. In our family of three I'm the only one working. It's hard for me."

"Then you didn't know they had anything valuable?"

"No."

"You just thought that with more people working they might own more?"

"Yes."

"But there are many other families that are not so badly off?"

"That may be, but I don't know them that well. I'm not familiar with them."

"But thieves often steal from people they don't know, so you had better say why you stole from your friends."

"I knew the house well, and I saw that the whole family was at the hall."

"Is that when the idea came into your head, when you saw Old Lady Li at the play?"

"Well, I always thought they were much better off than me, but I never thought of stealing anything."

"You didn't think of stealing that box?"

"No. I only wanted to open it up."

"How long had you had that idea?"

"Five or six days."

"Why?"

"Because they are so rich."

"What made you think you could get in the door?"

"Well, I saw one link in that chain patched with wire."

"If you only wanted to open the box, why did you walk out with it?"

"I was afraid they'd come back."

"So you were afraid you'd get caught?"

"Well, it was like a bad dream. I wasn't really afraid when I was there. Only afterward I began to be afraid."

"This morning when they arrested you, you said you found the box in the castor bean field. Why?"

"Well, I knew if I spoke frankly I'd get lenient treatment and if I resisted I'd get shot."

"So what sort of statement did you write?"

"A resist statement."

"Well, don't you want lenient treatment?"

"Yes."

"Then why such a statement?"

"That was my thinking at the time."

"What thinking? What sort of illusion did you harbor then?"

"Illusion? I don't know what 'illusion' means."

"Never mind. I only want to know what you were thinking."

"I only thought, if I didn't break the lock no one would know I entered the house."

"And now?"

"Well, now I have thought it through. I want to tell everything just as it happened, return home, and get back to work. Since I'm the only one working in the family I have to worry about that."

"That's good thinking. We can't think only of ourselves, but of socialist construction and world revolution. So how can you get home and back to work?"

"By speaking frankly and telling everything."

"Well, this time have you told everything?"

"Yes. Everything."

"Well, then," said Judge Kao with a note of true disappointment in his voice, "what about all those other things we found in your house?"

"Some of them my brother brought home."

"The chisel?"

"It's Old Ch'en Wan-t'ien's."

"The wrench?"

"I borrowed it from Little Yang at the Cement Plant."

"I don't think you're telling the truth."

"Well, I have another wrench of my own."

"Where did that one come from?"

"I bought it. Yuan-lin's wife bought it for me when she went to Yellow Mill. And Lin Yao-lung bought the light bulbs for me. Old Pei at the locomotive repair shop gave me the socket. He lives in my sister's house at the south end of the village."

"And the ax?"

"It's my own. I bought it in Changyi."

"How long ago?"

"A month or two."

"How much was it?"

"Three yuan, thirty fen."

"Is that the one you hid under the kang?"

"Oh, no, the one you took from the house wasn't mine at all."

That point had already been established. Under the kang in Chung-ch'i's house they had found an ax that had long ago been lent to the pig farm by Swift Li. The pig farm had paid Li 4 yuan for the axe. And here it was in Chung-ch'i's home.

"Obviously you are only telling part of the story," said Judge Kao. "You had better tell everything, including even those things that you think we don't know. That's the only way to ensure your future."

"As for the future I don't even think of it," said Chung-ch'i. "I figure I'm already done for."

At this point Smart Fan, of the Changchih Party Committee, intervened. "Why do you think we haven't already sent you to the police? It's because our policy is one of leniency. We could turn you over to the police but we haven't. You had better think that over and tell us everything. Is there anything else in your house?"

"A piece of iron pipe. I bought it from Lin Yao-lung for 27 fen."

"Is it worth that much?"

"They charge by the catty—3 fen per catty."

"Where did the insulating wire come from?"

"Hsiao Tu [Little Bald] gave it to me when he was putting up the broadcasting wires."

"What else is there in your house?"

"A light socket worth 50 fen. I bought it but I haven't paid for it yet."

"Is that all?"

"Well, there are other bits and pieces but I can't remember everything."

"What bits and pieces?"

"I can't remember."

"Well, remember this, if you conceal anything it won't go well with you."

"It's quite late now," said Security Office Shen. "Let's continue our talk after supper. Then you can try for lenient treatment by telling everything all at once!"

"Yes," said Judge Kao. "You had better go back and write down what you told us this afternoon."

"Can I go home?"

"No. Only when you have told everything and have thought it through and can return home without any burden."

"But I haven't had anything to eat since this morning."

"Didn't they send any food?"

"My father told my brother not to bring me anything. I don't deserve to eat anyway. But I need a drink. Is there any water? Can I drink?"

"Of course. We want you to eat and drink. We want to treat you well. And we want you to recognize your problem. We want you to learn to hate your dirty past."

"Even if I hated it, it wouldn't do any good now."

"Why say that? We'll talk to your father."

"Oh, no, don't talk to my father. He'll only be hurt by what I've done."

"But it won't be a bad thing. It will be an education for him."

"But he can't even look after himself. He has only one hand. He can't take care of himself."

"I see you know what shame is, but you never thought what a shock it would be to the Lis to lose their box. It's hard work, day after day, that earns the points to buy those things. Then you take it into your hands in the twinkling of an eye. Isn't that exploitation? Li's mother was so worried she couldn't even get to her feet. . . . Well, we'll see that you have supper, something to drink and a place to sleep. In the meantime you had better try your hand at another statement. This time let's make it complete."

When Chi Chung-ch'i finished writing, Pipefitter Huang of the propaganda team read his words aloud:

"Last night I made a serious mistake. When everyone was at the play I went to Li's home, broke the chain, took a box, and hid it in the castor bean field. Later I went back and tried to carry the box home, but Li caught me. After people talked to me I admitted stealing it and now I feel that I have made a bad mistake. I promise never to do such a thing again and ask only for a chance to turn over a new leaf and take the road of revolution under Chairman Mao Tse-tung."

The cultural level of this youth was remarkable, I thought. He had studied in school only a few years, yet, like most people his age in the village, he was able to sit down and write out what he wanted to say.

While I was marveling at the level of Chi's achievement, Pipefitter Huang was shaking his head over the content of the statement the poor fellow had written.

"That's much too simple," said Huang sternly. "You haven't said a word about your motives. You must write about what went on in your mind when you were breaking into people's houses. And you have to write about all those things that we found in your house, and about the fact that you ran away when we allowed you to go to the toilet. Most important, you have to recognize that the root of your problem is bourgeois thinking, getting something for nothing. By stealing you can gain property without any labor and thus take advantage of the labor of others. This is a class question."

"Yes," said Judge Kao, breaking in. "You have to think through your whole past, recall each problem and write each down, one by one, then analyze it. You can't wrap fire with paper. If you don't want people to know the wrong things you do, the only way is not to do those things. If you do anything wrong there will always be someone who knows about it. You may wish you hadn't done it, but since you have been poisoned by bourgeois thinking, the only way out is to speak honestly and change resolutely."

"We also have to repudiate your talk about not having any future," said Security Officer Shen, anxious to have his say. "Of course this theft will stain your history but that doesn't mean you have no future. You are still young, your class background is lower-middle peasant. If you make an effort, the future stands bright before you. If you tell everything frankly, the poor and lower-middle peasants will forgive you. If you don't, the less said the better. So think about it."

To classify Chi's act as class struggle and blame it on bourgeois ideology puzzled me. Crime, it seemed, was not simply crime, but a form of counter-revolution. Was this realism or revolutionary-romanticism gone wild? I felt very sorry for young Chi. It seemed to me that he lived under tremendous pressure. He could only earn seven points a day, hardly enough to support one person, yet he had to support three—a crippled, aging father, a young brother in primary school and himself. While he slid deeper and deeper into poverty his neighbors, with four people working, prospered, saved money and stored it in a trunk.

Perhaps the diverging fortunes of these two families had to be seen as an example of the polarization brought about by the application of the socialist principle—"to each according to the work performed." The equalitarian promise of "equal pay for equal work" could not but be undermined by unequal labor power and unequal needs and burdens. The able-bodied with few dependents tended to accumulate surpluses while the weak with many dependents gradually fell short and went under. Such polarization plagued the population wherever "bourgeois right" held sway, as Mao Tse-tung so forcefully pointed out a few years later. Yet no country could abolish "bourgeois right"—such things as equal pay for equal work—as long as the productive forces remained primitive. Also, whenever state, cooperative and private production existed side by side, society had to maintain a market, people had to be allowed to buy and sell commodities, and the prices of commodities had to reflect, in some approximate way, the labor power embodied in them.

The only thing that might help young Chi was for the brigade to guarantee, as it must for all its members, the basic minimum of per capita grain, a guarantee that amounted to free supply. But there was a catch even here. If Chi could not earn enough to feed three, and the brigade fed three anyway, according to the coop charter it had to charge the grain to Chi's account. The family would not starve, but Chi would go into debt for every pound of grain he failed to earn by his work points. If the brigade did not write off the debt at some future date, payments on it could plague him throughout his life. There was always the possibility, however, that once his brother began to work the two of them could liquidate the debt they owed by means of hard labor.

From the point of view of a twenty-year-old clearly unable to keep the family afloat, the future must have looked dark indeed. I saw Chi as a victim of "bourgeois right," and the nub of the problem seemed to me to be to find a way out for the family economically, perhaps by finding some easy work for the father to do. If the brigade could throw some additional income their way, the question of thievery would not arise.

But the brigade leaders, the members of the propaganda team and the rank-and-file of Long Bow disagreed. In their view the only victims in this situation were the members of the Li family who had temporarily lost a box. Young Chi was an incipient class enemy, and the nub of the problem was Chi's ideology, whether he was going to commit himself to the socialist or the capitalist road. What the brigade confronted here was a class question and the solution involved intensified class education. They asked Chi Chung-ch'i if he had a copy of The Quotations of Chairman Mao. When he said no, they found a copy for him to study. "Study the sections on class struggle," they advised. "And study the section on youth. You will see how far short you are of satisfying the demands made by Chairman Mao on the young people of China."

62

CONFRONT THE
TWO GEMS

 Most of the members of the propaganda team saw the apprehension of Chi Chung-ch'i, the thief, as a heaven-sent opportunity. To them his crime appeared to be a clear-cut example of continuing class struggle. If properly handled, the case could serve as a lever to take the lid off the class struggle in Long Bow.

The morning after Chi confessed, the team chose study material from Mao Tse-tung's essay "On the Correct Handling of Contradictions among the People." Among the quotes which Teacher Li read aloud were several that illustrated what Mao called the "first function of the dictatorship of the proletariat":

". . . to suppress the reactionary classes and elements and those exploiters who resist the socialist revolution, to suppress those who try to wreck our socialist construction, or in other words, to resolve the contradictions between ourselves and the internal enemy. . . .

"To maintain public order and safeguard the interests of the people, it is likewise necessary to exercise dictatorship as well over thieves, swindlers, murderers, arsonists, criminal gangs and other scoundrels who seriously disrupt public order. . . .

"Dictatorship does not apply within the ranks of the people. The people cannot exercise dictatorship over themselves, nor must one section of the people oppress another.

"Law-breakers among the people will be punished according to law, but this is different in principle from the exercise of dictatorship to suppress enemies of the people. . . .

"In ordinary circumstances, contradictions among the people are not antagonistic. But if they are not handled properly, or if we relax our vigilance and lower our guard, antagonism may arise."*

To study these quotes was timely indeed, for the meeting that began with seven fine dramatic interludes and ended with the real life drama of a bold theft in Long Bow raised very sharply the question of the nature of the contradiction between the Two Gems and the brigade, and the nature of the contradiction between the thief and the brigade.

*Selected Works of Mao Tse-tung (Peking: Foreign Languages Press, 1977), 5:387–91.

Those propaganda team members who saw a similarity between the two contradictions—to start with, they saw them both as class conflicts—wanted to arrange a mass meeting where the people publicly repudiated at one and the same time the thief Chi Chung-ch'i, former Militia Captain Fast Chin, and such militiamen as Splayfoot Tseng and Whiskers Shen. They thought that this would expose at one stroke the heart of class struggle in Long Bow, place the most important contradictions plaguing the community out in full view, and thus, merely by opening up problems, go a long way toward solving them.

In the middle of the study session Security Officer Shen, backed up with enthusiasm by Pipefitter Huang, proposed such a mass meeting. Veteran Wang opposed it, while Judge Kao, Donkey Meat Wang and the white-haired Chao Fu-kuei wanted time to study the matter.

Wang opposed multiple repudiation on the ground that it was politically unsound. They had not yet settled the nature of the contradiction between Fast Chin and the brigade. There was a possibility that Chin was a class enemy, but it was much more probable that he was simply a poor peasant temporarily on the outs with the present leadership and that conflict with him was just another conflict among the people that had not yet become antagonistic. If they handled it correctly, they might be able to solve it relatively easily. If they handled it badly, it could develop into a serious confrontation. Just as Chairman Mao had pointed out, when cadres handled contradictions improperly, they could transform them into dangerous antagonisms.

The idea that he himself might be responsible for something bad startled Security Officer Shen.

"A bad thing may turn into a good thing, but can a good thing turn into a bad thing?" he asked.

"Certainly," said Wang. "Remember that old brigade secretary who didn't want the city to transfer his village to Tunliu County? He was a good man, he had a tremendous war record and won great prestige during the land reform. When his fellow villagers protested the decision that they join Tunliu County, he agreed with them and challenged the transfer which the city had approved. His constituents rallied behind him, praised him, and made him feel like a hero again. So he fought back with ever greater energy, serving the people through defiance, as he had so often done in the past. The trouble was, this time he was defying friends and allies. When Tunliu cadres came to talk the matter over, he sent people to overturn their car. When they tried to call him up he said, 'Cut down the telephone poles. I won't listen to their stupid talk.' At that point the contradiction became antagonistic. A model brigade secretary ended up a common criminal, charged with the destruction of public property. Having refused to take the way out they gave him, he did himself in. He left himself no room to maneuver. And that's what we'll be doing if we carry through the repudiation meeting you propose."

"Why do you say that?" asked Shen, still puzzled.

"Isn't it clear enough?" said Veteran Wang, trying to think of another way to explain the matter. "Thievery is definitely a crime. The contradiction between the thief and the brigade is definitely antagonistic. In the long run, of course, we may not handle it as such. We can look on the thief as a misguided son of the people, persuade him to reform and forgive him his transgressions. But if we lump Fast Chin together with the thief, it is tantamount to a public declaration that the contradiction we have with Chin is antagonistic, and that he is a class enemy.

"If we go ahead and do that, we have no room to maneuver. How are we going to get off the horse later? We can't repudiate him as if he were an enemy one day, and then turn around and say he is one of the people, after all, on the next day. Black face [evil] is his, and red face [good] is ours! Then suddenly he turns out to have a red face, too."

"How could that happen?" asked Shen.

"Well, isn't it possible that the Party will eventually reinstate him? It's very possible. After all, he can criticize himself and reform. What are we going to tell the people then? We can't destroy him completely one moment, then turn around and ask the people to treat him as a Communist, as a vanguard of the revolution, the next. Right now, since we are still unsure of the nature of the case, we had better leave ourselves some room to maneuver."

Wang was already unhappy about the way the preceding mass meeting had gone. Judge Kao had stated flatly, "Class enemies are going around wrecking and spreading rumors." As an example he had mentioned a dispute over sowing rates and a nameless person who said, "Open your hand a little and you can sow sixty catties."

Then Shen had stood up and carried the attack a step further. He said, "Fast Chin is trying to *wreck* the harvest by calling for a sixty-catty sowing rate." The class enemy already had a name!

"If anyone thinks that class struggle is over, just let him look around," Shen had continued. "People are stirring up trouble about the relief grain. Some people are stealing corn right out of the field. Others are stealing coal from the railroad yards. And now someone has stolen a trunk right from under our noses. A lot of other bad tendencies have also begun to surface."

Shen had gone on to list them. He had criticized all those who left the hall before the meeting was over, and all those who brought their sewing and knitting to the meeting and preoccupied themselves with domestic work and small group gossip instead of listening to the speeches, and he had criticized all those young people who answered the call of a local dance troupe for dancers and singers and had run off in the middle of the wheat planting to try out for the coming performance.

Though he did not actually say so, Shen's point had been that all of these negative phenomena illustrated class struggle; certainly they illustrated two-line struggle, which was at bottom class struggle. Thus he had ended up making a sharp class attack on almost everyone at the meeting.

"The people hadn't even opened their mouths yet, and you were denouncing them, every one of them," said Veteran Wang in disgust. "Again you haven't left us any room to maneuver. You have targeted the masses!"

The crux of the matter still lay in the handling of Fast Chin, and the conversation kept returning to his case. After hearing himself denounced by name in the meeting, Chin had sought out the propaganda team cadres.

"Just because Fast Chin has made mistakes, does that mean that everything about him is bad?" he had asked, talking of himself in the third person. "Has Chin been wrecking the fall sowing?"

To that Wang had replied, "Well, at least you have a lot of resentment. What is it if not resentment that makes you blurt out remarks like your sixty-catty blockbuster?"

"I'd admit to resentment," Chin had answered, after a moment of thought, "but not to wrecking."

"But remarks like that can play a wrecking role, objectively. The results just can't be good," Wang had countered, trying to defend the extreme position taken by the propaganda team, at least for the record. "The real problem is that you are too bound up with yourself. Your individualism is too great. When you see people who oppose you, you can't refrain from striking back, and thus the confrontation becomes sharper."

"So you see," said Wang in the morning study session, "it's better not to name names. It's better to describe what happened in a general way. Then if Chin comes himself and says, 'Was it me you were talking about?' he has already made a step forward. But if you call the action wrecking and name him by name, you force him into a corner. He can't help but resist."

"But isn't it wrecking?" asked Shen. "After all, the Commune Party Committee issued a correct directive calling for a twenty-catty sowing rate."

"Correct or not, that still has to be proven," said Wang. "We still have to test it in practice. How can you say that twenty catties is absolutely right for Long Bow? The soil here is different and the weather back of this hill is not exactly the same as that of the rest of the commune. Maybe we need to adjust the rate for Long Bow. The commune issues directives as guides to action, not as absolute truths. Didn't they tell us to plant improved hybrid corn seed last spring? And look what happened. Twenty percent of our corn is rotten with leaf blight. Can you say now that this was good seed?

"The commune also raised those *six don'ts*. 'Without sending 200 tan of manure to the field, do not plant wheat!' And you passed them on. But we know very well there are teams that don't have that much manure piled up. Are they to forget planting wheat? So isn't it clear that we ought to test the twenty-catty directive over a period of time?

"But you, you want to raise this thing to the highest level and say if anyone says anything to oppose the CP Secretary of the brigade he is actually criticizing the CP Secretary of the commune, which means criticism of the CP Secretary of Changchih City . . . and on and on right up to the Central Committee, so that a remark that is actually rooted in simple resentment of the way we are running things locally ends up as counterrevolutionary wrecking! Suddenly the speaker becomes a counterrevolutionary!"

Wang concluded on his own that Fast Chin had a *szu-hsiang* (thought) problem. Chin was angry because higher authorities had removed him from office and he was dissatisfied with the new leadership of the brigade, a dissatisfaction that quite a few others shared. This was not a crime but a question of attitude, of outlook. Cadres should analyze it as such and treat it as such. If they did, they might find a solution to the man's problem. With his sixty-catty remark Chin had really meant, "Do as the brigade leadership says to do. If they say plant twenty catties, plant twenty catties; if they say plant sixty, plant sixty." He thus implied, "Since they think they are so hot, let them be responsible; just shut up and do as you are told."

"But by handling this thing the way we have, we made a lot of people afraid to talk," said Wang. "If we treat a thought problem as a crime, who will dare say anything? People will just shut up for fear we may take their remarks as evidence of class struggle. Thus we mix up contradictions among the people with enemy contradictions and our work goes from bad to worse."

In this way Wang argued his case against a repudiation meeting with Chung-ch'i the thief and Fast Chin as joint targets.

"Chin is a Communist," Wang continued. "Are you going to repudiate him on the same platform as a man caught stealing? How can that be right? One man has a thought problem. The other has actually committed a crime. They are not in the same category at all."

But Security Officer Shen did not agree. "Sure they are in the same category," he said. "They are both 'three fall' wreckers. We certainly can repudiate them together. When it comes to settling these two cases, of course we cannot settle them together. But we can certainly repudiate these two men together on the same platform."

The two team cadres thus ended up with diametrically opposed views, one saying that they could not repudiate the two men together, but that they could solve their cases together; and the other saying that they could repudiate the two men together but that they must solve their cases separately. The deadlock was complete.

Confronted with an intractable contradiction, Wang searched hard for a compromise. He finally came up with one: They might launch a joint repudiation, he suggested, if the meeting illustrated some overall principle such as the continuation of class struggle in various forms, with the stress on the word "various." There is this thief, for instance, the individualist out for himself and to hell with the collective, and there are the Two Gems leading the brigade down the capitalist road because of capitalist road thinking, and so on—each example illustrating a different form of two-line struggle and all linked in various degrees to bourgeois ideology.

But even though Wang suggested this, his heart was not really in it because he thought it a piecemeal, ill-digested, premature attempt to confront the Two Gems before the team members had arrived at clarity or consensus as to the true nature of the contradiction the brigade had with them.

"The basic question still remains: What is the nature of our contradiction with Chin?" he said.

"And the answer still is, I don't know," said Shen.

"Well, we've been at it ten months already and it's getting rather late. We are discussing how to handle it correctly but we haven't yet decided what kind of a contradiction it is. Since we don't know, how can we throw

Chin together with a thief? There is no political level in that kind of repudiation and *since it has no political level how can it raise consciousness?* The truth of the matter is that we are frustrated in dealing with those Two Gems. It would make us happy to see them bow their heads alongside a common thief. At one stroke we could bring them all down to the same humiliating level. But how can that solve the problem?

"If we want to repudiate Chin we have to analyze his mistakes, his wrong thinking and his wrong leadership, his revisionist political line. If we lump him with a thief he can't accept it and no one else can understand it or accept it either."

As I listened to the debate I thought of the great mass meeting at Tsinghua University, where at the height of the Cultural Revolution Liu Shao-ch'i's wife, Wang Kuang-mei, confronted several hundred thousand critics. Her mentors had humiliated her by forcing her to wear a tight-fitting long gown, high-heeled shoes and a string of gold-painted Ping-Pong balls about her neck to simulate pearls—all of which were supposed to caricature her alleged bourgeois style of life. But, as the Tsinghua students later realized, this attempt at ridicule backfired. It diverted attention from the real question at hand—Liu Shao-ch'i's political line. It turned a serious repudiation effort into a ribald farce where hundreds of thousands directed their attention at Wang Kuang-mei, the individual, instead of at her political platform.

My thoughts also wandered inadvertently to a certain man of an earlier age who was nailed to a cross between two thieves. Did the advisers to the omnipotent Procurator who condemned him debate the alternatives? Did anyone ask if their victim could be reduced to the level of a common criminal by crucifying him in dubious company? Did anyone suggest that the onlookers might draw the wrong conclusions, that the populace might not appreciate the flimflam, that the whole episode might backfire?

Unfortunately, Wang's arguments did not carry the day. On the evening of the twenty-first, the team called a second mass meeting to repudiate Fast Chin, several members of his "clique," and the unfortunate young man, Chi Chung-ch'i, whom a militiaman had caught in the middle of the night with the Li family trunk in his hands.

63

CRUSH ALL GHOSTS AND MONSTERS

1. Never forget class struggle.

2. All erroneous ideas, all poisonous weeds, all ghosts and monsters, must be subjected to criticism; in no circumstances should they be allowed to spread unchecked.

3. Socialist society is a fairly long historical stage. During this historical stage classes, class contradictions and class struggle continue to exist, the struggle between the road of socialism and the road of capitalism goes on, and the danger of capitalist restoration remains. It is necessary to recognize the protracted and complex nature of this struggle. It is necessary to heighten our vigilance.

4. To maintain public order and safeguard the interests of the people it is likewise necessary to exercise dictatorship over embezzlers, swindlers, arsonists, murderers, criminal gangs and other scoundrels who seriously disrupt public order!

These quotes from Mao Tse-tung set the tone for a meeting which seemed to do everything that Veteran Wang had feared and warned against.

The vice-chairman of the Brigade Revolutionary Committee, Shen Chi-ts'ai, opened the proceedings with a call to repudiate the theory that the class struggle had died out.

"On the contrary," said Shen, in his dour lifeless prose, "the class struggle has never stopped in Long Bow village. Since the rectification movement began, class enemies here have gone into hiding and started to use all kinds of tricks to prevent us from carrying out Mao Tse-tung's call. Opposing our proletarian dictatorship, they are wildly attacking."

What proof did he cite for this? The theft of corn from the field, of wire from the pumping station and of a trunk from the Li family house, wrecking remarks about sowing wheat and sharing pigs.

"We can give no quarter to these class enemies! We must struggle with them to the end. Until we have killed all the wolves we will never retreat."

When Shen Chi-ts'ai retired from the center of the stage, Shen Hsü-wen, the handsome new chief accountant who was also a member of the Party Committee, took the floor to assert that an excellent situation was developing in Long Bow in regard to repudiating Liu Shao-ch'i's reactionary theories, in promoting production through accumulating manure, in fixing up irrigation systems, and in buying pigs.

"But there are people among us who won't carry out Mao Tse-tung's line," shouted Accountant Shen.

"Fast Chin, stand up!" he commanded, taking the audience, and presumably his opponent, by surprise.

When Chin, from the middle of the floor, got gingerly to his feet, Shen attacked him in the strongest possible language.

"Chin speaks of 'black'-gangers and 'red'-gangers. He wrecks our efforts. With monsters like this, if you don't struggle against them they will overwhelm you. Revolution is the main stream. Counterrevolution is a pitiful side current. The only way out for people like you is to transform your world outlook. We will stink out and knock down whoever wrecks the fall harvest. If you persist in your rotten ways you will drown in a sea of people's war!"

Then, with Chin still standing in the middle of the hall, surrounded by the seated peasants of Long Bow, Shen called for slogans from the floor.

"Down with Liu Shao-ch'i's reactionary line!"

"Never forget class struggle."

"Crush all poisonous weeds, all ghosts and monsters."

As Shen Hsü-wen shouted the slogans at the top of his voice, they came back from the depths of the hall as a disabled echo. The young women and old mothers-in-law, the callow youths and gnarled old peasants there assembled, dutifully repeated the young accountant's words, but in monotones, without enthusiasm and without conviction. They all knew well how to conduct a mass repudiation. They went through the familiar motions without protest, but they failed to generate any repudiating emotion or any indignation. I had a feeling that as far as the people were concerned, they were acquiescing to a ritual because they could not avoid doing so, because the propaganda team and the brigade office had arranged it. They felt, it appeared, that it was a ritual in which they had no stake.

A young peasant named Yang Ch'eng-ping followed Shen Hsü-wen, the accountant, on the platform. Yang pulled his speech from his pocket and read it in that peculiar staccato style used for reading Chinese aloud that originated in shouting school,* each syllable standing by itself, as written on the page or blackboard, instead of flowing together in the polysyllabic rhythm that enlivens ordinary speech.

Yang, insisting that Fast Chin remain standing, repeated, one after another, the various wrecking remarks attributed to the former militia captain, and ended with a shouted threat:

"Fast Chin, your dream of capitalist restoration has failed! If you resist you will be crushed by the wheel of the revolution."

*As in the one-room schoolhouses of rural America, students in China shout back in unison the lessons written for them on the blackboard.

As each speaker retired another young person immediately replaced him or her on the stage. Each had a written commentary, replete with slogans, stock phrases, warnings and threats to contribute. It soon became apparent that these were not young people moved by the excitement of the moment, but the members of Long Bow's Youth League who had met, divided up the task, and each written out beforehand the content of an attack on the vicious "class enemies" who had dared to raise their ugly heads in the fall of 1971.

That they had invested considerable discussion and planning in this effort was illustrated by the variation in emphasis from one short talk to the next. Yang Ch'eng-ping concentrated mainly on the question of learning from Tachai and Chin's remark, "Tachai road, Long Bow road, what does it matter, so long as we produce the grain."

Lu Han-hua concentrated on the sorry state of pig raising in Long Bow and blamed it on the idea, alleged to be Chin's, that the "masses are backward."

Chi Yü-ken aimed at the 10,000-catty shipment of relief grain, and Chin's statement that "We black-gangers can't get any, but you red-gangers can all get your share."

Chin Fu-t'ien stressed the pig question again, while Shen Hung-chang repudiated the Two Gems for "blowing up an evil wind and lighting a devil's fire" by promoting the theory that "class struggle was dying out in Long Bow." To back up this charge he cited no evidence at all.

The sixth speaker, Shen Hung-fu, shifted the attack to the young thief Chi Chung-ch'i. Shen allowed Fast Chin to sit down, then directed Chi Chung-ch'i to stand up and charged that he had engaged precisely in class struggle.

"Chi Chung-ch'i," read Shen from his paper, "we want to tell you, no matter how slippery you are, you can't escape!" Then he offered Chi a way out. "Only through honest self-criticism can you become a new person. Now is the time to turn back."

Li K'ang-hsing continued the offensive against thief Chi. He characterized him as a young person influenced by Liu Shao-ch'i's black line.

Shen Ming-wang took the stage next. He startled the audience with a new command.

"Splayfoot Tseng, stand up!"

As Splayfoot obeyed and Chi Chung-ch'i sank to the floor, Ming-wang shouted:

"Bloody claw of Liu Shao-ch'i, riffraff Splayfoot Tseng, how can you so misjudge the future? How can you ever succeed in your aim?"

A young woman, Shen Hsiu-ying, carried this attack forward, only to yield to Chin Ch'eng-yuan, who focused on Lin Yao-lung, notorious for his profiteering while on sideline work at Changchih Steel Company.

In the middle of all this another young woman, Chang Hsien-hua, Hsin-fa's daughter, attacked Liu Shao-ch'i's views on the status of women. She did not venture to claim that anyone in Long Bow had supported Liu in this, but called on him to open his dog's eyes and see if women have strength or not. "What men can do, women can do," said young Chang with feeling. "We will prove that we hold up half the sky!"

A remarkable thing about this long succession of speeches was the fact that all these young people were literate. Each had taken up one aspect of the joint task and each had written out his or her own attack. It was a far cry from the days of the land reform movement in 1948 when poor peasant activists often began by apologizing for word blindness, for standing helpless before the documents. To me it seemed that by 1971 the study of the documents had gone a bit too far. All the young people were writing and speaking in stock phrases right out of the *Red Book* or the *People's Daily:* "If we don't follow Mao Tse-tung's line, we follow a bourgeois line." "The situation is excellent, a new high tide has come, waves are breaking, red flags are waving, high spirits rise up to the sky while great changes take place." "Class enemies blow up a devil's wind and light a devil's fire." I found myself ardently wishing that one, just one of the speakers, would throw away his or her notes and say something straight from the heart in the language that Long Bow people spoke day in and day out. But it was not to be. The ritual continued as planned and the people dutifully heard the speakers out, occasionally reacting to shouted slogans with the same half-hearted response they had supplied to Shen Chi-ts'ai.

Suddenly in the midst of one speech the Chairman, All Here Li, came forward to interrupt the proceedings with an announcement. Had some new crisis arisen, had another theft occurred? Silence spread quickly through the hall as private conversations ceased and listeners bent an ear for unexpected news.

"A child in the audience has lost a shoe," said All Here. "Whoever finds it please bring it up onto the stage."

A sigh of relief and a ripple of laughter greeted this "new crisis." The speaker of the moment hardly had time to resume before a little cloth shoe, bright red in color and beautifully embroidered, came flying up out of the crowd on the floor and landed, *plop,* in the middle of the stage. The speaker did not miss a word as All Here stepped quietly forward to retrieve the errant shoe. Was this simply a "peasant" way of returning the shoe, or did it reflect some real dissatisfaction with the content of the meeting? It was hard to say at this point, but as for me, I felt increasingly uncomfortable as one speech followed another, and so did my daughter Carma, who was translating.

She always found it hard to translate rhetoric, and the rhetoric this evening all but overwhelmed her. Only by an extreme effort of will was she able to listen to it and repeat it in English.

The final speaker, Pipefitter Huang, resplendent in his army uniform, outdid both in voice and emotion all the preceding speakers. He harangued the people in a high-pitched, strident, authoritarian tone that made it seem as if that supreme scoundrel, Liu Shao-ch'i himself, had appeared in our midst. As he paused between sentences he spoke a guttural "heh!" or "heh, heh!" for emphasis. The sound of these "hehs" was like the croak of a frog in a pond. If one stopped listening to his words and concentrated on those "hehs," each sounded more froglike than the one before and more menacing to boot. With his face contorted, his manner mean, and his voice overloud, his message was clear: "Stand aside, class enemies, or be crushed!"

"Never forget class struggle!" Huang shouted. "This meeting is very good! It has taken the spirit out of our class enemies . . . heh . . . But what is that capitalist roader with reactionary thinking, Fast Chin, doing? Heh. He is sitting there studying the little *Red Book,* heh, studying Mao quotes in order to resist us! Heh. Isn't this a case of using the Red Flag to oppose the Red Flag? Heh, heh. Isn't this his usual cover-up method while really he concentrates . . . heh . . . on future revenge?"

Pipefitter Huang then reviewed the recent crimes of Fast Chin, Swift Li, Lin Yao-lung, Splayfoot Tseng, Whiskers Shen and Chi Chung-ch'i, the thief. He called on the people to repudiate them all, and praised the evening's meeting as a *liu liu te shih* (a bright gathering) that had raised morale all around. He praised the brigade members for their accomplishments in planting wheat (400 out of 600 mou being already in the ground) and in buying pigs (190 pigs bought in two days), and wound up his performance with six shouted slogans:

> Down with Liu Shao-ch'i!
> Down with Liu Shao-ch'i's counterrevolutionary line!
> Support Mao Tse-tung's revolutionary line!
> Strengthen proletarian dictatorship!
> Unite to achieve still greater victories!
> Long live Mao Tse-tung Thought, Long live the Chinese
>   Communist Party, Long live Mao Tse-tung!

The response from the audience was, if anything, weaker than before, because a majority of the peasants had long since slipped away. Only a few dozen people remained in the hall and their enthusiasm for slogans at this hour of the night had reached its nadir.

On returning to my room I wrote the following words in my notebook:

"Puzzled by this meeting. So many empty words and no clear line! Is Chin supposed to be a class enemy or is he one of the people? What was the political content of the attack? Was he supposed to be in the same category as the thief? Is thievery an expression of class struggle? Why don't they ask Chin to make a self-criticism? Is he really wrecking the fall work? Objectively? Consciously?"

During the next few days Carma and I had some heated discussions with Lin T'ung and Smart Fan over the way in which the Party rectification movement had developed. I found myself more and more closely aligned with Wounded Veteran Wang's view that it was wrong to lump all these cases together for repudiation. Not only did the whole approach seem wrong, but the results seemed to me to be disastrous. The people were staying away in droves. Those who did turn up at production team meetings were few and had little to say. Wang's prediction, that if thought problems were handled in this manner few would ever dare to speak out, was rapidly being realized in practice.

Surely, I argued, the case of the Two Gems must be treated as a contradiction among the people. The possibility that the two had links to some counterrevolutionary underground should be thoroughly investigated, but unless and until some solid evidence showed up one must act on the assumption that they were two cadres from among the people—disaffected, perhaps; angry and resentful, certainly, at having been removed from office and labeled "black-gangers," but clearly not conscious wreckers, not capitalist roaders out to overthrow socialism, not reactionaries.

"Wasn't it Mao Tse-tung's policy," I asked, "to cure the disease and save the patient?" Yet no such spirit had surfaced at the mass meeting. Instead, almost every speaker had called the Two Gems "class enemies," thus blocking a way out for them and almost guaranteeing that an internal contradiction would be transformed, in time, into an external one.

In reply Smart Fan stressed the serious mistakes made by the two—their capitalist road, sideline occupation, grab-for-money line; their smashing and grabbing in the Cultural Revolution, the objective wrecking effect of their attitude and words in the present period. Smart Fan declared that he, for one, didn't find it hard to call them class enemies.

Lin T'ung backed him up with enthusiasm.

Carma and I both said that we did not see how any condemnation could go that far. Just because the Two Gems had made serious capitalist road mistakes did not make them capitalist roaders. If they had followed a wrong, reactionary line, this made them guilty of that mistake, but it did not make them reactionaries. If they were, in fact, undermining the village leadership and eroding the authority of the new responsible cadres, could it not be attributed to intense individualism, resentment at being overthrown, personal ambition and similar selfish motives, rather than to any conscious desire to wreck socialism? Would it not be more realistic to stop calling them class enemies and characterize them, instead, as cadres with serious mistakes, deep individualistic tendencies, cadres who, if they recognized their mistakes and changed their attitude, could still be won over?

Swift Li, we pointed out, had at least one current merit. He not only had raised pigs at home, but he had raised a sow that farrowed four little pigs. In actual practice he had thus outdistanced 98 percent of the village in carrying out Mao Tse-tung's line in pig raising. In this sphere at least, one had to give him some credit.

The discussion waxed hot and heavy but failed to resolve the issues. We left each meal feeling defeated, that is to say, feeling that Smart Fan had already made up his mind to attack the Two Gems as class enemies. Since this decision seemed to me to be extreme and ultraleft, I didn't see any way out of the current impasse in Long Bow. When would the "overthrow" cycle ever end? It was as if we were walking in a tunnel without any light in view. In a village where conditions were already quite bad, even the highest cadres were making the kind of mistakes that could only make the situation worse. My morale dipped to a very low point. How had political work in Long Bow ever fallen into such a morass?

One argument which Smart Fan kept throwing at us was that the rank-and-file would never catch the subtle distinction we were making between a person with serious mistakes and a counterrevolutionary. The important thing at the present time was to expose the culprits and rouse the people against them. When the time came to pass judgment on the case, then the cadres could draw all the fine distinctions necessary.

In rebuttal Carma and I made clear that we did not expect all the peasants to make a clear distinction between "class enemy" and "cadre with serious mistakes"; between "bourgeois man" and "man with strong bourgeois tendencies." But we felt that it was important for the leadership to make this distinction and make clear the Party policy of "cure the disease and save the patient" so that they could present the Two Gems with a way out and perhaps save them as cadres and revolutionaries. Why should the city cadres and the propaganda team tail behind the people?

In a very real sense, of course, the city cadres were not tailing the people at all. The people, sensing the ultraleft dogmatic thrust of rectification policy as applied by the propaganda team, were voting with their feet in droves. They were refusing to take part, just as they had in 1948. Then an extremist Poor-and-Hired-Peasant Line dominated events in Long Bow village. When the cadres tried to establish an absolute equality that was utopian in concept and reactionary in essence, the rank-and-file peasants expressed their displeasure by failing to show up at meetings, by refusing to talk when they did show up, by sleeping through the long-winded empty reports, or by quietly leaving when the opportunity presented itself. The people always appeared "backward" when leaders confronted them with half-baked, far-fetched policies which went beyond the realities of the moment, only to unite and push onward with enthusiasm when leaders came forward with a valid revolutionary policy.

This point we also argued, for one could hardly call the short papers presented at the last mass meeting an expression of popular thought. Those papers represented an organized effort on the part of the propaganda team, working through the Brigade Party Branch and the Youth League led by it, to mount a vigorous repudiation campaign against designated "class enemies." What the Youth League members expressed were not their own real thoughts, but a willingness to take part in such a campaign, once their organizational superiors had decided on mounting it. How many of the speakers actually believed the words they spoke was impossible to determine. Since the leadership was fanning up a repudiation wind, most loyal Party and Youth League members went along with it as a matter of course without asking too many questions. Only truly seasoned campaigners, like Wounded Veteran Wang, had the ideological maturity and political courage to go against the tide, and even he had to apologize constantly. He categorized his own views as "probably rightist" or even "revisionist," but nevertheless stuck to them.

Smart Fan, on his part, continued to counter our views with strong arguments to prove the "main direction" of the repudiation correct. The record of the Two Gems upset the masses, he said, so they had spoken out in the right direction. "What could the leading cadres do but express support?" he asked.

"But even if the main direction of the repudiation is correct," we replied, "the clublike nature and form of the attack is wrong. The people haven't really understood the nature of the problem they are dealing with. If the leaders just give 'full support' at that level how can the people avoid serious mistakes? The leaders need to go more deeply into the case, make valid distinctions between mistakes, mistaken thoughts and crimes, enemy disruption, wrecking, et cetera, . . . and properly evaluate the nature of what has happened."

Smart Fan, moved to a certain extent by these arguments, began to waver a little. At one moment he agreed that the critique was crude, only to reassert at the next moment that the men were in fact class enemies and deserved a crude critique. Thus he fluctuated between a certain amount of agreement with us and assertions that our ideas overthrew the whole repudiation attempt.

I felt more and more strongly that without some change in the attitude of the leaders Long Bow courted trouble. Lin T'ung, who constantly reminded one and all that she came from *Central,* had for obscure reasons decided to crush the Two Gems by whatever means came to hand. Smart Fan, wishing perhaps to impress Lin T'ung and win merit with *Central,* had gone along with her wishes and adopted an extreme position. The rest of the propaganda team split down the middle over the issue, with Security Officer Shen and Pipefitter Huang opting for a tough, class enemy policy, while Veteran Wang, Judge Kao and Donkey Meat Wang called for a "cure the disease, save the patient" line, a line of struggle over backward thinking. The other members of the team, less vocal than the leaders, were still trying to make up their minds.

Team members never thoroughly debated the issue, at least not in our presence. Who could say what the propaganda team would advise in the end? It would not be easy to overrule *Central* in the person of Lin T'ung, for the prestige of Peking and the Central Committee remained high. No one could lightly contradict a cadre who claimed to speak for such a level, a cadre, furthermore, who insisted that Central Committee decisions were objective truth.

On this question of objective truth Lin T'ung and I argued furiously through many a meal. What started the argument in each case was news of a change in the evaluation of some famous cadre or some well-known mass organization. Take Liu Ke-p'ing, the erstwhile chairman of Shansi Province. In January, 1967, the Central Committee had given him outspoken support as a good revolutionary cadre, a model for the rest of the country to follow. Suddenly, in 1969, the Central Committee removed him from his post, dropped him from the Shansi Party Committee, and transferred him to an obscure job elsewhere. Our mentor, Commander Li Ying-k'uei, argued that Liu had become involved with an alleged plot, known as the May 16 Conspiracy, an organization of counterrevolutionaries, and implied that this was the view held by the Central Committee in Peking.

As the evaluation of Liu Ke-p'ing underwent a 180-degree turn, the question arose: Which evaluation should be considered correct, the early positive one or the later negative one?

According to Lin T'ung, both had to be correct, not because a good person had changed into a bad person (quite the contrary; since Liu ended up bad, he must always have been bad), but because Central Committee decisions always reflected objective reality. If a new decision about a given matter clearly reversed an old one, she maintained that both the new one and the old one were correct just so long as each was based on all relevant information available to the decision makers at the time. With new, more comprehensive data old decisions could be revised, even reversed, but neither revision nor reversal could change the validity of the original decision as of the time it was made.

Leaving aside all questions relating to the possibility that both individuals and organizations can change, leaving aside also all questions concerning the possibility that a change in the context might cause a change in role, I certainly had no quarrel with the idea that information about people or organizations always amounted to approximations. New data could deepen understanding and cause the revision, even the reversal, of conclusions. To me this confirmed the relative, subjective nature of all knowledge and the difficulty of collecting enough valid data to arrive at conclusions that approximated objective truth. But to Lin T'ung approximate information, if it was the best information available to the Central Committee at any given moment, added up to objective truth. A new decision based on new information, even if it completely overthrew the old one, also added up to objective truth. What I saw as two subjective estimates of a reality existing outside of consciousness, estimates that improved as information accumulated, she saw as two objective truths separated by time, each one valid for the time it was made. For her, it seemed, any Central Committee decision based on the best information available was, by definition, valid. This applied with almost equal force to any decision of any Party Committee all the way down the line. After all, as the slogan everywhere proclaimed, "The Communist Party of China is a great, glorious and *correct* Party."

We never were able to bridge this gulf in understanding and/or approach. Lin T'ung felt that I did not appreciate the dialectical nature of truth—how it developed and changed—while I felt that she did not appreciate the central principle of philosophical materialism—that the world exists independent of man's will or his understanding of it. We both held that reality developed and changed, but what she was talking about I felt was not changing reality at all, but only man's perception of it. She was confusing truth with reflections of truth in men's minds.

If this had been merely a philosophical debate it would not have been very important. What made it important was that Lin T'ung was applying her concept of truth, her "theory of the absolute correctness of the present," to the political work going on in Long Bow, where a false estimate of the objective situation had enormous potential for mischief. What good, for instance, could come from mobilizing the whole community to expose class enemies if, in fact, such enemies did not exist or were not an important factor in the life of the village?

In thinking over the situation I could not help but marvel at how closely it resembled that of April, 1948, with the cadres of an earlier work team split over how to handle four difficult Long Bow leaders, some wanting to crush the "bad apples" by whatever means necessary and others stressing the need to save them. In 1948 Ch'i Yun and Hsieh Hung, the intellectuals from the University, advocated confrontation, while Hou Pao-pei, the reticent *fanshen* here from Sand Market Village, advocated salvation through education. At that time Comrade Wang Ch'ien, the subregional Party leader, came down strongly on the side of the peasant, Hou Pao-pei. He advocated rescuing the four embattled cadres by patient persuasion.

Where, I asked myself, was the Wang Ch'ien of today?

Where, for that matter, was the Wang Ch'ien of yesterday? According to rumor, that patient and compassionate cadre had risen to high office in Shansi Province, only to be cast out as a revisionist in 1967. People said that he was down in the countryside somewhere, raising crops by hand, one more casualty of a Cultural Revolution that loomed in the background of local history like the menacing shadow of a cloud larger than the horizon.

Part VII

BOMBARD THE HEADQUARTERS

All revolutionary struggles in the world are aimed at seizing power and consolidating it. The desperate struggles waged by counterrevolutionaries against the revolutionary forces are likewise for the sake of maintaining their political power.

Mao Tse-tung, *1967*

64

SHAKING THINGS UP

 According to custom the propaganda team members gathered at dawn in the Lu family courtyard for an hour of political study. Chilly as it was at that early hour, they preferred to sit outdoors, where they could catch the first warm rays of the sun, rather than to huddle in the damp gloom of the adobe room that the Lu family had loaned to Security Officer Shen and Donkey Meat Wang as living quarters. Inside that cavernous chamber the sun barely penetrated, even at noon, and nobody lit the fire under the kang until evening.

"In the course of the Cultural Revolution all the well-known Shansi people have gone down," said Security Officer Shen, his voice tinged with sorrow.

"That's true," said Judge Kao. "You only have to list them—Po Yi-po, An Tse-wen, P'eng Chen, Li Hsueh-feng—they have all gone down as capitalist roaders. Shansi seems to have got the worst of it."

"Well," said Veteran Wang, "there are a few Shansi men who rose up in the meantime."

"Who?" asked Little Li.

"Well, there's Chi Teng-k'uei, for one. He's from Wuhsiang County, not so far from here. It's the oldest anti-Japanese base in the Taihang Mountains. Chi went south in 1948 and eventually became vice-Party Secretary of Honan Province. When the Cultural Revolution began he supported the Red Guards. Mao met him, brought him to Peking and now he's an alternate member of the Political Bureau."

"I know another Shansi man who went up. He is vice-consul in Tanzania," said Security Officer Shen.

"So, not all Shansi cadres went down," said Wang. "A few went up."

"That doesn't help much," said Judge Kao morosely. "Shansi men played such a big role in the Liberation of our country, and now the famous ones have all messed up."

Silence followed this comment. Such a turn of events made all Shansi people sad. They had absorbed local pride with their mother's milk; they would most likely carry it with them to their graves.

The team cadres present, ten in all, sat on light folding stools, small piles of bricks or simply on their haunches, a position they had learned to hold hour after hour, as long as the occasion demanded. Representing the Communist Party and the government of the City of Changchih, they had come to Long Bow to review the results of the Cultural Revolution and salvage something from the debacle. They remained to conduct a Party rectification campaign and to reorganize the village administration to ensure, if possible, some progress in construction and production in a community where, for a decade at least, little progress had been made.

My daughter Carma and I continued to join the group each morning without fail. The informal discussions that flourished here revealed facets of life and politics that we could not hope to uncover or even to stumble on in the ordinary course of events.

On this particular September day in 1971 talk rolled more freely than usual because Lin T'ung, our guide and mentor from Peking, had sprained her ankle on the street the day before and had stayed in bed nursing her pain. When Lin T'ung joined a discussion group everyone took care before speaking because, who could tell, their words might reach Central. Better to think first and speak later, or not to speak at all under those circumstances. With Lin T'ung absent, such restraints fell away. Nobody seemed to care if their words reached America. What could America do about them in any case? To ask what Central might think about words that reached America did not occur to them. The prospect seemed remote indeed.

The official topic for discussion was the editorial published in the *People's Daily* on August 27. Little Li, the bob-haired young Russian teacher from the regional normal school, read the words aloud. A college graduate, she was the most literate member of the team and the one usually chosen by mutual consent to read weighty documents. The August 27 editorial concerned Party building, and the first paragraph declared that all the Provinces of China, with the exception of Taiwan, had now reestablished their provincial Party committees, a great victory. New Party committees laid the groundwork for moving ahead after the disruptions and disturbances of a Cultural Revolution, which had begun by dismantling Party committees everywhere.

The good news, read out so smoothly and precisely by Little Li, generated a lively exchange of opinion over the dates when the last committees finally appeared and over the cadres who played important roles as leaders. None of the group had ever heard of Jen Jung, the new First Secretary of the Tibetan Party Committee, and they were surprised to see that Pan Fu-sheng, who had long been prominent in Heilungkiang, was no longer a member of that province's leading body. They were sorry to see that Li Hsueh-feng, the North China Area leader who replaced P'eng Chen as First Secretary of the Peking Party Committee, had not won a place on the Hopei Provincial Committee at all. Most of the well-known area leaders earned notoriety by their absence. The propaganda team cadres ran through the names—T'ao Chu (South China), Li Hsueh-feng (North China) . . . and concluded that all had "gone down," along with Li Hsueh-feng and the other Shansi cadres whose names Judge Kao remembered so well.

When Little Li finally read out the second paragraph, it stimulated even more discussion than the first. The paragraph stressed the importance of

Party rectification, the need for every Communist to pass once more a "gate" manned by his or her peers and delegates chosen by the people.

"The Cultural Revolution was one big rectification movement," said Donkey Meat Wang. "It's easy to forget that, but that's what it was."

"Yes," said Chao Fu-kuei, "but it wasn't like anything we had before. In the past they always said, 'Shake things up, shake things up,' but who got shaken up? Only the rank-and-file. Secretaries of county committees, city committees and regional committees never got shaken up. But this time the students aimed the arrow at the higher-ups. That's why they all rushed out to suppress the student movement in 1966."

"Remember Wang Cheng [Changchih City Party Secretary in 1966]?" said Little Li. "His wife was a teacher in the middle school. When the students rose up against her, he ran over to shut them up."

"Yes, and he ordered Mao quotes painted large on walls all over the city," said Shen. "That was to keep the people quiet. Who would dare paste a poster over a Mao quote?"

"Things changed soon enough after that," said Veteran Wang. "I remember one high-level meeting for the study of Mao Tse-tung Thought. Two students from the normal school broke it up. They said they represented the *Red Detachment of Women.* 'You say you are for Mao, but all you do is suppress the people!' they shouted. Nobody dared challenge them, but later we found out that their *Red Detachment* had a membership list of two [they represented only themselves]."

"For a while the young people ruled the roost but their factionalism soured everything," said Donkey Meat Wang. "I knew a son who opposed his father. When they quarreled he slapped his father's face!"

To Wang this was worse than the news that a student had been shot on the threshing floor of Long Bow's Fourth Team.

"I knew a pair of brothers who were on opposite sides," said Veteran Wang. "When their father died they negotiated a truce so they could go home together and pay their respects. But on the road home they began to quarrel. They had to separate, then show up on alternate days to display their filial respects."

"Well, nobody could stay out!" said Shen. "You had to join one side or the other. There was no such thing as taking a middle position. Once a city cadre came to Horse Square. He said, 'I hear they're investigating some of these posters. Please look into it, they look like middle faction posters to me.' He said 'middle faction,' can you beat that! If there ever was a 'middle faction' it sure didn't last long. It either fell apart, split or went lock-stock-and-barrel to one side or the other."

Rectification, all agreed, would never end. The Party had launched such movements again and again over a long period of time but in each historical period the content had been different. In 1948 the central issue had been each cadre's attitude toward land reform, then in 1952 it was how each felt about cooperation. The Cultural Revolution started out as another big open-door rectification concerned with social consciousness, but many cadres couldn't really understand or accept it.

"Remember Old New Year Wang?" asked Veteran Wang. "He passed through the Four Clean Movement with flying colors and wrote a rhyme about it:

> In '65 came the great Four Clean
> And a work team 23 strong and mean.
> Back-to-back, face-to-face,
> Accusations all over the place,
> For a whole year the movement boiled,
> But not one hint of graft ever spoiled
> The reputation of Old New Year Wang.

"In 1967, when the people of Anyang suddenly began to criticize him, he couldn't understand it. Since his birthday had rolled around once more he wrote another rhyme:

> On the first day of January,
> The dawn of the year, my anniversary,
> Not half a bowl of millet did I eat
> Before they dragged me down to the street.
> There, pretending to speak for the masses,
> Stood rows of cows' heads and horses' asses.

"Cows' heads and horses' asses, what right did they have to question him? With the majority behind him, what right did a minority have to haul him out for a struggle meeting?"

"Well, that's the way Swift Li, Fast Chin and Wang Wen-te feel now. They don't see why anyone should have the right to criticize them," said Judge Kao. "They don't see what right 'cows' heads' and 'horses' asses' have to question Party members."

Bits and pieces, scraps, fragments and tailings led us inevitably toward the Cultural Revolution through a side door. It was high time, we decided, to come to grips with it in a more direct and systematic way. In the intervals left to us between urgent "three fall" production tasks we set up long hours of interviews that led outward and upward from village to city, to region, to province, and finally to the national capital, Peking. Informants at each level opened cracks and apertures on a series of intertwined events so surreal and bizarre, so involved and complex, that no novelist could hope to dream them up, and no reporter could hope to reconstruct them in full. What follows in the chapters to come is a description of a few currents in the vast cataract of the Cultural Revolution that we were able to chart, the stories of a few people and a few events that we were able to record even if we could not fully comprehend their meaning.

65

STUDENT REBELS
RISE AND SPLIT

 When in the middle fifties collective agriculture, coopera-
tive handicrafts and cooperative petty commerce finally
emerged to join forces with the country's state-owned
industry, trade and banking, thus squeezing private enterprise almost entirely out of the economy, China's leaders
could say with some justification that they had established socialism
economically. But for Mao socialism in the economic sphere was hardly
enough. He immediately turned his attention to the revolutionary transformation of the superstructure.

Far from assuming that public ownership of the factories and cooperative
ownership of the fields could, by themselves, guarantee the development of
socialism and open the way to Communism, Mao held that only further
radical changes in social relations, institutions, culture and ways of thinking
could consolidate what had been built and propel society forward. While the
opposition claimed that the disparity between the newly created, advanced
social relations and inherited backward productive forces constituted the
principal contradiction in China, Mao claimed something very close to the
opposite. Outmoded, tradition-bound social institutions, he said, still hin-
dered the development of China's productive forces, and this was at the
bottom a class question. He saw the primary obstacle to change and development as the existing party-state apparatus manned by a class of bureaucrats
who seemed far more likely to lead China to capitalism than to socialism.

As summed up by Meisner, Mao based his position on two propositions:
"The first was that officials in the upper echelons of the party bureaucracy,
by virtue of their power and prestige in the state apparatus, were acquiring
material privileges and exploiting society as a whole; in effect they were
becoming a functional bourgeoisie, albeit one whose privileges derived from
political power rather than from property. . . . The second proposition was
that an entrenched bureaucracy had acquired a vested interest in preserving
the social order over which it ruled and from which it derived its privileged
position, and thus was opposed to radical social changes and willing to
tolerate (and perhaps even promote) capitalist forms of socio-economic
relations and ideologies in society at large."*

*Maurice Meisner, *Mao's China* (New York: The Free Press, 1977), pp. 354–55.

This line of thinking placed Mao in direct opposition to most of the other power holders in China and caused him, again and again, to confront the status quo by appealing directly to the people to launch mass movements that either bypassed all the "normal" procedures approved by orthodox economic planners and organization men, or directly challenged their expertise and control.

The failure of such mass movements as the Hundred Flowers campaign and the Great Leap to achieve the goals Mao had set for them led directly to the confrontation at Lushan. Having lost heavily there to Liu Shao-ch'i and Teng Hsiao-p'ing, Mao held his fire while he prepared the ground for a comeback. Granting his rivals enough time and authority to make some serious mistakes of their own, he concentrated, with Lin Piao's help, on building up a strong enough base in the army to ensure freedom of action at a later date and on preserving and building up his personal prestige in the form of the "Cult of Mao."

Mao's first counterstroke was, as we have seen, the Socialist Education Movement, but when this failed to break Liu's grip on the Party organization he decided on a much bolder and more decisive strategy. Instead of returning to the countryside, raising a new guerrilla army and renewing peasant war, as he had threatened when his back was to the wall at Lushan, he launched a counterattack in 1966 that did not duplicate past history at all. To match an unprecedented situation Mao created a unique and far more formidable method—a nationwide political offensive that he called a "Cultural Revolution." Since no one had ever heard of such a "revolution," most people did not take it seriously at first. They thought Mao had launched some sort of protracted, but nevertheless benign, educational campaign, a new rectification movement capable of producing a plethora of speeches and articles, but precious little in the way of real social or political challenge.

Mao, on his part, launched the movement in a modest way with an article by Yao Wen-yuan, a Shanghai journalist, that criticized the play *Hai Jui Dismissed from Office*. Yao charged that this play, written by the vice-mayor of Peking, Wu Han, far from being the straightforward historical reconstruction that it pretended to be, was in reality an attack on Mao for dismissing General P'eng Teh-huai. This charge certainly came close to the truth. Yao followed up his first article with several attacks on the Peking journalist Teng To for a series of essays innocently entitled *Notes from Three-Family Village*. Among other things they accused Mao of amnesia and recommended hitting him over the head with a blunt instrument to restore his memory.

These articles stimulated some academic debate about Hai Jui's role in history and some polemics on educational policy. In the meantime Mao persuaded one of his prime targets, P'eng Chen, a Political Bureau member and concurrently the mayor of Peking, to head a five-man group to take charge of the proposed "Cultural Revolution." P'eng used his position to censure Yao for making a political issue out of an academic problem. With army support and a barrage of polemics aimed at P'eng's "Black Gang," Mao counterattacked, dissolved the Group of Five, and pushed through the dismissal of Mayor P'eng; Vice-Mayor Wu Han; the head of the Propaganda Department, Lu Ting-yi; and the man in charge of culture for all China, Chou Yang. Then he recommended Li Hsueh-feng, a trusted comrade, for the post of Peking's mayor and appointed an entirely new Cultural Revolution Group, this one headed by his old secretary Ch'en Po-ta; his wife, Chiang Ch'ing; and the long-time security chief, K'ang Sheng. With these moves Mao reasserted his authority over Peking City and all the media then under central control. Firmly entrenched at the nerve center of the nation, Mao launched what can only be called a surprise attack on his outmaneuvered and ill-prepared opponents. With little or no warning he backed a call for a student rebellion against "counterrevolutionary revisionists" and set off a chain of events which neither he nor anyone else ever managed to bring under effective control thereafter.

In the countryside, cadres and peasants ground through the second phase of the Socialist Education Movement, the Big Four Clean, without paying much heed to events in Peking. They could hardly help snapping to attention, however, when Mao's "Cultural Revolution" suddenly exploded in direct political action.

On May 25 six staff members at Peking University put up a poster charging their university president with counterrevolutionary acts. President Lu P'ing, they declared, had banned mass meetings, ordered the destruction of big-character posters, and set up all sorts of restrictions and taboos that tied the "revolutionary masses" hand and foot.

"All revolutionary intellectuals, now is the time to go into battle! Let us unite, hold high the great banner of Mao Tse-tung Thought, unite around the Party's Central Committee and Chairman Mao, and break down all the various controls and plots of the revisionists; resolutely, thoroughly, totally and completely wipe out all ghosts and monsters and all Khrushchev-type counterrevolutionary revisionists, and carry the socialist revolution through to the end."

This call to action, put up by a group of cadres, headed by the woman Nieh Yuan-tzu, a functionary in the philosophy department of Peking University, alerted the nation.

Lu P'ing and the university authorities reacted by mobilizing the majority of students and staff against the rebel group, hauling them before mass meetings to be denounced in turn as counterrevolutionaries. The original poster went up on May 25. The week of sharp confrontation that followed ended with a staggering surprise on June 2. For on that day the *People's Daily* published Nieh Yuan-tzu's poster for the whole country to read, and Peking Radio broadcast it to the nation. Chairman Mao himself, it seemed, had studied the poster. He had given it his full approval, called it the "first Marxist-Leninist poster of the Cultural Revolution," and asked for its nationwide dissemination.

This poster had an extraordinary effect. Approved by Mao Tse-tung and given the widest publicity in the press and on the air, it amounted to a call for rebellion on the part of students everywhere against teachers and school administrators whom they saw as conservative, revisionist or counterrevolutionary. Within hours of the first broadcast not only university students, but middle-school students as well, went into action from Heilunkiang to

Kwangtung. With the dissemination of the contents of Nieh's poster on June 2 the Cultural Revolution reached into every county, district and community in China where any institution of higher learning existed— including Long Bow village where militant students of the Luan Middle School, housed in the old grounds of the Catholic orphanage, rose up to challenge the school administration.

The first few days of June, 1966, brought a euphoric time indeed to students. Rebellion spoke to their condition. In response to Chairman Mao's call, they would sweep away everything old and reactionary in China and clear the road to a bright Communist future. As events actually developed, however, this first burst of euphoria did not last very long. Early in June Mao Tse-tung left Peking for the south on an extended trip, placing the direction of the Cultural Revolution in Liu Shao-ch'i's hands. Liu responded to the student revolt by sending work teams made up of city cadres organized by the Peking Party Committee into the universities and middle schools of the capital and ordering them to "carry the revolution through to the end." But the real purpose of these work teams, it soon became clear, was to contain the student movement. Under cover of extraordinarily radical rhetoric they closed university gates, stopped public display of big-character posters, called all students and staff into closed meetings for political study, and urged everyone to hunt out the counterrevolutionaries in their midst. The effect of this strategy, so well known in the Socialist Education Movement, diverted criticism away from leading cadres toward the rank-and-file and broadened vastly the target of attack as people mobilized to examine and expose one another. Those student rebels who had responded to Nieh's poster with a massive barrage of anti-Lu P'ing material of their own suddenly came in for extreme criticism and suppression. Now it was their turn to wear the label "counterrevolutionary." They earned this label from the work teams not because they had attacked Lu P'ing but because they were now resisting orders to turn their attention away from such glamorous targets and concentrate on cleansing their own ranks.

The work team period lasted for fifty days, until Mao's return from the south, and later became known as "fifty days of white terror." Contrasting responses to this "white terror" laid the groundwork for a split in the student movement that was to have a devastating effect, not only on the students themselves, but on millions of workers and tens of millions of peasants who followed them into the conflict.

That minority of students who stood together as rebels at Peking, Tsinghua and other major universities, institutes and middle schools during those days, defying all the attacks and slanders of the work teams, came to think of themselves alone as true revolutionaries, as the genuine Marxist vanguard. These early "rebels" rejected as opportunists those middle-of-the-roaders who couldn't make up their minds as to who was right—student challengers or the work teams that suppressed them. They condemned as outright counterrevolutionaries those "loyalists" who stood by the work teams because they thought they represented the Communist Party and Chairman Mao himself. Yet most of these rejected or condemned students and staff members, whatever their position during the "fifty days," also stood up and called for revolution in August once Mao clarified the objectives of the movement and made his support for it clear.

By that time it was too late for unity. The militants of the "fifty days" who rallied around the famous rebel Kuai Ta-fu of Tsinghua rejected all "fair-weather" friends. The latecomers had no choice but to form organizations of their own.

These organizations, once formed, entered into fierce competition with their early "rebel" rivals for merit and credibility as revolutionaries, but found it increasingly hard to consolidate themselves in the face of the offensive launched by Kuai Ta-fu against them. Rank-and-file members tended to fall away and join the Third Headquarters established by Kuai, effectively obscuring all distinctions between "rebel" and "loyalist." By the time open warfare broke out over control of the Tsinghua campus in 1968 it was two factions from within Third Headquarters that fought it out, each containing within its ranks students and staff who had joined the revolution early and others who joined in later. What divided them had very little to do with choices made during the "fifty days." They broke ranks over which members of the overthrown faculty and staff to recruit or reject.

There were 4,000 middle-school students and 300 college students in Southeast Shansi, most of them in and around Changchih City. For them the Cultural Revolution began in the winter of 1966 with organized study on the problem of Peking Vice-Mayor Wu Han's play *Huai Jui Dismissed from Office* and writer Teng To's essay series, *Notes from Three-Family Village*. Once the Shanghai journalist Yao Wen-yuan had denounced these writings as vicious attacks on Chairman Mao, students and literate people all over the country studied not the original writings, but Yao Wen-yuan's overheated polemics refuting and deriding them. They found in this form of political study nothing new or unfamiliar. A series of political and cultural debates designed to educate people and raise consciousness had enlivened the preceding years. This one, even though it targeted such prominent people as Peking's vice-mayor and a popular essayist on the *Peking Evening News,* did not seem to promise anything qualitatively different.

The sudden reorganization of the whole Peking Party Committee in April and the fall of P'eng Chen and Wu Han alerted everyone to the fact that the debate could go beyond mere matters of theory. High positions and prominent careers were also at stake. But this too had happened before. There had been a Kao Kang–Jao Shu-shih case, and there had been a P'eng Teh-huai case. So, outside the capital, study continued on an even keel until the beginning of June, when Nieh Yuan-tzu's poster appeared.

Here indeed was something qualitatively different. The six dissidents had issued a call for students and ordinary staff to rebel outright. Mao had backed them up with a statement that "rebellion is justified," and the whole educational establishment of the capital had responded with drastic and irreversible upheaval.

Middle-school administrators in Changchih, fearful of direct challenge from local students, first tried to ride out the storm by calling on their charges to mount a poster campaign against certain teachers, teachers who had suppressed worker-peasant students, or teachers who had controversial political or social connections.

This poster campaign, launched on June 14, proceeded according to plan until suddenly, on June 23, an "incident" occurred. On that date a physical education instructor at the First Middle School directed his criticism not at some ordinary faculty member but at the head of the whole school, Party Secretary Chang himself. The authorities immediately denounced the poster. They herded the physical education instructor and those associated with him into the school library and placed them under supervision. They mobilized the rest of the students and staff to surround the library and criticize the helpless targets inside. Thus students, faculty members and government leaders in Changchih duplicated in virtually every detail the Peking events of May 25 through June 2, events that transpired before Nieh's poster won public support from Mao Tse-tung.

The local press blew up the whole affair at the First Middle School as the "June 23 Counterrevolutionary Incident." The Party Committee of Changchih City had no choice but to send a group of cadres to investigate. As they began their work a veritable flood of news and comment pouring out of Peking made clear that the worst mistake of all was to suppress the student movement. In the middle of the investigation the press dropped the word "counterrevolutionary" from accounts of the "June 23 Incident." Soon the "Incident" itself disappeared from the front page altogether. Militant students and Communist leaders confronted one another in relative peace for a few days. With all classes suspended and the poster-writing campaign temporarily abandoned, nobody dared decide what the next move should be.

Then in July two separate but linked events coincided. Militant students from the capital, flushed with the success of the Peking movement, arrived in Changchih anxious to fan a real local rebellion. At the same time the Party Committee of Changchih, following the lead of the Peking Party Committee, sent work teams into the schools to lead the Great Proletarian Cultural Revolution.

At the First Middle School both of these new forces picked Party Secretary Chang as their target. They clamped a tall hat on his head and paraded him around the campus for criticism and ridicule. They charged him with neglecting his duties in favor of bird hunting in the mountains, with hiring questionable reactionaries as teachers, and with suppressing the study of Mao Tse-tung Thought.

The treatment meted out to Secretary Chang divided students and staff. One group of individuals, rallying around the head of the physics department, spoke out against dunce caps and the use of force. Another group of students and staff sympathetic to the physical education instructor who had launched the "Incident," and the work team as well, all immediately denounced this teacher and his followers as conservatives. They transferred the tall cap to the head of the physicist and paraded him around the schoolyard just as they had Party Secretary Chang a few days before.

In Peking the work teams sent by Liu Shao-ch'i withdrew from all campuses on July 28, a day or two after Mao's return from the south. On August 5 the work teams sent by the Party Committee of Changchih also quietly withdrew, leaving behind a badly divided campus. On the one side stood a faction of students and staff called the "Yao Wu" or "Want Violence" Brigade and on the other side an equal number of students and staff who called themselves the "Hung Pao" or "Red Storm" Brigade.

The *Want Violence Brigade,* though prone to extreme action and not averse to parading people around the campus with dunce caps on their heads, had not really organized itself around a program of violence. The name came from an incident that occurred at the Gate of Heavenly Peace, when Mao Tse-tung first met with one of the Red Guard groups that flocked to Peking in August for vast, million-strong rallies. Mao Tse-tung had asked one enthusiastic young girl from the provinces what her name was.

"My name is Sung P'ing-p'ing [Sung Peace and Calm]," said the girl.

"Sung P'ing-p'ing," mused the Chairman, savoring the contrast between the quiet name and the defiant posture of the fiery-eyed young woman before him. "How come your parents didn't name you Sung Yao-wu [Sung Want Violence]?"

From that moment "Yao Wu" became a very popular name among radicals all over China.

Not to be outdone by the militancy of the opposition, the other group, insisting that it, too, wanted revolution, chose the name *Red Storm.*

Later both sides changed names. The *Want Violence Brigade,* after merging with several smaller groups, finally settled on *Red Union,* while the *Red Storm Brigade,* also after merger, shifted to *Peking Commune.* More reasonable names did not, however, lead to more reasonable attitudes. For the next two years the differences between the two groups widened and sharpened until their members ended up, as did their prototypes in the capital, in open and violent warfare for control of their respective campuses and of their respective cities.

The course of events at the Luan Middle School in Long Bow village closely paralleled the events at the First Middle School. Only at Luan two science teachers named Kao and Wang led the first "rebel" faction while the "loyalists" temporarily sided with their school principal, one Fan Hsiu-ch'i, whom the opposition called "Fan the Landlord." Those who supported Kao T'ai-sheng and Wang called themselves simply *Red Guards,* while those who supported Principal Fan called themselves *Mao Tse-tung Thought Red Guards.* In the alliances that developed between students in Long Bow and students in Changchih City the *Red Guards* linked up with *Red Union* and the *Mao Tse-tung Thought Red Guards* linked up with *Peking Commune.*

66

SIXTEEN POINTS ON HOW TO REBEL

Just as these regional student organizations were forming and the differences between them were crystallizing, national leaders in Peking issued a most important document: "The Decision of the Central Committee of the Chinese Communist Party Concerning the Great Proletarian Cultural Revolution." Adopted on August 8, 1966, this extraordinary statement defined in a few words what the Cultural Revolution was supposed to be about, named its motive forces and its targets, its organizational forms and its methods, warned specifically against the kinds of excesses that were already taking place, took up some special questions such as the role of intellectuals and scientists, the army and the schools, and ended with a call for universal creative study and application of Mao Tse-tung Thought. Its key paragraphs repeated and restated in various ways the central theme that the great masses of the Chinese people should rise up, challenge whatever stood in the way of transforming society, enter into lively contention and serious debate, learn by doing, and liberate themselves not only from Party members in authority who were taking the capitalist road, from bourgeois academic authorities, and from cadres guilty of commandism, but also from all the old thoughts, customs, culture and habits of the exploiting classes so as to establish the thought, customs, culture and habits of the working class. Furthermore, as a corollary of this theme, Party leaders should under no circumstances stand in the way of this movement but should welcome it and help it along, even when it meant their own downfall, their own removal from office.

The third paragraph of the opening point stressing class struggle deserves to be quoted in full:

"Although the bourgeoisie has been overthrown, it is still trying to use the old ideas, culture, customs and habits of the exploiting classes to corrupt the masses, capture their minds, and endeavor to stage a comeback. The proletariat must do exactly the opposite: it must meet head-on every challenge of the bourgeoisie in the ideological field and use the new ideas, culture, customs and habits of the proletariat to change the mental outlook of the whole of society. At present our objective is to struggle against and overthrow those persons in authority who are taking the capitalist road, to criticize and repudiate the reactionary bourgeois academic 'authorities' and the ideology of the bourgeoisie and all other exploiting classes, and to transform education, literature and art and all other parts of the superstructure not in correspondence with the socialist economic base so as to facilitate the consolidation and development of socialism."

The Decision went on to praise the young people who had already moved into action, excused their excesses and mistakes as the inevitable shortcomings of inexperienced youth in a complex revolutionary situation, and confirmed the main thrust of the struggle.

"Since the cultural revolution is a real revolution, it inevitably meets with resistance" both from targets like the capitalist roaders in power and from the force of habit of the old society. Such resistance would be overcome in the course of struggle and setbacks, and from this the working people and particularly the younger generation would learn.

The Decision condemned those party leaders who in one way or another stood in the way of the movement, some because all these new challenges simply overwhelmed them, some because they had made mistakes themselves and feared criticism, and some because they actually recognized themselves as "Party people in authority taking the capitalist road" and feared exposure and overthrow. In contrast, the Decision directed high praise toward those leaders who stood in the vanguard of the movement and boldly aroused the people to criticize and expose. "What the Central Committee of the Party demands of the Party committees at all levels is that they persevere in giving correct leadership, put daring above everything else, and boldly arouse the masses."

Point four stressed the need for the mass of the Chinese people to liberate themselves. "Trust the masses, rely on them and respect their initiative. Cast out fear. Don't be afraid of disturbances. . . ." Big-character posters and great debates to argue matters out would allow the people to "clarify correct views, criticize wrong views and expose all ghosts and monsters."

Point five defined the target as "those within the Party who are in authority and are taking the capitalist road." It also defined them as "a handful of ultrareactionary bourgeois rightists and counterrevolutionary revisionists."

Revolutionaries should isolate these enemies by discovering and mobilizing the Left, winning over the middle forces, and uniting with the great majority so that 95 percent of the cadres and 95 percent of the masses could join together as one.

Revolutionaries should take care, of course, not to lump people who had made a few mistakes with the anti-Party, antisocialist rightists, and not to lump academics who had a few ordinary bourgeois academic ideas with the "scholar despots" or "bourgeois academic authorities."

Revolutionaries should also take care not to confuse differences arising among the people with conflicts between the people and their enemies. The Decision characterized conflicting views among the people as normal. Disputants should resolve differences through debate, by presenting facts and reasoning things out. They should also protect minority views because "sometimes the truth is with the minority" and "even if the minority is wrong they should be allowed to argue their case and reserve their views."

"When there is a debate, it should be conducted by reasoning, not by coercion or force."

Because the authorities had almost universally attacked the early rebels among the students as counterrevolutionaries and because they had used certain mistakes made by the rebels as excuses for such attacks, point seven specifically warned power holders against this tactic and called those who indulged in it "pickpockets."

Point seven refuted as a *line* error (an error of principle) and castigated unconditionally the attitude assumed by many people in power, that opposition to the leaders of a given unit or work team meant opposition to the Party and to socialism.

Power holders should resort to police action only when they uncovered clear evidence of crime such as arson, murder, the use of poison, sabotage or theft of state secrets. Holding opinions, this document declared, could not be classed as criminal activity.

Point eight defined again the target in regard to cadres. It classed them as falling into four categories: good, comparatively good, mistaken but not Rightists, and Rightists. Most cadres fell into the first two categories. Revolutionaries should expose, refute and overthrow only the last category, the rightists. Even then they should give their targets a chance to turn over a new leaf.

Point nine defined the organizational models for carrying out the Cultural Revolution as cultural revolutionary groups, committees and congresses such as many schools, administrative and productive units had already formed. It called them the "organs of power" of the revolution. The organizations set up in the schools, while consisting mainly of students, should include representative teachers, staff members and campus workers. Because the revolutionary transformation of society must surely take a long time, the committees should be permanent, not temporary, and they should periodically reconstitute themselves through a system of general elections similar to that of the Paris Commune.

Point ten identified the transformation of education as a most important task and listed several specific goals: "The period of schooling should be shortened. Courses should be fewer and better. Teaching material should be thoroughly transformed, in some cases beginning with simplifying complicated material. While their main task is to study, students should also learn other things. That is to say, in addition to their studies, they should also learn industrial work, farming and military affairs, and take part in the struggle of the cultural revolution to criticize the bourgeoisie as these struggles occur."

The concluding points of the decision called for education in ideology through criticism of typical examples of bourgeois and feudal ideology, but forbade the naming of people as targets in the press without the permission of the Party Committee responsible, or, in some cases, of the Party Committee at a higher level. Another point called for handling scientists, technicians and ordinary members of the working staffs of advanced institutes who did not oppose the Party and socialism through a policy of "unity, criticism, unity." Revolutionaries should help them to transform their outlook and their working style. Still another point declared the concentration points of the Cultural Revolution to be the leading organs of the Party and government in the large and medium-size cities. The countryside should continue to carry out the Socialist Education Movement and gradually merge it with the Cultural Revolution where appropriate. The Decision defined the overall goal of the Cultural Revolution to be, through a revolution in ideology, to achieve greater, faster, better and more economical results in all fields of work and especially in production. *"Any idea of counterposing the great cultural revolution to the development of production is wrong."* One further point specifically exempted the armed forces from the influence of the mass movement. Army, navy and air force personnel should carry out the Cultural Revolution and the Socialist Education Movement "in accordance with the instructions of the Military Commission of the Central Committee of the Party and the general Political Department of the People's Liberation Army."

The final point, number sixteen, called for the creative study and application of Chairman Mao Tse-tung's works among workers, peasants, soldiers, cadres and intellectuals. *"Mao Tse-tung Thought should be taken as the guide to action in the cultural revolution,"* and "Party committees at all levels must abide by the directions given by Chairman Mao over the years, namely, that they should thoroughly apply the mass line of 'from the masses, to the masses' and that they should be pupils before they become teachers. They should try to avoid being one-sided or narrow. They should foster materialist dialectics and oppose metaphysics and scholasticism."

Looking back on this document with some knowledge of all that has happened since, one must admit it still stands out as something extraordinary in history. Where had there ever been a *ruling* party that called on the people to rise up, criticize and expose anything and everything that seemed to stand in their way, a ruling party that called on the people to clean out the alien elements in its own ranks? The Cultural Revolution clearly started out to be a vast and decisive Party rectification movement, a movement that would mobilize hundreds of millions of ordinary people, remove all the restraints of established authority, and allow these people to organize in any way they saw fit to transform their Party leadership, their government, their culture and their lives.

On the surface, at least, the basic assumption underlying this call was faith in the Chinese people, faith that they truly wanted to build a new socialist society, and that once mobilized they would find ways to expose and criticize everything that interfered with this goal, and ways to reorganize and educate themselves so that the goal could be reached.

Again, on the surface, Mao based his decision to take this extraordinary step on the failure of all previous limited mass campaigns and Party rectification movements to solve the problems of basic line and direction. As Mao was reported to have said in February, 1967, "In the past we waged struggles in rural areas, in factories, in the cultural field, and we carried out the Socialist Education Movement. But all this failed to solve the problem because we did not find a form, a method to arouse the broad masses to expose our dark aspect openly, in an all-around way and from below."

In 1966, with the great upsurge of the student movement, with the spread of revolutionary mass organizations from the schools to government units and factories, and with the Sixteen Point Decision of the Central Committee on the Cultural Revolution promulgated everywhere, the Party and the people, it seemed, had finally found this method. All over China people harbored profound feelings of excitement and optimism. They sensed that a historic turning point had come within reach and that if only hundreds of millions would rise up as activists and if only they sustained their struggle, the future of China as a strong, socialist country would be assured.

If indeed the people of China could have put into practice the Sixteen Points of that famous Decision, if they could have settled disputes by debate and through reasoning, if Party activists could have united with 95 percent of the cadres and 95 percent of the people to isolate, expose and remove from office a handful of bureaucrats and timeservers designated as "capitalist roaders," then the Chinese people could have won at least a partial victory and cleared away some of the barriers to economic and cultural progress that had developed in the course of socialist transformation. On the one hand, the constant expansion of the huge, increasingly inept, centralized bureaucracy menaced everyone. On the other hand, high-level opposition to Mao's "socialist road" undermined all efforts to consolidate that road. Since those in power could hardly be expected to reform themselves, why not put the matter in the hands of the people at large and help them rectify both Party and state?

In real life the remaking of China was by no means simple. Since from the very beginning no one proposed an objective standard for determining who the "capitalist roaders" might be, people disagreed sharply over the targets to be attacked and soon began to attack one another.

The very thing that point eight so strongly opposed—"to prevent the struggle from being diverted from its main target, it is not allowed, under any pretext whatever, to incite the masses or the students to struggle against each other"—was the very thing that developed unchecked. No sooner did rebellion break out anywhere, no sooner did the rank-and-file overthrow authorities in power, than the mass movement invariably split, and rebels began to fight one another, not so much over the shape of the new power to come as over who in fact had the right to hold and wield it.

With few exceptions every negative phenomenon which the Sixteen Point Decision warned against proliferated. Point six clearly stated that "contradictions among the people must not be made into contradictions between ourselves and the enemy"; and point five stated categorically that "anti-Party, antisocialist rightists should not be confused with people who support both the Party and socialism but have made mistakes," and that "bourgeois scholar despots should not be confused with ordinary scholars who held some bourgeois academic ideas."

Yet these confusions arose almost immediately. Small contradictions among the people quickly escalated in the rhetoric of ambitious activists into contradictions with enemies. They called thousands and tens of thousands of cadres who had made a few mistakes rightists and counterrevolutionary revisionists, and called thousands of teachers and specialists bourgeois academic authorities.

The government disseminated the Sixteen Points to the whole country, urging millions to study them. It is doubtful if any document ever received such intensive perusal as did this "magna carta" of the Cultural Revolution, but as with the Magna Carta, people found in it what they wanted to find. They used its various passages to justify what they wanted to do, especially after Mao Tse-tung cranked up the tension by declaring that the Great Proletarian Cultural Revolution was in fact "a great political revolution carried out by the proletariat against the bourgeoisie and all other exploiting classes; it is a continuation of the prolonged struggle waged by the Chinese Communist Party and the masses of revolutionary people under its leadership against the Kuomintang reactionaries, a continuation of the class struggle between the proletariat and the bourgeoisie."

By this definition, people who found themselves on one side of a factional split easily convinced themselves that the opposition did in fact represent not another segment of the people or of popular opinion, but the dreadful Kuomintang, and that therefore they should fight it by all means at hand, and thoroughly defeat it forever. Clearly what amounted to nothing more than contradictions between various groups of revolutionary people were here being mistaken for or deliberately promoted as contradictions with class enemies.

Once the Cultural Revolution began, drastic escalations of antagonism, both spontaneous and rigged, infected almost all of China. Yet few, if any, reflected questions of principle. In the provinces as well as Peking the original divisions arose primarily out of challenges to the revolutionary legitimacy of various groups based on their date of origin. Splits developed between those who rebelled against the status quo first and those who rebelled against the same thing later. At the time, of course, these distinctions seemed vital. Those who had rebelled earlier, when it was more dangerous, considered this their most valid credential. Hoping to preempt all authority, they would have nothing to do with those who had stood neutral at the beginning or even remained loyal for a time to the old administration. The latter, once they decided to join the revolution, had no choice but to form organizations of their own, and these organizations, once formed, tended to harden in hostile contradiction to those that had preceded them into the fray.

Mao's call, issued after he returned to Peking from his first southern trip, for all mass organizations to unite with faculty, staff and cadres who were good or comparatively good (some 95 percent of the total, in Mao's estimation), only served to deepen and widen the splits that already existed, because those contending could not agree on any estimate of the overthrown teachers and cadres. People whom one side regarded as good revolutionaries, the other side often regarded as hopeless revisionists. People whom one side regarded as mistake-prone but capable of reform, the other side most likely denounced as counterrevolutionaries. As the splits developed, mere adherence to one side or the other brought down condemnation by the opposition. If a certain teacher, in response to overtures from, say, the *Red Guards* at Luan Middle School, agreed to work with that group, students from the other headquarters, the *Mao Tse-tung Thought Red*

Guards, automatically opposed that teacher and dug into the record for any adverse material that could be found on him or her in an effort, not so much to discredit the individual, as to discredit the collective which the individual had joined. From digging out adverse material to creating adverse material was but one short step. In the contest for revolutionary legitimacy that developed, frame-up and counterframe-up crowded the agenda.

As rivalry between student factions boiled up into seething contradictions that often led to physical fighting, and ended finally in armed fighting, the original issues of the Cultural Revolution sank in a mire of violence and counterviolence. A naked struggle for power came to the fore in the local institution, the city, the region, the province and the nation as a whole, with each side doing whatever seemed necessary to take and hold high office while making sure that the other side could never do the same.

Mao denounced this battle over power as *bourgeois factionalism*—bourgeois because it was unprincipled; because it was like the struggle between various commercial interests under capitalism for control of the marketplace, for power to pursue self-interest. Having overthrown the old authorities, each group felt that it and it alone had earned the right to take office and rule. Furthermore, each faction convinced its adherents that if they failed as a group, Mao Tse-tung could not hope to retain his position in Peking and this would endanger the whole Chinese revolution. This seemingly solid revolutionary reasoning was in fact specious rhetoric used to cloak a raw struggle for power in a situation where there was very little "room at the top," and the top stood temporarily vacant.

The above description implies that the factionalism arose spontaneously from below as an inevitable trend rooted in the mass consciousness of the time. Factionalism did indeed break out at the grass roots, much of it a revival of old family clan sectarian and sectional rivalries, but there is reason to believe it would never have spread widely at this time had it not been provoked from above by rival groups inside the Central Committee of the Communist Party in Peking, who were themselves vying for supreme power and attempting to gather the kind of mass support necessary to win and consolidate their power against others.

Only the naive ever believed that Nieh Yuan-tzu's poster came spontaneously from below. She and her colleagues in the philosophy department at Peking University wrote it with direct support from Mao Tse-tung, or at least with support from several individuals very close to Mao, including his favorite general of the moment, Lin Piao; his longtime personal secretary, Ch'en Po-ta; and his wife, Chiang Ch'ing. It was common knowledge in Peking that Nieh formulated her list of grievances against Lu P'ing long before her "Marxist-Leninist" poster came out, and that she had suffered for it. A work team under the leadership of Peking's mayor, P'eng Chen, had summoned her and her colleagues to a rectification session in the International Hotel, and held them there for several months in 1965. Yet all the team's efforts to modify or suppress her obnoxious views failed because these views had the support of a second powerful clique in the Central Committee that the Chairman himself backed. When Kuai Ta-fu stepped forth at Tsinghua as a student rebel and steadfastly denounced the work teams sent by Liu Shao-ch'i to suppress the student movement, he did so not simply as a brave young student committed to revolutionary idealism, but as a young man with connections to powerful figures on the Central Committee who stood behind him, encouraged him, and fed him information that he could use as ammunition.

When higher cadres with something to fear from the upheaval saw the effective use which Mao and his supporters made of the student movement and the Red Guards, they quickly formed student organizations and Red Guard units of their own, so that they, too, might have a mass base with which to contend for and hold power. Some people went even further. It now seems clear that those who finally emerged as the "Gang of Four" quite early saw how useful factional contention *as such* could be to them. They were not interested in simply building factions as a mass base of support for specific goals of their own, but saw endless, spiraling factional confrontations as an ideal environment for preventing the consolidation of popular revolutionary power,* while they moved to transfer all power to their own hands. They did everything, therefore, to play off one side against the other, feeding each with ammunition against the other, flattering each with assurances that the revolution could never stand without the victory of that side, and finding endless material that could be used to tarnish reputations and frame the members of each side when used by the other.

The marvelous rhetoric of the Sixteen Points cloaked, in the end, a venal contest of all against all that harked back to imperial times. It did not take the average power holder long to catch on to this new/old form of infighting unleashed by the Cultural Revolution. Quick to perceive that what was at stake in the first instance was power and power alone, and that this had very little to do with the capitalist road or the socialist road, the whole bureaucratic apparatus of China fell to with a will, playing the centuries-old game of bowing to whatever wind blew most strongly from the center while jockeying ruthlessly for whatever power or position came within local grasp. The unprincipled quality of Mao's attack on P'eng Teh-huai, now renewed as he put down Liu and Teng, set the standard for strategy and tactics in this free-for-all. While everyone carefully adopted the rhetoric of the Sixteen Points because it had some prestige among the people, professional practitioners, in true mandarin style, set out to pull down anyone who stood in the way of their own climb to the heights.

Although Mao's program unleashed a surge of enthusiasm and hope for new forms of popular democratic rule at the village level, insiders quickly discovered that seizing and holding power remained the heart of the matter, that anything went as long as it contributed to that nefarious end. The Cultural Revolution soon became, as one Peking cadre so frankly explained, "a contest to see who could send whom to the cadre school."

Mao prepared May Seventh Cadre Schools, ostensibly for the political education of functionaries who had immersed themselves too long in urban

---

*There was always a possibility that fresh young forces, responding to Mao's challenge, might manage to join together on some national scale and actually carry through some part of the transformation of the superstructure that Mao was calling for.

offices and isolated themselves too long from the realities of life. Here they were supposed to reestablish contact with the people, do manual work, raise crops and pigs, study politics, repudiate revisionism, take part in self- and mutual criticism, and prepare themselves for the huge tasks of the socialist construction to come. Too often, however, those chosen for the honor found that they had simply been sent away to practice frugal living and hard labor at a spot so isolated that they could not hope to hold their forces together or ever mount a counterattack on their rivals who had sent them down.

Given the unprincipled nature of the infighting unleashed by the publication of the Sixteen Points, unity at any level was out of the question. Had there been a unified student movement in Peking, there might well have been a unified student movement in the schools of the hinterland, but since factionalists, contending for the highest stakes at the very core of the Communist Party itself, split the student movement in the capital, they doomed the student movement elsewhere in the country to similar division. This fractured student movement in turn guaranteed that the great mass movement of workers and peasants developing under its influence and inspiration down below must likewise split asunder.

67

FROM RINGSIDE
TO ARENA

 At the start the fractured student movement did not seem like a very serious matter to the peasants of Long Bow. Throughout 1966 and into 1967 the Cultural Revolution meant to them primarily a ringside seat for observing the activities and antics of the student movement at Luan Middle School, which occupied the old Catholic Compound at the very heart of their community. In the evening, when the peasants returned from hard labor in the fields, they had no choice but to listen to the interminable debates between the factions that both sides broadcast to the world by loudspeaker. To many peasants this incessant broadcasting was a nuisance and an insult. How could one hold a quiet conversation, think or rest, not to mention sleep, under that endless noisy assault? The Cultural Revolution, they concluded, was for people with culture, so why not carry it on in a cultured manner and leave peasants, who had no culture, in peace. Others, inspired by Mao Tse-tung's pronouncement that everyone, including peasants, should pay attention to state affairs, took an interest in the struggle going on at the school, and did their best to learn something from the debates.

Paying attention was not always easy, because the loudspeakers on both sides often blared forth simultaneously, each trying to drown out the other with superior volume. As a result, they canceled each other out. At other times one side or the other had trouble with the electronic equipment, thus giving the opposition a monopoly of the sound waves, an opportunity which it made the most of.

Among those peasants who took an interest was Kuo Cheng-k'uan, vice-secretary of the Brigade Party Branch and chairman of the Peasants' Association. He would have been miserable if he had not, because his house was built against the schoolyard wall. He and his family could hardly ignore the avalanche of sound that poured, night and day, over that adobe barrier. Cheng-k'uan talked about that time.

> Since I lived so close, I couldn't help but listen to their charges and countercharges. Once I even got involved in the struggle between them. This happened because the *Red Guards* stopped some army trucks on their way to the cement plant. Kao T'ai-sheng, one of the

science teachers at the middle school, led this group. When the students went out to stop the trucks, he led the way. Some of us peasants and a few workers saw them and we didn't like what they had done. The *Mao Tse-tung Thought Red Guards,* the other faction, didn't like it either. We joined up and went to find Kao. He was in the school grounds, surrounded by loyal supporters. But we came in force. We pushed right through and seized him. Then the soldiers criticized us. They said it was wrong to use force, we should debate instead. So right then and there we held a meeting that lasted all afternoon. We decided to determine, on the spot, what was right and what was wrong. We criticized the *Red Guards* for stopping the trucks and they didn't have any good answer. In the end the Liberation Army men said they'd like to take Kao along, talk with him, and return him the next day. But his supporters wouldn't let him go. Some held him by the legs while others grabbed his body. The army men said, "Don't worry, we'll take good care of him. It is our responsibility to help him think things out more clearly." But that didn't convince the students of his faction, so the army men let him go.

After that the debate really grew hot. The *Mao Tse-tung Thought* members yelled, "Down with Kao and Wang!" [the two science teachers] while the *Red Guards* yelled back, "Down with Fan Hsuich'i!" [the principal of the middle school].

At that time people talked a lot about seizing power. Those among us who could read knew that there was such a thing, but the rest of us who were illiterate didn't know what it was all about. You find power standing there and you seize it? It didn't make much sense.

But the students at the middle school took it very seriously just the same. The *Red Guards* threatened to seize power. The school accountant and the janitor identified power with the school seals, so each one took a seal along in his pocket for safekeeping. The janitor's wife lived at the cement plant. One day when her husband went to see her the *Red Guards* ambushed him on the road. They took the seal from him, then rushed back to the school and broadcast that they had seized power from the capitalist roaders in charge of the school.

Immediately the *Mao Tse-tung Thought* crowd cursed them over their loudspeaker and charged that the act was completely illegal— not a power seizure, but a power grab. For myself I couldn't figure out how anyone could seize power by grabbing a seal, but the deed had been done and there they were cursing each other. The *Mao Tse-tung Thought* crowd said their opponents must repudiate their wrong thinking and abandon their bourgeois reactionary line, but the *Red Guards* responded that they had only done what had to be done. Thus they carried on, each side defending its own position and denouncing the other.

After the *Red Guards* seized power in the middle school, some of the *Mao Tse-tung Thought* group who had retreated to Changchih came out from the city to search the grounds. In one of the teacher's desk drawers they found a picture of Liu Shao-ch'i. On the strength of this they accused the *Red Guards* of protecting Liu Shao-ch'i. "While we are all busy overthrowing Liu, you are supporting him!"

They came in some twenty big trucks, equipped with several loudspeakers. As soon as they found this picture the loudspeakers all began to blare the news. To prevent the *Red Guards* from answering back they seized the loudspeaker the *Red Guards* had been using in the middle school. They also went out into the village and seized a second loudspeaker that the *Red Guards* had given to one of the Long Bow peasant organizations. Young members of a rival organization had tipped them off about it.

All afternoon chaos ruled in the school grounds. The *Mao Tsetung Thought* group wanted to take power back. They looked everywhere for the official seal. They seized one girl and beat up several people. But *Red Guards* passed the seal from hand to hand. Since they had more than a hundred pairs of hands, the Changchih people never found it. In the end they retreated with the two loudspeakers they had grabbed and the picture of Liu Shao-ch'i.

No sooner had the city people left than the student factions started to accuse one another. One side charged, "You protect bad people like Kao!" The other side countercharged, "You stand behind Fan the Landlord!" After supper a big confrontation took place. Many people gathered to debate, others gathered just to listen. According to Mao Tse-tung, nobody should curse others or use violence, but in this debate both sides cursed the other for protecting the wrong people. Nobody understood what it was really all about. But at least they didn't beat each other up.

Every night these debates went on until after midnight. After we had eaten our supper we peasants had nothing to do, so we went to the middle school grounds, sat on the sidelines, and listened.

Events such as those described by Kuo Cheng-k'uan—strident, ludicrous, and at the same time threatening—went on until a decision by the Party Center in Peking brought peasants all over China into active participation in the Cultural Revolution. Almost overnight Central Government action transformed Long Bow residents from onlookers, both willing and unwilling, into deeply engaged protagonists.

The document that precipitated this shift was called "Directive of the Central Committee on the Great Proletarian Cultural Revolution in Rural Districts (Draft)." Underneath this imposing title the subheading read: "For discussion and trial application." The Central Committee issued it on December 15, 1966, after most of the fall harvest work throughout China had been completed. It represented a radical departure from previous official announcements, such as a Central Committee Directive of September 14, 1966, which emphasized the overriding importance of the coming harvest and warned *Red Guard* activists not to carry their revolutionary activities into the countryside or, except in very special circumstances, to go into the countryside at all.

Significantly, the directive of December 15 began with a paragraph urging the implementation of Mao Tse-tung's call to "grasp revolution and promote production," and advised peasants to "revolutionize their minds" *and* "move agricultural production forward." "As a rule, no work teams will be sent," said the directive. The masses should take responsibility, educate themselves, liberate themselves and rise on their own to make revolution. They should do all this according to the principles laid down in the Sixteen Points of August 8, combined with the Ten Points and the Twenty-three Points issued during the Socialist Education Movement. In fact, they should bring the Four Clean campaign of the Socialist Education Movement "into the orbit of" the Cultural Revolution and solve all remaining problems as part of this great new movement, the target of which should be "the small handful of capitalist roaders in authority within the Party and the *landlords, rich peasants, counterrevolutionaries, bad elements and rightists not well reformed.*"

Significantly, the document underlined and singled out the last named "five bad categories" as if everyone understood that such people posed the principal contradiction in the Chinese countryside in 1966—a very doubtful proposition that helped lay the groundwork for all manner of excesses, frame-ups, false charges and political detours in the ensuing months and years.

Next came the inspiring sentence that had earlier so moved the youth of Peking and other cities to smash monuments, invade homes, break records, burn books and demand red as the color for "go" in traffic lights —"Destroy the old thought, old culture, old customs and old habits of the exploiting class and establish the new thought, new culture, new customs and new habits of the proletariat." This basic revolutionary command, so seminal to the whole transformation of China, became an excuse for attacking anything and everything that activists didn't like, often resulting in the imposition of traditional feudal standards in the name of proletarianization.

This same point, number three of the ten in the December directive, advised the peasants to rectify bureaucracy and commandism among the cadres and to implement the system of cadres' participation in productive labor, a crucial ongoing requirement vital to the success of cooperative agriculture.

And who was to do all these things? The poor and lower-middle peasants uniting with the middle peasants and gradually uniting more than 95 percent of the masses and 95 percent of the cadres.

Using what organizational form? Cultural Revolution committees of poor and lower-middle peasants elected democratically by congresses of poor and lower-middle peasants. These committees were to take the lead in reorganizing, streamlining and reelecting production leadership groups "through mass discussion." That is, the peasants should democratically reappraise and reform their production teams.

In addition, young people should form *Red Guard* units. The sons and daughters of leading cadres should not hold leading positions in the units, nor should children of landlords and rich peasants now residing in other places return home to establish revolutionary ties. This last prohibition became necessary because the next point gave consent for revolutionary students from the cities to form groups to go to the countryside, build "revolutionary ties," eat, live and work together with the peasants, and take part in the Cultural Revolution so long as they did not monopolize the movement or act in place of the peasants.

Point number seven stressed "big democracy" or "extensive democracy," defined as the "four bigs"—big contending, big blooming, big character posters and big debates. The directive asked for a wide-open, no-holds barred, free-for-all mass movement of the people that was democratic and nonviolent. "Struggle must be waged by placing facts on the table and reasoning things out." A variant of this slogan, "Persist in struggle by reasoning and refrain from struggle by force," enjoyed wide and persistent repetition. Point seven also included permission to establish "revolutionary ties" between brigades and communes coupled with a warning against factional strife "stirred up by bad characters." All of which, in the light of the real struggle that developed, bears today a wistful, utopian flavor, something of the innocent idealism of the revolution in its infancy.

In order to make possible the widest use of big character posters and big debates, the document held communes responsible for distributing free paper, ink, writing brushes and poster paint to all participants in the Cultural Revolution.

Point eight absolutely forbade retaliation against rank-and-filers who expressed dissident views, specifically naming a reduction in work-point earnings as a common means of counterattack by brigade and commune leaders. Anyone labeled "counterrevolutionary" or "saboteur" for having expressed such views should be vindicated. But at the same time the document designated the "five bad" categories—landlords, rich peasants, counterrevolutionaries, bad elements and rightists—as the targets of mass dictatorship. It specifically enjoined them from rebelling, in the name of the Cultural Revolution, against the working class and the poor and lower-middle peasants. These two provisions, in fact, canceled each other out, for in practice, when a dissident wished to express his views, all that was necessary in order to suppress him was to label him or her as belonging to one of the "five bad" categories, in which case the individual had no rights at all that anyone need respect, and obviously no right at all to free paper, ink and writing brushes with which to dispute the label already applied, and vindicate himself or herself.

Point nine concerned education. It declared intermediate schools to be on vacation until the following summer. It instructed work-study universities and middle schools to work out on their own an appropriate method for "grasping revolution and promoting production." It asked commune and brigade leaders to guide primary schools in making revolution.

The last point, point ten, like the last point of the famous Sixteen Point Decision of August 8, raised the question of Mao Tse-tung Thought. "During the Great Proletarian Cultural Revolution, Chairman Mao's works must be studied and applied in flexible ways, the class struggle taken as the leading theme, and emphasis placed on 'application.' " A final, stirring call —"Through the Great Proletarian Cultural Revolution, change the rural districts into big schools for studying the Thought of Mao Tse-tung!"—

wound up the document. This exhortation laid the groundwork for a vast increase in the study of Mao Tse-tung's writings in the countryside. It also set the stage for dogmatic memorization of Mao Tse-tung quotes from the famous *Red Book,* which passed for study in some places. In the following period "flexible study" and "flexible application" were often conspicuous by their absence. Confucian rote learning applied to a new set of "analects" —the wisdom of Chairman Mao—took their place.

The leaders of Long Bow took the December 15 Decision quite seriously and immediately implemented it with the formation of a new administrative body called the *Cultural Revolution Committee,* and a mass organization called the *Revolutionary Rebel Regiment.* The *Cultural Revolution Committee* was made up of seven elected delegates, one from each agricultural production team and one from the Sidelines Team. In theory, each delegate satisfied the five standards for revolutionary successors laid down by Chairman Mao in his polemic against Khrushchev in 1964. But because the Party branch strictly adhered to the Directive's caution against acting in place of the rank-and-file and leaned over backward not to influence peasant choices, the elections brought forward some disappointing delegates, most notably Whiskers Shen, a man regarded by virtually everyone as a notorious rascal. He was chosen by the First Production Team.

Other delegates on the committee were Chou Cheng-lo, a Party member, as chairman; Lin Ling-chih, a teacher in the village primary school, as vice-chairman; and Chi K'uan-shun, Wei Tzu-kuang, Huai Teng-k'e and Li Lin-feng as ordinary members.

Led by this newly elected group, the seven teams met separately to choose who could enter the mass organization, the *Revolutionary Rebel Regiment.* The committee passed final judgment on all names approved by the rank-and-file and opened membership to all citizens not under supervision, regardless of age or sex. However, each had to fill out a form regarding class origin and current status, and the committee allowed only poor and lower-middle peasants without any stain on their history and their children to join. Not even all of these were welcome because, since the Cultural Revolution was obviously another "gate" for the examination of leading cadres, the committee disbarred cadres and cadres' wives, husbands and children. It also disbarred people who fell into any of six categories listed by the Public Security forces as undesirable. These included anyone whom the revolutionary regime had jailed since 1945 and any of their immediate relatives, including children; also the immediate relatives or children of anyone sentenced to death by the revolutionary regime since 1945.

The application of these standards, very strictly interpreted, excluded from the *Revolutionary Rebel Regiment* a large number of people, and amounted to a surrender to the inheritance theory that had inspired so many of the early *Red Guard* organizations in Peking:

> A dragon begets a dragon,
> A phoenix begets a phoenix,
> The son of a rat, from the day of his birth,
> Knows only how to dig a hole in the ground.

What are the requirements for worthy successors to the revolutionary cause of the proletariat?

1. They must be genuine Marxist-Leninists and not revisionists like Khrushchev wearing the cloak of Marxism-Leninism.

2. They must be revolutionaries who wholeheartedly serve the overwhelming majority of the people of China and the whole world and must not be like Khrushchev, who serves both the interests of the handful of members of the privileged bourgeois stratum in his own country and those of foreign imperialism and reaction.

3. They must be proletarian statesmen capable of uniting and working together with the overwhelming majority. Not only must they unite with those who agree with them, they must also be good at uniting with those who disagree and even with those who formerly opposed them and have since been proved wrong in practice. But they must especially watch out for careerists and conspirators like Khrushchev and prevent such bad elements from usurping the leadership of the Party and the state at any level.

4. They must be models in applying the Party's democratic centralism, must master the method of leadership based on the principle of "from the masses, to the masses," and must cultivate a democratic style and be good at listening to the masses. They must not be despotic like Khrushchev and violate the Party's democratic centralism, make surprise attacks on comrades, or act arbitrarily and dictatorially.

5. They must be modest and prudent and guard against arrogance and impetuosity; they must be imbued with the spirit of self-criticism and have the courage to correct mistakes and shortcomings in their work. They must never cover up their errors like Khrushchev, and claim all the credit for themselves and shift all the blame on others.

Successors to the revolutionary cause of the proletariat come forward in mass struggles and are tempered in the great storms of revolution. It is essential to test and judge cadres and choose and train successors in the long course of mass struggle.

> Mao Tse-tung, "On Khrushchev's
> Phoney Communism and Its
> Historical Lessons for the World"
> (July 14, 1964), pp. 72–74.

Or, more succinctly:

> Father a hero, son a great fellow,
> Father a reactionary, son a rotten egg.

So it happened that this first attempt to implement the Cultural Revolution in Long Bow resulted in the selection of a core group of peasants approved and trusted by a hastily chosen Cultural Revolution Committee, which in turn had the support and confidence of the Communist Party Branch. People whose primary commitment was to the status quo would carry out the great "rebellion" under the supervision of those already in power.

By contrast, the rhetoric accompanying all this organizing sparkled with revolutionary words and phrases. The masses were going to rise up against Party people in authority who were "taking the capitalist road"; they were going to criticize and repudiate the ideology of the bourgeoisie and all other exploiting classes; they were going to root out all vestiges of capitalism and revisionism. In the words of the famous January 1, 1967, editorial, the Great Proletarian Cultural Revolution in factories and rural areas must "firmly adhere to the line of letting the masses educate themselves, liberate themselves and rise up to make revolution by themselves. No one should take everything into one's own hands." Furthermore, the movement must "fully develop extensive democracy under the dictatorship of the proletariat. This extensive democracy means mobilizing hundreds of millions of people under the command of Mao Tse-tung's Thought to launch a general attack on the enemies of socialism and, at the same time, criticize and supervise leading organs and leading cadres at all levels." Democracy on such a scale had to be guaranteed, of course, by the army, the militia and the police. "Our organs of proletarian dictatorship must resolutely and unswervingly guarantee the democratic rights of the people and guarantee that free airing of views, the posting of big character posters, great debates and large-scale exchange of revolutionary experience proceed in a normal way."

The leaders of the Party Branch in Long Bow assumed that after studying the Sixteen Points on the Cultural Revolution put out by the Central Committee on August 4, and the Ten Points for carrying out the revolution in the countryside issued on December 16, members of the *Revolutionary Rebel Regiment* would seize the "four big democracies" and complete the Cultural Revolution with dispatch.

"We originally thought," said Swift Li, at that time vice-secretary of the Long Bow Party Branch, "that one organization was enough and that it could solve the problems left over by the Four Clean Movement and solve all the problems of the cadres." To put it mildly, he suffered under an illusion.

Events outside of Long Bow had already rendered an orderly, Party-led rectification movement in the village obsolete. In the period between August 8, when the Central Committee first defined the Cultural Revolution, and the end of the year, when the peasants began to act on the December 16 Decision, a militant rebellion spread beyond the schools into all levels of the government and into the factories, mines, railroads, shipping companies and other enterprises as well. Middle-school and college students no sooner formed their *Red Guard* organizations than they began to travel. Aided by free railroad tickets for all activists, Peking students fanned out to distant provinces, and students from other parts of the nation flocked to Peking, where Mao Tse-tung, Lin Piao, Chou En-lai and other leaders met them at huge rallies, a million or two at a time. The excitement generated by these rallies and the publicity that accompanied them soon broke down the barriers which many communities had built against *Red Guard* penetration. Students joined young workers, young workers contacted older workers and staff members, and soon the factories, mines, mills, railroads and truck depots of China seethed with as many activities, were decorated with as many big character posters, and were deafened with as many loudspeaker debates as the campuses continued to be. When the Cultural Revolution reached the working class, and particularly the working class of Shanghai (the only city in China where large numbers of people were born into this class, as distinct from being recruited into it from the countryside), political activity soon burst the bounds of popular agitation, debate, criticism and exposure and moved on to the seizure of power.

During the week that Long Bow peasants sat down to discuss who was qualified under the five standards for election to a Cultural Revolution Committee, one faction of workers and students in Shanghai, calling themselves the *Shanghai Workers' Revolutionary General Headquarters,* actually took control of the city by deposing the mayor, Ts'ao Ti-ch'iu, the Party Secretary of the East China Region, Chen Hsi-lien, and many other Communists on the City and Regional Party committees. Press and radio presented this power seizure, the culmination of a long and complex battle between the Revolutionary General Headquarters and the Shanghai Party leaders, to the nation as a rising of the working class, a victory of the people over "capitalist roaders" and counterrevolutionary revisionists. Official publicity conveniently glossed over the fact that at least half of the working class of Shanghai and its student allies didn't agree with the action and had long been organized in units that tried to block it. Inspired by this dubious example, power seizure by "the masses" became the order of the day.

Shanghai Workers' Revolutionary Headquarters took over that city on January 6 with stirring rhetoric. On January 11 a group of higher cadres took over from their superiors in Taiyuan, Shansi Province, and a few days later, on January 31, a similar upheaval occurred in Heilungkiang. Each toppling, which in reality more closely resembled a coup by one group at the top against another group at the top than it did a revolution from below, received noisy supportive publicity and turned attention throughout the country to the possibility of underlings overthrowing anyone currently holding position above them.

In this atmosphere the prosaic, step-by-step measures adopted in Long Bow for carrying out the Cultural Revolution from above broke down. Ten days after a well-organized series of elections and recruitments established the *Cultural Revolution Committee* and the *Revolutionary Rebel Regiment,* they both collapsed. Seven mass organizations, each formed by a different production team, took their places. These organizations represented the rank-and-file team membership more faithfully than the politically immaculate *Rebel Regiment,* and the members set up each one to attack a specific target, that is to say, a specific leading cadre in the brigade. Disagreement among the seven on who the real targets should be made it impossible to unite as one body, but they were able to merge, as did myriad competing organizations all over China, into two headquarters.

The seven organizations were the *Defend Mao Tse-tung Thought Platoon* of the First Team, the *Defend Mao Regiment* of the Second Team, the *Truth Champions* of the Third Team, the *Defend the East Guards* of the Fifth Team, the *Expose Schemes Fighting Corps* of the Sixth Team, the *Stormy*

Petrels of the Fourth Team and the *Shankan Ridge Fighting Team* of the Sidelines Team. The first five groups chose names common to mass organizations all over China. The last two chose more original labels. The *Stormy Petrels* called themselves after the wild birds celebrated in Gorky's poem "Rising Storm." The poet had watched petrels welcoming an impending sea storm as revolutionaries must welcome the imminent Russian revolution. Primary school pupils all over China memorized his poem. The *Shankan Ridge Fighting Team* named itself after a famous ridge in North Korea that a detachment of Chinese volunteers held for months against heavy odds during the seesaw war against the American forces fought in the mountains of Central Korea.

With the formation of several conflicting organizations a turbulent and exciting period began for Long Bow. In the first flush of enthusiasm all seven organizations mounted poster attacks on a variety of targets, often within their own team. The *Petrels* of the Fourth Team, for instance, attacked their team leader, Wang Wen-te, because of his high-handed methods. Whiskers Shen, who worked on the Sidelines Team but always considered himself a member of the First Team, wanted to attack Chu Hsi-ch'ing, leader of his own team, and Chi Shou-hsi, its political director. Dissident forces inside the First Team had already elected Whiskers to the *Cultural Revolution Committee*. When this collapsed he joined *Shankan Ridge* as a sidelines worker. But when *Shankan Ridge*'s ninety members refused to launch an attack on the First Team's leaders, Chu and Chi, he left *Shankan Ridge* and formed the *Mao Tse-tung Thought Platoon* inside the First Team to conduct rebellion there. *Shankan Ridge*, greatly influenced though not formally led by Sidelines Team leader Little Shen, first attacked an absolutely safe target—four "bad elements" under supervision, on the grounds that the four of them, Yen Lai-shun, Lin Ho-shun, Yang Kuang-hung and Chin Pao-ch'uan, were not behaving properly. A few days later, however, they mobilized against more serious quarry, joined a meeting of the *Petrels* to help them confront Wang Wen-te, and then launched a mass meeting to confront Lu Chin-jung, the Chairman of the Communist Party Branch.

When they attacked the prestigious brigade cadres Wang and Lu, the southend "rebels" split the community. With the removal of Chang Hsin-fa in the Big Four Clean, Lu Chin-jung had become, in fact as well as in name, the leading cadre in Long Bow. For many years Wang Wen-te had served not only as a team cadre of the Fourth Team but also as head of public security for the brigade as a whole. As soon as the *Shankan Ridge Fighting Team* began to attack Lu and Wang, other groups came to the two cadres' defense. They soon divided five to two, with *Shankan Ridge* and the *Petrels* lined up on one side, insisting on overthrowing Lu Chin-jung and Wang Wen-te, and with the other five organizations, headed by the *Defend Mao Tse-tung Thought Platoon*, insisting on retaining them.

A meeting to criticize Wang Wen-te took place on February 2, 1967. It was a joint meeting sponsored by both the *Petrels* of the Fourth Team and *Shankan Ridge* of the Sidelines Team. Initially they charged Wang Wen-te simply with arrogance, high-handed methods and repeated rejection of criticism. But once his team comrades decided to overthrow him, they raised other, potentially more serious charges. Some people said that he maintained links with counterrevolutionaries, because, when he built his new house, he borrowed grain from Lin Ho-shun, one of the bad elements under supervision, and accepted a plate of cookies sent over by Yen Lai-shun, also under supervision. As an illustration of his questionable attitude, some young people charged that he showed lack of respect for Chairman Mao. Only a few days earlier a film shown in Long Bow had depicted Mao Tse-tung at a mass rally in Peking receiving *Red Guards* from all over the country. It caused great excitement, especially among the young. "Seeing Chairman Mao in the film is like seeing him ourselves," they said. "Wouldn't it be great if we could go to Peking and see him in the flesh!"

"So what," said Wen-te, displeased with the way the young people were neglecting their jobs to talk about revolution all the time. "What if you did see him? You couldn't eat the sight or wear it. You'd still have to work hard here."

"This," said the young people, "was no way for a poor peasant to talk."

At the meeting Wen-te, arrogant as ever, refused to accept any of the criticisms that his teammates made. This caused resentment among the people and the atmosphere grew tense. Kuo Cheng-k'uan's stepson, Kuo Ming-en, a leader of the *Petrels,* chaired the meeting. As questions, in the form of written notes, were handed up thick and fast, Kuo Ming-en read them aloud.

Suddenly a question came up that influenced the whole course of the Cultural Revolution in Long Bow. In 1971 I heard several different versions of the incident. Some said the question had been written on a note that Kuo Ming-en destroyed. Others said the question came from the floor, voiced by Chin Yun-sheng, son of Chin Shen-yi, a notorious speculator and go-it-aloner. No one agreed on the exact wording of the question, but all agreed it concerned the fate of Wang Hsiao-nan, the middle peasant beaten to death in 1946 in an effort to find out if he had concealed more than one cache of gold coins for his landlord brother-in-law. Some said the question was, "How was Wang Hsiao-nan beaten to death?" Some said there was a second question, "How many people did you, Wang Wen-te, beat to death in the land reform?" Others said the question was, "How can you say when rebels criticize you that they are trying to reverse the case on Wang Hsiao-nan?" Whatever the exact form of the question, and whatever its source, it did bring back on the agenda an ugly incident dormant now for twenty years, a matter that was supposed to have been settled in the rectification movement of 1948.

Some people immediately took exception to the question. They said it should be ruled out of order. Others pressed for an answer. They began to shout at one another. Kuo Ming-en, finding it impossible to restore order, broke up the meeting. That is one version. Another version alleges that after the question was asked, Wang Wen-te rejected it, as he had all other questions, and the meeting continued on to a normal conclusion. Whatever the truth, on one thing everybody agreed: the meeting to challenge Wen-te ended in a standoff that led, for the time being, only to a hardening of position on both sides. But the fact that at least one question had challenged a major settlement of the land reform movement continued to rankle in some people's minds. Several months later, after the factions began to attack one another, the question served as extraordinary ammunition in the hands of one side.

The very next day a second mass meeting brought people together to confront the secretary of the Long Bow Party Branch, Lu Chin-jung. Because the loyal village majority felt that Lu Chin-jung was a good cadre, this meeting likewise came to no satisfactory conclusion. Lu had been closely scrutinized during the Four Clean Movement, had been judged and approved by the masses, and had been reconfirmed as Communist Party Secretary. How could he suddenly turn into a capitalist roader?

Those who opposed Lu insisted that he was a capitalist roader because of a whole series of mistakes, some of which they had brought out during the Four Clean Movement. During the movement a few people had held Chang Hsin-fa responsible for the death of Little Four P'ei, the young man caught stealing tools at the railroad yards who had died at the bottom of a well. Now suddenly they charged Lu Chin-jung with responsibility for this because he had been Party Secretary at the time. They also held him responsible for the death of Wang Tien-p'ing's mother, a woman who had died of a simple illness because, some charged, the brigade leaders had not taken her condition seriously. A third death occurred when an itinerant sieve maker stumbled across a hot electric wire that was down in the street. The wire accidentally electrocuted him.

As if responsibility for three deaths were not indictment enough, the opposition charged Chin-jung with taking advantage of his high position in the brigade to eat more, enjoy more, and win special favors. In 1965 the Long Bow crop had been good enough to enable everyone to eat more while at the same time the brigade sold more to the State Grain Trading Company. In recognition of this achievement, the Changchih City government awarded a bicycle to the brigade. Lu Chin-jung, some said, expropriated this bicycle for his personal use.

Also in 1965 the city asked the brigade leaders to recommend someone to serve on a Four Clean Work Team in another village. Long Bow's leading group recommended Chin-jung's sister, Lu Feng-chen, a schoolteacher in Changchih City, for this honor. Why should Long Bow's Communist Party Secretary recommend his own sister? And why should Lu Chin-jung help a former puppet policeman, Tseng Chung-hsi, to build a shed on land that was distributed to the poor peasant All Here Li in the land reform? Wasn't this reversing the case on land reform? And wasn't it because this particular person was the father-in-law of the Communist Party Secretary? And why should Lu Chin-jung recommend the former rich peasant Yang Ch'eng-tao, of the Western Mountains, as a settler in Long Bow? Why make him the buyer for the Sidelines Team? Why allow him to embezzle hundreds of yuan and lose outright another 9,000? Wasn't it because this Yang Ch'eng-tao was husband to Chin-jung's aunt? Wasn't this showing special consideration for a relative?

To top it all off, there was the case of Lu Ch'eng-hai, like Tseng Chung-hsi a puppet policeman under the Japanese occupation, who fled to Hung-tung at the time of land reform, married there, fathered a son now in his teens, and then came back to Long Bow in 1960. Lu Chin-jung had allowed him to go out and make bricks for another organization as long as he turned money in to the Long Bow Brigade. During the Four Clean the brigade chose him as an activist in the study of Mao Tse-tung Thought. He went about relating his experiences as if he were a model, but in fact he was a traitor.

The opposition posted these eight charges against Lu Chin-jung all over Long Bow. Lu himself could not avoid appearing before the mass meeting called by *Shankan Ridge* and the *Petrels,* but he effectively took the edge off this meeting by supporting a diversionary attack launched by Whiskers Shen against the leaders of the First Team, Chu Hsi-ch'ing and Chi Shou-hsi. Whiskers Shen's *Defend Mao Tse-tung Thought Platoon* concentrated its fire on Chi, the People's Liberation Army veteran and a Communist Party member who was the political director of their team. Huge posters calling him a capitalist roader and counterrevolutionary revisionist were pasted on the walls in competition with those attacking Chin-jung. Meanwhile Yang Szu-ho, another well-known rascal on the First Team who had served as team accountant, came forward to charge that Chi, the middle peasant, had oppressed him, a poor peasant, by forcing an examination of his accounts during the Four Clean Movement. In the end, he charged, the campaign had illegally forced him to turn over five sections of house in settlement for money grafted. Both Whiskers Shen and Yang Szu-ho claimed that they had been framed by Chi, and that he, not they, had stolen the goods and money in question. They demanded that Chi be expelled from the Party. Lu Chin-jung stood up to speak in support of this demand.

As charges and countercharges grew in bitterness, the Cultural Revolution in Long Bow gradually polarized the population, with everyone sooner or later lining up either as "rebels" behind the *Petrels* and *Shankan Ridge* in their demand for the overthrow of Lu Chin-jung, or as "loyalists" behind the *Defend Mao Tse-tung Thought Platoon* and its allies in his defense.

I use the terms "rebel" and "loyalist" with some hesitation and place them in quotes for good reason. No one should assume any important ideological or political differences between the two groups. The peasants who challenged Lu Chin-jung's right to the job of Party Secretary were neither more nor less revolutionary than he. Their challenge expressed no underlying programmatic dissent and certainly not any class contradiction. It was a case of the "outs" expressing dissatisfaction with the performance of the "ins," in part because that performance was flawed, but mainly because this expression gave the "outs" a chance to get in.

This distinction must be stressed because there is a notion widespread in the West that Mao urged political radicals to rise up, then betrayed and suppressed them. It would be unfortunate if the terms "rebel" and "loyalist" gave credence to this myth. I use these terms for convenience only, to describe two sets of activists, with essentially the same politics, who quarreled over power.

68

SEIZE, COUNTERSEIZE

By the beginning of February, power seizures were occurring in China every day, every hour, every minute, in all the provinces between the Amur River and the South China Sea and at all levels—provincial, regional, municipal, commune, brigade and team. Sometimes higher-level seizures led to lower-level seizures, but sometimes the process reversed itself, with upheavals at the bottom inspiring upheavals at the top. Horse Square Commune was typical of the latter. Rebels threw leading cadres out of office in several of its brigades, including Long Bow, before the commune leadership changed hands, and rebels at the commune level carried out this latter coup only with the help of successful insurgents from the village level.

Members of *Petrel* and *Shankan Ridge* seized power in Long Bow on February 8, sent a contingent on to Anyang on the tenth in support of an abortive coup there, and on the twelfth went en masse to Horse Square to threaten Party Secretary Shih Chao-sheng and Commune Chairman Chang Ai-ch'i. The head of the Commune Militia Department, Yang Hsiu-shan, riding a rebel tide, charged Shih Chao-sheng with eight crimes and got people from as many brigades as possible to confront him face to face. Not the least active in this endeavor were members of Long Bow's *Petrel* and *Shankan Ridge*, but this time around they failed.

Helping others take power was an extravagant gesture on the part of *Petrel* and *Shankan Ridge*. Their own power at home was far from secure, for they represented only a minority of Long Bow peasants and not a very prestigious minority at that. When the leaders of these two organizations first decided to challenge Long Bow's status quo they tried hard for a broad coalition. They invited the *Defend Mao Tse-tung Thought Platoon* of the First Team, the *Truth Champions* of the Third Team and the *Defend Mao Regiment* of the Second Team to join in, but only some individual members of the last group agreed to take part.

They had more success with outside organizations. The *Red Guards* from the cement plant, the *Rebel Regiment* from the locomotive repair shop, the *Mao Tse-tung Thought Red Guards* from the Luan Middle School, and a group of workers from the power station at Anyang all sent representatives to take part in decisive action on February 8. This hastily collected force converged on the brigade office after dark, intent on taking over the official seals and declaring a new administration for the brigade.

To seize power meant, concretely, to seize the seals used in the transaction of brigade business. The task of seizing the seals was simplified, to some extent, by the fact that Shen Chi-ts'ai of the Fourth Team, a member of *Shankan Ridge* and brother to Shen Chin-ts'ai, served as chief accountant for the brigade and held the seals as part of his job. The "rebels," however, did not simply want to possess the seals. They wanted the responsible leaders of the brigade to hand power over to them by handing over the seals. Unfortunately, they could not find Lu Chin-jung. According to the rebel account, he had run away. In Lu's absence they rounded up Chang Kuei-ts'ai, then vice-chairman of the brigade, so that Shen Chi-ts'ai could hand the seals over to him. Then they demanded that Kuei-ts'ai in turn hand the seals to the "rebels."

All this went smoothly. When Kuei-ts'ai finally put the seals in "rebel" hands, they passed them on for safekeeping to a young *Petrel* member whom they thought no one would search—Hsin-fa's daughter, Hsien-hua. Then everyone went home to bed.

As the following narration shows, many older peasants in Long Bow regarded any rebellion on their home grounds with skepticism. Chang Hsin-fa, who in 1967 still nursed a grudge against the whole community for having set him aside as a leader, deprecated his own daughter's role.

> My daughter Hsien-hua joined *Petrel*. She told me about an important evening meeting.
>
> "What meeting?" I asked.
>
> "The meeting where we talked about seizing power."
>
> "How was it discussed?"
>
> "We just decided to seize power."
>
> "But don't you have to have a three-in-one combination—poor peasants, support from the militia and all that?" I asked.
>
> "Well, we didn't really have much of a meeting," she said. "Only Shen Chin-ts'ai, Chi Wan-ch'ang and Yang Chi-wang were there. We got together in the drugstore at the south end of the village."
>
> "And what were you doing there?" I asked.
>
> "They want me to be a rebel team leader."
>
> "My, you really are climbing up fast," I said. "As soon as you go to the meeting they give you a big position. But I wouldn't go and seize power if I were you."
>
> I was afraid for her. If she goes and seizes power and everything goes well, that's all right. But if things go wrong they'll all say, "See, Hsin-fa has lost power after twenty years and now he has put his daughter up to taking it back for him!"
>
> At 10:00 P.M. they sent someone to get her. Their power seizure was about to begin.
>
> "Why do they want you?" I asked.
>
> "To seize power."
>
> "Don't you dare go!" I said firmly.
>
> She heard me. She didn't leave, so I went to bed. But the next

morning I heard that the *Petrels* had already taken power and had given the brigade seal to my daughter for safekeeping. At noon when she came home to eat I asked her what she was holding the seal for and who gave it to her. Chi K'uan-shun had given it to her; he said, "She's a young girl. It's safer with her than with others. She can keep it for a day and a night. Then we'll hold a meeting and elect a new brigade committee."

That afternoon my daughter wanted to go out but she didn't know what to do with the seal.

"You had better give that back to whoever gave it to you," I said. "We don't want to get involved in these affairs. They have nothing to do with us."

She came back at suppertime.

"Did you give the seal back?"

"Yes."

"Let's just forget the whole thing," said my wife. "Let's not quarrel at New Year's."

But I didn't let the matter rest.

"Do you have it on you?"

She patted her pocket.

"It's empty," she said.

A few days later I told my daughter again, "Don't stay in that organization. We don't want to get involved. If you get into trouble I'll be pulled into it."

Li Yü-hsi had joined the organization with her but soon started to waver. When he decided to get out she got out at the same time. She put up a poster that said, "I'm not a *Petrel* anymore. I've given up my armband."

Later, when she went out she met Yang Chi-wang.

"You've withdrawn?" he asked.

"Yes, I don't want to be in now."

"Well, you had better think it over," he said. "You could risk your Communist Party membership that way."

So my daughter came home worried.

"Never mind," I said. "None of them represents the Branch. They can't expel you."

Once she withdrew from the *Petrels* I stopped worrying.

Kuo Cheng-k'uan, longtime head of the Peasants' Association, shared Hsin-fa's doubts and hesitations about the strange business of grabbing power; but his stepson, Kuo Ming-en, played a leading role nevertheless:

On the eve of the Chinese New Year the *Petrels* and *Shankan Ridge* joined forces. They called all the cadres into the brigade office that night and announced, "We're seizing power. You had better hand it over." So the cadres gave them "power"—the brigade seal.

On New Year's Day my son Kuo Ming-en didn't come home because he and others were in the office guarding "power." The next day most of the members of the two organizations went to Anyang because a fraternal organization there asked for help. They marched out under a red flag singing at the top of their voices. Ming-en didn't go because he was guarding "power" at home. When he came home to eat I asked him where all the people had gone.

"To Anyang to seize power," he said.

"You haven't done anything here yet," I said. "How come you go running off to Anyang? You're flying all over the place. One day you pass the seals around, the next day you watch the office, the third day you rush off to Anyang. What for?"

"We went to help the people there seize power."

But things didn't go so well in Anyang. The Communist Party Secretary, Old New Year Wang, stood up on a platform. He held up the brigade seal and waved it in the air.

"Here's the seal," he said. "Who wants it? You'll have to elect somebody to take charge. If you don't, I won't give it up."

Since those who had gone to seize power were few and most of the peasants of Anyang rallied around New Year Wang, the "rebels" there called on the Long Bow "rebels" for help. But when our people got there and saw what the situation was, they hesitated.

Old New Year Wang was holding the seal up with two fingers. It would have been easy for anyone to grab it. But nobody moved.

"Why don't they seize power themselves?" the Long Bow people asked. Then they turned around and marched home again.

No one seized power in Anyang that day.

My daughter, Kuo Ming-yin, went to Anyang. When she came back I asked her where she had been.

"Anyang."

"Did you seize power?"

"No, the Communist Party Secretary stood there holding 'power' up in the air, but nobody dared take it. We thought they ought to seize it themselves."

"You're just like a toad that wants to eat swan meat," I said. "You haven't done anything in Long Bow yet, but you run off to Anyang!"

Both son and daughter began to debate with me then.

"Our two organizations are helping each other," they protested.

"Whenever they ask you to go, you go?"

"Yes, if they ask us, we go. We want to back them up. But if they won't take power, we can't do anything. We are only there to help."

"In the future don't meddle in other brigade's affairs," I warned. "Here you can join whoever takes the correct direction, but if the direction is not correct, don't join."

At this point they brought out their *Red Books* and began reading quotations to me: "Power is to serve the poor and lower-middle peasants. The bourgeoisie can't serve the poor and lower-middle peasants. They are capitalist roaders."

"Who are capitalist roaders?"

"Some people in power who don't take the socialist road."

"What do you know about it?" I said.

That made them mad.

"We won't listen to you. We're on top of the main trend. If you don't want to listen, to hell with you."

When they left I felt that these young people didn't think things through very well. They just wanted to do something, to act. And as for me, I couldn't make head or tail of what was going on.

Two or three days later some people from the commune headquarters called on the young people to go and seize power there. They wanted the support of the *Petrels.* So our young people went off and stayed away all night. All the detachments belonging to that faction, from Long Bow, Anyang, Horse Square, Horse Square Primary School—they all went to the commune headquarters and debated in the darkness. At sunrise they finally got hungry and came home to eat.

Those young people, they really had energy. They talked all night without food.

"What did you accomplish there?" I asked.

"We debated."

"Who was taking the right direction?"

"We were. We debated against them."

"Did you seize power?"

"No. We just went to debate."

"Now it's the commune comrades who ask your help to seize power. What if some group in the city does the same?"

"To say nothing of the city, if the Central Committee asks our help, we'll go. We'll seize power from Liu Shao-chi'i and the capitalist roaders."

"All right," I said, and shrugged my shoulders. "Go ahead and stir things up."

News of a power seizure by "rebels" in Long Bow ran like an electric shock through the village, and immediately generated strong opposition. Nobody went to work the next day, or for several days thereafter. Production came to a complete halt throughout the brigade. Lu Chin-jung's supporters rallied for a counterattack and went to the commune for help in mounting it. Commune headquarters in Horse Square gave them copies of a brand-new editorial from the Party's theoretical journal *Red Flag,* entitled "On the Proletarian Revolutionaries' Struggle to Seize Power." They studied and discussed it avidly. As with so many of the major documents of the Cultural Revolution, all factions could interpret this article to support their special interests. The forces loyal to the old brigade leadership seized on those paragraphs that urged discrimination, when seizing power, between Party people in authority taking the capitalist road and those leading cadres who have always firmly adhered to the proletarian revolutionary line and "are the treasure of the Party." "To regard all persons in authority as untrustworthy is wrong," the editorial said. "To expose, exclude and overthrow all indiscriminately runs counter to the class viewpoint of Marxism-Leninism-Mao Tse-tung Thought." Lu Chin-jung, they claimed, was obviously not a capitalist roader, but one of the "treasures of the Party."

Furthermore, the editorial warned, "at the present stage of the decisive struggle being waged by the proletariat against the bourgeoisie and its handful of agents within the Party, the landlords and rich peasants, who persist in their reactionary stand, the bourgeois rightists, bad elements, counterrevolutionary revisionists and the U.S.–Chiang Kai-shek special agents all emerge. These ghosts and monsters spread rumors to confuse people, and deceive and mislead those who are not aware of the true facts into forming counterrevolutionary organizations to carry out frenzied counterrevolutionary activities."

The editorial went on to advocate firmness in exercising dictatorship over these counterrevolutionaries. "For reactionaries even limited democracy is not allowed, not to speak of extensive democracy, not one iota. Toward them we should carry out only dictatorship!"

People of dubious origin and devious motives, people born of landlord and rich peasant parents, sons and daughters of counterrevolutionaries, bad elements of all kinds who were rising up to seize power from poor and lower-middle peasants led both *Petrel* and *Shankan Ridge,* the loyalists charged. To prove their case they wrote up material on five of the leading rebels that made it sound as if, indeed, counterrevolution had raised its ugly head in Long Bow.

Did the vice-secretary of the Party branch, Swift Li, and Militia Captain Fast Chin, who worked behind the scenes mobilizing members of the *Defend Mao Tse-tung Thought Platoon* to compile and distribute this slanderous material, really think that landlords were making a comeback in Long Bow? It seems unlikely. Their reason for condemning the overthrow that had occurred was that it annihilated their own power and that of close relatives. Personal interest compelled them to discredit the "rebels" by all possible means. The most effective method was to smear "rebel" leaders as class enemies. As they developed a case on class grounds they soon began to believe a substantial part of it, but the underlying reason for opposing what had happened had nothing to do with class politics.

The truth of the matter was that Long Bow, though not clan-ridden like many traditional Chinese communities, had long been divided north and south on old clan lines. The division had created two competing temples. The Lu family dominated the northern and larger section of the village, where the old North Temple, built by the Chi family, stood until *fanshened* peasants knocked it down in the fifties. The Shen family played a major role in the southern section, where the old South Temple had disappeared much earlier but left behind persistent remnants of sectional pride. The Lu family, since Liberation at least, and possibly for a long time prior to that, had played an increasingly dominant role in village government. People in the know had long called Long Bow the "Lu Family Kingdom." To the ruling Lus an uprising based on the Fourth Team in the south and the Sidelines Team led by Little Shen meant that southerners, instigated by Shens, were on the rampage and meant to take over. Obviously, self-respecting Lus had to stop them. They could not allow upstarts to get away with any such thing.

A personal feud that had broken out years before between Little Shen, the moving spirit behind the takeover, and Fast Chin, the overthrown militia captain who was the Lu family's closest ally, made this "upstart" rebellion even more intolerable. The feud began when Little Shen married the girl Fast Chin claimed as his—the widow of his dead brother Chin Ts'ai-pao. Fast Chin blamed Little Shen and not his widowed sister-in-law for this stunning reversal of fortune and bitterly resented the sight of him. When young people counseled by Little Shen rose up to seize power, their action deeply affronted Fast Chin. He saw it as another dastardly plot by the bride-snatcher. This time, however, something more important than a bride was at stake. Power to direct Long Bow Brigade hung on the outcome. As far as Chin was concerned, the challenge had to be smashed.

As the saying went in Long Bow, "two big cases" and "two big hates" dominated local politics. The Wang Hsiao-nan case (the case of the middle peasant who died of blows during the land reform) and the Little Four P'ei case (the case of the thief who jumped into the well), joined with hatred over "power seizure" and hatred over "wife seizure" as sources of dissension.

These were some of the more pressing reasons why, when the Cultural Revolution began, the people of Long Bow split into "loyalist" and "rebel" factions and then contested so bitterly for supremacy. But the struggle as it developed in 1967 obscured such venal motives more or less completely. What people talked about was the socialist road and the capitalist road, revolution and counterrevolution, poor and lower-middle peasants mobilizing to defend their power and landlords and rich peasants conspiring to overthrow it.

The case made by the "loyalist" *Defend Mao Tse-tung Thought Platoon* against the "rebel" *Petrel* and *Shankan Ridge* sounded quite convincing: Young Kuo Ming-en commanded the *Petrels,* chaired the meetings to critize Wang Wen-te and Lu Chin-jung, and led the group that seized power on February 8. Kuo Ming-en, said the "loyalists," was the son of Meng Hsien-chung, a notorious counterrevolutionary who headed the puppet security bureau under the Japanese occupation and hounded many people to death during the Resistance War. When peasants rose to take revenge after Liberation, they cut Meng to pieces with a fodder chopping knife. After the matter of his father came up for review, the village school fired Ming-en as a teacher.

Young Yang Chi-wang was vice-commander of the *Petrels* and an active participant in all of its program. According to the "loyalists," his mother was a Catholic nun. Worse still, she was the daughter of the notorious landlord Fan Pu-tzu and sister of Fan Tung-hsi, leader of an irregular Kuomingtang detachment that had avoided conflict with the Japanese but harassed the resistance forces, while robbing, raping and killing the common people at will. A detachment of Eighth Route Army soldiers cornered Fan Tung-hsi and ten of his men in a Long Bow compound and set it afire. Fan Tung-hsi climbed into an earthen crock filled with water, but the heat boiled the water and cooked him to death. Peasants found his charred remains in the crock after the fire burned itself out. Yang's grandmother, on the other side, though a poor peasant, once hid some wealth for a landlord and was beaten for her pains.

Young Chou Lai-fu was a leader of *Shankan Ridge.* According to the "loyalists" his bad background overshadowed that of the other two. He was the son of Shih Jen-pao and the grandson of landlord Shih La-ming. Shih Jen-pao had not only been a member of Fan Tung-hsi's marauding Kuomintang detachment, he had married Fan Tung-hsi's sister, Chien-chang, and this made him a cousin of the suspect *Petrel* Yang Chi-wang. After Fan Tung-hsi's fiery death, Jen-pao had led the remnants of Fan's group into the puppet Fourth Column and fought thereafter on the side of the Japanese. At the time of Liberation he ran away, but his wife, who remained in Long Bow, died of internal injuries after a beating inspired by the land reform campaign.

Shang Yin-k'u was an active member of *Petrel*. The "loyalists" stressed that he was the son of Shang Shih-t'ou, puppet village head under the Japanese, who was condemned to death by the Liberated Areas County Court. Several Eighth Route Army soldiers executed him in a daring midnight raid in 1942.

Chin Ken-so was also an active member of *Petrel*. The "loyalists" never failed to point out the rich peasant status of his father.

Then there was Tai Mao-hsiang, son of a puppet *pao chang* (head of a 100-family security group in which a transgression by one member was held to be the responsibility of all). "Loyalists" pointed out many others with similar blood ties to bad elements; most, if not all of them, had failed to qualify for membership in the officially sponsored *Revolutionary Rebel Regiment,* but when the *Regiment* broke down they flocked into *Petrel* and *Shankan Ridge* in order, said the "loyalists," to "reverse the case" on land reform, bring about a restoration of gentry rule, and avenge the sufferings of their parents.

The "loyalists" of the *Defend Mao Tse-tung Thought Platoon* also attacked the record of Little Shen, the man they considered the *hou t'ai* or backstage prop of the rebellion. Without encouragement from this older Communist Party member, Sidelines Production Team leader, and former Commune Credit Union cadre, the young rebels of the *Petrel* and *Shankan Ridge* would never have taken such bold action. But was Little Shen really the solid revolutionary he claimed to be? Of course not, said the "loyalists." For one thing he had a jail record. The six points issued by the security forces, as their supplement to the call for a Cultural Revolution in the countryside, proscribed ex-convicts from taking an active part. County police had arrested Little Shen in 1960 for beating up a poor peasant who resented attentions paid to his wife, and had jailed him for two months. Not only had Shen spent time in jail, he had once given a gun to the son of the notorious counterrevolutionary Kao Hsi-hsui. Because Little Shen found the son, young Kao Ming-wang, standing guard over the threshed grain at harvesttime, he gave him a gun to hold, a gross violation of procedure. Furthermore, the Four Clean Movement had exposed Little Shen as a speculator in cooking oil. He bought oil at 1 yuan per catty and sold it to people in another brigade for 2 yuan per catty, not as part of any brigade project but as a private deal.

From the very first day of the power seizure, the wide publicity given to these alleged transgressions stirred up tremendous controversy in Long Bow. Worse, the social and class background of the *Petrels* and *Shankan Ridge* generated repercussions during the very first hour. Even the young rascal Yang Szu-ho, who headed a small group of *Shankan Ridge* rebels, walked out of the "seize power" meeting when he saw Shang Yin-k'u, Chin Ken-so and Tai Mao-hsiang patroling the ground as sentries. "If these are the people who are seizing power," said Yang Szu-ho, "I can't stomach it." He left the meeting and the organization.

During the next few days, as the outcry against the *Petrel* and *Shankan Ridge* mounted, other young people like Hsin-fa's daughter Hsien-hua and the poor peasant Li Yü-hsi decided to get out. They formed an *Earn Merit Battle Group,* which defected with a resounding proclamation. But a loyal core of about eighty people remained in the two groups and steadfastly defended their class backgrounds, their political records, and their right to rebel against Lu Chin-jung and other men of his clique who held office in Long Bow.

The facts, as the "rebels" saw them, were not what the "loyalists" were making them out to be. To begin with, several leaders of the "loyalist" majority, including Party Secretary Swift Li himself, had class connections that were not above suspicion. The middle peasant Li, who adopted Ts'eng-pao as a child, was related to Wang Lai-hsun, the second-largest landholder in Long Bow. When Wang Lai-hsun died in a distant county, the whole family went into mourning. When Ts'eng-pao's mother by adoption (also his aunt, since she was his true mother's sister) died, he invited all her husband's relatives to the funeral, including those descended from the landlord Wang Lai-hsun. Was this a proper invitation for a poor peasant leader to send out?

Then there was Fast Chin, the militia leader. He was descended from a whole family of Catholics. His father had been a member of the reactionary Catholic organization, the Legion of Mary, and his uncle (his mother's brother), Chi Hsiang-yun, had been a group leader in the Legion. Could one trust the descendant of such Catholic fanatics with control over the brigade militia?

People said that Swift Li had two barrels to his gun, both of them "black," or bad. There was the "black pen" barrel—Chi Lung-ch'en—and the "black gun" barrel—Whiskers Shen. Chi Lung-ch'en was the best-educated peasant in Long Bow. Swift Li used him as a brigade secretary whenever there were letters to write and as the leader of the agricultural research group because he had studied science. Yet everyone knew that his father had once been a member of the Kuomintang. How could the son of a Kuomintang member play such an important part in brigade affairs? No one questioned Whiskers Shen's background as a genuine poor peasant. His problem was a suspicious personal history, the way he hung around the blockhouse when the Japanese occupied the village, the way he led the Japanese to North Rock when they wanted to seize grain, and the way he and Li Shou-p'ing, another militiaman in the Two Gems clique, helped the Japanese uncover resistance fighters. Was Whiskers Shen the kind of man to trust with a gun? Could he enforce law and order?

So much for the purity of the *Mao Tse-tung Thought Platoon.* When it came to the charges against members of *Petrel* and *Shankan Ridge,* most of them would not hold any water at all, said the "rebels." Take Little

Shen, for instance. Was he actually an ex-convict, a man with a jail record? No. While it was true that he had been held in a jail for two months on assault charges, his was a pretrial detention pending investigation of the incident. The court released him without any action, never brought his case to trial, and never sentenced him to anything. How, then, could he be regarded as a criminal? A brigade that barred from political activity every peasant who had spent some time in jail would seriously deplete the ranks of its activists.

Or take Kuo Ming-en. It was true that his real father was Meng Hsien-chung, a corrupt and ruthless puppet district leader. Meng, however, had never been a big shot, but only a minor official who smashed and grabbed, killed and looted but never got rich. At the time of Liberation the people's court had condemned him to death and sentenced him to execution by dismemberment with a fodder chopping knife. At that time his son, named Meng Yung-sheng, was one year old. His wife, widowed by the execution, married the bare-poor peasant Kuo Cheng-k'uan, from the very beginning of land reform head of the Peasants' Association. She made Cheng-k'uan a good wife, was classed thereafter as a poor peasant, and never told her son, now named Kuo Ming-en, that he was a foster child or that his real father was an executed counterrevolutionary. Ming-en grew up a poor peasant in a poor peasant household, a household in which the father was not only a Communist Party member but served as a leading cadre in the new revolutionary regime throughout the intervening years. When Ming-en graduated from primary school, he became a schoolteacher in Long Bow, but earned so little as a teacher (less than 300 workdays) that he asked to be transferred to the Sidelines Team so he could better support his wife and two children. Working a day at sidelines could often earn a day and a half or two days' worth of points and thus add up to 400 or more a year. The school had never thrown Ming-en out. He had requested a transfer.

As for Chou Lai-fu, he was not Shih Jen-pao's real son at all. He was the son of a peasant family so poverty-stricken that they sold him in the famine year for a few bags of grain to Shih Jen-pao, who was childless. He was seven years old at the time. He lived in this family for less than two years. Then came Liberation. His foster father ran away and his foster mother died of a beating, leaving him to shift for himself as a hungry orphan until Chou Cheng-lo, a Communist Party member and brigade activist, adopted him. From birth to the age of seven he knew only abject poverty. After the age of nine he grew up in the home of a liberated poor peasant who was a Communist. How could he be called a counterrevolutionary with blood on his hands?

Yang Chi-wang descended, on his father's side, from several generations of poor peasants. Before Liberation his father was much too poor to buy a wife even at the low prices charged by the Catholic orphanage. After Liberation, when the Church collapsed and the orphanage broke up, the nuns of that institution lost their means of support. Here was a chance for a poor peasant. Yang's father moved quickly, married a nun who happened to be Fan Pu-tzu's daughter, and started a family. This woman, serving as a good wife to the elder Yang, won reclassification as a poor peasant. Their son, Yang Chi-wang, born into a poor peasant family, of a poor peasant father and a poor peasant mother, could hardly be denied poor peasant status.

As for Shang Yin-k'u, he was the son of Shang Shih-t'ou, a poor peasant appointed to the post of village head under the puppet regime. Eighth Route Army men killed this man when he refused to cooperate with the resistance forces. He had two sons—Shang Chin-k'u (structure of gold) and Shang Yin-k'u (structure of silver). Both these boys joined the People's Liberation Army during the Liberation War. Shang Chin-k'u met death at the front. Shang Yin-k'u fought through until victory, was demobilized, and came home to farm. He married a young woman, Chi Ching-hsien, who was a member of the Communist Party and played an active role in brigade life. True, the people's court had this young man's father executed as a traitor, but he himself was a People's Liberation Army veteran, the brother of a revolutionary martyr, and the husband of a Communist. Could he be called a monster with blood on his hands?

There remained Chin Ken-so. Members of both *Petrel* and *Shankan Ridge* agreed that Ken-so was the son of a rich peasant, but they found him, in practice, to be a revolutionary, one of those who "turned the tables" on their reactionary class origin. Since this was the case should they not unite with him, and struggle together with him to transform China? Not to do so would be to follow the reactionary "inheritance" theory which even the New Year's editorial had denounced.

"The slogan 'A hero's son is a real man! A reactionary's son is no damn good!' has been turned into something contrary to the proletarian revolutionary line," said the editorial. "It should be pointed out that the way those people with ulterior motives have made use of the slogan is in essence to advertise the exploiting classes' reactionary 'theory of family lineage.' This is exactly the lineage theory spread by the feudal landlord class, that 'a dragon begets a dragon, a phoenix begets a phoenix, and those begotten by rats are good at digging holes.' This is out and out reactionary historical idealism."*

What was "reactionary historical idealism" to the members of the *Petrel* and *Shankan Ridge* looked like a commonsense, poor and lower-middle peasant "class stand" to the *Mao Tse-tung Thought* faction. They were not about to let any "rich peasant bastard," no matter what his or her record might be, share power in Long Bow. And so the split developed and hardened with a minority made up of Fourth, Fifth and Sidelines Team "rebels" stoutly maintaining their right to rebel and seize power (according to them, they were acting in harmony with the mainstream of history) and a majority made up of First, Second, Third, and Sixth Team "loyalists" vociferously denouncing the rebellion as a counterrevolutionary restoration carried out by class enemies, notorious *ti fu fan huai* (landlords, rich peasants, counterrevolutionaries and bad elements). Many Fifth Team members at first joined *Petrel,* only to withdraw as pressure mounted, leaving the rebel units even more isolated.

As a minority action led by people, so many of whom were vulnerable

*Peking Review, January 1, 1967.

to political attack, the power seizure never had much chance of success. The "rebels' " hold on the village office and their possession of the seals lasted only a few days. Unable to rally any other section of the population to their side, unable to set up any acceptable leading body, unable to mobilize production work at any level, *Petrel* and *Shankan Ridge* had to admit defeat.

They seized power on February 8, but before the week ran out, they had to give it up. On February 14, 1967, they turned the village seal over to a "takeover" committee headed by Short Shen, a six-foot-tall army veteran and Communist Party member who represented the other side in this burgeoning struggle. The "takeover committee" was made up of delegates elected by the teams (six production teams and one sidelines team). It contained many former brigade cadres such as Wang Man-hsi, and thus could be said by the "rebels" to represent a restoration even though they themselves had representation on it. On the one hand, the "takeover committee" represented progress for the "rebels" because Lu Chin-jung and Swift Li (the Party Secretary and Vice-Secretary) were excluded from it. On the other hand, it represented defeat because the majority of the delegates elected to it were supporters of these full brothers with different surnames.

The "takeover committee" served only as a provisional organ of power. Both sides recognized this. Under its temporary leadership brigade members went back to work while the jockeying over who should really hold power continued and sharpened. Both sides put up posters in profusion. Study sessions, mobilization meetings, strategy consultations and mass meetings followed one another in dizzying succession.

A large mass meeting packed the library of the middle school in Long Bow on March 15. *Petrel* and *Shankan Ridge* called it to review Lu Chin-jung's record and hear his self-criticism. The "rebels" mobilized not only their supporters in Long Bow but all the support they could muster from other places such as the *Maoism Red Guards* of the middle school, the *Rebel Regiment* from the railroad shops and the grain transportation station, and sympathetic fraternal groups from the cement plant.

Lu Chin-jung and Swift Li invited their allies from Anyang, Hsin Chiu-ch'uan, the commander of the Horse Square rebels who now controlled the Commune Committee, and other individuals and mass organizations sympathetic to their side. Chang Ching-hai, commander of Changchih City Militia Headquarters, who had previously led a Four Clean Work Team in Long Bow, came in response to invitations from both sides. His role was to chair the proceedings.

According to Little Shen, the "rebels" carried the day at this meeting. Their supporters outnumbered those invited by the opposition. Commune leader Hsin Chiu-ch'uan, though invited by the other side, joined in the criticism of Lu Chin-jung, supported the "seize power" line of *Petrel* and *Shankan Ridge,* and refuted those who called Little Shen a capitalist roader.

"At this big meeting," Little Shen said, "all the people from the railroad shops, the grain station and the cement plant supported *Petrel* and *Shankan*

Ridge. As a result the other side did not welcome any more such great debates."

Whether this was true or not is very hard to say. Presumably there was some truth to Shen's statement. Almost all of the "rebels" I talked to said that they won the public debates and the poster confrontations but lost out in the battle for power. The strong "seize power" wind that blew throughout the Province and the nation in the months that followed the January storm in Shanghai greatly enhanced their strength in debate. Seizing power, ostensibly from capitalist roaders, actually from anyone who happened at the time to hold it, dominated the order of the day in the early months of 1967. All the media, press, radio, Party propaganda and word of mouth celebrated power seizure at every level everywhere and fanned up such a gale that no one could easily oppose it directly.

Even Swift Li had to agree. He said to me in 1971: "On February 8, 1967, we had power seizure from below. This was the correct direction. It was in accord with instructions issued by Mao Tse-tung. No one opposed the power seizure because this was obviously the thing to do. But afterward differences arose over how to judge the cadres." And, one might add, over how to judge those who seized power.

"Power seizure was obviously the main direction," said Swift Li, "but still it created disunity. People who disagreed with the power seizure here went to militia headquarters to complain. They held that Long Bow Brigade had successfully concluded a Four Clean Movement carried out according to Mao Tse-tung's Twenty-three Points. It had set up a good leading group. It had chosen all leading members on the basis of the five standards for revolutionary successors. Those who had seized power, on the other hand, had all been targets of attack at the time of land reform, or the children of such targets. They also harbored social elements banned from leadership by the six points drawn up by the Security Department. These included people whose relatives had been killed as targets of the revolution and people jailed by the revolution. Since exactly such people led the power seizure in Long Bow, people didn't agree with this takeover."

Peasants who went to militia headquarters to complain received copies of the Third Red Flag Editorial for 1967, a statement celebrating the "seizure of power by the proletariat." Whose power should be seized? The power of a small handful of capitalist roaders, and not the power of revolutionary cadres, who are "the precious possession of our Communist Party." The people must always be on the alert against landlords and rich peasants taking advantage of the situation to seize power from the poor and lower-middle peasants.

"Loyalists" pounced on this material from the Third Editorial as the basis for their counteroffensive. They propagated it in the streets, in the fields, on the walls and in meetings. They organized a Mao Tse-tung Thought propaganda team to spread their position far and wide, wrote skits, read the editorials aloud, and plastered the village walls with posters. In debate and propaganda the defenders of the status quo refused to take a back seat. If, as Little Shen and his comrades said, the "loyalists" lost out in the big public confrontations, they nevertheless retained the initiative on village streets and walls, showed greater organizational clout, and success-fully stalled production until the "rebels" turned the brigade seal over to a "Takeover Committee" that included no "rebels" at all. Under the new committee's temporary umbrella, "loyalists" worked hard for a more per-manent Revolutionary Committee that could, in the long run, reestablish the rule of those who had been overthrown.

Organizationally the confrontation came down to five groups against two, with only *Petrel* of the Fourth Team and *Shankan Ridge* of the Sidelines Team joining hands as "rebels" to challenge the other five organizations coalescing as one *Revolutionary Alliance Fighting Team.*

A seesaw battle, primarily a battle of words, went on from the middle of February, when the Takeover Committee took charge, until the end of March. Then, after a new Revolutionary Committee assumed control in Changchih City, a cadre team known as the "Grasp Revolution, Promote Production Work Team" came to Long Bow to help establish a satisfactory revolutionary committee at the brigade level. This work team was led, as the previous team had been, by the Changchih City Militia commander, Chang Ching-hai.

With the arrival of the new work team polarization in Long Bow reached the point of no return. Chang Ching-hai established close liaison with Yang Hsiu-shan, commander of the militia in Horse Square Commune. Yang, having already decided to back the Long Bow "loyalists," convinced Chang that the "rebel" leaders were indeed a bunch of counterrevolutionary "ele-ments." The work team demanded that *Petrel* and *Shankan Ridge* expel Chou Lai-fu, Chin Ken-so, Yang Chi-wang, Shang Yin-k'u and others under suspicion, or face dissolution as legitimate mass organizations. When *Petrel* and *Shankan Ridge* refused, the commune *Seize Power Headquarters* expelled them as counterrevolutionary groups.

The expulsion of the "rebels" occurred on March 31. On April 1, a so-called "Three-in-One Revolutionary Committee" of old cadres, military representatives (in this case, militia representatives) and leaders of mass organizations took over Long Bow. This was not an elected committee, but a group designated by the work team after consultation with representatives of the five recognized mass organizations, the old Peasants' Association and the Party branch. The new Revolutionary Committee was supposed to be a committee of ten. Actually, the work team designated only nine members, holding one seat in reserve for a representative of the eighty or so peasants who belonged to *Petrel* and *Shankan Ridge,* when and if they ever agreed to clean house by expelling their leaders.

Brigade leaders, describing the situation much later, tended to forget the demand made on the "rebels" to expel their leaders, and simply stressed that they had held a seat in reserve to be occupied by "rebels," whenever they recognized the Revolutionary Committee as legitimate; a stand they never took, because to do so meant they had to condemn their own organi-zation and its leaders.

Members of *Petrel* and *Shankan Ridge* remained steadfastly loyal to each other and to the principles they professed. They refused to expel their leaders as landlords, rich peasants and counterrevolutionaries. They also refused to recognize the new Revolutionary Committee as legitimate. In their eyes it was nothing but a restoration of the old leading group—a "big mixture of reaction."

However, no one paid any attention to their objections. Swift Li, vice-secretary of the Party branch and head of the Youth League, came back to power as chairman of the Committee. Fast Chin, captain of the brigade militia; Chang Kuei-ts'ai, chairman of the brigade; and All Here Li, another vice-secretary of the Party branch, joined him as vice-chairmen. Lu Chin-jung, Communist Party Secretary; Li Hsiao-hua, vice-chairman of the Peasants' Association; Lu Shu-yun, chairwoman of the Women's Association; Sun Jing-fu, newly appointed head of the Sidelines Team; and Li Kuang-ching, a returned army veteran and respected Party member, filled out the other five committee posts.

Quite clearly, with some slight shuffling of positions, the old leading group had returned to power, just as the leaders of *Petrel* and *Shankan Ridge* said. But was it in fact a "big mixture of reaction?" Were these people capitalist roaders or revolutionary cadres, "the precious possession of our Party?" On this question the two sides continued to hold exactly opposite opinions, just as they did on the question of the political character of the leaders of *Petrel* and *Shankan Ridge,* the question that had led to the whole conflict in the first place. The contention between them had begun as a debate, but as factional differences in the region, the province and China as a whole deepened, *wen tou* (verbal or cultural struggle) transformed itself, step by step, into *wu tou* (physical or armed struggle), and the rights and wrongs of all divisive questions sank into obscurity. The more force replaced reason, the harder the two positions became, the more real injury each side inflicted on the other, and the more difficult they found it to arrive at any lasting solution.

69

HITTING, SMASHING AND ROBBING

 The establishment of the new Revolutionary Committee and the expulsion of *Petrel* and *Shankan Ridge* from the *Seize Power Headquarters* led to a drastic restriction on free debate. Once excluded from legitimacy, *Petrel* and *Shankan Ridge* could no longer draw on public supplies of paper, ink and paint for posters, leaflets and wall bulletins. Once the commune leadership designated them as "reactionary," it terminated their right to the free writing materials and paste guaranteed to all mass organizations. They had to finance by individual contributions any further written material which they wanted to put out. To an American this may seem like a small problem indeed; paper and writing materials are not, after all, very expensive here. But the peasants of Long Bow, committed to the cause of *Petrel* and *Shankan Ridge,* considered the ban a major blow. They pooled what resources they had, bought what paper and ink they could afford, wrote on walls with substitutes such as colored clay, made paste from flour contributed by member households, and carried the struggle forward as best they could. But for all intents and purposes the ban shut down free debate between the two opposing sides.

Meanwhile the "rebels" lost no opportunity to protest to the Commune Committee and the Changchih City Committee against the action that had been taken. They sent notes of protest, letters demanding reversal of verdict, and delegations to plead their case in person. They demanded the restoration of their rights as a mass organization, cited chapter and verse in regard to Central Committee policy—"no one has a right arbitrarily to dissolve any people's organization"—but they were rebuffed again and again. Invariably the answer came back, "If you will expel Chou Lai-fu (adopted son of a Japanese collaborator), Kuo Ming-en (son of a Kuomintang officer), and Yang Chi-wang (son of a landlord's daughter) and other questionable members from your organization, then your rights will be restored." Hsin Chiuch'uan and Yang Hsiu-shan of the Commune Committee demanded that the "rebels" turn these suspects over to the commune to be placed under supervision. But *Petrel* and *Shankan Ridge* refused to consider denouncing these members and turning them in. In their eyes the accused had done nothing wrong. Thereafter the pressure, especially the pressure against

Little Shen, the one old Party member and cadre in the "rebel" organization, increased.

During the first week in August the question of materials for putting out publicity on behalf of *Petrel* and *Shankan Ridge* became acute. The "rebels" had run out of paper, ink and paste altogether. Contributions of cash and kind had also slacked off. On August 8 they again sent a delegation to the commune to argue their case and ask for material support. The delegation members met with Militia Commander Yang.

"We appeal to you because you took a hand in dissolving our organization," they said. "Mao Tse-tung himself started the Cultural Revolution. Everyone has a right to speak out and put up posters. Why do you deny us?"

Yang rebuffed them.

On August 18 a larger group, more than a dozen people, went back to the commune. A Secretary Wang had replaced Secretary Yang in the office. Since this cadre had played no role in the exclusion of their organization, they appealed to him for help.

"Let us have some paper on loan," said Little Shen. "The City Committee doesn't agree to the commune's decision. When the case is settled, then we can settle accounts."

But Wang did not dare acquiesce without consultation. He called Party Secretary Shih Chao-sheng, the leader overthrown in February but now back in office. Shih said no.

In the meantime some of the young people from Long Bow made their way into the west yard, where they found an office secretary named Chang.

"What are you looking for?"

"We want to borrow some paper."

"There's a whole pile of it," said Chang, pointing to the cabinet. "Take what you want."

The young people took 500 sheets of white paper, 100 sheets of red paper, a bottle of black ink, a copying screen and three brushes. With these materials in hand they rushed home and began writing posters.

The "rebel raid" on the commune office created a stir throughout the suburban area. Militia Commander Yang mobilized supporters in ten brigades to write posters condemning the counterrevolutionary element Little Shen for looting. Early in the morning Yang closed down the commune office, locked the doors, and descended on Long Bow with his whole staff. Crowds gathered in the street in front of brigade headquarters to hear the commune cadres denounce *Petrel*, *Shankan Ridge* and their behind-the-scenes leader. Members of the Long Bow Revolutionary Committee joined in. While some people talked others prepared to put up posters.

"A handful of counterrevolutionaries led by Little Shen went to Horse Square to *ta, tsa, ch'iang* [hit, smash, rob]."

Undaunted, Little Shen went before the crowd himself.

"In the Sixteen Points Mao Tse-tung says we should use reason to convince people. He has given four rights, the four big democracies, to all poor peasants. If they are allowed to put up posters, we are allowed to put up posters. If they put up a poster against us, we can put one beside it defending ourselves. Let the masses see both. Let the masses judge who is a revolutionary and who a counterrevolutionary."

While Shen talked, his supporters fanned out to put up the posters. Visitors from the commune joined Long Bow "loyalists" who moved in to stop them. Fighting broke out as each side tried to place its posters in the most advantageous position and prevent posting by the other side.

In Long Bow that day the speeches, the debates, the rivalry over posters, the sporadic fist fighting, jostling, shouting and milling about went on all day. Toward evening, in the course of one scuffle two young people from *Petrel* grabbed an office messenger from the commune staff who had attacked them and hustled him off to the Fourth Team's stable yard. They held him there all night, then released him in the morning. When he got back to the commune he said he had been beaten, threatened with a knife, and denied both food and water.

The "rebels" stoutly denied this.

"As soon as I heard that we had captured a messenger, I went to the stable yard," said Little Shen. "I told the young people they must not hit their prisoner. Anyone who harmed him in any way must bear full responsibility. It was starting to get dark. The commune people were heading back for Horse Square. The captive wanted to go home but I was afraid they would attack us if we took him home in the dark. If we let him go and something happened to him, they would surely blame us. 'It's already dark,' I said. 'You had better stay over.' We cooked for him, fed him, and asked him to study Central Committee policy with us. In the morning we saw him safely back to Horse Square."

It seems unlikely that the young man's sojourn in Long Bow was as pleasant as Little Shen claimed. Whatever the truth about the treatment he received, this "kidnapping" incident added more fuel to the fire. Not only had *Petrel* and *Shankan Ridge* raided the commune office to hit, smash and rob, they had seized and beaten a commune staff member. This reactionary gang, complained their opponents, would stop at nothing.

Now the charges against *Petrel, Shankan Ridge* and Little Shen, as their real leader, escalated day by day. In August the question raised in the February meeting to criticize Wang Wen-te—the question about the death of Wang Hsiao-nan during the land reform—developed into a *cause célèbre*. Now, "loyalists" charged, Little Shen and his group blamed Wang Wen-te for Hsiao-nan's death. They were trying to reverse a case settled during the land reform movement. This was equivalent to trying to reverse the land reform itself. This gang of "landlords, rich peasants, reactionaries and bad elements" was trying to overthrow the revolution in Long Bow and restore feudalism. Vituperative posters went up all over the village and throughout Horse Square Commune. Not only had the "rebels" confronted Wang Wen-te with false charges at a meeting, but afterward they had tried to cover the whole thing up. At a secret meeting of twelve people held after the big February meeting was over, Little Shen, so it was charged, had demanded silence from everyone about the case, and had threatened reprisal against anyone who broke ranks. The original written note, sent up during the meeting, had mysteriously disappeared. Kuo Ming-en, son of a Kuo-mintang officer, had saved other written questions but had conveniently lost this one. He was clearly bent on revenge for his father's death at the hands of the revolution. Had he not chaired the meeting, received all the questions, and read them out? By misplacing or destroying this note he had joined with Little Shen in a conspiracy to conceal the whole incident. Everyone involved, everyone responsible should be arrested, investigated and punished.

To drive their point home the "loyalists" created a large mud statue of Little Shen. They placed it right beside two defamatory statues that appeared on the main street just south of the drug dispensary only a few weeks before. These depicted Liu Shao-ch'i, ex-president of China, and Chang Lien-ying, ex-secretary of the Commune Party Committee, as beasts on all fours. An anonymous sculptor had modeled Little Shen in the same pose, substituting hooves for feet and hands. The faces on all three monuments bore an uncanny likeness to the individuals under attack, the outstanding feature of the caricature of Little Shen being an exceptionally long nose. The life-size statues looked particularly frightful at night, as if three huge dogs were lurking in the shadows under the mission compound wall.

Not content with slanderous and insulting propaganda the *Defend Mao Tse-tung Thought Platoon* called on the security forces to take action. According to Little Shen, three members of the Changchih City Police Department actually came to look into the affairs of Long Bow, prepared to make arrests. They came secretly and stayed at the city-owned cement plant across the highway from the brigade. No one in Long Bow knew they were there until some members of the *Mao Tse-tung Thought Red Guards* of the Regional Middle School in Long Bow, who sympathized with *Petrel* and *Shankan Ridge,* learned of their presence through contacts in the city and plastered protest posters on the main streets of Changchih.

Armed with one of these posters, Little Shen sought out the three policemen at the cement plant. He tried to impress on them that he was a poor peasant who greatly admired Mao Tse-tung, had survived the last twenty years only because the land reform had saved him and his family from starvation, therefore he could not possibly want to "reverse the case" on land reform, kidnap commune cadres against their will, or steal commune property. His pleas had little effect, but when Shen brought out a protest poster and proved to them that he and his organization did in fact have ties to the *Mao Tse-tung Thought Red Guards* of the middle school, the policemen decided that they had been wrong in judging him. Without taking any action or making any arrests, they went back to the city.

Emboldened by the fact that the city authorities had declined at the last minute to take action against them, the members of *Petrel* and *Shankan Ridge* launched a counterattack of their own against the Horse Square Commune leaders who had made them such a target. Concentrating on Militia Commander Yang Hsiu-shan and the restored Communist Party Secretary Shih Chao-sheng, their posters read:

"Bombard Yang Hsiu-shan! Warn Shih Chao-sheng!"

"You do not carry out the directives of the City Committee."

"You press down ever harder on our organization."

"You are carrying out a bourgeois reactionary line [a line suppressing the masses]!"

Strong words averted eyes ignored.

For Long Bow peasants to appeal for redress to authorities in the City of Changchih at this time was an exercise in futility. It demonstrated a certain naive faith in salvation from above, in the correctness and goodwill of a Communist leadership so badly fractured and so deeply mired in fratricidal trials of strength as to be all but incapable of rational action. In the summer of 1967 the city, the region and the province as a whole, not to mention the nation, fell into a state of upheaval and disarray that intensified week by week. Hastily formed coalitions of higher cadres and grassroots organizations that represented, at best, only a small fraction of the people they claimed to speak for, everywhere wrested power from established authority.

In response to directives from Peking that reversed the original call for elections along the lines of the Paris Commune of 1871 and opted instead for new organs of power called "revolutionary committees," "rebel" forces attempted to set up such committees from three elements—representatives of the mass organizations, old cadres considered to be revolutionary, and representatives of the armed forces. Mass organizations were supposed to form great alliances from below, then after forging political consensus, set up their three-in-one committees. Many groups knocked together such alliances for the purpose of setting up revolutionary committees, but they scarcely concealed the enmity and suspicion with which the various "allies" regarded each other, and the ink on the announcements scarcely had time to dry before old splits revived and new splits came about, primarily over conflicting estimates of the quality and integrity of old cadres. The makeup of the new revolutionary committees was usually enough out of balance, one side of the coalition holding more posts than the other, to cause the side that was slighted to feel aggrieved. Thereafter what one side considered to be "proletarian power," the other side called "a big mixture of reaction." Those who thought they were wielding "proletarian power" considered anyone who attacked them to be by definition reactionary. Those who considered the ruling committee illegitimate thought renewed rebellion absolutely essential to save the revolution. Thus a new issue arose to aggravate and deepen existing splits—"for or against the revolutionary committee." And since the armed forces were involved in forming these committees and in making decisions either to support or oppose them, this issue developed into another one that was equally divisive—"For or against the armed forces, for or against the PLA." Thereafter anyone who opposed a new revolutionary committee that the PLA supported was in danger of being labeled "anti-PLA," which was only slightly less damaging than being called "anti-Mao Tse-tung" or "anti-Communist Party." The political consensus in China that had been developing throughout the country since the 1920s had three unshakable pillars: support for the Communist Party, support for the People's Liberation Army and support for Mao Tse-tung, the founder and leader of both. To fall into a position of opposition to any of the three amounted, in the popular mind, to falling into counterrevolution, to becoming an enemy of the people.

The Industrial Department of the Changchih City Government administered the coal mine at Wuchuang. This department had more power, a far larger budget and cadres with more prestige than its sister, the Agricultural Department, which always got whatever favors, money and personnel remained after the city took care of industry. Perhaps this was the reason why the contest for control over the Industrial Department outdid in bitterness all other contests, and why that bitterness spilled over into all subordinate units, such as the Wuchuang Mine.

One of Long Bow's more ambitious young men, Shen Chung-t'ang, got a job as a contract worker in the mine in 1967, just as the factional strife engendered by the Cultural Revolution began to heat up. He learned very little about mining but a great deal about political agitation, debating, poster writing and, finally, street fighting.

As Shen Chung-t'ang described the miners' life:

> Fighting began early in the year. In those days we fought with fists and sticks. If we began debating, we ended up fighting. If we put up posters, we fought over their content. Once I spoke up at a meeting and they beat me up. Sometimes, when we sat down to eat in the dining room, we began to argue. The arguments led to brawls. We threw stools at each other and smashed all the lights. Nobody got killed, but a lot of people got hurt.
>
> One night two or three of us were eating in the dining room along with four or five opponents. They began to talk about how good their faction was. When we disagreed they grabbed our bowls and smashed them on the floor. Then we all took hold of stools and went after each other. I got whacked twice on the back. Since we were outnumbered, we already had a plan. We would knock out the lights, then skip out, leaving the opposition to fight among themselves. As soon as the fracas began I got it on the back, but when the lights went out I managed to sneak to the far end of the hall and escape. I hid among the crops in the fields until I found my companions. Then, at 2:00 A.M., I ran back to Long Bow.

What this confrontation was all about no one could really explain. In early 1967 a plethora of organizations still maintained independent status, and the shifting of coalitions and alliances back and forth confused all but the most dedicated. Several of Shen Chung-t'ang's friends were members of the *Mao Tse-tung Thought Red Guards* at Luan Middle School, a group that adhered to an umbrella organization called *General Headquarters,* a loose coalition of units that supported the revolutionary committee in Changchih City but didn't like the Liberation Army Commander Wu T'ien-ming who headed it. This put them in opposition to another umbrella organization called *Red General Headquarters* that "resolutely defended" Wu T'ien-ming. A staunch component of this second headquarters, the *May Fourth Railroad Workers' Regiment,* dominated the locomotive shops at

Long Bow and tied up in turn directly to the *February Seventh Commune* based on the railroad yards at Chengchow, Honan, a freight hub of national importance. Shen Chung-t'ang couldn't even remember why his *General Headquarters* opposed army man Wu, but the issue soon became academic because another loose coalition of units joined together to attack the whole revolutionary committee over which Commander Wu presided. Their first act was to block his military units from hauling any water. Shocked by this "sabotage," *General* and *Red General* promptly settled their differences, agreed on a long joint name that ended in *United,* and went into action in support of the City Revolutionary Committee then in power. Trying to make sure that the army got its water, they started fights on the streets of Changchih that soon spread to all units under city control, including Wu-chuang Mine.

At that time *United* had no organization at all at the mine. The opposition with a long name that ended in *Red* controlled every department. But three or four contract workers from Long Bow, including Shen Chung-t'ang, and five or six from Horse Square, all followed the majority in their home communities in opposing *Reds* of whatever stripe and began to put up posters refuting the *Red* posters inside the mine headquarters. Posters led to fighting in the dining hall and *Reds* drove Chung-t'ang and his comrades from the grounds. But not for long. Shen described what happened next:

> Since they outnumbered us, we didn't dare go back to the mine for almost two weeks. During that time we got in touch with the *United* forces at the Wuyang Mine and the Changchih Steel Plant and formed the *Wuchuang Red Cliff Regiment.* Then we went quietly before dawn and posted up a declaration outside our mine gate. When the *Reds* saw this poster they sent people to debate with us. They urged us to join their organization and come back to work. Since we were so few in number, we refused. But later we decided to go back to work and to try and build up our forces.
>
> After I worked at the coal face for a while the manager assigned me to guard duty. Since we were *United,* while the mine was dominated by *Reds,* we didn't fit in. I always drew endless hours of stationary sentry duty. I had to stand still so long my legs swelled. My comrades got the same kind of treatment. Whatever the work, we always had to take the hardest assignments. When we met we all complained about how tired we were. When we couldn't bear it any longer we decided to open up a debate.
>
> By that time we had won over a few friends from our own area and we had solid support from the miners at Wuyang and the steelworkers at Changchih Steel. When any one of us started a debate the others came and mingled in the crowd. Nobody recognized them or knew what side they were on, but in case of trouble they would pitch in along with us. So we put up some posters and began a debate. The debate lasted all afternoon, then broke into a fight in the evening. This time we had so many friends in the crowd that we did well. As soon as the fighting began we sent out a call

for more help from Wuyang Mine. The outside miners came in trucks, all armed with big sticks, and as soon as they arrived they began laying about with enthusiasm. Thus we drove the *Reds* out.

Although most of them got away, we captured a few. We kept them prisoner in the mine guesthouse and named it our "high-class jail." We beat up everyone we captured. One of these was the *Red* leader. We put him on public trial day after day. When we "tried" people, we hauled them before big mass meetings, "holding their heads up to show their big ugly features and dragging their heads down to make them confess their crimes." If they didn't talk well or we thought they didn't tell the truth, we made them lean over a table and beat them on the rump. We took those who confessed before other mass meetings for repudiation. Actually we beat most of the confessions out of them. There was no question of right and wrong, we simply wanted to punish them.

As you can see, bad fighting disrupted Wuchuang Mine and lots of outsiders were drawn into it. After that first fight when we ran away, we never lost again. Everyone we captured we beat up.

The PLA assigned to our area demanded again and again that we free our captives. We finally had to let them go—the hurt, the wounded and the bleeding. The army men took them to the hospital in trucks and we criticized them for this. We thought that by saving our enemies they were suppressing us.

Once our captives were taken to the hospital, we controlled the mine completely. We then held meetings to bring the fighting to an end and start up production again. Since we had driven all the *Reds* out, we had no one left to beat up and the mine became peaceful. Then the Liberation Army men went through the miners' home villages with trucks and loudspeakers urging all those who had run away to come back to work. The soldiers asked them to take up their shifts with confidence.

But when they came back they couldn't help but be frightened. Sometimes fights broke out underground. The army decided to call a mass meeting aimed at creating a big alliance so that we could all concentrate on production. At this meeting the soldiers sat in the center while the *Reds* occupied one side and *United* the other. But before the meeting got well underway fighting broke out. We of *United* began shouting "Down with Ch'en" [the *Red* leader]. Someone threw a rock and soon both sides were throwing rocks and bricks at each other. Since the army men were in the middle, some of them got hit. They kept pushing outward from the middle, pushing the fighters apart. In the end they succeeded in breaking it up.

That night after supper quarreling began again in the dining hall. Since many *Reds* had defected to our side, those who remained *Reds* made up a small minority. When the fighting broke out once more a large group of them ran away for the second time. Of those who remained some were persuaded to join us. Others, unrelenting, worked on without speaking up. So the mine was still solidly in the hands of *United*.

We all went to work; production recovered. The army men asked us to call back all those who had run away, but we didn't do it. The army men also asked us not to mix in city politics but to stay in the mine and work, but our leaders continued to go to meetings in the city anyway and we got involved in lots of fights there.

It was only a matter of time before the fighting at Wuchuang Mine and in Changchih City spread to Long Bow village.

70

DEATH AT
LONG BOW'S
FRONT DOOR

On August 24, long after dark, more than 1,000 (some said 1,600) students and workers riding in dozens of trucks came to a halt on the main highway where it passed between Long Bow village to the west and the railroad shops to the east. The combatants who clambered off the trucks carrying clubs, spears and knives assembled on the threshing floor of Long Bow's Fourth Team, then broke into three groups—one to raid the Luan Middle School, their primary objective; one to guard the northern flank, the heavily populated North Station area; and one to guard the eastern flank, a source of possible counterattack because of the proximity of the railroad shops and the known alliance between the railroad workers of the *May Fourth Regiment* and the *Mao Tse-tung Thought Red Guards* who dominated the middle school.

The raiders launched this expedition for a very mundane purpose—the capture of grain and grain tickets from the middle school so that the *Red Guard* students, who had lost control of the campus, would have something to live on. In 1966 the *Red Guards* rallying in support of teachers Kao and Wang in a challenge to the principal, whom they called Fan the Landlord, had won control of the school grounds. Most of the members of the rival *Mao Tse-tung Thought* faction had been forced to withdraw. If they came back, they came back as raiders. But by midsummer, 1967, intense fighting had completely reversed this situation. The *Mao Tse-tung Thought Red Guards,* having started out life as "loyalists," eventually linked up with other "loyalists" in the area who had joined together under the banner of *United.* This made them part of a majority coalition, at least in the North Station area. With the backing of their new allies they took back the campus of the Luan Middle School by force.

Then it was the *Red Guard* students who could no longer stay in Long Bow. They fled en masse to Changchih, where they allied themselves with the industrial *Reds,* who by that time were the dominant force inside the city. By fleeing they cut themselves off from their livelihood, the grain and monthly stipends that all middle-school students received from the government. Without grain, or grain tickets that could be exchanged for grain at the State Grain Trading Company, these students could not long survive as an organized unit. No one in Changchih had more than a few days' grain to spare. Once this was gone the uprooted *Red Guards* would have no choice but to disperse to their homes throughout the region and seek food from their parents. Neither the students themselves, involved as they were in a heavy struggle for the future of China, nor the factional leaders in the city for whom the middle-school *Red Guards* represented an important source of mass support, wanted dispersal.

With their backs to the wall the logical thing for the Red Guards to do was to mount a raid on the middle-school grounds in Long Bow and take back what was rightfully theirs, the grain and grain tickets to which they were entitled as students in good standing. Such a raid, a life-and-death matter for the students, dovetailed neatly with the interests of the factional leaders in the city, so they assembled a force adequate to the task, as they conceived it. No one foresaw what the raid might lead to.

Aided by the element of surprise, the contingent assigned to enter the middle school quickly overran the whole campus. Strong forces then headed for the supply department to seize grain tickets and whatever grain could be found. They really wanted fine grains—wheat, wheat flour or rice—but they had to be satisfied with millet, which they found in some abundance. This they hauled out, bag after bag, and began to load on the trucks.

Meanwhile the *Mao Tse-tung Thought Red Guards,* stunned by the unexpected and overpowering attack, sent messengers to ask for help from the railroad shops across the highway and the tracks. To forestall any counterattack the *Red Guards,* in their turn, decided to take the railroad shops as well as the middle-school grounds.

The railroad shops themselves were not heavily defended. Altogether only about fifty workers lived there, but they were well organized and well led and they put up a defense in depth. While one group manned loudspeakers that called on the *Red Guards* to go away, another group fired up a steam locomotive and deployed it on the track between the highway and the repair shops.

As the steam locomotive moved up and down, it sprayed live steam right and left, threatening to scald anyone within fifty feet. This lethal new weapon forced the attackers to regroup. A detachment of stalwarts split off to find some rocks, which they piled on the track after the locomotive went by going north. When the locomotive returned, it stalled on the massive barrier, giving the attackers time to climb aboard, overpower the crew, and wreck the machine.

As *Red* attackers swarmed across the railroad tracks into the factory yard, the defenders, all workers from Honan, retreated. The majority ran to the upper floors of the buildings there and began to throw down whatever they could find. Meanwhile a small detachment ran out the east gate, made a big circle behind Great Ridge Hill, and came up the highway below the line of parked trucks.

By this time it was quite dark. The defenders switched on the yard lights so that they could see their attackers moving down below and make every missile count. Hsu Piao, the leader of the attacking force, packed two pistols as he went into battle. He shot out the lights. Under cover of darkness his stalwarts then rushed the buildings, confident of victory. According to the intelligence they had received, the defenders had no firearms, so it was just a question of who could overpower whom in hand-to-hand combat. Since the forces from the city had come in overwhelming numbers, they had no doubt about the outcome.

Unknown to the student *Red Guards* and their worker allies, however, the railroad workers had armed themselves only a few days before. As their situation became desperate, several of them began firing at the attackers from the windows on the second story. One bullet soon hit home.

The sudden shift from "cold" to "hot" weapons threw the invading forces into a panic. With one of their number hit and dying, they turned and ran for their trucks, only to find that an important segment of their transportation had been disabled. The small detachment of railroad workers that had circled behind the hill to the highway had reached the line of trucks from the south and slashed the tires on at least nine of them. The trucks that could still travel soon overflowed with people. They roared off toward the city in the darkness, leaving behind hundreds of frightened workers who had no way to flee but on foot. Some of these took to the highway. Others, afraid of being caught by their pursuers in the open, hid out in the fields, waiting for dawn. Railroad workers rounded up some of these the next day and took them to the shops as prisoners.

When news of this incident reached higher levels of the government the city forces excused themselves, saying they had gone to Changchih's North Station with printed copies of a provincial directive. There railroad workers had stopped them and had seized their trucks. Later, when they asked for their trucks back, the railroad workers beat them.

The railroad workers had a different story—the story of a major offensive mounted by their city rivals to take the railroad shops, the story of how fifty valiant defenders routed 1,600 determined assailants.

No Long Bow peasants took part in the famous battle of the railroad yards; or if they did, they didn't admit it. However, all of them could talk at length about what they saw and heard. They couldn't avoid sights and sounds that invaded their very dooryards. Chao T'ung-min, a brigade accountant in 1971, gave the most complete description.

> I came back home from work at the brigade office about 11:00 P.M. and went to bed. About midnight I heard a knock at my window.
> "Who is it?"
> "A *Mao Tse-tung Thought Red Guard* from the middle school."
> I opened the window and shone my flashlight in a man's face. I recognized one of the teachers from the school but didn't know his name.
> "Hurry and get up," he said.
> "What's up?"
> "*Red Guards* have come to attack."
> "Did they beat you up?"
> He pulled up his sleeve. I shone my light on his arm and saw purple welts.

"Why did they beat you?"

"They went to take the grain tickets from the Supply Department. They grabbed all the grain tickets and all the millet in the warehouse. The cadres and clerks didn't want to release it, but the invaders outnumbered them and beat up anyone who disobeyed them."

This teacher wanted me to get a group of people together to go out and spread the word that students mustn't come to the middle school to smash and rob, that if they did Long Bow peasants would retaliate.

I got up and started back to the brigade office. I asked him to go first while I followed. First I checked to see if the brigade office gate was shut. I knew there wasn't any cash there but all our accounts and records were there. We couldn't afford to lose them.

When I saw that the gate was shut I was relieved. I tried to rouse the barber, Mao-sheng, who lives inside, but even though I shouted a long time no one answered. While we were standing there, about thirty people came down the street going south. We didn't have any idea who they were, so we ran away. Chi-te was still up and let us into his yard. When we told him about the strangers he said we had better not try to rouse any more people, so we just sat there. Finally the teacher left.

Fifteen minutes later we heard shouting coming from the railroad shops. A locomotive whistle sounded and loudspeakers began to blare. Over the loudspeakers came the message, "Deceived masses of the *Red* faction, don't come here anymore. Don't allow yourselves to be cheated by bad leaders."

After a lot more shouting and broadcasting, we heard people yelling, "Attack, attack!" After that we heard shooting. Many shots were fired but they were all single shots—rifle fire, no machine guns.

Soon after that everyone ran away. We heard many footsteps pounding down Long Bow streets. I didn't dare go home. I talked for a while with Chi-te, then went to sleep at his place. When I woke up it was breakfast time. My family was looking for me. I had left home at midnight and had not come back. They heard that someone had been killed on the playground at the middle school and they were afraid it might have been me. My wife's brother finally found me. He woke me up and said the whole family was worrying.

After I got home I went out to see the dead person. He didn't die on the playground but on the threshing ground of the Fourth Team. He was a youth only seventeen or eighteen years old. A bullet had blown half of his safety helmet away and had smashed his head. A pool of blood darkened the ground beside him. Out on the road we saw nine trucks with slashed tires. A few days later we learned that the dead youth was a middle-school student from Changchih.

Old Kuo Cheng-k'uan's house was built against the wall of the middle school. He was one of the first to wake up after the raid began. As he described that night:

The sound of breaking glass woke me up. Then I heard the school guard blowing his whistle. I was frightened. I heard windows cracking and doors splintering. They broke every pane of glass in the schoolyard and forced every door open. After a student jumped over the wall into my yard I heard people shouting, "Don't let him get away! Catch him alive, catch him alive!" He ran off down the street. His pursuers caught a lot of other people and beat them up. I could hear their victims screaming.

"Now we are done for," I said to my wife. "It's too bad!"

Suddenly I heard the train whistle blowing. It didn't stop. It kept on and on. Just as suddenly the whistle stopped blowing. Then shooting started. Guns fired one after the other. It was three or four o'clock in the morning.

The raiders thought the defenders had no guns but they were wrong. The railroad workers had armed themselves a few days before. When the attack came they started to shoot back. Unprepared for live ammunition, the attackers started to run. Some ran toward Natienkung, some toward Tungtao, and some ran from Horse Square to Futsun around the hill. I heard several running past my door. People hid in village homes, in summer kitchens or storehouses. Three hid in the strawstack on the Third Team threshing ground.

On top of everything else it rained in the night. While it was raining and afterward many people ran through the village. They left odd articles lying all over the place. They lost shoes, hats, knives, pens, shovels and everything else in the muddy street.

Just before dawn I got up. Everyone was already out on the street. Just as I went out of my gate several railroad workers came along saying, "Don't come out! Go back to your homes!" I ignored them and ran to the place where our team keeps its draft animals. Right there a donkey started to give birth. I stopped to see how the donkey was faring and just then a man told me two people had been killed, one on the Fourth Team's threshing floor and one at the crossroads east of the railroad shops. Someone said a third had died at our brick kiln but that wasn't true. Only two died.

The railroad workers combed our village looking for people who had hidden away. I followed them to the Third Team's threshing ground and watched them pull three people out of the strawstack there. They took them back to their shop. They questioned them and set them free. Some of them knew all about the plan of attack. Others didn't know anything. They didn't know what they were doing or why they had come. As soon as the shooting started they ran in all directions.

The dead body on the Fourth Team's ground belonged to a student. His family came for his body. Family members wore a strip of adhesive tape on their faces for identification. Someone also put a strip of tape on the dead boy's face.

The railroad workers won this battle and afterward a lot of people came to look at everything. It was just like our autumn fair. All the villagers from Long Bow, Horse Square, Futsun and other places came to see the nine trucks with their slashed tires. And everybody praised the *May Fourth Regiment.* They had won a battle against enormous odds.

As victors, the *May Fourth Railroad Workers' Regiment,* a detachment of the *February Seventh Commune* of Honan Province, a nationally known left organization supported directly by the Cultural Revolution Group and Mao's wife, Chiang Ch'ing, became famous throughout the Southeast Region and even far beyond it. But if people who sympathized with *United* admired the fighting regiment, people who supported *Red* feared and criticized it. One of the *May Fourth* commanders called himself Fang Yang-kou (sheepherding dog, shepherd dog or sheep dog). He was notorious for the long whip he used when "repairing" people. He had made it out of a coiled steel spring, and used it with devastating effect to bite into raw flesh as he slashed it down across a limb or a back. Sheep Dog's second-in-command also won fame for brutality. He chose his own pseudonym, Hu Lu-ken (hooligan). It came from abroad, but how such a word ever reached the heights of the Shangtang Plateau remains a mystery.

The student who died on the Fourth Team's threshing floor and the worker who died at the crossroads east of the railroad shops were among the first, if not the first, casualties of the Cultural Revolution in all of Shansi Province. Their deaths, far from calming things down, only fueled the conflict. Now that "hot" weapons had come into use for the first time, all sides realized that the future depended on firepower. Any group that did not already possess arms had to find ways to make or seize them.

Peasant militiamen who supported the factional bias of their commanders had no problem. Militia captains passed out guns whenever they felt threatened with serious confrontation. Workers in plants that boasted machine tools quickly developed techniques for making not only rifles and hand grenades, but heavy artillery and artillery shells as well. This left students, peasants who did not belong to militia units or peasants who opposed the politics of their militia commanders, and workers in ordinary plants at a distinct disadvantage. They had no recourse but to raid other units and seize weapons wherever they could find them.

In Long Bow the majority faction had no problem securing arms. Swift Li's closest friend and ally was Fast Chin, captain of the brigade's militia battalion. At the first sign of conflict Fast Chin called out the stalwarts whom he trusted, issued arms to one and all, and confronted the opposition with overwhelming force. Members of *Petrel* and *Shankan Ridge,* even though they had originally belonged to the militia, lost their right to bear arms and had to redress the balance by illegal means. Charges that they were stealing arms soon reinforced the charges about "reversing the case on land reform" and "kidnapping commune cadres" that their enemies used to prove they were counterrevolutionaries. After August 28, 1967, the opposition blamed *Petrel* and *Shankan Ridge* for the notorious weapons raid on Kuyi Brigade, Horse Square Commune, even though as organizations they had nothing to do with it. Luan Middle School students who were members of the *Mao Tse-tung Thought Red Guards* mounted the Kuyi raid. Having survived the grain raid of August 24 and the battle of the railroad yards, they decided to arm themselves as quickly as possible. They linked up with the *May Fourth Railroad Workers' Regiment* at the railroad shops and the *Red Guards* of the Changchih Transportation Company, a trucking unit with headquarters at Changchih North Station, for a daring attack on the well-armed militia unit at Kuyi. They chose this distant brigade as a target because its members could not easily identify them.

Since no one in the raiders' ranks knew Kuyi well, they wanted Wan T'ien-shui, a young man from Long Bow's Fourth Production Team, to be their guide. Wan worked out on contract at the irrigation station in Luchia-chuang on the banks of the Chang River, so lived temporarily in Kuyi. First, however, the raiders had to lure Wan back to Long Bow. They sent a messenger to tell him that his mother had died. The alarmed youth came home in a hurry, only to find his mother alive and well and himself under heavy pressure to lead a raid on Kuyi. In the end he accepted. Since the members of his family had all joined *Petrel*, Wan's capitulation amounted to a member of that embattled unit joining the other three organizations in their quest for arms.

The raiders gathered at the Changchih Transportation Company to board a company truck for Kuyi. But the truck no sooner started out than it broke down. Everyone had to get off. At this point the railroad workers and the transportation workers lost their enthusiasm for the raid and decided not to go on. The middle-school students, more desperate for arms, said, "We're going anyway," and set off on foot, taking Wan T'ien-shui with them.

When they arrived at Kuyi, Wan led them straight to the brigade head-quarters, where they found the militia battalion head K'ung Chang-ying, and the Revolutionary Committee head, Chung Hu-ch'uan. As the raiders blindfolded these two, they told them that they were *Reds* from the Huai-hai Arsenal south of Changchih City. They ordered K'ung to take them to his home, where they seized ten rifles and a machine gun, then retreated to the outskirts of the village, where they led their captives around in circles so they wouldn't know one direction from another and ordered them to lie down in a dry irrigation ditch.

"Lie quiet or we'll beat you to death," they said as they departed.

The two Kuyi cadres lay quiet for a long time. Finally, as dawn broke, one of them managed to pull the bandage off his eyes. He saw his companion lying unharmed only a few yards away. Afraid that the raiders might still be in their village, the two set out in the opposite direction toward Lucheng County Town. Meanwhile their wives and children had mobilized the whole community, including the militia, to search for them. The women, surrounded by weeping children, arrived at commune headquarters before dawn to report their menfolk missing. It was two days before the militia located the men in Lucheng and convinced them that it was safe to go home.

When the Luan Middle School raiding party returned home, its leaders gave the machine gun they had seized to the *May Fourth Railroad Workers' Regiment* and turned the rifles over to their own organization, the *Mao Tse-tung Thought Red Guards*.

After investigating the incident for four or five days the leaders of Horse

Square Commune decided that it was not Huai-hai Arsenal workers but students from the Luan Middle School who had seized the weapons. They sent Security Office Shen to get them back. He found it hard to get into the school grounds. Students had converted their quarters into an armed camp. Guards with rifles manned every entrance. Once inside, tense attendants herded him from office to office at the point of a gun. When his hosts said "go here" he went, and when they said "come here" he came. He had no choice. If he hadn't been from the same political faction, they would never have let him in the gate. His request for the guns drew only blank stares.

"We've borrowed them for a while," said the students. "When we get through with them we'll return them."

A young activist named Li K'e-hai led the student raiders. When Long Bow's Swift Li and Fast Chin learned of the raid, they conducted a village-wide search for K'e-hai, arrested him, and beat him. Then they sent him to Kuyi for criticism. There the villagers beat him again. The beatings so incensed K'e-hai that many months later, at a meeting presided over by army officers negotiating the return of the guns, he attacked Swift Li with a meat cleaver.

Li K'e-hai felt that he had been betrayed. He considered himself not only to be on the same side of the factional split as Swift Li, but even to be related to Swift Li's forces by marriage. While studying at the Luan Middle School he had boarded in mine guard Shen Chung-t'ang's home, had courted his sister, and finally married her. After that he had joined his brother-in-law Chung-t'ang in many "smashing and robbing" expeditions on behalf of the "loyalists" of Long Bow. In the end, what he got for his pains was beatings.

"Loyalists" knew the true story of the Kuyi raids, but nevertheless managed to fasten the blame on *Petrel,* on *Shankan Ridge* and ultimately on Shen Chin-ts'ai. They concentrated their fire on Wan T'ien-shui, the guide, whom they classed as a *Petrel* because his relatives were *Petrels.* They also used Li K'e-hai's leading role as evidence, constantly bringing up reminders that the student firebrand had once been a *Petrel,* and conveniently passing over the sudden midsummer switch in allegiance he had made after he set eyes on Chung-t'ang's sister. The more *Petrel* and *Shankan Ridge* protested this flagrant distortion of the evidence, the more firmly the other side pushed it. Members of the "loyalist" *Defend Mao Tse-tung Thought Platoon* never hesitated to push whatever was necessary to discredit the opposition and lost no sleep at all over turning the truth inside out or upside down. Needless to say, their victims, led by Little Shen Chin-ts'ai, used the same tactics whenever a suitable opportunity presented itself.

Pursuing the history of the Cultural Revolution in Long Bow through August, 1967, convinced us that in order to understand it we had to review developments in the city, the region and the province. Most of the political currents that battered the brigade and set its members at loggerheads came from above and outside. We had to track them to their source. To accomplish this we made appointments with higher leaders for the following week.

Part VIII

ALL-OUT CIVIL WAR

There must be an immediate and unconditional cessation of hostilities between the two camps; all special fighting groups in any form and under whatever name must be dissolved; all combat bases must disappear; all arms and equipment must be returned. . . . The Central Committee is convinced that the two factions are equally dedicated to the revolution.

Warning to Shansi issued by the Central Committee of the Chinese Communist Party, July 23, 1969

71

SOUTHEAST SHANSI—CORN, COAL AND IRON

Commander Li Ying-k'uei was chief of staff and acting commander of the provincial troops assigned to Southeast Shansi. He impressed us as an officer who combined intellect, ambition, rhetoric, guile and charm in fascinating proportions.

In the military sphere Shansi Province made up an army *district,* the Southeast Region an army *subdistrict.* Li Ying-k'uei presided over the Southeast Shansi Army Subdistrict Headquarters. That was his military job. He also held a civilian job as vice-chairman of the Regional Revolutionary Committee, and a Party job as vice-secretary of the Regional Party Committee. The top spot in each of these categories he yielded to Commander Wu T'ien-ming. Holding so many posts simultaneously was part of a new system universally applied during the Cultural Revolution called *yi yuan hua* or "unified administration." At every level the leading Party functionaries held lesser government posts, all graded according to rank; this was true, almost without exception, from team and brigade level in the countryside right up to the ministries at the heart of the Central Government. The big exception, of course, was at the very top where Mao held the post of Chairman of the Party, but not that of Head of State. Once Mao engineered the overthrew of Liu Shao-ch'i, he would neither assume that post himself nor allow anyone else to assume it. The Central Committee abolished the post.

Commander Li Ying-k'uei had the short stature of a Cantonese, a very small head and a wizened face badly twisted to one side. The right side of his mouth thrust over and down, forcing his right eye into a permanent squint. Whether this was the result of some wound or injury, or whether this was a defect suffered since birth, I do not know, but it made a deep impression on all who saw him. Li's was a face one could not easily forget. When he was in a good mood, joking and laughing, this sharp twisted face seemed like the countenance of a mischievous elf. When, on the other hand, Li Ying-k'uei became serious or angry his contorted features took on a sinister quality more devilish than elflike and one could sense a hard, ugly streak behind the jovial front of the man. With us, in 1971, he almost always managed to maintain a friendly, jovial stance, polite, calm and brilliant—intellectually brilliant.

He was by nature quick and voluble. He talked more rapidly than most Chinese, certainly than most northerners, and rarely if ever found himself at a loss for words. He loved to tell stories, often giving them a humorous twist, and the words rolled out quite freely in what sounded to anyone addicted to Peking speech like a most atrocious distortion of Mandarin, a distortion so severe as to be all but unintelligible.

Stories about Li Ying-k'uei's terrible accent circulated widely in Southeast Shansi. We heard that he once lectured his troops on the "left" opportunist mistakes made by Wang Ming and Po Ku in the days of the old Kiangsi Soviet (1931). His listeners thought he was talking about *bai-ts'ai* (cabbage) and *lo po* (turnips). On another occasion he told his men to *chen chueh shen ju chua* (earnestly and deeply take hold). What they heard was *na chen tse chih chieh tsa* (take a needle and puncture it).

Li Ying-k'uei was smart enough, however, to turn weakness into strenth. He put his aptitude for southern coastal dialects to good use. In order to talk to colleagues in Peking without anyone monitoring his words, he found two soldiers from Fukien, sent one to the capital and kept one in Changchih. When they talked to each other on the phone no one else on the line stood a chance of understanding anything. Messages went through as if they had been in secret code.

In 1977 I learned that Li Ying-k'uei was not always jovial and that his stories were not always humorous. Those who replaced him in power in the region said that he was notorious for his bad temper and that he kept his staff in fear and turmoil—cursing, swearing and denouncing.

Although an outsider to Southeast Shansi, Commander Li always spoke proudly of the region and knew it fairly well. He loved to recite Mao's description of the civil war battle there: "The Shangtang area, rimmed by mountains, is like a tub. This tub contains fish and meat. Yen Hsi-shan sent thirteen divisions to grab it. Our policy was set long ago—to give tit-for-tat, to fight for every inch of land. This time we gave tit-for-tat, fought, and made a very good job of it. In other words, we wiped out all thirteen divisions."

Commander Li also loved to recite certain basic facts and figures that summed up the special character of his domain:

Southeast Shansi, Li said, consisted of a high plateau, called the Shangtang, surrounded on all sides by mountains—the Taihang to the east, the Taiyueh to the northwest and the Chungtiao to the southwest. High ranges and the steep hills leading up to them dominated 85 percent of the 23,500-square-kilometer area. Valley land filled in the remainder. Only small segments of the valley land, such as the old lake bed around Long Bow, lay flat.

The plateau, standing at 2,600 feet above sea level, linked mountain ranges that rose to 6,000 feet. Behind them Huapo Mountain in Chingyuan County towered to 8,000 feet. Three rivers trisected the plateau. Two smaller streams, the Chin and the Tan, plunged southward into Honan, while the mighty Muddy Chang dumped its waters eastward into Hopei where they merged with the Clear Chang and finally the Wei to form the Grand Canal near Tienstin. The south branch of the Muddy Chang flowing north past Changchih filled the city reservoir and supplied irrigation water to Long Bow village.

The climate of the Southeast was relatively mild but it was also dry. More than 150 frost-free days each year encouraged agriculture, but a 23-inch average rainfall limited plant growth. Most of the rain fell in July and August. When these months failed to supply their quota, even the reservoir dried up, causing crop failures on the valley floor.

In 1971 3,730,000 people inhabited the region, 3,500,000 of them peasants. They lived and worked in 22,700 production teams, organized into 4,965 brigades and 341 communes. They tilled 1,286,666 acres of land planted to corn, wheat, millet, grain sorghum, cotton, hemp and ginseng. This amounted to a third of an acre per capita, but they had to feed, in addition to themselves, some 230,000 city residents. Twenty-five years after land reform and fifteen years after collectivization they had succeeded in doubling grain production. But since the population, too, had almost doubled, grain and people remained evenly matched at levels close to those of the past.

The industrial accomplishments of twenty-five years were much more impressive. Southeast Shansi, with rich mineral resources that included coal, iron, sulfur, copper, magnesium and aluminum, had attracted heavy state investment between 1949 and 1970. As a result the value of minerals extracted and commodities produced had multiplied ten times. Coal mines alone numbered 564 and most of them were new. The total value of industrial production in the region had reached 616,660,000 yuan.

Commander Li boasted of the variety and vitality of the region's social and economic life.

The Nancheng brigade leader, Li Ping-pi, had won fame as a mechanical genius. In 1954 he swapped two mountain mules for a burned-out Ford tractor, hauled it home from Hopei behind donkeys, then fixed it up to run on wood gas. This tractor, shipped to China in 1946 by the United Nations Relief and Rehabilitation Administration (UNRRA), he converted back to gasoline fuel in 1971. In the sixties Li Ping-pi bought enough new, Chinese-made tractors to plow and fit most of the land of his brigade. Defying male supremacy, he put girls under eighteen on a dozen walking tractors and set them to hauling supplies and crops to and from the fields. Young men and women in a brigade-financed foundry and machine shop cast blocks for tractor engines and turned out lathes and drill presses that found a ready market nearby. In the open fields a group of peasants formed bricks for baking with an electrically powered press.

Nancheng also boasted disease-free pigs, heavy draft horses, pens of cattle raised for the manure they dropped, community rather than household grain storage, a brigade middle school, facilities providing free baths once a week and free haircuts once a month to all. On top of that brigade leader Li Ping-pi rose at four each morning, drove a truck to a local mine, and brought home coal for every household that had run low. Families paid for the coal but not for the hauling. Nancheng, it was clear, had something to teach Tachai.

The Tung Szu-yi brigade, taking an entirely different path, specialized in medicinal herbs, sanitation and all-around health care. Cooperators there raised domesticated herbs in a special garden, gathered wild herbs in the mountains in season, and processed herbs for shipment to Peking during the long winter months. They had stocked and equipped an excellent clinic, they had paved their streets with slabs of stone, and they had dammed the muddy stream that flowed past their village gate and lined the body of water thus created with masonry walls so that it looked like the lake at the Summer Palace in Peking. Outside the village they fitted a brick kiln with a tower that cracked nitrogen fertilizer from the fumes given off by burning coal.

Tayang, a brigade in Chincheng County, specialized in iron smelting. Iron mines dotted the hillsides there. From well-like holes in the ground peasant miners brought up ore in baskets by winding rope on simple wooden reels. Above ground they trundled the ore to furnaces in the village by wheelbarrow, by donkey cart or by ore wagons pushed by hand down a narrow-gauge track. Brigade members lived in a cluster of stone houses huddled below a steep bluff. On top of the bluff a 1,000-year-old temple dominated the countryside. Iron furnaces, scattered among the houses, poured smoke night and day across the face of the temple, soaking its beams and intricate carvings with corrosive acid and turning them black as soot.

Tayang furnaces demonstrated three levels of technology. At the brigade level members dug pits in the loess soil, installed cold-air fans, and turned out a ton and a half of white iron per pit a day. White iron, too brittle to machine, could still be cast into cooking pots and other household utensils. Commune-level technicians and workers had built a large, cone-shaped adobe furnace with a hot air blast that turned out six tons of gray iron a day. County employees, not to be outdone, had put up two steel towers that rivaled the temple in height, if not in beauty. They turned out forty tons of gray iron a day.

Tayang peasants had smelted local ore as a sideline for hundreds of years. Long before the Great Leap promoted backyard furnaces everywhere, they had built their own. That is why they were still making iron there long after peasants abandoned Great Leap furnaces elsewhere. At Tayang 600 people worked at the iron trade all year round. They dug ore in the east, coal in the west, and smelted pig iron in the shadow of the temple in between. Each year Tayang's fifteen furnaces turned out 20,000 tons of metal.

Rich in coal and iron, Chincheng County specialized in small industries. In the county town an industrial exhibit displayed hundreds of local products and demonstrated indigenous ways to make everything from fertilizer to barber's shears. One Chincheng County man invented a gravity system for unloading railroad wagons that allowed the running gear and wagon bed to drop away from the loaded gondola, then rejoin it once the load had dropped. Models of this and many other inventions, all original and practical, packed the exhibit hall.

Commander Li Ying-k'uei convinced us that socialist transformation, far from imposing uniformity and mediocrity on the region, had unleashed great stores of energy and inventiveness. The depth, breadth and variety of creative talent in Southeast Shansi could not help but impress any visitor.

But as Commander Li and other regional and city cadres went on to talk about the Cultural Revolution, we could not help but conclude that local talent, energy and inventiveness had deepened, broadened, enriched and complicated factional strife to a degree unmatched in these mountains since the days of the warring states, several centuries before Christ.

Our questions concentrated on the critical year 1967.

72

THREE-RING TWO-STEP

 In the summer of 1967 the Revolutionary Committee of Southeast Shansi represented a "grand alliance" that was an alliance in name only. Unity had become a convenient charade to be acted out tongue-in-cheek while two hostile factions of cadres inside the ruling committee gave primary attention to mobilizing all possible allies and all possible resources for a showdown over power.

In the regional arena both sides covertly backed not only slanderous propaganda against each other, but raids seeking documents, kidnappings, physical assaults, power seizures and coups in subordinate units. Dissension and infighting at higher levels required each side to mobilize support down below, a mobilization that polarized the population at the village level and spread dissension and infighting far and wide. Since neither side could allow itself to be isolated or outflanked, every move kindled countermoves that tended to go beyond the provocation that had inspired them. Action led to overreaction, overreaction to violence. Once violence broke out, it was almost impossible to return to rational negotiation, not to mention peace. As grievance generated grievance, injury generated injury, and conquest generated conquest, people on opposite sides could no longer stand to look at each other, much less talk to each other. They took up fighting almost with relief.

The origin of the split at city and regional levels, like the origin of the split in Long Bow Brigade, could be traced back to the student movement of 1966. An early band of "rebels" at the First Middle School called the *Want Violence Brigade* found allies and formed a coalition called *Red Union* in order to overwhelm an early band of "loyalists" called *Red Storm*. In retaliation Red Storm formed *Peking Commune.*

By the time the *Workers' Revolutionary Rebel Headquarters* seized power in Shanghai in January, 1967, two more or less comprehensive networks of mass organizations existed in Southeast Shansi. Each had crystallized around one of the student coalitions and each continued to compete for membership below and recognition above. At this early date, however, organizational lines still showed fluidity, alignments constantly shifted, and units formed, dissolved or switched allegiance, as did "alliances," "headquarters," "battle stations" and all other special forms of mass activity, thus thoroughly mixing those who had once been "rebels" and those who had once been "loyalists" to the point where such distinctions no longer had meaning. Through it all Red Union and Peking Commune could still be traced with some consistency, but the large, hostile coalitions that finally emerged came to be known simply as *Red* and *United.* *

While *Red* and *United* were forming they carried on only desultory activity—a period of calm before the storm. Changchih students who went out to the mining towns in Honan came back with tales of bitter confrontation, but they failed to stir up anything comparable on the Shangtang. A detachment of students that came down from the provincial capital at Taiyuan found the inertia in Changchih depressing. Before they had even selected a place to sleep they put up posters comdemning the Southeast Region as stagnant. They called for action that would stir things up and create a little chaos. Without sharp debate, fighting and chaos, the old order could not be torn down or the new order built. If no one aroused the masses, if groups failed to fight each other, the Cultural Revolution could not succeed. To celebrate violence and chaos proved not only popular, it was mandatory in those days. Those who hesitated to speak in favor of it were automatically labeled conservative, revisionist, reactionary, even counter-revolutionary. To stir things up, to slander, to denounce and in the end to fight—that was revolutionary.

The militants of the Southeast Region soon rose to the challenge posed by their mentors from Taiyuan. News of the power seizure in Shanghai reached Shansi on January 7. On January 14 high-level "rebels" overthrew the government in Taiyuan. Less than a week later *Red Union,* better known as *Red,* mobilized all possible allies in Changchih and surrounded the offices of the City Party Committee and the Regional Party Committee simultaneously. Armed squads took the official seals into custody, but they failed to get support from local Liberation Army units, opposition organizations refused to recognize the coup, and within a few days *Red* power collapsed.

On January 25 the rival coalition, *Peking Commune,* better known as *United,* mounted a second assault on the cadres in power. Fifty-two organizations representing 10,000 people sent thousands of fighters onto the streets. This time, when the leaders seized the seals, the army ordered crack units to march back and forth in front of City Hall. Stiffened by the "atmosphere of legitimacy" thus created, the coup succeeded. *United* ruled the roost in the city and the region.

Chain-smoking Smart Fan (Fan Wen), whom we came to know so well in Long Bow, played a key role in the takeover of City Hall. Formerly a clerk in the State Grain Bureau, he rose to prominence in June, 1966, when he wrote a poster attacking Bureau leaders for failing to mount a mass campaign of criticism and exposure aimed at Peking journalist Teng To's essays *Notes from Three-Family Village.* He followed this up with a slashing

*In telling about it people used these terms retroactively, calling units that eventually ended up on one side or the other *Red* or *United* even though these terms had not been invented at the time some of the events described took place.

attack on Yang Ching, the Grain Bureau head, for writing a handbook about how to buy, store, treat, keep track of and sell grain, without including a word about Mao Tse-tung Thought, proletarian dictatorship or class struggle. Smart Fan's polemic won support particularly among the grain station workers who resented having to master the intricacies of grades, weights, moisture levels and prices that defined the grain trade. They denounced all this as "technique in command."

Taking Smart Fan's poster as his platform, Vice-Bureau Head Chao gathered a group around himself and went after Bureau Head Yang. To strengthen his attack he threw in a charge that Yang had a suspicious history. Not to be outdone, Yang mobilized some supporters and went after Chao, with an accusation that the Vice-Bureau Head had collaborated with the Japanese, sold heroin for a Korean capitalist, and covered up for an alleged renegade named Wu, a man who, after he was freed from a Japanese jail, parlayed his war record into a post as vice-mayor of Changchih.

As the two bureau heads slugged it out, rank-and-file Party members joined hands with Smart Fan and threw them both out of office. A newly elected Party committee asked Fan to lead the Cultural Revolution in the Grain Bureau. The ex-clerk took up the task with enthusiasm, turned his fire on former Vice-Bureau Head Chao, and developed the charges against him into a major renegade case. In 1968 Chao, in despair, hanged himself in a broom closet.

In the meantime Smart Fan's activism and literary talent brought him to the attention of city leaders. Student militants with outside support had mobilized a rebellion against the city newspaper, the *Changchih Daily,* and the Party Committee needed someone with "rebel" credentials to cope with the crisis. They picked on Smart Fan, promoted him to the City Party Committee, and put him in charge of the paper. Thus they brought in the man who eventually threw them all out.

The big organization formed to carry out the Cultural Revolution in the City Committee was called the *Red Flag Fighting Team.* At its height it numbered 180 members, all of them Communist cadres. Even though it established ties with the *Reds* who claimed to be the original "rebels," it supported the Party Secretary of the City and was therefore dubbed "loyalist" by Smart Fan. *Red Flag* set strict standards for membership. Every recruit had to prove cadre, worker or poor and lower-middle peasant origin and a faultless revolutionary history. Of the eighteen Party members under Smart Fan's leadership at the newspaper, only two qualified by class origin and past record to join the group entrusted by the majority to make the new revolution. Smart Fan was one of the two, but *Red Flag's* exclusive by-laws repelled him, and he decided to set up his own organization, the *Red News Rebels,* with thirteen founding members. This so-called "mass" organization later expanded its membership to seventeen. Its goal was to carry out "struggle, criticism, and transformation well at the newspaper office, support student demands, and create public opinion for the Cultural Revolution in Changchih."

Another group of eight Party members, also excluded from *Red Flag,* organized a *Red Rebel Team* and vowed to "stir up the dead water of the

City Party Committee, settle accounts with its reactionary line, and remove all stumbling blocks to the Cultural Revolution in Changchih."

These two minority groups established ties with a wide range of student and worker organizations loosely affiliated with the so-called "loyalist" *United* coalition, among them detachments of workers from Changchih Steel, the Diesel Engine Works, the State Construction Company and the Printing Shop that printed the newspaper. Allied student detachments included groups from the Taiyuan Engineering School, Shansi University, Changchih First Middle School, Changchih Second Middle School and Luan Middle School in Long Bow.

After news of the big revolution in Shanghai reached Shansi, seven *United* organizations led by Smart Fan's *Red News Rebels* and the *Red Rebel Team* seized the city newspaper that the *Red News Rebels* already controlled, sealed up its doors, and then, from the back door, issued an inflammatory sheet called the *Changchih Battle News*. Its program: denounce the City Committee and prepare to wrest away its power.

Smart Fan described how the conflict developed:

> After we took over the newspaper we asked why it was that the City Committee could suppress both students and cadres and decided that it was because they held state power. The obvious solution was for us to take over both at the city and the regional level.
>
> We sent out two *Red Rebels* to sound out our allies and they came back saying, "Tonight is the night."
>
> I was confused. How could it be done?
>
> They said all we had to do was to get all the leading cadres together, tell them they had no right to rule, order them to step aside, and set up a command headquarters of our own.
>
> I asked if that was the way it had been done at the provincial level in Taiyuan.
>
> They said it was.
>
> But I still had a few doubts. Was this what the Central Committee in Peking was calling for? Whom did we really represent? What sort of an administration could we organize? How would we handle power once we had it in our hands?
>
> The outside students repeated what they had said before. The Taiyuan rebels had copied the Shanghai pattern. We ought to copy the Taiyuan pattern. There was nothing to worry about. Everything was in line with Central Committee directives.
>
> Some of my newspaper group taunted me for being afraid to tackle such a big job. The outside students got impatient. They said, "We'll go ahead without you."
>
> That did it. I thought, if they are going to act, I had better join them, even if I can't see what the future will bring. So I said, "OK. Let's not worry about whether it's right or not. Let's just discuss how to carry it out."
>
> Having agreed on that approach, we set up a Command Head-

quarters and made our assignments. My group undertook to get all the Party secretaries of the city together in one place, hold them, and shut down the building so that no one else could get in. It sounded easy but how could a mere seventeen of us corner all five of them at one spot and seal off the building at the same time? More than 500 people worked in that building. How could we cope with them all?

The others said if we could handle the Party secretaries they would help patrol the building, so we accepted the task. Then we decided that everyone involved in the action should wear a white towel on his left arm. That way we could be sure what side any person sighted was on.

On the afternoon of the twenty-fifth the City Party Committee called a plenary meeting. We walked in and challenged its members to say whether or not it was right for us to close down the *Changchih Daily*. Some of them, suspecting a plot, walked out right away. They escaped. We ordered those who remained to stay put. The Mayor, Wang Ching-sheng, the Vice-Mayor and the three standing committee members obeyed. Old Kuo [of the standing committee] asked if he could go out for something to eat but we wouldn't allow it. We said he had to answer our questions first. The rest didn't even suggest leaving. They were afraid we would start a fight.

The opposition group, *Red Flag,* sent a contingent to block the entrance of the building. A few members came inside to argue with us. They said we at least ought to let the older members out to eat, but we didn't agree. Instead, we divided our forces. Half of us talked with the *Red Flag* members and the other half talked with the city cadres. That way we kept them all busy from six in the evening until after eight. By that time some 3,000 students and workers, mobilized by the *Red Rebels* [a unit of eight members], had surrounded the building. They began to shout in unison, "Down with Mayor Wang Ching-sheng."

That's when the Mayor realized he was in trouble. He asked, "What's going on?"

We said we didn't know.

The *Red Flag* members went out to have a look. They never came back. They didn't have any white armbands on, so our people arrested them and sent them to a ground-floor room under custody.

We grabbed the three most important city officials and, holding them by the arms, hauled them down the stairs to the front door.

There a worker from the Railroad Shops organization named Hsu Chih-yu and a student from Peking named Lo Ting-chan, representing our *Seize Power Command Headquarters,* announced that we had removed the three from their posts and that our headquarters was now in charge. A tremendous cheer went up from our supporters outside.

We hustled the three city officials into a car and drove them to the Regional Guest House, where we held them for several days. While we were seizing the offices of the City Party Committee, other contingents seized the regional offices so in the course of a single day both the city and the region fell into our hands.

The bold coup carried out by organizations affiliated with *United* forced many who adhered to the other side to question their own stand. Seizing power was, after all, the main current of the time. If they opposed it, where would they end up? Scores of city-level cadres left *Red Flag* and set up new organizations, some fifteen in all. Some of these asked to join the new "rebel" *Command Headquarters,* but others felt that though taking power was proper, the action had been premature, that *Command Headquarters* had not won enough support down below, and some of the contributing organizations did not meet the standards required of allies. They appeared to be "unclean," even reactionary. Those who felt this way linked up to form a *Revolutionary Rebel Liaison Station* and set up headquarters in the south end of the City Hall. Their office became known as the *South Station* and linked up with *Red* in the Region. Those who supported the power seizure set up a *Proletarian Revolutionary Alliance Liaison Station,* with headquarters in the north end of City Hall. Their office became known as the *North Station* and linked up with *United* in the region.

South Station members held a clandestine meeting to plan the overthrow of *Command Headquarters* but before they could act word got out. Under relentless attack for their "January 29 Black Meeting," they had to drop their plan.

From January 25, when city and regional offices changed hands until April 5, when the *North* and *South* stations finally forged an alliance, turmoil ruled in Changchih. Students from outside, especially students from Shansi University in Taiyuan, who arrived as two hostile cliques, constantly fanned up new controversies. They brought the rupture in the provincial student movement down with them to the region and contested their differences with an intensity that reflected their fratricidal rivalry for dominance on the home campus.

Several members of the *Shan Ta Pa Yao Szu* (Shansi University August 14)* threw in their lot with the *South Station.* They could not stand the sight of the twelve members of *Shan Ta Pa Pa* (Shansi University August 8)† who had thrown in their lot with the *North Station. August 14* accused *August 8* of opposing Kuan Feng, a member of the Central Cultural Revolution Group in Peking who was much in the news as a leading leftist in those days. Defying Kuan Feng, *August 8* had pulled out of the coalition that seized power in Taiyuan, thus exposing its own reactionary nature in the eyes of its opponents. How could such an organization claim the right to share power in Changchih? Its very presence called into question the legitimacy of *Command Headquarters.*

What with *August 14* versus *August 8, Red Flag* versus *Red News Rebels,* and *South Station* versus *North Station,* the polarization of the mass move-

---

*August 14 was the anniversary of the first big gathering of Red Guards reviewed by Mao at Tien An Men Square.
†August 8 was the anniversary of the Sixteen-Point Decision.

ment seemed complete. For a while, however, a few maverick independents still hovered in the wings. One of these was the *Tsunyi Sharp Sword Team,* formed by six section-level cadres of the City Government. They supported *Command Headquarters* but *Command Headquarters* refused to have anything to do with them, so they wandered aimlessly about looking for an organizational home.

Conflict in the early months of 1967 still boiled up primarily as verbal debate. Night and day hot arguments dominated the foyers of City Hall and the streets around it. Since most people had to work during the day, students carried on from eight to four, but toward evening when plant workers came off shift and government cadres left their desks, half the city joined in. Surging polemics reached their peak around 9:00 P.M., then fell off sharply until about two in the morning when the diehards finally gave up and went home to bed.

The huge crowds milling about in the streets formed numerous small clusters that constantly dissolved and re-formed. A dozen activists debating hotly in one spot could draw an audience of twice that number as long as they kept their altercation at a high pitch. As the pitch fell off bystanders drifted away, only to crowd some other spot. Partisans of one side might lose out in one location but win the argument decisively in another. In the confusion, fights broke out frequently, many of them provoked.

Members of one faction would surround a debating group, then send people in to take part. Once they had dispersed themselves throughout the crowd, they would pick up bricks and start throwing them out. Thus "provoked" into "self-defense," their comrades on the outside would hurl rocks and bricks back. The heavy fighting that followed appeared to generate spontaneously, but in fact one collective or another stage-managed each such incident. Lone debaters could also provoke fights. A youth would hold his *Red Book* high overhead with one hand and shout, "Use reason, not force!" With his other hand he would punch one of his opponents in the stomach and simultaneously step on his feet. Most of the people on the street wore cloth shoes, but many plant workers wore heavy leather boots. When they put their feet down they could break bones. If the victim said, "Hey, what was that all about?" the speaker would deny everything.

"Were you hit? I didn't hit you. What are you getting excited about?"

Most bystanders couldn't tell what was going on.

From a group named *East Is Red* everyone learned a sure-fire method for turning a debate into a fight; it could be called the *Three-Ring Two-Step.* A group of militants would lead several opposition leaders to one side to talk things over, then surround them. The cluster that formed looked casual but was actually well organized. In the inner ring stood young women. A second ring made up of men of the same organization backed them up, while behind them more men and women of fraternal organizations, especially mobilized for the occasion, formed a third layer of encirclement. As the debate waxed hot, the young women in front would start to shout, poke people with their fingers, even prick them with knitting needles. Sooner or later one of the opposition would retaliate by slapping one of the women. Then the men would jump forward to defend the "weaker sex." As the women ducked out, the stalwarts from the fraternal organizations would wade into the fray while the small group at the center quietly slipped to one side. By the time the fighting reached its height, those who provoked it had long since left the scene.

East Is Red was a faction of Medical School students who adhered to *Red.* They chose as leader one Wang Ch'ing-chieh. His enemies said he was a hooligan type who knew how to talk and also how to cry. When the army commander called him in to question his rough tactics, he started to cry and all thirty of his followers burst out crying with him. Some of them even fainted, a trick they learned to carry out on command.

"Would young people weep and faint if they were not persecuted?" asked Wang.

In the free-for-all on the streets, posters supplemented debate. Contending organizations put up temporary billboards, one touching the other, all the way from the north to the south end of Main Street, and on many side streets as well. The various groups were supposed to use their own billboards, but they soon learned to disregard that rule and paste posters wherever they felt like displaying them. Poster writers wrote "leave for five days" all around the edge of their latest creations but nobody paid any attention. Rivals pasted new posters over the old long before the old ones had a chance to dry on. At the start people wrote their posters at home, then brought them out and pasted them up, but they soon abandoned this method in favor of carrying paper, ink and paste right onto the street and slapping up each message as fast as they could write it. Even then, by the time they got to the north end of the street, rivals were already beginning to cover what they had left behind at the south end.

The poster war soon spread beyond the city. The *Red Rebel Team,* still boasting only eight members, placed posters up the highway all the way to Taiyuan. This zeal earned them the label "Iron Loyalists" from those who opposed the power seizure and the new *Command Headquarters* in Changchih. *Red Rebel* leader Li Chih-chung was also known as the "black stooge of Wei Heng," a charge that linked him to the overthrown chairman of the provincial government, who, it was rumored, had sent followers to take power in Changchih after he lost power in Taiyuan.

Poster writing and poster pasting often led to fighting, and this grew more frequent and more serious as time went on. However, the most serious fights did not originate over posters in the streets, but as the result of planned marches and raids. On February 29 members of Shansi University *August 14* marched on City Hall with 200 supporters. They wanted to seize the twelve members of *August 8* and "repair" them, which meant to give them a serious beating.

Singing defiantly, the *August 8* dozen locked themselves in their North End Office. Their ally Smart Fan ordered his supporters to defend the building, then to make sure of victory, notified the headquarters of the Liberation Army in the city. The army sent two squads, one on motorcycles, the other on horseback, to maintain law and order. The mere sight of this half-mechanized, half-mounted force was enough to deter the 200. They retreated in disarray.

On April 5, in response to nationwide calls for unity and the insistent demands of local army commanders, the North Station *United* coalition joined the South Station *Red* coalition in a "grand alliance." On April 8 leaders of the grand alliance chose a Revolutionary Committee composed of army officers, old cadres, and key leaders of mass organizations to run the city. On April 17 a grand alliance of the Region chose a similar Revolutionary Committee to run Southeast Shansi. Once the new governments took over at both levels they declared political struggle outmoded, called on all mass organizations to dissolve, and urged everyone to join hands to reform society and develop production.

By May it became clear that no such peaceful progress was possible. Setting up grand alliances and unified committees resembled pasting paper over an active volcano. All the jealousies, hard feelings and rivalries that had set people against one another from the beginning continued to fester, to multiply, and to escalate. It was only a matter of time before the flames of the old conflagration broke through.

The first sign of dissension came with the creation, early in May, of a new center for opposition to the power seizure of January 25. It was called the *Red Liaison Station to Repudiate Liu and Teng,* and rallied not only those members of the *Red* coalition who still could not accept the status quo but various groups of defectors from the opposing *United* coalition. Workers from the Huai-hai Arsenal, the Region's most important industrial plant, made up one large contingent. They had supported the original attempt at power seizure mounted by *Red,* but had not turned out at all for the second successful attempt carried through by *United.* When the Revolutionary Committee was finally chosen, this opposition called it "a big mix-up, a mishmash, a tub of mud and sand, a restoration, not a revolution." In their view what had really come to power was the army, an army they perceived as a conservative force.

There was no question that the army had played a decisive role in all the events of that strange season. The January 25 power seizure succeeded primarily because it had the support of the army units assigned to the region. The commander of these troops, Wu T'ien-ming, and his Chief of Staff, Li Ying-k'uei, failed to cooperate with the first seizure (it is possible that no one even asked them), but gave full support to the second, even sending armed units into the streets to create "an atmosphere of legitimacy." Much later, when the factions joined to set up their new Southeast Shansi Revolutionary Committee, both Wu T'ien-ming and Li Ying-k'uei automatically assumed leading roles on it. They played such an active part that many people concluded "the gun is in command." If they had been evenhanded in their relations with disaffected people and groups they might have won broad support, but from the very beginning they played favorites, working closely with those cadres and movement leaders who obeyed and flattered them while isolating the others.

The Chairman of the new Revolutionary Committee, Ch'en Hsiu-ch'uang, was not a military man but a Communist Party cadre originally designated by the Provincial Party Committee to head up a "core leading group" for the Region. Because he was an outside appointee, *United* rebels simply bypassed him when they seized power. Then, because he was the highest ranking Party official in the Region, and did not oppose the January 25 Coup, they chose him to head the Revolutionary Committee that emerged.

But Ch'en Hsiu-ch'uang very early fell out with Commander Wu T'ien-ming and Chief of Staff Li. Differences arose, as might have been predicted, over the evaluation of old cadres who had been overthrown. By May antagonism over the issue of which ones to rehabilitate and which ones to set aside had developed to such a point that Ch'en helped organize a breakaway detachment called the *North China Rebel Army to Take Revenge for Wang Hsiang-chih.*

Wang Hsiang-chih, former secretary of the Regional Party Committee, and head of its Four Clean Work Team, had been assigned to Southeast Shansi from a post in Inner Mongolia less than a year before the Cultural Revolution began. City police found him dead at the bottom of a well on December 31, 1966. Six months later they were still investigating the cause of his death. Had he committed suicide, or had the members of some hostile faction thrown him into the well? Nobody knew. But Ch'en Hsiu-ch'uang, who had been the political director of Wang's Four Clean Work Team, blamed his death on the People's Liberation Army.

On July 19 several thousand demonstrators, including a large contingent of workers from the Huai-hai Arsenal, surrounded army headquarters in downtown Changchih. They accused the army of monopolizing power in the region, of suppressing the left (themselves), of supporting a revisionist restoration, and more concretely of causing the death of Wang Hsiang-chih. They called for the dissolution of the ruling Revolutionary Committee and the selection of a new one staffed with people they could approve.

On July 21 another group of demonstrators, assembled around a militant core of Huai-hai Arsenal workers, surrounded the Regional Medical School, a *United* stronghold, and tried to break in. In the fighting that ensued, *United* later charged, Huai-hai workers beat up 200 of the defenders, injured more than ninety, seventeen of them seriously, and damaged property to the value of 100,000 yuan.

On July 22 Red units surrounding the Army Subdistrict Headquarters demanded that Commander Wu T'ien-ming come before them for criticism. They questioned him roughly for several days and, *United* said, "conducted a struggle" against him. Hsu Piao, the workers' leader who led the abortive attack on the railroad shops at Long Bow, said, "Wu T'ien-ming must be overthrown. If we can't do it in a week I'll see that my severed head is hung in front of his headquarters."

On July 23 Commander Li Ying-k'uei took the West Gully labor hero Li Hsun-ta with him to Peking to find the Chairman of Shansi Province, who had been called to the capital for discussions on the chaotic situation in the Southeast. Chairman Liu said that even though it was not wrong for the *Revenge Army* to surround the Army Subdistrict Headquarters, he would advise it to break off the action. The next day, July 24, the *Revenge Army* did call off its demonstration.

A few days later members of the Standing Committee of the City Revolutionary Committee sharply questioned *Red* sympathizer Ch'en Hsiu-ch'uang about the antiarmy demonstration and the fighting at the Medical School. This time it was he who responded by going to Peking to seek out the Provincial Chairman. When he got there Chairman Liu invited him to take part in the discussions on Shansi. A Sixty-ninth Army escort brought him back to Changchih on August 11, whereupon *United* supporters called him before a mass meeting and, according to *Red* partisans, "conducted a struggle" against him in turn.

In the seesaw conflict the most extraordinary confrontation took place as the Huai-hai workers surrounded the Army Subdistrict Headquarters. According to Commander Li Ying-k'uei, their demonstration built up to a shocking climax on the afternoon of the last day. Only one soldier stood guard. As the hostile crowds marched by shouting antiarmy slogans, those who passed near the soldier spat on him. The lone sentry never changed his position, or even, so far as anyone could see, moved a muscle. The saliva from thousands of hostile workers landed on his face, his hands, his gun and his uniform, wetting him from head to toe. As the spitting continued, excess fluid began to run down the front of his body to the ground. When the last of the demonstrators had passed, the sentry, still motionless, stood in a pool of saliva that spread slowly outward from his feet. After a few minutes Commander Li relieved the sentry, but the sight of that uniformed man, soaking wet and standing in an expanding pool of spit, did not quickly fade from the mind of anyone who saw it.

In 1977 regional leaders denied that any such incident had taken place. I tend to believe, however, that Chief of Staff Li spoke the truth. Even his fertile imagination could not easily have conjured up such a bizarre scene, such a shameful form of attack. Assuming that it really did happen, could the death of a former Party Secretary have brought thousands of workers to the point where they wanted to spit on a soldier of the People's Liberation Army? What else lay behind this contempt? Why were the workers attacking the army in the first place?

The first and most compelling reason for these workers to hate the army in Southeast Shansi was that its commanders were at loggerheads with the faction to which the workers belonged and had effectively excluded them all from any positive role in the politics of the region. Their grievance on this score was reinforced by an antiarmy wind that blew through the whole nation that spring. In April, 1967, Wang Li, Kuan Feng's militant colleague on the Cultural Revolution Group in Peking, had warned of imminent danger to Mao Tse-tung's proletarian headquarters from a four-tiered bourgeois encirclement that specifically included a "right-wing trend backed up by the army in Shansi." On July 14 one of the "capitalist road" army commanders he castigated, General Ch'en Ts'ai-tao, arrested Wang Li himself. When Ch'en Hsiu-Ch'uang's *Revenge Army* militants surrounded military headquarters in Changchih and proceeded to spit on the sentry, their hero Wang Li still sat incommunicado in a room in Wuhan, Central China.

We could now understand how rank-and-file workers, dissatisfied with the way power had been seized in the first place, angry at the slanderous accusations hurled against them, denied a place in the sun, and alarmed by events in Wuhan, might fall in with the political wind blowing so strongly from Peking and decide that they indeed confronted counterrevolution in military garb right in the heart of Changchih.

We could also understand how the local commander, Wu T'ien-ming, and his chief-of-staff, Li Ying-k'uei, might see the revolting demonstration at army headquarters as part of a nationwide antiarmy plot fanned by ultraleft conspirators. The march of the *Revenge Army* coincided with numerous assaults on army installations and army commanders from Shen-yang to Canton. Such a many-sided offensive could hardly be spontaneous, the army commanders reasoned. Cherishing the Liberation Army as the bulwark of the revolution, they convinced themselves that organized counterrevolutionaries planned the attacks on army units. When, on September 5, Mao's wife, Chiang Ch'ing, denounced the national antiarmy wind and blamed it on a group of unnamed conspirators called the *May Sixteenth Group,* Wu and Li felt vindicated. Clearly it was they who had been defending revolution all along while others were attacking it. The opposition leaders who opposed them were dangerous counterrevolutionaries. They must be exposed.

In the ensuing weeks Wu T'ien-ming and Li Ying-k'uei launched a counterattack designed to discredit the opposition once and for all. Their strategy was to zero in on Ch'en Hsiu-ch'uang, Chairman of the Regional Revolutionary Committee and leader of the opposition forces, discredit him as a renegade, a counterrevolutionary and a Kuomintang agent, and by this method discredit his entire organization and all the major and minor groups that had joined together under his leadership.

The mastermind behind the counterattack was Commander Li Ying-k'uei.

73

ANATOMY OF A FRAME-UP

When Commander Li sat down to tell us about Ch'en Hsiu-ch'uang in September, 1971, his characteristic informal, voluble style suddenly gave way to a curious hesitation. He talked extremely slowly, pronounced a single sentence, then paused, looked at the ceiling for what seemed like an interminable interval, then added a second sentence. It was as if he could not make up his mind what word to use next or what sentence to say next, and this was so even though he had plenty of time, while Carma translated his words, to formulate whatever was to follow. It seemed to me that he was not at all sure of himself, that he was groping his way, trying out one idea after another, marking the effect of each on his hearers, then proceeding with the development of his case.

This uncharacteristic performance lasted throughout Li's basic presentation, then gradually gave way to more normal talk as he elaborated on the significance of the "facts" laid out. When he came to his own views on how this case should be settled no hesitation at all marred his delivery. Speaking forcefully, he said, "Ch'en Hsiu-ch'uang should be sentenced to death, but he should be given a two-year stay of execution to give him a chance to reform. If, during the two years, he makes no more mistakes he may win a reprieve. Otherwise the sentence should be carried out."

The first thing Commander Li Ying-k'uei described for us was the investigation he had conducted into the background, work record and Party history of *Red* leader Ch'en Hsiu-ch'uang. He told how he sent teams of fact finders throughout the region and the province and even into neighboring provinces to look into every facet of the Regional Chairman's past.

But, said Commander Li, as soon as teams from one side went forth to pick holes in Ch'en Hsiu-ch'uang's record, other teams went forth from the other side to bring out the best possible side of Ch'en's record. When Ch'en's opponents found ten documents that called his record into serious question, his supporters countered with eighty-six documents that proved he was a solid revolutionary cadre.

Chen's supporters, he charged, went even further. They did everything possible to block, even to wreck, the fault-finding investigation of the other side. When *United* sent people to Licheng County to look into enemy and puppet files, *Red* mobilized its supporters to seize the county town by force so that no one could get at the files. *United* people made their way to Licheng several times but each time they were beaten, arrested and imprisoned. When supporters of Ch'en from the *Regiment* of Taiyuan City went to Licheng, on the other hand, they had no trouble gaining access to all pertinent material. *United* investigators who went to Loyang and Taiyuan for evidence met *Red* harassment at every step. In Loyang *Red* made an attempt to kidnap them, but local Liberation Army forces foiled the plot.

Commander Li Ying-k'uei charged that the *Red* investigators themselves unearthed damning material about Ch'en, but lied about it and suppressed it, just as they suppressed the efforts of the *United* investigators to find any evidence at all.

"Thus," said Li Ying-k'uei, "the investigation and counterinvestigation initiated a sharp and complicated class struggle."

In spite of all difficulties Li's men soon compiled a dossier of damning evidence, which they divided into several categories:

1. Ch'en's bad class background and social connections;
2. his fraudulent career as a patriot in the war against Japan;
3. his overt counterrevolutionary activity;
4. his subsequent misleading record as a revolutionary cadre;
5. his rise to power in the Cultural Revolution;
6. his divisive activities and many crimes during the Cultural Revolution.

Here are some of the "data" that General Li compiled on his adversary Ch'en:

Ch'en Hsiu-ch'uang was born in 1919. He said that his parents were poor peasants, but actually they were rich peasants. With only four members in the family they owned eighty mou of land, a mule and a horse. From 1935 to 1947 they hired laborers on a long-term basis and took in over 10,000 catties of grain in land rent. Chen's father headed the family clan and practiced geomancy (the "science" of picking propitious sites for ancestral graves, buildings, etc., thus guaranteeing good fortune). His mother headed the Taoist Sun Worship Society. His older sister, Ch'en Ai-t'ien, first married a landlord, then had an affair with the Kuomintang Party branch secretary, Chao Pan-chen. His second sister, Ch'en Chang-p'ing, also married a landlord.

Ch'en, at an early age and by arrangement, married a girl named Sung. While he was away from home, his wife became pregnant by another man, so his mother sold her and arranged for him to marry a second Sung girl from the same village whom they called Sung Yi-huan, or Sung In-Exchange. This second Sung was the widow of the head of the local Yi Kuan Tao, the gentry-dominated secret society, who had taken part in an uprising against the Liberated Areas Government in 1942. After the Eighth Route Army captured and killed her first husband, she married Ch'en. Said Li Ying-k'uei, "In his whole family background there is not one clean person!"

In 1936 Ch'en became warden at the Licheng County Jail, recommended for this post by a Kuomintang special agent, Yang Cheng-fang. In 1937 he joined the National Army Officers' Training Team organized by the Shansi warlord Yen Hsi-shan as part of his New Model Army. This was the force that under Po Yi-po's leadership turned into the Dare-to-Die Column in the Anti-Japanese War. Ch'en started out as a squad leader in the Fifth Company, First Regiment. He won promotion to the post of political cadre in the Fifth Company and finally became the political director of the Company. In 1939 he was wounded fighting Japanese troops in the battle for P'ingyao County and went to the hospital.

According to Ch'en's own statements, he was already a Communist when he entered the hospital, having joined the Party in 1937. He named two members who he said had introduced him. In 1967 when the investigation was made, one of the men was already dead. The other claimed that he himself had not joined the Party until 1943, so could not possibly have introduced Ch'en in 1937. "Thus Ch'en wormed his way into the Communist Party," said Li Ying-k'uei.

In 1943, in the most difficult year of the Resistance War, Ch'en went home for twelve months. Li Ying-k'uei said it was because he lost his nerve in the face of the Japanese offensive. While at home, Li charged, Ch'en linked up with Kuomintang agents who ran a cooperative in the village. It was ostensibly under Communist leadership but actually served as cover for an organization of agents. Enemy files showed that Ch'en had joined the Kuomintang Party Branch in November, 1944. They also contained a letter from Ch'en to the branch giving information about revolutionary cadres. A Kuomintang agent, later executed, named Ch'en as a fellow agent. Two other Kuomintang agents, one of them in Ch'en's home village, another in Szechuan, verified that he had introduced Ch'en and his wife to the Kuomintang on November 6, 1944.

Further investigation showed that Ch'en's wife's home served as the liaison station for Kuomintang agents in Tunliu County, part of a network of stations leading from Southeast Shansi down into Honan.

"So," said Li Ying-k'uei, "investigation showed that Ch'en Hsiu-ch'uang was a false Communist and a true Kuomintang."

Late in 1944 Ch'en became a member of the Military Committee of the Second District of Lucheng County, and in 1946 was transferred to the County Militia Department. While serving in this capacity he stole four rifles and one pistol and grafted 24,000 yuan. As a result the Communist Party placed him under supervision for a year. "The most severe punishment short of expulsion," said Li Ying-k'uei.

In March, 1948, Ch'en transferred to the Military District of the Third Subregion of the Taihang Region, with headquarters in Changchih. This militia command merged with the People's Liberation Army command on August 1, 1949, when the army set up its Southeast Shansi headquarters. Ch'en fell ill while serving in Changchih and went to the Liberation Army Hospital in Tientsin to recuperate. He spent two years under medical care. In 1951 the regional government assigned him to the Shangtang Coal Company as Party Secretary. In 1952 the government transferred him to the Enterprise Company as manager. In 1953 it appointed him head of the Changchih City Industrial Bureau. In 1954 city workers elected him a delegate to the Changchih People's Congress and the Congress appointed him vice-mayor of Changchih City; in 1956 he became mayor. In 1958 provincial officials promoted him to the post of vice-liaison officer for the Southeast Shansi Region, a provincial appointment making him responsible for the work of the whole region. After the power seizure of January, 1967, when the "rebels" failed to knock him down, he became head of the Regional Communist Party core leading group. When rebel groups established their new Regional Revolutionary Committee on April 17, 1967, they chose him as chairman.

This looked like a record of steady promotion based on merit, but Li Ying-k'uei didn't interpret it that way. "From 1937 when he slipped into the Communist Party he transferred twenty-nine times and filled in eleven false histories. He often wrote down higher levels of office than he had actually held, saying that he was chairman when in fact he was only vice-chairman. Concerning those places where his work raised questions he often wrote nothing at all. In 1943, for instance, he made no mention of going home, but claimed to have served as section head in the Subdistrict Army office that year. In fact there was no such office that year."

How then could he assume so high a post?

"Because he made up his history. As a cadre transferred from the Liberation Army to the local region he was able to deceive people for a while. The Liberation Army Subregional Staff didn't know him well and the people didn't know him well either. He claimed he was a cadre who had been under attack by the old Party leadership. So this gave him prestige. It was necessary to appoint representatives of the old cadres to every Revolutionary Committee (a three-way combination of leaders of the mass movement, army men and old cadres), so the committee chose him."

After January, 1967, Ch'en's record, according to Li Ying-k'uei, went from bad to worse. First came the death of Wang Hsiang-chih. While the case was still under investigation, before anyone could determine whether the Party Secretary had been killed or had committed suicide, Ch'en demanded a memorial meeting for him. Since he died while under fierce attack from certain mass organizations, a memorial meeting meant, in fact, a repudiation of those organizations. It was an effort to use the dead to suppress the living.

Commander Li alleged that Ch'en had acted ruthlessly against people who knew or revealed information about his past; also that he had ordered a mass organization to seize and beat to death a county Communist Party Secretary who put up a poster containing adverse historical material.

Ch'en supporters also beat to death an accountant from his home village named Yang Chih-cheng who had publicized some material unfavorable to Ch'en. Yang was targeted for retaliation.

While Ch'en professed on many occasions that the army was his "mother" and his "home," he attacked the army stationed in the region at every opportunity. Was it not Ch'en who had organized the demonstration of July 19, 1967, when thousands spat on a lone sentry?

And was it not Ch'en who organized an attack on the Medical School on July 21, when Huai-hai workers beat students and staff with iron rods, slashed them with sawblades, and cut them with knives? Seventeen were seriously sounded. Ch'en tried to cover up this atrocity by asking the army to say that no one had been beaten at all.

On August 11, after he returned from a high-level meeting in Peking, Ch'en Hsiu-ch'uang divided the mass movement and personally launched the whole factional struggle that led to armed fighting. According to Li, before Ch'en pulled his faction together in the summer of 1967, factionalism didn't exist in Southeast Shansi. Once Ch'en got the factions going, Li charged, he initiated one atrocious incident after another.

"Allow me," said Li Ying-k'uei, "to give my views on this man Ch'en.

"I think he is a renegade, a Kuomintang agent, a diehard capitalist roader and an acting counterrevolutionary!

"After he joined the revolution he joined the counterrevolution. This makes him a renegade.

"He joined a group of Kuomintang special agents and exposed some of our anti-Japanese fighters. This makes him an agent.

"During the period of socialist construction he wildly pushed Lui Shao-ch'i's revisionist line, hence he is a diehard capitalist roader who won't change.

"During the Cultural Revolution he gathered together all sorts of landlords, rich peasants and so-called leaders of mass organizations, including people just released from jail after serving sentences, Kuomintang agents and all the dregs of society, and together with them planned a whole series of counterrevolutionary incidents. He directed assassination plots to do away with witnesses who had evidence against him. The blood of revolutionary martyrs is on his hands. He owes the people a blood debt. This makes him an active counterrevolutionary!"

Every time Commander Li Ying-k'uei succeeded in expanding his dossier on the Chairman of the Regional Revolutionary Committee, Ch'en Hsiu-ch'uang, he congratulated himself. His goal was to prepare an airtight case that could stand up to cross-examination in Taiyuan or even in Peking. As his collection of documented charges grew, it approached the point where he would be able to discredit and crush completely the forces under Ch'en, consolidate the forces led by himself and Commander Wu, and take unchallenged control of the region.

When anyone asked whether the alleged counterrevolutionary record of one man constituted sufficient grounds for condemning half the people's organizations in the Shangtang Plateau, Commander Li emphatically defended his choice of target and his method.

"We are solving a problem of revolutionary tactics," he said. "In battle one has to concentrate forces against the weakest link and make a breakthrough. Exposing Chen's record as an enemy agent gives us a place to stand, a solid foundation for solving whatever difficulties may arise. If we start discussing policy questions we can only provoke a big debate and bog down in recriminations over our own mistakes as well as those of others. But if we concentrate on Ch'en we can avoid such digression and go straight to the heart of the matter. Ch'en, the agent, is the crucial factor, the main stumbling block to progress in the whole region. Remove this stumbling block and we can get at all the other problems. In any struggle you have to take hold of the principal contradiction, the main point, and battle it out. Basing ourselves on such a main point we become invincible. We can maintain our footing in front of the Central Committee and never be defeated."

Commander Li needed a particularly strong case against the opposition because he did not have a monopoly of legally constituted armed power in the region. Although he commanded all the units of the People's Liberation Army, he had no control at all over any unit of the navy. To his dismay, the naval unit 0115 under Commander Hsu Li-shen challenged every move he made. True, the navy could not boast any major presence in the landlocked Taihang Mountains. The first handful of naval personnel came to Changchih in the fifties to man a weather station. Later, navy men came, it was said, for "construction work." By 1967 they numbered several hundred, too few to control the region, but enough to upset the local balance of power and give the navy, if not a decisive voice, at least some veto power over local politics.

Problems arose early in 1967 when the Military Commission in Peking ordered all the armed forces to "support the left." Commander Hsu Li-shen never did see eye to eye with Commander Li Ying-k'uei on the question of who represented the "left." By jumping in on the opposite side of the factional struggle, he broke Li's mandate as the final arbiter of all local quarrels and stiffened the resistance of all those whom the army officer proposed to crush. Outnumbered ten to one, twenty to one, even, in the end, one hundred to one, by army personnel, navy men could not hope to turn the tide in their own favor. Nevertheless, by merely existing as armed units in opposition, they undermined the influence and the credibility of the army and its commanders and made difficult any overt action against those the army considered hostile.

Clearly, in the short run, the presence of the navy had a moderating influence. One thing Commander Li Ying-k'uei wanted to avoid at all costs was a direct clash with any naval unit, no matter how weak. Mao Tse-tung and the Central Military Commission had taken a strong stand against fighting between regular units of the armed forces and especially between units of the separate services. No commander wanted to court disgrace by being the first to initiate such fighting, regardless of the provocation.

The reluctance of the army to attack the navy also had a moderating influence, for the time being at least, on factional strife at the civilian level. Placing armed units in a solid block across the middle of Hero Square, army units on one flank, navy units on the other, made it possible for vast contingents of hostile civilian forces to gather on the same parade ground without making contact and consequently without assaulting each other.

A group of army commanders who called themselves the "Support the Left Leading Body" organized a huge unification meeting for September 5, 1967. The purpose of the meeting was to demonstrate to higher authorities that the army was at least trying to breathe new life into the grand alliance formed in April. By bringing opposing forces together in one place the army could demonstrate progress toward formal unity and thus make a case that it was carrying out Mao Tse-tung's instructions even while, behind the scenes, it maneuvered for a political showdown.

The mine guard from Long Bow, Shen Chung-t'ang, attended the September 5 meeting and described what happened.

> The crowd divided into hostile camps. The armed forces occupied the middle of the square with the army contingent and the navy contingent dividing the space between them. *United* supporters filled the ground north of the army while *Red* supporters filled the ground south of the navy. Both sides agreed that neither Commander Wu T'ien-ming, who was in fact a leader of *United,* nor Chairman Ch'en Hsiu-ch'uang of the Regional Revolutionary Committee, who was the acknowledged leader of *Red,* should appear. They also agreed that neither faction should shout any slogans. The Support the Left Leading Body advised *United* to drop its demand for the overthrow of Ch'en, and *Red* to drop its support for Ch'en. "Put aside the issue of Ch'en Hsiu-ch'uang temporarily and get together!"
>
> As the meeting opened the *Red* delegate spoke first. While he was still making his introductory remarks, Ch'en Hsiu-ch'uang suddenly appeared in a navy truck and, guarded by twenty naval personnel, rode round the square once.
>
> "Firmly support Ch'en Hsiu-ch'uang!" shouted the *Red* speaker, breaking the rules.
>
> Members of *United* immediately began to throw rocks. *Red* partisans responded in kind. Ch'en, startled by the sudden violence, quickly drove away. The rocks from both sides fell, for the most part, on the servicemen in the middle of the square. But the soldiers and sailors were under strict orders. They could not leave their posts. Under a mounting barrage of rocks, bricks and other hard missiles they stood their ground. Over 100 were hurt.
>
> This big meeting, called to revive the grand alliance, ended in one nasty brawl!
>
> We Wuchuang miners and Changchih Steel Plant workers ran for our trucks under a hail of bricks and stones. When bricks and stones ran out, *Red* partisans grabbed pieces of fruit and garlic from the stalls on the street. We kept our heads down but our driver couldn't start the truck. The attackers moved in and broke all the glass. We had come prepared for a fight. We had stout sticks stacked on the truck bed. When the windshield broke we grabbed our sticks, jumped down, and drove the *Red* attackers away. Soon after that our driver managed to start the truck and we got out of the city altogether. It was about 5:30 P.M.
>
> We went into the city several times after that to put up posters and got involved in fighting but never anything as serious as that incident in Hero Square. The army leaders knew that we were going into the city not to work or to debate, but to fight, so they tried to keep us at home. When our group went on shift at night they sent a soldier along with each guard to make sure that he stayed on duty where he belonged and they kept close watch on the gate so that no one could go out. They were also very strict about home leave. They wanted to know exactly where we were

going, how many days we would be gone, and what day we planned to come back.

Sometimes I took a few days off to come home to Long Bow. Then my father cursed me for taking part in the fighting.

If the presence of the navy cooled the ardor of the army and helped put off overt military action in support of *United,* it also polarized the conflict between *United* and *Red* and made escalation all but inevitable. Since each side could claim military approval and support, neither saw any reason to back down. Quite the contrary, each side felt justified in raising the level of its demands and the violence of its attacks.

The single most divisive element in the conflict in Southeast Shansi was the case Commander Li Ying-k'uei continued to build against Ch'en Hsiu-ch'uang. Since Li Ying-k'uei clearly planned to deliver a knockout blow, Ch'en Hsiu-ch'uang had no choice but to plan an equivalent counterblow, and so, step by step, the antagonism intensified. Confrontations, denunciations, mass mobilizations and open fighting surged to such heights that the authorities in strife-torn Taiyuan became alarmed. In the fall of 1967 the Chairman of the Revolutionary Committee of Shansi Province, Liu Ke-p'ing, decided to tour the Southeast Region in one final effort to patch up a peace.

74

EVERGREEN LIU SUCCEEDS TO A PROVINCE

For Provincial Chairman Liu Ke-p'ing to set out for Southeast Shansi as a peacemaker struck most observers as ironic, to say the least. In the fall of 1967 the conflict between irreconcilable factions in Taiyuan was, if anything, more virulent and extreme than the conflict anywhere else, including Changchih. The antagonisms in the Southeast continued to sharpen in large part because of the encouragement each side received from fraternal units in Taiyuan that had to build bases in outlying regions in order to maintain their footing in the capital. Just as regional and city groups sought support in the communes and brigades under their leadership, thus spreading their quarrels to the village level, so provincial groups sought support in the regions, thus spreading their quarrels to cities and towns in the four corners of the province. It goes without saying that groups in the national capital spread their rivalries to the provinces in the same manner and for the same reason.

The Cultural Revolution at the provincial level in Shansi as described for us by such varied informants as General Ts'ao Chung-nan, vice-chairman of the Provincial Revolutionary Committee; Commander Wang Chih-p'ing, member of the Standing Committee of the Provincial Revolutionary Committee; and Ma Chieh, vice-secretary of the Taiyuan City Committee, was complicated, bitterly fought out and bizarre.

In a briefing given us by Premier Chou En-lai, in Peking, we had been forewarned.

"Shansi," said the Premier, "was one of the first provinces where rebellion led to power seizure. But neither faction that grew out of the mass movement did well.

"At first they challenged the old provincial Communist Party leaders and seized power. This was correct. Two key leaders rose up in rebellion. The first was a member of the old provincial Party Committee and vice-head of the provincial government—Liu Ke-p'ing. The second was the political director of the Shansi Military District—Chang Er-ch'ing.

"At the start these two men worked together. But later they fell out, built antagonistic factions, and quarreled fiercely. I don't know how many times they quarreled. Both of these men opposed the old Shansi leadership right back to Po Yi-po. They were both new faces, not old faces. But this only goes to show that new forces can also fall out.

"As a result of their split, factionalism influenced the whole of the Cultural Revolution in Shansi. I can't begin to tell you how many times we held meetings right here in the Great Hall of the People in an effort to solve the Shansi problem. We used this room and many other rooms. We wanted those two leaders to unite. At the meetings they talked well and promised to unite, but when they went back to Taiyuan they fell to quarreling again and instigated armed fighting.

"In Taiyuan, on Liu Ke-p'ing's side, there was a leader who was very fierce, a real rascal. His father once worked for the Japanese and he himself had a bad record in puppet Manchukuo. His name was Yang Ch'eng-hsiao. I once met him face to face in the Peking Hotel. This Yang was then commander-in-chief of the Shansi 'rebels.' The political director of his unit was none other than Liu Ke-p'ing's wife, Ting Lei, and she also served as chief of staff.

"We invited all these factional chiefs to come and study in Peking. But to get the Shansi factions to cooperate was very difficult. In the end we had to send a new army to take over from the old army. At the Ninth Congress of the Communist Party the delegates elected Liu to the Central Committee and Chang Er-ch'ing as an alternate member. But after the Ninth Congress they still quarreled. They quarreled until they destroyed their political support. This time when we held a Party Congress of Shansi Province no one supported either of them. Even though one of them was a Central Committee member and the other an alternate, not a single person voted to have them on the Provincial Committee. And this shows the strength of the Cultural Revolution. No matter who you are, if you oppose the proletarian revolutionary line, you will collapse.

"In the end we transferred both Liu and Chang from Shansi. We sent them to work in other places. Then conditions in the province began to turn for the better. The Shansi problem lasted a long time. The quarrel went on for more than two years, longer than anywhere else in the whole country. It was 1970 before the situation began to improve. Therefore, whoever goes to Shansi should first look into the underlying situation."

The Premier had given us good advice, but it was far from easy to carry out.

Chairman Liu Ke-p'ing's support in Southeast Shansi came from the *Red* faction. By 1971 *Red* members in the Southeast and their allies at the provincial center had suffered such thorough defeat and suppression that no one with the courage to speak for them could be found. Most of the cadres in power who were eager to tell us about the struggle came from *United.* They were loyal supporters of Chang Er-ch'ing. The military commanders who were supposed to be "above the battle" also supported Chang Er-ch'ing, some of them covertly, others openly and brazenly. As a result, everything we heard tilted outrageously to one side. We heard no criticism at all of Chang Er-ch'ing, the military man, but heard many fascinating and lurid descriptions of Liu Ke-p'ing, the civilian, who seemed to be a universal target, not so much of hatred as of contempt. In 1967, when he came to power, he was entering his sixty-eighth year. Absent-minded, hard of hearing and a hesitant speaker, he blurted out short sentences that faded into long silences.

One cocky army officer, T'ien Huai-pao, described Chairman Liu as half-dead. "He coughed after each spoken phrase. 'Live air, dead smoke' describes his spirit. He preceded every sentence, every phrase, with a *che ke* [meaning this or this thing], at least one *che ke* if not more. Listening once and timing his speech I counted eighty-six *che kes* in ten minutes! First comes a *che ke,* then he clears his throat and with each half-sentence throws in a *ma* [syllable indicating a query]. In ten minutes he can get through only four or five sentences, especially when he doesn't have a script. You get so bored, so anxious, so impatient when you hear him."

Our friend Smart Fan loved to imitate the old man's style:

"Some people call Ting Lei *che ke* old broken shoe [prostitute]. Comrades . . . ahem, aha [throat clearing, long pause] . . . *che ke, che ke* attitude is no good. Ahem, aha . . . [long pause]. You shouldn't say things like *che ke, che ke* this . . . ahem, aha . . . [long pause]. Ting Lei is my wife . . . ahem, aha . . . [long pause]."

Or:

"Some say *che ke, che ke* Ch'en Hsiu-ch'uang is a bad person . . . ahem, aha . . . [long pause]. He's not a bad person, he's a *che ke, che ke* good person . . . aha . . . [long pause]. If he were a bad person would I support him? . . . *ma* . . . ahem, aha [long pause] . . . If he were a *che ke, che ke* bad person he'd fall by himself . . . aha . . . you wouldn't need to push him over!"

Even the factional names *United* and *Red* indicated a certain dullness of wit on Liu's part. In the beginning these two coalitions had long revolutionary titles that reflected some of the complexity of their origins. Liu was unable to remember these titles or even to distinguish one group from the other, but he did notice that a majority on one side had *Red* in their title while a majority on the other had *United* in theirs, so he said, "Let's call them by their trademarks, their brand names, *United* and *Red.* That way we'll keep them straight." And so they came to be known throughout the region by two words each, the *United Brand* and the *Red Brand.*

In 1971, remembering Chairman Liu's halting, long-winded speeches and the pedestrian character of his thought processes, people delighted in imitating him and holding him up to ridicule, but in 1967, after Liu led the group that seized power in the provincial capital, Taiyuan, these were not laughing matters. The coup of January 14 and the Revolutionary Committee Liu established on January 28 received almost immediate support from the Central Committee in Peking, which held it up as a model for the "rebels" of other provinces to follow. Liu soon won an ardent band of supporters who named him Liu Wei Lao ("never old," "eternally young" or, with poetic license, "evergreen"), after those youths described in Mao's famous poem *Huichang* who wandered over the green hills of Kiangsi and never grew old.

> When the east lights up
> It is not too early to march.

> Everything here
> Is so fair to see.
> Wandering these green hills
> We do not grow old.

As Liu's fame spread, his admirers even issued a *Red Book* of his most pithy sayings in imitation of the famous *Red Book* compiled for Chairman Mao by Lin Piao. They printed it in thousands of copies and distributed it far and wide. They culled the "Quotations of Chairman Liu" from the halting speeches he delivered while traveling through the Southeast. Since his words gave all-out support to the embattled *Reds,* members of that faction did their best, thereafter, to immortalize them.

When I visited the famous West Gully Brigade in 1971, labor hero Li Hsun-ta showed me a copy of the quotation book, but he considered it so atrocious an attempt at deification, so monstrous an example of arrogant folly, that he would not allow me to have a copy, to hold it long enough to record any of the quotations or even to savor their flavor. In China, to this day, when a man falls into disgrace his detractors must wipe him out completely. They feel compelled to bury the wrong or foolish things he has said or has done, lest they contaminate the present and the future. And this is particularly true of the written word, which, simply because it is written down, tends to become sacrosanct and worthy of the most pious respect. Most people cannot afford to deal with suspect reality and certainly not with any unvarnished tainted record, but only with that part of the record that currently pleases "Heaven"—something like "hear no evil, see no evil, speak no evil," and evil will go away. This formalistic approach, passed down through the ages, makes it hard for anyone to examine what really has happened, even that which they themselves have directly experienced, if it is currently under attack.

Evergreen Liu's main claim to fame rested on an exercise in formalism that had tremendous influence on the course of the Cultural Revolution. Liu, it turned out, was one of the young North China Communists whom the Kuomintang arrested in the thirties and held prisoner in Tientsin.

As the Japanese threat to China escalated, some sixty-five of these prisoners, on the advice of their Party organizer, Liu Shao-ch'i, reportedly signed anti-Communist affidavits and won release. This alleged "sellout" enabled them to carry on their revolutionary work and mobilize the Chinese people for resistance to Japan. The most famous of those released was Po Yi-po, who, at Shansi warlord Yen Hsi-shan's invitation, organized large numbers of students and progressive intellectuals into a "Dare-to-Die Corps" that became the nucleus of Yen's anti-Japanese "New Army." When the Japanese invaded Shansi and Warlord Yen retreated southwestward, Po Yi-po led five columns of the "Dare-to-Dies" eastward into the mountains, where they eventually merged with units of the Old Workers' and Peasants' Red Army, the survivors of the famous Long March that General Liu Po-ch'eng brought across the Yellow River from Yenan. This merger sparked the development of the huge Eighth Route Army of 300,000 that eventually liberated large parts of Shansi and far larger parts of North China as a whole.

In 1966 the leaders of the Cultural Revolution Group, in full control of all media in China, suddenly attacked Po Yi-po and sixty-four of his fellow prisoners who reportedly had signed anti-Communist affidavits, as renegades, thus wiping out with one stroke lifetimes of devoted soldiering, organizing, planning and building for a new, revolutionary China.

Never mind that, under dangerous and complicated circumstances, Po Yi-po built a progressive armed force under the very nose of Yen Hsi-shan; never mind that this force later served as the backbone of the People's Liberation Army in the north; never mind the role that this force, and Po Yi-po personally, played in the resistance to Japan and the liberation of Shansi, North China and China as a whole, not to mention their respective contributions to socialist construction later on; the signing of an anti-Communist affidavit by a young Communist under orders from his Party superior was apostasy, an absolute, inexcusable betrayal which turned day into night, white into black, hero into villain, forever and ever, amen. The final twist to this episode was the charge that the sixty-five renegades, quite aware they had done wrong and fearing exposure, clung together as a criminal clique under Liu Shao-ch'i's leadership and, when the time was ripe, helped him mount his "revisionist" offensive against socialism.

Behind the wholesale frame-up of the "North China Renegades" lay Mao's drive to win back the decisive control over the whole of the Communist Party lost to Liu Shao-ch'i and his allies at the Lushan meeting. To do this it was necessary completely to wipe out and discredit the record which Liu had, in the main, built up as leader of underground work in the White (Kuomintang-dominated) areas of China in the thirties. While Mao led the early guerrilla campaigns in the old Soviet bases, the Long March and the consolidation of the Yenan Border Region, Liu assumed the slow, dangerous and complicated task of organizing the Party and the Party-led mass movement behind enemy lines. The united Party that took command of all China after 1949 was an amalgam of individuals from these two distinct and diverse spheres, with people from Liu's underground gradually assuming a dominant position in the organization department and consequently the inner life of the Party as a whole. When Mao, with Lin Piao's help, undertook to reassert control over the whole party in 1966, the most direct and effective method available was to cast doubt on the Party history of all the individuals from the underground wing, starting with Liu himself. This was easy to do because the backgrounds, social connections and careers of people living and working in the White areas were necessarily complex and poorly documented. Their biographies often contained gaps or activities and relationships that could be invidiously interpreted to suit the bias of the investigator. Those who had been imprisoned by the Kuomintang, and particularly those who had been released by the Kuomintang, were saddled with the burden of proof that they had not defected in a situation where, as often as not, no witnesses existed or all witnesses had died. Taking advantage of such opportunities for slander and distortion, Mao's cohorts, possibly without his specific approval, had a field day concocting cases to prove the victims renegades, cases the victims found almost impossible to combat. Starting with the famous "North China 65," Party prosecutors manufactured literally thousands of indictments with devastating effects on the lives of the people against whom they drew the indictments and also on the lives of close comrades, wives, children, relatives and friends, in ever-widening circles.

But every cloud has its silver lining, and every disaster benefits someone. One outstanding beneficiary of the "North China" renegade cases was Evergreen Liu. Liu, so the story went, had been in the same prison as Po Yi-po but had refused to sign, or at least had *not* signed, any anti-Communist affidavit, and so had saved himself from eternal damnation. How, under the circumstances, Evergreen Liu survived imprisonment and eventually won release remains obscure. In Shansi nobody talked about that. In 1967 it was enough that he alone, or he among a select few, had not been emmeshed in Liu Shao-ch'i's "diabolical plot." As one cadre with a clean record in an administration dominated by exposed "renegades," he won automatic acclaim as a "rebel" leader.

Evergreen Liu had other claims to fame. First and foremost, he was a Hui, a Moslem from a small Moslem settlement in Central Hopei, one of the few minority people who came forward to play a leading role nationally in a revolutionary movement dominated by Hans. As a Hui he had once served as Chairman of the Nationalities Commission for All China, and had also served as Chairman of Ninghsia, a Moslem Autonomous Province lying along the western bend of the Yellow River.

Secondly, Evergreen Liu won fame because of his wife, Ting Lei, a beautiful if plump woman twenty-eight years younger than her husband, who stepped forward to play a very active role in the factional struggles of the province. Her admirers called her "the Plum Blossom of Shansi," "an until now undiscovered bright star of the Milky Way," a buried talent that came into its own only in the great proletarian Cultural Revolution. Parallels between the political careers of Ting Lei and Chiang Ch'ing, Mao's wife, are striking.

The stories we heard about Ting Lei rivaled in number the stories about her husband. Her beauty, her vanity, her conquests provided stuff for legends. According to Shansi people, she put on all the airs of a Shanghai merchant's wife. Troubled by an inappropriately dark complexion, she used light powder liberally on her face and splashed so much perfume over it that people could smell her twelve yards away. She smoked cigarettes, one after the other, by placing them into the end of a long cigarette holder. When living in Peking during the long study meetings held to resolve Shansi problems, she went by car every third day to the Tungan market to buy meat and vegetables. Each time she spent more than 40 yuan—a month's earnings for a skilled worker. She curried favor with the market attendants by handing out Mao badges left and right. Her pet dog went to the market with her, but was not allowed to ride in the car. He followed, running hard, in the street behind. Since few Chinese have ever kept dogs as pets, the very presence of a dog aroused hostility.

Ting Lei used her wiles on the men around her as needed, particularly if it would advance her husband's career. On Commander Li Ying-k'uei, the opposition army leader with the twisted face from Southeast Shansi, she lavished notorious attention, flattering him at every opportunity, lighting his cigarette for him, and trying to win his sympathy with jokes, stories and fluttering eyelids.

Her personal preference, however, was for younger men. Peking residents often saw her with a Shansi student leader named Yang who went about, even at important gatherings, in an undershirt, shorts and a pair of slippers. On the street this Yang wore dark glasses. A pipe protruded from the corner of his mouth. To see this pair coming home from the Tungan market was an unsettling experience—a Volga car, Yang in his undershirt holding a watermelon in his lap, beside him Ting Lei, powdered and perfumed, her cigarette dangling from a long holder, and behind them in the street her pet dog running.

Another favorite Ting Lei companion was Yang Ch'eng-hsiao, notorious military commander of the Taiyuan steel workers' fighting unit known as the "Dare-to-Dies." He called himself "Old Dare." As Chou En-lai had informed us, Ting Lei served as political director of this famous "smash and rob" outfit. During the Peking study classes she used to skip the afternoon session to go swimming with Yang Ch'eng-hsiao in an exclusive suburban pool. Seated in style in Ting Lei's chauffered limousine, Yang the warrior, like Yang the student, wore dark glasses, but his taste in clothing ran not to underwear but to tailored shirts in the latest style. After their swim the two were wont to repair to the Great Western Guest House, the hotel built for army commanders, there to enjoy a gourmet supper with Evergreen Liu. The managers of the Great Western Guest House chose waitresses and room attendants for their beauty. The gambling casinos of Las Vegas never assembled more perfect young women for staff work than did these army innkeepers, a selection that Evergreen Liu presumably appreciated as much as anyone.

By contrast, Chang Er-ch'ing, the leader of the other faction in Shansi, hovered in the background as a gray eminence, without vices, or for that matter virtues, worth recording. Was it that he could hardly compete for attention with such colorful characters as Evergreen Liu, his "plum blossom" consort and "Old Dare" Yang? Or was it that his followers had no interest in spreading tales and gossip about him? I have no way of knowing, for I heard nothing at all about Chang's personal life, his appearance or his style. By omission he seemed to stand as a model commander, forced against his better judgment into factionalism by the arrogance, chicanery and sheer flair of the opposition.

The factional bias of our informants showed itself in the double standard they used on so many occasions. From July to December, 1967, they said, Chang Er-ch'ing had nothing to do with factionalism in Shansi because he was assigned to Peking for study classes, hence could hardly be blamed for what happened in Taiyuan during those months. But in 1968, when Evergreen Liu and Ch'en Hsiu-ch'uang went to the capital for study, the charge circulated that they manipulated the Shansi struggle from their guesthouse rooms by telephone, telegram, letter and personal messenger. Perhaps Chang did not meddle in Shansi while he studied in Peking, but if so it wasn't because he found such meddling impossible from a distance. Others managed well enough—so well, it seems, that huge battles boiled up at their instigation and on their behalf.

The struggle in Shansi, so we learned, began in a more subdued manner in 1966. Leading the mountain province at the time was a triumvirate known as "Wei-Wang-Wang": Wei Heng, Party Secretary and chairman of the Province; and Wang Ch'ien and Wang Ho, both vice-Party Secretaries and vice-chairmen of the Province. Wang Ch'ien had been Party Secretary of the Third Administrative District of the Taihang Subregion in 1948, with headquarters in Changchih. He had led the land reform in Lucheng County, and had come to Long Bow village more than once to resolve problems, and especially the problem of Wang Yü-lai, Wang Wen-te and Shen Chin-ts'ai while these three faced false charges concerning the alleged assault on Little Ch'uer. Wang Ch'ien won fame throughout China as the author of memoranda concerning the polarization of classes after land reform, based on statistics from the Southeast Region of Shansi Province. His findings helped persuade Mao Tse-tung to advocate an early upsurge in cooperative farming before polarization led to a rural economy dominated by rich peasants. But in the sixties, and particularly during the Socialist Education Movement, Wang Ch'ien followed the lead of Liu Shao-ch'i, and made "revisionist" or "capitalist road" errors. He acknowledged these errors to me in 1977, but with shrewd reluctance to talk about himself, he gave no details concerning what they were.

In 1966 certain forces inside the Party leadership launched accusations against Wei, Wang and Wang. They called all three "Party people in power taking the capitalist road," and denounced them as stooges of Po Yi-po, An Tse-wen and others of the Liu Shao-ch'i clique in the national capital. These Shansi natives, they charged, had long dominated the politics of their home province, and made of it an independent kingdom of reaction.

The first inner-party challenge to Wei and the two Wangs came from a cadre named Yuan Chen, who had transferred to Taiyuan after several years of service in Anshan, Liaoning, the famous steel center of Northeast China. Yuan Chen was already well known as an organizer of the steel industry and claimed responsibility for the famous Anshan Constitution, the charter of the Anshan Iron and Steel Corporation. This charter, drawn up to suit Chinese conditions and Chinese political goals in opposition to the Magnitogorsk Charter imported from the Soviet Union, won the approval of Mao Tse-tung and the Central Committee in 1964 and was promoted all over China as a model for socialist organization. As a consequence, Yuan Chen gained considerable prestige and a mass following. After coming to Shansi he felt strong enough to challenge the provincial leaders on a number of points of policy. In 1966, at a meeting of the North China Bureau which began in May, outraged provincial leaders subjected Yuan in turn to sharp counterattack as a careerist, oppositionist, seize-power element, and anti-Communist plotter on the Shansi Provincial Committee.

In November, 1966, as the Cultural Revolution moved toward a showdown in several major Chinese cities, Shansi Province held a three-level (county, regional and provincial) cadre meeting at the vacation complex built by the Central Committee near the Chin-tze, that marvelous temple, more than 2,000 years old, which remains one of Shansi's most notable

> ### The Anshan Constitution
>
> Persevere in putting politics in command; strengthen Party leadership; develop the mass movement in a big way; institute a system under which cadres take part in productive labor, workers take part in management, irrational and outdated rules and regulations are revised, and leading cadres, workers and technical personnel work in close cooperation and vigorously carry out the technical revolution.

historic sites. Modern architects conceived the villas, hotel accommodations and meeting halls at the Chin-tze so grandly and furnished them so lavishly that the buildings earned the ironic label "Antirevisionist Dance Hall" from visitors who expected frugality from Chinese leaders and felt shocked at the sight of such luxuries as sixteen-foot ceilings, wall-to-wall carpeting, king-size innerspring mattresses, and a choice of three types of toilet in each elite suite. In the sixties everyone blamed Liu Shao-ch'i for this decadence, but in the seventies people came forward to claim that Mao had enjoyed even grander villas.

At the Chin-tze, Yuan Chen mounted the offensive against Wei Heng and the two Wangs for a second time, and quickly succeeded in reversing the tables on them. The provincial leaders made self-criticisms which they hoped would get them by, but Yuan Chen renewed his attack and sustained it until he temporarily forced all three of them from office. They were suspended pending investigation. What gave Yuan Chen such clout that fall was the united support he received from two powerful factions of Taiyuan students, both of them founded and led by students from the national capital, Peking. A student named Hsiao from Tsinghua University's famous *Regiment* had settled in Taiyuan City's First Guest House and helped form a *Revolutionary Rebel Regiment,* which chose as its leader one Liu Hao. Other students from rival Peking organizations settled in Taiyuan City's Second Guest House and formed a *Red Rebel Liaison Station,* which chose as its leader one T'uan Li-cheng.

As long as the three Shansi chairmen Wei, Wang and Wang loomed as targets, the rival organizations from the two guesthouses did everything possible, separately and in unison, to confront them. They packed the Chin-tze night and day with chanting thousands, plastered posters on every available wall, and set up loudspeakers that dominated the air. Back in Taiyuan they also mobilized street demonstrations that included masses of workers. Feeling themselves in tune with the spirit of the times, convinced that they had the backing of Chairman Mao, the students mounted an irresistible political offensive that in the end completely overwhelmed the Shansi leaders. They forced Wei-Wang-Wang out of office and paralyzed the Shansi Provincial Committee and government, but this did not yet amount to a power takeover.

In January, 1967, after the *Shanghai Workers' Revolutionary General Headquarters* overthrew the Party Committee and Government of China's greatest industrial city, the situation in Taiyuan, Shansi, became ripe for a more decisive coup. On January 14 a loose coalition of old cadres and army officers, who had very little in common except a desire for more power, rose in rebellion. This coalition thrust Evergreen Liu into the limelight as the "seize power" leader, because his rank was high (fourteenth grade) and because he had a revolutionary record that spanned several decades. No one considered him the moving force behind the action, however. He had come to Shansi Province from Ninghsia only a few months earlier as a complete stranger, and few citizens of Shansi had ever heard his name. By contrast, Yuan Chen was well known and, what was more important, had a mass following both among the students led by Liu Hao and among the steelworkers. By his side stood Liu Kuan-yi, a native son who was a vicechairman of the provincial government, and Ch'en Shou-cheng, secretary of the Taiyuan City Party Committee.

Other members of the original civilian group included Ho Ying-ts'ai, Chairman of the Standing Committee of the Provincial Political Consultative Conference, and Liu Tse-lan, head of the Rural Work Department of the Provincial Party Committee. The latter was a woman, quite famous in Shansi as the "White-Haired Girl" (heroine of China's most popular revolutionary opera) because of her graying locks. What gave this indifferent collection of functionaries clout and won it the support of the Central Committee in Peking was the backing of General Chang Er-ch'ing, a Long March veteran and the political director of the armed forces in the Shansi Army District. (In peacetime the political director of each unit served as the leading officer; the commander held a subordinate position.)

Composed of old cadres, propped up by the army and supported by several organizations of militant workers, the new committee seemed to be a three-in-one combination of the kind advocated by Mao Tse-tung and the leaders of the Cultural Revolution Group after they backed away from the idea of an elected government of the Paris Commune type. They approved it almost at once. With legitimacy thus established, the new committee gripped power securely and the situation in Shansi seemed to stabilize.

Crucial mass support came from the steelworkers, or at least that part of the steelworkers led by Yang Ch'eng-hsiao, the adventurer from Anshan in the Northeast who had known Yuan Chen for years. Steelworker Yang was, however, completely unprincipled. On the day set for the power seizure he detained both Wei Heng and Yuan Chen, then waited to see which one of the two would "stand"—that is, which one of them would receive support from the Central Committee in Peking and thus actually succeed in holding on to power in Shansi. When it became clear that Yuan Chen, by linking up with Evergreen Liu, had found the key to Central support, Yang threw his forces to their side but never let them forget that the real power, as the leader of the mass movement in the steel mills, was his. When the Central Committee finally confirmed Evergreen Liu as Chairman of Shansi's new Revolutionary Committee, Yang said to him, "Don't forget, we gave you this seat. If we don't want you in it, we can throw you out."

What gave Yang such self-assurance? Sheer nerve, it seemed, for his record was far from pure. A foster father who once served the Japanese in the Northeast as a puppet policeman had raised him. As a young man he had worked in the steel mill at Anshan, then had moved to Taiyuan in 1958.

He arrived as a Third Grade or journeyman worker in the Thirteenth Metallurgical Company, an organization set up for capital construction projects at Taiyuan Steel. In 1966 he organized a faction of "rebels" in his construction unit but it was vigorously suppressed at first by the unit director, with support from the Provincial Committee, so his "rebels" only became "legitimate" after the promulgation of the Sixteen Points in August of that year. Thus, like Kuai Ta-fu, Tsinghua's famous student rebel, Yang was regarded as a victim of the "bourgeois reactionary" line and "fifty days of white terror." When Mao finally exposed and smashed this suppression, Yang stood forth as a hero and seized the leadership of the militant worker forces by virtue of his daring and his predilection for rough tactics. His "core group" never hesitated to beat or even to kill those who got in their way.

Yang never joined the Communist Party. Because of his foster father's bad record in the Northeast he was not even eligible for membership. But he turned this weakness into strength at the time when radicals were exposing the so-called "bourgeois reactionary" line by claiming that all attacks on his record represented unwarranted suppression. He claimed successfully that the authorities had framed him. Opponents later said that his men forced a comrade in the Security Bureau who knew of Yang's real record out of an office window, where he fell to his death.

In its heyday Yang's worker column numbered some thirty to forty thousand people organized in 160 regiments, some with over 1,000 members each and some with only 100 or so. These regiments controlled thousands of trucks and so gained extraordinary mobility. When they rallied for a mass meeting they could bring several hundred thousand people to their side in a few hours.

While Yang called himself "Old Dare," and his regiments "Dare-to-Dies," the people after experiencing their disfavor learned to call them the "Dare Bandits." In one instance the "Dare-to-Dies," seeing an opposition faction pasting unwelcome posters on the wall, picked them off one by one with sniper fire. On another occasion they attacked Liberation Army sentries with hand grenades and rifle fire, killing one and wounding four.

Some people thought that Yang had made Evergreen Liu his political captive. But in reality the situation was not so one-sided. Liu needed Yang for the mass support the steelworker brought him. This was especially important in the rough-and-tumble factional fighting that developed after April, 1967. But Yang needed Liu for the recognition that Liu, as an old cadre of prestige and experience, had won from the Central Committee. As a member of Liu's clique Yang won a legitimacy which he never could have earned on his own. Thus the relationship was one of mutual support, mutual convenience. Neither man could do so well without the other.

In the game of musical chairs that inevitably followed seizures of power, allies were all-important. Evergreen Liu learned that he could count on Yang Ch'eng-hsiao's *Dare-to-Dies* and on Liu Hao's student *Revolutionary Rebel Regiment*. Relations did not develop so smoothly, however, with student T'uan Li-cheng's *Red Rebel Liaison Station*. On the day that Evergreen Liu emerged as the head of the "seize power" coalition, T'uan Licheng withheld support. Unlike Old Dare Yang, he refused to change his stand even when the Central Committee approved the new leading core. Evergreen Liu retaliated by denouncing T'uan and his *Red Rebels.* He ordered all its members to appear en masse in Taiyuan's Central Square and bow their heads before a portrait of Chairman Mao. This humiliation solved the problem of allegiance temporarily, but Commander Chang Er-ch'ing, the military prop of the new regime, criticized it, and T'uan and his followers deeply resented it. Thus Liu, early on, sowed seeds of dissension that waited only for favorable circumstances to sprout, take root and grow.

75

ATTACK WITH REASON, DEFEND WITH FORCE

 Evergreen Liu, basking in the light of the favorable publicity given to a power seizure of the Shanghai type and universally recognized as a cadre who represented the "genuine left," presided over a united mass movement and a united government for a month or two. Then his Shansi "proletarian headquarters" began to crumble. Of the several factors leading to disintegration, the most important perhaps was the loose-knit and diverse character of the leading group. The main reason these individuals formed a group at all, it seemed, was that they happened to be on hand when the old government fell and they jumped off its collapsing frame soon enough to avoid going down with it. None of them had any real plan for reforming Shansi. Their seize-power poster, renowned for its revolutionary rhetoric, mounted a general attack on the alleged revisionism of Po Yi-po, An Tse-wen and other old Shansi cadres who had fallen, along with Liu Shao-ch'i, early in the Cultural Revolution. The poster called on the masses to rise up, but it was vague about what they should do, having risen. Neither before nor after the coup that brought them to power did any of these men or women take seriously the task of mobilizing people down below. Only a fraction of the population in the capital joined any group, to say nothing of the population of the province as a whole. Instead of creating a base of support, these leaders made deals with whatever groups emerged, thus putting themselves at the mercy of the first "rebels" who came along.

In March Shansi's civilian vice-chairman, Liu Kuan-yi, made a speech calling for a grand alliance of all the organizations at the grass roots so that peace could prevail and the population could complete the Cultural Revolution by July. Organization leaders immediately denounced his call as counterrevolutionary. What seemed eminently reasonable to any impartial observer was anathema to the *hsiao t'ou t'ou* (the little bosses) of almost every citizens' or cadres' group, presumably because none of them had yet achieved the positions of power they aspired to. To conclude the Cultural Revolution at that point could only mean (perish the thought) the perpetuation of the status quo. Fortunately for all concerned, someone unearthed —or, more than likely, created—a renegade past for Liu Kuan-yi. On April 14 Evergreen Liu, still the preeminent "Mr. Clean" in North China, accepted the charges against his second-in-command and took the issue to the people with a series of strident posters denouncing him as an upstart. The surprise attack split the Revolutionary Committee at the top and the mass movement down below. Up to that point Old Dare Yang had led a united movement called the *Seize Power Headquarters*. With the open attack on Liu Kuan-yi this movement broke into a *Repudiate Liu-Teng* Liaison Station*, better known as the *Red General Station* under Old Dare, and a *Red Rebel Liaison Station* under the student leader T'uan Li-cheng. Strange as it may seem, both these groups rose to denounce Liu Kuan-yi. What they fell out over was their appraisal of Evergreen Liu. Old Dare Yang and the *Red General Station* adherents defended Liu against all comers, but T'uan Li-cheng and the members of the *Red Rebel Liaison Station*, still smarting from the humiliation they suffered in the city square, felt there were some facets of the new Shansi chairman's own past that ought to be looked into.

This difference might not have developed into anything serious if Chang Er-ch'ing, the army commander, without whom no revolutionary committee could stand, had remained neutral. But Chang sided with the *Red Rebel Liaison Station*, giving all-out support to those who doubted Evergreen Liu. Chang appeared to do this out of concern for the purity of the revolution, but his motives became suspect when he used the developing rift to build a popular movement loyal to himself, a movement that could rival Liu's steelworker battalions and contest their domination over the streets of Taiyuan.

Right at this time the three most celebrated "radicals" on the Cultural Revolution Group in Peking put their hand in. Wang Li, Kuan Feng and Ch'i Pen-yu threw their support to Evergreen Liu and the *Red General Station*, thus fanning the split from above. July, 1967, was the heyday of the Wang-Kuan-Ch'i trio, a group later charged with responsibility for the ultraleft May 16 conspiracy and summarily removed from office. Their 1967 program was to carry into the army the campaign against "Party people in power taking the capitalist road," and they denounced Chang Er-ch'ing as a reactionary military man who was trying to take power in order to reverse the victory of the Cultural Revolution in Shansi.

The confrontation with army commander Ch'en Ts'ai-tao at Wuhan on July 20 played into their hands. In the light of today's knowledge it would not be stretching credibility too far to say that they probably provoked the events there.

In the book *Turning Point in China*, I described the Wuhan Incident thus:

> In Wuhan as in other areas mass organizations of rebels came into conflict with established Party authorities and the mass organizations supporting them. Ch'en Tsai-tao, Governor of Hunan, under vigorous attack from rebel students and three organizations of steelworkers from the Wuhan mills had helped organize yet another worker organization called the Million Heroes. When the rebels became strong enough to present a real challenge Ch'en not only

*Liu for Liu Shao-ch'i, Teng for Teng Hsiao-p'ing.

encouraged the Million Heroes to physically suppress them, he ordered Independent Division 8201, the local garrison troops under his command, to break up rebel demonstrations and arrest rebel leaders. The rebels defended themselves with arms and serious fighting broke out.*

At this point the Cultural Revolution Committee in Peking sent two members, Hsieh Fu-chih† and Wang Li to Hupei to investigate the cause of the trouble and work out a solution. After looking into the matter these two leaders severely criticized Ch'en's use of troops against the rebel masses and advised him to work for an alliance between the Million Heroes and the organizations of the opposition. Instead of accepting this advice, Ch'en arrested the two delegates and held them incommunicado. Wang Li was apparently even beaten up.

In this impasse Chou En-lai himself flew down to Hupei to try to settle the affair. As his plane approached the landing field he saw that it was surrounded by large contingents of the Million Heroes plus troops armed with tanks and automatic weapons. Chou En-lai decided not to land there, lest he himself be arrested and held. Instead he flew on to another field where troops loyal to the Cultural Revolution Committee were stationed. Then with an army at his side he drove overland to confront Ch'en Tsai-tao. At this meeting Chou En-lai arranged for the release of Hsieh and Wang. Later, after naval units had sailed up the Yangtze and parachute troops had been dropped at strategic locations around the triple cities (Hankow-Wuchang-Hanyang), Ch'en himself surrendered and went to Peking for criticism and re-education.‡

In the following months the press universally vilified Ch'en Ts'ai-tao§ as a reactionary military man who opposed revolution in China. When Wang Li returned to Peking he warned everyone that there were Ch'en Ts'ai-taos and Li Ts'ai-taos lurking in the wings everywhere, just waiting for an opportunity to defy Mao Tse-tung and suppress the mass movement.

Mao Tse-tung, Wang Li said, as he met with the most militant student leaders in Peking, faced a dangerous multitiered encirclement. The first tier was made of conservative peasant organizations in the countryside (groups like those that dominated Long Bow); the second tier was the right-wing trend backed up by the army in Shansi (the movement led by Chang Er-ch'ing); the third tier was made up of capitalist-road commanders holding power in the main military regions of the country (among them Ch'en

---

*Later information indicates that Ch'en's troops killed 250 and wounded 1,500 "rebels."

†In 1980 the Communist Party expelled Hsieh Fu-chih posthumously from its ranks, along with K'ang Sheng.

‡*Turning Point in China* (New York: Monthly Review Press, 1972), pp. 69–70.

§Ch'en Ts'ai-tao is listed in the Indictment of the special procuratorate of November 2, 1980, as one of the high PLA cadres "framed and persecuted by the Lin Piao and Chiang Ch'ing counterrevolutionary cliques."

Ts'ai-tao in Wuhan, Hau Hsien-chu in Fukien, Hsu Shih-yu in Nanking); and the fourth was the ring forged by the reactionaries on Taiwan, their imperialist backers in Japan and the United States, and social imperialist USSR on the northern border—a formidable array, to say the least.

One of the most ardent proponents of the encirclement theory was Mao's wife, Chiang Ch'ing. She went about in the summer of 1967 actively agitating for student exposure of military leaders and for student arms raids on military bases. "Attack with reason, defend with force" was her slogan, but in the confusion of those months attack and defense could hardly be differentiated. Every group claimed to act in self-defense. Promoting this campaign behind the scenes was none other than Commander-in-Chief Lin Piao, who found it a convenient method for ruining the careers of military men who were not in his clique so that he could consolidate his personal command over all the armed forces.

Toward the end of July, adjutational effort culminated in a rash of confrontations between citizens' organizations and various military units and commanders. The march of the *Revenge Army* on the army subdistrict in Changchih took place on the same day that a fraternal group assaulted the army district headquarters in Taiyuan, and a similar group tried to break into the army hotel known as the Great Western Guest House in Peking. These incidents preceded by only a few days the armed seizure of the Liberation Army Reception Center in Shanyang, Liaoning Province, the student raid on the home of Marshal Hsu Hsiang-ch'en, vice-chairman of the Military Commission in Peking, and a mass mobilization led by the Regiment Faction of Tsinghua University against Han Hsien-chu, commander of the Fukien Coast, and Hsu Shih-yu, commander of the Nanking Military Region.

Each of these incidents added fuel to the factional fires that already burned so fiercely throughout the country. They confirmed the radicals in their theory that the revolution was indeed endangered by reactionary military men and they confirmed the military men and their supporters among the masses in their countertheory that a dangerous ultraleft conspiracy, bent on destroying the armed forces and with them the revolution, was abroad in the land.

As the assaults and the army's response to them continued, the violence with which the opposing forces confronted each other increased. In August "hot" weapons (firearms) began to take the place of "cold" weapons such as fists, sticks and stones. Soon on far-flung battlefronts death reports began to circulate. Among the first deaths reported from Shansi were those of the Changchih student who died on a threshing floor in Long Bow and the worker who died at the crossroads near the Long Bow locomotive shed, both casualties of the famous August 24 battle for the railroad shops.

A few days later two more people died violent deaths in Shansi, this time as casualties of a pitched battle in Taiyuan. The killings climaxed a drama that began on September 5 when Evergreen Liu, Chairman of the Provincial Revolutionary Committee, called the Provincial Army District Headquarters in great excitement. His car, he said, had been smashed, his secretary seized, his documents raided. To forestall anything worse Headquarters sent soldiers to guard the chairman's house. An angry crowd surrounded the military vehicle as soon as it drove up and pelted it with stones. Liu's supporters blamed the attack on the opposition *Red Rebel Liaison Station.* But the *Red Rebels* had a different story. According to its leaders Liu's *Red General Station* had arranged the whole incident as a provocation to put them in a bad light.

Whatever the truth about this incident, Old Dare Yang used it as an excuse to mobilize 100,000 stalwarts. Armed with sticks, stones, iron bars, bicycle chains and fifty kilograms of dynamite, they marched on the headquarters of the *Red Rebels* located on the grounds of the Number 10 Middle School in the heart of the city, and prepared to blow it up.

Chang Er-ch'ing, commander of the Shansi Army District, was still in Peking undergoing reeducation. Even if he had been in Taiyuan he would have found it hard to take any action. He had already compromised his neutrality by lining up politically behind the *Red Rebels.* To call out troops on their behalf would have exposed him as a crass and unreconstructed military meddler in civilian affairs. Fortunately, the Central Committee, fearing anarchy in Shansi, had dispatched a new armed force to the province, the Sixty-ninth Army of the Peking Military District, commanded by Hsieh Chen-hua and Ts'ao Chung-nan. For the time being, at least, these two, even though they were old army colleagues of Chang Er-ching's, could claim to be above the battle.

Commander Ts'ao called in Evergreen Liu and "Old Dare" three times in a row, each time demanding that they call off their attack on *Red Rebel* headquarters. The militants refused to do so, but in deference to the newly arrived commander Old Dare decided not to use dynamite on the middle school buildings. Instead, his forces launched a human wave assault with "cold" weapons. In the melee that ensued a seventeen-year-old girl student and a worker lost their lives. These casualties served as a legitimate excuse for counterviolence on the part of the *Red Rebels,* who then besieged the *Red General Station* with all the forces they could muster. Both factions stepped up the recruitment of supporters and involved them in confrontations wherever possible. Whole factories shut down as their workers took to the streets in support of one side or the other.

Ironically, September 5, the day this urban civil war began, was the very day that Chiang Ch'ing, at Mao's insistence, publicly reversed her position and came out against "pulling a handful of capitalist roaders out of the army." Attacks on the army, she said, were part of an ultraleft plot mounted by the May 16 conspiratorial group to destroy the army, overthrow the Premier and undermine Mao Tse-tung's leadership. Chiang Ch'ing did not deny that the army, once it was ordered to intervene in the mass struggle, had made mistakes, but these mistakes, she said, should never be used as excuses for attacks on army officers, for "plucking a handful of capitalist roaders" from their ranks or for stealing weapons. Could we "come to the Hall of the People for this talk if we didn't have the army?" she asked.

Not long after this stunning reversal by Chiang Ch'ing, Mao Tse-tung issued his famous directive against factionalism. "There is no conflict of fundamental interest within the working class," Mao said. "Under the dictatorship of the proletariat there is no reason whatsoever for the working class to split into two big irreconcilable groups." Both press and radio publicized these words on September 14 after Mao returned from an extended trip into Central and South China. He came back saying that the overall situation in the Cultural Revolution was "excellent," and this was because the people in their hundreds of millions had been politically aroused and were actively engaged in changing the world. It is hard to avoid the conclusion that though Mao deplored the antagonism and dissension he found everywhere, he tended to discount it when balanced against the enthusiasm and commitment which so many people so amply demonstrated. Even the senseless, fratricidal fighting seemed to give him a certain amount of satisfaction because it was so boldly conceived and cleverly executed. The Chinese people were clearly no passive serfs, no mindless automatons, but creative activists who dared to storm the very walls of Heaven.

Whatever the positive aspects of the fighting might be, in September, 1967, Mao could hardly afford to let it continue. Fighting was disrupting production and diverting the army from its political tasks. Worse still, militants were concentrating their most ferocious attacks against the army itself as a target, a trend no government could tolerate for long. The army was the only centrally directed, organized force left in the country. If the army ever broke up or drifted into civil war, one unit against another, there could be only one result—unbridled anarchy. Given the centrifugal tendencies so deeply rooted in Chinese society and culture, once central direction broke down no one could guarantee the continued existence of the nation, socialist or otherwise. For Mao the integrity of China had to take precedence over any other consideration. Publicly he threw the whole weight of his political authority behind an effort to block the endless fracturing of the mass movement and stop the fighting that was its inevitable result. He urged all sides to fill the power vacuum with grand alliances of popular forces that could join old cadres and military commanders in the work of transforming society.

Unfortunately, by September factionalism throughout the country had reached such heights that no leader at any level could apply Mao's directives. Most people paid no serious attention to them in any case. They had already convinced themselves that the struggle in progress was a continuation of the decades-old struggle between the Communist Party and the Kuomintang and knew that the opposition represented the Kuomintang. Even though they had all studied the Sixteen Points of August, 1966, and had memorized the injunction that all conflicts should be resolved through reason and not through force, they held that in the local situation this injunction did not apply because they were not dealing with a contradiction among the people that was amenable to argument and compromise, but with a contradiction between themselves and a class enemy that was amenable only to force. All ordinary rules, all customary standards of conduct, must be abandoned as they mobilized the full strength of the people to defeat venal class enemies by all means at hand. And even if, at the bottom of their hearts, they didn't really believe this, they nevertheless believed that they and not their opponents deserved to rule, and that any argument which contributed to that end was justified. In the final analysis, no argument carried more weight than the one stating that the opposition was, in fact, a class enemy.

In Shansi the Sixty-ninth Army, the Provincial Revolutionary Committee and the Provincial Army District went through the motions of compliance with Mao's call. Commanders Hsieh and Ts'ao, Evergreen Liu and Old Dare Yang, Commander Chang Er-ch'ing and T'uan Li-cheng all gave wide publicity to Central directives, led study classes that inveighed against factionalism, and advocated the formation of grand alliances, but all to no avail. On the one hand, a succession of violent incidents inflamed feelings and provoked equally violent retaliations. On the other hand, all responsible leaders, whether military or civilian, continued to practice the very factionalism which they so ardently criticized. In every confrontation Hsieh and Ts'ao gave tacit support to their comrade from the Peking Military District, Chang Er-ch'ing, as he mobilized a mass movement based on the army units under his command and on the vast network of militia that in the normal course of things followed the lead of these same unit commanders. To counter this formidable array Evergreen Liu mobilized a less-extensive but nevertheless still quite formidable network of dedicated and militant civilian contingents that for one reason or another had fallen out with the military in their locality.

As these two networks squared off to challenge each other throughout the province, fighting spread to each region in turn. At no time did general civil war rage north, south, east and west across the whole territory at once. Nevertheless, it touched almost every part of it, breaking out first here, then there, hopping from one county to another, from one city to another in response to pressures and in accordance with a pattern that nobody could control. Conflicts resolved in one place flared up again in another, or, after smoldering unnoticed for a time, flared up with greater intensity in the same place.

In the whole of Shansi there was only one county that did not witness major armed fighting—Hsiyang, the home of the model Tachai Brigade. During the seize-power phase of the Cultural Revolution, rebels chose Ch'en Yung-kuei as the Party Secretary of Hsiyang. He replaced a man, Chang Jung-huai, with whom he had long been in conflict. Premier Chou En-lai, appalled at the damage done by factional conflict and aware of the disastrous consequences that factionalism could have if anyone dragged Hsiyang County and the Tachai Brigade into it, took steps to defuse conflict there. Chou called Ch'en Yung-kuei in for a long talk. Ch'en had already come forward in public as a supporter of Evergreen Liu, but in the course of this talk the Premier convinced the famous brigade leader that the quarrel between Liu and Chang Er-ch'ing was not some conflict between the Communist Party and the Kuomintang but an unprincipled struggle for personal power which Ch'en and Hsiyang County ought to steer clear of. Chou urged Ch'en to stay out of the conflict himself and to insulate the whole county from it as much as possible. This was a very unpopular position at a time when commitment to the Cultural Revolution tended to be judged by how much conflict and upheaval a leader could generate, but Ch'en stuck to it, at least in the version of events he presented to us:

> In many parts of Shansi, bourgeois factionalism was serious. Violent fighting ensued. Some people were proud of their hitting, smashing and grabbing. They put pressure on us. "Your mother's ———," they said. "There is no armed fighting in your county. How can you carry out the Cultural Revolution?"
>
> "That's easy for us to understand," we replied. "The Cultural Revolution should be carried out without violence. To whom do you listen? To Chairman Mao, or someone else? When Chairman Mao says to use reason and not violence, he is talking about the whole country. When you say we are wrong, what you are actually saying is that Chairman Mao is wrong. We firmly stand for using reason and not force."
>
> During this period, in the whole of Hsiyang County all the guns of the militia remained in the hands of the rank-and-file. We did not collect any guns, nor did anyone use them. No outsider seized our guns nor did any of our people go out to fight. Not only did we not lose any guns, we actually gained one. Some people came to start a fight. When we confronted them, they ran away so fast they dropped one of their guns. People often came and tried to start fights. We didn't fight them. We just sent lots of people to debate with them and persuade them to leave. We mobilized all 400 brigades in the county to do this work. Whenever people came and tried to start something, we urged our members to go out and convince them to leave. We did this because we saw the damage done by all this fighting. In other places some cadres were badly beaten.
>
> As violent fighting in Shansi spread and grew fiercer, some people without weapons took refuge here. We used local grain to feed them. Then it was said, "Hsiyang County is an air-raid shelter. It is a nest of bad people."
>
> But how could there be so many bad people?
>
> We didn't know who came from what group or faction, we only knew that most of them were workers, peasants or students. Maybe there were some bad people among them. If so, they were certainly a minority. We can't say that the ordinary people taking refuge here were bad or against Mao's line.
>
> Among those who came seeking safety were some who asked our help to put down the other side. But we refused and only gave them some grain to eat. We would not help them carry on their violent fighting.
>
> Those who came in were panic-stricken—severely wounded, weeping, clothes torn and worn out. We gave them food and asked them to live in peace here.
>
> Because of this, outsiders applied more and more pressure on us. They played dirty, mean tricks. Some people put on PLA uniforms, then came to search for their factional enemies.
>
> Tens of thousands took refuge here, among them some who

wanted to start up the struggle on the spot. Sometimes they started fights, or they took a shot at someone passing by. Sometimes when our own members left the county to visit relatives, factionalists beat them up or even fired on them. They did this to provoke fighting in Hsiyang. Outsiders hoped we would respond. But I would never allow any response. Once fighting started here hundreds would be hurt.

With all the weapons in the hands of the militiamen a rumor spread that a so-called anti-PLA faction had seized weapons in Hsiyang. But this was a lie. How could we supply weapons to enable others to fight when we refused to fight ourselves?

Slanders were also spread about Ch'en Yung-kuei. They said I turned over arms and food to the "anti-PLA" faction. Hence I must be anti-PLA. But could we allow refugees to starve? No. So they called me an anti-PLA element. Since some runaways belonging to the faction called anti-PLA took refuge here and we fed them, then we must oppose the PLA. Is this logic? The fact of the matter was, we didn't know what side they were on. We didn't know if they were supporters of Liu Ke-p'ing [chairman of the Provincial Revolutionary Committee] or of Chang Er-ch'ing [commander of the provincial armed forces]. All we knew was that these people could not go home. As soon as they went home, the opposition would beat them up.

In the end a directive came from the Central Committee saying that all refugees must go home. They should not be afraid to go home. After they left we don't know what happened to them. But anyway, they left here as individuals and not as organized groups. When they arrived home some people asked them what kind of poisonous influence they had met up with in Hsiyang County. People charged that we poisoned them, then sent them back to make trouble. "What kind of poison did you soak up from Ch'en? What task has Ch'en given you to do?" It was so bad that when they ran away a second time they didn't dare come to Hsiyang County. They were afraid they would give us a bad reputation.

Later some said that Ch'en was a bad guy; rumor had it that I was a landlord from Hopei who ran away to settle in Tachai. Here indeed was a class enemy! Then it was discovered that this Ch'en was not born in Hopei but in Honan, thus I became a tyrant from Honan. So, speaking of class struggle, I myself became a class enemy.

In those days, if I started for Taiyuan, the provincial capital, the factional leaders would get word of it. They would order their henchmen to guard the highway with fixed bayonets and hand grenades. They told everyone a class enemy was coming. Whenever a big car came along, the guards jumped out and yelled, "Stop!"

They yelled "stop" at me.

"I won't move," I said. "I'm not a class enemy."

When the people opened the car door and saw that it was only me, they said, "Sorry, so sorry. It's only old Ch'en."

So I sighed and went on my way.

How could I say that these people engaged in counterrevolution?

I only saw that they had been tricked into some bad activity by bad people. If they had been counterrevolutionaries, they would have stuck me with their bayonets.

Sometimes they fired a few shots at my car. But regardless of the pressure applied to me, I would never support any faction. Even at the risk of death, I didn't waver. If they followed Mao Tse-tung's policy, I supported them. If they didn't, I opposed them.

At the time of the power seizure in Shansi Province, when the Revolutionary Committee was formed, the Central Committee in Peking supported Liu Ke-p'ing as Provincial Chairman. So I supported Liu Ke-p'ing also. Afterward, he made mistakes, but that happened later. When Liu first came to power, we followed the Central Committee and supported him. How could we support the opposition? But since we gave that support at that time, we are now called bad and wrong. The opposition says we should have opposed him from the start instead of joining the Central Committee in giving support. All this led to rumors that Ch'en Yung-kuei supported Liu Ke-p'ing and was therefore immersed in factionalism.

They put lots of pressure on me. Once at a meeting of 100,000 people [a mass meeting of both factions called by the Shansi Revolutionary Committee], the whole crowd surrounded me six or seven times. They tried to get me to say which faction I supported, but I refused. They said, "If you supported the wrong side, it doesn't matter. Just correct your mistake." But I said, "I've never done any such thing, I've never supported either side."

So then I was labeled the *ting men kuar* of Shansi.*

Finally, after dark, a car came to get me out, but I refused to leave because there were twenty or thirty people who had come with me and I wouldn't go without them.

Once Ch'en established a reputation for neutrality, he became very useful as an arbitrator and peacemaker between factions and was often sent to difficult spots when all else failed. Ch'en continued his recital.

Once the Central Committee sent me to P'ingyao County to try to end the violent fighting there. One armed faction surrounded me for twenty-four—no, thirty-six—hours. They closed the gates of the town wall† so I couldn't get out and they cut all the telephone lines. Then they blew bugles all night long and shouted, "Charge!" and "Capture Ch'en alive!"

*Because he would not support either faction against the other and particularly opposed violent fighting between factions, Ch'en was accused of blocking the development of the Cultural Revolution in Shansi just as a wooden brace behind a door blocks access to a peasant's house. People on both sides of the factional split who hoped to come to power through armed struggle—a process that was alien to the whole concept of the Cultural Revolution as envisioned by Mao Tse-tung—made this accusation.

†P'ingyao's wall has been preserved as a historical monument.

Before I went to P'ingyao I sent a person from central Shansi to announce that the Central Committee had asked me to visit the city to try and solve the factional conflict. But instead this person reported that I had come to support one side and suppress the other. He didn't say that the Central Committee had sent me to try and stop the violent fighting, but only that I had come to support one side against the other. Those who feared suppression were very upset. Since I came with 120 soldiers, all fully armed, members of the apprehensive faction surrounded us. People surrounded the house where I stayed, and people manned the city wall on all sides. Outside the city wall more people gathered. These people didn't really oppose me, only some of their leaders. The soldiers with me were frightened. It looked as if the struggle would be very sharp.

When the masses outside the city learned that I was surrounded there, they sent for help. They sent a cable to the Central Committee. The Central Committee sent a Liberation Army battalion to save me and take me out. Soldiers dispersed all the people who surrounded me. At the same time, both province-wide factions set out to save me. They sent 1,200 trucks to P'ingyao. The trucks came from both sides. This proved that I was no factional leader. Both sides sent forces to save me. So many people and so many trucks. They almost crushed the city.

People elsewhere sent cables saying they, too, wanted to rescue me. By that time I could answer that the problem was already solved.

76

EVERGREEN LIU GOES TRAVELING

 If, in the summer and fall of 1967, Hsiyang County remained relatively calm, the same could not be said for Changchih City, its surrounding suburbs and such nearby counties as Lucheng, Licheng, Hukuan, P'ingshun, Kaoping and Chinhsien. With the army backing *United* and the navy backing *Red,* the entire region boiled with controversy, charges and countercharges flew thick and fast, fights broke out almost daily, and the all-pervading turmoil brought industrial production to a near standstill. Nor did agriculture escape. At a time when fall planting, fall harvesting and fall plowing could not be postponed without serious damage to the current year's crops, not to mention those of the next year, tens of thousands of peasants neglected their work to drill with guns, join protests and marches, and clash with rivals.

The confrontation in the Southeast forced the provincial government in Taiyuan to look beyond the anarchy in the streets of its own capital, and focus attention on Changchih. On August 29, the very day that Evergreen Liu returned to Taiyuan after the long peace talks in Peking, he called an enlarged meeting of the Provincial Core Leading Group (an executive committee of high Party and government cadres) and drew up a Seven Point Program for the Southeast. Commander Li Ying-k'uei never did tell us what the Seven Points contained. He was angered by point number three, a criticism of his army units for backing a coup by *United* after *Red* had failed, and by point number seven, which urged everyone to unite behind Regional Chairman Ch'en Hsiu-ch'uang. According to Commander Li all Seven Points boiled down to this last one, "Support Ch'en," a piece of advice that he found intolerable.

Red partisans labeled the provincial program the "red Seven Points." Having printed up the points in tens of thousands of copies, *Reds* went everywhere loudly declaiming, "Our direction is correct. The provincial government supports us." The navy sent personnel to give protection to mass organizations as they paraded under the slogan, "Firmly carry out the Seven Points." Drama groups performed plays and skits about the points on stages everywhere. *Red* headquarters printed the points on huge posters just as both sides had earlier printed Mao's Twenty-three Points, and they distributed them throughout the countryside with the same admonition that usually accompanied directives from Chairman Mao: "Enthusiastically propagate and study, bravely defend and protect, and loyally carry out the Seven Points." In keeping with this exalted spirit, *Red* organized study classes around the points and called on all cadres from factories, communes and government offices who had not yet taken a stand to join the classes. Those who were ambitious enough to attend learned that the Seven Points were absolutely correct, that the *United* faction, with army support, had taken a wrong turn, and that all good revolutionaries should act accordingly.

Some leading cadres who had joined *United,* intimidated by the quasi-official backing given to this offensive, withdrew and went over to the *Reds.* Others, who stood firm in opposition to the Seven Points, found themselves under attack by name in posters everywhere. *Red* charged them with opposition to Evergreen Liu, who was Mao's good student. To oppose the Seven Points was to oppose Evergreen Liu. And since Liu was an outstanding, loyal pupil of the Party Chairman, to oppose Evergreen Liu was to oppose Mao Tse-tung. Clearly anyone who opposed Evergreen Liu deserved to die 10,000 deaths.

The campaign for the Seven Points coincided with and reinforced the period of Evergreen Liu's greatest renown. In the fall of 1967 the new provincial chairman reached the pinnacle of his career. The pitched battles in and around Taiyuan in August and September, the victories of that formidable new breed of *Dare-to-Dies* under Old Dare Yang, and the tremendous publicity given to every word and act of Liu's created for him a "golden age," which his supporters hoped to perpetuate and consolidate with the publication of two books that rolled off the presses in October. The first was a biography of Liu written in his own home by a group under the direction of his wife, Ting Lei. The text "proved" that Liu had, throughout his life, followed a "correct" political line. The second was a panegyric entitled *Clear 1,000 Li of Mist from the Jade Palace.* The "Jade Palace" turned out to be that venerable cadre, Evergreen Liu himself, "clearing away the mist" (a euphemism for setting the record straight) on this "great genius" now leading the struggle in Shansi, but constantly subject, nevertheless, to the attacks and slanders of reactionaries.

The cult of Mao Tse-tung, blown up in the sixties to huge proportions by Lin Piao, served as a model for provincial and regional factions trying to develop cults around local leaders. That they were able to develop these cults so easily can be partially explained by the remnants of traditional outlook still embedded in the popular mind. Abandoning, under prolonged bombardment, their own reason and judgment, people surrendered to the a priori judgment of others, particularly those high in rank, on questions of genius. In Chinese this word is literally "heavenly talent," "heaven-sent talent" or "talent from on high." Belief in the genius bestowed on a chosen few by the will of heaven, by the arrangement of the planets on the day of birth, or by the benign influence of some properly chosen ancestral burial site, satisfied the need so many felt for certainty, for some secure focus for their loyalties in an age of upheaval and transition.

Reinforcing "genius" as a reason for popular support was Liu's legitimacy as a Provincial Chairman who had won the approval of the Central Committee in Peking. His supporters played up "legitimacy" as their second major theme and in the end backed it up with an alleged quote from Mao Tse-tung: "The Sixty-ninth Army's position in Shansi is very important. Tell the Sixty-ninth Army comrades they must stand with Liu Ke-p'ing and firmly support comrade Liu Ke-p'ing."

From July through December, 1967, *Reds* spread this "quotation" throughout the province. Mass organizations, when they met, studied, repeated and even memorized the sentence, word for word. Influenced by them many cadres took a stand on Evergreen Liu's side. When groups sponsored meetings to hear Liu talk they plastered the "quotation" all over the walls. Evergreen Liu, when he spoke, even read it aloud. *United* charged that this Mao quote was made up out of whole cloth, that Mao had never said any such thing, but this did not dampen the enthusiasm of those who wanted to believe it, particularly those whose careers it benefited.

United partisans labeled Liu's vaunted provincial program the "black Seven Points." They responded to the *Red* mobilization with an intensive countercampaign of slander and derision that they hoped would knock the Seven Points down, and Ch'en Hsiu-ch'uang along with them. The Seven Points became the axis around which the regional struggle developed; as the weeks passed, confrontation grew sharper and sharper. Far from solving the problems of the Southeast Region, the provincial resolution gave most of them a new lease on life.

In mid-October Evergreen Liu decided to tour parts of Central and Southeast Shansi. The provincial press announced his tour as a peace mission, an effort to bring the warring factions together for negotiations that could create those elusive "grand alliances" that all the meetings in Taiyuan and Peking and all the directives and proposals issued by higher bodies had failed to conjure into being.

With all army district and subdistrict troops committed to the support of their commander, Chang Er-ch'ing, and with most of the militia units at the village level likewise committed because their military advisers were officers under Chang Er-ch'ing's command, Liu had a problem assembling a military escort. For a trip into the hinterland he required more than a bodyguard or two. He needed an armed convoy large enough to uphold the prestige and independence of a Provincial Chairman. As long as he remained in Taiyuan Liu had no trouble filling the streets with fighting men. The *Dare-to-Dies* could mass and march at a moment's notice to any part of the city. But once he left Taiyuan the military balance shifted strongly against him, particularly in the countryside. Without guns and troops of his own he would be, in effect, a hostage in the hands of whoever held local power.

As Chairman of the province and political director of all its armed forces, two positions that were customarily linked, Liu had the right to request a detachment of provincial troops to guard him, but since their loyalty was the last thing he could count on, he also requested 500 rifles from the army district warehouse in Taiyuan. He used some of these rifles to arm 200 cadets from the Air Force Academy and held the rest in reserve to be distributed where they would do the most good. He formed the cadets into an elite personal guard. As students in a military school and not soldiers in a regular army unit, they did not have to obey the order of any unit commander outside the classroom. They had the right to practice the "four democracies" (free airing of views, free writing of posters, big debates and unrestricted liaison with outside groups). They also had the right to form mass organizations, to join alliances, to rebel, to seize power—in a word, to act like the students of any other school in China. From the very first moment that Evergreen Liu fell out with Chang Er-ch'ing, the majority faction in the school had sided with Liu and had taken over the campus. When he decided to travel, they were ready and willing to form a loyal escort, and neither Chang Er-ch'ing nor Hsieh Chen-hua of the Sixty-ninth Army could do anything about it.

Liu's first stop was Yangch'uan, a Central Shansi coal-mining town of 50,000 people, 10,000 of whom worked in the mines. In the fall of 1967 the miners, after a complicated period of factional maneuvering, had patched together a "grand alliance" based on some fragile unity pacts in individual mines and shops and the formal dissolution of industry-wide and city-wide hostile factions. This development was based on the experience of workers in Kweichow Province where a grand alliance so formed had won the approval of Mao Tse-tung and a generous measure of nationwide publicity. In reality the Yangch'uan grand alliance only confirmed the domination of the city by Chang Er-ch'ing's faction. As soon as Evergreen Liu arrived with his armed cadets, the other side took heart. A group of workers from Coal Mine #4 led by miner Liang Pao-kuei linked up with a group of chemical workers led by ex-army commander An Ke to challenge the uneasy status quo. The grand alliance collapsed. The minority faction obtained forty rifles from Liu's surplus stocks, rose up and drove the majority faction, several thousand people in all, out of the city altogether. Those driven out survived in the hills as best they could on grain they managed to carry with them and on the charity of local peasants. Needless to say, production in the mines fell off sharply and Yangch'uan took on the appearance of an armed camp.

On his return from Yangch'uan Evergreen Liu immediately traveled to Changchih in the Southeast Region, accompanied, as before, by his "palace guard" of armed cadets, a few token soldiers, and a truckload of extra rifles. The whole city shut down production, administration and study to welcome this unprecedented delegation from the capital. One hundred thousand people turned out in the streets. Their welcome cut across factional lines. Both sides welcomed Chairman Liu because both sides nurtured illusions about his influence and intentions. Once the "great man" appeared in person, many argued, he would quickly resolve outstanding issues and make it possible for the vast majority to unite to carry the revolution forward.

The expectations of the two sides were very different, however. Each expected Liu to support its own views and convert the other side. Even if he did not win over all the leaders, surely he would win over most of the masses and thus solve the problem, if only from below. The *Reds,* who already had his public support, counted on Liu to create a high tide of opinion in their favor. *United* members, busy preparing a dossier on Ch'en Hsiu-ch'uang, thought that Liu, once he was informed of the true facts of the case and realized that Ch'en was indeed a Kuomintang agent, would switch his allegiance, denounce the *Red* leadership, and swing the masses to the side of *United*.

The *United* research group, which included Smart Fan, expected Liu to call on it for a report as soon as he settled into his quarters. Instead, Liu summoned thirty people from each side and gave them a long lecture about carrying out the Seven Points and uniting under the leadership of Ch'en Hsiu-ch'uang. After this meeting a disappointed *United* member said, "Liu Ke-p'ing doesn't want our report. He thinks he understands the situation already." A delegation of two, dispatched to present the case directly to Liu, could not get past his secretary. They left their written report in the secretary's hands, expecting Liu to read it and react immediately. Whether Liu ever read it or not is unclear. What he did was call a meeting in the regional auditorium to which he invited not thirty, but 500 people from each side.

Ch'en Hsiu-ch'uang himself came out on the platform to introduce Liu. As soon as he appeared all the *United* members present began to shout, "Down with Ch'en Hsiu-ch'uang," while the *Reds* responded with "Support Ch'en, support Evergreen Liu."

Smart Fan, sitting at the back of the balcony, actively proposed the anti-Ch'en slogans and led *United* in shouting them. But cadets from the Air Force Academy took responsibility for order in the hall. When someone informed them that Smart Fan was directing the hostile sloganeers, the cadet in charge of the balcony said, "Arrest him."

This suited Fan, who thought, "If you arrest me, we will have all the more reason to oppose you. We will have a solid grievance."

He stood up on his seat and yelled, "My name is Fan Wen. Come and arrest me!"

This threw the whole meeting into confusion.

United supporters shouted, "Go ahead, arrest him. Why don't you?"

Reds stood up and yelled, "You are disturbing the meeting, you should be arrested."

Evergreen Liu, who saw the meeting collapsing in disorder, took the center of the stage and said, "Comrades, please sit down. We came here to have a meeting. Please look at me, look at my face—"

He repeated these words over and over again, expressing the same thought with only slight variations, until finally the people calmed down. Then Ch'en Hsiu-ch'uang again came forward and said, "Welcome Political Director Liu, who has come to make a report."

No sooner did Ch'en appear again, however, than *United* members began denouncing him a second time, and so it went the whole afternoon. Evergreen Liu began his report but it was disrupted by slogans, shouts and disorders from all parts of the floor and the balcony.

Liu spoke in his slow, halting style.

"You want to overthrow Ch'en. . . . This is wrong. . . . He has no problem. If he had a problem I wouldn't be his host at the gambling table. . . . You must carry out the Seven Points. . . . Some people say we should carry out only six and a half points and down with Ch'en. . . . Comrades, that's no good. . . . We must have Seven Points, not six and a half points. . . . That's my position. . . . Ch'en is the head of your Revolutionary Committee. How can you casually overthrow him? . . . The *Red* faction is very good. They seized power first in January. . . . You *United* folk were against power seizure at the start, but now you put up so many posters calling for Ch'en's overthrow. . . . You even put them up in Taiyuan. . . . But one can't be overthrown by posters or slogans alone. If posters can overthrow someone that person must be made of paper.

"Some say Chen's wife has problems. . . . I know her personally. She had a husband before. Her husband was an agent. . . . We suppressed him. Is this what you want to use to say that Ch'en has problems? Comrades, it's just the opposite. . . . If he were a bad element he would fall even if we didn't knock him down."

The old man talked all afternoon, repeating himself again and again. According to the partisans of *United* all of his points added up to one point —support Ch'en.

Red photographers took lots of pictures, most of them of Liu in various poses. Ch'en Hsiu-ch'uang, when he saw this going on, made sure to stand close by. Later, when the press office posted the enlarged photographs, two feet high and a foot and a half across, on bulletin boards all over the city, there was Ch'en side by side with Liu, basking in his glory.

Red propagandists also recorded Liu's speeches on tape and later broadcast them endlessly to the people over the loudspeaker system in the city. They also published some of these speeches in pamphlet form and collected excerpts from them for the volume of Chairman Liu's quotations which later flooded the region. The quotations even included remarks Evergreen Liu made to labor hero Li Hsun-ta while both men visited the toilet.

About Li Hsun-ta, who had thrown his great prestige behind *United,* Evergreen Liu was quoted as saying, "He is a peasant. What does he know? He knows nothing."

To the army subdistrict commander, Wu T'ien-ming, Liu said, "You should support Ch'en Hsiu-ch'uang. If you don't support Ch'en it is a line mistake [a mistake in principle]."

On Chang Er-ch'ing, his rival for leadership of the province, Liu said, "Some people say Chang Er-ch'ing has a high level of political understanding. Actually, he has a high level of mistake making. On the other hand, people say my political level is low. But I support revolutionary cadres as I support Ch'en Hsiu-ch'uang."

As the final stroke in their campaign in support of Evergreen Liu, *Red* faction propagandists made up thousands of Liu Ke-p'ing buttons. In Shansi they definitely succeeded in adding the cult of Evergreen Liu to the cult of Mao Tse-tung.

United leaders, somewhat overwhelmed by this avalanche of Liu materials, redoubled their efforts to counter it. Unsuccessful in getting their Ch'en Hsiu-ch'uang dossier back from Liu's secretary, they proceeded to compile a dossier on Evergreen Liu himself which added up to 300,000 words. They collected all twenty-five of Liu's speeches, Liu quotes, several Liu photos and a collection of Liu buttons, and forwarded these to the Central Committee in Peking on the assumption that these materials themselves discredited the man completely. Leaving nothing to chance and realizing that their ace in the hole was the Ch'en Hsiu-ch'uang dossier, they sent Li Hsun-ta, the labor hero, to Liu's headquarters to retrieve it. Then Chief of Staff Li Ying-k'uei took it personally to Peking for the perusal of the Central leadership.

Objectively Evergreen Liu's trip brought disaster on Southeast Shansi. Far from bringing the two sides together, his speeches solidified the divisions in the region and provoked a showdown. Prior to Liu's visit both camps had their share of internal divisions. *United* counted in its ranks groups that wanted to overthrow Ch'en Hsiu-ch'uang and groups who only wanted to subject him to severe criticism. *Red* included groups that wanted to overthrow Wu T'ien-ming and groups that only wanted to "bombard" him, which meant to criticize him. In addition to these "major" differences, many minor differences divided the numerous units that made up the two coalitions. Many people did not yet see the two as clearly defined sides already set on a collision course. But as soon as Liu identified himself with Ch'en Hsiu-ch'uang and came up with the brand names *United* and *Red*, he quickly polarized the situation. He pushed those on each side who only wanted to bombard into unity with those who wanted to overthrow. Thus two antagonistic camps hardened at an accelerated rate.

In fairness to Evergreen Liu, it must be said that he did not create the splits, small or big, nor did his codification of them do anything more than slightly speed the process of contrariety. Throughout the Cultural Revolution the widest spectrum of organizations, large and small, always tended to coalesce into two (not three, not four, but two) opposing headquarters. Coalescence occurred with such regularity and persistence that it had to be recognized as some sort of law of the political sphere as universal as Boyle's law in chemistry or Newton's law in physics. Once rebellion dismantled the original power structure, the coalition that brought it down inevitably split, at first into many pieces. But later these pieces, merging, changing places, breaking up and re-forming, always finally coalesced into two. If some outside force did not stop them, they fought it out until one ruled the roost and the other went under. Evergreen Liu's trip served as a catalyst for consolidating two opposite poles in Southeast Shansi, but the same basic process manifested itself all over China, and had the same result.

To be realistic, the army subdistrict position that Ch'en Hsiu-ch'uang was a Kuomintang agent, that *United* supported a "correct" revolutionary line while the *Reds* supported an "incorrect" counterrevolutionary line, acted as a much greater spur to polarization than any stand taken by Evergreen Liu. Army commanders tended to play with two hats. On the one hand, they posed as impartial arbitrators sent in from outside to solve problems and promote unity; on the other, they played factional politics to the hilt, identified with one side against the other, and acted as the de facto leaders of one against the other. Far from being an impartial mediator above the fray, Li Ying-k'uei functioned as the prime instigator of the *United* faction in the Southeast Region. He entered the factional fray, however, not simply as another player, but as a representative of the Central Government, as a Liberation Army soldier with all the glory and prestige that that implied. He never lost an opportunity to stress Lin Piao's view, later expressed at the Ninth Congress, that the Cultural Revolution could succeed because of the leadership of Chairman Mao Tse-tung and the existence of the People's Liberation Army. In his opinion the army stood above criticism. He helped to create an atmosphere in the region equating criticism of the army with counterrevolution. In his opinion, to criticize the army, to oppose any army leader, was ipso facto to oppose the revolution. In conversations in 1971 both Li Ying-k'uei and Ts'ao Chung-nan did admit that the army had made mistakes. That is, they admitted this in principle. But nowhere did they admit any actual, concrete mistakes. Nor, in fact, did they admit any important mistakes on the part of the *United* faction. All problems, in their eyes, stemmed from the activities of *Red*. It was the *Reds* who wanted to break up the Revolutionary Committee, it was the *Reds* who were disatisfied with the army, it was the *Reds* who smashed and robbed everywhere and seized guns, it was the *Reds* who started the violence and kept escalating it, it was the *Reds* who chose Kuomintang agents and counterrevolutionaries as leaders, it was the *Reds* who, when called to Peking for months of education and study, fomented factionalism back home by playing on all their connections.

When *United* opposed several important members of the Revolutionary Committee, including its chairman, and demanded their ouster, army leaders called this not opposition but a demand for reasonable adjustment. When *United* brought guns into play, they called this not unwarranted escalation but only self-defense. When *United* brought armed militiamen into battle, they called this not reliance on armed struggle but simply reliance on the masses. When *United* leaders went all the way to Peking for education and study, they argued that they could not be accused of factionalism back home because they were too far away, too cut off to influence events.

It seemed quite clear that they were applying a double standard here. *United* could do no wrong. *Red* could do no right.

77

CITY UNDER SIEGE

Starting with the principle that *Red* fomented all the trouble in Southeast Shansi, the army subdistrict commanders blamed the trouble that followed Evergreen Liu's trip to the Southeast on the Provincial Chairman's insistence that some form of unity with *Red* be forged. The one concrete result of Liu's trip, they charged, was the arming of the *Red* faction and, as a direct consequence, open civil war. Although he stayed in Changchih only one week he managed to hand out 110 automatic rifles to various *Red* units and arranged for them to steal 1,500 more. The armed forces had confiscated 1,500 rifles from various militia units and stored them in the navy compound. While the navy looked the other way *Red* militants raided the compound and made off with enough arms to give them offensive capacity. After that they raided opposition units and even regular army units and seized vast quantities of arms and ammunition.

Whether or not *Reds* solved the arms question in this straightforward manner, the fact remains that not long after Evergreen Liu left for Taiyuan the *Red* faction did undertake to challenge *United* for control of the region. It was a curious rebellion, led by the chairman of the regional government himself, Ch'en Hsiu-ch'uang. Well aware of the case being prepared against him by the Sixty-ninth Army commanders, he knew he had to take power or be eliminated. In November and December the *Reds* moved by force of arms to liquidate whatever strongholds *United* held in Changchih. In retaliation, *United* forces in the suburbs and out in the countryside combined to liquidate any *Red* strongholds that survived. The two sides never completed this mopping-up process because neither side had the strength to crush the other entirely, but in the main *United* seized the suburbs and the rural hinterland while *Red* seized the city. Inside *Red* Changchih, *United* still held the Handicrafts Building, the Construction Company Second Team building, the Medical School compound and the Red Star Machine Company. Outside the city, *Red* still held Hsiao Sung Brigade, the Taihang Sawblade Works and a few other communities and factories that *United* had not yet mobilized sufficient forces to challenge, but these were minor pockets of resistance that could not change the overall alignment. *Reds* held the city, *United* held the countryside, and *United* took this very alignment as the basis for hurling more charges at *Red*. To hold the countryside, surround the cities, and eventually liberate them, they said, was to follow Mao Tse-tung's revolutionary strategy. To hold the cities, on the other hand, and from them to attack the countryside was to follow the reactionary, counterrevolutionary strategy of Chiang Kai-shek. What further proof was needed that this struggle was indeed a continuation of the decades-old struggle between the Communist Party and the Kuomintang?

As mutual liquidation of pockets of resistance continued, the use of heavy weapons grew commonplace. Both the Red Star Machine Company under *United* control and the Huai-hai Arsenal, which was the *Reds'* main base, began to manufacture heavy machine guns and artillery. By December the bore of the guns in use had increased from 60 millimeters to 160 millimeters. Heavy shelling led to a need for tanks. Factory workers created them by welding steel plates on farm tractors of the crawler type. No sooner did these slow-moving tanks appear in the streets than antitank rockets came forth to stop them.

Early in January *Red* forces in the city overwhelmed the Handicrafts Building, killing one of its defenders and capturing several others. On January 6 these same forces occupied the Construction Company Second Team building. In that battle another *United* defender died. Perhaps even more devastating than these victories on the battlefield was the decision made by *Red* to take control of all grain tickets in the city and stop issuing them to cadres who still adhered to *United*. This meant that scores of people in scattered pockets could no longer obtain grain and could not, in the long run, survive. *United* leaders, who had set up their regional headquarters in the railroad shops across the highway from Long Bow village, had to send scouts into the city to help their stranded adherents escape. *Red* bands captured some of these emissaries and tried to block all escape routes. Their efforts succeeded in the main. Soon it became difficult to move anywhere in the city.

A cadre from the Normal College who was a *United* sympathizer decided to go back to his home in Tunliu. He no sooner stepped out into the street than some men in uniform accosted him. Thinking that they must be *Reds* he said, "I'm *Red*."

That was a serious mistake. The men were *United* commandos on an inner city raid. They beat him up and left him lying in the street.

After he managed to pick himself up and set out again he came face to face with another group of uniformed men. Deciding to play it safe he said, "I have no trademark."

"That's impossible," they said.

"Well, I'm *United*."

This time the men turned out to be *Red*. They beat him up more severely than the *United* raiders had.

When he got home to Tunliu he complained bitterly.

"Walk one damn li. Get beaten twice!"

In spite of the frequent patrols quite a few *United* people did manage to get out of the city. After checking in at the railroad shops they were assigned to quarters at the Luan Middle School in the middle of Long Bow. Soon the Luan Middle School became an integral part of *United Regional Headquarters.*

One of the city cadres who played a prominent role at the Headquarters was Smart Fan. Even though the organization of Party cadres that he founded never numbered more than thirty-two members, he was considered a leader of the masses and rose to be Chairman of the Taihang Workers' Rebel Headquarters, a coalition of tens of thousands that grew into an important component of *United.* In the fall of 1967, because he had journalistic experience, he joined the Special Case Investigation Team assigned to look into the history of Regional Chairman Ch'en Hsiu-ch'uang and played a key role in assembling the documents that enabled Commander Li Ying-k'uei to denounce Ch'en. When the situation in the city became dangerous for *United* partisans, Investigation Team members moved to the railroad shops at Long Bow and took over some dormitories south of the main shop as their living quarters. Smart Fan, in addition to his duties as an investigator, assumed responsibility for the daily welfare of all *United* cadres. On January 10, 1968, he decided to make a trip into the city to see how those remaining there were faring. The following is Smart Fan's account of his trip from Long Bow to Main Street:

> I decided to go into the city. It was very dangerous. Many people urged me not to go. But I said, "I'll just go and have a look." Ho Po-wen said, "I'll go with you."
>
> We both dressed as ordinary factory workers. We wore black padded coats, black padded caps, white face masks and dark glasses. This concealed our faces.
>
> Why dress like that? Almost everyone who took part in the fighting dressed like that. In such clothes nobody could tell what faction you belonged to.
>
> Properly clad, we rode our bicycles into the city. We had to pass one particularly dangerous place. This was the Electricity Bureau. It was a *Red* base, but we had to pass in front of it. There was no way to go around.
>
> As we approached it, Ho said, "I'll go first."
>
> But I said, "No, let me go first."
>
> I took the lead while Ho followed about fifty meters behind. If I got caught he would have time to turn back. They would not capture us both.
>
> As I rode past the building I saw that the guards had automatic rifles at the ready. I rode very slowly, as if bent on legitimate business.
>
> "Get down," ordered a guard.
>
> If I stop you'll grab me. If I don't stop you'll also grab me, I thought.
>
> It seemed safer just to keep going. I rode on past and the guard did nothing. He didn't even call out again. So we both passed that spot smoothly. (The guard thought we must be factional comrades when we rode by so slowly and confidently.) But I broke out in sweat all over. My heart was really jumping!

Once we got into the city we decided to ride only on the wide streets. We had no idea what the alleys might be like. The wide streets were bad enough. It was as if the city had been through a Japanese Army Three-All Campaign—rubbish everywhere, all the windows broken and all billboards toppled or half toppled, and no posters on them. We found it hard to take in all this destruction. Think of our city looking like this!

At one big cross street we caught sight of Ho Hsiao-ken, a street regiment leader with five or six of his strong-arm men. He was patrolling from west to east with an automatic rifle in his hand.

Now we're finished, I thought.

But he didn't see us. Just as he came out on our street from the west we turned off south toward the Medical School and he didn't notice us.

As we passed the door of the South Street Food Shop we heard gunfire at the crossroads. Later, when we got to the Medical School, we heard that right at that moment Ho had captured a student from the Second Middle School who belonged to the *United* faction.

United still held the Medical School and we continued to hold it right through the period of heavy fighting. When I went in on January 10, 1968, 150 people still lived there. I got there at noon and ran to the dining hall to get something to eat. I found five or six big holes in the roof—holes blown by artillery shells—and no food at all. So I went over to the dormitory to ask what could be done about food.

"We can't use the kitchen," said the occupants of the dormitory. "As soon as smoke rises from the chimney the artillery over at the Huai-hai Arsenal goes into action. So we have to cook our food in our drinking cups in the dormitory rooms. If you want to eat you'll have to do the same. There's meat in the big hall. Help yourself."

Sure enough, I found four big pigs, killed but not cleaned, in the hall. If you wanted meat you could cut off a piece of raw flesh.

One look at this place was enough to frighten anyone. Shell craters scarred the yard, while shell casings stuck up from the dirt like cornstalks in a field.

"I'd better get out of here," I said.

"Don't worry," said the others. "You don't have to be afraid of the artillery. Shells hit the compound five or six times a day but they have never killed anyone. True, they wounded two, but that was because those two were careless."

"How could that be?"

Two old soldiers among the *United* residents explained that the explosive part of the shell is the tip. As soon as it hits the building it goes off, blowing most of its force backward and outward. In a two-story building the roof and the upper floor take the brunt of the shelling. Down below, on the ground floor, people are safe.

So I stayed and began cooking in a big tin cup. At about 1:00 P.M. *Red* opened fire. Some shells hit the roof above me, others landed in the yard or on the meeting hall. But inside the rooms, on the ground floor, people cooked and played cards as if nothing were happening. Girl students, seventeen and eighteen years old, showed no fear, so why should I be frightened? The windows were all bricked in, so shells in the yard couldn't come through and neither could shells on the roof. Thus I underwent baptism by fire. I went from being scared to death to being just plain scared.

In the afternoon I managed to get across to the Regional Irrigation Bureau. I found a friend there who loaned me some money and I decided to get out of the city as fast as possible. But my first attempt failed. When I got to the Changchih Normal School I found the road blocked by *Red*. I had to go back to the Medical School and spend the night. Without electric power the yard was pitch-black. Some people had a few candles, but to light a candle meant to invite a *Red* attack, so everything was dark. Only a few had quilts. The rest of us wrapped ourselves in our black padded coats and tried to sleep, but nobody slept very much. The cold bothered me but mainly it was the fear. I shut my eyes for a while, but it was no use. I was wide awake. I thought morning would never come. That was a long night, my first night.

On the second day I found the road still blocked and I had to stay over again. I stayed there at the Medical School under daily shelling until the fifteenth. Then I managed to get across to the army's Regional Guest House. Militia leaders from various factories and communes now held by *Red* filled it. Since they couldn't return to their own units they lived at army headquarters. Two of them were old friends of mine—the leader of the militia at the Transportation Bureau and the leader of the militia at the 543 Plant. I stayed with them and slept very well for a change.

Just before dawn I heard a loud explosion. A very heavy artillery bombardment began. Looking across at the Medical School compound, I could see dust and dirt flying. I was afraid everyone inside would be killed. I ran out of the army headquarters and followed the wall until I came opposite the Medical School. There was a flat spot there sheltered by a wall. I no sooner reached this spot than several tanks came from the south and turned into the gate of the Medical School. The gate was made of steel rods but the lead tank just drove right through them into the yard. It advanced on the main building.

If that tank knocks the building down, everyone inside will be buried alive, I thought.

But before the tank reached the building it stopped, turned around, and started back. Just as it reached the gate two people ran up behind it with grenades. The grenades exploded against the tank but did no harm. It drove off down the street. Then I saw one of the attackers bleeding from a wound in the head. He had been hit by a grenade fragment.

From my vantage point across the street I could see right through the gate to the back of the Medical School compound and beyond to the Southeast Regional Hospital and the printing plant beside it.

I saw that *Red* had occupied the hospital but my comrades inside the Medical School didn't know that. I wanted to warn them but I was afraid I would be caught if I left cover, so I stayed where I was.

Artillery fire fell north and south of the main building and gradually zeroed in on their target. A group of attackers gathered in the south and started to move on the building. Suddenly a shell fell very close to them, wounding several. They withdrew. We heard later that these infantrymen went back and cursed the artillerymen in the rear. They had shelled their own forces.

That day, between six and eight in the morning, the arsenal fired over 1,000 shells at the Medical School. Yet not a single shell killed anyone, because the *United* forces all hid deep inside the building. One of their number died that day, but not by shellfire. He was hit by a rifle bullet. While everyone else stayed under cover he lost his head and ran into the yard. *Reds* on the upper floor of the Regional Hospital shot him down.

Large-scale fighting continued unabated from the fifteenth to the twenty-first. I went back to the Medical School on the night of the fifteenth and stayed there until the twenty-first. Why couldn't I get away? Well, every time I came out on the street I found people patrolling with rifles and steel helmets. They had hand grenades, many of them homemade, hanging at their belts. They had barricaded the roads all around the Medical School. The road south led to the Huai-hai Arsenal. I couldn't go that way. The road leading to the Regional Revolutionary Committee Headquarters led past the Army Guest House and this, too, was held by *Red.* The road north went past the Immunization Center, also a *Red* stronghold. The only way out was to slip east toward the old city wall. But the *Reds* patrolled day and night outside the wall, so I couldn't go that way either.

On the twentieth in the middle of the night I was awakened. Tuan Chin-wen had sent a messenger from the North Station to find me. He wanted me to come back immediately. He had an urgent task for me.

"But how can I get out?" I asked. "I've been trying for days."

"Just get out of bed and I'll take you," said the messenger.

It was 3:00 A.M. on the morning of the twenty-first. He led me out toward the east in the darkness. Once past the East City we took a path through the fields that finally brought us to the North Station. We dared not appear on any road until we had put at least ten li between us and the city.

I got back to the North Station at about 10:00 A.M. Then Tuan Chin-wen told me that a lot of new troops had arrived for "Support-the-Left" work. They needed grain and vegetables, and the Revolutionary Committee wanted me to handle supplies. Thus I undertook a new task.

From the eleventh through the twenty-first, in the course of ten days in Changchih City, I lived through a miasma of war that I could not have imagined even in my wildest dreams. I went into the city to make contact, borrow money, and have a look at the situation. But no sooner had I got there than I wished I had wings to fly out!

Violent as the fighting was in Changchih when Smart Fan slipped into the city, it was not yet all-out war. The two factions were still only feeling each other out, maneuvering for position and trying to consolidate their gains. Their confrontation placed the whole region in an extreme state of factional tension, engendered raids and counterraids for arms, forced the liquidation of alien pockets in otherwise solid territory, set factories to manufacturing heavy artillery, tanks and even rockets, but the showdown, the full mobilization of the forces available on either side for the war that would decide who would in the end hold power, had not yet begun. The region resembled a forest where many small fires smoldered and burned, waiting only for a wind to come up that could set the whole area ablaze.

At this point two things happened that brought matters to a head. Toward the end of January a meeting of the Central Committee in Peking took up the question of Southeast Shansi, and basing itself on the materials supplied by Commander Li Ying-k'uei, publicly declared that Ch'en Hsiu-ch'uang was a "bad person," a counterrevolutionary. The Central Committee ordered the *Red* faction leaders themselves to arrest him, and turn him over to the Sixty-ninth Army so that he could be sent to Peking to be tried and punished.

The response of the *Red* faction to this ultimatum was not long in coming. On January 16, while Smart Fan still sheltered at the Medical School, *Red* patrols ambushed a convoy of vehicles carrying cadres into the center of Changchih and kidnapped 125 of them at gunpoint.

The *Red* patrols kidnapped six members of the Regional Revolutionary Committee, all of them leaders of the *United* faction, several county leaders also linked to *United,* and several dozen lower level activists, a few of whom were *Reds.* Most famous of the regional leaders was Li Hsun-ta, the labor hero from West Gully, known throughout China for production miracles long before Tachai Brigade won recognition anywhere. The others, well known locally as movers and shakers in various mass organizations, included Chia Mao-tung, Li Szu-yuan (an unusual, long-nosed vegetarian), Chang San-mao and Tai Chin-chung, a rising journalist who headed the general affairs office of the Regional Party Committee.

The regional and county leaders had been to a high-level meeting in Taiyuan to discuss the future of Southeast Shansi. The activists had attended a study session on Mao Tse-tung Thought. All of them were returning to Changchih under military escort. A company of army subdistrict soldiers commanded by Chief of Staff Li Ying-k'uei led the way and a company from the Independent Division brought up the rear. The soldiers, with the exception of Li Ying-k'uei in his command jeep, rode in trucks, the activists and county cadres in buses, while behind them came the soldiers of the Independent Division in trucks. Altogether this convoy contained seventeen vehicles. They drove straight down North Street, the most direct route to army subdistrict headquarters. Since they came in such strength and were escorted by the military, *United* leaders assumed that they could pass through the main thoroughfare of a city tightly held by

Red without being molested. This was a serious miscalculation fostered in part by the cloak of neutrality which Li Ying-k'uei and the local armed forces had thrown over themselves for public display. According to their own rhetoric they were an outside force doing everything possible to unite the two factions and bring peace to the region. Who would dare interfere in such a noble endeavor?

Who indeed but the *Reds*, fighting for their political lives, in some cases their physical lives, against an offensive that demonstrated over and over again strong links to "Heaven." (In 1971 Li Ying-k'uei assured us many times that he had cleared his strategy and his tactics with the Central Cultural Revolution Group and particularly with Chiang Ch'ing.)

As the seventeen-vehicle convoy came down North Street in the dark— it was 1:00 P.M. in midwinter—a farm tractor suddenly pulled a four-wheeled trailer across the road sideways and stopped. Li Ying-k'uei, recognizing an ambush, ordered his driver to speed up. The command jeep shot through the small opening still left between the trailer and the wall on the left and careened on to army headquarters. Several army trucks smashed their way through behind the jeep but the first bus loaded with activists stalled as it brushed the wall and blocked the street completely.

As the main body of the convoy came to a halt snipers on the rooftops peppered it with rifle fire. Hand grenades, lobbed from above, exploded in the street. In the background loudspeakers sprang to life with a crackle that gave way to hoarse voices shouting, "Welcome to the Sixty-ninth Army, which has come to support the left," "A shameless gang of *United* criminals has launched an armed attack," "Highway Regiment, Highway Regiment," and "The devil gets carried out!" As this shouting filled the air *Red* fighters rolled a large pipe into the gap behind the trailer so that the street was doubly blocked. Then they placed another barricade north of the convoy so that no vehicle could back out.

Shouting, rifle fire, exploding hand grenades, and busy action in the street kept the convoy tied down until *Red* reinforcements arrived from the East Gate of the city. Then a large number of armed men came down the line smashing the windows of the buses, pulling the passengers out and beating them up as they emerged.

The soldiers of the Independent Division, under strict orders not to fight back, tried to rescue the regional leaders by persuading them to leave their car, hide in the back of the trucks with the soldiers, and cover themselves with greatcoats. But the attackers saw the men climbing into the trucks and insisted on searching each one. They found Chang San-mao in the third truck, pulled him out roughly and knocked him down in the street. Then they found Chia Mao-tung and Li Szu-yuan. Finally, in the lead truck they uncovered Li Hsun-ta, the main target of the whole exercise. This is how he described the next few hours:

> They pulled the coat off my head and asked, "Who is this?" Actually there was no need to ask. They knew very well who I was. They threw me off the truck, but I broke my fall by holding on to the sideboard slats with my hands. Then a bunch of scoundrels surrounded me, hand grenades and rifles in hand. They took my hat and

coat off and began to beat me with their rifle butts. Several hit me with grenades. One used a steel strap as a whip. I got hit on the head. My head started to bleed and I put my hand up to feel the wound. Just then a grenade wielded as a club hit me on the hand. The finger that the grenade hit is still sore, but most of the blows landed on my back and shoulders.

After the first assault they drove us inside the office of the Fourth Transportation Company and tied us up. They took the blood-soaked scarf from around my neck and plastered it on my head, stuffed a face mask in my mouth, then tied my hands behind my back with a hemp rope that passed once around my neck. Then they pushed and shoved us from the Fourth Transportation Company to the Regional Transportation Company, which is several blocks down the street. They locked most of their prisoners in a vegetable cellar. But I was bleeding badly, my coat was soaked with blood, so they put me in a little room at the gatehouse along with one of the bus drivers who also had a bad cut on his head.

A doctor came to see us. I was still bleeding, so he went to find our captors. When he came back he took off my blindfold and loosened the rope. He found a wound on my scalp big enough to put a finger in. He put medicine on it and bandaged it. He did the same for the bus driver. Then he said, "Old Li, they've really messed you up. I can't give you the treatment you ought to have."

The guard at the gatehouse wasn't so bad. After the doctor had gone he asked me, "Old Li, where did they beat you?"

"All over," I said. "Maybe they broke some bones."

He felt my whole body and decided that no bones were broken.

So I lay on the bed and he covered me up. But I couldn't sleep. I was sore all over—persistent throbbing pain.

A man came. He wanted a statement from me in support of Ch'en Hsiu-ch'uang. I ignored him.

Then three came together. One hit me between the eyes with a flashlight. The second hit me in the stomach with his rifle butt. The third slapped my face with his bare hands several dozen times.

Suddenly something exploded in the yard.

"Who fired the shell?"

"I don't know."

"Put him out in the yard where the shells are falling."

"No. Shoot him."

They put my blindfold back on, tied me up tight, and took me into the yard. I thought they were going to shoot me. These people were capable of anything! Instead, they grabbed me by the legs and arms and threw me onto a truck. I landed face down on the steel plate that covered the bed of the vehicle. It was very cold. I could hear them hauling people out of the vegetable cellar and loading them all on the truck. Then I heard San-mao near me. He was not gagged. They were sitting on him, holding him down. He couldn't breathe. He cried out that he could never hold out in that position. So the man on top eased up a little and let him take a breath.

The truck traveled very fast, moving southward from the Regional Transportation Company toward the Huai-hai Arsenal. When we got there they pulled me off the truck and dragged me to the second floor of the technical building. I couldn't see, I was still blindfolded. After a lot of discussion among themselves they took me downstairs again and pushed me into a car. The car drove around several turns, then stopped. They led me down into a cellar and way to the end of it, then they threw me into the very last room, a place full of dirt and dust. I landed on the floor. After that my clothes, my hair, my face, my hands were covered with gray dust that I could not wash off.

In the next few days *Red* commandos alternately beat and interrogated Li Hsun-ta and his comrades and demanded that they forswear their allegiance to Chang Er-ch'ing and line up behind Ch'en Hsiu-ch'uang.

News that Li Hsun-ta and other regional leaders had been kidnapped spread rapidly throughout the whole of Southeast Shansi. The leaders of the *United* faction, meeting in the railroad repair shops across the highway from Long Bow village, decided to concentrate their forces for an offensive against Changchih, an offensive to "liberate" the city and free the captives. Word went out to all loyal militia units to assemble in the North Station area and prepare for battle. Simultaneously, the leaders took measures to strengthen the security of *United* headquarters. They ordered brigade and commune leaders to arrest and interrogate anyone suspected of past loyalty or ties to *Red*.

As *Red* security squads harassed and beat Li Hsun-ta and his colleagues in the cellar at Huai-hai in an attempt to make them sign statements in support of Ch'en Hsiu-ch'uang, *United* rounded up *Red* suspects all through the suburbs and out in the countryside and harassed and beat them in an attempt to make them confess their counterrevolutionary loyalties, expose their accomplices, and if possible switch their allegiance to Wu T'ien-ming and Li Ying-k'uei.

In the meantime word of the "unprovoked" kidnapping flashed over the wires to Peking. The Central Committee responded on January 28 by ordering General Hsiao Hsuan-chin of the Sixty-ninth Army into the region with a regiment and a brigade of new troops. The Central Committee also advised the provincial leaders to demand the release of the kidnapped cadres. On February 5 helicopters dropped thousands of copies of an order signed by General Hsieh Chen-hua, military commander of the province, and Liu Ke-p'ing, Revolutionary Committee Chairman, over the city of Changchih. The order stated that unless *Red* immediately released the prisoners taken on the night of January 16, the Central Committee would declare the *Red* faction as a whole to be a counterrevolutionary organization and its members would have to suffer the consequences.

All of this activity only further inflamed the situation. As the militiamen under *United* leadership gathered for their all-out offensive, the date for which they had already set as February 20, the *Reds* struck back whenever and wherever they could. They surrounded twelve companies and two squads of the new forces moving in under General Hsiao and seized all their arms. In this action they wounded a department head of the Sixty-ninth Army and many rank-and-file soldiers. They killed the vice-commander of a brigade of the Independent Regiment under subregional command and a squad leader in the same unit. Army units, still under strict orders not to fight with civilians, found no effective way to counter such raids.

A small battle on the west side of Changchih resulted in the shelling by *Red* artillery of a grain station where large amounts of grain were stored. At some point in this battle some buildings at the grain station caught fire and the blaze, before it could be put out, destroyed some six million catties of wheat and corn. Li Ying-k'uei charged *Red* with deliberate destruction of huge quantities of grain.

A much more serious incident occurred on February 4 outside the gate of the Huai-hai Arsenal. A handcart full of unexploded shells, being pushed through the street toward the local PLA barracks by some members of the *Red* faction, exploded without warning, killing forty-two people.

The explosion left a scene of terrible carnage. Old people, women and children who had crowded around the handcart to see what was going on lay dead in the street, some of the bodies mangled beyond recognition. Arms, legs, torn flesh, pieces of clothing hung on nearby trees; blood splattered everywhere; and after a few hours an obscene smell induced nausea in all who approached.

Li Ying-k'uei seized on this accident as a *Red* plot to blow up the military unit stationed at the Huai-hai Arsenal, a plot that backfired at the last moment because the shells exploded before zero hour, killing civilians instead of soldiers. He ordered the awful details of the resulting carnage to be written up, published, broadcast and distributed by leaflet to the far corners of the region, supplying further incentive, if incentive were needed, for the massive offensive already under preparation.

Inside the city, living conditions deteriorated. *Red* at first cut off electricity, water and food from army headquarters and such units as the Medical School where *United* held out. The cutoff gradually spread to include the entire city. The army blamed all shortages on the *Reds*, but no one ever explained why they would inflict such grievous injury on themselves.

78

THE ARMY
ENFORCES PEACE

On February 17 the Central Committee in Peking issued an order calling on the opposing factions in Southeast Shansi to cease fire and meet for peace talks. Under no illusion that either faction would in fact listen to reason, the Central Committee further commanded Generals Ts'ao Chung-nan and Hsiao Hsuan-chin of the Sixty-ninth Army to enforce a cease-fire, arrange peace talks, and build a great alliance in the region. To ensure that these officers had sufficient forces to back up their demands, the Central Military Commission arranged the transfer of four additional regiments from three neighboring provinces. A few days later they backed these up with three more—altogether ordering seven new regiments into the Shangtang.

General Ts'ao Chung-nan, placed in overall command of the operation, arrived at the Changchih airport at 3:00 P.M. and immediately set about coordinating the movements of the newly assigned army units. All of them, whether they arrived by truck or by train, were scheduled to be in place by 6:00 P.M., thus effectively blocking that other huge army of *United* militiamen that waited in the northern suburbs of the city, poised for an all-out offensive.

Army commanders carried out this whole movement in strict secrecy. On instructions from the Central Committee none of the members of the Core Leading Group of Shansi Province heard the least hint of what was about to happen. Neither Evergreen Liu nor Chang Er-ch'ing had any forewarning, so that neither could alert their respective forces in the region to do anything to hamper or divert the Central action.

General Ts'ao had orders to set up headquarters in Changchih, but because the fighting was already so heavy there, with several hundred artillery pieces in constant action, and because the hostile populace was likely to oppose any army initiative, he set up temporary headquarters at Horse Square, one mile north of Long Bow. From there he deployed each newly arrived army unit in such a manner as to encircle the city completely. With his troops all in place he began a propaganda offensive to publicize the Central Committee Order of February 17.

Ts'ao's forces printed the order on tens of thousands of leaflets, handed them out everywhere on the outskirts of the city, and dropped them over the center of the city by helicopter. They also read the leaflet aloud from dozens of broadcasting trucks that roamed all open roads and penetrated as far as possible into the city itself. This was dangerous work, given the intensity of the fighting. Rifle fire and hand grenade attacks wounded several soldiers the very first day.

One widely publicized point called on the leaders of both sides to meet at the airport waiting room for peace negotiations. On the first day, a *United* delegation came and waited but no *Red* delegation showed up. Ts'ao finally sent messengers into the city to speak directly to the *Red* leaders. On the second day they, too, sent a negotiating team.

The Central Committee leaflet made three demands: 1. Cease fire. 2. Turn in all arms. 3. Exchange all prisoners. Neither side wanted to be the first to implement any of these points.

The *Red* forces inside the city argued that they had been encircled, that they were the target of a major offensive and had taken up positions purely in self-defense; therefore the other side should stop firing and hand over weapons in order to show sincerity. The *United* forces countered with the argument that those who had fired first—that is, the *Reds*—should be the first to quit firing and lay down their arms. Since neither side would give in, the talks dragged on for two tense days.

The army insisted on a cease-fire. Since enough forces had been assembled to force compliance, the two contending factions had no choice in the end but to agree. On Ts'ao Chung-nan's insistence they verbally agreed to an eight-point contract that called for simultaneous cease-fire, mutual surrender of weapons and full assumption of responsibility by anyone who violated the agreement—that is, the violator would be in the wrong.

But when the time came to sign this agreement another stumbling block arose. The *Red* negotiators would not accept Hsu Chih-yu, commander-in-chief of the January 25 power seizure, as a cosigner. Hsu was from the Railroad Shops, an organization under the direct leadership of the Railroad Bureau in Honan. He was a person without local political rights. The *Red* faction refused to negotiate with anyone from Honan. The *United* delegation denounced this as a preposterous position. Hsu Chih-yu was their commander; how could he possibly be barred? He had played a leading role throughout the struggle. Furthermore, *Red* forces had come in trucks to try and take over the Railroad Shops. It was the *Reds* who involved Hsu Chih-yu in local struggle. How could they refuse to settle with him now?

But the *Reds* remained adamant. They refused to recognize the Honan man and withdrew their five-man delegation from the airfield. Both sides continued to fire, to attack and counterattack all around the city. Casualties mounted, not only among the contending factional forces, but among the soldiers who had come to stop the fighting.

Finally Ts'ao, negotiating separately with both sides, persuaded *United* to drop one man (Hsu Chih-yu) from their team on condition that the *Reds* drop one man from their team. With four rather than five delegates representing each side, they renegotiated an eight-point agreement and finally signed it.

After both sides signed the agreement, fighting more or less stopped, but no one handed in any guns. A whole day went by and not a single gun, bullet or hand grenade showed up at army headquarters at the airfield.

Since Ts'ao and Hsiao had set up offices in Horse Square, the headquarters of *United,* relied on *United* for food and other supplies, and in fact treated the *United* forces as reliable allies, Ts'ao suggested to *United* leaders that they take the initiative on the arms question. They should make the first move, give up some weapons, and start the reconciliation process.

After a period of intense persuasion *United* forces turned over several cannons, 200 rifles, and several thousand rounds of ammunition to the army units holding the airfield. They did this with considerable fanfare, beating drums and gongs, waving flags and marching in a big parade to the turnover point.

Then Ts'ao turned to the *Red* leaders and asked them for a similar gesture of goodwill. "Since *United* has taken action, you should match their action and earn some merit for your side." At this point the *Reds* could hardly refuse so they, too, sent some weapons, with great fanfare and publicity, to the army units at the airfield.

Actually this disarmament was more apparent than real. Both sides handed in broken weapons, worn-out guns and faulty ammunition. Each carefully retained whatever they found serviceable. Neither had confidence in the good faith of the other, and neither wanted to be at a disadvantage when fighting broke out again.

Nevertheless, the handing in of weapons, however token, led to a sharp decline in fighting. A de facto cease-fire gradually spread throughout the city. As the firing stopped, soldiers went farther and farther into the city to meet people face to face, urge them to give up whatever arms they had, and to restore essential supplies and services. By that time a severe supply crisis plagued Changchih. The city had no water except in local wells, no electricity, and very little food. Since no barbers had given any haircuts for months, most men had beards that concealed their chins and hair that covered their ears.

The army brought grain and vegetables into the city and opened public markets. It sent teams to restore water supplies and power, and also sent in teams of barbers to give haircuts. But in spite of this, many people did not welcome the army. The *Red* faction had opposed the army subdistrict leadership from the beginning. *Red* leaders looked on army intervention now as a form of suppression and they spread the word that the soldiers had come to impose martial law on the population. Thus on many back streets and in many courtyards, when soldiers appeared the people disappeared. The soldiers tried to win friends by filling empty water jars and sweeping cluttered courtyards, but it was a slow process.

They found the schoolyards held by *Red* students particularly hard to enter. Even though the soldiers came into the city without guns, they met cocked rifles and machine guns ready to fire at schoolyard gates. Only prolonged negotiations persuaded the students to lower their weapons and let the soldiers in.

Within a few days the army organized thousands of classes for the study of Mao Tse-tung Thought in schools, factories, streets, alleys, even single family units, but many people refused to attend. Some men sent their wives to sit in. Others sent daughters-in-law to report back on what they found. If the army instructor won the confidence of the young person, other members of the family gradually showed up.

Continued patient persuasion resulted in a gradual turnover of arms. At first a few guns showed up here and there. Then one person talking to another spread the word. Some people led the army men from door to door; "I turned in my gun, did you give up your hand grenade?" Thus the movement snowballed and within two weeks most people turned in the weapons in their hands. The army had made a rough estimate of the total arms available and was thus able to calculate when the bulk of them had been returned. Even so, large numbers of weapons could not be accounted for. More than 1,000 *Red* activists, rather than surrender their weapons, retreated to Kaoping County and went into the high mountains there, prepared for guerrilla war. The army let them go, content, for the time being, that the weapons had been removed from the city. Guerrilla units could be handled later. Rather than divide his forces and spread them too thin, Commander Ts'ao concentrated on pacifying the city, the focus of all the fighting in the region.

Once Ts'ao felt certain that the bulk of the weapons in people's hands had either been turned in or taken away, he made a determined effort to get the two sides to release their prisoners. Both sides had taken many prisoners and no real peace was possible until they had been exchanged. The *Reds* admitted to holding seventy *United* captives while *United* said it held some fifty *Reds*. Actually, both sides had originally held many more captive personnel, but the numbers had dwindled due to killings, untreated wounds that proved fatal and terminal illnesses.

Negotiating the prisoner issue was difficult because each side claimed that the other side held at least 100 of their people and would not accept the much reduced figure which the antagonist admitted to holding. An exhaustive check by army representatives showed that the disputed figures each side turned in did roughly correspond to the actual number of prisoners held alive. Since nothing could be done about those who had died, Commander Ts'ao insisted that both sides release everyone still held captive.

Finally, on February 26, in front of the City Revolutionary Committee offices the exchange took place. Both sides brought their prisoners in trucks and parked them in two lines about 100 meters apart on the main street. At a given signal the prisoners were supposed to climb down from their vehicles, walk across the open space that separated the two lines, and climb into the trucks on the opposite side. When the signal was given the *United* captives of *Red* got down and started walking, but the *Red* captives of *United* refused to move. They claimed that they had been too badly beaten to walk unaided. They demanded that the army send stretcher bearers to carry them across. Over this issue they blocked the exchange until about five in the evening.

The army had sent more than a platoon of troops to oversee the action. These troops refused to carry anyone. The commander said, "We are here following orders and you should all follow orders, too. This exchange must be completed by 5:00 P.M. Anyone who stays beyond that time does so at his or her own risk. We can't be responsible for anything that happens after that."

At 4:50 P.M. the commander said, "We are leaving in ten minutes." When they heard this warning the Red prisoners of United finally gave up, climbed down from their trucks and scrambled across the open space as best they could. Since most of them did, in the end, move on their own, the bystanders began to laugh and the Red faction lost some standing even among its own supporters.

After the exchange of prisoners had been completed, the atmosphere relaxed some more. The army stepped up its study classes and intensified its search for weapons. Soldiers found a large cache hidden between the roof beams in the Changchih Guest House, a Red stronghold. They found more in the cellar there, and in tunnels under the yard. They ripped hand grenades out of sofas and stuffed chairs. When the army added up the figures for weapons turned in, in and around Changchih the totals included 300 artillery pieces, 6,000 rifles, 400 to 500 grenades, 32 radio sets (some expropriated from the government, some handmade) and over 4 million rounds of ammunition.

Having pacified and disarmed Changchih, Ts'ao sent a regiment to Kaoping County to surround the runaways on East Mountain. Soldiers surrounded the mountain quietly in a surprise maneuver, then demanded talks. The thousand would-be guerrillas on the heights didn't know how many soldiers had actually come, nor did they know that the soldiers who displayed their weapons so prominently carried no ammunition. They decided that they were hopelessly surrounded and agreed to surrender peacefully. When they surrendered they turned in another 1,000 rifles.

The army brought the fighting to an end but not the factionalism. United members returned to the city as conquerors. Had not the Central Committee declared Ch'en Hsiu-ch'uang, leader of the Reds, a bad person and a Kuomintang agent? Had not the army arrested the second in command, Chao Ch'en-yuan, of the Huai-hai Arsenal, and charged him with capital crimes? Had not the army also charged Jen Yao-hsin and Kao K'e-kung and other prominent Red commanders with serious crimes? Had not the army openly said that United had followed a correct policy of support for the January 25 power seizure and support for the army, while Red had incorrectly opposed both? All this laid the groundwork for serious repression of Reds by members of United who felt vindicated in almost everything they had done.

United members, returning to factories and work units in the city where they had once been a minority, tried to redress all the grievances they felt at having been shut out, denied pay, refused fringe benefits such as padded clothes and safety goggles, and in the end denied access to the city altogether. United members joined forces, seized Red activists and beat them up. On several occasions they beat Reds to death. United workers in the bicycle factory killed a shopmate who had been a Red, then tried to cover up by saying that the man had jumped out of a window. Another group of United workers in the light bulb factory brought a Red shopmate back from

Hukuan, where he had been lying low, then beat him so badly that he died of internal injuries. *United* members of the Security Bureau (police) staff broke into the home of one of their fellow operatives, a well-known *Red,* and beat him to death.

The army tried to stop retaliatory beatings and revenge killings by arresting those who perpetrated the most violent crimes and conducting investigations into all such incidents, but the favoritism that most army men showed to their erstwhile allies in *United* undercut this campaign. Shen Chung-t'ang, the Long Bow mine worker who fought so hard to establish the preeminence of *United* at Wuchuang Mine, told about going into Changchih after the truce took effect:

> As soon as the armed fighting ended we went into town to put up posters celebrating the fall of Ch'en Hsiu-ch'uang—"Overthrow Ch'en," "Down with Ch'en," "*United* is bound to win," "Red is bound to fail."
>
> The city was full of *Reds* but they had been disarmed. They no longer had cannon, machine guns, rifles, hand grenades or even iron bars or wooden clubs. And army men everywhere maintained law and order. So we saw no fighting on the main streets, but on the side streets and in the small alleys fighting still went on. If you got into an argument *Reds* could grab you, drag you into an alley and beat you up. We once went to a victory celebration that was harassed by *Reds.* When we saw that the soldiers weren't looking our way we dragged the troublemakers into an alley and beat them soundly.
>
> Everyone said the army men would arrest brawlers and lock them up, but usually they just took us aside and gave us a long lecture.

The methods used by the army to pacify Changchih alienated *Red* partisans from the beginning. Army officers not only showed leniency toward *United* brawlers while punishing *Reds* severely, they publicized a rash of official charges against key *Red* leaders. Each day they charged Ch'en Hsiu-ch'uang with more serious crimes until he became known throughout the region as a renegade, a traitor and an acting counterrevolutionary—the biggest "case" in the province. Since Ch'en had run away, they launched a major search for him, and in the meantime arrested his leading assistants. They rounded up Chao Ch'en-yuan, former field commander of the *Reds* and their delegate to the talks at the airfield; Kao K'e-kung, a vice-commander; and Huo Hsiao-ken, a former city cadre. All three were promptly put on trial for murder.

Little wonder that many *Reds* decided to flee, making their way, arms in hand, if possible, to Shihchiachuang in Central Hopei, to Taiyuan or Yangchu'an in Central Shansi, or to any other place where mass organizations linked to their faction still existed and would take them in.

After army intervention stopped the fighting in Southeast Shansi, commander Ts'ao turned his attention to forming a grand alliance between the two sides. On the one hand he set up all sorts of study classes and training institutes at the local level, and on the other, he sent key leaders to study and negotiation sessions in Peking. The Peking sessions resembled a marathon in duration, for they began in May and concluded only in September.

The meetings in Peking constituted the fourth national conclave held to solve the Shansi problem. The first took place in April, 1967, shortly after the factional conflict between the forces led by Evergreen Liu and those led by Chang Er-ch'ing broke into the open. Chou En-lai called the two key leaders and some of their most important aides to the capital; after several weeks of study and discussion they agreed to work together. They no sooner returned to Shansi, however, than they renewed their rivalry with increased vigor. In July the Premier called the same people back to Peking for further education and negotiations. This time the Central Committee put most of the blame on Chang Er-ch'ing. Chou asked him to stay in Peking while Evergreen Liu went back to Taiyuan alone. But in spite of Chang Er-ch'ing's forced absence the factional struggle rose to new heights. In the wake of visits by Evergreen Liu the violent fighting described in the previous chapters broke out in Yangch'uan and Changchih. So in December Chou En-lai reprimanded Evergreen Liu and called him back to Peking for further education. Chang Er-ch'ing played a major part in the deliberations, as before, but this time criticism centered on Liu. Toward the end of the year a chastened Liu made his peace with Chang for the third time and both men returned to Shansi to "carry out Mao's line of unity and grand alliance." But their return did nothing to mitigate the conflicts in Shansi. Both sides concentrated instead on arming themselves. Chang Er-ch'ing's men rushed to distribute militia arms to worker and peasant units that supported them while Evergreen Liu's men attacked militia units, seizing arms wherever they could find them. In the seesaw struggle that this contest engendered many people suffered beatings, wounds, even death. The fighting so disrupted social order that Central Shansi and the western counties of South Shansi ran out of grain. The army appealed to the Central Government for 400,000 tons of food grain to tide people over until spring. Because forces engaged in factional maneuvers and open warfare had tied up most of the trucks in the province, the army also asked for 100 trucks to transport the huge tonnage to those in need. The government sent both grain and trucks but neither reached their destination. Each faction seized the loaded trucks that approached their roadblocks. Taiyuan Mechanical University students seized forty trucks in one operation and diverted both vehicles and cargo to factional use.

In Shansi the most serious situation developed in the Southeast, as we have seen. There only the intervention of a large number of troops restored peace in Changchih and its outskirts. With 800 people already dead and thousands wounded, the Central Government sought a political solution. Chou En-lai again called Shansi provincial and regional leaders back to Peking for study classes.

Chou demanded that each side first make a serious self-criticism, clean its own house, so to speak, and then unite with the other side to carry the revolution forward.

But the factional leaders brought no such spirit with them to Peking. From their point of view the talks were a place to expose the other side while defending themselves. This was especially true of the *United* leaders, who, with army support, considered themselves to have been right all along. In their minds the purpose of the talks was to get the *Red* faction to admit its guilt and promise to change. Many army officers assigned to the talks held the same point of view.

A glaring example of this was officer T'ien Huai-pao, the vice-director of the Political Department of the Southeast Military Region, a dashing young fellow full of confidence and rhetoric, who told us the story in 1971. He had taken part in the entire process of the negotiations at Changchih Airfield in February. "On the surface I was a leading army cadre trying to make peace. Actually, I was adviser to the *United* faction at the talks," he said proudly.

Smart Fan, of the Changchih Communist Party General Affairs Office, spoke with equal pride of his role. "I was picked to go to Peking for the national meeting when our *United* faction leaders found out that one of the delegates whom the *Reds* had picked once worked in our office. I went to the capital not to examine my own mistakes or to make a self-criticism, but to deal with this man. The purpose of my being there was, when the 'grabbing of facts' began, to counter his distortions and keep the record straight. We figured that he could never get too much on me because my work history spanned only ten years and I had not made very serious mistakes. In the Cultural Revolution I hadn't committed any crimes, so I could serve effectively as his opposite number."

T'ien Huai-pao had this to say about the conference:

> We had one yuan a day for food. None of the *Reds* got fat. They had too great a burden on their minds. Even though they wouldn't admit it, they knew that they had made mistakes and some had serious crimes on their conscience.
>
> The *United* members all got fat, especially Mao P'ei-chung. He got so fat that people dubbed him Khrushchev—his eyes and nose looked so much like Khrushchev's. He had always been quite thin but in Peking his weight went up to 190 catties.
>
> After all, the meeting and the one yuan a day food allowance lasted for six months. Lu You-wen got so fat he couldn't bear the summer heat.
>
> Smart Fan put on a lot of weight, too, all at the waistline. He was young, a worker, used to sports, and suddenly he had to sit for half a year, all the time, eating one yuan worth of food a day.
>
> Since the *Reds* wouldn't talk [admit their guilt] the *United* members gave up trying to move them. They ate, slept, played poker, and walked around Peking every day. Then they came home and ate some more. The schedule called for study until ten, take a break until lunchtime, then all out for a walk or a swim, and back for supper at six.
>
> As for me, I couldn't eat well. I shouldered such a heavy burden. I had to be the bridge to bring people together. I found it hard to sleep at night and so, while many grew fat, I lost four catties.

No one hung any signs on our necks. No one made us do any airplanes.* But still the meeting touched our souls.

The fourth Peking meeting may have touched some souls but it didn't touch them enough to cause any members of *Red* or *United* to admit mistakes.

In the meantime, back in Changchih *United* set out to educate *Red*. *United* leaders organized a study class at Wuyang coal mine and sent five *Red* leaders there for reeducation. City leaders recruited the five by arresting them, tying them well with ropes, and loading them on a Wuyang-bound truck. When they got them to the study class, they beat them up thoroughly.

The *Red* whom Smart Fan went to Peking to supervise came to him one day and asked, "How many people do you plan to arrest in our office?"

To show how tough he was, Fan replied, "As long as there are bad people we'll arrest all of them."

"Well, is Wang An-hui a bad person? What about Chao Hsüeh-chung? Yen Jou-chiang? Are they good or bad?"

When he heard this, Smart Fan knew something must have happened at home. The next morning he took the first bus to the city and made a long-distance call. He got a *United* comrade on the line.

"Has anyone seized any *Reds?*" he asked.

"We sent five *Reds* to a study class at Wuyang Mine."

"How?"

"We took them by truck."

"Did you beat them?"

"If the masses get angry they might well knock people about a little. We tied them up with ropes and sent them to the study class."

"You can't do that," protested Smart Fan. "That's not in accord with Mao Tse-tung Thought. It violates Communist Party policy. And it makes a lot of trouble for all of us representing you here in Peking. It makes it hard for us to speak. If you continue this way you had better come here yourself, for I can't represent you anymore."

"Well, they are already at the mine. What can I do now?"

"Guarantee that it won't happen again," said Smart Fan.

Guarantees were hard to enforce. *United* partisans repeatedly beat up *Red* faction people after the fighting ended in February, 1968. *Reds,* when they had a chance to retaliate, beat up *United* faction people in return. Thus violence continued, not out in the open as it had been in December and January, but in secret, behind closed doors, in back alleys and lonely lanes. Army men found the situation hard to police because the army itself had branded hundreds of thousands counterrevolutionary. Every time a new problem arose, *United* victors blamed these "class enemies," hauled them before public tribunals, asked them to confess, and beat them if they refused.

*To do an airplane was to stand bent over, head down, with arms held high above one's back, an attitude of enforced submission. Forcing the arms higher could cause extreme pain and ultimately dislocate them from their sockets.

After February, 1968, few people could be found in Southeast Shansi who dared admit that they had been part of *Red*. They either denied having taken an active part or claimed that they had actually been on the side of *United* all along. Because so many organizations had split, reversed position or reversed alliances once, twice or even more times, evasions and denials were easy to sustain. One could always claim to have been on the "right" side at a certain period regardless of what the real record showed, if it showed anything consistent at all.

Given this atmosphere in Changchih and the stubborn impasse in Peking, it seemed unlikely that the two sides could reach any agreement at the study session. Nevertheless, after six months, they did finally agree. This was because everyone had a stake in arriving at a compromise. Peking authorities told them that unless they signed a mutually agreed-upon document nobody could go home. This was threat indeed. The longer they stayed away from home, the less support they could muster, and this was particularly true of the *Reds*, whom all the higher levels of leadership held to have been in the wrong, almost from the beginning. If *Red* leaders could not soon return to Changchih to revive their organization, it would collapse. The pressure from all sides was too great. When news came that two factions from the Hsinhsien Region of Shansi had come to an agreement and had already left Peking, the delegates from Southeast Shansi made a determined last effort to match the Hsinhsien achievement.

On August 21 three delegates from each side met under the chairmanship of Officer T'ien Huai-pao, the "impartial" mediator who considered *United* to be a correct revolutionary mass movement, while *Red* was a conspiracy led by Kuomintang agents.

T'ien Huai-pao described the negotiations as follows:

> We talked, then wrote out what we had agreed on. The participants fought hard over each sentence. Since we could only write down what we all agreed on we wrote very slowly, sentence by sentence. Wu Huei-feng wrote for *Red*, Han Hai-ch'eng wrote for *United*, and Secretary Wang, of my office, wrote for the army.
>
> First we had to find a formula that summarized the overall situation and evaluated the two mass organizations in the region. I suggested a sentence that went like this: "Ch'en Hsiu-ch'uang wormed his way into the Revolutionary Committee, gathered together a handful of counterrevolutionary elements, obstructed Mao Tsetung's strategic plan and wrecked the excellent situation in the Southeast Region."
>
> The word "handful" made trouble. *United* delegates agreed to use it. *Reds* disagreed.
>
> "Doesn't this word 'handful' include all of us, especially those who are here?" asked the *Reds*.
>
> We debated this point for a long time.
>
> "What it means is: just a few," I said.
>
> But they felt, "anyway, we are included."
>
> So I suggested that we begin the sentence with "Bad people such as Ch'en Hsiu-ch'uang and others."

"Now you've run us in again!" said Wu Huei-feng.

We fought over this for two hours. We didn't rest. We didn't eat. Finally I suggested, "Bad people, Ch'en Hsiu-ch'uang, et cetera." But they wouldn't agree.

We said "et cetera" meant that it was more than Ch'en. "There was Hsüeh Liang, there was Kao K'e-kung, there was P'ei Ch'i-lung and Jen Yao-hsin, to name only the most important bad leaders."

"Then you have to name them all," they said.

"Such a list would be too long," we responded.

Over and over again we explained that this only meant Ch'en and other *bad* people, but they said, "In our minds it can also mean us."

United delegates said they wouldn't make any further concession on this point. We had to adjourn the meeting. I talked to *United* separately; Kuo Hou-liang, Yangch'uan County Political Director, talked to the *Reds*. I finally convinced the *United* delegates that "bad element Ch'en Hsiu-ch'uang" without any more words would do. [Since the Central Committee had already named Ch'en as a "bad element" and a "Kuomintang agent" no one could object to this solution without directly contradicting the Central Committee and consequently defying "Heaven."] The *Reds* accepted this, so we moved on to the next sentence.

I suggested, "Both factions should support the army. The army in Southeast Shansi was correct in the main in its support-the-left work. To oppose the army is to oppose our Great Wall of Steel."

But the *Reds* wouldn't agree to "correct in the main." They denied the great achievements of our army and opposed that key sentence.

Wu Huei-feng stood up to tell his family history. He came originally from Shenyang. Because his father couldn't stand the oppression of the Japanese he took his whole family north to Heilungkiang, where he worked as a hired laborer while his wife worked as a servant. Then Mao Tse-tung led our army to overthrow the three great mountains—feudalism, bureaucratic capitalism and imperialism—and liberated the Wu family. Wu had a chance to go to school. Before that he lived a hard life, eating wild vegetables and pumpkins. "I ate so many wild vegetables and pumpkins when I was a child that I can't stand the sight of them anymore. So how could I oppose the army? In my heart I don't oppose the army."

"Then how could you seize weapons from the army? How come your faction killed or wounded fifty-eight soldiers?" we asked.

"Those were worthless trash—bean-curd mash soldiers," he said. "When we took weapons from army men we had tears in our eyes."

What did he mean by all this? He meant that since we didn't support his faction we were wrong. If we had supported him, we would have been right. If not, we were wrong.

Another long debate ensued. Finally, when facts could no longer be denied, the *Reds* reluctantly agreed.

The 3,000-word contract took twenty hours to write. But we kept at it until we finished it. In the end there were only three people left awake—myself, Wu and Han. I spoke to them and we quarreled.

Fat Mao P'ei-chung fell asleep on my bed, snored like thunder, and annoyed us. Li Sung-nien leaned back in his chair and fell asleep sitting up. P'ei T'ung-lin got up and left. Meng Huai-pi fell asleep with his mouth wide open. The saliva ran out over his chin. Every so often he woke up with a jerk and his head hit the wall.

The *United* delegates sat through the night, bored. They had been hoping for a quick agreement. They had already written congratulatory letters to the people back home and had bought firecrackers for a celebration.

Finally, at 7:00 A.M. on the morning of August 22, 1968, we all signed the agreement. We celebrated with dancing, firecrackers and noise.

Under tremendous pressure from higher authorities in Peking, delegates from *Red* and *United* signed an agreement on August 22, but it was ten days before peace could be celebrated back in Southeast Shansi. Before the document could be declared official, Evergreen Liu, as Provincial Chairman, had to study and sign it. But for several days, nobody could find Evergreen Liu. Finally, on September 1 he showed up at the Great Western Guest House, and on September 2 gave his approval. Then the delegates returned in triumph to Changchih. All the leaders of the city and the region, at the head of a crowd of 10,000 citizens, came to the station to welcome them home. They brought enough cars to seat all thirty of the negotiators and give them a triumphal ride through the city. But when the speeches were over and the officials moved to get into the cars, it turned out that all but one of the *Red* delegates had already disappeared. They had climbed into Huai-hai Arsenal cars and driven off to *Red* headquarters. They were afraid, not without reason, of bodily harm. Their "crimes" as fighters and factionalists had received wide publicity and they felt safe only among trusted comrades.

The motorcade was supposed to terminate at the sports ground with a mass rally, but because most of the *Red* delegates had ducked out, the organizers of the reception postponed the rally until the next day. On September 3, 10,000 people showed up at the sports ground but the whole affair had to be low in key because, once again, most of the *Red* delegates and leaders failed to appear even though *United* officials had invited each of them personally. Still afraid they would be physically attacked, they stayed away in droves.

The army insisted on appointing *Red* leaders to join their *United* counterparts on a *Carry Out the Alliance Agreement Committee,* but after two days the chief *Red* representative, Meng Huai-pi, ran away and was not heard from again for more than half a year.

The new "grand alliance" was off to a very shaky start.

79

DECLINE AND FALL OF LIU AND CHANG

While peace talks continued to go forward in Peking, Commanders Hsieh and Ts'ao of the Sixty-ninth Army tried in various ways to get *Red* refugees to return to Southeast Shansi. Ts'ao estimated that the total number of runaways exceeded 6,000. The biggest single group settled in Taiyuan, the provincial capital, but quite a few found shelter in Hsiyang County, where no fighting ever developed, or in Shihchiachuang, on the Hopei plain, where food and work tended to be more plentiful. Another sizable group ended up in far Tientsin. Most of its members were leaders and activists from the *Red*-led mass organization at the Taihang Sawblade Works, a plant that had moved to Changchih City from Tientsin with most of its workers and staff in the early sixties. A few *Reds,* representing a variety of plants and units, hung about Peking to contest the verdict passed on Ch'en Hsiu-ch'uang by the Central Committee and to make the best possible case for their side. Other individuals scattered through various counties in Shansi where allied units, outspoken supporters of Evergreen Liu, still had forces in being. Li Ying-k'uei charged that they planned to organize new armed units, make or seize weapons, and at some point in the future mount a counter attack on the Southeast Region, an attack they would advertise as "liberation."

In midsummer, 1968, Hsieh and Ts'ao sent Commander Li Ying-k'uei and the labor hero Li Hsun-ta on a wide-ranging trip to find and talk to *Red* militants in "exile" and persuade them to return home. These two took along a staff of twenty, an indication of the size of the problem. They called their expedition the *Welcome Home Task Force.*

The *Task Force* had some success. It met with *Red* leaders everywhere, handed out grain tickets, food, money and railroad tickets, and guaranteed safe conduct to all returnees. But often, at the last minute, people who had agreed to go home refused. This happened on a mass scale in Taiyuan, where the two Lis distributed some 50,000 catties worth of grain tickets, 40,000 yuan in cash, and free rail tickets by the hundreds. A large group of people assembled at the station. But just before the train pulled out they suddenly changed their minds. "Don't get on," they called to each other. "There's fighting down there. If we go back we'll surely be killed." They threw their rail tickets away and ran out of the station.

Later, army officers saw many of these same people marching in a mass demonstration calling for the overthrow of Ts'ao Chung-nan, vice-commander of the Sixty-ninth Army. Li blamed their intransigence on rebellious *Red* leaders still able to mislead the unsophisticated.

When the task force reached Peking, Commander Li and labor hero Li Hsun-ta arranged to talk to the delegates of both factions who were still engaged in the long-drawn-out peace talks. They planned to report on the stable condition of the Southeast Region and urge the delegates to resolve their differences quickly and come home soon. The report meeting never materialized. When the *United* delegates assembled to greet Commander Li, the *Reds* refused to budge from their rooms. Section Head Ts'ui went to bring them out but they wouldn't come. A Secretary Wang tried his hand at persuasion, but to no avail. Finally officer T'ien Huai-pao went in person and spoke to each delegate individually, but none of them would leave his quarters. In the end Commander Li and Li Hsun-ta had to make a separate visit to the *Reds*. The episode ended in a confrontation.

T'ien Huai-pao described what happened:

> The two Lis and I met all the delegates in one room. Wu Huei-feng, a primary-school teacher at the Huai-hai Arsenal, spoke up. He was a short little man with eyes like a mouse. Let him so much as wink an eye, some devil's idea is sure to come out of his mouth. He stuttered badly but always managed to utter very logical words. He had the power to move people with his speeches—very persuasive.
>
> He said, "We have already been away from home for several months. We miss our homes and our families. We worry about the fate of our comrades. We thank you for coming with news from home, but we can't attend any meetings. We have been charged with so many serious crimes. We can't bear the weight of them and we can't bear the weight of the hat [the label] that has been put on our heads."
>
> To this Commander Li responded sternly: "The hat of a counter-revolutionary was not put on you by the army, the Revolutionary Committee, or the *United* faction. You earned it by your actions. Mao Tse-tung says, if you have made mistakes, correct them and everything will be all right. Since you put the hat where it is by bad acts in the past, you can remove it by good acts in the future."
>
> They greeted this statement with silence.
>
> The next to speak up was Wang Chang-yi. In the spring of 1968 his unit had raided a neighboring brigade and seized 20,000 yuan, new clothes from the tailor shop, 1,000 catties' worth of grain tickets and two pigs, already slaughtered and ready for the New Year feast. As Wang's men made off with their loot, brigade militiamen gave chase. They killed Wang's brother with machine-gun fire.
>
> "You directed violent fighting throughout the region," said Wang to Commander Li accusingly. "Your forces killed my brother, and they killed Little Yao and Big Shang. . . ."
>
> As Wang spoke he lost his temper and began to shout. All fifteen delegates jumped up and surrounded the three of us. They cursed

and screamed. Saliva from their mouths sprayed our faces. They gave us no chance to answer back. We had to get out.

The strong reaction from the *Red* delegates in Peking and the reluctance of *Red* activists everywhere to return to Changchih were understandable. In Southeast Shansi *United,* backed up by the army, insisted on treating *Red* partisans as conquered foe. *Red* had signed a peace agreement, not a surrender document, but that didn't seem to make any difference. While the fighting was still going on, the army blamed them for starting it. Now that the fighting was over the army blamed them for having prolonged it. All the violent incidents that had occurred in the course of fighting, if only they could be blamed on the *Reds,* the army tallied as crimes. Equivalent acts initiated by *United* the army overlooked. One notorious case involved a certain Pan Wen-hung, a well-known killer in the ranks of *United.* As soon as the factions declared peace, the Revolutionary Committee dominated by Li Ying-k'uei appointed him to a regional post. When thousands protested, Li transferred him to the Generator Plant. There, once protests died down, the factory committee recruited him into the Communist Party and made him a management cadre. Workers on the floor complained to no avail. In promoting Pan, the factory committee had followed orders from above.*

While the Party leaders busied themselves recruiting Pan and promoting him to a leading post in industry, they expelled at least 100 *Red* city cadres from the Party, removed them from their posts, and sent them down to labor in the countryside as ordinary team members in rural brigades. They did not allow these expelled cadres to settle in brigades administered by Changchih City or to return to the city on any pretext. They had to find homes in outlying counties and stay there—a form of local exile.

These 100 were the lucky ones. The regional committee charged most prominent *Red* leaders with counterrevolution. A national meeting of the steel-processing and arsenal industry, held in Shansi on August 16, 1968, served as a forum for settling accounts with the high command of the *Red* faction, most of whom had served as workers or cadres in the Huai-hai Arsenal. The organizers of the meeting directed six key *Reds* to appear before mass audiences for repudiation, then ordered them to cease all factional activity or face the consequences. After the meeting adjourned they turned the six over to the regional court for trial and punishment. Most of the punishments meted out were severe:

Hsüeh Liang, an arsenal cadre who had sworn to uphold Ch'en Hsiu-ch'uang, come what may: neither sentenced nor released, but held indefinitely pending further investigations.

Kao K'e-kung, former Party Secretary of the Huai-hai Arsenal, removed from office during the Four Clean Movement, later appointed to a new leading post. His worst mistake was that he married the adopted daughter

---

*In 1976, with Commander Li Ying-k'uei in disgrace, regional authorities arrested Pan as a murderer. His comrades denounced the arrest as a reversal of the Cultural Revolution, and a number of them went to Taiyuan to protest. They helped kidnap the new provincial governor, Wang Ch'ien.

of the famous Shansi leader Po Yi-po. This made him a prime target regardless of his record in any other respect: condemned as a renegade; sentenced to twenty years in prison.

Hao Cheng-hsiang, a worker who had risen to the post of director of the Huai-hai Arsenal: sentenced to life imprisonment.

Chao Ch'en-yuan, a former worker, leader of the mass movement in the plant and the man who assumed direction of the whole *Red* faction after Ch'en Hsiu-ch'uang went into hiding in December, 1967: sentenced to death, shot by firing squad.

Hou Hsiao-ken, a former cadre, once jailed for stealing, and a *Red* activist throughout the struggle: sentenced to death, shot by firing squad.

Liu Chou, charged with burning the wheat in the State Grain Company warehouse, after artillery fire set the wheat aflame: shot by firing squad.

The court meted out stiff sentences only to *Reds* who stood by their comrades. They gave "lenient treatment" to *Reds* who recanted. One of these was Wu Huei-feng. At the August 16 meeting he turned on his shopmates and denounced them, thus earning a post in the new administration.

Another turnabout was Chang T'ien-ts'ai. He had served as Ch'en Hsiu-ch'uang's personal secretary. He knew every detail of Ch'en's career as a regional leader. After Ch'en ran away he saw the light, denounced his former boss, and made himself valuable enough to the prosecution to earn a position as vice-director of the regional Financial Bureau. He also earned a seat on the standing committee of the regional Party Committee. Said Li Ying-k'uei of this Chang, "He turned over. He attacked Ch'en Hsiu-ch'uang, so we trust him."

Li Ying-k'uei learned to trust several other members of the standing committee of the *Red* faction who turned state's evidence. He assigned Wang Tsun-chieh, a medical student, to a doctor's practice; gave Kuo T'ien-ching, another medical student, a post in Hsiangyuan Hospital; and sent Chang Tse-jen, a political worker in a railroad construction unit, to serve in the railroad construction Command Post, Building 3202.

Said Li Ying-k'uei, "It's not a crime to make mistakes. It is only necessary to correct them. Those who come over to us are OK. This is Mao Tse-tung's line and it helps develop production." He talked of such matters as if he were expounding profound proletarian ethical principles which Chinese Communists had learned from Mao Tse-tung while the rest of the world wallowed in bourgeois moral turpitude, knowing only how to punish and not how to forgive, knowing only how to destroy and not how to use erstwhile enemies who recanted.

Sensitive to the charge that his administration might be partisan in any way, Li Ying-k'uei went out of his way to prove that he had dispensed justice evenhandedly. He cited the case of one notorious *United* chief of staff in Kaoping County. This man had once been an officer in Yen Hsi-shan's provincial army. On the basis of this military experience he had taken the lead when fighting engulfed Kaoping. He had personally killed a number of people and had been tried and executed for his crimes. Commander Li recalled one or two other cases of nameless "smashers and grabbers" on the

United side who received punishment, but these exceptions only seemed to confirm the rule that he reserved punishments primarily for *Reds.*

Little wonder, then, that large numbers of *Reds* preferred to keep their distance and even threw away the free railroad tickets that Li Ying-k'uei and Li Hsun-ta journeyed far and wide to hand out.

In 1968 thousands of people from Southeast Shansi were able to travel to other parts of the province and find temporary refuge, primarily because factional strife was on the rise everywhere they went and old allies welcomed them as reinforcements. Peace prevailed only in the Southeast, where the Sixty-ninth Army had suppressed all fighting; in the Northwest, where a stable leading group had managed to maintain unity at the top; and in Hsiyang County, where labor hero Ch'en Yung-kuei, forewarned by Premier Chou En-lai, never let fighting get started. Everywhere else confrontations between mass organizations linked to Evergreen Liu on one side and to Commander Chang Er-ch'ing on the other had developed into open armed fighting. Young militants with a commitment to Evergreen Liu, such as the *Red* refugees from Changchih, were a tremendous asset to the *Red General Station* in Taiyuan headed by Old Dare Yang. He saw to it that they received food, clothes, arms and training.

Evergreen Liu and Old Dare Yang had to begin worrying seriously about the isolation of their forces when the popular Yuan Chen, of Anshan Constitution fame, deserted them. Yuan's desertion occurred in October, 1967, while Evergreen Liu was traveling in Southeast Shansi trying to promote his Seven Point unity program. With Chairman Liu on safari, Yuan Chen came out with a ten-point plan for a grand alliance in the province. Liu, taken by surprise, denounced Yuan's plan as a "great mishmash of reaction." The denunciation so angered Yuan Chen that he immediately switched sides, came out in support of Chang Er-ch'ing, and carried student Liu Hao's *Revolutionary Rebel Regiment* with him.

This grand switch brought Shansi's two main student-led organizations together for the first time since they marched home victoriously from the villas at the Chin-tze in 1966. On November 8, 1967, they formed a new joint organization called the *Regiment Liaison Station* and chose Yuan Chen's wife as their political director. The merger brought the prestige of the student majority, with all its nationwide ties, onto Commander Chang's side. As Liu Hao put it, "The *Regiment's* correct politics, joined by the *Liaison Station's* masterful essays [*Liaison* was famous for the most literate and accomplished poster displays], now confront the *Red General Station's* smashing and robbing." He did not mention, though he could hardly have failed to note, that the merger also gave Chang, for the first time, an edge in the number of people who could be brought out on the street.

The loss of major student support in Taiyuan occurred only a few weeks before the Sixty-ninth Army crushed the *Red* faction, Liu's only prop in the Southeast. The new study meeting called by the Central Committee for Shansi cadres in Peking constituted a third grievous blow. Premier Chou called all the key leaders of both factions to the capital in May, 1968, for study sessions designed to end factionalism, and held them there until mid-September, almost five long months later. While these sessions lasted,

Chou entrusted power in Shansi to the commanders of the Sixty-ninth Army, Hsieh Chen-hua and Ts'ao Chung-nan. These two claimed to be working for unity on the basis of Mao Tse-tung Thought, but in fact all their sympathies lay with Political Director Chang Er-ch'ing, their old comrade from the Peking Military District. The longer they ran Shansi the less chance Evergreen Liu and Old Dare Yang had of salvaging any position at all.

When the renewed Shansi study sessions began in Peking, fighting still plagued the streets of Taiyuan. Vice-commander Ts'ao called Old Dare Yang and the student leader T'uan Li-cheng back to the city to patch up a truce between their rival mass organizations. After several weeks of study and negotiation Old Dare and T'uan signed a truce, whereupon they went back to Peking once more. Commander Ts'ao then printed up hundreds of thousands of copies of two Central Committee orders against armed fighting (the July 23 Order directed at Shensi and the July 24 Order directed at Kweichow), and put 10,000 soldiers to work handing them out in various trouble spots in the hinterland.

Ts'ao's tactics proved effective. Fighting began to die down and some contenders began to hand in their arms. In South Shansi, Central Shansi and in the capital city of Taiyuan fighting citizens turned over some 10,000 rifles, 100 artillery pieces and 100,000 rounds of ammunition to the army. The overall effect of this was to disarm Evergreen Liu's forces while leaving arms in the hands of Director Chang's forces. The authorities considered the latter to be legitimate arms in the hands of militia units.

Old Dare found it impossible to sit quietly in Peking while this process went on. Twice he climbed over the wall of the hostel to which he had been assigned and made his way back to Taiyuan to regroup his forces. The first time K'ang Sheng, adviser to the Central Cultural Revolution Group, and head of security nationally, sent a special plane after him and brought him back. The second time K'ang Sheng threatened to tie him up if he caught him, so he came back by himself.

According to Commander Ts'ao, by late September the army had almost succeeded in pacifying Shansi. "People had tired of the endless violence. They were beginning to understand that it had been provoked, in the main, by bad people, by ambitious schemers and counterrevolutionaries with ulterior motives. A big alliance wind began to blow as unity agreements were signed at the grass-roots level—in communes, factories and schools. In Taiyuan alone thirty units a day were signing pacts to create alliances."

But in October Evergreen Liu, Old Dare Yang, Political Director Chang, and the student firebrands T'uan Li-cheng and Liu Hao all returned to Taiyuan. In Peking they had signed a series of pacts eschewing violence and promising peace. But they had not been at home more than twenty days when fighting broke out once more in many parts of Shansi.

Late in 1968 neither side enjoyed the mass support that each had earlier taken for granted. Liu Hao, who had once been able to muster 1,000 truckloads of enthusiasts with one phone call, could now rouse only a few hundred. Old Dare Yang, who had once been able to call out 300,000 to 400,000 demonstrators, could now count on only 30,000 to 40,000. Since it was Old Dare and Evergreen Liu who experienced the sharpest decline in all-around support they launched a series of desperate actions to recoup prestige and influence.

The first of these came to be known as the *Shansi Daily* incident.

On November 24, 1968, Yang's *Dare-to-Dies,* with 10,000 members of the *Red General Station* held in reserve, surrounded the *Shansi Daily* newspaper plant, rushed the building, and seized a handful of army men who had been assigned to protect the paper and supervise its editorial content. Since the *Shansi Daily* was already in the hands of men who reported to Evergreen Liu, this whole action appeared to be irrational. But that was a simplistic, one-sided view. What Old Dare had in mind, according to his opponents, was to seize the army contingent, mistreat its members, and thus provoke a counterattack from the Sixty-ninth Army in the city. His forces could then appeal to the populace as victims of army intervention and revive some of the spirit of 1967 when people rose up en masse to challenge the "power of the gun." With 10,000 stalwarts in reserve, Old Dare also hoped to repulse the army counterattack with a surprise counterattack of his own.

Whether or not this was what Yang intended, the incident developed in a different direction entirely. The provocation failed to rouse the army. No confrontation with troops materialized. Instead, student T'uan Li-cheng's *Red Rebels* mobilized their full strength and surrounded their hated rivals in the streets around the newspaper plant. As this confrontation developed to the brink of all-out war the army rushed several commanders in to mediate. After ten days of tense negotiations both sides began to withdraw. Old Dare's men agreed to evacuate the *Shansi Daily* buildings and T'uan Li-cheng's men agreed not to launch a counterattack upon them. Thus, both sides narrowly averted a civil war of the sort that had engulfed Changchih earlier in the year.

Old Dare gave a bizarre reason for his all-out assault on the newspaper headquarters—missing ideographs. Much of the content of the paper consisted of reprints from the *People's Daily* in Peking. On this particular day the headline in the Peking paper read "Mao Tse-tung, Lin Piao and Chou En-lai." Reprinting this, the *Shansi Daily* left out the *and,* thus placing Chou En-lai on an equal footing with the other two. In the body of the article a second typesetting mistake replaced one ideograph with another of doubtful meaning. These two printing errors, according to Old Dare, constituted a serious "political incident," and he held the twenty-six army supervisors responsible.

How anyone could take seriously such minor changes in typesetting is hard to imagine. But there is in China an abiding fetishism about the printed word that leads to extraordinary interpretations concerning the placement, form, true meaning and intent of any ideograph. It is as if words on a page possess a life of their own, and indeed, with several thousand years of history behind them, they almost invariably do so. The way any individual reader understands a word is influenced by scores of cultural echoes that previous use has engendered, and all these echoes have political implications that can be elaborated into major challenges that the writer never had the capacity even to imagine. Such is the power of symbols in Chinese life.

Symbols of an exotic sort were responsible for real fighting that broke out only a few days later between the same forces that confronted each other before the newspaper office. This time conflict arose over a shipment of wax mangoes en route from Peking to Taiyuan.

To the people of Shansi the mangoes came laden with significance. The original mangoes (real, not wax) had been given to Chairman Mao by the Pakistani ambassador as a present. Mao received them at about the time the Peking Workers' Propaganda Team, 30,000 strong, succeeded in pacifying the campus at Tsinghua University, after suffering five killed and 750 wounded at the hands of the university's most militant student defenders. Mao sent the mangoes as a token of appreciation to the Propaganda Team, which had refrained from using violent methods in spite of extreme provocation and had finally subdued the campus by staying power, persuasive argument and sheer weight of numbers.

Thereafter mangoes became a national symbol of truce, peace, unity and great alliance between opposing factions. The Central Committee sent wax models of the original mangoes—symbolic fruit bearing, as it were, Mao's "blessing"—wherever people brought fighting to an end and managed to patch up some sort of alliance between mass organizations. After the *Shansi Daily* incident, alliance became the talk of the town in Taiyuan. The two sides drew up an agreement on paper and set a day for a mass rally. The Central Committee duly sent off a shipment of wax mangoes by rail from Peking.

Unfortunately, Evergreen Liu's forces, and especially Old Dare Yang, deeply resented the conditions laid down in the proposed agreement. Old Dare decided to protest the agreement, disrupt the rally, and possibly usurp Mao's "blessing" by intercepting the mangoes. He dispatched an armed force to Shihchiachuang, the main railroad junction that was the gateway to Shansi, in time to waylay the Peking train. But the army got wind of the impending raid and surrounded the wax fruit with a superior force. A strong armed escort then accompanied the mangoes to Taiyuan and turned them over to the new Provincial Revolutionary Committee at a rally attended by hundreds of thousands who poured out on the streets in a festive mood.

Having failed to seize the mangoes in Shihchiachuang, Old Dare decided to try once more in Taiyuan. He mobilized hundreds of trucks and without warning sent his forces to surround and attack the meeting. What had been billed as a celebration of unity turned into an all-out battle for mangoes on the streets of Taiyuan. In the course of the battle at least 100 people were badly wounded. Old Dare failed to seize the symbolic fruit but he did successfully destroy the alliance the fruit arrived to celebrate.

Desperate attacks such as these sowed disillusionment with Evergreen Liu, and more particularly with the "smashing and robbing" that had become the trademark of Old Dare Yang, Liu's military commander. People were already disillusioned with Director Chang Er-ch'ing, who always rejected shared power in his drive for supremacy; as for Yuan Chen, who shifted his forces from one side to the other, the less said the better. It became clear to millions that these men were not fighting for any principles at all but only for personal power.

A saying arose:

Liu Ke-p'ing pu p'ing,	Liu the just is not just,
Chang Er-ch'ing pu ch'ing,	Chang the clear is not clear [straightforward],
Yuan Chen pu chen.	Yuan the able is not able [spirited].

In each case the saying turned that element in the man's given name that was most laudatory into a negative that demonstrated the dissatisfaction of the people.

Popular disenchantment, however, did not have much effect on the militant core around each of these men. Just as, on the campus at Tsinghua University in July, 1968, a few hundred students on each side battled for supremacy with homemade tanks and rockets long after the majority of students, staff and faculty had fled the scene, so in late 1968, a few fanatic activists continued trials of strength on the streets even though they could rally only a fraction of the mass support they once took for granted. They gathered around themselves a motley assortment of brawlers, ruffians, misfits and common criminals for whom fighting was a way of life, a chance to loot, rape and bash people, and perhaps even end up as heroes. Whenever decisive battles loomed, leaders on both sides, like the counts and barons of medieval Europe, augmented their ranks by hiring reinforcements. They paid peasants 2 yuan a day plus a regular grain ration for armed service and this was at least twice, and sometimes three times, as much as the same young men could earn working in the fields.

Medievalism also raised its head when it came to the treatment of captives. In 1977 stories still circulated in Taiyuan about interrogators who cut and burned women's breasts or crucified male victims by nailing them to compound walls, a spike through the palm of each hand, and left them there to die. Another form of slow death was called "hot beef." Factional sadists placed their victims between steel plates that they slowly drew together by tightening nuts on bolts that joined the two sides. Once they had tightened the plates to all but unbearable pressure, they heated them with acetylene torches. Thus torturers improved techniques handed down from ancient times with the technology of a modern age.

As 1969 began, rumors of an impending national Party Congress gave new impetus to factional confrontation. Whoever controlled the province could control the selection of Congress delegates and thus consolidate a political network that would last for years. On January 5 Liu's forces issued a call for the overthrow of the Shansi Revolutionary Committee, where power had to be shared with Director Chang and his lieutenants, and for the establishment of a new committee composed of "revolutionaries"— Liu's diehard constituents. Old Dare Yang drafted and distributed the statement. He aimed it at Commanders Hsieh and Ts'ao of the Sixty-ninth Army, accused them of carrying out a new "February Current" (a replay of the alleged reactionary "adverse current" of February, 1967), and called on the people to rise up and smash their plot.

The Central Committee in Peking, already highly suspicious of Old Dare, denounced this January 5 "seize power" statement as counterrevolutionary. Its denunciation was tantamount to calling Old Dare Yang a counterrevolutionary element and seriously undermined Evergreen Liu and his whole movement. Mao's wife, Chiang Ch'ing, had already publicly denounced the miner Liang Pao-kuei and the chemical plant executive An Ke, to whom Liu had given arms at Yangch'uan, as troublemakers and "bad eggs." Now she suggested that Liu's forces in the provincial capital had linked up with the notorious May 16 counterrevolutionary conspiracy.

Evergreen Liu's forces responded to this provocation by going on the offensive militarily. As Shansi cadres gathered to choose delegates for the Ninth Party Congress, fighting broke out in several central districts. On April 1, as the Shansi delegates joined the formal sessions of the Congress in Peking, the fighting spread and intensified.

The opposition charged that Liu was using armed conflict as a form of pressure on the Congress. Liu, on his part, hurled the charges back. Many ordinary citizens hoped that the Ninth Congress, billed as a Congress of unity and transformation, would find a way to solve the Shansi problem, but the forces attacking and counterattacking in the field seemed to be saying, "You can't solve anything in Peking; you have to deal with us here."

The Congress met and adjourned, but fighting in Shansi raged on unchecked. Appalled, Premier Chou En-lai asked the Shansi delegates to stay on in Peking until they resolved their differences. He wanted them to draw up an agreement in the capital, then enforce a cease-fire as soon as they returned home. Once again the Premier's effort proved fruitless. Both sides talked well. They promised to form grand alliances when they got back to Shansi, but when they finally arrived on the scene no alliances materialized, only more warfare.

The most serious clashes developed in Chieh-hsiu County and at Liangtu Mine. In both cases Evergreen Liu's forces held the town, as they had in the Southeast, while Director Chang's forces held the surrounding hills. Chou En-lai asked the members of the provincial Core Leading Group to go together into the contested territory and negotiate truces on the spot. They formed an eleven-man truce team but had little success. When the team demanded that both sides cease firing and hand their weapons over to local army units, neither side would do so.

At Chieh-hsiu Chang Er-ch'ing said, "My people are outnumbered. How can they be the first to disarm?"

At Liangtu Mine Chang said, "With those people holding the town how can we come out of the mountains without guns?"

Arguments proliferated endlessly and even split the Core Leading Group of the provinces. Its members could not sit down together without fierce quarreling. Hsieh and Ts'ao claimed that they gave evenhanded support to all peace efforts and criticized disruption from whatever the source without fear or favor, but nothing worked. After a month of full-time cease-fire agitation, the fighting continued as fiercely as ever.

Finally the Central Committee in Peking decided on drastic action. The Premier called Evergreen Liu, Director Chang and Yuan Chen back to the capital, temporarily suspended them from office, and appointed seven new members—four army officers and three civilians—to the Shansi Core Leading Group. On the surface, the reorganization strengthened neutrality. Actually, it completed a power play that shoved Evergreen Liu's forces aside and packed the Group with sympathetic allies or outright supporters of Director Chang. The four army men—Hsiao Hsuan-chin, Wang Chih-p'ing, Hsu Hsiu-heng and Lu Kou-p'ing—were all officers of the Peking Army District, hence colleagues of Chang Er-ch'ing's. Three of them were from the Sixty-ninth Army that had always supported him.

As for the three civilians: Li Hsun-ta, the labor hero from West Gully, was a well-known supporter of the *United* faction in the Southeast; Wang Li, the miner from Yangch'uan, had a reputation as an independent, but nevertheless bitterly opposed Evergreen Liu; Han Ying, a cadre from the coal mines at Tatung, had never taken sides, but he had no trouble working closely with Commanders Hsieh and Ts'ao, thus helping to impose their pro-Chang outlook on the whole province.

The reorganization of Shansi's Core Leading Group, imposed from above, received support on July 23, 1969, from a special Central Committee order directed at Shansi.* The order was similar to those issued a year earlier to stop fighting in Shensi and Kweichow. It demanded, in the name of the Party's highest body, an end to all fighting and the surrender of all weapons. The Army printed it up in hundreds of thousands of copies, distributed it throughout the province by every available means, and dropped it over contested areas by helicopter.

The July 23 Order brought results. Within two weeks the army collected over 60,000 guns and 500 artillery pieces. Slowly the situation improved. An August 28 Directive from the Central Committee in Peking, calling on the Chinese people to prepare for possible invasion from the north, played a unifying role. By October, 1969, it became possible to form a great alliance from below. The new Core Leading Group members, all of whom leaned to one side, worked well together. The PLA troops under their direction imposed and vigorously upheld cease-fires, then stepped in as leading members of grand alliances at all levels.

Three months after the removal of Liu, Chang and Yuan from office in Shansi, the army succeeded in pacifying the whole province and production began to revive in mines and mills that had been all but shut down for months, even years. By the spring of 1970, when the Shansi Provincial Party Committee finally reestablished its authority, neither Evergreen Liu nor Director Chang nor Yuan Chen got a single vote. The next National Congress of the Party dropped Liu and Chang from the Central Committee on which the former had served as a full member and the latter as an alternate for years.

When Evergreen Liu lost his exalted office, Old Dare Yang fell from grace. He first lost his post as a standing committee member of the Shansi Provincial Revolutionary Committee. A few months later the army arrested him and put him on trial as a counterrevolutionary. Finally, in October, 1970, he was executed by firing squad in a rocky orchard on the road to the

*For the full text of the order, see Simon Leys, *The Chairman's New Clothes* (New York: St. Martin's Press, 1978), pp. 192–95.

famous temple at Chin-tze southwest of Taiyuan. The Central Committee approved the death sentence imposed on Yang after it had been discussed by local leading bodies throughout Shansi. Ninety-nine percent of the cadres polled voted for execution.

"Some people whose mistakes are small can be remolded," said Commander Ts'ao. "But this man had too much blood on his hands. Only a few close followers asked for a stay of execution for him, so we carried out his sentence without delay."

These words were spoken in 1971, but because the whole pacification procedure had been so flagrantly one-sided they could not be accepted at face value. In the ensuing years many verdicts had to be reversed. In 1977, after the fall of the "Gang of Four," I learned that both Hsieh and Ts'ao had been charged with factionalism and transferred from Shansi. I then asked once more about Old Dare Yang. Had he been framed or did he get the sentence he deserved? The answer, even then, was that Yang Ch'eng-hsiao, commander of the *Dare-to-Dies*, had earned his execution.

A fascinating character, this Yang. A journeyman worker, boss of a small gang of bullies, he suddenly vaulted by virtue of ability, audacity and ruthlessness to the forefront of a great province. In the power vacuum created by the collapse of the provincial government he parlayed a handful of *Dare-to-Dies* into an army of 40,000 and a mass movement of 400,000. He commandeered trucks by the thousands, put armed squads on wheels, assembled a headquarters staff and a communications center capable of monitoring the nation, hired secretaries, procured concubines. Yang, it must be admitted, was a veritable Ts'ao Ts'ao of the modern age. With a few changes the words used by Balazs to describe daredevils of the kind that "brought the Han dynasty down, transforming China in one generation, from a powerful empire into one vast cemetery," could well sum up this steelworker's career.

"Now it was the military who came into their own . . . adventurers, swashbucklers, condottieri, and military leaders of all kinds. With their bands of starving and ragged mercenaries, vagabonds, criminals, landless peasants, jobless intellectuals who had come down in the world—men of every variety, with neither creed nor code . . . they roamed about with their bands of freebooters, pillaging now one province, now another; if they were lucky they succeeded in seizing some fortress or town [substitute "factory" here] left standing and used it as a springboard for the next step toward victory."*

Reviewing Yang's life, bizarre images flash through the mind:

Yang, rifle in hand, picks off poster-pasting rivals—one shot, one corpse.

Yang, losing patience, orders a defiant captive thrown from a third-story window.

Yang, sporting dark glasses, tailor-made shirt and tropical shorts, speeds down a broad Peking avenue in Ting Lei's limousine.

Yang, addicted to the high life, swims in an exclusive Peking pool, then

*Etienne Balazs, *Chinese Civilization and Bureaucracy*, trans. H. M. Wright, ed. Arthur Wright (New Haven: Yale University Press, 1964), p. 194.

dines on sharks' fins and sea slugs at a mess reserved for commanding officers at the Great Western Guest House.

Yang, breaking out of a study session, climbs over the compound wall and makes his way home to Taiyuan to revitalize his private army.

Yang, apprehended, returns to Peking in a plane sent after him by K'ang Sheng, gray eminence of China's internal security.

Had he been on the winning side, he might now be a leading official of Shansi, perhaps even of all China. Losing, he became a vile bandit, fit only for a bullet in the head.

What medieval forces, in confluence, produced such a man? And how widespread was their influence? If adventurers of the Yang Ch'eng-hsiao type are any indication, their influence must have permeated a large part of the body politic, for once the Cultural Revolution broke out, numerous "Old Dares" flashed across the dark, chaotic firmament of the hinterland, like shooting stars, each blazing to astonishing brightness before fading away or suffering asphyxiation in the void.

The extraordinary careers of such people had their roots in powerful centrifugal impulses—provincial, regional, local, clan and sect—that survived after 1949 and constantly renewed themselves in spite of persistent efforts from the center to suppress and annihilate them. On such impulses factionalism fed and prospered, taking advantage of every rivalry, grievance and blood feud left over by history. But from the record in Shansi it seems clear that impulses from below would not have generated significant momentum, and would certainly never have driven an entire province to virtual civil war, had they not been fanned from above in each instance and, what is more, consistently provoked and cultivated from the very top by powerful individuals inside the Central Committee of the Party who were themselves contending for supreme power. By their contention these individuals succeeded in undermining all the normal processes of government and all normal political and social arrangements, whether at the center or on the farthest reaches of the land. Circle by circle, layer by layer, they pulled a large proportion of the population of China into the maelstrom whose dizzy spirals they helped to create but in the end found no way to control.

The outline history of the Cultural Revolution in Shansi Province that we were able to assemble—incomplete, confused and biased as it proved to be when presented by such active protagonists as Li Ying-k'uei and Ts'ao Chung-nan—gave us some basis at last for understanding, if not condoning, the strange happenings of 1967–68 in Long Bow village itself, when the *Defend Mao Tse-tung Thought Platoon* helped arrest, beat and drive into exile the leaders of *Petrel* and *Shankan Ridge*. Once we understood Long Bow's strategic importance as the headquarters of the whole *United* faction in the region, and understood also the scale and ferocity of the civil war that local factionalism unleashed, we could understand how young men raised in adjacent alleys by uniformly poor peasant parents, recruited into one Party branch by a single group of admiring peers, and elected to office by the same fraternal neighbors, might end up mortal enemies and find themselves one freezing winter night in a dimly lit room at the local middle school, split into two groups—one a handful of blindfolded prisoners defying their inquisitors, the other a handful of hard-faced guards acting as accomplices to the inquisition.

Part IX

NEVER FORGET
CLASS
STRUGGLE

*Some people say that the Chinese people are passion-
ately fond of peace. I don't think they are so fond of
it. The Chinese people are pugnacious.*

Mao Tse-tung, July 1967

80

GET LITTLE SHEN!

As the sun set one winter evening in January, 1968, armed detachments gathered on the grounds of the Luan Middle School in the center of Long Bow. Young militiamen from Anyang and Wuyang, workers from the railroad shops across the highway and peasants from Long Bow village crossed paths in silence. Over their shoulders, in lethal disarray, hung rifles, fully loaded cartridge belts and slings of hand grenades. Willing hands lifted machine guns and boxes of ammunition onto truck beds, some of which already carried mounted guns that could swivel full circle. Once the darkness became total, at least thirty truck engines sprang to life, propelling as many heavily laden vehicles onto the highway leading south. Half an hour later firing began at the edge of Changchih City—a staccato burst, a scattered response, another burst, then a more sustained response. Soon the sounds of battle merged into an ominous roar that only the giant crusher at the local cement plant could rival. Now and then the thunder of a grenade broke through above the tumult.

In a well-built house at the southern edge of Long Bow several men sat quietly, listening to the cacophony in the distance. They exchanged words sparingly. Suddenly the door flew open, propelled by a blow from a rifle butt. Three men, bayonets fixed, stormed into the house. Behind them pressed five more. Another dozen, all armed to the teeth, milled around the dark courtyard outside.

"Who is Shen Chin-ts'ai?" asked the leader, a stranger to Long Bow.

"I am," said Shen, standing up. As he rose he recognized two Long Bow cadres, Swift Li and Fast Chin, and several other members of the brigade's militia unit.

"Put your hands at your side," ordered the leader.

Little Shen put his hands down.

Militiamen bound them behind his back with wire.

When his companions also dropped their hands the intruders wired them tightly, then marched their captives to the primary school and locked them in separate rooms. Two men stood guard while the core of the arresting party went off to eat. When the men came back they blindfolded the prisoners with hand towels, then dragged them across the village to the middle-school grounds, where they secured the makeshift blindfolds with gauze and adhesive tape. Several men took Little Shen to an isolated chamber and began to beat him with the fan belt of a truck. They beat him until he fainted, then half dragged, half pushed him to a cold cubicle on the west side of the compound, where two strangers mounted guard over him until morning.

The next day several middle-school students came to get the battered sidelines cadre. They reinforced his blindfold with cloth and tape, then pulled him by the hair into a big gallery where many men stood in a circle, rifles in hand. They knocked him back and forth among them with their rifle butts until he fainted. When he came to his senses, they pulled him to a standing position and beat him from above with strands of number 8 wire bound at one end to form a whip. The wire ripped his light padded jacket to shreds and cut deeply into his neck and shoulders. Although the only voices he heard belonged to students, he could tell there were other people present by the sounds of heavy breathing that came from all sides. He felt certain that Swift Li was among them.

His captors demanded that he turn over his handgun.

"What handgun? I never had one. How can I turn over what I never had?" groaned Little Shen.

The more he denied owning a gun, the more his captors beat him. That night he lost consciousness three times. Finally, at two o'clock in the morning they dragged him back to the same cold cubicle and left him under guard to get some sleep if sleep he could.

The incident that triggered this fratricidal confrontation in Long Bow was the January 16 ambush in Changchih. When armed men of the *Red* faction kidnapped labor hero Li Hsun-ta, his colleagues of the Provincial Committee and scores of other cadres, and took them to the Huai-hai Arsenal as prisoners, the *United* faction responded by mobilizing for an all-out assault on Changchih City. As the leaders mobilized they decided they must take measures to secure the safety of their headquarters. They ordered commune and brigade cadres to arrest and interrogate anyone suspected of past loyalty or ties to *Red*. They enforced this order vigorously in Long Bow village because the Luan Middle School had long been integrated into the *United* command post, situated in the railroad shops across the tracks.

On January 24, in spite of stepped-up security measures, an alarming incident occurred at the middle school, confirming everyone's worst fears about infiltration and sabotage. In midafternoon a hand grenade came flying over the north wall of the huge compound. It landed near the kitchen. Fortunately for those inside, the grenade was a dud; it failed to go off. Nobody got killed; nobody even got hurt. Nevertheless the bouncing grenade badly frightened everyone. Were there *Reds* living right beside the *United* headquarters? If so, it was time to clean them out.

The leaders of *United* called in Swift Li, Party Secretary of the Long Bow Brigade, and Fast Chin, the militia captain.

"Are there any *Reds* in Long Bow?"

"Yes."

"Who are they?"

"The members of *Petrel* and *Shankan Ridge.*"

"Better round them up. Bring them here and we'll question them."

"Can't you send anyone with us?" asked Swift Li.

"We'll send eight men. Better hurry before something worse happens."

United headquarters quickly organized an armed group made up of eight men from *United* and a dozen or so from Long Bow's *Defend Mao Tse-tung Thought Platoon.* The latter contingent included Swift Li, Fast Chin, the notorious rascal Whiskers Shen, the street brawler Splayfoot Tseng and other stalwarts of the local militia.

The group went straight to Little Shen's house and arrested every man found there: Little Shen himself; the head of *Petrel,* Kuo Ming-en; the head of *Shankan Ridge,* Chou Lai-fu; rank-and-file members of both organizations like Huai Teng-k'e, Yang Yu-ts'ai, Ch'en Wan-t'ien, Shen Ch'i-ch'ang and Chi Yu-hsin; and a refugee from the fighting inside Changchih City, one Li Hung-nien. They also searched the house from top to bottom. They found eight hand grenades.

United headquarters personnel held all these Long Bow prisoners in the middle-school compound, questioning and beating them for three days and three nights in a row. While twenty miles to the south *Red* militants beat Li Hsun-ta and his comrades of the Regional Revolutionary Committee in the cellar of an obscure building at the Huai-hai Arsenal, trying to force them to say a few words in support of Ch'en Hsiu-ch'uang, *United* militants in Long Bow beat Shen Chin-ts'ai and his comrades from *Petrel* and *Shankan Ridge,* trying to force them to admit that they were dangerous *Reds,* committed to support Ch'en Hsiu-ch'uang and his counterrevolutionary restoration in Southeast Shansi.

Finally, on January 27, three men acquainted with Little Shen—a cadre from Changchih Transportation and two workers from the railroad repair shop—came to find him and get him out of the middle school. As members of *United* they convinced the people holding Shen that their prisoner was really no threat. *United* headquarters then let him go. "There has been a misunderstanding," said Chu, the man in charge. "It was people from the brigade who brought you here. You had better go home now. Try and see a doctor. You have been badly beaten. If you have any further trouble come and find me."

Little Shen could hardly walk. He staggered home a few steps at a time. When he finally got there he learned that he alone, of the nine men arrested, had been released. He called on two young friends and with one supporting each arm, immediately went back to the middle school to protest. But that day he couldn't find guard captain Chu anywhere. He gave up and went home.

The next day, guard captain Chu sent for Little Shen. When the badly beaten village cadre finally managed with another's help to hobble over to the school, Chu sent out word that he was too busy to talk. When Little Shen and his assistant tried to leave, they found they had been locked in. After several hours a new guard released them, but as they went out the gate, members of Long Bow's militia blocked their way. When Little Shen protested loudly, the militiamen consulted headquarters staff and finally let both men go on condition that they dissolve their organization. "If *Petrel* and *Shankan Ridge* continue any activities, look out for your life," they warned. When Little Shen finally got home that day he collapsed as he walked through the door. He fell down upon the kang in pain and couldn't get up even to pass water. He lay ill at home for two weeks.

United headquarters released the men arrested with Little Shen after about five days, but not before guards beat them all severely. In the meantime, other *United* activists caught and beat other members of *Petrel* and *Shankan Ridge* when they tried to put up posters protesting the detention of their comrades.

Just when Little Shen began to feel well enough to get off the kang, Huai Teng-k'e, Chou Lai-fu and Shen Ch'i-ch'ang came to him, greatly agitated. Swift Li and Fast Chin had ordered them to appear at the primary school for a meeting. They felt sure they would be beaten again.

Little Shen advised them to find a friend of his, Li Hsien-ching, at the cement plant, and with his help present their case to Li Hsun-ta, the famous labor hero, now a regional leader of *United,* who had the power and the prestige to do something about the situation in Long Bow. In compliance with an ultimatum from Peking, *Red* had just released Li Hsun-ta from the cellar of the Huai-hai Arsenal and he was resting up at *United's* offices in the cement plant.

That afternoon the three *Petrels* quietly slipped out of the village and made their way across the highway and the railroad tracks to the cement plant. When they failed to show up as ordered at the Long Bow primary school, the Long Bow militia shouldered their rifles and went after them. Leading the platoon that evening was Splayfoot Tseng.

Many months before, Splayfoot Tseng and a dozen or so other Long Bow peasants had worked in the cement plant as contract workers. While there they had joined a mass organization that later linked up with the *Red* faction. The guard at the cement plant didn't know that when the Long Bow men received layoff notices from the plant they had switched sides, linked up with *United,* and gone on to serve as stalwarts under Fast Chin.

When Splayfoot Tseng walked up with his rifle and demanded that the three men be turned over to him, the guard said, "Who are you?"

"I'm in command of the Long Bow militia. Some *Reds* have run into the cement plant. We want them back."

"We're *United* here," said the guard. "You must be *Reds.*"

With that he alerted the security forces inside the plant. A group of armed men dashed out, disarmed the Long Bow militiamen, then told them to run for their lives.

Just to make sure that the Long Bow men kept moving, the cement plant guards opened fire with machine guns. They aimed high enough to avoid hitting anyone, but the fleeing men didn't know that. The machine gun fire badly frightened the disarmed militiamen. It also made them angry. As they ran, Splayfoot Tseng fumed, "Let's get some dynamite and blow the place up!" Once they made it to safety they went straight to commune headquarters in Horse Square, where they found militia leader Yang Chiu-shih and vice-chairman Chang Ch'ang-fu of the commune. They persuaded the two officials to go immediately to the cement plant to talk to the leaders there.

They wanted their arms back and they wanted the three Long Bow runaways.

After a prolonged conference during which the commune leaders repeatedly guaranteed the safety of the refugees, cement plant men handed back the seized rifles to the Long Bow militiamen and turned over the three *Petrel* activists. But when Splayfoot Tseng got his prisoners back to the village, he didn't release them as he had promised, he took them instead to the primary school. As soon as the two commune officials Yang and Chang turned their backs and started for Horse Square, the Long Bow militia beat Huai Teng-k'e, Chou Lai-fu and Shen Ch'i-ch'ang unmercifully. They broke Teng-k'e's arm. The militiamen blamed the three for their own humiliation in front of the cement plant gate, their ignominious flight and the frightful machine gun fire. "Because of you we almost ate some bullets," they snarled. They also wanted their prisoners to admit that Little Shen had in fact tried to "reverse the case" on land reform. In the end, unable to stand the pain, the three *Petrels* admitted whatever their captors demanded of them.

After suffering serious beatings in the primary school the three members of the minority faction decided they had better get out of Long Bow. Little Shen, Kou Ming-en and Chi Yu-hsin decided to leave with them. Little Shen got letters of introduction for them all from Li Hsien-ching at the cement plant and from Ch'en Tse-wen at the railroad shop. He presented these to some railroad workers who lived along the highway opposite Horse Square. They took handcarts to Long Bow, carried the crippled men out, and took them to the Railroad Hospital for treatment. The doctor there set Teng-k'e's arm and placed it in a cast. He put Chou Lai-fu and Shen Ch'i-ch'ang to bed for observation. Railroad workers took Little Shen and his two other companions into their homes. Thus the six stayed near Horse Square, only a mile from Long Bow, for six weeks. During that time nobody in Long Bow dared come after them or attack them because Ts'ao's Sixty-ninth Army units had established their headquarters at Changchih North Station, next door. The army had also set up a reception station where civilians could bring grievances and ask for help. Little Shen went there frequently to report on the situation in Long Bow. Cadres from the Sixty-ninth Army, confronted with a major factional war for possession of Changchih City, were not in a position to do anything about disputes, however violent, at the village level, but they assured Little Shen that once the main fighting had been brought to an end, anyone guilty of violence would be criticized for wrecking Mao Tse-tung's great strategic plan.

In February, after the Sixty-ninth Army brought the fighting to an end, army headquarters moved south to a site closer to the city. Then Fast Chin came to Horse Square with a large detachment of militiamen hoping to arrest the *Petrel* and *Shankan Ridge* leaders there.

"You'd better come back with us," said Chin.

"How can we? You'll beat the hell out of us."

"Of course we'll beat you," said Chin. "It's right to beat bad people."

But a railroad worker's wife saw the militiamen coming and ran off to warn an army political director who still remained nearby. He arrived just in time.

"I am Commander Tung of the Sixty-ninth Army. My duty is to stop all violent fighting. If anybody continues to fight in Long Bow now that the truce is in effect, he is violating Chairman Mao's specific instructions."

"But this man is a counterrevolutionary from our village," protested Fast Chin. "He deserves to be beaten up."

"How can there be so many counterrevolutionaries everywhere?" asked Tung. "We don't believe he's any such thing."

"Well, if you are going to protect him," said Chin, "you had better protect him to the end."

With that the militia captain walked out.

Commander Tung also walked out.

"If you're going to beat them you have to take full responsibility," he shouted as he left.

The confrontation had resolved nothing. Little Shen and the *Petrel-Shankan Ridge* leaders still did not dare go home. They sent a messenger to ask Commander Tung's advice. He told them they had better leave the area altogether. If they stayed near Long Bow no one could guarantee their safety. They decided to join the stream of refugees that poured out of Changchih City once the fighting stopped, a stream that within a few days siphoned off more than 6,000 people.

One night after dark the Long Bow men slipped downstairs quietly, one by one, so that nobody would be alerted, and set out in the direction of Changchih. Since none of them could walk unaided, the railroad workers found sticks and canes for them to lean on. They hobbled off into the darkness, only to discover that fighting had again broken out near the city limits. Unwilling to risk their lives in the battle zone and afraid of being caught by the Long Bow militia if they tarried near home, they found an abandoned brick kiln in the fields and crawled inside it to sleep. In the morning they decided to head for Huai Teng-k'e's old home in P'ingshun County. Because Chou Lai-fu was in such pain they made only ten li (3⅓ miles) the next day. When they finally staggered into Hsinhsu Gully, an old friend of Little Shen's put them up for the night. They stayed through the next day and a second night because Chou Lai-fu felt too ill to go on. Finally, on the fourth day they walked thirty li to Wang Village and began to breathe more easily. On the fifth day they headed eastward toward Shihhui. Their route took them past Tu Street, the home of Kuo Ming-en's aunt. Leaving Kuo there they limped on to Ma Family Mountain in P'ingshun County, only to find that Huai Teng-k'e's widowed mother had remarried and moved to West Slope. Teng-k'e walked on to West Slope, found his mother, then sent for his companions. They all gathered in her house, planning to stay.

They no sooner arrived, however, than local commune headquarters sent militiamen to question them.

"Where are you from?"

"Long Bow."

"What are you doing here?"

"There was fighting in Long Bow. Reactionaries broke Huai's arm, so we brought him home."

"Are you *Reds?*"

"No. *United.*"

The militiamen didn't believe them. Shen had to name such prominent *United* leaders as Li Hsien-ching at the cement plant and Commander Ch'en Tse-wen at the railroad shop, and insist that they send a messenger to verify the facts, before they finally accepted his word.

Once they did accept it they immediately said, "Well, if you are *United* you had better get right back, grasp revolution, and promote production at home."

Obviously, they could not all stay with Huai Teng-k'e at West Slope. Little Shen and Chou Lai-fu traveled on to Hsiangching Village in Lucheng County, where Shen's old friend from the supply cooperative, Yang Fu-shan, lived. Fu-shan agreed to take a trip to Long Bow to size up the situation. When he got there, Little Shen's brother, Chi-ts'ai, told him that feelings were still running high and that the men should not try to come home yet. Chi-ts'ai gave Fu-shan twenty yuan and some grain coupons to take back with him. With this money and an assurance of grain Little Shen set off for Shihchiachuang, Hopei, a great rail hub on the plain more than 100 miles away. Shen's aunt, who had married an old Red Army man, and an uncle employed by a Liberation Army construction squad, lived in Shihchiachuang. Since two men traveling together always seemed to arouse suspicion, Chou Lai-fu set off in a different direction—toward Linhsien, where he had a grandmother who could be counted on for a few days' shelter.

Little Shen arrived in Shihchiachuang on March 20, 1968. He lived with his aunt for fifty days, then with his uncle for thirty more days. In mid-June both his money and his grain coupons ran out. He had no choice but to return home. He borrowed enough money for a train ticket right through to Horse Square (Changchih North Station) and bought a one-way pass. Once on the train he thought, If I get off the train at four in the afternoon just as the people are returning to the fields, and they see me walking home down the road, they're liable to grab me again before I even reach my door. So he jumped off early on the upgrade before the train went through the cut in Great Ridge Hill, hid in the fields, and then walked home after ten o'clock at night when everything was quiet.

As soon as he got home he sent for his brother, Chi-ts'ai. Chi-ts'ai said, "It's still not safe. They've beaten everyone else and they're trying to get everyone to put the blame on you. You had better get out and stay out for now."

"If it's just a question of a few beatings, I might as well stay," said Shen. "I can suffer through that."

"It's not just a question of a beating or two," said Chi-ts'ai. "Your life is at stake."

So Little Shen took to the road once more. At two o'clock in the morning he sought out two friends, one a student and one a worker, who helped him escape to Tunliu, where his grandmother lived. She had fed Shen and Chi-ts'ai during the famine year when they were still small boys. Now Shen again threw himself on her mercy. It was June 10, 1968.

On August 26 Chi-ts'ai and his uncle Big Shen went to Tunliu by bicycle to find Little Shen. Chi-ts'ai reported that a new detachment of the army, the 4733 Division, had come to the Horse Square area, and that they were propagating the July 3 and July 24 orders of the Central Committee, calling on people everywhere to stop fighting (this was the Tsinghua University order), and calling on all who had run away to return home. According to Chi-ts'ai, a new situation had developed, a real turning point. It was safe at last for Shen to come home. The two men took turns carrying Little Shen over the rear wheel of their respective bikes and he returned that very day to Long Bow.

Little Shen had a bad cold. As soon as he got home he fell asleep on his kang.

At 10:00 P.M. he once again heard loud banging on the yard gate—fists and gun butts. It was Whiskers Shen with a group of militiamen, all armed to the teeth.

"Open up!" they shouted.

"What for?"

"We've come to take you to the mass meeting!"

Before Little Shen could get off the kang they burst into the yard. He had just time enough to tell one of the railroad workers who rented a room in the courtyard to mark well who grabbed him. Then Whiskers Shen seized him and hustled him off to the brigade meeting hall.

He found himself at the center of the stage with a huge cardboard sign across his chest. The sign, hanging by a string from his neck, read "Counter-revolutionary."

Swift Li and Fast Chin questioned him sharply. "Chin-ts'ai, you have been away a long time. Where have you been? Did you go to join the fighting in Taiyuan?"

"How could I fight in Taiyuan when I haven't even been there?"

"Where have you been?"

"Tunliu. Shihchiachuang. If you don't believe me check it out your-selves."

"You're a *Red!*"

"No. I'm *United.*"

"But you linked up with Chang Lien-ying of *Red Cliff.*"

"That's right. Because Chang supported us when Militia Commander Yang went after us. But we never joined the *Reds.*"

According to Little Shen, Swift Li then began to shout, "Damn you, you counterrevolutionary! Why don't you ever say anything honest?" But all the shouting led to nothing. An army observer and a teacher from the Fourth Middle School, who represented a work team assigned to Long Bow to do political work, attended the meeting. Both the soldier and the teacher opposed coercion as a violation of Mao Tse-tung's instructions. They for-bade beatings or "airplanes." Frustrated, Long Bow cadres adjourned the meeting.

But that was not the end of the evening's proceedings. According to Little Shen, as he walked home past the brigade office gate, Whiskers Shen and Chang K'uan-hsin seized him and pulled him inside. They held him there and questioned him until dawn. Swift Li, Fast Chin and ten militiamen hung a heavy board from his neck with number 12 wire and weighted it with two large bricks from the Changchih City wall. As the wire cut into his neck Shen began to sweat. The pain became sharper and sharper. They demanded that he sign a statement that he had tried to "reverse the case" on land reform and had then held a meeting to cover up his tracks.

When the pain became unbearable Little Shen said, "I'll tell you all about it."

His interrogators immediately removed the bricks from the board, easing the pressure.

Then Shen reversed himself.

"I have nothing to say."

They replaced the bricks on the board.

This confrontation went on for hours, but since Shen refused to talk and refused to sign, Swift Li released him at five in the morning.

The next day he sought out the cadre from the middle school to report what had happened. That night militiamen carried him once again before a meeting in the brigade office. This time his interrogators added both bricks and rocks to the board. They pulled his hair to make him bow low and hit him from time to time with their rifle butts.

They wanted something new from him. They wanted his signature on a paper charging Yang Chi-wang and Chin T'ien-shui (young men from the Fourth Team) with responsibility for the "reverse the case" incident and cover-up.

"If you don't sign this, you won't live until morning," they said.

Seeing no way out, Little Shen finally signed. They released him and he went home, sore all over. When he lay down on his kang he couldn't get up.

On September 1 the work team withdrew. Little Shen himself then went to Changchih to plead with the Revolutionary Committee of the city to send another team. A few days later a group of cadres from the City Hospital arrived to act as a new work team. By that time the charges against Little Shen were flying thick and fast. He had stolen guns from Kuyi, he had received 500 yuan for blowing up a bridge, he had threatened to catch the commune militia commander, Yang Hsin-sha, alone in order to settle accounts with him.

The new work team investigated these charges, found nothing to implicate Little Shen, and left again on September 13. On the fourteenth, Long Bow Brigade members set up a new revolutionary committee. They confirmed Swift Li and Fast Chin in office. On the twentieth the Party branch began a rectification movement, targeted Little Shen as the enemy, and brought all the old charges against him. A few days later the Party branch members voted to expel him.

Little Shen went to the City Party Committee to protest this action. City Party leaders told him that Party rectification had not even begun in the region, and that the matter of his membership would have to be taken up at the commune level. But when he got home the Brigade Party Branch not only confirmed his expulsion, it ordered him out to work on the streets along with the other "elements" (landlords, rich peasants, counterrevolutionaries and bad eggs) still under supervision in the brigade. When he refused to work under such conditions, militiamen carried him before a mass meeting again. When he still refused to work under guard, *Mao Tse-tung Thought* activists criticized him before a third village mass meeting. They jerked his head down so sharply that tufts of his hair came out. They held his arms back so far that for a while he lost the use of them. He also lost track of time. After one such meeting, his family had to take him to the hospital. Because the North Station Hospital had no empty beds, the doctor there sent him on to the Changchih People's Hospital. He stayed in Changchih a week. Finally, when he still refused to work under supervision as an enemy of the people, Long Bow leaders sent him to a study class set up for all those who had been the targets of critical posters, some seventy people in all. There the struggle against him continued.

By this time it was January, 1969. The Commune Party Committee not only failed to reverse his expulsion, but finally confirmed it. The local branch began rejecting his Party dues; before a mass meeting of 10,000 people the Party Secretary of Horse Square Commune, Shih Chao-sheng, announced that he had been expelled as a counterrevolutionary.

The preceding paragraphs summarize Little Shen's story. The story as he told it was much longer and more detailed. Some of the details seemed irrelevant, but even the irrelevant material had its purpose. It made Little Shen appear reasonable—a hardworking, concerned cadre who even admitted mistakes and was anxious to work together with anyone who would agree to work with him.

When it came to self-criticism, Little Shen admitted at least two serious mistakes:

> Grabbing paper for posters from the commune office was one. This was in violation of the June 6 Directive from the Central Committee against smashing and robbing. But we had been suppressed and blocked for so long and we couldn't get the commune to help us. Our young rebels got angry and took what they saw. I didn't tell them to do it; they did it spontaneously. I didn't stop them from doing it either. I should have. I was older. I was a Party member. I should have done something when they went out and helped themselves.
>
> I also took some money. That was my second mistake. In April, 1967, the new revolutionary committee threw me out of my job as Sidelines Team leader. They came and told me I had to stop work. I quit, but the day I quit I took some of the Sidelines Team money and turned it over to *Shankan Ridge*. It wasn't a great deal of money —137.58 yuan to be exact—but I gave it to my group because we were in such bad shape financially. We spent some of it on our appeal to the City Party Committee. We spent some more—about 20 or 30 yuan—on paper and brushes. We spent the rest after they beat me so badly. We spent it on doctors' fees, medicine and travel so that they could not seize and beat me again. I kept a record of everything and reported it to the work team leader. I wrote a self-criticism and reported everything in detail.

I tried hard to confirm this story through other sources. Swift Li in 1971 and Splayfoot Tseng, much later, in 1977, denied that the Long Bow militia had ever physically abused Little Shen. Someone beat him badly in the middle school—yes. But this was the work of student leaders of *United* who feared that he was a dangerous *Red* element inside their fortress, so to speak. When Long Bow militia made Little Shen their target, they only hung a cardboard sign on his neck, made him bow his head low and hold his hands behind his back, but nobody beat him up, nobody pulled his hair out, and nobody twisted his arms.

This is what the cadres said, but some of their loyal supporters, in free conversation on the street, told a different story. At one meeting at least, an old man told me, the militia hung a board from Shen's neck, then pulled his head down so sharply against it that his front teeth knocked wood— *bang, bang, bang.* The teller of the tale re-created both the motion and the sound for me.

My own conclusion is that Little Shen exaggerated what happened, but that in fact he did suffer very rough treatment. Not outsiders but fellow villagers of Long Bow knocked out his front teeth, pulled tufts of hair out by the roots (his scalp is covered with scars), and twisted his arms so badly that they dislocated his shoulders. And they meted out this rough treatment to at least ten or more of the activists who led *Petrel-Shankan Ridge.* When I talked to Kuo Ming-en, his eyes filled with tears. "What they did to us should never have been done," he said. "I do not blame them for it now. It was a result of factionalism. Now we work together like brothers. But what they did should not have been done."

Chou Lai-fu suffered even more grievously. After he ran away, his wife divorced him and two of his children died. Fearing for his life, he hid out in Honan for a whole year.

Swift Li, while denying that he had personally beaten or abused anyone, still said, "When we think back on it now, it frightens us. Nobody got killed. Everyone survived. But we could so easily have killed someone. We could so easily have made an irreversible mistake. We do not like to think about it. It frightens me to think about it. It was all the result of factionalism."

What Little Shen left out of his story was the violence perpertated by his side. At the start, in the winter and spring of 1967, *Petrel-Shankan Ridge* could count on a fairly large number of members who saw their cause as just and deeply resented the reversal of the seize-power movement launched by their side. In the debate and poster war, when the two factions battled it out in the streets, *Petrel-Shankan Ridge* members often took the offensive, and sometimes won the fight. At night they sent squads out to look for Swift Li and Fast Chin, and threatened to beat them if they found them. It was for this reason, according to Splayfoot Tseng, that Li and Chin sometimes spent the night in homes that were not their own.

At the start, then, the two factions had been relatively well matched. Each had considered the other to be counterrevolutionary, or at least reactionary, and each had felt justified in beating up members of the opposition. It was only later—after the *Mao Tse-tung Thought* faction raised charges concerning "reverse the case on land reform," after its members began calling Chou Lai-fu, Kuo Ming-en and others "landlord and Kuomintang elements," after the commune committee expelled *Petrel* and *Shankan Ridge* from the seize-power headquarters—only then that many people felt constrained to reconsider their stand, decided they didn't want to become the targets of such abuse, and either dropped out or switched sides. Thus the *Mao Tse-tung Thought* faction isolated *Petrel-Shankan Ridge*, cut it down in size, and persecuted it as a minority unit, with its back to the wall. Later, when, in the region as a whole and in Changchih City, *Red* and *United* finally formed and the army denounced *Red* as counterrevolutionary while it upheld *United* as correct, the majority began to identify *Petrel-Shankan Ridge* as *Red*. Then everybody began to denounce it as a front for landlords, rich peasants, counterrevolutionaries and bad elements, and to hold it up for contempt. When this happened, it became hard for any *Petrel* or *Shankan Ridger* to hold his or her head up.

When I asked Swift Li if he had ever believed that Little Shen and the *Petrels* were counterrevolutionary, he said, "I don't believe it now, but at the time we convinced ourselves of it. We made a case, and it all seemed plausible. It frightens me to think of what might have happened."

Others were not as enlightened. In 1977, almost ten years after these events, Splayfoot Tseng, for instance, said, "Little Shen mobilized landlords, rich peasants and bad elements to reverse the case on land reform. We never beat him, but he deserved to be beaten. Bad people ought to be beaten."

81

THE BRIDE WHO
FELL FROM HEAVEN

In 1968 persecutions and beatings had one clear result.
They smashed "rebel" power and put Swift Li and Fast
Chin into uncontested control of Long Bow village at a
time when the faction to which they claimed allegiance,
United, established equally uncontested control over the
city and the entire region. Unchallenged power, coupled with the conviction
that they had always been right, that they were revolutionaries who had
steadfastly defended Mao Tse-tung Thought, went to their heads. They
considered themselves heroes and they began to think that the community
owed them a debt of gratitude. Step by step they began to abuse their
prestige and power, or at least so numerous critics later charged.

The ringleader in the abuse of power was Fast Chin. He was older than
Swift Li, more experienced in the ways of the world, more adept at manipulating affairs in his favor, and more attracted to pleasure, particularly
the pleasures of the flesh that he had pursued with enthusiasm as a bachelor militiaman. In 1968, however, Fast Chin was no longer a bachelor.
Losing out in the contest for the hand of his widowed sister-in-law had
apparently wounded his pride much more deeply than it had his heart.
When Little Shen married the woman Fast Chin wanted the most, the
jilted suitor joined the army. While serving far from home, he arranged a
match with a Linfeng woman he seemed to want very little, if at all. After
he brought her home to Long Bow she bore him a son, while he pursued
other women wherever he found an opening, whether in the courtyard
next door, in the inns of Changchih, or on the road in distant countries.
His most notorious liaison, as noted earlier, was with the famous "Songbird of Horse Square," the "Flower of Long Bow," the twenty-year-old
opera star Shih Kui-hsiang.

As a demobilized army man wearing three hats (vice-chairman of the
Brigade Revolutionary Committee, member of the Brigade Party Committee, and captain of the Brigade Militia), Chin felt politically secure enough
to court Shih even though her father was under surveillance as a member
of the Legion of Mary and her uncle the priest was in prison for life as a
notorious Catholic counterrevolutionary. Not only did he do nothing to
conceal this relationship, he seemed to go out of his way to flaunt it. When
he went to Changchih on business he took Shih Kui-hsiang along, treated

her to restaurant meals, bought theater tickets for two, and shared a room with her at the inn.

When Fast Chin's cronies dropped over to his house for the evening, Shih Kui-hsiang came across the yard to preside, just as if the house were her own. Dressed as she would have been for a role on the stage, she fixed and served all food and drink; rumor had it that Chin was so fond of her cooking that he would not eat a meal prepared by any other hand.

When not presiding at Chin's house, Shih turned her own dwelling into a reception center for brigade cadres, or at least for those cadres who could count as Chin's henchmen. These included Swift Li, the police captain Wang Wen-te, Splayfoot Tseng, Lin Yao-lung and Chi Yung-fu, all militiamen, and last but not least, Whiskers Shen, the most notorious scoundrel in the suburban area. Shih's husband, the cement plant worker Pei Chi-fa, when not required to work the night shift, also joined in the festivities.

Some years later, when the propaganda team accused Swift Li of eating and drinking in Shih Kui-hsiang's home, he denied that it had ever been his custom.

"I drank wine there only once."

"But everyone says that you and Fast Chin often ate food prepared by Shih and drank wine poured by her hand."

"In Chin's house, yes, many times, but in Shih's house, no. I only went there once."

Shih Kui-hsiang very much wanted a child but never conceived one. She applied to the commune authorities for the right to adopt a daughter. In the meantime she enjoyed looking after Chin's baby son. One day she took him out to the fields, dug up some potatoes, and tried to roast them over a fire made of cornstalks. This aroused a storm of criticism, but Fast Chin would not allow people to bad-mouth Shih. "It's not her fault. If you have to criticize someone, criticize me." Saying that, he went out, found a few potatoes, cut them up, buried them in the potato patch and said, "There, I've returned the spuds."

The advantage to Fast Chin of a liaison with Shih Kui-hsiang can readily be imagined. But what was there in it for her? Protection, for one thing. Because she was the niece of a "counterrevolutionary" and the daughter of a man under supervision, her position in society was patently insecure. Who could tell when another movement against the four bad categories (landlords, rich peasants, counterrevolutionaries and bad eggs) might suddenly blow up and pinpoint her as one of its targets? The better her relations were with the militia captain, and through him with the brigade Party Secretary, the safer she would be in a storm. Even if Fast Chin had been ugly, awkward and old, rather than handsome, dashing and young, self-preservation would have dictated a positive response to his advances. Furthermore, Shih's husband could hardly object. In these uncertain times the couple's right to live in the community could stand or fall with the fortunes of this illicit intimacy. Team Leader Pei Liang-shun also had a stake in the outcome. After all, he was married to Shih's cousin, Shih Kui-chen. If the case ever broke, the authorities might tar him with guilt by association.

Fast Chin's affair with Shih Kui-hsiang was reminiscent of that earlier liaison between Party Secretary Hsin-fa, and the rich peasant widow's spoiled daughter, Pu-ch'ao, at the time of the land reform in 1948. At that time Pu-ch'ao, though married to a poor peasant and classified as one, feared expropriation as a target of the final campaign for the distribution of wealth. She could not but welcome attention from the most important cadre in the brigade, a man with the power to uphold her rights as a poor peasant or to reverse all earlier decisions and call her a rich peasant. The fact that Hsin-fa was both handsome and charming only added spice to a liaison which self-interest propelled her to accept.

Fast Chin's triumphs in affairs of the heart deeply influenced Swift Li, his constant companion at work and at play. Though Li had married for love and was already the proud father of several fine children, once he became Party Secretary he began to show an interest in women other than his wife. Soon the village pulsed with rumors about the extramarital affairs of its leading citizen. While the rumors shocked some, they set others to shaking their heads in disbelief. Swift Li was not, after all, very handsome or dashing. He could hardly be expected to rush village belles off their feet as Fast Chin was wont to do. With his body slightly stooped, his shoulders humped and his head thrust awkwardly forward, he had always been shy and somewhat ill at ease in the company of women. A single female word, glance or gesture had often been enough to send a rush of blood to his face, suffusing its broad surfaces and high forehead with a bright red flush that he could not control. Nevertheless, attractive young women, many of them married, suddenly began competing with one another for his attention, and rumor had it that he carried on at one time at least eight different liaisons. How anyone kept track of all this is difficult to say, but people assumed that where there was so much smoke there must be some fire. Since eight girl friends at once was quite a lot, especially for a man with so many physical and social liabilities, some people began to call him *huen wang*—a term reserved for the most corrupt of emperors, for a ruler unsatisfied in spite of 1,000 wives.

The secret of Swift Li's sudden attractiveness to women was, of course, power over their daily lives. As the saying goes, "If you know someone in the kitchen, you can always be sure of a bowl of soup. If you know someone in the palace, you can always be sure of a lucrative post." Once he became Party Secretary, everyone interested in special treatment of any kind, every-one in need of a favor, set out to flatter him, to play on his youth, his impressionable nature and his deep attraction to the pleasure-loving life pioneered by Fast Chin.

But what special treatment, what favors, would young women want or need in socialist Long Bow?

To start with, of course, there were people like Shih Kui-hsiang who lived under a political cloud because their relatives had bad reputations or bad records. While Kui-hsiang's notorious relatives lived in Horse Square, Long Bow had its own quota of family heads under supervision as class enemies. One of the most notorious of these was Wu Kuo-fan, an ex-bandit classed as a counterrevolutionary. His beautiful daughter Yü-chen lived at home and looked after him. Whether she set her cap for Swift Li, or he picked her out for pursuit, is not clear. What many people began to notice was that he spent an unusual amount of time at her house and in her company. If you could not find Swift Li anywhere else in the village, the chances were good, if you went to Wu's house, you would not be disappointed. Such was the street gossip in those days. Obviously the arrangement was advantageous to old man Wu. How could he fail to be nice to the brigade Party Secretary?

But it was not only class enemies that could benefit from a friend "in the palace." If a young woman wanted to be accepted into the regional middle school, attend a training class, or win appointment as a delegate to a municipal meeting, a recommendation from the brigade Party Secretary was considered a necessity. Some people even depended on his word to eat. There were quite a few young women in the village whose husbands lived and worked outside, earning as little as 30 or 40 yuan a month. These women either did not work themselves or did not work as many hours as was necessary to earn their basic grain ration. They received their per capita grain from the brigade, but like the thief Chi Chung-ch'i always fell behind when it came to earning the work points needed to pay for it. If they had been real hardship cases, the brigade might have allocated relief funds for their survival, but since, like thief Chi, they themselves possessed labor power and since their husbands were unquestionably able-bodied, the brigade expected them, in the long run, to pay their own way. If they did not, the supply officer was supposed to cut them off. However, if the brigade Party Secretary said, "Give the woman her grain, let her pay for it later," the grain would continue to flow without more ado. What greater incentive could be imagined for being nice to the man in charge?

All talk of illicit liaisons upset Swift Li's wife, Kuan Hsiu-ying, very much. She didn't know how much of it to believe. After all, her husband's many rivals for the leading position in the brigade, and particularly the leaders of the faction he had helped suppress, not to mention all its ordinary members, would naturally make him the target of every kind of slanderous gossip. What better way to destroy a man's prestige? Nevertheless, the rumors persisted ominously. Swift Li spent little time at home and often stayed away from one day to the next. In 1967 his excuse was that *Petrel* and *Shankan Ridge* stalwarts were looking for him. If they found him alone they would beat him up. Therefore he slept at a different home every night, just as the puppet village head Shang Shih-t'ou had done during the Japanese occupation, when he knew that the Eighth Route Army wanted to settle accounts with him. At that time underground activists upset Shang's wife with stories of unbridled philandering. To pacify her, he had to return home. As soon as he did so, they caught and killed him.

In 1968 sleeping away from home for safety's sake could hardly be justified. Yet rumors persisted about Swift Li. None of them was very substantial. One day a neighbor told Hsiu-ying that she had seen her husband in a nearby house alone with a young woman. Hsiu-ying approached the building quietly and locked the door from the outside, then went to the neighbors for help. Nothing came of her efforts because Swift Li claimed that he and the young woman were only talking about village sanitation.

Chang Kuei-ts'ai, at that time vice-chairman of the brigade, once looked all over the village for Swift Li, only to find him, in the end, in the electrician's shop, lying on a kang in the dark. When Chang turned on the light Swift Li and a young woman sat up, their faces flushed red.

"What are you doing here?" Chang asked.

"Talking about the Youth League," both said at once.

How could anyone prove otherwise?

In time incidents and rumors involving Swift Li eroded Hsiu-ying's faith in her husband to the point of despair. She decided on a silent protest. She climbed to the loft of her house and lay there without making a sound for several days. Swift Li had no idea where to look for her. He searched every possible corner, even plumbed the village wells, fearful that her body might be floating in one of them. When this proved fruitless he sent a messenger to check out the Kuan family courtyard, thinking perhaps she had returned in anger to her mother's house, but to no avail. He also asked his mother (not his foster mother, but his real mother) for help. He felt certain Hsiu-ying was already dead and feared he himself might be held responsible. "Next thing you know, I'll be hauled into court!"

Finally he sent for his wife's aunt, an old woman whom Hsiu-ying dearly loved. This aunt broke down weeping in Swift Li's house. Hsiu-ying, already half delirious in the loft, heard the weeping and began to weep herself. She crawled over to the opening in the ceiling and fell down the ladder to the floor. Her aunt picked her up and they wept in each other's arms for a long time.

Thus began the Long Bow legend about the bride who fell from heaven. According to the tale we heard in 1971, Hsiu-ying had spent eight days in the loft without food or water.

What with the "Songbird of Horse Square" pouring wine for the cadres and "brides falling out of heaven," the moral atmosphere in Long Bow spiraled downward. Since leading cadres failed to set strict standards for themselves, others found it easy to tread the path of least resistance, and this was particularly true of certain militiamen under Fast Chin's command, who tended to become increasingly arrogant as time passed. As members of the great *United* movement which had been declared "correct," they saw themselves as staunch warriors upholding Mao Tse-tung's line, fearing neither hardship nor death as they carried the revolution through to the end.

They spent long hours standing guard, searching for suspects, maintaining order at meetings, running errands for brigade leaders, and polishing their skills as riflemen and hand grenade throwers. In return for their services they saw nothing wrong with cigarettes on demand, wine with their food, free meals at brigade headquarters and free haircuts in town. Since, in their minds at least, they cut dashing figures, they also expected favors from women and boldly pursued those who caught their fancy.

Chang K'uan-hsin set the whole village gossiping when he took up with a twenty-year-old whose husband worked on the railroad and spent most of his days far from home. Since K'uan-hsin was forty and had been in poor health for some years, it was hard to understand why a twenty-year-old would take any interest in him. But as the weeks passed K'uan-hsin's health improved remarkably. He regained weight, regained color and apparently regained the full vigor of his youth. Sometime later it turned out that K'uan-hsin, who was in charge of the brigade warehouse, had appropriated to himself a large stock of dried ginseng root and had regularly brewed and consumed enormous quantities of ginseng tea. Since the restorative ppowers of ginseng were well known to all, the mystery of K'uan-hsin's success with the maiden was cleared up and everyone had a good laugh. Whether or not he ever repaid the brigade for all of the expensive herbs he consumed remained unclear.

When it came to chicanery, however, K'uan-hsin was a rank amateur. He could not be compared to a professional rascal like Whiskers Shen. Four years of noble rhetoric had made no impression on Shen whatsoever. Quite the contrary, the free hand Fast Chin gave him to ride herd on the opposition and punish "bad people" had only made him bolder and more unscrupulous. The extraordinary upheavals and "left"–right swings of the Cultural Revolution helped him fine-tune his talent for political manipulation and developed his uncanny ability to play on the illusions and prejudices of ordinary mortals to the point where they found themselves handing out free what they would ordinarily charge a high price for, or would never part with at all.

Somewhere Whiskers Shen found a resplendent army uniform. He donned it whenever he wanted to go into town. Disguised as a trim soldier on urgent military business, he would stand outside the village entrance and hail the Changchih bus. When the bus came to a screeching halt, he would climb on with such verve and self-confidence that the driver never thought to ask if this new passenger was really a soldier. He took the uniform at face value and never asked for a fare.

Once he was inside the city limits Shen's options branched in all directions, but first on the agenda was always finding something to eat. During the spring festival fair he approached a comely out-of-town lass and invited her to share a meal with him at a booth operated by a donkey meat vendor from a distant commune. As soon as both had eaten their fill, Whiskers Shen excused himself, saying he would be right back with the money. He never showed up, of course, and the young woman had to pay the bill for two.

When Whiskers could not avoid work entirely, he joined the flatcart transport group that drove its donkeys wherever anyone agreed to pay for a load. Once the whole group hired out to haul cookies for the central coop in Horse Square. On his way through Long Bow, Whiskers managed to drop off several boxes of cookies at his own home and substitute a few bricks for the equivalent weight. When coop discovered the bricks, Shen pretended to be deeply shocked. He hinted that Lu Shui-ch'ang might be the man responsible. Shen's false charges and the subsequent investigation created hard feelings in the transport group for a long time.

It was only a few days later that Whiskers Shen stole the piece of brass that caused so much trouble for the propaganda team in 1971. What he stole was a worn-out brass bearing, but in the course of the investigation one of the cadres of the propaganda team went to the coop where brass was sold and prevailed on the clerk there to sign an affidavit that Whiskers Shen had taken a brand-new bearing and never paid for it. This affidavit provided ammunition for a case that could never be settled because it was based on false charges to start with.

Second to Whiskers Shen as a scoundrel and ne'er-do-well was the bachelor militiaman Splayfoot Tseng. During the height of the Cultural Revolution Splayfoot drew rations as a militia squad leader, but after the army suppressed factional fighting and imposed uneasy peace on the region, all militiamen were supposed to take up some honest work. Honest work did not exactly suit Splayfoot's temperament, however. He chose instead to try his hand at buying and selling. In 1968 the commodity that offered the best margin of profit was dried sweet-potato slices. Speculating in dried sweet potatoes meant jumping on the southbound freight, almost always made up of carloads of coal bound for the industries of Hopei, and riding it down into North Honan, where dried chips could be bought for 15 fen a catty. The chips were loaded on empty returning cars, and then swapped in Long Bow, pound for pound, for corn that could be sold for 40 fen a catty on the free market. This was approximately four times the official price.

In Honan dried sweet-potato slices, which were a grain substitute, could be freely bought and sold without ration coupons. They came under the same category as fresh vegetables and were sold on the open market by peasants who set up stalls for the purpose in the market towns, or traveled with their stocks from one local fair to another. It was illegal for outside buyers to purchase these chips in bulk, but no one objected to any individual who bought a pound here or two pounds there. What Splayfoot was wont to do, when he arrived in Honan, was to wander from place to place buying chips in small quantities wherever he ran across them, until he had accumulated at least 200 catties. Then he would pack them in two 100-catty sacks and carry them at night to the railroad yards where the northbound freight usually stopped for at least ten minutes. By using all his strength Splayfoot was able to toss these 100-catty bags over the side of an empty coal car and then jump in behind them himself. Train crews rarely caught anyone doing this because there were only four people on each train, two engineers and a firemen in the locomotive, and a brakeman in the caboose. They could hardly supervise the long coal trains effectively, even if they had wanted to, which seems unlikely, and peasants with wanderlust rode around China almost at will, carrying with them whatever they pleased.

People in the region as fast on their feet, agile and cunning as Splayfoot were few and far between. If anyone did surprise him he could always abandon his sacks and make a swift getaway. When I asked him if many people rode the trains he said, "No. Ours is a socialist society. Only a few people have any need to do anything like this, very few. I was one of the few who thought of it. There is no mass movement for riding freight trains."

Since there was no mass movement to cover his tracks, whenever Splayfoot made a trip into Honan, Swift Li heard about it. He sought out the wanderer and criticized him. "Why carry on all this illegal activity?" asked Li. "Why fall headfirst into the compost pile? Wouldn't it be better to come back to the brigade and do some honest work?"

Swift Li read selections from Mao Tse-tung aloud, reminded Splayfoot that his parents were famine victims and that he himself had been sold as a child for a peck of grain. Wasn't he taking advantage of other poor peasants? Wasn't he shamefully betraying his past and his class? Listening to the radio, Splayfoot also heard stories of past suffering. Once-destitute families, the radio said, now worked hard to transform society. Swift Li, backed up by the radio, shamed and moved him. He decided that he ought to do something for the brigade, make some contribution, take up some work, and drop his speculative adventures. When his eighty-one-year-old stepmother died, he asked the brigade for a job.

"I want to work," he said. "But I don't want anyone over me. I don't want anyone telling me what to do. I want to be my own boss and I want to come and go whenever I like."

This seemed like an impossible request, but Swift Li found a solution. He assigned Splayfoot to the Sidelines Team as a mulecart driver responsible for long distance hauls. This work from the very first day really suited the brawling militiaman.

"I took charge of a mulecart with three fine mules. I liked the work. It's hard. You are on the road day after day in all kinds of weather. But you can travel here and there, go everywhere, and have a look around. This suited me. I mean, I really liked it. I hauled coal, cement and many other goods, and I earned over 400 yuan a year. In addition to the work points that were worth 1 yuan a day, I got a 60-fen subsidy for expenses on the road. That's much better than any city worker can do. It's a very good job. And besides," said Splayfoot, returning to the aspect of the work that really attracted him, "I could wander around and see everything I wanted to see."

Alas, the job did not last.

Splayfoot drove the mulecart for almost three years. When he needed money for purchasing freight or for travel, he simply went to the brigade accountant and drew out 500 or 600 yuan, whatever amount the trip required. Then when he returned he handed in receipts for all of his income and his expenses. But without supervision he became careless about his accounts. Once he hauled coal for a man who paid him but did not ask for a receipt. This enabled Splayfoot to keep the 14.30 yuan hauling fee for himself. When the brigade accountant totaled up his ledger, he exposed this "take" and the brigade dropped Splayfoot Tseng as a driver. For a paltry 14 yuan he lost his chosen profession.

After that he started going to Honan again to look for sweet potatoes.

Notorious as Splayfoot Tseng was as a grafter, speculator and all-around rascal, there was at least one man whose reputation was far worse. This was Li Yü-ken, a brigade member of poor peasant origin who had always matched in daily life the old rhyme that ran:

> Ch'ih, ho, p'iao, tu, chueh,
> Hsiao t'ai t'an ke tsui!
> (Eat, drink, whore, gamble, and smoke dope,
> Then throw in a little stealing on the side.)

He had spent four years in jail for killing his wife with a blow to the head. He no sooner returned home than his daughter drowned in the privy cistern in the courtyard of his house. His reputation was so bad that many people found it easy to believe that this time he had done his daughter in. Li Yü-ken had it in for Secretary Chang Kuei-ts'ai because it was Chang who pressed the murder charges that sent him to jail in the first place.

Other militiamen in Long Bow with unsavory reputations included Li Yü-ken's son Li Shou-p'ing and Ch'en Liang-t'ien. The notoriety of the latter spread far and wide due, in part, to the flamboyant reputation earned by both his mother and his wife.

When Ch'en Liang-t'ien's father died, his mother never remarried. Feudal custom dictated that a widow should remain single and forever chaste in order to win from her sons, once they married, a plaque over the front door celebrating her virtue. In this case the plaque never went up. Ch'en Liang-t'ien's mother entertained many men, and though she had no use for children, periodically became pregnant. Once she wrapped a stillborn baby in a section of reed mat and threw it in the privy cistern. Ch'en Liang-t'ien spied the bundle in the gloom and pulled it out, only to earn a string of terrible curses for meddling in affairs that should not concern him. People called his mother "a broken-down donkey at a broken-down mill."

Ch'en Liang-t'ien's wife, well known for her beauty, played a different game entirely. She pioneered a revolving-door style of wedlock that was profitable indeed. She married three men in a row before she settled down with Ch'en. Each time she demanded a large cash settlement for her hand, honored her marriage contract for a month or two, then sued for divorce and went looking for a bigger offer.

When I asked why anyone would want her after such a string of tricks, I was told that if you posted a sign on each of the four gates of Changchih City stating what a "bad apple" she was, there would still be somebody that wanted her because he hadn't seen the sign. Beneath this marriage mill lay hard reality; men still outnumbered women in Southeast Shansi and attractive young brides could always command a premium price.

Party leaders assumed that rectification campaigns, reeducation movements, self- and mutual-criticism and community pressure would straighten out all reprobates and rascals in time. But taking the "long view" hardly solved the problem of how to restrain these elements in the interim, especially since so many of the unruly men were members of Fast Chin's militia. They stood guard at night, made arrests, kept order at meetings, and enforced the will of the brigade leadership when persuasion failed. And they gathered at Shih Kui-hsiang's house to eat, drink, sing and socialize without a bow, or even a nod, in the direction of traditional morality. How could the lawless uphold law and order? How could the self-indulgent put "public first, self second" and lead the way in building socialism?

These were the questions people were asking, privately at least, if not in public. And the answer was, of course, that they could not. Standing in the way of a deeper examination of this question was always factionalism. Swift Li and Fast Chin and all their supporters and retainers heard only that they had been on the right side of the battles of the Cultural Revolution, that they had upheld the revolutionary line. Why, then, should they criticize themselves? Why should they take their shortcomings seriously? Why, especially when the opposition, though defeated, had not been completely crushed, but still maintained a presence and a challenge in Long Bow and the region? Give the *Reds* the least opening, it was said, and they would certainly make the most of it.

THE DEVIL TAKE
THE COMMONWEAL

 In the strange political atmosphere that hovered over Southeast Shansi after the fighting had been brought to a close no true rectification was possible. No individual, no collective retained authority. Prior to 1966 the Communist Party had always set the tone. No matter what the abuses, no matter what the deviations, sooner or later the Party center had generated some cleansing wind. In spite of the strange goings on at Lushan, where Mao set out to destroy P'eng Teh-huai, faith in the Party and faith in its cause remained strong enough at the grass roots to cause some people, at least, to speak out in self-criticism and criticism of others that plumbed reality, confident that in the long run truth would be upheld and the cause of socialism would benefit. But now the entire Party organization had fallen into disarray. Half of the Party members were busy proving that the other half were counterrevolutionaries, and the army, the only place where the Party still remained intact in any meaningful sense, the only place where the authority of the Party still had clout, was busy backing one side against the other, an exercise that turned morality inside out and upside down and made rectification irrelevant. High-level hypocrisy elbowed people into cynicism. Since no center remained to which people could look for leadership, they fell back on their own resources, trying to make the best of a situation where all the rules had been bent and no one could be sure what the outcome of any action would be.

A journalist, overwhelmed by the endless possibilities of power seizure and counterseizure, wrote Mao a letter in the form of a poem, the essence of which, in rough translation, reads as follows:

> Round and round
> Spin the wheel,
> The devil take
> The commonweal.
>
> Rebels rise,
> Challenge all.
> Work teams come,
> Rebels fall.

Rebels rebound,
Work teams fall.
Rebel power
Crushes all.

Soldiers help,
Victims rise.
Victims rebels
Victimize.

Rebels rise,
Victims fall.
Soldiers rise,
Hold down all.

Round and round
Spin the wheel,
The devil take
The commonweal.

Through the decade of political drift that began in 1966 many individuals in Long Bow and the surrounding communities had little choice but to make their own way, not only in regard to personal morality but in regard to making a living. As political motivation receded, material incentive came to the fore. The trend showed up in many ways. One of them was the sharp rise in such budget items as the brigade entertainment fund. People who came to perform services for the brigade never did them well if they were not entertained well, which meant, in the main, if they were not well fed and liberally plied with tobacco and wine.

In 1968 Long Bow Brigade had no tractors of its own. Horse Square Commune had two big, seventy-five-horsepower track-tractors that could plow ten mou an hour and turn over the land to the depth of one foot. This was three times as deep as anyone could do it with a horseplow or a hoe. The speed and depth of tractor plowing made it advantageous to the brigade even though it required a cash outlay, and so the brigade leader invited the tractors in. But the brigade soon discovered that the open charges were only part of the cost of tractor plowing. There remained the question of entertaining the crew. Fed ordinary peasant fare, the tractor drivers did sloppy, uneven plowing. Fed better food, the drivers improved their work. Fed the best food available in the brigade, the drivers took great care, plowed the fields to a maximum depth, laid the furrows over evenly, and plowed out the ends and even the difficult corners.

This relationship between the level of hospitality and the quality of work became so notorious and so universal that it inspired some ironic verse:

Feed him porridge, he'll plow porridge land.
Feed him noodles, he'll plow noodle land.
Feed him wheat cakes, he'll plow wheat cake land.

Porridge land contained bumps, hummocks and hollows. Noodle land looked better, but the drivers failed to control the depth and neglected to plow out the corners. Wheat cake land satisfied all requirements. Local cooks fried wheat cakes in oil and often mixed in bits of meat and vegetables. When you fed the drivers wheat cakes, a form of large, flat pancake grilled over a very hot fire, they did their best work. Then the crops responded in kind.

It was not only tractor drivers who demanded good food, a special kitchen and quality cigarettes and wine. All skilled workers had the same demands, especially electricians and truck drivers. So demanding were they that the peasants classified them, along with tractor drivers, as the "three pests." They were "pests" who had to be bribed to do what they were supposed to do for ordinary wages. The airs put on by skilled workers and all their special demands underlay the coining of a new term by the peasants —"worker attitude." "Worker attitude" meant habitual arrogance, the arrogance of conscious superiority. In the latter half of the sixties, when anyone treated a brigade member abruptly or with disdain, it was said that "he pulled a worker attitude on me."

Skilled workers, of course, were not the only privileged beings who required special entertainment. Brigade leaders had to welcome and feed generously all buyers and sellers. If they did not, they could not make beneficial deals on behalf of the brigade. And the same was true of city or regional cadres who put in an appearance at the village level. Since they all held power, power that could hurt or help the brigade, the brigade had to entertain them royally. From 1967 through 1971, when Swift Li and Fast Chin ran the affairs of Long Bow, the amount of money spent on entertainment soared. Entertainment expenses which had been counted in the past by the tens reached 800 yuan in 1970. Cadres spent the money on wheat flour, eggs, bean curd, pork, cigarettes and wine.

People said that in order to handle outside contacts, official and commercial, it was necessary to arm oneself with a twenty-shot pistol (a pack of cigarettes), a hand grenade (a bottle of wine) and an explosive satchel (a carton of sweet cookies).

Brigade cadres called making a deal or solving a problem *yen chiu, yen chiu,* which meant literally to study things out. It also meant cigarettes and wine, since nothing could be studied out unless the main beneficiary of the deal provided cigarettes of high quality and good wine. The principals in any negotiation consumed ample quantities of both in the course of the long discussions required to resolve the fine details.

Brigade cadres, it was said, had to carry cigarettes in both pockets— ordinary brands in the left pocket to be smoked day in and day out, and in the right pocket a pack of Heavenly Gate cigarettes from Peking to offer visiting cadres and buyers.

From entertainment funds to small bribes made up of cigarettes and wine to outright embezzlement was not such a big step. During the period that the Two Gems led Long Bow, at least two people misappropriated more than 1,000 yuan apiece while more than a dozen others made off with amounts that varied from 100 to more than 500 yuan. The most serious charges involved Shen Chun-fu, the accountant for the Second Production Team who was said to have embezzled 1,641 yuan, and Lu Ho-hai, the accountant for the Sidelines Team, who was said to have embezzled 1,193 yuan. All the others accused of corruption were either accountants, buyers or materials handlers such as warehouse keepers. They all dealt with property or cash or both. No serious irregularities ever showed up in the accounts of the brigade leaders themselves, but Fast Chin was said to have warned Shen Chun-fu about the impending investigation of his accounts and came under suspicion as an accomplice.

During the Party rectification movement of 1971, the most serious financial irregularity attributed to Swift Li was the purchase, with brigade funds, of 1¼ catties of eggs to be taken along on an expedition by truck to buy and haul straw for community-owned draft animals. Some witnesses said that Swift Li ate the eggs, but Li said that the truck driver ate all of them and they should be written off as normal "entertainment" expense.

In the absence of significant corruption charges, the propaganda team charged that Swift Li had taken over a brigade with 20,000 yuan in the kitty, and so mismanaged things in the course of five years that the brigade fell 17,000 yuan into debt. This also proved to be untrue. When Li became Party Secretary in 1967, Long Bow owed the bank 17,000. In 1971 the debt remained the same. The brigade had paid nothing off, but neither had it borrowed more. From a management point of view, things could have been worse.

The most serious charge against Swift Li was that under his direction grain production fell year after year. Even if this had been true, and the figures seemed to belie it, one had to ask how much of the blame was his. Years of split, struggle, persecution, flight, return and further persecution for some, arbitrary, righteous power for others, and a steady inexorable drift toward the cash nexus that brought bribery and corruption in its wake, seemed to provide few of the conditions necessary for maintaining the relatively meager level of production that Long Bow had managed to achieve in the sixties, let alone any development of that production. But in the long run the factional struggle, severe as it was, involved only a small minority of the brigade's total membership. Furthermore, most of the confrontations occurred during the winter months, as did most of the armed fighting in the region as a whole. Throughout the growing season the vast majority of the population tilled, sowed, weeded, harvested and dried grain much as they always had before, and, strange as it might seem, production even rose a little.

In 1965, before the Cultural Revolution began, production had dropped below 20 bushels to the acre for the first time since 1960. In 1966, before the conflict at the middle school spread to the brigade, production rose above 20 bushels to the acre once more. In 1967, the year of the most intense political activity in Long Bow, the year of power seizure, counterseizure, north-south split, fist fighting in the streets and struggle meetings at night, production rose above 30 bushels for the first time in history. Though in 1968 yields fell back sharply due to bad weather, in 1969 they surged once again—this time to an all-time high of 32 bushels.

None of these fluctuations meant too much. In 1963 Long Bow peasants harvested just under 30 bushels to the acre. Eight years later, in 1971, they harvested almost 33. In between, the yields dropped sharply on three different occasions, but fluctuated around the 30-bushel mark the rest of the time. What this added up to was stability at a level three times that of the average production before Liberation. It also added up to stagnation because, while Tachai Brigade, under adverse conditions on mountain land, had already reached a production level of 100 bushels to the acre and the best brigades in Horse Square Commune had already surpassed 60 bushels, Long Bow was still producing as it had in the fifties at a 30-bushel rate. The brigade responded every year to mobilization from above with endless production meetings and cascades of stirring rhetoric but in the end, when it weighed in its crops, the results were about the same as in previous years.

These disappointing production figures were used as political ammunition in the factional strife that flared with such energy in 1967 and continued to smolder through the years that followed. In 1967 the *Mao Tse-tung Thought Red Guards* attacked the Fourth Team for neglecting production in order to engage in counterrevolution. They presented the charge with devastating effect in the form of a syllogism: Counterrevolutionaries sabotage production, hence poor production always follows counterrevolution. In this case the "counterrevolutionary" was Little Shen, who, once he was suspended from the Sidelines Team, took over the leadership of the Fourth Team, replacing Wang Wen-te, whose leadership the team members had rejected.

When the Fourth Team finally completed its harvest, however, the figures did not confirm the charges. Team members harvested 33 bushels of grain to the acre—the best record in the brigade—fulfilled their state grain quota, and distributed 370 catties of grain to each member. Furthermore, the grain they delivered to the state was of good quality and well cleaned—so good and clean, in fact, that the State Grain Company asked the commune to praise the Fourth Team. But the people in power had slandered the Fourth Team *Petrels* so persistently that they were unable to reverse direction. The charges of counterrevolutionary sabotage spread by Swift Li and Fast Chin continued to circulate throughout the commune. Li and Chin, now known to all as the Two Gems, repeated the charge that the Fourth Team had abandoned its land, neglected production, and put all its energies into counterrevolution. Confronted with a full quota of grain delivered to the state by the Fourth Team, the Two Gems said the grain turned in was poor in quality and dirty to boot.

"Let them talk," said Little Shen. "The crucial thing is whether we produce any grain or not.

"Our people really worked hard. They didn't even go home to eat at noon. They took their meals with them to the fields so that we easily came through the harvest rush. Then we cleaned our grain as we threshed it. We had a good harvest but our threshing ground lies in the shelter of the village. The breeze is not what it should be there. To overcome this we borrowed a winnowing fan from the Grain Bureau. We blew all of our millet nice and clean with electric power. When we turned it into the state we were told we had come in first in the whole of Horse Square Commune. Grain brought in by other teams had to be winnowed and recleaned, but not ours.

"So," said Little Shen, "in 1967 the Fourth Team carried out Mao Tse-tung's policy and worked hard. From backward we became advanced and this was due to the Communist Party, Mao Tse-tung Thought and the revolutionary masses. The people of the Fourth Team were happy, they made their state deliveries and harvested enough to eat!"

Whether the situation in the Fourth Team was truly that good is open to question. What seems certain is that slanders about the team continued to circulate in the face of much evidence to the contrary. How could anything go right in "Little Taiwan" (as Wang Wen-te called the Fourth Team)? He said this out of spite after the team rejected his leadership, but many brigade members, taking their cue from him, actually began to view it that way.

After another year passed and production continued to stagnate in the entire brigade, people began to hold Swift Li responsible. Then the political pressure on the Fourth Team eased. Even though Swift Li continued to make Little Shen the target of attack from time to time, it was harder and harder to blame him for the state of affairs in a village where he no longer held any power and to which, for long periods, he dared not even return. The Two Gems were clearly in charge in Long Bow. If things went well, they could claim the credit. If things went poorly, who but they should take the blame?

The authorities, from the level of the Central Committee on down, tried to spur production primarily by upholding the example of Tachai. What they stressed as most exemplary about Tachai was its spirit, the development of socialist consciousness, faith in the power of the collective, pride in community self-reliance and confidence in the ability of men and women to transform nature through hard labor.

Once people developed the Tachai spirit and the Tachai outlook, Party leaders said, great changes inevitably followed. Whenever a community succeeded in transforming itself, it was because, first of all, thinking had changed. Thus spirit, not objective reality, decided the future. A poetic comparison described this to Long Bow peasants over and over again:

> Tachai,
> High mountains,
> Rock-strewn slopes.
> Step out the door,
> Start climbing up or down.
> Yet Tachai people reap 1,000 catties per mou.

> Long Bow,
> Flat land,
> High water table.
> Step out the door,
> Walk five li without interruption.
> Yet Long Bow people harvest only 200 catties per mou.

Tachai people, it was said, went to work like a wall, then spread out like bees. Long Bow people went to work like bees, then spread out like a wall.

"Going to work like a wall" described how Tachai people reported to work together, on time and in a disciplined manner. "Spreading out like bees" described how they went their own way in the field so that each person could work at his or her own pace, each doing his or her best and paying no mind to the fact that others might be doing more or less. All this was possible because Tachai based work points on each individual's worth measured against criteria respected by all.

Long Bow people, on the other hand, came to work as they chose, some on time, most of them late. As they worked they formed a solid line across the field, a line that adapted to the pace of the slowest worker. Since their work points did not adequately express individual differences, no one wanted to be out front and no one wanted to fall behind. No wonder that yields suffered and work-point earnings remained low.

Another way of describing Long Bow people at work in the field was to say that they resembled a dragon—all bunched up. Since Long Bow people felt dissatisfied with their work points, they worked poorly without supervision. Leaders therefore drew back from a rational division of labor. Instead of sending people out individually or in small groups to accomplish distinct but complementary tasks, they bunched them up in gangs where they could more easily supervise them. But this could hardly be called good planning.

From above came the demand that Long Bow people study Tachai.

83

THE FAT OF THE LAND

 Truly Tachai had achieved results worthy of study. In one month there Carma and I had seen tremendous crops—corn yielding 150 bushels per acre, sorghum yielding 200 bushels—growing on terraced land created by knocking down loess ridges by hand. Tachai peasants used the rich loess to fill gullies with good soil, then held this soil in place with masonry walls all of which arched, horseshoelike, toward the mountain. The arching gave the walls enough strength to withstand the washouts brought on by the torrential rains of July. The labor required to build these terraces was enormous, amounting to thousands of man-days per acre, but the results fully justified the effort, especially since during the winter months people had nothing else to do.

A nitrogen fertilizer plant that fixed nitrogen from the air with coal gas helped guarantee high yields on the remade land. The county government built the fertilizer plant with money allocated by the Central Government after Tachai people had shown what they could do through self-reliance. It demonstrated the power of modern technology when linked to sound cooperative effort. As Premier Chou En-lai told us, Tachai was an example, not of absolute self-reliance, but of self-reliance in the main.

The brigades and communes of Hsiyang County, after transforming large areas of land at the community level, had turned their attention to the much larger, untapped resources of the county's five river valleys and the waste-lands on the mountaintops.

We saw dikes several kilometers long that held one great river to the south side of its flood plain while soil, carried in by hand, filled in the boulder-strewn space on the north side. The large flat fields thus created could be irrigated with river water and produced corn, millet, sorghum grain and even rice in abundance.

We saw a tunnel that pierced a perpendicular cliff and diverted a river from an entire half-mile loop. The peasants of one brigade had blasted the tunnel through several hundred meters of rock, built a dam to block the river, then carried in soil to create new fields in the riverbed all the way around the loop. With this one project they more than doubled the land available for tillage in their brigade.

We saw whole forests planted on mountaintops that had previously been barren. To ensure that the trees had a chance to grow, the brigade strictly controlled the areas to be grazed and the areas to be reforested. White-washed boulders, clearly visible for miles, marked the borders between the two.

With the exception of the terracing at Tachai Brigade itself, most of this work began in 1967 after Ch'en Yung-kuei assumed power in Hsiyang County as chairman of its revolutionary committee. Taking seriously Pre-mier Chou En-lai's advice to avoid choosing sides in the factional disputes that plagued Shansi Province, Ch'en concentrated on mobilizing the whole county to learn from Tachai. In brigade after brigade he helped bring forward a core group of leaders who believed in putting politics in com-mand, in putting public interest ahead of private interest, and in developing the full potential of their community through self-reliant capital construc-tion as Tachai had already begun to do. This reorganization stimulated a remarkable rise in productivity throughout the county.

After the peasants turned their attention to the riverbeds and the mountaintops, the scale of the projects soon surpassed the capacity of individual brigades to carry them through. They required concentrating the labor power of several brigades, of whole communes or of several communes working together. Ch'en therefore advised the formation of special teams for capital construction. The productive forces and wealth created at the commune and county level by these special teams opened up the possibility of higher levels of cooperation, higher levels of account-ing and sharing.

Organizing whole communes as functioning producer cooperatives, rather than as service centers for production brigades, suddenly became practical. Even the question of an eventual leap to state-owned agriculture by merging all production units into one large county farm came into focus as something that this generation and not some distant descendants might have to consider.

As Ch'en Yung-kuei spoke of his hopes and plans, he radiated an enthusi-asm that was infectious. Seeing things momentarily through his eyes, visi-tors caught a glimpse of the great potential of the Chinese countryside in the hands of a creative peasantry. The excitement of his vision of new levels of human relationship liberating untapped productive forces, which in turn must generate new human relations in a constantly rising and expanding spiral, swept them along.

"What I have really felt during these years," said Ch'en, "is optimism."

Listening to him, we found it easy to share this optimism and to recognize it as a significant social force in the Chinese countryside:

> Before 1966 the production of the whole county never exceeded 70 to 80 million catties of grain. No year's record went above this figure. Our 200,000 people farmed 400,000 mou of land that yielded 200 catties per mou or 400 catties per person. [1 mou = 1/6 acre; 1 catty = 1.1 pound.] This had to supply seed, feed, food, sales to the state and accumulation funds. If one took out the grain needed for all other purposes, the people were left with only 200 catties per year

to eat. Since production was low, sales to the state were also low. They amounted to only 7 million catties in 1966. We actually sold 14 million catties that year but had to ask for 7 million back in order to get through until the next harvest.

With 1967 things began to change. In 1967 we set up a new Revolutionary Committee, drew up a plan to change the backwardness of the whole county, and began to rearrange Hsiyang's mountains and rivers. After 1967 production went up year after year, and it went up in a straight line. From 200 catties per mou in 1966 to 650 catties per mou this year for the whole county; once you compare you can see what is involved.

By 1970 the production of the whole county reached 200 million catties, or more than 1,000 catties per capita, all this in only four years' time. We were able to sell 52 million catties to the state. Each year these sales have gone up and the amount of food for each person has also gone up. Now each person has 530 catties for consumption. In 1966 only Tachai Brigade made bean noodles for the state. Now there are over 300 bean noodle plants in the county, consuming more than 12 million catties of grain. We sell all the bean noodles to the state to help support factories in the city. This is in addition to the grain supplied to the state under the quota. Before 1966 we always held back 5 percent of our quota grain to make these processed food products. But now we don't hold back anything. We make noodles with the surplus grain held in each brigade and this amounts to much more grain than we used to sell to the state, several times more. All this goes to show that our surplus is rising. Our consumption is also rising, and all because our yields are rising. Only if this holds true can we say that we are really supporting the cities, new industries, national defense and world revolution.

This year, barring unforeseen disaster, our county should harvest 260 million catties, or 1,300 catties per person. We will sell about a third of this to the state as surplus. That amounts to 400 catties per person, or 80 million catties all told, which is equal to our total production in 1966. But even with these huge sales each person will have 900 catties left over. Even if they eat 600 they will still have 300 to spare. Can we order every peasant to eat 600 catties, eat it up come what may? Hardly. No one can eat 600 catties, or even 500 for that matter. Should they sell their grain on the free market just because they have a family surplus? No. We should educate people to save grain. Since we have a lot, we should save a lot. We'll order everyone to take his or her 600 catties home. Since they can't eat it, they must store it away, store it in their own homes. Here at Tachai we can't memorize quotations from Mao Tse-tung so well, but real grain is on hand in the people's homes.

In the course of the struggle, people have transformed their personal thinking. If you only talk about how good Mao Tse-tung's line is but the peasants have no grain stored away and no money to spend, you won't prove a thing. Political and economic struggle is very sharp. Line struggle is very sharp all around. All those who shout about boundless loyalty, saying whatever they like but doing no hard work every day, such people are not loyal.

Contradictions are always coming up. In our county we are already aware of the contradiction between advanced and backward units. Advanced units tend to become all the more advanced while some ordinary units meet trouble and find no way out.

One solution would be to merge small collectives into larger ones. But backward units that haven't done so well feel they should go the other way and try small-scale organization. They are discouraged and feel that they have fallen too far behind. They feel that the gap is too great, that things are too far out of balance. They want to go forward but they have fears. They fear that others will walk too fast and that they will lag too far behind.

So we have to come up with new ideas and develop new plans. We are thinking about how to solve problems of production based on new [higher] levels of organization. And we are thinking of how to help backward units catch up with advanced units in order to get balanced progress in the whole county. We are also thinking of more collective reserves as a means of capital investment. But some say that too great a collective reserve will violate the "Sixty Points."*

What we are experimenting with are special teams on the county, commune and brigade level. Such teams were popularized in 1968–69. Now every brigade has its special team and this has led to charges that we are blowing up a Communist wind. Rumors about this are widespread in Shansi. But really, this cannot be called a Communist wind. We have already been through all that. The Communist wind involves, besides false reports, the transfer of wealth without compensation, from individuals to the collective, or from lower collective levels to higher ones, as happened in the case of the pigs. First transfer the pigs to the commune and then transfer the feed. First ask for brigade labor power to build the commune pigpen, then take over brigade land to build the pigpen on.

Now that we have created special teams, people say the Communist wind is blowing again, but we don't agree.

Special teams pool labor power for basic construction of land, of dams, of reservoirs. When they fix up something, they obtain results right away, the very first year. They create a productive force that didn't exist before. There is no leveling and transferring in the old sense at all. These special teams are not transferring wealth; they are creating new wealth. This is not unreasonable. They are made up of people from the lowest units who are assigned to brigade-, commune- or even county-level projects. The group now working at the

---

*The "Sixty Points" is officially called "Regulations on the Work of Rural People's Communes—Central Committee (Revised Draft)," September, 1962; also known as the "Sixty Articles on Agriculture." That document lays down the rule that reserves set aside should be less than wealth distributed.

county farm at the river's edge is a case in point. Quite a few people are involved.

In 1967 we tried allocating 10 percent of the labor power of certain brigades to collective projects. We wondered what the effect of such an allocation would be on the brigade's own production. We didn't dare do this on a large scale, but only with the manpower of a few brigades. Not only were the results not bad, production inside the brigades increased. They worked better with 10 percent less labor to command.

Why would we want to transfer workers into special teams? There are all kinds of rivers and ravines in our county. How can they be fixed up in a short period of time? If you really want to fix them up you must find a workable method that will serve as a good example. When we transferred labor power out we did not undermine enthusiasm in the brigades. The 90 percent left behind worked harder than before and did a better job. When brigades have lots of labor power they figure that labor is no problem. There is plenty of time and there are plenty of people. But once we transfer some labor out we alert the brigade leaders. They no longer feel so confident. Labor shortage spurs their activism. Even though 10 percent doesn't amount to very much, its removal sends out a signal. As soon as we cut back labor power everyone becomes alert! All begin to ask, "How can we solve this problem? How can we mobilize the rank and file? How can we develop new techniques?" Cadres become active. They all use their brains. They all begin to think up good ideas. And the people come out to work more days each year.

To begin with, we chose two spots where we could reclaim land in the riverbed, one at Feng Chu, a commune project, and one at Chieh Tu Ho, a county project. The success of these two experimental projects had an immediate effect. People saw that in a short time great things could be built by concentrating labor. They recognized the advantage of special teams. The more labor power we transferred out, the better they did back home, the more their yields increased. It spurred the whole year's production. Thus these two projects created a model for the whole county.

At Chieh Tu Ho we built a long dike and reclaimed 3,000 mou. At Feng Chu we added land to the riverbank and created 1,000 mou. In one year we built dikes and dams, carried in soil, and reaped crops from the rocky riverbed! Chieh Tu Ho, with the help of labor allocated from all over the county, harvested more than 400,000 catties of grain. Feng Chu, with labor from the whole commune, harvested 140,000 catties.

We summed up this experience and organized visits to study these places. Then we asked the brigades to discuss the problems of labor-power shortages. Thus the lessons of these two examples spread. All over the county people began big projects fixing up the rivers and mountains. If one counts only the dams and dikes in the riverbed, we have built two million meters of stonework and filled in 50,000 mou of new land. From this new land alone we should get about 30 million catties of grain this year. I'm counting only the land already planted to crops. There is still more land under construction, land that has not yet been filled in or that has not yet been planted.

But did projects like these silence the critics?

No. In 1968 and 1970 some people still tried to slander us, saying we had blown up another Communist wind. Visitors from many different places all said they had heard such stories. We, on our part, were determined to stand by our plan and withstand this slander. But even though we stood firm we could not really relax. Sooner or later these stories would surely reach the Central Committee in Peking. We felt that if leading comrades from the Central Committee could come here and have a look it would be much better. If we had done wrong it could be corrected. If we had done right it could be confirmed. Last year, members of the Central Committee finally came. They liked what they saw. And we discovered that what we had organized was a "special team" system.

Central Committee members said, "You have 'special teams.' Big construction cannot be done without them."

Feeling that we had the full support of the Central Committee, we stood firm. We give no credence to that Communist wind talk. If there is no clarity as to what constitutes a Communist wind, what constitutes leveling and transferring, as distinct from the solid development of productive forces, one can't launch projects like this.

What happened in 1958, the year of the Great Leap Forward, was that the county took wealth from the commune and the commune in turn took wealth from the brigades. They transferred wealth from the strong places to fill in the weak spots. This was taking the wealth of the prosperous to give to the poor and the backward. This in no way increased the wealth of all, but only redistributed that which already existed.

If you see only this bad example and don't dare transfer any labor power from below, you cannot do any big projects. Those who accuse us of blowing up a Communist wind are not realistic. If that was what we were doing, how could our production go up so fast and so far? Those who don't dare concentrate any labor power are just sitting on resources. They are afraid to liberate productive forces.

Tachai people live very well. Why? As thinking changes, the land changes and yields change. If you want to increase production you have to liberate your thinking, transform the land and increase yields. You can't just sit there and hold the fort.

All this illustrates the superiority of the collective economy. If the collective doesn't dare carry on any projects to fix up land and reroute rivers, what can be said for the power of the collective? It is just as if large collective units had adopted go-it-alone, family-farm thinking. We must repudiate this hold-the-fort, go-it-alone, individualistic kind of outlook. We must set up examples of the superiority of our collective economy.

When all this came under attack our first reaction was, say what you want, we'll do what we want. Later the pressure got so great that we became upset. But we still did what we wanted. The more they attacked, the more we repudiated. And whom did we repudiate? Liu Shao-ch'i. We called all this talk "leftover Liu Shao-ch'i poison." That made these people very angry. So then we won a victory after all. We won on a new front and put down something wrong.

Now we are planning to build 800 reservoirs. Formerly we planned on the county and the communes doing most of the work. But now the brigades will do most of it. With 400 brigades, each will build two reservoirs. This includes large, medium and small reservoirs, but even the large ones will not be as big as the main reservoir on the river. As for the water storage basin on the ridge above Tachai, that is not a reservoir; it's just a pond, or a puddle. We call it a cistern.

When we started all this reclamation work, we quarreled over where to start. Should we start by fixing up some farm land in the riverbed, or should we first build reservoirs to hold back the runoff?

This was resolved in line with our old principle that practice should, first of all, suit the peasants. One must show some down-to-earth, practical achievement. This meant we had to start by fixing up some crop land. We created some new land in each of the riverbeds. Everyone watched happily as the new crops grew. All had but one worry. Will floods wash everything away? They couldn't help but worry over this. Everyone began to talk about the flood problem, talk that the county leaders fanned up. They helped spread the idea that the new land was bound, sooner or later, to be washed away by the river. As a result, the demand that reservoirs be built came from below. So today reservoirs are being built everywhere, quickly and well.

As the enthusiasm of the masses rose, we helped draw up plans for the reservoirs. Originally most of them were county- or commune-level projects to which we asked the brigades to contribute. But soon the brigades took over and now they work on their own. If people hadn't seen the good land in the riverbed they wouldn't have understood the importance of reservoirs.

All this goes to show that you must grasp the main problem to solve the secondary one. As soon as you build some land you start being afraid of floods. If there is no land to protect and you ask people to hold water back, they have no motive to do so and cannot be mobilized.

How are the special teams paid? They are paid primarily by earning work points in their own brigades; thus the brigades finance the project. When we allocate labor power from the brigades for reclamation work, nearby brigades contribute more labor power, and brigades farther away contribute less. Brigades that are still farther away don't contribute labor but earn work points from the county. They are paid out of public tax funds.

Actually, we financed the Chieh Tu Ho project in this way. Those who left home to work on it earned work points in their own brigades the first year, but as the project began to yield income the county paid the brigades back.

Up to now, workers on the county farm still count as members of their home brigades and earn work points at home. But as the farm is consolidated they will be transferred to it as farm workers and cut their ties to their home brigades. They will then set work points for each other based on mutual appraisal. Earnings will be paid out of the farm's income, but the amount will not be based on any proportionate share of that income as is usual in brigade distribution. They will get what amounts to a good average income in the county. If they were to be paid a proportionate share of the farm's income, their wages would be extremely large.

Through commune projects, the problem of commune accumulation funds has been solved. Brigades have always been required to contribute two to three percent of their income to the commune accumulation fund. But nobody has ever sent the money up. Brigades never liked to turn over money to the commune. On the other hand, they have been willing to allocate some labor power. If they send up labor power, they don't owe any money. With labor power the commune has the possibility of creating productive forces, reclaiming land, opening up livestock farms, et cetera, and thus the commune develops a source of income.

Even though our communes were set up long ago, as long as they had no income of their own the role they played was not outstanding. Now the commune plays an important role. It raises livestock, it raises crops, it has its own manure. It has its own income. It is in a position to help out weak brigades. This can't be called a Communist wind. Poor brigades and victims of disaster share the commune's wealth. This is indeed a Communist form of sharing according to need. But in this case the poor are not sharing the wealth of other hardworking brigades, but the collective wealth of the commune itself, a wealth they have helped to create.

These things must be analyzed properly. All sharing cannot be lumped together as a Communist wind. Whatever these poorer brigades need they can now get. If they need money, they can get money; if they need grain, they can get grain; if they need draft animals, they can get draft animals. In a sense the aid is very similar to state relief. But in this case there is no drain on the state. When a commune can relieve its members like this, then all members feel that the commune is good.

Of course, when the commune gives aid to a poor brigade, it tries to help out with means of production, not simply relief. In this way the commune helps the brigade get production going rather than merely giving brigade members something to eat or wear.

My idea at this point is to grasp the commune level. When a commune has a rich material base it can help the backward teams narrow the gap between them and the more advanced. At a certain point all can then merge at the commune level without dragging the more prosperous teams down. By helping the poor move up, the commune prepares the road to commune ownership and commune accounting. If we all merge in this way at the commune level, the rich brigades cannot object.

But if you talk about this too much, mentioning when and how, there are people who will start complaining that you are blowing up a Communist wind, that you want poor brigades to share the wealth of the rich. So even if you have a good plan in mind, it is better not to talk about it.

At Tachai Commune [of which Tachai Brigade is a part], we already have money to buy machines. We don't need money from the state or from the brigades. We have already created this kind of material base. Yet the accounting unit remains at the brigade level. Even maintaining it at the brigade level makes us subject to pressure because the whole country is learning from Tachai. When people learn that our accounting is done at the brigade level, it creates a similar demand on their part. But if a community moves to brigade-level accounting without having created the proper conditions, it will end up in a mess. Some places don't even have cooperative production at the team level yet, not to mention team-wide accounting. So when we take a step forward like this we have to do it quietly.

We must also consider the fact that our mountain brigades are small. Most of them have fewer than 100 families. If these were divided into production teams we couldn't possibly carry out the projects that we now undertake. Our brigades are really only about the size of production teams on the plains of Hopei.

We are also involved in controversy over private plots and the individual reclamation of wasteland.

At Tachai we have no need for private plots. Everything needed to sustain life is grown in the fields on collective land. We produce enough grain for all so there is no question of private plots.

In 1963 floods washed away the big fields of the collective, not to mention the private plots. In order to recover we had to fix up the collective land first. It would have been quite wrong to fix up private plots first. After conquering many difficulties and restoring the collective land to production, everything began to go well. So we said, "Let's fix up the private plots." But then the members all said, "This is wrong. We've been through such a disaster, we've overcome such hardship and famine, and it's all been by collective effort. If we had depended on individual, selfish thinking, how could we ever have stood up?"

The people equated private plots with selfish thinking, with individualism. Since all the crops, both high on the mountain and down below in the gullies, were growing well, since all the crops on large plots and small were growing well, we decided to do away with private plots. If you hand out private plots here now, people don't want them. They won't take them.

When visitors came and saw that the crops on all our land grew equally well, they were amazed. "At home," they said, "the private plots look better." Some of them, when they went home, confiscated private plots, expecting thereby to put all their land in top shape. But when they did this, the crops on collective land looked worse than before. Class enemies immediately spoke out:

"Don't study Tachai. It's a disaster. The more you learn the worse you get!"

The trouble was that these visitors looked only at the surface of our brigade and not at the essence, hence they brought disaster on themselves. We gave up private plots when the material conditions were ripe, when people no longer wanted them. But they confiscated private plots when the people still wanted them, and even wanted bigger plots. Conditions were unripe. Political consciousness was not high, therefore collective production did not go well either. Under such conditions you can't abolish private plots. People still think that their plots aren't big enough.

So now we don't talk about our brigade accounting or about the fact that we have given up private plots. Talking about it doesn't do any good; it only leads to criticism. We just say that our brigade is equivalent to a team elsewhere, that we can't divide our small unit further. It just wouldn't work.

Is brigade accounting universal in Hsiyang County? Let us just say we have quite a few units doing it. The important thing here is that collective consciousness has spread. When the big river is full, the little river overflows. When the big collective prospers, brigades, teams, families and individuals all prosper.

Actually we are running into a new type of problem. Our production is rising so fast that we are running out of labor power. We have given our mountaintop land and our sheep to the commune. We couldn't manage them all ourselves. In order to solve such problems we need mechanization and since the commune already has funds it is better for the commune to go ahead and buy machines rather than wait for the brigades to buy them. One big tractor, one big threshing machine, can do the work for several brigades.

As the water rises the boat goes up. Since production increases every year, so does income. Now in the commune as a whole each workday earns 1 yuan in cash. When it reaches 3 yuan there may well be a shortage of consumer goods. People could be standing in line all the way to Taiyuan. But if we didn't distribute the income to our members, and share it out with less-advanced units, wouldn't that be leveling and transferring again? Wouldn't that be the Communist wind? And wouldn't we be blowing it up ourselves?

In Tachai Brigade, for three years already, our workday has been held at the 1.5-yuan level. The people haven't complained about this fixed rate because our accumulation fund has gone up sharply. They know we are collecting capital and experience for a transition to commune accounting, which can be done when all workdays are worth 1.5 yuan but not when workdays are worth .5 yuan, or even 1 yuan.

We could probably afford to pay 3 yuan a day to Tachai Brigade members, but we couldn't reach commune accounting that way because we'd be too far ahead. With help from the commune the backward brigades now average 1 yuan. When they reach an average of 1.5 yuan, the level we are holding at, then the conditions will be ripe for commune accounting.

Once we have commune accounting, we can reorganize our whole plan of production. We can plant trees where they should be planted and grow crops where crops do best. We can concentrate on the larger fields and make full use of machines. Then everything will fall into its rightful place.

Now the commune has already reclaimed 300 mou along the river. The amount can be increased to 3,000 mou, all in one stretch. That one new field alone will equal three Tachai Brigades. Can the commune handle it? Maybe we Tachai residents will have to leave a few people up here to plant fruit trees while the rest move down to the riverbed to plant the flat land. Our brigade alone can't take care of all the new land that can be built. Neither can the commune take proper care of it. We may have to join forces with the other brigades, make a transition to commune ownership, and take care of everything together. If anyone says this is wrong and that we should split up again, let him explain how we are to solve this problem. We are not afraid to pool prosperity. We have too much. We have to share it. It's not the same as sharing poverty!

All this creates problems. Mao's slogan calls on the whole country to study Tachai. What is Tachai to do? We must move ahead. We must jump to a higher stage of organization. We are forced to do it by the development of production. But in relation to the situation in the country as a whole, it is premature.

What, then, is the next step? County-wide ownership [a form of state property recognized as property of the whole people]. The idea of making Hsiyang County a Tachai-type county contains the germ of this idea. When it materializes I could become the head of a farm that comprises the whole county.

Then the mountains will all be covered with trees while the big gullies and valleys will be covered with grain. By opening up the mountains and building all these reservoirs, we are preparing conditions for the creation of flat land. By creating flat land we are preparing conditions for mechanization.

Come back in a few years' time. We'll show you not only crops, but reservoirs. Hsiyang County will look like South China. Not only will we make it unnecessary to send southern grain north, we'll create southern-style yields in the northland! In the south the climate allows two or three crops a year. They add up to 800 catties per mou. Of course there are brigades there that raise more than 1,000 catties, but not many. There are not too many that have even reached the standard yield of 800, just as north of the Yellow River not too many have reached 400.

If we fix up our land and raise fertility we can easily get as much with one crop as they raise with three. Down there they start off short of labor. Raising three crops a year creates a very tight situation. They have to find time to plant and hoe three crops. We raise only one. We save more than half of the labor so we have manpower for new construction. If they plant rice, we can plant rice. If they have underground water, ponds and wells, we can build reservoirs all over the mountains. If the mountains of the South are covered with trees, we too can plant trees for timber and fruit. If we don't develop forestry, we can't catch up.

Before the Cultural Revolution I always wanted to go south to see for myself. Our yields were crossing the Yangtze [topping 800 catties per mou], but we ourselves never crossed the Yangtze to see what it was really like down there. During the Cultural Revolution I still couldn't go. Finally, this year, I made the trip: I saw the South and it gave me some ideas about what we must do. I also learned that the South has its shortcomings. I went there in winter. The days were either foggy or overcast. There was very little sunlight. In summer, they said, conditions are even worse. I thought to myself, at least we have sunlight. Once we fix up the land and raise fertility we can do more than they because we have the sun. I came back, thinking of Mao Tse-tung and his call: Make the North independent of southern grain.

But to accomplish this you have to carry out a revolution. Without revolution none of it is possible.

84

LEARNING
FROM TACHAI

 For Long Bow, bogged down in factional conflict and unable to push yields beyond the 30-bushel mark, questions concerning massive capital construction, special teams, commune accounting, or making the North look like the South could well seem premature if not wildly irrelevant. Nevertheless, Tachai had started out with much less in its favor than Long Bow. Most of what Tachai peasants had accomplished they had accomplished with their bare hands and a little dynamite. Surely there were some lessons there for Long Bow people to ponder. In any case, Party leaders were urging Long Bow people to study Tachai, so they embarked upon that task.

The best way to study Tachai was to go and visit the place. It was not so far away, only a day's ride by bus through some spectacular limestone mountains. A commune delegation, organized in 1969, held open ten places for Long Bow. Since there were eleven people who wanted very much to go, Swift Li, as Party Secretary, withdrew in favor of one of the team leaders. This was not because he didn't want to learn from Tachai, but because he was willing to give others the first chance. Critics later attacked him for stalling. Swift Li, they said, didn't care about Tachai. He refused to go there when he had the chance.

Fast Chin went to Tachai, but later, when someone criticized Long Bow methods, Chin replied, "The Tachai way, the Long Bow way, what difference does it make as long as we harvest the grain!"

People held this remark against Chin. They took it as a sign of defiance, a challenge to the commune leadership, the city, the region, the province and the Central Committee. But they never made the context of these remarks clear. It seems probable that Chin's words were no more subversive than Wang Wen-te's words about going to Peking to see Chairman Mao: "Even if you go, the grain won't grow in Long Bow unless you work hard here in the field."

Going to Tachai and bringing back something of value were two different things, however. Visits to model communities had developed as a custom in China ever since model peasants and labor heroes received publicity during the Anti-Japanese War. Over the years tens of millions of people had taken trips, long and short, to visit outstanding examples of production and creativeness. These visits often bore fruit, but apparently just as often they did not. Even if one was very impressed with what one saw it was not always easy to apply the lessons to one's home brigade. Already someone had written a poem about that, too:

> Moved when you see it,
> Moved again when it is explained.
> Motionless when you get back home.

In Long Bow we heard a story about a local peasant who visited the Red Flag Canal. He was so inspired by what he saw that he could hardly wait to get home. "The canal we have built is puny, it's not much better than scratching a groove in the ground with your toe. Just wait till you see what we can build!"

But on the way home everyday problems began to crowd into his mind. When he opened his door he found his wife yelling at the children, and the children, as usual, yelling at each other. Grand plans for canal building faded before the exigencies of the moment. He never got any large project off the ground.

This phenomenon, by no means unique, was summed up in another rhyme:

> At the meeting, wholeheartedly for it.
> On the road back, halfheartedly for it.
> At home, no heart for it. It is forgotten!

And the reason for this was that the advanced brigades were often so far ahead that the laggards had no way to catch up with them. Doing so in one big leap was obviously impossible. Small steps seemed grossly inadequate and soon faltered. What people needed was a long-range plan leading step by step to a higher level of achievement—concrete measures, solid work. Creating an enthusiastic atmosphere through public meetings, stirring slogans and individual mobilization ought to help, but very often such mobilization went forward without generating any concrete achievements. Enthusiasm then quickly dissipated and it became that much harder for the organizers to move people a second time.

This was exactly what happened when Long Bow people went to visit Tachai. They came back deeply impressed by such things as the fact that Tachai team leaders didn't ring any bell to wake people up in the morning, nor did they go from house to house knocking on doors. Tachai people showed up in the fields on their own and worked hard without supervision. They came back impressed by the fact that Tachai crops were a deep dark-green, reflecting ample fertilization and special care, and they attributed all this high morale and good crops to the Tachai work-point system, whereby all brigade members evaluated each other once a year through a system of self-report and public appraisal and then assigned each other points based on their work records, points that did not vary from day to day, and did not require any records other than attendance.

But when Long Bow people tried to hand out points this way, the system broke down. In Long Bow, people did not trust one another enough to speak from the heart. They made self-reports in the spirit of winning friends, influencing people and turning away wrath. Their public appraisals suffered from the same defects. The overall result was that they equalized their work points and smoothed out legitimate differences. This forced some people who always earned more than they deserved onto the defensive while it forced others, who always earned less than they deserved, onto the offensive. In the end everyone began to grumble and the crops suffered.

As one peasant summed it up, "We were impressed by the fact that Tachai's crops were green [good] but failed to grasp that this was because the people's hearts were red [revolutionary]. In Tachai they put politics in command. Here work points always take command."

After a second visit to Tachai, Long Bow peasants brought back a determination to improve housing. Tachai people had built solid stone caves for everyone, caves that were expected to last 2,000 years. Long Bow people were not so dogmatic as to decide to build caves for themselves—they did not, after all, live in a loess gully—but they did decide to build a lot of new houses, especially for the younger generation getting married, and these houses they built wider, longer, taller and better than the old housing had ever been. New housing improved the quality of life but generated criticism on all sides because it was not undertaken on the basis of any increase in production, any new level of prosperity. At Tachai the slogan had always been:

> Hsien hsiu p'o
> Hou hsiu wo.
> (First fix up the slopes,
> Then fix up the houses.)

But Long Bow people built dozens of new houses without any improvements on the land, and without any increases in yield. The new houses, in fact, cut down the crop because they occupied land on the periphery of the village that the brigade had always tilled before.

To visit Tachai was easy, to emulate Tachai was hard. People who went to see those five ridges and six gullies on the slopes of Tigerhead Mountain almost always learned something, but when they tried to apply it at home the results tended toward the extreme. To emulate the Tachai work-point system without the high level of unity and political consciousness that Tachai Brigade members possessed almost always resulted in ultraleft "leveling," in distortion of the distribution system based on the principle "to each according to his work," in the direction of extreme equalitarianism that distributed goods based on need, not work.

If, on the other hand, one came home impressed by good housing, and proceeded to emulate Tachai by investing heavily in housing, this became a rightist mistake, a premature emphasis on consumption under conditions where production could not sustain and did not warrant such consumption.

Wherever grain production remained low the resources of the community had to be concentrated on raising yields, on releasing productive forces in agriculture. Diverting funds to housing could only perpetuate stagnation.

Perhaps the primary lesson Tachai had to teach was to concentrate first on farm production and to treat sidelines as secondary. But even this obvious lesson was not well learned by peasant visitors from Long Bow. It was not that Long Bow's leaders failed to give lip service to the concept. Everyone knew enough to stress agriculture as the main task and grain production as the key link in agriculture, but when it came to actual practice, the best energies of the brigade, the most initiative, and the best labor power almost always ended up in sidelines. Sidelines developed whether anyone paid attention to them or not. And that was because labor expended in sidelines yielded both a more immediate and a larger return than labor expended in the fields. Central Committee guidelines limited the labor power assigned to sidelines to 15 percent of the total. In Long Bow there were times when 40 percent of the labor power went into sidelines.

Long Bow was no longer, in any sense, an isolated rural community. It was a suburban community situated at the heart of one of China's most rapidly developing industrial zones. The highway, the railroad, the railroad shops, the cement plant, the construction workers' encampment and the new east-west railroad they were building, the land set aside for the Taihang Sawblade Works, and the North Station complex one mile up the road all bespoke urbanization, industrialization and modernization. The industry, the transportation network and the frenzied pace of construction all created a demand for labor, both skilled and unskilled, and beyond that a demand for products, particularly building materials that nearby brigades could easily supply. Bricks, for instance, were in great demand. The soil of the Shangtang plain was well suited for brick making. Coal for firing brick kilns was cheap. Thus almost every brigade set up a brick kiln or two. These supplied bricks for home use and also on a major scale for the industrial construction proceeding on all sides.

The Long Bow brick kilns employed ten or twelve people on a year-round basis. Many more went out to do transport work as members of a flatcart brigade that could muster twenty carts. They hauled freight on contract for whatever the traffic would bear—raw rock to the cement plant, cement from the cement plant, freight to and from Changchih North Station, coal, pig iron, steel rods and bars, bricks, lots of bricks, tiles and countless other products. A much smaller group equipped with large carts powered by mules, three to a hitch, hauled similar freight on long-distance routes. A permanent crew of a dozen or more unloaded freight at Changchih North Station at so much a ton. Other crews, on a short-term basis, performed various industrial jobs on contract. Crews went out to Changchih Steel to cut steel rod, and to the Grain Mill Factory to cut iron bars.

Piecework jobs yielded the most profit. In 1970 the militiaman Lin Yao-lung led five people out to Changchih Steel to cut rods with acetylene torches. Lin's crew of six worked for three months and earned 7,041.75

yuan. The acetylene cost 1,311.85 yuan. They turned 3,538.90 yuan in to the brigade and got 181 workday credits apiece (more than two days for each day worked), and then divided the balance of the money, 2,191 yuan, among themselves for a bonus of 365.17 yuan per person. During the rectification movement critics charged them, not without reason, with profiteering.

All the projects described above fell into the category of brigade sidelines. The people who took part worked as a collective. They were supposed either to turn in their cash earnings for workday credits, or to turn in so many yuan per day for the right to work and keep the balance as personal earnings. When Lin Yao-lung went out to Changchih Steel he combined both these methods.

Other Long Bow natives worked outside, not in groups but individually, as so-called "temporary" workers. The plants that hired them paid their wages to the brigade. The workers themselves got credit for work points in their home teams. The brigade supplied such workers on contract to nearby industrial plants. Their work was not "temporary" in any usual sense but, rather, "long term." The contracts ran for two or three years. These workers were called "temporary" to distinguish them from regular plant workers who had what might be called "tenure" and enjoyed all the rights, privileges and fringe benefits of regular employees. The temporary workers had few rights and privileges and no fringe benefits because they did not "belong" to the factory where they worked, but to the brigade from which they came. That is to say, the city classed them as resident members of their local cooperative, not as factory staff. They had no residency permit, no ration book, no free medical care at the factory clinic and no right to send their children to the factory school. They registered as village residents, they got their grain as a share of the local crop based on work points earned, they paid a small fee every year for cooperative medical care, and sent their children to the village school. Any problems which they had they referred to their local brigade leader, not to the factory management. The factory had no responsibility for their welfare. As workers they were second-class citizens, but from the brigade point of view they were a sure and steady source of cash income.

Other peasants operated sidelines on an individual basis, as private enterprises. A few families still wove cloth at home, usually in their spare time, and sold it at retail. Chin Shen-yi continued to operate a repair shop that was so prosperous that he eventually acquired his own welding equipment and began to manufacture handcarts that he sold as far away as Hantan. Old Lady Wang's son, Jen-pao, all on his own, set up a bicycle repair shed beside the highway and did a thriving business. When the brigade could no longer ignore these "businesses," it incorporated them as concessions into the overall cooperative structure. Then Chin and Wang had to pay a concession fee of so many yuan a day to the brigade. Anything earned above that they kept as their own.

When one added up all these various nonagricultural endeavors they often absorbed as much as 40 percent of the total available labor power of the brigade. Since the sixty points issued by the Central Committee suggested 15 percent as a maximum, Long Bow was clearly out of line, and this was counting only the legitimate sideline and industrial employment. Above, beyond and between all these, various forms of buying, selling, speculation and commission-taking developed that were, if not overtly illegal, certainly illegitimate in a socialist society. I have already described Splayfoot Tseng's dried-sweet-potato racket. There were many others. Lin Yao-lung for many years bought silver coins in the Taihang Mountains and sold them as far away as Kaifeng and even Shanghai. Little Shen, as an adjunct to his legitimate efforts as sidelines manager, made private deals of all kinds that earned him commissions as a middle man.

There is no figure for the amount of income that came to Long Bow Brigade in this way because, since all such income was private, it went unreported. The figure for legitimate sideline income was reported as approximately 45 percent of the total. It played a role in the economy of the brigade out of proportion to its size because it represented a steady cash inflow that could be spent on production expenses such as seed, fertilizer and insecticides and thus guarantee the success of the main staple crops. It also gave the brigade cash that could be distributed to members prior to such major events as the annual fall fair and the New Year holidays. Most important of all, this large inflow of cash made it possible to distribute almost 1 yuan to each member for each day worked, a level of income not far below that of the industrial workers in the region and a level that made Long Bow an attractive place for immigrants to settle. If farming had provided the only income, a labor day in Long Bow would have been worth only 50 to 60 fen, which was about what many peasants in isolated mountain communities earned from their crops. Most people considered such incomes disastrously low.

Clearly, sidelines made Long Bow prosperous in spite of a stagnant agriculture. Sidelines grew by themselves without any major campaign to foster them, while all the campaigns to develop agriculture bore little fruit. Because sidelines absorbed so much energy and talent, Long Bow people had very little left over for application to their fields.

It would be wrong to put too much blame on sidelines for the stagnation of agriculture in Long Bow in the sixties. Sidelines diverted attention from agriculture, but there were many other problems, both technical and political, that made a breakthrough in farming difficult.

Technically, the character of the soil all around the base of the Great Ridge and Little Ridge hills presented the greatest problem. Most of the land on the Shangtang Plateau consisted of clay, laid down at the bottom of a great Shansi lake millions of years earlier, but the clay at the base of the ridge near Long Bow was particularly heavy and saline. Peasants found it harder to work, less productive and more subject to salt damage in the fall after the heavy evaporation of the summer months than any of the land nearby. Furthermore, nobody knew how to ameliorate this condition.

Long Bow clay presented a much more complex and stubborn challenge than that which confronted Tachai. Rich loess soil, some of it thirty feet deep, covered much of Tachai's Tigerhead Mountain. Over the years fierce torrential rains had badly eroded this loess, cut it into alternating sharp ridges and deep ravines, and washed thousands of tons of it away, but at the same time the loess that was left was marvelously fertile, not just at the surface in the layer known as the topsoil, but all the way down through to the bedrock. If one spread the loess out, all of it was fertile, or could soon be made so. Thus it was quite clear from the beginning what Tachai people had to do. They had to level the loess, build terrace walls to hold it in place, and bring water to the new fields thus created. If they did these things they could easily raise production year after year, cross the Yellow River and cross the Yangtze yieldwise, and serve as an example to all of China.

But what were Long Bow people to do? Most of their land already lay flat. Level fields stretched out from brigade doorsteps in every direction as far as the eye could see except to the south where the fields gradually rose to merge with the slopes of Great Ridge and Little Ridge hills—"Flat land, high water table. Step out the door, walk five li." Why, then, couldn't Long Bow surpass Tachai in yields?

The answer was obvious. Heavy soil, poorly drained, and subject to salt poisoning in the fall. "Fall salt land," they called it.

The advice that came from above, from the commune, from Changchih City, from the agricultural departments of the region and the province, was *irrigate*. Hadn't Chairman Mao called irrigation the lifeblood of agriculture? And couldn't irrigation double yields in almost every case? Higher cadres urged Long Bow peasants to irrigate, irrigate, and then irrigate some more. After the Great Leap in 1958, when peasant labor completed the Changchih Reservoir, irrigation suddenly became practical. Only a few li to the west lay an enormous body of water, many miles long and over a mile wide. After the region financed a pumping station on the bank of this man-made lake, all that was needed was a trunk canal to lead the water eastward onto Long Bow land. Through efforts jointly undertaken with other nearby brigades Long Bow completed this trunk canal by 1965. Thousands of people dug for a few weeks one winter and cut a channel through the heavy clay all the way to the highway. What remained for local peasants to do was to create a field canal system that could lead the water into the fields of the various teams and then level up the fields one by one so that these, in turn, could be irrigated.

As Long Bow people began this work, the problem turned out to be a little more complex than had at first appeared. The water in the trunk canal was too low to flow onto any Long Bow field. An intermediate pumping station had to be built to lift the water a second time. Since the best land lay to the east of the railroad, the brigade leaders decided to work at this first. They ordered pumps and pipes, built a pumping station, and constructed thousands of feet of secondary canal. Long Bow people invested some 6,000 yuan and 20,000 labor days on an irrigation system that was supposed to bring water to some 300 acres of their eastern land.

But things went wrong with the project from the very beginning. The engineers dispatched from the city made an error in the survey. The pumps, when they finally went into action, could not send enough water high enough actually to reach more than a fraction of the land. At the height of the growing season, when the crops most needed water, drought plagued Southeast Shansi and the water in the reservoir fell below the intake gates at the primary pumping station. Just when irrigation became critical, the pumps ran dry. When the water level at the reservoir recovered, other communities depleted the flow, leaving little or nothing for Long Bow in any case. Whatever reservoir water reached the fields brought results that were far from ideal. Irrigation caused the land to puddle. When the sun dried out the wet land, deep, wide cracks split it into cubelike blocks, thus exposing the roots of the small plants that were trying to establish a foothold there. As the season wore on, this irrigated land developed salinity. White crystals of salt formed across the surface, damaging or killing the few plants that survived. Then, before any of these problems could be studied or resolved, the city decided to locate the Taihang Sawblade Works right in the middle of the land serviced by the flawed system. The new Sawblade Works rendered the whole project obsolete. The pumping station and all its canals had to be abandoned. The Sawblade Works paid for the dismantling of the pumping station and the removal of the pumps to another site, but failed to pay anything for all the work that had gone into the rest of the canal system. Long Bow people lost 20,000 man-days, several hundred mou of land, and the potential irrigation of 2,000 mou, all in the space of a few days.

The dubious value of all irrigation on Long Bow clay made the losses easier to bear. If the system had been designed so that it really worked, if water had in fact doubled crop yields, the construction of a sawblade plant east of the railroad would have been nothing short of a disaster for Long Bow. As it was, the whole project had to be looked upon as an experiment that hadn't worked very well from the start. At least the sawblade plant would bring night soil to Long Bow and night soil could do more than water to increase yields. This night soil question was not a minor matter. Taihang Sawblade was planning to employ about 5,000 workers. Together with their families the new plant would create a community of more than 10,000, five times the population of Long Bow village. Since most of the night soil deposited by this huge mass of people must accrue to Long Bow, it opened the possibility of wonderful new crops on a reduced area of land.

The fiasco of the canal and the pumping station east of the railroad made no real impression on higher leaders, whether at the commune or the city level. They continued to stress irrigation as the lifeblood of agriculture and urged Long Bow Brigade to irrigate as quickly as possible. Every winter agitation for irrigation found an important place on the agenda of the village and by spring reached a climax in the course of which the whole community mobilized to dig new wells, create new channels, and level up individual fields so that in the coming crop season the irrigated area could be doubled, tripled, or made universal. The size of the goal fluctuated with the level of the euphoria in the minds of the cadres in charge.

And every year the results fell far short of the plans, for the simple reason that the peasants had no faith in irrigation as long as the problem of salinity remained unresolved. They never verbally contradicted irrigation plans (who wanted to contradict Chairman Mao?); they simply voted with their feet by not working very hard at implementing them. As a result, the area of irrigated field crops grew very slowly, if at all, and Long Bow village became known in the city and the region as a very backward place. This was nothing new. Long Bow had always been *lao, ta, nan* (old, big, diffi-cult). History was merely repeating itself.

If salinity presented an insoluble technical problem, land loss and the threat of land loss presented an equally insoluble political and social prob-lem. The two problems were linked because nobody wanted to go to great lengths to transform land that might soon be transferred out in any case. With uncertain land rights the incentives for a creative solution tended to evaporate. After 1958 Long Bow lost altogether over 2,000 mou, or two-fifths of the total area available. The land went to the highway, the rail-road, the railroad shops, the cement mill, Third Bureau construction battalions, and finally the Sawblade Works. Even though city cadres kept assuring one and all that they would divert no more land to industrial use, and categorically asserted that they would never divert land west of the highway, the peasants still felt uncertain about the future, unsure as to whether there really would be enough land to go around in another year or two.

Some foresaw that if industry kept developing as it had in the past they would suffer the same fate as the peasants of the inner city who no longer raised anything but vegetables on the small acreage that remained to them inside the perimeter of the old city wall. But Long Bow people had little experience as vegetable gardeners. The whole art was new to them. They did not understand it and they feared it. They were grain growers, corn, millet and bean experts, and the threat to traditional practices posed by the diversion of acreage worried them day and night. This worry underlay almost everything that happened in the fall of 1971.

On several occasions when we went out to work on fields in the east with Kuo Cheng-k'uan, he stopped in the middle of the railroad yards, looked around, sighed and said with deep feeling, "All this was our land. It all used to be in grain. The best land, the very best land!"

Paradoxically, at the heart of the stalemate in agricultural production an area of dynamism developed that contradicted the general trend. This was vegetable production. The rapid growth of the nonfarm population in the North Station area created a huge demand for fresh vegetables. To satisfy it, the city government directed Long Bow to divert land from grain to vegetable production. To ensure compliance, the city government canceled certain quotas for grain to be sold to the state and substituted vegetables quotas in their place. Even though they knew very little about market gardening, Long Bow peasants had little choice but to comply with the needs of the city. In so doing, they acted inadvertently in their own best interest. Since their land holdings were shrinking, they had to intensify production and concentrate labor on the acres that remained. Massive accumulations of night soil from the new residential quarters made intensifi-cation and concentration both practical and profitable. Since vegetable prices were not fixed but fluctuated seasonally with the supply, growers enjoyed a built-in premium for good management, an incentive to come up with preseason or postseason supplies on which extra profits could be made.

Responding to these pressures and incentives, each production team in

Long Bow set aside six acres for vegetables. Vegetable land put irrigation back on the agenda because there was no way to make garden land produce without ample supplies of water on a regular basis. This raised anew the question of the practicality of irrigation for Long Bow, the question of the availability of water, and the question of the damage done by water to "fall salt" land.

Since practice had shown that Long Bow people could not rely on water from the reservoir, they had to build their gardens around wells that tapped the vast water table underneath the village. With the construction of the reservoir, this water table had risen many feet and now lay, in an ordinary season, only a few feet below the surface of the land. Peasants learned to construct wells of large diameter and no more than twenty or thirty feet deep, each of which, when equipped with a power pump, could irrigate an acre or two. Thus they solved the problem of water resources.

As to the second problem, the problem of salinity, Long Bow people gradually discovered that on intensively cultivated garden land the salinity decreased and in the course of several years disappeared altogether. This had something to do with the heavy applications of night soil, with the continued use of "sanitary manure"—the name given to the kitchen waste from people's homes that was composed mainly of coal ashes and floor sweepings—and with the constant, intensive working of the soil by hand. When the sun cracked the land, hoeing healed the cracks, and this hoeing could be done on small areas of garden whenever necessary. After a year or two the land no longer cracked in the sun.

Clearly vegetable growing provided a road forward for Long Bow. With an assured market, with ever-expanding supplies of natural fertilizer, with water available only a few feet below the surface, and with a soil that could be transformed in the course of a few years of hard work, the diversion of more and more land to gardening became inevitable. Labor power for such an intensification presented no problem. In addition to the new hands provided by the natural growth of the population, electric power and power equipment were liberating old hands from daily chores. With grain grinding, fodder chopping and water pumping all done by machine, the people once required for these tasks could take to the fields.

In the late sixties and early seventies the breakthrough provided by vegetable gardening did not change the overall picture of stagnation in agriculture. At a time when the brigade still possessed over 3,000 mou of crop land, vegetables grew on only 180. At a time when there were over 1,000 able-bodied laborers available, vegetables provided employment for no more than sixty, and this employment was seasonal. People looked on the whole development of market gardening as a promising sideline that did not fundamentally alter the gloomy picture of poor yields on saline soil that no one had as yet found a way to alter except on a very small scale.

No one had really placed on the agenda the question of how to apply the lessons of Tachai to Long Bow, that is to say, how to put Long Bow people to work transforming nature so that they as a collective could tap the full potential of their environment. The general program that came from above —expanded irrigation—had proved clearly inadequate, yet no one systematically studied any alternative. Questions of political power—who should hold power and to what purpose?—had usurped the stage and still absorbed all the attention of the leadership, regardless of level.

While political rhetoric remained militantly socialist, reality tended toward the "capitalist road"—that is to say, toward individualism—because no clear leadership, no real unity and no consensus gave a lift to collective effort.

85

666 STAINS
THE PORRIDGE

One-sided and imperfect as the peace settlement was in Southeast Shansi, once the army enforced the peace all the normal functions of government at various levels quickly revived. Shih Chao-sheng, having returned to full power as Party Secretary of Horse Square Commune, decided to concentrate on the most severe problems left behind by the conflicts of the Cultural Revolution. This approach focused his attention immediately on Long Bow village, famous as an "old, big, difficult" place ever since land reform began in 1948. From a perusal of crop yields alone, Long Bow was obviously in trouble, for at a time when Horse Square was reaping more than 40 bushels to the acre, surpassing the standards in the national plan for North China, Long Bow was still reaping 30 bushels or less. Shih Chao-sheng concluded that Long Bow Brigade needed special help. To provide it he pulled together a work team of four, headed by himself, and set out for the village on June 8, 1970.

The Party Secretary of Horse Square Commune took with him Chang Ch'ang-fu, vice-head of the Revolutionary Committee of the commune, Ch'en Hsiao-kuan, commander of the commune militia, and Shen An-huai, the man in charge of commune security. This was the same Security Officer Shen whom we found in Long Bow in 1971. The efforts of these four to come to grips with Long Bow failed dismally. They could not understand the problems in the village, much less solve them. Shih Chao-sheng, with a whole commune to worry about, soon had to withdraw. A few days later he called back Chang Ch'ang-fu. In September Ch'en Hsiao-kuan went off to lead a commune delegation to Tachai, and Security Officer Shen, without any stomach for remaining in Long Bow alone, attached himself to that delegation and headed for Tachai as well.

By the time Shen came back from Hsiyang County the Changchih City Rural Work Department had formed another Long Bow-bound cadre group. Its leader asked Shen to join. After studying together for two weeks this group, known as a propaganda team, descended on the village in October. The head man, with the title of political director, was Chang Kuang-sheng, a leader of the Communist Party in the Luan Mining Bureau and a cadre of the thirteenth grade (considered extremely high in Southeast Shansi). The City Committee designated Security Officer Shen team leader, and Li Chin-t'ung, the theater manager from Changchih whom we met in 1971, a vice-team leader.

On reaching Long Bow, the new team set up a Party Rectification Group that consisted of the team leaders and Long Bow's Brigade Chairman Chang Kuei-ts'ai, the only local man they trusted enough to include. As Security Officer Shen said, "Whenever family history counts, Chang Kuei-ts'ai never loses out. He is a poor peasant and everyone related to him is a poor peasant, with the possible exception of his wife's mother. He is a Communist Party member from way back and so is his sister who now works at the Yumen oil field. His second sister and her husband are both Communists and live in Chaocheng Village. Every way you look at it, this is a reliable family, a family made up of 'basic elements.'

"And Kuei-ts'ai is as reliable as his family. Power has never corrupted him as it has some of the others. You cannot buy him with favors. He has even made up a poem about that:

> For landlords and rich peasants I don't give a fart.
> Where there's stealing and cheating I take no part.
> Sugar-coated bullets can't knock me down,
> So how can you take over this town?

"When relief grain is handed out he never takes any, even when his family qualifies for a share. He really loves the brigade and always draws a clear line between public and private property. And he always defends the interests of the poor peasants."

But as soon as the propaganda team showed support for Chang Kuei-ts'ai, his prestige started to unravel. Wall posters went up attacking him as a tyrant, and, as might have been expected by anyone familiar with Long Bow history, they accused him of having murdered Little Four P'ei. Little Four was the thief who stole tools and iron from the cement plant in 1963 and later was found dead at the bottom of a well. In Long Bow, it seemed, one thing could always be counted on—whoever rose to power sooner or later could expect to be blamed for the death of Little Four. When Chang Hsin-fa dominated village affairs he was held responsible for the tragic demise of the thief. When Lu Chin-jung replaced him Lu got the blame. Now the onus was transferred to Chang Kuei-ts'ai.

Just at this time a youth named San-mao lost his life under the wheel of a horsecart. Only two days earlier he had informed the propaganda team that he would not become an activist in their campaign on pain of death. He no sooner said it than he was killed. One of the chief mourners was the militiaman Ch'en Liang-t'ien. Ch'en's mother, "the broken-down donkey at the broken-down mill," suddenly went into a trance, emitted shrill cries, and flung her arms wildly about. San-mao's ghost possessed her body, she said, and he was talking through her to the world. His complaint was that he had been unjustly done in. He held Kuei-ts'ai responsible. Once Ch'en Liang-t'ien's mother started talking about ghosts, political study in the fields came to an abrupt halt. Whenever the members of any team took a break they began to discuss ghosts instead of Mao Tse-Tung Thought.

Voices from the dead served as a way for Ch'en's mother to get back at

Chang Kuei-ts'ai for harrassment that had nothing to do with poor San-mao. What she really resented was that the brigade leader had canceled some of her son's work points. Ch'en Liang-t'ien had been a member of a sidelines group, led by Splayfoot Tseng, which unloaded freight at Changchih North Station. The group worked so poorly and wasted so much time that the Railroad Bureau complained. At this point Chang Kuei-ts'ai, backed up by the demobilized parachutist Li Kuang-ching, recalled most of the men from the freight yards and sent them back to field work. Ch'en Liang-t'ien refused to leave. As punishment the brigade refused to credit him with work points earned, even though he claimed seventy. Kuei-ts'ai insisted that he make a self-criticism. Once he admitted that he had been in the wrong he would get his points. But Ch'en refused to admit anything, so Kuei-ts'ai withheld his points. Then Ch'en and his mother both cursed the brigade leader.

Splayfoot Tseng, who had also lost out at the railroad yards, was currently courting Ch'en Liang-t'ien's wife. He felt doubly aggrieved and declared, "If I can't overthrow Chang Kuei-ts'ai, I'll move right out of Long Bow." He not only said it, he wrote it on a village wall in letters two feet high. Two months later, when Kuei-ts'ai, far from stepping down, stepped up to the post of Party Secretary of the brigade, someone wrote above Splayfoot's angry words, "Kuei-ts'ai has not been overthrown. What are you going to do about it?"

"Move out," said Splayfoot Tseng.

The very next day he put his house up for sale.

Right at this moment Secretary Chang embroiled himself in an unfortunate quarrel with Chou Cheng-lo, a highly respected member of the Party branch. The quarrel arose between Chang's wife and her brother Chou Cheng-lo, but Chang was drawn into it through family solidarity and it soured his relations with a whole section of the village at a most inopportune time.

The quarrel concerned a quilt that belonged to Chou Five, the only one of six Chou brothers who had no children of his own. He had borrowed a daughter, who became Kuei-ts'ai's wife, from Chou Six, and a son, Chou Cheng-fu, from Chou Three. Chou Cheng-fu, as a dutiful son, was supposed to take care of him in his old age and see him safely buried, but Chou Cheng-fu was *pa mao* (eight dimes), which meant "not all there," and could hardly take care of his immediate family, not to mention an aging "father." So Chou Cheng-lo, who was the son of Chou Six and a full brother to Kuei-ts'ai's wife, undertook those filial duties—at a price. Chou Cheng-lo's price was that he be named sole heir to Chou Five's property. On his deathbed, however, Chou Five renegotiated the deal. He made Chou Cheng-lo agree to give his sister a trunk, a felt mat from the kang and one good quilt. After the old man's death, Chou Cheng-lo broke his word. He gave his sister the trunk and the mat but not the quilt. Chang Kuei-ts'ai told his wife to forget it, but she would not drop the matter. For months she talked of nothing else. She brought her brother up on charges before the brigade office and when brigade cadres failed to solve the problem she appealed her case to the commune committee. After weeks of investigation, altercation and litigation, the commune committee directed Chou Cheng-lo to turn over the quilt. When he refused, the committee directed the brigade to withhold 70 yuan from his annual income and cancel his cloth ration by denying him coupons. Faced with such severe economic reprisal, Cheng-lo finally gave in. He returned the quilt, but not before he had removed the high-quality cotton from the lining and replaced it with ragged, used cotton from a beat-up substitute quilt. When Kuei-ts'ai's wife discovered the rotten mess, she worked herself into a frenzy and took the case to court in Chang-chih City.

Kuei-ts'ai tried to calm her. One quilt, however well made, was not worth the destruction of family and community relations. But his wife felt that a principle had been violated. "I can't swallow this foul air," she said, denouncing her brother to the whole community. Her charges generated so much heat and ill will that they cast a shadow over everything her husband did and made it that much easier for the opposition to heap abuse on his head.

Attacks such as those aimed at Chang Kuei-ts'ai threatened everyone the propaganda team tried to work with. Anonymous posters denounced Li Pao-an and Chao T'ung-min on the walls as "middle peasants" (always suspect in Long Bow) and "bad elements" to boot. They accused Lu Kuang-han of having married a woman whose uncle had a bad history. Wang Yü-lai, Wang Man-hsi, Lu Tai-chen, Shen Hsü-wen, Shen Chi-ts'ai, Lu Ho-jen and Sun Jing-fu all confronted slanderous allegations as soon as the team showed an interest in them.

If the attacks had consisted only of words, the team might have been able to cope with them, but verbal fusillades often seemed to pave the way for bizarre and nasty physical assaults that bid fair to change the whole character of the confrontation. After Lu Yu-sheng testified in public that Chang Kuei-ts'ai had nothing to do with the death of Little Four, he found raw night soil dumped inside his courtyard gate. A few days later he reported that someone had dropped 666, a very poisonous fungicide (lindane), in his cooking pot. On that very same day he reported that a masked stranger had assaulted his daughter, Fang-ling. The girl had excused herself from a card game with friends in order to go to the toilet. While she was squatting in the darkness at the far corner of the courtyard, a man with a sack over his head suddenly appeared, grabbed her arm and tried to pull her away. Fang-ling screamed. The assailant pulled harder. She screamed more loudly. He dropped her arm and ran away.

One night Little Shen's brother, Chi-ts'ai, met with the team cadres for several hours. When he entered his own courtyard to retire, flying pieces of broken brick struck his head and shoulders.

Somebody used a big beam, like a battering ram, to pound on Li Kuang-ching's compound wall. Several of his neighbors reported finding the air in their homes saturated with mosquito repellent. A few even claimed that they heard "black shots" in the night. Out near the threshing ground of the Second Production Team a small temple mysteriously burned to the ground.

Fungicide poisoning, battering rams, arson and gunfire all added up to a serious confrontation indeed.

At the time, the propaganda team blamed all these incidents on Swift Li and Fast Chin. "We didn't think that they actually plotted such incidents," said Security Officer Shen, "but they complained loudly, made sarcastic remarks and thus set the tone. The members of the clique took whatever action they felt like taking. Li and Chin couldn't openly support such deeds, but they didn't suppress them either—or so we concluded.

"When we set up study classes, posters went up saying that we were only middle cadres. The higher cadres would never support our actions, the posters proclaimed.

"When we set up a class for people with problems—graft, speculation and the like—and asked the students to go out and labor with some of the activists who supported us, they wouldn't work. They only sat around in the field and cursed.

"One of the people they cursed was me. After all, I had been in the same faction as Swift Li. I had supported him from the beginning, but when he and Fast Chin found that they couldn't 'pull me over' they began to attack me. They even charged that *Reds* had come to Long Bow to 'Reverse the Verdicts of the Cultural Revolution.' "

In 1970 the Central Committee launched a big, nationwide campaign called *Yi Ta, San Fan* (Knock Down One, Oppose Three). This slogan stood for knocking down counterrevolutionaries and opposing graft, speculation and waste. But it also served as an umbrella for opposing private plots, free markets and individual enterprises conducted for profit, all of which the Central Committee denounced as speculative, capitalist road tendencies. Both the commune team that came in July and the city team that came in October paid special attention to the sidelines conducted by individuals. They suppressed them for the second time in a decade by confiscating the tools necessary to various trades, such as the pliers and small screwdrivers used by the watch repairmen Chin and Wu, and the wrenches and welding torch used by Chin Shen-yi. Peasants vigorously opposed the suppression of private trades and crafts. At the very first meeting called by the new team in October several people accused Security Officer Shen and Commune Secretary Chao of messing up the economy by shutting down sidelines. Without sideline earnings how could farming prosper? they asked.

The brigade leaders confronted the new team with a similar question and made an irrelevant demand:

Since individuals are not allowed to carry on sidelines, how are they going to survive?

Our sewing group has no accountant. Find one for us.

"We were amazed," said Shen. "We said, 'We didn't come here to solve small problems of daily life. Your own Revolutionary Committee can put people to work and find an accountant. We came here to solve big problems like the rectification of the Party.' But nobody was happy with an answer like that.

"Wang Wen-te, one of the Two Gems' staunchest supporters, began to spread all sorts of rumors. According to him, the propaganda team couldn't solve one simple problem. 'If you don't have any money, sell some eggs,' said Wang. 'If you don't have any coal, pick some up at the railroad shops.' His meaning was clear—since the team has nothing to offer, we peasants have to make the best of it. We have to look out for our own interests."

In Long Bow opposition to rectification seemed to be coming from all sides. The propaganda team members, pressed for time, failed to investigate all the incidents in depth. They took the peasants at their word and easily convinced themselves that class struggle was increasing daily in intensity. Wasn't that what Chairman Mao had suggested after all? Since the most vocal opposition to their work stemmed clearly from their primary target, the Party committee in power in the brigade, they continued to blame everything on Swift Li and Fast Chin, and girded themselves for serious combat.

In the meantime the three leading members of the team fell out among themselves. The Grade 13 cadre, Chang Kuang-sheng from the Mining Bureau, Theater Manager Li from Changchih, and Security Officer Shen from Horse Square, found it hard to agree on the simplest question of analysis or procedure. Over and over again they had to take their quarrels to higher levels for arbitration. In the end, toward the middle of March, the city committee transferred their entire team out. After four days of intense political study the prestigious thirteenth-grade cadre Chang Kuang-sheng and three others were reassigned. Security Officer Shen and Theater Manager Li were then sent back to Long Bow along with Liu T'ing-tung, the head of security at the Shihkechieh Coal Mine, and twelve new appointees, among them Donkey Meat Wang and white-haired Chao Fu-kuei, both of whom we came to know so well later in the year. We never met the man from the mine. He fell sick soon after he arrived, could not continue, and yielded in May to Judge Kao.

By the time Judge Kao showed up, relations between the propaganda team and the Two Gems had reached an impasse. The team, having found much to criticize in Long Bow, blamed all troubles on the leading body, while the Two Gems, finding much to criticize about the work of the team, blamed most of their trouble on outside intervention. What particularly galled them was that the team was made up primarily of *Reds*, most of whom eagerly sought to find fault with *United* stalwarts and apparently planned to stop at nothing to do them in. If, in the region as a whole, *United* had thoroughly suppressed *Red*, here in Long Bow it looked as if *Red* had turned the tables and was in a position to take revenge. It was not an attractive prospect for anyone committed to the other side.

Actually, the factional background of the team members was not entirely one-sided. While Judge Kao, Veteran Wang, Chi the Moslem and white-haired Chao Fu-kuei were all *Red*, Donkey Meat Wang was *United*, and Security Officer Shen was mixed—that is, he was a *Red* rebel who had gone over to *United* when it became clear that *United* would dominate the suburban area.*

A sprinkling of *United* members and turncoats, however, did not suffice

*Clearly, factional links had nothing to do with political stance. The most radical was Security Officer Shen, a *United* latecomer, while the most conservative was Chao Fu-kuei, a long-time *Red*.

to give the team balance. *Red* clearly predominated and controlled the key positions. It might be supposed that the new Revolutionary Committee of Changchih City had loaded the team with *Red* partisans as a means of combating factionalism, as a gesture of reconciliation that could lay the foundations for unity in the future, but I found no evidence that this was the case. The move was made out of pure expediency. There simply were not enough old cadres in the ranks of *United* to staff all city departments and simultaneously man all the political action teams required by a massive Party rectification movement. For lack of anyone else to send, the City Committee had sent *Reds*.

Having taken over all key positions of power in the city and the region, *United* leaders felt secure in the saddle and quite able to use defeated *Reds* as team members in the field. Many of the *Red* cadres had long since been sent down to cadre schools for reeducation through labor. As cadre school inmates they could be loaned out to propaganda teams to bring them up to strength. While undergoing what amounted to punishment for their "crimes" by serving long stints in the countryside as manual laborers, defeated *Reds*, it appeared, could also do some necessary organizational work.

The anomaly of placing *Reds* in charge of a brigade dominated by *United*, and the effect this almost certainly would have both on the outlook and the morale of the citizens of Long Bow after the long and complex struggle they had gone through, did not seem to bother the city authorities. The question of who held local power, which the residents of Long Bow tended to regard as a life-and-death matter and one worth fighting bitterly over for years, was considered minor, even inconsequential, by the city cadres in charge. What mattered to them was holding office in the city and region. As long as *United* dominated the center *Reds* would have no choice but to carry out *United* directives. Thus *United* could surely control all outlying districts.

Sending *Reds* to rectify Long Bow also illustrated what, for want of a better word, can be called class solidarity. In a society as hierarchical as China's, state cadres, regardless of origin, constitute a privileged group, caste or class that puts a high value on defending the common interests of its members. State cadres, whatever their factional loyalties, never want to be confused with ordinary workers or peasants. When there is an administrative job to be done, when state business is on the agenda, the people ordained to do the job are the ranking cadres and nobody else. They will tolerate a sprinkling of workers and peasant party members as assistants, but only if they clearly recognize who is in charge. The state cadres may fight bitterly among themselves over who should direct their efforts, over who—what faction—will give the orders, but they will defend to the death the right of their kind, people of their rank, training and expertise, to monopolize the business of governing. In a less hierarchical society the victors might have been tempted to recruit new forces from the ranks of those who supported them down below, but Chinese tradition being what it is, the normal thing for victorious *United* leaders to do was to put defeated *Reds* to work as underlings. Bonds of common Party membership reinforced the solidarity felt for those of equal rank. To be a state cadre one almost had to be a Party member (Chi the Moslem was a significant exception here). The two forms of status were but complementary sides to the same coin. It should be made clear, however, that the opposite did not hold true. To be a Party member one did not have to be a state cadre, and state cadres never allowed millions of Party members at village and shop level to forget it.

If it was natural for the city leaders to send *Reds* to lead Long Bow, it was not at all natural for the leaders of Long Bow, who had gone out on a limb as *United* activists, to accept them. They viewed the makeup of the propaganda team as a disaster. Swift Li and Fast Chin felt cornered, even betrayed. They had no confidence that any objective standard would be used to judge them, or that any explanation of theirs would be listened to. At the start, at least, these expectations were not disappointed.

Security Officer Shen, who had twice left Long Bow in frustration, was particularly anxious to achieve something on his third time around. Even though he claimed allegiance to *United,* he had no choice but to set about investigating the Two Gems with a vengeance.

To start with, Shen arranged a mass meeting at which he hauled Swift Li, Fast Chin and eighteen other members of their group before the people for "struggle." One of the slogans was, "Down with Swift Li." Li, standing on the stage, raised his arm and joined in the shouting, but each time said instead, "Swift Li will never be downed."

Li had a bad stomachache that day, so when Dr. Chi came near he asked for some medicine. When Dr. Chi came back with the medicine, he walked down behind the row of "struggle objects" and put some herbs in Li's hand.

When the meeting was over Shen announced adjournment, but Swift Li rushed to the speaker's stand and said, "You may be finished, but I haven't had my say." He poured out a glass of water, put the herbs in his mouth, then washed them down with one gulp. It was a gesture of defiance that needed no explanation.

Since the members of the Two Gems' group united so strongly behind their defiant leaders, Shen's first task was somehow to split it up. Without a few cracks and splits he saw no way to "take the lid off the class struggle." The obvious ploy was to concentrate on the weakest characters in the ranks, such rascals as Whiskers Shen and Lin Yao-lung. He hoped, by putting heavy pressure on them, to get them to talk and reveal the seamy side of the last four years—graft, corruption, rascal affairs—anything that would put the two leaders in an unfavorable light.

Putting on pressure meant nonstop interrogation—bringing people in at six in the evening and questioning them until dawn the next day. It also meant threats of dire consequences to be visited on the individual under scrutiny and on all his or her close relatives and descendants. Since all sides automatically assumed guilt by association, entire families took it for granted that they would suffer if any member provoked official ire. In the final analysis putting on pressure meant physical abuse, and before the first month had passed the propaganda team stood accused of severely beating several supporters of the Two Gems.

Those who were willing to talk about it said that neither Shen nor any other member of the team struck blows themselves, but team members were present as interrogators when "repairmen" whom they supervised laid into several victims. No one ever revealed the identity of the "repairmen" except to hint that they belonged to Little Shen's clique. The mine guard, Shen Chung-t'ang, was an obvious choice, for he was a "hit, smash and rob" specialist by his own admission. Just because he fought for *United* at the mine, there was no reason to suppose that he would refuse to take revenge on a dominant *United* in Long Bow that oppressed his own relatives.

"Repairmen" beat Lin Yao-lung most severely and hurt him so badly that he missed nine meals and had to be fed intravenously. One stalwart in heavy leather boots kicked Whiskers Shen in the ankle so hard that he couldn't walk for a week. Some said the kick broke his ankle, others that it only dislocated it.

When Chi Chin-yi, vice-head of the militia under Fast Chin, approached the team living quarters one night, several men grabbed him on the ground that he was trying to eavesdrop. They called the team members out and, in this case, according to all reports, both peasants and cadres beat Chin-yi.

The Two Gems and their supporters looked on confrontations with the work team as a continuation of the factional struggle they had been carrying on for years, only this time, due to a bizarre twist of fate, they were operating from a defensive rather than an offensive position. Under pressure, far from cracking and telling the propaganda team what it wanted to hear, the gang members drew more closely together and reaffirmed their loyalty to the Two Gems and to each other, a manifestation of a trend that Veteran Wang, for one, paid serious attention to; the more the team criticized the Two Gems, the more support the two won in the community.

One reason Swift Li gained support was that he stood up for his friends. When the propaganda team started beating people Li lost patience. He decided to lead a protest delegation to the City Party Committee. Contrary to what the propaganda team members told us at the city meeting, Swift Li, Fast Chin, Splayfoot Tseng and Wang Wen-te slipped into the city after midnight one day in May, not because they couldn't answer the charges against them, but because they indignantly rejected the protracted and increasingly violent interrogations they and their friends were being subjected to. Swift Li talked about it later:

> We felt great pressure from the outside. Pressure from the propaganda team and from the community drove us together; we couldn't help but form a little knot. The people in my group all had the same traits. First of all, we were stubborn. We were the sort who, on entering the south gate, have to walk all the way to the north wall just to bump our heads on it.
>
> That time four of us took off for Changchih, we prepared sixty or seventy *wo t'ou* [steamed corn rolls], tied our quilts to our backs, and set off down the railroad track. It was three o'clock in the morning. Splayfoot told an old neighbor that he was going to sell his house and everything else he owned. He was going to Changchih, to Tai-yuan, and if necessary, to Peking to seek justice.

Wang Wen-te joined us because he couldn't stand working in the Fourth Team anymore. He said it was an "enemy-occupied area," a "Little Taiwan." He vowed that if he wasn't allowed to transfer out, he would never return.

Halfway between Long Bow and Changchih we found the truck repair shop where Wen-te's sister works. We took a break there, rested a while, then finally got into the city at 7:00 A.M. But it was Sunday. We had forgotten about that. Not a single office was open. We had to split up and make plans to meet the next day. Splayfoot and I went to the dynamite factory at the East Gate, where I had some relatives. Fast Chin and Wen-te walked all the way back to the truck repair shop. We spent the day trying to put some of our grievances on paper. In the meantime all the members of the Long-Bow Propaganda Team and several commune cadres took to the road looking for us.

Monday morning, at 8:00 A.M., just as all the offices opened, we showed up at the gate of City Hall. Smart Fan was standing there waiting for us. The propaganda team cadres figured that we might go there to appeal our case, so they had alerted him.

"What are you doing here?" he asked.

"We came to tell you what's going on in Long Bow," we said. "We don't mind if the team looks into problems, but why do they have to beat people, and question them day and night? We don't deserve that."

Smart Fan questioned us briefly, then said, "You had better go back to Long Bow. If you don't, you'll harm the spring work."

But we all said, "No. We'll go to jail first."

I said, "If you won't send me to jail, just give me a ration book and let me go to work in Changchih. When I go to a meeting in Long Bow they won't even let me sit down!"

But Smart Fan said, "You had better go right back. If you don't, we can't discuss your case at all."

Confronted with such an ultimatum, we walked out, found a tree, sat down under it, and refused to leave. As we sat we conferred and as we conferred we quarreled. A messenger came out to say that vice-chairman Ts'ui of the Party Committee would see us. Splayfoot didn't believe it. Neither did Wen-te. Fast Chin and I wouldn't go without the other two, so the stalemate continued. After a while we got tired of sitting there, so we got up and set off on a walk around the city. When we came back in the afternoon, all worn out, we decided to go up and see Ts'ui after all.

He was sympathetic. He praised me as an activist in the Four Clean Movement and said we had all done well in the Cultural Revolution, but he criticized us for the way we led production, stressing sidelines instead of grain, not paying attention to Tachai, spending too much on entertainment, and making trouble for the rectification movement.

After a long talk we decided to go back. When we got home we all went back to work.

Two days later the propaganda team called a mass meeting in Wang Yü-mei's courtyard. Judge Kao announced that Fast Chin and I had been removed from office and suspended from the Party branch.

After the propaganda team removed Swift Li from office, the ex-cadre resumed an old trade that he had learned as a child from his real father and his father's brothers—carpentry. He knew both how to build houses and how to fashion tables, chairs, cabinets and chests of the highest quality. Swift Li never had to worry about unemployment; his skills were in too great demand. People sought him out when they wanted a house built not only because he knew how to lay out a structure and put it up so that it would endure, but also because he finished off each building with little flourishes of woodwork and tile that set it apart from other buildings. He stamped each structure with his personal trademark, so to speak, and people proudly showed off what Swift Li had created for them.

But even though he worked hard and earned enough cash to support his family, he could not get enough grain to feed them. The brigade's wheat crop, harvested in July, fell far short of expectations and the per capita shares distributed to many families were not enough to carry them through until fall. One way out was to take the train to Honan and buy dried sweet potatoes on the free market. So many family heads left home for this purpose that field teams fell short of labor power at the height of the hoeing season and weeds bid fair to smother the fall crops. In an effort to control the traffic, brigade committee leaders stopped issuing the official letters of introduction that Honan authorities required of all out-of-province buyers. They made exceptions only for proven hardship cases. When the committee violated its own standards by issuing letters to Ch'en Wan-t'ien and Chi Lung-fei, Swift Li applied. The committee turned him down even though he had more mouths to feed than either Ch'en or Chi. He got mad, went to Chang-yi Commune, his wife's old home, and persuaded the leading cadres there to write a letter for him. Then he and three companions set out for Honan, taking along some homegrown hemp for bargaining purposes.

The hemp proved unnecessary. Money talked in Linhsien, Honan. But Swift Li and his companions no sooner arrived than they were relieved of their money. They were sitting in the dining room at the railroad station having a bowl of noodles when a representative of the Market Management Office came up to their table and asked what they were doing there.

"We came to buy chips," said Swift Li.

"Do you have a letter of introduction?"

"Sure. Here it is."

"But this letter is from Chang-yi Commune, and you are from Long Bow Brigade, Horse Square. This won't do at all," said the official. He herded them to the Market Management Office, took away their money, and told them to go home. They sought out an old classmate of Swift Li's, who had married in Linhsien, left the hemp with her, and went home empty-handed. The Market Management Office mailed their money back to Long Bow, so they recovered every fen, but they still didn't have enough food for their families to eat.

The same official intercepted Ch'en Wan-t'ien and Chi Lung-fei. He told them to go home, too, saying Honan chips could not be exported, but since they had a proper letter, stamped with Long Bow's official seal, he did not take their money. They disregarded his orders, went from house to house, buying a few chips here and a few chips there, and came home well pleased.

The episode illustrated, if further illustration were needed, the tight control which the authorities exercised over the market in all its phases and over the entire peasant population. Opportunities for harassing anyone out of favor were legion. Swift Li, accustomed to wielding the powers of a brigade leader, found the restraint particularly galling. When on top of that team cadres accused him of traveling to Honan illegally and profiteering with hemp, he was beside himself. But he had no recourse other than sullen silence.

In the end, because the grain situation was so tight for so many families, old Chang Kuei-ts'ai got in touch with a Honan official who had been a district leader in Lucheng County at the time of the land reform. Through this old friend he arranged for a whole carload of dried sweet-potato slices to be shipped north by rail. The carload arrived in time, before the last of the wheat had been eaten, and Long Bow peasants were able to get through the summer without serious hardship.

The decision to remove the Two Gems from office in Long Bow, counter-stroke though it was, might have occurred in the normal course of the development of factional struggle in Changchih City and the Southeast Region, but it seems clear in retrospect that the event that tipped the scales toward removal was my sudden reappearance in China after an absence of seventeen years. I arrived in Peking with my family just in time for the celebrations marking the international day of labor, May 1. On May 24 Premier Chou En-lai invited us to the Great Hall of the People for a banquet and a long talk, in the course of which he said, "I know you want to visit Long Bow village, but I don't know if it can be arranged. You see, we don't know which class is in power down there." Not long after this, Premier Chou sent word that we could go to Long Bow after all. What happened in the meantime was that the propaganda team, under pressure to stabilize the situation and uncertain as to the nature of the contradiction between the Two Gems and the people of the brigade, decided to remove them from office and raise up in their place some individuals in whom it had more confidence, some individuals it felt sure represented the poor and lower-middle peasants. This drastic step, the second overthrow of Swift Li in five years and the twelfth reorganization of the village government since 1948, was undertaken after intense consultation between the leaders of the propaganda team and those at commune and city levels. All of these people already knew that I had arrived from America and that Premier Chou wanted me to revisit the community about which the book *Fanshen* had been written.

On June 8 the Long Bow Party Branch met in plenary session and elected a new secretary and four new vice-secretaries, a group of five that automatically took over not only the Party branch but the Brigade Revolutionary Committee as well. The entire reorganization was carried out inside the Party branch on the initiative of the propaganda team. The brigade rank-and-file took no part in the deliberations or the elections even though the newly established Revolutionary Committee was supposed to represent them.

Had general elections been held, Swift Li would probably have been confirmed in his post. As it was, the Party members chose Chang Kuei-ts'ai, who had served as brigade chairman under Swift Li, as their new Party Secretary. They chose to serve as vice-secretaries Li Kuang-ching, the demobilized paratrooper who had been political officer of his air force unit, and Shen Chi-ts'ai (Little Shen's brother), who moved up from the post of brigade accountant. Lu Ho-jen replaced Fast Chin as captain of the militia, and Shen Hsü-wen replaced Shen Chi-ts'ai as chief accountant.

Thus the community set the stage for my return.

Clearly that principle of particle physics that makes it impossible to measure subatomic events without changing them had here found a parallel in the social sphere. A village under scrutiny by a foreigner could not be left to its natural fate. Four thousand years of centralist tradition made intervention inevitable.

86

AN EGG CAN TURN INTO A CHICKEN

Veteran Wang usually arrived at meetings early, even the meetings devoted to morning study. While waiting for the rest of the team to show up he told stories. The point that he usually wanted to make was that there are many different ways to solve problems. One day in late September he started to tell about some brash young men in Sung Family Settlement who always made trouble. If their community brought in a film to show or scheduled a dramatic performance, they always rushed in and tried to grab the best seats. They pushed, shoved, fought and shouted, creating scene after scene.

One day the brigade leader called them in. He asked them what they thought should be done about disorderly conduct in public places. When the young men looked around, they realized that only brawlers had been invited. They winked at each other, smiled and stood silent. They said they had no opinions on the matter at all.

So the brigade leader decided on a new tactic. The next time a drama group came to town, he made sure that no one sat in the front row. "These fine seats are reserved for young Wang, Li Ch'un . . ." he announced in a loud voice, then proceeded to read off the names of all the troublemakers. Embarrassed, the young men shrank back.

"Don't read our names," they pleaded. "Let us sit in the back."

But the brigade leader insisted that they all move to the very front and take their seats from the middle of the row outward. As they sat down, he introduced them, one person at a time.

Later, when he called the brawlers into his office for the second time, they all apologized and promised to reform. From that day forward, the seating always went smoothly at public performances in Sung Family Settlement.

When Veteran Wang finished his story, Little Li, the Russian teacher, read through once again the editorial from the *Peking Daily* of August 27. This time she concentrated on paragraph three, dealing with the importance of asking every Communist to do manual labor on a regular basis. The editorial called on all cadres to do some manual labor every day and thus maintain close ties to ordinary people. In Long Bow, the team members said, ordinary peasants began to change very quickly as soon as they rose to positions of power. Take the new accountant, Shen Hsü-wen. Since taking over the job only two months earlier, he had spent his whole time in the office poring over the books and had not appeared in the fields even once. He was a Party member. He ought to know better. He ought to take the initiative and report to work on a regular basis. At the same time the brigade should set up some standards about manual work for cadres and enforce them. In the busy season everyone, including the brigade doctor, nurse, pharmacist and accountant, ought to work full time on the land. Abstention could easily corrupt anyone who didn't.

"How can the accountant busy himself in the office and never pick up a hoe?" asked Donkey Meat Wang. "An accountant's job is really not a full-time job. Whatever has to be done can easily be done in the evening. Students from the highest grade in school and cadres from the top jobs in the city all come out for manual work. Why should the accountant be an exception?"

"Some people always except themselves," said Shen. "And it's not just cadres. Why, over near Changchih Steel there's a crop production brigade that asks steelworkers and management cadres to help out during the rush season. But while the outsiders are sweating in the field, many able-bodied men of the brigade stay right on the highway hauling steel for big money."

"These young accountants in Long Bow are a law unto themselves," said Judge Kao shaking his head. "One day they arrived home with 4,000 yuan in cash just as the film show began on the street. They plunked the money down on the table in the brigade office and rushed out to see the film. I came by later, saw the money lying there, and had to comb the crowd to find the financial wizards. I criticized them for carelessness, but it remains to be seen if it did any good."

As Little Li started in on the fourth paragraph, Secretary Chang appeared in the doorway, cursing.

"What's the matter?"

"That Third Bureau bastard . . . His mother's ———!"

"What happened?"

"He pulled a worker attitude on me, that turtle's egg. I was there across the tracks looking at the land they want to take over. There was this cadre pulling up the sticky millet.

" 'What in the devil's name are you doing?' I asked.

" 'Just checking out the soil,' he said. 'We want to make bricks here.'

" 'But you can't make bricks here. This is our millet,' I told him.

" 'Horse Square Commune said we could have it,' he replied, looking right through me like I wasn't there.

" 'Well, you haven't got it yet,' I said. 'You'd better leave our crops alone.'

" 'Your mother's ———. Who are you to tell me off? You'd best send the brigade chairman out.'

" 'I'm the brigade Party Secretary,' I said.

"That stumped him for a bit. He stopped looking through me and began to look at the ground.

"Then he said, 'In that case, you'd better go find your superior. You'd better get someone from the commune.'

" 'I don't have time for that,' I said. 'By the time I run to Horse Square and back you'll have this millet uprooted.'

"Well, the man didn't pull up any more. He swore at me and turned away. I ran all the way here. You had better do something quick!"

The propaganda team members were shocked that anyone would pull up millet only a week or two before harvesttime. What possessed him to do that? The land wasn't even his yet. By law, if the Third Bureau wanted land, the transaction had to be cleared with the brigade, then the commune, then the city and finally the region. Only the regional government could approve the diversion of farmland to nonfarm use. If the region approved, then the Bureau had to give the brigade a sum equal to the value of three years' crops at average prices for each mou. Even then, once the land was paid for, if the Third Bureau didn't use it right away, the brigade still had the right to plant crops and harvest them. Once the crops were planted no one was allowed to destroy them at all. If it was necessary to destroy them, application had to be made through brigade, commune, city and region, as before, and the entire value of the crop—seed, fertilizer and labor-input—had to be paid for.

But in this case the land hadn't even been transferred. How could anybody start pulling up millet?

"We're not even sure they need the land," said Kuei-ts'ai.

"Some factories always take more land than they need," said Judge Kao, frowning.

"They certainly do," said Kuei-ts'ai. "When the Third Bureau came here they took 2,000 mou, and paid for every one of them. But at first they only used 200. One day they came and wanted their money back. I told them they would have to go through channels. If they take land and don't use it they have to give it back, but there is no regulation that says the brigade has to give them back their money. They thought differently, so I said, 'OK. Level it up. Put it back the way it was when we had it and I'll give the money back.' That stopped them. After they looked at all the pits and hollows, the places where they had removed fill for the embankment and the places where they had dug soil for bricks, they didn't say another word about money. They just stalked off."

"At the city court one Third Bureau man complained that you almost beat him up out here when he went to claim some land," said Judge Kao. "The City Party Secretary told him it served him right. 'You can't just go around condemning people's land. You're lucky they didn't tan your hide with a carrying pole.' "

"No matter what happens we seem to get the worst of the deal," said Kuei-ts'ai. "When the sawblade factory representatives came to negotiate we decided we had to turn over some land to support industry. But what did they do? First they put up a brick wall so we couldn't get in. Then they planted crops on the land. How do you like that! Your mother's ——! They can build houses and they can build shops, but if there is any grain to plant we are supposed to plant it. Our slogan is, 'Every day you don't use it, we use it.' So, you had better send someone with me to the Third Bureau. If we don't get there soon they'll start tearing up the sticky millet again."

Judge Kao asked Pipefitter Huang to go along with Kuei-ts'ai.

Then the team members began once more to discuss the main problem facing them, the case of the Two Gems.

Just as Veteran Wang had predicted, the meeting that repudiated the two cadres along with the thief had failed to solve any problem. It had only pushed all its targets more tightly against the wall, cutting off all avenues of escape. Unable to accept the labels placed upon them and seeing no way out, they had drawn together in defiance, less willing to accept criticism, less likely to criticize themselves, than at any previous time.

I had requested a chance to talk to Swift Li. Smart Fan and Lin T'ung had agreed. But when they went to ask Li he flatly refused. "Why should I talk to him? What good would it do? You have already decided that I have oppressed the people, wrecked production, and taken the capitalist road. What is there left to say?"

When they pressed him he weakened a little. "If I talk to him, can I say what I really think? Or do I have to say what you tell me to say? If I have to say what you want, then I won't talk. Why should I agree to talk under those conditions? No. Absolutely not. You are entitled to your opinions. I'm entitled to mine."

"Well, if we agree that you can say what's on your mind?"

"I'll think about it," said Swift Li.

Veteran Wang, who was responsible for all "special case" investigations, had been looking into the charges of violent retaliation against the city propaganda teams, all three of them, and against those who had collaborated with them. An important part of the case against the Two Gems had been that they mobilized people to harass anyone who approached the team in a friendly spirit. But Wang's investigations led to some surprising results.

"Analysis has to be all-sided," said Veteran Wang. "We listen to all the evidence, hear all sides, and then analyze what is right and what is wrong. Take the case of Lu Yu-sheng. Rumor had it that some saboteur had put 666 into the family cooking pot. That seemed like a clear example of wrecking, but when we looked into it from all sides we began to see the incident in a different light. What happened was that Lu Lu-sheng's daughter, Fang-ling, was molested in the privy after dark one night by a man with a sack on his head. When she screamed he ran away. She immediately came to find some propaganda team member, saying that a masked man had attacked her. When we started asking questions some family members said, 'And there was 666 in our cooking pot, too.' We assumed that the two things were linked, that the masked man was responsible.

"But the next day when Fang-ling's mother came back from Kuyi, where she had been visiting relatives, all the answers suddenly shifted focus. Instead of blaming the night prowler for the 666 in the pot, they said they themselves kept the 666 on the lintel over the door. It could have fallen into the pot by mistake. Close neighbors said the Lu family never kept any 666 in the house at all. No one seemed very anxious to go into detail.

" 'So, how did you know there was 666 in the pot?' I asked.

" 'The porridge had a queer, fungicide smell.'

" 'Was the 666 in the pot or was it in the grain to begin with?'

"No answer to that one.

" 'Do you still have some of the grain?'

" 'Yes.'

"But they never produced one ounce of tainted grain.

"When I tried to question Fang-ling I got nowhere. Each time I asked her a question her mother said, 'You mustn't ask. She blacks out whenever she thinks about it.'

"Fang-ling herself covered her face and refused to answer.

"I could see right away there was something fishy going on. One possible version came immediately to mind. The masked man might have been Lu Ho-hai [the accountant on the Sidelines Team who was charged with misappropriating 1,193 yuan]. He'd courted Fang-ling's mother in the past. This time, when he found that his paramour was not at home, he made a pass at her daughter.

"Why would he go after the daughter? Well, people like that have no morals at all.

"As for the 666 in the pot, the most likely explanation is that the family stole some seed grain. It had already been treated with 666 to ensure germination. When they started to cook it, the smell warned them.

"So the two incidents are not linked and the family has no interest in discussing either one. Fang-ling, when attacked, ran for help, but her mother, when she came home, tried to calm everything down. As far as she is concerned the propaganda team should never have entered the case.

"And so," said Veteran Wang, "there are several sides to the case of Lu Yu-sheng. There is *this* side, *that* side and *his* side. *This* side is the one that involves Li Shou-p'ing, who is one of Fast Chin's militiamen. It was Li Shou-p'ing who testified against Kuei-ts'ai and blamed him for the death of the thief Little Four. It was Lu Yu-sheng who testified for Kuei-ts'ai, refuted Li's case, and thus made Li look foolish. So there is reason to assume some hostility, some motive for revenge. Did he put 666 in the pot?

"*That* side is the side of Lu Ho-hai, who has long courted Yu-sheng's wife. He might well have tried to grab the daughter, Fang-ling, but why would he want to put 666 in the pot?

"*His* side is Yu-sheng's own side. Maybe he's responsible for the 666. Maybe he got hold of some seed wheat somewhere, and doesn't want to own up to it?

"At first we saw only *this* side. We suspected Li Shou-p'ing, who was hand-in-glove with Fast Chin, and this turned the case into a political vendetta—the old leading group against the new leading group, the 'black gang' against the 'red gang,' the bourgeoisie against the proletariat. But when we saw how reluctant the whole family was to press charges, even to discuss the case, we had to reconsider the evidence. Summing it all up, we had to put *his* side first, *that* side second and *this* side last. So there you have the *all-sided* outlook."

"But," said Shen, still bent on indicting the Two Gems, "you yourself said you had to have solid evidence in order to suspect someone. All you have here are a lot of conjectures."

"If I had solid evidence I could settle the case," said Wang. "My suspicions run in many directions, but so far clear proof doesn't exist. The outstanding fact is that Lu's family is trying to avoid discussing the matter. In the beginning they wanted to expose the attack on their daughter, so they threw the book at us—night attack, hooded man, 666 in the grain. They made a big hullabaloo, but we no sooner began to look into it than they began to make light of the whole thing. So I sum it up as *his* side in the first place."

Lu Yu-sheng, it seemed, had learned something from Whiskers Shen. "When in trouble, blame class struggle." It was a sure-fire way to divert attention from the true facts of life. And he might have gotten away with it had it not been for Veteran Wang's unflappable pursuit of "all sides."

"That fire in the temple appears to have nothing to do with politics either," said Wang. "I've talked to dozens of Second Team people and the root of the matter seems to be that Shih Hui-fang's pig died. Now, most Shansi people won't eat dead pig, but Hui-fang is from Shantung. He has a passion for pork. The premature death of his prized shoat didn't deter him at all. He decided to dress it, cook it, and eat it in some out-of-the-way place where no one would be the wiser. Of course, since the pig was big, he invited some friends to share it without telling them about its sad, unnatural, early death. He chose the old temple north of the Second Team threshing floor as the most secure site for his feast, but he paid too little attention to the dry reeds stored there. Sparks from his fire set them ablaze and most of the temple burned to the ground before anyone could come to the rescue. The fire, of course, had to be explained. What could be more credible than a tale of arson perpetrated by class enemies?"

As he deflated the most serious charges against the Two Gems, one after the other, Veteran Wang became more convinced than ever that he was dealing with a pair of disgruntled cadres, a contradiction among the people that had nothing to do with class enemies or class struggle. But as he deflated the old charges, Swift Li and Fast Chin, especially Chin, kept creating new incidents that added fuel to the flames. Remarks such as those made by Swift Li: "I don't have enough piglets for my 'black gang,' why should I share them with the likes of you?" and those made by Fast Chin: "We 'black-gangers' can't get any relief grain, but you 'red-gangers' shouldn't have any trouble," and "If you open your hand, you can sow sixty catties," provided Security Officer Shen, Pipefitter Huang, Lin T'ung from *Central* and Smart Fan with signs that a conspiracy was on foot to seize power in the brigade. When Splayfoot Tseng walked home half-drunk after midnight, singing "Curse in the Hall" at the top of his voice, his act confirmed their suspicions and seemed to supply the proof that they had all been looking for. Wasn't "Curse in the Hall" a song of protest against the emperor in power, an accusation of usurpation, a claim by disinherited heirs who considered themselves legitimate? What further proof of an impending power seizure did anyone need? If nothing had so far happened, wasn't it simply because the propaganda team was present? What would happen when the team withdrew? Who could vouch for the future of Long Bow then?

After looking into the history of the Two Gems, Lin T'ung had decided that they themselves were probably not class enemies, but she still held firmly to the notion that they might have been used by class enemies—by insidious Catholic plotters such as Songbird Shih's uncle or by Wu Yü-chen's father, the historic counterrevolutionary. The Two Gems mixed closely with the women, Lin T'ung always argued. How could one avoid the suspicion that class enemies might have used these *femmes fatales* to pull two unsuspecting cadres down into the black swamp water? How could one fail to ask if there was not some hidden counterrevolutionary clique manipulating them behind the scenes? And even if no such manipulation was actually going on, the deeds done by the Two Gems, the political lines they carried out, served the interests of landlords, rich peasants, counter-revolutionaries and bad elements, so they were doing what class enemies could not do, they were playing a role that class enemies could not play. How could one explain that, even after losing office, after subjection to the masses for investigation, after months of patient help and criticism, they not only still refused to admit any mistakes, still showed no sign of repentance, but continued to spread complaints far and wide and repeat the insidious rhyme:

Chao K'uang-yin conquered the realm but
Chao K'uang-yi has occupied the throne.

"Look closely," Lin T'ung was wont to say, "see how they go on plotting with their clique. They say they want to pull down the new leading body. Day by day they provoke disunity within it, trying to make it collapse, trying to create an opportunity for their own reentry onto the stage—such is their dream!"

Lin T'ung, with Smart Fan's help, even developed a general theory about the form of class struggle in the Chinese countryside fifteen years after the successful establishment of cooperatives. It was a theory to explain how and why two young men of undoubted poor-peasant origin and great ability, after holding power for only a few years, branched out on the capitalist road and jeopardized the revolution.

According to Lin T'ung, the socialist revolution had developed such strength and such depth that class enemies could no longer come out in the open and do their dirty work with impunity (of course, one could not say that it was impossible). Instead, they had created the "pull out and use" method, whereby they influenced cadres inside the Communist Party itself. They used women, money and special privilege to corrupt and pull down honest young people who were weak of will and whose experience in class struggle was minimal. In the villages and basic units in the seventies, she averred, this was likely to be the chief form of class struggle.

Her suggested cure was for those in power constantly to transform their world outlook, to pay attention to Mao Tse-tung's line, and to mobilize the rank-and-file brigade members to supervise and criticize the actions of the leaders. Education and struggle had to be carried out yearly, monthly, daily and hourly. "Never forget class struggle!"

While Lin T'ung was absent that day with a turned ankle, Security Officer Shen acted as chief spokesman for her views. As far as he was concerned, the Case of the Two Gems now rested squarely in their own hands. They could change their attitude, decide to listen to the opinions of others, begin to criticize themselves and transform their world outlook, or they could go on resisting the city leaders, the propaganda team, the brigade committee and the revolutionary masses and end up as counter-revolutionaries.

Veteran Wang, who had heard this view expressed countless times, questioned it this morning on the ground that it minimized the influence of external factors, such as the work of the team. Wang was not at all sure that everything rested with the Two Gems themselves. He was not at all sure that the team had done its work well. He felt that the process of change in a person was a prolonged one, that it could not occur overnight and that a lot of outside help was needed.

"You can't say that today I am one thing and tomorrow I turn into something else," said Wang. "It's true that the internal is the basis of change and the external is the condition of change. It's true that the external only works through the internal but . . ."

"But the external can only help," said Shen, interrupting. "They have to change themselves."

"What I was going to say," Wang went on, "was that you can't leave the external out. It's part of the process. An egg can turn into a chicken, but it's only under certain circumstances—the temperature, the moisture, all have to be right. If you give the egg proper conditions, it will turn into a chicken and not into a rock. A rock can also change, under certain conditions. With the right conditions a rock can change into cement."

"But an egg will not change into a rock," said Shen, still stressing the internal.

"Right. An egg and a rock have nothing in common," said Wang, still trying to concentrate on his own diagnosis. "What I think is that Swift Li can change in two ways. He can remain in low spirits, stop working for the revolution, and concentrate on his ax and his trowel. That way he can earn good money and to hell with everyone else. Or he can change for the good and join everyone else in carrying on the revolution. It's possible. The conditions exist for it. There's a struggle going on in his mind. Has he really decided not to make revolution any more? I doubt it. There are these two choices going round and round in his head—there's some unity and there's some contradiction."

"Well, what is this ax-and-trowel thought, anyway?" asked Donkey Meat Wang.

"It's the idea that I'll put technique in command and take the road of the 'white' expert. No more revolution, to hell with politics. I'll pick up my woodworking ax and my mortar-smoothing trowel and I'll earn good money building houses. In my free time I'll laze around. What it amounts to is loss of revolutionary will."

"Not bad," said Donkey Meat Wang, who had a few butchering skills himself. "I take my ax and my trowel and I go from house to house and I make good money and good connections all around. Not bad!"

"So how do you know Swift Li has this ax-and-trowel thinking? How can you say what's at the bottom of his mind?" asked Shen.

"Well, at least you can say it's one strand in his thinking," replied Veteran Wang. "I think it's an important strand. He tends to think of skilled work outside the village as an acceptable way of life. And he's not the only one. There are lots of people who have the same idea, especially old cadres who have made mistakes. They often see it as a way out. Chairman Mao says there are always two tendencies—one is to advance, the other is to slip back. Of course, if you slip too far back you can end up as a counterrevolutionary. But that's not where we're at today. On the one hand, Swift Li has a tendency not to make revolution; on the other hand, he has a tendency toward the opposite. So what is needed is some outside influence. And that's our work. If we do it well, if the masses undertake a correct policy to help him, he can still come around. Why not?"

Wang painted quite a different picture from the one painted by Lin T'ung, but it was a picture I could understand. I figured that if Swift Li went off to build houses it would be a cold day in hell before he overthrew the revolutionary committee of Long Bow, and a much colder one indeed before he turned into a counterrevolutionary. The real choice before the community, it seemed, was on the one hand to make life so difficult for the ex-Party Secretary that he went off to do carpentry, or, on the other hand, to deflate the rhetoric, treat mistakes as mistakes and not as political catastrophes, show some appreciation for the man's strong points, and offer him a way out. Either way, class struggle hardly figured in the equation. The real problem was factionalism. If Swift Li recognized that, he could take the initiative himself.

87

SMART FAN
CHANGES COURSE

 After the loudspeaker broke the predawn silence with "The East Is Red" and the last strains of that majestic hymn had faded away, we almost never listened to the Mao quotes that followed. For weeks they had been the same, starting with, "In agriculture learn from Tachai, in industry learn from Taching, people of the whole country learn from the People's Liberation Army," and ending with, "The force at the core, leading our cause forward, is the Chinese Communist Party. The theoretical basis, guiding our thinking, is Marxism-Leninism."

But on September 24, without explanation, the first quotation suddenly expanded. It began with the usual three phrases, "In agriculture learn from Tachai, in industry learn from Taching, people of the whole country learn from the People's Liberation Army"; but to the astonishment of everyone listening it didn't stop there. It continued with a new and long-neglected phrase: "Men of the People's Liberation Army learn from the people!"

The revised slogan alerted Carma immediately. "Something big has happened," she said as soon as we met, rubbing our eyes and preparing to wash our faces at the lone spigot in the middle of the courtyard.

"What do you mean?" I asked.

"Didn't you hear the slogan? They added a phrase."

"I heard it," I said. "The extra phrase jarred me, but I hardly heard the words and didn't pay much attention."

"It said 'Men of the People's Liberation Army learn from the people.' "

"What does it mean?" I asked. "Not what do the words mean, but what does the change mean? Why now? What has happened?"

"I don't know," Carma said, "but I know it's important. Any way you look at it, it's a criticism of the army. For years we have been learning from the army. Now suddenly the army is being told to learn from us."

Carma could not add more that morning. The news report contained nothing special—some examples of self-reliance in agriculture, a breakthrough or two in industry, the results of some national sports event, a long editorial on Party rectification. "Throw out the stale, take in the fresh; not throw out the stale, take in the favorites—nephews, nieces, uncles and aunts."

After the national news report vice-brigade leader Shen Chi-ts'ai's voice broke in to announce another village-wide meeting to sum up the Party rectification. He set the meeting for 8:00 P.M. in the brigade hall, but everyone knew that it was not likely to take place before nine because, after returning from the fields at sundown, the people still had to cook supper and eat their fill. Short of another performance by Long Bow's Drama Group, only a popular new film or regional opera could hurry them through that process, and in 1971 there was not much chance of either. Chiang Ch'ing's Eight Model Works dominated stage and screen, and everyone had seen and heard them so often that no one was likely to miss a bite or skip a rest for another immersion in her brand of "revolutionary romanticism." In any case, Chi-ts'ai didn't offer entertainment that night, only more speeches. If people came, they would come out of habit, out of a sense of duty, out of loyalty to the brigade and to its future even when that future could not be seen very clearly.

Like everyone else, Carma and I went to the meeting out of habit. All we expected to hear was more of the class struggle rhetoric that had dominated the previous meeting, leaving the audience both apathetic and confused. My own mood had sunk far below mere apathy. What I felt was deep despair. In summing up the Cultural Revolution Mao Tse-tung had said, "The problem is that contradictions between ourselves and the enemy and contradictions among the people are all mixed up together and it is difficult to sort them out." Difficult it certainly was. The more deeply one penetrated into the affairs of the community, the more complicated its contradictions and conflicts seemed to become. But instead of trying to sort them out, those in charge, as soon as they faced opposition, raised each contradiction to an antagonistic level and denounced the targets of their criticism as class enemies. It was as if the whole community and its outside mentors had been swept onto a giant Ferris wheel that lifted some up as it dropped others down, then flung those above into the abyss as it raised those below to the heavens.

First up, then down, then up again. Round and round turned the huge wheel. Up and down churned the antagonists. Hotter and hotter flared the tempers. Nobody, it seemed, could stop the wheel. And nobody could get off. Where was it all headed? How could it possibly end in anything but disaster?

The meeting hall seemed particularly shabby that night. A group of carpenters had been using the space to fashion some trusses for a new house and someone had swept the shavings they left behind into random piles in front of the stage. Several peasants found the sweepings soft to relax on, but as they sat talking, turning and twisting they dispersed shavings in every direction. Other people had brought the usual planks, bricks and small collapsible stools as seats. They formed little knots for socializing all around the hall. Carpenters' tools, benches and a table or two cluttered the back of the stage, even blocking from view part of the great plaster-stiff portrait of Mao Tse-tung that dominated the center of the back wall. On each side of the portrait hung a plywood board, painted bright red, as a backdrop for slogans in white—"Never forget class struggle" on the right, and "The force at the core, leading our cause forward, is the Communist Party" on the left.

By nine o'clock the hall seemed quite full, but Judge Kao, after counting heads quickly, told us that several production teams had showed up in token numbers only. He could see only thirty-five members from the Sixth Team, and only fifty from the Fifth. Since the Fifth Team had more than seventy families, not even one member per family had deigned to appear.

Security Officer Shen, the opening speaker, launched into the kind of long, dull report that people had learned to expect from him. Before he had finished his first point, quite a few people quietly got up and slipped out. Others slid their seats into more congenial conversational positions and began to talk in low tones. Many of the remaining heads in the crowd began to nod, and some of the nodders soon fell asleep. By the time Shen had warmed up to his third point people were sleeping all over the hall. One or two inadvertently slipped off their perches onto the floor, where they began to snore.

Shen Chi-ts'ai followed Security Officer Shen. He was famous for the most deadly oratorical formalism, strings of slogans strung together in erratic order. Well aware that nobody cared to hear him, he spoke very briefly, a strategy that brought him some applause.

Smart Fan followed Shen Chi-ts'ai. His appearance on the stage caused a stir across the floor. Some people stopped talking momentarily. Others woke up. The prominent city cadre had a reputation as a provocative speaker and the peasants were willing to give him a chance. But with his opening paragraph Smart Fan all but dissipated his welcome. He launched into a routine review of the rectification movement, praising the masses for the opinions offered at the production team meetings and promising that Long Bow's leading cadres would take those criticisms seriously. They would try to overcome their off-again-on-again working style, their tendency to push hard at one time only to relax at another, whether it be in production, in the repudiation of bad people and bad things, or in political education. Smart Fan then proceeded to give the new leading body some qualified praise. "Their line is correct. They are less selfish than the previous body. They work hard. Thus, in the main, they must be seen as good. People respond to this kind of leadership. The city committee and the commune committee trust these cadres and rely on them. But that doesn't mean they have no shortcomings. They must always review their work, develop their strong points, and overcome their weak points. . . ."

So far, so good—safe, routine and boring.

Smart Fan went on to ask the question that was on everybody's mind— what should be done to get Long Bow moving?

The question brought a few wandering minds to attention, but the answer turned them loose again. "First, brigade members must put Mao Tse-tung Thought uppermost in all work. Second, they must never forget class struggle."

Carma and I exchanged despairing glances. We knew what Smart Fan's position was but we hadn't expected it to be stated so flatly, so badly. Was he going to deliver another long harangue on the class enemies in our midst and drive what remained of the audience from the hall? For a moment it seemed so, for as the young city cadre talked quietly on, the conversations on the floor grew in intensity and volume, almost drowning him out. Soon someone would either have to call the meeting to order or adjourn the whole affair.

Suddenly Smart Fan stepped to the very front of the stage and raised his voice.

"What is the situation in the class struggle in Long Bow now?" he asked.

Hearing this, the majority on the floor cocked an ear.

"There are class enemies trying to stir up trouble behind the scenes. There are also some individuals who are objectively wrecking things by stealing and breaking into houses, and there are some ex-cadres who have been removed from their posts and resent it. They are trying to pull together some backward people, even some bad people, to oppose the new leading body and challenge its power in the brigade."

Suddenly listeners outnumbered talkers. Conversations on the floor died away. Sleepers awoke.

With one sentence Smart Fan had challenged the premise that had dominated the rectification proceedings from the beginning. There were class enemies, there were *also* people who were stealing things; there were class enemies, there were *also* resentful cadres. What immediately struck those who heard him was that Smart Fan had drawn a distinction between class enemies, thieves and disgruntled cadres. He had not lumped the thieves with class enemies and had not lumped the Two Gems with the other two categories. Here was something new and startling. People began to drift in instead of out the door.

Smart Fan launched immediately into a review of the activities of Swift Li and Fast Chin and some of their closest collaborators. He charged that they had tried to discredit Chang Kuei-ts'ai by dragging up the Little Four case; they had cursed the new administration by reviving classical opera and ridiculed the administration with extreme politeness, even greeting leaders on the street with "Official, how are you? Official, where might you be going?"; they had undermined the prestige of the propaganda team by spreading rumors that two seats on the brigade revolutionary committee were being held open for Swift Li and Fast Chin; they had started quarrels over emergency grain loans and the purchase of pigs by pitting "black gang" against "red gang."

"In spite of all this they haven't harmed our new leading body," said Smart Fan. "When 95 percent of the people support you, what does it matter if 5 percent of them curse you? But the question remains, Why are they so full of resentment? Why are they so full of hatred? Is it because they have been removed from power and can no longer work their will on the people? If we relax our vigilance and allow them to return to power, will we ever be able to learn from Tachai? Will we ever have enough to eat? Will we ever be able to make a proper sale of grain to the state?

"Mind you, I'm not saying that these two people can't change. What I am saying is that up to now they have not recognized their mistakes, let alone corrected them. They are still brimming with resentment and antagonism toward the help which the people are trying to give them."

This was close to Veteran Wang's theory of the Two Gems. Suspended cadres harboring resentment were a far cry from counterrevolutionaries trying to wreck the state. Carma could not repress a smile. As for me, I could hardly wait to hear what Smart Fan would say next.

Smart Fan began to analyze some of the arguments that the Two Gems had been using in support of their defiance. One was that they were not isolated, that they still had wide support in the village and, what was more important, still had support from higher cadres in the commune and the city.

"In saying this Chin and Li are only trying to comfort themselves. They are putting up a bold front. We cadres support actions in accord with Mao Tse-tung Thought. When the two act correctly, of course they find support from above, but when they make serious mistakes and refuse to recognize these mistakes, how can they claim support anymore?"

Another excuse put forth by the Two Gems was that the harsh measures which they had taken against so many people in the brigade, and especially against Little Shen and his comrades in *Petrel* and *Shankan Ridge,* were factional excesses, repressions carried out in the heat of the struggle for power and, as such, excusable. Such excesses, they argued, were common at the height of the Cultural Revolution.

"But can we excuse beatings on the ground of factionalism?" asked Smart Fan. "Hardly. What happens when mass organizations rise up and fight one another is one thing. That can be called factionalism. But you Two Gems were in power! You held power in the brigade. As commanders of the brigade militia you seized people and had them beaten. What's more, most of the people you seized and beat were poor peasants or lower-middle peasants. Can anyone call this simple factionalism? By no means! This is a form of bourgeois dictatorship over the masses. This is carrying out a *bourgeois reactionary line.* Once you hold power the whole situation is qualitatively transformed. You are responsible for carrying out the policies of the Communist Party and Chairman Mao Tse-tung. If you don't take the socialist road, unite all who can be united, grasp revolution and promote production, and carry the socialist revolution through to the end, you take the capitalist road, promote privilege for a few, divide the people and oppress them."

This, it seemed to me, was a most important point, a point which sorely needed making after all the confusion and chaos of the Cultural Revolution. But it was a point which Smart Fan would surely find difficult to square with his own record, with the record of *United* in the city and the region.

As Smart Fan explained his position the hall fell quiet, so quiet that one could hear people breathing, even the rustle of clothing as limbs shifted position. Looking around I saw that, in contrast to the situation when he started to speak, the hall was now full, absolutely full, and there were people unable to crowd inside the door who were leaning in at the windows, straining to catch every word that was spoken, just as if a play had started on the stage.

Smart Fan, on his part, had abandoned all effort at oratory, at dramatic gestures, at climactic crescendos. He was speaking in a quiet, matter-of-fact manner—no fierce looks, no "hehs," no shouts, no threats. He depended, instead, on rational analysis, on convincing argument to carry the day. He was trying, in Mao's words, "to touch the people to their very souls."

Having exposed the activities of the Two Gems and their "clique," having refuted the main arguments that they still used in their defense, he went on to make clear the attitude of the propaganda team and the city Party committee toward them.

"Our attitude is to save them for the revolution, to cure the disease and save the patient. But up to now they don't see it that way. They are still antagonistic and treat us as a hostile force. What can we do about that?

"Well," said Smart Fan, speaking directly to Li and Chin, who sat in front of him in the audience, "if you people refuse to see things as we do, we have no alternative but to struggle with you. We will carry on the struggle as long as it is necessary and we shall see who will be able to make out in Long Bow in the long run.

"We have a policy of lenient treatment for those who speak frankly and harsh treatment for those who resist. What counts the most is not how big or small your crime or mistake is, but what your attitude toward it is. In Changchih, a woman cadre grafted 300 yuan. Not only would she not admit it, she stole more money in order to cover up her crime. Since she behaved so badly we fired her. In another case a man confessed to the misappropriation of 2,000 yuan. But since his attitude was good we did not punish him at all.

"What road will the Two Gems take? They can choose themselves."

This led Smart Fan back to the question of basic Communist policy— the correct handling of contradictions, and the necessity to distinguish contradictions among the people from contradictions between the people and their enemies, and, having made such distinctions, the necessity of handling each case according to concrete circumstance.

"All those who make mistakes are not necessarily class enemies," said Smart Fan. "We must try to educate them to save them. Never push away people who can be pulled together, never make more enemies than is absolutely necessary."

Now these words were not mind-boggling in themselves. They expressed well-known principles that Mao Tse-tung had explained and advocated over and over again. They had lain at the root of the land reform, the cooperative movement and every successful rectification movement carried out since the revolution began. What was significant was that Smart Fan was suddenly applying them to Long Bow village and suggesting a sharp change in the direction of the rectification campaign of 1971. What had been building up for months as a tidal wave to swamp the errant cadres he meant to trans- form overnight into a gentle current designed to float them back into the mainstream. To return to the original metaphor, Smart Fan was applying brakes to the Ferris wheel, hoping to slow it down enough so that a few, at least, could dismount.

Having launched an attack on extremism, he decided to follow through. He spoke about several severe distortions of common-sense principles of unity that had plagued Long Bow ever since the land reform of 1945. "Our class line in the countryside is: rely on the poor peasants, unite with the middle peasants and isolate the landlords and the rich peasants. But to this day we still do not really apply this line in Long Bow. We still have ultraleft tendencies," said Fan Wen. "When we speak of various middle peasants, some of whom are even Party members, we say that their class origin is *hard* and we hesitate to use them as cadres simply because of their class origin. Now what kind of sectarianism is that?

"In dealing with people whom we illegally attacked and expropriated at the time of land reform, to this day we still do not call them simply poor peasants or middle peasants, or even wrongly struggled poor peasants or middle peasants, but we call them struggle objects and consider their class origin to be *hard* also! What kind of sectarianism is that?

"And then there are the sons and daughters of landlords and rich peasants. The policy of our Party is to treat them according to their political essence—that is, according to the way they actually think, feel and act. If they are sympathetic to socialism, we should work with them and educate them and unite with them. But instead, here in Long Bow we set them aside and deny them a future.

"In addition there are some people whose background is questionable, like one young man whose father was suppressed and killed as a counter-revolutionary, but whose mother later married a poor peasant. This person is willing to be the son of the poor peasant, in whose house he has lived since the age of one. But some people refuse to accept this and do not allow him to be a poor peasant's son, but only a counterrevolutionary's son! If this continues, if we cannot find a way to unite with such a person, how can we ever unite with 95 percent of the people to build socialism?"

The effect of Smart Fan's words was tremendous. From the moment when he placed the Two Gems in a category distinct from that of class enemies, I felt a great burden slipping from my back. As he went on to repudiate one ultraleft tendency after another, the sense of liberation intensified. It was as if I had been transported back to that day in 1948 when, in Lucheng County's great temple, Party Secretary Ch'en exposed and denounced the ultraleft, poor-and-hired peasants' line that had so distorted land reform policy for everyone. As Ch'en spoke that day, light had seemed to flood the dark tunnel where we had been confined, bent over, all but blind, groping for an ever-receding exit. All at once we had found ourselves walking upright onto a wide-open plain, able to move freely toward a rational and unifying goal.

The liberation that I again felt so strongly apparently moved the whole audience in the hall, for the peasants sat in rapt attention, some of them smiling quietly, some of them nodding. Not a single child whimpered, not a single baby cried.

Finally Smart Fan took up the case of Little Shen, the man whom the Two Gems had treated as a class enemy, the man whom the commune Party committee had expelled from the Long Bow Party Branch for "leading a gang of landlords, rich peasants and counterrevolutionaries to seize power."

"From the investigations we have made in the last few months we understand that most of the charges against Little Shen are false," said Smart Fan. "We are asking the commune Party committee to reopen this case. We would like to see a thorough discussion of it at both the Party committee level and among the masses."

Once again Smart Fan had broken through the endless talk about general principles and attacked a concrete case. He had made a bold political judgment that was bound to shake up the status quo not only in Long Bow village but in Horse Square Commune as well. For if the commune Party committee were to reverse its decision on Little Shen, people still in power would have to admit a serious mistake and take responsibility for a serious miscarriage of justice. People in power would have to admit participation in a frame-up that had held together for more than four years. The implications of such an admission were extraordinary. This was no isolated case. The frame-up of Little Shen was almost certainly linked to a whole series of frame-ups, a whole series of atrocious political settlements, all of which would be called into question by the reversal of this case.

Right here in this meeting Smart Fan, by publicly questioning the expulsion of Little Shen, had lit a fuse that could set off a series of explosions all up and down the highway from Yellow Mill at the northern end of the Changchih City administration right back to the City Party offices themselves, and almost certainly on up to the regional offices as well.

This was an extraordinary announcement to make, and the people treated it as such. Late as the hour already was, not a single person left the hall. All concentrated single-mindedly on Smart Fan's next words.

The young city cadre with the prominent forehead, tobacco-stained fingers and quiet platform manner wound up his speech with an appeal for learning from Tachai.

"This is a question of whether you want socialism or not.

"The City committee has decided to build a Tachai-type city in three years. But Long Bow, with a little success in the planting of wheat, has already started to grow complacent. We have done well planting wheat and we have earned the praise we received from the commune leaders, but it should never cause us to be self-satisfied and relax. . . . The way things are here we can't just walk slowly forward, we have to run and catch up. With conditions as they exist today we have neither the soil nor the manure to cross the Yellow River, to say nothing of the Yangtze. Only if we prepare all the conditions for crossing the Yangtze can we guarantee crossing the Yellow River. So the task ahead is heavy.

"Long Bow is now famous all over the world. But does the fact that Old Han has returned after twenty-three years to find us all so backward cause you to feel glory on your face? I should think not!"

When Smart Fan finished, his listeners applauded. They clapped for a long, long time and I clapped, too. I felt like doing more than clapping. I felt like rushing to the stage and hugging the man, for in one evening he had cleared away weeks of obscurantism and miasma; more than that, he had opened the door to clearing up injustices that had hung over the community for years. It was an extraordinary performance and I wondered what had brought it about. Could it be the arguments that had taken place on the propaganda team? Could it be the objections that Carma and I had so stubbornly pushed on Smart Fan and Lin T'ung over the last few days?

Or had something happened at the city level to cause this basic reappraisal?

While we remained in Long Bow I never did come close to an answer to these questions. But when we returned to Peking in October we learned through the "small broadcast" (the grapevine) that an extraordinary event had occurred, not at the city level, not at the regional or even at the provincial level, but at the highest pinnacle of national power. Between the time that the propaganda team in Long Bow began its offensive against the Two Gems as class enemies, in early September, and September 24, when Smart Fan reversed that thrust, Lin Piao had fled the country in a Trident jet and crashed somewhere on the steppes of Outer Mongolia. The defection and exposure of Lin Piao as an anti-Mao conspirator bent on seizing supreme power had been thoroughly suppressed as news but had been passed through internal channels as privileged information right down to the children in primary schools. It shook the Communist Party, the government bureaucracy and the people of China from top to bottom. On the surface it might seem that even this cataclysmic development could hardly have affected grass-roots policy in Long Bow within so short a time. Nevertheless, it had long been common knowledge that extremism, sectarianism and ultraleft dogmatism typified the Lin Piao line. Could it be sheer coincidence that left dogmatism met its first head-on challenge in Long Bow less than two weeks after Lin Piao fell? Could it be sheer coincidence that the day Smart Fan finally questioned the main decisions of the local Cultural Revolution was the same day that the Peking news broadcast suddenly added the phrase "and the People's Liberation Army learn from the people"?

Coincidence here seemed unlikely. What seemed likely was that Lin Piao's flight and death had unleashed a nationwide tide of moderation and common sense powerful enough to challenge the "class struggle" straitjacket that had universally been imposed in his name, and that this tide was already rising irrepressibly on the Shangtang. Cadres like Smart Fan, extremely sensitive to the slightest shift in political currents, were already trimming their sails and adjusting to a shift in the climate.

88

DEEP-DIGGING, SOFT CORN, HIGH DRAMA AND A RIGHTED WRONG

We were out on the great flat to the west of the village, seventy-four strong, each armed with a Tachai shovel, a long flat blade of steel on a stout wooden handle. Tachai people designed their shovel for deep-digging. By applying one foot to the projection of the blade a digger could force the steel nine or ten inches into the earth. With a sharp backward motion of the arms against the upright handle he could then break loose a complete block or divot of topsoil. Lifting this out intact, he could set it to the left, in the trench left open by a previous pass down the field. Then by taking a short step backward and repeating the sequence—thrust, break and lift—he could remove the next six-inch slice.

The long trench created by manhandling the soil to the left set the stage for the second half of the process. The digger turned completely around, stood at the bottom of the trench and again, with the aid of one foot, thrust the steel blade as deep into the hard subsoil as it would go, usually about two-thirds of the depth possible in the mellow soil of the surface layer. With the same backward motion of the handle he broke a divot loose, deftly turned it over and returned it, loose and crumbling, to the hole from which it came. By moving backward up the trench, step by step, he could turn over in place all the subsoil underfoot, thus completing a strip of deep-digging in the field to the width of one Tachai shovel, about eight inches.

Once the digger reached the upper end at last, he turned around once more, stepped up onto the undisturbed soil to his right and proceeded to move it, slice by slice, onto the overturned subsoil beside it. The whole process did to the surface of the soil what a good plow would do—throw a layer of topsoil upside down into the adjacent furrow; and did to the subsoil what a good agricultural chisel would do—stir and loosen a buried layer that no plow could ever reach. With a good Tachai shovel and lots of energy one person could deep-dig the land to a depth of fourteen or even sixteen inches. By working a long ten-hour day each digger could process one-fortieth of an acre. In the course of 40 days, 400 hours of digging, one person could turn over an acre. The goal set for the 72-member Deep-Digging Shock Brigade in Long Bow in October 1971 was just under two acres a day. By maintaining this pace for 70 days, the brigade could prepare 800 mou (133 acres) for a bumper crop in 1972.

Behind the deep-digging effort lay the assumption that stirring the soil increased yields, and that the deeper one stirred it, the higher the yields would be. Stirring the soil was supposed to incorporate air, increase water percolation, and hasten mineral decomposition to the great advantage of the crop to be planted the following spring. So far as I could determine no scientific, controlled experiments had ever been done to test out this theory one way or another. It was accepted by one and all on faith, a deep faith in tillage as the heart and soul of agriculture. *Shen kung, hsi tso* (deep tillage, careful tending) was the slogan raised by the peasants of Tachai to explain their success with crops, and from Tachai this slogan spread to every corner of the land.

Actually the deep-digging craze began long before Tachai became famous. It started in Honan at the time of the Great Leap and millions of peasants carried it to extremes as the leaders of county after county, region after region, tried to outdo one another in their demands for superior land preparation. At the height of the euphoria, ambitious tillers dug some fields to depths of three and even four feet. Indifferent results led to the conclusion that "irrational" deep-digging (three to four feet) was wasteful, probably even harmful, but this did not shake the universal faith in "rational" deep-digging (one to two feet) which Party committees suddenly placed on the agenda again in Shansi (and possibly many other provinces) in 1971.

Long Bow leaders met to discuss the matter after Horse Square Brigade went all out for deep-digging, and Commune Secretary Ho recommended the method to everyone. They decided to make a special effort and suggested a shock brigade of the strongest and healthiest young militiamen and women under the age of twenty-five. Militia members of each field team selected the twelve best from among their ranks and sent them to a mobilization meeting on October 11, where they laid their "battle" plans. Shock team members decided to try for one-fortieth of an acre per person per day; for twenty-two acres per platoon per season; for dawn to dusk digging, with both breakfast and lunch sent to the field; for team rather than individual preparation of meals; and for a socialist emulation contest between the various platoons to see which could dig the most and dig it best, day after day.

The meeting was lively, the liveliest we had attended since our arrival in August. The young people appreciated the challenge and the chance to work together as a special unit on a great task, especially the girls. They looked to be about twelve or thirteen but were really sixteen to eighteen years old. In bright, multicolored jackets of machine-made cotton cloth, they huddled together in tight little groups. Holding hands, leaning on one another, hugging one another, laughing and giggling, they challenged the boys to come over and start the discussion. How much could they do per shift? What platoon should they challenge? What food should they prepare? Who had shovels? By contrast the boys seemed callow, diffident, half awake. Nevertheless, by the end of the meeting they, too, were laughing, bright-eyed and eager, evidently turned on by the girls.

Judge Kao, in his introductory speech, had headed off any discussion of the value of deep-digging by making support for it a political issue. "When we try to dig deep, class enemies come out and say the land here is not good, that it can't be improved by tillage. The more you dig it, the worse it gets, they say. Others say only that the work is too hard, that deep-digging is not worth the trouble. This is lazy, cowardly, bourgeois thinking. Toward those who would try to wreck our three-fall work we have to carry on a campaign of repudiation. We dig deep for the revolution. Deep-digging is a revolution. This is class struggle in reality."

After that introduction no one dared raise a question about whether to do the job. The only question to ask was how. Everybody wanted high yields. The commune said deep-digging would prepare the way, so let's get on with it. Besides, who wanted to be called a class enemy?

The next day in the field everything went well. Militia Captain Lu Ho-jen saw to it that each platoon brought a large red flag. He divided the land up in such a way that seventy-two people could all fall to at once without getting in each other's way and without creating backfurrows, unfilled trenches, all over the place. Carma and I borrowed shovels from old Kuo Cheng-k'uan and joined the "battle." Under a gray, cloud-filled sky a strong west wind bore down on us, whipping the silk banners into frenzied motion, making them snap and slap like a muleteer's whip. Whenever the wind died down we could see our breath on the air, but nobody felt cold. How could they, digging at that pace? Thrust, break and lift; shove, heave and throw; minute after minute, hour after hour. If we took the time to look we could see the tilled land growing and the stubble land shrinking, first in checkerboard pattern as small squares expanded, then by leaps as the squares linked up. We vowed to stay with it, at least for the day, but no one ever said that we did our one-fortieth of an acre share, even after we returned for two more afternoons.

I joined because I wanted to be part of the effort, not because I had faith in deep-digging, and the longer I dug the less happy I felt about the whole project. The commune tractors could easily plow nine inches deep. With a chisel they could rip another five- or six-inch layer and accomplish in minutes what this crew could not do in days. What a waste! What a waste! But nobody had a tractor-drawn chisel, nobody had ever heard of one, and nobody, as far as I could see, showed any interest in one. So it was thrust, break and lift; shove, heave and throw; from dawn until just before dark, when the loudspeaker on the Brigade Meeting Hall, for the second time that day, blasted "The East Is Red" to the sky. This time it announced the end of the working shift. The way the wind was blowing past us toward the speaker, even the thunderous rendition of "The East Is Red" sounded faint and far away.

That night, after we had eaten our supper, we went to the Fifth Team threshing floor to see the start of the fall grain distribution. Powerful electric bulbs mounted high on poles lit up the area, which was bounded on the north and west by bundles of millet straw stacked shoulder-high to break the wind. Two piles of well-cleaned millet dominated the center. The larger pile, pale lemon in color, was regular millet; the smaller pile, bright golden, was high-quality "yellow" millet. Just for fun we took turns estimating the total weight of the big pile. The estimates varied from 8,000 catties to 28,000 catties. Then the warehouseman, who had already weighed it, gave us the figure—15,586. It was easy to see how estimates exaggerated yields during the Great Leap. Commune cadres looked at a pile, made a shrewd guess, and reported that. Pretty soon the government came looking for grain that wasn't there. The peasants, on their part, almost always underestimated. The more grain they reported, the larger the tax bite and the more they had to sell to the state as its legitimate share.

Veteran Wang said one year Kuyi Brigade failed to report 50,000 catties of wheat, but the commune secretary found out about it because several members talked out of turn. One Kuyi woman who had married outside, but refused to move away, received her regular per capita share but no part of the surplus, the hidden wheat. She went to the commune office to complain.

"I didn't get my share of the extra grain."

"What extra grain?"

"The grain they didn't keep any record of," she said, as if the whole scam was common knowledge.

The commune Party Secretary then invited the brigade chairman to a meal. He made sure to pass out plenty of sorghum liquor. In an unguarded moment the brigade chairman boasted of the excellent crop.

"My share of the surplus alone was 500 catties," he said.

The next day the commune Party Secretary dropped in for a chat.

"How about those 50,000 catties?" he asked.

"Who said anything about 50,000 catties?"

"You did, when you were drinking last night!"

"Well, I don't remember what I said last night, but I can assure you there is no hidden wheat here," said the brigade chairman, indignant.

Later, Horse Square Commune called a meeting for brigade cadres.

"We have reason to believe that some brigades are hiding grain," said the Party Secretary. "Whoever is guilty should report it now, make a clean breast of it, and we will not make an issue of it. But if it is not reported now, we can't guarantee the future."

Nobody spoke up, but when the meeting adjourned Kuyi leaders milled around, reluctant to leave the room.

Finally Kuyi's chairman said, "Add 50,000 to our production figure."

Thus the matter was cleared up.

On the Fifth Team threshing floor that night equal distribution ruled. Every person—man, woman and child—got eighty catties of regular millet and twenty catties of "yellow" millet. These were the amounts that had been distributed the year before. They represented not the individual's final share, but a preliminary distribution, pending the completion of the harvest, which included huge amounts of corn that still had to be dried and weighed. Final shares would not be equal, but would reflect workdays earned in the course of the year. In the meantime team leaders handed out millet to keep everyone going.

Checkers weighed the millet on a platform scale by pouring it into wooden boxes shaped much like the boxes Western masons use to mix mortar. Boards nailed to opposite sides of the boxes protruded at each end and served as handles so that once the proper weight had been recorded two people could lift the box, carry it to one side, and dump the grain in a pile that represented a given family's share. Family members then bagged it. Sometimes the family members were ready with a bag when the millet poured out. They tried to hold it so the grain went directly into their floppy container, but since the boxes were square and clumsy a lot of grain hit the ground anyway and had to be swept up.

To ensure fair weights, those who manned the scales came from another team. Fifth Team checkers weighed the grain for the Second Team. The theory was that outsiders, who had no stake in the amount distributed because it would not affect their own shares, would be unlikely to play favorites or to cheat.

Team chairman Kuo Cheng-k'uan was pleased with the way things were going. Millet yields had been comparatively high, about seventy catties per mou above the previous year, so the shares looked ample. Cheng-k'uan liked the collective harvest and the collective distribution. It was so much simpler than any procedure followed in the old days, when each family had to thresh and clean its own grain and keep the different varieties separate. Then, there were little piles crowding the threshing floor and it was hard to keep them straight. He wanted to make sure we understood the difference.

We wandered around to see how everything was done and talked to different family members as they filled their bags. Their morale was high because the millet was plentiful and would fill to the brim all the jars reserved for it in each home. But when we brought up the question of the corn crop, people shook their heads. The corn crop, just then being harvested, did not look good at all. In August everyone assumed that the corn would yield more than 300 catties per mou, thus breaking all Long Bow records and filling every jar in the village. But during the heavy rains, leaf blight struck and stopped plant growth in its tracks. It was just as if a hard frost had hit the fields. Many ears failed to mature. Many soft kernels shriveled as they dried, falling far short of normal weight. The worst-hit variety was the much-touted single-cross Nan Tan #15. (Nan for south, Tan for single). It was a new hybrid that experts had brought into the Shangtang at considerable expense. Secretary Chang, trying to break the conservatism of the past, had pushed it as a scientific breakthrough that revolutionaries should welcome and put to work. His own team, the Second, had planted a large acreage of it and now was suffering from the collapse of the variety due to leaf blight brought on by wet weather. Another single-cross, Wen Ke #1 (Wen for Culture, Ke for Revolution—politics was evidently in command in plant breeding), stood up better, but the most resistant varieties of all were the old open-pollinated Ching Huang Ho (Golden Queen) and Pai Ma Ya (White Horse Tooth), imported many years before from Lancaster County, Pennsylvania. In fact, if it hadn't been for these old standbys, the 1971 corn crop would have been close to a disaster and the brigade would have had to appeal to the state for help to get through the winter, as it had already done to get through the summer after a disastrous wheat crop.

What made the new hybrids susceptible to leaf blight was the incorporation into their breeding of the Texas Male Sterile gene, a technique that made it possible for big American seed companies to create hybrid corn without manual detasseling. They didn't have to hire people to go through the fields cutting the male tassels off the rows that would be used as female ear producers because Texas Male Sterile tassels produced no pollen. What they failed to realize was that the same gene that carried this sterility also carried low blight resistance. Their mistake threatened the entire American corn crop in 1970 and, in 1971, much of the corn crop in China, where Texas Male Sterile showed up a year later.

The collapse of Nan Tan #15 was a disaster not only for advanced hybrid corn but for the prestige of science. Many peasants had never wanted to plant the single-crosses anyway; they didn't trust them. They were persuaded to do so because it was "scientific." When the single-crosses failed, science failed, and it would take several good years and several good new varieties to overcome the bad reputation science gained for itself that season.

The propaganda team, oblivious to the importance of what had happened, failed to take the collapse of Nan Tan #15 seriously. Judge Kao refused to blame the seed corn for the near-disaster on Second Team land and blamed instead sloppy work, loose organization and conservative thinking. He argued that since every team had received the same amount of improved corn, every team had planted the same amount. If differences showed up at harvesttime, they had to be due to poor management. The Second Team had only itself to blame. He initiated an investigation into the allocation of seed corn to find out if the new varieties had indeed been distributed equally. But this investigation proved nothing because, although every team got the same amount of each variety, most of them didn't plant all the seed they received, certainly not all the single-cross seed. Skeptical, as they had a right to be, about depending too heavily on untried varieties, they had fallen back on open-pollinated Golden Queen and White Horse Tooth. All they needed to do for this seed was shell kernels off their own stored ear corn. But they didn't tell the higher cadres what they were doing because they didn't want to be accused of "conservatism." In the atmosphere of the times such a charge could easily be blown into counterrevolution.

As luck would have it, there was enough "conservatism" around in 1971 to ensure large areas of good crops. The teams that listened to the commune leadership, the brigade leadership and the Party leadership, and went in heavily for new varieties, headed for crop failure. The teams that kept their own counsel, planted only token amounts of the new varieties, and put their faith in old standbys had good to excellent crops. This should have been clear to anyone with any farming experience, but unfortunately it wasn't clear to the cadres of the propaganda team. They saw only the surface of the phenomenon and not its essence. They were so anxious for modern science, modern corn breeding and new technology to break through and win out over blind conservatism that they refused to grant the obvious, that in this case science had failed. It was all due to vagaries of the weather. If the weather had been normal that year, the crop picture would have been quite different. In a dry season the new hybrid varieties might well have outyielded the old standbys. Science would have recorded a straightforward triumph. But it would have been a questionable triumph, nevertheless, because the terrible weakness of the new strains in the face of leaf blight would have remained hidden, lying in wait for a wet year to come. By that time the peasants would have planted all or most of the land to blight-prone corn. Then the crop failure could easily reach catastrophic proportions.

What struck me was the independence of the peasants. Over and over again they made up their own minds and went ahead and did what they thought best, regardless of shrill instructions from on high. When things didn't work, or looked dubious, they simply held back, voted with their feet, did things their own way, and the less said about it the better. What the cadres didn't know wouldn't hurt them. Sometimes the gap between leaders and led widened to a veritable chasm.

Too often, when the cadres insisted on having their way, disaster struck. Down below Li Village Gulch on the road to Changchih City, Agricultural Department officials insisted on planting apple trees. They called the project the *State Apple Farm*. Many peasants said the soil was too wet, that the site was unsuitable for apples, but the city cadres, combating "conservatism," went ahead anyway. No apples ever set on the trees and after quite a few years had passed, cadres changed the name of the farm to *New Happiness Village*. What there was to be happy about they never made clear. Happiness, at least, could not be weighed on a scale like apples, and so who could say there was no happiness there?

In Hukuan, to the north, peasants had long planted beans in the corn after the last hoeing, and reaped a good crop. Commune cadres ordered them to plant millet instead. The peasants said, "It won't work." But the cadres said, "It works in Changchih." So in 1971 they all planted millet and harvested exactly nothing. They didn't have the irrigation water, the night soil and the chemical fertilizer available to the market gardeners inside the city limits.

Veteran Wang chuckled over peasant intractability. Sometimes the most backward showed the best sense, he said. As soon as a team or a brigade became "advanced," members felt they had a reputation to maintain; then if they went out to hoe, they made sure they hoed the crops near the road, where everyone could see the quality of their weed control. Anyone who was so unwise as to strike out into the middle of the field might find weeds in profusion. Backward teams, without any reputation to maintain, did some hard hoeing in the middle of the field, where it counted most, where it had the greatest influence on yields. If the fields looked a little ragged around the edges, who cared? Call them backward, they agreed. "OK, we're backward," they would say with annoying cheerfulness.

The anxious piling of half-shriveled corn ears for air drying, the division of threshed millet to tide people over until corn could be ground, and deep-digging aimed at bumper crops in the year to come all followed in the wake of a great fall harvest push that began the day after Smart Fan reversed his position in public and suddenly stopped calling the Two Gems class enemies. That crucial mass meeting had served as the last big event of the Party rectification—at least until the harvest could be completed—

and mobilization for the new campaign in the fields had begun the first thing the next morning even though some teams were still planting the last of their wheat.

The brigade leaders assigned about 15 percent of the labor power to finish up the wheat land and 85 percent to harvesting millet, sorghum, beans and corn. They urged everyone to turn out. The sideline workers at the brick kiln promised to take to the fields after their daytime shifts were done. The grain-grinding crew at the milling station sent two people out all day while one stayed home alone to grind far into the night. The accountants, all six of them, volunteered for full days in the field and promised to balance their accounts after hours. Even the doctor in the clinic and the druggist in the dispensary volunteered for field work, taking their first aid kits with them in case of need. The school staff temporarily suspended classes so that all schoolchildren could either join the harvest or glean what was left behind by the harvest crews. A directive came down from the Rural Work Department of Changchih City stopping all construction—no house building, no warehouse construction; all hands must report for the harvest. Another directive ordered all tractors off the roads; no more hauling until fall plowing on the land freed by the fall harvest had been completed. Any tractor found on the highway would be seized and impounded until further notice. A third directive ordered all city cadres and all city students into suburban fields to help. That some people at least responded was brought home to us when Commander Ts'ui of the People's Liberation Army and vice-chairman of the Changchih City committee stopped in Long Bow to have a chat. Ts'ui's windburned face and sweat-stained uniform testified to a day spent in the army rice fields on the open land to the east. There officers and soldiers had completed the harvest ahead of schedule.

Long Bow's vice-chairman, Shen Chi-ts'ai, announced over the loud-speaker that every team and every working group should take note of outstanding achievements and report them to the brigade office; then people could be praised by loudspeaker and encouraged to continue the good work. This would stimulate others to catch up. Every day thereafter during the noon broadcast he cited dozens of names.

It was after the bulk of the harvest had been gathered in that mobilization for deep-digging had begun. While seventy-two young militiamen and women concentrated their spades two days at a time on the land of each team in rotation, the rest of the manpower went on with what remained of the harvest.

In the midst of all this activity I felt once again the tremendous social and productive power of this cooperative community. Whenever there was a big job to do, whenever the direction was clear, Long Bow had the capacity to mobilize brains, muscles and enthusiasm on an unprecedented scale. Confronted by a challenge, Long Bow saw feuds, grievances and resentments fade away, factionalism lose its sting, and everyone turn out in high good humor to lend a hand. It was exciting to observe and exciting to take part in.

Of course, not even the harvest rush could proceed without a hitch, as Sixth Team leader Lu Yu-sheng found out. He set a group of schoolchildren to work in a bean field. He gave each boy three rows to cut. When he came back, there was no one in the field. Shih Nien-hsi's son had cut his finger, and since he himself could no longer work he persuaded all the boys to put down their sickles and join him in a ball game. When Lu Yu-Sheng found them, he criticized the ringleader. "It's OK for you to quit since you cut your finger, but why drag everyone else out of the field?"

Nien-hsi's son got angry. "You not only butt into our everyday work, you hold our family's life in your hands," he said and stalked off.

That same afternoon the boy disappeared.

Nien-hsi's wife came to the team headquarters cursing. She accused Lu Yu-sheng of driving her boy out. "He even claims to hold our lives in his hands!" These were her boy's words, not Yu-sheng's, but by using them she made a damaging case against the team leader. He felt so vulnerable that he borrowed 80 yuan from the brigade office and went out looking for the boy.

The next day Nien-hsi's son returned, on his own. His disappearance, it turned out, had been an accident. After he left the field he went to the railroad yard to play. He climbed onto a freight car that was sitting on a siding. Suddenly the car began to move. It moved so fast that the boy didn't dare get off. The car carried him all the way north to Hsinhsiang before the train that had coupled onto it stopped. He arrived there without food or money and it took him a whole day to get home.

His mother lost a lot of face. She had sworn at the team leader and blamed him for driving her son away, but her son was at fault, not the team leader. She had to apologize to Lu Yu-Sheng when he finally came home, distraught because he had not found any trace of the boy.

As the day approached for our scheduled departure, work in the fields eased somewhat and the drama group decided to put on one last evening of plays for our benefit. Anticipating an audience far larger than that which had jammed the Brigade Meeting Hall for the Party rectification meeting, the group decided to use the outdoor stage that still occupied the southern edge of the old North Temple site. This stage, all that remained at the site of the temple complex, resembled a small temple in its own right, a solid structure of upright beams, brick platforms, brick walls and a tiled roof with upturned corners. It faced a large rubble-strewn yard about the size of two basketball courts. The layout was ideal for local performances at any time when the weather was fair and the evening of October 20 brought fair weather indeed. There was just enough bite in the air to keep people alert.

An enormous crowd gathered long before the performance began, jamming the open space from that time until the last performer retired from the scene. Not only did almost the entire population of Long Bow turn out, including all the workers and their families from the rented rooms, but also all the soldiers from the Liberation Army tank unit, housed at the southern end of the village, and most of the staff and the students from the Medical School housed in the old Catholic orphanage compound. In addition, many people came across the tracks from the Railroad Third Bureau Construction Corps.

According to custom, the brigade reserved the best section of the empty yard for the Liberation Army tankmen. They occupied a solid block directly in front of the stage, and only the seats provided for Carma, myself, Lin T'ung from *Central* and the regional cadres in our entourage, broke this block. As honored guests, we enjoyed not only reserved seating space, but benches to sit on as well.

With such a huge audience before them, the Long Bow entertainers went all out with bright costumes, makeup and two long plays that they had not performed before. From my point of view the makeup was not necessarily an improvement. I thought the local girls quite beautiful enough in their natural state, each one unique, each distinct in character and features. Powdered and rouged, with their eyebrows and eyelashes blackened, they tended to look almost exactly alike, a row of painted mannequins with only one expression—a fixed and meaningless smile. But what is drama without makeup? What is theater without pretense? And so, with the aid of a dramatic adviser from the Changchih municipal theater, the Long Bow troupers plastered themselves with cosmetics, draped themselves with bright cloth, and prepared to recapture, if not overwhelm, the long tradition of rural opera that they loved so much.

The makeup, distasteful as it was to me, certainly did no harm to their dancing or acting. Stimulated by the outsize audience, skills honed by intense practice since the days of the fair, they put on a brilliant performance that held the entire audience spellbound. The young women did their hoe dance to perfection. The young men put their hearts into the Tachai skit with its delightful, heavy-footed chorus, but the real star of the evening was Wang Yü-mei, the pharmacist in charge of the dispensary, and the oppressed daughter-in-law of the Lu family in whose house the propaganda team met every day for morning study.

Yü-mei starred in two beautifully staged productions—one, a new version of *Brother and Sister Reclaim Wasteland,* an operetta from the early days of the revolution in Yenan; and the other, *Taking Gifts to the People's Liberation Army,* a play which the group presented as if the leading characters were Long Bow peasants. The play, already a little out of date considering the new slogan, "Men of the Liberation Army learn from the people," was about a young girl, Little Red, and her grandfather, who set out to devise a stratagem for persuading the local army unit to accept a gift on August 1, the birthday of the revolutionary armed forces. Knowing full well that because the "Three Disciplines and Eight Points for Attention" forbade soldiers to take even a needle or a piece of thread from the people, no soldier or commander in the unit will knowingly accept any gift from the people, the two practice various ruses, hoping to accomplish by indirection what they cannot accomplish by any frontal approach. They take turns playing the part of the alert army man and the dedicated gift-giver. The granddaughter is unsuccessful in pressing soap, made by the students of the local ten-year school, into her grandfather's hands. He repeatedly reminds her that army men take nothing from the people. But when the grandfather plays the part of the gift-giver he launches into such a lively monologue about the merits of the army and the people's gratitude that his granddaughter is quite carried away and inadvertently holds onto the soap which he places in her hands.

"Look, there you are," says the grandfather triumphantly. "You've taken it."

"Yes," says Little Red, crestfallen, knowing full well that no army man would ever let his guard down to that extent. "But after all, it's only I who have taken it, and not any soldier."

"That's right," says her grandfather. "There's no easy way to get around *them.*"

In the end Little Red decides to sneak into the barracks, make off with the army men's soiled clothing, and, together with a group of friends, wash all the clothes in the village pond. In that way the army men will have to accept the locally made soap without taking any material object into their hands. Elated by this idea, Little Red and her grandfather happily part company.

Wang Yü-mei threw herself into the part with enthusiasm. Her expression of disappointment and dismay when she found she had been tricked into holding onto the soap was poignant and her joy when she thought a solution to the problem had been found was contagious. Yü-mei, like the teenager whose song had so moved us during the previous performance, possessed facial features that were plain, yet added up to provocative beauty. Bulging eyeballs puffed her eyelids slightly outward, while protruding teeth held her lips forward. These features, combined with a receding chin, gave her a fishlike profile, but her animated face, from any other angle, framed her full, slightly puckered lips with flashing eyes and dimpled cheeks that complemented each other and blended to express unusual fire and energy. A heavy, jet-black braid of hair, hanging down her back all the way to her hips, alternately caressed and danced away from her slight body and by its motion projected her mood more convincingly than any play of her features or gesture of her hands.

Yü-mei's physical attributes, pleasing as they were, were not the secret of her success on the stage. That was the way she identified with the part she was playing and made every word and gesture contribute to an illusion of reality so apt that it was almost painful to experience. Since she was, after all, playing the part of a young woman very much like herself, it might be argued that this did not take much acting skill. Nevertheless, others with equal physical endowment who played themselves never approached her ability to create on the stage a believable liberated country girl. I, for one, was easily captivated.

The man who played the grandfather in this skit also played his part well. There is a tendency in China, at least among workers and students, to overplay the part of any peasant and particularly of any older peasant, turning the role into a caricature, rather than a character study of a real rural grandfather. But this young actor, far from overplaying the part, treated it with respect, thus providing a perfect foil against which Yü-mei could pit her talent. I later learned that the actor was still under a cloud in the village as a grafter sentenced to "supervision by the masses." That this supervision in no way interfered with his career as a member of the dramatic troupe was of more than passing interest. It turned out that he not only played various roles on the stage in Long Bow but also went on the road whenever the group traveled, and even performed in the great theater in Changchih when the Regional Drama Corps put on a major opera and needed a small play or two to round out its program.

The cast had introduced the play *Taking Gifts to the People's Liberation Army* with a strident declaration that "our Long Bow Brigade has undergone an earthshaking, sky-collapsing transformation."

When Wang Yü-mei came off the stage, Smart Fan called her aside to make a suggestion. As he talked she stood in the shadow cast by the old tiled roof, leaned back against the masonry, and with one hand readjusted her hair. Flushed with the excitement of her part and the prolonged applause, she looked particularly attractive, feminine, even coquettish, and this made it hard for Smart Fan to maintain his dignity.

"Why did the play start with such an unqualified declaration of earthshaking, sky-collapsing transformation?" he asked. "Wasn't that an exaggeration?"

"Well, yes," Yü-mei admitted. "That's not exactly what one would say about Long Bow. But for that matter we don't produce any soap, either, in our ten-year school."

"Then why do you pretend that this is our brigade? Why not just say it's a play about some other brigade?"

"Well," said Yü-mei, hesitating, her eyes looking at the ground, "we like to pretend that it is happening right here. It makes everything so vivid that way. And besides, we do make iron in our ten-year school. We could easily make soap."

"Well," said Smart Fan gently—who but her mother-in-law could be anything but gentle with this shy young woman?—"if you have to pretend that it's really Long Bow, at least change that 'earthshaking' statement to something like 'great change.'"

Wang Yü-mei agreed. Then, apparently quite impressed with Smart Fan, she turned to Security Officer Shen, who was standing nearby, and asked if the city cadre was older than he.

"I'm the little finger, he's the thumb," said Shen. "He led the rebels of the whole city!"

On this question—exaggerating the impact of the Cultural Revolution—Smart Fan was trying to follow through on the speech he had made at the mass meeting to sum up the Party rectification campaign. Once he became critical of things ultraleft, he found no end of targets to attack, and not the least of these was exaggerated rhetoric. Hyperbole had replaced common sense on almost every front for years. Never mind the actual situation; since Chairman Mao has called the situation excellent, we will call it excellent, too. Since the Cultural Revolution is supposed to transform us, we will celebrate transformation. What, after all, is the ultimate criterion of truth? Is it not to mark which way the wind is blowing and fashion a rhetoric to match?

I found Smart Fan's sudden penchant for understatement, or more accurately, for mild rather than outrageous overstatement, fascinating. It was one more straw in the wind to add to the sudden change in the slogans that had come over the radio from Peking.

I wasn't granted much time to think about it.

Our enjoyment of the play carried with it a price, so it seemed, and that price was heavy. Carma and I had to appear upon the stage and put on some sort of performance. I had made the mistake, during certain relaxed moments, of singing some American songs and doing a few clog steps for friends, particularly children. Now the whole community believed that I could both sing and dance, and the audience refused to take no for an answer. Someone thrust an accordion into Carma's hands and insisted that she play so her father could get on with his act.

In the end we had no way out. We had to accept the challenge or spend the rest of the evening refusing, for the audience, instigated by Security Officer Shen, showed no signs of giving up, no sign at all. When Carma finally agreed to play, I sang an old song about immigrant Irish railroad workers breaking up a ledge of rock somewhere in the Alleghenies.

> The boss came around and he said cape still
> And come down heavy on the cast-iron drill.
> Drill, ye tarriers, drill; drill, ye tarriers, drill,
> And work all day for sugar in your tay,
> Down behind the railway, and drill, ye tarriers, drill,
> And blast! And fire!
>
> The new boss's name was Jim McCann,
> By God, he was a damn mean man.
> Past week a premature blast went off
> And a mile in the air went big Jean Goff
> And drill, ye tarriers, drill. . . .
>
> Next week when payday came around
> Jean Goff a dollar short was found.
> When he asked what for, came this reply,
> You're docked for the time you was up in the sky.
> And drill, ye tarriers, drill. . . .
> And blast! And fire!

The audience loved it, particularly after Carma translated the lyrics. The peasants knew all about such meanness. There had been a landlord in Long Bow who would not hire anyone who lived nearby. A laborer with a house of his own always preferred to relieve himself in his own toilet cistern, thus depriving the landlord of night soil. An out-of-town hired man usually lived on the landlord's premises and contributed his bit to the landlord's own cistern, thus increasing both yields and profits.

I followed big Jean Goff's ripoff by capitalists with a rendition of an old Vermont clog, a heavy-footed jig that inspired several minutes of the wildest kind of applause. It was certainly no great dance. I performed it clumsily, but it was new, it was different, it was therefore marvelous.

On the following evening, our last in Long Bow, I invited all of the brigade's leading citizens to a banquet. It was a cheap gesture on my part since I paid for the affair with *Central* funds dispersed by Lin T'ung, but it satisfied protocol and delighted everyone in the village who took part.

Assembling the guest list proved to be a very delicate matter, for we could not possibly seat or feed everyone whom I knew well, enjoyed conversing with, owed hospitality to or simply wanted to include for old times' sake. The only principle I could think of was the tried-and-true, time-tested formula taken for granted in China—start at the top and work downward according to rank until the guest list is filled. It was an unfortunate formula for my purposes because many of the people I valued most in Long Bow had no rank at all, but if I departed from it there was no way to ensure leaving town with good feelings intact. Those left out could only accept being slighted if a clear-cut, traditional etiquette, an etiquette which they could easily understand if not admire, disciplined our decisions.

But when Lin T'ung came up with the list, she herself departed from this principle. She invited Yang Lien-ying, vice-chairwoman of the Women's Association, whom she liked, and left out Lu Shu-yun, chairwoman of the Women's Association, whom she did not like. Although I shared her preference for Lien-ying, I questioned her choice, and suggested that she invite both or neither. For some reason my disapproval enraged Lin T'ung. She cursed me, called me the most difficult foreign visitor she had ever had to deal with, said I was a troublemaker and a pain in the neck to boot. In one great flood all the frustrations that she had felt over the last six months while traveling with me and my family came pouring out in the form of bitter recriminations. It was an extraordinary surprise attack born of anguish at having been held so long in this rural backwater, at the postponement of important personal and state plans because I had been playing things by ear and following not some preconceived rational program but whatever path opened before me and showed the greatest potential for breaking through to reality. Why, asked Lin T'ung, couldn't I write a book according to plan like any other sensible person? In a socialist society everything had to be planned—tours, factory construction, the planting of crops, education, childbearing—why should I make an exception of my writing? And now, with the guest list all drawn up, I had to come up with my own absurd set of standards and create trouble when no trouble was called for.

I felt like saying that books could not be assembled like bridges, that it was hard to plan the study of a Cultural Revolution that nobody really understood, but I sensed that in matters such as these, as in matters pertaining to the objectivity of the real word, our basic assumptions would be so far apart that a month of talk would never bring us together, so I simply restated my proposal for the invitations—a straightforward hierarchical guest list would solve all problems. Nothing else was likely to do so.

Cursing and protesting, Lin T'ung left the room.

That night when the guests appeared both the chairwoman and the vice-chairwoman of the Women's Association were there. In addition, all the leading male officials of the brigade appeared—team leaders, Youth League leaders, Party leaders and Peasants' Association leaders, the head of the school, the village doctor, the chief accountant. It was a lively occasion, with lots of toasts and lots of fat pork washed down with sorghum liquor. Carma and I were not too keen on fat pork, but for Long Bow peasants that was the main attraction of any banquet. Living from day to day, month to month, and year to year on grain, cabbage and potatoes, they lacked fat in their diet. A good three-inch slab of pork belly looked to them far better than sea slugs or sharks' fins. After four or five "bottoms up" I lost my ability to tell fat pork from lean in any case.

After the banquet Secretary Chang convened a mass meeting in the Brigade Hall so that everyone would have a chance to say goodbye. The highlight of this meeting was an announcement by Smart Fan that on that very day word had come that the Commune Party Committee had cleared Little Shen of crime, had reinstated him with full rights in the Communist Party and in the brigade as a cadre. It was welcome news, extremely welcome news. When Smart Fan made the announcement, everyone in the hall began to talk at once. Little Shen's father, Old Shen Chi-ming, whom I had known for more than twenty years, came up to us afterward, bowed deeply from the waist three times, and thanked us for saving his son's life and his family's good name. He seemed to think that without our presence no one would have bothered to clear up the case and no one would have reversed the decision to expel this son, certainly not in 1971, and he may have been right. Because we were present, Shansi officials at every level had focused their attention on Long Bow, and because we intended to write about its history, historic justice had to be done.

We tried to tell Old Chi-ming that the reversal was not our doing but the work of responsible Party committees, but he would have none of it. He grasped my hand, thanked me profusely, and bowed low again and again. For me it was embarrassing and for him unwise, for the accepted mode of behavior would have been to thank Chairman Mao; under Chairman Mao's wise leadership his son had been cleared. But Shen did not seem to care. Tears came to his eyes as he thanked us again and again.

Little Shen, towering over his father, kept nudging him and saying, "Thanks to Chairman Mao, I have been cleared. You'd better remember Chairman Mao." But Old Chi-ming ignored him, grasped my hand, and would not let it go.

89

ONCE AGAIN,
LONG BOW, TSAI CHIEN

 We left Long Bow village on October 20. After a two-day stopover in Changchih that made it possible to interview Commander Li Ying-k'uei for more clarity on the Cultural Revolution, we set out by jeep for Hantan, a major station on the Peking-Hankou Railroad. Our route lay eastward through the mountains, down the very same road that I had traveled upward by truck on my first visit to the Shangtang in 1947; the same road, for the most part, that Ch'i Yun, Hsieh Hung and I had traversed by foot and mulecart when we left Long Bow in 1948 to rejoin the staff members of Northern University at their new home in Chengting, Hopei.

Road crews had improved the highway greatly in the intervening years. A heavily graveled surface, strong bridges, culverts, well-tended drainage ditches made of it an all-weather thoroughfare along which buses ran every hour on the hour in both directions between Changchih and Hantan. To the south at almost any point on our route we could see the heavy construction underway on the new East-West railroad—bridges and trestles of cut stone already in place, sections of roadbed nearing completion, piles of ballast, piles of ties, earthmoving equipment in all shapes and sizes. After Szehsien we tried to pick out the line of the narrow gauge track that had run down the valley in 1948, the first operating railroad in the Liberated Areas of North China, but the widened highway and new railroad construction had completely obliterated it.

In spite of improvements to the road, the countryside looked much as it had twenty-three years earlier, a fantastic region of high rock mountains, loess-covered hills, and endless gullies and ravines. A few of the villages, mixed constructions of stone and adobe, crowned the heights like medieval fortresses. Others hid in the bottoms of immense ravines or climbed the terraced slopes of canyon headwalls. These villages, some of them thousands of years old, did not disrupt or violate nature. On the contrary, they seemed to blend into their background, as indigenous an outgrowth of local terrain and climate as the eroded loess bluffs and the willows by the lowland streams. Almost all of them were surrounded by fruit trees that had blossomed with incredible beauty in the spring and now, in the fall, bore heavy

NOTE: *Tsai chien* is the Chinese equivalent of *au revoir*.

fruit. Most prominent as we rushed along, leaving in our wake a great cloud of dust, were the persimmon trees, spare branching giants as large as or larger than the oldest American apple trees and now laden with fruit like the fruit of the orange tree in color, but in shape more like tomatoes. Seeing this abundant harvest we understood why the Chinese word for tomato is "Western red persimmon." Next to the persimmon orchards stood the walnut groves. If there was any single product that typified the Taihang Mountains, it was walnuts. They were on sale from small stands in most of the settlements we roared through—unshelled, shelled, dyed red, candied and cracked.

The charm of these mountain villages has always been difficult to convey. Their color is that of the rock and the soil from which they are made, the alignment of their buildings as complex, multilayered and many-faceted as the highlands that determine their layout. Each dwelling with its yard, its pigpen, its scavenging chickens, its mangy dog and its glorious mountain view constitutes an independent kingdom and at the same time one unit of a complex and interdependent social community that is clearly more than the sum of its parts. I can't think of any place in the world to which I would rather retire. Anna Louise Strong was evidently of the same mind. She wept and could not be consoled when, because Hu Tsung-nan's legions drove in from the south, she had to leave Yenan. She knew in her heart that she would never return. Between the loess hills of Yenan and the loess hills of Licheng, there is not much to choose.*

Under the whiplash of the slogan "politics in command," the Communist Party campaigned vigorously in the late sixties and early seventies for the "new village," the destruction of all old, "haphazard" housing and its replacement with barracklike, identical units in blocks and rows, every wall, every roof, every courtyard the same, every front door facing due south and every back wall facing due north. Tachai peasants built stone caves in a line because their loess caves collapsed and there was only one direction for expansion in their gully. The rest of the country, in emulation of Tachai, imposed straight lines on the most diverse contours. At Wuchiap'ing peasant builders even wasted good crop land by condemning small clusters of traditional dwellings among their ravines and knolls and building new, dormitorylike blocks on the flats beside the river.

I found it hard to fathom where this all-pervasive impulse for uniformity had come from. Was it a gut reaction of the new leading cadres to the problem of controlling the peasant population? Was it a reaction based on an illusion that through standardization and mechanization the people could be mobilized for "great works of Communism"? Did it express the equalitarian thrust of the peasant radicals themselves, still intent on creating for every family exactly the same material conditions so that justice could prevail? Or did it reflect some inherited commitment to the "square, straight-line, north-south" beauty of the pre-Confucian well-field system? Whatever its source, the impulse posed a serious threat to the beauty of the

*The presence in Yenan of Chairman Mao and the Central Committee, of course, had something to do with Miss Strong's tears.

Chinese countryside and the quality of rural life. One could only hope that it would soon spend itself.

As we hurtled down the mighty staircase of the Taihang range, from Lucheng, to Licheng, to Szehsien, Wuan and Hantan, each county town occupying a plain significantly closer to sea level than the plain preceding it, I tried to make some sense of all we had seen and heard, but no matter how hard I tried nothing would fall into place. The Cultural Revolution that had seemed, from a distance, to be a watershed in history—a breakthrough that would enable people to shake up the superstructure of old China, all the inherited institutions and culture of an entrenched feudalism, and remold it into harmony with the new communal relations of production, a harmony that could propel production forward—now seemed to have degenerated into a most bizarre and Byzantine free-for-all, a no-holds-barred factional contest for power from top to bottom, where nothing mattered but getting the best of the opposition, and all means to that end seemed justified. If capitalism was an economic jungle, socialism, if that was what existed in China, looked like a political jungle, where because the only power that mattered was state power, getting it and holding onto it became not only more important than everything else, but the only activity of any importance at all. In the bourgeois West, those who controlled the most capital, the largest chunks of industrial plant, machine tools and resources, wielded real power. They dominated the state, moved in and out of state positions, or shuffled state positions around, supporting in office whoever best served their interests. Because they inherited their wealth their power loomed as relatively stable. Presidents came and went, but Rockefellers and Fords, Du Ponts and Mellons went on for generations. By contrast, in "proletarian" China power automatically concentrated in the hands of those who climbed into leading positions. There was no other locus for it, no independent material base, and consequently no objective standard for judging who could or should wield it. For five years the organizers of the Cultural Revolution had insisted that the deserving could be judged by the policies they followed, whether they took the "socialist" or the "capitalist" road, but in regard to these two roads no objective standard could be found. Was a private plot capitalist? Was brigade accounting socialist? Had Li Ying-k'uei advanced the revolution by calling Ch'en Hsiu-ch'uang a renegade? Had Ch'en Hsiu-ch'uang served the people by calling Li Ying-k'uei a reactionary military man? Had Swift Li taken the capitalist road when he fostered sideline earnings? Had Little Shen betrayed socialism when he recruited Chin Ken-so, the son of a rich peasant?

What worried me most at the time was the analysis put forward by Commander Li Ying-k'uei. After spending a month at the February Seventh Locomotive Works outside Peking and three weeks at Tsinghua University I had learned enough to realize that factionalism in China was unprincipled. Both Premier Chou En-lai and Chairman Mao Tse-tung regarded it as unconscionable. Where two huge factions composed of workers, peasants, students and cadres confronted each other, the only proper course was to insist on peace talks, to insist that each cease to magnify the mote in the eye of the opposition and look for the beam in its own eye, that each put grievances and enmities aside and reach out a hand in friendship and cooperation. But in Southeast Shansi, even though a peace-talk format had been followed, only armed confrontation and a surrender ultimatum had actually brought hostilities to a close. The People's Liberation Army, the only remaining arbiter of fate, had then declared one faction revolutionary and the other counterrevolutionary, had rewarded one faction with power and the other with supervision in cadre schools and "squat spots" in the countryside. Army officers had tracked the leader of the condemned faction to a commune outside of Hantan, arrested him there, and brought him back to Changchih to be held for trial as a Kuomintang agent. As they held him they beat him to extract a confession, and when they beat him they broke his arm. They had shot at least half a dozen of his lieutenants, tortured and imprisoned many more. And still Li Ying-k'uei insisted that he was following Mao Tse-tung's instructions, firmly defending the "socialist road," and uniting all who could be united for the transformation of China.

I had gone back to question Li in depth three different times, and each time had received the same answer in ever more detailed and elaborate form. Because I didn't believe what I heard and insisted on questioning him again, I was attacked as a rightist. Lin T'ung, from *Central,* told me she saw no difference between my approach and that of any reactionary bourgeois journalist who questioned what he heard in China.

"Haven't you placed all the blame on the *Red* faction in this struggle?" I asked Commander Li, the third time we met.

"Factional struggle, feudal clan struggle, class struggle and line struggle are all mixed up in the Cultural Revolution," said Li Ying-k'uei. "Here in Southeast Shansi our struggle has been line struggle. It revolves around one man, Ch'en Hsiu-ch'uang, support for him and opposition to him, and he is a class enemy who held great power. Before he organized his *Red* faction in the summer of 1967, factionalism didn't exist in Southeast Shansi. Power had been seized by a united group of mass organizations, and all of them had later more or less dissolved. Then Ch'en raised the banner of seizing power from the Revolutionary Committee and pulling a handful out of the army. This stirred up a storm. Those who did not agree had no choice but to organize in self-defense and they built a group opposed to Ch'en, in support of the Revolutionary Committee, and in support of the army. This line was correct. So here we had line struggle, not factional struggle."

"To hinge the whole evaluation of a mass movement on the character of one leading man and on the single charge that he is an enemy agent seems inadequate to me," I said, still puzzled.

"In battle one must look for the weak point in the enemy line and make a breakthrough. We understand that this is line struggle, but other people don't. In this period of the Revolution all kinds of people are raising the Red Flag to combat the Red Flag. So, to test whether one's line is correct or not, the first question to ask is whether one supports good people or bad people; that is the criterion for judging any line. The wrong line is to support capitalist roaders and capitalist restoration, to support bad elements.

"In the village it's the same. The poor peasants take the collective, the socialist road of frugality, hard work and the transformation of nature, while the landlords, the rich peasants and the bad elements try to take the capitalist road of profiteering. In order to judge whether a Communist Party Secretary is correct or not, look at whom he supports. If he supports bad elements, he has taken the wrong line. If he supports honest poor peasants, he is on the correct line.

"So we start out by proving that Ch'en himself is a Kuomintang agent and that the people under him are also bad—former convicts, et cetera, a whole clique of people whose goal is to oppose the PLA, the Revolutionary Committee and the popular masses. . . . Our enemies are Kuomintang agents, renegades and counterrevolutionaries. Just as Chairman Mao says, the people led by the Communist Party are carrying on the struggle between the Communist Party and the Kuomintang. So the breakthrough point lies right here, with this issue. Afterward, of course, there is a big long article to write, but we concentrate on this target and we have strength. This is the tactics of the struggle."

Commander Li concluded his presentation with a restatement of his basic position: "Ch'en the agent is the crucial factor, the main stumbling block to progress in the whole region. Remove this stumbling block and we can get at all the other problems. In any struggle you have to take hold of the principal contradiction, the main point, and battle it out. Basing ourselves on such a main point we become invincible. We can maintain our footing in front of the Central Committee and never be defeated."

Here bankruptcy of political principle found expression in its crudest form; the road to power lay through the denunciation of the opposition, the political assassination of its leading personalities, defining them at one extreme as class and national enemies, at the other, as common criminals. The tradition, it seemed, was as old as Chinese civilization, recorded and handed down from one generation to the other in story, song and, above all, opera. Were not all the exiled heroes on Liang Mountain, the rebel stronghold of the Water Margin epic, driven there by frame-ups of one kind or another? When Liu Ta-jen, the emperor's representative, undertook to investigate Shantung, was he not thrown into jail on false charges? And was he not amazed to discover that most of his jailmates had met a similar fate? In China the first step in engineering any political succession was to blacken the reputation of all who stood in the way, setting them up, if necessary, for the most serious charges. Wasn't Lin Ch'ung, another Water Margin hero, set up by being enticed into a prime minister's chambers, sword in hand, so that he could be accused of plotting the minister's assassination?

The appalling thing was the universality of the technique. What Li Ying-k'uei had done at the regional level, Smart Fan had done at the city level, Shih Chao-sheng had tried at the commune level, and the Two Gems had imitated at the brigade level. They all used Marxist rhetoric—principle contradiction, class struggle, line struggle, revolution, counterrevolution—but the action in each case was in the classical tradition of bureaucrats unable to coexist with any kind of pluralism, any grass-roots initiative, any lower-level dissent. Power that fell short of the absolute turned out to be power that was insecure. And the same held as true at all levels above the region as at various levels below. Evergreen Liu and Secretary Chang framed Wei-Wang-Wang in Taiyuan, then moved heaven and earth to undermine each other. For inspiration and instruction they had only to look to Peking, where, on a national scale, most of the leading figures kept busy waylaying their rivals. What was not so clear at the time was that Mao Tse-tung, at the very center, had himself shown the way with his "case" against P'eng Teh-huai and his "case" against Liu Shao-ch'i. Since Mao presided over the center he tended to define his own moves, however expedient, as legitimate, but whenever he acted in defense of power for power's sake his actions, regardless of subjective intent, had factional consequences.

In 1971 I felt that Mao truly deplored factionalism and saw it as a disaster. Time and time again he had taken measures to suppress it. What has become clear in the interim is that he didn't deplore it enough to refrain from actions that provoked it and increased it. Factionalism, the unprincipled struggle for power between individuals, cliques, bands and mass organizations, once launched at the center, soon burgeoned beyond control, expanded exponentially according to laws of its own, swept everything before it and swamped the country. I had no theory to explain it, no grasp of its magnitude, no true perception of the disaster it threatened. What I did see wherever I looked was irrational confrontation and, in society as a whole, frustration and the widespread stagnation of production.

Stagnation and stalemate—those two words summed up the situation in Long Bow. It was a community turned back upon itself, grinding through the same redundant cycle of the seasons without any apparent upward or forward thrust. Yet over and over again I had sensed the potential power of the village collective. I could not see anything fundamentally wrong, anything lethal, in the way it had been organized. The difference between the Long Bow of 1971 and the Long Bow of 1948 was extraordinary and almost entirely positive. Pick any measure of progress at random, apply it to Long Bow, and improvement was obvious. Take education—what was wrong with 480 children in school, over twenty full-time teachers, an entire generation of literates? The old society never educated more than eight or ten Long Bow children a year. Independent peasants after land reform could hardly finance universal schooling. The community, organized as a cooperative, set it up as a matter of course, set it up with one finger, so to speak, while the other nine fingers busied themselves with other important tasks.

Or take medical care. What was wrong with a well-staffed clinic, two doctors and a full-time pharmacist, with a cooperative plan that ensured medical care to all for one yuan per head, per year? Could independent producers have mobilized in one morning to wipe out every mosquito in the area? Physically it was possible, organizationally certainly not.

Or take tree planting. What was wrong with a forestry group for the community as a whole, with a central tree nursery, with the planting every year of tens of thousands of saplings? Without a cooperative, could this have been organized in any form?

Or take vegetable production. What was wrong with six gardens, each one several acres in size, each one pumping water from several wells and tended by a team of specialists? What was wrong with centralized seed buying, with fertilizers and insecticides ordered in bulk, with a cooperative produce market? Without a cooperative community such gardens could hardly exist. In pre-Liberation Long Bow only the priest grew vegetables. The rest of the population hunted herbs in the hills.

Or take housing. Even though house building and house ownership were still private in Long Bow, the brigade set housing standards, allocated land for new housing from community-held acres on the periphery of the settlement, and so in essence planned expansion on the basis of what was thought best for the entire community. Such planning would have been impossible given the fragmented holdings of a precooperative village.

But the greatest strength of the cooperative community still showed up in the sphere of production. Long Bow had the capacity to mobilize enormous labor power to accomplish whatever seemed necessary for the improvement of yields on the land or for new sideline enterprises. When higher cadres suggested deep-digging, seventy-two young people went at it full time and proceeded in the course of a protracted campaign to turn over 133 acres to a depth of fourteen inches. Whether or not deep-digging did any good, the drive proved the efficiency of the cooperative form. When a project required the concentration of labor, that could be done with a minimum of effort. When a project required the dispersal of labor, as for hunting herbs in the hills, or retrieving manure on the roads, that, too, could be accomplished. The only real problem arose out of the tendency of higher cadres at commune or city level to issue blind directives, to order unreasonable projects, and recommend impractical schemes. The very efficiency with which the cooperative responded to all mobilization made possible mobilization for foolish purposes, but this was not the fault of the cooperative form as such; it was the result of too much centralized power at the commune level and too little autonomy at the brigade level. It was also the result of political winds that castigated local initiative and local innovation as breaches of discipline and made them politically suspect.

When city leaders presented irrigation as a panacea for high-yield grain production, Long Bow peasants went out as teams to create a trunk canal, a pumping station and a secondary canal system. But when irrigation proved that it created as many, if not more, problems than it solved, major efforts in water conservancy collapsed and Long Bow's "fall salt" land continued to encroach on the crops. If and when some method could be found to modify the "fall salt" land, Long Bow had the human resources to apply it on a massive scale. The potential for a breakthrough had always existed. In the meantime, given a little leadership, the brigade could make progress in manufacturing. It could expand brickmaking and build a cement mill, and there was always the possibility that it could contract out important work from one of the new neighboring industrial plants. In each case the strength of the community, organized as a cooperative, made a successful response possible.

It seemed to me that Long Bow had everything necessary for rapid development and a prosperous future—an excellent location; flat, potentially fertile land; a committed, hardworking older generation; a vigorous, literate, younger generation; many talented craftsmen; many seasoned leaders. What the community lacked was unity and political vision. Long Bow peasants needed to choose a unified leading group, decide on some common goals, and then set to work.

What were the chances?

Given the state of political life in the province and the region, the chances didn't look good. How could individuals in Long Bow unite and work together when all up and down the line hostile factions were in the process of consolidating a flagrantly partisan settlement that castigated hundreds of thousands as counterrevolutionaries, or the dupes of counter revolutionaries, and upheld other hundreds of thousands as heroic defenders of Mao Tse-tung Thought? The disgrace of the *Red* faction was so complete that even people who had been militant *Red* activists did not dare admit it publicly. The cadres of the propaganda team, many of whom had been *Reds,* never dared talk about it. While doing their best to ease the pressure on rank-and-file *Reds* at the grass roots, they went along with the public denunciation of *Red* as revisionist and reactionary and thus helped perpetuate the myth of a clash in Southeast Shansi between the forces of good and evil, heaven and earth, God and the devil.

In Long Bow claims made by both sides that they had all along adhered to *United* complicated the situation, but no matter how many times Little Shen and his colleagues in *Petrel* and *Shankan Ridge* made that claim, the majority, who claimed membership in the *Defend Mao Tse-tung Thought Platoon,* denounced them as *Reds* and treated them as such. Under the circumstances the last-minute reversal of the verdict on Little Shen, his reinstatement in the Party and his reappointment as a cadre, constituted an important victory that cleared the way for breaking down factionalism. But at the same time, the stubborn refusal of the Two Gems and the members of their "black gang" to admit any mistakes, or hold out a hand in cooperation, threatened that victory and raised doubts about whether the road, once cleared, would ever be traveled.

A few days before we left Long Bow, Swift Li finally agreed to talk to me. He agreed because he was assured that he could say what was on his mind and not what the propaganda team wanted him to say. I tried to find out what he considered Long Bow's main problem to be. It quickly became clear from his answers to questions that Long Bow's main problem was rival leader Little Shen himself, and particularly the alleged effort made by that cadre to blame Wang Wen-te for the death of middle peasant Wang Hsiao-nan. To Swift Li this was a serious attack on the land reform and on the entire democratic revolution. It was a counterrevolutionary "reversal of verdict." He criticized the propaganda team sharply for not taking it seriously. "You can talk any way you want if you don't go by the facts. But from Mao Tse-tung we learn 'Never forget class struggle.' This 'reversal of verdict' is a big question. If you say it is not a big question, you deny class struggle. . . . Just because we didn't do well in leading production work later doesn't mean we were wrong in attacking this 'reversal of verdict.' "

By stressing the importance of this case he implied that Little Shen was a class enemy.

Not long after I talked to Swift Li I talked once more to Little Shen. I tried to find out what he thought the main problem in Long Bow might be.

He agreed with Swift Li—the problem was class struggle—but he reversed the role of the antagonists. He saw it as a confrontation between the Two Gems and their lieutenants, all of whom had betrayed their poor peasant background, on the one hand, and Little Shen and his colleagues, all of whom had consistently defended poor peasant interests, on the other.

"Mao Tse-tung teaches that no matter what position we hold, we are servants of the people," said Little Shen. "But the Two Gems, as brigade cadres, acted like the people's master. Everyone feared them. How could they go deep among the people and solve problems? Those who made trouble and messed everything up with beatings and false charges [primarily Fast Chin's militia stalwarts] numbered no more than twenty. The main body of the poor peasants never did things like that. They did not violate the Sixteen Points.

"If there is a mass movement and people rise up, beat me or beat each other, that's not such a problem. But the Two Gems, young as they are, they are cadres. They ought to carry out Party policy. When they don't, I have to conclude that the main problem here is not factionalism but class struggle."

How could these positions be reconciled? How could the young men on both sides, all of poor peasant background, all Communists, all capable and hardworking, find common ground in service to the community? How could they be brought together?

In October, 1971, the answer was not at all clear. With the whole region bogged down in factionalism, with the political tone set by an army general who was himself a leading factionalist, the prospect for unity among peasants at the grass roots seemed remote indeed. Factionalism alone appeared to have shattered the Great Proletarian Cultural Revolution, and in the political shambles thus created people found themselves unable even seriously to consider, let alone find answers to, the major questions raised by Mao when he organized the campaign with such hope and enthusiasm six years before. We left the region confused and disappointed, full of anxiety for the future of Long Bow and the whole Shansi countryside, and without any satisfactory analysis of what had happened.

In the decade that followed, I tried to fashion a coherent explanation for the course of events during those extraordinary years. As millions of Chinese made their own independent analyses, the Communist Party offered a series of pronouncements that gradually shifted from the cautiously positive to the overwhelmingly negative. While Mao lived, commentators began to admit serious mistakes but still called the Cultural Revolution "an absolutely necessary movement to defend and consolidate socialism." After Mao's death and the fall of the Gang of Four, new voices began to criticize certain excesses as ultraleft and blamed them on Mao's wife and her Shanghai clique. General Yeh Chien-ying, speaking for the Central Committee in October 1979, finally denounced the whole Cultural Revolution as an unmitigated disaster. "Ten lost years," the commentators said—and this formulation, which matched the personal experience of millions of people (especially large numbers of intellectuals, who had suffered grievous harm, long terms of labor in the countryside, even physical torture as political prisoners and the death of friends and relatives), swept the field.

General Yeh's pronouncement opened the way for a series of articles and speeches that laid the blame for the "false" revolution squarely on Mao's shoulders and classified the politics of his declining years as ultraleft. As they developed this theme, Mao's critics began to delve into pre–Cultural Revolution history. They then extended Mao's ultraleft period backward in time to include, first, the Socialist Education Movement, then the Great Leap Forward and the formation of communes, and finally the wholesale creation of higher-stage cooperatives in the countryside as well as the headlong merging of handcrafts and service establishments in the cities during the middle fifties.

This revision of history finally settled on a post-Liberation turning point for the revolution, a watershed between progress and decline, between correct and "left" politics, somewhere in 1956. By denouncing all Mao's subsequent initiatives, his critics avoided grappling in any concrete way with the questions Mao raised so insistently after that date—questions concerning the development and consolidation of China's new socialist relations of production.* Since they rejected the relations themselves, since they regarded communes, coops, even production teams as premature, they found it easy to reject a Cultural Revolution designed to solidify these innovations. "Ten lost years" needed no further analysis.

In 1956, what was socialist in China consisted primarily of a radical new system of cooperative and public ownership without an adequate supporting complex of new ideology, culture or institutions to bind it together. In the long run, Mao held, only by carrying the revolution into the superstructure; only by transforming old ideas, customs, culture and habits; only by remolding education, literature, art, social institutions and, above all, forms of government could a new social fabric in harmony with and supportive of the socialist economic base be brought into being. Without such a new social fabric, without what amounted to a coherent, evolving socialist civilization, the new economic base could neither develop nor long endure.

The subsequent experience of nation builders in China and other parts of the world lends credence to Mao's thesis. Many postrevolutionary regimes have brought large segments of industry and agriculture under public or collective control, yet have clearly failed to establish anything remotely resembling socialism in any other respect. Wracked with contradictions, stifled by bureaucracy, they remain inherently unstable and crisisprone. Mao's opponents, nevertheless, resisted all serious challenge to the status quo of the fifties. In their view, the allocation of land to the peasants and the takeover of industry by the state completed the revolution internally. Only one great problem remained, and that was technical—the contradiction between China's backward productive forces and her "advanced" social system. What the country urgently needed, they said, was certainly

*The term "relations of production" refers to the necessary, usually involuntary, relations with each other that men enter into in the course of making their livelihood, in the course of producing material goods or providing services. These relations are also called economic or property relations because their character depends on who owns the means of production—the land, the raw materials, the machinery, the manufacturing plant.

not more rebellion, more political and social transformation, but technical modernization, education for professional competence, fine-tuned industrial management and vast injections of capital, science and technology from abroad—from overseas Chinese communities in Asia, from Japan and from the West.

In the fifties and sixties Mao denounced these propositions as revisionist and vigorously pushed his own theory of continuing revolution. For a while his views prevailed. He made a shrewd estimate of the creative power of the Chinese people, particularly the peasants, and counted on unleashing that power to transform the countryside, transform the nation, and in the process transform the people themselves. Appealing to the people over the heads of the majority of Party leaders and government functionaries, he time and again set hundreds of millions in motion. They challenged authority, defied tradition, and broke down barriers, one after another. In the course of each movement, activists succeeded in creating new social, economic and governmental institutions. Land-pooling coops, themselves the product of a great mass movement, brought in their wake democratically elected community congresses. The Great Leap fanned communes to life: district-sized collective units that brought civil administration, military affairs, education, health care, social services and all production under unified, semiautonomous leadership for the first time in history. During the Cultural Revolution rebellious organizations overthrew all established officeholders and replaced them with revolutionary committees originally composed of delegates from mass organizations, military units and the ranks of the deposed cadres—a vast transfusion of new blood.

The mass movements inspired by Mao nevertheless fell far short of achieving their ultimate goals. Cadres high and low transformed reasonable directives into irrational dogma, solid accomplishments paved the way for extreme measures that undermined all accomplishment, young officeholders abused power as badly as the elders they replaced, unbridled regionalism threatened the integrity of the nation, production suffered, enthusiasm collapsed, and the movements, one after another, ground to a halt. The new institutions at the base managed to live on as set forms but failed to retain much of their innovative, democratic content. Pressure from above for a unified, centrally controlled, hierarchical chain of command always returned real power to the hands of appointed Party secretaries who, more often than not, set up "one-man speaking halls." They soon reestablished something very close to traditional rule, albeit far more heavily staffed, efficient and all-pervasive than anything known to the ancients.

When Mao's supreme effort, the Cultural Revolution, bogged down in unprincipled factional fighting, when Mao had to call in the army to forestall anarchy and chaos, it was clear that the revolution could not "continue" in any meaningful sense. The pain and folly of the Gang of Four challenge and the uncertain bravura of the Hua Kuo-feng interregnum unfolded as forlorn epilogues to a drama that had long since played itself out. It was only a matter of time before an opposition coalition of victims, targets, bystanders and reluctant collaborators in Mao's Great Strategic Plan assumed power—more or less by default—and proceeded to dismantle not only the ideological, cultural and institutional superstructure built under Mao's leadership, but also the basic economic relationships that had brought peasants, handicraftsmen and rural workers together for collective production, and peddlers and small tradesmen together for cooperative trade. By reviving all the pragmatic, profit-oriented policies that Mao had so vigorously condemned, China's new leaders opened the way to individual enrichment for those with the labor power and resources to take advantage of the new "freedom."

Clearly, the battles fought by Mao, warped as they were by clashes over naked power, were not battles to settle questions of power alone. They were battles to determine the direction of China's development, and no one could easily reconcile either the conflicting policies of the antagonists or the contrasting world views from which they sprang.

Did the defeat of Mao's initiatives prove his critics right? Was his program sheer voluntarism—impractical, utopian and ultraleft?

The most persuasive evidence to the contrary lies in the success of Tachai Brigade over three decades and the impact of the Tachai model on Ch'en Yung-kuei's home county, Hsiyang, and on the countryside as a whole.* By putting public first, self second, by nurturing strong collective units and stressing self-reliance, peasants in various parts of China mobilized the full power of their respective communities to conquer nature, remold the land and forge a prosperous life. Far from stressing grain at the expense of everything else, as critics now charge, they carried out Mao's full program; took grain as the key link; fostered livestock-raising, forestry, fisheries and a variety of small industries; developed their resources in an all-around way —and astonished the world by their creativity, their productivity and the high standards of living they achieved.

In the seventies, Long Bow Brigade followed suit. Solving, fairly quickly, problems of outlook, leadership and production, that "old, big, difficult" unit of Horse Square Commune forged ahead on the Tachai road and took the lead in sideline industries—soil transformation and the mechanization of crop production—a lead that posed a challenge to the peasants of the entire nation. *Li Chun,* the concluding volume of this history tells how Long Bow peasants created their own appropriate technology and broke out of the stagnation that plagued them throughout the sixties and early seventies. It is the story of a rapid and profound community transformation.

While Long Bow peasants remolded their economy, followers of Tachai on the national scene did not confine their mobilization efforts to the village level. They went on to organize the population of entire communes and counties for capital construction on a broad scale. Massive collective actions —big joint battles (now denounced as "leveling")—drained waterlogged lowlands, brought water to parched highlands, reclaimed rock-strewn riverbeds, and covered sterile gullies and ridges with rich garden soil. In the

*Even if we accept the charge that Hsiyang County officials inflated yield figures from 1973 to 1977, the corrected figures are still remarkable. If China as a whole could reach anything close to the production achieved throughout Hsiyang in the last decade, the grain problem would be considered solved.

mid-seventies as many as thirty million people took part in rural capital construction every winter and laid the foundations for a prosperous agriculture in the decades to come. Stories in the daily press, now full of praise for the progress made by families who are going it alone, almost never mention the debt these individual producers owe to the collective labor that prepared the ground. Nor do they explain how, now that capital construction has all but ceased, the expanded resource base required by future generations will be created.

One cannot, of course, ignore all the scattered ultraleft follies, the leveling extremes, the "blind directives" that led to the uprooting of fruit trees to plant grain, the suppression of handcrafts to enhance field work, the banning of rural markets to forestall speculation—all in the name of studying Tachai. Nor can one ignore the all-too-numerous cooperative communities that failed to find a way forward on the Tachai road, sank into apathy owing to mediocre leadership, or fell under the sway of local Party despots, only to degenerate into neofeudal backwaters. One can, however, question whether the breakup of cooperative production, the fragmentation of the fields and the individual contracting of all the scattered fragments—abandoning in the process all economies of scale—is a viable solution to the problems these failures posed.

While the rank-and-file of many backward brigades tend to look on the chance to contract land individually as a liberation, a method for getting out from under oppressive rule, the contract system, by putting each peasant in a one-to-one relationship with the state, threatens to destroy the autonomy achieved by the members of successful coops by virtue of having banded together. Unfortunately, this very autonomy—the self-reliant staying power demonstrated by well-run democratic collectives, their ability to resist intervention and find an independent course forward—poses a disturbing threat to the power of all officials who stand above them, and makes them feel insecure. And this is certainly one reason why many officials today are so energetically pushing every brigade to cease collective production and contract its resources out for individual exploitation. It seems clear, however, that any individual who liberates himself from the petty tyranny of a badly run coop will soon find that he has put himself at the mercy of several more-universal tyrannies—those of nature, of the market and of the arbitrary power of higher levels of government. Once the peasantry as a whole returns to its previous, unorganized state as a "mass of loose sand," individual peasants will rediscover just how powerless they are to influence their fate in any significant way.

The new slogan is: "Some must get rich first."

As tens of millions begin to implement it, polarization sets neighbors on divergent tracks, long-dormant class tensions revive and, along with them, the fetishism and fatalism that has always served to obscure and excuse such tensions. All the rejected and long-suppressed ideas, culture, customs and habits of the past burst forth with the vigor of common weeds and threaten to choke out whatever collective sprouts still survive the debacle. Already some peasants on the rise are hiring labor and lending out money at usurious interest rates. As harvesttime approaches, they are also finding it necessary to erect in the fields huts made of stalks to provide shelter for family members who must guard the crops night and day against less fortunate tillers. Here and there, graves appear in the very middle of fertile plots that liberated peasants had cleared of all impediments less than a generation ago. How long will it take for the dead to reoccupy the land so recently bequeathed to the living? Trees, telephone poles, power poles—even the doors, doorframes and window frames of schools and other community buildings —disappear in broad daylight, fair loot for whoever gets at the precious wood first. And the same holds true for collectively owned machinery that can be dismantled for parts or for scrap.

Soaring bride prices, lavish weddings, even more lavish funerals, now reviving as face-saving displays of filial piety, go hand in hand with a great boom in rural house construction. These expenditures may reflect a rise in income; they most certainly reflect a shift in priorities from accumulation and investment to consumption. As the market for consumer goods expands, the flow of wealth into the cities quickens, stimulated by a price scissors that heavily favors manufactured goods. Certain cities, Peking in the lead, explode with consumer-oriented high-rise apartment and hotel construction. Such frenzied building can only widen the gap between city and countryside. Similarly, a revived examination system that floats the sons and daughters of the new urban elite into the universities cannot help but widen the gap between mental and manual labor, between professionals and working people, while both these categories distance themselves further from peasants still irrevocably tied to the land. What tensions, what confrontations will these trends produce in five years? In ten?

The basic question remains—if Mao Tse-tung had a program for China that could forestall polarization and still ensure development, why did it fail?

The answer has to be many-sided and, as of now, far from complete. A few points seem relatively clear. Some of them pertain to subjective failings on the part of Mao and his supporters, others to the objective stability of the civilization that they tried to transform.

One important factor contributing to defeat for Mao's program was his reluctance or inability to launch any mass movements against "left" distortions of line and policy. Each time Mao mobilized people for action, large numbers of cadres and activists invariably pushed on to egalitarian extremes reminiscent of the poor-and-hired-peasant line of the land reform period. In later years, instead of responding with nationwide educational campaigns that could help millions understand the reactionary, destructive nature of these extremes, and thus inspire them to resistance, Mao handled the problem administratively, primarily by shuffling people from post to post at the top of the hierarchy. This reinforced the popular notion that left was better than right, that left was, in any case, revolutionary, while right was counterrevolutionary. All this stood in marked contrast to the many mass campaigns launched against rightist tendencies, in the course of which Mao tried to mobilize the greatest possible number of people for action and educate them politically. This discrepancy in tactics contributed to that strange impasse in 1973 when Mao lumped the notorious leftist Lin Piao— by then already dead—with Confucius, as a rightist. It also contributed to the political paralysis that long prevented any coherent response, inside or outside the Party, to the obvious excesses and atrocities perpetrated by the Gang of Four. Overall, Mao's failure to deal effectively with left excesses gave opposition forces extraordinary leeway to use left politics against the revolution and lay the blame where it would do the most damage.

Probably the most damaging excesses had their roots in Mao's constant reiteration of such slogans as "Never forget class struggle" and "Grasp class struggle, and all problems can be solved." While these calls laid bare the essence of the overall situation and defined the principal contradiction besetting society at each stage of development, they did little to illuminate most of the problems that came up from day to day. Cadres who treated all contradictions as class conflicts raised them artificially to absurd levels of antagonism, created "class enemies" where none existed, and ended up fighting battles that they never should have fought.

While Mao balanced his militant remarks with repeated advice about "uniting with all those who can be united," "uniting more than 95 percent of the masses and more than 95 percent of the cadres," and "the more of the masses we unite with the better," people down below found class-struggle slogans far more useful for advancing their careers (if nobody falls down, how can I climb up?) and therefore seized on them at every opportunity. In the tense atmosphere thus created, anyone who slighted "class struggle" not only forfeited the right to speak but also risked becoming a target for all those who professed greater militancy. In the long run, these tactics succeeded in distorting and obscuring what Mao cared most about —precision in sifting friends from enemies, a deep grasp of fundamental class issues.

Mao himself further obscured the class question by focusing primary attention on the bourgeoisie as the enemy. While it is hard to object to Mao's characterization of Liu Shao-ch'i's policy for the countryside as "capitalist road" (what better label could be devised for family contracts aimed at individual enrichment, profit in command of all endeavor and the primacy of the market?), it does not follow that those who advocated and implemented it from above were capitalists. Regardless of origin, once they achieved high government position, most of them behaved more like traditional, scholar-gentry bureaucrats than they did like modern businessmen. To call them bourgeoisie was to underestimate their finely honed capacity for political manipulation and intrigue and to overestimate their entrepreneurial expertise and commitment. They placed far more emphasis on maintaining territorial imperatives and hierarchical distinctions than they ever did on getting things done. They rarely made economic decisions based on objective factors relating to production and marketing. They made such decisions, instead, in the light of the influence each would have on their own careers, on their own prestige and clout on the national scene.

Shanghai leaders prevailed on the State Council to sign a contract with Japan to build a steel mill in their city, which, as it turned out, could not burn Chinese coke or smelt Chinese ore and was, furthermore, much too heavy to float on the mud flats of the Yangtze delta. They went ahead with it anyway, regardless of cost, because it enhanced their preeminence on the industrial front. It is unlikely that any bourgeoisie, under constraint to produce profits, would make such a decision. Some deeper analysis of the class situation in China seems necessary in order properly to place such people.

While concentrating his fire on the "bourgeoisie" in the Party, Mao himself sank progressively into the swamp of an imperial tradition that I have chosen to call, throughout this book, feudal. His very choice of Peking, a consumer city with an enduring bureaucratic infrastructure, as the revolutionary capital; his decision to reside at Chungnanhai, right under the wall of the old Imperial Palace; his tolerance of luxury in living quarters, personal service and travel arrangements; his fostering of a Mao cult that surpassed the emperor worship of old; his nepotistical reliance on wife, nephew, niece; his penchant for frame-up and other byzantine forms of infighting when power was at stake—all these certainly led to isolation, misinformation and warped judgment. They could not but undermine the struggle for enlightenment, democracy and socialism in China.

Hemmed in by institutional feudalism at the top of the hierarchy, Mao failed to give effective support to the popular institutions of self-government sprouting at the base, the place where democracy, however limited, had the most chance of success. Whereas, in theory, the members of peasant collectives had the right to elect their own leaders and run their own affairs, in reality, as this book shows, the Party organization could always intervene, throw out the individuals holding elective posts, and replace them with new candidates from below or even from outside the community altogether. Thus, higher bodies routinely usurped the sovereign power that should have resided in elected village congresses or revolutionary committees. Subject to all-pervasive "tutelage," most congresses and committees never exercised the autonomy that they had a right to claim by virtue of their economic success, the very real measure of prosperity and self-reliance that they had achieved. Nobody—not even Mao, apparently—was willing to trust villagers with substantive local power, and this made it all but impossible—short of major, centrally led mass movements of the sort initiated from the Party center—for people on the land to challenge bureaucracy at all. Once the movements ebbed, traditional rule always reasserted itself.

The list of subjective faults and/or omissions could be longer. Toward the end of Mao's life, creeping senility exacerbated all his failings. But it would be wrong to put too much emphasis on their importance. Objective factors —particularly the stubborn ability of China's traditional civilization to survive, revive, regroup and reassert itself—probably played the decisive role. As long as 80 percent of the Chinese people remain peasants, as long as they are tied to the land and farm it with hoes, an extraordinarily appropriate foundation on which to reerect an authoritarian, elite-dominated superstructure continues to flourish.

In the past I took it for granted that the old Chinese state grew up to serve and protect the interests of the landlord class. It now seems clear that this traditional state apparatus developed in time into an autonomous entity with a raison d'être and a destiny distinct from that of the class that had given it birth. The Chinese revolution of the twentieth century thoroughly uprooted and expropriated the landlords, destroying them as a class. It nevertheless re-created a bureaucratic infrastructure uncannily reminiscent of those built by past dynasties whose roots lay in landlordism. Communist functionaries had little trouble grafting the democratic centralism of the European workers' movement onto the bureaucratic centralist rule they had inherited from the ancients. Needless to say, not much of the democratic component of the former survived. Perfecting their role as modern mandarins, these functionaries now exhibit a solidarity, a tenacity, a flexibility, a competence and a guile that is formidable, especially when mobilized in defense of their career interests. Taken as a whole, the state apparatus resembles a self-renewing, myriad-celled coral massif, solidly attached to bedrock below and protected above by resilient, many-layered defensive screens. It can give ground before any alien force that makes so bold as to attack it, then surround and immobilize the attacker. Thus the embattled bureaucrats of the sixties succeeded, not without a certain amount of style and finesse, in stalling, breaking up and finally absorbing all the campaigns, massive as they were, that Mao launched against them. In part, at least, because people at the community level had no guaranteed rights and no institutionalized power, Mao could not make much headway mobilizing young workers, peasants and students alone. He had to use state cadres against the state, lower cadres against higher cadres, young cadres against old cadres, outside cadres against inside cadres—but rare indeed was the cadre who, having won a position of prestige and influence, failed to buttress it in every way known to tradition, and thereby in effect reinforced the very system that he or she had originally set out to transform.

Most state cadres, even if they gave lip service to the goals of the Cultural Revolution, saw Mao's freewheeling challenge to established institutions, culture and politics as a lethal threat to the orderly conduct of government and, worse still, to their careers. Alerted and alarmed, they dragged their feet to prevent any popular movement from getting off the ground. When that failed, they jumped in to organize "rebel" forces of their own, thus guaranteeing some leverage when the time for a settlement arrived. Enthusiastic followers dragged some of them into extreme action. Others pushed extremes as a diversion and a disruption. They understood that chaos, judiciously promoted, could ensure the revival of the status quo ante and preserve their own ability to maintain a foothold within it. When the revolution played itself out, when the inevitable debacle matured, they joined hands to orchestrate a return to "normalcy." A social complex armed with such formidable defenses cannot easily be led, cajoled or driven into change. Only a well-organized and aroused people with some economic independence can put change on the agenda at all.

To sum up, post-Liberation China developed by means of a series of wavelike advances and retreats. Mao time and again unleashed enthusiastic mass movements of the people. As they rushed forward, threatening everything in their path, they jeopardized the prerogatives and careers of innumerable officials who, drawing on tradition and counting on the solidarity of their peers, parried, misdirected, blocked or coopted every popular thrust. While Mao still lived, each confrontation ended in stalemate. After he died—*le déluge* in reverse.

The successive stalemates of the Maoist era resemble, in retrospect, the one described by Heine in his poem about God and the Devil.

"You can't create," says God to the Devil, scornfully.

"No," replies the Devil, "but I can spoil whatever you create."

Almost, but not quite.

Even though Mao-inspired mass movements fell far short of their goals, even though they failed to create institutional alternatives that could nourish the new socialist relations of production, the socialist culture and the continuing socialist development that Mao deemed essential, they nevertheless propelled hundreds of millions into unprecedented political action, set them to examining every facet of Chinese civilization, and drastically altered the set of their minds. Now when pronouncements come down from on high, ordinary people, especially the young, no longer accept them at face value. They want to know *why?* Asking *why* has created a new climate of opinion that will surely unsettle and may even unlock the future.

Complete Index